GLOBAL ANTITRUST COMPLIANCE HANDBOOK

AF679148

GLOBAL ANTITRUST COMPLIANCE HANDBOOK

Edited by

D. Daniel Sokol, Daniel Crane, and Ariel Ezrachi

OXFORD
UNIVERSITY PRESS

OXFORD
UNIVERSITY PRESS

Great Clarendon Street, Oxford, OX2 6DP,
United Kingdom

Oxford University Press is a department of the University of Oxford. It furthers the University's objective of excellence in research, scholarship, and education by publishing worldwide. Oxford is a registered trade mark of Oxford University Press in the UK and in certain other countries

© The Editors and Contributors 2014

The moral rights of the authors have been asserted

First Edition published in 2014
Impression: 1

All rights reserved. No part of this publication may be reproduced, stored in a retrieval system, or transmitted, in any form or by any means, without the prior permission in writing of Oxford University Press, or as expressly permitted by law, by licence or under terms agreed with the appropriate reprographics rights organization. Enquiries concerning reproduction outside the scope of the above should be sent to the Rights Department, Oxford University Press, at the address above

You must not circulate this work in any other form and you must impose this same condition on any acquirer

Crown copyright material is reproduced under Class Licence Number C01P0000148 with the permission of OPSI and the Queen's Printer for Scotland

Published in the United States of America by Oxford University Press
198 Madison Avenue, New York, NY 10016, United States of America

British Library Cataloguing in Publication Data
Data available

Library of Congress Control Number: 2013950789

ISBN 978–0–19–870384–6

Printed and bound by
Lightning Source UK Ltd

Links to third party websites are provided by Oxford in good faith and for information only. Oxford disclaims any responsibility for the materials contained in any third party website referenced in this work.

PREFACE

The proliferation of antitrust enforcement regimes around the world has transformed the enforcement landscape in recent decades. This trend has led to increased focus on the competitiveness of markets and the curtailment of anticompetitive activities, to the benefit of consumers. It has also led to increased bilateral, regional, and multinational cooperation resulting in a gradual process of assimilation of thought and law.

However, while record numbers of competition agencies progressively apply similar principles and law, competition law enforcement remains domestic in nature. Indeed, a look at the active jurisdictions reveals a range of substantive and procedural approaches. Differences in the competition agencies mandate, priorities, and enforcement powers, as well as different political, social, and legal environments are only several of the variants which underscore the heterogeneous enforcement landscape.

This reality presents challenges for companies and undertakings operating across borders. With increased globalization of business and increased extraterritorial application of competition laws, it is often the case that an activity, agreement, or transaction will be subjected to a range of overlapping competition regimes. Subsequently, the task of managing the legal and financial risks associated with competition law infringements requires a careful exploration of the law and practices around the world.

This multi-jurisdictional compliance guide addresses this complexity and offers a comprehensive and detailed multi-country review of critical antitrust compliance issues. The book outlines the laws and practice in forty three of the leading antitrust jurisdictions around the world. With compliance requirements in mind, this book provides businessmen, law firms, and in-house lawyers with the necessary information to explore the changing global antitrust landscape.

This book is a resource for those responsible for competition and corporate compliance programs and for those interested in the international enforcement landscape of competition law. It assists in tailoring global compliance programs while considering multijurisdictional effects and policies. In addition, it provides a clear and accessible benchmark for the consideration of agreements, activities and transactions on a case by case basis.

Contributions to this book have been authored by leading competition law practitioners from their respective jurisdictions. Chapters in this guide enable assessment of personal and corporate risk exposure. The reader will find information on each regime's laws and practice. Areas covered include enforcement procedure and substance. These include, among others, the enforcement environment and enforcement priorities, leniency programs, penalties, fines and individual sanctions. In addition chapters outline the laws applicable to horizontal and vertical agreements, market power, the abuse of a dominant position and merger control.

Information is this book has been updated to present the law as it stands on January 2014.

Danny, Dan, and Ariel
February 2014

CONTENTS

TABLE OF CASES

ARGENTINA

AUSTRALIA

ACCC and TPC refer respectively to the Australian Competition and Consumer Commission and to the Trade Practices Commission

AUSTRIA

BRAZIL

CANADA

CHILE

CHINA

COLOMBIA

CZECH REPUBLIC

DENMARK

ESTONIA

EUROPEAN UNION

General Court

Court of Justice of the European Union (CJEU)

European Commission

FINLAND

FRANCE

GERMANY

GREECE

HONG KONG

HUNGARY

INDIA

IRELAND

ISRAEL

ITALY

JAPAN

KOREA

LITHUANIA

MEXICO

NETHERLANDS

NEW ZEALAND

NORWAY

PERU

POLAND

PORTUGAL

ROMANIA

RUSSIA

SOUTH AFRICA

SPAIN

SWEDEN

SWITZERLAND

TAIWAN

TURKEY

UNITED KINGDOM

UNITED STATES

TABLE OF LEGISLATION

AUSTRIA

BRAZIL

CANADA

Federal

COLOMBIA

CZECH REPUBLIC

DENMARK

ESTONIA

FRANCE

GERMANY

GREECE

HONG KONG

HUNGARY

INDIA

INTERNATIONAL TREATIES AND CONVENTIONS

IRELAND

ISRAEL

ITALY

JAPAN

KOREA

LITHUANIA

MALAYSIA

MEXICO

NORWAY

PERU

POLAND

PORTUGAL

ROMANIA

RUSSIA

SWITZERLAND

TAIWAN

TURKEY

UNITED KINGDOM

UNITED STATES

LIST OF ABBREVIATIONS

REAPPEARING THROUGHOUT CHAPTERS

AAC	Average avoidable cost
ADR	Alternative dispute resolution
ATC	Average total costs
AVC	Average variable costs
CJEU	Court of Justice of the European Union
EC	European Commission
ECHR	European Convention on Human Rights
ECtHR	European Court of Human Rights
EUR	Euro
FRAND	Fair, reasonable and non-discriminatory
IT	Information technologies
JV	Joint venture
LRAIC	Long-run average incremental cost
MAP programs	Minimum advertised price programs
MFN	Most favored nation
OECD	Organisation for Economic Co-operation and Development
R&D	Research and development
RPM	Resale price maintenance
SLC	Substantially lessening competition
SMEs	Small and medium enterprises
SSNIP	Small but significant non-transitory increase in price
TFEU	Treaty on the Functioning of the European Union
USD	United States Dollar

1. ARGENTINA

ARS	Argentinian Peso

2. AUSTRALIA

ACCC	Australian Competition and Consumer Commission
BOM	Commonwealth Bureau of Meteorology
CCA	Competition and Consumer Act 2010 (Cth)
PAWA	Power and Water Authority
PD	Peritoneal dialysis
SPAs	State and territory purchasing authorities

3. AUSTRIA

CA	Austrian Cartel Act

4. BRAZIL

BRL	Brazilian Real
CADE	Administrative Council for Economic Defense (*Conselho Administrativo de Defesa Econômica*)
STJ	Superior Court of Justice

5. CANADA

CAD	Canadian Dollar
DPP	Director of Public Prosecutions
MAPPs	Minimum advertised pricing policies
PPSC	Public Prosecution Service of Canada
TREB	Toronto Real Estate Board

6. CHILE

BAT	British American Tabacco
FNE	National Economic Prosecutor's Office (*Fiscalía Nacional Económica*)
MVOs	Mobile Virtual Operations
SC	Chilean Supreme Court of Justice (*Corte Suprema*)
TDLC	*Tribunal de Defensa de la Libre Competencia*
UTAs	Annual tax units

7. CHINA

AIC	Administration for Industry and Commerce
AMC	Anti-Monopoly Commission
AML	Anti-Monopoly Law
AMEAs	Anti-Monopoly Enforcement Authorities
AUCL	Anti-Unfair Competition Law
CNY	Chinese Yuan
J&J	Johnson & Johnson
LCD	Liquid crystal display
Local AICs	Local Administrations for Industry and Commerce
MOFCOM	Ministry of Commerce
NDRC	National Development and Reform Commission
NDRC Procedural Rules	NDRC Procedural Rules on Administrative Enforcement against Price Monopoly
NDRC Rules	NDRC's Anti-Price Monopoly Rules
SAIC	State Administration of Industry and Commerce
SAIC Agreement Rules	SAIC Rules on the Prohibition of Monopoly Agreements
SPC	Supreme People's Court
SPC Rules	Rules on Civil Litigation under the Anti-Monopoly Law

8. COLOMBIA

ACEMI	Colombian Integral Medicine Association
COP	Colombian Peso

CRC	Commission for Regulation of Communications
HHI	Herfindahl–Hirschman test
ICPC	Colombia Cement Institute
SIC	Superintendence of Industry and Commerce
TII	Interbank Exchange Tariff

9. CZECH REPUBLIC

CZK	Czech Koruna

10. DENMARK

AFC	Average fixed cost
AIC	Average incremental cost
DKK	Danish Krone
SØK	Serious Economic Crime (*Statsadvokaten for Særlig Økonomisk Kriminalitet*)

11. ESTONIA

ECA	Estonian Competition Authority
EEK	Estonian Kroon

12. EUROPEAN UNION (EU)

DG Comp	Directorate General
DRAMs	Electronic memory chips
NCAs	National competition authorities
WMP	Windows Media Player

13. FINLAND

FCCA	Finnish Competition and Consumer Authority
SAC	Supreme Administrative Court
MC	Market Court

14. FRANCE

DGCCRF	General Directorate of Competition, Consumer Affairs and Fraud Control
EIG	Economic interest group
FCA	French Competition Authority
FCC	French Commercial Code
RRP	Recommended resale prices

15. GERMANY

ARC	German Act against Restraints of Competition
BER	Block Exemption Regulation 330/2010
FCO	German Federal Cartel Office
NPR	Non-binding price recommendations

16. GREECE

EETT	Hellenic Communications and Post Commission
EOPYY	National Organization for Health Care Provision
HCC	Hellenic Competition Commission
IMAP	Internet-operated minimum advertised price
RAE	Regulatory Authority for Energy

17. HONG KONG

COMPAG	Competition Policy Advisory Group
HKD	Hong Kong Dollar
Telco Guidelines	Guidelines to Assist Licensees to Comply with the Competition Provisions under the Telecommunications Ordinance issued byb the Office of Telecommunications Authority on December 30, 2010
Telco Rule	Telecommunications Ordinance
TVB	Television Broadcasts Limited

18. HUNGARY

GVH	Hungarian Competition Authority (*Gazdasági Versenyhivatal*)
HCA	Hungarian Competition Act (Act No. 57 of 1996)
HUF	Hungarian Forint
MÁV	Hungarian rail cargo company
VKK	Centre for Competition Culture (*Verseny Kultúra Központ*)
VT	Competition Council (*Versenytanács*)

19. INDIA

AAEC	Appreciable adverse effect on competition
AAI	Airports Authority of India
CCI	Competition Commission of India
CMA	Cement Manufacturers' Association
COMPAT	Competition Appellate Tribunal
INR	Indian Rupee
NSE	National Stock Exchange of India

20. IRELAND

DPP	Director of Public Prosecutions
BBS	Brazil Body Sports
ILCU	Irish League of Credit Unions
ComReg	Irish communications regulator (the Commission for Communications Regulation)

21. ISRAEL

IAA	Israel Antiquities Authority
ILS	Israeli Shekel

22. ITALY

AGCOM	*Autorità per le Garanzie nelle Telecomunicazioni* (the regulatory authority)
ANCL	National Association of Labour Consultants (*Associazione Nazionale Consulenti del Lavoro*)
ECN	European Competition Network
ICA	Italian Competition Authority (*Autorità Garante della Concorrenza e del Mercato*)
IVASS	Institute for Insurance Supervision (*Istituto per la Vigilanza sulle Assicurazioni*)
TAR Lazio	Regional Administrative Court of Lazio (*Tribunale Amministrativo Regionale del Lazio*)

23. JAPAN

ICN	International Competition Network
JAA	Act on Prohibition of Private Monopolization and Maintenance of Fair Trade
JARA	Japanese Arbitration Act (Law No. 138 of 2003)
JFTC	Japan Fair Trade Commission
JPY	Japanese Yen
UNCITRAL	United Nations Commission on International Trade Law

24. KOREA

MRFTA	Monopoly Regulation and Fair Trade Act
KFTC	Korea Fair Trade Commission
KFTMC	Korean Fair Trade Mediation Committee
KRN	Korean Won

25. LITHUANIA

LCC	Lithuanian competition council
VBER	EU vertical restraints block exemption regulation (330/2010)

26. MALAYSIA

BEO	Block exemption order
CHFA	Cameron Highlands Floculturist Association
FLFAM	Federation of Livestock Farmers Association of Malaysia
FMPOC	Federation of Malaysian Port Operators Council
GDP	Gross domestic product
LIAM	Life Insurance of Malaysia
LRIC	Long-run incremental cost
MASA	Malaysian Shipowners Association
MyCC	Malaysian Competition Commission
MYR	Malaysian Ringgit
SAM	Shipping Association of Malaysia

27. MEXICO

Canacar	National Chamber of Cargo Transportation

CFC / Cofeco	Federal Competition Commission
LFC	Federal Economic Competition Law (*Ley Federal de Competencia Economica*)
MXN	Mexican Peso

28. THE NETHERLANDS

ACM	Netherlands Authority for Consumers and Markets (*Autoriteit Consument en Markt*)
AFM	Netherlands Authority for the Financial Markets (*Autoriteit Financiële Markten*)
CBB	Trade and Industry Appeals Tribunal (*College van Beroep voor het bedrijfsleven*)
DCA	Dutch Competition Act
DCC	Dutch Civil Code
DCCP	Dutch Code of Civil Procedure
GALA	General Administrative Law Act (*Algemene wet bestuursrecht*)
NMa	Dutch Competition Authority (*Nederlandse Mededingingsautoriteit*)
OPTA	Netherlands Independent Post and Telecommunications Authority (*Onafhankelijke Post en Telecommunicatie Autoriteit*)
WCAM	*Wet Collectieve Afwikkeling Massaschade*
Wft	Financial Supervision Act (*Wet op het financieel toezicht*)

29. NEW ZEALAND

ACCC	Australian Competition and Consumer Commission
EDC	Exclusive dealing clause
ECPR	Efficient Component Price Rule
NZ Bus	New Zealand Bus Limited
NZD	New Zealand Dollar

30. NORWAY

EEA	European Economic Area
EFTA	European Free Trade Association
ESA	EFTA Surveillance Authority
NCA	Norwegian Competition Authority
NCA	Competition Authority (*Konkurransetilsynet*)
NOK	Norwegian Krone

31. PERU

INDECOPI	National Institute for the Defense of Competition and for the Protection of Intellectual Property

32. POLAND

DIY	Do-It-Yourself
DVB-H	TV digital video broadcasting via mobile phones
NG	New Gas
OPCC	Polish Office for the Protection of Competition and Consumers
PCW	Polifarb Cieszyn-Wrocław S.A.

PGNiG	Polish Oil and Gas Company
PLN	Polish Zloty
PTC	Polska Telefonia Cyfrowa
TP	Telekomunikacja Polska
URE	Office of Regulation of Energy

33. PORTUGAL

AGEPOR	Association of Navigation Agents of Portugal (*Associação dos Agentes de Navegação de Portugal*)
ANTRAM	National Association of Freighters (*Associação Nacional de Transportadores Públicos Rodoviários de Mercadorias*)
APETRO	(*Associação Portuguesa de Empresas Petrolíferas*)
MoU	Memorandum of Understanding
PCA	Portuguese Competition Authority

34. ROMANIA

CECCAR	Body of Expert and Authorized Accountants of Romania
FMCG	Fast-moving consumer goods
NSRT	The National Society "Romanian Tobacco"
RCC	Romanian Competition
TDG	Total Distribution Group Romania

35. RUSSIA

FAS	Federal Antimonopoly Service
IP	Intellectual property
JVA	Joint venture agreement
LPC	Federal Law No.135-FZ on the Protection of Competition dated July 26, 2006
RUB	Russian Ruble
RZD	Russian Railways
SHA	Shareholder agreement
ZMZ	Zavolzhskiy Motorniy Zavod (car and bus engine manufacturer)

36. SOUTH AFRICA

ANSAC	American Natural Soda Ash Corporation
BHF	Board of Healthcare Funders
CAC	Competition Appeal Court
CLP	Corporate leniency policy
HASA	Hospital Association of South Africa
SAMA	South African Medical Association
SCA	Supreme Court of Appeal
USAP	United South African Pharmacies
VANS	Value added network service providers
VESA	Vehicle Security Association of South
ZAR	South African Rand

37. SPAIN

NCC	National Competition Commission

38. SWEDEN

Afab	A Flygbränslehantering AB
BCM	Bring City Mail Sweden AB
EKAB	Ekfors Kraft AB
NÅRAB	Norra Åsby Renhållnings AB
NVSH	*Nordvästra Skåne Södra Halland Energi AB*
RKV	*Rationella Kontors Varuinköp AB*
SCA	Swedish Competition Authority
SAS	Scandinavian Airlines Systems
SEK	Swedish Krona
TPA	Trading Prohibitions Act

39. SWITZERLAND

CHF	Swiss Franc
ComCo	Competition Commission
RPW	Recht und Politik des Wettbewerbs

40. TAIWAN

ODD	Optical disk drive
TFTA	The Fair Trade Act of Taiwan
TFTC	The Fair Trade Commission of Taiwan
TWD	Taiwanese New Dollar

41. TURKEY

MFC	Most favored customer
TRY	Turkish Lira
TÜRSAB	Turkish Association of Travelling Agencies

42. UNITED KINGDOM

CAT	Competition Appeal Tribunal
CC	Competition Commission
CMA	Competition and Markets Authority
GBP	Great British Pound
HAL	Heathrow Airport Limited
LPP	Legal professional privilege
NG	National Grid
NHS	National Health Service
OFT	Office of Fair Trading
ORR	Office of the Rail Regulator
PPI	Payment protection insurance
RRP	Recommended resale prices

43. UNITED STATES

AMD	Advanced Micro Devices Inc.
CFR	Code of Federal Regulations
DOJ	Department of Justice
FAA	Federal Arbitration Act of 1925
FTAIA	Foreign Trade Antitrust Improvements Act
FTC	Federal Trade Commission's
HSR Act	Hart–Scott–Rodino Act
SEPs	Standard essential patents

1

ARGENTINA

Miguel del Pino and Santiago del Rio
Marval O'Farrell & Mairal

Introduction

The latest Antitrust Law No. 25,156 (the "Antitrust Law") passed in 1999 in Argentina prohibits certain acts relating to the production and exchange of goods and services if they restrict, falsify, or distort competition or if they constitute an abuse of dominant position, provided that in either case they cause, or may cause, harm to the general economic interest. Such behavior or conduct is not unlawful as such, nor must it cause actual damages; it is sufficient that the conduct is likely to cause harm to the general economic interest. **1.01**

The provisions of the Antitrust Law apply to all individuals and entities that carry out business activities within Argentina, and those that carry out business activities abroad to the extent that their acts, activities, or agreements may affect the Argentine market (known as the "effects theory"). **1.02**

While, in the past decade, a greater emphasis was placed on merger control procedures, over the last two years, the *Comisión Nacional de Defensa de la Competencia* (the "Antitrust **1.03**

Commission") has rekindled its interest in the analysis of anticompetitive conduct and has launched several high-profile investigations, with a special focus on price discrimination as well as any other conduct that may have a direct impact on the pricing structure of consumer goods. Regarding its relation with the government, in a high-profile investigation in 2012, the Antitrust Commission issued a resolution which stated that "...the competition policy in Argentina must keep in line with the economic policy of the last years," and included a description of the achievements of the current political administration.

I. Acting alone

1.04 In order to determine the existence of dominance, s. 4 of the Antitrust Law sets out that an undertaking holds a dominant position when: (i) it is the only buyer or supplier of a given product within the market; (ii) when, without being the only supplier or buyer, it lacks substantial competition or; (iii) it is able to determine the economic feasibility of competitors because of a certain vertical or horizontal degree of integration. In addition, s. 5 establishes three relevant factors for determining the existence of a dominant position: (i) the degree of substitution for a product or service; (ii) the existence of regulatory barriers; and (iii) the extent to which a company can unilaterally set prices or restrict output.

1.05 It is important to bear in mind that the Antitrust Law does not set out that a dominant position is anticompetitive per se, since its s. 1 states that the types of conduct sanctioned by law are those that may prejudice the general economic interest. A non-exhaustive list of abuses of dominant position is provided under s. 2 of the Antitrust Law, but this list must only be taken into account for illustrative purposes, since the threshold in all cases will be whether the conduct has had an impact on the general economic interest.

1.06 By itself, the fact of being a dominant participant in the market will not trigger an antitrust accusation, but a greater degree of care will have to be employed by the dominant company. Furthermore, the Antitrust Law does not set out a market share threshold on what should be considered a dominant position. Consequently, the analysis of the dominant position will have to be carried out on a case-by-case basis regarding each specific market.

1.07 Since the early 1980s, the Antitrust Commission has been investigating conduct that falls under the abuse of dominant position. Over the first decade of dominance abuse investigations, the Commission carried out extensive (and often repetitive) investigations in certain specific markets, such as real estate, bakery and, surprisingly, the connection between the hiring of electrical services and of funeral insurance. However, no significant sanctions were imposed until 1999 in the *Commission v. YPF*[1] case concerning price discrimination when a local petroleum company incurred a significant sanction for abuse of its dominant position by discriminating prices in the liquid gas market. As of currency exchange rate on that day, the fine imposed by the Antitrust Commission on the infringing company was of USD 109,000,000. In 2000–05, the Commission would shift its focus to collusive practices.

1.08 Presently, however, the Antitrust Commission is using its investigatory powers to monitor key sensitive markets, such as the oil industry where it is running two major investigations regarding price discrimination on bulk diesel sales and the provision of aerokerosene. Other sectors that are also under the probe are the provision of port services, commercialization of cars, and the dairy industry. Lately, the Antitrust Commission has also started analyzing the

[1] *Commission v. YPF and others*, Docket No. 064-002687/97 (1999).

software industry and, in particular, the relation between online search engines and mobile operative systems.

A. Predatory pricing

Predatory pricing is sanctioned under s. 2(m) of the Antitrust Law, which describes it as "[s]elling goods or providing services at prices below cost, without a reason based on commercial usual practices in order to exclude competition in the market. . . ." **1.09**

The Antitrust Commission has sanctioned a very limited number of cases relating to predatory prices, and in most cases the conduct was considered ancillary to another, principal type of anticompetitive conduct. For example, in *Tolaza v. Centro de Panaderos de Santiago del Estero*,[2] the Commission considered that the accused party had used predatory pricing techniques in order to enforce a price imposed by an industry association on certain members. **1.10**

In *Cámara Argentina de Papelerías y Librerías v. Supermercados Makro*,[3] the Antitrust Commission held that, should the sale be carried out for a limited amount of time (i.e. in this case for fifteen days) and for a promotional reason, no anticompetitive conduct could be construed. This "promotional" exemption was also used in *Cámara Empresaria de Olavarría v. Supermercados Toledo*,[4] *SRT v. Cable Charlone*,[5] *EMI Odeon v. Libertad*,[6] and *Caratzu v. Granaderos Market*,[7] among other cases. The Antitrust Commission has also stated that no predatory pricing can take place in public bids (pursuant to *Stella Marias Alvarez v. Cooperativa de Electricidad Bariloche Ltd.*[8]) and that lower pricing as a result of an industrial promotion regime could not be considered to be unlawful by the regulator, since it falls outside the scope of the Commission's analysis, as shown in *Cámara Argentina de la Motocicleta v. Zanella Hermanos y Compañía*.[9] **1.11**

The Antitrust Commission's current review process on predatory pricing was evidenced in *Decoteve v. Cablevisión*,[10] in which it set out the conditions that must exist in order to establish predatory pricing, namely (i) dominant position, (ii) intent to carry out a market exclusion of competitors, and (iii) barriers of entry so as to prevent the entry of new competitors after the pricing, so as to be able to recoup the losses caused by the predatory pricing. In the event those circumstances are met, predatory pricing liability may be established if the dominant firm's prices were below average total cost. **1.12**

B. Exploitative offenses

Excessive pricing has been analyzed regarding several sensitive markets such as medicine supplies in *Commission v. Bago*,[11] in which the Commission held that significant increases in price that had no foundation in legitimate commercial reasons could indicate an abuse of dominant position. **1.13**

[2] *Tolaza v. Centro de Panaderos de Santiago del Estero and others*, Docket No. 18.254/82 (1983).
[3] *Cámara Argentina de Papelerías y Librerías v. Supermercados Makro*, Docket No. 064-000962/97 (1997).
[4] *Cámara Empresaria de Olavarría v. Supermercados Toledo*, Docket No. 064-002856/2001 (2002).
[5] *SRT v. Cable Charlone and others*, Docket No. 064-010415//2001 (2002).
[6] *EMI Odeon v. Libertad*, Docket No. 064-000870/2001 (2003).
[7] *Caratzu v. Granaderos Market*, Docket No. S01:0109838/2004 (2005).
[8] *Stella Marias Alvarez v. Cooperativa de Electricidad Bariloche Ltd.*, Docket No. 064-002885/97 (1998).
[9] *Cámara Argentina de la Motocicleta v. Zanella Hermanos y Compañía*, Docket No. S01:0154237/2002 (2007).
[10] *Decoteve v. Cablevisión*, Docket No. S01:0130563/2005 (2010).
[11] *Commission v. Bago and others*, Docket No. 106.179/89 (1992).

1.14 As valid commercial reasons, the Antitrust Commission has accepted factors beyond the scope of the supplying company, such as the imposition of foreign surcharges for long-distance communications in *Smolensky v. Telintar*,[12] as well as specific industry factors, such as safety standards for handling radioactive material in *Autoridad Regulatoria Nuclear v. Search*.[13] It has also discarded accusations regarding abusive pricing when the prices were regulated by the state, as shown in *Torrisi v. El Popular*.[14]

1.15 Furthermore, the Antitrust Commission has also taken into account an Argentina-specific factor relating to its 2001 currency crisis. In *Bamenex v. Terminales Portuarias Rio de la Plata*,[15] *CAPCICA v. Terminales Rio de la Plata* and *Hospital de Pediatria Profesor Garrahan v. Laboratorios Northia*,[16] among other cases, it considered that steep price increases generated by currency exchange recalculations upon a devaluation cannot be considered as abusive.

C. Monopsony

1.16 The Antitrust Commission has held that the exercise of monopsony power is not, per se, a violation, but that it might be one if it entails an abuse of dominant position, thus harming the general economic interest. This can be seen in *Commission v. Industrias Welbers*[17] in which the Antitrust Commission determined that the use of this condition in order to impose credit conditions beyond the normal course of business was a clear abuse of dominant position, since it used its position in the sugarcane acquisition market to unnecessarily delay payments to its suppliers. Monopsony cases have been seldom adjudicated by the Antitrust Commission.

D. Price discrimination

1.17 Price discrimination falls under s. 2(k) of the Antitrust Law, which contains the following description: "To impose discriminatory conditions for the acquisition or selling of assets or services without reasons based on usual commercial practices of the corresponding market."

1.18 In *Unión General de Tamberos v. Cooperativa Popular de Electricidad de Santa Rosa*,[18] the Antitrust Commission stated that the freedom to buy or sell and of the manner to do so in the most convenient manner, is limited in the case in which a dominant position is held since a reasonable justification would be needed. A reasonable justification was found to be a shortage of production output, as decided in *Safety SACIF v. Carboquímica Argentina*[19] or the granting of volume discounts, as stated in *Castro*[20] and *Jacoubian v. Shell*.[21] In *Autrotransportes Cita*[22] the Antitrust Commission held that a price difference generated by a public regulation refund could not be construed as price discrimination.

1.19 The guidelines for the determination of price discrimination can be found in *Lafalla v. Juan Minetti*[23] in which the Antitrust Commission considered that for price discrimination to take

[12] *Smolensky v. Telintar and others*, Docket No. 609.259/92 (1995).

[13] *Autoridad Regulatoria Nuclear v. Search*, Docket No. 064-011746/99 (2000).

[14] *Torrisi v. El Popular*, Docket No. 064-019229/2001 (2002).

[15] *Bamenex v. Terminales Portuarias Rio de la Plata*, Docket No. S01:0148930/2002 (2003).

[16] *Hospital de Pediatria Profesor Garrahan v. Laboratorios Northia and others*, Docket No. S01:0214185/2002 (2005).

[17] *Commission v. Industrias Welbers*, Docket No. 106.403/81 (1983).

[18] *Unión General de Tamberos v. Cooperativa Popular de Electricidad de Santa Rosa*, Docket No. 104.084/81 (1982).

[19] *Safety SACIF v. Carboquímica Argentina*, Docket No. 10.307/81 (1984).

[20] *Carlos Alberto Castro*, Docket No. 307.353/91 (1992).

[21] *Jacoubian v. Shell*, Docket No. 064-009518/2001 (2002).

[22] *Autrotransportes Cita*, Docket No. S01:0250619/2005 (2006).

[23] *Lafalla v. Juan Minetti*, Docket No. 064-006002/2000 (2000).

place three factors were necessary, namely: (i) the possibility of effectively carrying out a segmentation of the market; (ii) the encumbering of, or restriction on, reselling the product; and (iii) the existence of market power. Additionally, an adequate geographical market definition proved to be essential as a factor to be taken into account in the differentiation in pricing, as shown in *Falcioni v. EG3*.[24]

The landmark case (and the most important fine imposed as of that moment) concerning price discrimination in Argentina was *Commission v. YPF*,[25] in which the Commission considered the following factors: (i) the dominant position held by the accused party; (ii) the non-essential market shares of its competitors; (iii) the tracking of YPF's prices by other participants in the market; (iv) high barriers on entry onto the relevant market; and (v) the prohibition on reimporting YPF's own exports to other countries in which it did not hold a dominant position and thus charged significantly lower for its products. The Commission imposed a fine of USD 109,000,000 as per the exchange rate on the day of the issuance of the fine. In a followup case in 2009,[26] the Antitrust Commission decided not to impose a sanction on the same company since it considered that the company no longer held a dominant position. **1.20**

In early 2012, the Antitrust Commission initiated two major investigations in fuel-related markets, namely an investigation into an alleged discrimination between bulk and retail diesel oil, and another concerning the aerokerosene fuel used to power aircraft. In both cases, the Antitrust Commission issued preliminary injunctions to preventively stop the alleged discrimination. These cases are currently on appeal. The Commission is also actively pursuing another investigation regarding the commercialization of cars in certain areas with tax incentives. **1.21**

E. Dictating or influencing resale prices

(i) Resale price maintenance

Resale price maintenance (RPM) is encompassed by s. 2(g) of the Antitrust Law, which defines it in the following terms: "To set, impose or carry out, directly or indirectly, in agreement with competitors or individually, in any manner, prices and conditions for the acquisition or sale of assets, rendering of services or manufacturing." **1.22**

The printing of recommended resale prices in the products has been considered by the Antitrust Commission as competitive, as long as the reseller retains the freedom to choose the final price, as stated in *Federación Argentina de Supermercados y Autoservicios v. Danone*.[27] **1.23**

The Antitrust Commission considered that maximum resale prices have a positive benefit on consumers since the consumers end up paying lower prices. In *FECRA v. YPF*,[28] the Antitrust Commission pointed out that, by recommending resale prices, the producer was trying to undercut downstream players selling the products at higher prices than those that were considered more convenient by the manufacturer in its competition against other players on the market. The Commission also took this position in *Cámara de Comerciantes de Derivados del Petróleo, Garages y Afines de Tucumán v. YPF*,[29] among other cases initiated against YPF. **1.24**

---

[24] *Falcioni v. EG3*, Docket No. 064-19885/2000 (2001).
[25] *Commission v. YPF and others*, Docket No. 064-002687/97 (1999).
[26] *Lafalla v. YPF*, Docket No. S01:0227185/2003 (2009).
[27] *Federación Argentina de Supermercados y Autoservicios v. Danone*, Docket No. S01:018144/2004 (2005).
[28] *FECRA v. YPF*, Docket No. 607.043/93 (1994).
[29] *Cámara de Comerciantes de Derivados del Petróleo, Garages y Afines de Tucumán v. YPF*, Docket No. 614.364/93 (1995).

In principle, pursuant to these precedents, the setting of maximum resale prices would not generate an antitrust concern.

1.25 While there have been precedents concerning minimum resale prices, their scarcity and lack of uniformity do not allow for a unified understanding of the conduct. In the *Recorridos de la Tarde v. AAE* case,[30] the Antitrust Commission held that the imposition of minimum resale prices was legal, while in *Commission v. TeleRed Imagen*,[31] it held that such minimum RPM allowed for collusion. In *TeleRed*, there was an agreement whereby the owners of the soccer matches broadcast rights agreed on the prices with the paid-TV operators. The Antitrust Commission considered that the fixing of minimum resale price in this case was a mechanism ensuring the collusion among paid-TV operators. However, *TeleRed* was ultimately revoked by the Court of Appeals, and the appeal decision was upheld by the Argentine Supreme Court of Justice. Both courts expressed that there was no effective restriction on competition evidenced in the case. They stated that there was no evidence that, as a consequence of the agreements among the paid-TV operators, the prices charged to consumers were maintained artificially high producing harm to consumers.

(ii) Minimum advertised price programs

1.26 While there have not been any major cases specifically dealing with minimum advertised price (MAP) programs, should a company try to prevent a distributor from advertising prices below the recommended resale price, the Antitrust Commission could initiate a case of abuse of dominant position based on the generic provisions regarding abuse of dominant position set out by the Antitrust Law.

F. Tying arrangements

1.27 Section 2(i) of the Antitrust Law characterizes these agreements as the act of "[c]onditioning the sale of an asset to the acquisition of another one or the hiring of a service or conditioning the usage of a service to the hiring of another one or the acquisition of an asset."

1.28 The first major investigation into tying arrangements was carried out by the Antitrust Commission in *Asociación de Empresa de Servicios Funebres y Afines de Villa María.*[32] In this case, the regulator uncovered the unlikely link between the provision of electrical light and funeral services insurance in one of the provinces in Argentina. The tying arrangement consisted in the fact that the electrical light users were being forced to also contract funeral services insurance provided by affiliated companies. The Antitrust Commission ordered the cease of the arrangement, and imposed fines. This case led to several other similar cases across the country on exactly the same grounds, effectively turning tying arrangements into one of the key conducts adjudicated by the Antitrust Commission, a trend that would later decrease.

1.29 In *Ferrari v. Supercanal*,[33] the Commission held that a supplier's offer of secondary supplemental services which could be freely rejected by the customer without termination of the primary contract could not be considered a tie-in sale. Further, in *Ferrari v. Plan Ovalo*,[34] it disregarded a claim regarding alleged restrictions to acquire insurance services in car financing schemes other than those suggested by the defendant company, since several separate insurance offers were available. The Commission also highlighted the interest of the party

[30] *Recorridos de la Tarde v. AAE*, Docket No. 600.221/92 (1992).
[31] *Commission v. TeleRed Imagen and others*, Docket No. 064-002331/99 (2001).
[32] *Asociación de Empresa de Servicios Funebres y Afines de Villa María*, Docket No. 106.213/81 (1982).
[33] *Ferrari v. Supercanal*, Docket No. 333.165/31 (1995).
[34] *Ferrari v. Plan Ovalo*, Docket No. 064-000802/2000 (2000).

providing financing to the prospective car buyer in setting out specific requirements that the buyer be duly covered in the event of an accident for the duration of the financing agreement.

A recent case[35] involved an alleged abuse of dominant position by a sports channel operator, whereby it tied the supply of a high-definition sport channel to the hiring of a new signal by a cable company. While the Antitrust Commission has not yet issued a decision on the matter, it has ordered a preventive injunction ordering that the operator refrain from tying one signal to another. It must be noted that, in *Telecentro*, the Commission has not yet adjudicated whether the sport channel exerted an abuse of dominant position in the tying market. **1.30**

G. Exclusive dealing

There have not been a great number of precedents on exclusive dealing. In *Commission v. Acfor*,[36] the Antitrust Commission prohibited granting two distributors of Ford vehicles exclusive distribution for sales to the Argentine government administration since the government agencies located within their territories had to acquire vehicles solely from those Ford distributors. The Court of Appeals overturned this decision arguing that the supplier had the right to choose how to carry out the distribution of its products and that it had done so in a competitive market. **1.31**

In a later case[37] concerning a sub-distributor that was prevented from contracting an agreement with a distributor because the supplier disallowed such sub-contracting, the Antitrust Commission held that if the market under analysis is duly supplied or competitive, producers and distributors must be guaranteed their freedom to conduct business in the manner of their choice. **1.32**

In *SADIT v. Massalin and others*,[38] the Commission held that the imposition of exclusive intra-brand distribution can have a twofold effect. On the one hand, it can be anticompetitive if it results in a market power increase, allows market power to be exercised in a more efficient manner, or restricts the entry of new competitors. On the other hand, exclusive distribution can also be pro-competitive if the parties had the prior option of contracting with other parties or if the exclusivity generates cost savings or increases the quality of the products. However, this investigation is still being carried out following a judicial order. **1.33**

As regards exclusive rights granted by official bodies, in *Executive Class S.R.L. v. Manuel Tienda León*,[39] the Antitrust Commission requested the annulment of an exclusivity agreement that had been granted to a transport company servicing the Buenos Aires international airport. The order was based on the fact that the transport company charged much higher prices to incoming passengers than any other company not allowed to operate within the perimeter of the airport. In a similar case, *Castro v. Catedral Alta Patagonia*,[40] the Antitrust Commission held that the enforcement of an exclusivity generated by a governmental authorization beyond the scope of the purpose for which the authorization had been granted was an abuse of dominant position. **1.34**

H. Refusal to deal

The conduct known as refusal to deal is defined as follows in s. 2(l) of the Antitrust Law: "To deny with no justification the provision of a specific request for the acquisition or sale of an **1.35**

[35] *Telecentro v. Fox Sports Latin America*, Docket No. S01:0316202/2011 (2011).
[36] *Commission v. Acfor and others*, Docket No. 100-6-22-0869/79 (1983).
[37] *Pregal v. Basualdo and others*, Docket No. 323413/91 (1994).
[38] *SADIT v. Massalin and others*, Docket No. 064-000960/97 (1997).
[39] *Executive Class S.R.L. v. Manuel Tienda León and others*, Docket No. 613.289/94 (1995).
[40] *Castro v. Catedral Alta Patagonia*, Docket No. S01:0343037/2005 (2012).

asset or hiring of a service which had been carried out in the current conditions of the corresponding market."

1.36 In the majority of cases that implied an alleged refusal to deal behaviour, the Antitrust Commission rejected the claims by stating that the real grounds for those allegations were commercial or business disagreements between the supplier and the purchaser of a product.

1.37 Furthermore, it has stated in several cases, such as *Casa Amado v. Massalin*[41] and *Kosloff v. IATA—JURCA*,[42] that an abuse of dominant position must be proved beyond the mere freedom of the parties to carry out a commercial agreement. Thus, in *Campos v. Buena Vista Columbia Tristar Films of Argentina*,[43] the Commission held that the lack of a commercial background for the specific market and unusually aggressive attitudes during the initial stages of negotiation could be considered as a justification for the refusal to deal. It has also accepted that a spotty credit history or preexisting debts can also be considered a legitimate justification for refusing to deal (as stated in *Axelirud v. Páginas Doradas*[44] and *Representaciones Siderúrgicas v. Siderar*[45]).

1.38 Another factor that has been taken into account by the Antitrust Commission in upholding refusals to deal is the existence of alternative and adequate sources of supply, as evidenced in *Ferretería Alborelli v. R.O.R. Mayorista.*[46]

1.39 However, the Commission has held that refusals to deal may be unlawful in cases where the supplier could offer no specific commercial reason for its refusal other than the connection of the rejected party to a competing group of the supplier.[47]

I. Essential facilities

1.40 While this anticompetitive behavior is not expressly described by the Antitrust Law, the Antitrust Commission may construct an essential facilities doctrine based on the general prohibition of abuse of dominance.

1.41 In its first case concerning a potential essential facilities claim, *A. Savant v. Matadero Vera*,[48] the Antitrust Commission held that the granting of a public authorization (in this case, to run a slaughterhouse in a small town) entails the responsibility to satisfy demands of all sorts, even from competitors in the downstream market, and that any denial to supply would have to be based on objective grounds. Other similar cases have involved a wide range of industries, such as access to ski resorts, the certification for the welding of metal coffins, or credit card network systems. Remedies have included granting access to the plaintiff firm as well as, in some cases, imposing moderate fines on the respondent.

1.42 In a recent case,[49] the Antitrust Commission considered that the owner of a transport company that also owned the sole bus terminal in a town had to allow other transport companies to have access to it on equal terms. As such, the Commission stated that, while companies had the freedom to determine their own agreements, dominant companies could not block

---

[41] *Casa Amado v. Massalin*, Docket No. 84.596/83 (1985).
[42] *Kosloff v. IATA—JURCA*, Docket No. 064-002855/97 (1998).
[43] *Campos v. Buena Vista Columbia Tristar Films of Argentina*, Docket No. 064-001065/98 (1999).
[44] *Axelirud v. Páginas Doradas*, Docket No. 064-007195/2001 (2003).
[45] *Representaciones Siderúrgicas v. Siderar*, Docket No. 064-0147/2001 (2005).
[46] *Ferretería Alborelli v. R.O.R. Mayorista*, Docket No. S01:0171584/2003 (2006).
[47] *Decoteve v. Pramer*, Docket No. 064-006301/99 (1999).
[48] *A. Savant v. Matadero Vera*, Docket No. 30.782/81 (1982).
[49] *Empresa Almirante Guillermo Brown and Others v. Terminal Salta*, Docket No. S01:0030739/2002 (2011).

access to their competitors in the downstream market without a valid commercial justification; it also stated for the record that the denial of access to the terminal would entail a monopoly in the downstream market.

Despite these cases, the main focus on the essential facilities doctrine has been placed on merger control decisions. **1.43**

J. Bundling (including loyalty and market share discounts)

The relation between discounts and exclusive dealing was analyzed by the Antitrust Commission in *Bieza v. Sierras del Mar*,[50] in which it stated that the granting of discounts was of no interest to the regulator, except in those cases in which the discounts were related to exclusivity provisions. **1.44**

Additionally, in *Compañía de Radiocomunicaciones Móviles S.A. v. Telecom Argentina Stet-France*,[51] the Antitrust Commission considered that bundling would generate concerns if it also entailed predatory pricing conduct. **1.45**

K. Standard-setting groups (disclosure requirements, licensing arrangements, and licensing pools)

The Antitrust Commission has not dealt specifically with these issues, but should they be proven to involve abuse of the dominant position, an investigation could be initiated pursuant to s. 1 of the Antitrust Law. **1.46**

L. Customer termination

While customer termination has not been identified as anticompetitive conduct, the Antitrust Commission has launched a series of investigations in order to determine whether the said terminations could point towards the existence of an abuse of dominant position, primarily in conjunction with the essential facilities doctrine. However, there have not been any relevant precedents that could provide guidelines for the Antitrust Commission to follow in dealing with the matter. **1.47**

A special sub-classification regarding customer termination can be considered as anticompetitive, as described in s. 2(ll) of the Antitrust Law, which prohibits "[t]he suspension of provision of a dominant monopolic service in the market to a public service or public interest operator." **1.48**

M. Termination of intermediaries (retailers, wholesalers, dealers, and value-added resellers, agents, and brokers)

Like the behavior with respect of customers discussed above, the termination of agreements with intermediaries has not been characterized as anticompetitive conduct, but it could indicate one, such as failure to comply with a supplier's RPM. The Antitrust Commission has launched investigations in answer to claims from intermediaries whose agreements had been terminated, in an effort to identify whether an abuse of the dominant position was committed. However, there have been no relevant precedents that could offer any guidelines for the Antitrust Commission to follow. **1.49**

[50] *Bieza v. Sierras del Mar*, Docket No. 107.337/81 (1984).

[51] *Compañía de Radiocomunicaciones Móviles S.A. v. Telecom Argentina Stet-France and others*, Docket No. 064-012623/2000 (2005).

N. Termination of relationships with competitors

1.50 The types of conduct that have been adjudicated by the Antitrust Commission have mostly pertained to situations that may have led to the termination of relationships with competitors, such as the lack of consensus regarding possible collusion or situations relating to the essential facilities doctrine. These cases have been largely deemed to be ancillary to the main anticompetitive conduct.

O. Exemptions

1.51 The sole parameter employed by the Antitrust Law is whether a particular conduct has harmed the general economic interest. There are no exemptions regarding the *de minimis* impact, or any other kind of impact, of the conduct.

1.52 However, pursuant to the provisions of s. 36 of the Antitrust Law, the alleged infringer may propose a "commitment" to the immediate or gradual cessation of the actions which originated the accusation. Such commitment can be submitted at any time prior to the Commission's issuance of a resolution on the matter. If the proposal is accepted, the investigation is automatically suspended, and the Commission must supervise compliance with the terms of the undertaken commitment.

1.53 In this regard, the Antitrust Commission has stated that "...the legal figure set forth in s. 36 of Law No. 25,156 should not be automatically granted, being reserved only for those cases in which the irrelevance of the conduct under analysis, measured by the near inexistent prejudice to the general economic interest...."[52] The Antitrust Commission has lately shown a tendency to accept commitments in non-essential cases but no major case has been concluded by means of a commitment.

II. Dealing with competitors

1.54 The Antitrust Commission has carried out an extensive probing regarding interactions with competitors in the past, but it has also run into problems while trying to uncover cartels. Thus, while its investigations have led to two major collusion cases, namely the *Cement*[53] and *Liquid Oxygen*[54] cases, the lack of a leniency program has held back these investigations.

1.55 However, the Antitrust Commission has been actively monitoring since its inception encouraged the interactions within trade associations and has made several findings of illegality in that regard.

A. Horizontal price fixing

1.56 Section 2(a) of the Antitrust Law describes this conduct as "fix[ing], agree[ing] or manipulat[ing] in a direct or indirect manner the price for the sale or acquisition of assets or services that are offered or demanded on the market, as well as exchanging information in this regard."

1.57 In the *Bariloche Liquid Petroleum* case,[55] the Antitrust Commission stated that the key factors that encouraged collusion included low elasticity of demand, the lack of close substitute products, low quantity of operators, the homogeneous product quality, the existence of trade

---

52 See e.g. *Petroquímica Cuyo v. PBB Polisur*, Docket No. S01:0468538/2010 (2012).

53 *Cement*, Docket No. 064-012896/99 (2005).

54 *Liquid Oxygen*, Docket No. 064-011323/2001 (2005).

55 *Bariloche Liquid Petroleum*, Docket No. 064-003996/98 (2003).

associations, and significant barriers to entry. The Commission also noted that long duration of the conduct was also a factor.

In *Federación de Clínicas Sanatorios, Hospitales y Otros Establecimientos Privados de la Provincia de Buenos Aires v. Rouc-OCEFA*,[56] the Antitrust Commission stated that an analysis of a possible horizontal price-fixing conduct must take into account whether the market-wide increase could have been generated by external reasons, as was the case in the 1995 "Tequila crisis," for example. The Commission has also noted that certain regulations set out by the state in sensitive markets as part of state economic policy and their subsequent impact on price homogeneity across the industry could be justified by an emergency situation in the economy, as evidenced in *Confederación de Asociaciones Rurales de Buenos Aires y La Pampa v. Bunge Argentina*.[57] **1.58**

However, external forces, such as an economic crisis, need not necessarily impact all the involved companies in exactly the same manner, as shown in *Administración General de Puertos Sociedad del Estado v. Centro Coordinador de Actividades Portuarias*,[58] in which the Antitrust Commission did not accept a defense based on the increase in variable costs in order to justify a market-wide fixed-price surcharge. **1.59**

In the *Cement* case,[59] the Antitrust Commission was not able to fully prove the existence of price coordination; however, since it had already been to verify the existence of a market allocation scheme as well as the coordination of production output between the undertakings, it did not delve into the issue in full. The Commission issued one of its most important sanctions as of today in the *Cement* case, in which the total amount of the fines surpassed the USD 100,000,000 mark as of the currency exchange rate of the date of issuance. **1.60**

Finally, there were cases concerning oligopoly markets in which the Antitrust Commission determined the existence of price parallelism, but was unable to prove that it had arisen from collusive practices.[60] **1.61**

B. Horizontal agreements to allocate customers or territories; agreements not to compete

Section 2(c) of the Antitrust Law defines market allocation by prohibiting the practice of "...horizontally allocate[ing] zones, markets, clients and sources of supply." **1.62**

In the *Sand Producers* case,[61] the Antitrust Commission uncovered a scheme mounted by sand producers in the Buenos Aires area that had the backing of naval sand transport unions. A cartel was found whereby the sand producers and the unions formed an agreement setting production quotas. If one of the competitors in that market decided to leave the cartel, the transport unions would block their transportation. **1.63**

Regarding the possible intervention by governmental bodies, in the *Liquid Petroleum Gas Investigation* case,[62] the Antitrust Commission held that, even though the accused parties had **1.64**

---

[56] *Federación de Clínicas Sanatorios, Hospitales y Otros Establecimientos Privados de la Provincia de Buenos Aires v. Rouc-OCEFA and others*, Docket No. 034-003749/95 (1998).

[57] *Confederación de Asociaciones Rurales de Buenos Aires y La Pampa v. Bunge Argentina and others*, Docket No. S01:0486731/2006 (2007).

[58] *Administración General de Puertos Sociedad del Estado v. Centro Coordinador de Actividades Portuarias and others*, Docket No. 602.494/94 (1996).

[59] *Cement* (n 53).

[60] *Asociación de Titulares de Taxis Independientes v. Servicios Gas Automotores*, Docket No. S01:0227995/2002 (2010).

[61] *Sand Producers*, Docket No. 70.332/84 (1986).

[62] *Liquid Petroleum Gas Investigation*, Docket No. 84.543/83 (1989).

invoked an official regulation in order to carry out a customer allocation scheme, the fact that the regulation had been issued by a body that did not deal with antitrust matters could not be considered as a defense.

1.65 In *Mayol v. Shell*,[63] the Antitrust Commission stated that a "hard core cartel" was prejudicial to the general economic interest without it being necessary to prove any actual harm. The Commission applied a per se rule, even though the Antitrust Law provides for a "rule of reason." The case originated in a claim filed by a distributor of liquid gas who stated that, after having switched suppliers, he was refused a sale by the new supplier due to an agreement the latter had with its former supplier, aimed to divide the clients in the city of Posadas. However, the Antitrust Commission was later challenged in court regarding its decision. The Federal Court of Appeals for the City of Posadas overturned the decision since it considered that the Antitrust Commission had not followed a real competitive analysis in order to evaluate whether an illegal conduct had been committed. The court stated that the Antitrust Commission did not specify the relevant market in which the participants offered their products, and therefore failed to analyze the real competitive effect of the conduct. Additionally, the court pointed out that the evidence gathered by the Antitrust Commission was not sufficient to impose a sanction. According to the Court of Appeals, the absence of a general analysis of the testimonies showed that there were not enough evidences to demonstrate the existence of a collusive agreement that may have harmed the general economic interest.

1.66 The best known case regarding these types of agreement in Argentina is the *Cement* case[64] in which six major cement-producing companies were accused of staging a nationwide market allocation and production output-setting framework which lasted almost 20 years. The Antitrust Commission's investigation began in 1999, when a disgruntled employee revealed to a newspaper that the cement companies were allegedly exchanging information and dividing their market shares through an agreement. According to the findings of the Antitrust Commission, the exchange of detailed confidential market information was performed via the cement trade association. The Antitrust Commission found records of real-time software that was used to exchange current commercial records between the cement companies. As mentioned above, the Commission issued in this case one of its largest fines to date.

1.67 In the *Liquid Oxygen* case,[65] after performing several raids on the liquid oxygen companies and obtaining documentary evidence, the Antitrust Commission unveiled an alleged cartel that had been rigging bids for liquid oxygen. The four members of this alleged cartel were thought to have actively set among themselves the amounts and conditions of their offers in each bid so as to determine who would be the supplier for each public hospital. This was considered as a division of market among competitors, and it lasted for five years. The Antitrust Commission seized emails that evidenced the information exchange corresponding to the bids to be offered by the accused parties to the public hospitals. As a result of the investigation, a major fine of over USD 30,000,000, as of the currency exchange rate of the date of issuance, in total, was imposed on the parties. A similar case, related to pathogenic waste disposal[66] was later adjudicated by the Antitrust Commission, which rendered a non-unanimous decision to accept a behavioral commitment and ordered the termination of the proceedings.

[63] *Mayol v. Shell*, Docket No. 064-004881/2001 (2006).

[64] *Cement* (n 53).

[65] *Liquid Oxygen* (n 54).

[66] *Eco-System v. Pelco and others*, Docket No. S01:0091114/2003 (2010).

A recent customer allocation scheme case[67] adjudicated by the Antitrust Commission involved the allocation of the infrastructure of the former operator between two new entrants in a cable TV market. The Antitrust Commission uncovered the market allocation scheme which was being carried out under the cover of a division of assets. **1.68**

C. Horizontal boycotts

While the Antitrust Commission has not rendered any specific decision in this matter, it must be taken into account that horizontal boycotts could be considered as an exclusionary collusion, and as such an investigation could be launched. **1.69**

D. Joint ventures and other competitive collaborations

The absence of case law regarding joint ventures and other competitive collaboration, as well as the provisions of the Antitrust Law, could lead to the conclusion that these types of behavior are not considered to be anticompetitive per se unless they entail harm to the general economic interest. As such, as long as collaboration among competitors cannot be determined to constitute collusion or produce any other anticompetitive effect, it cannot be considered as anticompetitive under the Antitrust Law. **1.70**

E. Trade associations

Over the past thirty years, the Antitrust Commission has been probing the recommendations and impositions by trade associations. In one of its earliest cases, *Commission v. Cámara Inmobiliaria Argentina*,[68] the Commission imposed a sanction on a realtor trade association due to an industry-wide communication that was intended to produce systematic price adjustments in real estate properties in Argentina. A similar approach was taken by the regulator, among other similar cases, in *Commission v. Cámara del Flete*,[69] *Commission v. Colegio Oficial de Farmaceúticos y Bioquímicos de la Capital Federal*,[70] and *Commission v. Centro de Industriales Panaderos*.[71] However, the Commission has accepted that the publication of "reference" prices is not anticompetitive per se, provided that pricing decisions would be independently taken by each member of the association.[72] **1.71**

The recommendation to set up a determinate minimum fee for the rendering of professional services was also considered to be anticompetitive in *Commission v. Colegio de Graduados en Ciencias Económicas-Consejo Profesional de Ciencias Económicas*[73] and in *Commission v. Colegio de Traductores Públicos de la Ciudad de Buenos Aires*.[74] Nevertheless, it must be taken into account that in *Cámara Argentina de Farmacias v. Colegio de Farmacéuticos de la Provincia de Buenos Aires*,[75] the Antitrust Commission stated that a trade association's functions of oversight do not necessarily entail an abuse of the dominant position. **1.72**

---

[67] *Sabella de Prina and others v. Video Cable 6 and others*, Docket No. 064-004218/98 (2011).

[68] *Commission v. Cámara Inmobiliaria Argentina*, Docket No. 100.676/81 (1981).

[69] *Commission v. Cámara del Flete*, Docket No. 10.031/81 (1981).

[70] *Commission v. Colegio Oficial de Farmaceúticos y Bioquímicos de la Capital Federal*, Docket No. 109.419/81 (1982).

[71] *Commission v. Centro de Industriales Panaderos*, Docket No. 109.696/81 (1982).

[72] *Commission v. Asociación Empresaria Hotelera Gastronómica de Mar del Plata y Zona de Influencia*, Docket No. S01:0251931/2002 (2008).

[73] *Commission v. Colegio de Graduados en Ciencias Económicas-Consejo Profesional de Ciencias Económicas*, Docket No. 20.548/82 (1983).

[74] *Commission v. Colegio de Traductores Públicos de la Ciudad de Buenos Aires*, Docket No. 22.963/82 (1983).

[75] *Cámara Argentina de Farmacias v. Colegio de Farmacéuticos de la Provincia de Buenos Aires*, Docket No. 115.462/81 (1984).

1.73 Another common thread running through trade associations was manifested in the healthcare industry, where medical associations forbade their members to negotiate directly with the healthcare providers instead of carrying out their negotiations within the association, as shown, among others, in *Dirección de Bienestar de la Armada v. Agremiación Odontológica de La Plata, Berisso y Ensenada y Sociedad Odontológica de La Plata.*[76]

1.74 In the *Cement* case,[77] the intervention of the trade association was considered to be vital to the market allocation scheme, since it allowed the parties to fully coordinate and oversee the operation of each one of its members.

F. Interlocking directorates

1.75 While there is no specific provision in the Antitrust Law pertaining to interlocking directorates, in *Unisys Sudamericana v. Impresora Internacional de Valores*[78] the Antitrust Commission stated that the presence of a preexistent link between the companies competing in a public bid resulted from a market structure issue rather than being a form of anticompetitive conduct. In *Ventachap v. Siderar*,[79] the Antitrust Commission examined whether there had been any collusive agreement due to the membership of a director appointed by a foreign competitor (which held a minor shareholding on the Argentine undertaking) in the Board of Directors of a local company, but found none.

1.76 A merger control decision shows a more recent approach taken by the Antitrust Commission in this matter. In the past, the Antitrust Commission had considered that joint control existed solely in the cases in which shareholders must reach an agreement regarding strategic commercial decisions. It further held that the existence of veto rights must be analyzed to determine the existence of joint control. Those veto rights might include the approval of a budget, business plans, regular investments, and appointment of key officers. The Antitrust Commission determined that holding one or more veto rights is sufficient to confer control.

1.77 However, the high profile *Telecom v. Telefónica* merger control decision[80] shows a clear departure from such interpretation, and includes a new factor to be taken into account: access to a competitor's information. As a result, joint control would take place not only when two shareholders have reached an agreement regarding strategic decisions, but also when a competitor—by means of the acquisition of a minority shareholding—could determine its competitive strategy based on its competitor's sensitive information.

1.78 While interlocking directorates have not yet been prohibited under the Antitrust Law, the Antitrust Commission has already stated that such arrangements can show a unity of control in certain cases, which could lead to collusion-based cases in the future.

G. Facilitating practices

1.79 Facilitating practices are not specifically covered by the Antitrust Law, and the Antitrust Commission cases have not specifically dealt with this issue. However, in the event that the Antitrust Commission should be able to prove that these practices might entail collusion

[76] *Dirección de Bienestar de la Armada v. Agremiación Odontológica de La Plata, Berisso y Ensenada y Sociedad Odontológica de La Plata*, Docket No. 614.897/92 (1997).

[77] *Cement* (n 53).

[78] *Unisys Sudamericana v. Impresora Internacional de Valores and others*, Docket No. 064-005104/2001 (2001).

[79] *Ventachap v. Siderar*, Docket No. 064-008057/1998 (2004).

[80] *Telecom v. Telefónica*, Docket No. S01:0014652/2009 (2009).

between competitors and thus prejudice the general economic interest, an investigation could be launched.

H. Information exchange

As mentioned above, exchange of information is specifically covered by s. 2(a) of the Antitrust Law. **1.80**

The key case concerning information exchange in Argentina was the *Cement* case,[81] in which the Antitrust Commission uncovered an alleged information exchange cartel carried out within a cement industry association thanks to which companies exchanged statistical data that provided detailed, up-to-date information regarding geographic areas, manufacturing output, types of client, types of commercialization packages, and other sensible data. **1.81**

The information exchange was considered to be anticompetitive since it deprived competitors of their independence when establishing their commercialization strategies; it also served to monitor companies' conduct to ensure compliance with the cartel. The Antitrust Commission held that shared information should not have included prices, client lists, productions costs, quantities, or manufacturing outputs. Furthermore, the degree of information as well as the fact that it was being constantly updated was taken into account by the Antitrust Commission. **1.82**

I. Joint purchasing agreements

Joint purchasing agreements are not considered as anticompetitive per se. However, in the event that such agreements lead to collusion in purchasing, the conduct would fall under the prohibitions of the Antitrust Law. Thus, in *Ventachap v. Siderar*,[82] the Antitrust Commission considered that the setting up of a joint venture with competitors in order to obtain an award on a foreign public bid was not anticompetitive as long as no collusion takes place and the public bid rules are duly followed. **1.83**

J. Joint lobbying/regulatory/legislative efforts

There are no joint lobbying exemptions under the Antitrust Law, and there are no specific precedents or provisions considering these types of conduct as anticompetitive. Nevertheless, it must be taken into account that the general standard regarding prejudice to the general economic interest remains in place and, should another anticompetitive practice take place while carrying out any of these practices, it would still be forbidden by the Antitrust Law. **1.84**

III. General issues

A. Jurisdiction and applicable law (including sector-specific competition regulation)

The current applicable body of law is the Antitrust Law which, pursuant to s. 3, is applicable to "all persons or companies, either public or private, that carry out economic activities, either with or without the purpose of obtaining a profit, in all or part of the national territory and those that carry out economic activities outside the country, as long as their acts, activities or agreements may generate effects in the national market." **1.85**

There is no sector-specific competition regulation but it is important to note that the recent Audiovisual Law No. 26,522 states that the Antitrust Commission will intervene in the **1.86**

[81] *Cement* (n 53).
[82] *Ventachap* (n 79).

provision of cable TV licenses should there be an objection to the setting up of a new player in a specific region. The focus that the current administration is placing on media and telecommunications will most certainly trigger a more extensive intervention on the part of the Antitrust Commission than ever before.

B. Antitrust system

(i) Name of agency/agencies

1.87 The Antitrust Law created the National Tribunal for the Defense of Competition within the scope of the Ministry of Economy, which would be the ultimate antitrust regulator in Argentina. This Antitrust Tribunal would be composed of seven members, including the minimum of two attorneys and two accounting professionals.

1.88 However, the Antitrust Tribunal has not yet been created. After several diverging cases, the Argentine Supreme Court ultimately set out a double-tier regulatory structure,[83] consisting of enforcement agencies that would decide antitrust cases until the Antitrust Tribunal has been formed. This double-tier regulatory structure follows the provisions of the prior Antitrust Law no. 22,262, passed on August 1, 1980.

1.89 Under this new interpretation, the Antitrust Commission, i.e. the regulator created by former antitrust regulations, performs a technical review of mergers and investigations, and issues a recommendation to the Secretary of Domestic Trade of the Ministry of Economy, which is the body that ultimately decides antitrust cases. For the purposes of this chapter, this double-tier regulator structure has been referred to as the "Antitrust Commission."

(ii) Staff size and budget

1.90 According to the 2012 annual budget approved for the Antitrust Commission, the latter has a staff of approximately 158 employees and a budget of ARS 23,000,000.

(iii) Recent enforcement actions and trends

1.91 The current Antitrust Commission has been very active over the past years trying to re-ignite its investigations, after almost a decade of focusing on merger control decisions. This upsurge in investigations has been targeting certain sensitive consumer markets so as to ensure price control over those industries, over specific conducts.

1.92 A major emphasis has been placed on the oil industry in which there have been several attempts in order to restrain possible increases in prices. Furthermore, the software industry and, more specifically, the search engine industry has been a major concern for the Antitrust Commission, a fact evidenced by several investigations that have been carried out in this area. The Commission also envisages focus on telecommunications and media in the upcoming years.

1.93 It has been noted over the past years that the analysis timeframe for anticompetitive investigations has been greatly increased, and that the vast majority of cases, even non-material ones, are not concluded during the initial instruction stage. Due to the lengthy investigation timeframe currently in place, the Antitrust Commission has resorted to issuing preliminary injunctions pursuant to s. 35 of the Antitrust Law. However, the preliminary injunctions issued have faced court challenge, and in some cases, it was decided that the Secretary of Domestic Trade would have the power of issuing them, while the Antitrust Commission would not be able to do so on its own.

[83] *Recreativos Franco*, Supreme Court, Case no. S.C., R.1172, L. XII (June 5, 2007) and *Credit Suisse First Boston*, Supreme Court, Case no. S.C.C. 1216, L. XLI (June 5, 2007).

The renewed interest in investigations would also explain the interest of the Antitrust Commission in its leniency program proposal, which is currently being analyzed by Congress. **1.94**

A recent development in the performance of the Antitrust Commission can be found in a pending case, *Secretaría de Transporte v. YPF*[84] in which the regulator stated that "... the competition policy in Argentina must keep in line with the economic policy of the last years." The statement was included in a resolution in which the regulator also described the achievements of the current political administration, implying a closer alignment of the regulator with the political administration. This situation has been the result of the non-implementation of the Antitrust Tribunal that was envisaged by the Antitrust Law back in 1999. **1.95**

C. Private litigation

Regarding private claims, s. 51 of the Antitrust Law states that individuals or companies affected by the conduct prohibited under the provisions of the Antitrust Law may invoke the right to compensation for the damages suffered before a competent court. **1.96**

As of today, there has only been one major case entailing private antitrust litigation, namely the *Auto Gas* case,[85] in which the plaintiff was awarded ARS 13,094,457 of compensation for the damages suffered as a result of an abuse of the dominant position. **1.97**

In *Auto Gas*, the court merely referred to the analysis carried out by the Antitrust Commission and established a connection between the conduct that the Commission found illegal and the damages suffered by the plaintiffs. However, the fact that the Civil Code already contains provisions allowing for private damages actions leaves the door open for courts to examine their own cases, namely to investigate anticompetitive acts in order to determine the conduct and then determine the appropriate reparation for damages. **1.98**

While there has been only one case to date providing damages, there are several cases currently pending. However, there have not been any other judgments in that regard due to lengthy court review times in Argentina. **1.99**

D. Follow-on litigation

In the *Auto Gas* case,[86] the most important antitrust damages award in Argentina, the court considered that the claimed abuse of dominant position had already been identified by the Antitrust Commission. As a result, the court would only review whether there was a factual connection between the identified conduct and the damages claimed by the plaintiff. To date, there have been no court cases determining whether the court could veer away from the Antitrust Commission's analysis in the matter. **1.100**

E. Arbitration and alternative dispute resolution

There is currently no arbitration nor alternative dispute resolution (ADR) regarding antitrust matters in Argentina. **1.101**

F. Remedies

(i) Civil liability

In addition to the s. 51 provision regarding private claims, s. 1109 of the Civil Code sets out that in order to seek reparations, the following conditions must be met: (i) there must be an **1.102**

[84] *Secretaría de Transporte v. YPF and others*, Docket No. S01:0013373/2012 (2012).
[85] *Auto Gas*, National Commercial Court No. 14, Clerk's Office No. 27, Judgment of September 16, 2009.
[86] *Auto Gas* (n 85).

illicit act; (ii) there has to be damage; (iii) there has to be a link between the former and the latter; and (iv) the act must have been performed either by negligence or by means of deceit.

(ii) Criminal liability

1.103 Pursuant to s. 300 of the Argentine Penal Code, any person that may generate a rise or a decrease in the price of a merchandise, public offer funds, or securities by means of false news, fake negotiations, or by an agreement among the main holders of the good, in order to sell or to refrain from selling it at a specific price, will be sanctioned with imprisonment, which may range from six months to two years. As can be seen, not all types of conduct are included, but mainly those related to price fixing. These types of conduct would be investigated by criminal prosecutors, but there have been no relevant cases to date.

1.104 The proposed leniency bill does not cover immunity from s. 300 of the Argentine Penal Code.

G. Leniency and immunity

1.105 On December 15, 2010 the Commission finalized a draft bill to include a Leniency Program in the Antitrust Law that makes available two different scenarios to infringing parties, namely an exemption scenario and a reduction scenario, both based on a "race-to-the-door" structure.

1.106 An infinging party must comply with the following requirements in order to be exempt from the sanctions under the Antitrust Law: (i) it must be the first party, among the participants in the conduct, which provides the Commission with information and evidence, regardless of whether the Commission has launched an investigation or not, but has not yet been able to gather sufficient evidence; (ii) it must immediately cease engaging in the infringing conduct, unless the Commission deems otherwise in order to preserve the investigation; (iii) it must collaborate until the end of the investigation; (iv) it must not destroy, forge, or conceal evidence of the anticompetitive conduct, nor make public the fact that it has filed for a Leniency Program, unless such communication is addressed to another antitrust regulator; and (v) it must not be the leader of the anticompetitive conduct.

1.107 Parties that are not the first to require the enforcement of the Leniency Program could request that the sanctions be reduced, if they are able to meet requirements (ii)–(v) and provide the Commission with information useful in the investigation. The bill sets out that sanctions can be reduced by 20 percent, 30 percent, or 50 percent. The reduction ratios are to be determined by the Commission by taking into account the chronological order of the filing, as well as the number of participants involved in the conduct.

1.108 The bill also includes a "leniency plus" provision, by means of which parties which are unable to request an exemption regarding anticompetitive conduct but which could provide information on a second instance of anticompetitive conduct can obtain an exemption on the latter, and a 30 percent reduction on the former.

1.109 Additionally, the bill specifically sets out that there can be no joint enforcement of the Leniency Program, the sole exception being if a company and its directors or other members of its staff request the enforcement of the program.

H. Document creation and retention

1.110 The Antitrust Law does not have any specific rules regarding document creation and retention. However, the Argentine Commercial Code sets out an obligation for the retention of commercial documentation for ten years.

2

AUSTRALIA

Gina Cass-Gottlieb, Elizabeth Avery, Emma Ringland, and Lena Vanmali
Gilbert+Tobin

Introduction

Competition law in Australia is enforced pursuant to the Competition and Consumer Act 2010 (Cth) (CCA). The CCA has the object of enhancing the welfare of Australians through the promotion of competition and fair trading and provision for consumer protection. The Australian Competition and Consumer Commission (ACCC) is responsible for the enforcement of the CCA. **2.01**

The CCA applies to all natural persons, corporations, and, to the extent that it carries on business, the Government. It has extraterritorial application and extends to conduct by corporations and/or individuals outside Australia with the requisite connection. **2.02**

The CCA regulates a wide range of conduct including the restrictive trade practices provisions in Part IV of the CCA, summarized below: **2.03**

- Division 1 of Part IV prohibits cartel conduct (defined in s. 44ZZD), which is subject to both civil and criminal prosecution;
- s. 45 prohibits making or entering into contracts, arrangements or understandings containing a provision with the purpose, effect or likely effect of substantially lessening competition;
- s. 46 provides that a corporation with a substantial degree of market power must not take advantage of that power in that or any other market for a prohibited purpose;
- s. 47 prohibits exclusive dealing if the purpose, or likely effect, of such conduct is to substantially lessen competition in any relevant market (and also prohibits third line forcing);
- s. 48 prohibits minimum resale price maintenance; and
- s. 50 prohibits any acquisition of shares or assets that has the effect, or likely effect, of substantially lessening competition.

2.04 The CCA also contains provisions relating to infrastructure access, consumer protection (including, for example, unconscionable conduct, misleading and deceptive conduct, and consumer warranties), and certain sector-specific regulation, most notably in relation to telecommunications.

2.05 Australia primarily has a judicial enforcement model in relation to competition law. That is, except in limited circumstances relating to consumer protection, penalties may only be imposed by the court (including where sought by the ACCC in the context of cartel proceedings). Proceedings may be commenced not only by the ACCC pursuant to its responsibility to prosecute conduct that contravenes the CCA, but also by private parties. Class actions are becoming increasingly common, though only single damages are available. Competition policy and enforcement is a key aspect of the Australian Government's economic policy. After attempts to introduce competition law in Australia in the early twentieth century were rejected on constitutional grounds, competition law first came into effect in Australia in 1971. In 1974, the Trade Practices Act 1974 (Cth) was introduced. Subject to some amendments, particularly in the late 1980s and early 1990s as part of the Government's microeconomic reform agenda, the provisions of the 1974 statute largely remain in force as the CCA with some significant additions, including the Australian Consumer Law and other sections such as criminal penalties for cartel conduct.

2.06 The ACCC Chairman has described the ACCC's role as "making markets work for consumers now and in the future," through a combination of education, voluntary and administrative measures and enforcement action to:

- maintain and promote competition and fix market failure—by preventing anticompetitive mergers, stopping cartels, and intervening when it identifies any misuse of market power;
- protect the interests and safety of consumers and support a fair marketplace—addressing misleading behavior, removing unsafe goods, and tackling unconscionable dealings; and
- drive efficient infrastructure—through industry specific regulation and access regimes.[1]

2.07 The ACCC Chairman recently indicated that the ACCC's strategic focus for competition law enforcement is on important theories of harm that produce "the most beneficial outcomes for competition and consumers." The three priority areas for enforcement activities identified by the ACCC are the online economy, cartels, and misuse of market power and other anticompetitive conduct, particularly in concentrated markets.[2]

---

[1] ACCC, "Australian Competition and Consumer Commission and Australian Energy Regulator Annual Report 2012–13," p.16. <http://www.accc.gov.au/publications/accc-aer-annual-report/accc-aer-annual-report-2012-13>.

[2] See ACCC (n 1) p. 34.

Recent prosecutions by the ACCC for which decisions are still pending (as at January 2014) include: **2.08**

- proceedings commenced in December 2013 against Colgate-Palmolive, Cussons and Unilever alleging cartel and other anti-competitive arrangements in relation to laundry detergent products;
- proceedings commenced in February 2013 against Visa Inc. and a number of related Visa entities alleging that it misused its market power and engaged in exclusive dealing in relation to the supply of dynamic currency conversion services;
- proceedings commenced in August 2012 against Renegade Gas Pty Ltd. and Speed-E-Gas (NSW) Pty Ltd. alleging an anti competitive cartel arrangement which included an agreement not to supply LPG cylinders for forklifts to each other's customers; and
- proceedings commenced in December 2012 against Yazaki Corporation, a Japanese company, and its Australia subsidiary, Australian Arrow Pty Ltd. alleging that it engaged in cartel conduct, market sharing and price fixing in relation to the supply of wire harnesses to Toyota.

This chapter provides a high-level overview of the operation of the CCA in relation to unilateral conduct (Section I) and interactions with competitors (Section II). Further details about the operation of the ACCC and competition law in Australia more generally are set out in Section III. **2.09**

I. Acting alone

A. The general prohibition against misuse of market power

The general prohibition in s. 46(1) of the CCA provides that a corporation with a substantial degree of market power in a market must not take advantage of that power in that or any other market for one of the following prohibited purposes (Prohibited Purposes): **2.10**

- Eliminating or substantially damaging a competitor;
- Preventing the entry of a person into that or any other market; or
- Deterring or preventing a person from engaging in competitive conduct in that or any other market.

In considering whether a corporation has contravened s. 46(1), s. 46(4A) provides that a court may consider any conduct by the corporation consisting of supplying goods or services for a sustained period at a price less than the relevant cost to the corporation of supplying such goods or services, and the reasons for that conduct. However, a court is not limited to considering only this factor. **2.11**

In considering whether a corporation has a *substantial degree of power* in a market, judicial consideration of the presence of "market power" has focused on an absence of constraint; that is, the ability to behave in a certain way persistently, free from the constraints of competition.[3] This is reflected in the terms of s. 46(3), which provides that, in determining the degree of power that a corporation has in a market, the court shall have regard to the extent to which that corporation's conduct is constrained by the conduct of competitors and persons from or to whom that corporation acquires or supplies goods or services. **2.12**

[3] See in particular the High Court decisions: *Melway Publishing Pty Ltd. v. Robert Hicks* (2001) 205 CLR 1; *Queensland Wire Industries Pty Ltd. v. BHP* (1989) 167 CLR 177, and *Boral Besser Masonry v. ACCC* (2003) 215 CLR 374.

2.13 In addition, s. 46(3C) provides that this may be the case even though the corporation does not substantially control the market, or does not have absolute freedom from constraint by the conduct of competitors (or potential competitors), suppliers or customers. Section 46(3D) clarifies that there can be more than one corporation with a substantial degree of power in a market.

2.14 In considering whether a corporation has *taken advantage* of its substantial degree of power, a court may take into account the non-exhaustive list of factors set out in s. 46(6A). These factors emphasize the requirement for a connection between a corporation's conduct and its substantial degree of market power:

- whether the conduct was materially facilitated by the corporation's substantial market power;
- whether the corporation engaged in the conduct in reliance on its substantial market power;
- whether it is likely that the corporation would have engaged in the conduct if it did not have substantial market power; and
- whether the conduct is otherwise related to the corporation's substantial market power.

2.15 The ACCC has observed that Australia is characterized by a large number of concentrated markets, often with two or three participants only. It is particularly focused on enforcement of competition law, including misuse of market power provisions, in those sectors where there are only two or three participants. The ACCC has highlighted current priorities involving unilateral conduct including:

- competition and consumer issues arising in highly concentrated sectors, and in particular, the supermarket and fuel sectors;
- cartel conduct, anti competitive agreements and misuse of market power, which the ACCC has identified as a high priority;
- issues relating to the treatment of suppliers by the major supermarket chains which include competition issues as well as allegations of unconscionable conduct, business-to-business; and
- online competition issues, including conduct which may impede competition between online traders or limit the ability of small businesses to compete online.[4]

B. Predatory pricing

2.16 In Australia, predatory pricing may be analyzed under:

- the general misuse of market power prohibition under s. 46(1) of the CCA; and/or
- the specific prohibition against below cost pricing in certain circumstances under s. 46(1AA) of the CCA.

2.17 The legislation does not define the relevant measure of costs, and case law has not clearly determined the issue. Courts consider the relevant cost on a case-by-case basis, and concepts such as "marginal," "average variable," and "avoidable costs" have been used.[5] More recently, emphasis has been placed on the particular facts of the case and whether there is an economic rationale for providing goods or services at a price less than the corporation's relevant cost other than eliminating a competitor.[6]

[4] See ACCC (n 1) pp. 34–39.

[5] For example, in *Boral Besser Masonry Ltd. v. Australian Competition and Consumer Commission* (2003) 195 ALR 609, the judge at first instance used "avoidable cost" as the relevant measure, but on appeal, the High Court of Australia cautioned against using this measure because there might be an economic rationale for selling below a corporation's avoidable cost.

[6] See e.g. *Australian Competition and Consumer Commission v. Eurong Beach Resort Ltd.* (2006) ATPR 42-098.

Section 46 was amended specifically to provide that there is no requirement to show recoupment is likely in establishing a breach under s. 46(1), where it is established that "a corporation supplies goods or services for a sustained period at a price that is less than the relevant cost to the corporation of supplying the goods or services." **2.18**

The prohibited purpose need not be the only purpose for engaging in the conduct, but it must be a substantial purpose (see s. 4F of the CCA). **2.19**

Section 46(1AA) of the CCA was specifically introduced to address a perceived inadequacy of the law in preventing below-cost pricing in light of the High Court's decision in *Boral Besser Masonry*.[7] The provision states that: "a corporation with a substantial share of a market must not supply, or offer to supply, goods or services for a sustained period at a price less than the relevant cost to the corporation," for any of the Prohibited Purposes referred to above in para. 2.10. **2.20**

There is no guidance in the legislative materials as to what constitutes a "substantial share," a "sustained period," or "the relevant cost to the corporation." To date, there have been no cases to provide any guidance. **2.21**

C. Exploitative offenses

In Australia, conduct such as monopoly leveraging, excessive/exploitative pricing, exploitative terms of acquisition or supply, or price squeezes may be a breach of s. 46 if and only if the elements of s. 46 are made out (that is, if a corporation with substantial market power engages in such conduct by taking advantage of that market power for one of the Prohibited Purposes set out in Section I.A). Importantly, the Prohibited Purposes are referrable to conduct directed at competitors rather than customers or suppliers, so a corporation may only be liable under s. 46 for misuse of market power if it also competes with the customer or supplier subject to the "exploitative conduct." **2.22**

In contrast, in relation to the telecommunications industry, the relevant misuse of market power test is effects-based, rather than purpose-based. Specifically, s. 151AJ (in Part XIB of the CCA) provides that a carrier or a carriage service provider engages in anti competitive conduct if it has a substantial degree of power in a telecommunications market, and takes advantage of that power in that or any other market with the effect of substantially lessening competition in that or any other telecommunications market. **2.23**

In addition, unconscionable conduct in relation to the supply or acquisition of goods or services may be addressed under ss. 20 to 22A of the Australian Consumer Law, contained in Schedule 2 of the CCA. Unconscionable conduct is defined in terms of the general law from time to time and includes a range of factors (such as the relativity of the bargaining positions of the parties, whether undue influence or pressure was exerted, and whether the conduct was reasonably necessary to protect legitimate interests). **2.24**

As noted above, the ACCC's enforcement priorities include treatment of suppliers and the competitive effects of fuel discounts based on grocery purchases from a related entity, both of which relate to allegations relating to exploitative conduct. **2.25**

D. Monopsony

An acquirer who exercises monopsony power may also contravene s. 46 if the elements of s. 46(1) are established (i.e. if the acquirer has a substantial degree of power in a market **2.26**

[7] *Boral Besser Masonry* (n 5).

and takes advantage of that power to engage in conduct with one of the three Prohibited Purposes): see further s. 46(4)(c) of the CCA.

2.27 For example, in *Australian Competition and Consumer Commission v. Australian Safeway Stores Pty Ltd.*,[8] the majority (Heerey and Sackville JJ) held that Safeway, the largest supermarket chain and the largest single retailer of bread in the state of Victoria, was found to have had a substantial degree of power in the wholesale market for bread, and to have taken advantage of it for a Proscribed Purpose. Safeway was held to have a market share of around 16 percent (if the wholesale market included bread supplied by independent bakers and in-store bakeries) or closer to 20 percent (if the wholesale market did not include in-store bakeries).

2.28 Emmett J, though dissenting on the question of whether Safeway had a substantial degree of power in the relevant market, observed that:

- monopsony power could be defined as the ability of a purchaser to obtain a market price lower than would otherwise be obtained in a competitive market, or to obtain more favorable terms of trade in the market than would otherwise be obtained in a competitive market;[9]
- the existence of barriers to entry was a prerequisite to the establishment of monopsony or near monopsony;[10] and
- exclusive dealing or refusing to deal might be a manifestation of monopsony power—that is, the ability to engage in such conduct persistently, without a loss of supply, might indicate market power if it could be shown that such conduct would have a different consequence if engaged in a "competitive market."[11]

E. Price discrimination

2.29 Although the price discrimination offense was repealed in 1995, practices that amount to price discrimination may still be in breach of the other provisions of the CCA in certain circumstances.

2.30 For example, if a supplier with a substantial degree of market power discriminates between customers by charging higher prices to a customer who is also one of its downstream competitors for the purpose of preventing that customer from competing in the downstream market (i.e. a price squeeze),[12] the conduct may constitute a misuse of market power in breach of s. 46 of the CCA. However, if the discrimination is for a legitimate purpose, for example cost differences between customers or based on volume discount incentives, then price discrimination would not be unlawful under s. 46 of the CCA.

2.31 In addition, if an agreement to charge discriminatory prices amounts to a contract, arrangement or understanding with the purpose or likely effect of substantially lessening competition, it could be in breach of s. 45 of the CCA. Also, if trading terms are discriminatory, this may be evidence of exclusive dealing under s. 47 of the CCA (see Section I.G).

---

8 *ACCC v. Australian Safeway Stores Pty Ltd.* [2003] FCAFC 149.

9 *Australian Safeway Stores* (n 8) para. 455 per Emmett J.

10 *Australian Safeway Stores* (n 8) para. 458 per Emmett J.

11 *Australian Safeway Stores* (n 8) para. 461 per Emmett J.

12 In the context of the telecommunications industry (referred to previously in Section I.C), the misuse of market power test is effects-based rather than purpose-based. In March 2004, the ACCC issued a "Part A Competition Notice" to Telstra in relation to an alleged price squeeze on the basis of Telstra's broadband pricing to its wholesale customers (who were Telstra's competitors at the retail level) compared to the broadband pricing offered by Telstra to its retail customers. This Competition Notice was subsequently revoked by the ACCC in February 2005.

There have not been any recent cases involving straightforward price discrimination conduct; however, price discrimination has been a side-effect of a variety of other conduct caught under s. 46 of the CCA. For example: **2.32**

- through a large buyer with substantial buying power forcing a supplier to give it more favorable terms with regard to price than charged to the buyer's competitors (as was the case in *ACCC v. Safeway Stores*[13]);
- through discriminatory price squeezes employed by a vertically integrated firm charging a higher input price to downstream rivals than it charges itself (as was the case in *Pont Data Australia Pty Ltd. v. ASX Operations Pty Ltd.*[14]); and
- through fidelity discounts granted by a corporation with substantial market power in return for securing all or an increased proportion of the business of particular customers (as was the case in *Cool & Sons Pty Ltd. v. O'Brien Glass Industries Limited*[15]).

F. Dictating or influencing resale prices

(i) Resale price maintenance

Minimum resale price maintenance (RPM) is per se prohibited in Australia under s. 48 of the CCA. (In contrast, *maximum* resale price maintenance is not prohibited in Australia.) **2.33**

Section 96 of the CCA explains the types of practices that constitute resale price maintenance, and s. 96A extends the practices described in s. 96 (relating to goods) to also apply to services. Specifically, s. 96(3) provides that a supplier engages in resale price maintenance if it: **2.34**

- makes it known that it will not supply goods/services unless the purchaser agrees not to sell those goods below a price specified by the supplier (i.e. the minimum price);
- induces or attempts to induce the purchaser not to sell goods/services supplied directly or indirectly by the supplier below a minimum price;
- enters or offers to enter into an agreement containing the term that the purchaser will not sell the goods/services at a price below the minimum price;
- withholds the supply of goods/services because the purchaser or a third person has sold, or has not agreed not to sell, below a minimum price ("withholding supply" is further described in s. 98); or
- uses a statement of a price that is likely to be understood by the purchaser as a minimum price (s. 99 provides further clarity about such statements).

In addition, s. 96(7) clarifies that a reference to selling goods below a minimum price includes a reference to advertising, displaying, or offering goods below a minimum price. **2.35**

However, pursuant to s. 97 of the CCA, it is not a contravention of the prohibition on resale price maintenance for a supplier to *recommend* a retail price, provided that this does not oblige or induce the setting of a retail price. **2.36**

A price is deemed to be specified if the supplier makes it known that the price below which goods/services are not to be sold is a price specified by another person, including in respect of those or similar goods, or if a formula is specified and a price may be determined based on that formula (see s. 96(4) of the CCA). In addition, the fact that a price is stated to be within a range, or that an element of approximation is introduced, does not mean that the price is not a specified price (see *Trade Practices Commission v. Bata Shoe Co. of Australia Pty Ltd.*[16]). **2.37**

---

13 *ACCC v. Safeway Stores* (2003) 129 FCR 339.
14 *Pont Data Australia Pty Ltd. v. ASX Operations Pty Ltd.* (1990) FCA 30.
15 *Cool & Sons Pty Ltd. v. O'Brien Glass Industries Limited* (1981) FCA 95.
16 *Trade Practices Commission v. Bata Shoe Co. of Australia Pty Ltd.* (1980) 44 FLR 149.

(ii) Minimum advertised price programs

2.38 The prohibition on maintaining a minimum advertised price (MAP) at which a purchaser resells the goods/services also extends to maintaining a minimum price at which a purchaser advertises, displays, or offers the goods/services for resale: see s. 96(7).

2.39 Accordingly, if a supplier requires a purchaser (e.g. a distributor or a reseller of its products) not to advertise products purchased from it below a specified price, including through the imposition of a minimum advertised price program or policy, this will contravene the prohibition on resale price maintenance.[17]

G. Tying arrangements

2.40 Tying or bundling arrangements may be unlawful in certain circumstances, under the exclusive dealing prohibitions of s. 47 of the CCA. Alternatively, where a corporation has substantial market power, tying or bundling may also be analyzed as a potential misuse of market power under s. 46, as described above in para. 2.10.

2.41 Under s. 47, requiring a customer not to buy from a competitor, or only to a limited extent, as a condition of supply, is unlawful if the purpose, or likely effect, of any such requirement is to substantially lessen competition in any relevant market. Similarly, refusing to supply to a customer unless the customer agrees not to acquire from a competitor is unlawful if for the purpose or likely effect of substantially lessening competition (see ss. 47(2)(d) and 47(3)(d) of the CCA).

2.42 In addition, "third line forcing," namely, tying of a sale of one product or service on condition that the customer acquires a second product or service from a third party is per se unlawful under s. 47 of the CCA (see ss. 47(6), (7), (8)(c), and (9)(d) of the CCA). The sale of the first product must be conditional on the purchaser acquiring another product from a second, specifically identifiable person, who need not be a single person, but must be specifiable and not unknowable (for example, as part of a panel).[18] However, immunity is available to allow a corporation to engage in third line forcing if the ACCC is notified of this conduct in advance pursuant to s. 93 of the CCA. The ACCC will allow the notification to stand if it considers that the likely public benefit outweighs any likely detriment of the third line force.

2.43 "Bundling" arrangements also may be considered as a subcategory of "tying" arrangements, since they constitute the sale of several goods or services as a single package, typically at a discount compared to the individual price of each of the goods or services within the package.[19]

H. Exclusive dealing

2.44 Section 47 of the CCA regulates exclusive dealing among corporations, i.e. vertical arrangements between corporations at different levels in the supply chain.

2.45 Exclusive dealing is generally prohibited only if the exclusive dealing has the purpose, or is likely to have the effect, of substantially lessening competition. See s. 47(10) of the CCA (note however that third line forcing, described in Section I.F above, is prohibited regardless of the purpose or effect on competition). One of the most significant, relatively recent cases considering exclusive dealing is *ACCC v. Australian Safeway Stores Pty Ltd*,[20] which concerned

[17] See e.g. *Trade Practices Commission v. Simpson Pope Ltd.* (1980) ATPR 40-169.

[18] See *ACCC v. Link Solutions Pty Limited (No 2)* [2010] FCA 919, para. 80; *ACCC v. Black & White Cabs Pty Ltd.* [2010] FCA 1399.

[19] See further Section I.J, and in particular *ACCC v. Baxter Healthcare Pty Ltd.* [2008] FCAFC 141 which is the most recent, significant case brought on this area of law.

[20] *Australian Safeway Stores* (n 8).

the imposition or attempted imposition of a condition on individual wholesale bread manufacturers preventing them from supplying cheap wholesale bread to certain independent retailers who were undercutting Safeway's retail prices. The court found that the conduct did not amount to exclusive dealing on the basis that the particular prohibition alleged to be contravened did not apply to conditions on the acquisition of goods that relate to the price of goods.[21]

On February 4, 2013, the ACCC commenced proceedings against Visa and its related entities alleging misuse of market power and exclusive dealing in relation to their distribution agreements for the supply of dynamic currency conversion (DCC) services to Australian banks and retailers. The ACCC is alleging that Visa engaged in exclusive dealing by supplying access to its payment network to Australian banks and, in turn, retailers, on condition that they did not acquire DCC services from other DCC suppliers. **2.46**

I. Refusal to deal

A corporation's refusal to deal with, or supply, another corporation may breach the CCA if it constitutes: **2.47**

- an exclusionary provision/collective boycott, i.e. an agreement among competitors with the purpose of preventing, restricting, or limiting the supply to, or acquisition from, particular persons or classes of persons (s. 4D/s. 45 of the CCA);
- an agreement with the purpose, effect, or likely effect of substantially lessening competition (s. 45 of the CCA);
- taking advantage of market power for a prohibited purpose (s. 46 of the CCA);
- third line forcing or exclusive dealing, subject to the effects test (s. 47 of the CCA, see Setion I.G above); or
- resale price maintenance (s. 48 of the CCA, see Section I.E).

In relation to s. 46, a refusal to supply is generally difficult to establish given the difficulty of establishing that a corporation's conduct constituted a "taking advantage of" substantial market power. Even where a corporation has substantial market power, Australian courts have found that a refusal to deal may be justified by a legitimate business rationale of a supplier; merely refusing to deal with a customer is not unlawful unless it is for a Prohibited Purpose.[22] **2.48**

However, if a corporation has substantial market power and takes advantage of that market power for a Prohibited Purpose by refusing to deal with a third party to prevent that party from competing with it, then the refusal to deal may be unlawful under s. 46(1) of the CCA. For example, in *NT Power Generation v. Power & Water Authority* (2004),[23] the High Court of Australia held that Power and Water Authority (PAWA), a vertically integrated statutory authority that owned electricity transmission and distribution infrastructure, breached s. 46(1) of the CCA by refusing to supply wholesale electricity to NT Power, which would enable NT Power to sell to customers, in competition with PAWA. The court held that in the transmission and distribution markets for electricity, PAWA had market power arising from its ownership of infrastructure (and this was a barrier to entry because it was difficult to duplicate), and by not granting access to the infrastructure, PAWA took advantage of this market power for the purpose of injuring NT Power and excluding NT Power from the market. **2.49**

[21] See further Section I.C.

[22] See e.g. *Melway Publishing Pty Ltd. v. Robert Hicks Pty Ltd.* (2001) 205 CLR 1 (termination of a distributor was not unlawful where the termination was not facilitated by the existence of the market power).

[23] *NT Power Generation v. Power & Water Authority* (2004) 219 CLR 90.

2.50 The most recent unilateral refusal to deal case was brought by the ACCC against Cabcharge in June 2009. The ACCC obtained a penalty of AUD 11 million against Cabcharge which admitted engaging in conduct amounting to a refusal to allow competing suppliers of electronic payment processing services for taxis to process Cabcharge-branded non-cash payment products in breach of s. 46 of the CCA.[24]

J. Essential facilities

2.51 If a refusal to grant access to a facility that was essential to compete were found to be a misuse of market power in breach of s. 46(1) of the CCA, then the court would have power to order access. The facts of the *NT Power* case referred to in Section I.H provide an example of a case where the court considered access to PAWA's infrastructure to be essential to enable NT Power to compete (although in that case, only damages were sought).

2.52 Other than the fairly limited possibility of obtaining access to an essential facility by establishing a breach of s. 46, the principles underlying the essential facilities doctrine have been legislatively enshrined in Australia in Part IIIA of the CCA.[25] Part IIIA enables third parties to obtain access to infrastructure owned by third parties, where the service provided by the infrastructure is "declared" by the Government Minister, subject to the criteria in s. 44H(4) being met, among other requirements. If the service is declared, then access is subject to a framework of negotiation of terms between the parties (and, in the event negotiations fail, binding arbitration by the ACCC).

2.53 The criteria of s. 44H(4) are as follows:

- criterion (a)–that access (or increased access) to the service would promote a material increase in competition in at least one market (whether or not in Australia), other than the market for the service;
- criterion (b)–that it would be uneconomical for anyone to develop another facility to provide the service;
- criterion (c)–that the facility is of national significance, having regard to:
  1. the size of the facility; or
  2. the importance of the facility to constitutional trade or commerce; or
  3. the importance of the facility to the national economy;
- criterion (e)–that access to the service is not already, generally, the subject of a regime in relation to which an effective access regime is in force; and
- criterion (f)–that access (or increased access) to the service would not be contrary to the public interest.

2.54 The access criteria outlined above were considered recently by the High Court of Australia in *The Pilbara Infrastructure Pty Ltd. v. Australian Competition Tribunal*,[26] in relation to attempts by an iron ore miner (Fortescue Metals Group) to seek access to dedicated iron ore railways owned by BHP Billiton and Rio Tinto in the Pilbara region of Western Australia to transport iron ore produced by its mines, rather than build its own railway lines in the same general location.

2.55 The court held that "Criterion (b)," being the test of whether or not it is "uneconomic" for anyone to develop an alternative facility, should be determined based on whether it is "economically feasible." This required a consideration of whether it was "feasible or practicable

[24] *ACCC v. Cabcharge* [2010] FCA 1261.

[25] Note that in relation to telecommunications, there is a specific access regime under Part XIC of the CCA.

[26] *The Pilbara Infrastructure Pty Ltd. v. Australian Competition Tribunal* [2012] HCA 36 (September 14, 2012).

taking into account the principles of economics," also known as the "private profitability test" (namely, whether there was sufficient prospect of a sufficient return on funds employed to warrant the investment).[27] The court considered that to "develop a duplicate facility where an existing facility can already meet reasonably foreseeable demand, and thereby to increase excess capacity, is neither feasible nor practicable when the principles of economics are taken into account."[28]

The court further held that in determining "Criterion (f)," being whether or not granting access to a third party would be contrary to the public interest, any review should be reluctant to interfere with any finding made by the Minister, since the regulation of significant economic infrastructure is not simply an economic or legal issue, but gives rise to significant political and national interest issues.[29] **2.56**

K. Bundling (including loyalty and market share discounts)

Bundling, including loyalty discounts and market share discounts, may breach the CCA if such conduct amounts to: **2.57**

- a misuse of market power (i.e. a breach of s. 46 of the CCA); or
- exclusive dealing with the purpose or effect, or likely effect, of substantially lessening competition (i.e. a breach of s. 47 of the CCA). Such conduct may amount to a breach of the exclusive dealing provisions if they have the purpose, effect, or likely effect of substantially lessening competition by foreclosing competitors.

In *ACCC v. Baxter*,[30] the Full Federal Court found that Baxter, a manufacturer and supplier of sterile fluids and peritoneal dialysis (PD) fluids, had offered a bundled package such that the "bundled" price of the sterile fluids and peritoneal dialysis fluids was significantly lower than the item-by-item of these products. **2.58**

The court held that Baxter had sought to prevent its competitors from supplying PD fluids to state and territory purchasing authorities (SPAs) as part of their tender process—that is, an improper *purpose*. In addition, since SPAs were the largest purchasers of PD fluids and only acquired these products through tenders, the court found that this would have a significant *effect* on the competition in the market. **2.59**

The court also found that Baxter had a substantial degree of power in the Australia-wide sterile fluids market and had taken advantage of this market power for the purpose of deterring or preventing its competitors (Fresenius and Gambro) from engaging in competitive conduct in the PD fluids market. In setting the "bundled" price of the sterile fluids and peritoneal dialysis fluids significantly lower than the item-by-item prices of these products to secure as much of the supply of sterile and PD fluids as it could, Baxter had the purpose of shutting out its competitors from being able to put forward bids which could not be accepted by customers without a significant cost penalty. **2.60**

Because under s. 46 of the CCA, a taking advantage of market power may be found in a market different from the market in which the anticompetitive purpose is alleged (i.e. monopoly leveraging), bundling cases may be more prevalent under Australian competition law than in some other markets where monopoly leveraging claims are not viable. **2.61**

[27] *Pilbara Infrastructure* (n 26) paras. 72–73.
[28] *Pilbara Infrastructure* (n 26) paras.179.
[29] *Pilbara Infrastructure* (n 26) paras. 108–114.
[30] *ACCC v. Baxter* (n 19).

L. Standard-setting groups (disclosure requirements, licensing arrangements, and licensing pools)

2.62 Although there have been no decided cases in Australia, if a corporation owns a patent that was adopted as a standard, and it imposed prohibitive license terms to block new entrants in the downstream market in respect of devices that require the patented technology, or by demanding royalty rates in excess of those it would normally be able to command, then such a refusal to grant access could be considered a misuse of market power in breach of s. 46(1) of the CCA, and the court could grant relief on terms requiring a compulsory license.[31]

2.63 For example, in December 1995, the ACCC commenced proceedings against the Bureau of Meteorology (BOM) alleging that it had breached s. 46 of the predecessor to the CCA (the Trade Practices Act 1974) by refusing to supply basic meteorological information to a competitor for the purpose of deterring the entry of that competitor into the market for enhanced meteorological services. The ACCC further alleged that BOM also provided specialized meteorological services on a non-commercial basis for the purpose of deterring competitive conduct.[32] In May 1997, the ACCC and BOM settled the court proceedings. One of the key elements of the settlement was a model license agreement which set out conditions applicable to the access and use of information held by BOM, provided dispute resolution procedures (including the option of mediation by an independent third party), and specified termination grounds and rights of parties.[33]

M. Customer termination

2.64 Mere unilateral termination of a customer is not a breach of the CCA. However, in certain limited circumstances, a unilateral customer termination may be a contravention, as follows:

- If the customer is also a competitor or potential competitor, the termination potentially may be a breach of s. 46(1) (misuse of market power), if the elements of that offense were established (see Section I.H above).
- If the termination resulted from the customer's refusal not to buy goods or services from the supplier's competitor, then the termination could breach the exclusive dealing prohibitions under s. 47, if the purpose, effect, or likely effect of the supplier's exclusive dealing was to substantially lessen competition (see Section I.G above).
- If a distributor/wholesale customer was terminated for reselling goods or services supplied below a specified price in breach of the prohibition on resale price maintenance (see Section I.E above).

2.65 A customer termination could also constitute a breach of the unconscionable conduct provisions under the Australian Consumer Law, if the relevant elements were satisfied (see Section I.B above). The ACCC has recently identified that enforcement of the Australian Consumer Law and protecting vulnerable consumers are among its priorities; accordingly, we anticipate that more cases may be brought under the unconscionable conduct provisions of the Australian Consumer Law in the future.

---

[31] Kylie Pappalardo and Nicolas Suzor, "Standardisation and patent ambush: potential liability under Australian competition law," 18(3) *Competition and Consumer Law Journal* (2011), 276.

[32] See "Weather bureau misused market power ACCC claims," Australian Competition & Consumer Commission (December 14, 1995), <http://www.accc.gov.au/media-release/weather-bureau-misused-market-power-accc-claims>.

[33] See "Weather court case settled," Australian Competition & Consumer Competition (May 21, 1997), <http://www.accc.gov.au/content/index.phtml/itemId/87108/fromItemId/622289>.

N. Termination of intermediaries (retailers, wholesalers, dealers and value-added resellers, agents, and brokers)

Mere termination of an intermediary is not a breach. However, for the same reasons as outlined in Section I.L above, in certain circumstances, the termination of an intermediary could give rise to a breach of the CCA, for example if the prohibition on resale price maintenance is breached. **2.66**

By way of illustration, the facts of *Trade Practices Commission v. Sony (Australia) Pty Ltd.*[34] involved two retailers discounting Sony's products, and Sony refusing to supply those two retailers. The Federal Court of Australia held that it was possible to breach the resale price maintenance prohibition not only by withholding supply for the reason that the acquirer had sold goods below a specified price, but also by withholding supply by reason that the acquirer was likely to do so. **2.67**

A more recent example is the resale price maintenance undertaken by a supplier, Dragon Alliance South Pacific Pty Ltd. ("Dragon"), in respect of the online sales of its sports and ski equipment and accessories by retailers. The relevant conduct involved Dragon circulating an email to its online retailers, attaching an order form containing recommended retail prices and stipulating "the requirement to adhere to recommended retail pricing on-line." When brought to Dragon's attention by the ACCC, Dragon admitted that the relevant conduct contravened the prohibition on resale price maintenance, ceased the prohibited conduct and offered the ACCC court enforceable undertakings pursuant to s. 87B of the CCA.[35] **2.68**

O. Termination of relationships with competitors

Termination of relationships with competitors may be a form of "refusal to deal," as explained in Section I.H. Whether or not such conduct amounts to a breach of the provisions of the CCA will depend on whether it can be characterized as conduct under the specific sections set out above in Section I.H, and whether the circumstances give rise to a breach. **2.69**

If such conduct is engaged in by a corporation with market power, and the termination of the relationship with the competitor is to take advantage of the corporation's market power for an improper purpose (e.g. to stop supplying goods or services to a customer that is a downstream competitor in order to affect that competitor's ability to compete), such conduct may be a breach of s. 46 of the CCA. **2.70**

P. Exemptions

Exemptions for unilateral conduct that would otherwise breach the provisions are as follows. **2.71**

Q. Express exemptions in s. 51 of the CCA

Section 51(1) of the CCA provides that something specifically authorized or approved by legislation or legislative instruments, such as regulations (except for legislation relating to patents, trademarks, designs, or copyright) should not be considered when deciding whether a person has contravened the provisions relating to anticompetitive conduct, which are dealt with under Part IV of the CCA. This power to grant an exemption is subject to the limitations **2.72**

---

[34] *Trade Practices Commission v. Sony (Australia) Pty Ltd.* [1990] ATPR 51, 479.

[35] See further "Undertaking [Given] to the Australian Competition and Consumer Commission for the purposes of section 87B [of the CCA] by Dragon Alliance South Pacific Pty Ltd ACN 090616005, accepted by the ACCC on 24 February 2011," <http://www.accc.gov.au/content/item.phtml?itemId=974709&nodeId=340036a2a0e9d6e272ad45e6433d3790&fn=Undertaking.pdf>.

in s. 51(1C). In particular, the legislation or legislative instrument referred to in s. 51(1) must specifically refer to the CCA.

2.73 In addition, s. 51(2) of the CCA provides for certain exemptions from Part IV of the CCA (except to the extent that there is a contravention of the prohibition on resale price maintenance):

- agreements relating to employees' remuneration, conditions of employment, hours of work or working conditions;
- restrictions on work following the termination of a contract of service or a contract for the provision of services;
- obligations to comply with or to apply standards of dimension, design, quality or performance prepared or approved by Standards Australia or by a prescribed association or body;
- provisions relating to the terms or conduct of a partnership;
- provisions relating solely to the protection of the purchaser in respect of the goodwill of the business that is being sold; and
- provisions exclusively relating to the export of goods from Australia or supply of services outside Australia, if detailed notification is made to the ACCC within 14 days of the conduct.

2.74 Further, but of less relevance to unilateral conduct offenses, s. 51(3) provides for exemptions for conduct that would otherwise be in breach of provisions of Part IV of the CCA (other than the misuse of market power and resale price maintenance provisions), including:

- imposing, or giving effect to, a condition of a license or assignment of a patent, registered design or copyright to the extent that the condition relates to the underlying invention, goods, or work;
- including an agreement, or giving effect to an agreement, authorizing the use of a trade mark in accordance with the Trade Marks Act 1955; and
- including a provision in an agreement (between the registered proprietor of a trade mark, and a registered user of that trade mark), or giving effect to that provision, relating to the types of goods bearing the mark that may be produced or supplied.

R. Authorization

2.75 Section 88 of the CCA provides the ACCC with the power, upon application by a corporation, to grant the corporation an authorization to undertake conduct that would otherwise be a contravention of Part IV of the CCA. Broadly speaking, the test that is applied to assess whether authorization should be granted is whether the public benefit would exceed the anti-competitive detriment arising from the conduct. Once authorization is granted, the conduct will not constitute a breach of the provision of Part IV for which the authorization is granted. While authorization cannot be granted for conduct that breaches s. 46, authorization may be granted for conduct that could be caught as exclusive dealing under s. 47 of the CCA.

S. Notification

2.76 In addition, in respect of exclusive dealing, notification may also be available under s. 93. Notification involves a corporation (which engages or proposes to engage in conduct that would amount to exclusive dealing under s. 47) giving the ACCC a notice setting out particulars of the conduct or proposed conduct. Once this notification is lodged, the conduct is deemed not to have the effect of substantially lessening competition and the corporation is permitted to engage in that conduct until otherwise notified by the ACCC. The ACCC will allow the notification to stand unless it determines that any benefit to the public that has resulted or is likely to result from the conduct, or would result or be likely to result from the proposed conduct, would not outweigh the detriment to the public constituted by any lessening of competition that has resulted or is likely to result from the conduct, or would result or be likely to result from the proposed conduct (see s. 93(3) of the CCA).

II. Dealing with competitors

A. Horizontal price fixing

In Australia, horizontal price fixing may be a contravention of the prohibitions on cartel conduct (s. 44ZZRD of the CCA) and the prohibition against making or entering into contracts, arrangements or understandings containing a provision with the purpose, effect, or likely effect of substantially lessening competition (s. 45 of the CCA). As described in further detail below, there is both a civil and criminal regime in respect of cartel conduct, and the ACCC has identified cartel conduct as a key focus for enforcement. **2.77**

B. Cartel conduct

Horizontal price fixing may be caught by the cartel conduct prohibitions under Division 1 of Part IV of the CCA, which came into effect in July 2009 (which also apply to horizontal agreements to restrict output, allocate customers or markets, and bid rigging). Civil and criminal penalties (including imprisonment) apply in relation to making (s. 44ZZRJ) or giving effect to (s. 44ZZRK) a cartel provision, with the criminal provisions requiring the additional fault element of "knowledge or belief" to be established. **2.78**

A cartel provision relating to price fixing is a provision of a contract, arrangement or understanding between competitors or potential competitors that has the purpose or likely effect of fixing, controlling, or maintaining prices (or discounts, allowances, rebates, or credits) for the supply or acquisition of goods or services. Price fixing is per se prohibited (that is, prohibited irrespective of its effect on competition). **2.79**

In certain circumstances, conduct may be exempt from the application of the cartel conduct prohibitions, including if an authorization has been granted, if the provision is contained in a contract for a joint venture, if the conduct constitutes exclusive dealing under s. 47, if the provision is a collective acquisition, or if the provisions concern employee remuneration and employment. **2.80**

As of January 2014, the ACCC has not brought proceedings under the criminal cartel provisions and there have been only two decided cases in relation to the civil cartel conduct prohibitions.[36] However, as noted at para. 2.78, the ACCC has identified cartel conduct as a key enforcement area, and its focus on cartel conduct has also manifested in the development and dissemination of a short film entitled "The Marker," intended to educate businesses and employees about criminal penalties attaching to cartel behavior.[37] **2.81**

Prior to the introduction of the cartel provisions, the ACCC prosecuted price fixing conduct under the now repealed s. 45A of the CCA,[38] and much of the case law relating to the prior **2.82**

---

[36] See *Norcast S.ár.L. v. Bradken Limited (No. 2)* [2013] FCA 235. This case was appealed, but prior to the appeal hearing (which had been set down to commence on 4 November 2013) the matter was resolved by consent and the appeal discontinued: see *Bradken Limited v. Norcast S.ár.L* [2013] FCAFC 123. See also *Australian Competition and Consumer Commission v. Koyo Australia Pty Ltd.* [2013] FCA 1051. This case was settled by way of consent of the Parties, subject to the court being satisfied that the orders, including the terms of any pecuniary penalty, were appropriate.

[37] The ACCC's short film, "The Marker," available at <http://www.youtube.com/watch?v=louVP9VvFlg>.

[38] Section 45A deemed a provision with the purpose or likely effect of fixing, controlling or maintaining price to substantially lessen competition under s. 45.

provision will be relevant under the cartel conduct prohibitions.[39] In particular, the concepts of "contract, arrangement or understanding" have been the subject of much judicial consideration under the previous provision. Australian courts have strictly construed the terms "arrangement" and "understanding," as discussed in more detail in Section II.C.

C. Anticompetitive contracts, arrangements, or understandings

2.83 Horizontal price fixing can also be caught under s. 45. Section 45 prohibits certain anticompetitive contracts, arrangements or understandings, including the making of or giving effect to a contract, arrangement or understanding (i.e. an agreement) which contains a provision which has the purpose, effect or likely effect of substantially lessening competition in a market.

2.84 Section 45 applies not only to "contracts" in the traditional sense, but also to "arrangements" which involve a "meeting of the minds" which gives rise to certain expectations and the acceptance that parties to the arrangement will act in a particular way, and also to "understandings" (a concept that is understood to be something less formal and a looser concept than an "arrangement"). Whether mutuality is a necessary component of an understanding is yet to be resolved; however, the courts have generally considered that there must be an element of commitment or sense of moral obligation to engage in the conduct subject of the alleged contract, arrangement or understanding. Notably, the ACCC has been unsuccessful in a series of alleged petrol price fixing cases[40] because of a lack of evidence sufficient to prove a commitment between the parties to engage in the alleged arrangement to fix prices.

2.85 It is also necessary to establish an anticompetitive purpose or likely substantial lessening of competition in a relevant market. This assessment can be in respect of any market in which the parties to the agreement supply or acquire goods (or would do so but for the arrangement), and in making this assessment, two or more provisions of an arrangement may be aggregated (see ss. 45(3) and 45(4) respectively).

2.86 There are a number of exceptions to s. 45, including where the agreement is caught by s. 47 (in which case the anti-overlap provision in s. 45(6) means that s. 45 will not apply). Also, as described in "Section I.R" authorization may be granted by the ACCC under s. 88 of the CCA.

D. Horizontal agreements to allocate customers or territories; agreements not to compete

2.87 The prohibition on market sharing under the cartel provisions in Division 1 of Part IV of the CCA is expressed broadly to include all agreements between competitors (or potential competitors) with the purpose of restricting or allocating supply to customers, acquisition from suppliers, and/or the geographic areas of supply and acquisition of goods and services.

[39] A recent example of such a case is *ACCC v. TF Woollam & Son Pty Ltd. and others* [2011] FCA 973 which related to "cover pricing." In that case, it was held that the request for a "cover price" by Builder A, and the giving of it by Builder B, was a relevant arrangement or understanding within the meaning of s. 45. Builders A and B were considered to be in competition with each other within the meaning of s. 45A. The purpose of the provisions was to put a ceiling on the price at which Builder A tendered and a floor on the price at which Builder B tendered (i.e. an intention to "control" the price for the goods or services supplied, pursuant to s. 45A).

[40] See e.g. *ACCC v. Leahy Petroleum Pty Ltd.* [2007] FCA 794 and *Apco Service Stations Pty Ltd. v. ACCC* [2005] FCAFC 161. See also *Australian Competition and Consumer Commission v. Australia and New Zealand Banking Group Limited* [2013] FCA 1206 (appeal pending) but see in contrast *Australian Competition and Consumer Commission v. Flight Centre Limited* (No. 2) [2013] FCA 1313.

Amongst other conduct, this encompasses agreements that provide for geographic market sharing between competitors in relation to trading locations and trading relationships. It is not necessary to define a relevant market.

Since market sharing agreements involve an arrangement between competitors to restrict the supply of goods or services, they may also fall within the definition of an exclusionary provision in s. 4D (in which case they are per se prohibited under s. 45(2)—see Section II.E). As noted earlier, conduct may be exempt from cartel conduct as a result of "anti-overlap" provisions that test the conduct under other sections. For example, exclusive distribution territories between a supplier and a distributor would be tested under s. 47, and thereby exempt from the cartel prohibitions. **2.88**

Bid-rigging between competitors is also prohibited cartel conduct under Division 1 of Part IV of the CCA. **2.89**

E. Horizontal boycotts

Horizontal boycotts, or collective boycotts, are prohibited under the CCA under s. 45 where they contain an exclusionary provision as defined in s. 4D of the CCA. They may also be prohibited as cartel conduct in that they may amount to market allocation. **2.90**

An exclusionary provision is a contract, arrangement, or understanding between two or more actual or potential competitors with the purpose of preventing, restricting, or limiting the supply or acquisition of goods or services from a particular person or particular classes of persons, or in particular circumstances or on particular conditions. Making or giving effect to an exclusionary provision is prohibited, irrespective of the effect or likely effect on competition. **2.91**

Common collective boycott issues that have been addressed in Australian case law include market sharing conduct (e.g. *TPC v. TNT Australia Pty Ltd*[41] concerned an agreement between freight companies not to poach each other's customers), non-compete provisions in agreements, industry agreements on standard practices, joint venture agreements preventing joint venturers from acquiring goods or services elsewhere, and collective acquisition arrangements. **2.92**

One of the more significant cases in this area is *News Ltd. v. South Sydney District Rugby League Football Club Ltd.*[42] which concerned the decision of Rugby League competition organizers to exclude a particular club from the competition. Ultimately, this agreement was held to not contain an exclusionary provision including because the agreement did not have the purpose of excluding any particular club. **2.93**

F. Joint ventures and other competitive collaborations

Without authorization or exemption, joint venture arrangements, particularly between competitors, may give rise to a range of breaches of the CCA, including relating to price fixing and other cartel conduct prohibitions, collective boycotts and other anticompetitive agreements. **2.94**

The CCA contains a number of joint venture-related exceptions, defenses, and immunities to the provisions of the CCA, described in Section II.K. **2.95**

The joint venture exceptions to the civil and criminal cartel provisions apply where the relevant provision is contained in a contract, the relevant provision is for the purpose of the joint venture and the joint venture is for the production of goods or services. **2.96**

41 *TPC v. TNT Australia Pty Ltd. and others* (1992) ATPR 411-375.

42 *News Ltd. v. South Sydney District Rugby League Football Club Ltd.* (2003) 200 ALR 157.

2.97 The joint venture defense for exclusionary provisions applies in relation to exclusionary provisions which are for the purpose of the joint venture and do not have the purpose or effect of substantially lessening competition.

2.98 The conduct of the joint venture that may give rise to a breach of the CCA may be authorized by the ACCC under s. 88 of the CCA, in advance of entering into the joint venture, if the ACCC considers that the benefits of the joint venture (e.g. efficiencies) outweigh any potential anticompetitive effects.

2.99 Informal clearance may be available under the ACCC's merger review process if the joint venture involves an acquisition of shares or assets. Under s. 50 of the CCA, any acquisition of shares or assets that has an effect or likely effect of substantially lessening competition is prohibited. The ACCC has a well-established informal clearance process, whereby the ACCC will review the proposed transaction based on the facts presented, and if it decides not to oppose, will provide written notification of this based on the circumstances presented. Accordingly, parties to a joint venture may obtain a "letter of comfort" in relation to the entering into, and operation of, the joint venture on the basis of the facts presented. If the operation of the joint venture were to depart from the facts presented, the ACCC may nevertheless intervene.

G. Trade associations

2.100 Membership of a trade association is not unlawful under the CCA, and there are many legitimate and pro-competitive reasons why competitors may wish to collaborate through an industry body. However, industry associations may give rise to a risk of anticompetitive conduct between competitors (including cartel conduct and collective boycotts). Examples of conduct in the context of a trade association that has been prosecuted under Australian competition law include:

- bid rigging through a trade association (e.g. *ACCC v. ABB Power Transmission Pty Ltd.*[43] where total penalties of AUD 35 million were enforced for tender rigging by manufacturers of power transformers and distribution transformers throughout Australia);
- any agreement between competitors to adopt standard forms, terms of trade, or products may raise collective boycott issues, and parties will either need to avoid agreement, or seek authorization from the ACCC to do so;
- a trade association, which may facilitate price fixing or other anticompetitive agreements between members and including by means of a "hub and spoke conspiracy." For example, in *TPC v. Service Station Association Ltd.*,[44] a service station association began as an educational campaign to teach petrol operators to run their businesses profitably by publishing a minimum profit margin. Although ultimately this was not found to be price fixing because of the particular market circumstances the behavior of service stations resulted in prosecution for price fixing; and
- information exchanges: since many associations seek to collect and distribute information, including pricing information, there is a real risk of a price fixing contravention unless appropriate precautions are taken.

H. Interlocking directorates

2.101 Under Australian competition law, there is no limit on the number of boards on which an individual may serve as a director, or any prohibition on interlocking directorates. However,

[43] *ACCC v. ABB Power Transmission Pty Ltd.* [2001] FCA 38.
[44] *TPC v. Service Station Association Ltd.* (1993) 44 FCR 206.

multiple directorships across competitors or in vertical relationships may give rise to investigation risk due to their potential to facilitate anticompetitive behavior if used as a conduit for information or other anticompetitive purposes (e.g. collusion). In such circumstances, this behavior would be investigated under the cartel provisions or the other horizontal or vertical arrangements discussed above.

The ACCC has identified that minority interests may raise competition concerns when the same party has an interest in a number of otherwise independent competitors (including interlocking directorates). If such circumstances give rise to a likelihood of coordinated effects, this may be a basis of investigation by the ACCC in relation to a proposed transaction under s. 50 of the CCA. **2.102**

I. Facilitating practices

Facilitating practices (such as exchanging information) are generally not subject to specific prohibitions under Australian competition law except to the extent that such conduct is a provision of a contract, arrangement or understanding that has the purpose or effect, or likely effect, of substantially lessening competition, or is in breach of the cartel provisions. As noted above, to establish an arrangement or understanding between parties requires proof of commitment by the parties to the alleged cartel provision (e.g. price fixing). Concerted action or parallel conduct is not sufficient. **2.103**

Partly due to this perceived "gap" in the law, legislation to prohibit certain unilateral information disclosures was introduced in June 2012. This legislation is contained in Division 1A of Part IV of the CCA and prohibits: **2.104**

- private disclosures of pricing information to one or more actual or potential competitors where the disclosure falls outside the ordinary course of business (see s. 44ZZW—this is a per se breach); and
- general disclosures (whether public or private) relating to price, capacity or commercial strategy where the purpose of the disclosure is to substantially lessen competition (see s. 44ZZX).

The prohibitions only apply to goods and services as prescribed by regulation. Currently, the prohibitions only apply to deposit taking and lending activities of Authorized Deposit-taking Institutions (which are, generally speaking, banks). **2.105**

The prohibitions are subject to a range of exceptions intended to exclude certain legitimate information disclosures. **2.106**

J. Information exchange

A mere exchange of information between competitors is generally not unlawful under the CCA. However, information exchanges between competitors in Australia may risk investigation under a range of prohibitions under the CCA relating to dealings between competitors (including prohibitions in relation to cartel conduct, collective boycotts and anticompetitive agreements and, in the banking sector, the new laws prohibiting private disclosures of price information to competitors outside the ordinary course of business)—see further Section II.I. **2.107**

As noted above in Section II.A, because of the need to establish that a contract, arrangement or understanding involved a "commitment" between the parties to engage in the alleged conduct (e.g. to fix prices), it will not be sufficient to establish a price fixing offense merely because price information is exchanged between the parties. **2.108**

However, an information exchange may also be alleged to constitute a contract, arrangement or understanding for the purpose or likely effect of substantially lessening competition under **2.109**

s. 45 of the CCA. Whether or not information exchange indicates conduct that may give rise to a breach of the CCA will depend on a case-by-case assessment, and will largely depend on:

- the nature of the information exchanged (particular care needs to be taken account of price-related information, and the currency and aggregated/disaggregated nature of such information);
- the purpose for which that information is being exchanged; and
- the context in which information is exchanged.

2.110 Particular care will need to be taken in the context of information provision during merger discussions and it may be appropriate to establish a "clean team" and protocols which provide guidance as to the composition of the "clean team" and the type of information to be exchanged.

2.111 A current example of an information exchange being investigated by the ACCC is the publicly announced, ongoing ACCC investigation of price information sharing arrangements in the retail fuel industry.[45] In December 2013, Mr Sims indicated that the investigation was nearing completion.

K. Joint purchasing agreements

2.112 Joint purchasing agreements might contravene the CCA to the extent that they constitute cartel conduct, an exclusionary provision (if the joint purchasing agreements relate to more than just the price of goods), or otherwise manifest an anticompetitive agreement.

2.113 However, if the relevant provision being considered relates either to the price for goods or services to be collectively acquired, or joint advertising of the price for the resupply of those goods or services, s. 44ZZRV provides a collective acquisition exception to the cartel conduct prohibitions in relation to price fixing (but not other cartel conduct prohibitions). Parties are also able to seek authorization for joint purchasing agreements (see further Section I.R).

2.114 Where relevant, parties may seek a collective bargaining notice from the ACCC, which means that the prohibitions on price fixing (both in s. 45 and under the cartel provision prohibition) and exclusionary provisions under s. 45 will not apply. Collective bargaining notices may be sought where the value of the transactions proposed to be conducted under the collective bargaining arrangement will not exceed AUD 3 million and operate for a maximum of three years. The ACCC may approve a collective bargaining notice for collective arrangements that involve price fixing or exclusionary arrangements (the test requires a benefit to the public that would result or is likely to result, and which does not outweigh the detriment to the public). By way of example, the ACCC granted a collective bargaining notice on November 15, 2012 (specifically, interim approval was granted to Queensland coal producers to collectively bargain for water supply, allowing them to collectively negotiate the arrangements while the Nathan Dam project is constructed in Northern Queensland).

L. Joint lobbying/regulatory/legislative efforts

2.115 Unlike the United States, Australian competition law does not generally afford any express immunity in relation to joint lobbying by competitors, or other efforts to jointly petition Government. However, if the joint lobbying efforts do not involve any purpose or effect of substantially lessening competition, or have any effect of excluding third parties, the joint conduct should not raise any competition concerns under the CCA. If the joint lobbying

[45] See e.g. Rod Sims, "Competition and consumer issues: State of play in the food and grocery sector," Paper presented at the Australian Food and Grocery Council Industry Leaders Forum, Canberra, October 11, 2012, <http://www.accc.gov.au/content/index.phtml/itemId/1084119/fromItemId/8973>.

efforts (e.g. by an industry association) involve additional elements of joint or coordinated conduct, it may be possible for the group to obtain authorization to facilitate such joint conduct that may be of public benefit (see further Section I.R).

III. General issues

A. Jurisdiction and applicable law

The CCA applies to anti competitive conduct, acquisitions of shares or assets that substantially lessen competition, infrastructure access issues, and consumer protection issues. Australia has adopted an integrated model where all firms are generally subject to the anti-competitive conduct and merger rules in Part IV of the CCA. In addition, most sectors are subject to the generic access regime in Part IIIA of the CCA. There is some sector-specific regulation, most notably in relation to telecommunications (e.g. Telecommunications Act 1997) and energy (e.g. National Electricity (South Australia) Act 1996), and currently, banking (the information disclosure prohibitions). A single national body, the ACCC, oversees the administration of competition law, access issues and consumer protection issues under the CCA, as well as sector-specific regulation in the telecommunications and energy sectors. **2.116**

The CCA applies to all natural persons, corporations (being trading, financial, or foreign corporations) and to the government, insofar as it carries on business. The CCA also has extraterritorial application such that it extends to conduct outside Australia with the requisite connection: **2.117**

- for corporations being that the corporation must be incorporated in Australia, carry on business in Australia or be registered as a foreign corporation in Australia; and
- for individuals, that the person must either be an Australian citizen or ordinarily resident in Australia (see s. 5 of the CCA).

B. Antitrust system

(i) Name of agency/agencies

The ACCC is responsible for the enforcement of the CCA. It promotes competition and fair trade in the marketplace to benefit consumers, business, and the community. It also regulates national infrastructure industries. Its primary responsibility is to ensure that individuals and businesses comply with Australia's competition, fair trading, and consumer protection laws.[46] **2.118**

Some of the ACCC's decisions relating to authorizations, clearances, grants of immunity, and arbitration decisions involving access to essential facilities can be appealed to the Australian Competition Tribunal. Additionally, many of the ACCC's decisions are also subject to review under Commonwealth administrative law principles.[47] **2.119**

(ii) Staff size and budget

In the 2012–13 financial year, the ACCC had 798 staff members[48] and a net cost of services of AUD 176.3 million.[49] **2.120**

---

[46] See ACCC, About us <http://www.accc.gov.au/about-us>.

[47] See ACCC, Decision making processes <http://www.accc.gov.au/about-us/australian-competition-consumer-commission/decision-making-processes>.

[48] This number has grown from 702 in 2008–9, to 732 in 2009–10, to 790 in 2010–11 (it has fallen since 2011–12 when staff numbers were at 807).

[49] See ACCC, "Australian Competition and Consumer Commission and Australian Energy Regulator Annual Report 2012–13," <http://www.accc.gov.au/publications/accc-aer-annual-report/accc-aer-annual-report-2012-13>.

2.121 The ACCC has five committees composed of full-time members and/or associate and *ex officio* commissioners who have expertise on particular matters.[50] These committees comprise:

- the enforcement committee, which meets weekly and oversees the enforcement program. Its recommendations are referred to the ACCC for decision;
- the mergers committee, which meets weekly and considers most mergers matters. It refers major matters to the ACCC and reports to it on others;
- the communications committee, which meets as required and oversees functions on telecommunications, including matters arising under Part XIB and XIC of the CCA and authorizations. It coordinates with the enforcement committee;
- the regulated access and price monitoring committee, which meets as required and oversees access and price monitoring issues; and
- the adjudication committee, which meets weekly and considers authorizations and notifications, and reports to the full ACCC.

(iii) Recent enforcement actions and trends

2.122 The ACCC's 2012–13 Annual Report identified the following four goals:

- promoting vigorous, lawful competition, and informed markets;
- encouraging fair trading, protection of consumers, and product safety;
- regulating national infrastructure and other markets where there is limited competition; and
- delivering results through the ACCC's investment in its people and systems.

2.123 The ACCC is conducting active enforcement in respect of all areas of its jurisdiction under the CCA. This includes:

- enforcement in relation to cartel conduct (for example, in relation to the air cargo cartel matter, the ACCC penalized Korean Air Lines Co. Ltd., Malaysian Airlines Cargo Sdn Bhd, and Emirates AUD 5.5 million, AUD 6 million, and AUD 10 million respectively for price fixing);
- investigations and proceedings in relation to consumer protection (for example, its proceedings against Optus for misleading broadband advertising resulted in the Full Federal Court ordering Optus to pay civil pecuniary penalties of AUD 3.61 million; and its proceedings against Apple for misleading advertising in relation its promotion of the "iPad with WiFi + 4G" resulted in the Federal Court ordering Apple to pay civil pecuniary penalties of AUD 2.25 million); and
- a range of decisions opposing the grant of informal merger clearances, or requiring divestitures (e.g. in the Asahi/P&N Beverages transaction) or undertakings (e.g. in the FOXTEL/Austar transaction) as a condition of clearance.

C. Private litigation

2.124 Third parties may bring private enforcement actions for contraventions of Part IV or Part IVB of the CCA. Third parties may seek injunctions (but not in relation to mergers), declarations, and damages. In relation to the latter, the CCA contains two general provisions under which third parties are able to seek compensation for loss or damage as a result of a contravention of Part IV.

2.125 Section 82 of the CCA provides that a person who suffers loss or damage due to another's conduct in contravention of Part IV or IVB may recover the amount of the loss or damage by bringing an action against that person or any other person involved in the contravention.

---

[50] See ACCC, Decision making processes (n 47).

Such an action may be commenced within six years after the day on which the cause of action that relates to the conduct accrued. There is no restriction on private actions against parties who have been subject to criminal or civil enforcement proceedings, nor is there any restriction against bringing a private action against a party who receives immunity or leniency in an ACCC prosecution, or who has already paid a civil penalty.

Section 87 of the CCA also provides a legislative basis to seek remedies including compensation and/or rectification but is broader in application than s. 82. It provides the court with the power to make orders "as it thinks appropriate" against a person who engaged in or was involved in the conduct, including orders for damages in respect of a person who has suffered loss and damage. In addition, under s. 87(1B) of the CCA, the ACCC has the power to commence representative proceedings on behalf of a group that has suffered loss or damage as a result of cartel conduct. The remedies that may be sought for this are very wide-ranging. **2.126**

Unlike in the United States, Australia does not have treble damages for third party enforced contraventions. **2.127**

Third party actions can be brought: **2.128**

- simultaneously with any ACCC proceedings (but heard by separate judges);
- after the ACCC proceedings have been heard and determined; and
- on a standalone basis (i.e. even if there is no ACCC investigation or proceeding on foot or completed).

Since no private cartel litigation (in the sense of a third party action) has been completed without settlement prior to a decision, key principles in this area are as yet unresolved (for example in relation to the calculation of damages and the existence of the passing-on defense). **2.129**

Over time, private cartel litigation is likely to become more significant because the Federal Court has streamlined procedures for commencing class actions, and further interest from litigation funders is likely. By way of illustration, after Visy was fined AUD 36 million by the ACCC in 2007 for engaging in cartel conduct, private litigation was commenced against Visy and also against Amcor, the cartel member that originally informed the ACCC about the cartel conduct. The amount claimed exceeded AUD 1 billion, but on the first day of trial the parties settled for AUD 95 million plus legal costs. Although this amount is significantly less than the initial AUD 1 billion that had been claimed, it is still significantly higher than the ACCC's AUD 36 million fine and is the largest private price-fixing settlement amount to date in Australia. **2.130**

D. Follow-on litigation

Apart from private parties being able to make claims under the CCA for s. 82 damages or s. 87 remedies (see further Section III.C), there is an increasing trend of class actions after the ACCC commences proceedings, particularly in relation to cartel conduct. There is no requirement that the class action be stayed pending resolution of the ACCC proceedings. While there is no specific provision for class action proceedings under the CCA, the Federal Court of Australia Act 1976 (Cth) sets out the requirements for bringing class action proceedings. **2.131**

By way of example, there is currently a large cartel class action proceeding on foot in Australia in relation to the air cargo cartel proceedings commenced by the ACCC—*De Brett Seafood Pty Limited & Ors v. Qantas Airways Limited & Ors.* **2.132**

Findings of fact in enforcement proceedings are admissible as prima facie evidence of those facts in private litigation (s. 83 of the CCA). However, this position is complicated by the prevalence of tightly drafted agreed statements of facts, as well as uncertainty under Australian **2.133** law as to whether admissions constitute findings of fact. However, the ACCC may disclose or be compelled to disclose information unless an exception applies (e.g. the ACCC would not be required to disclose information that falls within the protected cartel information scheme in the CCA, if it is obtained under the ACCC's compulsory information-gathering powers, or if privilege or confidentiality applies).

E. Arbitration and alternative dispute resolution

2.134 The role of arbitration and ADR in Australian competition law is generally limited to telecommunications access disputes and access disputes for declared services under Part IIIA of the CCA.

2.135 Private parties to an agreement may stipulate that all disputes (including in relation to competition law) must be subject to arbitration. To date, Australian courts have not considered whether such clauses would be effective to preclude judicial review.

F. Remedies

(i) Civil liability

2.136 The maximum penalties that can be imposed for each contravention of the civil prohibitions under Part IV of the CCA are as follows:

- for corporations:
  - when the value of the illegal benefit to one or more parties can be ascertained, the greater of AUD 10 million or three times the total value of the illegal benefit; or
  - when the value of the illegal benefit cannot be ascertained, 10 percent of the Australian turnover of the corporate entity (including related bodies corporate) in the preceding twelve months; and
- for individuals: AUD 500,000. When proceedings are taken against an individual company officer, the company is prevented from indemnifying the individual for legal costs and any financial penalty. The court may also disqualify directors and officers from managing a company.

2.137 The Australian Consumer Law also contains distinct pecuniary penalty provisions applicable to Australian Consumer Law contraventions.

2.138 In addition to penalties, the ACCC may also seek injunctions, non-punitive orders (e.g. community service orders, probation orders, disclosure of information, or publication of an advertisement), undertakings, or divestitures for a contravention of the civil prohibitions.

(ii) Criminal liability

2.139 For contravention of the criminal cartel provisions, penalties may include gaol sentences of up to ten years and/or fines of up to AUD 340,000 (being 2,000 penalty units) for the individuals involved, as well as other court orders.

G. Leniency and immunity

2.140 The ACCC has both an immunity policy and a leniency (cooperation) policy.

2.141 Although applications for immunity can be made under the ACCC's policy in relation to both civil and criminal liability, the ACCC can only make a determination as to whether or not to grant immunity from civil liability (the decision about whether to grant immunity from criminal liability lies solely with the Commonwealth Director of Public Prosecution, see further para. 2.144).

Both corporations and individuals may apply for immunity. In order to be eligible, applicants: **2.142**

- must be or have been a party to a cartel;
- must admit that their conduct in respect of the cartel may constitute a contravention of the CCA;
- must be the first person or corporation to apply for immunity (subsequent applicants may be offered leniency);
- must not be the clear ring leader of the cartel or have coerced others to join the cartel;
- must have ceased involvement in the cartel or agree to cease involvement; and
- must undertake to provide full disclosure and cooperation to the ACCC.

Additionally, the immunity applicant will only be eligible for immunity if at the time of applying for immunity the ACCC has not received written advice that there is sufficient evidence to commence court proceedings. **2.143**

The decision about whether to grant immunity from criminal liability lies solely with the Commonwealth Director of Public Prosecution, although the ACCC can make recommendations about whether the requirements under its immunity policy have been met. The same criteria apply in the assessment of whether immunity from criminal liability should be granted. **2.144**

Leniency is available to applicants who are not "first in," and is available to both corporations and individuals. This cooperation policy is designed to encourage participants who may be in breach of the CCA to assist the ACCC in its investigation, and by doing so, potentially to benefit from joint submissions to the court and an agreement as to any penalty for conduct that is in breach of the CCA. Informal cooperation may also be available to those who admit cartel conduct early on in an investigation or proceedings. **2.145**

H. Document creation and retention

Australian competition law does not include any explicit rules on document creation and retention. However, the ACCC has wide powers under s. 155 of the CCA to compel the provision of information, documents, and evidence when investigating possible contraventions of the CCA. Generally these powers are used if it is not appropriate or effective to seek voluntary cooperation in the circumstances of the case or if potential respondents are uncooperative. **2.146**

In exercising its powers under s. 155, the ACCC considers whether there is a risk that the information, documents or evidence may otherwise be destroyed, not provided, or provided only on terms unacceptable to the ACCC. Failure to comply with any notice issued under s. 155 requiring the production of information, documents or evidence is an offense under the CCA, as is knowingly providing false or misleading information. **2.147**

The ACCC also has search and seizure powers under Part XID of the CCA which can be utilized if there are reasonable grounds for suspecting that there is a document or thing which may afford evidence of a contravention of the CCA located at particular premises or that will be located at premises within the next 72 hours. There are significant penalties for failing to comply with the ACCC in conducting such a raid. **2.148**

3

AUSTRIA

Astrid Ablasser-Neuhuber and Heinrich Kühnert
bpv Hügel Rechtsanwälte

Introduction

3.01 While Austria has a long history of rather strict antitrust legislation, modern legal and enforcement standards have been only gradually introduced after Austria's accession to the European Union in 1995. This is perhaps one of the reasons why Austria's antitrust practice is considered somewhat "younger" than that of most of its West European counterparts. Legislative and enforcement trends in recent years, however, clearly show that Austria has embraced modern antitrust law, with both complex economic analysis and intrusive public enforcement (in particular via dawn raids) becoming increasingly prevalent. Austria thus is right in the center of Europe also with regard to competition law.

3.02 One of the reasons for this is that Austrian substantive competition law is now closely based on EU principles. Thus, the law broadly distinguishes between "behavioral" restrictions of competition and the "structural" provisions of merger control. Among behavioral restrictions, which are the focus of this chapter, Austrian law prohibits both concerted and unilateral restrictions on competition. Some of the most serious restrictions on competition are concerted restrictions, in that they involve agreements between competitors. These restrictions are described in Section II. By contrast, Section I deals with unilateral conduct, as well as with agreements between firms that do not compete.

Austrian law, however, differs from the EU model as regards its institutional and procedural setup. Under Austrian law, there is a strict separation between the investigating authority and the ultimate decision maker: investigative powers are vested in the Federal Competition Authority, an administrative agency, while all decisions in antitrust matters are made by the Cartel Court. **3.03**

Historically, Austria does not have a strong record of actively enforcing its competition regime, in particular due to an understaffing of its enforcement agencies. While the increases to its resources granted by the government have been rather limited, the Federal Competition Authority has still succeeded in significantly stepping up its enforcement since the mid to late 2000s, relying both on the leniency regime and on its investigative powers (in particular, dawn raids) to uncover and prosecute anticompetitive practices. Public enforcement by the Authority focuses in particular on hard core cartels, such as price fixing, market or customer allocation, and bid-rigging. In addition, the Authority's recent practice reveals a focus on certain vertical restraints in distribution relationships, in particular on resale price maintenance. **3.04**

By contrast, unilateral conduct has not been a main focus of public enforcement in recent times, even though the Austrian rules on such conduct are comparatively strict (see Section I). The rather low level of enforcement by the agencies is somewhat mitigated by the fact that private parties may directly apply to the Cartel Court, a specialized court which is the decision-maker in all antitrust cases (see Section III). **3.05**

I. Acting alone

Antitrust law only applies to purely unilateral conduct if the business in question holds significant market power. Businesses holding market power may infringe antitrust law by harming customers directly, in particular by charging excessively high prices. Furthermore, they may infringe the antitrust rules by foreclosing competitors, thus harming the competitive process. Examples of such exclusionary practices include exclusivity arrangements with customers, pricing schemes which keep competitors out of the market, and refusal to supply competitors with an indispensable product or service. **3.06**

The concepts underlying Austrian law with regard to unilateral conduct draw heavily on EU law. In particular, unilateral conduct is only caught by Austrian antitrust law if it is carried out by a business in a "dominant position." Furthermore, Austrian law does not prohibit businesses from attaining or holding a dominant position as such, but only covers its "abuse." However, Austrian law is stricter than EU law in a number of respects. **3.07**

In particular, businesses will more easily be considered as holding a dominant position under Austrian law than under EU law. This is due to the very wide presumption of dominance laid down in s. 4 of the Austrian Cartel Act (CA). In particular, a business will be presumed to be dominant if it holds a market share of 30 percent or more. Under a number of additional presumptions, businesses may be presumed to hold a "collective dominant position." These statutory presumptions are rebuttable, but give rise to a reversal of the burden of proof, i.e. the business in question will have to prove that it is not dominant. **3.08**

Austrian law also contains some stricter rules regarding the existence of an abuse, which will be referred to in para. 3.15. In addition to these competition law rules, Austrian law also **3.09** provides for a more general ban on discrimination among business partners. This non-discrimination requirement also extends to businesses which are not dominant. Non-dominant businesses, however, do not face the risk of very high fines, which may be imposed on dominant entities.

A. Agreements with non-competing businesses

3.10 The Austrian competition rules also cover agreements with non-competing businesses. This includes, in particular, vertical agreements with businesses that operate at a different level of the supply chain. The Austrian Federal Competition Authority has recently been quite active in this field, having carried out a number of dawn raids in cases of suspected resale price maintenance (RPM).

3.11 Like coordination with competitors, agreements with non-competitors are assessed under the prohibition of anticompetitive agreements and concerted practices, laid down in s. 1 CA. These rules also apply to non-dominant businesses. Section 2 CA, however, provides for a safe harbor rule: in line with the *de minimis* rules at the EU level, agreements between non-competing businesses are exempted from the prohibition of restrictive agreements if neither of the parties holds a market share of more than 15 percent. Notably, however, this exemption does not cover cases of resale price maintenance.

3.12 While, pursuant to the CA, further exemptions may be enacted by regulation of the Federal Minister of Economic Affairs, no such regulation has in fact been passed. In practice, the Austrian courts however, follow the assessment laid down in the European Commission's Block Exemption Regulations and Guidelines, which de facto leads to the exemptions laid down at EU level being applicable under Austrian law (see Section I.O).

B. Predatory pricing

3.13 A dominant business may harm consumers by pricing below cost, if it thereby weakens competitors or forces them to exit the market. A business engaging in such practices runs the risk of its pricing being considered predatory. Predatory pricing is one of the examples explicitly mentioned in s. 5 CA which contains a non-exhaustive list of practices that will be considered abusive if carried out by a dominant firm.

3.14 The Austrian Supreme Court has fleshed out the requirements for prices to be considered predatory in a number of cases since the late 1990s. Pursuant to this case law, a dominant business will abuse its dominant position if it prices below average variable cost (AVC), i.e. below the sum of those costs which vary with output, divided by the number of units produced. Furthermore, a dominant business may also commit an abuse if it prices above AVC but below average total cost (ATC), if this is part of its plan to eliminate a competitor. Austrian courts have so far not ruled on whether the more precise concepts of "average avoidable cost" (instead of AVC) and "long-run average incremental cost" (instead of ATC) should also be adopted under Austrian law. Given the fact that the European Commission has adopted these concepts in its Guidance on exclusionary abuses, it is, however, quite likely that Austrian practice will follow suit.

3.15 Predatory pricing is often difficult to prove by private complainants, since they do not have sufficient information on the dominant business's cost structure. This is partly addressed by s. 5(2) CA, which sets out a rebuttable presumption that the sale of goods below the price at which they were purchased is abusive. While this statutory presumption only applies to the distribution of goods,[1] the courts have alleviated the burden on complainants in other cases

[1] *Attorney Software*, Austrian Supreme Court, Case no. 4 Ob 60/09s (July 14, 2009).

as well. Effectively, private applicants in the Cartel Court are only required to adduce *prima facie* evidence demonstrating that the dominant business is likely to price below cost. If the private complainant succeeds in making out such a *prima facie* case, the burden of proof switches to the defendant.[2] In spite of this, both public and private enforcement of predatory pricing remain rather low, probably due to the complex legal and economic analysis required in such cases.

C. Exploitative offenses (excessive pricing, monopoly leveraging)

Austrian law does not prohibit businesses from attaining or holding a dominant position as such. By virtue of their market power, dominant businesses have the ability to price above the competitive level. In line with the situation at EU level, Austrian law, however, prohibits them from charging "excessive" prices. **3.16**

There is little case law as to when prices are so far off the mark as to be considered "excessive." The most significant exploitative abuse case decided in Austria related to the decision of the Austrian Post to cut the commission made by distributors of postal stamps by approximately 70 percent. Based on a comparison of the remaining commission with the distributors' related costs, the Cartel Court held that the decision to cut the margin amounted to an abuse of the Austrian Post's dominant position, as it forced distributors to make losses on the sale of stamps.[3] **3.17**

While the Austrian competition authorities rarely enforce the rule against excessive pricing, they have been involved in efforts to increase price transparency for consumers on the retail fuel market, by publishing a monthly "fuel price newsletter." Similar services are also provided by sectoral regulators, for example in the energy sector. **3.18**

D. Monopsony

The rules regarding abuse of a dominant position apply to dominant buyers as well as to sellers. In practice, monopsony cases are rare though. In the early 2000s, a number of monopsony cases were brought by private applicants against the Austrian social security carriers, which are state bodies in charge of public healthcare. These cases collapsed when the Austrian Supreme Court held that the social security carriers could not be qualified as "undertakings" engaged in an economic activity, but served a social purpose, and hence were not subject to the competition rules.[4] **3.19**

The only Austrian case in which fines were imposed on monopsony grounds involved Europay Austria, the largest acquirer on the Austrian market for debit card systems. In a complex case, one of the grounds on which Europay Austria was found to have engaged in an abuse of its dominant position was the agreement, with its member banks (issuers), that the banks should charge higher interchange fees to competing acquirers than to Europay Austria itself. Europay Austria was fined EUR 7 million, which to date is the highest fine imposed in Austria for abuses of a dominant position.[5] **3.20**

E. Price discrimination

Section 5 CA prohibits dominant businesses from applying different conditions to equivalent transactions with other trading parties, if they thereby put those trading parties at a competitive disadvantage. While pure discrimination cases are rare, discrimination is sometimes relied **3.21**

---

[2] *Newspaper Subscription*, Austrian Supreme Court, Case no. 16 Ok 6/00 (October 9, 2000).
[3] *Stamp Commission*, Austrian Supreme Court, Case no. 16 Ok 14/03 (November 17, 2003).
[4] *NÖ Gebietskrankenkasse*, Austrian Supreme Court, Case no. 16 Ok 5/04 (June 14, 2004).
[5] *Europay Austria*, Austrian Supreme Court, Case no. 16 Ok 4/07 (September 12, 2007).

on as an additional consideration in foreclosure cases. By way of example, the Cartel Court's review of the Austrian Post's pricing for services offered to a competitor (whose application was finally rejected) addressed the issue of discrimination, but clearly also involved concerns of anticompetitive foreclosure.[6] While there is some private enforcement of the antitrust rule against discrimination, public enforcement by the Federal Competition Authority is rare.

3.22 In addition to the non-discrimination requirement under antitrust law, Austrian statutory law provides for a more general ban on discrimination between business partners, which also applies to non-dominant businesses. This obligation of equal treatment applies to the resale of (processed or unprocessed) goods at all levels of trade with the exception of end consumers.[7] Infringements of this provision, however, do not carry the risk of high fines which is associated with violations of competition law.

F. Dictating or influencing resale prices

(i) Resale price maintenance

3.23 Resale price maintenance is assessed under the prohibition of anticompetitive agreements (s. 1 CA), which also applies to non-dominant undertakings. Indeed, in line with the strict treatment of RPM at the European level, businesses risk running afoul of the Austrian competition rules by engaging in RPM even if they hold very moderate market shares.

3.24 Fixed or minimum RPM is regarded as a serious infringement of the competition rules. This prohibition covers both direct agreement on the resale price and indirect means to achieve the same end, for example rebates conditional on the maintenance of a price level determined by the supplier. The prohibition also covers price recommendations, unless the recommendation explicitly makes it clear that it is not binding, and is not in fact enforced by the supplier. In its recently published draft Guidance on RPM,[8] the Federal Competition Authority indicated that it would regard repeated "reminders" by the supplier regarding compliance with the recommended resale price as going beyond the scope of a non-binding recommendation.

3.25 While parties may rely on economic efficiencies to justify restrictions of competition, in the case of RPM, it is generally regarded as unlikely that the conditions of this defense will be met. A sectoral exemption exists regarding RPM in the sale of books, art prints, music notes, magazines, and newspapers to end users. In practice, however, this exemption will often be ineffective, as many cases of RPM will come under the ambit of EU competition law, which does not provide for a similar exception.

3.26 RPM has recently been a major enforcement priority of the Austrian competition authorities. In the press sector, the Federal Cartel Procurator brought proceedings before the Cartel Court, arguing that the pricing schemes agreed between German magazine publishers and their Austrian distributors amounted *inter alia* to illegal RPM. The Cartel Court, however regarded RPM as justified in this case, as it was linked to the right of Austrian press distributors to return unsold copies, which was found to be beneficial to press circulation.[9] Furthermore, the Federal Competition Authority is investigating alleged RPM and hub-and-spoke practices between DIY stores and producers of insulating materials, as well as between supermarkets and branded goods manufacturers. In these cases, the Federal Competition Authority carried out a number of dawn raids. While several investigations are still pending, a

[6] *Austrian Post*, Austrian Supreme Court, Case no. 16 Ok 9/04 (October 11, 2004).

[7] *Lumber mills*, Austrian Supreme Court, Case no. 16 Ok 3/08 (July 16, 2008).

[8] Federal Competition Authority, *Standpunkt zu vertikalen Preisbindungen*, draft of June 13, 2013, p. 8, <http://www.bwb.gv.at/Aktuell/Seiten/LeitlinienzuvertikalenPreisbindungen.aspx>.

[9] *Wholesale press distribution*, Austrian Cartel Court, Case no. 26 Kt 17, 18, 27, 28/07 (March 20, 2013).

number of undertakings, including Austria's largest retail chain, have already agreed to settled solutions, involving the payment of a reduced fine.

(ii) Minimum advertised price programs

Minimum advertised price (MAP) programs involve the unilateral determination of a MAP by the supplier, coupled with a policy of refusing to support resellers who do not respect this price. For example, the supplier may make the payment of advertising subsidies to resellers conditional on respect of the MAP. While there is no practice on MAP programs in Austria, such programs will, in all likelihood, be considered as a form of indirect RPM under Austrian competition law, and are thus likely to be found in violation of the competition rules. **3.27**

G. Tying arrangements

Tying may constitute an abuse of a dominant position if the supplier is dominant on the market for the tying product, and if the practice forecloses competition on either tying, the tied, or on both markets. **3.28**

For tying to be anticompetitive, there needs to be a separate demand for the products in question. This requirement can sometimes give rise to difficulties. For example, in 1996, the Austrian Supreme Court held that the combination of rental agreements for liquefied petroleum gas tanks with exclusive purchasing obligations for the gas itself had become a general trade practice, and hence did not constitute an abuse.[10] Nevertheless, in 2009, the Federal Competition Authority brought new proceedings before the Cartel Court in relation to this practice, arguing that it amounted to unlawful tying. These proceedings are still pending. **3.29**

Other than by contract, tie-ins may also be achieved by technical measures, for example by making the dominant business's tying and tied products work together, but limiting interoperability with substitutes for the tied product produced by competitors. By way of example, the Austrian Supreme Court held that the Austrian telecommunications incumbent, Telekom Austria, had abused its dominant position by selling phones for fixed-line telephony which automatically pre-selected its network. While, in reality, customers could have easily disabled this pre-selection, the operating instructions informed customers that the phones were only suitable for use in Telekom Austria's network.[11] **3.30**

Enforcement of the rule against tie-ins has largely focused on regulated industries, in particular telecommunications. Recently, an application by the Federal Competition Authority alleging an illegal tie-in in the rail freight industry was rejected by the Cartel Court. **3.31**

H. Exclusive dealing

Exclusive dealing will usually be considered an infringement if carried out by a dominant business. This prohibition also applies to indirect means of achieving exclusivity. Thus, Austrian courts held that the terms and conditions offered by the Austrian Post for newspaper distribution, which provided for lower prices if the customer agreed to a five-year contract, and provided that a reference quantity (based on the customers' previous purchases) was reached in each year, constituted an abuse of a dominant position.[12] **3.32**

In certain circumstances, exclusive dealing may also be prohibited if entered into by non-dominant businesses, under the rules on anticompetitive agreements (s. 1 CA). In the case of exclusive dealing obligations imposed on the buyer, the competition law assessment will **3.33**

---

[10] *LPG*, Austrian Supreme Court, Case no. 16 Ok 12/96 (December 9, 1996).

[11] *Wireless phone*, Austrian Supreme Court, Case no. 16 Ok 11/03 (November 17, 2003).

[12] *Redmail*, Austrian Supreme Court, Case no. 16 Ok 46/05 (February 27, 2006).

depend on a number of factors, including the market position of the supplier and its competitors, the overall coverage of exclusive arrangements and their duration, as well as the existence of entry barriers and countervailing buyer power. Agreements which would benefit from exemption under the Vertical Block Exemption at EU level are considered to also be in line with Austrian competition law. Thus, obligations on the buyer not to sell competing goods or services will pass the competition law test if both the seller's share of supplies and the buyer's share of purchases do not exceed 30 percent, and if the duration of the obligation is limited to no more than five years.

3.34 A number of applications brought before Austrian courts involved so-called "radius clauses." These arrangements are often included in contracts for rental space in shopping centers, and require the tenant not to open stores in competing centers within a certain distance of the mall in question. In the only case which to date has reached a final verdict, the Cartel Court concluded that the radius clauses in question did not infringe the competition rules. This decision was based, in particular, on the consideration that rental space outside of shopping centers was a sufficiently close substitute for space in shopping centers to be considered part of the same market. Upon appeal, the decision was upheld by the Supreme Court.[13]

3.35 Conversely, Austrian competition law also limits granting exclusive rights (namely, territorial or customer exclusivity) to customers, as suppliers should not completely bar their remaining customers from selling in a particular territory or to a particular customer group. In line with EU law, while suppliers may require their customers to refrain from "active" sales, they may not restrict "passive" sales (i.e. broadly speaking, unsolicited sales initiated by the purchaser). Suppliers also have to allow their customers to sell on the internet, but may require them to meet certain standards.

3.36 Detailed rules and guidelines regarding the assessment of various distribution schemes (exclusive dealing, selective dealing, franchising, etc.) exist at EU level. As the Austrian rules are based on the EU model, these rules also inform the assessment under Austrian law.

I. Refusal to deal

3.37 Under Austrian law, businesses are generally free to choose their trading partners. Certain exceptions to this rule exist, in particular for dominant businesses. On the face of the law, these exceptions are somewhat broader than in many other competition law regimes. In recent years, refusal to deal, however, has not ranked high in the enforcement priorities of the Austrian competition authorities.

3.38 Austrian case law regarding dominant companies provides for an obligation to contract, provided certain requirements (set out in para. 3.39) are met. While the case law does not explicitly distinguish between specific categories of cases, it appears that these requirements may be more or less strict, depending on the prior use of the resource in question by the dominant business.

3.39 If the resource in question has previously been used only internally by the dominant business, refusal to deal will not violate competition law other than in exceptional circumstances. In contrast, if the resource has been sold to third parties, courts apply a stricter test, generally requiring refusal to deal to be objectively justified. This requirement applies both in cases regarding the termination of existing commercial relationships, and in cases involving the establishment of new relationships (see Section I.M).[14] Objective justifications accepted by

[13] *Radius clause IV*, Austrian Supreme Court, Case no. 16 Ok 8/10 (December 12, 2011).

[14] *Railway handbook*, Austrian Supreme Court, 16 Ok 1/12 (October 11, 2012).

the Austrian courts include *inter alia* capacity constraints[15] and breaches of trust by the business seeking to be supplied, such as prior violations of contract[16] and refusal to provide ordinarily accepted collateral.[17]

The scope of the obligation to contract is extended by the concept of "relative dominance" enshrined in the Cartel Act. Pursuant to s. 4 of the Act, a business may be considered dominant if its customers or suppliers are dependent on the maintenance of their commercial relationship. This resulted in businesses being considered to be dominant and subject to an obligation to contract even when they held very modest market shares, e.g. in the case of a film distribution company holding a market share of only 12 percent.[18] **3.40**

Further obligations to contract may arise, in particular, under the Act on Local Supplies, which is also enforced by the Austrian competition authorities. Violations of this Act, however, do not carry sanctions as serious as those attached to competition law proper. **3.41**

J. Essential facilities

Based on the Court of Justice of the European Union's (CJEU) judgment in *Bronner*,[19] Austrian courts have held that dominant businesses may in some cases be required to grant access to "essential facilities" in order to allow other businesses to compete. The circumstances in which dominant businesses are required to do so have been defined narrowly: the resource (usually, an infrastructure or IP right) must be indispensable to compete, and the refusal must be likely to eliminate competition on the market. The dominant business may also rely on objective justifications. Based on these criteria, Austrian courts rejected *inter alia* an application by a newspaper publisher demanding access to another publisher's early morning distribution network.[20] **3.42**

A related question is whether the same criteria apply when refusal of access is not explicit but constructive, for example, if the margin between the cost of the resource and the price of the downstream product is insufficient for other businesses to compete ("margin squeeze"). This question has arisen, in particular, in the telecommunications industry. Austrian case law suggests that, in such cases, it is sufficient to demonstrate that the margin is insufficient to cover the related costs of an equally efficient competitor, without there being a need for the general criteria for access to essential facilities (indispensability and elimination of competition) to be met.[21] As the CJEU took a similar position in the *TeliaSonera* case,[22] it is likely that the essential facilities criteria will not apply in margin squeeze cases. **3.43**

K. Bundling (including loyalty and market share discounts)

Austrian courts have laid down a rather broad test for bundling by dominant businesses. According to the Austrian Supreme Court, bundling is unlawful if competitors are unable to replicate a bundle that is similar to and competitive with that offered by the dominant businesses. If this is the case, bundling is considered to be in violation of competition rules even if no part of the bundle is offered at a predatory price.[23] **3.44**

---

15 *Penicillium*, Austrian Supreme Court, 16 Ok 23/04 (December 20, 2005).
16 *Mobile phone exchange*, Austrian Supreme Court, 16 Ok 22/97 (December 17, 1997).
17 *Pharmaceutical data*, Austrian Supreme Court, 16 Ok 1/03 (March 10, 2003).
18 *Film distribution*, Austrian Supreme Court, 16 Ok 20/04 (April 4, 2005).
19 Case C-7/97 *Bronner v. Mediaprint* [1998] ECR I-7791.
20 *Bronner*, Austrian Supreme Court, 16 Ok 4/00 (May 15, 2000).
21 *KombiPaket*, Austrian Supreme Court, 16 Ok 13/08 (January 19, 2009).
22 Case C-52/09 *Konkurrensverket v. TeliaSonera* [2011] ECR I-527.
23 *Minimum fee*, Austrian Supreme Court, 16 Ok 11/04 (October 11, 2004).

3.45 Rebates granted by dominant businesses have not been addressed frequently in Austrian case law. Pursuant to a 1999 court decision, a dominant business abuses its position if it offers rebates in exchange for the customer's agreeing to exclusivity.[24] While there is no case law regarding rebates which reward loyalty without requiring exclusivity (e.g. market share or volume growth discounts), it is likely that such rebates would be considered to be in violation of antitrust rules, without evidence of actual foreclosure being required (in line with the *Intel* and *Tomra* cases at EU level).[25]

3.46 While there is no practice in Austria regarding the assessment of volume discounts, it is likely that the Austrian courts will follow EU practice in this regard. Generally speaking, individualized discounts will therefore be more objectionable than general rebate schemes, and retroactive rebates (i.e. rebates which apply to all purchases once a volume or value threshold has been reached) will be more objectionable than incremental rebates (i.e. discounts which apply only to purchases made above the threshold).

L. Standard-setting groups (disclosure requirements, licensing arrangements, and licensing pools)

3.47 While standard setting has recently received significant attention at EU level, there has been no relevant practice in Austria. It is, however, likely that any enforcement of the competition rules in relation to industry standards would be informed by the European Commission's practice. The safe harbor rule and additional considerations provided in the European Commission's Horizontal Cooperation Guidelines, while not binding on Austrian authorities, nevertheless provide useful guidance on the potential analysis under Austrian competition law.

M. Customer termination

3.48 Termination of existing customers is assessed within the framework of refusal to deal. Termination of customers by a dominant business will be considered abusive unless it is objectively justified. While the legal test is the same for the termination of existing customers as for the refusal to supply new customers, it is often assumed that it will be applied more strictly in the former case.

3.49 As discussed in Section I.I, Austrian courts have accepted that dominant businesses are entitled to terminate customers based on a breach of trust. In practice, this is the most common objective justification. Since the burden of proof is on the dominant undertaking, the justification of the termination should be clearly documented, both internally and in external correspondence with the customer. In the case of terminations that are not objectively justified, the main risk is private enforcement by the customer, who may apply for a cease-and-desist order before the Cartel Court or ask for damages in ordinary courts. By contrast, customer termination has received relatively little attention in public enforcement by Austrian competition authorities.

N. Termination of intermediaries (retailers, wholesalers, dealers, and value-added resellers, agents, and brokers)

3.50 Termination of intermediaries by dominant businesses is another case of refusal to deal (see Section I.I) and is assessed within that framework. If used to support or enforce other anticompetitive practices, termination of intermediaries may, however, fall within the scope of

[24] *Roof bricks*, Austrian Supreme Court, 4 Ob 90/99k (June 22, 1999).

[25] Case C-549/10 P *Tomra v. Commission*, April 19, 2012; *Intel*, EC Case COMP/C-3/37.990, 13 May 2009.

rules on anticompetitive agreements which also apply to non-dominant business. The most prominent case is where (a threat of) termination is used to enforce a recommended resale price, which will be considered as RPM.

O. Termination of relationships with competitors

Businesses are generally not required to trade with their competitors. In exceptional cases, termination of a relationship with a competitor by a dominant business may, however, infringe competition law (see Sections I.I and I.JI). **3.51**

P. Exemptions

Austrian competition law applies to all sectors of the economy, with limited exemptions for the finance and transport industries: circumstances which fall within the remit of sectoral regulators in these fields fall outside the scope of competition law. In other regulated industries, such as energy and telecom, competition law applies in conjunction with sectoral regulations. **3.52**

In addition, the law provides for a number of specific exemptions which cover only the rules on anticompetitive agreements (but not any other prohibitions of competition law). Limited sectoral exemptions from the prohibition on anticompetitive agreements exist in particular within the agricultural sector. More generally, anticompetitive agreements will be considered lawful if they give rise to economic efficiencies, provided that a number of requirements stipulated by the Cartel Act are met. **3.53**

Austrian law also provides for a safe harbor rule for agreements of minor importance. A recent amendment to the Cartel Act has brought this *de minimis* exemption in line with the EU model. Horizontal agreements are exempted if the combined market share does not exceed 10 percent, and vertical agreements—if the market share on either of the vertically related markets does not exceed 15 percent. The exemption does not apply to certain serious violations, such as price fixing, market sharing, or RPM. **3.54**

Unlike the European Commission, Austrian authorities have not enacted any safe harbor regulations for specific types of agreements. The European Commission's block exemption regulations, which provide safe harbor under EU law for certain types of agreements (see Chapter 12), however, also inform Austrian practice. **3.55**

II. Dealing with competitors

Horizontal agreements with an anticompetitive object, such as price or quantity fixing or market sharing, rank among the most serious violations of competition law. While, historically, Austria did not take a tough stance against cartels, the Federal Competition Authority has considerably stepped up its enforcement record in this regard since the mid-2000s, relying in particular on its leniency program and on its power to carry out unannounced inspections ("dawn raids"). These activities have led to significant fines being imposed on businesses by the Cartel Court. **3.56**

Horizontal agreements which do not directly aim to limit competition, such as agreements on joint purchasing, production, R&D, and information exchange, may also be prohibited if they produce anticompetitive effects. Horizontal agreements may, however, be justified based on economic efficiencies, provided that a number of requirements laid down by law are met. **3.57**

A. Horizontal price fixing

Price fixing among competitors is one of the most serious violations of competition law, and attracts very high fines. Since the mid-2000s, the Federal Competition Authority has been very active in pursuing these types of cartels, and, in a number of cases, has successfully **3.58** applied for fines before the Cartel Court. The highest fine to date (a total of EUR 75.4 million) was imposed in 2007 on five producers of elevators and escalators, for an infringement comprising customer allocation, price fixing, and exchange of sensitive market information.[26] Fines have also been imposed, *inter alia*, on distributors of specialty chemicals[27] and printing chemicals.[28] The latter case is notable because it involved the imposition of a fine on the first leniency applicant, who had failed to meet all of the requirements for full immunity.

3.59 Advance price announcements may be an instrument used by cartelists, and may thus serve as evidence of an underlying price cartel. Parallel announcements will not, however, always be sufficient proof of an "agreement" or a "concerted practice" between competitors. Pursuant to the CJEU's judgment in *Wood Pulp*,[29] which concerned simultaneous quarterly price announcements in the trade press, parallel announcements will not be regarded as sufficient proof of concerted action unless concerted action constitutes the only plausible explanation for the conduct in question.

3.60 Recent investigations by the Federal Competition Authority in the supermarkets[30] and insulation materials[31] businesses relate, *inter alia*, to hub-and-spoke practices. In this type of cases, producers use their distributors as intermediaries to exchange information and arrive at a common understanding, for example regarding pricing (or *vice versa*, producers serve as intermediaries for distributors). As all cases decided to date have been settled against the payment of a fine, no reasoned decision on hub-and-spoke practices is available in Austria.

B. Horizontal agreements to allocate customers or territories; agreements not to compete

3.61 Like price fixing, market and customer allocation rank among the most serious violations of competition law. Most of the hardcore cartels which have been fined by the Cartel Court also involved elements of market or customer allocation (such as the elevators, specialty chemicals, and printing chemicals cases[32]). However, in a recent case, the Federal Competition Authority's application to impose fines for alleged market sharing among providers of sanitary installation services was rejected by the Cartel Court, which considered that the arrangements were *de minimis*.[33]

3.62 In some cases, agreements not to compete, such as joint production or specialization agreements, may, however, give rise to economic efficiencies. Austrian law provides no safe harbor for such agreements. However, the safe harbor rules laid down in the European Commission's block exemption for specialization agreements (which provides for an exemption of up to a combined market share of 20 percent, subject to certain additional requirements) as well as the additional considerations set out in the Horizontal Cooperation Guidelines will also inform Austrian practice with regard to such agreements.

---

[26] *Elevators and escalators*, Austrian Cartel Court 25 Kt 12/07 (December 14, 2007), upheld by Austrian Supreme Court, 16 Ok 5/08 (October 8, 2008).

[27] *Industry chemicals*, Austrian Cartel Court, 29 Kt 132, 133/07 (October 24, 2008), upheld by Austrian Supreme Court, 16 Ok 4/09 (March 25, 2009).

[28] *Printing chemicals*, Austrian Cartel Court, 29 Kt 5/09 (March 26, 2010), upheld by Austrian Supreme Court, 16 Ok 5/10 (October 4, 2010).

[29] Joined Cases C-89, 104, 114, 116, 117, and 125–129/85 *A. Ahlström Osakeyhtiö and others v. Commission* [1993] ECR I-1307.

[30] See e.g. Federal Competition Authority, Press Release of May 14, 2013, <http://www.bwb.gv.at/KartelleUndMarkmachtmissbrauch/Entscheidungen/Seiten/K-252.aspx>; Federal Competition Authority, Press Release of October 3, 2013, <http://www.bwb.gv.at/KartelleUndMarkmachtmissbrauch/Entscheidungen/Seiten/KartellgerichtverhängtGeldbußeimLebensmittelhandel.aspx>.

[31] See e.g. *bauMax*, Austrian Cartel Court, 27 Kt 32/13 (May 13, 2013).

[32] See *Elevators and escalators* (n 26); *Industry chemicals* (n 27); and *Printing chemicals* (n 28).

[33] *Sanitary installation services*, Austrian Cartel Court, 27 Kt 20, 21/09 (July 13, 2012).

C. Horizontal boycotts

Agreements between competitors not to deal with certain customers or suppliers may violate the prohibition on anticompetitive agreements. In a recent case, members of the Austrian Association of Brewers agreed to a settlement involving a EUR 1.1 million fine for their decision not to supply wholesale traders with beer in casks.[34] Boycott cases, however, are rare under competition law; more commonly, such practices are challenged under the commercial fairness rules of the Unfair Competition Act. **3.63**

D. Joint ventures and other competitive collaborations

Joint ventures which are "full-function," i.e. which operate on the market as independent economic entities, fall within the scope of merger control rules. There is some uncertainty as to whether Austrian merger control rules also cover joint ventures which are not full-function, such as purchasing joint ventures. In 2011, the Cartel Court rejected an application for review of a purchasing joint venture in the telecoms sector under merger control, holding that the creation of JV did not qualify as a reviewable merger.[35] **3.64**

Cooperation in joint ventures which is not caught by the merger control rules will be subject to the prohibition of anticompetitive agreements. This rule is applicable to a wide variety of joint ventures which involve cooperation in R&D, production, purchasing, etc. Such joint ventures will be prohibited if they have an anticompetitive object or give rise to anticompetitive effects, but may be justified based on economic efficiencies. **3.65**

There is limited case law in Austria that analyzes such joint ventures. In 2005, the Cartel Court prohibited a production joint venture involving a number of large Austrian construction companies, which operated a joint asphalt-mixing plant.[36] On appeal, the decision was set aside by the Austrian Supreme Court,[37] and later settled based on commitments aimed at limiting the information flow between the joint venture and the parent companies.[38] As the Supreme Court's decision reveals,[39] the assessment of joint ventures under Austrian law will essentially be guided by the block exemption regulations and guidelines issued by the European Commission (see Section II.B). **3.66**

E. Trade associations

While participation in trade associations in itself is not objectionable under competition law, anticompetitive activities conducted by such associations are caught by antitrust rules. The Cartel Court may impose fines on a trade association for such activities. In the mid-2000s, the Federal Competition Authority actively reviewed decisions issued by a number of trade associations (in particular in the liberal professions), which resulted in these associations abandoning the publication of price lists in favor of more general calculation guidelines.[40] Since then, enforcement of competition law against trade associations has not been a main priority in Austria. **3.67**

---

[34] Federal Competition Authority, Press Release of April 10, 2012, <http://www.bwb.gv.at/KartelleUndMarkmachtmissbrauch/Entscheidungen/Seiten/BWBK-212.aspx>.

[35] See the information made available at the Federal Competition Authority's website, <http://www.bwb.gv.at/Zusammenschluesse/Zusammenschluesse_2011/Seiten/BWB_Z-1506.aspx>.

[36] *Asphalt mixing plant*, Austrian Cartel Court, 25 Kt 183, 184/04 (September 5, 2005).

[37] *Asphalt mixing plant*, Austrian Supreme Court, 16 Ok 51/05 (June 26, 2006).

[38] *Asphalt mixing plant*, Austrian Cartel Court, 25 Kt 41/06 (July 15, 2009).

[39] *Asphalt mixing plant* (n 37).

[40] *Building engineer fee guidelines*, Austrian Cartel Court, 16 Ok 45/05 (December 20, 2005). In addition, a number of industry associations (e.g. furniture transporters, financial service providers, technical bureaus, freight forwarders, and logistics providers) voluntarily modified their recommendations, see Federal Competition Authority, Annual Report, May 1, 2004 to June 30, 2005, pp. 26 ff.; Federal Competition Authority, Annual Report, July 1, 2005 to June 30, 2006, pp. 23 ff.

3.68 Trade associations, however, may also serve as a platform for concluding anticompetitive agreements or exchanging sensitive information. If members of a trade organization engage in such conduct, they violate competition law (just as they would if they did the same outside the organization), and are liable to incur fines. It is therefore important to avoid this kind of conduct within trade associations. Particular care should be taken with regard to information exchange (see Section II.H). In order to avoid running antitrust risks, trade associations sometimes invite specialized antitrust counsel to monitor high-level meetings.

3.69 Business representatives who remain passive in association meetings while anticompetitive discussions take place run the risk their company will be held liable for the conduct. In order to avoid that risk, they should actively dissociate themselves from such discussions by leaving the meeting, and making sure that the reason for their departure is recorded in the minutes of the meeting.

F. Interlocking directorates

3.70 Interlocking directorships fall within the scope of the Austrian merger control rules if they lead to a minimum 50 percent overlap between the executive or supervisory boards of two businesses (irrespective of whether these businesses are competitors).

3.71 While the presence of management interlocks which fall short of the 50 percent threshold may constitute an infringement of antitrust law, there is no case law on this issue in Austria. More importantly, overlaps in management may facilitate anticompetitive practices, such as cartels or exchange of sensitive information. In such cases, infringing businesses will be held liable.

G. Facilitating practices

3.72 Practices which facilitate anticompetitive conduct are not subject to regulation in their own right under Austrian competition law. An exception exists for interlocking directorates (see Section II.F) and for acquisitions of non-controlling minority interests which may be subject to merger control scrutiny.

H. Information exchange

3.73 Information exchange violates Austrian antitrust law if it has an anticompetitive objective, or gives rise to anticompetitive effects, unless it can be justified based on economic efficiencies. Austrian courts have held that information sharing is objectionable when it concerns recent data which is not readily available to the parties and is of relevance to competition between them.[41] While no detailed guidance on information exchange is available in Austria, reference can be made to the European Commission's Horizontal Cooperation Guidelines (see further Chapter 12, Sections I.K and II.H).

(i) Exchanges of historic pricing information

3.74 Exchange of price information is generally problematic, unless the information is historic such that its sharing can no longer result in coordination between the parties.

(ii) How old, anonymous, and aggregated pricing information needs to be

3.75 There are no hard and fast rules regarding the characteristics of data that may be exchanged. Rather, the assessment of information exchange will depend on the characteristics of the market (such as market concentration and the frequency of price negotiations), as well as of the exchange itself (level of aggregation, frequency of the exchange, openness of the exchange to third parties such as customers).

[41] *Loss sharing agreement*, Austrian Supreme Court, 16 Ok 12/06 (March 21, 2007).

(iii) What pro-competitive purposes, if any, exchange needs to help participants achieve; pre-merger due diligence

Information exchange that does not restrict competition need not produce pro-competitive effects. However, undertakings may rely on pro-competitive effects (such as efficiency gains through benchmarking) to justify information exchange that otherwise would be prohibited. **3.76**

Competition law also applies to information disclosed in the course of pre-merger due diligence. In transactions involving competing businesses, sensitive data may therefore not be disclosed. In order to allow for a meaningful due diligence assessment, parties may establish "clean teams" and adopt safeguards to prevent further circulation of sensitive information. **3.77**

I. Joint purchasing agreements

Joint purchasing agreements may infringe competition law, in particular if they give rise to significant buyer power vis-à-vis suppliers, or facilitate coordination between the parties on the market where they sell their products. The parties may, however, rely on the efficiency defense in order to justify joint purchasing agreements. Limited case law on these issues is available in Austria, but guidance may be found in the European Commission's Horizontal Cooperation Guidelines (see Chapter 12, Sections I.K and II.H). **3.78**

J. Joint lobbying/regulatory/legislative efforts

Joint lobbying activities generally do not give rise to liability under antitrust law. However, lobbying activities are subject to regulation in their own right under the Austrian Lobbying Act, which sets out in particular registration requirements (s. 5) and certain obligations relating to the conduct of lobbying activities in good faith and with sufficient transparency (ss. 6 ff.). **3.79**

III. General issues

A. Jurisdiction and applicable law (including sector-specific competition regulation)

The substantive provisions of Austrian competition law are laid down in the Cartel Act, while the Competition Act provides for investigative powers on the part of the Federal Competition Authority. Sectoral regulation in a number of sectors, such as telecoms, energy, and rail, also sets out rules which are of relevance to competition (e.g. access to infrastructure, pricing, etc.). **3.80**

Ratione personae, Austrian competition law applies to all natural or legal persons that are the owners of an "undertaking." Undertakings include any entity involved in economic activities, regardless of its legal form and whether or not it operates for profit. **3.81**

In terms of geographic scope, Austrian competition law explicitly enshrines the effects doctrine: it applies to all conduct that produces effects on the Austrian market, irrespective of where the conduct itself has taken place. In cases which affect trade between the EU member states, the jurisdiction of the Austrian competition authorities, however, is subject to certain limitations. In particular, a decision by the European Commission to initiate proceedings relieves national authorities already working on the case of their jurisdiction. **3.82**

B. Antitrust system

(i) Name of agency/agencies

Unlike the EU model, the Austrian antitrust system is based on a strict division between the investigating authority and the ultimate decision-maker. Investigative powers are vested in the Federal Competition Authority (*Bundeswettbewerbsbehörde*), whereas all decisions in **3.83** antitrust matters are made by the Cartel Court (*Kartellgericht*). In addition to the Federal Competition Authority, the Federal Cartel Procurator (*Bundeskartellanwalt*) also is *ex officio* party to all proceedings before the Cartel Court, and may bring proceedings before that court. Unlike the Federal Competition Authority, however, the procurator has no investigative powers.

3.84 Finally, the Cartel Court may also be applied to by a number of other public bodies (such as sectoral regulators), as well as by any persons having a legal or economic interest in the matter at issue. Applications for fines, however, may be brought only by the Federal Competition Authority or the Federal Cartel Procurator.

3.85 Decisions by the Cartel Court are subject to judicial review by the Superior Cartel Court (*Kartellobergericht*), a division of the Austrian Supreme Court. Appeal lies on points of law only.

(ii) Staff size and budget

3.86 With a staff of about thirty (including four support staff) and a budget of approximately EUR 2.4 million, the Federal Competition Authority is a comparatively small enforcement agency.

(iii) Recent enforcement actions and trends

3.87 While in the first few years since its creation in 2002, the Federal Competition Authority focused mostly on merger control work, it has considerably expanded its enforcement record in the antitrust field since the mid-2000s. The authority's focus has been on cartels as well as, more recently, on RPM and hub-and-spoke practices. In bringing cases, it relies primarily on dawn raids and on information received under its leniency program. The efforts made by the Federal Competition Authority to step up enforcement are evident when considering data on dawn raids: the authority did not conduct any dawn raids of its own in 2010, but carried out fourteen in 2011 and eighteen in 2012.[42]

3.88 The Federal Competition Authority has been less active in bringing cases for abuse of dominance. Such cases, however, continue to be brought by private applicants, who are entitled to apply directly to the Cartel Court (where the burden of proof on them is somewhat lower than in the ordinary civil courts, since the Cartel Court can gather evidence *ex officio*).

C. Private litigation

3.89 Private applicants can apply to the Cartel Court for orders putting a stop to infringing activity, as well as for injunctive relief, provided they have a legal or economic interest in the matter. Private applicants may also apply for cease-and-desist orders in ordinary courts under the Unfair Competition Act, since violations of antitrust rules will often (but not always) qualify as unfair conduct under that Act.

3.90 Since the late 2000s, private litigation for damages is also increasingly common. Typically, it takes the form of follow-on litigation after an infringement decision by the Cartel Court (for the status of these cases, see Section III.D). Damages claims cannot be adjudicated by the Cartel Court, but must be brought before ordinary courts. Under Austrian law, courts cannot award punitive damages to private claimants.

[42] Excluding dawn raids in support of the European Commission or foreign competition authorities. See Federal Competition Authority, Annual Report 2012, pp. 11, 47; Federal Competition Authority, Annual Report 2011, p. 51.

D. Follow-on litigation (includes role of agency determinations of liability for follow-on litigation)

Since the 2007 decision in the elevators and escalators cartel,[43] follow-on litigation has become increasingly common in Austria. So far, however, there has only been one award of damages in a case involving negligible amounts (a test case brought by the Federal Chamber of Labor for a driving school student against a driving school),[44] while a number of cases involving significant damages claims are currently pending. **3.91**

In a number of interim judgments, Austrian courts have clarified that private claimants can base their claims directly on the violation of antitrust law at issue (which has several advantages compared to contractual claims), and that the members of a cartel may be held jointly and severally liable for the damage caused.[45] Other issues, such as the availability of the passing-on defense, are yet to be clarified under Austrian law. **3.92**

While infringement decisions previously were not legally binding on civil courts, this has been changed by a recent amendment to the Cartel Act. Pursuant to s. 37a(3) of the Act (as amended), final decisions rendered by the Cartel Court, the European Commission, as well as by the national competition authorities of other EU member states, now have binding effect on Austrian civil courts. **3.93**

E. Arbitration and alternative dispute resolution

Pursuant to CJEU case law, the rules of competition law are public policy rules. If an arbitral panel ignores competition law, for example by enforcing a contractual provision which is in violation of the antitrust rules, its award may be challenged on public policy grounds. In practice, competition law issues sometimes arise in arbitration, for example in cases involving energy supply contracts. **3.94**

F. Remedies

(i) Civil liability

For anticompetitive agreements and abuses of a dominant position, the Cartel Court may impose fines of up to 10 percent of a business's group-wide annual turnover. Similar fines apply in the case of violations of commitments which have been declared binding by the Cartel Court. Violations of procedural orders, such as the order to comply with an information request, also carry fines (albeit lower). In addition, the Cartel Court also has the power to impose periodic penalty payments of up to 5 percent of the average daily turnover to compel a business to end certain infringing activities. **3.95**

The statutory maximum amounts (5 or 10 percent, respectively) are based on the turnover achieved by the business group in the last fiscal year. The maximum amount therefore is to be determined based on the worldwide turnover achieved by the entire group, rather than just the revenues achieved in Austria, or the turnover achieved by the subsidiary which is party to the proceedings.[46] **3.96**

Only the Federal Competition Authority and the Federal Cartel Procurator may bring applications for fines or period penalty payments. The Cartel Court may not impose a fine or penalty higher than that applied for by the requesting authority. While no guidelines **3.97**

[43] *Elevators and escalators* (n 26).

[44] *Graz driving schools*, Regional Court for Civil Matters Graz, 17 R 91/07p (August 17, 2007).

[45] See e.g. *Elevators and escalators III*, Austrian Supreme Court, 7 Ob 48/12b (October 17, 2012); *ATM agreement III*, Austrian Supreme Court, 4 Ob 46/12m (August 2, 2012).

[46] *Manner*, Austrian Supreme Court, 16 Ok 8/07 (January 21, 2008).

have been published under Austrian law, in practice, in determining the level of fines, the Federal Competition Authority relies on the European Commission's 2006 Guidelines on the method of setting fines. Within the limit of the fine applied for by the requesting authority, the Cartel Court has a broad discretion in determining the actual fine to be imposed.

3.98 Violations are subject to a limitation period of five years, within which the application for fines must be lodged. Investigative measures by the Federal Competition Authority do not interrupt the limitation period.

3.99 In its decision bringing the infringing activity to an end, the Cartel Court may also impose remedies, which may be behavioral or—if behavioral remedies are not equally effective or would be even more burdensome—structural. Similarly, the court may make binding the commitments proposed by a business that is subject to Cartel Court proceedings. Upon application, the Cartel Court is also competent to impose interim measures.

3.100 In addition to any measures imposed by the Cartel Court, contractual provisions which violate antitrust rules will be considered void, pursuant to Austrian statutory provisions and case law. Austrian courts have held that provisions affected by nullity may, however, be severable from the rest of the contract.[47] Whether a provision is severable will depend on the circumstances of the case.

(ii) Criminal liability

3.101 Pursuant to the Austrian Criminal Code, bid-rigging amounts to a criminal offense and is punishable by imprisonment of up to three years. It is unclear whether this provision applies only to public procurement proceedings, or whether it also includes private calls for tenders. In some older decisions, the Austrian courts also qualified participation in a cartel as criminal law fraud.[48] Serious cases of fraud may give rise to prison sentences of up to ten years.

G. Leniency and immunity

3.102 Leniency is available in Austria for all violations of the prohibition of anticompetitive agreements. Unlike at EU level, leniency is therefore not restricted to secret horizontal cartels, but may also be granted, for example, in vertical cases. While no leniency is available for dominance, contributions by the dominant business to fact-finding will be taken into account as an attenuating circumstance.

3.103 Leniency applications are submitted to the Federal Competition Authority, which may grant the applicant full immunity from fines, or apply for a reduced fine. While the material standard to be met by immunity applicants so far has been relatively unclear, a recent amendment to the Competition Act has brought requirements in line with the EU model: immunity will be granted to the first applicant, allowing the Federal Competition Authority to apply for the authorization of a dawn raid or (if the authority already has sufficient information for a dawn raid) allowing the Authority to submit to the Cartel Court a reasoned application for the imposition of a fine. In addition, the applicant for immunity is required to cease the infringing activity, and to fully cooperate with the Federal Competition Authority throughout the investigation. Immunity is not available for businesses which coerced other participants to take part in the infringement.

[47] See e.g. Austrian Supreme Court, 10 Ob 10/12m (March 13, 2012); Austrian Supreme Court, 6 Ob 322/00x (February 22, 2001).

[48] See e.g. Austrian Supreme Court, 13 Os 135/03 (October 10, 2004); Austrian Supreme Court, 13 Os 34/01 (September 26, 2001).

Businesses that fail to meet the material standard for full immunity may nevertheless qualify for a reduction in fines. Evidence provided by applicants must represent significant added value in order to qualify for a reduction. The other conditions for full immunity (cessation of infringement, full cooperation, and no coercion of other participants) also apply to fine reductions. **3.104**

The Federal Competition Authority has published a "Leniency Handbook" in which it sets out its interpretation of the statutory conditions for leniency, as well as the main procedural steps in leniency proceedings.[49] **3.105**

H. Document creation and retention

Austrian competition law does not provide for rules on document creation or retention. In its "Leniency Handbook," the Federal Competition Authority explains that it will regard the suppression, tampering with, or destruction of evidence as incompatible with the duty of full cooperation which is incumbent upon leniency applicants. In addition, it is very likely that, even outside of leniency cases, the authority would regard such conduct as an incriminating circumstance when determining the amount of the fine applied for before the Cartel Court. Finally, the provision of incomplete information in response to a formal information request is subject to fines in its own right. **3.106**

[49] Leniency Handbook, <http://www.bwb.gv.at/KartelleUndMarkmachtmissbrauch/Kronzeugenregelung/Seiten/default.aspx>.

4

BRAZIL

*Barbara Rosenberg and José C. M. Berardo**

Barbosa, Müssnich & Aragão

Introduction

4.01 Brazil has had competition-related laws since at least 1937, and the country's main competition authority, the Administrative Council for Economic Defense (CADE), was created in 1962. Strong government control of the economy, however, relegated these competition laws and the authorities' activities to a secondary role. Only after the enactment of the Brazilian 1988 Constitution and the initial steps of the modernization of the economy in the early 1990s did competition become legally and economically relevant. In December 1990, a Law criminalizing cartel behavior was passed, and in June 1994, Law no. 8,884 entered into force.

4.02 From 1995 through 2002, most of CADE's actions were focused on merger control, with cartels and other anticompetitive behavior dealt with reactively, even on the criminal side.

* The authors thank Bruno Bastos Becker for his assistance in the preparation and review of this Chapter.

An amendment passed in 2001 authorized CADE to enter into leniency agreements and the competition authorities to conduct searches, and it was only from 2003 onwards that the Government optimized its work in merger cases, reducing the amount of duplicated work, and started to concentrate its enforcement actions against cartels, with leniency agreements, searches, and closer work with the criminal authorities (police, federal, and state prosecutors) becoming increasingly more common.

On May 29, 2012, Law no. 12,529 entered into force, strengthening CADE's position as an independent agency, first by consolidating investigative and decision powers that were previously held by a body within the Ministry of Justice; and, second, by adopting a suspensory merger control regime. Even though there were no meaningful changes to substantive rules regarding the prohibition of anticompetitive conduct (art. 36 of Law no. 12,529), there are no relevant precedents issued by the CADE or reviewed by the Courts under the new Law; our analysis of substantive issues herein, therefore, relies mostly on precedents that were adopted by CADE or the courts on the basis of article 20 of Law no. 8,884. In 1999, the CADE adopted a regulation (Resolution no. 20) which set forth guidance framework rules for the economic assessment of anticompetitive conduct. Although this regulation might have been implicitly cancelled by Law no. 12,529, its value as orientation persists. **4.03**

Enforcement activities have been particularly focused, after the issuance of Law no. 12,529, on clearing merger control dockets and making the pre-merger notification system work as expected. Nonetheless, the CADE has also dedicated a lot of effort in fighting cartels, especially in the infrastructure sectors; unilateral behavior is generally not seen as an enforcement priority even if the number of cases and decisions is not relatively small. **4.04**

I. Acting alone

Brazilian law sets forth a general prohibition to any conduct having the limitation of competition as its object or its potential effect (art. 36, I, of Law no. 12,529/2011); this prohibition derives directly from the constitutional rule stating that "the law shall punish the abuse of economic power aimed at dominating markets, at eliminating competition or at arbitrarily increasing profits" (art. 173, s. 4 of the Brazilian Constitution). The competition law also sets forth that market growth "resulting from a natural process founded on the increased efficiency of an economic agent in relation to its competitors" is not unlawful. **4.05**

These rules compose the framework for the prosecution of both horizontal (i.e. conducts involving contacts with competitors) and unilateral (mostly abuse of dominance cases) conduct and vertical restraints (i.e. conduct that involves firms' relationships with their customers and suppliers). Despite the authorities' focus on the prosecution of cartels, there is a growing body of administrative precedents in Brazil regarding conduct that does not involve competitors, on a wide range of sectors, from beverages to automotive parts, including pharmaceutical products, electronics, media, credit cards, and shopping malls. Court decisions on the merits of the proper interpretation of the law (confirming or denying the authorities' instance on the law), however, are still rare,[1] but should appear more often as the judicial review of the first administrative decisions come to an end.[2] **4.06**

[1] See Superior Court of Justice (STJ), Case REsp 1181643, decision of March 3, 2011, per Justice Herman Benjamin.

[2] See e.g. the cases involving exclusivity (*Shopping Iguatemi*, CADE Case no. 08012.006636/1997-43, decision of September 2007, under Court review) and loyalty discounts (*AmBev*, CADE Case no. 08012.003805/2004-10, decision of July 2009, under Court review).

4.07 Within this framework, the authorities' decision practice indicates that, in general, investigations and decisions of unilateral and vertical conduct generally follow an effects-based approach (sometimes referred to by the authorities as a "rule of reason" approach), which takes into consideration the balancing of both the potential or actual anticompetitive effects of the conduct and its potential economic benefits (efficiencies). Some precedents, however, seem structured as form-based, and they either implicitly impose some type of special responsibility on dominant firms or are mainly based on the alleged anticompetitive "object" (intent) of the conduct, giving less emphasis to the balance of its competitive effects.

4.08 The assessment of dominance is a central element of the authorities' analysis in unilateral conduct or vertical restraints, and the finding of an unlawful conduct under Brazilian Law in those types of cases depends on a finding of dominance. In general, dominance in Brazil is identified following conventional antitrust wisdom (definition of the markets affected by the conduct, assessment of concentration levels, analysis of entry barriers and imports etc.), and, in essence, the concept of dominance is seen as corresponding to the finding of "market power," in the usual sense this expression is adopted by the literature and other jurisdictions—the ability of a firm, profitably and unilaterally, to increase prices for a reasonable period. Although the authorities have more than once recognized that market power and dominance are not necessarily linked to market shares, the competition law sets forth a rebuttable presumption of dominance if a firm's market share exceeds 20 percent (art. 36, s. 2 of Law no. 12,529/2011).

4.09 The standard of proof adopted by the authorities for a finding of dominance and for the assessment of the conduct's competitive effects, however, is not consistent from case to case, and parties' are sometimes faced with an illegal shift in the burden of proof on the basis of the dominance finding during the proceeding (i.e. the investigations are carried out such as to give the parties the opportunity to show the benefits of the practice under investigation).

4.10 The law sets forth a list of examples of conducts that could be distinguished as infringements (art. 36, s. 3 of Law no. 12,529/2011). This list, however, is merely illustrative and the finding of an infringement does not depend on the conduct being expressly cited by the competition law. Although not systematically, enforcement activities on unilateral behavior in the recent past included RPM, exclusivity and fidelity discount cases.

A. Predatory pricing

4.11 Even though cited by the competition law as a potential infringement (art. 36, s. 3, XV of Law no. 12,529/2011), decisions finding infringements because of predatory pricing are rare in Brazil.[3] To find a violation, the authorities assess not only the claim of underselling, but also market conditions for recoupment of the losses (Ordinance no. 70/2002, issued by the Secretariat of Economic Monitoring of the Ministry of Finance). Therefore, they generally require evidence that the dominant firm has easy access to financing and either (i) that it priced below its average variable cost, or (ii) that it (a) priced above its average variable cost but below its average total cost and (b) that it is purposefully neglecting price increase opportunities (sacrificing revenues/profit) in view of relevant demand and supply variables (sudden demand shifts, sudden supply excess capacity, etc.).

4.12 The authorities may assess similar predatory behavior in connection to other types of conduct (e.g. loyalty discounts), and they are bound to follow the same dual approach with respect to (a) cost analysis and profit/revenue sacrifices and (b) possibility of recoupment.

[3] See e.g. *Drogaria São Paulo*, CADE Case no. 08012.000219/2005-02, decision of August 2006 and *Fresenius Kabi Brasil*, CADE Case no. 08012.011596/2007-21, decision of November 2012.

B. Exploitative offenses (excessive pricing, monopoly leveraging)

Exploitative offenses are no longer cited by the competition law as an infringement, as it used to be under Law no. 8,884. Nonetheless, the authorities have consistently pointed out that they are ill equipped to assess the lawfulness of pricing practices, even if exploitative ones could harm consumers. The prevailing understanding is that excessive pricing and similar conduct are probably the result of other types of anticompetitive behavior or induced by particular market structures than isolated infringements. There were no findings of pure exploitative infringements under the competition law in Brazil.[4] **4.13**

C. Monopsony

There have been no isolated investigations of abuse of monopsony power, even though it theoretically could be a competition infringement under Brazilian law in view of the general prohibition set forth by article 36, I. Some investigations emphasizing monopsony power have occurred in the context of merger reviews, but there are not enough decisions that would allow a clear framework of how the matter shall be dealt with, especially in the context of a conduct investigation. **4.14**

D. Price discrimination

Price discrimination is cited as a possible infringement of the competition law under article 36, s. 3, X of Law no. 12,529/2011. However, there are no relevant precedents in which price discrimination was found as an isolated violation. Generally speaking, the authorities tend to recognize that "price discrimination is not intrinsically anticompetitive, even if it increases the supplier's profits, as it may not restrict, or even increase, output," as long as the discrimination is based upon criteria that take into consideration relevant differences among different groups of customers, and they require a detailed assessment of the particular concrete conduct. The authorities recognize that price discrimination may at times be used to conceal some form of refusal to deal or tying, the competitive effects of which should be considered separately.[5] **4.15**

E. Dictating or influencing resale prices

Despite the relevance of the matter and widespread adoption of methods to influence retail prices, the Brazilian authorities have had very few precedents over the years regarding resale prices. The law cites that an infringement can be found if a "company imposes to distributors, retailers and agents resale prices, discounts, payment conditions, minimum or maximum quantities, profit margins, or any other sale conditions regarding the relationship of these distributors, retailers or agents with third parties" (article 36, s. 3, IX of Law no. 12,529/2011). **4.16**

The most relevant case in this area was a majority decision issued in January 2013, after more than ten years of investigation, in which the prevailing opinions asserted, in brief, that a dominant company may only implement a retail price maintenance policy with its distributors—no matter how limited or specific—if the practice entails relevant cost-savings, in view of the coordination risks they imply in the upstream and downstream market, and the availability of less restrictive means for obtaining economic efficiency.[6] **4.17**

Even though this decision does not expressly formulate the issue as such, currently, there is a rebuttable presumption of unlawfulness of resale price (margins, discounts, sales terms **4.18**

---

[4] See *White Martins*, CADE Case no. 08012.003648/1998-05, decision of August 2008. The CADE also assessed similar claims regarding intellectual property rights in *Koninklijke Philips Electronics N.V.*, Case no. 08012.001315/2007-21, decision of May 2009.

[5] See CADE Resolution no. 20/1999.

[6] *SKF do Brasil*, CADE Case no. 08012.001271/2001-44, decision of January 2013.

and conditions, etc.) maintenance arrangements among producers and distributors/retailers. Price suggestions, in whatever form they appear (minimum advertised price (MAP), manufacturer's suggested retail price (MSRP), etc.), however, have been considered lawful and pro-competitive if there are no explicit or tacit mechanisms for punishing deviations of distributors and retailers, and the authorities generally take into consideration the level of inter-brand competition as a benchmark to assess the actual competitive effects of these suggestions.[7]

F. Tying arrangements

4.19 Article 36, XVIII of Law no. 12,529/2011 cites tying as a potential anticompetitive practice, but it is difficult to identify a decision from the CADE actually finding this type of violation. Resolution no. 20/1999 used to limit the anticompetitive effects of tying practices to leveraging of market power from one market to another—in a very similar fashion to the rationale adopted by other jurisdictions—and to the foreclosure effects associated to the tied product. Even though precedents are sparse, the rationale for the assessment of unilateral practices in Brazil naturally requires dominance in the tying product as condition for the finding of a violation. Scope economies are often deemed to be valid as an efficiency-based defense in tying cases.

G. Exclusive dealing

4.20 The CADE has already reviewed several exclusive dealing cases, but the findings of anticompetitive effects are generally rare; the law does not cite exclusivity as an example of anticompetitive behavior, and in the past it was generally framed under the residual example of "creating difficulties for competitors."

4.21 The framework of analysis is more established in comparison with other types of unilateral conduct and, in addition to dominance, a violation requires the demonstration that the exclusive agreement forecloses a substantial part of the demand/supply of the exclusive product, either by preventing competitors from accessing a substantial part of the consumers or distribution channels or by relegating competitors to less efficient distribution channels. The authorities have not up to now established safe harbors for assessing foreclosure levels, but decisions generally refer to a 20–30 percent level as acceptable.

4.22 The authorities generally place great value on the business rationale offered for the adoption of exclusivity clauses and related economic efficiencies are consequently taken into consideration for the finding of a violation. Depending on the size of the efficiencies verified and the extension of the anticompetitive effects, exclusivity clauses may be deemed as lawful.

H. Refusal to deal

4.23 Although the CADE reviewed a number of cases involving refusal to deal claims,[8] no infringement decision has been issued as of the time of this writing. CADE decisions, however, highlight that this type of claim should be assessed on the basis of the effects of the conduct competition in the upstream or downstream markets and ultimately to consumers. Harm to an individual customer or supplier is not deemed to be relevant for purposes of assessing refusal to deal claims.[9]

---

[7] See e.g. *Several book publishers*, CADE Case no. 08012.001743/2002-40, decision of July 2011, and in *Puma, Nike, Asics, Adidas and others*, CADE Case no. 08012.008443/2007-04, decision of December 2009.

[8] See e.g. *Several hospitals in São Paulo*, CADE Case no. 08012.011924/1999-17, decision of September 2012; *Sumitomo Corporation do Brasil*, CADE Case no. 08012.000416/2005-13, decision of July 2012; and *Santa casa de Arcos*, CADE Case no. 08012.011463/2007-54, decision of January 2011.

[9] See e.g. *Globosat Programadora*, CADE Case no. 08012.003048/2001-31, decision of May 2006.

I. Essential facilities

The CADE has reviewed very few cases involving claims regarding access to essential facilities, and no general rule can be extracted as a basis for the assessment of practices involving essential facilities. Generally speaking, however, the CADE has adopted as a basis for its analysis the framework adopted by relevant decisions abroad (mainly in the US and Europe). It is possible to say, however, that the CADE has more than once expressed its concern about the existence of essential facilities as this may result in excessive intervention that may be harmful for investment and development. **4.24**

J. Bundling (including loyalty and market share discounts)

In the *AmBev v. Tô Contigo* case[10] the CADE found an infringement on the basis of the aggressive adoption of loyalty rebates inducing exclusivity, on the basis that supporting evidence revealed anticompetitive intent in the implementation of the loyalty program. On the basis of this isolated decision and on a provisional opinion regarding another case,[11] it seems the Brazilian authorities tend to lean towards an European-based interpretation of loyalty discounts as object (per se) violations, even if they should—because of the legal framework discussed in para. 4.7—assess these discounts on the basis of their ability to lessen competition, the dominant companies' costs and related efficiencies. **4.25**

K. Standard-setting groups (disclosure requirements, licensing arrangements, and licensing pools)

There have been no cases involving standard-setting groups in Brazil, especially regarding disclosure requirements. Licensing arrangements and licensing pools, however, have been reviewed at least once[12] as possible anticompetitive practices, but no violation was found because the CADE could not establish whether the licensing arrangement excluded competitors from the market. In the same sense, the CADE considered the licensing pool (collective sale of licensing IP rights) to produce relevant efficiencies. **4.26**

L. Customer termination

The CADE reviewed several cases involving customer and intermediaries termination, but it rarely, if at all, found a violation. The authorities' decisions are largely based on the fact that the cases brought regarding terminations did not imply in any type of harm to competition (lack of potential anticompetitive effects or object), but only private decisions which did not affect competition. As a rule, to the extent that the termination is based on objective criteria (profitability, brand positioning, etc.), the CADE generally views termination as an exercise of business discretion not affecting competition. **4.27**

M. Termination of intermediaries (retailers, wholesalers, dealers, and value-added resellers, agents, and brokers)

See Section I.L. **4.28**

N. Termination of relationships with competitors

See Section I.L. **4.29**

---

[10] *AmBev* (n 3).

[11] Settlement decision between the CADE and Infoglobo signed in August 2013 regarding Case no. 08012.003064/2005-58.

[12] *Philips*, CADE Case no. 08012.001315/2007-21, decision of May 2013.

O. Exemptions

4.30 There are no general exemptions from unilateral behavior being viewed as an anticompetitive practice, even if sparse laws might allow for the adoption of certain practices which would otherwise be objectionable. For instance, copyright laws authorize publishers to set retail prices for books. These exceptions, however, are generally not adopted as an antitrust exemption, but as sector-specific rules which end up superseding competition rules.

II. Dealing with competitors

4.31 The fight against collusive practices among competitors has been the top priority of the CADE since at least 2002, and as a result any type of conduct that involves dealings with competitors tends to receive a lot of attention from the authorities.

4.32 Recent cases from the CADE have reaffirmed the dichotomy of the legal standards for anticompetitive conduct, distinguishing between (a) conducts based on the object and (b) conducts based on the effects.[13] In the first set are conducts related to classic cartels, such as price fixing, joint restrictions of output, bid-rigging, market sharing, and allocation agreements. These conducts are considered illegal regardless of their actual or potential effects on the market, and they have as their main character the inherent restriction of the competition, normally associated with secrecy and deception elements. The second set, in turn, includes conducts that may be considered anticompetitive according to their potential effects on the market and final consumers. These are mostly commercial practices that may be considered anticompetitive depending on the market share of the involved companies, specific market dynamics and the type of practice.

4.33 The CADE has been very aggressive in the investigation of cartels, imposing penalties that tend to be among the highest allowed by the law.[14]

A. Horizontal price fixing (including advanced announcements of price or product changes)

4.34 Agreements among competitors to manipulate or adjust the prices of goods or services are a violation of the competition law by object and expressly referred to as the classical example of anticompetitive conduct (art. 36, s. 3, I of Law no. 12,529). In cases of price fixing conduct, the CADE is not required to assess the market share of the companies involved; simple evidence of agreements among competitors (or potential competitors) on price increases or restrictions of output (or the defendants' willingness to jointly increase prices or restrict output) tend to be sufficient for the finding of an infringement and the imposition of fines.

4.35 Price fixing is the most classical form of cartels and, thus, the most common in the history of CADE's condemnations. Announcements of price or product changes as a facilitating practice for price fixing have not been yet been reviewed in-depth as an isolated conduct (see Sections II.G and II.H).

[13] See e.g. *Gas stations cartel of Caxias do Sul/RS*, CADE Case no. 08012.010215/2007-96, decision of March 2013.

[14] See Section F for information on remedies.

B. Horizontal agreements to allocate customers or territories; agreements not to compete

The allocation of customers or territories is also considered a violation, according to article 36, s. 3, I(c). Most of the time, this practice goes hand in hand with price fixing or boycotts. **4.36**

Non-compete agreements are generally assessed as a restriction by object (as almost every other practice involving agreements among competitors). However, whenever these types of covenants are ancillary for purposes of another, legitimate agreement (i.e. an acquisition or merger), the CADE accepts these restrictions on competitions but imposes certain limits to the scope of the relevant covenants: (a) duration cannot be longer than five years, (b) products may not exceed those that are related to the transaction, and (c) area must be limited to the relevant market involved.[15] **4.37**

C. Horizontal boycotts

Boycotts are also considered violations. In a recent precedent,[16] the CADE identified a boycott of customers alongside other exclusionary practices (price fixing and market allocation) as the basis of a cartel infringement, and imposed heavy fines. **4.38**

D. Joint ventures and other competitive collaborations

The incorporation of joint ventures (and other associative contracts) may be subject to merger control rules, as set forth by article 90, IV of Law no. 12,529, if the relevant turnover (revenues) thresholds are met by the parties to the joint venture. **4.39**

The CADE has not yet defined what may be considered as associative contracts under Law no. 12,529/2011. However, precedents under the former law (Law no. 8,884/1994),[17] as well as a few indications under the new law,[18] indicate that associative contracts may include a number of different types of agreements, regardless as to whether they are or not full-function joint ventures. **4.40**

Collaborations among competitors that are not inherently anticompetitive (restrictions by object) are nevertheless assessed on the basis of their potential effects on competition, either as merger cases (in which CADE's approval is a condition for closing) or as conduct investigations. **4.41**

E. Trade associations

Trade associations are traditionally in the spotlight of the CADE's investigations.[19] According to the CADE, the following are the main concerns related to trade associations: (a) information exchange, (b) meetings among competitors, (c) price lists, (d) codes of conduct ("*códigos de ética*"), (e) standardization and certification, (f) criteria for adhesion and exclusion of members, (g) non-members treatment, and (h) joint acquisitions.[20] **4.42**

In relation to trade association meetings, the CADE emphasizes that they cannot be an occasion for debating commercially sensitive issues, such as prices, discount practices, clients, suppliers, market allocation. In order to prevent any discussion, the meetings should have a public agenda with clearly itemized points. Price lists, which have been the object of several **4.43**

---

[15] See CADE Decision nos. 4 and 5, issued in 2009.

[16] *Hydrogen Peroxide Cartel*, CADE Case no. 08012.004702/2004-77, decision of May 2012, under Court review.

[17] See e.g. *Líder Táxi Aéreo and Helicopteros do Brasil*, CADE Case no. 08012.002442/2004-03, decision of December 2004.

[18] See. e.g. *Petrobras and MPEC*, CADE Case no. 08700.008736/2012-92, decision of November 2012.

[19] For example, the CADE has recently condemned several Gas Station Trade Associations for promoting anticompetitive conducts among their participants: see e.g. *Gas stations cartel of Teresina/PI*, CADE Case no. 08700.000547/2008-95, decision of March 2013.

[20] According to the CADE's Brochure on Fighting against Cartels in Trade Unions and Associations.

investigations, are a very controversial topic, and the CADE has several decisions identifying these lists as infringements because, in sum, they may facilitate and influence the adoption of uniform price by the members of an association.

4.44 Regarding information exchange, please refer to Section II.H.

F. Interlocking directorates

4.45 The CADE has never identified interlocking directorates as a competition infringement, although it is known that it has recently engaged in the analysis of the relation between the members of competing or vertically related companies' boards of directors, normally in the context of merger cases.[21]

G. Facilitating practices

4.46 There are no clear rules regarding so-called facilitating practices, although any type of conduct that, directly or indirectly, benefits, aids, or abets collusive behavior among competitors may be an infringement if the CADE finds the conduct to limit competition, and there are no pro-competitive benefits to offset the potential harm to consumers (i.e. there are no legitimate business reasons or upfront efficiency gains associated with those practices).

H. Information exchange

4.47 Exchange of information among competitors is generally considered as a practice that may facilitate collusion, although the authorities also recognize that increased market transparency may enhance competition. In this sense, the CADE has defined some "safe harbors" regarding information exchange mechanisms among competitors.[22] The authorities advise that the exchange of information that meets the following requirements are less likely to be considered anticompetitive: (a) historical data; (b) aggregate data that does not identify individual companies' commercial information (e.g. production costs, clients, suppliers, strategy); (c) confidential and independent data gathering (e.g. "black box" agreements); (d) information must be publicly available.

(i) Exchanges of historic pricing information

4.48 For an exchange of information to be lawful, the information exchanged must be considered historic, which the authorities interpret as information that is over one year old; at the same time, the authorities acknowledge that this timeframe may vary depending on the markets involved.

(ii) How old, anonymous, and aggregated pricing information needs to be

4.49 Pricing information preferably needs to be more than one year old, and aggregated (annonymized) in order to prevent identification of the individual participants.

(iii) What pro-competitive purposes, if any, exchange needs to help participants achieve; pre-merger due diligence

4.50 The CADE will consider pro-competitive purposes and welfare-enhancing effects of information exchange mechanisms in its review of this type of case. The burden of proof regarding these positive effects, however, is generally on the participants.

---

[21] See *Mr. Diniz Consultation*, CADE Case no. 08700.003340/2013-30, decision of October 2013.

[22] See *Photograpy Companies' Labor Union of São Paulo*, CADE Case no. 08012.005994/2004-65, decision of November 2009, and *Driving Schools' Labor Union of Minas Gerais*, SDE Case no. 08012.003874/2009-38, technical opinion of August 2010, CADE's decision still pending.

Pre-merger due diligence is authorized by law, as long as the merging parties (or the acquirer) do not have access to information that may be relevant for competitive purposes, such as production costs, strategies, suppliers, and clients, prior to closing. There is a general prohibition that prevents merging parties from modifying their competitive relationships prior to closing, and detailed information exchanges may be seen as resulting in prohibited modifications.[23] **4.51**

I. Joint purchasing agreements

Joint purchasing agreements are generally reviewed under the merger control regime. The review is normally based on the effects of the agreements on the market and it is related to the buying power and the market share of the companies involved. In the limited assessments it pursued, the CADE has usually considered joint purchasing agreements to be pro-competitive, as long as they do not relate to purchases of non-strategic inputs, do not give rise to significant monopsony power and, in cases involving competitors, there are strong governance mechanisms to avoid unnecessary information exchanges.[24] **4.52**

J. Joint lobbying/regulatory/legislative efforts

There have been several investigations regarding joint lobbying and regulatory efforts by competitors. However, at the time of writing, none of them resulted in the imposition of sanctions by the CADE strictly for the joint efforts.[25] This type of behavior will be assessed on the basis of its potential effects; they are acceptable if the competitors' joint efforts have a welfare-enhancing or pro-competitive justification without increasing barriers to entry or the costs for non-participating competitors. **4.53**

III. General issues

A. Jurisdiction and applicable law (including sector-specific competition regulation)

The Brazilian competition law is applicable (a) to practices carried out in Brazil and (b) to practices that potentially affect the Brazilian territory (art. 2 of Law no. 12,529). The stated purpose of the competition law is to "prevent and prosecute violations of the economic order, under guidance of the constitutional rules of freedom of enterprise, free competition, social function of property and prosecution of the economic power" (art. 1 of Law no. 12,529). **4.54**

There are no legal or constitutional sector-specific exemptions or specific competition regulation[26] in Brazil; therefore, the law is applicable to any person or entity, even if unincorporated. Certain governmental acts and decisions are beyond the scope of the competition authorities' activities. However, the Brazilian competition authorities have powers to issue requests to governmental bodies, and provide advice to promote competition and remedy potential anticompetitive rules and regulations issued by the public administration. **4.55**

---

[23] See Law no. 12,529, art 88, ss. 3–4 and CADE Resolution no. 1/2012, art. 108.

[24] See *Bimbo and Bertin*, CADE Case no. 08012.009537/2008-73, decision of June 2009; *Ambev and Suzano*, CADE Case no. 08012.006980/200-35, decision of November 2001; and *MAN and Scania*, CADE Case no. 08012.008025/2010-12, decision of June 2011.

[25] See *Public transport companies in São Paulo*, CADE Case no. 08012.004989/2003-54, decision of August 2010.

[26] Even though there is no exception in the Law, there is a controversy with respect to the application of competition law to the banking (financial) sector, because of the powers of the Brazilian Central Bank to oversee this specific sector. The competition authorities have strongly rebutted this understanding in more than one case (see e.g. settlement between the CADE and Banco do Brasil signed in October 2012 regarding Case no. 08700.004988/2012-42, and REsp 1094218).

B. Antitrust system

4.56 Brazilian competition law is enforced at the administrative level by the Administrative Council for Economic Defense (*Conselho Administrativo de Defesa Econômica* or "CADE"), an independent government agency defined as quasi-judicial (*entidade judicante*, art. 4 of Law no. 12,529). The CADE is made up of two main bodies: the Directorate General (*Superintendência Geral*) and the Board (*Tribunal*). These two bodies are supported by a Legal Services Division (*Procuradoria*) and an Economic Studies Division (*Departamento de Estudos Econômicos*).

4.57 Within the CADE, the Directorate General is responsible for carrying out administrative investigations, which, once completed, are submitted to the Board for review and decision. The Director General is appointed by the President for a two-year term.

4.58 A Chairman and six Commissioners compose the Board of the CADE. The Board adopts decisions by majority, assuming at least four Commissioners are present at a hearing. The Chairman, who has the casting opinion and is responsible for the legal representation of the CADE, and the Commissioners receive the results of the investigation carried out by the Directorate General, usually in the form of a non-binding opinion, upon which they may either decide the case in a public hearing or supplement the investigation through any legal means.

4.59 The CADE has a team of approximately 150 officials and, in 2012, it had a budget of approximately BRL 20 million (approx. USD 10 million)—more than double the previous years' amounts. This is because of the entering into force of Law no. 12,529 on May 29, 2012, which increased the authority's budget.

4.60 Any decision issued by the CADE regarding the enforcement of competition rules can be subject to a court review, as the Brazilian Constitution does not allow administrative authorities to issue definitive decisions. Decisions regarding fines, therefore, may be challenged on both their merits and on procedural grounds. Research has shown that Courts tend to uphold CADE's decisions, although proceedings are generally very long.[27]

C. Private litigation

4.61 Parties harmed by anticompetitive conduct may request that the courts order violators to cease their activity, regardless of the administrative investigation carried out by the competition authorities (art. 47 of Law no. 12,529). This this type of case, however, is still uncommon in Brazil. Usually, private litigation regarding competition violations takes place as follow-on damage claims based on earlier cartel infringement decisions issued by the competition authorities, because of the reduced burden of proof of those types of claims.

4.62 As a general rule under Brazilian law, any harm caused by an unlawful act must be redressed in the form of compensation for the damages suffered. Damages are therefore awarded if the harmed party successfully proves the existence of the unlawful conduct and the extent of the damages it caused. The burden of proving the unlawful conduct tends to deter stand-alone private litigation and stimulates follow-on cases, even if it is uncertain that courts will uphold the administrative authorities' decisions.

4.63 Competition law includes a specific provision authorizing compensation for damages suffered in connection with competition violations (art. 47 of Law no. 12,529). Any harmed

[27] See Fabricio Antonio Cardim de Almeida (ed.), *Revisão Judicial das Decisões do Conselho Administrativo de Defesa Econômica (CADE), Pesquisa empírica e aplicada sobre os casos julgados pelos Tribunais Regionais Federais (TRFs), Superior Tribunal de Justiça (STJ) e Supremo Tribunal Federal (STF)* (Sociedade Brasileira de Direito Público (SBDP), 2010).

party may seek individual compensation; public prosecutors and certain consumer associations may, in turn, seek collective redress.

Even with a growing number of cases involving damages deriving from cartel cases, mostly because the authorities have increased cartel enforcement since the early 2000s, there are very few non-appealable precedents regarding private enforcement of the competition rules. As a result, several issues remain unsettled, such as the applicable statute of limitation for claims, standards and burden of proof for damages (especially in hard core cartels), and standards or references for the calculation of damages in cartel cases. **4.64**

Generally speaking, the statute of limitation is three years for damage claims, but the concealed nature of most competition violations and the constitutional presumption of innocence pose a question as to the start of this period. There seems to be no consensus on whether this period starts with the start of the conduct itself, at the moment the harmed party becomes aware of the conduct, or on the date the authorities find the conduct unlawful. **4.65**

D. Follow-on litigation (includes role of agency determinations of liability for follow-on litigation)

See Section III.C. **4.66**

E. Arbitration and alternative dispute resolution

Enforcement of competition rules is generally regarded as a matter of general interest ("public order"), and therefore arbitrators and alternative dispute resolution (ADR) methods generally refrain from finding violations or awarding damages for violations. Private litigation could theoretically migrate to arbitration for damage claims, if the relationship between the parties was regulated by an agreement containing an arbitration clause, what is currently uncommon. The finding of a violation and the imposition of fines, however, can only be carried out by the authorities or by the courts. **4.67**

F. Remedies

(i) Civil liability

Pursuant to current competition law, a company deemed liable for a violation is subject to a fine ranging from 0.1 percent to 20 percent of the gross turnover excluding taxes (pre-tax revenues) of the "company, group or conglomerate" in the "sector of activity" (*ramo de atividade*) in which the violation occurred, for the year prior to the formal initiation of the investigation. This fine cannot be lower than the gain obtained from the violation, if this is assessable (art. 37, I of Law no. 12,529), and it may be doubled in case of recidivism. **4.68**

The CADE issued a rule (Resolution no. 3/2012) clarifying the concept of the "sector of activity," implying that it is different from the concept of "relevant market." The rule includes a list of 144 different sectors. If a defendant fails clearly and accurately to indicate its revenues within one specific sector of activity, the CADE will consider the total revenues "of the company or group of companies." **4.69**

There is a yet unsettled controversy regarding the correct interpretation of the expression "turnover of the company, group or conglomerate" used in the legal text, as it implies that the revenues of other entities of the same group (i.e. entities under common control) in the same "sector of activity" may be considered as the basis for the calculation of the fine, even if those other entities were not involved in the conduct. In addition, a company involved in the conduct, its directors and officers (*dirigentes* and *administradores*), as well as other entities of the same group, are all jointly liable for the payment of fines incurred for competition violations (arts. 32 and 33 of Law no. 12,529). In the cases of abuse, fraud, bankruptcy, or **4.70** discontinued activity resulting from bad management, shareholders may also be held liable for the payment of fines as a result of the lifting of the corporate veil doctrine (*desconsideração da personalidade jurídica*) (art. 35 of Law no. 12,529).

4.71 Companies may also be subject to ancillary penalties, such as: (a) publication of a summary of the decision in the newspapers; (b) the prohibition to enter into contracts with public banks; (c) the prohibition to take part in public bids or to enter into agreements with the government, for a minimum of five years; (d) the inclusion of the violator in a list of consumer offenders; (e) the recommendation for the compulsory licensing of patents held by the offender; (f) the recommendation for public authorities not to grant, or to revoke if already granted, tax payment schedules, public subsidies, or tax incentives; (g) the spin-off, transfer of control, sale of assets, or any other measure necessary for the complete cessation of the illicit behavior and its effects (art. 38 of Law no. 12,529).[28]

4.72 Officers (*administradores*) directly or indirectly responsible for the violation are subject to fines of 0.1 percent to 20 percent of the fines applied to their respective entities if intent (*dolo*) or fault (*culpa*) is proven (art. 37, III of Law no. 12,529). Other individuals or entities that do not conduct corporate activities (trade associations, for instance) involved in violations are subject to fines that range from BRL 50 million to BRL 2 billion (art. 37, II of Law no. 12,529). Individuals may also be subject to a disbarment decision, with a prohibition on running a business under their own name or becoming legal representatives in corporations for a period of up to five years (art. 38, VI of Law no. 12,529).

4.73 The imposition of fines must take into account the violator's good faith, the severity of the violation, the extent of the harm caused, the advantages obtained by the violator, the violator's financial situation, whether the violation was consummated, and the harm to the economy, consumers or third parties. The CADE, however, is not entirely consistent in its application of these criteria, but in the recent years there has been a clear trend that imposes fines in cartel cases in the higher spectrum of the applicable fines.

(ii) Criminal liability

4.74 Pursuant to the language of article 4 of Law no. 8,137/1990, which was revised by Law no. 12,529, hard core cartels are considered criminal violations in Brazil. As criminal liability under Brazilian Law is generally only applicable to individuals (and not corporate entities or associations), individuals—regardless of their corporate ranking—found guilty of cartel crimes are subject to imprisonment, from two to five years, and to a criminal fine.

4.75 The finding of criminal liability in Brazil generally demands a stricter standard of proof and evidence than at the administrative level; the current language of the Law seems to require proof "beyond reasonable doubt" at least (a) of anticompetitive intent (*dolo*) and (b) of the existence of the agreement, in order to allow for a conviction (consequently, "parallelism plus" type of cases and information exchange agreements are extremely unlikely to imply criminal liability).

4.76 It is important to highlight that there are relatively few final decisions on the merits of criminal cartel violations and possibly none since the current Law entered into force. The lack of decisions in the past is probably due to the fact that prosecutors and courts were relatively comfortable in entering into criminal settlements (mainly through payment of contributions to charities and social work periods etc.) with defendants; as a result, the cases were dismissed without a decision on the merits.

[28] See *Gas stations cartel of Manaus/AM*, CADE Case no. 08012.002959/1998-11, decision of March 2013, and *Teresina/PI* (n 21).

G. Leniency, immunity, and settlements

The first company to report a violation under the leniency program may receive full administrative immunity; individuals implicated in the conduct may benefit from immunity from administrative penalties and from criminal liability. A "leniency plus" alternative allows an applicant that is not eligible for full immunity for a certain violation to benefit from reduced fines (in the range of one-third to two-thirds) for the violation in question if it reports a second violation and qualifies for full immunity. **4.77**

The authorities may grant immunity only if the violator is the first to come forward; if the violator confesses and ceases the conduct; and if it effectively cooperates with the investigation by identifying the other violators and by submitting documents and information regarding the conduct (art. 86 of Law no. 12,529). In addition, a leniency agreement may be entered into only if the authorities lack evidence to convict the parties at the time they are approached by the leniency applicant. The benefits of a leniency agreement may accrue to the involved employees (or former employees) of the applicant, as well as to the involved officers, directors, managers, and other affiliated entities, as long as they enter into the leniency agreement along with the corporate entity and fulfill the legal requirements—confess, cease, cooperate (art. 86, s. 6 of Law no. 12,529). **4.78**

Markers are made available to secure the place in line for the leniency application, but they depend on the disclosure—even if on an oral basis—of basic information regarding the conduct (e.g. identity of the applicant and the implicated competitors, business and territories affected, and the estimated duration of the conduct). Markers statements issued by the authorities grant the interested party 30 days to file a proposal for leniency and may be kept by the applicant itself, assuring the interested party its place in line as the first comer. After a marker is issued, the applicant formally submits its interest by applying for a leniency agreement and, if accepted, it enters into the leniency agreement with the authorities, which then pursue the investigation in a formal proceeding. **4.79**

The authorities generally observe a strict regime of confidentiality as to the leniency, marker documents, and the identity of the leniency beneficiary, but there are no rules preventing their disclosure by third parties (e.g. other violators) or protecting them from discovery rules applicable abroad. **4.80**

A leniency application that does not result in an agreement (because, for instance, it does not meet the legal requirements) cannot be adopted by the authority as the basis for further investigation (i.e. constitute a confession of the facts or acknowledgement of the unlawful conduct). This is to ensure that potential applicants come forward, even if the outcome of the negotiation is not necessarily a final and effective leniency agreement. **4.81**

H. Settlements

The authorities may enter into settlements (referred to by the Law as "cease-and-desist commitments") during the investigations of the anticompetitive conduct, including cartel violations. Parties may submit a settlement proposal at any time during the proceedings, and the authorities have ample discretionary powers to accept it. These settlements show some similarities to "direct settlements" in the EU or "plea bargains" in the US, and they basically consist in a settlement between the investigated party and the competition authorities. **4.82**

In cases involving unilateral behavior, the settlement consists in the investigated party agreeing to cease the conduct in exchange for the dismissal of the investigation. The settlement prevents the authorities from issuing a decision regarding the merits of the case, even though the authorities may—at their discretion—require the payment of a contribution or the adoption of behavioral remedies to address competition-related problems deriving from or stimulating the conduct. **4.83**

4.84 Especially in cartel cases, the CADE has been criticized for the uncertainty that surrounded settlement procedures, especially in relation to the calculation of the monetary contribution to be paid. The same occured in relation to confession and collaboration requirements.

4.85 In this context, CADE has very recently adopted changes to the settlement proceeding and requirements (CADE Regulation No. 5/2013) in order to eliminate the uncertainty regarding the authorities' position on certain topics (especially the size of contribution and cooperation requirements), bringing the settlement possibility closer to the so called "second in" and "third in" types of settlements.

4.86 According to the new Regulation, defendants willing to settle in cartel cases would be required: (a) to pay an amount as a contribution, which cannot be lower than the lowest applicable fine; (b) cease the conduct (if applicable); (c) confess the unlawful conduct; and (d) collaborate with the investigation. According to CADE, these are required allegedly to maintain the correct incentives for leniency applications. Defendants that cooperate with the authorities and provide useful information, would benefit from a reduction of the applicable fines depending on the extent and utility of the information, and on the order of settlements: discounts from fines would range from 30 to 50 percent for the first defendant to settle, 25 to 40 percent for the second defendant to settle, and up to 25 percent for the remaining defendants. The authorities have been especially concerned with concluding cartel investigations only after having made sure that the payable contribution is still capable of having deterrence effects; this concern remains valid under the new regulation as well.

4.87 Even though the bases for the calculation of the contribution are yet to be clarified, due to the lack of a consistent set of precedents of how fines are to be applied (especially for international cartels), there is an expectation that the new rules and levels of discount will help create a more predictable set of settlements. Time will tell whether this is the case.

4.88 One issue yet to be cleared is the potential negative effect that a confession before the CADE may have on the criminal investigations involving individuals.

I. Document creation and retention

4.89 There are no specific rules regarding document creation and retention in Brazil, but the parties in an administrative investigation, for example conducted by the competition authorities, have the general duty to provide accurate and truthful information, to act in good faith, and to collaborate with the investigations (art. 4 of Law no. 9,784/1999).

4.90 The authorities have substantial powers to request information and documents from third parties, whether the latter are being investigated or not, including governmental entities; they may also ask courts for the authorization to perform surprise inspections (searches) and wiretapping. The authorities also have powers to make announced inspections on a company's premises; if a person obstructs an inspection, he or she may be subject to a fine of up to BRL 400,000.

4.91 If a person refuses to provide information required by the competition authorities or delays its submission, he or she is subject to a daily fine of up to BRL 1 million (art. 40 of Law no. 12,529), whereas the submission of misleading information or declarations, or the submission of tampered documents may result in fines of up to BRL 5 million (art. 43 of Law no. 12,529). Under certain circumstances, the destruction or concealment of relevant documents could imply civil and criminal liability, but the observance of the right to avoid self-incrimination is unlikely to be seen as a failure to cooperate or to produce required evidence.

5

CANADA

Mark Opashinov and Devin Anderson
McMillan LLP

Introduction

When Melanie Aitken, who retired as Canada's Commissioner of Competition effective September 21, 2012, was appointed to the post in 2009, she announced that the hallmark of her tenure would be enhanced enforcement efforts. She did not disappoint on that score. Ms. Aitken advanced cases against Canada's largest telecommunications carriers;[1] settled a civil advertising case for a seven figure amount;[2] brought cases to the Competition Tribunal for abuse of dominance in the waste disposal[3] and real estate brokerage businesses;[4] fought a contested case before the Competition Tribunal against Visa and MasterCard under Canada's new **5.01**

[1] *Canada (Commissioner of Competition) v. Rogers Communications Inc.*, 2011 CarswellOnt 13550 (Ont. S.C.J.).

[2] *The Commissioner of Competition v. Bell Canada, Bell Mobility Inc. and Bell Expressvu Limited Partnership*, CT-2011-005 (Comp. Trib.).

[3] *The Commissioner of Competition and IESI-BFC Ltd., BFI Canada Inc., Waste Services Inc., and Waste Services (CA) Inc.*, CT-2010-005 (Comp. Trib.).

[4] *The Commissioner of Competition v. The Canadian Real Estate Association*, CT-2010-002 (Comp. Trib.).

price maintenance provisions;[5] commenced a contested abuse of dominance case involving the Toronto Real Estate Board;[6] tested the new civil provisions of the Competition Act with respect to agreements amongst competitors;[7] brought the first prosecution for breach of a consent agreement;[8] and has prosecuted numerous cartels, including those involving retail gasoline.[9] Canada is expected to remain a jurisdiction notable for vigorous competition law enforcement, with Ms. Aitken's successor, Commissioner of Competition John Pecman, confirming on multiple occasions that the Bureau's active enforcement will not abate under his leadership.[10]

I. Acting alone

5.02 Abuse of a dominant position in Canada occurs when a dominant firm or a dominant group of firms in a market engages in a practice of anticompetitive acts, with the result that competition is, or is likely to be prevented or lessened substantially.

5.03 Subsection 79(1) of the federal Competition Act[11] (the "Act") defines the constituent elements of abuse of dominance, each of which must be established for the federal Competition Tribunal to grant a remedy:

> Where, on application by the Commissioner, the Tribunal finds that:
> - one or more persons substantially or completely control, throughout Canada or any area thereof, a class or species of business,
> - that person or those persons have engaged in or are engaging in a practice of anticompetitive acts, and
> - the practice has had, is having, or is likely to have the effect of preventing or lessening competition substantially in a market,
>
> the Tribunal may make an order prohibiting all or any of those persons from engaging in that practice.

5.04 Section 78 of the Act enumerates a non-exhaustive list of acts that are deemed to be anticompetitive for the purposes of s. 79:

> For the purposes of section 79, "anti-competitive act," without restricting the generality of the term, includes any of the following acts:
>
> - squeezing, by a vertically integrated supplier, of the margin available to an unintegrated customer who competes with the supplier, for the purpose of impeding or preventing the customer's entry into, or expansion in, a market;
> - acquisition by a supplier of a customer who would otherwise be available to a competitor of the supplier, or acquisition by a customer of a supplier who would otherwise be

[5] *The Commissioner of Competition v. Visa Canada Corporation and MasterCard International Incorporated and others*, CT-2010-010 (Comp. Trib.).

[6] *The Commissioner of Competition v. The Toronto Real Estate Board*, CT-2011-003 (Comp. Trib.).

[7] *The Commissioner of Competition v. Air Canada, United Continental Holdings Inc., United Airlines Inc., and Continental Airlines Inc.*, CT-2011-004 (Comp. Trib.).

[8] Competition Bureau, *Charges Laid Against Waste Services Company for Breaching Consent Agreement* (September 11, 2012).

[9] Competition Bureau, "List of Charges and Sentences in the Quebec Gasoline Price-fixing Cartel" (September 28, 2012), <http://www.competitionbureau.gc.ca/eic/site/cb-bc.nsf/eng/03079.html>.

[10] See e.g. Competition Bureau, "Remarks by John Pecman, Interim Commissioner of Competition" (February 7, 2013), <http://www.competitionbureau.gc.ca/eic/site/cb-bc.nsf/eng/03529.html>; Competition Bureau, "Remarks by John Pecman, Commissioner of Competition" (October 24, 2013), <http://www.competitionbureau.gc.ca/eic/site/cb-bc.nsf/eng/03622.html>; and Competition Bureau, "Remarks by John Pecman, Commissioner of Competition" (November 14, 2013), <http://www.competitionbureau.gc.ca/eic/site/cb-bc.nsf/eng/03629.html>.

[11] Competition Act, RSC 1985, c C-34.

available to a competitor of the customer, for the purpose of impeding or preventing the competitor's entry into, or eliminating the competitor from, a market;

- freight equalization on the plant of a competitor for the purpose of impeding or preventing the competitor's entry into, or eliminating the competitor from, a market;
- use of fighting brands introduced selectively on a temporary basis to discipline or eliminate a competitor;
- pre-emption of scarce facilities or resources required by a competitor for the operation of a business, with the object of withholding the facilities or resources from a market;
- buying up of products to prevent the erosion of existing price levels;
- adoption of product specifications that are incompatible with products produced by any other person and are designed to prevent his entry into, or to eliminate him from, a market;
- requiring or inducing a supplier to sell only or primarily to certain customers, or to refrain from selling to a competitor, with the object of preventing a competitor's entry into, or expansion in, a market; and
- selling articles at a price lower than the acquisition cost for the purpose of disciplining or eliminating a competitor.

When assessing whether an act is anticompetitive, the purpose of the act may be proven directly by evidence of subjective intent, or inferred from the reasonably foreseeable consequences of the conduct. An additional factor in the determination of whether an act is anticompetitive is whether it was in furtherance of a legitimate business objective. A business justification is not a defense to an allegation that a firm has engaged in anticompetitive conduct. Rather, it can act as an alternative explanation for the overriding purpose of the impugned conduct, where the Competition Bureau (the "Bureau"), the administrative unit of the federal Department of Industry that supports the Commissioner of Competition (the "Commissioner") in his enforcement of the Act, alleges that the purpose of the conduct was an anticompetitive one. **5.05**

In considering enforcement action under s. 79 of the Act, the Bureau evaluates allegations of abuse on a case-by-case basis in the context of structural and other market-specific characteristics. **5.06**

In the course of an examination or inquiry, the Commissioner will generally afford parties the opportunity to respond to the Bureau's concerns regarding alleged contraventions of s. 79 and to propose an appropriate resolution to address them. Firms proposing voluntary revisions to existing business practices should be aware that, while such proposals will be given due consideration by the Bureau, any approved proposal will generally be embodied in a Consent Agreement and registered with the Tribunal pursuant to s. 105 of the Act. Upon registration, a Consent Agreement has the force of an order of the Tribunal (per s. 74.12(4) of the Act). Where a resolution cannot be reached on consensus with the Bureau, the Commissioner may file an application for an order of the Tribunal. Where an abuse of dominance is established, the Tribunal has the power to make a variety of orders, including ordering the conduct to stop or for the offending firm to pay an "administrative monetary penalty" (that is, a fine) of up to CAD 10 million (CAD 15 million for subsequent orders) per s. 79(3.1) of the Act. **5.07**

In assessing whether a particular act is likely to be anticompetitive, the Bureau is of the view that anticompetitive conduct generally falls into two broad categories: (a) exclusionary conduct; and (b) predatory conduct.[12] **5.08**

[12] Competition Bureau, *Enforcement Guidelines on the Abuse of Dominance Provisions* (September 20, 2012), http://www.competitionbureau.gc.ca/eic/site/cb-bc.nsf/eng/03497.html.

A. Exclusionary conduct

5.09 In general, the Bureau is not concerned with conduct that forces competitors to be more effective, but rather with conduct that makes it more difficult for competitors to be effective. Exclusionary conduct is designed to make current and/or potential rivals less effective at disciplining the exercise of a firm's market power, to prevent them from entering the market, or to eliminate them from the market entirely.

5.10 Section 78 describes various means by which a firm may engage in exclusionary conduct. These include, for example: margin squeezing of a downstream competitor by a vertically integrated supplier; vertical acquisitions; preempting scarce facilities or resources; adopting incompatible product specifications; and exclusive dealing. Other exclusionary strategies can include tying and bundling, and conduct that increases customer switching costs and makes customers more difficult for rivals to acquire. All such activities can, in certain circumstances, serve to increase a rival's costs and may force that rival to raise its prices, which in turn may make it more difficult for the rival to compete or result in its exclusion from the market. This may allow the dominant firm to maintain or increase its prices, which can be profitable if the costs of the exclusionary strategy are offset by the ultimate increase in revenue, or by the preservation of revenues that would otherwise be lost, owing to competitive entry or expansion.

B. Predatory conduct

5.11 Predatory conduct, including predatory pricing, involves a firm deliberately setting the price of a product below an appropriate measure of cost (and irrespective of any consequential losses on the sale of such product) in the relevant market for a period of time sufficient to eliminate, discipline, or deter entry or expansion of a competitor, in the expectation that the firm will thereafter recoup its losses by charging higher prices than would have prevailed in the absence of the impugned conduct. Predatory pricing may be implicit (e.g. through discounts or rebates) or explicit.

5.12 The Bureau's view is that "average avoidable cost" is the most appropriate cost standard to use when determining if a dominant firm's prices are below cost.[13] Avoidable costs refer to all costs that could have been avoided by a firm had it chosen not to sell the product in question during the period of time the policy was in place. The Bureau will examine whether an alleged predatory price is able to cover the dominant firm's average avoidable cost of supplying the product in question during the time period over which the alleged predation has occurred.

5.13 As there are difficulties inherent in applying a price–cost test and in distinguishing between predatory and competitive pricing (as both involve lower prices in the short term), the Bureau generally uses various "screens" prior to conducting an avoidable cost analysis.[14] Specifically, the Bureau will examine whether the alleged predatory price can be matched by competitors without incurring losses (suggesting that discipline or exclusion, and subsequent recoupment, is unlikely to occur), as well as whether the alleged predatory price is in fact merely "meeting competition" by reacting to match a competitor's price.

C. Recent enforcement highlight

5.14 On April 15, 2013, the Tribunal dismissed an application brought by the Commissioner under the Act's abuse of dominance provisions against Canada's largest real estate board, the Toronto Real Estate Board (TREB).[15] The Commissioner's application specifically sought

[13] Competition Bureau, *Enforcement Guidelines* (n 12) s. 3.2.2.

[14] Competition Bureau, *Enforcement Guidelines* (n 12).

[15] *The Commissioner of Competition v. The Toronto Real Estate Board*, 2013 Comp. Trib. 9.

an order pursuant to s. 79 of the Act requiring TREB to eliminate rules imposed on its real estate agent members that allegedly denied them the ability to introduce internet-based real estate brokerage services by limiting the use the members could make of the Multiple Listing Service listings and related data.

The Tribunal turned to the Federal Court of Appeal's *Canada Pipe* decision[16] for the principle that in order for anticompetitive conduct to be caught by s. 79, the conduct must have had a negative effect on a competitor that is predatory, exclusionary or disciplinary. The Tribunal's primary holding pertained to the fact that TREB did not compete with its members in the market and therefore the alleged anticompetitive membership rules could not by definition satisfy the requisite need for a resulting negative effect on a competitor. The Tribunal did not accept the Bureau's position that based on the language of s. 78, which sets out a non-exhaustive enumerated list of anticompetitive acts, s. 79 could cover abusive conduct by entities other than competitors. The Tribunal, stating that the determinative issue was the fundamental question of whether the Commissioner's application met the requirements of s. 79, disposed of the matter on that basis. **5.15**

D. Predatory pricing

The Act no longer contains specific provisions dealing with predatory pricing. Rather, to establish that a firm has engaged in predatory pricing, the elements of s. 79 of the Act must be established by the Bureau on an application to the Tribunal. It is a species of abuse of dominance. **5.16**

E. Exploitative offenses

Nothing in the Act prohibits a competitor—even a dominant competitor—from "exploiting" its position in the market. Rather, the Act, as noted, prohibits abuse of dominant position comprising a practice of acts that has had, is having or is likely to have the effect of preventing or lessening competition substantially in a market. See the discussion above in this connection. **5.17**

F. Monopsony

Nothing in the Act expressly applies to monopsonists. However, the exercise of monopsony power may amount to abuse of a dominant position in circumstances where, for example, the exercise limits competition in a downstream market. A lack of meaningful guidance from the Bureau and an absence of monopsony cases before the Tribunal within the past twenty years makes it difficult for advisers to apply analytical frameworks with confidence that the Bureau will adopt similar frameworks for its investigation and assessment of conduct that raises monopsony issues. **5.18**

G. Price discrimination

Previously, price discrimination had been a standalone criminal offense. In 2009 the offense was decriminalized and is now dealt with exclusively under the abuse of dominance provisions. **5.19**

H. Dictating or influencing resale prices

(i) Resale price maintenance

Previously, resale price maintenance (RPM) had been a standalone criminal offense. In 2009 the offense was decriminalized and is now dealt with under the abuse of dominance and civil price maintenance provisions. This legislative change to Canada's price maintenance **5.20**

[16] *Canada (Commissioner of Competition) v. Canada Pipe Co.*, 2006 FCA 233.

provision more closely aligns the US and Canadian standards by removing practices that do not constitute criminal activity from the criminal law and placing them in a context where such practices are dealt with by the Tribunal only when anticompetitive effects result.

5.21 For the price maintenance provision to apply, the following requirements must be met:

- a supplier, by means of a threat, a promise or an agreement, influences upward, or discourages the reduction of, the prices charged or advertised by another business that is either a customer of that supplier, or a competitor;
- a supplier refuses to supply a product to, or discriminates against, another person because of that other person's low pricing policy; and/or
- any person, as a condition of doing business with a supplier, induces that supplier to refuse to supply a product to another person because of that other person's low pricing policy; and
- the conduct described above has had, is having or is likely to have an adverse effect on competition in a market.[17]

5.22 At the time of writing, the scope of the new civil price maintenance provision is being considered by the Tribunal in *The Commissioner of Competition v. Visa Canada Corporation and MasterCard International Incorporated.*[18] The Tribunal's decision in the case is expected sometime in 2013.

(ii) Minimum advertised price programs

5.23 Unilateral minimum advertised pricing (MAP) policies are now permitted in Canada. These have long been used in the United States, but were problematic under the pre-2009 Canadian price maintenance rules. While MAP policies are presumed to be lawful, provided they do not have an adverse effect on competition, firms doing business in Canada should still be cautious, especially if they enjoy market power.

I. Tying arrangements

5.24 Tying arrangements are considered for their potentially anticompetitive effects pursuant to s. 77(2) of the Act. Specifically, tying constitutes an offense in circumstances where the conduct (a) impedes entry into or expansion of a firm in a market, (b) impedes introduction of a product into or expansion of sales of a product in a market, or (c) has any other exclusionary effect in a market, with the result that competition is or is likely to be lessened substantially.

5.25 Tied selling is defined as any practice:

- in which a supplier, as a condition of supplying the product requires the customer to either (i) acquire any other product from the supplier or the supplier's nominee, or (ii) refrain from using or distributing, in conjunction with the tying product, another product that is not of a brand or manufacture designated by the supplier or the nominee, and
- whereby the supplier induces a customer to meet one of the conditions set out in (a)(i) or (ii) by offering to supply the tied product on more favorable terms if the customer agrees to those conditions.[19]

5.26 In addition to enforcement actions taken by the Bureau, the Act allows a person to apply directly to the Tribunal for a hearing when the actions of a supplier are alleged to meet all the requirements under the tied selling provision. Where the requirements of the provision

[17] Competition Bureau, *Price Maintenance* (October 4, 2011), <http://www.competitionbureau.gc.ca/eic/site/cb-bc.nsf/eng/h_03210.html>.

[18] *The Commissioner of Competition v. Visa Canada Corporation and MasterCard International Incorporated and others*, CT-2010-010.

[19] Competition Act (n 11) s. 77(1).

are satisfied, the Tribunal may make an order prohibiting the supplier(s) from continuing to engage in the impugned conduct and containing any other requirement that, in its opinion, is necessary to overcome the effects thereof in the market or to restore or stimulate competition in the market.

J. Exclusive dealing

Like tying arrangements, exclusive dealing arrangements are considered for their potentially anticompetitive effects pursuant to s. 77(2) of the Act. Where the conduct (a) impedes entry into or expansion of a firm in a market, (b) impedes introduction of a product into or expansion of sales of a product in a market, or (c) has any other exclusionary effect in a market, with the result that competition is or is likely to be lessened substantially, a finding of exclusive dealing will follow. **5.27**

Exclusive dealing is defined as any practice: **5.28**

- in which a supplier, as a condition of supplying the product, requires the customer to either (i) deal only or primarily in products supplied by or designated by the supplier or its nominee, or (ii) refrain from dealing in a specified product or class of product except as supplied by that supplier, and
- in which a supplier induces a customer to meet a condition set out in (a)(i) or (ii) by offering to supply the product to the customer on more favorable terms if the customer agrees to those conditions.

Similar to the tied selling provision, the Act allows a person to apply directly to the Tribunal for a hearing when the actions of a supplier are alleged to meet all the requirements under the tied-selling provision. Where the requirements of the provision are satisfied, the Tribunal may make an order prohibiting the supplier(s) from continuing to engage in the impugned conduct and containing any other requirement that, in its opinion, is necessary to overcome the effects thereof in the market or to restore or stimulate competition in the market. **5.29**

K. Refusal to deal

Section 75 of the Act addresses unconditional cases of refusal to deal (e.g. refusals that are not simply conditional on exclusivity or tying arrangements). A refusal to deal will be found where: **5.30**

- the person denied supply is substantially affected in its business or is unable to carry on its business because of an inability to obtain adequate supplies of a product anywhere in a market on usual trade terms;
- the person denied supply is unable to obtain adequate supply in the market because of insufficient competition among suppliers;
- the person is willing and able to meet the usual trade terms of the suppliers;
- the product is in ample supply; and
- the refusal has resulted in an adverse effect on competition.

Satisfying the requirements of the refusal to deal provision have proven to be challenging. In the event the requirements are satisfied, the Tribunal may order that one or more suppliers of the product in the market accept the person as a customer within a specified time on usual trade terms. The Act allows for a private right of action when the actions of a supplier are believed to meet all of the requirements under the refusal to supply provision.[20] **5.31**

[20] See e.g. *The Used Car Dealers Association of Ontario v. Insurance Bureau of Canada*, 2011 Comp. Trib. 10.

L. Essential facilities

5.32 While there is no essential facilities doctrine in Canadian law, the preemption of scarce facilities or resources required by a competitor is explicitly recognized as a species of abuse of dominance in s. 78(1)(e) of the Act. According to now superseded draft enforcement guidelines issued by the Bureau in 2009,[21] preemption of scarce facilities could occur in cases of both actual and constructive denial of access to a facility. These draft guidelines defined constructive denial as "a practice that has the equivalent effect of an actual denial, *e.g.*, by charging a prohibitively high access price or offering prohibitively poor quality of service for the facility."[22] Unfortunately, clarification of the Bureau's interpretation of s. 78(1)(e) was removed from the final version of the draft guidelines.

M. Bundling

5.33 See Section I.I concerning tying arrangements.

N. Standard-setting groups

5.34 Standard-setting groups risk attracting Bureau scrutiny where standards have the effect of restricting entry into an industry, deterring innovation, or otherwise inhibiting the ability of persons to compete and those goals are not consistent with the legitimate goals and purposes of the organization.[23]

O. Customer termination

5.35 Terminating customers may attract Bureau scrutiny in circumstances where the termination amounts to a refusal to deal pursuant to s. 75 of the Act. See Sections I.H and I.B.

P. Termination of intermediaries

5.36 Terminating intermediaries may attract Bureau scrutiny in circumstances where the termination amounts to a refusal to deal pursuant to s. 75 of the Act. See Sections I.H and I.B.

Q. Termination of relationships with competitors

5.37 Terminating relationships with competitors may attract Bureau scrutiny in circumstances where the termination amounts to a refusal to deal pursuant to s. 75 of the Act.[24]

R. Exemptions

5.38 In connection with the abuse of dominance provision, s. 79(5) of the Act provides that an act engaged in pursuant only to the exercise of any right or enjoyment of any interest derived under the Copyright Act, Industrial Design Act, Integrated Circuit Topography Act, Patent Act, Trade-marks Act, or any other act of Parliament pertaining to intellectual or industrial property is not an anticompetitive act. Stated differently, the Bureau will apply the more general provisions of the Act where conduct involves something more than the mere exercise of an intellectual property right. The Bureau defines the mere exercise of an intellectual property right as the "the exercise of the owner's right to unilaterally exclude others from using the IP."[25]

---

[21] Competition Bureau, *Updated Enforcement Guidelines on the Abuse of Dominance Provisions of the Copmetition Act (sections 78 and 79)* (January 2009).

[22] Competition Bureau, *Updated Enforcement Guidelines* (n 21) fn 77.

[23] Competition Bureau, *Draft Information Bulletin on Trade Associations*, s. 3.7 (September 8, 2008), <http://www.competitionbureau.gc.ca/eic/site/cb-bc.nsf/eng/02730.html>. See also Section I.E.

[24] See Sections I.K and I.E.

[25] Competition Bureau, *Intellectual Property Enforcement Guidelines*, para. 4.2.1 (September 2000), <http://www.competitionbureau.gc.ca/eic/site/cb-bc.nsf/eng/01286.html>.

Additionally, no order shall be made pertaining to otherwise prohibited conduct among affiliates as defined by s. 2(2) of the Act. **5.39**

II. Dealing with competitors

Section 45 of the Act is the core of Canadian cartel law. Section 45 provides that any person who, with a competitor in respect of a particular product, conspires, agrees or arranges any of the following is guilty of an indictable offense and liable to imprisonment for a term not exceeding 14 years or to a fine not exceeding CAD 25 million or to both: **5.40**

- fixing, maintaining, increasing or controlling the price for the supply of the product;
- allocating sales, territories, customers or markets for the production or supply of the product; or
- fixing, maintaining, controlling, preventing, lessening or eliminating the production or supply of the product.

Price fixing, market allocation, and output restriction conspiracies are per se illegal in Canada. Notably, there is no statute of limitations for s. 45 offenses. As with most other criminal offenses in Canadian law, a conviction under the Act requires the prosecution to prove beyond a reasonable doubt both the *actus reus* and the *mens rea* of the offense. The *actus reus* is established by demonstrating that the accused was a party to a conspiracy, agreement, or arrangement with a competitor to fix prices, allocate markets or customers, or lessen production or supply of a product in the manner described above. To establish the *mens rea* of the offense, the prosecution must demonstrate that the accused subjectively intended to enter into the agreement and had knowledge of its terms. **5.41**

Sections 46 and 47 of the Act prohibit Canadian corporations from implementing directives from a foreign corporation for the purpose of giving effect to conspiracies entered into outside of Canada and bid rigging, respectively. **5.42**

Agreements between competitors that fall outside of the prohibitions of s. 45(1) or that satisfy the elements of the ancillary restraints defense[26] can be reviewed under s. 90.1, the civil analogue to s. 45's criminal prohibition of competitor collaboration. Section 90.1 of the Act permits the Tribunal to issue certain remedies in respect of existing or proposed agreements between competitors or potential competitors that are likely to substantially lessen or prevent competition in any relevant market. Subsection 90.1(1) states: **5.43**

> 90.1 (1) If, on application by the Commissioner, the Tribunal finds that an agreement or arrangement—whether existing or proposed—between persons two or more of whom are competitors prevents or lessens, or is likely to prevent or lessen competition substantially in a market, the Tribunal may make an order
>
> - prohibiting any person—whether or not a party to the agreement or arrangement—from doing anything under the agreement or arrangement; or
> - requiring any person—whether or not a party to the agreement or arrangement—with the consent of that person and the Commissioner, to take any other action.

As noted above, over the last three years, the Commissioner has adopted an aggressive approach to enforcement, particularly in respect of improper competitor collaborations. Since the 2009 amendments were passed, the Bureau has worked at issuing new competitor collaboration guidelines, a memorandum of understanding with the Director of Public **5.44**

[26] Competition Act (n 11) s. 45(4). See also the discussion in Section II.D.

Prosecutions (DPP), and updated immunity and leniency bulletins. The most obvious recent example of that increased enforcement activity in this area is the ongoing global investigation into the auto parts industry. According to public record documents filed by the Bureau to obtain subpoenas in that investigation, it has at least ten cooperating parties across a range of different products and has issued more than 160 "markers." This inquiry appears to be shaping up to be one of the largest cartel investigations in history.

A. Horizontal price fixing

5.45 Section 45(1)(a) of the Act makes it a criminal offense "to fix, maintain, increase or control the price for the supply of the product." The offense extends beyond the setting of prices and also includes arrangements that result in the control of prices—for example, agreements on price formulas, transportation costs, or discounts.

5.46 Notably, the price fixing offense is committed when competitors enter into a conspiracy, arrangement, or agreement. The planned conduct need not actually be carried out. Likewise, if the conspiracy, agreement or arrangement is not successful in fixing prices (for example, if cartel members cheat), the offense has nevertheless been committed and is open to prosecution. The same is true of the other s. 45(1) conspiracy offenses, in relation to market allocation and output restriction (discussed in Section I.B).

5.47 The existence of an agreement or arrangement may be established through direct evidence, or it may be inferred through circumstantial evidence (though in any case, it must be proved beyond reasonable doubt).[27]

B. Horizontal agreements to allocate customers or territories; agreements not to compete

5.48 Other agreements or arrangements not to compete that are not strictly based on price fixing can be prohibited by s. 45(1)(b) and (c). Section 45(1)(b) makes it an offense to allocate customers, sales, customers or markets. In essence, agreements among firms not to compete in particular areas or for particular customers are prohibited. Section 45(1)(c) prohibits the restrictions on output of a product. The elements these offenses are the same as the price fixing provision discussed in Section II.A.

5.49 The Act has a separate provision that specifically addresses bid-rigging. Under s. 47, it is a per se criminal offense to enter an agreement or where one or more of the parties undertakes not to bid or tender, withdraw a bid or tender, or submit a bid or tender arrived at by agreement. Unlike the s. 45 offenses, the bid-rigging provision applies to agreements and arrangements between "two or more persons" and not specifically to "competitors." Interestingly, no offense is committed if the person requesting the bid or tender has knowledge of the agreement or arrangement at the time the bid or tender is submitted (or withdrawn, as the case may be).

5.50 There are also other types of agreements or arrangements between competitors that may be subject to review if they are likely to prevent or lessen competition substantially (or do, in fact, prevent or lessen competition substantially), but are not the kind of "hard core" offenses described in ss. 45 and 47. Section 90.1 of the Act creates a civil "reviewable practice" and may apply to agreements such as non-competes, joint purchasing agreements, joint production, joint selling and commercialization, or information sharing agreements. Bureau

[27] Competition Bureau, *Competitor Collaboration Guidelines*, para. 2.2 (December 23, 2009), <http://www.competitionbureau.gc.ca/eic/site/cb-bc.nsf/vwapj/Competitor-Collaboration-Guidelines-e-2009-12-22.pdf/$FILE/Competitor-Collaboration-Guidelines-e-2009-12-22.pdf>.

guidelines on this provision suggest that the type of economic analysis applicable to merger reviews will also be used in the review of such conduct.[28]

C. Horizontal boycotts

A horizontal boycott or a group boycott between competitors generally involves a concerted refusal to deal that has the effect of preventing one or more firms from competing in the market. Group boycotts are not expressly addressed by the current Act or the *Competitor Collaboration Guidelines*. What constitutes a "group boycott" is also not addressed. However, it was generally understood that prior to the 2010 amendments, group boycotts could constitute a conspiracy under the previous version of s. 45(1) for unduly restricting competition. **5.51**

D. Joint ventures and other competitive collaborations

The conspiracy offenses in the Act apply to agreements or arrangements between "competitors," which "includes a person who it is reasonable to believe would be likely to compete with respect to a product in the absence of a conspiracy, agreement or arrangement to do anything referred to in paragraphs (1)(a) to (c) [of s. 45]." Joint ventures will often be between two parties who compete or would be likely to compete. **5.52**

In its *Competitor Collaboration Guidelines*, the Bureau takes the view is that the per se criminal cartel offenses are intended to apply to agreements that constitute "naked restraints" on competition. The Bureau recognizes that joint ventures and other strategic alliances may be legitimate forms of competitor collaboration. Parties may be hesitant to participate in a joint venture without some kind of explicit restraint on competition; absent such a restraint one party to the joint venture could compete with the joint venture independently. Section 90.1 is the expected means by which joint venture will be analyzed. **5.53**

Furthermore, to the extent that joint ventures or other such collaborations fall within the prohibited conduct in s. 45(1), they may be protected by the ancillary restraints defense. Section 45(4) carves out an exemption for an agreement or arrangement that would otherwise contravene the s. 45(1) criminal offenses, but is ancillary to, and necessary for giving effect to a broader or separate agreement or arrangement which does not, on its own, contravene s. 45(1). The Bureau's perspective is that joint ventures and other forms of competitor collaborations may be subject to review under the s. 90.1 civil provision where they are likely to substantially lessen or prevent competition and has proceeded against proposed joint ventures under this provision.[29] **5.54**

E. Trade associations

Trade associations can have a legitimate purpose, but are open to significant risks since, by their nature, they bring together competing businesses to discuss topics of common interest. As such, they may create opportunities to engage in anticompetitive conduct. Discussions on topics such as proposed new legislation, product standards, packaging, and industry promotion are usually innocuous. However, risks increase when members start engaging in informal discussions ancillary to the trade association meetings, or exchange sensitive information.[30] **5.55**

The Bureau has commented that trade associations may be considered a principal party to a s. 45 contravention (or other provisions of the Act such as s. 79).[31] Private plaintiffs have **5.56**

---

28 Competition Bureau, *Competitor Collaboration Guidelines* (n 27) s. 3.1.

29 See e.g. *The Commissioner of Competition v. Air Canada, United Continental Holdings, Inc., United Airlines, Inc. and Continental Airlines Inc.*, CT-2012-001.

30 See Section I.G.

31 Competition Bureau, *Draft Information Bulletin on Trade Associations* (n 22) part 2.

also initiated proceedings against trade associations based on alleged breaches of s. 45. The *Competitor Collaboration Guidelines* indicate[32] that where members of the trade association are not agreeing to fix prices, allocate markets or reduce output, the Bureau would examine the agreement or arrangement under the s. 90.1 civil provisions. However, the Guidelines are not binding on the Commissioner or private parties.

5.57 In 2008, prior to the 2010 amendments to the Act, the Bureau released a *Draft Information Bulletin on Trade Associations*,[33] but ultimately never finalized the Bulletin. In the draft Bulletin, the Bureau identified a number of trade association activities that could raise concerns including information sharing, meetings and agendas, association membership, fee guidelines, or advertising restrictions.

F. Interlocking directorates

5.58 Unlike in the United States, Canada's Act does not address the issue of interlocking directorates. An interlocking directorate may arise where a director of one company also serves as an employee, executive, partner, owner, or board member of another company. The Bureau has indicated through its *Merger Enforcement Guidelines* that its interest in interlocking directorates generally pertains to mergers and proposed mergers.[34] The Bureau's concern is that an interlocking directorate may prevent or lessen competition, for example, by effective pricing or inducing one or both companies to compete less aggressively. But it is also conceivable that interlocking directorates could raise issues concerning facilitating practices, on which see the next section.

G. Facilitating practices

5.59 Certain practices enhance the ability of rival firms to coordinate conduct and avoid vigorous competition. In the context of criminal conspiracy provisions, such facilitating practices, coupled with other conduct, may point to an arrangement or agreement under the conspiracy provisions.

5.60 The *Competitor Collaboration Guidelines* discuss the role of facilitating practices in conjunction with "conscious parallelism." While it is not usually an offense for competitors to choose independently a common course of conduct based on an awareness of the likely response from competitors, such "conscious parallelism" in conjunction with facilitating practices may provide sufficient evidence that there was an agreement between the parties. The facilitating practices may consist of sharing sensitive information, or conduct that assists the companies in monitoring each other's prices.

H. Information exchange

5.61 Prior to the 2009 amendments, the Act included an exemption for the exchange of certain types of information including statistics and credit information, so long as the arrangement did not lessen competition unduly. This provision is now repealed.

5.62 Information may be exchanged between competitors under information sharing agreements or as part of other collaborative efforts such as joint purchasing agreements or trade associations. The Bureau is generally not concerned about information exchanges where competitively sensitive information is not shared. Concerns arise where the information shared is competitively sensitive.

---

[32] Competition Bureau, *Competitor Collaboration Guidelines* (n 27) para. 2.3.1.
[33] Competition Bureau, *Draft Information Bulletin on Trade Associations* (n 22).
[34] Competition Bureau, *Merger Enforcement Guidelines* (October 6, 2011) at para. 1.16.

Both ss. 45 and 90.1 may be engaged by the exchange of information amongst competitors. While s. 45 does not criminalize the exchange of information in and of itself, the conduct may be used as circumstantial evidence by a court (or private plaintiff—see s. 36 of the Act) to infer the existence of an agreement to fix prices, allocate markets, or restrict output. The exchange of information may also be reviewed under s. 90.1 if it is likely to prevent or lessen competition substantially. Under the civil offense, the Bureau will consider, *inter alia*, the following factors: **5.63**

- the nature of the information (i.e. whether the information is competitively sensitive);
- the timing of the information exchange (e.g. whether the information relates to historical, current or future activities);
- whether the parties participating in the information exchange have market power or will likely have market power;
- the manner in which the information is collected and disseminated (e.g. whether the information is shared directly between competitors or aggregated by a third party);
- whether any anti competitive effects are offset and outweighed by the efficiencies generated through the information sharing agreement.

(i) Exchanges of historic pricing information

Exchanges of historic pricing information are less likely to raise alarms than the exchange of information regarding current or future activities since the latter is more likely to impair competition. On the other hand, pricing is generally considered competitively sensitive information that can result in the substantial lessening or prevention of competition. The Bureau's concern is that the sharing of competitively sensitive information can make it easier for competing companies to act in concert. As such, the disclosure of information relating to current or future pricing would be more likely to raise concerns than the sharing of historic pricing information. However, the *Competitor Collaboration Guidelines* caution[35] that competition could be negatively affected where historical information provides a "meaningful indication" of intended future pricing. **5.64**

(ii) How old, anonymous, and aggregated pricing information needs to be

In addition to historic data, information that is aggregated in a way that does not disclose firm-specific details is less likely to raise concerns than disaggregated information. Furthermore, information supplied to an independent third party is less likely to create issues than information exchanged directly between competitors. For example, the Bureau suggests[36] that if businesses wish to determine costs relative to industry averages, they may provide sales information to a third party, who then can disclose it in an aggregated, anonymous, form. **5.65**

(iii) What pro-competitive purposes, if any, exchange needs to help participants achieve, pre-merger due diligence?

Due diligence conducted as part of mergers and acquisitions requires the sharing of information. However, these activities have the potential to raise Bureau concerns depending on the nature and manner of information exchange. In evaluating an agreement to exchange information, the Bureau will consider the safeguards that are directed at preventing or minimizing the disclosure of competitively sensitive information. For example, the communication of competitively sensitive information in the context of merger diligence should be conducted in a strictly one-way manner from vendor to prospective buyer. Additional mitigation in this context may be achieved by staging the disclosure of competitively sensitive information such **5.66**

35 Competition Bureau, *Competitor Collaboration Guidelines* (n 27) para. 3.7.2.
36 Competition Bureau, *Competitor Collaboration Guidelines* (n 27) para. 3.7.4.

that less disclosure occurs early in the diligence process (i.e. when there are more prospective buyers) and gradually increasing as the transaction progresses and the number of prospective buyers is reduced.

5.67 In addition, in the pre-merger stage, the parties must continue to compete. They should not combine activities or exchange competitively sensitive information. The Bureau seeks to prevent "gun jumping," where the merging parties combine their activities before the merger has been reviewed, or disclose competitively sensitive information beyond the requirements of due diligence. If the transaction is not successfully completed, competitively sensitive information may reveal to the parties how to behave in the future in a way that impairs competition.

5.68 To reduce the risks of raising Bureau concerns, competitively sensitive information should be exchanged through a third party and only information necessary to the merger should be exchanged.

I. Joint purchasing agreements

5.69 Businesses sometimes agree to purchase some or all of a product from a particular supplier. These arrangements can be pro-competitive, as they enable smaller firms to aggregate their purchase quantities in order to receive discounts from suppliers, and share the delivery, distribution, or other costs.

J. Joint lobbying/regulatory/legislative efforts

5.70 Lobbying and other such joint legislative efforts are not dealt with by the Act expressly, but are generally considered to have beneficial effects. The *Draft Information Bulletin on Trade Associations* (which was never finalized) had expressly recognized lobbying by associations to be a beneficial activity. Lobbying and discussions of proposed legislation are often undertaken by trade associations on behalf of their members. Trade associations commonly collect information, which is used for lobbying or other legitimate purposes such as industry benchmarking.[37]

III. General issues

A. Jurisdiction and applicable law

(i) Applicable law

5.71 Canada has only one statute governing all aspects of competition law: the federal *Competition* Act.

(ii) Jurisdiction

5.72 Canada's competition law enforcement regime applies to Canadians and non-Canadians alike. To take jurisdiction over activities occurring outside of Canada, a Canadian court must find that it has both "subject matter" (or substantive) jurisdiction with respect to the alleged offense, and personal jurisdiction over the accused person. The Supreme Court of Canada's 1985 decision in *R v. Libman* sets out the following test for substantive jurisdiction:

> This country has a legitimate interest in prosecuting persons for activities that take place abroad but have an unlawful consequence here... all that is necessary to make an offence subject to the jurisdiction of our courts is that a significant portion of the activities constituting that offence took place in Canada.[38]

[37] See Sections II.E and II.H for further discussion.

[38] *Libman v. The Queen* [1985] 2 SCR 178, pp. 67 and 74.

The issue of substantive jurisdiction over cartel conduct taking place outside Canada with effects in Canada has not been specifically canvassed in a contested criminal proceeding. Some uncertainty remains regarding the jurisdiction of Canadian courts over such conduct. **5.73**

The Commissioner has demonstrated a willingness to adopt an expansive interpretation of *Libman*.[39] The Bureau can be expected to argue that a foreign cartel that affects Canadian consumers triggers substantive jurisdiction. Recent document production orders have sought documents located abroad, and expressed an interest on the Bureau's part in claiming jurisdiction over indirect sales into Canada. This theory is currently being tested before the Canadian courts in connection with the multijurisdictional London Interbank Offered Rate (LIBOR) investigation. **5.74**

(iii) Personal jurisdiction

The general principle governing a Canadian criminal court's assumption of personal jurisdiction is that a person who is outside Canada and not brought by any special statute within the jurisdiction of the court is *prima facie* not subject to the process of that court. If there is no special statutory provision for the service of a summons outside the jurisdiction, then the court does not have jurisdiction and cannot try the accused, unless the person is present in Canada or voluntarily submits to the jurisdiction of the court. For persons who are not resident in Canada, a summons compelling attendance before a Canadian court cannot be served abroad for an offense under the Act. If no service has occurred, then Canadian courts will not have jurisdiction. **5.75**

The case of foreign corporations with no Canadian presence or assets in Canada is more complex. Where the accused is a corporation, a notice of an indictment must be served on the corporation pursuant to the *Criminal Code* by delivering it to "the manager, secretary or other executive officer of the corporation or of a branch thereof."[40] Service upon the Canadian "affiliate" of a foreign corporation is unlikely to be sufficient, given that an affiliate is a separate legal person and service outside of Canada on a foreign corporation is not specifically authorized. However, a corporation that does not have a branch in Canada may still be properly served if one of its executive officers is present in Canada to carry on the business of the corporation. If there is a Canadian affiliate of a foreign corporate conspirator, a prosecution may also be instituted against the local subsidiary under s. 46 of the Act,[41] regardless of whether charges under s. 45 are pursued against the foreign parent. **5.76**

B. Antitrust system

(i) Name of agency/agencies

The Act is administered and enforced by the Commissioner of Competition (the "Commissioner") who serves as the head of the Bureau, a unit of Industry Canada. **5.77**

[39] *Libman* (n 36).

[40] Criminal Code, RSC 1985, c C-46, s. 703.2.

[41] Section 46 of the Act provides that:

> Any corporation, wherever incorporated, that carries on business in Canada and that implements, in whole or in part in Canada, a directive, instruction, intimation of policy or other communication to the corporation or any person from a person in a country other than Canada who is in a position to direct or influence the policies of the corporation, which communication is for the purpose of giving effect to a conspiracy, combination, agreement or arrangement entered into outside Canada that, if entered into in Canada, would have been in contravention of section 45, is, whether or not any director or officer of the corporation in Canada has knowledge of the conspiracy, combination, agreement or arrangement, guilty of an indictable offense and liable on conviction to a fine in the discretion of the court.

5.78 **Commissioner of Competition** The Commissioner, a federal cabinet appointee, has statutory responsibility for the administration and enforcement of the Act. The Commissioner is the chief executive of the Bureau which itself operates within the federal Department of Industry.

5.79 **Competition Bureau** The Bureau provides all necessary logistic support to permit the Commissioner to carry out his responsibilities. For many years, the Bureau was organized internally along sectoral lines. The Bureau's principal office is located in Gatineau, Quebec, across the river from Ottawa, the federal capital, at Industry Canada, Place du Portage, Phase I, 50 Victoria Street, 21st Floor, Gatineau, Quebec K1A 0C9, telephone: (819) 997-4282 (or 1-800-348-5358), fax: (819) 997-0324. Regional offices are maintained throughout Canada.

5.80 The Commissioner is responsible for investigating alleged breaches of the criminal provisions of the Act. The criminal matters branch of the Bureau, consisting of the senior deputy Commissioner, two assistant deputy Commissioners and approximately 40 officers, investigates all matters relating to cartels and conspiracies. The Bureau is supported by a team of approximately 20 lawyers from the Public Prosecution Service of Canada (PPSC) who are responsible for the conduct of prosecutions under the Act. Canada's attorney general has ultimate discretion and authority to initiate criminal proceedings under the Act, and the discretion of the attorney general is effectively exercised by the DPP, who is head of the PPSC. In practical terms, cartel prosecutions are initiated only upon the Commissioner's recommendation to the DPP. Although the criminal provisions of the Act relating to cartels and conspiracies date back to 1889, until the 1960s successful prosecutions were rare. Prosecutions have become significantly more frequent since amendments to the Act were adopted in 1986 and the Supreme Court of Canada clarified the law in a 1992 decision. Numerous cartels have been uncovered and cases resolved through the use of an immunity program that was developed in the early 1990s, revised in September 2000, and most recently revised again in 2010. As a result of amendments to the Act in March 2009, significant changes to the criminal provisions of the Act came into force on 13 March 2010.

(ii) Staff size and budget

5.81 The Bureau maintains a well-organized and comprehensive website containing volumes of resource materials such as news releases, backgrounders, enforcement guidelines and legislative commentary. The Bureau's total staffing strength (for all branches) exceeds 400 people. Of these, the vast majority are located at the Bureau's headquarters in Gatineau, Quebec (opposite Ottawa, Ontario). The Bureau's operating budget for 2009–2010 was CAD 50.8 million.

(iii) Recent enforcement actions and trends

5.82 Since the 2009 amendments to the Act were passed, the Bureau has diligently worked at issuing new competitor collaboration and abuse of dominance guidelines, a memorandum of understanding with the DPP and updated immunity and leniency bulletins.

5.83 While not an exhaustive list, recent Bureau enforcement actions include commencing cases against Canada's largest telecommunications carrier; settling a civil advertising case for a seven figure amount; bringing cases to the Tribunal for abuse of dominance in the waste disposal and real estate brokerage businesses; fighting a contested case before the Tribunal against Visa and MasterCard under Canada's new price maintenance provisions; bringing a contested case involving the Toronto Real Estate Board for abuse of dominance; testing the new civil provisions of the Competition Act with respect to agreements amongst competitors; and prosecuting numerous cartels, including those involving retail gasoline.

C. Private litigation

5.84 Section 36 of the Act grants private parties the right to recover in the ordinary civil courts any losses or damages suffered as a result of a breach of the criminal provisions of the Act, as well as their costs of investigation and litigation. The Act expressly provides that a prior conviction for an offense is, in the absence of any evidence to the contrary, proof of liability. However, the absence of a conviction, or even the refusal of the Commissioner to commence an inquiry, does not bar or provide a valid defense to such a private litigant's action pursuant to s. 36. Such claims cannot be launched on the basis of an alleged violation of the civil provisions of the Act.

Historically, private enforcement played a limited part in formal competition law and policy in Canada. While Canada has had competition legislation since 1889, for much of that time, competition laws were primarily enforced by public officials. A private civil cause of action, allowing parties to seek damages for conduct contrary to the Act's criminal provisions or contrary to an order of the Tribunal, was introduced into the legislation in 1976, but relatively few private party court proceedings were initiated and even fewer were successful. However, Canada has more recently seen increasing importance placed on the role of private civil actions as a tool for enforcement of competition law and policy. This has been due in large part to the increased prominence and availability of class actions as a means of seeking redress for alleged anti competitive wrongs. In particular, recent developments in Canadian class action jurisprudence are widely perceived to have both lowered the threshold for bringing a competition law class action and increased the scope and availability of collective civil redress for alleged anticompetitive conduct. **5.85**

In 2002, private parties were granted a limited ability to seek leave from the Tribunal to bring an application before that body in respect of a handful of the Act's provisions. Only a small number of applications have been initiated and no applicant has been successful in a contested hearing on the merits. **5.86**

D. Follow-on litigation

Follow-on class actions are now a virtual certainty in multiple provinces in Canada before or after a conviction under the Act in matters where cartel activity may have occurred. A vigorous and effective plaintiffs' bar has evolved in Canada, often acting in conjunction with US plaintiffs, and this is a rapidly developing area of practice. Class action procedures are available in each Canadian jurisdiction. Most Canadian jurisdictions now have specific class action legislation.[42] Even in jurisdictions without comprehensive class action legislation, the Supreme Court of Canada has confirmed that class action procedures are available.[43] **5.87**

E. Arbitration and alternative dispute resolution

Arbitration and alternative dispute resolution (aside from the immunity and leniency programs) do not form part of the enforcement landscape in Canada. **5.88**

F. Remedies

(i) Civil liability

Cartel cases are prosecuted under the criminal provisions of the Act and are primarily subject to the criminal sanctions of fines and imprisonment discussed in para. 5.40. It is also possible for the prosecution to seek a prohibition order to prevent future repetition of the offense. **5.89**

[42] Class Proceedings Act, 1992, SO 1992, c 6 (Ontario); Class Proceedings Act, SA 2003, c C-16.5 (Alberta); Class Proceedings Act, RSBC 1996, c 50 (British Columbia); Class Proceedings Act, SNS 2007, c 28 (Nova Scotia); Class Proceedings Act, RSNB 2011, c 125 (New Brunswick); Class Actions Act, SNL 2001, c C-18 and Rules of the Supreme Court, 1986, SNL 1986, c 42, Sch D, Rule 7A Class Actions (Newfoundland and Labrador); Class Proceedings Act, CCSM c C130 (Manitoba); Class Actions Act, SS 2001, c C-12.01 (Saskatchewan); An Act respecting the class Action, RSQ, c R-2.1 (Québec) and Quebec Code of Civil Procedure, R.S.Q., c C-25 (Book IX Class Action); Federal Courts Rules, SOR/98/106 (Federal).

[43] *Western Canadian Shopping Centers*, 2001 SCC 46.

5.90 For cases that do not fall into the traditional hard core cartel pattern, s. 90.1's civil reviewable practices provisions governing competitor collaboration permits the Bureau to pursue a prohibition order from the Tribunal against the conduct in question. Alternatively, it might be possible for the Commissioner to bring an application under the joint abuse of dominance provisions in the non-criminal part of the Act. Such applications would be heard before the Competition Tribunal, an administrative body that considers the evidence on a civil standard of a balance of probabilities. Since 2009, the Competition Tribunal can impose administrative monetary penalties under the abuse of dominance provision of the Act of up to CAD 10 million for a first order and of up to CAD 15 million for subsequent orders.

(ii) Criminal liability

5.91 Given their status as the most serious indictable offenses under the Act, cartel prosecutions attract very significant penalties—up to CAD 25 million per count charged for companies, and up to CAD 25 million and/or fourteen years imprisonment for individuals—together with prohibition orders made after a conviction. Courts have emphasized that, in the competition law context, fines must be large enough to deter powerful companies and must not become simply a cost of doing business. CAD 10 million is the highest fine to date for a single count conspiracy under s. 45. This amount (the previous statutory maximum) was imposed for the first time in January 2006.[44] However, it is common for the prosecution to proceed on multiple counts. As a result, the Commissioner has obtained much larger fines following guilty pleas in a number of conspiracy cases. These include the highest fine in the history of Canadian criminal law, CAD 50.9 million, against F. Hoffmann-La Roche in the vitamins case.[45]

G. Leniency and Immunity

5.92 The Commissioner's bulletin entitled "Immunity Program under the Competition Act" sets out the circumstances in which the Commissioner will make a recommendation of immunity. This bulletin reflects the current practice of the Commissioner and, by extension, the DPP. The Bureau has also released FAQs to elaborate on areas of practice under the program. The current bulletin was published in June 2010 and replaces former versions. In September 2010, the Commissioner published a finalized information bulletin and FAQs on leniency in cartel cases available online.[46]

H. Document creation and retention

5.93 The Act does not contain provisions dealing expressly with document creation and retention obligations. However, exposure to obstruction of justice charges for failing to retain documents relevant to an investigation underscores the need for a cautious approach to records management in Canada.

[44] See Competition Bureau, Press Release, "Competition Bureau Investigation Leads to Record Fine in Domestic Conspiracy" (January 9, 2006).

[45] See Competition Bureau, Press Release, "Federal Court Imposes Fines Totalling $88.4 Million For International Vitamin Conspiracies" (September 22, 1999).

[46] See Competition Bureau, *Leniency Program* (September 29, 2010), <http://www.competitionbureau.gc.ca/eic/site/cb-bc.nsf/vwapj/LeniencyProgram-sept-2010-e.pdf/$FILE/LeniencyProgram-sept-2010-e.pdf>.

6

CHILE

Paulo Montt Rettig and Sander Van Der Voorde

Ferrada Nehme, Michael Jacobs, Fiscalía Nacional Económica

Introduction

Chile's successful implementation of its competition law and establishment of supporting institutions are often considered a model for other countries in Latin America and for small, developing nations around the world. As part of Chile's accession to the Organisation for Economic Co-operation and Development (OECD), a review was undertaken of the country's competition law and policy to assess its coherence with that of other OECD member nations. The Accession Review, published in 2010, concluded *inter alia* that Chile's laws and institutions "support... effective policy and enforcement against restrictive agreements and concerted actions, unilateral abuse of dominance, predatory exclusion and anticompetitive mergers."[1] **6.01**

While Chile was among the first countries in Latin America to adopt a competition law—enacting its initial Competition Act in 1959—the law saw little use during its first decades, **6.02**

[1] OECD "Competition Law and Policy in Chile" (2010) p. 3.

which were characterized by significant state involvement in the Chilean economy. Following the *coup d'état* in September 1973, the military regime enacted a new Competition Act (Decree Law No. 211 of 1973, "Competition Act" or "DL No. 211") as part of its program to liberalize the Chilean economy.

6.03 The 1973 Competition Act, as amended, still embodies the general rule of Chilean competition law. With remarkable simplicity and generality, the Competition Act establishes as its objective the promotion and defense of "free competition" in the marketplace. Under the law, anticompetitive conduct is to be corrected, prohibited, and sanctioned in accordance with the rules established in DL No. 211.

6.04 Nevertheless, it was not until the creation of the Competition Tribunal (*Tribunal de Defensa de la Libre Competencia*, TDLC) in 2003 that the "modern" Chilean system was established. The TDLC replaced the Competition Commission (*Comisión Resolutiva*) and central and regional Consultative Commissions (*Comisiones Preventivas*)—whose members were empowered to impose sanctions, issue injunctions, and make recommendations. Decisions of the Competition Commission, which largely focused on vertical restraints and similar market foreclosures, followed a formal, legalistic approach. The TDLC, in contrast, is comprised of five full-time members (*ministros*), and its decisions have become more "effects-based" and less formalistic. Therefore, this Chapter focuses largely on developments since 2003.

6.05 Article 3 DL No. 211 is the central provision of the Competition Act, which delineates anticompetitive practices. It stipulates that whoever executes or enters into any act, agreement, or contract, either individually or collectively, which hinders, restricts, or impedes "free competition," or that tends to produce such effects, may be penalized with the measures set forth in the Competition Act, notwithstanding any preventive, corrective, or prohibitive measures that could be ordered with respect to said acts, agreements, or conventions. Three subsections provide a non-exhaustive list of examples of such anti competitive conduct, covering explicit or tacit agreements or concerted practices between competitors (art. 3(a)), abusive exploitation of a dominant position (art. 3(b)), and predatory or "unfair competition" practices to attain, maintain, or strengthen a dominant position (art. 3(c)).

6.06 US and European jurisprudence has influenced the interpretation of the Competition Act's simple and general substantive provisions. While the US and Europe have seen significant convergence in recent years, important differences nevertheless remain, particularly with respect to abuse of dominance. The influence of these two sometimes divergent systems, along with other factors, has sometimes resulted in uncertainty regarding the application of the Competition Act to a particular conduct, as discussed in more detail below.

6.07 In addition to substance, the Competition Act establishes the respective responsibilities of the principal entities charged with enforcing Chile's competition laws: the National Economic Prosecutor's Office (*Fiscalía Nacional Económica*, FNE) and the TDLC. The respective roles of these entities are described in more detail below (see Section III.B (i)).

6.08 Moreover, the Competition Act also specifies the principal procedural rules that will govern investigations by the FNE and proceedings before the TDLC. Rulings by the TDLC are subject to appeal before the Chilean Supreme Court of Justice (*Corte Suprema*, SC).

6.09 Although the majority of the cases decided by the TDLC and the Supreme Court are still related to abuse of dominance—more specifically exclusionary practices such as predatory pricing and exclusive dealing—the number of cartel cases has increased in recent years. This trend likely will continue, given the FNE's current focus on cartel enforcement, its new investigative powers, and the authorities' growing interest in merger review.

I. Acting alone

Article 3 DL No. 211 prohibits abuse of dominance and exclusionary conduct with the object of obtaining, maintaining, or strengthening a dominant position. Article 3 (b) DL No. 211 mentions resale price maintenance and tying, as well as "similar" exploitative abuses, as examples of abusive conduct. Article 3 (c) DL No. 211 refers to exclusionary or "predatory" practices.[2] **6.10**

In line with the international case law, it is not in itself illicit to have a dominant position, and a dominant company is allowed to compete on the merits. A company with a dominant position, however, has a special responsibility not to restrict already weakened competition or to impair genuine competition. Subjective intent as to the anticompetitive impact is not required, and liability may arise as long as the conduct itself was intended. Article 3 DL No. 211 applies to abuse by a firm holding a single dominant position, as well as dominance by two or more entities. The FNE thereby seems to focus on exclusionary practices such as tying, refusal to supply, exclusive dealing, and rebates. **6.11**

A. Predatory pricing

The TDLC has stated that illicit predation requires actual or potential dominance, likelihood or reasonable expectation of future recoupment of short-term losses, and some indication or evidence of sales below marginal costs.[3] **6.12**

The standard for loss-leading prices—i.e. repeated offers for selected groups of critical products at reduced promotional (below-cost) prices—is not clear. The Supreme Court held in one case concerning joint price undercutting by several bus operators that average avoidable costs are a more appropriate standard for predation than average variable costs.[4] The court, however, did not analyze the issue further in that case. The court assumed a predatory/exclusionary intent because the economic sacrifice resulting from the coordinated action did not correspond to efficient production or legitimate competition. **6.13**

In the supermarket context, the TDLC has held that loss-leading is not per se abusive.[5] Such a pricing strategy can be commercially justified when temporary price reductions on products with high elasticity increase the demand for other products for which the margin is sufficient to recoup the loss on the low-priced items. In upholding the decision on appeal, the Supreme Court reiterated the relevance of recoupment as a requirement, i.e., that the company will be in the position to raise its prices above the competitive level in the future. **6.14**

[2] Article 3 DL No. 211: "...Among others, the following shall be considered as acts, agreements or conventions that hinder, restrict or impede free competition, or which tend to produce such effects: (b) Abusive exploitation by an economic agent or a group of economic agents, of a dominant position in the market, fixing sale or purchase prices, tying a sale to the sale of another product, allocating territories or market quotas or imposing other similar abuses. (c) Predatory practices, or unfair competition practices, carried out with the purpose of attaining, maintaining or increasing a dominant position." The references are non-exhaustive, and other conduct may constitute abuse as well.

[3] *Sociedad Will S.A. v. Claro Chile S.A.*, TDLC Ruling No. 110/2011 of January 28, 2011. Dominance is not a condition *sine qua non* for illicit predation as art. 3(c) DL No. 211 also prohibits predation with the object of attaining a dominant position (*Producción Química y Electrónica Quimel S.A. v. James Hardie Fibrocementos Ltda*, SC Ruling No. 39/2006 of November 29, 2006).

[4] *FNE v. Asociación Gremial de Dueños de Mini Buses Agimal (Agimal)*, SC Ruling No. 102/2010 of January 14, 2011.

[5] *Comercial Arauco Ltda. v. D&S and another*, TDLC Ruling No.103/2010 of September 8, 2010.

6.15 Fine-tuning of the conditions for predation should come from future cases, although it isn't an area of specific enforcement concern.

B. Exploitative offenses

6.16 Article 3(b) DL No. 211 explicitly prohibits exploitative abuses, and the TDLC has used this in the past to condemn excessive prices. In some cases, the TDLC has found exploitative abuse by examining the pricing methods employed in concession contracts when those contracts or tender documents provided for a price cap or price indexation, or by using prices charged by companies in similar situations as a benchmark.[6] In other cases, the TDLC has evaluated whether the prices charged were economically justified, taking into particular account the costs involved.

6.17 The TDLC, however, is increasingly reluctant to interfere in the pricing behavior of companies, whether they are dominant or not, provided that there is no issue of predation or other exclusionary conduct. The court recently held, for instance, that it lacks competence—as a general competition court—to decide in a particular matter whether prices were excessive.[7] The TDLC is likely to interfere only in exceptional cases, for example in markets characterized by natural monopolies, or in situations in which an explicit legal provision authorizes such interference. The TDLC's intervention in earlier cases may be explained by the challenged conduct's effect on social welfare and/or the protected position of the companies concerned.

C. Monopsony

6.18 The TDLC has dealt with alleged discrimination or exploitation by supermarkets vis-à-vis suppliers in various cases. Over time, the court's approach to monopsony has changed "from a more legal and pro-competitor view (economic dependence) towards an economic oriented and pro-competition conception, based on monopsony theory and welfare effects."[8] In an earlier case, the TDLC stated—without examining the level of competition in the downstream market and the consequent effects of the challenged behavior—that using the buying power to lower purchase prices has the same effect as using a dominant position to increase prices, and may lead to a variation in prices, lower output, and reduced social welfare. In a subsequent supermarket merger case, however, the TDLC applied a more economic analysis, stating that further market concentration, while it may increase buying power, affects competition only when it has a non-transitory effect on supply, whether through the reduction of total output, the increase in prices, or the reduction of investments in innovation and development of new products.[9] The relatively high concentration in the supermarket sector and possible effects on competition resulting thereof remain an area of continued significant enforcement concern.

D. Price discrimination

6.19 Stand-alone discrimination claims are rare, and such claims are generally made in connection with accusations of other competition law infringements. There are examples in which pricing or distribution models were deemed discriminatory and economically unjustified. Companies ordered by the TDLC to modify their pricing and distribution models include

---

[6] *Atrex and others v. SCL*, TDLC Ruling No. 75/2008 of September 30, 2008, upheld on appeal.

[7] *FNE v. Empresa Eléctrica Atacama S.A.*, TDLC Ruling No. 93/2010 of January 6, 2010, upheld on appeal.

[8] OECD, "Roundtable on Monopsony and Buyer Power, Note by Chile" (2008) (DAF/COMP(2008)82), <http://ec.europa.eu/competition/international/multilateral/2008_oct_direct_settlements.pdf>.

[9] *FNE v. D&S S.A. y Cencosud S.A.*, TDLC Ruling No. 65/2008 of May 8, 2008.

a credit card operator owned by the main banks in Chile, which was charging discriminatory prices to card issuers;[10] and EFE, the state-owned railway company, which was charging telecommunication companies discriminating and economically unjustified fees for crossing railways so they could interconnect with their networks.[11] The companies were required to base their tariffs on objective, general, and non-discriminatory criteria. In a recent instruction by the TDLC, mobile communications companies were prohibited from discriminating between their *on-net* and *off-net* calls—i.e. calls made to customers of the same company and calls made to customers of other mobile companies—given the exclusionary effect of such differentiation on new (smaller) entrants.[12]

E. Dictating or influencing resale prices

(i) Resale price maintenance

Article 3(b) DL No. 211 mentions resale price maintenance (RPM) as abusive conduct, and the authorities have recognized that use of RPM by a manufacturer in a market characterized by increasing vertical integration and barriers to entry, for instance, may pose competitive risks. Jurisprudence or extensive doctrine on resale price maintenance, however, is currently lacking in Chile. The FNE did, however, recently publish two papers regarding vertical restraints.[13] **6.20**

(ii) Minimum advertised price programs

There are no decisions by the TDLC regarding the requirement imposed by suppliers on their distributors to refrain from advertising prices below a certain minimum. **6.21**

F. Tying arrangements

Tying is mentioned explicitly in article 3(b) DL No. 211 as an example of abusive conduct. That provision recognizes, however, that tying and bundling are common commercial practices and generally constitute an infringement only when (a) the products or services offered are distinctive but are not offered separately; (b) the company concerned has a dominant position in the tying product's market; (c) the conduct has the ability or effect of foreclosing the tied market by limiting or eliminating competitors' expansion or entry; and (d) there is no objective justification for the conduct concerned. **6.22**

Recent cases on tying all relate to the communications sector. In one recent example, Telefónica's subsidiary, CTC, was sanctioned for bundling broadband services to fixed telephone services and a certain amount of free minutes, thereby foreclosing operators of Voice over Internet Protocol (VoIP) services. CTC was ordered to make an unbundled broadband offer and price its bundled offer above the price of the product/service having the highest value.[14] Similar obligations were imposed by the TDLC on all communications companies offering packages of fixed and mobile telephony, broadband services and/or pay television.[15] **6.23**

---

[10] *Transbank S.A.*, TDLC Ruling No. 29/2005 of September 12, 2005,

[11] *GTD Teleductos S.A. v. EFE*, TDLC Ruling No. 76/2008 of October 14, 2008, upheld on appeal.

[12] TDLC Instruction No. 2 of December 18, 2012.

[13] Patrick Rey, "Vertical restraints—an economic perspective, Revised draft report" (October 13, 2012), <http://www.fne.gob.cl/wp-content/uploads/2013/11/Patrick-Rey.-Vertical-Restraints.pdf>; and Michael E. Jacobs, "Legal treatment of vertical restraints: some lessons from the ongoing international debates, A Research Paper for the *Fiscalía Nacional Económica*" (October 25, 2012), <http://www.fne.gob.cl/wp-content/uploads/2012/10/Legal-Treatment-of-Vertical-Restraints.pdf>.

[14] *Voissnet S.A. v. Compañía de Telecomunicaciones de Chile S.A.*, TDLC Ruling No. 97/2010 of March 4, 2010, upheld on appeal.

[15] TDLC Instruction No. 2 of December 18, 2012.

G. Exclusive dealing

6.24 The various TDLC rulings on exclusive dealing and loyalty-enhancing rebates follow an effects-based approach. While exclusive dealing and de facto exclusivity are not per se anti-competitive, a dominant company—and especially a quasi-monopolist in a market in which publicity is already restricted due to regulation—has a special responsibility not to harm the already weakened competition.

6.25 In a case brought by Philip Morris, for example, the Chilean subsidiary of British-American Tobacco (BAT) was sanctioned for classic exclusionary conduct (exclusivity clauses and exclusivity enhancing incentives) towards both high-trade customers and low-trade customers given the significant exclusionary effect of its conduct (the company held a 98-percent market share).[16]

6.26 In another case, the largest producer of matches in Chile (which accounted for 90 percent of security matches) was sanctioned for its use of exclusivity clauses and loyalty discounts with the main distributors. The TDLC held that the discounts, granted in exchange for exclusivity or purchases in excess of the total amount purchased in the preceding calendar year, were predatory because they lacked any objective economic justification.[17] In its decision, the court referred explicitly to European case law (*Michelin II* and *British Airways*)[18] and US case law (*LePage's Inc. v. 3M* and *JBDL Corp Wyeth v. Ayerst Labs Inc.*).[19]

6.27 Other exclusive dealing and loyalty rebate cases concerned the distribution of beer, carbonated soft drinks, and ice cream, and were settled by the FNE (and the settlements were subsequently approved by the TDLC). The settlements suggest that price discounts tied to a customer's purchases, or sales reaching a particular market-share level, may be seen as anti-competitive, but that volume discounts generally are explicitly allowed.[20]

6.28 The request to reserve space in sales dispensers—in line with similar solutions by, for example, the European Commission in the *Coca-Cola* case[21]—was rejected in the first tobacco case.[22] In a subsequent case regarding the foreclosure effects of exclusive publicity, however, BAT's Chilean subsidiary was ordered to reserve 20 percent of its cigarette displays for competing brands in outlets where the competition does not have its own displays.[23] Similarly, the reservation of coolers' capacity was part of a settlement reached by the FNE with two of the three Coca-Cola bottlers in Chile.[24]

6.29 Exclusive dealing remains an area of significant enforcement concern in Chile.

---

[16] *Philip Morris v. Chiletabacos* (*Tabacos I*), TDLC Ruling No. 26/2005 of August 5, 2005, upheld on appeal.

[17] *FNE v. Cia. Chilena de Fósforos S.A.*, TDLC Ruling No. 90/2009 of December 14, 2009, upheld on appeal.

[18] Case T-203/01 *Manufacture française des pneumatiques Michelin v. Commission of the European Communities* [2003] ECR II-04071; Case C-95/04 P *British Airways plc v. Commission of the European Communities* [2007] ECR I-02331.

[19] *LePage's Inc. v. 3M*, 324 F.3d 141 (3d Cir. 2003); *J.B.D.L. Corp. v. Wyetch-Ayerst Labs., Inc.*, 485 F.3d 880 (6th Cir. 2007).

[20] *FNE v. Cervecera CCU Chile Ltda.*, TDLC Decision no. 62/2008 of July 23, 2008 approving settlement; *FNE v. Embotelladora Andina y Coca Cola Embonor*, TDLC Decision no. 92/2011 of November 22, 2011 approving settlement; *Alimentos Trendy S.A. v. Nestlé Chile S.A.*, TDLC Decision no. 97/2012 of March 8, 2012 approving settlement.

[21] *Coca-Cola*, EC Case Comp/A.39.116/B2, commitments decision of June 22, 2005, OJ L 253-2005.

[22] *Tabacos I* (n 16).

[23] *FNE contra Cía. Chilena de Tabacos S.A.* (*Tabacos II*), TDLC Ruling No.115/2011 of November 17, 2011, upheld on appeal.

[24] *Coca-Cola* (n 20).

H. Refusal to deal

It is generally accepted that any person, regardless of its market position, is free to choose its trading partners. Restrictions on this right therefore require careful consideration and usually are allowed only when (a) a firm is unable to obtain, under normal commercial conditions, the input necessary to develop its economic activity, (b) the firm therefore is substantially affected in its capacity to act in the market, and (c) a single provider, or various providers in coordination, refuse to supply the input, although the firm is willing to accept the commercial conditions generally established by the provider.[25] Justified refusals to deal, which can include scarcity of resources or insufficient qualifications of the requiring party, are allowed. **6.30**

Margin squeezes can be seen as a species of refusal to deal. Margin squeeze cases that have been decided by the TDLC all relate to the telecommunications sector. In one case, a claim concerning discriminatory charges for intermediate wireless data transmission—the input necessary to provide GPS location services—was rejected due to lack of dominance by the mobile operator concerned.[26] In contrast, a margin squeeze was condemned in *OPS v. Movistar*[27] when the prices charged by Movistar to the cellulink service provider,[28] OPS, were higher than the prices cellulink providers charged to their own clients for on-net calls, which left them without any margin. **6.31**

I. Essential facilities

Both the TDLC and the Supreme Court have characterized certain installations and inputs as "essential," after considering whether the facility or service in question is practicably replicable, if there were other economically viable alternatives, and whether the facility or input is indispensable for participating in the downstream or secondary market.[29] These essential facilities generally consist of infrastructure or inputs from vertically integrated entities. **6.32**

Applying the essential facilities doctrine, three mobile operators were required to offer capacity at wholesale to Mobile Virtual Operators (MVOs) based on general, uniform, objective, and non-discriminatory criteria, with the objective of facilitating the entry of MVOs in Chile. Notwithstanding the general criteria described above, the Supreme Court did not clarify how the input of any individual operator could be deemed essential and why inputs of the other operators would not constitute economically viable alternatives for the MVOs.[30] **6.33**

Refusal to supply and customer termination do not appear, however, to be areas of specific enforcement concern. **6.34**

J. Bundling (including loyalty and market share discounts)

See Sections I.F and I.G. **6.35**

---

[25] *Agrícola Verde Sur Ltda. v. Petróleos Transandinos S.A.*, SC Ruling No.1174/2011 of June 14, 2011.

[26] *GPS Chile S.A. v. Entel PCS S.A.*, TDLC Ruling No. 78/2008 of December 4, 2008, upheld on appeal.

[27] *OPS Ingeniería Ltda. and others v. Telefónica Móviles de Chile S.A.*, TDLC Ruling No. 88/2009 of October 15, 2009, upheld on appeal.

[28] "Cellulink" or "fixed–mobile on-net" service is a service whereby calls from fixed networks are converted into mobile calls to avoid high Mobile Terminating Access fees.

[29] *FNE v. Sociedad Punta de lobos S.A.*, TDLC Ruling No. 47/2006 of December 6, 2006, on the indispensability of a port to export salt.

[30] *FNE v. Telefónica Móviles de Chile S.A. and others*, SC Ruling No. 104/2010 of December 23, 2011.

K. Standard-setting groups (disclosure requirements, licensing arrangements, and licensing pools)

6.36 There is currently no Chilean jurisprudence on standard-setting groups. The FNE, however, has issued guidelines on trade associations and competition[31] which deals with, among other issues, the setting of technical standards and standard contracts (see Section II.E).

L. Customer termination

6.37 Customer termination is a type of refusal to supply (see Section I.H). When the customer is not competing with the supplier, most likely, the termination does not constitute abuse (unless there is a case of discrimination which affects the customer's competitive position).[32]

M. Termination of intermediaries (retailers, wholesalers, dealers, and value-added resellers, agents, and brokers)

6.38 Termination of intermediaries is a type of refusal to supply (see Section I.H). When the intermediary is not competing with the supplier, the termination is unlikely to constitute abuse (unless there is a case of discrimination which affects the customer's competitive position).

N. Termination of relationships with competitors

6.39 Termination of relations with competitors may constitute abuse in cases of vertically integrated suppliers of essential inputs (see Section I.I and the case law referred to).

O. Exemptions

6.40 There are no block exemption regulations or sector-specific exemptions for unilateral conduct or vertical agreements in Chile. Unilateral conduct restricting competition may fall outside the scope of article 3 prohibition if there are objective justifications for such conduct, or when it results in economic efficiencies that outweigh any restrictive effects.

II. Dealing with competitors

6.41 Article 3(a) DL No. 211 refers to classic cartel behavior such as price fixing, market sharing, production limitation, group boycott, or bid-rigging.[33] Actual restrictive effects are not required; the wording of article 3 DL No. 211 and the case law demonstrate that the object and potential (referred to as "objective ability" or "causal ability") to restrict competition is sufficient for a violation to occur. Subjective intent regarding the restrictive effects is also not required; liability may arise when the conduct itself was intended.

6.42 Chilean competition policy generally emphasizes market power, and article 3(a) speaks in terms of horizontal agreements or concerted practices that confer market power on the parties.

---

[31] FNE, Trade Associations and Competition (*Associaciones Gremiales y Libre Competencia*) (August 2011), <http://www.fne.gob.cl/wp-content/uploads/2011/08/guia_-asociaciones_-gremiales.pdf>.

[32] *Fundación Chile Cuidadano and another v. VTR B.A. Chile S.A.*, upheld TDLC Ruling No. 98/2010 of March 18, 2010, on appeal.

[33] DL No. 211, art. 3: "...Among others, the following shall be considered as acts, agreements or conventions that hinder, restrict or impede free competition, or which tend to produce such effects: (a) Express or tacit agreements between competitors, or concerted practices between them, which confer to them market power and which consist of fixing sales prices, purchase prices, or other commercial conditions, restricting production, allocating territories or market quotas, excluding competitors or affecting the results of tender processes." The reference is non-exhaustive; other restrictive agreements fall within the scope of the subsection as well.

While *de minimis* or per se rules, or equivalent doctrines, have not yet been explicitly recognized in Chile, the Supreme Court seems to have made a move towards a per se interpretation in its most recent joint price fixing decision.[34] Future cases should elaborate on this point.

Until recently, the sanctioning of cartels was rather rare in Chile. Circumstantial evidence generally did not meet the standard of proof required by the courts, and prior to 2009, the FNE had limited investigative powers. The 2009 amendments to the Competition Act, however, granted the FNE new investigative tools (subject to approval by the TDLC and Court of Appeal), including the power to perform dawn raids and conduct telephone taps. Moreover, political momentum towards the prosecution of cartels has generated an increase in the prosecution of collusion cases in Chile, which has become a priority for the FNE. There are currently various cases pending before the TDLC involving alleged price fixing, market sharing, and production quotas. **6.43**

A. Horizontal price fixing

Horizontal price fixing agreements and other arrangements that have as their object or effect the prevention or the diminishing of price competition are generally held to infringe the Competition Act. The public transport sector has faced various convictions—and a number of new cases have been recently brought by the FNE—for classic illegal conduct such as price fixing, market sharing, and restrictions on output. **6.44**

The highest-profile recent case, which generated a political and public debate and a legislative proposal to criminalize cartels, concerned coordinated price increases for some 206 prescription medicines by the three main pharmacies and drugstore chains in Chile. The coordination occurred through a "hub-and-spoke" mechanism (also referred to as a "1-2-3" information exchange model) whereby the first increase of a certain medicine was executed on "day 1" upon the recommendation by the pharmaceutical company supplying that medicine, the second by another company on "day 2," and the third by a third company on "day 3." The pharmaceutical companies facilitated the information exchange between the chains regarding, for example, the actual starting date of an increase etc.[35] The TDLC dismissed the chains' arguments regarding lack of direct evidence of coordination. There was, according to the court, no reasonable alternative explanation for the pharmacies' pricing behavior, especially given the parallel pattern of the increases. Moreover, the court credited the supporting evidence including internal emails, declarations by the executives of both the pharmacies and the pharmaceutical companies involved, and extraordinary price-monitoring activities undertaken by the pharmacies in the period when the collusion occurred. Two of the pharmacy chains were sanctioned with fines of USD 20 million each, the maximum penalty available under the law at the time of the conduct. The third chain settled with the FNE during the proceedings and, as part of the settlement, paid the equivalent of USD 1 million in fines.[36] **6.45**

B. Horizontal agreements to allocate customers or territories; agreements not to compete

Although market sharing is deemed anticompetitive, given the likely effects on prices, it has not always been sanctioned, generally due to lack of evidence. Cases concerning production **6.46**

[34] *FNE v. Abercrombie & Kent S.A. and others* (*Explora*), CS Ruling No. 113/2012 of November 20, 2012.

[35] *FNE v. Farmacias Ahumada S.A. and others* (*Farmacias*), TDLC Ruling No. 119/2012 of January 31, 2012, upheld on appeal.

[36] The settlement was reached despite the fact that Chilean competition law didn't explicitly provided for such possibility at the time. Both the Constitutional Court and the Supreme Court determined that the decision of the TDLC to approve the deal was lawful.

quotas or other limitations on output are equally rare, and generally, such conduct is part of a wider anticompetitive scheme to stabilize prices. The case pending against the three largest poultry producers in Chile and their trade association is basically about alleged market sharing and production limitation. This is the first case brought by the FNE based on evidence obtained during dawn raids, and therefore is a novelty in Chilean competition enforcement.[37]

C. Horizontal boycotts

6.47 Coordinated pressure on suppliers with the purpose of foreclosing a competitor has been sanctioned on several occasions. Several cases relate to actions by trade associations. A threatened boycott to pressure a client (luxury hotel chain Explora) into accepting a fee increase proposed by several travel agencies was recently sanctioned by the Supreme Court.[38]

D. Joint ventures and other competitive collaborations

6.48 Joint ventures and other collaborative agreements are treated differently than cartel agreements or other unlawful concerted practices. The Competition Act does not provide specific regulations for cooperation agreements or "non-structural" joint ventures; there are no block exemptions or guidelines on the subject; and precedents are scarce and often predate the establishment of the TDLC. Nevertheless, these cooperation agreements are generally seen as not impeding, restricting, or hindering competition, but instead as having pro-competitive effects because of the efficiencies that they may generate. Examples include agreements on specialization, joint purchasing, and joint production.

6.49 The only joint production agreement examined by the TDLC is the emblematic *HidroAysén* project, a joint venture between the two major electricity providers *Colbún* and *Endesa* for the financing, construction, and operation of five hydroelectric plants in southern Chile and the construction of a transmission network to connect the plants with the central interconnection network (supplying the vast majority of electricity consumers in Chile). Under the agreement, the five plants will be productive units, while commercialization will be done independently by the joint venture's parent companies working in competition with each other. The TDLC accepted the parties' position that the joint venture was (economically) the most efficient form to construct and operate both the plants and the ancillary transport infrastructure. After analyzing the effects on competition between the parent companies, and the possible impact on third-party competitors, the TDLC approved the project subject to conditions ensuring rivalry in the commercialization of electricity and guaranteeing third-party access to water rights and the transport network.

E. Trade associations

6.50 Because of the nature of their activities, which entail certain competitive risks, trade associations have been a subject of interest in the Chilean competition system, both in matters brought before the TDLC, and in the FNE's promotional activities.

6.51 The TDLC has held that a trade association may be charged and sanctioned for illicit collusion when its members use the association as a vehicle for coordinating anticompetitive behavior.[39] Indeed, the law governing trade associations explicitly considers conduct in violation of the Competition Act as a particular subject of reproach,[40] something that the TDLC has noted in various rulings.[41]

---

[37] *FNE v. Agrícola Agrosuper S.A. and others*, Case No. C 236-11 (pending).
[38] *Explora* (n 34).
[39] *Agimal* (n 4).
[40] See DL No. 2.757/1979, art. 26.
[41] *FNE v. la Asociación de Buses Interbus and others*, TDLC Ruling No. 82/2009 of January 22, 2009.

In the pending case involving the poultry industry, the FNE argues that the trade association played a central role in coordinating and maintaining the alleged cartel. In addition to a monetary fine, the FNE is requesting the dissolution of the trade association.[42] The FNE is similarly seeking the dissolution of a trade association in a pending complaint relating to alleged price fixing by bus operators in Valdivia.[43] **6.52**

In August 2011, the FNE published a guide on Trade Associations and Competition, which identified risks relating to coordinated conduct and other conducts and practices (ranging from membership and affiliation with the association, to the establishment of technical standards) that can affect competition. The FNE stipulates that these types of conduct are generally pro-competitive but may cause concerns in exceptional circumstances when the object or effect is to restrict entry by new competitors or to frustrate innovation, thereby shielding a certain product or technology from competition. Such anticompetitive harm is less likely when the standards or technical norms are based on objective elements, participation in certification schemes is voluntary, and the conditions to participate are non-discriminatory. The use of standard contracts or standard conditions should also be on a voluntary basis. **6.53**

F. Interlocking directorates

While the Competition Act does not explicitly address the question of interlocking directorates, Chile has some experience with the potential competitive effects that might arise. In one example, the FNE recently decided not to submit a consultation to the TDLC in connection with the acquisition of a department store chain by one of the country's largest retail conglomerates when the former committed to eliminate ties with another retail competitor. One of those ties in question involved common directors.[44] **6.54**

These competitive concerns are equally reflected in the conditions imposed by the TDLC in certain merger cases, prohibiting the controlling entity of the merged company to participate in the ownership of any company competing with the merged entity. For instance, in a recent merger of two supermarket chains, SMU and SDS, the TDLC required the merged entity to divest its ownership of another supermarket.[45] **6.55**

G. Facilitating practices

Facilitating practices are not subject to specific rules under the Competition Act. As discussed in Section II.A, conduct such as exchange of strategic information about current or future pricing, cost structures, current or future production volumes, among others, may be considered violations of the Competition Act if they have the aim or the effect of restricting competition.[46] **6.56**

H. Information exchange

As discussed in greater detail in Section II.A, the high-profile retail pharmacies case involved a "hub and spoke" or "1-2-3" information exchange arrangement. The pharmaceutical companies facilitated information exchange between the retail chains regarding coordinated price increases of numerous prescription drugs. This arrangement, which was condemned by the TDLC in a ruling upheld by the Supreme Court, resulted in fines of USD 20 million against two of the three retail pharmacies, with the third pharmacy chain paying the equivalent of **6.57**

---

42 *Agrígola Agrosuper S.A.* (n 37).

43 *Sociedad de Transportes Línea Uno Collico S.A.*, Case No. 244-12 (pending).

44 See *Operación de concentración Cencosud-Johnson's*, Case No. 1978-11 FNE(A).

45 *SMU–SDS*, TDLC Resolution No. 43/2012 of December 12, 2012, upheld on appeal.

46 See e.g. FNE, Trade Associations and Competition (n 31).

USD 1 million in fines.[47] The FNE's guide on Trade Associations and Competition has also recognized the role that trade associations can sometimes play in facilitating the exchange of strategic information.[48]

I. Joint purchasing agreements

6.58 Although the TDLC has not issued any decisions regarding joint purchasing agreements, the Competition Act mentions in article 3(a) express or tacit agreements among competitors that fix purchase prices, provided that the agreement confers market power. Thus, the analysis is likely to follow the approach taken in the EU, and consider the effects of such agreements, including whether the purchasers have sufficient market power to force their suppliers to reduce the range or quality of their products, or to foreclose a competitor's access to suppliers.

J. Joint lobbying/regulatory/legislative efforts

6.59 While joint lobbying in connection with regulation or legislation in and of itself should not generally raise any red flags under the Competition Act, such efforts could become the occasion for anticompetitive exchanges of information or other illicit conduct that raise competitive concerns.[49]

6.60 Further, in a case involving lobbying efforts regarding tariffs and other import restrictions on sugar, the TDLC concluded that the fact that those efforts fell within the jurisdiction of other agencies acting within the scope of their legal responsibilities, did not preclude the TDLC from exercising its powers to analyze the markets in question.[50]

6.61 Thus, depending on the particular regulatory environment, the outcome of a lobbying effort may become the subject of a subsequent challenge by the FNE, either by way of a request that the TDLC propose a regulatory change to the President of the Republic, or—when the regulatory decision is not expressly protected by a legal provision or the state entity adopting the decision has latitude to ensure that its decision conforms to competitive norms—the lawfulness of the resulting decisions could be challenged before the TDLC.[51]

III. General issues

A. Jurisdiction and applicable law (including sector-specific competition regulation)

6.62 As indicated above, the Competition Act is the central legislation in Chile establishing a broad prohibition against conduct that impedes, restrains, or hinders competition, or that tends to produce those effects. The Competition Act was amended in 2003 (Law No. 19.911) and 2009 (Law No. 20.361) in view of improving competition enforcement. The 2003 amendment created the TDLC and gave new investigative powers to the FNE. The 2009 amendment further strengthened the investigative powers of the FNE by granting it the authority (subject to judicial oversight) to perform dawn raids, and by establishing a leniency program.

6.63 The Competition Act applies generally to the Chilean economy, without sector-specific exemptions. It covers economic activity by private and public entities. As to the territorial scope of Chilean competition law, the relevant factor in the application of Chilean

[47] *Farmacias* (n 35).

[48] See Section II.E.

[49] See Section II.E.

[50] *AGIP A.G.*, TDLC Ruling No. 27/2005 of August 23, 2005, upheld on appeal.

[51] See FNE, The Public Sector and Free Competition (*Sector Público y Libre Competencia*) (July 2012), <http://www.fne.gob.cl/wp-content/uploads/2012/06/Guia-final-sector-publico.pdf>.

competition law is the actual or potential effect in the Chilean market. This position was recently confirmed in a claim brought by the FNE against Mr. John Malone, a US resident without legal domicile or residence in Chile, holding interests in Liberty Global Inc. and Liberty Media Inc. Mr. Malone was sanctioned for breaching one of the conditions set by the TDLC when clearing a merger between the two major cable TV operators in 2004.[52]

The TDLC has issued various executive regulations ("*Auto Acordados*") on administrative procedure, the form, content, or other conditions of applications and submissions, as well as general instructions. The general instructions—such as the instructions establishing the basic criteria for bidding procedures in the collection, transportation, and disposal of household waste[53] and the prohibition on mobile operators to discriminate between *on-net* and *off-net* tariffs[54]—are binding upon the companies or individuals concerned. **6.64**

The FNE has issued guidelines and notices to clarify the scope and direction of certain aspects of its policy. These include, among others, Guidelines on the Analysis of Horizontal Mergers and Guidelines on Leniency and Reduction of Fines in Cartel Cases.[55] The FNE has also stated publicly that it plans to issue guidelines on vertical restraints. **6.65**

Certain sectors of the economy, including telecommunications, electricity, water and waste disposal, transport and port operations, are subject to sector-specific rules. These regulations use familiar tools to correct resource misallocation created by natural monopolies or market distortions, including price regulations, access obligations, interconnection duties, limitation of vertical integration, separation of operations, resource allocation, etc. The Competition Act remains fully applicable in these sectors and sector regulators have no concurrent powers with the Chilean competition authorities. **6.66**

B. Antitrust system

(i) Name of agency/agencies

The two primary institutions that comprise the Chilean competition system are the FNE, the national economic prosecutor's office, and the TDLC, a specialized competition court competent to hear and decide on matters of competition law. **6.67**

The FNE is empowered to investigate violations of the Competition Act and to bring actions before the TDLC. The prosecutor's office is an autonomous agency (but subject to supervision of the President of the Republic through the Ministry of the Economy), charged with representing "the general economic interests of the community," independent of any other public authority. It is headed by the National Economic Prosecutor (*Fiscal Nacional Económico*), who is responsible for the management of the agency as well as its representation in and out of court. **6.68**

The TDLC is the decision-making court with jurisdiction over complaints brought by the FNE and others regarding violations of the Competition Act. It is an independent court comprised of five "ministers," three of whom are lawyers and two economists. The TDLC **6.69**

---

[52] *FNE v. Sr. John C. Malone*, TDLC Ruling No. 117/2011 of December 29, 2011. The parties reached a settlement in appeal, SC Ruling No. 117/2013 of July 10, 2013.

[53] General Instruction TDLC No. 1 of 08-06-2006, modified by General Instruction No. 3 of 21-03-2013.

[54] General Instruction No. 2 of 18-12-2012.

[55] FNE, Horizontal Merger Guidelines (*Guía Interna para el Análisis de Operaciones de Concentración Horizontal*) (October 2012), available in English at <http://www.fne.gob.cl/english/wp-content/uploads/2013/01/Guia-fusiones-traducida-final-2.pdf>; FNE, Internal Guide on Benefits of Immunity (*Guía sobre Beneficios de Exención y Reducción de multas en caso de Colusión*) (October 2009), available in English at <http://www.fne.gob.cl/english/wp-content/uploads/2012/03/Guide_benefits.pdf>.

can impose fines, behavioral or structural relief, or both by way of a ruling (*Sentencia*) (see Sections III.E and III.F).

6.70 In addition to adversarial proceedings, non-adversarial "consultative" proceedings can be brought before the TDLC to determine the legality of particular contractual provisions or other practices (predominantly structural conduct including mergers). The TDLC will rule by way of resolution (*Resolucion*) which may set conditions under which the conduct falls outside the scope of article 3 DL No. 211.

6.71 Moreover, the TDLC is empowered to issue general instructions, which are binding upon the addressees, and can propose legal and regulatory changes to the Government that it considers to be in the interests of promoting competition. Rulings of the TDLC are subject to review by the Supreme Court.

(ii) Staff size and budget

6.72 The FNE has a non-administrative staff of more than 75 people, largely attorneys and economists, working on competition enforcement. The agency's budget for 2012 was approximately USD 7.3 million. The five TDLC ministers (judges) are supported by a staff of professionals, both lawyers and economists, headed by the Secretary of the TDLC.

(iii) Recent enforcement actions and trends

6.73 Along with abuse of dominance cases, the FNE has placed an increased emphasis on cartel detection and enforcement in recent years, in particular with respect to products and services that directly impact the lives of Chilean consumers.

6.74 Amendments to the Competition Act in 2009 greatly strengthened the FNE's ability to pursue and prosecute cartels, and increased the maximum available fines that could be imposed by the TDLC in collusion cases.[56] As a result of those reforms, the FNE has implemented a leniency program,[57] and the agency now has the ability, with court authorization, to conduct wiretaps and perform dawn raids when there are serious suspicions of collusion.

6.75 The FNE already has used these new investigative tools to initiate proceedings against a number of suspected cartels. The compressors cartel ruling of June 2012, for instance, marked the first time the TDLC imposed fines in a case initiated on the basis of a leniency application.[58] In an investigation of five inter-city bus transport companies, a leniency application resulted in the first use by the FNE of its wiretapping authority.[59] The agency's dawn raid powers were first used during an investigation of an alleged cartel in the poultry industry involving three producers and a trade association.[60]

6.76 Recent years have also seen some of the largest fines ever imposed for cartel activities. In the compressors case, for instance, the TDLC imposed a fine of approximately USD 10 million on the non-leniency applicant.[61] In a cartel case against the three main pharmacy chains accused of fixing prices of prescription drugs, the TDLC imposed fines of US$20 million on two defendants, the maximum penalty available at the time of the challenged conduct.[62]

---

[56] See Section III.F(i).

[57] See Section III.G.

[58] *FNE v. Tecumseh do Brasil Ltda and another* (*Tecumseh do Brasil Ltda*), TDLC Ruling No. 122/2010 of June 14, 2012, upheld on appeal although the SC lowered the fine imposed.

[59] *Pullman Bus Costa Central S.A.*, Case No. 234-11.

[60] *Agrígola Agrosuper S.A.* (n 37).

[61] *Tecumseh do Brasil Ltda* (n 58).

[62] *Farmacias* (n 35) .

C. Private litigation

In addition to complaints by the FNE, the TDLC is empowered to hear complaints initiated by private entities regarding violations of the Competition Act (art. 18 DL No. 211). Indeed, private parties have accounted for more than half of parties to adversarial proceedings before the TDLC in recent years. Damages, however, cannot be awarded by the TDLC, but only by civil courts in indemnification actions following a finding of an infringement by the Competition Tribunal.[63] **6.77**

D. Follow-on litigation

Since 2003, the Competition Act has allowed for indemnification actions to be brought before general civil courts to recover damages incurred as a result of competition law violations found by the TDLC (art. 30 DL No. 211). The civil court must decide on the basis of factual and legal assessments made by the TDLC, hence its powers are limited to questions of damages and causation mainly. Civil damage actions must be brought within four years following the TDLC decision (art. 20 DL No. 211). **6.78**

To date, only a few damage actions have been filed by affected competitors. The first successful damages case tried under article 30 was *Cementa v. Volcán*, a matter involving claims of predatory pricing that were recognized by the Supreme Court. In the damages proceedings, the civil court concluded that, because a competition infringement had been established by the TDLC, it was unnecessary to prove negligence during the civil trial. Instead, the court limited its judgment to legal standing of the plaintiff, injury-in-fact, causation, and quantification of damages based on the infraction already found, and awarded the plaintiff approximately USD 13.5 million. The case was settled while on appeal.[64] Large damages awards based on Competition Act violations, however, remain exceedingly rare in Chile. Moreover, damages claims by consumers in cartel cases have been virtually non-existent, as an effective mechanism for collective proceedings in competition matters has not yet been established. **6.79**

E. Arbitration and alternative dispute resolution

Competition law cases can be dealt by the TDLC and the Supreme Court on appeal. These are the only two courts empowered to deal with cases concerning competition law violations. Competition law is considered a matter of public policy under Chilean law and can therefore not be enforced by arbitrators. Any clause submitting a competition law conflict to arbitration would be deemed null and void. However, it is completely lawful to submit civil claims arising from competition law violations to arbitration. **6.80**

F. Remedies

(i) Civil liability

The TDLC can impose fines of up to 30,000 UTAs (annual tax units, approximately USD 30 million) for unlawful collusion, and up to 20,000 UTAs (roughly USD 20 million) for other violations of the Competition Act (art. 26(c) DL No. 211). In establishing the amount, the TDLC considers a variety of factors, including the economic benefit obtained, the seriousness of the breach, and whether the violator is a recidivist. Collaboration provided to the FNE before or during an investigation can be considered a basis for decreasing a fine (Article 26 DL No. 211). In the retail pharmacies case, as indicated above, early and substantial **6.81**

---

63 See Section III.D.

64 See on this issue also OECD, "Roundtable on the Quantification of Harm to Competition by National Courts and Competition Agencies, Note by the Delegation of Chile" (DAF/COMP/WD(2011)1), <http://www.fne.gob.cl/wp-content/uploads/2011/03/oecd_0001_2011.pdf>.

cooperation with the FNE by one of the defendants resulted in a commitment to pay USD 1 million as equivalent of a fine, while the other defendants were condemned to pay fines close to USD 20 million each.

6.82 Fines may be imposed not only on the companies involved in the infringement, but also on their directors, managers, or any other person involved in the unlawful conduct. The Competition Act prohibits individuals' fines from being paid by the company or by its shareholders or partners.

6.83 In addition to fines, the TDLC may impose behavioral or structural remedies. For instance, the tribunal may order the modification or termination of acts, contracts, or agreements that are in violation of the Competition Act (art. 26(a) DL No. 211), and the dissolution of companies, corporations, and other private entities involved in the unlawful conduct (art. 26(b) DL No. 211). Indeed, the Competition Act seems to give the TDLC authority to impose case-appropriate remedies even beyond those explicitly mentioned in it (art. 3 DL No. 211).

6.84 Penalties might also be levied for failure to abide by the rulings of the tribunal. In one case the TDLC imposed a fine of nearly USD 4 million on a major shareholder of a parent corporation of a Chilean cable television provider when that shareholder also acquired an interest in a satellite television provider, thus violating the conditions of an early ruling that cleared a merger in the cable market.[65]

6.85 The limitation period is, as a general rule, three years from the occurrence of the challenged conduct. In collusion cases, the limitation period is five years since the effects of the conduct ceased in the market (art. 20 DL No. 211).

(ii) Criminal liability

6.86 Although the Competition Act does not include criminal liability for competition violations (criminal liability under DL No. 211 was abolished with the modifications in 2003), Chile's Criminal Code includes a prohibition against altering the "natural price" of goods or services "by fraudulent means" (art. 285 Criminal Code). The Criminal Code provides for imprisonment of up to three years and fines capped at less than USD 1,000. This provision, enacted in 1874, was never applied to competition-related conducts prior to 2009. While the object of the law, which is not part of the Competition Act, is arguably limited to unilateral conduct, charges were brought by a criminal prosecutor (not the FNE) against several executives of the pharmacy chains involved in the case brought by the FNE in 2009.[66] The criminal case is still pending.

6.87 A commission of experts appointed by the President to study possible modifications to the Competition Act considered, among other questions, the potential negative impact that the application of article 285 to violations of the Competition Act might have on Chile's incipient leniency program. The commission recommended that if penal sanctions were to be established for collusive conduct, the FNE should be the agency charged with requesting criminal penalties in particular cases. Whether criminal penalties for certain violations of the Competition Act should be re-introduced has been a subject of continued discussion recently, including by the Presidential commission. In reaction to the pharmacies case, a group of senators submitted a bill that would make imprisonment available as a sanction in collusion cases. At the time of writing, however, the bill has not yet been discussed by the Chilean Congress.

---

[65] *John C. Malone* (n 52).
[66] See Section II.A.

G. Leniency and immunity

The 2009 amendments to the Competition Act included reductions in or exemptions from fines that may be extended to participants in unlawful collusive conduct under certain circumstances. In order to qualify, a leniency applicant must: (a) supply the FNE with precise, veracious, and verifiable information that provides sufficient grounds to initiate a proceeding before the TDLC; (b) abstain from disclosing the fact of the application until a complaint has been filed; and (c) immediately terminate its participation in the unlawful conduct, unless the FNE deems that continued participation is necessary for attaining the objectives of the investigation (art. 39bis DL No. 211). **6.88**

The first applicant to satisfy these requirements is eligible for full exemption of civil fines. Subsequent applicants may obtain fine reductions of up to 50 percent provided that information about the unlawful conduct is supplied to the FNE beyond that turned over by the first applicant. The FNE has published detailed guidelines (available in English and Spanish on the agency's web site) regarding the leniency program. **6.89**

Leniency is available to anyone who is or has been involved in a cartel, including individuals and legal entities. In the case of a leniency application by legal entity, any resulting benefits apply equally to the entity itself and to any of its executives, employees, counsel, or other individuals identified in the application, provided they did not act as independent economic agents in the market at the time the collusion took place. An application by an individual is strictly personal and does not extend to other persons or entities. **6.90**

Notwithstanding the benefits available to applicants with respect to civil fines, the leniency provision of the Competition Act does not provide immunity from any criminal liability that might attach to certain conduct. It does not shield from civil damage claims either. **6.91**

H. Document creation and retention

The Competition Act does not include any explicit rules on document creation and retention, and there have not been any TDLC rulings on the subject so far. The FNE, however, has the authority to request information and documents regarding ongoing investigations (art. 39(h) DL No. 211). Given that the TDLC, in setting fines, can consider the seriousness of the respondent's behavior and its collaboration with the FNE before or during an investigation (art. 26 DL No. 211), failure to retain relevant documents carries the risk of adversely affecting any penalties ultimately imposed. **6.92**

7

CHINA

Peter Wang, Sébastien Evrard, Yizhe Zhang, and Baohui Zhang
Jones Day

Introduction

7.01 Chinese antitrust law is still very new.[1] Its principal statute, the Anti-Monopoly Law (AML), came into effect in August 2008, and most public decisions and rulemaking under the AML have come in the merger control area. Other key laws that contain antitrust-related provisions, notably the 1997 Price Law, are somewhat older, but their antitrust provisions were seldomly enforced prior to the passage of the AML.

7.02 The Chinese antitrust laws are enforced by three Chinese ministries, known in this context as Anti-Monopoly Enforcement Authorities (AMEAs), all of which pre-date the AML and have regulatory responsibility for broad portfolios of which antitrust is only a small part. The

[1] For a detailed analysis of the PRC Anti-Monopoly Law, see generally H. Stephen Harris, Peter J. Wang, Mark A. Cohen, Yizhe Zhang, and Sebastien J. Evrard, *Anti-Monopoly Law and Practice in China* (Oxford/New York: Oxford University Press 2011).

principal enforcement agencies for anticompetitive conduct (i.e. non-merger) issues are the National Development and Reform Commission (NDRC), which also serves as the national price regulator and a key industrial policymaker, and the State Administration of Industry and Commerce (SAIC), which is also responsible for most company registration functions as well as administrative anticorruption and IP/anti-counterfeiting enforcement. Article 50 of the AML also provides for private civil enforcement through the Chinese court system.

The AML is divided into four substantive components. First, certain "monopoly agreements" between competitors (horizontal) or trading partners (vertical) are prohibited by articles 13 and 14, subject to possible exemptions under article 15. Second, for firms with dominant market positions as defined in article 18, certain "abusive" conduct is prohibited by article 17, albeit generally subject to potential "valid justifications." In both of these areas, the AML essentially provides a sort of "rule of reason" analysis, balancing anticompetitive against pro-competitive effects, and on its face does not contain any per se prohibitions. 7.03

In addition, mergers and acquisitions meeting the reporting thresholds issued by the People's Republic of China (PRC) State Council require pre-merger clearance by a third anti-monopoly enforcement agency, the Ministry of Commerce (MOFCOM), under chapter IV of the AML. Certain administrative monopoly acts by government entities or departments also are prohibited by chapter V of the AML. 7.04

Unusually, from the perspective of most Western antitrust practitioners, Chinese antitrust law in practice (and not only in theory) requires antitrust enforcers and courts to weigh antitrust issues alongside other industrial and government policy considerations. For example, article 15 of the AML directs NDRC and SAIC to consider whether an otherwise prohibited restraint serves the objective of "enhancing the competitiveness of small and medium-sized enterprises" when evaluating eligibility for exemption. Similarly, article 27 requires MOFCOM to consider, *inter alia*, "the effect of the concentration on national economic development" when reviewing proposed mergers and acquisitions (M&A) transactions. 7.05

Other relevant Chinese competition-related laws include the Price Law, the Anti-Unfair Competition Law (AUCL), the Bidding Law, the Contract Law, the Foreign Trade Law, the Patent Law, and related regulations. 7.06

The Price Law sets forth China's price regulation mechanism (also overseen by NDRC), but it also includes prohibitions on several forms of "unfair pricing behavior" such as price-fixing, dumping at below cost, spreading false rumors of price increases (implicated in a case involving Unilever in 2011[2]), price discrimination, and "seeking excessive profits in violation of laws and regulations." The AUCL includes prohibitions on predatory pricing, tying, and bid-rigging, in addition to provisions addressing other unfair competition issues such as counterfeiting, commercial bribery, false advertising, trade secret theft, and trade disparagement (all overseen by SAIC). The Bidding Law prohibits both horizontal and vertical bid-rigging. The Contract Law and a related judicial interpretation prohibit a number of restrictive clauses in technology-related agreements. The Foreign Trade Law and related regulations prohibit other restrictive clauses involving technology licensing from foreign to Chinese companies. Finally, the Patent Law provides for compulsory licensing if the exercise of a patent right is determined to be monopolistic and anticompetitive. 7.07

[2] NDRC Press Release, "National Development and Reform Commission official to investigate and fine Unilever (China) for disturbing the market order by spreading information of price increase" (May 6, 2011), http://www.ndrc.gov.cn/xwfb/t20110506_410543.htm (in Chinese).

7.08 Over the past four-plus years, merger control has been the principal focus of AML enforcement, although non-merger enforcement by NDRC and SAIC also has steadily increased, especially against domestic cartels. In addition, the Chinese Supreme People's Court set out a framework for civil antitrust litigation in June 2012 that is expected to increase private enforcement.

I. Acting alone

7.09 Chapter III of the AML addresses unilateral conduct, focusing on anticompetitive abuses of a company's dominant market position. Some types of unilateral conduct, such as tying and predatory pricing, are also prohibited by other laws, such as the AUCL, regardless of whether a company has a dominant position. There has been little enforcement in this area so far other than some private litigation.

7.10 Under article 17 of the AML, dominance means a market position that "enables a competitor to control the price or quantity of products or other trading conditions in the relevant market or to impede or affect entry of other competitors into the relevant market." Article 18 lists a number of factors that can be considered in that evaluation, including market shares, ability to control the sales market, financial or technical strength, the reliance of other companies or trading partners, and the difficulty of entry. Interestingly, article 17 of the NDRC Anti-Price Monopoly Rules and article 3 of the SAIC Rules on Prohibition of Abuse of Dominant Market Position each state that "impeding or preventing entry means preventing or deferring other undertakings' entry into the relevant market, or significantly increasing the market entry cost, thus making it impossible for the new entrant to compete effectively with incumbent undertakings although entry into the relevant market is possible."

7.11 Article 19 of the AML creates a rebuttable presumption of dominance where one competitor accounts for more than 50 percent of a relevant market. A similar presumption also applies where the top two firms in a relevant market together exceed two-thirds share, or the top three firms exceed three-quarters share, except that a firm with less than 10 percent share will not be presumed dominant. There does not appear to be a requirement, as in Europe, that the firms be acting in coordination in order to be found collectively dominant.

7.12 So far, courts have been relatively conservative and have in most cases refused to accept the existence of a dominant position in cases of abuse of dominance. For example, in a lawsuit against the Chinese search engine and internet company Baidu,[3] PRC courts held that the plaintiff had failed to prove Baidu's dominant position. Although in this case, the plaintiff submitted statements from third parties evidencing Baidu's substantial market share, the courts viewed them as insufficient, apparently because such statements were not based on reliable data and did not include any details about the methods used for calculating the market shares. In a lawsuit against another Chinese internet company, SNDA,[4] which operated a literature website, the court also found that the defendant did not have a dominant position

[3] *Renren v. Baidu*, Beijing No.1 Intermediate Court, Case No. 845, December 18, 2009 (first instance ruling), <http://blog.sina.com.cn/s/blog_e12c8cce0101apdy.html> (in Chinese); *Renren v. Baidu*, Beijing Higher Court, Case No. 489, July 9, 2010 (second instance ruling), <http://www.lawyee.org/Case/Case_Display.asp?ChannelID=2010100&RID=733219&keyword=> (in Chinese). A summary of the court's judgment is available in Chinese at <http://bj1zy.chinacourt.org/public/detail.php?id=675>.

[4] *Sursen v. SNDA*, Shanghai No.1 Intermediate Court, Case No. 113, October 23, 2009 (first instance ruling), <http://ipr.court.gov.cn/sh/bzdjz/201001/t20100104_126336.html> (in Chinese); *Sursen v. SNDA*, Shanghai Higher Court, Case No. 135, December 15, 2009 (second instance ruling), <http://www.lawyee.org/Case/Case_Display.asp?ChannelID=2010100&RID=349178> (in Chinese).

in an alleged "online literature market." Although the plaintiff submitted as evidence a page from Shanda's website stating that Shanda had more than 80 percent of the Chinese online literature market, the court found that this did not constitute proof of market share, as the statements merely were for promotional purposes.

Accordingly, market definition is critical to the analysis of potentially anticompetitive conduct under the AML. The rules for market definition are stated by the *Guidelines on the Definition of Relevant Markets* issued by the Anti-Monopoly Commission (AMC) of the State Council in 2009. In general, they follow international practice, focusing on both supply and demand substitutability, and considering product and geographic market definition. The Guidelines discuss in detail the hypothetical monopolist (or small but significant non-transitory increase in price, SSNIP) test, but also emphasize more general product characteristics, such as appearance, features, price differences, sales channels, customer preferences, and other factors. **7.13**

Of course, in China, as in other important antitrust jurisdictions, the possession of a dominant market position alone does not violate the AML. Rather, a dominant firm must engage in prohibited "abuses" of its dominant position to violate article 17 of the AML or similar prohibitions in the AUCL. Specific types of anticompetitive conduct are explained in further detail below. **7.14**

Article 6 of AML suggests that an abuse of a dominant position also requires anticompetitive effects,[5] a view confirmed by, *inter alia*, article 3 of NDRC Anti-Price Monopoly Rules (the "NDRC Rules"), article 2 of SAIC Rules on the Prohibition of Abuses of Dominant Position (the "SAIC Abuse of Dominance Rules"), and the *Johnson & Johnson* litigation discussed in Sections I.E and I.M. **7.15**

So far, very few non-merger decisions under the AML from courts or regulators have been published. It is therefore too early to say whether China will impose broad obligations on dominant firms; adopt a more moderate approach, like the European Union; or adopt a relatively lenient one, like the United States. In this respect, it is important to understand that China's AML, while borrowing from foreign jurisdictions (and in particular the European Union), has some specific Chinese features and, in particular, must serve to promote the healthy development of the socialist market economy. Given the importance of industrial policy considerations, it would not be surprising to see China's position on unilateral conduct as well as other antitrust issues be different from that of other jurisdictions. **7.16**

A. Predatory pricing

Article 17(2) of the AML prohibits "without valid justification, selling products at prices below cost." Article 14(2) of the Price Law similarly prohibits dumping merchandise below cost to force out competitors or monopolize the market. And article 11 of the AUCL prohibits selling products below cost "for the purpose of forcing out competitors." **7.17**

There has been little if any public enforcement of the AML and Price Law prohibitions on predatory pricing by NDRC. As such, little clarity exists regarding, for example, what would constitute an appropriate measure of cost (such as using average variable cost as a proxy for marginal cost) for Chinese enforcement authorities or courts to evaluate possible predatory pricing. NDRC's enforcement rules provide no detail on this. **7.18**

[5] See e.g. "The issues in determining the abuse of dominant market position" (August 10, 2008), SAIC expert opinions, <http://www.saic.gov.cn/gzfw/zjgd/200808/t20080810_50394.html> (in Chinese). SAIC's interpretation of the AML provisions on abuse of dominant market position seems to suggest that only abuses that have the effect of eliminating or restricting competition are prohibited by the Law.

7.19 However, the NDRC Rules do suggest several possible valid justifications for pricing below cost, including disposing of expiring or overstocked products, repaying debts, closing down a business, or sales promotions for new products. Article 14(2) of the Price Law similarly includes exceptions for lawful disposal of fresh, live, seasonal, or overstocked merchandise. The AUCL provision also specifically excludes from prohibition several of the same scenarios listed as valid justifications in the NDRC Rules.

7.20 Notably, the AUCL and Price Law prohibitions extend to all companies, not merely those with dominant market positions. It is understood that SAIC has had a number of enforcement cases in this context—some reported in a book the agency published in 2007[6]—but few have been publicly reported.

B. Exploitative offenses (excessive pricing, monopoly leveraging)

(i) Excessive pricing

7.21 Under article 17(1) of the AML, firms with dominant market positions are prohibited from "selling products at unfairly high prices, or buying products at unfairly low prices." This is the only item in article 17—the list of prohibited abuses of dominance—not qualified by the phrase "without valid justification," implying that the prohibition is absolute even while undefined. Article 14(7) of the Price Law similarly prohibits "seeking exorbitant profits in violation of laws and regulations."

7.22 Article 11 of the 2011 NDRC Anti-Price Monopoly Rules provides some elaboration about what may support a finding of unfairly high pricing, but unfortunately most of the elaboration is worrisome and does not appear to be market-based. Thus, the NDRC Rules in part base consideration of whether a price is excessively high on a comparison with the prices of competing products, finding a violation if a selling price is "obviously" higher than that charged by competitors selling similar products. This leaves little apparent room for competitors to price higher for legitimate reasons, such as to reflect higher quality products or better service, or even simply to differentiate products at higher price points. The NDRC Rules also seek to peg selling prices to costs, rather than supply and demand—finding as evidence of unfairly high pricing any time when pricing increases "above normal levels" while costs remain "basically stable," or when pricing increases at a rate "obviously higher" than increases in costs.

7.23 Excessively high pricing also may constitute a disguised refusal to deal, as discussed in Section I.H, but so far there has been no published case in this context.

(ii) Monopoly leveraging

7.24 There is no specific prohibition in Chinese antitrust law addressing monopoly leveraging, or the use of monopoly power in one market to create or enhance a company's position in another market.

C. Monopsony

7.25 Under the Chinese antitrust laws, the issue of monopsony power (or market dominance as a purchaser) is handled exactly the same as monopoly power. Article 17 of the AML specifically prohibits a firm with a dominant market position from "buying products at unfairly low prices," just as it prohibits firms from selling at excessively high prices.[7] Similarly, article

[6] SAIC & Chinese Academy of Social Sciences (CASS), *Selected Anti-Monopoly Cases and the Investigation and Analysis on the Chinese Administrative Anti-Monopoly Enforcement* (Beijing: Law Press 2007) 96–9.

[7] See Section I.B, as well as the NDRC Rules, art. 11.

18(2) states that consideration of market dominance requires evaluation of, among other factors, the ability of a competitor to control the raw material purchasing market, as well as the sales market. However, article 17(2) does not specifically mention "predatory buying" in addition to predatory pricing, and it remains to be seen whether and how the enforcing agencies and court will apply the AML provisions in this regard.

D. Price discrimination

Discrimination as to price or other terms is prohibited by the AML for dominant firms. **7.26**

The issue of discrimination is taken very seriously in Chinese antitrust law. Article 17(6) of the AML prohibits dominant firms from "according different treatment in regard to transaction conditions such as price to equivalent trading partners." This is repeated, with respect to prices, in article 16 of the NDRC Rules. **7.27**

Article 7 of the SAIC Abuse of Dominance Rules provides more specific guidance on non-price discrimination, stating that dominant firms may not offer different trade volumes, grades, qualities, preferential conditions (such as volume discounts), payment terms, delivery methods, or after-sales service conditions (such as warranty services, periods, maintenance terms, spare parts supply, and technical assistance) to similar counterparties. Price discrimination also is prohibited by article 14(5) of the Price Law. **7.28**

Similarly, the August 2012 draft SAIC Guidelines on AML Enforcement in the Area of Intellectual Property Rights also lists differential royalty rates to similar counterparties as a potential abuse of dominant position in the context of IP licensing. **7.29**

There have been only a handful of published cases involving price discrimination. In 2009, a customer filed a lawsuit against state-owned telecom company China Mobile alleging, *inter alia*, that the firm had abused its dominant position in the China cellular telephone service market by charging subscribers different fees for substantially similar services.[8] Several months later, the parties settled, and the customer withdrew its complaint. **7.30**

In November 2011, the NDRC announced an investigation into China Telecom and China Unicom, the other two major state-owned telecommunications companies, for alleged abuse of dominant position in broadband backbone networks. The two companies also are engaged in the downstream broadband market and allegedly charged higher fees to rivals in the downstream market. The parties reportedly submitted commitments that were deemed sufficient to terminate the investigation, but there have been no further public announcements regarding this case. **7.31**

E. Dictating or influencing resale prices

Unlike other unilateral conduct, which is covered by article 17 of the AML, resale price maintenance (RPM) is prohibited by article 14 of the AML concerning vertical agreements with other trading counterparties. The prohibition in article 14 includes both "fixing resale prices to a third party" and "restricting the minimum price for resale to a third party." The AML also prohibits maximum resale prices where they result in "fixing" resale prices, as likely would be the case if all retailers use the maximum price as a de facto price. Article 8 of the NDRC Rules provides no more detail about this prohibition, but article 10 of those rules makes clear that such resale price maintenance agreements may be eligible for exemption if they satisfy the criteria of article 15 of the AML, as discussed further in Section II. **7.32**

[8] *Ze Zhou v. China Mobile*. The lawsuit was originally filed in the Beijing No. 2 Intermediate Court and was later settled by the parties during the course of litigation on October 23, 2009, <http://www.lawyee.org/Case/Case_Display.asp?ChannelID=2010100&RID=1423339> (in Chinese).

7.33 The issue of RPM has been raised in some well-publicized cases. In February 2012, Johnson & Johnson (J&J) was sued by a distributor alleging that J&J set minimum resale prices for medical equipment and wrongfully terminated its distributor agreement after the plaintiff sold equipment below that minimum resale price. In May 2012, the Shanghai No. 1 Intermediate People's Court ruled in favor of J&J, finding that the plaintiff had failed to prove anticompetitive effects from the RPM restraint.[9] In August 2013, the Shanghai Higher People's Court reversed that decision on appeal, finding that Johnson & Johnson had a "strong market position" giving rise to anticompetitive effects from the RPM restraint, and assessing damages of CNY 530,000.[10] In February 2013, NDRC, through its local counterparts, issued total fines of around CNY 450 million (around USD 70 million) on two premium alcohol companies, Moutai and Wuliangye, for setting minimum resale prices for their distributors and punishing those selling below those prices.[11] In August 2013, NDRC issued a record set of fines totaling CNY 670 million (USD 107 milion) against a group of six leading producers of infant formula, while exempting from penalty three other producers that had proactively reported their violations, cooperated with the investigation, and actively implemented corrective measures.[12]

F. Tying arrangements

7.34 Tying arrangements have long been prohibited—without regard for market position—under article 12 of the AUCL, which states that "business operators may not link sales to the sale of other products against the purchaser's wishes, or attach other unreasonable conditions." SAIC has reported taking a number of enforcement actions against alleged tying under the AUCL, including some cases that appear to place a very low burden on any finding of coercion in the tying process.

7.35 A prominent pre-AML litigation in 2004 filed against Sony by a maker of replacement batteries for Sony camcorders and digital cameras reportedly involved allegations of "technical tying," where through technical means Sony prevented the plaintiff's replacement batteries from being compatible with Sony's electronic products.[13] Media reports stated that the suit was brought not under article 12 of the AUCL, but rather under the broad requirement in article 2 of the AUCL that companies "observe the principles of voluntariness, equality, equitability, honesty, and trustworthiness and abide by generally accepted business ethics."[14] The case was reportedly rejected by the Shanghai court in 2007, just prior to the AML's coming into force.

7.36 Article 17(5) of the AML now prohibits dominant firms from, "without valid justification, tying products or imposing other unreasonable trading conditions." The SAIC Abuse of Dominance Rules, in article 6(1), elaborate that this prohibition includes "forcibly tying or

---

[9] *Rainbow v. Johnson & Johnson*, Shanghai No. 1 Intermediate Court, Case No. 169, May 18, 2012 (first instance ruling), <http://www.hshfy.sh.cn:8081/flws/text.jsp?pa=ad3N4aD0xJnRhaD2jqDIwMTCjqbum0rvW0MPxzuUo1qops/XX1rXaMTY5usUmd3o9z> (in Chinese).

[10] *Rainbow v. Johnson & Johnson*, Shanghai Higher Court, Case No. 63, August 1, 2013 (second instance ruling), <http://www.hshfy.sh.cn:8081/flws/text.jsp?pa=ad3N4aD01JnRhaD2jqDIwMTKjqbumuN/D8cj9KNaqKdbV19a12jYzusUmd3o9z> (in Chinese). See further discussion in Section I.M.

[11] See "Moutai and Wuliangye incurred the largest fines in the history of China antitrust enforcement," *Xinhua News Agency* (February 22, 2013), <http://www.gov.cn/jrzg/2013-02/22/content_2338339.htm> (in Chinese).

[12] NDRC Press Release, "Infant formula manufacturers including Biostime were fined a total of CNY 668.73 million for restricting competition against AML" (August 7, 2013), <http://www.sdpc.gov.cn/xwfb/t20130807_552991.htm> (in Chinese).

[13] *Dexian Technology v. Sony*, Shanghai No. 1 Intermediate Court, Case No. 223, December 20, 2007 (first instance ruling), <http://www.cnipr.net/article_show.asp?article_id=20529> (in Chinese).

[14] *Dexian Technology* (n 13).

bundling different products in violation of trade practice or consumer habits, or in disregard of the functions of the products."

In August 2010, NDRC investigated a company in Hubei province with a monopoly for the sale of salt. NDRC ordered this salt company to cease tying salt and certain washing powders when selling to retailers. However, NDRC did not impose a fine in view of the defendant's cooperation.[15] Also in 2010, a customer alleged that Dongfeng-Nissan and its authorized sales and service shop operator monopolized the supply of Dongfeng-Nissan spare car parts, charged excessively high prices and refused to sell the parts and offer repair services separately. The Changsha Intermediate People's Court ruled in favor of the defendants in December 2011 on the ground that the plaintiff failed to define the relevant market or prove the defendants' dominance.[16] **7.37**

Finally, in early 2013, the Intermediate Court in Xi'an ruled in favor of an individual plaintiff who sued Shaanxi Broadcast and TV Network Intermediary Group, a state-owned company and the only supplier of cable TV transmission services in Shaanxi Province, for tie-in sales of basic services (cable TV) and value-added services (e.g. digital TV). The court held that basic TV services and value-added services are separate services addressing different customer needs, and that the defendant had abused its dominance in the market of cable TV transmission services by offering the two kinds of services together without giving customers the opportunity to choose.[17] This reportedly is the first successful private antitrust lawsuit for a plaintiff in China, albeit for a very low damages award. **7.38**

G. Exclusive dealing

Exclusive dealing by dominant firms is prohibited by article 17(4) of the AML, absent valid justification. Article 5 of the SAIC Abuse of Dominance Rules merely restates this prohibition. Article 14 of the NDRC Rules adds that dominant firms may not, without valid justification, "restrict by means of price discounts or otherwise a trading counterparty to trade exclusively with it or another undertaking designated by it." The NDRC approach appears somewhat to expand the concept of exclusive dealing to encompass exclusivity that results from better economic terms offered by the seller. Moreover, the NDRC Rules also provide several possibilities for valid justifications of exclusive dealing: to ensure product quality and safety; to maintain brand image or improve service; or to lower costs or improve efficiency (if those benefits are shared with consumers). To date there have been no published cases involving the exclusive dealing provision of the AML. **7.39**

A similar provision (art. 6) in the AUCL prohibits state utilities or other enterprises that possess a state-granted monopoly from exclusive dealing. For example, in 2003, a company that produces and sells electricity meters in Beijing filed a lawsuit against a public utility **7.40**

---

[15] NDRC Press Release, "Hubei Price Bureau investigated and fined Wuchang Branch of Hubei Salt Group for tying the sales of washing powder" (October 15, 2010), <http://jjs.ndrc.gov.cn/gzdt/t20101115_380421.htm> (in Chinese).

[16] "Automobile components monopoly—why customer lost the antitrust lawsuit against Dongfeng-Nissan?" *People* (Feburary 16, 2012), <http://auto.people.com.cn/GB/1050/17134294.html> (in Chinese). *Dahua Liu v. Dongfeng-Nissan*, the first instance ruling decided by the Changsha Intermediate Court on December 15, 2011.

[17] For discussion and analysis of this case, see Jianjun Yao, "The legal nature and constituents of a tying sale," *Chinacourt.org* (February 28, 2013), <http://www.chinacourt.org/article/detail/2013/02/id/903920.shtml> (in Chinese). The defendant was ordered to repay the plaintiff CNY 15, representing one month's fee for the tied service. *Xiaoqin Wu v. Shaanxi Broadcast & TV Network*, Shaanxi Higher Court, Case No. 38, September 12, 2013 (second instance ruling), <http://sxfy.chinacourt.org/public/paperview.php?id=1220547> (in Chinese).

enterprise that was in charge of the selection and installation of electricity meters in the city. The plaintiff alleged that the defendant, by issuing a so-called selection document without applying any selection criteria, excluded the plaintiff as potential supplier and forced the power plants to use meters produced by five companies designated by the defendant, without justification. The Beijing No. 1 People's Court ruled in December 2003 in favor of the plaintiff, holding that the defendant's act constituted unfair competition.[18]

H. Refusal to deal

7.41 Article 17 of the AML also includes a prohibition on dominant firms refusing to deal with trading partners, absent valid justification. This prohibition on refusals to deal is not limited to outright refusals to supply. For example, article 4 of the SAIC Abuse of Dominance Rules provides that the following conduct, without valid justification, shall constitute a refusal to deal:

(1) reducing the current volume of trading with the counterparty;
(2) delaying or terminating its current transaction with the counterparty;
(3) refusing to have a new transaction with the trading party;
(4) imposing restrictive conditions which make it difficult for the trading party to continue its dealing with the [dominant firm]; or
(5) refusing to allow the counterparty to use its necessary facilities under reasonable conditions in the course of production and operations.

7.42 The NDRC Rules also provide that the imposition of "excessively high prices" can amount to a "disguised" refusal to deal (or an excessively low price in the case the buyer has a dominant position and tries to extract low prices from a supplier).[19] It remains unclear what constitutes an "excessively high price."

7.43 According to article 13 of the NDRC Rules, a refusal to deal does not amount to an abuse of a dominant position if the customer is able to purchase the same type of products or alternative products from other undertakings at a reasonable price. The Rules also recognize a justification based on "bad credit standing or continued worsening of operations, which may pose significant risks for the transaction." In contrast, the SAIC Rules do not provide for a list of possible valid justifications for refusals to deal, but rather (according to art. 8) state that SAIC should take the following into account when assessing whether a refusal to deal can rely on a valid justification:

(1) whether the conduct is based on normal operations and for normal benefits of the undertaking; and
(2) the effect of the relevant conduct on economic efficiency, public interest, and economic growth.

7.44 These elements seem to indicate that SAIC will perform a sort of rule of reason analysis when assessing the compatibility of refusals to deal with the AML. But as there is little public information on SAIC's enforcement in this regard, it is unclear how much weight SAIC will give to the pro-competitive elements listed in article 8 compared to the possible anticompetitive effects. There has been no published case so far regarding refusals to deal.

---

[18] *Saien (Tianjin) New Technology v. Beijing Power Supply*, Beijing No.1 Intermediate Court, Case No. 2876, December 18, 2003 (first instance ruling), <http://www.lawyee.org/Case/Case_Display.asp?RID=33831> (in Chinese); *Saien (Tianjin) New Technology v. Beijing Power Supply*, Beijing Higher Court, Case No. 215, May 27, 2004 (second instance ruling), <http://www.lawyee.org/Case/Case_Display.asp?ChannelID=2010100&RID=57781&keyword=> (in Chinese).

[19] See the NDRC Anti-Price Monopoly Rules, art. 13, which provides that "without valid justification, an undertaking with a dominant market position shall be prohibited from refusing to deal with a trading counterparty in a disguised form by setting excessively high selling prices or excessively low buying prices."

I. Essential facilities

Pursuant to the SAIC Abuse of Dominance Rules, refusals to permit access to essential facilities may constitute abuses of dominant market position. Article 4(5) of the SAIC Rules refers to refusal to "allow a counterparty to use a company's essential facilities under reasonable conditions in the course of production and operations." The SAIC Rules list a series of factors that can be considered in the case of a claim of a refusal to grant access to such an essential facility. First, SAIC will assess the feasibility in separately investing and building or developing an alternative facility. Second, SAIC will assess the "degree of reliance of the counterparty on such facilities in effectively running its production and operations." Third, SAIC will take into account the possibility for the dominant firm to grant access to its facility, suggesting that in the case there is no spare capacity, no access should be granted. SAIC also will assess the impact of the access on the production and operations of the dominant firm. **7.45**

There have been no published enforcement cases or court decisions in this area so far. **7.46**

J. Bundling (including loyalty and market share discounts)

See discussion of tying in Section I.F. **7.47**

Chinese antitrust law does not specifically address the issue of bundling at this time, but it can be relevant to questions not only of tying but also effective refusals to deal, effective exclusive dealing (such as with market share discounts *a la AMD/Intel*), and predatory pricing, among other topics. **7.48**

K. Standard-setting groups (disclosure requirements, licensing arrangements, and licensing pools)

The AML seems to recognize the pro-competitive effects of standard setting and indeed specifically lists "unifying product specifications and standards" as one of the beneficial purposes potentially justifying an exemption from the prohibition of monopoly agreements under article 15. Draft rules on the Administration of Patents Incorporated into Standards require mandatory disclosure of patents and the election of free use or licensing fees for patents to be incorporated into mandatory national standards. **7.49**

If a patent is incorporated into a standard, the patentee may not be able to sue third parties for infringement (as opposed to for the payment of a reasonable royalty) of the relevant patent when implementing the standard. An advisory opinion by the Supreme People's Court (SPC) in a patent infringement case in 2008 involving IP rights in a national construction standard provides that: **7.50**

> ...if a patentee engages in standard setting or agrees that the patent be incorporated into a national, industrial or local standard, the patentee would be deemed to have permitted others to exploit the patent while implementing the standard. Such exploitation of the patent by others does not constitute patent infringement under Article 11 of the Patent Law. The patentee may charge the exploiter or implementer of the patent a fee for use of the patent, but the amount of such fee should be significantly lower than the normal license fee.

The SPC advisory opinion is case-specific, and the principles contained therein do not appear to have been applied in practice in any high-profile cases to date.

L. Customer termination

Customer termination may constitute a refusal to deal, as discussed in Sections I.H and I.I. Termination may also constitute exclusive dealing, if the termination is punishment for dealing with the dominant firm's competitors. The AML is unclear whether the elimination of competition could occur within the market in which the supplier (i.e. the dominant firm) is **7.51** active, or within the market in which the customer is active (even if the supplier is not active in the customer's market). It is also unclear whether elimination of the customer from the market (in case it cannot find alternative sources of supply) would amount to an "elimination or restriction of competition" if there remain enough other competitors in the customer's market. So far, there is no case law to provide guidance in this respect.

M. Termination of intermediaries (retailers, wholesalers, dealers and value added resellers, agents, and brokers)

7.52 Unilateral termination of intermediaries (i.e. not by agreement with other distributors or competitors) and for legitimate business reasons in general is not prohibited by the AML. However, termination due to intermediaries' dealing with the dominant supplier's competitors or for failure to implement resale prices might be prohibited as conduct reinforcing exclusive dealing or RPM.

7.53 The Court's first instance ruling in the Johnson & Johnson case,[20] although not a refusal to deal case, indicates that the "elimination or restriction of competition" at least can happen in the market of the customer. In February 2012, Johnson & Johnson (J&J) was sued by a distributor alleging that J&J had violated the AML by setting minimum resale prices for medical equipment and wrongfully terminating its distributor agreement after the plaintiff sold equipment below that minimum resale price. In May 2012, the Shanghai Intermediate Court ruled in favor of J&J on the basis that the plaintiff had failed to prove anticompetitive effects from the RPM restraint. The Court's decision stated that the plaintiff failed to provide evidence to show the market share of the products concerned in the distribution agreement and the supply structure of those products, while J&J submitted evidence to show that there were many other suppliers of the same kinds of products. In August 2013, the Shanghai Higher People's Court reversed that decision on appeal, finding that Johnson & Johnson had a "strong market position" giving rise to anticompetitive effects from the RPM restraint, and assessing damages of CNY 530,000.[21]

N. Termination of relationships with competitors

7.54 There are no explicit rules dealing with termination of relationships with competitors, except those discussed in Section I.H and I.I.

O. Exemptions

7.55 All prohibitions (other than unfairly high pricing) constituting abuses of dominance under article 17 of the AML are subject to the defense of valid justification. In this sense, valid justification might be considered as an exemption to an otherwise illegal agreement. The NDRC Rules list valid justifications for each type of abusive conduct, while the SAIC Rules list some factors to be considered in evaluating whether a justification is "valid," as discussed in Section I.H with regard to refusals to deal.

7.56 Agreements otherwise prohibited by article 13 of the AML (agreements among competitors) can benefit from an exemption from the prohibition under article 15 if they can be proved to have been entered into for one of the following objectives: (1) improving techniques or

[20] *Rainbow v. Johnson & Johnson*, Shanghai Intermediate Court, Case No. 169, May 18, 2012 (first instance ruling), <http://www.hshfy.sh.cn:8081/flws/text.jsp?pa=ad3N4aD0xJnRhaD2jqDIwMTCjqbum0rvW0MPxzuUo1qops/XX1rXaMTY5usUmd3o9z> (in Chinese).

[21] *Rainbow v. Johnson & Johnson*, Shanghai Higher Court, Case No. 63, August 1, 2013 (second instance ruling), <http://www.hshfy.sh.cn:8081/flws/text.jsp?pa=ad3N4aD01JnRhaD2jqDIwMTKjqbumuN/D8cj9KNaqKdbV19a12jYzusUmd3o9z> (in Chinese). See further discussion in Section I.M.

researching and developing new products; (2) upgrading product quality, reducing costs, improving efficiency, unifying product specifications and standards, or realizing division of work based on specialization; (3) improving operational efficiency and enhancing the competitiveness of small and medium size enterprises (SMEs); (4) realizing public welfare, such as conservation of energy, protecting the environment, and providing disaster relief; (5) mitigating the severe decrease in sales volume or excessive overstock during economic recessions; (6) protecting "legitimate interests in foreign trade and economic cooperation," or (7) other circumstances stipulated by law or regulations. Companies seeking exemptions under article 15(1)–(5) must also prove that the agreements in question do not substantially restrict competition and will enable the consumers to share the benefits derived from the agreement.

The AML and its supplementary antimonopoly rules do not provide sector-specific rules, and the law itself is silent on whether AML prevails over other laws or whether sectoral regulators should cede jurisdiction to antimonopoly authorities. **7.57**

In addition, article 7 of the AML exempts certain state-owned companies from the application of the AML, in particular in industries that have a vital bearing on the national economy and national security or in industries where monopolies are granted by law. The scope and application of this exemption have not been addressed in any publicly reported cases or enforcement actions. **7.58**

II. Dealing with competitors

Article 13 of the AML prohibits the following categories of "monopoly agreements" between competitors:[22] (a) price fixing, (b) restricting output or sales volume; (c) allocating sales markets or raw material purchasing markets; (d) restricting the purchase of new technology or new equipment, or restricting the development of new technology or new products; (e) boycotts; and (f) other agreements as determined by the enforcement agencies. Unlike the abuse of dominance provisions, which must be supplemented by article 6 for the requirement of anticompetitive effects, article 13 expressly states that such monopoly agreements are prohibited only where they eliminate or restrict competition. **7.59**

Article 13 further states that prohibited monopoly agreements can include "agreements, decisions or other concerted practices." The definition of what constitutes concerted practices sufficient to reach the level of a monopoly agreement is not further defined in the AML itself. The enforcement agencies have taken slightly different approaches to the issue. Article 6 of the NDRC Rules states that "a finding of other concerted practices" in the pricing context shall be based on (1) uniformity of pricing conduct and (2) some communication of intention between the undertakings involved. That article also requires that market structure, market changes, and "other conditions" be taken into consideration in evaluating any concerted practice. Similarly, article 2 of the SAIC Rules on the Prohibition of Monopoly Agreements (SAIC Agreement Rules) states that "other concerted practice" means "collusive coordination in practice between undertakings without express oral or written agreements or decisions." Article 3 of the SAIC Rules states that, in finding concerted practices, SAIC will consider: (1) uniform market conduct; (2) intention of contact or information exchange between the competitors; and (3) any reasonable justification for the uniform conduct. The SAIC Rules also require that market structure, competitive conditions, market changes, and **7.60**

[22] Article 14 of the AML prohibits certain vertical agreements relating to resale price maintenance. See para. 7.32.

industry conditions be considered. While NDRC and SAIC have been active in cracking down cartels, there has been little information about their enforcement against "concerted practices." NDRC's investigation in the *Unilever* case indicates that the signaling of price increases may constitute engaging in prohibited concerted practices.[23]

7.61 The AML does not treat "hard core" violations or "naked" restraints any differently than other types of anticompetitive agreements, meaning that no agreements expressly are per se illegal and without any recourse to possible exemption under article 15. However, it would appear difficult for companies to demonstrate that otherwise hard core or per se violations (such as price-fixing cartels) could satisfy all of the criteria in article 15 and actually benefit from exemption.

A. Horizontal price fixing

7.62 Agreements to fix or change prices of products expressly are prohibited by article 13(1) of the AML. They also are covered by article 14(1) of the Price Law, which prohibits collusion to manipulate market prices. Further details are provided in article 7 of the NDRC Rules, which extends the prohibition to, *inter alia*, agreements relating to fixing prices, ranges of price changes, discounts, price formula, and "fixing or changing price in a disguised form by other means."

7.63 There have been several reported enforcement cases taken by NDRC or its local affiliates against price-fixing cartels. Many have been under the Price Law, but in recent years NDRC also has begun to prosecute such actions using the AML. For example, in October 2012, NDRC imposed fines totaling approximately CNY 760,000 (USD 120,000) on three leading participants in a price cartel relating to sea sand—an important component in concrete used for construction—in Guangdong Province, after more than twenty companies together raised their prices for sea sands, doubling the market price. In January 2013, NDRC imposed fines of CNY 353 million (approx. USD 56 million) on six international manufacturers of liquid crystal display (LCD) panels for price-fixing in connection with the so-called global LCD cartel. Both of these decisions were based on the AML.

7.64 There has been no published case law on the issue of when parallel pricing behavior and price signaling can constitute "other concerted practices" prohibited by article 13(1) of the AML. However, in March 2011, NDRC issued a fine of CNY 2 million (USD 300,000) to the international company Unilever for publicly announcing a potential price increase of approximately 10 percent for various household products. These announcements led to consumer "panic" buying in a number of Chinese cities. NDRC found Unilever's behavior in violation of article 14(3) of the Price Law as "spreading price increase information" that disrupted market order.

B. Horizontal agreements to allocate customers or territories; agreements not to compete

7.65 Agreements not to compete, or otherwise to restrict output or sales volume, are prohibited by article 13(2). Article 4 of the SAIC Agreements Rules provides more detail, including that competitors may not agree to restrict sales volume by refusing to supply.

[23] NDRC Press Release, "National Development and Reform Commission official to investigate and fine Unilever (China) for disturbing the market order by spreading information of price increase" (May 6, 2011), <http://www.ndrc.gov.cn/xwfb/t20110506_410543.htm> (in Chinese). See further discussion in Section II.A.

Horizontal agreements to allocate markets are prohibited by article 13(3) of the AML. These are elaborated on in article 5 of the SAIC Agreement Rules. **7.66**

There have been some reported enforcement actions against cartels that restricted output or allocated markets. For example, in early 2011, SAIC imposed fines of CNY 530,000 (USD 83,000) on a concrete association in Jiangsu Province and five of its member companies for market allocation under the AML.[24] **7.67**

C. Horizontal boycotts

Horizontal boycotts are prohibited by article 13(5) of the AML. Article 7 of the SAIC Agreements Rule states that joint boycotts include "concerted refusals to supply or sell products to a specific undertaking, concerted refusals to purchase or sell products of a specific undertaking, and concerted restraints on a specific undertaking from dealing with a competing undertaking." At this stage, there are no published cases on boycotts under the AML. **7.68**

D. Joint ventures and other competitive collaborations

Joint ventures and other forms of collaborations among competitors that may restrict competition but also have pro-competitive benefits may be compatible with the AML if they meet the criteria for exemption set forth in article 15. In addition, MOFCOM practice and the most recent version of its merger reporting filing form make clear that joint ventures are subject to pre-merger reporting and clearance under chapter IV of the AML. Indeed, many key MOFCOM conditional merger clearance decisions have involved joint ventures, which are a common form for foreign investment into China. **7.69**

E. Trade associations

The AML contains several potentially ambiguous provisions regarding trade associations. Article 11 of the AML provides that trade associations "shall strengthen self-discipline of industries, provide guidance for undertakings in industries to compete lawfully, and maintain the order of market competition." Article 16 of the AML then provides that trade associations "shall not organize undertakings in the relevant industry to engage in any monopolistic conduct prohibited [by the AML provisions governing anticompetitive agreements]." This approach is required by the unique role that trade associations historically have played in organizing and coordinating the behavior of Chinese companies. **7.70**

Article 9 of the SAIC Agreement Rules provides that trade associations are prohibited from "formulating and issuing articles of association, rules, decisions, notices or standards, eliminating or restricting competition" or "convening, organizing or promoting undertakings in the relevant industry to reach agreements, decisions, minutes and/or memorandum eliminating or restricting competition." Article 9 of the NDRC Rules contains similar language regarding price-related trade association activities. **7.71**

In one publicized case (the outcome of which is yet unknown), a consumer association filed a lawsuit against several publishing trade associations, which jointly had promulgated rules limiting the discounts that their members could offer on publications during the first year after publication. **7.72**

[24] Jiangsu Concrete Cartel, Jiangsu AIC, Case No. 37 (2020), Administrative Penalty Decision of August 31, 2010, <http://www.saic.gov.cn/zwgk/gggs/jzzf/201307/t20130726_136749.html> (in Chinese). The sanctioned parties include: the Concrete Commission of the Lianyungang Contruction Materials and Construction Machinery Association, Lianyungang Xindian Concrete Co., Ltd., Lianyungang Sujin Concrete Product Co., Ltd., Lianyungang Dongsheng Commercial Concrete Co., Ltd., Lianyungang Zhonggang Concrete Co., Ltd., and Lianyungang Runfeng Concrete Co., Ltd.

F. Interlocking directorates

7.73 There is no specific provision in the AML that covers interlocking directorates. Nevertheless such arrangements could in theory fall under article 13 of the AML (regarding monopoly agreements between competitors) if they have the effect of restricting competition and do not meet the criteria of article 15 for an exemption. Moreover, companies that arguably might acquire sole or joint control of another company by way of interlocking directorates should be aware that they may be required to obtain pre-merger clearance under chapter IV of the AML.

G. Facilitating practices

7.74 Unlike s. 5 of the US Federal Trade Commission's Act, the AML does not prohibit "facilitating practices" per se. Rather, such practices may violate the general prohibition of antimonopoly agreements if the conditions under article 13 are met.

H. Information exchange

7.75 Exchanges of competitively sensitive information may in some circumstances violate the AML. So far there is no specific case law or guidelines setting out under what circumstances such exchanges may be unlawful in themselves.

7.76 However, as discussed above at the start of Section II, the fact of information exchange between competitors may, under the SAIC and NDRC Rules, be sufficient, when combined with evidence of parallel conduct, to justify a finding of "concerted practices" constituting an illegal monopoly agreement in violation of article 13 of the AML.

I. Joint purchasing agreements

7.77 Joint purchasing agreements may arguably violate the AML if the conditions set out in article 13 are met, and the agreement does not qualify for an exemption under article 15. However, article 13(1) of the AML does not make it clear whether its prohibition on price fixing agreements extends to joint purchasing by competitors. At this stage, there is no published case law or detailed guidance setting out, for example, safe harbors within which joint purchasing agreements are deemed legal.

J. Joint lobbying/regulatory/legislative efforts

7.78 There is no specific provision under the AML covering joint lobbying or similar efforts, nor is there in China an equivalent to the US Noerr–Pennington doctrine. Therefore, such collaboration between competitors only will be illegal if it otherwise is prohibited by article 13 of the AML and does not qualify for an exemption.

III. General issues

A. Jurisdiction and applicable law (including sector-specific legislation)

7.79 Article 2 of the AML provides for extraterritorial application of the law, stating that "[t]his Law is applicable to monopolistic conduct outside the territory of the People's Republic of China that eliminates or has restrictive effects on competition in the domestic market of the People's Republic of China." This contrasts with other PRC antitrust-related laws, such as the Price Law, which do not contain express statements concerning extraterritorial application (but do not generally exclude the possibility of such application). The extraterritorial reach of the AML does not have a substantiality requirement, i.e. article 2 does not require that the anticompetitive effect be direct, substantial, or foreseeable.

B. Antitrust system

The AML authorizes three existing ministry-level Anti-Monopoly Enforcement Authorities (AMEAs) to enforce the law: the State Administration for Industry and Commerce (SAIC), the National Development and Reform Commission (NDRC), and the Ministry of Commerce (MOFCOM). These three agencies each have established new internal antimonopoly offices or bureaus to perform their AML-related functions, but their staffing and budgets are not published. **7.80**

SAIC is responsible for enforcement of AML provisions relating to monopoly agreements, abuses of dominant market position, and abuses of administrative power, excluding price-related monopolistic conduct. It operates through provincial, subprovincial, and local Administrations for Industry and Commerce (local AICs). SAIC may delegate to Provincial AICs enforcement powers on a case-by-case basis, except for enforcement against administrative monopolies for which there is a blanket delegation. As noted above, SAIC also is responsible for the enforcement of other laws, including laws with antitrust components such as the AUCL. **7.81**

NDRC is responsible for price-related monopolistic conduct, including price cartels and price-related abuses of dominance. NDRC has delegated its enforcement powers to provincial-level price authorities, which can also prescribe penalties specified in the AML. NDRC also is responsible for the enforcement of other antitrust-related laws, notably the Price Law. **7.82**

MOFCOM is in charge of concentrations and merger review. Unlike SAIC and NDRC, MOFCOM has not delegated its AML-related enforcement powers to its local counterparts. However, it sometimes engages its local counterparts to assist in verifying case facts when it sees appropriate. MOFCOM currently does not have enforcement responsibility for other antitrust-related laws. **7.83**

There remains uncertainty as to the precise allocation of responsibilities among the three AMEAs, especially between NDRC and SAIC, which frequently need to deal with cases involving both price-related and non-price aspects of potentially anticompetitive conduct. The two agencies have used formal and informal methods to coordinate their activities so far. For example, SAIC's procedural rules provide for information sharing and case transfer mechanisms, MOFCOM regularly solicits comments from NDRC and other relevant authorities, and the three agencies have reportedly applied a principle of "whoever initiates a case first must investigate." **7.84**

So far, SAIC and NDRC have only publicized a dozen of selected decisions, mainly cartel cases, because neither of them is required to publish its enforcement decisions. By contrast, MOFCOM must and has published its prohibitions and decisions imposing remedies. In addition, in late 2012, MOFCOM started to publish a list of unconditional approval decisions (albeit with very limited information) issued since the AML came into force in August 2008 and stated that it will disclose such information on a quarterly basis going forward. Through the end of 2012, MOFCOM had closed 534 merger reviews, including sixteen with conditions imposed and one prohibition (*Coca-Cola v. Huiyuan*[25]). **7.85**

In the context of investigations by NDRC, SAIC, and MOFCOM, it appears that the companies subject to investigation must bear the burden of proof to demonstrate to the agency **7.86**

[25] *Coca-Cola v. Huiyuan*, MOFCOM No. 22, March 18, 2009, <http://fldj.mofcom.gov.cn/article/ztxx/200903/20090306108494.shtml> (in Chinese).

that their conduct or proposed transaction will not have the effect of eliminating or restricting competition.

C. Private litigation

7.87 Article 50 of the AML states that "[u]ndertakings that implement monopoly acts and cause damage to others shall bear civil liability according to law." This provision is understood to provide for the possibility of private civil litigation to redress violations of and damages under the AML.

7.88 The Chinese Supreme People's Court (SPC) set out a framework for civil antitrust litigation in its Rules on Civil Litigation under the Anti-Monopoly Law (the SPC Rules) in June 2012.

7.89 Private plaintiffs who suffer damages caused by monopoly conduct, or have other disputes due to violations of the AML (e.g. arising out of contracts or the activities of industry associations), can bring civil antitrust lawsuits before the PRC court. Although there is no notion of "class action" under the Chinese laws, the SPC Rules provide that, where two or more plaintiffs file lawsuits against the same defendant for the same alleged monopoly conduct, the courts may combine the cases together for hearing.

7.90 For horizontal monopoly agreements, the defendants bear the burden to prove that their agreements do not have anticompetitive effects. The SPC Rules are silent as to which party should prove whether other kinds of monopoly agreements are anticompetitive or not, but presumably the burden of proof is on the plaintiff. For abuses of dominance, plaintiffs bear the burden to prove both the existence of a dominant position and abuse by the defendant, while the defendants (i.e. dominant firms) must prove the existence of "valid justifications." The SPC Rules do not state which party must demonstrate or disprove the existence of anticompetitive effects, or set forth what is the standard of proof for each party.

7.91 A plaintiff seeking damages arising out of violations of the AML must prove its damages and causation between the damages and the violations. The courts may order defendants to bear civil liability, including orders to cease the violations and the payment of compensating damages. They also can invalidate contractual terms or trade association articles that are in violation of the AML.

7.92 The AML is not the only Chinese antitrust-related law that provides for private litigation. Article 41 of the Price Law states that "a company whose illegal pricing act results in overpayment by a consumer or other business operator shall refund the overpaid portion of the price and, if damage is caused, assume liability for damages according to law."

7.93 Between the August 1, 2008 entry into force of the AML and the end of 2011, Chinese courts reportedly accepted sixty-one AML-related cases and closed fifty-three of them. From public reports, it appears that very few plaintiffs have been successful so far—with one exception being the cable TV service tying case discussed in Section I.F. It is understood that a principal reason for this is the high burden of proof faced by plaintiffs prior to issuance of the SPC Rules on private litigation. It is expected that those rules will increase private litigation as they, among other things, lessen plaintiffs' burden of proof in most types of AML litigation. For example, the rules require defendants to prove that horizontal agreements are not anticompetitive and permit plaintiffs to use information published by defendants as evidence to prove their dominant market position, in apparent contrast to the *Shanda* case described in Section I above.

D. Follow-on litigation

7.94 According to the SPC Rules, private plaintiffs must wait until after the AMEA's decision regarding an AML violation becomes effective to file a follow-on lawsuit. As the SPC Rules do not provide further detailed provisions, and so far there has been no published follow-on litigation, it remains to be seen to what extent the courts will defer to final AMEA decisions. In practice, however, the Chinese courts at least will take into consideration administrative authorities' decisions, unless the decisions are based on clear errors in fact finding or application of the law.

E. Arbitration and alternative dispute resolution

It is unclear whether antitrust claims arising under the AML or other PRC antitrust law provisions but relating to contracts containing broad arbitration provisions can properly be arbitrated under the PRC Arbitration Law. There are no specific provisions in the AML, the Arbitration Law, or other supplementary rules addressing this issue to date. **7.95**

F. Remedies

(i) Civil liability

The AML provides for civil liabilities for various types of violation of the law. For monopoly agreements and abuses of a dominant market position, under articles 46 and 47 of the AML, the AMEAs can order cessation of the unlawful conduct, confiscate the illegal gains and/or impose a fine not more than 10 percent of the total sales achieved in the previous year. Penalties may be mitigated or foregone for companies that report a monopoly agreement and provide important evidence to the AMEA according to the circumstances (further discussed in Section III.G). **7.96**

Violators whose acts have caused damage to others also may be required to compensate the injured pursuant to article 50 of the AML, as discussed in paras. 7.87 to 7.93. However, the law is not clear on how to calculate damages, for example, whether they should include only actual losses or also expected profits of the victim. As there have been very few published cases, it remains to be seen how the AMEAs and the court will address these issues. There are no "punitive damages" under the Chinese antitrust law system. **7.97**

Conduct that violates the unfair pricing (including antitrust) provisions of the Price Law may be subject to different, or additional, sanctions under article 40 of the Price Law, including the confiscation of any "illegal gains" fines of up to five times those illegal gains (or, if illegal gains cannot be proven, then a fine of up to CNY 5 million); and, in serious circumstances, revocation of the violator's business license. In addition, such conduct may give rise to civil liability under article 41 of the Price Law. **7.98**

(ii) Criminal liability

There is no criminal liability under the AML, except that officials of the AMEAs may be subject to criminal liability if their unlawful handling of the cases (for example disclosure of trade secrets) constitutes a crime. **7.99**

However, several articles of the PRC Criminal Law potentially apply to antitrust violations, including article 223 (for bid-rigging) and article 225 (for illegal business operations that "disturb market order"), as well as article 226 (for buying or selling through violence or threat, or forcing others to provide or accept service). All of those provisions include potential jail terms of up to three years (up to five years under article 225). There is no public record of the imposition of such criminal penalties for antitrust violations under these provisions. **7.100**

G. Leniency and immunity

Under article 46 of the AML, if a company reports its participation in a cartel to the antitrust agencies and "provides important evidence," the antitrust agencies "may" grant reduced **7.101** penalty or exemption from penalty at their discretion. This is consistent with article 27 of the PRC Administrative Punishment Law, which provides for reduced administrative penalties when parties voluntarily mitigate the consequences of their illegal acts, were coerced into their illegal acts, or assist in the administrative investigation of their illegal acts.

7.102 Both agencies have issued more detailed regulations about their leniency programs in January 2011, namely the NDRC Procedural Rules on Administrative Enforcement against Price Monopoly (NDRC Procedural Rules) and the SAIC Rules on the Prohibition of Monopoly Agreements (SAIC Agreement Rules).

7.103 So far, there has been no published case law enabling companies to get a better understanding of the leniency process.

7.104 In addition, the agencies may terminate an investigation once a suitable remedy is proposed. They also have some discretion to impose mitigated penalties outside the framework of formal leniency or remedies.

7.105 NDRC Procedural Rules: article 14 of the NDRC Procedural Rules provides that "when a business operator voluntarily reports to [NDRC] about the circumstances of the price monopoly agreement reached and provides important evidence, [NDRC] may discretionally reduce or exempt the penalty for that business operator."

7.106 The first entity to report the existence of a cartel (and provide "important evidence") may receive total immunity. "Important evidence" is defined as "evidence which plays a key role for the [NDRC] to ascertain the existence of a price monopoly agreement."

7.107 The second applicant to submit important evidence may be granted at least a 50 percent reduction in the fine. Subsequent applicants may be granted a reduction of at most 50 percent, provided they submit "important evidence."

7.108 The main issue with the NDRC rules is that they seem to give the agency a certain level of discretion in granting immunity or leniency, even if the applicants have submitted the required "important evidence." Indeed, both the AML and the NDRC rules indicate that it *may* grant immunity or leniency.

7.109 SAIC Agreement Rules: article 11 of the SAIC Agreement Rules provides that "business operators that report to [SAIC] a monopoly agreement and provide important evidence on their own initiative may be granted by [SAIC] a mitigated penalty or be exempted from penalty."

7.110 Important evidence is defined as evidence "that is sufficient to initiate an investigation or that plays a key role in finding a monopoly agreement by the [SAIC] including information of the parties to the agreement, the products involved, the form and content of the agreement, and specific details of implementation of the agreement."

7.111 The first applicant to submit such "important evidence" "should" be granted immunity, which seems to indicate a lower level of discretion compared to the NDRC rules described above.

7.112 For subsequent applicants, the penalty "shall" be mitigated discretionally. There are no prescribed ranges of fine reductions in the SAIC Rules. Rather, they provide that "exemption or mitigation of the penalty...shall be determined in accordance with the time sequence of voluntary self-reports by the business operators, the importance of the evidence provided, relevant information about concluding or implementing the monopoly agreement, and its cooperation with the investigation."

H. Document creation and retention

When SAIC and NDRC investigate into a potential AML violation, they have the power to copy relevant corporate documents such as agreements, business letters, and electronic data, as an important sources of evidence. Companies should properly maintain their agreements, meeting minutes, emails, and other documents which may be helpful in establishing justifications for conducts that are allegedly in violation of the AML. **7.113**

8

COLOMBIA

Alfonso Miranda Londoño[1]
Esguerra Barrera Arriaga

Introduction

8.01 Colombia is a country with well-established democratic institutions and a constitutional history that spans more than two hundred years. The country is organized as a centralized republic under a presidential system of government based on the rule of law and the exercise of checks and balances by the different branches of power.

[1] Alfonso Miranda Londoño is a lawyer from the Javeriana University Law School in Bogotá, Colombia. Specialized in Socioeconomic Sciences at the same University, in Banking Law at Los Andes University (also in Bogotá) and with a Masters Degree in Law (LLM) at Cornell University (1987). Director of the Law and Economics Department at the Javeriana University Law School, the co-founder and Director of the Centre for Studies in Competition Law—CEDEC, and a Professor of Competition Law at the Javeriana University. He is also the partner that leads the Competition Law practice at Esguerra Barrera Arriaga.

Since the mid-1930s, the country has incorporated into its constitutional doctrine the possibility of state intervention in the economy; such intervention has permitted the exercise of economic freedom. The 1991 Constitution calls for a "social market economy." **8.02**

Like most countries in Latin America, Colombia issued its first antitrust legislation in the late 1950s, under the political and academic influence of the US and the European Union. However, the laws were not applied in this first era, mainly due to the economic protectionism of the governments in the region before the 1990s, which was at odds with a truly competitive environment.[2] **8.03**

The evolution of antitrust laws in Colombia can be divided into two main phases, which, in turn, can be subdivided into many others depending on the depth and detail of the analysis. **8.04**

The first phase began with Law no. 155 of 1959 ("Law 155"), which contained the first comprehensive regulation of antitrust law in Colombia, and ended with Special Decree 2153 of 1992 ("Decree 2153"). The 1991 Political Constitution was issued during this first phase. This event had an enormous significance for competition law in Colombia, because the new Constitution established free economic competition as a key political principle. **8.05**

The second phase began when Decree 2153 was issued, and it continues to this day. This second phase is marked by a consistent progress in the enforcement of the law, and in the development of case law, the doctrine, and the technical capability of the National Competition Authority (the "Authority"), which is now more experienced and mature, showing an interesting position among its peers in Latin America. **8.06**

Decree 2153 reorganized the Competition Authority and structured the scheme of competition infringements into several categories including: (a) the general prohibition; (b) anticompetitive agreements; (c) anticompetitive acts; (d) abuse of a dominant position; and (e) violation of merger control regulations. **8.07**

In 2009, Law 1340 was issued ("Law 1340") and made significant changes, not least by giving the Superintendence of Industry and Commerce (SIC) the status of National Competition Authority, increasing the levels of fines that can be imposed, expanding the statute of limitations, encouraging stricter enforcement, and introducing a leniency regime. Taken together, Law 155, Decree 2153, and Law 1340 govern most competition issues in Colombia. **8.08**

Nowadays, anticompetitive practices are analyzed under the general prohibition contained in article 1 of Law 155, and the prohibitions against specific actions in articles 47 (horizontal and vertical agreements), 48 (unilateral conducts), and 50 (abuse of the dominant position) of Decree 2153. The National Competition Authority, the Superintendence of Industry and Commerce (SIC) is in charge of enforcing these provisions. **8.09**

The main focus of the Authority has been in the fight against cartels; but there are, however, cases on unilateral conduct and abuse of dominance. Some of the most significant cases have been related to the agricultural sector and to other key economic activities such as cement and telecommunications. It seems that in the immediate future the authority will focus on **8.10**

---

[2] Colombia, like other Latin American countries applied for the most part of the twentieth century a development strategy based on "Protectionism" fostered by the Economic Commission for Latin America and the Caribbean—ECLAC. (The Spanish acronym for the ECLAC is CEPAL.) The institution was initially created as "the ECLA" by Economic and Social Council Resolution no. 106(VI) of February 25, 1948, and began to function that same year. Later on, its scope was broadened to include the countries of the Caribbean, and its name was changed to ECLAC by Resolution no. 1984/67 of July 27, 1984. The Spanish acronym, CEPAL, was kept.

the application of the so called Anti-Corruption Statute, which makes bid-rigging in public contracts both an anticompetitive agreement and a criminal offense.

I. Acting alone

8.11 Unilateral action is governed by three articles in the law: (i) article 1 of Law 155 which contains the general prohibition together with article 46 of Decree 2153; (ii) article 48 of Decree 2153 on unilateral conducts or anticompetitive acts; and (iii) article 50 of Decree 2153 which prohibits the abuse of a dominant position.

8.12 The conduct of abuse of dominance requires a prior proof of the dominant position of the investigated company. According to article 45(5) of Decree 2153, a company has a dominant position when it has the possibility of affecting directly or indirectly the conditions of the market.

8.13 The structure of Colombian competition laws allows for the application of two different systems of analysis to the investigation of anticompetitive conduct; these systems resemble the *per se rule* and the *rule of reason.*[3]

8.14 While the legislation specifically lists certain types of prohibited conduct, anticompetitive conduct that does not fall under the specific categories may be investigated by the SIC as an infringement of the general prohibition against anticompetitive behavior using a system that resembles the *rule of reason.* Accordingly, the SIC will take into consideration the relevant market, the nature, purpose, and effect of the conduct, and balance the pro-competitive against the anticompetitive effects of the conduct in order to establish if it violates the general prohibition. On the other hand, the types of conduct specifically described in the legislation are investigated according to the specific characteristics and elements of each conduct in a sort of per se rule of analysis. This means that when the Authority studies a specifically prohibited conduct, it focuses on the demonstration of the elements of a type of conduct considered as anticompetitive under the law; and will not accept explanations of legal or economic nature trying to demonstrate that the investigated conduct is not illegal. For example, article 48(2) of Decree 2153 prohibits influencing a company to increase its prices or abstaining from reducing them. The Authority will not accept evidence or arguments trying to demonstrate that the conduct caused no harm or that it was done with a beneficial intent or effect, because the law has defined such conduct as anti competitive.

8.15 The three kinds of anticompetitive acts specifically described in article 48 of Decree 2153, are: (i) violation of the advertisement regulations contained in the consumer protection laws;

[3] Even though there has been some academic debate around the application of the so-called per se rule of analysis in Colombian competition law, the issue appears to be settled both for the authorities and the Council of State. In 2000, the SIC decided to sanction ANDEVIP (*ANDEVIP*, Case no. 29302/2000), a group of surveillance companies that agreed upon the price charged for their services. Once accused, the companies argued that they entered into this agreement because the Superintendence of Surveillance and Private Security issued a regulation stating that whoever charged less than ten (10) minimum monthly wages for the surveillance service, was against labour and tax laws. The SIC considered that this was nevertheless a price fixing agreement and sanctioned the companies. In their reconsideration plea and later, before the administrative jurisdiction, the surveillance companies argued that the fact that they concluded an agreement did not mean that they were acting against the law, because their intention was not to restrict free competition. In the first instance decision, the Administrative Tribunal annulled the SIC decision on the grounds that it was not sufficient to enter into a price fixing agreement, but the SIC also had to demonstrate that the objectives of the law were damaged (efficiency, consumer welfare, and access to market) in order to impose a sanction. This position threatened the root of the per se analysis in Colombian antitrust law. However, the decision was appealed and the Council of State reversed the first instance decision, saying that in these cases the demonstration of the prohibited conduct was sufficient in order to impose a sanction.

(ii) influencing a company into increasing its prices or abstaining from reducing them; and (iii) unilateral refusal to deal or discrimination against a company, as a retaliation for its price policies.

The six kinds of conducts of abuse of dominance described in article 50 of Decree 2153, are: (i) predatory pricing; (ii) vertical discrimination or exploitative abuses; (iii) tying; (iv) horizontal discrimination or anticompetitive abuses; (v) regional predatory pricing or leveraging; and (vi) obstruction or blocking access to market or distribution channels. **8.16**

So far, the Authority has focused more on the repression of cartels and horizontal agreements in general, than on the investigation of unilateral conduct. However, there have been important cases in the areas of predatory pricing and influencing price increases. In the past few years, the Authority has been investigating cases of discrimination as an abuse of dominance of the gas distributors over the companies that compete with them in the construction of the internal installations needed in each household in order to connect the gas appliances. **8.17**

A. Predatory pricing

Predatory pricing is a conduct of abuse of dominance specifically prohibited by article 50(1) of Decree 2153. It consists in pricing below cost with the intention of eliminating competitors or deterring them from entering the market or expanding their business. There is a structural requirement for this conduct: only dominant undertakings can infringe article 50(1). **8.18**

According to article 45(5) of Decree 2153, a company has a dominant position when it has the possibility of affecting, directly or indirectly, the conditions of the market. In order to establish if a company has a dominant position, the SIC will first define the relevant market in its product, geographic and temporal dimensions, using conventional economic tools such as the SSNIP (small but significant non transitory increase in price) test.[4] Once the relevant market is defined, the SIC will analyze the concentration in the market with the help of concentration indexes such as the HHI, NEE, CR2, and CR4,[5] and others. The authority will then proceed to analyze barriers to entry and the contestability of the market in order to establish if the accused company enjoys a dominant position. **8.19**

In the General Competition Regime[6] there is no law, regulation, case law, or doctrine that allows for the presumption of dominance in the presence of a defined percentage of market concentration. However, pursuant to article 14(13) of Law 142 of 1994 (Public Utilities **8.20**

---

[4] Also called the "hypothetical monopolist test." The test is designed to measure the elasticity of demand of the selected product in the face of an increase in price. The test assumes that the market of the product under analysis is a monopoly. If in the face of a small but significant increase in price ordered by the monopolist, the consumers turn to consume other products, it means that those products also form part of the relevant market.

[5] The Herfindahl–Hirschman (HHI) test is a measure of the concentration of a market based in the sum of the squares of the participations of the companies in the market. It is therefore considered that a market with low concentration will have an HHI of less than 1000; a market with moderate concentration will have an index between 1000 and 1800 and a highly concentrated market will have an index above 1800.

The NEE Index represents the number of companies with similar size before and after of the merger transaction and reflects the diminution of competitor of equivalent size after the transaction.

The CR2 and CR4 Indexes show the market participation of the first two and first four firms that participate in the market.

[6] Pursuant to article 4 of Law 1340, the General Competition Regime is recognized as the set of general antitrust laws such as Law 155, Decree 2153, and Law 1340, applicable to all economic sectors and activities. If there are special competition laws, they will be applied in the first order to the specific sector or activity they regulate.

Law) a public utility company with a market participation equal or superior to 25 percent is considered as dominant. However, this is applicable only to public utilities.

8.21 When investigating predatory pricing, the SIC assesses pricing against total average costs,[7] and not variable costs. However, there is no binding requirement on the SIC or the courts to use this measure or apply the economic calculation thereof. It is then possible that the authority or the courts will use other definitions of costs for the determination of predatory pricing in the future. As to the requirement of the intention (*intenti*) to eliminate a market competitor or to prevent it from entering the market or expanding its business, the SIC considers that the agent's intent should be deduced from its behavior, taking into account its economic rationality. In the *Setas Colombianas* case, the SIC concluded that the economic behavior of the investigated company was reasonable because the reduction in its prices was not prolonged in time or unreasonable in the context of the market, and therefore did not amount to a predatory campaign.

8.22 In 2005, the SIC decided a case against Cadbury Adams,[8] a manufacturer of chewing gum with national presence and a dominant position in the market for mint flavored gum. In this category, Cadbury Adams participated with its product "Chiclets Adams," presented in a box priced at COP 200. When Confiteca, an Ecuadorian company entered the Colombian market with a low-cost mint-flavored chewing gum "Tumix" priced at COP 100. Cadbury Adams responded with a new product "Chiclets Clarks" priced at COP 50. The SIC concluded that Cadbury Adams was a dominant firm and that its conduct amounted to an abuse of dominance in the form of predatory pricing, because the price of COP 50 did not cover the cost of production of "Chiclets Clarks."

8.23 There is also a more specific prohibition against *regional predatory pricing*, as a conduct of abuse of dominance, in article 50(5) of Decree 2153. A company will be accused of regional predatory pricing when it sells its products at different prices in different regions with the intention, or the effect, of diminishing or eliminating its competitors in that region. Here, the SIC is not concerned with pricing below costs, but with pricing differentials not based on the costs of the transactions in different regions. This conduct can therefore be seen as a form of price discrimination.

8.24 In 2001 the SIC decided a case against a manufacturer of ice cream cones based in Medellín, with national presence and a dominant position based on its superior technology.[9] When a new company in Barranquilla started to compete aggressively, Induga started to sell its products on the Atlantic coast at a price lower than the one applied in the rest of the country, including Medellín. The SIC concluded that Induga was a dominant firm and that its conduct amounted to an abuse of dominance in the form of regional predatory pricing, for it was not reasonable that the price of the cones in Medellín (the company headquarters) was higher than the price on the coast, taking into consideration the cost of transportation. The decision was challenged before the administrative jurisdiction and the Council of State annulled the decision of the SIC on May 23, 2013.[10]

The Council of State considered that when delimiting the relevant market, the SIC did not consider other products with which consumers tend to replace ice cream cones, such as plastic recipients. If those products were considered the SIC would have concluded that Induga did not have a dominant position. The Council of State established that even if Induga had a

7 *Setas Colombianas S.A.*, SIC Case no. 30835/2004.

8 *Adams*, SIC Case no. 22624/2005.

9 *Induga S.A.*, SIC Case no. 15653/2001.

10 Council of State, Case File no. 25000-23-24-000-2001-01029-01.

dominant position, it did not sell its products in the Atlantic coast at a lower price than the one applied nation-wide. Hence, there was no infraction of any Colombian competition law. It must be noted that, as said earlier, the SIC focused on price discrimination and did not refer to prices below cost.

While article 50(5) of Decree 2153 requires dominance before an infringement can be found, non-dominant companies may be caught by the general prohibition under Law 155. In this case, the Authority will analyze the conduct using an approach similar to the rule of reason, and consider all aspects of the conduct and weigh its pro-competitive and anticompetitive effects. So far there have been no investigations regarding this conduct. **8.25**

This type of conduct could also be analyzed under the general prohibition of the unfair trade law, contained in article 7 of Law 256 of 1996 (Unfair Trade Law). The authorities that have jurisdiction over this type of case, that is, the SIC or the civil circuit judge, would consider if such a conduct is against the principle of good faith and honest commerce practices, and whether it can affect the decisions of consumers and the general operation of the market. **8.26**

Finally, it must be said that there have not been many investigations related to predatory pricing during the previous years. **8.27**

B. Exploitative offenses (excessive pricing, monopoly leveraging)

Article 50(2) of Decree 2153, prohibits companies with a dominant position from applying discriminatory conditions to equivalent transactions that put a supplier or a consumer at a disadvantage in relation to other suppliers or consumers. **8.28**

Excessive pricing is not specifically included as a form of abuse of dominance. However, the general prohibition contained in article 1 of Law 155 together with article 46 of Decree 2153, makes a reference to (unilateral or bilateral) types of conduct that serve to establish or maintain inequitable prices. That last sentence of article 1 of Law 155 was added by Special Decree 3307 of 1963 ("Decree 3307"), but had not been used to investigate excessive pricing until 2011. In 2011, the SIC opened an investigation against the Concessionaire of the San Andrés and Providencia Airports and the supplier of jet fuel to those airports, for allegedly entering into an agreement to indirectly fix an excessive price on the "access to platform fee" and for tying the supply of jet fuel to the airlines to the payment of such fee. The investigation is ongoing. It is important to note that in this case the SIC is investigating an alleged agreement and not a unilateral conduct. However, it is interesting that this case is not proceeding only on the grounds of price fixing and tying, described in Sections II.A and I.F respectively. This suggests that excessive pricing may be investigated as a standalone infringement in the future. **8.29**

Monopoly leveraging conduct is prohibited by article 98(1) of Law 142, which sets out one of the most important special competition regimes in Colombia. The SIC has investigated many undertakings for monopoly leveraging resulting in abuse of dominance. Specific investigations are ongoing against gas distributors and mobile carriers involving a violation of public utilities regulations and abuse of dominant position. **8.30**

C. Monopsony

Abusive conduct is usually committed by a business in a dominant selling position. However, Colombian competition law also considers the possibility that a buyer with enough power to influence market conditions can engage in abuse of dominance in similar terms as happens with companies in a selling position. These kinds of conduct will generally fall under article 50(2) of Decree 2153 which prohibits the abuse of dominance for vertical discrimination (discrimination against providers or clients). **8.31**

8.32 The SIC has carried out very few investigations related to abuse of dominance by a firm in a dominant purchasing position. The most important case investigated by the SIC was against Cooperativa Colanta Ltda.[11] This manufacturer of dairy products was exonerated after the authority found that the different conditions offered to suppliers of milk where justified by the quality of the products they had to offer.

D. Price discrimination

8.33 The standard for discrimination in Colombian competition law is drawn from article 13 of the Political Constitution, which guarantees equality under law. The Colombian Constitutional Court has derived this principle from the Aristotelian concept of distributive justice, encapsulated in the maxim "equality for equals." Reference to discrimination is found in the list of agreements and types of conduct of abuse of dominance.

8.34 Article 47(2) of Decree 2153 prohibits agreements that set sales or marketing conditions that are discriminatory against third parties. Article 50(2) prohibits vertical discrimination (exploitative abuses), that is, the application of differential conditions to equivalent transactions in such a way that providers or consumers are put in at a disadvantage as compared with other providers or consumers under similar conditions. Article 50(4) prohibits horizontal discrimination (anticompetitive abuses), that is, the imposition of different purchase conditions to different consumers when done with the purpose of diminishing or eliminating competition.

8.35 Further, article 50(5) of Decree 2153 prohibits regional predatory pricing as a conduct of abuse of dominance. This conduct allows the dominant firm to leverage a predatory campaign while charging monopolistic prices in other zones of the country. Discrimination arising from unilateral conduct is only punished as an abuse if carried out by a business in a dominant position. Where price differences, and differences in other conditions, can be explained by an objective factor, such as volume discounts, transportation costs, or any other market circumstances, there will be no infringement. As an example, the competition authorities investigated mobile phone companies for charging higher prices to consumers for calls from landlines to mobiles than for calls from mobiles to landlines.[12] The cellular companies offered a guarantee to the SIC in order to obtain the anticipated termination of the investigation without sanctions. The SIC accepted the proposal and the investigation ended without sanctions.

E. Dictating or influencing resale prices

8.36 In Colombia horizontal and vertical price fixing agreements are considered per se illegal under article 47(1) of Decree 2153.

8.37 There is no per se prohibition of unilateral resale price maintenance (RPM); this conduct is studied by SIC under the rule of reason.

8.38 Pursuant to article 48(2) of Decree 2153 a conduct is considered as anticompetitive if it aims to influence another company to increase its prices or to abstain from lowering them.

(i) Resale price maintenance

8.39 There has been intense debate in Colombia regarding the legality of unilateral RPM, for article 9 of Law 155 explicitly allowed manufacturers to set final resale retail prices, case in which the manufacturers, their distributors, and or independent retailers had an obligation

---

[11] *Cooperativa Colanta Ltda*, SIC Case no. 00588/2003.

[12] *Celumovil-Comcel*, Case no. 19444/2001.

to apply those prices. Further, the former Consumer Protection Statute, Decree no. 3466 of 1982 ("Decree 3466") explicitly allowed manufacturers and wholesalers to set retail prices.

Even though article 9 of Law 155 has not been expressly abolished, the SIC, backed by the Council of State, has interpreted that it was tacitly abrogated by the 1991 Constitution. On the other hand, Decree 3466 was entirely replaced by the new Consumer Protection Statute, Law no. 1480 of 2011 ("Law 1480") which does not refer to RPM. **8.40**

Finally, as mentioned earlier, article 48(2) of Decree 2153 prohibits a company from influencing another to increase its prices or abstain from lowering them. Article 48(3) of Decree 2153 further prohibits the conduct of unilateral refusal to deal as retaliation against a company's price policies. **8.41**

In 1999 the SIC concluded an investigation against a wholesaler of water measurement equipment.[13] Medidores Tavira was sanctioned by the SIC, for forcing its distributors to increase, or refrain from reducing, their prices. The decision was challenged before the administrative jurisdiction, and the Council of State upheld the SIC's decision. **8.42**

In 2001 the SIC decided a case against a Chocolate company.[14] Casa Luker was sanctioned by the SIC for influencing Makro, one of its distributors, requesting it to maintain the prices of their products, even though the products had been sold by Luker at a 7 percent discount. Luker was fined by the SIC. The decision was challenged before the administrative jurisdiction, and the Council of State upheld the SIC's decision. **8.43**

In summary, in Colombia it is per se illegal to enter into vertical agreements to set prices, and unilateral RPM is no longer considered lawful. As a matter of fact, the SIC considers that at each level of the production chain there should be an independent decision with regard to prices. Furthermore, it is expressly forbidden to influence a company to increase prices or to abstain from lowering them; the conduct of unilateral refusal to deal is also illegal when applied as retaliation against a company's price policies. Consequently, it is considered risky to enter into unilateral RPM and companies are advised to go as far as suggesting retail prices. For instance, in Colombia, many laboratories advertise a maximum suggested retail price on medication packaging, and this practice is accepted as legal by the SIC. **8.44**

(ii) Minimum advertised price programs

In Colombia, minimum advertised price (MAP) programs can be considered as a violation of article 48(2) of Decree 2153 in the sense that they prohibit distributors or retailers from applying lower prices than those set by the program. Even a minimum suggested retail price could be considered as a violation to this statute. **8.45**

F. Tying arrangements

In Colombia, tying is prohibited both as an agreement and as a unilateral conduct, case in which it is considered as an abuse of dominance only when committed by a company that enjoys a dominant position. **8.46**

Pursuant to article 47(7) of Decree 2153, it is considered as per se illegal to enter into agreements with the purpose, or the effect, of subordinating the supply of a product to the acceptance of additional obligations that were not naturally the object of the transaction. **8.47**

According to article 50(3) of Decree 2153, when a company enjoying a dominant position engages in tying conduct, as described above, it is liable for abuse. **8.48**

---

[13] *Compañía Colombiana de Medidores Tavira*, SIC Case nos. 27263/1999 and 13514/2000.

[14] *Casa Luker*, SIC Case nos. 8231/2001 and 20229/2001.

G. Exclusive dealing

8.49 Pursuant to article 47(3) of Decree 2153, it is considered per se illegal to enter into horizontal market distribution agreements. Vertical market distribution agreements are not explicitly prohibited by the law, which does not mean that they are always legal. Any such agreements will have to be analyzed using the rule of reason, under the general prohibition contained in article 1 of Law 155 in conjunction with article 46 of Decree 2153, in a way similar to the rule of reason analysis used by the US Supreme Court in the case of *Continental TV. v. GTE Sylvania*.[15]

8.50 Exclusive dealing clauses can also be considered a violation of article 47(10) of Decree 2153 which prohibits entering into agreements with the purpose or effect of obstructing or impeding third parties' access to markets or commercialization channels. This conduct is also considered as an abuse of dominance when performed unilaterally by a company that enjoys a dominant position.

8.51 Finally, it must also be considered that under article 19 of Law 256, entering into exclusive dealing clauses in supply contracts, with the purpose or effect of impeding competitors' access to the market or of monopolizing distribution channels, is unlawful.

H. Refusal to deal

8.52 In principle, businesses are free to choose with whom to engage in trading activities; in that sense, a refusal to deal hardly appears to be an antitrust violation. Nevertheless, article 48(3) of Decree 2153 specifically prohibits the conduct of unilateral refusal to deal when applied as retaliation against a company's pricing policy. The SIC imposed a financial penalty on veterinary laboratories Gabrica Ltda because Gabrica refused to supply distributors who had not followed the company's price policy.[16] It is important to notice that the Superintendence established that such retaliation is an infringement of antitrust law even if it is carried out with the objective of preventing distributors from pricing products below costs.

8.53 The conduct of unilateral refusal to deal is considered illegal under article 48(3) of Decree 2153, when the refusal to deal is real and not just a threat. However, the threat of refusal to deal can also be a violation of article 48(2), as seen in the *Gabrica* case,[17] when the threat is aimed at influencing a company to raise its prices or to abstain from lowering them.[18]

8.54 Finally, the unilateral refusal to deal performed by a company that enjoys a dominant position, can be considered as horizontal or vertical discrimination abuse, or an impediment to access to the market, in violation of article 50(2), (4), and (6) of Decree 2153.[19]

I. Essential facilities

8.55 The doctrine of essential facilities is not expressly developed in the General Competition Regime. It is however, a fundamental principle of the Information Technologies Law no. 1341 of 2009 ("Law 1341"). Pursuant to article 4(9) of Law 1341, State intervention is needed in order to guarantee access to network elements and essential facilities. Article 22(3) of Law 1341 grants the Commission for Regulation of Communications (CRC) the capacity to issue a regulation related to the access and use of essential facilities in the IT sector. Article 22(6) and (10) of Law 1341 grant the CRC the power to define the essential facilities and

---

15 *Continental TV. v. GTE Sylvania* 433 U.S. 36 (1977).
16 *Gabrica*, SIC Case no. 8310/2003.
17 *Gabrica* (n 12).
18 See further Section I.E.
19 See Section I.D.

to impose easements (mandatory rights of use) of such infrastructure. During the last two decades, there have been numerous procedures aimed at imposing easements in the IT sector.

Refusal of the use of an essential facility could be interpreted by the SIC as an abuse of dominance in the IT sector, or in any other economic sector. In the 1990s, the SIC launched an investigation against Drummond Ltd., one of the most important coal producers in Colombia. Drummond obtained a contract from the national railway company Ferrovías, which granted it priority in the use of the northern railway connecting Bogotá (in the center of the country) and Santa Marta (on the northern coast) in order to transport coal from the coal mine in Cesar to the coast. Prodeco, a new competitor in the coal market accused Drummond of abuse of dominance based on the priority it enjoyed in the use of the railway. Prodeco argued that discriminatory conditions were applied to equivalent operations, which placed Prodeco and other users of the railway in a disadvantageous position. The SIC accepted the guarantees offered by Drummond and Ferrovías. Specifically, these companies agreed to modify the priority clauses that originated this situation in the contract. The outcome was that Drummond began to share the railway, and the investigation was terminated without sanctions. **8.56**

J. Bundling (including loyalty and market share discounts)

In general terms, bundling is permitted and even considered as pro-competitive when it is used as a means of offering new products or a combination of products that will satisfy consumer needs. A unilateral bundling strategy can be analyzed under the general prohibition contained in article 1 of Law 155, together with article 46 of Decree 2153. However, a horizontal or vertical agreement to offer bundles of products or services can infringe various antitrust statutes. **8.57**

It is important to distinguish bundling from tying. Article 47(7) of Decree 2153 prohibits tying agreements, and article 50(3) prohibits tying as an abuse of dominance. Under Colombian law, tying is an agreement or abusive conduct aimed to subordinate the supply of a product to the acceptance of additional obligations that are not a natural part of the business transaction. **8.58**

In 2001, the SIC decided an abuse of dominance case against Bavaria S.A., the biggest manufacturer of beer in Colombia, owned by SABMiller,.[20] Heineken accused Bavaria of abuse of dominance, in relation to the launching of the Peroni beer brand. Heineken accused Bavaria of engaging in an abusive tying scheme that forced high-end bars and restaurants to advertise exclusively Bavaria beers as a condition for the sale of the Bavaria products. Bavaria was able to demonstrate that the sponsor contracts it used to promote the Peroni beer were temporary, that they required exclusivity of advertisement but not exclusivity of sales, and that they were used in a very limited number of bars and restaurants in Colombia. The investigation ended without sanctions for Bavaria. **8.59**

The Authority has discussed loyalty discounts in the past. They can be considered illegal if they amount to tying of some sort. **8.60**

K. Standard-setting groups (disclosure requirements, licensing arrangements, and licensing pools)

As will be explained in Section I.O, article 49 of Decree 2153 contains explicit exceptions to Colombian competition law. One of those exceptions is contained in article 49(2), which **8.61**

[20] *Bavaria*, SIC Case no. 33361/2011.

excludes from the scrutiny of the antitrust laws agreements involving compliance with non-mandatory standard settings and measures adopted by the competent body, provided that they do not create artificial barriers to the entry of new competitors to the market.

8.62 As can be seen, Colombian competition law recognizes the pro-competitive effects standard-setting groups can have. They can lead to increased market transparency, which in turn leads to lower transaction costs and higher market efficiency. However, these groups create an antitrust risk due to information exchange between competitors (dealt with in Section II.H), or even actual cartel activity arising under the auspices of a standard-setting group. Further, these groups can agree standards that effectively exclude non-abiding undertakings from the market.

8.63 The SIC has recognized the advantages of standard-setting groups.[21] However, it has made clear also that the authority will not tolerate the abuse of the setting groups as the cover for the planning or executing of anticompetitive conducts.

8.64 The SIC has also made it clear that some of the activities of the standard-setting groups can limit competition, or even infringe on the interests of consumers and other economic agents. Thus, those entities must refrain from activities that have the potential of restricting competition.[22]

8.65 The greatest concern of the Superintendence regarding standard-setting groups is the information exchange that takes place within them. Section II.H has further explanations regarding this conduct.

8.66 To reflect this concern, article 2(49) of Decree 2153 establishes that standard-setting agreements should respect certain parameters. In particular, standard-setting agreements should not be mandatory and should not exclude new competitors from the market.

L. Customer termination

8.67 Customer termination can be the valid consequence of contractual conditions between a company and its clients. However, it can also amount to anticompetitive conduct in the form of anticompetitive agreements (art. 47 of Decree 2153) or abuse of dominance (art. 50 of Decree 2153).

8.68 A horizontal or vertical agreement to terminate a certain customer can violate article 47(2) of Decree 2153. When a dominant company decides to terminate a customer without a valid business reason, it may be liable for an abuse of dominance in the form of a vertical discrimination in violation of article 50(2) of Decree 2153.

8.69 Patterns of customer termination may also suggest the existence of market allocation or a production quota agreement between upstream competitors, and both of those types of conduct are banned under article 47 of Decree 2153.

M. Termination of intermediaries (retailers, wholesalers, dealers, and value-added resellers, agents, and brokers)

8.70 As was pointed out with respect of customers, termination of intermediaries can be the valid consequence of contractual conditions between a company and its vertical allies. However,

---

[21] *Fendipetróleo*, Case no. 71794/2011.

[22] *Asociación de Hospitales de Risaralda (ASORALDA)*, Case no. 56311/2011.

it can also amount to anticompetitive conduct in the form of anticompetitive acts (art. 48 of Decree 2153) or abuse of dominance (art. 50 of Decree 2153).

Unilateral refusal to deal, as retaliation against a company's pricing policy, infringes article 48(3) of Decree 2153. As in the case of customers, when a dominant company decides to terminate an intermediary without a valid business reason, it can be liable for an abuse of dominance in the form of a vertical discrimination in violation of article 50(2) of Decree 2153. **8.71**

The situation of a producer that engages in direct sales, and at the same time uses an independent distribution channel, raises interesting competition issues and concerns related to the vertical intra-brand competition created between the producer and its distribution channel. **8.72**

The intra-brand competition between a manufacturer that engages in direct sales and its independent distribution channel creates a delicate situation in which the agents or distributors can easily feel that the producer is discriminating against them or that its conduct amounts to unfair trade. **8.73**

From the perspective of the Colombian Competition Authority, vertical relationships between the manufacturer and the distributors raises questions related to vertical agreements, abuse of dominance, unfair trade, and merger review. **8.74**

In 2011, Holcim terminated its relationship with one of its distributors in Medellín (Department of Antioquia), Colcementos, based on the latter's defaulting on the payment of its invoices. Colcementos accused Holcim of abuse of dominance and unfair trade.[23] **8.75**

The SIC acquitted Holcim in both cases at the level of the preliminary investigation: the first case related to abuse of dominance and the second related to unfair competition. In the abuse of dominance case, the SIC concluded that, with only 6 percent of market participation, Holcim's conduct was not significant and had no capacity to affect competition. The SIC took into consideration the fact that Colcementos continued in the market selling other brands of cement. **8.76**

In the unfair competition case, the SIC stated that the conflict between the parties, rather than a conflict of unfair competition, was a contractual conflict, and if the distributor wished to claim an indemnification pursuant to the alleged damages, it should file a contractual liability action. **8.77**

N. Termination of relationships with competitors

Relationships with competitors must always be considered carefully for they can be interpreted by the SIC as anticompetitive agreements. There are however, many relationships of this kind that are perfectly legal, such as joint procurement, supply of raw materials, use of essential or joint facilities, logistic services, etc. Such relationships may have a vertical dimension, and in those cases the analysis in Section I.M applies to the termination of relationships with competitors. **8.78**

O. Exemptions

There are two kinds of exemptions under Colombian competition law: (i) the so-called block exemptions contained in article 1 of Law 155 and article 5 of Law 1340, including a general block exemption, applicable to all economic sectors and industries, and a block exemption for the agricultural sector; and (ii) the specific exemptions contained in article 49 of Decree 2153. **8.79**

[23] *Colcementos v. Holcim—Abuse of Dominance*, Case nos. 56821/2011 and 7287/2012; *Colcementos v. Holcim—Unfair Competition*, Case nos. 56823/2011 and 7285/2012.

8.80 Pursuant to article 1 of Law 155, the government can authorize agreements that, despite being anti competitive, are aimed at defending the stability of a basic sector producing goods or services of importance to the general economy of the country. Later on, article 1 of Decree 1302 of 1964 ("Decree 1302") defined the basic sectors producing goods or services of importance to the general economy and social welfare of the country. The definition covered all economic activities that are, or may be in the future, of fundamental importance in rationally structuring the country's economy, as these activities supply goods or services indispensable for the general well-being of the population, such as production and distribution of food, clothing, basic sanitation, and housing. This category also includes production and distribution of fuel, and services such as banking, education, transportation, electricity, aqueduct, telecommunications, and insurance.

8.81 As a result of the rise of the antitrust cases in the agriculture sector, in 2009, Congress decided to include in article 5 of Law 1340 a special block exemption provision specifically for the livestock and agricultural sector. According to this article, the livestock and agricultural sector is a basic sector of importance to economy in general. Article 5 further orders the Ministry of Agriculture and Rural Development to issue a motivated and binding report before the SIC can authorize the agreements aimed at the stabilization of the sector.

8.82 Finally, in 1992, article 49 of Decree 2153 introduced three specific exceptions to the application of competition laws in any economic sector. Article 49(1) excludes conducts aimed at the research and development of new technology. Article 49(2) excludes agreements related to the adoption of set standards (see Section I.K) as long as they are adopted by the competent body, are not mandatory, and do not create barriers to the entry of new competitors. Article 49(3) excludes conduct involving procedures, methods, and systems for the use of joint facilities.

II. Dealing with competitors

A. Horizontal price fixing

8.83 As in many other jurisdictions, in Colombia, horizontal price fixing agreements represent the most basic infraction to Competition Laws. In that regard, article 47(1) of Decree 2153 defines as per se illegal all agreements entered into with the purpose or effect of fixing prices directly or indirectly. The law does not distinguish between minimum and maximum prices or between horizontal and vertical price fixing agreements, and for that reason, as pointed out earlier, it is considered that both kinds are expressly prohibited and therefore per se illegal.[24]

8.84 The SIC considers agreements that fix prices indirectly just as harmful as those that fix them directly. In 2010, the SIC investigated several sugar manufacturers for entering into a horizontal agreement to fix the price of the sugar cane they buy to the producers.[25] In this case, the SIC claimed that the manufacturers set the price of the sugar cane using a formula based on the final price at which sugar was sold. The Authority questioned the fact that the application of the different formulas used by the manufacturers, resulted in sharing with the sugar cane producers no more than 50 percent of the income gained from the sale of the sugar. The Authority considered that despite the different prices paid for the sugar cane at different points in time, the formulas applied by the manufacturers amounted to an indirect agreement to fix the price of sugar cane.

[24] See Section I.

[25] *Sugar Cane Mills*, SIC Case no. 6839/2010.

The SIC considered agreements fixing maximum or minimum prices are equally harmful. In 2004, the SIC imposed fines on a group of transportation companies that entered into an agreement in order to protect customers from excessive pricing.[26] **8.85**

Consistent with the per se illegality of horizontal price fixing under Colombian law, other defenses have also been ineffective. In 2000, the SIC decided a case against real estate agents for an agreement to fix the commission they charged their clients at 3 percent.[27] In this case, the defendants argued that there was a mercantile use or custom in Bogotá, which was mandatory under the Commercial Code. The SIC concluded that mercantile uses or customs cannot go against the law, and imposed fines on all the companies that participated in this price fixing agreement. The decision was challenged before the administrative jurisdiction, and the Council of Stated upheld the decision taken by the SIC. **8.86**

It is also important to underscore that, pursuant to article 45(1) of Decree 2153, for antitrust purposes an agreement is defined as a contract, convention, concerted practice, or conscious parallelism. The SIC has investigated both express and tacit agreements. There have been investigations into tacit collusion based both on concerted practices and on conscious parallelism. **8.87**

In 2008, the SIC decided a case against the cement manufacturers Cementos Argos, Holcim Colombia, Cemex Colombia, and Cementos Andino.[28] In this case, the SIC imposed a fine on the investigated companies for entering into a price fixing agreement. According to the Authority, there was no reasonable economic explanation for the pricing conduct of the companies, and as a result, there was a high possibility that the companies in question had entered into a concerted practice in order to fix their prices. **8.88**

In 2009, the SIC decided another case on the grounds of concerted practice. This case involved Derilac and Colanta, two manufacturers of dairy products accused of fixing milk prices.[29] The SIC deduced the existence of the agreement from the fact that the investigated companies printed the same retail price on milk bags during 1997, 1998, and 1999, and it was clear that the prices were raised by the same amount at the same time. The SIC concluded that a contract or agreement was not necessary for a concerted or consciously parallel practice to exist. The mere existence of the conduct proved that there was, indeed, a price-fixing agreement. The SIC sanctioned these companies. The decision was challenged before the administrative jurisdiction, and the Council of Stated upheld the decision taken by the SIC. **8.89**

In 2009, the SIC decided a case against several gas stations, including "La Pedregosa" owned by Rafael Ortiz Mantilla, for a price-fixing agreement that lead to an increase in the price of four-star gasoil.[30] It was relevant for the SIC's analysis that the price increases took place at the same time. The decision was challenged before the administrative jurisdiction, and the Council of State upheld the decision taken by the SIC. **8.90**

There have been price fixing investigations in many economic sectors, but it seems important to highlight the investigations related to the agricultural sector, where the SIC decided cases against the industries that acquire the crops from the producers: **8.91**

- Investigation against the rice mills for an agreement to fix the price of the green *paddy* rice.[31]

[26] *Cooperativa Colombiana de Transportadores Ltda*, SIC Case no. 21821/2004.
[27] *Realtors*, SIC Case no. 27759/1999 and 7508/2000.
[28] *Cement*, SIC Case no. 51694/2008.
[29] *Derilac—Colanta*, SIC Case no. 27762/1999.
[30] *Gas Stations*, SIC Case no. 08732/2002.
[31] *Rice Mills*, SIC Case no. 22065/2005.

- Investigation against the Chocolate companies for an agreement to fix the price of the cocoa beans.[32]
- Investigation against the sugar manufacturers for an agreement to fix the price of the sugar cane.[33]

8.92 It must be said, that to this date, horizontal price fixing remains the main cause for investigations in Colombia.

B. Horizontal agreements to allocate customers or territories; agreements not to compete

8.93 Horizontal market allocation agreements, including customer, supplier, or geographic market allocation are considered per se illegal under article 47(3) of Decree 2153 which expressly prohibits agreements with the purpose or effect of allocating markets among producers or distributors. In 1999, the SIC launched an investigation against cement manufacturers and their association, the Colombian Cement Institute—ICPC, for an alleged horizontal market distribution agreement in violation of article 47(3) of Decree 2153, and an agreement to share confidential and commercially sensitive information through the ICPC in violation of the general prohibition contained in article 1 of Law 155. The SIC aimed to demonstrate that the cement companies had divided the country among themselves, and that they controlled this agreement by sending the ICPC a weekly report of the locations and clients where they made sales and by receiving from the Institute a report that provided each company with the same information. The companies explained that, due to its character and to the cost of transportation, each manufacturer sells its product mainly in the area closer to the plant. The companies offered a guarantee consisting *inter alia* in a protocol of information that did not allow them to monitor the sales of their competitors. The SIC accepted the guarantees, and the investigation was terminated without sanctions.

8.94 Article 47(5) of Decree 2153 also prohibits agreements entered into with the purpose or effect of assigning, distributing, or limiting the supply sources of raw materials. In the case against the Sugar Manufacturers,[34] the SIC accused the companies of concluding an agreement to divide among themselves the sugar cane growers, so that they could sell their crops only to the assigned mill. In this case, the Sugar Manufacturers were also accused and sanctioned for an agreement to indirectly fix the price of the sugar cane by using a formula; however, they were able to demonstrate to the SIC that there was no agreement to allocate the lands planted with sugar cane. The defense argued that the character of this industry demanded that each mill buy crops from the closest farms possible, for once the cane has been cut it has to be taken to the mill as soon as possible because sugar starts to degrade very quickly. The SIC accepted this argument and the investigated companies were acquitted of this accusation.

8.95 It must be noted that Colombian law does not prohibit vertical market distribution, for example, vertical territorial exclusivity granted by a manufacturer to its distributors. This does not mean that such vertical agreements can be considered as always lawful; what it means is that they are not illegal per se, but they can be always investigated under the general prohibition contained in article 1 of Law 155 in conjunction with article 46 of Decree 2153, using the rule of reason analysis.

8.96 In 1999, the SIC began an investigation against the three soft drinks manufacturers in Colombia: Postobon, Panamco (Coca-Cola), and Bavaria.[35] The SIC accused the producers

[32] *Chocolate Manufacturers*, SIC Case no. 52202/2009.
[33] *Sugar Manufacturers*, SIC Case nos. 6839/2007 and 42411/2010.
[34] *Sugar Manufacturers* (n 33).
[35] *Soft Drinks*, SIC Case no. 19644/2000.

and their distributors of horizontal and vertical price fixing agreements in violation of article 47(1) of Decree 2153; and of horizontal and vertical market allocation in violation of article 47(3) of Decree 2153. The investigated companies explained that they had not entered into horizontal or vertical price fixing. They argued that the manufacturers unilaterally imposed on the distributors the price at which they had to sell the product to the retailers. Regarding market allocation, the manufacturers argued that they did not have a horizontal agreement but that they awarded territories to their distributors in order to reduce costs and increase efficiency in their distribution channel, therefore increasing inter-brand competition in the market. The companies were able to convince the Authority that there were no per se violations, and that under the rule of reason, their conduct to unilaterally impose prices on their distributors and award territories for logistic purposes had pro-competitive effects and fostered inter-brand competition. The SIC accepted the guarantees offered by the companies and terminated the investigation without sanctions. The SIC accepted the unilateral RPM imposed on the distributors and the vertical market allocation for logistic purposes.

As shown in Section I.G, exclusivity clauses between a manufacturer and its distributors can **8.97** also be investigated as an unfair trade practice under article 19 of Law 256. According to this article, including exclusive dealing clauses in supply contracts, with the purpose or effect of impeding access of the competitors to the market or monopolizing distribution channels, is considered to constitute unfair competition.

Non-competition agreements will be investigated under the general prohibition contained in **8.98** article 1 of Law 155, in conjunction with article 46 of Decree 2153 using the rule of reason analysis. Even though there is not much development or conceptualization on the part of the SIC, it is considered that non-competition clauses can be accepted in certain circumstances when they are reasonable, limited in time, and can serve a meritorious purpose. For instance, it is only natural that a non-competition clause is included in a merger deal in order to avoid the risk of confusion or unfair trade on the part of the seller.

There are however, other restrictive agreements that are specifically prohibited and are con- **8.99** sidered as per se illegal:

- Agreements entered into with the purpose or effect of assigning production or supply quotas are considered per se illegal under article 47 (4) of Decree 2153.
- Agreements entered into with the purpose or effect of limiting technical developments are considered per se illegal under article 47 (6) of Decree 2153.
- Agreements entered into with the purpose or effect of abstaining to manufacture a product or provide a service or to affect the levels of production, are considered per se illegal under article 47 (8) of Decree 2153.

C. Horizontal boycotts

An agreement between competitors boycotting specific businesses or under specific condi- **8.100** tions is an antitrust infringement that can be investigated under the general prohibition contained in article 1 of Law 155, in conjunction with article 46 of Decree 2153, as well as under article 47(2) of Decree 2153, which specifically prohibits and considers entering into agreements with the purpose or effect of establishing conditions of sale or commercialization that are discriminatory to third parties, per se illegal; and finally, under article 47(3) and (8) of Decree 2153, which refer to market allocation and restriction to production, respectively.

In 2001, the SIC sanctioned the agricultural wholesaler Corabastos and a number of onion **8.101** producers for entering into an agreement not to allow other onion retailers to distribute their products in Corabastos.[36] The companies were accused of the infraction described in article 47(3) and (8) of Decree 2153.

D. Joint ventures and other competitive collaborations

8.102 Joint ventures and other forms of horizontal or vertical collaboration are legitimate ways of doing business. The SIC has even prepared the *Draft Guidelines for Collaboration Agreements between Competitors* (2012), which have not been officially issued.

8.103 The main problem when studying joint ventures is to draw the line between those that amount to an economic integration subject to merger review; and those that do not have that implication. The test for deciding whether a joint venture amounts to an economic integration or not refers to the response of four questions: (i) whether the interested companies participate in the same economic activity (horizontal) or belong to the same value chain (vertical); (ii) whether the economic and market participation thresholds are met;[37] (iii) whether the joint venture subordinates the corporate policy of the participating companies, to the authority of one decision making body; and (iv) whether this subordination is permanent in time. If the answer to these questions is affirmative, then we are confronted with an economic integration subject to merger review under articles 9 to 13 of Law 1340.

8.104 All collaboration agreements must avoid the specific prohibitions contained in articles 47, 48, and 50 of Decree 2153. They will be analyzed under the general prohibition contained in article 1 of Law 155, considered in conjunction with article 46 of decree 2153, using the rule of reason. The SIC will consider, *inter alia*, whether competition in the industry in general and among the participating companies in particular is therefore reduced; whether the companies gain market participation; whether a new participant will be therefore admitted into the market; whether there will be benefit to the consumers, etc.

8.105 Some of the most common collaboration agreements are: collaboration for production; collaboration for marketing; collaboration for procurement; collaboration for research and development (which is specifically exempt under article 49(1) of Decree 2153); and collaboration for information sharing.

E. Trade associations

8.106 Articles 38 and 39 of the Political Constitution guarantee "...the right to free association for the development of the various activities that people carry out in society" and also the creation and operation of associations "...without the intervention of the State." As can be seen, trade associations are legal and have the protection of the Constitution, but this does not mean that they are exempt from the application of Competition laws, for article 333 of the Constitution protects free competition as a right of all people, which implies responsibilities. This means that trade associations, legal as they are, cannot be used as an instrument for engaging in anticompetitive practices. As a matter of fact, pursuant to article 2 of Law 1340, competition law is applicable to "...anyone that develops an economic activity or affects or may affect such activity, independently of their form or legal nature." In this sense, trade associations can also be guilty of unfair trade practices, pursuant to article 22 of Law 256.

---

[36] *Corabastos-Onion Producers*, SIC Case no. 8233/2001.

[37] The economic threshold is met if the world wide operational income or the assets of the interested companies, individually or jointly considered, amount to 100,000 times the minimum monthly wages (around USD 30,000,000). If the economic threshold is not met, then the transaction does not need to be reported to the SIC. If it is met, then it is important to define whether the market participation of the companies, individually or jointly, in any of the markets affected by the transaction is of 20 percent or more. If the answer is negative, then the transaction is only subject to a short-form *notification* (no waiting period). If the answer is affirmative, then the transaction is subject to a long-form *information* (waiting period).

Trade associations are in fact economic agents that have impact in the markets in which the associated undertakings perform their activities. It is important that the behavior of the association and of the companies respect antitrust regulation, especially as recent trends show SIC's growing interest in the way this entities work. The draft trade associations guidelines prepared by the SIC recommend that these entities (i) avoid setting or recommending commercial conditions or a specific way of conducting businesses; (ii) abide information exchange guidelines; (iii) abstain from coordinating actions among its associates; and (iv) abstain from discriminating their members based their commercial conduct or nature. **8.107**

Associations must be careful in order to avoid infringements, particularly when taking actions that may directly or indirectly influence the way their members make decisions, which in principle should be taken freely and individually. **8.108**

The SIC has investigated several cases involving trade associations: **8.109**

- The SIC investigated the Colombian Cement Institute—ICPC[38] for an alleged agreement to share confidential and commercially sensitive information through the ICPC, in violation of the general prohibition contained in article 1 of Law 155. The case was settled without sanctions.
- The SIC imposed sanctions to the Association of Television Channels[39] for limiting access of competitors to a necessary procurement of certain inputs for their businesses.
- The SIC imposed sanctions to the Colombian Integral Medicine Association (ACEMI) for facilitating information exchange between the HMOs, aimed to influence the amount of money granted by the social security system to the HMOs for the health plan of each affiliated person.[40]
- The SIC investigated the Colombian Banking Association and other financial institutions for allegedly entering into an anticompetitive agreement to fix the Interbank Exchange Tariff (TII by its initials in Spanish) for the handling of credit cards between financial institutions.[41] The case was settled without sanctions.

F. Interlocking directorates

Article 5 of Law 155 expressly prohibits the legal representatives and members of the board of directors of companies in the industrial and commercial sectors[42] from holding similar positions in companies dedicated to the same economic activities, in order to avoid a conflict of interest and prevent anticompetitive conduct among the companies. Even though there is no express exception in the Law, the SIC has interpreted that this prohibition does not apply to companies that respond to the same control or form part of the same economic group[43] as defined by Law no. 222 of 1995 ("Law 222").[44] **8.110**

---

[38] *Cement-ICPC*, SIC Case no. 17464/1999.

[39] *UCEP*, SIC Case no. 23890/2011.

[40] *ACEMI*, SIC Case no. 41611/2011.

[41] *TII*, SIC Case no. 40478-53990/2012.

[42] There are special rules for interlocking directorates in the financial sector regulation and in other special legislation. For instance, in the public utilities sector, art. 21 of Law no. 142 of 1994 ("Law 142") allows a person to participate in the boards of directors of two companies dedicated to the same kind of service (water, electricity, sewage, etc.), provided that the companies do not participate in the same city or geographical zone.

[43] This is similar to the decision of the US Supreme Court in *Copperweld Corp. v. Independence Tube Corp.* 467 U.S. 752 (1984).

[44] *La Camisa Alemana Ltda*, SIC Case no. 31965/2003. Pursuant to Article 28 of Law 222, there is an economic group when in addition to control, there is unity of purpose and direction among the companies that integrate the group.

8.111 Article 6 of Law 155 forbids the legal representatives and members of the board of directors of companies in the industrial and commercial sectors, to participate directly or indirectly in companies that distribute the products or services of the company they serve.

8.112 Finally, pursuant to article 23 of Law 222, members of the board of directors of any company, have a duty not to compete against the company that they serve, and to avoid any conflict of interest. When a conflict of interest arises, the board member's obligation is to reveal it to the company's general assembly, so that the maximum body of the company can decide whether the board member should be separated from the matter that gave place to the conflict.

G. Facilitating practices

8.113 Facilitating practices are not considered as standalone offenses. See further Section II.H on information exchange.

H. Information exchange

8.114 Information exchange normally is not just legal but desirable as long as it allows agents to compete on equal footing, taking into account that one of the assumptions for perfect competition is perfect information sharing among suppliers and customers. However, private information exchange may also be likely to restrict competition when it concerns sensitive information that facilitates anticompetitive cartel-like behavior. The SIC considers that even the most casual or informal exchange may lead to agreements or tacit behaviors that affect market functioning. For example, information exchange is likely to constitute an antitrust infringement when it concerns sensitive matters such as pricing, production quantities, cost structure, or marketing policies.

8.115 Information exchange is not specifically prohibited under the General Competition Regime: it is not included within any of the types of conduct prohibited by articles 47 (ten kinds of agreements), 48 (three kinds of acts), or 50 (six kinds of abuse of dominance conducts) of Decree 2153. Information exchange is therefore not considered illegal per se and must be studied as a violation of the general prohibition, under the rule of reason analysis.

8.116 In the *Cement* case decided by the SIC in the 1990s,[45] the SIC investigated cement manufacturers and the Colombian Cement Institute—ICPC for an agreement to share confidential and commercially sensitive information in violation of the general prohibition contained in article 1 of Law 155. The SIC established that, though the exchange of detailed and daily information was not per se illegal, it was preferable for the companies to have only consolidated information, which would allow them to elaborate free and independent tendencies and projections. The investigation ended with a settlement and without fines because the companies offered guarantees consisting, *inter alia*, in an information protocol that did not allow them to monitor the sales of their competitors.

8.117 The SIC has allowed information exchange between competitors where the information is aggregate and historic. What constitutes "historic information" will largely depend on the particular dynamics of the relevant market under study.

8.118 Information exchange is also caught by sector-specific regimes (see Section III.A). The SIC sanctioned the Colombian Integral Medicine Association (ACEMI) for information exchange that led to anticompetitive agreements between the HMOs, aimed to influence the amount of money granted by the social security system to the HMOs for the health plan of each affiliated person.[46]

[45] *Cement–ICPC*, Case 17464-546/1999.
[46] *ACEMI* (n 40).

In the *Draft Guidelines for Collaboration Agreements Between Competitors*[47] prepared by the SIC, there are recommendations regarding information exchange. For example, the Guidelines establish that the exchange of information related to actual or future situations is more likely to constitute an infringement; it is therefore recommended that information exchanges refer to historical information. This is especially relevant for the information handled within trading associations. **8.119**

I. Joint purchasing agreements

Joint purchasing agreements are not specifically prohibited under the General Competition Regime, but they are not included within any of the conducts prohibited by articles 47 (ten kinds of agreements), 48 (three kinds of acts), or 50 (six kinds of abuse of dominance conducts) of Decree 2153. They are therefore not considered illegal per se and must be studied as a violation of the general prohibition, under the rule of reason analysis. **8.120**

Pursuant to the *Draft Guidelines for Collaboration Agreements Between Competitors*,[48] the SIC considers that Joint Purchasing Agreements can reduce transactional costs, but must be done carefully so that the participant companies do not engage in illegal conduct such as price fixing or market distribution agreements. Joint purchasing agreements reduce transactional costs as they centralize the offer or demand of a certain product or service. Nonetheless, the latter cannot lead to the standardization of prices, commercial conditions, and as a scenario to access strategic commercial information of competitors. **8.121**

Thus, it is important that the company or entity in charge of joint purchasing has strict confidentiality standards and abides by the *Draft Guidelines for Collaboration Agreements Between Competitors*.[49] **8.122**

J. Joint lobbying/regulatory/legislative efforts

Colombian competition law has not developed the equivalent to the *Noerr Pennington Doctrine* in the US. **8.123**

However, as with trade associations and joint purchasing agreements, there is no specific prohibition related to joint lobbying, but undertakings should be careful to make sure that their cooperation does not mutate into illegal agreements or practices. **8.124**

In the case that the SIC ruled against the health care sector, the HMOs and the Colombian Integral Medicine Association (ACEMI) were investigated for exchanging information that led to anticompetitive agreements between the HMOs, aimed to influence the amount of money granted by the Social Security System (the Government) to the HMOs for the health plans of every affiliated person.[50] **8.125**

III. General issues

A. Jurisdiction and applicable law (including sector-specific competition regulation)

As explained earlier, article 333 of the Political Constitution (1991) protects free competition as a right of all the people. Pursuant to article 2 of Law 1340, legislation related to the protection of competition includes references to anticompetitive agreements, acts, abuse of **8.126**

---

47 *Draft Guidelines for Collaboration Agreements Between Competitors* (2012), <http//www.sic.gov.co>.
48 *Draft Guidelines for Collaboration* (n 47).
49 *Draft Guidelines for Collaboration* (n 47).
50 *ACEMI* (n 40).

dominance, and merger control. This legislation is applicable to "...anyone who develops an economic activity or affects or may affect such activity, independently of their form or legal nature."

8.127 According to article 4 of Law 1340 the General Competition Regime created by Law 155, Decree 2153, Law 1340, and amendments, applies to all economic sectors and activities. The application of specific sector competition regulation will prevail in the specific sector.

8.128 The reference to the application of the General Competition Regime to all economic sectors and activities is one of the most important achievements of Law 1340. Prior to the enactment of this law, it was utterly impossible to amend or interpret the less technical complete sector-specific regulations using the more solid and complete concepts and principles contained in the General Competition Regime.

8.129 The most important sector-specific competition regulations are contained in the following laws and decrees:

- Law 142, 1994: Public Utilities Law.
- Decree 663, 1993: Financial and Insurance Sector Statute.
- Decree 1663, 1993: Competition Statute for Health Services.
- Law 1, 1991: Ports Law.
- Law 1341, 2009: IT Law.

B. Antitrust system

8.130 As in most Latin American countries, in Colombia the main weight in the application of Competition Laws depends on the activity of the National Competition Authority, the Superintendence of Industry and Commerce.

8.131 The SIC conducts preliminary investigations that are launched by decision of the authority, or following accusations from any citizen. If the Authority finds a possible infraction, it will issue a resolution with a formal accusation against identified persons and companies. This resolution is notified to the accused persons who will have a term of twenty working days to present and request evidence and, if they decide so, to offer "guarantees"—a procedural benefit that allows the investigated parties to request the anticipated termination of the investigation, without sanctions, by guaranteeing the Authority that they will behave in a way consistent with competition laws and in compliance with a set of obligations, including a collateral in the form of a bond. The Superintendent can accept or reject the guarantees at his discretion, depending on their ability to convince the Superintendent of the compliance of the investigated companies with competition law.

8.132 If guarantees are not offered or accepted, the SIC will gather the evidence in the form of administrative visits, depositions, expert opinions, interrogations, documents, and the like. Once the evidence is gathered, the attorneys for the investigated parties will be invited to present their case orally, following which, the Superintendent Delegate for Competition will file a "Motivated Report" with the Superintendent, assessing the evidence and recommending fines or acquittal of the investigated parties. The report will be communicated to the companies under investigation, and they will be able to present their final arguments to the Superintendent.

8.133 The Superintendent will evaluate the motivated report presented by the Delegate as well as the final allegations presented by the companies. After consulting with the Competition Council (a consulting body formed by five persons appointed directly by the President), the Superintendent will issue a final decision in the form of a resolution in which he will sanction or acquit the investigated persons. Against this decision the parties can present a reconsideration plea. Once the Superintendent decides on this plea, the case is over before the administration. The decision is final and can be enforced by the Authority, including the collection of the fine.

The final resolution issued by the SIC can be challenged before the administrative judges in order to obtain its annulment and the indemnification of the damages produced by the decision. Therefore, the final authority in any antitrust case is the Council of State. **8.134**

(i) Name of agency/agencies

Perhaps the most important feature of Law 1340 was to name the Superintendence of Industry and Commerce (SIC) as the National Competition Authority in Colombia, with exclusive jurisdiction to decide all administrative investigations for the breach of competition and unfair trade laws (article 6 of Law 1340). **8.135**

The SIC is also in charge of applying the merger control regulation in all sectors of the economy with the exception of economic integrations between financial institutions, which are decided by the Financial Superintendence, and economic integrations between aircraft operating companies, which are decided by the Aeronautic Authority. **8.136**

It must be noted that the SIC is also the authority in charge of both administrative and jurisdictional cases under the new Consumer Protection Statute, Law no. 1480 of 2011 (Law 1480), and shares the jurisdiction with civil circuit judges in decisions concerning unfair trade brought under Law 256. **8.137**

There is some criticism of the many functions assigned to the SIC. In addition to what has been said, the SIC is the Industrial Property Authority, in charge of deciding over trademarks and patents; data protection; weights and measurements; and supervises the chambers of commerce. **8.138**

In regard to the structure of the Competition Authority, some reforms are in order and should be introduced: **8.139**

- The authority should be plural and not dependent on the opinions of only one person, the Superintendent, as happens nowadays. The authority could be structured, for instance, in the form of a Competition Commission, which would add independence and impartiality to the institution, and would allow it to resist the attempts of different economic or political sectors or, by the State itself to capture or influence its decisions.
- The authority must be independent from the Government. Its members must be appointed using a system of checks and balances, based on their academic standing and their professional experience. The members of the Commission must have fixed term that does not depend on the decision of the President of Colombia as happens today.
- The authority or public official that makes the decision to open and handle the investigation (actually the Superintendent Delegate for Promotion of Competition) should be different and independent from the authority or public official that issues the final decision (Actually the Superintendent of Industry and Commerce). Currently, the Superintendent Delegate for the Promotion of Competition is a subordinate of the Superintendent of Industry and Commerce who can appoint and remove him freely.
- Additionally, the Delegate participates in the preparation of the final decisions that will be signed by the Superintendent, situation that impedes the absolute independence that should exist between the entity that investigates and the entity that decides if there was an infraction. This principle of independence and neutrality is consistent with article 10 of the Universal Declaration of Human Rights. According to this article "Everyone is entitled, in conditions of full equality, to be heard publicly and with justice, by an independent an impartial tribunal, for the determination of its rights and obligations o for the examination of any accusation against him...".

- In order to accomplish this objective, a Competition Tribunal should be created. The Commission would present the investigations to the Tribunal in order to give the investigated parties a greater assurance regarding the independence and neutrality of the final decision maker, as happens in several jurisdictions.

(ii) Staff size and budget

8.140 According to the latest report, the SIC has a general budget of COP 125,071 million (approx. USD 60 million). This budget refers to all the issues that are attended to by this entity, i.e. data protection, consumer protection, trademarks and patents, and unfair trade issues.

8.141 The budget for monitoring and regulating anticompetitive practices is likely to increase as Law 1340 of 2009 provides that the fines recovered in enforcement should be paid directly to the SIC and not to the national treasury. This means that with increased fines the SIC will see a significant increase in its budget in upcoming years.

8.142 As can be seen this is a terrible mistake that was pointed out to Congress early in the discussions of Law 1340, for it creates a perverse incentive for the authority to find the investigated parties guilty and to impose heavy fines in order to finance its operations.

8.143 The Antitrust Investigation Group is conformed by approximately 40 professionals: mainly lawyers, economists, and accountants. There is now a chief economist, and it must be said that the quality and sophistication of the economic analysis has greatly improved in the past few years.

(iii) Recent enforcement actions and trends

8.144 Recently, the SIC has focused on trade associations, bid-rigging agreements, and public utilities sector. The agency has dealt specifically with competitors sharing information and other facilitating practices, and bid-rigging. It is important to note that bid-rigging is the only antitrust offense in Colombia that has criminal implications.

8.145 Given the prevalence of enforcement action against trade associations, the SIC has recently published *Draft Guidelines on Trade Associations*[51] in order to make associations aware of their obligations under competition law.

C. Private litigation

8.146 As described at the beginning of Section III, the enforcement of Colombian competition law depends heavily on the activity of the National Competition Authority, the Superintendence of Industry and Commerce. The Authority has been granted high administrative police functions, and conducts investigations in protection of the free competition principle and the whole community. These investigations, administrative in nature, conclude with a decision regarding the violation of the law, ordering a stop to the illegal conduct, and imposing fines on the investigated parties. The decision is not judicial in nature, and does not refer in any way to the damages that third parties may have suffered as a consequence of the anticompetitive conduct.

8.147 The victims of any anticompetitive conduct have to seek indemnification using other actions different from the antitrust investigation. For that purpose, they can file a civil lawsuit, a class action, or an unfair trade action since many instances of anticompetitive conduct are also unfair trade violations; and in any event, there is always article 18 of Law 256. Pursuant to this article it is considered unfair competition to obtain a significant competitive advantage over the competitors through the infraction the law. This means that private parties can file

[51] *Draft Guidelines on Trade Associations*, <http//www.sig.gov.co>.

an unfair trade lawsuit, which runs under a judicial procedure, in order to recover damages caused by anti competitive conducts that are considered also as unfair trade conducts under article 18 of Law 256.

Having said that, it must be recognized that to date probably no one has obtained indemnification of the damages caused by antitrust infraction and this is therefore an area in which the Colombian system of competition law is far behind. **8.148**

D. Follow-on litigation

As noted earlier, the SIC cannot refer to damages resulting from the antitrust conducts it investigates. Nevertheless, a fine imposed by the SIC serves as a very solid evidentiary support on which to base a civil or class action. **8.149**

E. Arbitration and alternative dispute resolution

As defined in article 19 of Law 155 and article 46 of Decree 2153, conduct that infringes antitrust statutes has an illegal object, and therefore any contractual clauses or unilateral acts against competition can be declared null and void by a judge. It is important to convey that the decision of the Superintendent at the end of an antitrust investigation will not refer to the validity or nullity of contracts or any other acts, for such decisions belong to the judges. The SIC will only examine if competition laws have been violated. If there was a violation, the authority will declare it, will also prohibit the offending conduct and impose fines. **8.150**

There has been some discussion as to the possibility for judges to decide on the nullity of contracts and other acts for antitrust reasons, when the SIC has not conducted an investigation. However, judges and arbitration tribunals have rightfully decided that they are competent to decide these kinds of cases and have indeed declared the nullity of contractual clauses for violation of the competition laws. In 2000, an arbitration tribunal declared the nullity of a non-competition clause included in a contract between two cement companies, for violation of the competition laws.[52] **8.151**

F. Remedies

(i) Administrative and civil liability

As noted earlier, the SIC can rule on the violation of competition laws, order the investigated companies to cease their illegal conduct, and impose fines both on the companies and on the natural persons involved. **8.152**

One of the improvements to Law 1340 was the notorious increase in the capacity of the SIC to impose fines. Under Decree 2153, the maximum fine imposed on companies could reach 2000 times the minimum monthly wages (approx. USD 500,000) and the fine imposed on natural persons, 300 times the minimum monthly wages (approx. USD 70,000). Under Law 1340, however, the SIC can impose fines on the companies of up to 100,000 times the minimum monthly wages (approx. USD 30,000,000) or up to 150 percent of the profits obtained from the anticompetitive conduct, and fines on natural persons involved of up to 2000 the minimum monthly wages (approx. USD 500.000). There is an important addition regarding the express prohibition on the investigated companies to pay for the fines imposed to the natural persons. **8.153**

It must be noted that the SIC can impose fines for anticompetitive conduct, but also for obstructing the investigations; infringing the merger control regulations; failure to comply **8.154**

[52] *Cementos Hércules v. Cementos Andino* (2000).

with orders; for the failure to comply with obligations acquired pursuant to guarantees accepted in view of the anticipated termination of investigations or the conditions accepted for the approval of a merger transaction. There are also circumstances that allow the Authority to impose harder or softer sanctions depending on different factors.

(ii) Criminal liability

8.155 Colombian Antitrust Law has no criminal liability tradition. Nevertheless, in 2010 Law 1474 of 2010 (Anticorruption Statute) determined that bid-rigging in government contracts is both an antitrust and criminal infraction. This means that the conduct prohibited under article 47(9) of Decree 2153 can lead to administrative, civil, and criminal liability.

G. Leniency and immunity

8.156 One of the features of Law 1340 is the introduction of leniency programs into Colombian competition laws. Pursuant to article 14 of Law 1340, the SIC can grant benefits to the participants in an anticompetitive conduct, provided that they collaborate with the Competition Authority by providing information and evidence of the existence of the conduct and its characteristics including the identification of the participants, even if there is already an investigation under way.

8.157 The benefits can include total or partial exoneration of the sanctions and are not available for the leaders and instigators of the illegal conduct. The SIC will award the benefits based in the quality and opportunity of the information and evidence provided by the applicants to the leniency program.

8.158 In 2010, the Government issued Decree no. 2896 in order to regulate the functioning, the requisites, and procedure for applying to the leniency programs. Despite these efforts, to date there has been no leniency application made in Colombia. The reason for this is that there is much uncertainty as to the application of the benefits and the reliability of the immunity that the program offers. There are also cultural issues, such as the resistance of the entrepreneurs to be identified as informants or traitors in the eyes of their companies or their colleagues.

8.159 As shown above, in criminal cases related to bid-rigging in public contracts, the SIC and the office of the Attorney General cannot grant total immunity with regard to the criminal sanctions, but only a reduction. This is also a factor that reduces the incentives for application to the leniency programs.

H. Document creation and retention

8.160 The Colombian Commercial Code imposes on all companies the obligation to retain all mail and documents relating to their business activities. This obligation has the term of ten years. The documents can be stored by any means that allow for their truthful reproduction.

8.161 Antitrust regulation doesn't refer to this issue specifically. Nevertheless there are severe administrative and criminal consequences for companies under investigation that refuse to provide information required by the SIC. The obligation to provide the information requested is independent of any other fact or circumstance.

9

CZECH REPUBLIC

Arthur Braun

bpv Braun Partners s.r.o.

Introduction

The Czech Act on Protection of Competition No 143/2001 (Competition Act)[1] distinguishes between concerted (cartels) and unilateral (abuse of dominant position) restrictions of competition. The most serious types of cartel agreements/concerted practices involve agreements and practices between competitors, which aim to increase price, limit output, or allocate markets or customers (hard core cartels). Cartels are described in Section II. **9.01**

[1] Consolidated Act on the Protection of Competition No. 143/2001 Coll. of 4 April 2001, as amended. Unofficial English translation, <http://www.compet.cz/fileadmin/user_upload/Legislativa/HS/CR/Act_143_2001_consolidated.pdf>.

9.02 Intensity of enforcement has been very different in the last decade. In the early 2000s, the Office for the Protection of Economic Competition was not afraid of investigating into unchartered territories and hand out considerable sanctions. In the last years, partly due to a change in leadership of the office, other political priorities, and various lost court cases, the Office seems to be more cautious in its approach, supporting competition advocacy and agreeing on settlements and commitments rather than handing out penalties.

I. Acting alone

9.03 In its ss. 10 and 11, the Competition Act covers exclusively the unilateral conduct of businesses which hold significant market power. Such businesses may infringe antitrust law by harming other businesses or customers directly, and are therefore subject to increased investigative pressure both from the Czech competition authority (the Antitrust Office), regulators (if applicable), and the European Commission (the *CEZ* investigation in 2009[2] being one of the major recent examples).

9.04 The concepts underlying Czech law with regard to unilateral conduct draw heavily on EU law. In particular, unilateral conduct is only covered by Czech antitrust law if carried out by a business in a "dominant position." Czech law does not prohibit businesses from attaining or holding a dominant position as such, but only covers its "abuse" to the detriment of other competitors or consumers.

9.05 Competitors will be considered to hold a dominant position under Czech law if they fulfil the definition in the Competition Act. A presumption of dominance is laid down in s. 10 of the Competition Act stating that one or several competitors jointly have such position if their market power enables them to behave independently to a significant extent of other undertakings or consumers. In particular, a competitor will already be presumed to be dominant if it holds a market share of 40 percent or more. This presumption is rebuttable (for instance if one or two other competitors have an equally large market share or if it can be proven that strong competition and no significant market entry barriers exist), but the competitor in question will have to prove that it is not dominant. In the past, the Office has assumed dominance with market shares considerably below 40 percent (decisions in *Eurotel*[3] and *RadioMobil*[4] for granting lower rates for telephone calls between their networks than with a third mobile phone operator).

9.06 Section 11 of the Competition Act contains, besides a general prohibition (General Clause), a non-exhaustive list of abusive behavior which is explained in detail below.

9.07 For a few years, the Czech Republic has had, in addition, a separate law (Act No. 395/2009) regulating specific abuses of market power by retailers of food and agricultural products. This Act contains a detailed list of practices such as listing fees or opening fees that retailers must not request from their suppliers. Moreover, it intervenes into contractual relations, stipulating for instance payment terms. The Antitrust Office is the enforcement agency under that Act.

9.08 A special Czech feature not belonging to competition law but regulating to a large degree the same matter is the Prices Act No. 526/1990, dating from the first year after the 1989 revolution. It is still in effect despite being considered largely obsolete and having been replaced by the subsequent Competition Acts. In its s. 2, the Prices Act prohibits the abuse of the

---

[2] *ČEZ and others* COMP/39.727.

[3] *Eurotel,* Case no. S 18/01.

[4] *RadioMobil,* Case no. S 19/01.

economic position of a seller by charging exaggerated prices or, on the other hand, selling below cost. On the other hand, purchasers must not use their economic position to obtain prices that by far do not reach justified costs. A penalty of up to CZK 1 million, or in the amount of the entire unjustified profit from such transaction, may be levied by the tax authorities for an abuse. After a short renaissance of this provision a few years ago, this Prices Act has again lost in practical importance; still, it should not be forgotten when discussing unilateral behavior in competition.

Czech law also provides some antidiscrimination provisions between business partners for reasons such as nationality of race. This non-discrimination requirement also extends to businesses which are not dominant, but no significant fines are to be expected. **9.09**

Practicing usury could also be considered when discussing abusive pricing: such practice would be both a criminal act and would render a contract invalid under the Civil Code. **9.10**

While the Czech rules on unilateral conduct are quite strict in their wording, such behavior by dominant businesses has not in recent times been a main focus of enforcement by the Czech Antitrust Office, as opposed to many cases in the early 2000s (in particular seven proceedings against *Český Telecom*, the then incumbent telephone operator). Between 2009 and 2011, only two administrative proceedings were started for abuse of a dominant position—for instance 2011 against *Telefonica O2*,[5] formerly *Český Telecom* for various allegedly abusive conduct in the matter of access to broadband ADSL. **9.11**

This recent, rather low, level of enforcement by the Office, despite the high demand, can only to a small degree be explained by the wide use of competition advocacy in which the Office takes pride. In the opinion of many in the Czech antitrust community it can be rather better explained by some indirect political influence—despite the formal full independence of the Office. **9.12**

A. Agreements with non-competing businesses

Further to agreements with competitors and unilateral conduct, the Czech competition rules also cover agreements with non-competing businesses. This includes, in particular, vertical agreements with businesses that operate at a different level in the supply chain. The Office has traditionally been quite active in this field of suspected resale price maintenance (RPM)—usually cases that are easy to prove. **9.13**

Agreements with non-competitors are assessed under the prohibition of anti competitive agreements and concerted practices, laid down in ss. 3–7 of the Competition Act. These rules also apply to non-dominant businesses. **9.14**

Czech soft law is in line with the *de minimis* rules at EU level, exempts vertical agreements from prohibition if neither of the parties holds a market share of more than 15 percent. **9.15**

B. Predatory pricing

Predatory pricing is one of the examples of illegal behavior explicitly mentioned in s. 11(1)(e) of the Competition Act. **9.16**

The first decision by the Office on predatory pricing dates from 2010 (*Student Agency*[6]) and derives many arguments from European cases (*AKZO*[7] and *Tetra Pak*[8]). Despite having been **9.17**

[5] *Telefonica O2*, 11/035/HS014.
[6] *Student Agency*, Case no. 10/123/HS035.
[7] Case 62/86 *AKZO Chemie v. Commission* [1991] ECR I-3359.
[8] C-333/94P *Tetra Pak International S.A. v. Commission* [1996] ECR I-05951.

able to prove the intent and detailed economic analysis to push a competitor out of the market defined as an overland coach line, the decision was reversed by the Administrative Court in Brno in November 2012 due to wrong definition of the relevant market, and therefore still is not final.

9.18 In order to establish predatory pricing, the Office will investigate prices of the dominant competitor to determine whether they lie below "average variable costs" (AVC); in this respect, the Office is thus fully in line with European practice. A dominant competitor may also commit an abuse of its position if it prices above AVC, but below "average total costs" (ATC), if this is part of a plan for the eliminating of a competitor.

C. Exploitative offenses (excessive pricing, monopoly leveraging)

9.19 As pointed out above, Czech law does not prohibit businesses from attaining or holding a dominant position as such. By virtue of their market power, dominant businesses have the ability to price above the competitive level which would qualify as enforcement of unfair conditions, especially enforcement of performance, which at the time of contract conclusion is conspicuously inadequate to the counter-performance provided (s. 11(1)(lit a) of the Competition Act).

9.20 Such behavior was fined various times in particular in the 1990s when electricity, gas, and water providers charged inappropriate fees for connection to the grid (i.e. *Středočeská energetická*[9]).

D. Monopsony

9.21 The rules on the abuse of a dominant position by enforcing unfair conditions (s. 11(1)(lit a) of the Competition Act) apply to dominant buyers as well as to sellers. In practice, monopsony cases are rare, however. Some academic discussion is at present being led in the Czech Republic as to what degree the few health insurers in the country act as dominant buyers when it comes to issues such as number of hospital beds or reimbursing pharmaceuticals. Nevertheless, at present, the status of medical insurers would probably not be qualified as that of competitors.

E. Price discrimination

9.22 Section 11(1)(lit c) of the Competition Act prohibits dominant competitors from applying different conditions to equivalent transactions with other market participants, if thereby they put those at a competitive disadvantage. This becomes relevant in particular with rebate systems. Nevertheless, this does not mean that the same prices must always be granted to everyone. Matters such as financial strength of the business partner may serve as an argument for justifying discrimination.[10]

9.23 While pure discrimination cases are rare, discrimination is sometimes relied on as an additional consideration in foreclosure cases. In the field of rail cargo, the railways incumbent Česke Drahy received one of the highest fines issued so far (approx. EUR 10 million) in 2008 for price discrimination against competitors.[11]

F. Dictating or influencing resale prices

(i) Resale price maintenance

9.24 Resale price maintenance (RPM) may constitute a prohibited behavior which applies both to dominant as well to non-dominant undertakings.

---

[9] *Středočeská energetická*, Case no. S 25/96. High Court abolished the fine later.

[10] *Eurotel* (n 3).

[11] *Česke Drahy*, Case no. 09/066/HS021 (2009).

Fixed or minimum RPM is regarded as a serious infringement of the competition rules and has been penalized frequently by the Office.[12] **9.25**

RPM has recently been a major enforcement priority of the Office, possibly also due to the lack of defenses by the violator. **9.26**

(ii) Minimum advertised price programs

Minimum advertised price (MAP) programs will, in all likelihood, be considered as a form of indirect RPM under Czech competition law, and are thus likely be found in violation of the competition rules if applied by a dominant competitor. **9.27**

G. Tying arrangements

Tying may constitute an abuse of a dominant position under s. 11(1)(lit b) of the Competition Act, if the supplier is dominant on the market for the tying product, and if the practice forecloses competition on either the tying, the tied, or on both markets. A defense used by the dominant business could be that such tying is customary in that specific business, or that the tied products are connected. **9.28**

For tying to be anticompetitive, there needs to be a separate demand for the products in question. Of the seven proceedings against the incumbent Český Telecom until 2004 (combined fines of EUR 16 million), many were related to tying telecoms services (for which the monopoly existed) with other services. A spirits company dominant for Fernet-type drinks was already earlier under the old competition act held to have violated its position by tying its product to other purchases of alcoholic beverages where it was not dominant.[13] **9.29**

H. Exclusive dealing

Exclusive dealing will usually be considered an infringement under the General Clause on abuse (s. 11(1), first sentence) if carried out by a dominant business. This prohibition also applies to indirect means to achieve exclusivity, for instance the decisions *Linde Technoplyn* 2003/repeated 2008[14]—where the dominant business forced customers to have their entire consumption of gas bought from the dominant competitor. **9.30**

Contractual prohibitions to export may also be considered to be an abuse of dominance, for instance in the *Sokolovská Uhelná* case.[15] Moreover, such behavior could have a community dimension, and as such be evaluated under European rules if it could affect trade between the member states of the European Union. **9.31**

Detailed rules and guidelines on the assessment of various distribution schemes (exclusive dealing, selective dealing, franchising, etc.) exist at an EU level. As the Czech practice is strongly based on EU practice, these rules also help in the self-assessment of clauses required for competitors under Czech law. **9.32**

I. Refusal to deal

As in any market economy, also in the Czech Republic, businesses are generally free to choose their trading partners. Certain exceptions to this rule exist. In particular for dominant businesses, such behavior may be considered to be a breach under the General Clause of s. 11 of **9.33**

[12] See *Kofola*, Case no. 08/091/HS057 (2008) (settlement); *Tupperware*, Case no. S 9/05 (2005).

[13] *Fernet Stock*, Case no. S 21/95 (1995).

[14] *Linde Technoplyn*, Case no. S 199/02 (2003, 2008).

[15] *Sokolovská Uhelná*, Case no. S 255/07 (2010).

the Competition Act. In recent years, refusals to deal, however, have not ranked high in the practice of the Office.

9.34 Czech case law regarding dominant companies provides for an obligation to contract, provided that certain requirements are met. If the resource in question has previously been used only internally by the dominant business, a refusal to deal will not violate competition law other than in exceptional circumstances (see Section I.I). The decision in *SPT Telecom*[16] as early as 1999 saw for instance a violation of the General Clause in the refusal to deal with a competitor for internet connection.

J. Essential facilities

9.35 The Czech Competition Act has a very detailed description of illegal behavior when the dominant competitor is considered to operate an essential facility.

9.36 According to s. 11(1)(lit f) of the Competition Act, a refusal to grant other undertakings access, for a reasonable reimbursement, to transmission grids or similar distribution networks or other infrastructure facilities, which are owned or used on other legal grounds by the undertaking in a dominant position are an abuse of the dominant position. The condition, however, is (a) that the other undertakings are unable, for legal or other reasons, to operate in the same market as the dominant undertaking without being able to jointly use such facilities, and (b) that such dominant undertakings fail to prove that such joint use is unfeasible for operational or other reasons, or that they cannot be reasonably requested to enable such use. This applies also in the event of refusal of access for a reasonable reimbursement.

9.37 The same rules apply explicitly for the use of intellectual property or access to networks owned or used on other legal grounds by the undertaking in a dominant position, provided such use is necessary for participating in competition in the same market as the dominant undertakings or in any other market.

9.38 Decisions by the Office already before the clause was introduced into the law in 2004 (such as *Český Telecom* in 1999) allowed a rather extensive interpretation of the indispensability of the facility. Court decisions still showed that the existence and the indispensability of the essential facility must be proven by the Office in its decisions.

9.39 In some industries such as energy or postal services non-discriminatory access to the networks or at least some services is expressly contained in the sector-specific laws.

K. Bundling (including loyalty and market share discounts)

9.40 Czech practice will consider bundling to be prohibited if competitors are unable to replicate a bundle that is similar to, and competitive with, that of the dominant businesses. Bundling was an occasional topic in particular in telecommunications. If this is the case, bundling will be considered to be in violation of the competition rules even if no part of the bundle is offered at a predatory price. Rebates granted by dominant businesses have not been frequently addressed in Czech case law. There are no cases in this area.

L. Standard-setting groups (disclosure requirements, licensing arrangements, and licensing pools)

9.41 While standard-setting has recently been the subject of significant attention at EU level, there is as yet no practice in the Czech Republic. It is, however, likely that any enforcement in the Czech Republic would be informed by the European Commission's practice.

[16] *SPT Telecom*, Case no. S 104/99 (1999).

The safe harbor rule and additional considerations provided in the European Commission's Horizontal Cooperation Guidelines, while not binding on the Czech authorities, provide useful guidance on the potential analysis under Czech competition law (see Section 12.56 of Chapter 12).

M. Customer termination

Termination of existing customers is assessed under the General Clause.[17] In particular, sudden termination of customer contracts by a dominant business will be considered to be abusive unless it is objectively justified. Such justification could for instance be the non-payment of advance payments to an electricity provider.[18] **9.42**

N. Termination of intermediaries (retailers, wholesalers, dealers, and value-added resellers, agents, and brokers)

Termination of intermediaries would be considered under the General Clause, though no sanctions have been published. **9.43**

O. Termination of relationships with competitors

Businesses are generally not required to trade with their competitors. In exceptional cases, termination of a relationship with a competitor by a dominant business may, however, infringe the General Clause, in particular if it is a sudden termination. **9.44**

P. Exemptions

Czech competition law applies to all sectors of the economy, with limited exemptions for the agricultural sector and activities having effect solely in other countries. In other regulated industries, such as energy and telecom, competition law applies in parallel with sectoral regulation. **9.45**

In addition, the law provides for a number of specific exemptions which only cover the rules on anti competitive agreements (but not the other prohibitions of competition law). More generally, anti competitive agreements may be saved if they give rise to economic efficiencies, provided a number of requirements stipulated by the Cartel Act are met. **9.46**

Czech law contained a safe harbor rule for agreements of minor importance (but never for the most serious infringements, the *hard core* cartels), but these provisions were abolished in 2009. Horizontal agreements were exempted if the combined market share did not exceed 10 percent, and vertical agreements if the market share on either of the vertically related markets did not exceed 15 percent. Since 2009, such exemption with the same market shares is no longer directly derived from the Competition Act but applied as soft law in the form of the Notice on *de minimis* Rules. **9.47**

An important aspect when discussing exemptions is that it is always the competitor who is obliged to provide evidence that requirements for implementation of such exemption are fulfilled. Self-assessment was introduced in 2004, and despite the possibility in practice of discussing individual issues on an informal basis with the Office, this has considerably increased the relevance of having all relevant matters practiced in strict accordance with the Competition Act. **9.48**

[17] See *Česká Rafinérská*, Case no. S 227/06 (2007); *Dopravní podnik Ústeckého kraje*, Case no. S 142/02 (2002).

[18] See *Východočeská energetika*, Case no. S 44/94 (1994).

9.49 Specific types of agreements are, however, excluded from the general prohibition of cartels in s. 3(4) of the Competition Act if they (a) contribute to improving the production or distribution of goods or to promoting technical or economic progress while allowing consumers a fair share of the resulting benefit; (b) do not impose on the undertakings restrictions which are not indispensable to the attainment of the objectives pursuant to (a); and (c) do not afford the competitors the possibility of eliminating competition in respect of a substantial portion of the market concerned.

9.50 While, pursuant to the Act, further block exemptions may be granted by the Office, no such regulation has at present been passed. The European Commission's block exemption regulations, which provide safe harbor for certain types of agreements (see Sections 12.65–12.66 of Chapter 12) are directly applicable, s. 4(1) of the Competition Act. Even though the Office would have the competence (under s. 4(3) Competition Act), at present no additional national block exemptions have been granted.

II. Dealing with competitors

9.51 The Competition Act contains a general prohibition on agreements between undertakings, which have as their object or effect the prevention, restriction, or distortion of competition. In fact, s. 3(1) is almost identical to part of article 101 of the Treaty on the Functioning of the European Union (TFEU).

9.52 Horizontal agreements with an anticompetitive object, such as price fixing, fixing of production and market sharing, rank among the most serious violations of competition law. The worst cases of such behavior ("hard core cartels") are (together with others) also criminal acts.

9.53 Horizontal agreements which do not directly aim to limit competition, such as agreements on joint purchasing, production, R&D, and information exchanges, may also be prohibited if they give rise to anticompetitive effects. Such agreements may, however, be justified based on economic efficiencies, provided a number of requirements laid down by the Act are met. Other than *hard core* cartels, "normal" horizontal cartels have so far not been one of the main targets of enforcement.

A. Horizontal price fixing (including advanced announcements of price or product changes)

9.54 Price fixing among competitors is one of the most serious violations of competition law, attracts very high fines, and is in addition to criminal prosecution for which both prison sentences and fines may be issued. Such price fixing may take the form of setting of minimum and maximum prices, margins, discounts or parallel price adjustments. The highest fine pre-EU accession (a total of EUR 18 million) was imposed in 2004 on savings and loans[19] but was later quashed by the courts. The gas-insulated switchgear cartel was fined for activity before EU-accession in 2004, and the fine amounted to almost EUR 40 million; this decision is also not final. In 2012, the Court of Justice of the European Union (CJEU),[20] deciding in a preliminary question, confirmed the parallel sanctioning by the Czech Office for activities prior to EU-accession. Nevertheless, the Office's case was refused by the Supreme Administrative Court for other reasons in the summer of 2013.[21] Fines have also

[19] Case no. S 067/04.

[20] C-17/10 *Toshiba Corporation and others v. Úřad pro ochranu hospodářské soutěže*, February 14, 2012.

[21] *2Afs*, Supreme Adminsitrative Court, Case no. 50/2012-241.

been imposed, on distributors of fuel, undertakers, but also coffee retailers[22] as early as in 1994—to be refused by the court later) of in chicken prices.[23]

Advance price announcements may be an instrument used by cartelists, and may thus serve as evidence of an underlying price cartel. Parallel announcements will not, however, always be sufficient proof of an "agreement" or "concerted practice" between the competitors in question. In 2004, the Office as one of the few antitrust authorities in Europe, issued fines for fuel companies arguing a concerted increase of retail prices of fuel; the decision still is not final after seven court and administrative decisions.[24] **9.55**

B. Horizontal agreements to allocate customers or territories; agreements not to compete

Like price fixing, market sharing (both for purchases as well as for sales) ranks among the most serious violations of competition law (s. 3(2)(lit c) of the Competition Act) and is a criminal act. Several of the hard core cartels which have been fined by the Cartel Court also involved elements of market or customer allocation. Such cases may later be qualified as information exchange (in the case of *Eastern Sugar*,[25] the conduct originally evaluated as market allocation and leading to a considerable fine was on appeal requalified as information exchange (2006)). **9.56**

In some cases, agreements not to compete, such as joint production or specialization agreements, may, however, give rise to economic efficiencies. Czech law provides no safe harbor for such agreements. However, the safe harbor rules laid down in the European Commission's block exemption for specialization agreements (which provides for an exemption of up to a combined market share of 20 percent, subject to certain additional requirements) will be of some support with regard to such agreements. **9.57**

C. Horizontal boycotts

Agreements between competitors not to deal with certain customers or supplies may violate the prohibition of anticompetitive agreements and are explicitly forbidden (s. 3(2)(lit f) of the Competition Act). In a recent case (*Alliance Healthcare*[26]), the four most important wholesale suppliers of pharmaceuticals announced at a press conference their decision to stop supplying with pharmaceuticals several hospitals which owed them considerable amounts. They were fined some EUR 4.5 million, not because of the individual boycott for enforcing their justified claims for payment, but for having done so in a coordinated way. **9.58**

D. Joint ventures and other competitive collaborations

Joint ventures which are "full function," i.e. which operate on the market as independent economic entities, are assessed under the merger control rules. **9.59**

Cooperative joint ventures—which are joint ventures that have as object or effect the coordination of competitive behavior of competitors controlling such joint venture—that remain independent in the market and are not caught by the merger control rules, will be subject to the rules on anticompetitive agreements (s. 12(6) of the Competition Act). These rules are applicable to a broad variety of joint ventures which involve cooperation in R&D, **9.60**

---

22 *Tchibo/Douwe Egberts*, Case no. S 40/94.

23 See e.g. *Agrodruzstvo*, Case no. S 014B/07 (2007). The case still has not been finally settled.

24 See e.g. *AGIP*, Case no. S 011/03.

25 *Eastern Sugar*, Case no. S 142/04 (2007).

26 *Alliance Healthcare and others*, Case no. S 60/06 (2007).

production, purchasing, etc. Such joint ventures will be prohibited if they give rise to anticompetitive effects, but may be justified based on economic efficiencies.

9.61 There is limited case-law in the Czech Republic on the analysis of such joint ventures. However, the assessment will likely be guided by the block exemption regulations and guidelines issued by the European Commission (see Section II.B above and Sections 12.75–12.77 of Chapter 12).

E. Trade associations

9.62 While participation in trade associations in itself is not objectionable on the grounds of competition law, anticompetitive decisions taken by such associations are caught by the antitrust rules. The Czech Chamber of Pharmacists has in various instances been fined, for instance for issuing an internal order that required its approval for every new pharmacy,[27] for regulation advertising and customer cards,[28] prohibiting cash paybacks to customers in its code of ethics,[29] or charging excessive registration fees thus banning new competitors. The Chamber of Dentists was fined in 2004 for stating it its code of ethics that no customer should be accepted if the dentist knows that a particular customer owes unpaid fees to another dentist, and also the chamber of veterinarians were fined.[30]

9.63 Since then, enforcement of the competition rules against trade associations has not been a main priority of the Czech authorities anymore, even though the enforceability of claims has been improved and the assessment of fines allowed for higher fines. In 2011, the Czech Bar Association managed to avoid a fine directing the ordering of gowns from only one company in competition advocacy by allowing the cuts for gowns to be bought from the firm for independent procurement.

9.64 Trade associations may in practice also serve as a platform for its members to conclude anticompetitive agreements or exchange sensitive information. If members of a trade organization engage in such conduct, they violate the competition rules (just as they would if they did the same outside an association), and are liable for fines. It is therefore important to avoid conduct of this kind in trade associations. Particular care should be taken with regard to information exchanges (see Section II.H), because awareness of these issues has increased in recent years, as probably every major company has a compliance program including competition issues.

F. Interlocking directorships

9.65 Interlocking directorships are assessed under Czech merger control if they lead to an overlap of at least 50 percent in the executive or supervisory boards of two businesses (irrespective of whether these businesses are competitors). Measures to avoid leaking of information could well be part of commitments or conditions in the proceedings.

9.66 While the establishment of management links which fall short of the 50 percent threshold may constitute an infringement of the antitrust rules, there is no case law on this issue in the Czech Republic. More importantly, overlaps in management may facilitate anticompetitive practices such as cartels or exchanges of sensitive information. In such cases, the businesses in questions will be liable for that infringement. Nevertheless, so far, no proceedings have been reported for such matters.

[27] Case no. S 125/04.
[28] Case no. S 006/05 (2006).
[29] Case no. S 284/2007 (2008).
[30] Case no. S 070/00; Case no. S 074/03.

G. Facilitating practices

Practices which facilitate anticompetitive conduct are not expressly regulated in Czech competition law. An exception exists for interlocking directorships (see Section II.F) and for acquisitions of non-controlling minority interests, which may be subject to merger control proceedings. There are no cases in this area. **9.67**

H. Information exchange

Information exchanges are regulated by the General Clause (s. 3(1) of the Competition Act). They violate Czech law if they have an anticompetitive objective, or give rise to anticompetitive effects, unless they can be justified by economic efficiencies. **9.68**

Information exchange is often connected to price fixing agreements (and easier to prove). Thus, a cartel incurred a fine of some EUR 2 million in 2010 for behavior between 1998 and 2004,[31] while the well-known gas-insulated switchgear cartel was also fined for its activity before the Czech Republic joined the EU. *Billa* and *Julius Meinl*[32] serve as similar examples where a price fixing cartel also involved illegal information sharing. **9.69**

Exchanges of price information are generally problematic, unless the information is so historic that it no longer may result in coordination between the parties. **9.70**

There are no rules given either by the Office or courts on the characteristics of data which may be exchanged. Rather—as generally under the TFEU and the practice of the European Commission—the assessment of information exchanges will depend on the characteristics of the market (including market concentration and the frequency of price negotiations), as well as of the exchange (state of aggregation, frequency of the exchange, openness of the exchange to third parties such as customers). Generally, a cautious approach would use anonymous, old data aggregated by an independent source. **9.71**

Information exchanges which do not restrict competition need not produce pro-competitive effects. However, undertakings may rely on pro-competitive effects (such as efficiency gains through benchmarking) to justify information exchanges which otherwise would be prohibited. **9.72**

I. Joint purchasing agreements

Joint purchasing agreements, as frequent as they are in many sectors of business, may infringe the competition rules, in particular if they give rise to significant buyer power vis-à-vis suppliers, or facilitate coordination between the parties on the market on which they sell their products. The parties may however rely on the business efficiency defenses as used in European case law in order to justify joint purchasing agreements. However, no Czech examples of efficiency defenses have been published. **9.73**

J. Joint lobbying/regulatory/legislative efforts

Joint lobbying activities do not give rise to issues under Czech antitrust law. **9.74**

---

31 *Toshiba*, Case no. S13/09/KD (2010).

32 *Billa and Julius Meinl*, Case no. S 94/02.

III. General issues

A. Jurisdiction and applicable law (including sector-specific competition regulation)

9.75 The substantive provisions of Czech competition law are laid down in the Competition Act, which gives the Antitrust Office full investigative power under national law. The Antitrust office with its seat in Brno (www.compet.cz) is an independent Central State Authority with a Chairman named for a term of six years.

9.76 Sectoral regulation exists in a number of sectors, such as telecoms (covering also postal communications) and energy. The cooperation between the authorities after several years of friction seems to work better now.

9.77 *Ratione personae*, Czech competition law applies to all natural or legal persons who are competitors. In practice, the expression "competitor" is applied very broadly to cover the "undertaking" as defined in European Competition law. Recent decisions by the Office (*Agel/Hutnická*[33] in a merger control case) made clear that also health insurances are in a limited area to be considered a competitor subject to the competition rules but not when signing a memorandum in October 2011 together with the Ministry of Health reducing the number of hospital beds.

9.78 In terms of geographic scope, the Competition Act explicitly (s. 1(5)) reflects the effects doctrine: it applies also to any actions of competitors, occurred abroad, which distort or may distort competition in the territory of the Czech Republic. In cases which affect trade between the EU's member states, the jurisdiction of the Antitrust Office is subject to certain limitations. In particular, a decision by the European Commission to initiate proceedings relieves national authorities already working on the case of their jurisdiction.

B. Antitrust system

(i) Name of agency

9.79 The Czech Republic has for twenty years followed the EU model, with the Czech Antitrust Office being both investigating authority and decision-maker. The Office also applies Articles 101 and 102 TFEU.

9.80 Decisions by the Antitrust Office are subject to internal appeal procedure by the Chairman of the Office and subsequent judicial review by the Administrative Court (*Krajský Soud)* in Brno, and subsequent division of the Czech Supreme Administrative Court. Recent years have shown that chances of appeal in court procedures are quite high and that it may well take some ten years until a sanction becomes final.

(ii) Staff size and budget

9.81 With a staff of about 150, the Antitrust Office is a comparatively large competition enforcement agency for a small country. Nevertheless, a large part of the staff are busy with the increased competences in public procurement with all appeals going first to the Office. No significant enlargement of staff has taken place in the field of protection of competition, except for the building up of economic capacity.

[33] *Agel/Hutnická*, Case no. S 118/09.

(iii) Recent enforcement actions and trends

In the first years since its creation in 1993, the Antitrust Office (formerly a Ministry) focused mostly on merger control work, thresholds being quite low at that time (not being turnover-based) and approvals of privatizations. In recent years, since the increase in the turnover thresholds in 2004 and the growing number of mergers that are subject to EU proceedings, the number of merger control proceedings is between 40 and 50 per year, mostly approved in the first phase with very few prohibitions, and a few more cases where commitments were offered or the merger was approved with conditions. **9.82**

In the new millennium, the Office has considerably expanded its enforcement record in the cartel field. Penalties issued per year have grown from a few hundred thousand Czech Koruna to billions in the early 2000s; since then the numbers have been decreasing again, partially due to the low number of cases actually decided (in 2009–11 at maximum three cartel proceedings were actually started in a year), partially due to the strong use of competition advocacy in which the Czech Office was one of the first strong proponents in the region. **9.83**

Of vertical cases, the share of RPM proceedings does not correspond to their small importance in business. In practice, hard core cartels are still hardly tackled. Most of the cases in the past (including the first leniency cases) piggybacked on cartel investigations at the EU level which led to it being established that cartels had existed in the Czech Republic before the jurisdiction in these cases went to the European Commission after the EU accession in May 2004 (such as the gas-insulated switchgear cartel with the highest fine ever). Courts have so far held that such dual punishment (one at the EU level, one at the Czech level for behavior prior to the EU accession) does not violate the *ne bis in idem* rule. **9.84**

The 2012 amendment[34] also established the right of the Office not to open administrative proceedings for cartels that have no relevance on the market (below 1 percent market share shall never to be considered too have such relevance), a hotly discussed issue, also considering the very low number of cartels actually prosecuted but which might bring some relief in the field of RPM. **9.85**

C. Private litigation

Victims of cartels or abuse by a dominant player can apply to the Office for orders bringing infringements to an end, as well as for injunctive relief, provided they have a legal or economic interest in the matter. They may also apply for cease-and-desist orders with the ordinary courts under the Commercial Code and Civil Procedure Code, since violations of the antitrust rules will often (but not always) qualify as unfair conduct under that law as well as under general tort provisions. Nevertheless, in practice, this is still a rather theoretical possibility as the courts would certainly wait for the administrative proceedings at the Office to be completed. In particular, due to low economic understanding of the matters involved and the lack of really specialized judges, the courts will show reluctance to decide any such matters within the short timeframe needed by the victims. There have been some private conduct cases involving economic analysis of restraints. **9.86**

D. Follow-on litigation (including role of agency determinations of liability for follow-on litigation)

Private enforcement of damage claims by victims of anticompetitive behavior, despite being a possibility under Czech civil law, and encouraged by the Antitrust Office, still has not led to any published court decision. Such reluctance to pursue damage claims in civil courts **9.87**

[34] Act 260/2012.

(except for arguing invalidity of a one-sided contract violating competition law) has many reasons, including the still extremely long duration of court proceedings; under international standards, very high court and lawyer costs; and a certain distrust in the business community to solve commercial disputes at state courts.

9.88 The passing-on defenses would probably be accepted by Czech courts, decreasing motivation to pursue private enforcement even further.

9.89 Damages claims cannot be adjudicated by the Antitrust Office, but must be brought in the ordinary courts or in criminal proceedings as an adhesive claim. Under Czech law, the courts cannot award punitive damages/treble damages to private claimants. Class actions are not known either.

E. Arbitration and alternative dispute resolution

9.90 Czech competition law is public law, and as such competition disputes are not to be decided in arbitration proceedings (despite the frequency of the use of arbitration courts in the Czech Republic). In practice, however, competition law issues sometimes arise in arbitration, for example if one party invokes invalidity of an entire contract or just of a provision due to violation of the Competition Act.

F. Remedies

9.91 For anticompetitive agreements and abuses of a dominant position, the Antitrust Office may impose fines of up to 10 percent of a businesses' group-wide annual turnover.

9.92 Violations of procedural orders, such as the order to comply with an information request, carry (lower) fines. The Office has the power to impose fines of up to CZK 300,000, or 1 percent of a company's group-wide annual turnover, for a variety of procedural infringements such as disturbance of seals or breach of commitments.

9.93 Public bodies (which may also be competitors as defined by the Act) may be fined up to CZK 10 million (about 400,000 EUR).

9.94 The Office has published guidelines on setting fines, very similar to the European Commission's 2006 Guidelines on the method of setting fines in determining the amount of the fine applied for.[35]

9.95 Starting in 2013 when the leniency policy which before had only been soft law, had been transposed into the Competition Act, some rules have been directly contained in the law.

9.96 In its decision bringing an infringement to an end, the Office may (but usually would not) also impose remedies, which may be behavioral or—if behavioral remedies are not equally effective or would be even more burdensome—structural. Similarly, it may accept commitments offered by a competitor. In the practice of recent years, competition advocacy would, in most cases, be the first attempt to end behavior that is considered to be an infringement.

9.97 Interim measures may be imposed but this is rarely done.

9.98 Whereas bid-rigging has always been a criminal offense in the Czech Republic, hard core cartels are criminal acts since 2010 and the acting persons may face imprisonment of up to eight years if the damage is higher than CZK 5 million (about EUR 200,000)—easily reached in cartel cases. Since the 2012 Amendment to the Antitrust Act, the conflict between leniency

[35] They are also available in English: <http://www.compet.cz/en/competition/antitrust/guidelines-on-the-method-of-setting-fines.html>.

and prosecution of criminal offenses has been resolved, a leniency application will protect the applicant from criminal proceedings if leniency has been granted.

Criminal law issues have even increased in importance as in 2012 the criminal liability of legal entities had been introduced into Czech law. Penalties include, among others, forced liquidation ordered by court against violators. So far no sentences have been published. **9.99**

Competitors that were held violators may also, since December 2012, for three years be prohibited from taking part in Czech public procurement proceedings, including public–private partnership (PPP) projects. **9.100**

G. Leniency and immunity

Whereas leniency had for many years been part of Czech competition law as *soft law* through a self-binding notice by the Office, the 2012 amendment introduced the leniency policy into the Competition Act. Full leniency will be granted to the first comer, up to 50 percent reduction in fines to the second applicant who brings substantial new evidence that was not known to the Office. A marker system exists. **9.101**

Unlike at EU level, leniency is therefore not restricted to secret horizontal cartels, but may also be granted for example in vertical cases. While no leniency is available in cases of dominance, contributions by the dominant business to fact-finding will be taken into account as a mitigating factor in setting fines. **9.102**

Leniency applications are submitted to the Office, which may grant the applicant full immunity from fines, or apply a reduced fine. In addition, the immunity applicant is required to cease the infringement and to fully cooperate with the Federal Competition Authority throughout the investigation. Immunity is not available for businesses which coerced other participants to take part in the infringement. **9.103**

Competitors who fail to meet the material standard for full immunity may nevertheless qualify for a reduction in the fine of up to 50 percent. Admittance of a violation in form of a settlement will grant a reduction of 20 percent. The other conditions for full immunity (cessation of infringement, full cooperation, and no coercion of other participants) also apply to reductions of the fine. **9.104**

H. Document creation and retention

Czech competition law does not provide for rules on document creation or retention. However, competitors under investigation by the Commission are under a duty actively to cooperate in the Office's investigative measures and to provide accurate information (*Kofola*:[36] original fine of EUR 450,000 for incomplete and false information, later reduced to EUR 200,000). Any negligent or intentional destruction of potentially relevant documents or otherwise tampering with evidence will be treated as a serious failure to cooperate, and may result in significant fines: a fine of up to 1 percent of the competitor's total turnover can be imposed repeatedly for non-cooperation. **9.105**

Moreover, such action may lead to loss of any claim under leniency. **9.106**

[36] *Kofola*, Case no. S 095/2008/KD (2008).

10

DENMARK

Morten Kofmann, Jens Munk Plum, and Erik Bertelsen
Kromann Reumert

Introduction

10.01 The Danish competition regime consists of two separate legal orders that effectively run parallel to each other—EU law and Danish law. EU law always applies if the relevant conduct has an effect on trade between member states, even if the conduct occurred in Denmark. On the other hand, Danish law applies if the conduct has an effect on Danish soil. In the event that both sets of laws are applicable, the EU law will always take precedence over national law. The Danish competition regime is modeled on EU law. However, Danish legislators reserve the right to create differences where special or unique conditions in the local Danish market justify such deviations. In the following Section, the focus will be on the Danish Competition Act and case law from the relevant Danish authorities and the courts. In recent years, the Danish authorities have focused their enforcement on the horizontal aspects of industry organizations' activities; cases involving possible links between resale price maintenance (RPM) and prevention of parallel import; and, finally, incumbent operators' possible abuse of dominant positions in fields such as electricity, post, and airport terminal activities.

I. Acting alone

Section 11 of the Danish Competition Act prohibits abuse of dominance. Whether or not an undertaking is dominant is assessed in accordance with EU practice. **10.02**

Section 11 only applies to the acts of: (a) an undertaking; (b) where that undertaking is dominant; and (c) abuses its dominant position; and (d) the abuse impacts effective competition in Denmark. Section 11(1) states broadly that any abuse of a dominant position by one or more undertakings is prohibited. Examples of "abuse" for the purposes of subsection (1) are provided in subsection (3) as: (i) directly or indirectly imposing unfair purchase or selling prices or other unfair trading conditions; (ii) limiting production, sales, or technical development to the prejudice of consumers; (iii) applying dissimilar conditions to equivalent transactions with trading partners, thereby placing them at a competitive disadvantage; or (iv) making the conclusion of contracts conditional on acceptance of supplementary obligations which, by their nature or according to commercial usage, have no connection with the subject of the contracts. **10.03**

Subsection (4) of s. 11 provides the Danish Competition Council with powers to bring infringements of subsection (1) to an end. In turn, subsection (4) refers to s. 16, a non-exhaustive list of enforcement tools that can be used not only to bring an abuse of dominance to an end, but also for anticompetitive agreements and articles 101 and 102 of the Treaty on the Functioning of the European Union (TFEU) infringements. The preparatory works to the Act state that "dominance" should be interpreted in accordance with the decisions of the Commission and the case law of the Court of Justice of the European Union (CJEU) regarding article 102 TFEU. Similarly, in general terms, the Danish definition of "abuse" is in line with the corresponding term under EU rules. Section 11(2) states that an undertaking can request the Danish Competition Council to declare whether or not it holds a dominant position. Declarations in the negative, confirming that no dominant position is held, are binding until revoked. Undertakings can also request the Council to make a declaration that certain conduct does not fall under the prohibition in subsection (1) and therefore, will not be subject to an order under subsection (4). **10.04**

The section's final provision, subsection (7), confers upon the Council a right to refrain from making such declarations where it may have implications for abuse of a dominant position in the common market or an essential part of it, and trade between the EU member states may be appreciably affected. However, in practice, s. 11(7) is rarely invoked. The scope of the Act is regulation of the Danish market. Both national and foreign companies can be subject to s. 11 if they engage in activities that restrict competition and the effects of their behavior extend to Denmark. In the field of unilateral/single-firm conduct, the Danish authorities have in recent years targeted excessive pricing in the field of electricity generation, exclusionary pricing strategies in for postal products and the access to essential facilities in the form of land for an airport terminal. **10.05**

A. Predatory pricing

Price predation is governed by s. 11(3)(i). Several Danish cases involving pricing practices have provided insight into the Danish rules. The cases show that when determining whether an undertaking has engaged in predatory pricing, the Danish Competition Council will **10.06** apply the so called *AKZO*-test set out by the European Court in *AKZO.*[1] Accordingly, prices below average variable cost (AVC) are per se abusive, whereas prices below average total cost (ATC) but above AVC will only be considered abusive if the prices form part of a plan for eliminating a competitor. It is likely that the Danish competition authorities will adopt the EU model, which uses the average avoidable costs (AAC) and the long-run average incremental cost (LRAIC) as the appropriate starting point in predatory pricing cases. After the model, it may also be investigated whether the undertaking's short-term conduct resulted in lower net revenues than could be expected from a reasonable alternative product. Regarding the requirement to show intent, the Danish competition authorities will rely on direct documentary evidence. Recent case law such as *Post Danmark* shows that the burden of proof is strict. In the preliminary ruling in *Post Danmark*, submitted by the Supreme Court, the CJEU stated that a dominant undertaking's selective below-cost pricing policy does not automatically constitute an abusive practice. On the basis of the preliminary ruling, the Supreme Court did not find sufficient evidence that Post Danmark had abused its dominant position. Thus, Post Danmark was acquitted.[2]

10.07 Since it can be quite difficult to prove intent, the case law concerning predation will often be decided by examining whether the dominant undertaking's prices are set below AVC. Variable costs are defined as costs that change with the amount of goods or services that an undertaking produces, whereas fixed costs are defined as the costs that an undertaking incurs regardless of the amount of goods or services produced. Costs may be classified as variable even though they do not vary with output, if an efficient undertaking is able to adjust the costs concurrently with changes in production. Whether costs are classified as variable or fixed costs will also depend on the period over which costs are assessed, since on a short-term basis most costs will be fixed, and vice versa. Often the relevant period over which to assess the costs will be the period within which the dominant undertaking has set its prices at predatorily low levels, but it has to be determined on a case-by-case basis. However, the AVC and average fixed cost (AFC) measures are not always appropriate for assessing predatory prices. Case law shows that the relevant cost measure can also, under certain circumstances, be the average incremental cost (AIC).

10.08 Danish case law prior to the Commission's decision in *Wannadoo Interactive* in 2003 recognized *de lege ferenda* the defense of meeting competition.[3] Accordingly, a dominant undertaking was entitled to set prices below AVC in order to meet the competition and defend a market position; that is, price reductions were allowed in response to competitors' price adjustments. In light of *Wannadoo Interactive*, and subsequent affirmation of that decision by both the General Court and the European Court of Justice, it is not a foregone conclusion that the Danish competition authorities will allow parties to invoke the meeting competition defense in cases where prices are set below AAC. However, the authorities have in earlier Danish cases accepted the defense under certain circumstances.

B. Exploitative offenses (excessive pricing, monopoly leveraging)

10.09 A price may be unfair in terms of s. 11(3)(i) if it is excessive. In line with the decisions of the CJEU in *General Motors* and *United Brands*,[4] among others, and the European Commission in *Scandlines Sverige AB v. Port of Helsingborg*, a price is deemed excessive for the purposes

---

[1] Case 62/86 *AKZO Chemie v. Commission* [1991] ECR I-3359.

[2] C-209/10 *Post Danmark A/S v. Konkurrencerådet*, March 27, 2012; *Post Danmark A/S v. Konkurrencerådet*, Supreme Court, Case no. 2/2008, February 15, 2013.

[3] *Wannadoo Interactive*, EC Commission, Case no. COMP/38.233, July 16, 2003.

[4] Case 26/75 *General Motors Continental v. Commission* [1975] ECR 1367; Case 27/76 *United Brands v. Commission* [1976] ECR 425.

of s. 11 if it exceeds the economic value of the product or service being provided.[5] Like the Commission, the Danish Competition and Consumer Authority is generally reluctant to find prices excessive. As a general starting point, a product or service's sale price should be compared with its production costs, and the calculation of costs should be made on a single-product basis, which means that if the undertaking manufactures several products or offers several services, the calculation of costs should be made for each of the products or services. According to the preparatory works to the 1998 Competition Act, an evaluation of the cost structure should be made with the assumption that conditions in the undertaking are as they would be where the undertaking is being run expediently, both from a technical and commercial perspective, and as a starting point valuation principles usually used in the industry should be applied. According to the preparatory works to the Act, this is likely to lead to the use of the cost method.

The calculation of costs on a single-product basis can be deviated from if there are considerations that justify it. Such considerations could be production methods which require substantial research and development efforts. The Danish Competition and Consumer Authority has not adopted a consistent approach to determining whether prices exceed a product or service's economic value. While the preparatory works to the 1998 Competition Act provide some guidance, the Authority takes a flexible approach in these cases and may develop its own, modified test instruments for application in a specific sector. Therefore, no clear rule on calculating the cost exists. Formally, the powers of the Danish Competition and Consumer Authority extend to granting an order that determines how a dominant undertaking should price its products. But in practice, the Authority will always refrain from telling an entity how to amend a price that is abusive. The power to issue a price order is therefore extremely rarely exercised. The unusual nature of such cases was noted by the Competition Appeals Tribunal in *Elsam II* when it stated that the instrument should only be used under very specific circumstances because it is, inherently, detrimental to competition for an authority to dictate an undertaking's pricing.[6] A different type of set price limit relate to tobacco, where the law explicitly provides that tobacco may only be sold at the price on the revenue stamp. However, certain restaurants are permitted to charge higher prices for tobacco. **10.10**

C. Monopsony

Monopsony falls within the scope of s. 11; hence it is prohibited for a dominant undertaking on the buying market to abuse its position. The situation has only been applied in one case under Danish law. In *Kædesamarbejdet i Inbogulve*, the Danish Competition Council found that an undertaking possessing less than 25 percent of the buying market was not dominant.[7] **10.11**

D. Price discrimination

According to s. 11(3)(iii), it is abusive for a dominant undertaking to apply dissimilar conditions to equivalent transactions with trading partners, thereby placing them at a competitive disadvantage, unless such behavior can be objectively justified. Price discrimination generally takes place in two different situations: when purchasers are charged different prices for the same goods or services and the prices are not justified by different cost structures; or when the same price is charged in circumstances where the cost for the supply of identical goods or services would justify a difference in price. Most discrimination cases also involve foreclosure **10.12**

[5] *Scandlines Sverige AB v. Port of Helsingborg* [2004] COMP/36.568

[6] *Elsam II v. Konkurrencerådet*, Competition Appeals Tribunal, Case no. 2005-0004688, November 14, 2006.

[7] *Kædesamarbejdet i Inbogulve*, Competition Council, Case nos. 2:8032-693-20 and 964-967, May 31, 2000.

elements. The Danish authorities are likely to analyze discrimination along the same lines as the Commission.

10.13 In Denmark, discrimination has often been actively pursued by the Danish Competition and Consumer Authority—perhaps more actively over time in comparison with authorities from other countries. The Danish authorities have a tendency to view discrimination from a relatively formalistic point of view. This approach has been supported by the courts that are arguably even more rigid in their analysis of what constitutes discrimination, and have been reluctant to carry out an effects-based analysis of the allegedly abusive behavior.

10.14 One explanation is that the courts are influenced by a more generally applicable principle of equal treatment, derived from administrative law that provides that everyone must be treated equally. The courts tend to adopt an analysis that is only based on whether dissimilar conditions have been offered by the dominant undertaking, and they refrain from analyzing whether the behavior leads to any anticompetitive effects viewed as discriminatory in nature. Typically, s. 11(3)(iii) covers price discrimination where the dominant undertaking offers rebates or discounts to some but not all of its customers for the same goods or services. It is important to notice that not all differences in pricing conditions constitute an abuse of dominance. Section 11(3)(iii) is not limited to be applied on price discrimination; it does also apply to other types of discrimination.

E. Dictating or influencing resale prices

10.15 RPM and minimum advertised price (MAP) (both covered below) constitute a borderland between acting alone and dealing with competitors, since the agreements covered under this paragraph are most commonly not concluded between competitors. Furthermore, an undertaking can infringe these rules alone. Nevertheless, the problems are explained in Sections I.E(i)–I.E(ii).

(i) Resale price maintenance

10.16 Unique to the Danish rules is a specific legislative provision addressing resale price maintenance. Subsection (2)(vii) of s. 6 was inserted into the Act in 2004 after the Eastern High Court's narrow reading of the s. 6 prohibition in *Levi Strauss*.[8] Expressly designed to preserve uniformity with EU case precedents relating to article 101, the subsection explicitly extends the scope of s. 6 to cover agreements made to "determine binding resale prices or in other ways seek to induce one or more trading partners not to deviate from recommended resale prices"—effectively, RPM. Resale price maintenance is considered a hard core infringement. There is no *de minimis* exemption, either explicitly in s. 7 or on account of an assessment of appreciable effects. According to the preparatory works to the Act, the purpose behind the insertion of s. 6(2)(vii) is to avoid a restrictive interpretation of the prohibition against certain anticompetitive agreements, as occurred in *Levi Strauss*. The subsection makes clear that the prohibition extends to single, isolated instances of RPM that occur without management's knowledge, and only affect a single reseller. It is also plain that agreements between the supplier and the distributor that provide for manufacturer's discounts or other incentives for maintaining certain resale prices will fall within the prohibition.

10.17 A distributor's explicit attempts to force resellers to follow its recommended resale prices can be sanctioned, even where resellers refuse to follow them, as long as an "agreement" can be established. The explicit wording of the provision and the first part of the preparatory works to the amendment both suggest that a distributor will be subject to fines in that particular

[8] *Anklagemyndigheden v. Levi Strauss*, Eastern High Court, Case no. S-2826-02, October 23, 2003.

situation. The second part of the preparatory works explicitly states that no revision of the concept of "agreement," which is to be interpreted in accordance with EU competition law, is intended. According to EU competition law, an attempt to force a reseller to follow recommended resale prices will not always constitute an "agreement" in restraint of competition. Correspondingly, it will not be an agreement under the Danish Competition Act and will fall outside the scope of s. 6. *OK/DK* suggests a relatively low threshold for consent before an agreement is ascertained.[9]

Efforts to make distributors enter into an agreement can be penalized as an attempt under s. 21(3) of the Danish Criminal Code, since such an infringement under aggravating circumstances can result in imprisonment. In practice, the scope of the prohibition against resale price maintenance has been interpreted widely. **10.18**

In *Levi Strauss* the Eastern High Court held that threats against a single distributor were not an infringement of s. 6.[10] It was considered that advice on prices was legal if it was not followed up with a threat of sanction for noncompliance. Further, an isolated occurrence did not amount to an infringement of s. 6. However, legislators did not agree with the Court's interpretation and the Danish Competition Act was amended to expressly include resale price maintenance. Almost all cases where the Danish Competition and Consumer Authority considers that resale price maintenance has occurred will be submitted to the State Prosecutor for Serious Economic Crime for further action. One notable exception, however, is the *OK/DK* case. The Authority's website states that it considers the case closed with the decision of the Danish Competition Council.[11] This seems extremely difficult to reconcile with the fact that the prohibition against resale price maintenance has otherwise consistently been applied very strictly in a large number of cases, even for cases where little effect could have been expected. **10.19**

(ii) Minimum advertised price programs

MAP programs fall within the scope of the prohibition in s. 6(2)(vii). Another situation which is covered by the prohibition is agreements on maximum rebates. Such agreements have the effect of limiting the resellers own price determination, and are therefore also limiting the free competition on the market. **10.20**

F. Tying arrangements

According to s. 11(3)(iv), a dominant undertaking will be found to have abused its dominant position if it uses contractual preconditions to impose supplementary obligations on other parties that, by their nature or according to commercial usage, have no connection with the subject of such contracts. The abuse described in s. 11(3)(iv) can consist of either tying or bundling. Tying occurs when a dominant undertaking conditions the sale of one product (the tying product) on the sale of another product or service (the tied product). Few EU cases have addressed tying and bundling and, similarly, Danish case law is also limited. However, it is clear that s. 11(3)(iv) must be interpreted in accordance with article 102 TFEU and corresponding decisions from the CJEU and the Commission, and in particular the *Microsoft* case which also forms the basis for the legal test that the Commission proposed in its Guidance paper.[12] The Danish Competition Council's decision in *Unimerco*[12b] confirms **10.21**

---

[9] *OK/DK*, Competition Council, Case no. ITE 4/0120-0289-0072, April 29, 2009.

[10] *Levi Strauss* (n 8).

[11] *OK/DK* (n 9). See also the text of the decision: <http://www.kfst.dk/Indhold-KFST/Nyheder/Pressemeddelelser/2009/~/link.aspx?_id=E0BFC31F405142B29839C1AEE78BC7CD&_z=z>.

[12] *Microsoft*, EC Commission Case no. COMP/C-3/37.792, March 24, 2004.

[12b] *Unimerco*, Danish Competition Council, Case no. 4/0120-0100-0512, October 29, 2008.

the applicability of the *Microsoft* test to the Danish rules and also reflects the latest views of the Danish competition authorities on tying practices.[13]

G. Exclusive dealing

10.22 Unless special circumstances apply, exclusive dealing will often give rise to concerns and can quite easily be found to constitute an abuse of dominance under s. 11(3). Consistent with the approach of the European Commission, exclusive dealing is likely to be considered abusive by the Danish competition authorities if the dominant undertaking, through *single branding obligations* or *English clauses*, generally commits purchasers to source all or most of their requirements from the dominant undertaking. It is a delicate balance as to how much volume a dominant undertaking will be able to tie without violating s. 11(3). The Danish competition authorities are unlikely to intervene if the single-branding obligations do not exceed 60 percent to 70 percent of the purchaser's requirements. However, this will also depend on the circumstances of each case and in particular, the dominant undertaking's market share, the duration of the agreement and the size of the customer. Even if the tied volume exceeds 60 percent to 70 percent, single-branding obligations may nonetheless be accepted if only a limited part of the market will be tied to the dominant undertaking. In *Carlsberg*, the Danish Competition Council accepted commitments that allowed Carlsberg to enter into exclusive agreements for the supply of draught beer provided that the volume supplied under these agreements would not exceed 4.5 percent of the total annual sale of beer to the HORECA channel.[14]

H. Refusal to deal

10.23 Refusal to deal is regulated by s. 11(3)(ii). The number of Danish cases on this issue that were decided prior to the Commission's Guidance paper is extensive. However, those cases show that there are three requirements that must be satisfactorily met before the authorities will order a dominant undertaking to supply: (1) the supplier must have a dominant position in the relevant market; (2) the supply must be of considerable importance to the purchaser; and (3) the supplier must be unable to provide any objective, fair, and non-discriminatory justification for the non-supply, and be unable to show that the refusal to supply has been applied objectively and, in a legal and economic sense, in accordance with the principle of proportionality. Despite the Commission's Guidance paper, it is likely that the Danish competition authorities will maintain their position on refusal to deal as expressed in previous case law. Therefore, the Guidance paper will have a limited effect on Danish practice.

10.24 An assessment as to whether the supply is of considerable importance to the purchaser can prove difficult where the purchaser is a retail chain. In a 1978 case, the Danish Supreme Court stated that the delivery of high-end electronic goods to a large supermarket was not of considerable importance to the operation of a retail chain with a wide range of goods, despite the retail chain having a commercial and economic interest in obtaining supply. [15]

10.25 Case law from the 1980s has established that the competition authorities can order supply to retail chains when the products concerned are linked to the retail chain's business areas and opportunities for growth. Cases also demonstrate that an order to supply can be issued even though the products concerned are intended for resale. The reasons for non-supply must be consistently observed and differences in the treatment of trading partners which cannot be justified will usually be unacceptable. Previous decisions show that the assessment of the

[13] *Unimerico*, Competition Council, Case no. 4/0120-0100-0512, October 29, 2008.
[14] *Carlsberg*, Competition Council, Case no. 3/1120-0204-0170, October 26, 2005.
[15] Supreme Court, Case no. U1987.361H, 1978.

supplier's reasons for non-supply will be made on a case-by-case basis. The fact that there are a sufficient number of other suppliers in the market will not qualify as an objective reason, but the authorities have accepted a refusal to deal on the basis of a purchaser's lack of professional qualifications, where the cost of the supply means that it is inefficient for the supplier; on the basis of capacity, with regard to the level of the branding of the goods or technical complexity; or on the basis of the competitive relationship between the purchaser and the supplier and the competitive behavior of the purchaser.

Assessment of a refusal to supply will take into consideration whether or not the refusal relates to an essential facility. In this respect, a 2006 Danish Competition Council decision regarding the taxi service industry is relevant.[16] The Council found that several taxi companies in Greater Copenhagen had abused their collective dominant position by excluding another taxi company from a mutual clearing arrangement covering taxi checks and taxi debit cards primarily issued to business customers. Although the Council did not specifically classify the abuse as a refusal to deal, the case is generally regarded as such. The Council ordered the taxi companies to readmit the excluded taxi company as a member of the mutual clearing arrangement on objective, fair and non-discriminatory conditions. The decision is in line with the Commission's Guidance paper since admission to the clearing arrangement was objectively necessary in order to effectively compete in the market, because non-admission to the arrangement would lead to the elimination of effective competition in the market, and because the refusal was likely to lead to consumer harm. **10.26**

I. Essential facilities

The concept of essential facilities established in EU competition law is recognized in Denmark too. An unusual situation involving essential facilities arose in the context of a complaint to the Competition and Consumer Authority against Copenhagen Airports over the latter's refusal to rent a piece of land for a competing airport terminal. By its decision of January 25, 2012, the Competition Council found that "law or public regulation" in the area of aviation constituted an obstacle for the project. Pursuant to s. 2 of the Competition Act, the provisions of competition law could not, therefore, be enforced to secure the land for the complainants. Very unusually, however, the Competition and Consumer Authority published an apparently final draft decision of 266 pages partly based on the essential facilities doctrine (Annex 2 to the Competition Council's decision).[17] **10.27**

J. Bundling (including loyalty and market share discounts)

Bundling generally describes the situation where two (or more) products are only offered for sale as a package but not separately, or where the products are sold both as a package and separately but it is more attractive to buy the package. A multi-product rebate can have the same anticompetitive effects as bundling where it is sufficiently large. Such rebates can constitute de facto bundling. In the 1999 case *Netto I/S*, it was held that the insistence by Egmont Magasiner A/S and Aller Press A/S that supermarket chain Netto must acquire *both* weekly tabloid magazines *Her & Nu* and *Kig Ind* if it wanted to market just *one* of the magazines constituted an abuse of the companies' collective dominant positions in the Danish market for the sale of weekly magazines to distributors. The Danish Competition Council also found that the companies had abused their collective dominant positions by threatening to disrupt delivery of all weekly magazines unless *Netto* purchased *Kig Ind*. The Council considered that **10.28**

[16] *Clearing af taxiboner og kontokort i Storkøbenhavn*, Competition Council, 4/0120-0100-0086, May 31, 2006.

[17] *Konkurrencerådets beslutning om at rette henvendelse til transportministeren*, Competition Council Case no. 4/0120-8901-1064, January 25, 2012.

Aller Press A/S had abused its dominant position in the overall market for weekly magazines by requiring Netto to purchase the full product portfolio of both companies. Further, Aller Press A/S had abused its dominant position by threatening to stop the deliveries of all weekly magazines unless Netto purchased *Kig Ind.* Despite the Council's reference to s. 11(3)(i) (unfair general terms and conditions), the decision is probably better classified as abuse by bundling.[18]

K. Standard-setting groups (disclosure requirements, licensing arrangements, and licensing pools)

10.29 There have been no cases on standard-setting activities in the administrative practice or case law.

10.30 As in other areas of Danish competition law, the practices of the Commission and the European Court of Justice are to be used as an interpretative guidance for the application of the provisions of competition law. Of particular relevance in this connection are the Commission's guidelines on the applicability of the Treaty on the Functioning of the European Union to horizontal cooperation agreements ("Horizontal Cooperation Guidelines"). It may be assumed that the Danish Competition and Consumer Authority as well as the Competition Council will apply the Horizontal Cooperation Guidelines' "safe harbor" from s. 6 for standardization agreements which satisfy the criteria outlined in the guidelines.

10.31 As a practical observation, it should also be borne in mind that the activities of standard-setting groups are likely to have an effect on inter-state trade. To the extent, therefore, that such activities comply with the provisions of EU competition law, they cannot be found illegal under corresponding national competition law provisions pursuant to article 3(2) of Regulation No. 1/2003.

L. Customer termination

10.32 A supplier's termination of a customer may be regarded as a special case of refusal to deal (as discussed in Section I.H). Refusal by a dominant company to supply customers may amount to an abuse unless there are objective, fair, and non-discriminatory justifications for the behavior and unless it can be shown that the behavior has been applied objectively and, in a legal and economic sense, in accordance with the principle of proportionality.

10.33 The principle expressed in the Commission's Guidance paper in relation to abuse of a dominant position that the termination of an existing supply arrangement is more likely to be found to be abusive than a refusal to commence supplying the requesting undertaking will also be applied under Danish competition law.

M. Termination of intermediaries (retailers, wholesalers, dealers, and value-added resellers, agents, and brokers)

10.34 In a decision of May 25, 2005, the Danish Competition Council found that Toyota A/S had abused its dominant position in the market for authorized servicing of Toyota cars by imposing unreasonable terms. Under the threat of termination/annulment of the repairer's status as an authorized repairer, Toyota Danmark had pressed him to change his marketing policy and trademark usage. Without leaving the repairer a fair opportunity to bring the case before a court or arbitrator, Toyota had also pressured him into paying various sums of money, which Toyota Danmark described as compensatory (for violation of marketing and trademark rights)—but which the repairer perceived as fines of a punitive nature. The

[18] Netto I/S, Competition Council, 1999.

Council also found that Toyota had abused its dominant position in terms of discrimination.[19] The Council's decision was later overturned by the Competition Appeals Tribunal on the basis that enforcement of remedies for breach of contract did not constitute an abuse of a dominant position unless the actions could be considered unusual business behavior or harassment. The Tribunal did not find that this was the case in the three incidents where Toyota had claimed damages.[20]

N. Termination of relationships with competitors

Termination of a relationship with competitors can only constitute a competition law infringement for an undertaking with a dominant position. The situation resembles refusals to deal and customer termination (as described in Sections I.H and I.L). However, it is accepted in Danish legal theory that it may be legitimate for a dominant undertaking to refuse to supply its competitors unless for example the essential facilities doctrine applies. There is no recent case law on the subject—with the possible exception of an unusual case (with no pre-existing relationship), where the Competition and Consumer Authority decided to publish a draft decision involving the Copenhagen Airports: Annex 2 to the Competition Council's decision of January 25, 2012.[21] **10.35**

O. Exemptions

The Danish Competition Act contains no general rule of exemption. Besides the specific exemptions mentioned earlier, there are no exemptions to anticompetitive behavior. **10.36**

II. Dealing with competitors

Section 6 of the Danish Competition Act prohibits restrictive agreements. The section must be read in the context of the provisions that follow it—ss. 7–10. Together, these sections provide a coherent system on restrictive agreements. Section 6(1) states that it is "prohibited for undertakings etc. to enter into agreements that have restriction on competition as their direct or indirect object or consequence." Read together with s. 6(3), the prohibition also extends to decisions made by an association of undertakings and concerted practices between undertakings. **10.37**

Section 6(2) provides a non-exhaustive list of examples of restrictive agreements. The list largely corresponds to article 101(1) TFEU, but also includes two unique additions that have their origins in Danish case law: joint venture coordination and resale price maintenance. Agreements will fall within the prohibition if they: (i) fix purchase or selling prices or other trading conditions; (ii) limit or control production, sales, technical development or investments; (iii) share markets or sources of supply; (iv) apply dissimilar conditions to equivalent transactions with trading partners, thereby placing some trading partners at a competitive disadvantage; (v) make the conclusion of contracts subject to acceptance of supplementary obligations which, by their nature or according to commercial usage, have no connection with the subject of the contracts; (vi) coordinate the competitive practices of two or more undertakings through the establishment of a joint venture; or (vii) determine binding resale prices, or in other ways seek to induce one or more trading partners not to deviate from recommended resale prices. Where a restrictive agreement falls within the s. 6(2) prohibitions, **10.38**

[19] *Toyota Danmark A/S*, Competition Council Case no. 3/1120-0100-1128, May 25, 2005.
[20] Toyota, Competition Appeals Tribunal.
[21] *Konkurrencerådets beslutning om at rette henvendelse til transportministeren*, Competition Council Case no. 4/0120-8901-1064, January 25, 2012.

and none of the exceptions or exemptions are applicable, the agreement will be void and unenforceable from the time it was created.

10.39 With s. 6(4), the Danish Competition Council is granted broad powers to "issue orders" to bring an infringement of s. 6(1) to an end. In turn, s. 6(4) refers to s. 16, a non-exhaustive list of the types of enforcement tools that the Council may use. The four examples given are orders with regard to contractual obligations, prices, divestment, and access to infrastructure. Specifically, the Council can terminate agreements, decisions, trading conditions, or similarly demand that stated prices or profits may not be exceeded or that prices or profits are to be calculated in accordance with specific rules, require one or more undertakings to divest assets to specific buyers, or order parties to grant access to important infrastructure. The Council can enforce these orders as well as commitments made by undertakings.

10.40 Subsections 6(2)(i) through (v) correspond to article 101 TFEU, whereas 6(2)(vi) and (vii) are unique to the Danish legislation. According to the preparatory works, s. 6 is to be interpreted in accordance with the EU regulation. Therefore, the practices of the Commission and the Court of Justice of the European Union are to be used as interpretative guidance for the provision, subject to the particularities of the market conditions (and importantly, only to the extent that the factual circumstances are similar).

10.41 With effect from 1 March 2013, s. 18b(1) provides for the Competition Council to issue interim injunctions, in case the competition would otherwise suffer from severe damage. While the acting together area accounts for the majority of the Danish competition authorities' enforcement activities, it is believed that these new powers will be used rarely.

A. Horizontal price fixing (including advanced announcements of price or product changes)

10.42 Section 6(2)(i) expressly prohibits price fixing. The scope of the prohibition includes agreements made to "fix purchase or selling prices or other trading conditions." Price fixing is a hardcore infringement. The lack of a *de minimis* exemption for price-fixing offenses is explicitly confirmed by s. 7(1)(i). Earlier, the Danish competition authorities took a comparatively lenient approach to pricing instructions from trade associations, but since the implementation of the EU regulations, this is no longer the case. A stricter approach is also consistent with the preparatory works to the Danish Competition Act, where it is stated that all restrictive agreements are encompassed by the s. 6 prohibition, including agreements of an instructive nature. As a consequence of this stricter approach, several trade associations have received fines for recommending minimum prices to their members.

10.43 The practice of the Danish Competition and Consumer Authority demonstrates that it is extremely difficult to obtain an exemption for a price-fixing agreement under s. 8. A rare example of an exempted price-fixing arrangement for purchase prices is the horizontal cooperation between twenty-seven small and medium-sized motor vehicle insurance companies, *Taksatorringen*.[21b] According to the Danish Competition Council, the cooperation restricts competition but can be exempted for its pro-competitive effects.

10.44 Bid-rigging is also a hard core infringement, for which there is no *de minimis* exemption. *El-kartellet* (the *Electricity Cartel* case) is the leading Danish case concerning bid-rigging. *Fælleslicitationskontoret og Varmebranchens Licitationsforening* shows that it is not only traditional bid-rigging that is prohibited by s. 6, but also agreements on additional charges limited to covering actual costs.[22]

[21b] *Taksatorringen*, Danish Competition Council, Case no. 4/0120-0301-0041, April 29, 2009.

[22] *Fælleslicitationskontoret og Varmebranchens Licitationsforening "Jermer" v. Konkurrencerådet*, Competition Appeals Tribunal, Case nos. 99-80.612 and 99-80.618, January 20, 2000.

B. Horizontal agreements to allocate customers or territories; agreements not to compete

Section 6(2)(iii) prohibits the allocation of market segments or customers. The preparatory works to the Act state that allocation of geographical areas, quotas, or customer categories are examples of horizontal agreements prohibited by s. 6. Like price-fixing and bid-rigging practices, customer or market allocation cannot any longer qualify for a *de minimis* exemption. **10.45**

C. Horizontal boycotts

Agreements between two or more undertakings to stop delivering to a specific buyer or to stop buying from a specific provider constitute horizontal boycotts. Section 6(2)(ii) prohibits such boycotts. Even though a boycott is not agreed on, the same effects can come through due to very unbeneficial conditions. Such a situation also falls within the scope of s. 6(2)(ii). **10.46**

D. Joint ventures and other competitive collaborations

For joint production, joint distribution, and joint selling, the application of Danish law is basically consistent with EU competition law. An agreement will most likely not contravene s. 6 where the commonality of total costs between the cooperating parties is low, for example, because only a minor part of the final product was produced in cooperation, or because the cooperation only concerned a minor part of the parties' total output of the final product. **10.47**

Agreements between competitors that fix prices for market supplies, limit output, or share markets or customer groups will fall within the scope of s. 6. However, if the agreement regarding output is limited to the output covered by the production agreement, this will not contravene s. 6. The same follows where a production joint venture also carries out the distribution of the products covered by the production agreement and sets the sales price for the produced goods. **10.48**

To test whether a production agreement restricts competition, the authorities will analyze the effects of the agreement and examine the parties' market shares, the number of competitors in the market and other relevant factors. An agreement concerning both specialization and joint production will be exempted under the block exemption concerning specialization agreements as long as the parties' combined market share does not exceed 20 percent. **10.49**

Following the Tribunal's decision in *Asphalt*, the Danish Competition Act was amended to include an express provision stating that coordination between competitors through a joint venture is contrary to s. 6.[23] However, full-function joint ventures are still classed as mergers, and as such will fall outside of the scope of s. 6. **10.50**

GDC A/S shows that parties who cooperate to jointly sell their products tread a fine line between permissible and illegal activities.[24] Joint selling is an area that, on some levels, approaches cartel activity. Since it can involve revenue sharing, and in some instances market sharing, it is often given harsh treatment by the authorities, or even directly condemned. **10.51**

Joint selling agreements between non-competitors cannot create any horizontal restraints, and will generally not infringe s. 6. Any vertical issues will usually be assessed under the block exemption for distribution agreements. **10.52**

---

[23] *Viborg Asfaltfabrik I/S m.fl. v. Konkurrencerådet*, Competition Appeals Tribunal, Case nos. 99-193.956, 99-193.964, 99-193.969, 99-195.116 and 99-195.125, April 25, 2001.

[24] GDC A/S [2002].

10.53 Where creating a joint selling agreement is, objectively, the only way for a competitor to enter a new market, the agreement will not create any restrictions as the parties are not actual or potential competitors. If, on the other hand, the joint selling agreement has as its object or effect to fix or otherwise coordinate prices between the competitors, the agreement will contravene s. 6 because it eliminates price competition between the parties.

10.54 The same goes for restrictions on the parties' production volume and for the allocation of markets and/or customer groups. Price fixing and volume restrictions will infringe s. 6 even where the joint selling agreement is not exclusive and the parties are free to sell to others outside of the agreement. Even if a joint selling agreement does not aim to fix prices, limit output or allocate markets or customer groups, it may infringe s. 6 if it allows the competing parties to exchange sensitive commercial information or if it influences a significant part of the parties' total costs. However, where the parties' combined market share does not exceed 15 percent, the agreement is unlikely to cause any competitive restraints. Joint selling is an area where activities are generally presumed to be permissible, providing parties with no reason to approach the authorities.

10.55 While in practice the authorities can give informal approval to cooperative activities, there is often no need for a formal decision. In any event, the authorities do not seem to allocate a significant amount of resources to law enforcement in this particular area—they tend to focus on more significant and harmful cooperative activities, such as cartels.

E. Trade associations

10.56 In a 2007 Competition Report,[25] the Danish Competition and Consumer Authority issued a set of guidelines expressing its views on information exchanges in trade associations, and consequently began a systematic survey of the statistics compiled by Danish trade associations. This led to a number of cases before the Danish Competition Council, some of which can only be interpreted as a general toughening of the stance taken by the authorities towards information exchanges in trade associations.

10.57 In the guidelines, the Authority lists a number of criteria for the assessment of information exchanges. But unfortunately the guidelines are not particularly clear and only describe the "grey zone" without providing guidance as to what is acceptable to the Authority and what is not. Therefore, the guidelines cannot meaningfully be applied by a trade association intending to comply with the competition rules. Combined with the Authority's general attitude that it will not provide positive reassurance to parties seeking informal guidance, the general effect is that trade associations have had to seek legal counsel for interpretation of the guidelines.

10.58 The Danish Competition and Consumer Authority states in the 2007 Competition Report that trade organizations are forbidden to exchange information taking the form of recommended prices, rebates and the like. As a general rule, it is very clear that the publishing of maximum prices will also violate the Act.

10.59 Two other types of prices are, as a general rule, not allowed to be published: future prices and actual prices (with the exception of certain price portals aimed at consumers). On the other hand, publishing historical prices can be legal if the prices are sufficiently outdated and aggregated.

10.60 For sales and production information, the Danish Competition and Consumer Authority suggests that publishing information which reveals the future sale prices and production

---

[25] *Konkurrenceredegørelse* (June 2007), <http://www.kfst.dk/Indhold-KFST/Publikationer/Dansk/2007/~/media/KFST/Publikationer/Dansk/2007/Konkurrenceredegoerelse%202007%20analyse%2020070612.pdf>.

levels for single companies is prohibited. However, publishing such information can be legal if the information is sufficiently outdated and aggregated.

In collecting the information, trade associations must ensure strict confidentiality so that members of the trade association do not receive confidential business information about each other. Further, trade associations are not permitted to publish information regarding members' costs if the information can in any way be perceived as a price recommendation. Information about an individual company's costs may only be published if there are associated and ascertainable efficiency gains, and if the information is depersonalized. **10.61**

As a starting point, the Danish Competition and Consumer Authority takes the view that recommendations that might amount to substantial competitive parameters are not allowed. Whether or not this is the case depends on a number of factors—such as the type and age of the information exchanged, the aggregation level, the concentration in the market and how the information is published and to whom. With regard to recommendations on pricing conduct, it is likely that the Danish Competition and Consumer Authority's views are more restrictive than the Danish and European case law in this area. **10.62**

In practice, it seems that the general rules are not applied as rigidly as the Authority states. In a number of cases, the Danish Competition Council has deemed information exchanges illegal by object. Previously, the authorities had shown a tendency to assess the legitimacy of information exchange practices from an "effect on competition" point of view. Also, the criterion used to establish whether or not an information exchange practice has the restriction of competition as its *object*, seems to be wider than under general EU law. This shift is seen in two landmark cases, *ITD* and *DTL*.[26] **10.63**

The prohibition is subject to the *de minimis* thresholds in s. 7(1). The s. 6 prohibition against restrictive agreements still applies even where the *de minimis* thresholds are not met if the agreement can be classified as hardcore. In *Dansk Juletræsdyrkerforening*, the Eastern High Court held that s. 7(2) does not only cover horizontal agreements but also agreements or concerted practices with the (lesser) purpose of guiding pricing.[27] It was held that agreements or concerted practices do not have to be binding to constitute a violation of the s. 6(1) prohibition. In recent case law, the Council has stated that an information exchange practice will have the restriction of competition as its object if it is "objectively suitable" to restrict competition. **10.64**

Taken at face value, this implies that it would never be necessary to conduct an effects-based analysis and ascertain whether information exchange practices had any practical effect because such practices would always be caught by the other test—"objectively suitable to restrict competition." However, in both cases, the Council concluded that there seemed to be no other objective purpose than to restrict competition. **10.65**

F. Interlocking directorates

The competition law concerns in relation to interlocking directorates have so far arisen in the context of the acquisition or holding of minority interests and/or board representation in competing undertakings. There is no practice or case law on the subject neither under ss. 6 or 11 nor under the provisions on merger control. In practice, the main concern is information exchange and possible collusion or coordination between competitors, and relevant precaution to remedy **10.66**

[26] *International Transport Danmark (ITD)*, Competition Council Case no. 4/0120-0289-0079, February 25, 2009; *Dansk Transport og Logistik (DTL)*, Competition Council Case no. 4/0120-0289-0080, December 17, 2008.

[27] *Anklagemyndigheden v. Dansk Juletræsdyrkerforening*, Eastern High Court Case no. SS-2-7791/07, February 17, 2009.

the situation is to erect Chinese walls and appoint the relevant representatives from different parts of the organization with different functions in combination with confidentiality obligations.

G. Facilitating practices

10.67 Concerted practices are a sort of coordination between undertakings which are not a specific agreement, but willfully replace the competition risk with a practical cooperation. According to s. 6(3), s. 6(1) is also covering concerted practices.

H. Information exchange

10.68 Agreements to exchange information can, in certain circumstances, amount to restrictive agreements or concerted practices in violation of s. 6(1). Some information exchange agreements—such as agreements that are ancillary to a cartel—clearly violate s. 6(1). Information agreements that are ancillary to a cartel and relate to price-fixing or market-sharing activities are naturally covered by s. 6(1) and will not be further elaborated on in this Section.

10.69 On the other hand, other information exchange agreements can occur in the absence of a cartel. These kinds of information exchanges can fall within or outside the scope of the prohibition in s. 6, depending on factors such as the nature of the information exchanged (whether it is prices, market shares, costs, etc.), the market structure (such as oligopolistic or fragmented), the frequency of the information exchanges, and the age of the information.

10.70 During the 1990s, the Danish competition authorities took a somewhat lenient approach to this issue. As a consequence, there were several cases where information exchange agreements regarding price fixing were found to be compliant with the Danish competition rules. Since 1998, the Danish Competition and Consumer Authority has taken a significantly stricter line on information exchange agreements—intervening in more than fifty cases. The issue has most frequently arisen in connection with information exchanges within trade associations. If there is a natural need for the information exchange, or if there exists a general contractual duty of loyalty, the information exchange practice can be exempted from the prohibition in certain cases: see for example, *Foreningen af Filmudlejere i Danmark*.[28]

I. Exchanges of historic pricing information

10.71 It is recognized that pricing information becomes less sensitive and even obsolete as time passes. In general, therefore, the exchange of up-to-date information has to be made at a highly aggregated level and without creating transparency into individual undertakings' information. With time, however, such information may be regarded as historic as a result of which the exchange no longer raises competition law concerns.

(i) How old, anonymous, and aggregated pricing information needs to be

10.72 The assessment of how old, anonymous and aggregated pricing information needs to be legally exchanged has to be determined on a case-by-case basis. As in many other jurisdictions, there has been an informal rule of one year, but the Competition and Consumer Authority have often stated that this is not a universal rule that always applies, and that it can be less as well as more.

(ii) What pro-competitive purposes, if any, exchange needs to help participants achieve; pre-merger due diligence

10.73 Information exchange even between competitors can have a pro-competitive purpose. An example is the performance of a pre-merger due diligence which is indispensable to enable a

[28] *Foreningen af Filmudlejere i Danmark*, Competition Appeals Tribunal Case no. 01-234.553, December 21, 2002.

contemplated transaction. In such cases, the parties are generally advised to conclude a non-disclosure agreement, limit the number of individuals involved (and perhaps avoid persons from certain commercially sensitive areas), and limit the information to what is reasonably necessary at the given stage of the transaction process.

J. Joint purchasing agreements

Joint purchasing agreements may affect two different markets: the purchasing market in which the agreement will have its direct effect, and the downstream selling market where the parties will sell the purchased goods. Agreements regarding joint purchasing will almost always be concluded between competitors, at least in the purchasing market. If the parties are not active in the same downstream market, the agreement will generally fall outside the scope of s. 6 unless the parties have particularly strong market positions in the purchasing market. **10.74**

As a general rule, joint production agreements only contravene s. 6 per se if the agreement in effect not only concerns joint purchasing, but also serves as a method for maintaining a cartel between the parties, for example, with regard to price fixing, market or customer allocation, or the limitation of output. The assessment of whether a joint purchasing agreement is contrary to s. 6 will first and foremost take into account the buying power of the parties. If the parties have significant buying power (e.g. where they account for a significant part of the total volume of the purchasing market), the agreement can lead to a foreclosure of the market and therefore run contrary to s. 6. Significant buying power can also have the result that lower prices are not passed on to downstream customers, which in turn can lead to cost increases for other competitors, or to supplier inefficiencies. This will often be the case where the parties have significant combined market power in both the purchasing and selling markets. If the parties have a combined market share of below 15 percent in both the purchasing and the selling markets, it is unlikely that a joint purchasing agreement will lead to a restriction of competition. **10.75**

K. Joint lobbying/regulatory/legislative efforts

Industry organizations' joint lobbying activities, involvement in regulatory processes, and other legislative efforts do normally not give rise to competition law concerns. It is important, nevertheless, for the members of the industry organizations, and in particular for their representatives, to be aware of the narrow boundary between such legitimate policy orientated activities and the risk of illegal information exchange, collusion, or coordination. **10.76**

III. General issues

A. Jurisdiction and applicable law (including sector-specific competition regulation)

The Danish Competition Act only applies to restrictions that have an effect on Danish territory. All restrictive actions that have an effect on the Danish market can be targeted by the Competition Act, regardless of the nationality or place of business of the parties involved. If the EU competition rules apply to the conduct, these rules will take precedence over the Danish Competition Act, and the Danish competition authorities will be obliged to transfer the case to the European Commission. **10.77**

Greenland and the Faroe Islands have their own competition laws and are not subject to the Danish Competition Act. Several sectors of the Danish market are subject to specific rules that deviate from the general provisions of the Competition Act. **10.78**

Some statutory barriers to entry still exist in the Danish market, a majority stemming from legal requirements to acquire state authorization before exercising certain professions, for example, lawyers, doctors, and accountants. Also, some market sectors are still controlled **10.79** by the state, and in those sectors only state-licensed undertakings can compete. The energy, public transport, and postal service sectors have all traditionally been controlled by the state. However, it is the telecommunications and insurance sectors that have retained special legal provisions unique to their areas.

10.80 The telecommunications sector is governed by the Tele Competition Act, which applies as *lex specialis*. The rules are based on EU directives, and differ from the provisions in the Competition Act, reflecting the traditionally monopolistic nature of this market. The most notable divergences are intercommunication provisions. Under the Tele Competition Act, a provider of a telecommunications network with significant market power—a provider that holds a dominant position—has an obligation to give competing providers access to its network so that consumers will be offered a wider variety of telecommunication services. Compliance with the act is supervised by the Danish Business Authority, in some cases in cooperation with the Danish competition authorities.

10.81 The Commission's new block exemption on agreements in the insurance sector provides that certain agreements between insurance companies are exempted from article 101 TFEU. Due to the parallel nature of the prohibitions in article 101 TFEU and s. 6 of the Danish Competition Act (the corresponding prohibition against restrictive agreements), the practical result of the block exemption is that it also operates to exempt certain agreements under Danish law.

10.82 The block exemption sets out two categories of agreements which are exempted per se. Compared with the previous block exemption which expired on March 31, 2010, the new regulation narrows the scope of application of the exemption significantly—from four categories of agreements to two. However, the Commission has made it clear that the amendments do not intend to reflect a significant change in the substantive approach.

10.83 The exempted agreements include:

- where created for reference purposes, the joint creation and distribution of certain calculations regarding the average cost of covering specified risks and certain mortality tables and tables showing the frequency of illness, accident, and invalidity, and the joint carrying out and distribution of studies on the risks and probable impact of general circumstances external to the interested undertakings or on the profitability of different types of investment;
- the setting up and operation of groups of insurance and reinsurance undertakings in the form of co-insurance or co-reinsurance for the common coverage of new risks or certain risks where the pools' aggregate market share is below certain thresholds.

10.84 The Danish executive order implementing the block exemption on insurance directly into Danish law is basically following the Commission's approach.

B. Antitrust system

10.85 The legal framework of the Danish antitrust system is the Danish Competition Act, supported by articles 101–109 TFEU. The rules are primarily enforced by the Danish Competition Council, see Section III.B.(i).

(i) Name of agency/agencies

10.86 The Danish Competition Council is the principal enforcer of competition law in Denmark. In practice, however, the Danish Competition and Consumer Authority, which is the secretariat of the Competition Council, is in charge of the day-to-day administration of the Competition Act and prepares the decisions of the Council. The decisions of the competition authorities can be appealed before the Competition Appeals Tribunal. The Appeals Tribunal forms part of the administration and its decisions can in turn be appealed by the undertakings to the ordinary courts.

(ii) Staff size and budget

10.87 The Danish Competition Council consists of a chairman and seventeen members appointed by the Minister for Business and Growth. The chairman and eight of the members must be independent of commercial and consumer interests while, of the remaining nine members, eight are nominated by various commercial interest organizations and one by a consumer organization. The Danish Competition and Consumer Authority has a total of about 300 employees of whom approximately 45 percent are employed within the competition area. The Danish Competition and Consumer Authority has a total yearly budget amounting to approximately DKK 200 million. The Competition Appeals Tribunal is made up of a Supreme Court Justice who is functioning as chairman and four other members with expertise in economics and law, respectively.

(iii) Recent enforcement actions and trends

10.88 The Danish Competition Act was recently amended, and entered into force on March 1, 2013. The amendments consisted primarily in raising the levels of fines and introducing imprisonment of up to six years for cartel participants under aggravating circumstances. Further to that, minor procedural issues were amended. Yet another amendment recently entered into force on August 1, 2013. This amendment introduced a filing fee of up to DKK 1.5 million in merger cases.

C. Private litigation

10.89 Undertakings can go directly to the civil courts to have an infringement determined, possibly in combination with a claim for damages. In practice, it is uncommon for an undertaking to directly pursue a claim in the civil courts. Instead, undertakings wait until they have a decision from the competition authorities stating that there has been an infringement of the Competition Act. Denmark's district courts hear cases at their lowest level. However, it is the Danish Maritime and Commercial Court that is competent to hear cases where the application of the Competition Act has "significant importance" or where cases involve the application of article 101 or 102 TFEU.

D. Follow-on litigation (includes role of agency determinations of liability for follow-on litigation)

10.90 The vast majority of damages actions in the field of competition law arise as follow-on litigation from administrative decisions (possibly after appeal before the Competition Appeals Tribunal or the ordinary courts). Such preexisting decisions are regarded as (an important) part of the relevant facts of the damages case, but not necessarily proof of the prerequisite legal basis for liability to pay damages (*culpa*).

10.91 Furthermore, the plaintiffs in damages actions need to establish the size of their losses as well as the necessary connectivity. An example of a case where this failed is *T.W. Autodele ApS v. Scandinavisk Motor Co. A/S*[29] in which the allegedly injured party, who claimed to be foreclosed by the dominant competitor's loyalty rebates, was unable to substantiate the magnitude of the lost business (in spite of the court's statement that a lenient standard of proof applied in the circumstances).

[29] *T.W. Autodele ApS v. Scandinavisk Motor Co. A/S*, City Court of Glostrup Case no. BS 1-161/2007, November 17, 2008.

E. Arbitration and alternative dispute resolution

10.92 Where a case proceeds by way of arbitration, it is most likely that the nominated arbitral tribunal will have competence to decide whether an agreement or part of an agreement should be considered null and void.

F. Remedies

(i) Civil liability

10.93 The Competition Act does not contain any provisions regarding damages. According to the preparatory works to the Act, it already follows from the general principles found in Danish law that when a legal or natural person suffers a loss due to an illegal restriction of competition, that loss can form the basis for a civil claim in damages.

10.94 The first condition for awarding damages as a result of an infringement of the Danish Competition Act is a basis of liability. This is determined by the general Danish rule of *culpa*, which means that the infringement must be intentional or due to negligence (including gross negligence). Infringement of a legal precept such as the prohibition against restrictive agreements or the prohibition against abuse of dominant position is an intentional or negligent act that provides a basis of liability.

10.95 The second condition for awarding damages is that the loss is foreseeable and there is a causal connection between the infringement and the loss. The *Ekko II* case shows that damages can be awarded where a concerted practice infringes the Danish Competition Act and losses are not passed on to customers.[30]

(ii) Criminal liability

10.96 Section 23(1) states that infringements will be sanctioned by fines imposed by the civil courts. An exception to this is s. 23b which authorizes the Competition Council to issue administrative fines in cases where the defendant has admitted guilt. Criminal penalties have previously formed the subject of debate. It is the State Prosecutor for Serious Economic and International Crime (*Statsadvokaten for Særlig Økonomisk og International Kriminalitet*, also abbreviated to *SØIK*) that conducts criminal cases, usually on request from the Danish Competition and Consumer Authority.

10.97 The Public Prosecutor initiates cases on its own where undertakings apply for leniency (see Section III.G). The Director of the Danish Competition and Consumer Authority decides whether or not the Public Prosecutor should be contacted for the purposes of prosecution. The Director also makes a recommendation regarding the size of any fine to be imposed. If the Public Prosecutor decides that there is sufficient evidence showing that either a natural or legal person has intentionally or by gross negligence infringed one or more of the provisions listed in s. 23(1), then it will draft an indictment. If the accused person does not admit the infringement and is not willing to pay the fine that the Public Prosecutor proposes, the Public Prosecutor will initiate a criminal case at one of the district courts. It is usual practice for the Public Prosecutor to prosecute both the company and a member of management (the CEO or director of the company) unless it is very clear that the CEO or director was not involved in the infringement.

10.98 Legal persons can only incur criminal liability if an infringement has been made within the undertaking, and this infringement is caused by one or more persons affiliated with the

[30] *Ekko A/S v. Elektrolux Home Products Denmark A/S, Miele A/S and BSH Hvidedvarer A/S Home Appliance Group (Ekko II)*, Maritime and Commercial Court Case nos. V-174-02, V-175-02, and V-176-02, October 15, 2004.

undertaking. "Legal persons" covers persons that can act in legal matters, including public authorities where they carry out activities analogous to those carried out by private entities. Section 23(4) states that legal persons can be subject to criminal liability under the provisions of Part 5 of the Criminal Code.

Natural persons can also incur criminal liability (see para. 10.100). As mentioned above, in practice the Public Prosecutor usually charges both the undertaking and a director of the undertaking. Subordinate-level associates in the business are rarely prosecuted unless the infringement amounts to a gross infringement and the lower-level associate has intentionally breached the competition rules. **10.99**

With effect from March 1, 2013, s. 23(3) states that natural persons, who have participated in cartel infringements, can be subject to imprisonment for up to one and a half years. "Cartel infringements," according to s. 23(3), covers (a) coordination of prices, margins, etc.; (b) limiting productions or sales; (c) market or customer sharing; and (d) bid-ridding. Cartel participants can under aggravating circumstances be imprisoned for up to six years under s. 299c of the Criminal Code. Aggravating circumstances can especially be a significant extent of the infringement or the fact that the infringement has been suitable to entail severe damages. **10.100**

There are two pre-conditions for legal or natural persons to incur criminal liability: **10.101**

(1) the elements of the crime in one of the sanctioned provisions must be met; and
(2) the infringement must have been committed intentionally or by gross negligence. An infringement is committed intentionally if the person knew that their actions constituted an infringement. Intent is also present if the person had the purpose of infringing a provision of the Competition Act or could reasonably foresee that an infringement could occur. When determining the scale of penalty applicable, the level of the infringement and the duration of the infringement—in that order—are significant.

With regards to fines, the explanatory notes to the Competition Act classify infringements as "less serious" (e.g. vertical agreements with limited effects), "serious" (e.g. vertical agreements regarding minimum prices), or "very serious" (e.g. horizontal agreements regarding prices or market sharing). **10.102**

The notes further state that since infringements governed by the Act will usually impact the Danish market, the level of any fine should be appropriate for the size of the Danish market. Generally, this means that fines will be lower than those imposed for a similar breach of the EU competition rules. The notes indicate that fines for "less serious" infringements should commonly amount up to DKK 400,000; fines for "serious infringements" between DKK 4 million and DKK 20 million; and "very serious" infringements should incur fines upwards of DKK 20 million. **10.103**

The explanatory notes classify the duration of infringements as "short," "medium-length," and "long." The duration of the infringement determines whether the base amount of the fine (set according to its level) will be increased. An infringement is of short duration where it subsists for less than one year. By and large, infringements of short duration will not give rise to an increase in the base amount of the fine. "Medium-length duration" generally describes infringements of between one and five years, usually resulting in a 50 percent increase in the base amount of the fine. The duration of an infringement is "long" if it continues beyond five years. In this case the base amount of the fine is likely to be increased by 10 percent for each year of the infringement (i.e. 60 percent for six years; 70 percent for seven years; and so on). **10.104**

Section 23(5) provides that turnover must be considered when determining the size of any fine. After assessing the level and duration of the infringement, the base fine can be adjusted up or down to reflect turnover levels. The explanatory notes list certain aggravating circumstances that **10.105** should be taken into account when determining the penalty, for example: recidivism (where the same undertaking has previously been penalized for a similar infringement); obstruction (if the undertaking has obstructed the investigation); or for a leading role (if the undertaking has played a significant part in the infringement or has encouraged or coerced others into participating in the infringement). There may also be mitigating circumstances. The Danish rules allow for a reduction in the fine if the undertaking has played a passive role in an infringement, has not adhered to (or implemented) a restrictive agreement, or if the undertaking has cooperated with the authorities or delivered information to help prove the infringement.

10.106 Provisions in the Competition Act that are subject to sanction can be divided into two groups: material infringements and formal infringements. These provisions are listed in s. 23(1). Material infringements are violations of the prohibition against restrictive agreements (s. 6(1)) and the prohibition against abuse of a dominant position (s. 11(1)). Formal infringements include contravention of or failure to comply with a condition attached to a decision that granted an exception to the prohibition against restrictive agreements; violation of an injunction issued by the Competition Council; or failure to adhere to commitments made binding in accordance with s. 16a.

10.107 A number of provisions regarding merger control allow for penalties to be imposed. The failure to notify a merger is the most significant, but failure to comply with a demand for information made by the Competition and Consumer Authority under s. 17 or the provision of incorrect or misleading information to the Competition and Consumer Authority, Competition Council or Competition Appeals Tribunal will also be subject to penalty.

G. Leniency and immunity

10.108 The key principles of Denmark's leniency program for cartel infringements mirrors the EU rules, though with some differences, e.g. the lack of a marker system for leniency applicants (all relevant information must be submitted at the time of the application for leniency). Cooperation with the authorities in a cartel investigation can lead to a reduction in any fine of up to 100 percent (for the first applicant), up to 50 percent (for the second applicant), up to 30 percent (for the third applicant), and up to 20 percent (for later applicants). The amount of the reduction is left to the authorities' discretion.

10.109 The first undertaking must—if applying for full immunity—provide the Danish Competition and Consumer Authority with information that it did not have at the time of the application and which enables the Authority to carry out a targeted inspection (a dawn raid). If a targeted inspection has already been carried out, the information must enable the Danish Competition and Consumer Authority to find an infringement.

10.110 All applicants seeking a fine reduction must submit information which represents significant added value compared to the evidence already in the possession of the authorities.

10.111 In addition, the following conditions must always be satisfied in order for an undertaking to qualify for immunity or a fine reduction:

- the undertaking must cooperate with the authorities on a continuous basis throughout the procedure;
- the undertaking must end its involvement in the cartel immediately following its application; and
- the undertaking must not have coerced other undertakings into joining the cartel.

10.112 If the requirements are not satisfied, the undertaking will not benefit from any favorable treatment.

10.113 There is no "right of advancement" for subsequent applicants if a preceding applicant, as a result of non-compliance with the requirements, loses its place in the leniency order.

Applicants cannot improve their position in one leniency exercise by participating in or initiating another. If multiple applications for immunity or fine reduction are made in the same cartel case, the decisive factor in determining the order of priority is the point in time when the authorities receive the information provided of course that all of the applicants *qualify* for leniency.

"All information" about the cartel infringement that the applicant has access to, comes into possession of, or which the undertaking can reasonably obtain must be supplied with the application for leniency. However, the Authority does accept a summarized application if a full application has been submitted to the European Commission. An applicant must provide prompt answers to any questions the authorities have during the investigation. Immunity or fine reductions are not available to applicants that took steps to coerce other undertakings to participate in the cartel. However, ringleaders are not excluded from the leniency program. **10.114**

The leniency program applies equally to persons and undertakings. An undertaking's application for leniency automatically includes all current and former employees and members of the board of directors and/or the management. Applications by former or current employees that do not have authority to act on behalf of the undertaking will not bind the undertaking. Applications from current employees with representative authority will only bind the undertaking if this is explicitly mentioned in the application. Immunity may only be granted by the Public Prosecutor after consultation with the Danish Competition and Consumer Authority, whereas fine reductions can be granted by either the Authority or the Public Prosecutor after consultation with the other authority. **10.115**

The Danish Competition and Consumer Authority will only be able to issue fines where: (a) the undertaking has admitted an infringement; (b) there exists an established court practice for the calculation of fines for similar infringements; and (c) the Public Prosecutor has consented to the case being settled in this way and has approved the level of fines. The competence to impose fines for cartel infringements generally lies with the criminal courts. However, the court must always act upon a proposal from the Public Prosecutor and take account of leniency granted by either the Danish Competition and Consumer Authority or the Public Prosecutor during the administrative procedure. **10.116**

H. Document creation and retention

When drafting documents, it is very important to be aware of risks of misinterpretations; is an outsider such as a competition authority able to read and understand texts in the way intended? **10.117**

Privileged material—such as correspondence with external legal advisors—is excluded from the investigation. However, legal professional privilege does not extend to internal material written by in-house lawyers or counsel. Legal professional privilege is not explicitly and comprehensively addressed by Danish legislation, but is a principle developed by the case precedents of the Community Courts. Subject to legal privilege, natural persons will be obligated to disclose information if they perform business activities or represent an undertaking. **10.118**

The right to request information is also limited by the privilege against self-incrimination, and it must be applied in accordance with EU law. Also, if a criminal offense is suspected then the special requirements in the Danish Criminal Act must be adhered to. **10.119**

If the necessary information is denied, the Danish authorities can impose penalties that accrue on a daily or weekly basis. An intentional or grossly negligent failure to comply with a request for information will also be penalized. Similarly, a party who provides incorrect or misleading information to the Danish Competition Council or Authority can be penalized with fines where that party's conduct is intentional or amounts to gross negligence. **10.120**

10.121 Disputes regarding the legality of the Council's information request cannot be brought before the Competition Appeals Tribunal. However, such requests are subject to judicial review by the courts. The power to request information extends to all information, regardless of the medium in which it is stored. It may include accounts and accounting records, paper files, books, correspondence, and other business documents. Also searchable are private bags, pockets, electronic calendars, mobile telephones, and similar items, but the investigation does not extend to documents covered by legal privilege—such as purely private correspondence, or legal advice given by external lawyers. Further, relevant employees and board members may be required to provide oral statements explaining document content, incidents, or events. If the information is stored or processed by an external data processor, the Authority is entitled to demand access to that entity's premises. However, a precondition to access is that it is not possible for the Authority to obtain the information concerned directly from the undertaking subject to the control investigation.

10.121 If it is not possible to take copies of the required information, the Danish Competition and Consumer Authority may seal off parts of the business premises and affected information for up to three working days after the initial inspection. Alternatively, the Authority may take relevant information away for copying and return it within three working days from the day of the inspection. In the latter case, the company must be provided with copies of the information that the Authority has extracted for further examination.

10.122 The Authority may take identical electronic copies (mirror images) of the electronically stored data covered by the investigation, and is permitted to take the copied material away for further examination. The mirrored material must be sealed when it leaves the premises, and the undertaking (or a representative of the undertaking) has the right to be present when the seal is broken and the mirrored material is reviewed.

10.123 As a general rule, the review must be finished within twenty-five working days from the dawn raid. It is within this same time limit that the undertaking must be given copies of the information that the Authority has extracted from the mirrored material. If there is any dispute about whether materials should be classified as legally privileged and excluded from the investigation, the documents in question will be placed in a sealed container for later review before the ordinary courts.

10.124 When the review of the mirrored material is complete, the material must be resealed. If there is no evidence of an infringement of the competition rules, the mirrored material must be deleted. But if the Authority decides to proceed further in the matter, the mirrored material will be stored and only deleted when the case is finally decided.

10.125 An undertaking has the right to seek legal assistance during the inspection. However, it is not a prerequisite to carrying out the dawn raid that the company is represented by legal advisors, and the Danish Competition and Consumer Authority does not have to wait for legal advisors to arrive before they begin their inspection. At the end of the investigation, the Authority and the undertaking's legal advisers will briefly review the seized materials. The Authority will store all of the seized materials as hard copies or electronically.

10.126 In the period following the dawn raid, it will scrutinize the material, but due to the volume of information that is often collected, this can take up to several months. If irregularities are found, the seized information will be passed on to the Danish Competition Council who will issue an enforcement notice. The State Prosecutor for Serious Economic and International Crime may also initiate criminal proceedings. Just as information requests under s. 17 can be used to gather information for other national competition authorities or for the European Commission, the same applies to inspections carried out under s. 18. Procedural questions such as disputes regarding the legal privilege attached to a document will follow a similar path before the courts.

11

ESTONIA

Elo Tamm and Liina Käis
LAWIN

Introduction

The substantive rules established by the Estonian Competition Act ("the Act") and applied by the Estonian Competition Authority (ECA) and courts are very similar to respective EU rules. There are only minor variations that in practice may not have much significance. In the view of the Estonian Supreme Court the EU competition law principles should be followed even in purely national cases with no cross-border effect. Most of the norms in the Act are based on EU law. Nevertheless, with regard to provisions that differ from EU norms, solely these provisions should be taken into account without applying EU principles.[1] Therefore, **11.01**

[1] *KPK Teedeehitus*, Estonian Supreme Court, Case no. 3-1-1-12-11, Judgment of May 4, 2011.

as the rules are very similar, most of the EU competition law principles are also applied in Estonia.

11.02 On the other hand, procedural aspects clearly distinguish Estonian competition law enforcement from many other countries. The most serious competition law violations are criminalized; however, competition law violations can also be subject to misdemeanor and administrative proceedings. Misdemeanor proceedings are very similar to criminal proceedings. As a general rule, all provisions of the Code of Criminal Procedure are also applicable to misdemeanor proceedings. One of the most important differences relevant in competition law cases concern surveillance activities permissible in collecting evidence in criminal proceedings but not in misdemeanor proceedings. Further, the limitation period for misdemeanors is considerably shorter than that for criminal offenses—limitation periods are three years and five years, respectively. The enforcement system is complicated as some of the infringements may be subject to different proceedings depending on the circumstances. Abuse of dominance can be subject to any of the different types of proceedings; however, criminal procedure applies only in exceptional cases.[2] Agreements, concerted practices, and decisions of associations of undertakings may be subject to either criminal or administrative proceedings. The exact scope of application of these procedures and their specific features are further analyzed below.

11.03 Since 2008 there has been a rise in criminal enforcement of competition law regarding cartels; however, there have been only a few final decisions, and many of those have resulted in acquittals. There is even less practice with regard to the abuse of dominant position. This is most likely caused by the enforcement difficulties related to misdemeanor proceedings.[3] Additionally, the ECA has been actively carrying out sector reviews and issuing non-binding recommendations for the improvement of competitive situation in certain sectors (e.g. waste management, pharmaceuticals).

I. Acting alone

11.04 Estonian competition law applies to unilateral conduct only when the undertaking adopting this practice holds a dominant position. Therefore some aspects on the definition of dominance are explained first.

11.05 Article 13(1) of the Act defines an undertaking or undertakings in a dominant position as "an undertaking or several undertakings operating in the same market whose position enables it/them to operate in the market to an appreciable extent independently of competitors, suppliers and buyers." Besides this definition, the same provision sets out a rebuttable presumption: "Dominant position is presumed either if an undertaking accounts for at least 40 percent of the turnover in the market or if several undertakings operating in the same market account for at least 40 percent of the turnover in the market." Additionally, undertakings having special or exclusive rights or having control over essential facilities are considered to hold a dominant position according to article 13(2) of the Act.

11.06 The ECA has confirmed that it will not decide over the existence of dominant position solely on the basis of the 40 percent market share threshold. For example, the ECA found that funeral parlor Kristin was not dominant, although it held a market share exceeding 40 percent. The ECA reasoned that the decrease of its market share by 2.2 percent could

[2] See Section II.F(ii).
[3] See Section II.B(iii).

be compared to the simultaneous slight increase of the market share of its competitor by 2.2 percent. In the ECA's view, this fact indicated lack of barriers to entry into the market and, therefore, despite the presumption of dominance, the funeral bureau Kristin was not considered as dominant. The small differences in the market shares of three operators in the market also indicated lack of dominance according to the ECA's view.[4]

Procedural norms applicable to abuse of dominance as well as other competition law infringements have been subject to constant change—cases of abuse of dominance have been subject to administrative proceedings in the past. Currently, abuses of dominance may be subject to criminal, misdemeanor or administrative procedure. Article 62(1)(5) of the Act provides that the ECA may impose an injunction in the case of abuse of dominant position, and a penalty payment in the case of failure to comply with the injunction. On the other hand, article 73[5] of the Act condemns abuse of dominance as a misdemeanor. Second-time abuse may be subject considered as a criminal offense.[5] Therefore, it has been difficult for the ECA to pursue rigorous and consistent enforcement activities. **11.07**

A. Predatory pricing

No specific test for evaluating whether an undertaking is implementing predatory pricing policy is clear, and the EU predatory pricing cost-based tests have not been adopted. Nevertheless, it is possible to draw some conclusions on the basis of some specific cases. **11.08**

For example, the ECA has held that the price of the service must cover at least the costs necessary for the rendering of the service. Otherwise, the pricing policy harms a competitor, or might even squeeze the competitor out. As the ECA did not draw a distinction between different costs (e.g. variable or incremental costs), it seems that total costs were taken as a basis.[6] In another case, the ECA found that the price must also include reasonable profit.[7] The ECA also compared the prices of the service provider with the prices of a competitor and noted that the selling prices must not fall below the total cost price of the service.[8] **11.09**

In a more recent case, the ECA analyzed whether Metrosert (a company offering verification and calibration services) had applied excessive discounts for verification of scales and fuel pumps, which would have been possible due to cross-subsidizing on account of calibration and certification services. Based on the calculations submitted by Metrosert, the ECA found that providing discounts was normal and even necessary, especially when the client had multiple measuring devices to verify. This prevented Metrosert from charging excessive prices. The calculation demonstrated that costs of transport and other activities, which are part of the calibration service price, are distributed over a larger number of measuring devices, which provides economies of scale. Therefore it is possible to charge lower prices. The ECA terminated the proceedings without imposing any sanctions. Since the ECA did not find an infringement, the existence of dominance was left open in this case.[9] **11.10**

B. Exploitative offenses (excessive pricing, monopoly leveraging)

According to article 16(1) of the Act, unfair sale prices are considered abusive. Regarding excessive pricing, there is a landmark case from earlier practice where the Supreme Court ruled that unfairly high prices are considered to restrict competition, notwithstanding their **11.11**

[4] *Matusebüroo Kristin*, ECA Case no. 43-L, September 18, 2006.

[5] See Section II.F(ii).

[6] See *AS STV*, ECA Case no. 20, July 30, 2004; and *AS Telset*, ECA Case no. 19, July 30, 2004.

[7] *AS Elion*, ECA Case no. 18-L, June 28, 2004.

[8] *AS Tallinna Lennujaam*, ECA Case no. 18, July 2, 2004.

[9] *Metrex Mõõtekeskus OÜ/AS Metrosert*, ECA Case no. 5.1-5/09-0052, December 30, 2009.

effect on competition in general, since consumers have to pay a higher price. With regard to establishing excessive prices, the Supreme Court held that a price is excessive if it has no reasonable relation to the economic value of the service provided. The economic value is in turn related to the costs necessary for rendering the service. Cost is necessary if it is incurred as essential to render the service. In order to analyze whether the pricing is excessive, it is at first necessary to find out to what extent the costs have been covered by the fees charged. The Supreme Court found that a price can be excessive even if the undertaking does not make any profit because it is not fair to charge additional costs arising from inefficient operation. To justify the profit, one appropriate criterion would be the comparison of the following: profit of the dominant service provider and the average profit in the economy and profits in analogous markets in other states. At the same time, it should be considered that the smaller the investment risk in the relevant sector, the smaller the justified profit.[10]

11.12 More recently, the ECA analyzed prices charged by Levira for broadcasting services.[11] The ECA held that the provisions of the Act prohibiting abuse of dominant position would not be applicable if sector-specific regulation granted more favorable treatment to an undertaking. Prior to this case, the ECA had compiled a methodology for calculating weighted average cost of capital (WACC) for communications service providers under the competence provided by the Electronic Communications Act. The ECA had held that a reasonable WACC in this case was 13.5 percent. The ECA admitted that this value of WACC is significantly higher than in many other regulated sectors, but considered the higher value as justified, given that Levira operated in a somewhat more risky area of activities.

11.13 Another interesting aspect of the case is that the ECA gave a detailed guidance on how to calculate the value of a company. In relation to older equipment, the ECA held that the book value of the assets should be taken as a basis, rather than the reappraised value as claimed by Levira. Levira claimed that since they were using old equipment which, according to their accounting data, had already depreciated and had no value in the bookkeeping terms, it was not correct to use the book value of the assets. The ECA in turn explained that it would not be justified if Levira were to earn additional profit without making any additional investment. The ECA held that this could be justified only in competitive markets where most of the undertakings own new equipment, and an undertaking using old equipment may use it as an opportunity to earn higher profit. The ECA also held that the ratio of Levira's current assets to its total assets was excessive. This implies that Levira was ineffective, and Levira's clients should not be obliged to pay more because of the excessive volume of current assets. Further, the ECA found that a reasonable current assets-to-sales ratio should be 5 percent, that is similar to that in other regulated sectors. The ECA found that in the period from 2007/2008 to 2009/2010, Levira's prices were unfair. Levira justified the higher prices by evoking exceptional circumstances, namely that both analog and digital broadcasting platforms were used simultaneously. The ECA did not accept this justification, as higher demand did not justify higher profit during three years. Moreover, the ECA held that three years is not a short time period as claimed by Levira; during this time, Levira should have considered making changes to its activities when setting the price for its services.[12]

C. Monopsony

11.14 There are no special rules regulating the conduct of dominant or monopolistic buyers. The authors are also not aware of any relevant practice in that regard.

---

[10] *AS Eesti Telefon*, Estonian Supreme Court, Case no. 3-3-1-66-02, Judgment of December 18, 2002.
[11] *AS Levira*, ECA Case no. 5.1-5/11-020, September 16, 2011.
[12] *AS Levira* (n 11).

D. Price discrimination

Article 16(3) of the Act prohibits a dominant undertaking from offering or applying dissimilar conditions to equivalent agreements with different trading partners, thereby placing some of them at a competitive disadvantage. The ECA has explained the relevant criteria in establishing price discrimination as abuse of dominance in the context of the ECA's response to an inquiry from Eesti Loto. State-owned dominant lottery company, Eesti Loto, submitted its new standard terms with retailers for ECA's review and approval. Although the ECA clarified that this analysis should be carried out by undertakings themselves, it nevertheless gave some guidance, stating that volume sale discounts are permitted, when they are based on cost saving resulting from selling larger volumes.[13] **11.15**

The ECA initiated misdemeanor proceedings against Eesti Post concerning price discrimination in two episodes. Eesti Post is the largest postal operator in Estonia, and owns the only nationwide postal network. In public procurement organized by the Ministry of Finance, aimed at several postage-related services, two tenders were submitted: one from Itella and a joint tender from Eesti Post and Eesti Elektronpost (subsidiary of Eesti Post). Both Itella and Eesti Elektronpost needed to buy postal carrying services from Eesti Post to participate in the procurement. The ECA established that the price offered by Eesti Post to Eesti Elektronpost was significantly lower than the price offered to Itella for the same services. The ECA established that materials supposed to be transferred to Eesti Post for home delivery needed to be prepared equally for Itella and Eesti Elektronpost. Therefore, there was no reason for the price difference. The ECA concluded that by offering different prices to Eesti Elektronpost and Itella, Eesti Post put the latter at a competitive disadvantage. The circumstances and conclusions were analogous concerning another public procurement organized by Estonian leading energy company Eesti Energia and are not further explained here. The court of first instance upheld the finding of abuse of dominance but reduced the fine imposed by the ECA on Eesti Post from EUR 36,000 to EUR 18,000.[14] The decision was upheld by the Supreme Court by its ruling not to accept appeal of Eesti Post. **11.16**

Another case that was recently upheld by the Supreme Court concerns the wholesaler and retailer of magazines Lehepunkt, which from the perspective of magazine publishers offered wholesale service. Lehepunkt charged a different percentage of a magazine cover price as a service fee and different transport fees from different publishers, favoring in particular publishers that belonged to larger groups. The ECA found that Lehepunkt abused its dominant position as it was not justified to apply different fees which were not based on different costs.[15] **11.17**

There is a case concerning higher license fees charged to night clubs than to bars/restaurants by the Estonian Authors' Society, the Estonian Association of the Phonogram Producers, and the Estonian Performers Association. The ECA found that the associations had the right to differentiate in the level of fees based on the importance and level of intensity of the music in the venue. The ECA acknowledged that license fees are always to some extent subjective, and measures usually applied in competition law for assessing prices are not applicable in this case. Therefore, the ECA found no abuse of dominance. In addition, the ECA stated that if it is in the public interest to monitor license fees, it should be done by amending the state regulation and not through competition law infringement proceedings.[16] **11.18**

---

[13] *AS Eesti Loto*, ECA Case no. 5.1-1/10-0006-087, October 1, 2010.

[14] *AS Eesti Post*, Harju County Court, Case no. 4-11-4656, Judgment of April 27, 2012.

[15] *AS Lehepunkt*, ECA Case no. 5.1-4/09-0020, April 29, 2009.

[16] *Eesti Autorite Ühing, Eesti Fonogrammitootjate Ühing, Eesti Esinejate Liit*, ECA Case no. 5.1-5/09-0043, October 28, 2009.

E. Dictating or influencing resale prices

(i) Resale price maintenance

11.19 Giving resale price recommendations (RPMs) and setting maximum resale prices is allowed, whereas setting minimum or fixed resale prices is considered as a hard core restriction under article 3(1)(1) of the Government of the Republic Regulation No. 60 of May 27, 2010 on Grant of Permission to Enter into Vertical Agreements which Restrict or May Restrict Free Competition (Vertical Block Exemption). Giving resale price recommendations and setting maximum resale prices is allowed, provided that the other conditions of Vertical Block Exemption are met (threshold of 30 percent for both the buyer's and the seller's market shares).

11.20 All restrictive agreements, whether horizontal or vertical, are considered criminal offenses under Estonian law.[17] The procedural aspects of competition enforcement have created considerable lack of clarity in the ECA and Public Prosecution enforcement actions. In some cases where vertical RPM was considered to be an infringement, the ECA has taken a rather lenient approach by not initiating criminal proceedings and imposing only an injunction as a sanction in administrative proceedings.

11.21 Even though the ECA has shown leniency in the context of administrative proceedings, its substantive assessment of the prohibited activities has been rather strict. The ECA has concluded that printing the recommended price on the product or on the advertising leaflet is not in conformity with the Vertical Block Exemption because the retailer is not motivated to change the price that is already advertised to the consumers.[18] In *AS Ottender & Valgmäe*, the ECA took the fact of price advertising as a conclusive evidence of price fixing. It is important to note that article 3(1)(1) of the Vertical Block Exemption explicitly sets out that printing the resale price on the product is a type of a practice that makes the recommended or maximum resale prices operate as minimum or fixed resale prices.

11.22 More recently, the Harju County Court issued a judgment in criminal proceedings regarding minimum RPM. Although, the infringement was qualified by the court as an agreement between competitors, it could also be viewed as a vertical agreement because the accused company (car tire seller), which imposed restrictions on several retailers, was simultaneously a wholesaler and a retailer of the same products. It is interesting that although the infringement was qualified as an agreement, the retailers involved—besides the one who had allegedly imposed the restriction—were not accused or punished.[19]

(ii) Minimum advertised price programs

11.23 Establishing minimum resale prices is considered as a hard core restriction under the Vertical Block Exemption. There are no special rules for minimum advertised price (MAP) programs, nor is there any relevant practice, but in principle MAP programs should be treated the same way as minimum RPM.

F. Tying arrangements

11.24 Tying falls under article 16(4) of the Act which prohibits a dominant undertaking from making entry into an agreement subject to acceptance by the other parties of supplementary obligations which have no connection with the subject of such agreement. The ECA has analyzed tying in a case where an investment company and pension fund LHV filed a complaint

[17] See Section II.A.

[18] *AS Ottender & Valgmäe*, ECA Case no. 5.1-5/09-0009, March 20, 2009.

[19] *OÜ Rehvid 24*, Harju County Court, Case no. 1-12-5650, Judgment of June 12, 2012.

against three largest Estonian banks claiming that the banks were tying their services by requiring their loan customers to transfer their funded pension to the pension funds of the same banks, or by offering more favorable loan terms in return for the transfer. LHV based its arguments on abuse of dominant position and restrictive agreements. The ECA rejected the arguments concerning abuse of dominant position. The ECA did not establish an infringement in that case, stating that tying is objectively justified if the aim of the behavior is not to exclude competitors from the market, but rather to give consumers a bonus on the account of the economies of scale from selling multiple products together.[20] In this case, the ECA considered the intent of the dominant undertaking as a determining factor in establishing abuse. The principle that the ECA seemed to follow in this case clearly makes it easier for the dominant undertaking to avoid liability—in the case of absence of anticompetitive intent, there is no abuse regardless of the anticompetitive effects. Nevertheless, the application of this principle might as well be an isolated case, as the ECA has not taken this kind of approach in abuse of dominance cases since then.

G. Exclusive dealing

There are no special rules regulating exclusive dealing. Vertical agreements containing exclusive dealing provisions would be allowed as long as they are in compliance with the Vertical Block Exemption (analogous to EU rules). The authors are also not aware of any relevant practice in that regard. **11.25**

H. Refusal to deal

Refusal to deal is considered abusive if it cannot be objectively justified—unjustified refusal to sell or buy goods by a dominant undertaking is prohibited under article 16(6) of the Act. There is some case law on this specific type of abuse of dominant position; however, there has not been thorough competition law assessment. In *SEB Bank*, for example, the ECA did not find an infringement where the bank terminated an agreement for providing its bank link system to identify the instant loan provider Monetti's loan clients. The ECA found that the refusal to provide the service was not contrary to the Competition Act, since the provision of such service to Monetti would have been in breach of the Money Laundering and Terrorist Financing Prevention Act.[21] In another case, the ECA made a recommendation to local water supplier, AS Pärnu Vesi, to develop an internal procedure for the prevention of conflicts with regard to connection point in case of accidents. The ECA reasoned that the public water supplier is not entitled to refuse fixing problems or restoring the water supply if the client does not pay an advance fee or does not agree with the water supplier's view on the location of the connection point.[22] **11.26**

I. Essential facilities

According to article 15 of the Act, an undertaking is deemed to control an "essential facility" if it "owns, possesses or operates a network, infrastructure or any other essential facility which other persons cannot duplicate or for whom it is economically inexpedient to duplicate but without access to which or the existence of which it is impossible to operate in the goods market." According to article 13(2) of the Act, undertakings in control of essential facilities are also considered as undertakings in a dominant position. Therefore, all the restrictions applicable to dominant undertakings are also applicable to these undertakings. **11.27**

[20] *AS Hansapank, AS SEB Ühispank, AS Sampo Pank*, ECA Case no. 58-L, December 18, 2006.

[21] *SEB Bank*, ECA Case no. 5.1-5/10-0004, January 5, 2010.

[22] *AS Pärnu Vesi*, ECA Case no. 5.1-1/09-0805-004, February 5, 2010.

11.28 Additionally, article 18 of the Act provides the main obligation of the undertaking in control of an essential facility which is to allow other undertakings access to its network, infrastructure, or any other essential facility under reasonable and non-discriminatory conditions. Article 18^1 concerns an obligation to keep separate records on revenue and expenditure. Access may be refused if the refusal is based on objective reasons, mostly if giving access is technically impossible or impractical. Article 18(2) of the Act gives a non-exhaustive list in that regard, which covers mostly restrictions enacted in other acts (e.g. refusal to grant access is justified if the undertaking applying for the access does not hold the permit prescribed by law for the corresponding activity).

11.29 The ECA's decision concerning activities of waste station operator AS Cleanaway gives important guidance on the use of essential facilities generally. According to the decision, a waste station (a technically equipped facility that includes collection containers for the collection and initial management of various type of recyclable waste) was not an essential facility and, hence, the operator of a waste station did not have to grant access to every waste management organization. There were alternatives to waste stations for collecting waste, and the mere fact that the other options were more costly was not a sufficient reason to consider a waste station as an essential facility. Because of the available alternatives, the waste stations were not indispensable for competing in the collection of waste from end consumers. The building of waste stations at issue was financed by state and local government funds. The ECA did not consider this fact as a relevant criterion for the assessment of whether these waste stations were essential facilities. Instead, the infeasibility of alternatives to waste stations was the relevant criterion. Additionally, the ECA noted that although, taken as a whole, all waste stations in Estonia could be considered as an essential facility, this would not be in compliance with the definition provided in article 15 of the Act which refers to one undertaking. This in turn means that one essential facility cannot be possessed by several undertakings. As in this case waste stations in Estonia are owned by different undertakings, these waste stations could not be considered as an essential facility.[23]

J. Bundling (including loyalty and market share discounts)

11.30 There is no distinction among different categories of discounts. There are no legal presumptions applying to particular types of discounts, and the case law on discounts is rather limited. Nevertheless, there is one important precedent in that matter that made its way to the Supreme Court. In *AS Eesti Post v. ECA*, the Supreme Court stated that an undertaking holding a dominant position is prohibited from implementing loyalty discounts conditioned on the client obtaining 100 percent of its supplies from the dominant undertaking. The Court clarified that this practice, implemented by Eesti Post, amounted to excluding competitors by its object and it might have the effect of market foreclosure.[24]

K. Standard-setting groups (disclosure requirements, licensing arrangements, and licensing pools)

11.31 There are no special rules regulating issues related to standard-setting groups in the context of competition law. The authors are also not aware of any relevant practice in that regard.

[23] *AS Cleanaway*, ECA Case no. 5.1-5/09-0023, May 22, 2009.

[24] *AS Eesti Post v. Estonian Competition Authority*, Estonian Supreme Court, Case no. 3-1-1-64-07, Judgment of December 5, 2007.

L. Customer termination

There are no special rules regulating customer termination. The authors are also not aware of any relevant practice in that regard. 11.32

M. Termination of intermediaries (retailers, wholesalers, dealers, and value-added resellers, agents, and brokers)

There are no special rules regulating termination of intermediaries. The authors are also not aware of any relevant practice in that regard. 11.33

N. Termination of relationships with competitors

There are no special rules regulating termination of relationships with competitors. The authors are also not aware of any relevant practice in that regard. 11.34

O. Exemptions

There are no explicit provisions for exemption regarding the unilateral conduct by a dominant undertaking. Nevertheless, the conduct that would at first sight appear abusive may be objectively justified or may bring about overriding efficiencies, and therefore would not be considered abusive. For example, the ECA has found that economies of scale may be such a justification.[25] 11.35

Outside the context of unilateral conduct by dominant undertakings, there are some block exemption regulations adopted by the Government. Besides Vertical Block Exemption,[26] there are block exemptions for research and development agreements, specialization agreements, and vertical motor vehicle distribution agreements. 11.36

II. Dealing with competitors

Dealing with competitors may be subject to criminal or administrative proceedings. There are relevant regulations in both the Act and the Penal Code. 11.37

Since 2008 there has been a rise in criminal enforcement of competition law; however, there have been only a few final decisions, and a majority of those have resulted in an acquittal. Although each case is different, it could be said that the lack of convictions may relate to the fact that criminal enforcement in these complicated matters was and still is a relatively new area. The legislation needs amending and the officials need specific training to ensure effective enforcement. 11.38

Article 4(1) of the Act contains a non-exhaustive list of prohibited agreements between undertakings, concerted practices, and decisions by associations of undertakings which have as their object or effect the restriction of competition. These include: 11.39

(1) directly or indirectly fixing prices or any other trading conditions, including prices of goods, tariffs, fees, mark-ups, discounts, rebates, basic fees, premiums, additional fees, interest rates, rent or lease payments applicable to third parties;
(2) limiting production, service, goods markets, technical development, or investment;
(3) sharing goods markets or sources of supply, including restriction of access by a third party to a goods market or any attempt to exclude the third party from the market;

[25] See Sections I.A and I.B.
[26] See Section I.E(i).

(4) exchanging information which restricts competition;
(5) agreeing on the application of dissimilar conditions to equivalent agreements, thereby placing other trading parties at a competitive disadvantage;
(6) making entry into an agreement subject to acceptance by the other parties of supplementary obligations which have no connection with the subject of such agreement.

11.40 Article 400(1) of the Penal Code states that entering into agreements, making decisions or concerted practices between undertakings which have as their object or effect the restriction of competition is punishable by a pecuniary punishment or imprisonment of up to one year. Article 400(2) condemns hard core cartels (the list is analogous to paragraphs 1–3 of the above list from article 4(1) of the Act), stating that these infringements are punishable by a pecuniary punishment or imprisonment of one to three years.

11.41 Additionally, article 62(1)(6) of the Act provides that the ECA may impose an injunction in the case of violation of a prohibition against agreements, practices, or decisions restricting competition, and a penalty payment in case of failure to comply with the injunction. Therefore, the same kinds of infringement may be subject to either criminal or administrative proceedings. According to the principle of mandatory criminal proceedings, the pre-trial investigator is required to conduct criminal proceedings upon the appearance of facts referring to a criminal offense provided there are no grounds precluding criminal procedure or requiring termination of the criminal procedure (e.g. application of leniency).

11.42 It is not entirely clear what cases are covered by article 400(1) of the Penal Code and in what cases by article 62(1)(6) of the Act. Article 400(2) of the Penal Code lists hard core infringements. In the case these offenses occur, the criminal proceedings should be conducted based on the principle of mandatory criminal proceedings. On the other hand, article 400(1) of the Penal Code does not provide any specific type of agreements; therefore, this provision and article 62(1)(6) to some extent overlap. There is no clear practice on whether the principle of mandatory criminal proceedings is infringed if administrative proceedings are conducted instead of criminal proceedings in these cases.

11.43 Harmful cooperation between undertakings has been punishable under criminal law since 2002. Prior to 2002, all competition law infringements were considered to be administrative offenses. Presently, there is no concept of administrative offense: in the case of administrative proceedings, injunctions are issued, and penalty payments are imposed in the case of failure to comply with the injunctions.[27] The ECA may issue injunctions in administrative proceedings in the case of abuse of dominance, as well as of anticompetitive agreements, concerted practices, or decisions of associations of undertakings, as explained above. During the recent years, the ECA has not used this opportunity, but there were several administrative proceedings which the ECA has terminated without issuing an injunction. The increased criminal enforcement started in 2008, after the reorganization of the ECA.[28] In 2008, two investigations in criminal matters (there were only a few cases from earlier practice) were completed and several cases were pending. The courts ruled in these matters in the subsequent years.

11.44 Particular features of criminal proceedings have influenced the development of competition law in the area of cooperation between competitors. In several cases, aspects of criminal law and criminal procedure law were decisive for the outcome of the case, rather than specific issues in the competition law.[29]

[27] See Section II.F(i).
[28] See Section I.B(ii).
[29] See Section II.A.

11.45 Other cases concerning mostly procedural aspects are analyzed in Sections II.A, II.B, II.C, II.H, and II.I, but there is one case that escapes classification, because it concerns attempts at several infringements—market sharing, price fixing, and boycott. In *Oleg Ossinovski and AS Spacecom*, Harju County Court convicted a railway freight service provider, Spacecom, and a member of its management board, of an attempt to agree on restrictions of competition with the competitor Eesti Raudtee (Estonian Railways).[30] The ruling was upheld by the Tallinn Circuit Court. The case is interesting because a certain type of surveillance activity was used—staging a crime. A member of the management board of Spacecom, met several times with the representatives of the management of Eesti Raudtee who did not agree with the proposals to conclude anticompetitive agreements. The last meeting was held under the surveillance of the enforcement authorities, and the representatives of Eesti Raudtee participated in the meeting by way of staging, which had been authorized by the Tallinn City Court. In this meeting, Spacecom and Eesti Raudtee seemingly concluded anticompetitive agreements. The County Court imposed a monetary penalty of 40 daily wages on the member of the management board of Spacecom (approx. EUR 11,500) as well as detaining him for three days during the criminal proceedings. The punishment was reduced to approximately EUR 9,000 by the Circuit Court. The company incurred a penalty of approximately EUR 32,000.[31] There are other notable procedural aspects about this case besides the act of staging of a crime that are beyond the scope of this Chapter and will not be analyzed.

A. Horizontal price fixing (including advanced announcements of price or product changes)

11.46 In Estonia, as in most other jurisdictions, price fixing between competitors is considered as one of the most serious infringements of competition law, and there is little to say in justification. Even the *OÜ Liivikas Varad and others* case concerning price fixing agreements with little relevance and influence on the wider market situation, was investigated and prosecuted in Estonia. The *OÜ Liivikas Varad and others* case concerned an agreement between consultancy services providers to simultaneously increase prices of ready-made companies. The court held that the agreement was illegal, and the participants were convicted. The defendants claimed that, since the market share of all the companies involved was only 5–7 percent, and that it was also possible for Estonian residents to establish companies in simplified proceedings in a fast and easy manner, their price increase had no anticompetitive consequences on the market. The court rejected their arguments.[32]

11.47 *KPK Teedeehitus*, a price fixing case which made it all the way to the Supreme Court, can be considered a landmark case in relation to the burden of proof of individual exemption criteria.[33] The case concerned two construction companies that participated in public procurement of road construction. Prior to submitting tenders, the companies agreed the price for the intended joint tender. The companies also intended to cooperate when performing the construction work, and the intended price was calculated based on this plan. The companies were able to offer a lower price as they had complementary equipment and competence at

[30] *Oleg Ossinovski and AS Spacecom*, Harju County Court, Case no. 1-05-689, Judgment of December 21, 2007.

[31] *Oleg Ossinovski and AS Spacecom*, Tallinn Circuit Court, Case no. 1-05-689/13, Judgment of March 11, 2008. The Supreme Court did not grant a leave for cassation.

[32] *OÜ Liivikas Varad and others, Harju* County Court, Case no. 1-10-2979, Judgment of September 24, 2010; Tallinn Circuit Court, Case no. 1-10-2979/52, Judgment of December 17, 2010. On February 21, 2011, the Supreme Court did not grant a leave for cassation.

[33] *KPK Teedeehitus*, Estonian Supreme Court, Case no. 3-1-1-12-11, Judgment of May 4, 2011.

their disposal. Nevertheless, both companies submitted separate tenders after having discussed the intended price.

11.48 Two aspects are important in the context of this case. First, the Supreme Court reached a conclusion that—although, in administrative proceedings, the burden of proof regarding compliance with the cumulative exemption criteria provided in article 6 of the Act (analogous to individual exemption criteria of art. 101(3) TFEU) is placed on undertakings party to the alleged breach—the burden of proof should be reversed in criminal proceedings. This finding was based on the principle of criminal law, namely, presumption of innocence. Nobody is obliged to prove their innocence in criminal proceedings; and proving that the exemption criteria have been satisfied would constitute proving one's innocence. Therefore, the Court held that it is for the prosecutor to prove that the exemption criteria provided in article 6 of the Act have not been met. Another notable aspect relating to this case is the relatively low standard in the fulfillment of these criteria applied by the Supreme Court. Regardless of the likely absence of any anticompetitive effect, it is notable that the Court exempted a clear-cut price fixing agreement, finding that all the exemption criteria had been met. It is not clear why the Court presumed that indispensability criterion was fulfilled—the efficiencies claimed could be achieved by submitting a joint tender; instead, the companies agreed on prices and submitted separate tenders.[34] The case demonstrates the difficulties in the criminal enforcement of competition law. Still, it remains to be seen whether this case will serve as an important precedent in the future. The reversed burden of proof established by this judgment is expected to have a strong impact on future cartel investigation and may already have some influence on the activities of the ECA and prosecutors.

11.49 Another important case that clarifies procedural aspects related to illegal agreements concerns an alleged price fixing agreement between alcohol producers. The accusation was based on telephone call records obtained during covert surveillance activities. There was communication between the representatives of two alcohol producers which was conducted through an intermediary. This communication concerned Liviko's proposal for setting a minimum price for half-liter vodka and Forgola Group's confirmation. The Supreme Court found that the lower courts had not provided sufficient grounds for the finding that the prosecution's version of the circumstances was more reliable than the defendant's. The Supreme Court held that the intermediary might have misunderstood Liviko's proposal or arbitrarily misled the Forgola Group about the proposal (the person who allegedly made the proposal stated that by referring to the price of vodka, he merely drew attention to the possible tax law infringement and unfair competition related to Forgola Group's pricing policy). Because the Supreme Court questioned the objectivity of the statements of the intermediary made in the aforementioned phone records, and because, in the context of criminal law, these doubts should be interpreted in favor of the defendant, the defendants were acquitted.[35] Therefore, as in many cartel cases, procedural aspects were here again decisive for the outcome.

B. Horizontal agreements to allocate customers or territories; agreements not to compete

11.50 The first competition law infringement to incur criminal sanctions was a market sharing agreement. Estonian distributor of film on video, V&K Holding, agreed with a Lithuanian distributor of videos to divide the Estonian and Lithuanian market for videos. The Estonian subsidiary of the Lithuanian company agreed not to distribute videos in Estonia, and vice

[34] *KPK Teedeehitus* (n 32).

[35] *AS Liviko, Forgola Group OÜ*, Estonian Supreme Court, Case no. 3-1-1-10-11, Judgment of July 1, 2011.

versa (V&K Holding was operating in the Lithuanian market prior to the agreement). Since V&K Holding cooperated with the ECA and the Prosecutor's Office throughout the proceedings, a settlement was reached between the prosecutor and the company which the court approved. The sum of the pecuniary punishment was EEK 150,000 (less than EUR 9,600), which could be considered as a very small price to pay for an explicit market sharing between competitors.[36]

More recently, the court of first instance found two security service providers guilty of anticompetitive behavior: one of these undertakings was found guilty of violating article 400(2) of the Penal Code, while the other was found guilty of an attempt to commit the same crime. The case concerned allocation of customers. Namely, two security service providers agreed not to provide their services to customers who already had a purchase contract with the other party to the agreement. The case concerned several attempts to commit a crime (proposals to conclude anticompetitive agreements) as well as one instance of committed crime. A peculiar aspect is that, although the court established an agreement between the undertakings, only one of them was found guilty of the offense, while the other was found guilty of attempts to conclude an agreement in other instances. Pecuniary punishment of EUR 20,000 was imposed on both undertakings.[37] **11.51**

C. Horizontal boycotts

Horizontal boycotts concern the exclusion of competitors from the market, and are prohibited under Estonian competition and criminal law.[38] **11.52**

The court of first instance found a producer responsibility organization MTÜ Rehviliit whose main activities are collecting and organizing the recovery of old tires, guilty of violating article 400(2) of the Penal Code. MTÜ Rehviliit had concluded an agreement with waste management companies, whereby the latter were obliged not to buy tires from certain firms listed in the agreement. The case was settled, and a pecuniary punishment of EEK 200,000 (approx. EUR 12,800) was imposed on MTÜ Rehviliit.[39] **11.53**

An interesting case, from a procedural point of view, concerns the agreement between the municipality of Tartu and an outdoor advertising company, JCDecaux Estonia. The municipality of Tartu granted JCDecaux Estonia an exclusive right to use municipally owned land for outdoor advertising and erection of public transport pavilions. The ECA concluded that the exclusive right to advertise on municipal land cannot be considered as an exclusive right in the meaning of the Act, because the municipality of Tartu acted as an undertaking when concluding the agreement. Thus, the ECA concluded that the agreement was an exclusive agreement governed by competition law provisions relating to agreements, and not by competition law provisions concerning exclusive rights. All anticompetitive agreements are subject to criminal proceedings, and based on the criminal procedure principle of mandatory criminal proceedings, it is not clear whether administrative or criminal proceedings should have been applied in this case.[40] Following the ECA's initial assessment, parties to the agreement shortened the term of the agreement, which allowed the ECA to conclude that the individual exemption criteria had been met, and the proceedings were terminated since the competitive situation had been significantly improved.[41] **11.54**

---

36 *AS V&K Holding*, Tallinn City Court, Case no. 1-1939/04, Judgment of October 7, 2004.
37 *AS Securitas Eesti, AS Pristis*, Harju County Court, Case no. 1-12-3302.pdf, Judgment of April 25, 2012.
38 See paras. 11.37–11.45.
39 *MTÜ Rehviliit*, Harju County Court, Case no. 1-10-4332, Judgment of April 27, 2010.
40 See paras. 11.37–11.45.
41 *JCDecaux Eesti OÜ/Tartu LV*, ECA Case no. 5.1-5/09-0022, May 8, 2009.

D. Joint ventures and other competitive collaborations

11.55 The authors are not aware of any practice outside the merger control.

E. Trade associations

11.56 There are no special rules regulating competitors' collaboration or communication through or within trade associations. However, there is a specific provision, article 4(1)(4) of the Act addressing information exchange practices that might become relevant with respect to information exchange practices in trade associations.[42]

F. Interlocking directorates

11.57 There are no special rules regulating interlocking directorates outside the merger control context. The authors are not aware of any relevant practice in that regard.

G. Facilitating practices

11.58 The authors are not aware of any practice relating to facilitating practices other than those analyzed in other Sections.[43] Nevertheless, any type of practice that has as its object or effect the restriction of competition falls under the prohibition of anticompetitive agreements.

H. Information exchange

11.59 Information exchange continues to be a topical subject among competition law practitioners, but it has not received much attention from the ECA or courts. There are only a few cases on pure information exchange, concerning the analysis of whether information exchange in itself can infringe competition rules without any proof of any other harmful cooperation. Thus, no definite case law has developed regarding the type of information exchange that could be considered as exchange of historical or aggregated information or acceptable on the basis of other characteristics.

11.60 The ECA handled information exchange issues in a case that mainly concerned abuse of dominance. The ECA concluded that exchange of historical information is not a per se violation. Exchange of future information that enables the undertakings to plan sales and/or production strategy generally restricts competition. Exchange of past data may restrict competition only if special circumstances create a possibility of restricting competition. In *MTÜ Eesti Liikluskindlustuse Fond*, the ECA did not establish such special circumstances. The information exchanged included quantities of car insurance policies sold on a particular date, and specific data regarding clients of the insurance broker IIZI was presented. The data sent by the chairman of Eesti Liikluskindlustuse Fond (all Estonian insurance companies are members of this organization) to all the insurance companies was only a few days old (exchanged data was dated May 9, and the information exchange took place on May 12, 2008).[44]

11.61 In an earlier decision, the ECA found the infringement of article 4(1)(4) of the Act in a case concerning packaging waste collection, but it granted individual exemption on the basis of article 6 of the Competition Act (there is no individual exemption granting possibility after 2006). This was not purely an information exchange case since it involved the exchange of collection prices, coordination of these prices, and exchange of companies' costs as well as coordination of waste disposal fees. The intended information exchange and coordination were planned to be conducted by the beverage packaging recovery organizations created in

[42] See Sections II.H and II.I.

[43] See Sections II.H and II.I.

[44] *MTÜ Eesti Liikluskindlustuse Fond*, ECA Case no. 5.1-5/09-0035, August 17, 2009.

view of fulfilling obligations set out by the EU directive on packaging and packaging waste. Information exchange was not analyzed in detail, and it is not known whether the planned conduct involved exchange of individual data or whether an independent data collector was supposed to aggregate the information. Whether that particular exchange of information would have restricted competition or not has no practical importance in the context of the case. The coordination and ancillary information exchange were considered to satisfy all the criteria of individual exemption on the basis of the obvious positive impact of the coordination on environmental protection. Nevertheless, it was the coordination that received attention, and information exchange was not analyzed by the ECA in detail.[45]

The lack of practice in the field of information exchange may be considered peculiar since article 4(1)(4) of the Act specifically addresses information exchange practice stating that it is prohibited to exchange information which restricts competition. The rationale as well as the actual content of the provision is unclear. The Supreme Court briefly dealt with the issue in a case concerning price fixing. The court held that in the case of price fixing, the unlawful nature of the exchange of price-related information is already covered by article 4(1)(1) of the Act. Therefore, article 4(1)(4) of the Act refers to other kinds of anticompetitive information. That kind of interpretation results from a narrow concept of price-related information. The Supreme Court only concentrated on future pricing intentions and failed to consider that information could also be exchanged about current or past prices. Therefore, the implications of the case should be considered in the context of the facts, and it is possible that in future cases the conclusions may be different. Another important aspect of this case is that the Supreme Court confirmed its previously stated view that the practices listed in article 4(1) of the Act are infringements by object.[46] The Supreme Court also stressed that since article 101(1) TFEU contains no provision regarding restrictive information exchange practices, information exchange analyzed in this case would not be infringement by object under this provision.[47] The Supreme Court failed to consider that article 101(1) TFEU provides a non-exhaustive list, and that other practices not mentioned in the list might be infringements by object. In terms of legal certainty, the conclusions of the Supreme Court are highly problematic: information exchange practices could be infringements by object but it is not clear on what conditions. **11.62**

There is another case that did not explicitly concern information exchange but it might be of some relevance. In *AS Astro Raamatud*, the ECA found that restricting price comparison harms competition, and lawful price comparison benefits competition by improving consumer price transparency.[48] Therefore the ECA is probably not seeing public information exchange in the form of a price comparison website as problematic in itself. **11.63**

I. Exchange of historic pricing information

Exchange of historic pricing information has not been assessed in practice. Nevertheless, the ECA's position in *MTÜ Eesti Liikluskindlustuse Fond*, concerning exchange of historical information on quantities, may help shed some light on the issue. According to the ECA, the practice implies that information exchange is anticompetitive if confidential information regarding the future is exchanged. Exchange of past information is anticompetitive only in special circumstances. The wording of the ECA's decision implies that in the case of exchange of past information, regardless of the content of the information, there must be special **11.64**

[45] *MTÜ Taara Liit*, ECA Case no. 38E, July 14, 2005.
[46] See also Estonian Supreme Court, Case no. 3-1-1-32-10, Judgment of May 7, 2010.
[47] *KPK Teedeehitus*, Estonian Supreme Court, Case no. 3-1-1-12-11, Judgment of May 4, 2011.
[48] *AS Astro Raamatud*, ECA Case no. 25-L, July 28, 2003.

circumstances present to conclude that there is an infringement of article 4(1)(4) of the Act.[49] The ECA has not provided further guidance on the notion of "special circumstances" in its practice since *MTÜ Eesti Liikluskindlustuse Fond*. There are other aspects about the ECA's conclusions that remains unclear. The ECA uses the notions of "historical information" and "past information" interchangeably (information a few days old was considered "historical" in this case). The ECA refers to competition law practice as a basis for its conclusions without specifying the type of practice. Assuming that it was EU competition law practice, the conclusions may be based on a wrong interpretation.

(i) How old, anonymous, and aggregated pricing information needs to be

11.65 There is not enough practice to draw any certain conclusions with regard to how old, anonymous, and aggregated pricing information needs to be in order not to fall under prohibition of anticompetitive agreements, concerted practices, and decisions by associations of undertakings.

(ii) What pro-competitive purposes, if any, exchange needs to help participants achieve; pre-merger due diligence

11.66 In the *MTÜ Taara Liit* case[50] the environmental protection objective was considered as sufficient to fulfill the individual exemption criteria. The authors are not aware of any practice regarding other pro-competitive purposes. There are no special rules for the pre-merger due diligence situation in that regard.

J. Joint purchasing agreements

11.67 There are no special rules regulating joint purchasing agreements. The authors are also not aware of any relevant practice. Nevertheless, the provision addressing information exchange[51] might be relevant, alongside the list in article 4(1) of the Act, if parties to the agreement go further than needed for the purpose of joint purchasing.

K. Joint lobbying/regulatory/legislative efforts

11.68 See Section II.I.

III. General issues

A. Jurisdiction and applicable law (including sector-specific competition regulation)

11.69 The rules of competition law are designed by the Act and regulations issued under the Act. The rules of the Act apply to all sectors of the economy (with a limited exception of agriculture). Nevertheless, the Act is not the only Estonian piece of legislation laying down rules for the protection of competition on the market. There are some specific pieces of legislation containing special provisions applicable to specific industries and sectors with the purpose of protecting competition (e.g. the Energy Market Act in the energy sector, the Electronic Communications Act in the electronic communications sector).

11.70 The rules of competition law apply to all undertakings. The notion of "undertaking" includes any entity engaged in economic activity, whatever its legal form. To the extent that

[49] *MTÜ Eesti Liikluskindlustuse Fond* (n 42).
[50] *MTÜ Taara Liit* (n 43). See also para. 11.61.
[51] See Section II.H.

undertakings are engaged in economic activity, competition law applies to public as well as to private entities.

Because the Estonian competition law enforcement system is complicated—administrative, misdemeanor, and criminal proceedings are possible (for some infringements several types of proceedings may be applicable)—there are different rules with regard to applicable law. **11.71**

According to article 6(1) of the Penal Code, Estonian penal law applies to acts (both crimes and misdemeanors) committed within the Estonian territory. It is also important to consider article 11(1)(3) of the Penal Code which states that an act is deemed to have been committed in the place where the consequences of the act, constituting a necessary element of the offense, are being felt. Therefore, if an act of abuse of dominance or restrictive agreement, decision or concerted practice, is committed outside the territory of Estonia, the Penal Code applies if it restricts competition in the territory of Estonia. Article 1(2) of the Act establishes an analogous principle—the Act applies if an act or omission directed at restricting competition is committed outside the territory of Estonia but restricts competition within the territory of Estonia. **11.72**

If the Penal Code is not applicable under the concept of territorial applicability, it might still apply in accordance with the personal jurisdiction provision (applicability of penal law by reason of person concerned), i.e. article 7 of the Penal Code. This possibility may widen the Estonian jurisdiction, but because it has little practical relevance, especially in competition cases, this concept is not further analyzed for the purposes of this chapter. There are no personal jurisdiction rules in the Act. **11.73**

B. Antitrust system

(i) Name of agency/agencies

The ECA is a governmental agency within the administrative jurisdiction of the Ministry of Economic Affairs and Communications which runs administrative proceedings, and acts as a body conducting extrajudicial proceedings in misdemeanor proceedings and as pre-trial investigator in criminal proceedings. The ECA has broad powers in the context of misdemeanor and criminal proceedings—to conduct interrogations, confrontations, and carry out observations and searches. In administrative proceedings, the ECA can request information, documents and other materials, and search a company's location and place of activity (in contrast to criminal and misdemeanor proceedings, it has no power to conduct searches in other places, e.g. private homes or cars). **11.74**

If it is necessary to collect evidence through surveillance (e.g. covert surveillance of people, things, or places; wiretapping; staging a crime; using a police agent), the ECA has to involve the police (officers of the Security Police Board or the Police and Border Guard Board) as the ECA has no authority to carry out surveillance activities. **11.75**

The Prosecutor's Office is a government agency within the Ministry of Justice. The prosecutor leads pre-trial proceedings. The prosecutor guides the pre-trial investigator in collecting evidence, and decides whether to bring charges against a person on the basis of the facts established. **11.76**

There are three court instances: county courts and administrative courts as the courts of first instance; circuit courts as the appellate courts; and the Estonian Supreme Court as the highest court. The courts hear criminal matters and serve as appellate bodies for the decisions of the ECA in misdemeanor and administrative cases. Administrative cases are heard in administrative courts which are separate from the general court system only in first instance. Also, courts have competency to hear civil matters concerning competition law violations relating to damages claims. **11.77**

(ii) Staff size and budget

11.78 It is important to note that the ECA has other functions besides those related to its role as a competition authority. In 2008, regulatory agencies responsible for energy, water, railway, and communication sectors, as well as three surveillance departments, were merged into one agency—the ECA. Since then, the ECA has acted both as the competition authority and the sector regulator for the above sectors. The approximate size of the staff is sixty people, whereas about a third of the staff is employed in the Competition Division. In 2011 the budget of the ECA was EUR 1.83 million.[52]

(iii) Recent enforcement actions and trends

11.79 Since the reorganization in 2008, the ECA has noted that the fight against hard-core cartels is one of its main priorities. The ECA has referred to the inappropriateness of misdemeanor proceedings in the context of abuse of dominance, since cases are complicated but sanctions are small compared to other countries. Also, the limitation period for these infringements is two years from the moment the infringing act is first committed. The ECA regards the ineffectiveness of sanctioning the incumbents as one of the biggest shortfalls in its supervisory activities.[53] Based on all these difficulties related to the misdemeanor procedure, it is likely that cartels will remain the main focus, and the ECA will concentrate only on those cases of abuse of dominance where a strong public interest is at stake.

11.80 Currently ongoing court proceedings in cases investigated by the ECA concern public procurements of State Forest Foundation with regard to the transport of raw timber, and anti-competitive agreement between flour mills.[54]

C. Private litigation

11.81 There is no established case law on private litigation in Estonia. Claims for damages arising from infringements of competition law are not subject to any special rules. According to article 78 of the Act, proprietary or other damage caused by activity prohibited by the Act shall be subject to compensation by way of civil procedure. In the framework of the Law of Obligations Act, damage arising from competition law infringement may be classified as unlawfully caused damage. This type of damage shall be compensated provided that three preconditions are met: (i) existence of an act, damage, and a causal relationship between the act and the damage; (ii) unlawfulness of the act; (iii) culpability of the person who caused the damage.

11.82 There is an additional procedural possibility for a victim in the context of criminal proceedings—to file a civil action in criminal proceedings with the court of first instance through the intermediary of an investigative body (including the ECA) or through the Prosecutor's office. Filing this kind of claim is exempt from state fee. Nevertheless, the authors are not aware of any practice in that regard in the context of competition law infringement. The lack of practice may be caused by the fact that the concept of victim may be problematic in the context of competition infringement, as damage has to be directly caused by a criminal offense in order to meet the definition of a victim.

[52] See Estonian Competition Authority, Annual Report 2012, p. 8, <http://www.konkurentsiamet.ee/public/Aastaraamat/ECA_Annual_Report_2012.pdf>.

[53] See Estonian Competition Authority, Annual Report 2011, p. 7, <http://www.konkurentsiamet.ee/public/Aastaraamat/ANNUAL_REPORT_2011.pdf>.

[54] *Kaupo Nõmmemees and others*, Viru County Court, Case no. 1-10-3815; Tartu County Court, Case no. 1-11-9300 (pre-trial proceedings no. 099921000002).

D. Follow-on litigation (includes role of agency determinations of liability for follow-on litigation)

There are no special rules regulating follow-on litigation. Follow-on litigation and litigation based on "stand-alone" claims are subject to the same regulation. **11.83**

The *AS Levira* case concerning the issue of follow-on litigation that cannot be considered as a precedent for private litigation but might have some implications for further developments in this area. Tallinn Administrative Court issued a ruling according to which the reasoning of ECA decisions is not contestable in administrative proceedings. In this case, Levira claimed that, although the ECA closed the proceedings and did not impose any sanctions, its reasoning suggested that there was a period when Levira abused its dominant position by setting unfairly high prices. Levira claimed that its rights were violated because Levira's clients may bring civil actions for damages cases against Levira and base their claim on the ECA's decision establishing the existence of an illegal conduct. The court found that the possibility that the references to the infringement in the ECA's decision can be used as a proof in civil damages case does not violate claimant's rights. The court explained that the reasoning behind the ECA's decisions is not binding on civil courts.[55] **11.84**

E. Arbitration and alternative dispute resolution

There are no special rules regulating the application of Estonian competition law in case competition law issues arising in arbitration. The authors are also not aware of any precedent according to which an arbitral award not in conformity with the Act was overturned on the basis of the conflict with public policy. **11.85**

F. Remedies

(i) Civil liability

In administrative proceedings, the ECA may impose an injunction as a remedy. Upon failure to comply with an injunction, the ECA may impose a penalty payment of up to EUR 3,200 on natural persons and up to EUR 6,400 on legal persons. Additionally, the ECA may make recommendations to state agencies, local governments, and natural and legal persons as to the improvement of the competitive situation. **11.86**

(ii) Criminal liability

Actions listed in article 400(1) of the Penal Code—all agreements, decisions, and concerted practices which have as their object or effect the restriction of competition are punishable by a pecuniary punishment or imprisonment of up to one year. Certain "hard core" restrictions provided in article 400(2) of the Penal Code (price fixing, market sharing, and limiting production, service, goods markets, technical development, or investment) are subject to harsher penalties—a pecuniary punishment or imprisonment of one to three years.[56] The punishment by imprisonment concerns natural persons only. With regard to companies, the respective pecuniary punishments are 5 percent and 10 percent of the company's turnover. **11.87**

If the offender has already incurred a punishment for a misdemeanor offense for the same act—abuse of dominant position or violation of other obligations of monopoly undertakings—then these violations are considered as criminal offenses under articles 399 and 402 of the Penal Code respectively. According to these provisions, a pecuniary punishment or imprisonment for up to three years may be imposed in case of these offenses. **11.88**

[55] *AS Levira*, Tallinn Administrative Court, Case no. 3-11-2471/8, Judgment of November 29, 2011.

[56] See para. 11.40.

11.89 According to the general part of the Penal Code which applies to all criminal offenses, natural persons (company executives) may be punished by a fine of 30 to 500 daily wages or imprisonment of up to three years, and legal persons (companies) can face a fine of up to EUR 16 million. A pecuniary punishment may be imposed on a legal person also as a supplementary punishment together with compulsory dissolution. In addition, the gain obtained through illegal activities should be confiscated by the court. In the case of infringement of article 400 of the Penal code (prohibited agreements, decisions, and concerted practices) a prohibition to engage in entrepreneurial activity for a term from one to five years may be imposed on natural persons.

11.90 No imprisonment has been imposed for offenses relating to competition in practice. Also, pecuniary punishments have been considerably lower than the maximum limit of EUR 16 million or the turnover limit would allow. For example, in the *AS Securitas Eesti, AS Pristis* case,[57] which was a clear-cut market sharing agreement—the pecuniary punishment of EUR 20,000 was imposed on both companies involved, which is considerably lower compared to the above mentioned maximum limits. The settlement proceedings were applied in this case as in several competition cases in recent years.

11.91 In settlement proceedings, the Prosecutor's Office and the defendant and his or her counsel negotiate the legal assessment of the crime, the nature and extent of the damage caused by the criminal offense, and the type and the category or term of the punishment which the prosecutor will pursue in court. As the punishment is negotiated as an exchange for the waiver of examination of evidence in the court, the punishments are more lenient compared to those imposed in convictions in general procedure.

(iii) Misdemeanor liability

11.92 In the case of a first-time offense, abuse of a dominant position or violation of obligations of an undertaking with special or exclusive rights or in control of essential facilities, are considered as misdemeanors under the Act. A fine of up to EUR 32,000 may be imposed on legal persons (companies) and a fine of up to EUR 1,200 or detention for up to thirty days on natural persons (company executives). If a punishment for a misdemeanor has been imposed on the offender for the same act, then the offender is punished under the Penal Code—this is a pecuniary punishment or up to three years' imprisonment for natural persons, and a pecuniary punishment for legal persons.[58]

G. Leniency and immunity

11.93 The leniency program was introduced in Estonia on February 27, 2010. Some form of immunity was available before that in criminal proceedings—a so-called crown witness regulation, which means that criminal proceedings are terminated with regard to a person who assists the prosecutor in proving the facts of the crime. The ECA noted in its 2010 annual report that several leniency applications were submitted to the ECA already in the first year of the leniency program, in 2010. On the basis of leniency applications criminal procedures were initiated to investigate relevant anticompetitive cooperation and this increased the number of criminal proceedings handled by the ECA.[59]

11.94 Because of the special features of the rules of criminal procedure the characteristics of the leniency program are slightly different from EU framework. There are three different forms

---

[57] *AS Securitas Eesti, AS Pristis* (n 36). See also paras. 11.50–11.51.

[58] See para. 11.88.

[59] Estonian Competition Authority, Annual Report 2010, pp. 16–17, <http://www.konkurentsiamet.ee/public/AnnualReports_/ANNUAL_REPORT_2010_ECA.pdf>.

of immunity depending on the state of proceedings and when the leniency application is submitted:

(1) *Termination of criminal proceedings with regard to the first applicant before the proceedings have commenced.* According to article 205(1) of the Code of Criminal Procedure, the Public Prosecutor's Office shall terminate criminal proceedings with regard to the first leniency applicant who complies with the conditions for application of leniency provided for in the Act (see para. 11.96). There is an additional condition that the information contained in the leniency application must enable the prosecutor to commence criminal proceedings.
(2) *Termination of criminal proceedings with regard to the first applicant when the proceedings have commenced before submitting the leniency application.* According to article 205(2) of the Code of Criminal Procedure, the Public Prosecutor's Office shall terminate criminal proceedings with regard to the first leniency applicant who complies with the conditions for application of leniency and who provides evidence which, according to the Prosecutor's Office, contribute significantly to bringing charges.
(3) *Reduction of punishment.* According to article 205(3) of the Code of Criminal Procedure, the punishment imposed on a person for a criminal offense in accordance with article 400 of the Penal Code shall be reduced in proportion to the assistance received from that person in criminal proceedings if no other form of leniency is applicable. This might be the case for the applicants who are not the first to submit leniency applications.

Article 205(4) of the Code of Criminal Procedure provides that the Prosecutor's Office may **11.95** grant the leniency applicant a deadline of one month for submitting evidence. If the investigative body and the Prosecutor's Office find after the evaluation of the evidence received from the leniency applicant that there is no basis for the application of leniency under any of the three options (para. 11.94), the Prosecutor's Office shall notify the leniency applicant of the rejection of the application. Article 205(5) of the Code of Criminal Procedure grants the Prosecutor's Office the possibility of resuming proceedings with regard to the leniency applicant if, following the issuance of the order terminating the proceedings, circumstances become evident which prevent application of leniency.

Article 78(5) of the Act lists conditions necessary to fulfill when applying for leniency, in **11.96** addition to the timely submission of the application:

(1) the leniency application has been submitted on the initiative of the applicant;
(2) the leniency applicant shall terminate, with the approval of the Prosecutor's Office, his or her participation in the activity, unless he or she is involved in surveillance activities;
(3) on the conditions established by the Prosecutor's Office, the leniency applicant shall disclose and make available all evidence known to him or her regarding the offense;
(4) the leniency applicant shall cooperate with the investigative bodies and the Prosecutor's Office until the termination of the proceedings;
(5) the leniency applicant has not induced other persons to commit an offense or conducted either the preparation for or the commission of an offense;
(6) the leniency applicant has not destroyed or hidden in bad faith any evidence relevant to the criminal proceedings, or disclosed facts relating to the leniency application or the criminal proceedings without the permission of the Prosecutor's Office.

There is an important precedent with regard to some procedural aspects of contesting the **11.97** application for leniency. Namely, the Supreme Court established that a leniency applicant whose is denied leniency has the right to contest the termination of criminal proceedings, although the Code of Criminal Procedure does not explicitly address this issue.[60]

H. Document creation and retention

11.98 According to the Estonian Penal Code, fraudulent creation of evidence (including documents) is a necessary element in some criminal offenses. Removal and fraudulent creation of evidence constitute criminal offenses in themselves: according to article 316 of the Penal Code, removal or fraudulent creation of evidence with the intention of obstructing the ascertainment of the commission, or the absence, of an act punishable as a criminal offense, or of any other facts relating to the subject of proof, is punishable by a pecuniary punishment or imprisonment of up to five years. Also, in the case of false accusation (art. 319), false testimony, or perjury by a victim or a witness (art. 320), as well as false expert opinion or false translation or interpretation (art. 321), the punishment is more severe if it involves fraudulent creation of evidence.

11.99 In criminal and misdemeanor proceedings, the companies or persons under the investigation have no duty to cooperate in the investigative measures. This principle derives from article 22 of the Constitution of the Republic of Estonia, according to which no one has the duty to prove his or her innocence in a criminal procedure and no one shall be compelled to testify against himself or herself, or against those closest to him or her. According to the Code of Criminal Procedure, the accused or the suspect have a right to present evidence but no duty to do that. Nevertheless, it should be noted that, as employees of the company, who are not suspects or accused, are not allowed to remove or create evidence, if they do remove or create evidence, they may be held responsible for committing criminal offenses described above (see para. 11.101).

11.100 In administrative proceedings, there is a duty to cooperate with the ECA. The ECA may issue an injunction if a company or a natural person has committed any of the acts specified under article 62(1) of the Act. The list in article 62(1) of the Act includes failure to submit information or materials within the term specified in a written request by the Competition Authority, and hindering an inspection at the seat or place of business of the undertaking. Based on these provisions, the ECA may oblige the person who failed to submit documents to submit these documents by issuing an injunction. Upon failure to comply with the injunction, the ECA may impose a penalty payment of up to EUR 3,200 on natural persons and up to EUR 6,400 on companies.

[60] *Uuno Lausing and AS Tartu Mill*, Estonian Supreme Court, Case no. 3-1-1-10-12, Ruling of March 30, 2012.

12

EUROPEAN UNION

Uta Itzen, Andreas von Bonin, and Joanna Goyder
Freshfields Bruckhaus Deringer

Introduction

The most serious antitrust infringements in the European Union (EU) involve cartels entered into between competitors, and much enforcement activity concerns these. But there is also a broad range of other types of conduct that can infringe antitrust law, some of which can attract heavy sanctions. This range includes agreements or understandings entered into with other, non-competing, businesses in the supply chain (e.g. resale price maintenance (RPM), exclusive supply agreements, quantity forcing, non-compete clauses). These are analyzed under article 101 of the Treaty on the Functioning of the European Union (TFEU). For example, in recent years, there has been a focus on patent settlements and other arrangements which delay market entry of generic products in the pharmaceutical sector, and on certain practices in financial services markets. Attention has also been given to supply chains in the food sector, with the Commission cooperating closely with national competition authorities (NCAs) of the EU member states which carry out the majority of enforcement in these markets. **12.01**

12.02 The range also includes purely unilateral conduct characterized as "abusive" (e.g. predatory or exploitative pricing, refusal to deal). Unilateral conduct is only illegal if it is carried out by a business in a "dominant position," in which case it infringes article 102 TFEU. Recent enforcement action has involved a broad range of sectors, but some sectors have received particular attention. Among these are financial services markets, where the Commission has brought proceedings concerning such issues as access to information or services, standard setting, IP rights, and interoperability between different products or services. There have also been a number of cases in energy and telecommunications markets concerning behavior that excludes competing suppliers, or involves charging excessive prices. Innovation industries have also attracted much attention, and one of the current highest-profile Commission abuse cases concerns allegations of illegal practices used by Google to put competing search service providers and advertising platforms at a competitive disadvantage.

12.03 In the context of both articles 101 and 102 TFEU, although the main focus of enforcement action at EU level has been on situations which harm consumer welfare, the political aim of creating a single European market remains influential. This means that priority will be given to cases in which cross-border trade is hindered; and in some cases interference with exports appears to be a key factor in finding infringement.[1]

12.04 Cartels have long been the top enforcement priority in the EU, and many very high fines have been imposed in recent years. Fines imposed by the Commission in the five years from 2007 to 2011 totaled well over EUR 10 billion, and although some of these fines were reduced on appeal, the sums involved remain extremely high. The highest cartel fines ever imposed were those in *Car glass* (2008),[2] where total fines were EUR 1.38 billion, and St. Gobain alone was fined EUR 896 million. In cartel cases, the Commission has made increasing use of its settlement procedure (Commission Regulation 622/2008[3]), introduced in 2008 to facilitate more rapid case resolution, minimize the risk of lengthy appeals, and free up resources for further investigation. Also, substantial resources have been put into improving investigative procedures and technology, and into enhanced international cooperation with other cartel enforcement bodies.

12.05 Since the start of the economic crisis, Competition Commissioners and Commission officials have frequently stressed in strong terms that economic difficulties are not a reason to be more lenient in enforcing antitrust rules. Under Commissioner Almunia, who took over from Commissioner Kroes in 2010, there has been an increase in the number of settlements, as compared with the number of full infringement decisions, both for cartels and other anticompetitive conduct. But this should be seen not as a softening of approach, but rather as an attempt to make effective use of finite enforcement resources. The total of EUR1.47 billion in fines imposed in May 2012 for two cartels in television and computer monitor tubes respectively is evidence of a continuing hard line in cartel enforcement. The trend towards use of settlement, especially in cases involving fast-paced technology markets, can also be seen as a preference for obtaining quick behavioral commitments to ensure or restore competition

---

[1] See e.g. Case 26/75 *General Motors v. Commission* [1975] ECR-1367, in which an excessive charge for an export license inhibited cross-border car purchases and was found to infringe art. 102 TFEU; Case C-439/09 *Pierre Fabre Dermo-Cosmétique* [2011] ECR I-09419, where an absolute ban on distributors selling via internet was held to infringe art. 101 TFEU, in part because it reduced the scope for cross-border purchases of cosmetics.

[2] *Car glass*, Commission Decision C(2008) 6815 final relating to a proceeding pursuant to article 81 of the EC Treaty and article 53 of the EEA Agreement OJ 2009 C 173, p. 13 (November 12, 2008).

[3] Commission Regulation No. 622/2008 amending Regulation (EC) No 773/2004, as regards the conduct of settlement procedures in cartel cases (June 30, 2008), OJ L 171/3.

in the market within a relatively short timeframe. A good illustration of this is the current settlement proceedings concerning Google.

EU competition law applies to all sectors of the economy, with limited exceptions for agriculture, military equipment and nuclear energy. There are also other situations in which the EU antitrust rules will not apply, even to agreements or conduct which might appear anticompetitive. These include: (1) agreements or conduct which do not have an effect on trade between EU member states; (2) agreements which do not cause an "appreciable prevention, restriction or distortion of competition"; and (3) certain agreements between a principal and agent. These situations are discussed in turn below. **12.06**

An effect on trade between EU member states is a condition for the application of article 101 or 102 TFEU. The condition will be satisfied in most situations where the market involved covers a whole country or a large region of a country. Guidance on this concept is provided by the Commission Guidelines on the effect on trade concept contained in articles [101 and 102] (2004). These Guidelines further provide a rebuttable presumption that there is no appreciable effect on trade if the company has fewer than 250 employees or an annual turnover not exceeding EUR 50 million, or if the aggregate market share of the parties does not exceed 5 percent and certain turnover thresholds are not exceeded. **12.07**

Article 101 TFEU only applies to agreements if there is an "appreciable prevention, restriction or distortion of competition." This is sometimes referred to as a "*de minimis*" requirement. Guidance on its meaning can be found in the Commission Notice on agreements of minor importance which do not appreciably restrict competition under [article 101(1) TFEU] (*de minimis*) (2001). This Notice sets market share thresholds (10 percent for agreements between competitors and 15 percent for agreements between non-competitors) below which the Commission will not take infringement proceedings. But note that these "safe harbors" do not apply to cartels, RPM, or export bans; so called "hard core" restrictions. **12.08**

Finally, to the extent that an agreement fixes the scope of activity of an agent in relation to its principal's goods or services (e.g. resale prices and conditions, territory where, or customers with whom, the agent may deal), article 101 TFEU does not apply. For these purposes it is essential that the agent bear no more than insignificant commercial and financial risk, in particular in relation to contracts concluded or negotiated for the principal, or to any market-specific investments.[4] **12.09**

All twenty-seven member states have antitrust laws which are very similar in substance to EU antitrust rules, and which apply only to anticompetitive behavior affecting their national markets. They also have their own national, and in some cases also regional, enforcement bodies. These bodies, and national courts, must apply EU law in cases where there is an effect on trade between member states. (Where an agreement has no appreciable effect on trade between member states then it falls outside the scope of EU law and national law may be freely applied to the agreement.) In cases where EU law applies, either national bodies or the Commission may take enforcement action, but a national body may not do so if the Commission is already investigating the case. In practice, the Commission tends to deal with cases which affect several member states, and leaves national enforcers to deal with cases primarily affecting one or two member states. **12.10**

[4] Case T-352/01 *Daimler Chrysler AG v. Commission* [2005] ECR II-3319; Case C-217/05 *Confederación Española de Empresarios de Estaciones de Servicio (CEEES) v. Compañía Española de Petróleos SA (CEPSA)* [2006] ECR I-11987; Case C-279/06 *CEPSA v. Tobar* [2008] ECR I-06681.

I. Acting alone

12.11 Article 102 TFEU prohibits any unilateral abuse of a dominant market position. Dominant position means "a position of economic strength enjoyed by an undertaking, which enables it to prevent effective competition being maintained on the relevant market, by giving it the power to behave to an appreciable extent independently of its competitors, customers and ultimately of its consumers."[5]

12.12 Market shares are often used as an important first indication: dominance is unlikely where the market share is below 40 percent, but at 50 percent dominance may be presumed,[6] and if the share is over 70 percent, it will in practice be extremely difficult to rebut the presumption. Apart from market shares, the main relevant factors are the strength of existing and potential competition, including barriers to entry, and the constraints imposed by the bargaining strength of customers. So, for example, a business which is an unavoidable trading party for other businesses will probably be considered dominant.

12.13 It is not illegal for a business to have a dominant position, but only to abuse such a position (though the acquisition or strengthening of a dominant position may be subject to either EU or national merger control provisions). In its Guidance on the Commission's enforcement priorities in applying article [102 TFEU] to abusive exclusionary conduct by dominant undertakings ("Article 102 Guidance") the Commission sets out its enforcement priorities for exclusionary abuse.[7] The types of abuse it most commonly investigates include predatory pricing, exclusive purchasing, loyalty rebates, tying and bundling, refusal to supply, price squeeze, and imposing exploitative pricing or conditions.

A. Predatory pricing

12.14 Predatory pricing is an abuse and thus infringes article 102 TFEU if engaged in by an undertaking (business or other entity involved in economic activity) with a dominant position. Predation consists of pricing below cost so as to cause competitors to be weakened or to leave the market. In its Article 102 Guidance, the Commission states that in the case of price-based exclusionary conduct, such as predatory pricing, it will focus on pricing practices which may hamper competition from competitors which are *as efficient* as the dominant company. In 2003 the Commission fined Wanadoo EUR 10.35 million for predation.

12.15 According to European Court case law, the cost against which the allegedly predatory price must be compared is the "average variable cost" (the cost of making one additional item) or, if a plan to eliminate a competitor is shown, the "average total cost" (the total cost of each item).[8] The Commission's Article 102 Guidance refers instead to the concepts of "average avoidable cost" and "long-run average incremental cost," respectively. The use of these concepts has the advantage (in the case of average avoidable cost) that it takes into account the fact that, the longer the period considered, the more of the various costs should be treated as variable rather than fixed, and (in the case of long-run average incremental cost) that it excludes common costs incurred by a company producing more than one product.[9] It is

---

[5] Case 27/76 *United Brands and United Brands Continentaal v. Commission* [1978] ECR 207.

[6] Case 62/86 *AKZO Chemie v. Commission* [1991] ECR I-3359.

[7] Guidance on the Commission's enforcement priorities in applying [Article 102 TFEU] to abusive exclusionary conduct by dominant undertakings, OJ C 45, February 24, 2009, para. 23.

[8] *AKZO* (n 6).

[9] Article 102 Guidance (n 7) para. 26.

uncontroversial that in economic terms these cost benchmarks are generally more appropriate than those set out in *AKZO*, and they are now the most likely to be used.

EU law does not require actual proof that the dominant company will later be able to recoup the losses it incurs as a result of predation.[10] **12.16**

The same test is applied where a dominant company makes selective price cuts in order to target its competitors' customers: there will be an abuse if the prices offered to those customers are predatory.[11] If the prices are not predatory then there should be no abuse finding. **12.17**

Predation cases brought by the Commission are not common. The most recent infringement finding is that made against Wanadoo in 2003 which gave rise to the France Télécom judgment referred to above.[12] **12.18**

B. Exploitative offenses

Excessive pricing or imposing other exploitative conditions can constitute abuse and so be an infringement of article 102 TFEU if engaged in by a business with a dominant position. **12.19**

Pricing will be considered an abuse if it bears no reasonable relation to the economic value of the product supplied.[13] This value is established either by looking at prices in other geographic markets (in *United Brands* the Commission had compared prices in Germany to prices in Ireland, but the decision was annulled because a cost-based analysis had not been applied), or in similar product markets (in *Deutsche Post AG* the prices for cross-border mail were compared with domestic tariffs),[14] or alternatively by considering the cost of producing the product, though this can be a complex exercise. **12.20**

The Commission rarely brings exploitative pricing cases, probably because it does not wish to get involved in price regulation. However, it did recently bring proceedings concerning excessive royalty rates for DRAMs (electronic memory chips), and the case was settled on the basis of binding commitments including a cap on royalty rates.[15] **12.21**

C. Monopsony

Abusive conduct by a business in a dominant purchasing position constitutes an infringement of article 102 TFEU just as does conduct by a business in a dominant selling position, but the Commission has rarely used article 102 to combat buyer power. **12.22**

A rare example is the case in which British Airways was held to commit an abuse as a dominant purchaser of travel agency services. The abuse consisted in a system of commission payments to agents which increased as various sales targets were reached, and were applied to all sales, even those already made, and which had a strong exclusionary effect on British Airways' competitors.[16] **12.23**

---

[10] Case C-202/07 P *France Télécom v. Commission* [2009] ECR I-02369.

[11] Case C-209/10 *Post Danmark A/S v. Konkurrencerådet*, Judgment (March 27, 2012).

[12] *France Télécom* (n 10).

[13] *United Brands* (n 5).

[14] *Deutsche Post AG*, Commission Decision C(2001) 728 relating to a proceeding under Article 82 of the of the EC Treaty OJ 2001 L 125, p. 0027 (March 20, 2001).

[15] *Rambus*, Commission Decision C(2009)7610 relating to a proceeding under Article 102 of the Treaty on the functioning of the European Union and Article 54 of the EEA Agreement OJ 2010 C 30/17 (December 9, 2009).

[16] Case C-95/04 *British Airways plc v. Commission* [2007] I-02331.

D. Price discrimination

12.24 Article 102(c) TFEU stipulates that an abuse may consist in "applying dissimilar conditions to equivalent transactions with other trading parties, thereby placing them at a competitive disadvantage." Article 102(c) TFEU has been used in cases concerning abusive discount strategies as well as in cases concerning geographic price discrimination.

12.25 Price discrimination as between customers is potentially exclusionary, in that selectively low prices may exclude competing suppliers by taking away their customers. However, there will not be an abuse if the low price is not predatory i.e. not below cost.[17] Nor will it be an abuse if the lower prices can be justified as volume discounts, or as reflecting different market circumstances. On the other hand, discrimination is more likely to be found to be abusive if it is being used to partition the single European market along national lines.[18]

12.26 Price discrimination is also potentially an exploitative abuse if it is used by a dominant company to extract higher than normal prices.[19]

E. Dictating or influencing resale prices

(i) Resale Price Maintenance

12.27 Fixed or minimum resale price maintenance (RPM) is one of the few types of agreement with non-competitors to be considered a serious infringement of article 101 TFEU. It is presumed to restrict competition and so to infringe article 101(1). It is not exempted by Commission Regulation 330/2010 ("Distribution Block Exemption"),[20] and its inclusion in any agreement will prevent other terms of the agreement from benefiting from that block exemption. RPM infringes article 101 TFEU even where the companies in question have relatively low turnover and market share, provided that cross-border trade is affected.

12.28 The prohibition on RPM extends to both direct and indirect means of influencing the resale prices charged by distributors. The Commission's 2010 EU Guidelines on restrictions in vertical agreements ("Vertical Guidelines") give as examples of indirect RPM:

> fixing the distribution margin, fixing the maximum level of discount the distributor can grant from a prescribed price level, making the grant of rebates or reimbursement of promotional costs by the supplier subject to the observance of a given price level, linking the prescribed resale price to the resale prices of competitors, threats, intimidation, warnings, penalties, delay or suspension of deliveries or contract terminations in relation to observance of a given price level.[21]

12.29 RPM is also unlikely to satisfy the economic efficiency conditions of article 101(3) TFEU. The Vertical Guidelines (unlike earlier editions of these guidelines) acknowledge that it is possible for efficiencies arising from RPM to justify an exemption. The examples given in the Vertical Guidelines of justifications which might make exemption available are: (1) the need to induce distributors to promote a new product during an introductory period; (2) the organizing of a short-term low-price campaign (say two to six weeks) in a franchise or similar

---

[17] *Post Danmark A/S* (n 11).

[18] See e.g. *Swedish Interconnectors*, Commission Decision relating to a proceeding under Article 102 of the Treaty on the Functioning of the European Union and Article 54 of the EEA Agreement OJ 2010 C 142, p. 28 (April 14, 2010).

[19] See Section I.B.

[20] Commission Regulation 330/2010 on the application of Article 101(3) of the Treaty on the Functioning of the European Union to categories of vertical agreements and concerted practices (April 20, 2010), OJ L 102/1.

[21] European Commission, Guidelines on Vertical Restraints, OJ C 130/1, (May 19, 2010), para. 48.

distribution system; or (3) the need to provide an incentive for distributors to provide additional pre-sales services, particularly for experience or complex goods.[22] However, a case has yet to be argued successfully on this basis at EU level, so fixed and minimum RPM remains illegal in all but very exceptional cases.

12.30 Currently RPM cases are much more commonly brought by NCAs than by the Commission. However, in the past, the Commission imposed high fines for RPM,[23] and NCAs continue to do so.

12.31 Maximum or recommended resale price clauses will not necessarily infringe article 101(1) TFEU, provided they do not in practice operate as fixed or minimum RPM, because of pressure from or incentives offered by the supplier. In other cases, even where "maximum" or "recommended" resale price clauses do operate as fixed or minimum RPM, and so if they do infringe article 101(1) TFEU, they may benefit from exemption under article 101(3) TFEU. The Distribution Block Exemption exempts agreements with maximum or recommended resale price clauses, if the general requirements of that block exemption are satisfied: the main requirement is that neither the market share of the supplier (on the market where it supplies) nor that of the buyer (on the market where it purchases) exceeds 30 percent.

(ii) Minimum advertised price programs

12.32 As mentioned in Section I.E(i), in EU law, the concept of RPM extends beyond explicit resale price fixing to include also indirect forms of achieving a similar result. Therefore any requirement by a supplier that a distributor refrain from advertising any resale price below the minimum price set by the supplier will be treated in the same way as direct RPM.[24]

F. Tying arrangements

12.33 In principle, such practices may constitute restrictive agreements which infringe article 101 TFEU, but in practice the Commission now only brings infringement actions on the basis of article 102 TFEU. This means that it is only if a business has a dominant position that tying (or bundling) is likely to raise antitrust concerns. Both tying and bundling are analyzed in the same way under article 102 TFEU.

12.34 To establish an infringement, the company must be dominant in the tying market (or market for part of the bundle). The Commission has said that it will prioritize enforcement in cases in which the tying and tied goods are two distinct products, and the tying causes anticompetitive foreclosure of equally efficient competitors, and there are no objective justifications or overriding efficiency benefits. The Commission considers the risk of anticompetitive foreclosure to be particularly high where the tie is long-lasting, or where the company is dominant on the markets for more than one product in a bundle. It also states that in the case of multi-product rebates it will examine whether the incremental price paid for each of the dominant undertaking's products is above the long-run average incremental cost for that product.[25]

12.35 In 2004 the Commission fined Microsoft a total of EUR 497 million for two types of abuse, one of which was tying Windows Media Player (WMP) to its Windows operating system. Windows is the dominant operating system, and WMP was held to be a separate product to the operating system. The General Court rejected Microsoft's argument that the integration

---

[22] Vertical Guidelines (n 21) para. 225.

[23] See e.g. Case C-167/04 P *JCB Service v. Commission* [2006] ECR I-08935: EUR 39.6 million, reduced on appeal to EUR 30.9 million.

[24] See Vertical Guidelines (n 21) para. 226.

[25] Article 102 Guidance (n 7) paras. 50–62. See further Section I.A.

of media functionality in Windows is indispensable.[26] In an earlier case, the Court of Justice upheld the Commission's finding of an abuse by Tetra Pak consisting in requiring that customers for its liquid packaging machines also buy cartons and repair and maintenance services from it.[27]

G. Exclusive dealing

12.36 A business in a dominant position which imposes an exclusive dealing (also called "exclusive purchase" or "non-compete") requirement on a customer, normally commits an infringement of article 102 TFEU if it expressly requires the customer to make most or all of its purchases from it, or offers discounts or engages in other practices that have this effect. The largest antitrust fine ever imposed by the European Commission was one of EUR 1.06 billion (*Intel* (2009), appeal pending) for applying discounts and exerting other forms of pressure on customers not to make purchases from its competitors.[28]

12.37 In its Article 102 Guidance, the Commission states that it is particularly likely to take enforcement action in the case of exclusive dealing imposed by a dominant company when actual or potential competitors of the dominant company are not in a position to compete for customers' full requirements, either because the dominant company is an unavoidable trading partner, for example because it has a "must-stock" brand, or because of the competitors' capacity constraints. Also, the longer the duration of the exclusive dealing obligation, the more likely it is to cause anticompetitive foreclosure of competitors.[29]

12.38 In some circumstances non-dominant companies may infringe article 101 TFEU by entering into an exclusive dealing agreement covering all, or a large proportion, of the purchaser's total needs. Whether or not there is an infringement will depend on (1) whether the market in question is characterized by substantial barriers to entry or is for other reasons foreclosed to new entrants or growing competitors and (2) whether the supplier's agreements themselves make a substantial contribution to that foreclosure.[30] In these cases, an exclusive dealing clause, or restriction with a similar effect, which does not cover more than 80 percent of the purchaser's total needs, is exempted under the Distribution Block Exemption, provided the general requirements of that block exemption are satisfied. The main requirement is that neither the market share of the supplier (on the market where it supplies) nor that of the buyer (on the market where it purchases) exceed 30 percent of their respective markets. However, even if the exclusive dealing clause is not covered by the Distribution Block Exemption, its inclusion in an agreement does not prevent the rest of the agreement from benefiting from the application of that exemption.

12.39 Restrictions on the territories in which, and the customers to whom, distributors may sell, may infringe article 101. Any absolute prohibition on exports or on internet selling, or on selling outside a specified territory, or any practice aimed at discouraging such sales, such as the granting of discounts only if goods are used for domestic sales, will infringe article 101(1) TFEU, and is unlikely to be exempted under article 101(3) TFEU.

[26] Case T-201/04 *Microsoft Corp. v. Commission* [2007] II-03601.

[27] Case C-333/94 *Tetra Pak v. Commission ("Tetra Pak II")* [1996] ECR I-5951.

[28] *Intel*, Commission Decision D(2009) 3726 final relating to a proceeding under Article 82 of the EC Treaty and Article 54 of the EEA Agreement OJ 2009 C 227, p. 13 (May 13, 2009). For more on discounts see Section I.J.

[29] Article 102 Guidance (n 7) para. 36.

[30] Case C-234/89 *Delimitis v. Henninger Brau AG* [1991] ECR I-935.

Some lesser forms of territorial or customer restriction are exempted under the Distribution Block Exemption, again, provided the general requirements of that block exemption are satisfied. It exempts: **12.40**

(1) a prohibition on active sales into an exclusive territory or customer group allocated to another buyer or exclusively reserved to the supplier (the concepts of "active" and "passive" sales are explained in the Vertical Guidelines: the distinction is essentially between sales made as a result of active approaches to customers, and sales made in response to unsolicited orders made at the initiative of the purchaser). For this exemption to apply, there can only be one exclusive distributor for each territory, and the supplier must impose prohibitions on active sales in that territory on all of its other EU distributors. However, partial exclusivity, where exclusivity in a given territory is shared between two or more distributors, benefits from the exemption, provided no territorial protection is given beyond the assurance that the supplier will not supply another distributor in that territory;
(2) a prohibition on wholesalers supplying end-users;
(3) a prohibition on members of a selective distribution system selling to unauthorized distributors; note that, in the case of selective distribution, both active and passive sales by retailers to any end-users must be permitted; and
(4) a prohibition on the buyer reselling components, which have been sold to it for incorporation into another product, to competing manufacturers.

European Court case law and the Distribution Block Exemption both provide some special rules for the territorial and customer restrictions in selective distribution systems[31] and franchising networks.[32] **12.41**

If a territorial or customer restriction infringes article 101 TFEU and is not covered by the Distribution Block Exemption then, like an RPM clause, its inclusion in an agreement prevents the rest of the agreement from benefiting from that block exemption. **12.42**

H. Refusal to deal

In principle a business is free to choose its trading partners, and so refusal to deal infringes EU antitrust law only in very specific circumstances, and this is normally the case only if practiced by a dominant company. **12.43**

Article 102 TFEU only applies if a number of conditions are satisfied. These are that (i) the input which is being refused is indispensable, because duplication is impossible or extremely difficult; (ii) the refusal excludes any competition on a secondary market; and (iii) there is no objective justification for the refusal.[33] In addition, if the refusal to supply relates to an intellectual property right, the refusal must prevent the emergence of a new product for which there is consumer demand, though it is not necessary that a market for that service actually exists: a potential or even hypothetical market suffices.[34] **12.44**

When in 2004 the Commission fined Microsoft a total of EUR 497 million for two types of abuse, one of these consisted in the refusal to supply certain interoperability information which other market players needed in order to develop compatible products. This decision, upheld in *Microsoft Corp.*,[35] appears to lower the threshold for intervention, as it does not **12.45**

[31] E.g. Case 26/76 *Metro v. Commission ("Metro I")* [1977] ECR 1875; Case 75/84 *Metro v. Commission ("Metro II")* [1986] ECR 3021.

[32] E.g. Case 161/84 *Pronuptia de Paris GmbH* [1986] ECR 353.

[33] Case C-7/97 *Oscar Bronner GmbH v. Mediaprint* [1998] ECR I-07791.

[34] Case C-418/01 *IMS Health GmbH v. NDC Health GmbH* [2004] ECR I-05039; *Microsoft Corp.* (n 26).

[35] *Microsoft Corp.* (n 26).

require that the refusal prevent the emergence of a completely new product, but only of some innovation ("technical development").

12.46 It should be noted that a non-dominant company may infringe article 101 TFEU if it uses refusal to deal to enforce a separate anticompetitive practice, for example, by cutting off supplies to distributors which do not respect the resale price fixed by the supplier.[36]

12.47 A separate form of abuse under article 102 TFEU, which is closely related to refusal to supply, is margin squeeze, also called price squeeze. A number of cases have been brought in recent years, both at EU and national level, and a large proportion of these concern telecommunications markets.

12.48 Margin squeeze occurs when a company which is dominant in an upstream market (e.g. wholesale telecommunications network access) also competes on a downstream market (e.g. retail telephony services). If the difference between the wholesale price at which it supplies its downstream competitor and the retail price it charges its own customer is such that an equally efficient downstream competitor could not compete on a long term basis, then article 102 TFEU is infringed.[37] This is an independent head of abuse, and it is not necessary to demonstrate that the dominant company's pricing is either excessive at wholesale level or predatory at retail level. Nor is it relevant whether the purchaser is an existing or a new one.[38]

I. Essential facilities

12.49 "Essential facilities" is not an expression used in article 102 TFEU or in European Court case law. However, it is sometimes used informally in refusal to deal cases (most often when discussing access to infrastructure such as a newspaper distribution network, or a port or airport), as an alternative way of expressing the requirement that even a dominant company is under no obligation to deal with another company unless the input is indispensable.[39]

12.50 In any case, the concept is construed narrowly[40] and the Commission now rarely brings cases of this sort. The Article 102 Guidance says that an input is indispensable for these purposes when "there is no actual or potential substitute on which competitors in the downstream market could rely so as to counter—at least in the long-term—the negative consequences of the refusal."[41]

J. Bundling (including loyalty and market share discounts)

12.51 Bundling involves selling two or more products at a price lower than the total price that would be charged for the products if bought separately. In principle, it may constitute a restrictive agreement which infringes article 101 TFEU, but in practice infringement actions are normally only brought on the basis of article 102 TFEU. This means that it is only if a business has a dominant position that bundling, or granting loyalty or market share discounts, is likely to raise concerns. Analysis of bundling under article 102 TFEU is similar to that of tying.[42]

12.52 The Commission has brought several cases relating to rebates in recent years. It treats a broad range of rebate schemes as abuses of dominance, on the grounds that they tend to exclude

[36] See Section I.M.
[37] Case C-280/08 *Deutsche Telekom AG v. Commission* [2010] ECR I-09555.
[38] Case C-52/09 *Konkurrensverket v. TeliaSonera Sverige AB* [2011] ECR I-00527.
[39] See Section I.H.
[40] *Oscar Bronner* (n 33).
[41] Article 102 Guidance (n 7) para. 83.
[42] See Section I.F.

competing, and equally efficient, suppliers. Where a rebate induces a customer to make most or all of its purchases from a dominant company, in practice it will be difficult to avoid an infringement finding. Individualized volume or value targets, and retroactive schemes (in which the rebate applies on condition that a certain level of purchases is reached, but is then applied to both previous and future purchases), are also highly likely to be found to be an abuse. On the other hand, standardized volume rebates for individual deliveries, or cash discounts for prompt payment, are unobjectionable.[43]

In its Guidance Paper,[44] the Commission has stated that it will prioritize enforcement in the case of rebate systems most likely to foreclose equally efficient competitors, such as retroactive rebate systems where the rebate amounts to a high proportion of the total price and the threshold is high. This is because such systems create a very strong incentive to purchasers to continue to buy from the dominant company as they approach the threshold, because the price effectively being offered is very low, or even below zero. The Commission has explained how it will calculate the "effective price" that the dominant company is charging and whether that price is predatory. It will assess predation with reference to average avoidable cost and long-run average incremental cost.[45] **12.53**

In practice, the Commission's most recent decisions have included an increasing level of such quantitative economic analysis. However, when Tomra sought annulment of the article 102 infringement decision against it on the grounds of flaws in that analysis, it met with the courts' view that the Commission was not required to show quantitative proof of predation, but that it was sufficient for it to show that the rebate was capable of limiting competition.[46] **12.54**

All recent Commission rebates decisions have been appealed to the European Courts. They span a range of industries including air travel ticket agency services,[47] reverse vending machines,[48] and computer chips.[49] So far the courts have only given judgments reviewing Commission decisions taken prior to the publication of the Guidance Paper, and in recent years they have upheld all these decisions, even though the Commission has been taking a traditional, formal, approach and has not established by means of quantitative assessment whether the rebate system amounted to predation. It remains to be seen to what extent the courts will, in the future, when they get the opportunity, endorse the approach to rebates set out in the Guidance paper. **12.55**

K. Standard-setting groups (disclosure requirements, licensing arrangements, and licensing pools)

The Commission has given significant attention to standard-setting activities in recent years, and it published new guidance on this subject in 2011. Chapter 7 of its Guidelines on the applicability of the Treaty on the Functioning of the European Union to horizontal cooperation agreements ("Horizontal Cooperation Guidelines") recognizes the benefits of standard setting, but states that it can raise antitrust issues. The three main concerns the Commission has are the possibilities of (1) anticompetitive collaboration between competitors, (2) reduced innovation through the setting of detailed technical specifications, and (3) exclusion of certain competitors from access to the results of the standard-setting process, **12.56**

[43] E.g. Case 85/76 *Hoffmann-La Roche* [1979] ECR 461.
[44] Article 102 Guidance (n 7) paras. 37–45.
[45] See Article 102 Guidance (n 7) paras. 40–44. See further Section I.A.
[46] Case C-549/10 *Tomra Systems ASA v. Commission*, Judgment, April 19, 2012.
[47] *British Airways* (n 16).
[48] *Tomra* (n 46).
[49] Case T-286/09 *Intel v. Commission*, pending.

for example because a necessary intellectual property license is too expensive.[50] Examples of anticompetitive collaboration would be if certain manufacturers set a standard and pressurized third parties not to market non-compliant products, or if producers colluded to exclude new technology from an existing standard.[51]

12.57 The Horizontal Cooperation Guidelines provide a safe harbor from article 101 TFEU for standardization agreements which satisfy certain criteria. These are that (1) participation in standard-setting is unrestricted, (2) the procedure for adopting the standard in question is transparent, (3) there is no obligation to comply with the standard, and (4) access to the standard is provided on fair, reasonable and non-discriminatory (FRAND) terms. Agreements not meeting these criteria are not necessarily illegal, but will need to be assessed on a case by case basis.[52] The Horizontal Cooperation Guidelines also provide guidance on how it may be determined whether terms are FRAND, saying that cost-based methods are generally not helpful because of the difficulty in assessing the costs attributable to the development of a particular patent, but that it may be possible to compare the licensing fees charged by the company in question for the relevant patents in a competitive environment before the industry has been locked into the standard, with those charged after the industry has been locked in.[53]

12.58 While it is not essential that potentially relevant intellectual property rights be required to be disclosed at the start of the standard-setting process, such disclosure does make it more likely that there is effective access to the standard adopted, and so that article 101 TFEU is not infringed.[54]

12.59 It should be noted that a holder of an intellectual property right essential to a standard may find that it is in a "dominant position" in relation to the licensing of that right, and therefore must be careful when dealing with licensees.[55]

12.60 While the holding or exercising of an intellectual property right essential to a standard does not necessarily give the holder a dominant position, it may do so in some circumstances. The Commission has taken article 102 TFEU enforcement action in a few cases, but none have resulted in infringement decisions. One case arose out of concerns that Rambus, a technology development company, had abused its dominant position by claiming excessive royalties for certain computer chips. The case was settled on the basis of binding commitments by Rambus, including a cap on its royalty rates.[56]

L. Customer termination

12.61 Customer termination is a special case of "refusal to deal."[57] Refusal by a dominant company to supply an existing regular customer is likely to be treated as an abuse, unless there are good reasons for termination of supply.[58] To some extent, protection from losses caused by parallel trade will be treated as justification for refusal to supply, even to a longstanding customer.[59]

12.62 In setting out its enforcement priorities, the Commission states that although the same principles apply in the case of *disruption* of previous supply as to *refusal* to supply, an abuse is

[50] Guidelines on the applicability of Article 101 of the Treaty on the Functioning of the European Union to horizontal co-operation agreements, OJ C 11, January 14, 2011, paras. 264–268.

[51] Horizontal Cooperation Guidelines (n 50) para. 273.

[52] Horizontal Cooperation Guidelines (n 50) paras. 277–286.

[53] Horizontal Cooperation Guidelines (n 50) paras. 287–291.

[54] Horizontal Cooperation Guidelines (n 50) para. 268.

[55] See Section I.H.

[56] *Rambus* (n 15).

[57] See Section I.H.

[58] *United Brands* (n 5).

[59] Joined Cases C-468/06–C-478/06 *Sot. Lélos kai Sia ("Syfait II")* [2008] ECR I-07139.

more likely to be found in the case of termination of an existing supply arrangement. This might be, for example, because the purchaser had made relationship-specific investments, in which case the input is more likely to be considered indispensable.[60] A recent example of alleged abuse consisting of constructive refusal to supply an existing customer is a settlement reached by the Commission with IBM. IBM committed to ensuring prompt availability of certain spare parts and technical information to third parties carrying out maintenance under reasonable and non-discriminatory terms and conditions.[61]

M. Termination of intermediaries (retailers, wholesalers, dealers, and value-added resellers, agents, and brokers)

Termination of intermediaries is a special case of "refusal to deal"[62] and is not likely to infringe article 102 TFEU if the intermediaries are not competing with the dominant company. Nor will it infringe article 101 TFEU, unless termination is used to enforce a separate anticompetitive practice, for example, by cutting off supplies to distributors who do not respect the resale price fixed by the supplier, or who breach an export prohibition.[63] **12.63**

N. Termination of relationships with competitors

Termination of a relationship with a competitor can only constitute an antitrust infringement if engaged in by a business with a dominant position, in circumstances in which the termination is abusive. In this case there will be an infringement of article 102 TFEU.[64] **12.64**

O. Exemptions

Article 102 contains no express provision for exemption, but conduct which would otherwise be considered an abuse will not be prohibited by article 102 TFEU if it is shown to bring about economic efficiencies which outweigh its anticompetitive effects or can otherwise be objectively justified. The burden of proof in establishing justifying circumstances lies on the party wishing to rely on them. The Article 102 Guidance summarizes the law on such justification.[65] **12.65**

There are several block exemption regulations. These list certain types of clauses which, if the conditions set out in the regulation are satisfied, are exempted. One of the most important block exemptions is the Distribution Block Exemption, covering certain distribution agreements.[66] Commission Regulation 772/2004[67] covers certain patent and know-how licensing agreements, and there are also some sector-specific block exemptions applicable to motor vehicle aftermarkets (Commission Regulation 461/2010[68]), insurance (Commission Regulation 267/2010[69]), and liner shipping (Commission Regulation 906/2009[70]). **12.66**

---

[60] Article 102 Guidance (n 7) para. 84.

[61] *IBM*, Commission Decision C(2011) 9245 relating to a proceeding under Article 102 of the Treaty on the Functioning of the European Union and Article 54 of the EEA Agreement OJ 2012 C 18, p. 6 (December 13, 2011).

[62] See Section I.H.

[63] Case 107/82 *AEG Telefunken v. Commission* [1982] ECR 1179.

[64] See Sections I.H. and I.L.

[65] Article 102 Guidance (n 7) paras. 28–31.

[66] See Sections I.E and I.G.

[67] Commission Regulation (EC) No. 772/2004 on the application of Article 81(3) of the Treaty to categories of technology transfer agreements (April 27, 2004), OJ L 123.

[68] Commission Regulation (EU) No. 461/2010 on the application of Article 101(3) of the Treaty on the Functioning of the European Union to categories of vertical agreements and concerted practices in the motor vehicle sector (May 27, 2010), OJ L 129/52.

[69] Commission Regulation (EU) No. 267/2010 on the application of Article 101(3) of the Treaty on the Functioning of the European Union to certain categories of agreements, decisions and concerted practices in the insurance sector (March 24, 2010), OJ L 83/1.

[70] Commission Regulation No. 906/2009 on the application of Article 81(3) of the Treaty to certain categories of agreements, decisions and concerted practices between liner shipping companies (consortia) (September 28, 2009), OJ L 256/31.

II. Dealing with competitors

12.67 Article 101 TFEU provides for a two-stage analysis of agreements and understandings.

12.68 First, there is the prohibition on agreements which have an anticompetitive object (e.g. price-fixing or bid-rigging cartel, exchange of information on future pricing, export prohibition, minimum RPM) or effect (e.g. exclusive supply, joint purchasing, standardization or licensing agreements, franchising, selective distribution). "Agreements" means both written and oral agreements, and formal contracts as well as informal "gentlemen's agreements."

12.69 Second, article 101(3) TFEU provides an exemption from this prohibition in some circumstances if the agreement brings about economic efficiencies. The European Commission has adopted a number of block exemption regulations. If an agreement falls within the scope of one of these block exemptions, then there is no need to analyze it to decide whether it infringes article 101(1), or to analyze it under article 101(3), because the block exemption provides a presumption that it brings about efficiencies, and the agreement is automatically valid. If no block exemption applies, then the parties themselves have to analyze the agreement and all the surrounding market circumstances in order to assess whether it is prohibited by article 101(1) and, if so, whether it satisfies article 101(3) TFEU. Detailed guidance on the type of evidence needed can be found in the Commission's Guidelines on the application of Article [101(3) TFEU] (2004).

12.70 Agreements and arrangements entered into between competitors for clearly anticompetitive purposes such as price-fixing, fixing of other trading conditions, market-sharing, bid-rigging (collusive tendering), or collective boycotts, are prohibited by article 101 TFEU. In practice, they are unlikely to be exempted under article 101(3). They are the most serious type of infringement of EU antitrust law and are often referred to as cartels. Cartels have long been the top enforcement priority in the EU, and many very high fines have been imposed in recent years. Other types of agreements and arrangements between competitors, such as production joint ventures, joint purchasing, information exchange, or standard-setting systems, cannot be said to have an anticompetitive object. They may still infringe article 101 TFEU, depending on their precise terms and their market effects. There is limited enforcement in these types of cases, and when it does occur it tends to result in settlement on the basis of behavioral commitments,[71] rather than in a formal decision.

A. Horizontal price fixing

12.71 Horizontal price fixing always infringes article 101 TFEU and price fixing cartels are among the most serious of all antitrust law infringements. The Commission brings many cases and imposes very high fines. Recent examples of fining decisions are *Freight forwarding*[72] in which fourteen international corporate groups were fined a total of EUR169 million for fixing prices and other trading conditions in four separate cartels in the international air freight forwarding market; and *Washing powder*[73] in which two companies reached a settlement

[71] E.g. *Oneworld Alliance*, Commission Decision C(2010) 4738 relating to a proceeding under Article 101 of the Treaty on the Functioning of the European Union and Article 53 of the EEA Agreement OJ 2010 C 278, p. 14 (July 14, 2010).

[72] *Freight forwarding*, Commission Decision C(2012) 1959 relating to a proceeding under Article 101 of the Treaty on the Functioning of the European Union and Article 53 of the EEA Agreement OJ 2012 C 375, p. 7 (March 28, 2012).

[73] *Washing powder*, Commission Decision C(2011) 2528 final relating to a proceeding under Article 101 of the Treaty on the Functioning of the European Union and Article 53 of the EEA Agreement OJ 2011 C 193, p. 14 (April 13, 2011).

with the Commission and paid total fines of EUR 315 million for coordinating prices in the European washing powder and detergents market. Another is *Air cargo*[74] in which eleven air cargo carriers were fined a total of EUR 799 million for fixing surcharge levels. In each of the three cases there was also a corporate group which received full immunity.

B. Horizontal agreements to allocate customers or territories; agreements not to compete

Market sharing cartels, including geographic market and customer sharing, are, like horizontal price-fixing cartels, among the most serious of all antitrust law infringements. The Commission brings many cases and imposes very high fines. Recent examples of fining decisions are *Animal feed phosphates*[75] in which total fines of EUR 176 million were imposed for market-sharing and other illegal coordination in the animal feed phosphates market, and *Prestressing steel*[76] in which 16 corporate groups were fined a total of EUR270 million for market-sharing and price-fixing in the prestressing steel market. In both cases there was also a corporate group which received full immunity. **12.72**

C. Horizontal boycotts

Agreements between competitors not to purchase from, or supply to, specific businesses, if entered into for an anticompetitive purpose, are a serious infringement by object of article 101 TFEU. The agreement may be intended to hinder the entry or growth of new competitors, or to punish competitors who do not cooperate in cartel arrangements (e.g. *Pre-insulated Pipes*,[77] where cartel participants devised a strategy to eliminate a competitor who refused to participate in their bid-rigging scheme). **12.73**

D. Joint ventures and other competitive collaborations

Joint ventures which are "full function"—that is, autonomous economic entities which operate independently on the market—will normally be analyzed under the EU merger control rules, or similar national rules, and not under article 101 TFEU. But the terms of non-full function joint ventures—such as strategic alliances and agreements to cooperate in certain areas, such as research and development—are subject to article 101 TFEU. **12.74**

Joint ventures can take a wide variety of forms, but in each case the essential question is whether the joint venture agreement has anticompetitive effects on the market. Relevant factors include: whether the parent companies are actual or potential competitors; what the relationship is between the parent companies' market activities and those of the joint venture; the range of the joint venture's activities; and in particular whether these are close to the market (e.g. joint selling) or far from the market (e.g. early-stage research and development); and the extent to which the parent companies agree not to compete with the joint venture. **12.75**

---

[74] *Air cargo* (2010), unreported.

[75] *Animal feed phosphates*, Commission Decision C(2010) 5004 relating to a proceeding under Article 101 of the Treaty on the Functioning of the European Union and Article 53 of the EEA Agreement OJ 2011 C 111, p. 19 (July 20, 2010).

[76] *Prestressing steel*, Commission Decision C(2010) 4387 final as amended by Commission Decision of 30 September 2010 C(2010) 6676 final and Commission Decision of 4 April 2011 C(2011) 2269 final relating to a proceeding under Article 101 of the Treaty on the Functioning of the European Union and Article 53 of the EEA Agreement OJ 2011 C 339, p. 7 (June 30, 2010).

[77] *Pre-insulated Pipes*, Commission Decision C(2010) 4387 final as amended by Commission Decision of 30 September 2010 C(2010) 6676 final and Commission Decision of 4 April 2011 C(2011) 2269 final relating to a proceeding under Article 101 of the Treaty on the Functioning of the European Union and Article 53 of the EEA Agreement OJ 2011 C 339, p. 7 (June 30, 2010).

12.76 If article 101(1) TFEU is infringed, an exemption under article 101(3) TFEU may be available. There are two block exemption regulations[78] in this area which cover specialization agreements (Commission Regulation 1218/2010[79]) and research and development agreements (Commission Regulation 1217/2010[80]) respectively.

12.77 The Commission also gives a detailed summary of the general principles and the case law in this area in its Horizontal Cooperation Guidelines. It includes separate chapters on information exchange, research and development agreements, production agreements, purchasing agreements, marketing agreements, and standardization agreements.

E. Trade associations

12.78 Participation in trade associations is in principle perfectly legal. However, in practice trade association meetings and contacts can be fertile ground for anticompetitive activity and so it is important to ensure that legitimate meetings and communications do not become the occasion for anticompetitive cooperation or exchange of information. For example the price-fixing cartel in *Washing powder*,[81] in which two companies paid total fines of EUR 315 million for coordinating prices, started out as a trade association initiative to improve the environmental performance of detergents.

12.79 Trade association gatherings should not be used as an opportunity to agree with any competitor on prices or other trading terms, or even discuss prices with them. Nor should price information or other commercially sensitive information be exchanged. It is important to avoid any meetings with competitors where prices (including recommended retail prices) or components of prices (including rebates, discounts, credit terms, or allowances), or other trading terms are discussed. Anyone finding themselves present at such a meeting should leave, and ensure that it is recorded in the minutes of the meeting that they left because prices or other trading terms were being discussed by competitors.

F. Interlocking directorates

12.80 Interlocking directorates as such have not so far been the subject of article 101 or 102 TFEU enforcement. To the extent that they, and the acquisition of minority interests, have been considered by the Commission, this has normally been in the context of merger control proceedings.

12.81 If an acquisition is not covered by EU merger control legislation—for example because the turnover thresholds are not reached—it may still constitute an infringement of article 101 or 102 TFEU.[82] If the acquisition of a minority interest gives the acquiring company actual or legal control over the target's commercial conduct, or for some other reason would reduce competition between the two companies, or on the market more generally, then article 101 TFEU could apply to the agreement between acquirer and target. Article 102 TFEU could apply if a dominant firm acquires an interest in another business in circumstances in which this weakens the competitive structure of the market.[83]

12.82 But the Commission has not brought such antitrust cases in recent years, largely because even where acquisitions fall outside the scope of EU merger control rules, they will normally be subject to review under national merger control rules.

---

78 See Section I.

79 Commission Regulation No. 1218/2010 on the application of Article 101(3) of the Treaty on the Functioning of the European Union to certain categories of specialisation agreements (December 14, 2010).

80 Commission Regulation No. 1217/2010 on the application of Article 101(3) of the Treaty on the Functioning of the European Union to certain categories of research and development agreements (December 14, 2010).

81 *Washing powder* (n 73).

82 Case 142/84 *BAT Co. Ltd. v. Commission* [1987] ECR 4487.

83 Case 6/72 *Continental Can v. Commission* [1973] ECR 215.

G. Facilitating practices

Facilitating practices are not subject to specific rules in EU law. Conduct such as exchange of information about intended future pricing, or agreements to limit advertising, will only infringe article 101 TFEU if they have the aim or the effect of restricting competition. **12.83**

H. Information exchange

Information exchange has received considerable attention recently, and the Commission's Horizontal Cooperation Guidelines (unlike previous versions of this text) have a chapter giving a detailed summary of the general principles and the case law in this area.[84] **12.84**

Information exchange covers a broad range of practices. At one end of the spectrum are private, reciprocal exchanges between competitors on their individualized intentions regarding future prices or output, which the Commission has said it will treat as cartels. Even if an exchange occurs on a single occasion, it may be enough to establish prohibited collaboration.[85] One-way disclosure of strategically sensitive information by one firm to a competitor (whether by mail, email, phone, or orally at a meeting) in circumstances where the latter requests the information or accepts it is likely to be treated in a similar way. **12.85**

At the other end of the spectrum are economically neutral or beneficial information exchanges which will generally not infringe article 101(1), such as exchanges of purely historic pricing information. **12.86**

In between, there are many more nuanced situations, which need to be analyzed in terms of their effects in order to determine if article 101 TFEU is infringed. The Commission's main concerns focus on exchanges that enable competitors to coordinate their market behavior, and those which result in anticompetitive foreclosure of a market. Key factors will be the characteristics of the market (the extent to which it is transparent, concentrated, non-complex, stable, and symmetric): in *John Deere v. Commission*,[86] the General Court noted that collusive outcomes are more likely where supply and demand levels are relatively stable. However, in *Woodpulp II*,[87] the ECJ held that factors such as an oligopolistic market, product homogeneity, and market transparency meant that the woodpulp producers' conduct could be explained as the result of conscious parallelism, and that the Commission had therefore been wrong to infer that there must have been an agreement or concerted practice. **12.87**

Also very relevant are the characteristics of the information exchange (whether the information is strategic, the extent of market coverage, how aggregated or individualized the information is, its age, the frequency of exchange, and the extent to which both the information and the exchange are public). **12.88**

Even indirect disclosure to competitors, for example, through public announcements, may infringe article 101 TFEU. The question of when such indirect disclosures or exchanges establish or form part of a prohibited concerted strategy between competitors is a complex one, but the Commission has indicated that even public announcements made by one firm may be enough to establish a strategy for reaching a common understanding with competitors, in particular when it is followed by public announcements by those competitors. **12.89**

Pro-competitive purposes may provide justification for exemption under article 101(3) TFEU. Examples given in the Horizontal Cooperation Guidelines include allowing companies to **12.90**

---

[84] Horizontal Cooperation Guidelines (n 50) paras. 64–110.

[85] Case C-8/08 *T-Mobile v. NMa* [2009] ECR I-04529.

[86] Case T-35/92 *John Deere v. Commission* [1994] ECR II-00957.

[87] Joined cases C-89/85 etc. *Ahlström v. Commission ("Woodpulp II")* [1994] I-99.

benchmark their performance or to allocate production to enable them to be more efficient, and reducing consumer search costs.

12.91 Companies engaging in pre-merger due diligence need to ensure that any information exchange is carried out in such a way that article 101 TFEU is not infringed. It is frequently helpful to establish "clean teams" for these purposes, with strict rules regarding the type of information to be exchanged, the use to which it may be put, and the persons who have access to that information.

12.92 Information exchange is becoming an increasing focus of enforcement, with the Commission tending to treat it, when it occurs between competitors, as an "object" infringement.[88]

I. Joint purchasing agreements

12.93 Joint purchasing potentially infringes article 101 TFEU, both in terms of the relations between purchasers, and the relations between a joint purchasing organization and its members. The Commission's Horizontal Cooperation Guidelines have a chapter giving a detailed summary of the general principles and the case law on joint purchasing.

12.94 Such agreements are not generally considered as having an anticompetitive object under article 101(1) TFEU, and so need to be analyzed in terms of their effects. The Commission's main concerns focus on whether the purchasers may together have sufficient market power to reduce competition on their selling market; whether the purchasers may force their suppliers to reduce the range or quality of their products; and also whether competing purchasers may have their access to suppliers foreclosed.[89] If members are prohibited from participating in competing organizations, there may be an infringement of article 101 TFEU unless the prohibition is restricted to what is necessary to ensure that the organization functions properly and maintains its negotiating strength in relation to producers.[90]

12.95 If article 101(1) TFEU is infringed, exemption under article 101(3) TFEU may be available.

J. Joint lobbying/regulatory/legislative efforts

12.96 Joint lobbying in connection with regulation or legislation does not normally raise antitrust issues. However, as in all contacts with competitors, it is important to ensure that legitimate meetings and communications do not become the occasion for anticompetitive cooperation or exchange of information.[91]

III. General issues

A. Jurisdiction and applicable law (including sector-specific competition regulation)

12.97 EU antitrust law applies to all sectors of the economy (with a limited exception for agriculture, military equipment, and nuclear energy). In addition certain sectors which have been run as state monopolies in the past, such as telecommunications, postal services, energy and rail transport, are also subject to market liberalizing legislation.

---

[88] E.g. *Bananas Cartel*, Commission Decision C(2008) 5955 final relating to a proceeding under Article 81 of the EC Treaty OJ 2009 C 189, p. 12 (October 15, 2008).

[89] Horizontal Cooperation Guidelines (n 50) paras. 200–204.

[90] Case C-250/92 *Gottrup-Klim* [1994] ECR I-5641.

[91] See Section II.E.

The law applies to all "undertakings," which includes any entity engaged in economic activity, whatever its legal form. This includes any independent economic actor or entity: a company, partnership, association, trust company, individual, or group of individuals may therefore be an undertaking for these purposes. An undertaking does not have to be profit-making, and it is irrelevant whether it has legal personality. This means that public entities such as government bodies and local authorities may be classified as undertakings for these purposes, if they are engaged in a commercial activity for payment.[92] **12.98**

Member states have national competition laws. These are very similar in substance to EU antitrust rules, though there is more variety in the procedural rules and sanctions. Regulation 1/2003[93] provides that, whenever national bodies apply national competition law to an agreement or practice which affects trade between member states, they must also apply article 101. In such cases, application of national law must not lead to the prohibition of agreements which do not infringe article 101(1), or which fulfill the criteria of article 101(3), or fall within the scope of a block exemption. When there is an effect on trade between member states and national courts or authorities apply national law to an abuse prohibited by article 102, they must also apply article 102. However, in this case, national law may impose stricter national rules prohibiting unilateral conduct. This means that in the case of unilateral conduct there is a "double barrier": a practice must be permitted by both article 102 and the relevant national law if it is to be legal. **12.99**

B. Antitrust system

(i) Name of agency/agencies

The European Commission and NCAs are responsible for enforcing EU competition law. (NCAs may also apply their own national law in parallel to EU law, provided this does not interfere with proper application of EU law. Application of EU and national law by NCAs is covered in the relevant country chapters.) **12.100**

The Commission has the power to issue requests for information, conduct interviews with employees, carry out inspections of company premises and (with a judicial warrant) private homes, impose fines of up to 10 percent of group wide turnover and periodic penalty payments, and order behavioral or structural remedies. **12.101**

While antitrust decisions are taken by the European Commission (either by the full college of all 27 Commissioners or by the Commissioner for Competition), the investigations and all preparatory work are carried out by the Directorate General for Competition, one branch of the European Commission services. **12.102**

(ii) Staff size and budget

The part of the Commission which deals with competition law and policy is the Directorate General known as DG Comp. DG Comp has about 440 professional staff (lawyers and economists) and about 290 administrative and other staff, making a total of around 730. This number includes those responsible for merger control and state aid enforcement, as well as those working in the antitrust area. Its budget for 2012 was around EUR 92 million. **12.103**

(iii) Recent enforcement actions and trends

Cartels have been for a long time, and remain, the top priority. Commission fines for cartels in 2010 totaled EUR 2.9 billion, and although the 2011 total was only EUR 614 million, **12.104**

[92] E.g. running an employment agency: Case C-41/90 *Höfner & Elser v. Macrotron* [1991] ECR I-1979.

[93] Council Regulation (EC) No. 1/2003 on the implementation of the rules on competition laid down in Articles 81 and 82 of the Treaty (December 16, 2002).

there is no doubt that cartels remain the most important enforcement target, and that international cooperation is becoming more frequent. In the cartel area the Commission has made increasing use of its settlement procedure (see Section II) and eight cartel cases, resulting in fines around EUR 3 billion in total, have now been settled in this way.

12.105 The Commission has improved its technical capacity to detect and prove cartel cases, and now uses powerful software in dawn raids that allows it to perform extremely thorough and far-reaching searches of vast volumes of data in a very few days. This in turn means that a company under investigation itself needs to obtain and analyze the information within a very tight timeframe, and take key strategic decisions such as whether and where to apply for leniency far faster than was the case in the past. At the same time, more companies are now bringing challenges against some of the Commission's practices. For example, Deutsche Bahn brought a case questioning whether the Commission was entitled to enter its company premises to carry out an investigation without having obtained a judicial warrant.[94] So far the Commission has only sought such a warrant where private homes are concerned. Another controversial issue is the seizure during dawn raids of copies of hard disks or other computer material.

12.106 As far as abuse of dominance is concerned, the Commission regularly brings cases, not only in markets where it has traditionally focused, such as telecommunications, energy, and pharmaceuticals, but now also in sectors such as financial services and information technology. It has formally stated that, when looking at exclusionary abuses, it will give priority to types of conduct that are most harmful to consumers, whether in terms of higher prices or otherwise, for example reduced quality or choice.[95] One current high profile case is the investigation into Google, and another concerns the conduct of a number of financial institutions on the credit default swaps market.

C. Private litigation

12.107 A party who has suffered loss as a result of any anticompetitive agreement or conduct may claim damages, or other forms of relief such as an injunction, in the national courts of EU member states. Until recently the number of such actions was small, but over the last few years it has increased steadily. The vast majority of such actions relate to cartels, rather than other types of restrictive agreements and abuse of dominance. It is now routine for the subjects of Commission cartel decisions to face, often multiple, damages claims. Although very few claims result in judgments, there are grounds to believe that very substantial sums are being paid in confidential settlements in many of the actions being brought.

12.108 The Commission has for some years been exploring what measures it might take to encourage private litigation. It published a Green Paper (2005)[96] and a White Paper (2008)[97] which identified obstacles to claims and suggested some ways forward. Though few concrete measures have since been adopted (in 2013, the Commission adopted a Communication on quantifying harm in actions for damages for competition law infringements,[98] and a draft directive is currently under discussion), the debate generated by the Green and White Papers appears itself to have stimulated private litigation. An area of particular political importance is the possible introduction of EU rules on some form of collective or class action. However, progress has been slow, not least because this is an issue of relevance in many areas beyond competition law, and so involves a broad range of interests. So far EU action on collective

[94] Currently on appeal, Case C-583/13P.
[95] Article 102 Guidance (n 7) paras. 5 and 19.
[96] Green Paper on Damages actions for breach of the EC antitrust rules, COM(2005) 672, December 2005.
[97] White Paper on Damages actions for breach of the EC antitrust rules, COM(2008) 165, April 2008.
[98] OJ 2013 C 167/19 (June 13, 2013).

redress has been limited to a non-binding recommendation.[99] More detailed discussion of private litigation is included in the relevant country chapters.

D. Follow-on litigation

A large proportion of private litigation, and especially damages claims, is follow-on litigation. National courts, when ruling on an agreement or conduct which is already the subject of a Commission decision, cannot take a decision running counter to an existing Commission decision.[100] They are therefore required to treat Commission infringement decisions as proof of the existence of an infringement, but not necessarily of all the factual and legal findings included in the decision. More detailed discussion of follow-on litigation is included in the relevant country chapters. **12.109**

E. Arbitration and alternative dispute resolution

Competition issues, and in particular disputes as to the enforceability of contractual terms, increasingly arise in commercial arbitration. Though it is not established that arbitrators are required to apply EU competition law, it is clear that the competition rules are public policy rules. This means that if an arbitral award may be appealed on public policy grounds, it may be overturned if, for example, it upholds a contract which infringes article 101 TFEU.[101] **12.110**

F. Remedies

(i) Civil liability

Administrative fines of up to 10 percent of a company's group-wide annual turnover can be imposed by the Commission for breach of articles 101 or 102 TFEU.[102] The limitation period is five years from the end of the infringement, but any Commission enforcement action interrupts the running of the limitation period (Council Regulation 2988/74[103]). The way in which fines are calculated is set out in the Commission's 2006 Guidelines on the method of setting fines imposed pursuant to article 23(2)(a) of Regulation No 1/2003. Periodic penalty payments of up to 5 percent of average daily turnover can also be imposed to compel a company to end an infringement.[104] **12.111**

In addition to making an infringement finding, the Commission may impose behavioral or, if there is no equally effective behavioral remedy or it would be more burdensome for the company concerned, structural, remedies.[105] **12.112**

As well as the fines that may be imposed for infringement of articles 101 and 102 TFEU, the Commission has the power to impose fines for a variety of procedural infringements. Fines of up to 1 percent of a company's group-wide annual turnover can be imposed in certain circumstances for the intentional or negligent supply of incorrect, incomplete or misleading information.[106] **12.113**

---

99 Commission Recommendation on common principles for injuctive and compensatory collective redress mechanisms in the Member States concerning violations of rights granted under Union law (June 11, 2013).

100 Regulation 1/2003 (n 93) art. 16.

101 Case C-126/87 *Eco Swiss China Time Ltd.* [1989] ECR 643.

102 Council Regulation 1/2003 (n 93) art. 23.

103 Regulation (EEC) No. 2988/74 of the Council concerning limitation periods in proceedings and the enforcement of sanctions under the rules of the European Economic Community relating to transport and competition (November 26, 1974).

104 Regulation 1/2003 (n 93) art. 24.

105 Regulation 1/2003 (n 93) art. 7.

106 Regulation 1/2003 (n 93) art. 23.

12.114 The Commission can close a case with a formal commitments decision, rather than an infringement decision. Commitments do not involve an infringement finding or any fine, and so do not provide a basis for follow-on damages claims. Breach of commitments entered into can lead to fines of up to 10 percent of turnover, or daily penalty payments of up to 5 percent of average daily turnover.[107] This procedure should not be confused with cartel settlement proceedings, which result in infringement findings and fines.[108]

12.115 Further, once an investigation has been initiated, the Commission can impose interim measures which require a business to suspend its conduct or the operation of an agreement pending the conclusion of their investigation. Breach of an interim measures decision can lead to fines of up to 10 percent of a company's group-wide annual turnover.[109]

12.116 (See relevant country chapters for the fines and other remedies that may be imposed by NCAs for breach of articles 101 or 102 TFEU.)

12.117 In addition, any agreement term which infringes article 101 TFEU is automatically void and unenforceable. Contractual terms infringing article 102 TFEU are also unlikely to be enforceable. The validity of the remainder of the agreement will depend on its terms and on the national law applicable to the contract. Even if the rest of the contract remains enforceable, the voidness of the anticompetitive clause may have a severe impact on the commercial balance of the agreement.

(ii) Criminal liability

12.118 EU law does not allow the Commission to impose criminal liability, either for companies or for individuals. However, some member states' laws provide for criminal sanctions for some types of anticompetitive conduct.[110]

G. Leniency and immunity

12.119 Leniency and immunity are available from the European Commission only in the case of "secret cartels...between two or more competitors aimed at coordinating their competitive behaviour...and/or influencing the relevant parameters of competition."[111] Examples are given, including fixing of prices or other conditions, application of production or sales quotas, market-sharing, and bid-rigging. This means that leniency and immunity are not available in the case of non-cartel agreements between competitors, such as joint production or research and development agreements, or for agreements between non-competitors, such as distribution or licensing agreements. Nor do they apply in the case of abuse of dominance. Difficult questions can arise as to the availability of leniency or immunity, for example, in the case of certain information exchange cases. Note that member states may provide for leniency and immunity in a wider or narrower range of cases than does the European Commission.[112] Although a certain degree of streamlining has been achieved through agreement by all NCAs on a Model Leniency Programme, this still falls some way short of providing a "one-stop shop." This means that parallel leniency applications need to be made to the Commission and to all NCAs in jurisdictions which might deal with the cartel in question.

12.120 The full terms of the leniency and immunity program are set out in the Leniency Notice. Total immunity, meaning no fine at all, is available to the first company which provides information

[107] Regulation 1/2003 (n 93) arts. 9, 23, and 24.
[108] See para. 12.4.
[109] Regulation 1/2003 (n 93) arts. 8 and 23.
[110] See relevant country Chapters in this volume.
[111] Commission Notice on Immunity from fines and reduction of fines in cartel cases, OJ C 298 (December 8, 2006), para.1 ("Leniency Notice").
[112] See relevant country Chapters in this volume.

to the Commission that allows it either to carry out an inspection, or to make an infringement finding with respect to the cartel. The immunity applicant will have to make a detailed corporate statement containing all relevant evidence in its possession. There is also the possibility of putting down a "marker" with the Commission, and providing the necessary information later, but the Commission will allow only a short period for the marker to be perfected. The statement is normally made orally at the Commission's offices, to reduce the risk of its becoming available to damages claimants. From that time the company must cease participation in the cartel, unless the Commission gives permission for it to continue, and must cooperate "genuinely, fully, on a continuous basis and expeditiously"[113] with the Commission. This last obligation is likely to last over a period of years and can be very burdensome.

Other companies which subsequently supply the Commission with evidence of "significant value" to the investigation can obtain reductions in the fines which they would otherwise have paid. Like an immunity applicant, they will also have to provide a corporate statement and cooperate continuously. The second applicant (that is, the first in after immunity has been secured) is eligible for a fine reduction of 30–50 percent, the third to 20–30 percent, and any later applicants to up to 20 percent. **12.121**

There are currently many unresolved questions concerning the extent to which leniency materials may be disclosed to damages claimants. A recent judgment holds that that when disclosure of leniency materials—whether the leniency statement itself or related material—is sought, national courts have to balance the need to protect the effectiveness of the program against the right of individuals to claim damages for losses caused by a competition law infringement.[114] This requirement to take a "case-by-case" approach is already leading to diverging approaches across the member states' courts. This may soon be resolved by legislation. **12.122**

H. Document creation and retention

EU antitrust law does not include any explicit rules on document creation and retention. However, companies under investigation by the Commission are under a duty to actively cooperate in the Commission's investigative measures.[115] Any negligent or intentional destruction of potentially relevant documents will be treated as a serious failure to cooperate, and may result in significant fines: a fine of up to 1 percent of the firm's total turnover can be imposed for the supply of incomplete information following a request made by decision, or during an inspection. Periodic penalty payments of up to 5 percent of average daily turnover can also be imposed to compel provision of complete information which has previously been requested by decision.[116] **12.123**

In addition, destruction or concealment of documents when an investigation is ongoing may lead to an increased fine for the antitrust law infringement. In *Industrial Bags*[117] the Commission increased the fine imposed on Bischof & Klein GmbH by 10 percent because an employee of the company deliberately destroyed a document during an investigation. This may be the case even for destruction or concealment taking place prior to the opening of any investigation, if this is done in circumstances which suggest a deliberate attempt to hide evidence. **12.124**

---

[113] Leniency Notice (n 111) para. 12(a).
[114] Case C-360/09 *Pfleiderer* [2011] ECR I-05161.
[115] Case 374/87 *Orkem SA v. Commission* [1989] ECR 3283.
[116] Regulation 1/2003 (n 93) arts. 23 and 24.
[117] *Industrial Bags*, Commission Decision C(2005) 4634 final relating to a proceeding pursuant to Article 81 of the EC Treaty OJ 2007 L 282, p. 41 (November 30, 2005).

13

FINLAND

Sari Hiltunen and Anna Kuusniemi-Laine
Castrén & Snellman Attorneys Ltd.

Introduction

13.01 The main source of competition law in Finland is the Competition Act (948/2011). The Competition Act is compatible with the EU competition rules and forms the basis of the Finnish Competition policy. The authority responsible for the enforcement of competition law is the Finnish Competition and Consumer Authority (FCCA).[1] The decisions taken by the FCCA may be appealed to the Market Court and the Supreme Administrative Court.

13.02 The provisions of the Competition Act correspond to articles 101 and 102 TFEU. However, in 2013 the Finnish Parliament amended the Competition Act and added a new provision, according to which grocery chains with a national market share exceeding 30 per cent are

[1] The FCCA was created on January 1, 2013 by combining the Finnish Competition Authority (FCA) and the Finnish Consumer Authority. When referring to cases before 2013, the abbreviation FCA is used.

considered to hold a dominant position. This amendment entered into force at the beginning of 2014.

During recent years, the FCCA has publicly announced that it will direct its resources against the most harmful hard core competition restrictions. However, within the last couple of years it has only taken a few cases to the Market Court. The most significant recent enforcement cases concern cartels and resale price maintenance. **13.03**

I. Acting alone

In Finland, as at EU level, only dominant undertakings are subject to the competition rules that concern unilateral conduct. Having a dominant market position is not illegal as such, but dominant undertakings have a specific obligation to ensure that competition is not unfairly distorted due to their actions. Hence, the abuse of a dominant market position constitutes an infringement of competition rules. **13.04**

The substantive rules concerning the abuse of a dominant position are contained in s. 7 of the Competition Act, which states: **13.05**

> Any abuse by one or more undertakings or association of undertakings of a dominant position shall be prohibited. Abuse may, in particular, consist in:
>
> - directly or indirectly imposing unfair purchase or selling prices or other unfair trading conditions;
> - limiting production, markets or technical development to the prejudice of consumers;
> - applying dissimilar conditions to equivalent transactions with trading partners, thereby placing them at a competitive disadvantage; and
> - making the conclusion of a contract subject to acceptance by the other contract party of supplementary obligations which, by their nature or according to commercial usage, have no connection with the subject of such a contract.

The wording of s. 7 of the Competition Act is generally in line with that of article 102 TFEU. According to the government bill that resulted in the adoption of the Competition Act, the section shall also be interpreted in accordance with the EU rules. **13.06**

The Competition Act includes a specific definition of dominance. A party is dominant when its position in the national or a regional market for a given product is such that it is able to significantly control the price level or terms of delivery for that product, or otherwise influence the competitive conditions on that market. Whilst a large market share or the holding of an exclusive right are both key indications of a dominant position, the FCCA also looks at several other factors, such as market structure, market power of competitors and customers, entry barriers, etc., when assessing whether a company has a dominant position. However, the interpretation of dominance in Finland is generally the same as under EU competition rules. **13.07**

There is quite a lot of case law concerning abuse by dominant companies in Finland. However, the interpretation of abuse of dominance has been somewhat formal, and it is expected that the FCCA will concentrate more on the market effects in its future assessments. Based on the recent enforcement of the FCCA, the greatest concern of the authority has focused on rebates, refusal to deal, discriminatory pricing and predation. **13.08**

A. Predatory pricing

Predatory pricing refers to the practice of a dominant undertaking selling its products below production costs and so sacrificing its profits in order to foreclose a competitor from the market. Predatory pricing constitutes an infringement of s. 7 of Competition Act. **13.09**

13.10 The FCCA seems to follow the principle noted in the Court of Justice of the European Union's (CJEU) *AKZO* decision,[2] i.e. that pricing below average variable total costs can be considered indicative of abuse of dominant position unless objectively acceptable grounds can be shown for it, and that pricing above average variable costs but below average total costs shall only be deemed abusive if the intent to exclude an as efficient competitor from the market can be shown.

13.11 The case law and guidelines of the European Commission and the CJEU are followed in Finland when establishing whether a dominant company has engaged in predatory pricing. In 2012, the FCCA made a proposition to the Market Court to impose a fine of EUR 70 million on Valio, a Finnish dairy company. According to the FCCA, Valio had engaged in predatory pricing in the pricing of its fresh milk in the wholesale market. The main disagreement between the FCCA and the company concerned the calculation of costs. The matter is currently pending before the Market Court.[3] Thus far, the proposed fine is the highest in Finland imposed on a single company for a breach of competition law.

B. Exploitative offenses

13.12 Excessive pricing constitutes a competition law infringement if engaged in by a dominant undertaking. Typically this includes the charging of unreasonably high prices, but could also include charging of discriminatory prices or otherwise setting discriminatory terms to customers.

13.13 In order for a pricing system to be exploitatively high and so prohibited, it must be manifestly unfair.[4] In practice, pricing may be assessed with reference to pricing in similar markets or for similar products, as well as the undertaking's profitability and production costs. The pricing must be compared with the production costs of the company under scrutiny, allowing for a reasonable profit margin typically achieved within the industry in question.

13.14 Finnish case law also includes cases in which the raising of prices significantly in a sudden and exploitative way has been deemed an abuse of a dominant market position. For instance, the Supreme Administrative Court (SAC) found in the *Helsinki Harbour* case,[5] that raising the harbor passenger charges suddenly by 400 percent amounted to an abuse. In a case concerning the Finnish Composers' Copyright Society, the Competition Council stated that the copyright compensations collected by the association were unreasonable, because after a price increase they were unreasonably high especially when compared to the turnover of the customers and the value provided by the Society to the customers.[6] During the recent years, the FCCA has not conducted any investigations of this kind; therefore it is difficult to assess whether and how an effects-based approach would affect the enforcement.

C. Monopsony

13.15 Abusing a dominant position with respect to suppliers constitutes a competition law infringement in Finland, just as abusing a dominant position does with respect to customers. However, there is no case law concerning the abuse of a buyer's dominant position.

---

[2] Case 62/86 *AKZO Chemie v. Commission* [1991] ECR I-3359.

[3] *FFCA v. Valio Oy*, MC Case nos. 458/12/KR and 36/13/KR.

[4] *Elisa*, Competition Council Decision no. 150/690/1999, and *Helsingin Energia*, Competition Council Decision no. 151/690/1999.

[5] *Helsinki Harbour*, SAC Case no. 1993-A-57.

[6] *Visual Data Oy*, Competition Council Decision no. 96/690/2000.

However, as of the beginning of 2014 there is a new provision in the Competition Act stating that grocery chains with a national market share exceeding 30 per cent in the retail sales of daily goods are considered to hold a dominant position both in the sales and purchasing markets of such goods. **13.16**

D. Price discrimination

Dominant undertakings are required to treat their customers equally with respect to pricing (and other trading conditions). The prices do not, however, need to be identical. A dominant undertaking may differentiate prices when there are differences in costs or other acceptable reasons. The discount system of a dominant undertaking must be transparent and clear, and the pricing must not artificially distort competition between customers. Price discrimination is nowadays interpreted in Finland in line with EU jurisprudence. **13.17**

In a case concerning ATM operators, the FCCA considered that the three main Finnish banks had a joint dominance in the cash distribution market and that their pricing was discriminatory, because the difference of prices of on-us and off-us withdrawals was higher than their cost difference.[7] On-us withdrawal refers to a cash withdrawal made using the ATM's owned by the joint venture of the banks having joint dominance and off-us withdrawal to a cash withdrawal made using competing operators' ATM's. **13.18**

Discount systems that are based on cost savings are usually acceptable. Discounts must generally be given indiscriminately to all similar clients who, for example, reach a specific level of purchases. Discounts may, however, also be based on objective client-specific cost savings if this is justifiable in the particular situation.[8] However, despite the general requirement to treat its customers in a non-discriminatory manner, a dominant undertaking is allowed to protect its commercial interests by lowering prices for specific customers when responding to competition. This is the so-called "meeting competition defense." In the recent *Valio* case, the FCCA has not accepted this argument but has considered that targeted rebates offered by Valio were used as a tool of predation.[9] **13.19**

A specific form of price discrimination is margin squeeze. Margin squeeze refers to a practice whereby a vertically integrated dominant undertaking weakens the position of its competitors in the downstream market by charging them excessive prices on the upstream markets. Margin squeeze constitutes an infringement of s. 7 of the Competition Act if the difference between the price that the undertaking charges its downstream competitors on the wholesale upstream market and the retail price that the undertaking charges its own downstream market customers is such that an equally efficient downstream competitor could not compete with it on a long-term basis. **13.20**

Margin squeeze may arise in all sectors of the economy, but certain infrastructure sectors, like the telecommunication sector, where bottlenecks exist are typical examples. In the *Elisa* case, a major telecommunications company was found to have abused its dominant position by charging its downstream competitors substantially higher prices than what the company charged its own service operator, a practice that had rendered entry into the downstream market economically unviable for competitors.[10] In order to establish the existence of margin squeeze, a price comparison needs to be made between similar products. In a recent case, the Supreme Administrative Court dismissed a claim of margin squeeze when the undertaking under scrutiny had offered its downstream customers a product based on an Internet **13.21**

[7] *Automatia Pankkiautomaatit Oy*, FCA Decision no. 964/61/2007.
[8] *Neste Oy/SEO*, SAC Decision no. 1995-A-49.
[9] *Valio* (n 3).
[10] *Elisa* (n 4).

Protocol (IP)-wholesale product while offering its competitors asynchronous transfer mode (ATM)-based products. The court found that since the two products were different as to their pricing, technology, and maturity, it was not possible to assess whether margin squeeze had taken place. The company also refused to deal the other product based on the other technology to its competitors.[11]

E. Dictating or influencing resale prices

(i) Resale price maintenance

13.22 Resale price maintenance (RPM) refers to a practice whereby the resale price of a product is controlled by an upstream producer or seller of the product. In addition to outright stipulations of the resale price, RPM may take the form of fixing the distribution margin as well as many indirect ways of influencing the resale price by, for example making the reimbursement of marketing costs subject to the maintenance of certain price level.

13.23 Resale Price Maintenance falls within the scope of s. 5 of the Competition Act concerning restrictive agreements between undertakings and constitutes a competition law infringement. This concerns especially fixed or minimum price maintenance, which usually does not benefit from the efficiency exemption provided by s. 6 of the Competition Act. However, the maintenance of maximum resale prices is normally accepted, provided that it does not in practice lead to a fixed or minimum resale price maintenance scheme.

13.24 RPM is seen as a one of the hardcore competition law infringements, and it carries significant consequences for those engaging in prohibited RPM. In recent case-law, the Market Court (MC) imposed a EUR 3 million fine on Iittala Group Oyj for RPM practices that were systematically applied to the company's most significant household products (including, e.g. the Moomin products, the Aalto glassware, and the Teema series) and a number of distributors and that lasted for two and half years. The fine amounted to approximately 3 percent of the relevant Finnish turnover of Iittala Group Oyj.[12] However, the distributors can also be fined and this was also considered by the FCA in the *Iittala* case. This demonstrates that while RPM is dealt with under the s. 5, it is usually the result of pressure by a dominant upstream undertaking, and is treated as such. Other RPM cases concern *Kesko* (setting of maximum prices)[13] and *Topfield* (offering marketing compensation on the condition that recommended price was used).[14]

(ii) Minimum advertised price programs

13.25 It is not necessary for the arrangement to be a direct RPM in order to it fall under the scope of the prohibition. Hence, indirect mechanisms that have similar effects as direct RPM, such as minimum advertised price programs (MAPs), are forbidden as well.

F. Tying arrangements

13.26 Tying falls under the scope of s. 7 of the Competition Act and may constitute an infringement if entered into by a dominant undertaking. In the *Digital Equipment Corporation* case,[15] the company sold software updates at a lower price to customers who also bought maintenance services from Digital. Digital had a monopoly on its updates, and the position of its competitors in the maintenance market was significantly weakened by Digital's conduct.

13.27 A similar arrangement is "bundling."[16]

---

[11] *Lännen Puhelin*, SAC Decision no. 2011:40.
[12] *Iittala*, MC Case no. 594/11.
[13] *Kesko*, MC Case no. 648/09.
[14] *Topfield*, FCA Decision no. 1114/61/2006.
[15] *Digital Equipment Corporation*, Competition Council Decision no. 4/359/92.
[16] See Section I.J.

G. Exclusive dealing

Exclusive dealing arrangements are likely to infringe s. 7 of the Competition Act if a dominant undertaking requires its customers or suppliers to deal exclusively with it, and the practice leads to exclusionary effects on the market. In addition to outright requests for exclusive dealing, indirect methods, such as abusive rebate systems, can also have similar effects.[17] **13.28**

There are no cases concerning exclusive dealing. It can be estimated that there haven't been many agreements including these kinds of terms or that such clauses have been in line with EU law and have not had harmful effects from the competition law perspective. **13.29**

H. Refusal to deal

Section 7 of the Competition Act includes a prohibition on limiting production or markets to the prejudice of customers. A dominant undertaking may be deemed to infringe competition law if it terminates deliveries to a customer or terminates the business relationship without an objective justification. The prohibition on refusals to deal generally only applies to dominant undertakings. However, a similar type of an infringement could be constituted by a collective boycott between competitors. **13.30**

The obligation to deal goes counter to the prevailing freedom of contract, and applying s. 7 of the Competition Act to refusals to deal calls for striking a balance between the dominant company's freedom of contract and the need to protect the functioning of the markets. The factors that are taken into account in this balancing act include the dependency of the customers on the dominant undertaking and the availability of alternative sources of supply or alternative products fit for the same purpose. A dominant undertaking may refuse to deal if there is an objective justification for the refusal. An objective justification can be, for instance, capacity constraints or the inability of a particular customer to meet their obligations (e.g. to pay for the product). In addition to outright refusals to deal, similar effects may be achieved indirectly by offering terms so onerous that make it commercially impossible for the customers to continue dealing with or to enter into a delivery contract with the dominant undertaking. Hence, refusal to deal is often closely linked to charging excessive prices or margin squeezing,[18] and in practice, these infringements overlap considerably. **13.31**

Refusals to deal typically take place in situations where the dominant company is active both in the upstream and downstream markets and where the dominant undertaking may attempt to foreclose its competitors from the downstream market. In assessing refusals to deal, it is necessary to assess whether the refusal may in fact remove all competition from the market.[19] For instance, Suomen Numeropalvelu Oy was found to have abused its dominant position when it refused to sell telephone subscriber information to Eniro Finland Oy, which offered subscriber information services on the Internet free of charge and without requiring user registration. Suomen Numeropalvelu Oy was the only maintainer of the national database of such subscriber information. Suomen Numeropalvelu Oy defended its refusal by stating that Eniro's conduct violated Finnish data protection legislation. However, the FCCA and the Market Court considered that the data protection was the responsibility of relevant authorities and that Suomen Numeropalvelu Oy could not justify its refusal with such arguments.[20] **13.32**

In assessing refusals to deal, the FCCA assesses whether the refusal could remove all competition from the market. In a recent case concerning access to broadband infrastructure, **13.33**

[17] See Section I.J.

[18] See Section I.D.

[19] *Lännen Puhelin* (n 11).

[20] *Suomen Numeropalvelu*, MC Case nos. 178–179/09.

a dominant undertaking had refused to supply its competitors in the downstream market with a wholesale ADSL broadband product that was necessary for providing certain end-user broadband services. However, as two competitors had managed to construct their own network infrastructure covering 30 and 50 percent, respectively, of the dominant undertaking's network coverage, the dominant undertaking was found not to have infringed competition law when it had refused to supply the wholesale ADSL product.[21]

13.34 Based on the recent enforcement of the FCCA and the courts, it can be said that this area of competition law is one of the key priorities of the authorities.

I. Essential facilities

13.35 The competition law issues that arise in relation to essential facilities are refusal to deal[22] or discrimination in access.[23] Finnish authorities follow the EU doctrine concerning essential facilities.[24]

J. Bundling (including loyalty and market share discounts)

13.36 Bundling is assessed in essentially the same way as tying. It falls under the scope of s. 7 of the Competition Act, and it may constitute an infringement if entered into by a dominant undertaking.

13.37 In one case, a news agency was found to have abused its dominant position when it sold news stories only as part of a wider package containing news on all areas—a practice which forced customers to purchase far more than just the news they wanted or needed.[25]

13.38 As for rebates, a discount arrangement may be prohibited if it brings about similar effects as tying. Fidelity rebates that reward a customer for purchasing a certain percentage of all its purchases may be considered abusive if the required percentage is particularly high. In addition, rebates that tie the discounts offered on one product to the purchase of another product are highly likely to be deemed abusive and forbidden.[26]

K. Standard-setting groups (disclosure requirements, licensing arrangements, and licensing pools)

13.39 There is currently no case law in Finland that concerns standardization and other or the activities of standard setting groups and organizations.

L. Customer termination

13.40 Customer termination is a specific form of a refusal to deal.[27] Termination of supplies by a dominant undertaking to a customer can be found to constitute an abuse and be caught by s. 7 of the Competition Act unless there is an objective justification for the termination.

13.41 Customer termination is only in itself an infringement if the supplier is a dominant undertaking. However, refusal to deal may be used to enforce other competition law infringements as well, for instance, to ensure an RPM scheme is followed by distributors. In such cases, refusal to deal may be a part of conduct that is prohibited even when engaged in by a non-dominant undertaking.

---

[21] *Lännen Puhelin* (n 11).
[22] See Section I.H.
[23] See Section I.D for price discrimination.
[24] See e.g. *Lännen Puhelin* (n 11).
[25] *STT*, FCA Decision no. 129/01/2000.
[26] *Valio III*, SAC Decision no. 1998:65.
[27] See Section I.H.

M. Termination of intermediaries (retailers, wholesalers, dealers, and value-added resellers, agents, and brokers)

Termination of intermediaries is a specific form of a refusal to deal[28] and is prohibited if it is conducted by a dominant undertaking without an objective justification. **13.42**

Termination of intermediaries falls under the scope of s. 7 of the Competition Act. However, refusal to deal may also be used to implement other competition law infringements, for instance in order to punish a distributor who is not following recommended prices. **13.43**

N. Termination of relationships with competitors

Termination of relationships with competitors is a specific form of a refusal to deal.[29] It can constitute an abuse of a dominant position if the competitor is also a customer, or if it is a coordinated action of several companies, the practice may be a collective boycott and so an infringement under s. 5. The Supreme Administrative Court has recently given a decision concerning a collective boycott that was punishable under s. 5. The case concerned the market for automobile spare parts. According to the SCA, five spare parts wholesaler had by mutual agreement decided to boycott a major Finnish spare parts retailer. The boycott was organized by cutting the discounts granted to the company and the aim was to force it to abandon the alliance with the cartel participants' competitor.[30] **13.44**

O. Exemptions

Section 6 of the Competition Act including the exemption is only applicable to conduct falling under the scope of s. 5 (anti-cartel) of the Act, and not to behavior that falls under the scope of s. 7 (abuse of dominant position) of the Competition Act. The arrangement is similar to that of article 102 TFEU as compared to article 101(1) TFEU. However, as the Finnish competition rules are interpreted in a manner similar to EU rules, and the FCCA also applies the guidelines and notices given by the EU authorities, the FCCA will take into account the efficiency defense doctrine regarding the abuse of dominance formulated by the Commission and EU courts. **13.45**

II. Dealing with competitors

The proper functioning of a market economy relies on the effective competition between competitors. In order to ensure that competitors compete in the markets, competition law applies to any anticompetitive cooperation and agreements between competitors,—i.e. to "cartels." **13.46**

The substantive rules concerning prohibited cooperation and agreements are contained in s. 5 of the Competition Act, which states: **13.47**

(1) All agreements between undertakings, decisions by associations of undertakings, and concerted practices by undertakings which have as their object the significant prevention, restriction or distortion of competition or which result in a significant prevention, restriction or distortion of competition shall be prohibited.

(2) In particular, agreements, decisions, or practices which:
   1. directly or indirectly fix purchase or selling prices or any other trading conditions;
   2. limit or control production, markets, technical development, or investment;
   3. share markets or sources of supply;

[28] See Section I.H.

[29] See Section I.H.

[30] *Osaset*, SCA Case nos. 797, 939, 942, 947, 952, and 953/2/09, May 31, 2012.

4. apply dissimilar conditions to equivalent transactions with other trading parties, thereby placing them at a competitive disadvantage; or
5. make the conclusion of a contract subject to acceptance by the other party of supplementary obligations which, by their nature or according to commercial usage, have no connection with the subject of such a contract

shall be prohibited.

13.48 The wording of s. 5 of the Competition Act is in line with that of article 101(1) TFEU. According to the government bill that resulted in the adoption of the Competition Act, the section shall also be interpreted in accordance with the EU rules.

13.49 According to s. 5 of the Competition Act, it is required that the conduct "significantly" affects competition for the prohibition to apply. Hence, anticompetitive conduct must have an appreciable effect on competition for it to be prohibited. The FCCA follows the principles set out in Commission's *de minimis* notice[31] in its assessment of the appreciable effect.

13.50 Further, s. 6 of the Competition Act provides for a set of exemptions from the application of s. 5 (anti-cartel) of the Act. Hence, even if conduct would be caught by s. 5, it is not prohibited if it fulfills the criteria of s. 6. The relationship between ss. 5 and 6 is similar to that between articles 101(1) TFEU and 101(3) TFEU. The substantive stipulations of s. 6 are also similar to article 101(3) TFEU, and an exemption is provided if the conduct brings about economic efficiencies and allows the consumers to enjoy a reasonable share of the benefits so created.

13.51 Finnish authorities will consider the Block Exemptions adopted by the European Commission. However, as the national authorities are not directly bound to the EU rules when assessing purely national competition matters, they may depart from the exemptions on a case-by-case basis if competition would otherwise be restricted in practice in a specific case. The Competition Act also empowers the FCCA to formally withdraw the benefit of a block exemption in cases to which the EU competition rules are directly applicable, a power also foreseen in article 29(2) of Regulation 1/2003.

13.52 While EU competition rules only prohibit conduct that may affect trade between member states, there is no similar requirement in Finnish law. It is adequate that competition is distorted in Finland or any part of Finland. In practice, the competition authorities have also shown interest in investigating purely regional or local competition law infringements, and there is case law where such territorially limited infringements have resulted in competition law sanctions.[32]

13.53 The FCCA has publicly stated that hard core cartels form a basis of its key enforcement priorities. The FCCA may commence investigations on its own initiative or based on leniency applications or market contacts.

A. Horizontal price fixing

13.54 Price fixing is a hard core infringement of the Competition Act, and the FCCA takes a strict approach in enforcement against all types of price-fixing cartels. Price-fixing has also attracted the highest fines ever imposed in Finland, as detailed below.

---

[31] Commission Notice on agreements of minor importance which do not appreciably restrict competition under Article 81(1) of the Treaty establishing the European Community (*de minimis*), OJ 2001/C 368/07.

[32] E.g. *Lännen Puhelin* (n 11).

In 2009, final court rulings were given in two major price-fixing cartel cases: the "asphalt cartel" and the "raw wood cartel." Both of these cases faced fines vastly exceeding in magnitude any prior sanctions in the history of Finnish competition law enforcement. Both of these cases are also currently subject to a set of follow-on litigation by third parties that are seeking significant damages. 13.55

(i) Asphalt cartel

The asphalt cartel is the most significant of all Finnish cartel cases to date. The case dates back to 2002 when the FCA carried out dawn raids in major Finnish asphalt companies. On the basis of its investigations, the FCA concluded that seven asphalt companies and the Finnish Asphalt Association had been involved in long-lasting cooperation in pricing, bidding, and market sharing. According to the FCA, the cooperation had existed both on the national market as well as on a number of local markets. On the nation-wide market, the cooperation concerned state projects during the years 1996–2000, and on the local markets the cartel had been in effect in 1994–2001 with respect to local government and private customers. The aggregate market share of the parties to the cartel had reached approximately 70 percent of the total Finnish asphalt market. On the basis of its findings, the FCA proposed that the Market Court in 2004 impose fines totaling EUR 97 million. 13.56

The Market Court issued its decision in 2007 and imposed fines totaling EUR 19.4 million. This was much lower than what the FCA had proposed.[33] The Market Court decision was appealed to the Supreme Administrative Court by the FCA and by six of the asphalt companies. 13.57

The Supreme Administrative Court issued its decision on September 29, 2009, dismissing the appeals of the asphalt companies and approving many of the FCA's proposals.[34] The Supreme Administrative Court found that the cartel had involved bid-rigging and market sharing and that it had been nation-wide and long-lasting. The court also found that the directors of the companies had known about the cartel. As a result, the Supreme Administrative Court imposed significant fines amounting to almost EUR 82 million in total. The biggest individual fine, EUR 68 million, was imposed on Lemminkäinen Oyj found to have led the cartel. The fine amounted to approximately 4 percent of the company's turnover. For some participants of the cartel, the imposed fine amounted to 10 percent of their turnover. 13.58

Hence, the asphalt cartel case attracted both the highest single fine as well as the highest total amount of fines ever imposed in the history of Finnish competition law enforcement. Given that the highest single fine imposed prior to the asphalt cartel case had been only EUR 4 million, the case also signaled a significant change in attitudes towards detrimental competition restrictions. Moreover, the Supreme Administrative Court confirmed that a fine may be imposed in accordance with economic succession, i.e. a fine may also be imposed on an undertaking that has acquired an undertaking or business activity that had taken part in the cartel even if the acquiring undertaking was not aware of this fact. 13.59

Further, the asphalt cartel case shed light on a number of issues relating to competition law enforcement and the appraisal of competition law cases in the courts of law. In its decision, the Supreme Administrative Court emphasized the importance of "free consideration of evidence" by which the court is entitled review all evidence submitted to it, regardless of the form of the evidence and the way in which the evidence has been gathered, and to determine the grounds on which the resolution can best be based. In practice, the Supreme 13.60

[33] *Asfalttikartelli*, MC Case no. 441/07

[34] *Asfalttikartelli*, SAC Decision no. 2009:83.

Administrative Court accepted evidence that the Market Court had rejected as inadmissible (e.g. matters heard from third parties). The Supreme Administrative Court further noted that evidence shall be assessed as a whole; that, in cartel cases, extensive evidence is not always available to cover all aspects of the illegal activity; and that the burden of proof is lower in competition law cases than in criminal law cases. The Court also referred extensively to the case-law of the CJEU and European Court of Human Rights (ECtHR).

(ii) Exchange of raw wood purchasing prices

13.61 The raw wood case involved three major Finnish forest industry companies active in the procurement of raw wood. The companies were found to have exchanged information on their costs and purchasing prices as well as information on market conditions. The companies had not agreed on pricing, but they had discussed how to influence the price of raw wood. The infringement lasted from 1997 to 2004 and was nationwide.

13.62 The Market Court gave its decision on December 3, 2009 and imposed a fine of EUR 30 million on Stora Enso and EUR 21 million on Metsäliitto Cooperative (MC:614/09). Metsäliitto's fine was reduced by 30 percent, as the company had assisted the FCA in its investigations. The third company involved in the infringement, UPM-Kymmene, avoided fines altogether, as it had exposed the infringement to the FCA and had sought immunity. When determining the level of the fines, the Market Court took into account the fact that the cartel had been operational for a long period of time and that the companies involved were significant players with extensive knowledge of competition law. The Court further took into account the fact that the very same companies had already been fined for illegal cooperation in the procurement of timber.

B. Horizontal agreements to allocate customers or territories; agreements not to compete

13.63 Agreements on the allocation or division of markets are covered by s. 5 of the Competition Act and are prohibited regardless of whether geographical markets, product markets, or customers are allocated. There have been a few cases that involved market allocation, the most important of these being the asphalt cartel case.[35]

C. Horizontal boycotts

13.64 It is not necessary for horizontal boycotts to involve an outright refusal of supply or purchases. In the *Automobile spare parts case*, the boycott was arranged by cutting the discounts a group of spare parts wholesalers offered to a retailer with the aim of forcing the retailer to abandon a strategic alliance that it had entered into with a competitor of the parties to the boycott.[36] In this way, the groups' competitor was being foreclosed from a downstream market.

D. Joint ventures and other competitive collaborations

13.65 Joint ventures are subject to an obligatory merger control notification if they are "full function" in nature and if the statutory turnover thresholds are met.

13.66 Non-full function joint ventures are not subject to merger control, but they may be caught by s. 5 of the Competition Act, for example in situations where the owner companies use joint ventures as a vehicle for illegal cooperation.

[35] See Section II.A(i).

[36] *Automobile spare parts*, MC Case no. 91/09, and *Automobile spare parts*, SAC Decision no. 1429, May 31, 2012.

E. Trade associations

Trade associations have traditionally played an important role in the Finnish economy, and there is a long history of cooperation between competitors within the trade associations. The EU rules applicable to the exchange of confidential information between competitors are applied in Finland. Exchange of information within trade associations has also been a target of FCA investigations. **13.67**

In the "hairdresser case," the FCA found that the Finnish hairdressers association had given recommendations for price increases in 2000–2006. The FCA proposed to the Market Court that it impose a competition infringement fine on the association. The FCA considered that the recommendations of the association were given in order to influence competition in the hairdresser sector by raising the price level and harmonizing the level and timing of price increases. The Market Court imposed a fine of EUR 33,000 on the association, which corresponded to approximately 10 percent of the relevant turnover of the association. At the time of the decision, less than 20 percent of the Finnish hairdressers were members of the association.[37] **13.68**

In a recent case, the Supreme Administrative Court imposed a fine also for the member companies of the association. In 2006, the FCA proposed to the Market Court the imposition of a cartel fine to a trade association and to 17 companies that had participated in the association's board of directors during the infringement. The infringement consisted in fixing prices for services offered to companies for warranty repair services. The infringement essentially took place at the meetings of the trade association. In 2009, the Market Court imposed a EUR 5,000 fine on the trade association, but considered that the companies active in the trade association's board of directors could not be considered to be liable for the infringement as there was no proof that they had engaged in price fixing outside the association's meetings. **13.69**

In its judgment, the Supreme Administrative Court analyzed in detail the board meetings in which the representatives of the seventeen member companies were present and, where the companies had participated in price fixing, the court also found them liable for the infringement (excluding time barred instances). The court, however, reduced fines proposed on the companies as the administrative proceedings in the case had dragged on excessively long.[38] **13.70**

The Competition Act is not applicable to arrangements or agreements concerning the labor market. Hence, activities of employees' trade unions as well as agreements such as collective bargaining agreements are generally outside the scope of competition law. **13.71**

F. Interlocking directorates

The Competition Act does not include a provision that would directly prohibit interlocking directorates, and they have not been subject to competition law enforcement as such. However, interlocking directorates may facilitate cooperation between competitors and they may lead to competition issues, for example exchange of information. In addition, the creation of new interlocking directorates may be seen as acquisition of control for the purposes of merger control and may result in an obligation to notify the arrangement as a concentration. **13.72**

Finnish authorities are likely to treat interlocking directorates in line with EU jurisprudence. **13.73**

[37] *Suomen Hiusyrittäjät*, MC Case no. 289/07.

[38] *Suomen Kodinkonehuoltojen Liitto*, SAC Case no. 2013:8, register no. 278/2/10.

G. Facilitating practices

13.74 Facilitating practices refer to behavior that does not, per se, constitute a cartel, but helps competitors coordinate their actions by eliminating uncertainty about the competitors' plans or future strategy. Facilitating practices often take the form of information exchange.

13.75 The FCA issued a bulletin in 2010 where it drew attention to price signaling practices in the Finnish markets. Price signaling refers to practices whereby competitors make public announcements concerning their future pricing policies or production. If signaling is carried out by a number of companies, and if the information made public is detailed enough, the practice may facilitate silent coordination of pricing among competitors. As an example, price signaling may take the form of companies claiming publicly that prices of raw materials have increased and that there are "pressures" on them to increase prices of the end-products as well (e.g. oil companies could claim that increases in crude oil prices puts "pressure" on them to increase petrol and diesel prices as well).

13.76 There is no relevant case law concerning facilitating practices in Finland.

H. Information exchange

13.77 Information exchange between competitors constitutes an infringement of s. 5 of Competition Act if the information exchanged is sensitive. Such information may relate, for example, to pricing, customers, costs, market conditions, and strategy. The information is considered sensitive if an undertaking would normally consider similar information to constitute trade secrets. The prohibition to exchange sensitive information applies regardless of whether the information is exchanged directly between competitors or indirectly through intermediaries like trade associations.[39]

13.78 Information exchange is prohibited for two main reasons: it enables the participants to coordinate their market behavior and it may facilitate enforcement of a cartel. For example, it might reveal deviations from agreed-upon actions and enable retaliation by other cartel participants.

13.79 Information exchange has been the subject of a number of cases. The most important information exchange case in Finland is the *ScanTrack* case. The case concerned an information service called ScanTrack, which was maintained by AC Nielsen Finland Oy. Three major Finnish consumer goods retailers, Kesko, SOK, and Tradeka, with a combined market share reached approximately 85 percent of the retail market of daily goods, used the ScanTrack service to exchange detailed and current information on sales and prices. The companies had not entered into an agreement concerning the exchange of information, but they all had separate agreements on the provision of information with AC Nielsen. However, as the system relied on reciprocity and ScanTrack information was only available to companies that also supplied the system with their respective data, the FCCA considered that, taken as a whole, the arrangement constituted continuous information exchange between the undertakings involved and an infringement of competition law. However, since the companies had abandoned the information exchange system during the investigation, the FCCA did not take the matter to the Market Court and no fines were imposed.[40]

13.80 In another case, a trade association of record companies had collected sales information from its members on a monthly basis. On the basis of the information collected, the trade association had created statistics that showed not only the market shares of the member companies,

[39] See Section II.E.
[40] *ScanTrack*, FCA Decision no. 154/61/2007.

but also included detailed information on the sales of each of the companies. In practice, pricing information could be derived from the statistics. The FCA considered the conduct as an infringement of the competition law.[41]

The exchange of purely historic information is not likely to infringe competition law. Historic information generally does not enable competitors to coordinate their market behavior, nor does it facilitate the enforcement of a cartel. **13.81**

There are no exact limits on how old, anonymous, or aggregated pricing information needs to be for the exchange of information to be lawful. Instead, a case-by-case analysis is required, taking into account the specific characteristics of the market in question and, for example the frequency of actual price negotiations in the market concerned. However, annual exchange of company-specific information would normally be infrequent enough to be permitted. It should be noted that in certain circumstances the exchange of more current information (and thus more sensitive) can be accepted, but this depends on market factors.[42] **13.82**

Pro-competitive purposes and effects may constitute a justification for exemption under s. 6 of the Competition Act, and efficiency may be entered as a defense for information exchange. However, where the same efficiency benefits are attainable by less restrictive methods the efficiencies defense would not apply.[43] Moreover, exchange of information that results in, or significantly facilitates, a hard core anticompetitive behavior, such as price fixing, cannot benefit from the exemption. **13.83**

I. Joint purchasing agreements

Joint purchasing refers to a practice where two or more undertakings cooperate in their purchases. The cooperation affects two distinct markets: the relevant purchasing markets and the downstream selling markets on which the purchasers are active. Joint purchasing agreements are concluded between undertakings that are competitors at least in the purchasing market. The agreements generally only give rise to concern when made between companies that are also competitors on the downstream market. **13.84**

Joint purchasing agreements are generally appraised in Finland in the same way as they are under EU competition rules. Nonetheless, FCCA decisions on negative clearance and individual exemption decisions are still of guidance in the application of the Competition Act, even though the system of negative clearance and individual exemption decision was formally abandoned in 2004. The FCCA historically exempted arrangements that exhibited four characteristics: **13.85**

- efficiency gains were created by the arrangement;
- downstream selling markets were not significantly affected by the arrangement (because, e.g. the parties to the agreement were not active in the same downstream market or the market shares of the parties were small);
- the parties' aggregate market share in the purchasing market was insignificant; and
- the arrangement was non-exclusive.

J. Joint lobbying/regulatory/legislative efforts

Joint lobbying on regulatory and legislative issues is usually lawful and is often carried out by trade associations.[44] Nonetheless, care should be taken to ensure that no prohibited exchange **13.86**

[41] *ÄKT*, FCA Decision no. 740/61/2002.
[42] *ÄKT* (n 40).
[43] See e.g. *ScanTrack* (n 39).
[44] See Section II.E.

of information takes place in the course of the joint efforts and that the cooperation does not extend to anticompetitive cooperation in the markets.

III. General issues

A. Jurisdiction and applicable law (including sector-specific competition regulation)

13.87 The Competition Act forms the basis of national Finnish competition law. The Act came into force on November 1, 2011, and it replaced the previous Competition Restrictions Act. The Competition Act is applicable to agreements restraining competition, abuses by dominant undertakings, as well as to merger control. The Act applies to all sectors of the economy, with certain exemptions concerning the labor market and agriculture. The substantive provisions of the Competition Act are in line with the EU competition rules.

13.88 The Competition Act does not include an explicit stipulation on its territorial application. In case law, it has been established that the "effects doctrine" is generally followed. Finnish competition law is applicable even in situations where an agreement was entered into abroad, but has effects within the Finnish markets. Concerning restraints that may affect competition between the EU member states, the Competition Act includes an explicit stipulation that both EU and Finnish competition rules are applied simultaneously.

13.89 Although the Competition Act does not explicitly authorize the FCCA to issue guidelines on its remit, it has been accepted that it has such power. The FCCA has issued:

- Guidelines on merger control;
- Leniency Guidelines;
- Guidelines on the assessment of the amount of fine; and
- Guidelines on prioritization in the handling of competition restrictions.

13.90 The Competition Act also applies the European Commission's Guidelines to purely national competition restrictions.

13.91 The FCCA's guidelines are not legally binding. However, they serve to clarify the approach that the FCCA normally takes in its investigations and in its interpretation of the law.

13.92 In addition to general competition law, there are sector-specific regulations applicable to amongst others, the electricity, natural gas, TV and radio operations, telecommunications, transportation, postal and financial services markets. Sector-specific regulations stipulate licenses that may be required to operate in these sectors. In certain sectors, licenses are not freely transferable, and any subsequent transfer of a license may require the prior approval of the competent authority. Such approval does not generally relieve the parties of the need to also obtain merger control clearance in accordance with the Competition Act.

13.93 Case law does not have binding authority in Finland. However, the decisions of the Supreme Administrative Court and those of the European Union Courts are very influential on the FCA and lower courts' interpretation of Finnish competition rules.

B. Antitrust system

(i) Name of agency/agencies

13.94 **Finnish Competition and Consumer Authority** The Finnish Competition and Consumer Authority (FCCA) is responsible for enforcing competition law. However, supervision of the sector-specific legislation is generally the responsibility of other authorities. In order to carry out its tasks, the FCCA is vested with powers to conduct dawn raids and to issue interlocutory injunctions. The FCCA is not, however, empowered to impose fines for competition law infringement; instead, it may propose that the Market Court do so.

Regional State Administrative Agencies Regional State Administrative Agencies may independently investigate instances of competition law infringement, and they are empowered to conduct dawn raids with or without the FCCA. The Regional State Administrative Agencies are not empowered to propose sanctions or to issue injunctions, but they may refer a case to the FCCA for further actions. The role of the Regional State Administrative Agencies in the enforcement of competition law is limited in practice. For example, the officials of the Regional State Administrative Agencies may assist the FCCA in dawn raids, conducting market surveys and gathering information concerning regional markets. **13.95**

The Market Court The Market Court (MC) is a specialized court of law dealing with, among other things, cases concerning competition, public procurement, and special regulated sectors (electricity and natural gas markets). Furthermore, starting from September 1, 2013, cases concerning intellectual property rights (IPRs) fall under the jurisdiction of the Market Court. The Market Court is empowered to, upon the proposition of the FCCA, impose sanctions for competition law infringements and to review the legality of FCCA decisions. Decisions of the Market Court can be appealed to the Supreme Administrative Court. **13.96**

The Supreme Administrative Court The Supreme Administrative Court (SAC) adjudicates on appeals from the Market Court. Decisions of the Supreme Administrative Court are final. **13.97**

(ii) Staff size and budget

The total number of FCCA staff is about 150 people, fifty of whom work in competition enforcement. Roughly half of the officials are lawyers and half economist. Net annual expenditure of the FCA, the predecessor of the FCCA responsible for competition enforcement, in 2011 was circa EUR 5.5 million. **13.98**

(iii) Recent enforcement actions and trends

Recent years have seen a significant increase in the amount of fines imposed for hardcore anticompetitive cartels.[45] In its action plan for 2010–13, the FCCA has also announced that anti-cartel work will remain its priority. In addition, resources will be put into the investigation of arrangements employed by dominant undertakings in the protection of their market position, with a focus on infrastructure and service sectors which are vital to the economy. **13.99**

C. Private litigation

Private litigation is available, and a prior FCCA or Market Court procedure is not a prerequisite for private procedure. The Competition Act explicitly provides for the possibility of damage claims in the event that competition law is infringed and a party has suffered loss as a result. **13.100**

Private litigation in the field of competition law falls under the jurisdiction of the general courts as opposed to administrative courts. A case must be first brought to a district court. Judgments of the district courts are generally appealable to courts of appeal. A leave to appeal is required for an appeal to the Supreme Court. In case of private litigation, the general courts **13.101**

[45] See e.g. Section II.A for asphalt and raw wood cartel.

will adjudicate both on the question of infringement as well as on the amount of damages (if any).

D. Follow-on litigation

13.102 More common is follow-on litigation. These claims are still brought before courts of general jurisdiction.

13.103 There is no explicit statute on the role of FCCA or Market Court decisions in follow-on litigation. Hence, it appears that the general courts are not formally bound to prior findings of infringement by the FCCA or the Market Court. However, the courts have not, so far, revisited the question, and have instead accepted the final decisions of the Market Court or the Supreme Administrative Court as adequate proof of infringement.

13.104 The number of follow-on cases has risen significantly in the last couple of years. There are major competition damages cases pending before the District Court of Helsinki resulting from both the asphalt cartel and the raw wood case.[46] The asphalt cartel has spawned over fifty damages claims from municipalities and the State Road Administration, and the raw wood case over 700 damages claims from private forest owners, municipalities, private companies, and Metsähallitus (a state enterprise that administers state-owned land and water areas).

E. Arbitration and alternative dispute resolution

13.105 Competition law-related private claims are regularly dealt with in arbitration proceedings. Arbitration tribunals have in the past dealt with questions relating to the validity of restrictive contract terms and the consequences of the invalidity of a contract term. Where a restrictive term has caused damage to the other party, arbitration tribunals have also ruled on compensation for the damage. Arbitral tribunals have also decided on damages in situations where the buyer of a company that has infringed competition rules has claimed compensation from the seller due to fines imposed on the target company. In line with the growth in follow-on litigation cases, it may be foreseen that also the amount of arbitration and ADR in competition cases will rise in the future.

F. Remedies

(i) Civil liability

13.106 Administrative fines are imposed for infringements of the Competition Act unless the conduct is deemed to be minor or the imposition of the fine otherwise unjustified in respect to safeguarding competition. Pursuant to s. 12(2) of the Competition Act, the fine may also be imposed on an undertaking to which business activities involved in the infringement have been transferred. Under the previous Act on Competition Restraints, the Supreme Administrative Court confirmed that this principle of economic succession is applicable and that a fine may be imposed even if the acquiring undertaking had not been aware of the participation in the prohibited competition restraint.

13.107 Administrative fines are imposed by the Market Court upon a proposal by the FCCA. In practice, the Market Court conducts full legal proceedings, and it is not bound by the maximum level of fines proposed by the FCCA. Decisions of the Market Court are appealable to the Supreme Administrative Court. The fine is payable to the state. No fine may be imposed unless the FCCA has proposed one within five years from the termination of participation in a competition restraint by the undertaking in question or from the beginning of

[46] See Section II.A.

FCCA investigations, whichever is later. However, no fine may be imposed unless the FCCA has proposed one within ten years from the termination of participation in a competition restraint by the undertaking in question.

The maximum amount of the fine is 10 percent of the undertaking's worldwide turnover during the last year in which the undertaking was involved in the infringement. Hence, subsequent divestments or acquisitions do not affect the amount of the fine. In the assessment of the actual amount of the fine, the nature, the extent, the degree of gravity, and duration of the infringement are taken into account. The amount of fines imposed in Finland were relatively low until the landmark cases of the asphalt and raw wood cartels brought about substantial increases in the amount of fines.[47] The FCCA has welcomed these fine decisions and stated that its intention is to raise fines to assure the deterrent effect of competition policy on the detrimental behavior of the companies. Cartels have traditionally attracted the highest fines. **13.108**

The FCCA is also empowered to issue interlocutory injunctions. The FCCA may order an undertaking to terminate conduct that is prohibited under the Competition Act. The FCCA may also oblige an undertaking to deliver a product to another undertaking on similar terms as offered by the obliged undertaking to other undertakings in a similar position as the benefitting undertaking. Injunctions of the FCCA have immediate effect, unless the Market Court prohibits their implementation. The FCCA must propose a sanction within sixty days from the issuance of the injunction. Should the FCCA fail to do so, the injunction is automatically rendered void. The Market Court may extend the time limit if the FCCA applies for an extension within the sixty-day limit. **13.109**

In addition, any term of an agreement that infringes the Competition Act is automatically null and void. If the term cannot be separated from the rest of the agreement, the whole agreement will be null and void. **13.110**

(ii) Criminal liability

There is no criminal liability for breaches of competition law in Finland; and the sanctions which may be imposed are of an administrative nature only. However, submitting false or misleading information to the competent authorities during a competition law investigation may be a criminal offense, punishable by civil district courts as courts of first instance. In connection with the legislative reform which led to the entering of force of Competition Act in 2011, the question of whether competition infringements should lead to criminal sanctions was raised. However, the final outcome was to exclude explicit criminal liability, and the change in this respect cannot be deemed likely in the near future. **13.111**

G. Leniency and immunity

The leniency system was first introduced in the previous Act on Competition Restrictions in 2004. The leniency system is currently applicable to agreements between competitors that are caught by s. 5 of Competition Act and that involve the fixing of selling or purchase prices or other trading conditions, the limitation of production or sales, or the sharing of markets, customers or sources of supply. **13.112**

Immunity from fines is available to the undertaking that first produces information and evidence that either enables the FCCA to conduct dawn raids or, after a dawn raid, enables the FCCA to establish the existence of a cartel. In practice, the information and evidence normally consist of written documents, oral statements and computer data. In order for the immunity to be available, the information and evidence must be provided before the FCCA **13.113**

[47] See Section II.A.

has acquired the same information from other sources, for example from its own investigations. Immunity is not available to an undertaking that has pressured another undertaking to take part in a cartel.

13.114 A member of a cartel that does not qualify for full immunity may benefit from a reduction in the fine if it produces information and evidence that is significant for establishing the existence of the cartel or the extent and nature of the infringement. The information and evidence must be produced before the FCCA has acquired the same information from other sources. The fine is reduced by 30–50 percent for the undertaking that first produces such information and evidence, by 20–30 percent for the second undertaking to do so, and by a maximum of 20 percent for any subsequent undertakings.

13.115 In addition to producing the required information and evidence, there are additional obligations for the undertaking to follow in order to benefit from immunity or reduced fines. These obligations include keeping the leniency application confidential, cooperating with the FCCA during the investigation, and not destroying any evidence prior to or after filing the leniency application. Although the undertaking must generally cease any participation in the cartel immediately, the FCCA may also instruct the undertaking to continue its participation in the cartel under the direction of the FCCA in order to ensure successful investigations in the case.

13.116 In non-cartel cases, reduced fines are available if the undertaking involved has significantly assisted the FCCA in the investigation of the competition restraint. The FCCA may also refrain from proposing, or the Market Court may refrain from imposing, sanctions in such a case. The application of this rule is in the authorities' full discretion, since there are no specific rules or case law on the conditions for reduced fines or the amount of possible reductions.

13.117 In practice, the FCCA has received approximately a dozen leniency applications. Around half of the applications have led to FCCA investigations and two to court procedures. Full immunity has been granted in two cases.[48]

H. Document creation and retention

13.118 According to s. 33 of the Competition Act, undertakings and associations of undertakings are obliged to cooperate with the competition authorities. At the request of the FCCA or a state regional administrative agency, an undertaking or an association of undertakings must provide the authorities with all information and documents needed for the investigation of the content, purpose and impact of a competition restraint. Similarly, undertakings and associations of undertakings are obliged to provide all necessary information and documents needed to assess the competitive conditions on the market and the existence of a dominant position. Section 33(4) of the Competition Act provides that upon the request of the FCCA, any information required by the authority must be provided in writing. In addition, the FCCA is empowered to oblige a representative of an undertaking or association of undertakings, or a person who may for a justified reason be suspected of having acted in the implementation of a competition restraint, to appear before it. The FCCA may record such hearings.

48 *Raw wood cartel*, MC Case no. 614/2009 and *Automobile spare parts* MC Case no. 91/2009.

14

FRANCE

Jérôme Philippe, Maria Trabucchi, and Aude Guyon
Freshfields Bruckhaus Deringer

Introduction

French antitrust law aims at protecting the market and thus prohibits practices such as abuses of dominant position, anticompetitive vertical or horizontal agreements, and mergers that restrict competition. **14.01**

Other provisions prohibit "unfair competition" (such as brand imitation, disparagement, parasitic behavior etc.) and "restrictive practices" (such as resale below cost, resale price maintenance, sudden termination of commercial relationships, threat of termination of commercial relationships). Those rules seek to impose fairness between competitors and commercial partners and thus prevent them from acting in a way that has an excessively detrimental impact to their partner or competitors. **14.02**

14.03 Cartels are, in France, the most serious violation of competition law[1] and the French Competition Authority (FCA) which has jurisdiction to enforce both French and EU competition rules, repeatedly reaffirms its commitment to detect and punish cartels, increase the number of its investigations, and impose record fines.

I. Acting alone

A. Anticompetitive agreements

14.04 Pursuant to article L.420-1 of the French Commercial Code (FCC) agreements and concerted practices are prohibited when they have the object or effect of restricting competition on the market. Article L.420-1 FCC is the French equivalent of article 101(1) of the Treaty on the Functioning of the European Union (TFEU), which is also directly applicable in France when anticompetitive conduct may affect trade between member states.

14.05 This FCC prohibition includes anticompetitive agreements or practices between competitors (horizontal agreements) or between non competing undertakings, if they operate at a different level of the supply chain (vertical agreements). Anticompetitive practices imply the intent of at least two parties to enter into an agreement. Agreements can be oral or written, formal or informal.

14.06 With regard to vertical agreements, practices such as resale price maintenance (RPM) are in practice always prohibited: although theoretically available, exemptions are hardly ever granted.

14.07 Agreements between competitors such as joint purchasing agreements or agreements between non-competing undertakings such as exclusive distribution, which are not considered as having an anticompetitive object may be considered anticompetitive depending on their effects on the market.

14.08 Acting alone mainly encompasses situations where an undertaking holding a dominant position abuses its position, or where an undertaking has entered into an anticompetitive or restrictive vertical agreement vis-à-vis its commercial partners.

B. Abuse of dominance

14.09 Under French law, abuse mainly encompasses three different types of infringement: (i) abuse of dominant position provided for by article L.420-2(1) FCC (French equivalent of article 102 TFEU); (ii) abuse of economic dependence provided for by article L.420-2(2) FCC; and (iii) abusively low pricing provided for by article L.420-5 FCC. In addition, a number of "restrictive practices" deal with situations where an operator unfairly exploits a favorable business position.

(i) Abuse of dominant position

14.10 Article L.420-2(1) FCC prohibits the abuse of a dominant position, not the dominant position in itself. In line with EU law, a dominant position means "a position allowing the undertakings that hold it to behave to an appreciable extent independently of its competitors, customers and ultimately of consumers."[2] There is no formal dominance threshold set by the FCC or French case law.

---

[1] See Section II.

[2] FCA, *Annual report* (2011), <http://www.autoritedelaconcurrence.fr/user/standard.php?id_rub=450>.

Whether a company is dominant is assessed by considering various factors such as the holding of significant market shares or of a legal or de facto monopoly. Hence, an undertaking with market shares above 40 to 50 percent may be one of the key factors for indicating a dominant position.[3] Other factors relevant to the assessment of dominance include the discrepancy in market shares between the leading company and its competitors, the economic structure of the market (the strength of existing and potential competition, and the existence of barriers to entry), or a specific competitive advantage (the possession of advanced technology or specific know-how). Collective dominance for undertakings which have a number of structural links in common also is possible. **14.11**

Once it is established that a company has a dominant position, the conduct engaged in by that company must be anticompetitive by object or by effect to be considered abusive. Article L.420-2(1) sets out a non-exhaustive list of abuses that may be prohibited, such as refusal to sell, tied sales, or discriminatory conditions of sale. Although there is no French official guidance on abusive conduct, EU guidance and case law are also used by the FCA to conduct its analysis. French law on abuse of dominant position is based on case law. **14.12**

(ii) Abuse of economic dependence

French law contains specific rules prohibiting the abuse of economic dependence. This applies to a company which, without having a dominant position as such, holds significant economic power which it uses to impose abusive commercial conditions on other trading parties.[4] **14.13**

(iii) Abusively low pricing

French law prohibits abusively low pricing applied by a non-dominant company to consumers.[5] **14.14**

C. Predatory pricing

As under EU law, predatory pricing is an abuse and so infringes article L.420-2(1) if engaged in by a business in a dominant position. **14.15**

Predatory pricing is traditionally defined along the lines of the EU *AKZO*.[6] As for any abuse, the first step is to establish the dominant position on a market and then to prove predation. **14.16**

In its *GlaxoSmithKline* decision, the FCA defined predation as "a practice in which a company in a dominant position fixes its prices at such a level that it sustains losses or renounces profit in the short term with the aim of evicting or disciplining one or more competitors, or of making more difficult the entry of future competitors on the market, so as to later increase its prices in order to recoup its losses."[7] In this decision, the FCA also detailed the methodology to assess such predatory practices. **14.17**

Thus, the FCA applies a "cost test," which consists in comparing the price implemented during the alleged predation period and the costs incurred by the company in supplying products or services. **14.18**

If the sale price falls below the "average variable cost" (the cost that varies in direct proportion to the activity), the anticompetitive object of the dominant company's conduct is presumed. **14.19**

[3] *Road signs*, FCA Decision no. 10-D-39 (December 22, 2010), available at <http://www.autoritedelaconcurrence.fr>.

[4] See Section I.D.

[5] See Section I.C.

[6] Case 62/86 *AKZO Chemie v. Commission* [1991] ECR I-3359.

[7] *GlaxoSmithKline*, FCA Decision no. 07-D-09 (March 14, 2007), para. 164.

Consequently, such prices are not absolutely prohibited. The presumption may be rebutted by the dominant company providing for instance an alternative explanation of its behavior backed by verifiable data, or explaining the necessity, for a limited period of time, of sustaining costs indispensable for entering a new market or for launching a new product.

14.20 When the cost test leads to the finding that the price is comprised between the variable cost and the "average total cost" (the total cost of each item), a plan to eliminate, discipline, or discourage a competitor must be shown. The dominant company may put forward defense arguments.

14.21 The variable cost test can be substituted with an incremental cost test,[8] or even with an opportunity cost test,[9] depending on the nature of the activity.

14.22 Obviously, a cost test showing that prices are above average total costs is sufficient in itself to disprove the predation.

14.23 Unlike in EU law, in order to prove predatory prices it is also necessary that it be possible for the dominant company to recoup the losses initially incurred. It is not necessary to prove a real recoup of the loss by the dominant company, but that this recoup is just possible.

14.24 A non-dominant company may also be held liable for charging abusively low price to consumers (end users) compared to costs of the products (art. L.420-5 FCC) when this has the object or effect to eliminate an undertaking from or entry to the market.[10] Unlike other anti-competitive practices, this cannot be exempted.[11] Predatory cases are not frequent since the conditions that must be satisfied for observing predatory prices are very strict.

D. Exploitative offenses

14.25 Exploitative conditions may constitute an abuse of dominant position (art. L.420-2(1)) or an abuse of economic dependence (art. L.420-2(2)), although this is very rare. They can also constitute a restrictive commercial practice (art. L.442-6 FCC).

14.26 Exploitative conditions, such as excessive pricing to customers may be considered abusive either when the price level is not comparable to prices in equivalent markets (similar product markets or other geographic markets) or, alternatively, when there is a significant disproportion between the price offered by the dominant company and the value of the corresponding service (cost price).[12]

14.27 In addition, imposing exploitative conditions could fall within article L.420-2(2) (abuse of dependence) when this has an effect on the market. This provision aims at regulating abuses between commercial partners. Although it is not necessary to demonstrate that the company holds a dominant position, this provision applies to undertakings that possess considerable economic power. Abuse of economic dependence requires (i) the existence of economic dependence, (ii) an abuse (such as refusal to deal, termination of relationship or discriminatory terms of sales), and (iii) a distortion of competition. Economic dependence is characterized by either a lack of alternative for the economic partner, or a situation where the economic partner has made a huge specific investment in the relationship.

---

[8] *Transportation of passengers*, FCA Decision no. 04-D-79 (December 23, 2004).
[9] *EDF*, FCA Decision no. 11-D-09 (June 8, 2011).
[10] *Tourism sector*, FCA Decision no. 06-D-23 (July 21, 2006).
[11] See Section I.Q.
[12] *GLEM*, FCA Decision no. 03-D-18 (18 April 2003).

Finally, any company may also be held liable for restrictive commercial practices pursuant to article L.442-6 FCC, when it abuses its power, for example by obtaining a benefit from its partner without consideration, or imposing conditions which create a significant imbalance between the parties, or threatening termination of the relationship if it is not granted specific prices, or payment periods. No evidence of a distortion of competition is required. Only French courts have jurisdiction to award damages. Such conduct may also be sanctioned by a civil fine up to EUR 2 million upon request of the Minister for the Economy or the public prosecutor. In practice, such civil fines are quite rare. A decision dated October 29, 2009 of the Appeal Court of Versailles notably imposed on the central purchasing body of Leclerc (Galec) a civil fine of EUR 500,000.[13] **14.28**

E. Monopsony

Abusive conduct by a business holding a dominant purchasing position may fall within the scope of article L.420-2(1) prohibiting the abuse of a dominant position. To date, there has been no case sanctioning a monopsony. **14.29**

Abuse by a business holding a purchasing power is more likely to fall within the scope of article L.420-2(2) prohibiting the abuse of economic dependence. Abuse of economic dependence is established if the three aforementioned conditions are met.[14] The FCA has sanctioned distributors who imposed discriminatory prices in exchange for granting access for the supplier to a distribution network.[15] In practice, article L.420-2(2) is rarely applied in case of economic dependence of the supplier vis-à-vis its distributor since suppliers often fear delisting in retaliation. **14.30**

A company with a purchasing power can be liable for damages on the grounds of article L.442-6, for instance if it obtains payment or other advantages as a precondition for placing orders without any counterpart for the other party, or threatens delisting. **14.31**

F. Price discrimination

Discriminatory sales conditions—which include price terms—are expressly listed by article L.420-2 amongst the practices possibly constituting an abuse of dominance. A dominant undertaking may abuse its dominance by applying dissimilar prices or conditions to purchasers placed in the same situation. Conversely, a dominant undertaking may treat differently purchasers placed in different situations, without committing any abuse.[16] The FCA does not prohibit the application of different conditions to clients as such, but determines whether such practices have an anticompetitive object or effect and whether they can be objectively justified. **14.32**

Application of low prices to select clients will not be abusive if the price differentiation is justified by an economic incentive such as volume discounts or a service rendered by the client benefiting from the lower price.[17] Discrimination is abusive when it aims at excluding a competitor from the market (primary-line discrimination) or when the clients of the dominant company have been disadvantaged on their own market (secondary-line discrimination).[18] This latter case remains pretty exceptional. **14.33**

[13] *Leclerc*, Appeal Court of Versailles, Case no. 08/07356 (October 29, 2009).
[14] See Section I.D.
[15] *Héli-Inter Assistance*, FCA Decision no. 96-D-51 (September 3, 1996).
[16] *NMPP*, FCA Decision no. 07-D-23 (July 12, 2007).
[17] *Apple*, FCA Decision no. 02-D-56 (September 17, 2002).
[18] *NMPP*, FCA Decision no. 09-D-04 (January 27, 2009).

G. Dictating or influencing resale prices

(i) Resale price maintenance

14.34 RPM is mainly approached through unlawful agreements rather than abuse of dominance.

14.35 RPM most often falls within the prohibition on anticompetitive practices if included in distribution agreements, as it restricts competition between retailers (art. L.420-1). The prohibition on RPM covers both direct and indirect means of establishing a fixed or minimum price or of influencing the resale price charged by distributors. Thus, fixing the price level or the distributor's margin falls under the prohibition.

14.36 Pursuant to case law, recommended resale prices (RRPs) are not prohibited as long as the supplier does not implement any price fixing policy and the retailers do not apply RRPs on a compulsory basis.[19]

14.37 There is no prohibition on maximum resale prices provided that they do not have the characteristics of "minimum prices or fixed prices" or lead to RPM.

14.38 The highest fine imposed by the FCA for RPM has been EUR 63 million.[20] Most recently, in March 2012 the FCA fined companies a total of EUR35.3 million for RPM in the animal food sector.

14.39 RPM may also fall within the abuse of a dominant position prohibition where minimum retail prices are imposed on resellers by an operator holding a dominant position in the relevant market.[21] The FCA has held that a company abused its dominant position when it granted rebates subject to the observance of a given price level by the distributor.[22]

14.40 RPM is also a specific offense under article L.442-5 FCC that courts may sanction by a penalty of up to EUR15,000 per offense.

(ii) Minimum advertised price programs

14.41 Any requirement by a supplier that a distributor refrain from advertising resale price below the minimum price set by the supplier will be treated in the same way as RPM.[23] In practice, MAP cases are not frequent.

H. Tying arrangements

14.42 Tying is expressly prohibited by article L.420-2(1) if engaged in by a business with a dominant position.

14.43 The FCA uses the term "tying" to cover the notions of tying and of bundling. Tying refers to a practice where a dominant undertaking ties the supply of two separate products or services. It could be by imposing the selling of one product (the tying product) only on the condition that the buyer also purchases another product (the tied product) ("tying"), or by providing the incentive for a joint purchase by granting a rebate ("bundled discounting").

14.44 As under EU law, both tying and bundled discounting are not prohibited as such. The anticompetitive nature of the practice is assessed by the FCA on a case-by-case basis, and depends

---

[19] *Parisian palace*, FCA Decision no. 05-D-64 (November 25, 2005); *Luxury perfume*, FCA Decision no. 06-D-04 (March 13, 2006); *Toys*, FCA Decision no. 07-D-50 (December 20, 2007).

[20] *Orange Caraïbe*, FCA Decision no. 09-D-36 (December 9, 2009).

[21] *Royal Canin*, FCA Decision no. 05-D-32 (June 22, 2005).

[22] *Toys*, FCA Decision no. 99-D-45 (June 30, 1999).

[23] *Luxury perfume* (n 19); *Toys* (n 19).

on whether the following criteria are fulfilled: (i) the tie is applied across two distinct markets, (ii) the undertaking has a dominant position on the tying market, (iii) an anticompetitive object or strategy or effect on the tied market must be proven, (iv) and there is no objective justification for the practice.[24] An anticompetitive effect is presumed when the tying product is sold by a monopolistic undertaking.

When the practice targets consumers rather than commercial partners, the conditioning of the sale of one product or service to consumers on the purchase of a second different product or service could also be prohibited by article L.122-1 of the French Consumer Code if it is analyzed as an unfair commercial practice. This provision applies to any undertaking (dominant or not) but only with regard to their relationships with consumers. In case of infringement, only courts have jurisdiction to impose a fine, of up to EUR 1,500 per offense (e.g. per unit sold). **14.45**

I. Exclusive dealing

Exclusive dealing may fall under the prohibition on abuse of dominant position (art. L.420-2(1) FCC) if engaged by a dominant company, or under the prohibition on anticompetitive agreements (art. L.420-1 FCC), or restrictive commercial practices (art. L.330 FCC). **14.46**

For the first two prohibitions above, and in accordance with EU law, exclusivity is considered when more than 80 percent of the transactions are concerned. **14.47**

With regard to abuse of dominance, article L.420-2(1) does not expressly include exclusive dealing arrangements among the abuses. However, a non-compete or an exclusive purchase agreement under which clients are required to buy all or most of their purchases from the same supplier, or any other arrangements which may have the same effect, may constitute an abuse. The FCA has ruled that the granting of global reductions on sales volume with the purpose of becoming the exclusive supplier or being referenced with distributors' for the maximum of the products constitutes *de facto* exclusivity.[25] **14.48**

Exclusive dealing does not in itself constitute an abuse. For it to constitute an abuse, the FCA assesses whether it creates exclusionary effects on the market. Although there is no standard checklist, to ensure that exclusivity dealings do not create artificial barriers to entry, the FCA relies on several criteria that include in particular the level of market power of the dominant company, the scope of the exclusivity (what is the objective, and who is excluded from which market), its duration (the longer the duration the more likely foreclosure is), the possible early termination of contracts, the existence of potential technical justifications, and efficiencies passed on to consumers.[26] Although exclusivity will not be deemed illegal only because of a high market share, this often constitutes the most important criterion. **14.49**

Exclusive dealing may also constitute an anticompetitive vertical agreement falling within the scope of article L.420-1. As under EU law, the FCA may consider that exclusivity is anticompetitive if it covers all or a large part of the seller's needs, or where it restricts the territories in which, and the customers to whom, the distributor may sell. Such conditions are not required for dominance. Even when trade between member states may not be affected, the EU block exemption serves as a guideline to assess whether the exclusivity could be anticompetitive. **14.50**

[24] *France Télécom*, FCA Decision no. 08-D-10 (May 7, 2008); *Publishing of newspapers*, FCA Decision no. 04-D-56 (November 15, 2004).

[25] *Roquefort cheese*, FCA Decision no. 04-D-13 (April 8, 2004).

[26] *KalibraXe*, FCA Decision no. 07-MC-01 (April 25, 2007).

14.51 When these practices are not likely to have an appreciable effect on competition in France, the FCA may decide to apply the *de minimis* rule.[27]

14.52 Moreover, pursuant to article L.330 FCC, exclusivity clauses under which the purchaser undertakes not to source its products from any other suppliers than the seller is limited to ten years. Only French courts have jurisdiction to decide that this clause is void.

J. Refusal to deal

14.53 Refusal to deal is expressly listed among abusive practices in article L.420-2(1). Whether a refusal to deal is abusive is assessed by the FCA with regard to the other credible alternatives that the victim of the refusal to deal have for its supply.

14.54 The FCA has held that a refusal to deal is abusive if: (i) the product or service to which access is refused is objectively necessary to efficiently compete on the downstream market; (ii) the refusal is likely to lead to the elimination of effective competition on the downstream market; (iii) the refusal is likely to harm the consumer; and (iv) there is a likelihood of anticompetitive foreclosure.[28]

14.55 Refusal to deal can take the form of refusal by the dominant company to allow interoperability that is necessary for the development of products, to grant access to an essential facility,[29] or to supply its rival except on unreasonable terms (e.g. extremely high price or degraded service).[30]

14.56 Another form of refusal to deal is "margin squeeze" which occurs when a dominant company in an upstream market also competes on the downstream market and sets prices in such a way that is impossible for a competitor on the downstream market to compete without suffering loss. The FCA applies the "equally efficient operator" test, assessing whether the dominant company could trade profitably on the downstream market if it was charged the same wholesale price as the one paid by downstream competitors. The margin squeeze is established when the test shows that the dominant company would not be able to make a profit. However, a margin squeeze is not in itself an abuse. There is a presumption that margin squeeze is an abuse when (i) the vertically integrated company holds a monopoly or a dominant position on the upstream market; (ii) the upstream product or service is objectively necessary for competitors to compete on the downstream market; and/or (iii) there is a sufficient level of coordination between the dominant firm's upstream and downstream arms. In this case, the undertaking may justify the practice by efficiency gains. Sanctions of margin squeeze have mainly concerned liberalized markets (e.g. energy and telecommunications). In 2004, the FCA fined France Télécom EUR 20 million for a margin squeeze.[31]

14.57 A company, dominant or not, may also be held liable before courts for sudden termination of commercial relationship.[32]

14.58 Refusal to sell a product or supply a service to a consumer is also prohibited by article L.122-1 of the French Consumer code.[33] Refusal to sell to a consumer cases are very exceptional in practice.

---

[27] See Section I.Q.
[28] *TDF*, FCA Decision no. 10-D-09 (March 9, 2010).
[29] See Section I.K.
[30] *Medical imaging device*, FCA Decision no. 06-D-36 (December 6, 2006); *SNCF/Expedia*, FCA Decision no. 09-D-06 (February 5, 2009).
[31] *France Télécom*, FCA Decision no. 04-D-48 (October 14, 2004).
[32] See Section I.O.
[33] See Section I.H for details regarding the sanction.

K. Essential facilities

Essential facilities are defined as "infrastructures or equipment which are indispensable to ensure a relationship/link with clients and/or allow competitors to carry out activities, and which would be impossible to reproduce using reasonable means."[34] Not only refusal of access to these facilities, but also access on not oriented costs or discriminatory terms may be abusive. **14.59**

To decide whether there is an abuse, the FCA assesses whether the following cumulative conditions are met: (i) the facility must be operated by a dominant undertaking; (ii) use to the facility must be strictly necessary to access a market; (iii) the facility cannot be reproduced in economically reasonable conditions by competitors; (iv) access to the infrastructure is denied, or granted only under unjustifiably restrictive conditions; and (v) access to the facility would be technically possible.[35] **14.60**

The FCA applies this doctrine to both physical (for example a heliport[36]) and non-physical facilities (for example, a list of telephone subscribers[37]). Cases regarding essential facilities are quite rare. **14.61**

L. Bundling (including loyalty and market share discounts)

Bundling if engaged in by a dominant company may raise concerns in the same circumstances as tying.[38] **14.62**

Moreover, loyalty rebates or market share discounts (which are defined as discounts or rebates on units purchased of a single product conditioned upon the level of purchase) when granted by a dominant undertaking are not illegal as such but may be considered abusive under article L.420-2(1), especially when they apply retroactively. Their legality is assessed by the FCA on an effects-based analysis. **14.63**

The FCA examines whether the rebate or discount schemes have a foreclosure effect on the market because they exclude competitors by other means than competition on the merits or by creating barriers to entry[39] and whether they exceed a simple passing on of economic gains to consumers. **14.64**

The FCA often considers whether, were the customer to switch to another supplier, that supplier would be forced to decrease considerably its prices or offer economically unviable discounts to compensate the customer for the loss of rebate that he had from his original supplier.[40] **14.65**

When rebates are not retroactive, the test is conducted as a predation test.[41] When rebates are retroactive, the FCA conducts an analysis of their actual loyalty effects based on the rate, the duration of the reference period.[42] Cases regarding rebate schemes are not frequent. **14.66**

M. Standard-setting groups (disclosure requirements, licensing arrangements, and licensing pools)

Standard setting may in some cases fall under the prohibition of article L.420-1 FCC if, for example, it leads to anticompetitive coordination between participating undertakings **14.67**

[34] *Héli-inter Assistance*, Paris Appeal Court, Case no. 1997-022854 (September 9, 1997).
[35] *NMPP*, FCA Decision no. 03-MC-04 (December 22, 2003).
[36] *Héli-inter Assistance*, FCA Decision no. 96-D-51 (September 3, 1996).
[37] *France Télécom*, Supreme Court case no. 99-16.642 (December 4, 2001).
[38] See Section I.H.
[39] *Cement*, FCA Decision no. 07-D-08 (March 12, 2007).
[40] *Roquefort cheese* (n 25).
[41] *La Poste*, FCA Decision no. 04-D-65 (November 30, 2004).
[42] *NMPP*, FCA Decision no. 06-MC-01 (February 23, 2006).

or excludes competitors from the market (e.g. if the access to the results obtained are too expensive or strict).

14.68 The FCA has held that the development of common standards may also be pro-competitive provided that it leads to efficiencies (such as cost reduction, or an open standard which allows better compatibility of competitors' equipment), that the efficiencies are passed on to consumers, and that the products and services can still be sold in a competitive market.[43]

14.69 In 2010, in an opinion, the FCA stated that it welcomes the new EU Guidelines concerning standardization, and notably the creation of a "safe harbor" for standardization agreements which satisfy the following criteria: (i) the participation in standard setting is unrestricted; (ii) the procedure for adopting the standard is transparent; (iii) there is no obligation to comply with the standard; and (iv) the access to the standard is provided on fair, reasonable and non-discriminatory (FRAND) conditions. The FCA would use these Guidelines, even when the trade between members states is not affected.

14.70 The holding of an intellectual property right essential to a standard may in certain circumstances lead to an abuse of dominance. To date, there is no case law by the FCA.

N. Customer termination

14.71 Termination of an ongoing commercial relationship is expressly listed in article L.420-2(1) FCC as an example of abuse of dominance. Termination of an agreement where prior contractual relationships exist between the victim of the termination and the dominant undertaking are assessed in the same way as situations where the parties have never entered into any relationship prior to the refusal to deal or when access is refused to an essential facility.[44]

14.72 Termination by a non-dominant undertaking of a relationship with a customer that is economically dependent on its supplier may be prohibited by article L.420-2(2) if it restricts competition on a market and it is considered abusive.[45] For the conduct to constitute an abuse, the victim of the termination must have no credible alternative than to purchase from the dominant undertaking to supply on the downstream market, and there must be no objective and non-discriminatory reasons for the termination.[46]

14.73 Termination of an agreement may in any case be challenged under article L.442-6 FCC which holds liable for damages any company, dominant or not, which suddenly terminates or partially terminates ongoing commercial relationship without reasonable prior notice or threats to terminate it to obtain certain advantages. This provision is only applicable to relationships between business partners. Only courts have jurisdiction to apply this provision and award damages. In practice, cases for sudden termination are very frequent.

O. Termination of intermediaries (retailers, wholesalers, dealers, and value-added resellers, agents, and brokers)

14.74 French law does not make distinction on the direction in which the refusal to deal flows, for example towards a competitor, or an intermediary, or a customer.[47]

[43] *Electronic wallet*, FCA Opinion no. 03-A-17 (September 18, 2003).
[44] See Sections I.J and I.K.
[45] See Section I.D.
[46] *Blood products*, FCA Decision no. 04-D-26 (June 30, 2004).
[47] See Sections I.J, I.K, and I.N.

P. Termination of relationships with competitors

Termination of a relationship with a competitor may constitute an abuse under article L.420-2(1) FCC if engaged in by a dominant undertaking. It is assessed in the same way as refusal to deal or refusal to access an essential facility.[48] **14.75**

Q. Exemptions

All practices falling within the scope of article L.420-1 (anticompetitive agreements) or of article L.420-2 (abuse of dominance and of dependence) may theoretically benefit from an exemption. There is no per se prohibition. However, even if it is always theoretically available, the test for the individual exemption is very demanding. This differs from EU law where only anticompetitive agreements may obtain such benefit. **14.76**

The exemption can be either individual or collective ("block exemption"). Block exemptions are based on a number of EU or French regulations and concern only some types of agreements (vertical, transfer of technology, R&D, agriculture, automobile). There exists no block exemption for abuse of dominance or dependence. **14.77**

Individual exemption can benefit to every anticompetitive practice provided that it meets the following set of cumulative criteria: **14.78**

the practice contributes to economic progress;
consumers receive a fair share of the resulting efficiencies;
it does not eliminate competition; and
the restriction of competition is indispensable for achieving the economic progress.

These conditions are narrowly interpreted by the FCA, and so the benefit of article L.420-4(I) FCC is rarely granted. **14.79**

In addition, the FCA may decide to apply the *de minimis* rule, but only to agreements which might be anticompetitive under article L.420-1 where these are not likely to have an appreciable effect on competition in France, and not to abuse of dominant position. The *de minimis* rule is only applicable if the infringement does not relate to a public tender, and the aggregate market share held by the concerned parties does not exceed 15 percent on any of the markets affected by the practices if they are not competitors, or 10 percent if they are competitors. **14.80**

In any case, the *de minimis* rule is not available if the restrictions relate to RPM, or restrict passive sales, or limit sales by the members of a selective distribution network, or restrict cross-deliveries between distributors within a selective distribution network. **14.81**

All exclusive restraints that may affect trade between member states fall within the scope of article 101(1) TFEU and have to be analyzed under the European exemption rules.[49] **14.82**

II. Dealing with competitors

Like EU law, article L.420-1 prohibits agreements and arrangements between competitors for anticompetitive purposes such as price fixing, fixing of margins, market-sharing, bid-rigging (collusive tendering), or boycotts. They are the most serious types of infringement. In practice, these agreements are not exempted under article L.420-4 FCC or article 101(3) TFEU. **14.83**

[48] See Sections I.J, I.K, I.N, and I.O.

[49] See Chapter 12 (European Union).

14.84 Combating cartels has been and is still the priority of the FCA. The FCA imposes significant fines in order to dissuade companies from entering into a cartel. In 2011, the FCA sanctioned the main laundry detergent manufacturers in France with a total fine of EUR 367.9 million for having agreed on sales prices and promotions. To date, the highest fines ever imposed are those in the *Steel cartel* (2008),[50] where total fines were EUR 575.4 million. In this case, the total fine was however reduced to one eighth of this amount on appeal.

14.85 Many additional resources and tools have been introduced and developed by the FCA in order to minimize the number of decisions which are challenged before the Appeal Court, and to speed up resolution of cases, thus allowing the FCA to handle more cases. The FCA issued a notice on the method of setting fines in 2011, and a procedural notice on settlement proceedings in 2012.[51]

14.86 Other types of agreements between competitors, such as joint purchasing and information exchange may infringe antitrust law (art. L.420-1 FCC or art. 101(1) TFEU), depending on their precise terms and their effects.

A. Horizontal price fixing

14.87 Horizontal price fixing is considered as an anticompetitive practice which infringes article L.420-1 and is among the most serious of all antitrust law infringements. Very high fines are imposed for this type of infringement. For instance, in the *Packaged flour* case the FCA has imposed a total fine of EUR 242.4 million for price fixing and other collusive practices.[52]

B. Horizontal agreements to allocate customers or territories; agreements not to compete

14.88 Very high fines are imposed for market sharing cartels, including geographic market and customer sharing. These types of cartel are among the most serious of all antitrust law infringements. For instance, the FCA fined eight firms for a total of EUR 52.7 million for market sharing in the road signs sector.[53]

C. Horizontal boycotts

14.89 In line with EU law, agreements between competitors not to purchase from, or supply to, specific businesses, if entered into for an anticompetitive purpose, are a serious infringement of article L.420-1. The agreement may be intended to hinder the entry or growth of new competitors, to punish competitors who do not cooperate in cartel arrangements, or to eliminate a competitor not part of the cartel which practice low pricing.[54]

D. Joint ventures and other competitive collaborations

14.90 Joint ventures which are "full-function"—that is, autonomous economic entities which operate independently on the market—shall be analyzed under the EU or national merger control rules. Inversely, non-full-function joint ventures—such as strategic alliances and agreements to cooperate may fall within the scope of article 101 TFEU and/or article L.420-1 FCC. French competition law does not provide for specific guidelines but refers the European Guidelines.

14.91 The FCA assesses notably whether the creation of joint venture serves as a vehicle for a cartel, for instance for organizing market allocation.

---

50 *Steel cartel*, FCA Decision no. 08-D-32 (December 16, 2008).
51 See Section III.
52 *Packaged flour*, FCA Decision no. 12-D-09 (March 13, 2012).
53 *Road signs* (n 3).
54 *Opticians*, FCA Decision no. 02-D-36 (June 14, 2002).

Competing or related companies may also create an economic interest group (EIG) aiming at pooling their efforts—such as technical and resources complementarities—for various reasons such as joint bids, manufacturing agreements. Such agreements will be authorized as soon as they are implemented for technical reasons and that they do not have the object to eliminate competitors. 14.92

In some cases where large industries have merged to provide services to all competitors and thus permit the access to the market, access to EIG must be based on objective, transparent and non-discriminatory criteria.[55] EIGs may be caught by article L.420-1 FCC if they restrict competition and, notably, if the EIG membership is a condition for access to a market.[56] Thus, it is possible to limit the access to EIG membership when such membership is not a condition to access the market. 14.93

If article L.420-1 FCC has been infringed, exemption under article L.420-4 FCC (French equivalent of art. 101(3) TFEU) may be available. 14.94

The EU block exemption regulations are also applicable.[57] 14.95

E. Trade associations

Participation in trade associations is legal. However, it may provide opportunities for competitors to exchange views on the market, which could easily spill over into illegal coordination. Casual discussions on business strategy or on pricing can become anticompetitive agreements. Therefore trade associations are always subject to close scrutiny of competition authorities. Even if trade associations are not considered as entities with an economic activity, they are subject to French competition law. There are a large number of decisions sanctioning trade associations for anticompetitive agreements. For instance, the FCA fined taxi unions for fixing a license resale price.[58] 14.96

Competitors participating in trade associations will be at risk if they discuss commercially sensitive information.[59] 14.97

The FCA has held that, under French law, participation in even only one meeting where anticompetitive matters are discussed is sufficient to prove participation and liability of the company for an antitrust infringement, even if the meeting is not followed by actual anticompetitive practices.[60] In this context, a competitor attending a meeting where prices or other trading terms are being discussed by competitors can only avoid being held liable by publicly distancing himself or herself by immediately leaving the meeting, and ensuring that it is recorded in the minutes of the meeting that he/she has left. 14.98

F. Interlocking directorates

French corporate law has special provisions and limits for instance the number of mandates that could be held by a director in joint-stock company or a CEO, or a member of the executive board. 14.99

Interlocking directorates do not raise as such anticompetitive concerns provided that they do not lead to a coordination of commercial strategy or to an exchange of sensitive information between competitors. 14.100

Structural links between competitors in the form of the acquisition of a minority interest could be subject to article L.420-1 if they facilitate or lead to express or tacit collusion, or 14.101

---

[55] *Taxi*, FCA Decision no. 10-D-15 (May 11, 2010).
[56] *GIE Rhum*, FCA Decision no. 01-D-70 (October 24, 2001).
[57] See Chapter 12.
[58] *Taxis in Marseilles*, FCA Decision no. 06-D-30 (October 18, 2006).
[59] See Section II.H.
[60] *Electrical equipment*, FCA Decision no. 11-D-13 (October 5, 2011).

if the minority shareholder is given access to sensitive information about the target or may control the target's adherence to common agreed conduct. Safeguards may be put in place to ensure that the competitors keep their respective strategies separate and independent. Internal Chinese walls should be set up to prevent information leakage between the competitors.

14.102 In the case of public procurement, Chinese walls may, however, appear insufficient since any information exchange, even the slightest one, between the tenders prior to a bid is prohibited.

14.103 Article L.420-2 FCC could also theoretically apply if a dominant firm acquires an interest in another business in circumstances in which this weakens the competitive structure of the market. So far, there has been no French case law on this point.

G. Facilitating practices

14.104 Facilitating practices are not subject to specific rules in French law. However, conducts such as "hub and spoke"—exchange taking place between competing distributors via a common supplier, or between competing suppliers via a common distributor—may facilitate anticompetitive practices and thus infringe article L.420-1 FCC. Although there is no FCA decision to date, the FCA held in an opinion in 2010 in the food sector that it could sanction such practices.

H. Information exchange

14.105 Exchange of information is not as such prohibited by article L.420-1 FCC. To be sanctioned, it must have an anticompetitive object or effect.

14.106 Information exchange can constitute a concerted practice if it reduces strategic uncertainty for a competitor. Hence, exchange of sensitive information may as such amount to collusion.

14.107 Information exchange may be illegal when the information is:

- sensitive (relates to price, rebates, volumes, investments, costs, commercial strategy);
- individual (in the sense that at least one competitor can read, compute or restore another competitor's individual data based on the information exchanged); or
- recent or future (in the sense that information exchange can influence current or future strategy and is not purely historic).[61]

14.108 An isolated exchange will not generally be seen as an infringement since the case law targets regular systems of exchange of information.

14.109 In the pre-merger due diligence context, antitrust authorities recognize some latitude for information exchange. However, companies have to ensure that they do not infringe article L.420-1 FCC. In order to reduce any competition risk, companies usually use a "clean room" to which only restricted people have access and with strict rules governing the information that people may and may not have access to.

14.110 In case of public procurement, the FCA has a stricter approach regarding information exchange. It considers that any exchange of information, even isolated, prior to the submission of bids is anticompetitive.[62]

I. Joint purchasing agreements

14.111 Joint purchasing agreements are not considered as having an anticompetitive object as such. However, they may through their effects infringe article L.420-1.

[61] *Luxury hotel sector*, FCA Decision no. 05-D-64 (November 25, 2005).
[62] *Landscape designs*, FCA Decision no. 10-D-10 (March 10, 2010).

The FCA assesses whether: (i) the parties remains free to purchase from other suppliers; (ii) the suppliers' capacity to access consumers is not limited; and (iii) the advantage obtained does not lead to a significant distortion of competition in the resale market (if any).[63] The FCA has considered that a joint purchasing agreement infringes article L.420-1 if the additional rebates obtained have the object or effect of restraining access by certain suppliers to consumers. **14.112**

J. Joint lobbying/regulatory/legislative efforts

In line with EU practice, joint lobbying related to regulation or legislation does not normally raise antitrust concerns provided that meetings or communications between competitors do not lead to anticompetitive cooperation or exchange of information.[64] **14.113**

III. General issues

A. Jurisdiction and applicable law (including sector-specific competition regulation)

Anticompetitive practices are regulated by articles L.420-1 to L.420-7 FCC. Articles 101 and 102 TFEU are also applicable when trade between member states of the EU is or might be affected. **14.114**

Antitrust law applies to all sectors of the economy and to all "undertakings" engaged in economic activity. State-owned as well as private entities are subject to these rules. The law also applies to individuals and to entities such as corporations, trade associations and trade unions. **14.115**

Telecommunications, postal services, energy, and rail transport sectors are also subject to market liberalizing legislation. There exist specific sector regulators—in post and telecoms, energy, train, bank, insurance, and media sectors—that are not empowered to enforce competition law, but communicate with the FCA for any questions which may raise competition concerns. **14.116**

The FCA has full power to apply French and European competition law and sanctions companies which infringe competition law.[65] **14.117**

The Paris Court of appeal has exclusive jurisdiction on appeal of the decisions of the FCA. Rulings of the Paris Court of appeal may be brought before the French Supreme Court. **14.118**

In addition, a list of eight French courts (judicial) set by a decree are also competent to apply French and EU antitrust law.[66] Administrative courts may also have jurisdictions to apply French and EU antitrust law. **14.119**

B. Antitrust system

(i) Name of agency/agencies

The FCA is an independent administrative body. Its role is to ensure fair competition in all markets. The FCA may notably initiate, carry out inspections in company premises and impose sanctions to undertakings. **14.120**

The Minister of Economy—through the General Directorate of Competition, Consumer Affairs and Fraud Control (DGCCRF)—enjoys injunctive and settlement powers as regards local anticompetitive practices, provided that: (i) article 101 or 102 TFEU is not applicable; (ii) the annual turnover of each offender does not exceed EUR 50 million; and (iii) the aggregate **14.121**

63 *Heating industry*, FCA Decision no. 06-D-03 (March 9, 2006).
64 See Section II. E.
65 See Section III.B.
66 Marseille, Bordeaux, Lille, Fort-de-France, Lyon, Nancy, Paris, Rennes.

turnover achieved by all the offenders does not exceed EUR 100 million. Should a further investigation be required, the DGCCRF refers the case to the FCA. The DGCCRF's agents may also launch inspections in company premises and may assist the FCA in its inspections.

(ii) Staff size and budget

14.122 The FCA board comprises seventeen members: the President (appointed for five years by a decree of the President of the French Republic), four vice-Presidents, and a collegiate board of twelve members.

14.123 Following a European Court of Human Rights (ECHR) ruling, the investigation services are separate from the Board. A general case handler heads the FCA's investigation services. The investigation services have five antitrust units, an inspection unit, a merger unit, a Chief Economist team, and a leniency officer. Each of the antitrust units as well as the merger control unit is headed by a deputy general case handler. The investigation services employ ninety-three people, including eighty-three case handlers who are allocated amongst the different units. In total, the FCA has about 190 people. Its budget is around EUR 20 million.

(iii) Recent enforcement actions and trends

14.124 In 2011 and in 2012, the FCA released guidelines regarding sanctions and providing more transparency for companies.

14.125 In 2011, it issued a notice explaining the method followed by the FCA when setting fines. The notice is largely in line with EU law and constitutes a significant increase in transparency for companies. It may also reduce the number of challenges to the FCA's decisions, since until now the apparent lack of method for setting fines has led to regular challenges before courts. Although this is denied by the FCA, it may be considered that these guidelines tend to increase fines.

14.126 In 2012, the FCA released a procedural notice on settlement proceedings. This procedure enables companies to waive their right to challenge the charges made against them by the FCA in exchange for a fine reduction of 10 percent. In addition, companies can submit behavioral commitments (in particular by setting up a compliance program) or structural commitments which could result in a fine reduction of up to 15 percent. In contrast to EU settlement proceedings, this procedure is applicable to all types of antitrust cases, including abuse of dominant position. The settlement procedure could also be combined with leniency proceedings. Settlement proceedings are intended to shorten cases and to reduce the number of the FCA's decisions that are challenged before the courts.

14.127 In 2012, the FCA published a guide for companies wishing to set up a compliance program. Thus, with respect to the conditions provided for by the guide, companies committing to set up or to upgrade an existing compliance program in the context of a settlement with the FCA, may expect a reduction of their fine of up to 10 percent, which will be added to the reduction of up to 15 percent corresponding to the settlement procedure, and to an additional reduction of up to 5 percent that may be awarded in return for other commitments undertaken in accordance with the procedural notice regarding the settlement procedure.

14.128 Cartels remain the priority of the FCA. The French leniency program has been very successful. Since its introduction, the FCA has received almost sixty applications. In 2011, the FCA appointed a leniency officer whose role is to explain companies the procedural steps and to ensure cooperation with other competition authorities concerned with leniency applications.

14.129 Since 2011, the retail, banking, agri-food, transport, internet/telecommunication sectors have been particularly under the FCA scrutiny. Since 2009, the FCA has carried out several sector inquiries, some of which have led to litigation.

Class actions are not admissible yet but a draft bill introducing class actions is expected in early 2013. 14.130

C. Private litigation

Civil actions for damages for antitrust infringements are based on the rules applicable to tort actions. Damages claims can be brought before judicial courts by and against companies and individuals. 14.131

Damages are awarded to compensate actual loss as well as loss of profit suffered as a result of an antitrust infringement. French courts only grant compensatory damage. No cap is imposed on the amount of damages. 14.132

Since 2008, the limitation period has been reduced from ten years to five. The limitation period is calculated from the day when the claimant becomes aware (or should have become aware) of the infringement. Any judicial action interrupts the running of the limitation period. 14.133

The burden of proof lies on the claimants, who are required to prove the three following conditions: (i) fault; (ii) loss suffered by the claimant which must be direct, actual or foreseeable, and definite; and (iii) causal link between the fault and the loss. In 2010, the French Supreme Court ruled that no compensation is due if the claimant has passed on its loss to its client.[67] 14.134

The number of private actions has significantly increased in France in recent years. However, only a limited number of decisions awarding damages on the basis of antitrust infringements are publicly available. There are potentially many decisions of courts awarding damages but there is no system of centralized access to them. Also a very large number of disputes are settled out of court and there is no public information available on these private settlements. 14.135

On the basis of public decisions issued by French courts, the highest amount of damages granted to a private claimant was EUR 10 million for abuse of dominance.[68] With regard to cartel cases, the highest amount awarded to a claimant was EUR5.2 million for being excluded from a tender as a result of its competitor's anticompetitive practices.[69] 14.136

Since the assessment of harm and of its compensation is a question of fact, French judges have a large discretion to assess damages. 14.137

Class actions are not admissible yet. The only "collective" action currently allowed in France is the "joint representation" action, which allows approved consumer associations to bring an action on behalf of individuals who have suffered damages caused by the same practices (art. L.422-1 FCC). However, the conditions that must be satisfied for such action to be admissible are very strict and are strictly applied by courts. So far there are no cases in which a joint representation action as regards competition matters was eligible and succeed. In a decision dated May 26, 2011, the Supreme Court rejected the claim initiated by the association UFC Que Choisir. The Supreme Court considered that the association actually initiated the action instead of the individuals notably because it made appeal to the public by means of mass communication or personalized letter in order to initiate the claim.[70] 14.138

D. Follow-on litigation

The likelihood of private claims increases when there is a pre-existing decision of the FCA sanctioning an infringement of competition law. The majority of damages claims are such 14.139

[67] *Ajinomoto*, Supreme Court, Case no. 09-15.816 (June 15, 2010).

[68] *France Télécom Orange*, Paris Commercial Court, Case no. 2009073089 (March 30, 2011).

[69] *Mors S.A. v. Labinal S.A.*, Regional Court of Appeal, Paris, 1st chamber, Case no. 1998-022264 (September 30, 1998).

[70] *UFC Que Choisir*, French Supreme Court, Decision no. 10-15.676 (May 26, 2011).

follow-on litigation, since the proof of fault is not easy and in such cases the claimant can rely on the decision to establish fault.

14.140 However, a decision of the FCA, unlike European Commission decision is not binding.[71] In other words, the FCA decision is not sufficient to prove the fault.

E. Arbitration and alternative dispute resolution

14.141 Companies may raise competition law arguments in arbitration. An arbitral tribunal is bound to apply rules of competition law as they are matters of public policy. Moreover, if the arbitral award is not compliant with competition law, companies may seek to annul the award and/or oppose its enforcement on the grounds that it violates public policy. A large number of disputes are settled out of court, in particular as regards follow-on claims.

F. Remedies

14.142 Agreements and practices infringing antirust can trigger administrative, penal, and civil sanctions.

(i) Civil liability

14.143 The FCA may impose various types of sanctions for antitrust infringements. The limitation period is five years from the end of the infringement, but any FCA action interrupts the running of the limitation period. Additionally an action is time barred ten years after the end of the infringement if no decision of the FCA has been issued whatever steps are taken in the meantime.

14.144 The FCA can impose administrative fines of up to 10 percent of the highest worldwide consolidated turnover achieved by the infringing company in any one of the financial years preceeding the financial year before the implementation of the anticompetitive practices. Entities that are not undertakings, such as public bodies or natural persons, may be fined up to EUR 3 million. In 2011, FCA issued guidelines on the method of setting fines which is binding for the FCA. According to the guidelines, the FCA will in most cases rely on the turnover achieved by the company concerned on the relevant market during the last full year of the infringement. The basic amount of the fine will be constituted, depending on the seriousness of the infringement by a share of this turnover of up 30 percent for the first year of the infringement, and then apply a ratio of 0.5 for each additional year of this infringement. The FCA adjusts the basic amount downwards or upwards depending on aggravating and mitigating circumstances.

14.145 The FCA may also order infringing companies to cease their anticompetitive practices within a determined period or impose behavioral injunctions.

14.146 The FCA may also accept commitments proposed by the infringing company in order to remove the competition concerns. Like EU law commitments, these enable the FCA to close the case without a fine provided that the commitments bring an end to competition issues.

14.147 Periodic penalty payments of up to 5 percent of average daily turnover can also be imposed to compel a company to end an infringement. The FCA may also require publication of its decision.

14.148 Also, upon request by the Minister of Economy or by a company or a professional body, the FCA can impose interim measures if the practices at stake seriously and immediately harm the general economy, the economy of the sector concerned, the consumer interest, or the claimant's interest. The FCA may require the parties concerned to suspend the conduct, and to restore the original situation.

[71] French Supreme Court, Case no. 99-17251 (July 17, 2001).

In case of obstruction of an investigation by the FCA (including notably the supply of incorrect or incomplete or misleading information), the FCA may impose a fine of up to 1 percent of worldwide consolidated turnover. **14.149**

As regards small-scale anticompetitive practices, the Minister of Economy is empowered to order an undertaking to cease anticompetitive practices, notably when the market concerned is of local dimension. The Minister of Economy may also propose a fine settlement to the infringing parties (not exceeding EUR 75,000, or 5 percent of the turnover achieved by the infringing party in France). **14.150**

In addition, any agreement or provision which infringes article L.420-1 or L.420-2 FCC is void and unenforceable. **14.151**

(ii) Criminal liability

Individuals who fraudulently play a decisive role in the conception, organization, or implementation of anticompetitive agreements are liable to a maximum of four years of imprisonment and a fine of EUR 75,000. Companies may also be held criminally liable for a maximum fine of EUR 375,000. The FCA cannot impose a criminal sanction but it may pass the case file on to the French State Prosecutor's office for criminal courts to impose criminal sanctions. The State Prosecutor has no obligation to take legal action on receiving the file. **14.152**

With regard to criminal sanctions, case law has been rare and also rarely reported. In practice, cases prosecuted as a consequence of an anticompetitive behavior have been almost exclusively bid rigging cases. No case related to an abuse of dominant position has ever been brought to a criminal court. **14.153**

G. Leniency and immunity

Full or partial exoneration from fines may be granted by the FCA to an undertaking involved in certain anticompetitive practices, if it has contributed to establishing the existence and the extent of the concerted practices and to identifying those involved, by providing information that the FCA or the Minister for the economy did not previously know. While undertakings may apply to either the FCA or the DGCCRF, only the FCA is competent to grant full or partial exoneration of fines. **14.154**

The 2009 Procedural notice relating to the French Leniency Program indicates that the infringements concerned by the leniency program are those covered by article L.420-1 FCC and, where applicable, by article 101 TFEU. The Procedural notice targets in particular anticompetitive or cartel agreements between undertakings, which involve price fixing, or market sharing, including bid-rigging or any other similar anticompetitive behavior among competitors. Even though the FCA has not clearly stated that vertical agreements may be denounced to the FCA, the broad wording used in the law to describe the leniency applicant—"a company which, together with others, has implemented a practice prohibited by Article L.420-1"—suggests that this is possible. The leniency program does not apply to abuse of dominance. **14.155**

Full immunity is granted to the first company that provides information to the FCA, provided that the FCA does not already hold sufficient information on the reported anticompetitive practices to carry out an investigation. The information and evidence submitted by the applicant must be sufficient to carry out an investigation. The immunity applicant has to make a detailed corporate statement mentioning the legal entity applying for full immunity, the other members of the anticompetitive practices, a detailed description of the practices, information regarding any leniency application that has already been transmitted or is to be made to other competition authorities, and containing all relevant evidence in its possession. In order to minimize possible discovery risks under foreign laws, the statement is generally made orally. **14.156**

14.157 If the FCA already has information on the reported anticompetitive practices, the company may still be granted full immunity if no one had been granted immunity based on the above paragraph and if the company is the first to provide sufficient evidence to establish an infringement. However, full immunity cannot be granted to an undertaking which coerced another undertaking into participating in the infringement.

14.158 Applicants who are not the first, and do not meet the conditions for full immunity, may, subject to certain conditions, be eligible for a fine reduction proportional to the added value they provide; the reduction shall not exceed 50 percent. In order to determine the level of fine reduction, the FCA will take into account the added value—whether the evidence strengthens, by its nature and/or level of detail, the ability of the FCA to prove the existence of the alleged practices, and the ranking (date and time) of the applicant.

14.159 The Authority permits "markers" which temporarily guarantee the company's place in the leniency "queue." The undertaking applying for leniency will have to supply, at least, certain general information notably regarding the circumstances which led to its leniency application, the market sector concerned, the product(s)/service(s), and the anticompetitive practices. The applicant may be granted a time period—usually a few weeks—during which the position in the queue is maintained. During this period of time, the applicant must provide all relevant available information and evidence.

14.160 To qualify for immunity from fines or reduction, the applicant must in principle end its participation in the anticompetitive practice(s) immediately. However, the FCA may postpone this requirement in order to maintain confidentiality and to protect the effectiveness of the investigation. The applicant must cooperate on a continuous basis with the FCA, throughout the initial inquiry and the full investigation.

14.161 Full or partial exoneration from fines does not protect undertakings from the risk of private litigation.

14.162 Even though the leniency program does not cover personal criminal exposure, the FCA has undertaken not to request criminal prosecution of individuals whose employer company benefited from the leniency procedure. But the French State Prosecutor still has the power to instigate a procedure on its own volition.

14.163 The French leniency program has been very successful. To date, approximately sixty leniency applications (excluding the thirty-one summary leniency applications made in the framework of the European Competition Network) have been introduced by French and foreign companies. At the moment, only six leniency decisions have been issued by the FCA. The FCA will accept summary applications if the European Commission is particularly well placed to deal with the case and if the undertaking has filed or is about to file an application for full immunity with the European Commission.

H. Document creation and retention

14.164 There are no specific rules regarding the creation and the retention of documents.

14.165 However, the documents and emails must be cautiously created and written by any employers in order to avoid any misunderstanding in case of an FCA investigation or a dawn raid of competition authorities.

14.166 Even though there are no special rules, it is highly recommended for companies to define a clear retention or archiving policy.

15

GERMANY

Nadia Esken, Albrecht von Graevenitz, Dimitri Slobodenjuk, Miriam Kammer, Ruth Jorias, Tatjana Lemmens, and Achim Gronemeyer

German Antitrust Group
Clifford Chance

Introduction

The German antitrust regime is codified in the German Act against Restraints of Competition (ARC), first coming into force in 1958. During its existence, it was amended several times and is nowadays widely aligned with the European regulations, prohibiting both agreements between undertakings which restrict competition (see Section II) as well as the abuse of a market dominant position and other unilateral behavior (see Section I). In addition, it contains regulations with regard to diverse topics, such as merger control, competition rules of trade or industry associations, award of public contracts, as well as procedural aspects. **15.01**

The 8th amendment to the ARC, containing several changes and alignments to the European regulations especially with regard to the abuse of market dominance, several sector-specific regulations, as well as merger control, came into force on June 30, 2013. **15.02**

15.03 The German Federal Cartel Office (FCO) has been very active in recent years, conducting both proceedings in cartel prosecutions as well as in abuse cases. In 2012, the FCO imposed fines in fourteen cartel proceedings, in 2011 in as many as seventeen cartel cases. Affected economic sectors were, for example, stones and pipes, fire engines, railway rails, automatic door systems, power transformers, paper plates, mills, and hydrants. It is, however, impossible to draw a conclusion with regard to a potential focus of the FCO as most of the cartels were detected due to whistle blowers.

15.04 With regard to abuse proceedings, the FCO is regularly conducting investigations in energy-related industries such as power and gas supply, water supply, electricity wholesale, and district heating. Other sectors such as telecommunications, food retail, or retail banking have, however, been in the focus of the FCO as well.

I. Acting alone

15.05 In Germany, unilateral conduct can be caught by the prohibition of abuse of dominance, under ss. 18 ff. of the ARC.

15.06 While the definition of dominance in Germany is—since the coming into force of the 8th amendment to the ARC on June 30, 2013—to a great extent similar to the concept of dominance under EU competition law, some of the regulations on the behavior of dominant undertakings are stricter in Germany.

15.07 Sections 18 ff. ARC prohibit undertakings with a dominant market position to abuse this position.

15.08 A company is taken to be dominant if it is able to behave to an appreciable extent independently of its competitors or customers. Market share is an indicator of dominance. According to s. 18 (4) ARC, companies will be refutably deemed to be dominant, if they hold a market share of at least 40 percent. In addition, companies are deemed to have collective dominance if two or three undertakings have a combined market share of 50 percent, or if five or fewer undertakings together comprise two thirds of the market. The undertakings might, however, demonstrate that due to the specific market circumstances the dominance assumption of the ARC is not applicable to their case.

15.09 Whereas it is in itself not illegal for undertakings to have a dominant market position, it is illegal to abuse this dominant position. Undertakings having a dominant market position should not, as a general rule, engage in, among other practices, excessive, discriminatory, or predatory pricing; refuse to supply services or products and should exercise particular care when withdrawing its services from an existing customer; tie the sale of one product to the sale of another product; impose high penalty charges on its customers wishing to change suppliers; provide loyalty rebates except in certain circumstances; or impose exclusive terms on certain supply contracts.

15.10 Unlike at the EU level, in Germany, similar—and in some respect even stricter—rules might apply to non-dominant companies, insofar as small or medium-sized companies (SMEs) depend on them in such a way that the SME has no reasonable possibility of finding another trading (s. 20(1) ARC). One example is the manufacturer of well-known brand products whose products are a "must-have" for retail stores.[1] Companies facing obligations to SMEs

[1] *Adidas Sportschuhe*, Bundesgerichtshof (BGH), Case no. KZR 19/80 (June 30, 1981).

are described as having a "relative market dominance." However, undertakings having a dominant market position might also have a relative market dominance with regard to SMEs.

A. Predatory pricing

An abuse is assumed if undertakings with relative market dominance offer goods or commercial services below its cost price unless there is, in each case, an objective justification for this pricing.[2] Reference for the cost price is the net purchase price of the undertaking. Occasional below-cost pricing is allowed. **15.11**

For food retail, there is an even stricter regulation in place which prohibits even occasional offers below cost price, unless necessary to prevent the deterioration or the imminent unsaleability of the goods by promoting a timely sale, or for similarly convincing reasons. This special regulation for the food retail sector will terminate on December 31, 2017. **15.12**

B. Exploitative Offenses (excessive pricing, monopoly leveraging)

Excessive pricing by a dominant undertaking, i.e. if the undertaking demands payment or other business terms which differ from those which would very likely arise if effective competition existed, is prohibited by s. 19(2) ARC. The FCO especially compares the price or business terms to those imposed by undertakings in comparable markets, for example, neighboring regional markets in the electricity or gas retail markets, where effective competition prevails. Such a reference price, however, has to be significantly exceeded to constitute an abusive behavior. In contrast to the EU approach, under German competition law there is—apart from the below mentioned rules for the energy sector—no reference to cost price in excessive pricing cases. **15.13**

Section 29 ARC contains special rules for excessive pricing in the energy sector. It provides that the burden of proof is changed for administrative proceedings, so that an energy supplier (gas or electricity) has to prove that a deviation of its own prices from prices on a comparable market is objectively justified. In addition, s. 29 ARC prohibits energy suppliers from demanding fees which unreasonably exceed the costs, i.e. the FCO does not even need to compare the prices of an energy supplier with other prices but is allowed to conduct a pure cost analysis. **15.14**

C. Monopsony

The ARC does not differentiate between a dominant position on the purchasing markets or on the sales markets. Therefore, if a company holds a dominant purchasing position, an abusive conduct vis-à-vis its suppliers constitutes an abuse of its dominant position according to s. 19(2) ARC.[3] This also applies to companies having a relative market dominance. **15.15**

D. Price discrimination

Dominant undertakings are not allowed to charge less favorable prices (or offer less favorable terms) to similar customers in comparable markets, unless there is an objective justification for such differentiation. Such differentiation with regard to prices creates a presumption of abuse. **15.16**

It is, however, possible for the dominant undertaking to justify the differentiation. One of the justifications accepted by the courts is that lower prices may need to be offered to customers **15.17**

---

[2] *Netto Marken-Discount*, FCO, Case no. B 9–77/07 (October 25, 2007).

[3] In *Milchaustauschfuttermittel*, KG Berlin, Case no. Kart 35/82 (November 9, 1983), the court stated that a dairy cooperative abuses its dominant buying position if, by means of a reward system, it coerces its members to buy its own milk replacement feeds.

in a market which the undertaking tries to enter as a new player, though this justification is only temporary until the new entrant is settled.

E. Dictating or influencing resale prices

(i) Resale price maintenance

15.18 Over the last years, resale price maintenance (RPM) has been one of the enforcement priorities of the FCO. There have been several cases in which the FCO saw the seller's efforts to "convince" the purchasers of a certain non-binding price recommendation (NPR) as an illegal agreement on RPM and/or the illegal exertion of pressure. The authority issued several decisions imposing severe fines in this context. Based on these decisions and a letter issued by a panel of the FCO in April 2010 (never officially published, but publicly available[4]) it seems that in the view of the authority it takes very little to turn a legal NPR into illegal RPM, in particular in the relationship between producers/importers and wholesalers/retailers.

15.19 Under German law, RPM is dealt with looking at respective (vertical) agreements or concerted practices (this is similar to EU law) and/or looking at unilateral abusive practices the seller is using vis-à-vis its customers. In what follows these two possibilities are outlined.

15.20 In many cases, agreements or concerted practices on RPM risk being deemed by courts or authorities as an unjustified hard core restriction of competition, in particular as regards fixed or minimum prices, and in some cases also in relation to maximum prices. The respective legal provisions under German antitrust law and their interpretation are very near and partly identical to EU law. Thus, the interpretation of EU law by the European Commission and the EU courts heavily influences the interpretation of German law in this respect.

15.21 It should be noted that NPRs are deemed legal in this context, if the accompanying circumstances and conditions do not lead in effect to fixed or minimum prices. The same applies to vertical agreements not to exceed a certain maximum price, if the Block Exemption Regulation 330/2010 (BER)[5] is applicable. Even if the BER is not applicable, maximum RPM often has good chances to qualify as justified or *de minimis*.

15.22 Agreements on or concerted practices leading to fixed or minimum prices (i) are not exempted by the BER; (ii) make the BER inapplicable for the relevant overall agreement; and (iii) are presumed to be a restriction of competition which is likely not justifiable (regardless of the parties' market shares). However, there can be circumstances in which such agreements or concerted practices on RPM can be deemed legal as being *de minimis* or justified (as ancillary restraint or in the context of art. 101(3) TFEU). German courts and authorities are likely to take into consideration the Vertical Guidelines of the European Commission[6] in this respect, in which some limited scenarios of RPM are declared to be justifiable under certain circumstances.

15.23 As noted above, German law goes further than EU law as it does not only cover agreements and concerted practices on RPM; it also expressly prohibits unilateral pressure or the offer of inducements by the seller to reach (illegal) RPM (even if the seller is not market dominant or relatively dominant). The FCO applies this prohibition, for example, if a seller tries to force or induce their customers to resell the goods at the NPR price level.

---

[4] WuW 2010, 786.

[5] Commission Regulation 330/2010 on the application of Article 101(3) of the Treaty on the Functioning of the European Union to categories of vertical agreements and concerted practices (April 20, 2010), OJ L 102/1.

[6] European Commission, Guidelines on Vertical Restraints, SEC(2010) 411, paras. 223–229 ("Vertical Guidelines").

Given that RPM is deemed a hard core restriction, courts and authorities generally treat RPM with considerable skepticism, and there seems only narrow scope to argue for legality. Furthermore, companies need to thoroughly consider how to communicate in relation to their NPR as in view of the FCO the borderline towards illegal RPM is easily crossed. 15.24

(ii) Minimum advertised price programs

As is the case at the EU level, the German system in relation to RPM does not only cover direct agreements in relation to RPM, but also indirect measures and concerted practices. A German court or authority would check whether minimum advertised price (MAP) programs would lead directly or indirectly to effects of RPM and if the principles referred to in Section I.E(i) would apply. An obligation of a distributor not to advertise prices below a certain price level is very likely to be deemed as a measure of RPM. The FCO already fined companies for putting pressure on their retailers to apply a certain "recommended" price. 15.25

F. Tying arrangements

The definition of the term "tying" under German antitrust law does not significantly differ from the definition on the EU level. 15.26

The relevant theory of harm considered by the FCO is that an undertaking which is dominant in one product market (tying market) can harm consumers through tying or bundling products in that market with products in another separate market (tied market). This can lead to foreclosure concerns for competing products in the tied market. 15.27

In general, tying practices can also benefit from an objective justification.[7] Where the tying undertaking is dominant in both markets, the objective justification would not be possible, if the tying practice led to further stabilization of the market structure.[8] In any event, any potential foreclosure effects resulting from a particular tying practice have to be determined on a case-by-case basis. 15.28

G. Exclusive dealing

Exclusive obligations can be reached contractually, for example, if the customer is required to purchase his overall demand of the relevant products from the market-dominant undertaking.[9] Such exclusive purchase obligations are also referred to as "non-compete" obligations. However, exclusive dealing is also possible on a factual basis, for example via respective loyalty rebates.[10] 15.29

Many of the published decisions in Germany relating to exclusive dealing concern the gas supply sector. In this respect, a prohibited "exclusive purchase" obligation does not necessarily mean that 100 percent of the overall demand is purchased from the market-dominant supplier. In fact, depending on the duration of the particular arrangement, contractual obligations in the gas market under which the purchaser was required to purchase 50 percent of his overall gas demand for a period of four years, or 80 percent for two years, were found to infringe antitrust law provisions.[11] 15.30

---

[7] See *Strom und Telefon I*, BGH, WuW/E DE-R 1206 (November 14, 2003); *Strom und Telefon II*, BGH, WuW/E DE-R 1210 (November 4, 2003).

[8] *Stadtwerke Düsseldorf*, OLG Düsseldorf, WuW/E DE-R 2287 (April 16, 2008).

[9] *Fuchs Gewürze GmbH&Co*, FCO Case no. B2-12/00 (July 19, 2002).

[10] See Section I.J.

[11] *E-ON Ruhrgas*, BGH WuW/E DE-R 2679 (February 10, 2009), and *Stadtwerke Aachen*, OLG Düsseldorf WuW/E DE-R 854 (November 7, 2001).

15.31 Even though the decisional practice cited above relates to the infringement of s. 1 ARC, it can be assumed that the FCO and the competent courts would apply the same standards as regards the assessment of exclusivity clauses in cases referring to market dominance as well.

15.32 In any event, even if the exclusive dealing clause is not exempted under the BER, its inclusion in an agreement does not prevent the application of the block exemption to the rest of the agreement. In addition, an exclusivity clause which does not fall under the BER may still benefit from the individual exemption under s. 2 ARC and article 101(3) TFEU.

H. Refusal to deal

15.33 In general, any undertaking is free to choose its contractual partners. However, refusal to supply which is practiced by market dominant undertakings can constitute an abuse of a market dominant position.

15.34 A prohibited refusal to deal generally requires that the input which is being refused by the market dominant undertaking is indispensable to its customer, and that there are no other alternative sources available.[12] Refusal to supply can be objectively justified, a good example being a lack of creditworthiness of the customer. However, even if refusal to supply is objectively justified, it still has to be determined whether the supplies can be stopped immediately or only after a certain grace period.[13] In any event, refusal to supply would presuppose a comprehensive weighing of interests of both the supplier and the customer.[14]

15.35 Refusal to deal practiced by a non-dominant undertaking may infringe s. 1 ARC and article 101(1) TFEU if an undertaking uses refusal to deal or threatens to do so in order to enforce another prohibited practice. This is, for example, the case when the supplies to a distributor are cut off or limited simply because the distributor does not follow the resale price fixed by the supplier.

15.36 A separate form of abuse of a market dominant position under the German antitrust law regime, which closely relates to refusal to deal, is margin squeeze, also called price squeeze. In Germany, this form of abuse has been most prevalent in the telecommunications and fuel sectors. The latter was subject to a comprehensive sector inquiry by the FCO between 2008 and 2011, which lead to the respective investigations of the FCO against some of the market players.[15]

I. Essential facilities

15.37 Refusal to grant access to “essential facilities” constitutes a form of refusal to deal. The concept of essential facility is used mostly in cases relating to infrastructure such as electricity, railway, and telecommunication networks, or a port, airport, etc. The access to essential facilities can be denied directly, by expressly refusing access, or indirectly, for example, by demanding excessive fees.[16]

15.38 However, refusal to grant access may be objectively justified, for example due to the lack of capacities. Therefore, the holder of the essential facility is not obliged to grant access to third parties as long as his own demand for the respective infrastructure has not been satisfied.

---

[12] *Kälteanlagen-Ersatzteile*, KG, WuW/E OLG 4951 (January 23, 1992).

[13] *Ölbrenner I*, BGH, WuW/E BGH 1729 (February 12, 1980).

[14] *Sportschuhe*, BGH, WuW/E BGH 1885 (June 30, 1981).

[15] *Shell Deutschland/Lorenz Mohr*, FCO, Case no. B8-32/09 (May 8, 2009); *Rheinland Kraftstoffe/Honsel*, FCO, Case no. B8-31/09 (June 8, 2009).

[16] See *Reisestellenkarte*, BGH WuW/E DE-R 2708 (March 3, 2009).

In any case, the concept of essential facility is construed narrowly and requires a comprehensive weighing of interests of the parties involved on a case-by-case basis. **15.39**

J. Bundling (including loyalty and market share discounts)

Bundling closely relates to tying and presupposes a situation in which a market dominant undertaking sells two or more products below the total price it would charge for the products if they were bought separately.[17] The antitrust concerns described above in relation to tying practices fully apply to bundling as well. **15.40**

As for rebate schemes, the decisional practice in Germany relates to a wide range of practices which are considered to constitute abuses of market dominance. In general, the principles established at the national level in Germany are in line with those at EU level. An abuse of a dominant position is possible if the rebate schemes tend to exclude equally efficient competing suppliers. Where a rebate scheme induces a customer to make most or all of its purchases from the dominant company (so-called loyalty or fidelity rebate), in practice it will be difficult to avoid an infringement finding due to the likely foreclosure effects with regard to other suppliers of the same product. Individualized volume or value targets and retroactive rebate schemes in which the discounts apply on the condition that a certain level of purchases is reached within a certain reference period, for example, of one year, are also likely to be found to constitute an abuse of a market dominant position.[18] Such rebate schemes are often referred to as target rebates. **15.41**

However, standardized quantity rebates for individual deliveries which reflect gains in efficiency and economies of scale, or cash discounts for prompt payment, are generally unobjectionable. The same also applies to functional rebates. The commercial justification for these types of schemes is the fact that the customer is rewarded for the particular task(s) he has accepted. As indicated above, the main antitrust concerns resulting from rebate schemes relate to foreclosure of equally efficient competitors. This, in particular, applies to retroactive rebate schemes where the rebate amounts to a high proportion of the total purchase price.[19] In such cases, the purchaser will be inclined to continue to purchase the products from the dominant undertaking as he approaches the target threshold. **15.42**

K. Standard-setting groups (disclosure requirements, licensing arrangements, and licensing pools)

There are no guidelines or official statements of the FCO concerning the assessment of standard-setting activities under competition law. However, the FCO, although it is not obliged to take the European Commission's Horizontal Cooperation Guidelines into consideration, usually follows these Guidelines. Therefore, for the legal practice chapter 7 ("Standardisation Agreements") of the Guidelines serves as a starting point. **15.43**

Further, in a patents case that involved refusal to deal, the Federal Supreme Court held that a company may be given a compulsory license to use necessary intellectual property (IP) where (1) the prospective licensee has made an unconditional offer on usual market terms to the patent holder which the latter could not refuse without infringing the antitrust prohibition of discriminatory or impedimentary practices, and (2) the licensee complies with the conditions of his own offer, especially regarding the payment/deposition of the license fee.[20] **15.44**

---

[17] See e.g. *Zwangskombinationstarif II*, OLG Stuttgart, WuW/E OLG 2126 (April 30, 1979).

[18] *Fertigfutter*, KG, WuW/E OLG 2403 (November 26, 1980).

[19] *TUI-Partnerschaftsbonus*, KG, WuW/E OLG 3656.

[20] See *Orange Book Standard*, BGH, Case no. KZR 39/06 (May 6, 2009).

15.45 These conditions set by the Court also apply to rights which have become the subject of industry standards and which, therefore, are essential for the manufacture of certain products.[21]

L. Customer termination

15.46 The German Federal Supreme Court's case law with regard to customer termination is generally based on the idea that a company has a legitimate interest in freely designing its distribution system and its contractual relationships. Consequently, even long-term contractual relationships of a dominant undertaking may be ended if the undertaking intends to change its distribution system, for example switch from running its own distribution activities to distribution via sales agents.

15.47 However, besides the issue of termination, the length of the cancellation period applied is also subject to the German courts' review. Due to the general principle of prohibition of discrimination (ss. 19–20 ARC), an extended period for cancellation applies in cases where the (contractual) period of notice is inappropriately short. If, for example, an exclusivity clause within an agency agreement has the effect of economically binding the agent to his contractor (economic dependency)—especially because of large and specific investments made by the agent—the agent has a legitimate interest in regaining at least a part of the expenses in the course of the economic relationship. Therefore, German Courts usually grant the dependent party a sufficiently long period of time before the contract is brought to an end. The length depends on the individual case. Factors which are taken into account are the duration of the business relationship and the amounts invested in it, as well as the possibility of reutilizing these investments in other business relationships. However, in some cases, a period of one to two years was deemed to be reasonable.

M. Termination of intermediaries (retailers, wholesalers, dealers, and value-added resellers, agents, and brokers)

15.48 In principle, undertakings are free to restructure their distribution systems by terminating relationships with intermediaries. However, the termination of intermediaries can, under certain circumstances, be a version of the abusive refusal to deal.[22] Termination is therefore only permissible from a German antitrust perspective, if certain conditions are met. This includes in particular the obligation of the terminating undertaking to give notice of the termination sufficiently in advance in order to enable the intermediaries concerned to adapt their business to the intended changes.[23]

N. Termination of relationships with competitors

15.49 For terminating an agreement with a competitor the same principles apply as for the termination of an agreement with non-competitors.[24]

O. Exemptions

15.50 Section 2 ARC is the German equivalent of article 101(3) TFEU. The clause exempts agreements between undertakings, decisions by associations of undertakings, and concerted practices from the applicability of s. 1 ARC if the relevant behavior contributed to improving the production or distribution of goods or the promotion of technical or economic progress while allowing consumers a fair share of the resulting benefit. At the same time, no hardcore

[21] See *MPEG-2-Standard XXIII*, Regional Court of Düsseldorf, Case no. 4b O 54/10 (August 4, 2011).
[22] See Section I.H.
[23] See Section I.L.
[24] See Section I.L.

restriction may be justified in this way. The respective assessment has to be conducted by the parties to the relevant behavior, i.e. there is no guidance by the competition authorities.

Section 2 ARC, however, does not authorize the German competition authorities to grant general block exemptions. Section 2(2) ARC includes a dynamic referral to the European Commission's block exemption regulations. Therefore, the European block exemptions also apply to cases which are limited to Germany, without requiring a European dimension. **15.51**

Section 3 ARC contains special regulations for cartels of small or medium-sized enterprises. Those cartels whose subject matter is the rationalization of economic activities through cooperation among enterprises are exempted if the competition on the relevant market is not significantly affected and the agreement serves to improve the competitiveness of small or medium-sized enterprises. **15.52**

II. Dealing with competitors

Section 1 ARC prohibits agreements between undertakings, decisions by associations of undertakings, and concerted practices which have as their object or effect the prevention, restriction, or distortion of competition. As such, the section is generally aligned with European Competition law—article 101 TFEU. Similarly, s. 2 ARC corresponds to article 101(3) TFEU. **15.53**

In recent years, the FCO has had a particular focus on the investigation and prosecution of cartels. While between 1994 and 1997 only seven proceedings were initiated, the number increased to twenty proceedings between 2006 and 2009. In the year 2010, approximately EUR 255 million in fines were imposed on thirty-five companies in a total of eleven cases; in 2011, the FCO imposed EUR 193 million in fines on forty-two companies in a total number of seventeen cases; and in 2012, fines amounting to EUR 248 million were imposed on fifty-seven companies and thirty-one individuals in fourteen cartel proceedings. The highest cartel fines were imposed in *Cement*[25] where total fines amounted to EUR 660 million (the original fine was reduced by the Higher Regional Court Düsseldorf) and *Liquid gas*[26] with fines totaling EUR 250 million. More recent fines imposed in *Coffee*[27] and *Ophthalmic lenses*[28] amounted to EUR 159 million and EUR 115 million (because some cases, in particular in relation to *Liquid Gas* and *Ophthalmic lenses*, are still pending before court, not all of the fines are yet legally binding). **15.54**

Like the European Commission, the FCO has made increasing use of its settlement procedure in recent years by which proceedings are brought to an end more rapidly following confessions by the suspected undertakings. **15.55**

A. Horizontal price fixing (including advanced announcements of price or product changes)

As already indicated above, similar to EU level, horizontal price fixing always infringes s. 1 ARC and has been sanctioned by the FCO with severe fines. In the year 2010, the FCO imposed a fine of EUR 115 million on five leading producers of ophthalmic lenses in **15.56**

[25] *Cement*, press release FCO (April 14, 2003); in general confirmed by BGH WuW/E DE-R 3861 (February 26, 2013).

[26] *Liquid Gas*, FCO Case no. B11-20/05 (December 14, 2007; February 26, 2008; February 12, 2009; April, 9, 2009).

[27] *Coffee*, FCO Case no. B11-18/08 (December 18, 2009).

[28] *Ophthalmic lenses*, FCO Case no. B12-11/08 (May 28, 2010).

Germany, which had engaged in a price-fixing cartel, almost completely preventing any effective competition for years. The FCO was able to prove that, in 2005, the cartel members had disclosed the calculation model for their recommended retail prices, thus allowing them to fix prices for the next three years. The FCO proved that the cartel members had had regular meetings over a ten-year period in which information concerning rebates and conditions was exchanged.

15.57 Five months before that decision, the FCO had imposed a fine of EUR 159 million against three coffee roaster companies. The impetus for the investigations which led to this case was a leniency application by one of the undertakings which had participated in the cartel. The FCO was able to prove that the members of the cartels had had at least twenty meetings in a period of nine years which served as a forum to fix sale prices and special offer prices for their most important products. In both cases, cooperation with the FCO resulted in reduced fines at least for some of the undertakings involved.[29]

15.58 Most recently (January 2013), the FCO imposed fines of more than EUR 60 million on confectionary manufacturers, *inter alia*, for agreements on price increases for chocolate products.[30] The proceedings were initiated after a leniency application filed by one of the manufacturers. In February 2013, the FCO concluded proceedings against flour mills and imposed fines of approximately EUR 65 million on 23 milling companies for their involvement in illegal agreements in the sale of flour.[31] The FCO initiated the proceedings after receiving information from the market about agreements on prices and quantities.

B. Horizontal agreements to allocate customers or territories; agreements not to compete

15.59 As is the case with horizontal price fixing cartels, horizontal agreements allocating customers or territories have also been sanctioned by the FCO with severe fines. In March 2012, the FCO imposed a fine of EUR 30 million on a manufacturer of fire-engines[32] that was part of a price-and-quota cartel. Fines totaling EUR 20.5 million were imposed on three other manufacturers of fire-engines, the proceedings against which were ended by settlement in 2011.[33] Unlike most other cases, this procedure was not triggered by a leniency application but by an anonymous tip-off. The FCO was able to establish that the members of the cartel agreed both prices and quotas, thereby dividing the German market for fire engines and preventing price and rebate competition. One remarkable aspect was the involvement of an external accountant, who played an integral role by compiling data for the manufacturers in order to assure adherence to the agreements and who was also imposed a fine.

C. Horizontal boycotts

15.60 Under s. 21 ARC, undertakings or associations of undertakings are prohibited from requesting other undertakings not to purchase from, or supply to, specific third undertakings (which need not necessarily be a competitor of the undertaking launching such a request) with a view to damaging the latter in an unfair manner. It is important to note that the mere request to do so may be sufficient to infringe s. 21 ARC, provided that the relevant undertaking making such a request has the intention to damage the undertaking which is the addressee of the boycott in an unfair manner. This does not apply in cases where the launch of such request is

[29] See Section III.G.
[30] FCO, Case no. B11-11/08 (January 31, 2013).
[31] FCO, Case no. B11-13/06 (February 19, 2013).
[32] FCO, press release (March 7, 2012).
[33] FCO, Case no. B12-11/09 (February 10, 2011).

in the undertaking's legitimate interest, for example if the undertaking launching the request asserts a contractual claim because of an existing exclusivity agreement under which a certain territory is exclusively allocated to another supplier, or in case the boycott is targeted against illegal activity of another undertaking.

D. Joint ventures and other competitive collaborations

According to German law, joint ventures may be subject to both merger control and s. 1 ARC. If 25 percent or more of a company's shares are acquired simultaneously or consecutively by at least two undertakings, the acquisition is not only deemed the establishment of a joint venture within the meaning of s. 37(1) ARC but also a concentration on the part of the acquiring entities with regard to those markets where the acquired undertaking is active. Such fiction, referred to as a "partial merger" by the parent companies on the joint venture's market enables the FCO, when reviewing the notified merger, not only to deal with the vertical effects of the concentration but also with its horizontal effects, i.e. coordinated effects in relation to the parent companies' business conduct, which are to be assessed according to s. 1 ARC. **15.61**

In principle, in all joint venture cases that are subject to merger control reviews, the FCO will consider whether there are any indications that the parent companies will coordinate their future business conduct in an anticompetitive way. Such review will normally be superfluous if the parent companies are neither actual nor potential competitors. Moreover, the FCO normally refrains from initiating cartel proceedings if the combined market share of the parent companies does not exceed 10 percent. The same applies if it appears likely, in the view of the FCO, that an exemption under s. 2 ARC (corresponding to art. 101(3) TFEU) may be available. In the case that the FCO is not able to assess potential coordinated effects resulting from the proposed establishment of a joint venture *ex ante*, it will initiate separate cartel proceedings to assess compliance of the proposed joint venture with s. 1 ARC. **15.62**

E. Trade associations

Because they involve regular contacts between competitors, trade associations can be a natural and convenient forum for anticompetitive behavior. Meetings of trade associations, committees, or working parties between industry participants are perfectly legal under German law, but they become illegal if they lead or encourage the participants to coordinate their business activities and decisions, thereby infringing s. 1 ARC. In view of this, it is important that meetings of trade associations are not used as a forum to fix or even discuss prices (including components of prices such as discounts or allowances), recommended retail prices, trading terms, or customers with competitors, or to exchange any other commercially sensitive information. **15.63**

Before attending a trade association meeting, it is therefore advisable that the agenda of the meeting and other relevant documents are obtained and reviewed to be sure that the meeting does not involve any anticompetitive practices. Should such practices nevertheless occur, participants are certainly free to leave the meeting, which might indeed be advisable. However, in this case, they should make sure that their departure is recorded in the minutes of the relevant meeting to avoid any suspicion of being part of any anticompetitive practices. **15.64**

F. Interlocking directorates

Unlike in the US, there exists no explicit statutory rule under German competition law pursuant to which interlocking directorates between competitors are prohibited. Moreover, interlocking directorates as such have not so far been the subject of s. 1 ARC enforcement over the recent years. **15.65**

15.66 The main concern that could arise is the fact that the respective director usually becomes aware of information that might be competitively sensitive such as the content of the business plan, sales strategy, or any information regarding strategic acquisitions. The risk of such "exchange" of competitively sensitive information in breach of s. 1 ARC could be mitigated by implementing suitable measures. Such measures for instance include appointing only directors who are retired executive employees as they are no longer involved in the company's day-to-day management. In addition, such directors should be properly trained in competition compliance and information barriers should be established.

G. Facilitating practices

15.67 Unlike US antitrust law, German law does not treat "facilitating practices" as a specific infringement. Actions that would fall under the term "facilitating practices" as used in US practice (such as price fixing, exchange of competitively sensitive information, etc.) are, however, covered by the general principle of anticompetitive behavior within the meaning of s. 1 ARC.

H. Information exchange

15.68 An exchange of information—even one-way disclosure—might constitute an infringement of s. 1 ARC, should the information exchanged reduce or remove the degree of uncertainty as to the operation of the market player in question with the result that competition between undertakings is restricted. The underlying principle is that all market players must determine autonomously the policy which they intend to pursue on the market.

15.69 Whether an exchange of information might have the effect of restricting competition depends mainly on the type and sensitivity of information being exchanged. Information will generally be considered competitively sensitive if it enables the recipient to lessen its competitive efforts, because in practice it allows the recipient to predict the other party's or third parties' future market behavior.

15.70 As a rule of thumb, the more current and the more strategic the information provided is, the higher the risks will become that the disclosure/exchange of such information may infringe s. 1 ARC. The disclosure of data that is aggregated (i.e. grouped together to prevent identification of individual sales, specific customers, etc.), publicly available or historic (e.g. older than the average length of contracts in the industry, if the latter are indicative of price renegotiations) is unlikely to raise concern.

15.71 In recent years, the FCO has taken increased enforcement activity against information exchanges between competitors. In 2008 the FCO imposed a fine against four manufacturers of branded drugstore products and their sales managers for exchanging information about the state of annual talks with retailers.[34] Also in 2008, the FCO imposed substantial fines against nine manufacturers of luxury cosmetics for the implementation of an illegal market information system.[35] In relation to market information systems, the FCO found in its milk sector inquiry that the implementation of a market information system may infringe s. 1 ARC even if the participants do not automatically commit themselves to a certain behavior by participating in the information system. According to the FCO, the "mere" publication of milk prices in a trade journal, on the homepage of an association, or the collection and distribution of company-related information by the association to its members may constitute a concerted practice within the meaning of s. 1 ARC.[36] Further, even the exchange

[34] FCO Decision no. B 11-17/06 (February 19, 2008).

[35] "*Castle Round*," FCO, press release (July 10, 2008)

[36] *Milk Sector Inquiry*—Final Report, January 2012.

of information in vertical relationships may appear suspect to the FCO, if information is then passed on to a competitor of one of the parties (in what is known as a hub-and-spoke scenario).

As regards pre-merger activities, involved undertakings should be aware of potential risks emerging from information exchange. The exchange of competitively sensitive information from a target to a potential acquirer can to a certain extent be understandable as the potential acquirer needs information on the target business to evaluate the target and the transaction. Indeed, the exchange of competitively sensitive information can be justified on these grounds. However, any such possible justification needs to be carefully assessed on a case-by-case basis. Limiting disclosure to a "clean team" may help to mitigate the risk. **15.72**

I. Joint purchasing agreements

Joint purchasing agreements between competitors may lead to a restriction of competition under German antitrust law. The FCO approaches joint purchasing agreements in a similar way as the European Commission.[37] **15.73**

As such, joint purchasing agreements are assessed with regard to their objects and effects as any other agreement between competitors. According to the FCO's guidelines a restriction of competition is unlikely where the participating undertakings' combined market share does not exceed 15 percent on both the purchasing and the selling markets. **15.74**

Even if a joint purchasing agreement constitutes a restriction of competition, it may be exempted according to s. 2 ARC (particularly in the case of cartels of small and medium sized undertakings within the meaning of s. 3 ARC). **15.75**

The FCO examines joint purchasing cooperations thoroughly on a case-by-case basis, as such cooperations are often subject not only to general competition law but also to merger control law (e.g. in case of joint ventures). Current examples of the FCO's examination practice are the cooperation between RWE Group and Wasgau AG[38] and the strategic alliance between General Motors and Peugeot-Citroen.[39] **15.76**

Note that joint purchasing agreements are prohibited where they do not primarily concern joint purchasing, but instead serve as a tool to engage a disguised cartel. **15.77**

J. Joint lobbying/regulatory/legislative efforts

German antitrust law does not provide for special rules with regard to joint lobbying or joint regulatory and legislative efforts. It is not illegal if competitors jointly approach regulatory or legislative bodies. However, the background activities of such joint efforts may be illegal if they encourage the participating undertakings to infringe s. 1 ARC (e.g. by coordinating their business activities and decisions).[40] **15.78**

[37] See Commission Notice on agreements of minor importance which do not appreciably restrict competition under [Article 101 TFEU] (*de minimis*), OJ C 368 (December 22, 2001), and Bundeskartellamt, Information leaflet on the possibilities of cooperation for small and medium-sized enterprises (March 2007). <http://www.bundeskartellamt.de/SharedDocs/Publikation/EN/Merkblaetter/Leaflet%20-%20Cooperation%20for%20SMUs.html?nn=3591462>.

[38] FCO, press release (October 31, 2011).

[39] FCO, press release (October 26, 2012).

[40] See Section II.E.

III. General issues

A. Jurisdiction and applicable law (including sector-specific competition regulation)

15.79 German competition law governing cartels and abuse of a dominant position is set out in the ARC. The principal rules on cartels are found in ss. 1 and 2 ARC. Since these rules effectively mirror article 101(1) and (3) of the TFEU, the same standards as under the TFEU are generally applicable under German law. Section 1 ARC prohibits all agreements, concerted practices, or decisions by associations of undertakings, which have as their object or effect the restriction of competition. The abuse of a dominant position is prohibited by s. 19 ARC. In addition, discrimination and unfair hindrance by dominant undertakings and certain non-dominant undertakings with superior market power is restricted by s. 20 ARC. Hence, the German rules governing unilateral conduct are to some extent stricter than their EU counterpart (art. 102 TFEU).

15.80 The provisions of the ARC apply to all restraints of competition having an appreciable effect within Germany (s. 130(2) ARC). To the extent that the German market is affected, foreign undertakings might therefore be subject to German antitrust law even if they do not have offices or direct business activities in Germany.

15.81 The ARC applies to both private and public entities irrespective of their legal form. However, there are several exemptions and specific provisions for certain industry sectors. The prohibition of cartels does not apply to distinct agreements in the agricultural sector, the water industry and as regards the wholesale of newspapers and magazines. An industry specific provision regarding the abuse of dominance applies to suppliers of electricity or natural gas.

B. Antitrust system

(i) Name of agency/agencies

15.82 The enforcement of the national competition rules primarily falls within the remit of the FCO, based in Bonn. The FCO is a higher federal agency below the Federal Ministry of Economics and Technology which takes its decisions through 12 Decision Divisions which are organized along industry sectors. Apart from the FCO, there are state cartel offices (*Landeskartellämter*) at the level of the different federal states (*Bundesländer*) prosecuting competition law infringements with effects limited to a specific federal state. In practice, their role is limited to very few cases in particular with a local nexus. In addition, the Federal Network Agency (*Bundesnetzagentur*) is competent for assuring non-discriminatory access to networks in the energy, gas, telecommunications, postal, and railway markets. Finally, criminal prosecution of cartel offenses involving bid-rigging or fraud relating to bids lies within the responsibility of the public prosecutor.

(ii) Staff size and budget

15.83 The FCO's annual budget was EUR 25 million in 2012. Its total number of staff is approximately 320, comprising 223 staff working on competition enforcement (58 percent lawyers, 36 percent economists, and 6 percent others).

(iii) Recent enforcement actions and trends

15.84 Cartel enforcement remains the main priority of the FCO. It carried out fourteen dawn raids and issued fourteen cartel decisions with total fines of EUR 248 million against fifty-seven companies and thirty-one individuals in 2012. At the structural level, it added another specialist cartel unit (its third pure anti-cartel division) and recruited IT analysts as well as former state prosecutors, demonstrating clearly that cartel enforcement will remain an enforcement focus. In addition, the FCO set up an electronic whistle blowing system allowing it to receive anonymous tip-offs of competition law infringements via the internet. The whistle blowing system offers the possibility of continuing reciprocal communication via a secure electronic mailbox while guaranteeing full anonymity of the informer. The FCO also intensified its efforts to prosecute bid-rigging and its cooperation with the public prosecutors.

The FCO continues to carry out sector inquiries in order to get an insight into market activities and structures of specific markets suspected to be restricted or distorted. Recently, investigations have been conducted in the milk, rolled asphalt, district heating, food retail, fuel, refineries, and oil wholesale sectors. Sectoral priorities of the FCO in 2012 were TV rights for the German Soccer League, water supply, food retail, fuel, and manufacturing. **15.85**

The 8th amendment to the ARC came into effect on June 30, 2013. Key changes pertaining to antitrust enforcement include a clarification of successors' liability for infringements committed prior to a restructuring and the right to plead of consumer and industry associations in private litigation. **15.86**

C. Private litigation

Third parties who suffered a loss due to, or are affected by, an anticompetitive agreement or conduct are entitled to claim damages or injunctive relief pursuant to s. 33 ARC. This includes indirect customers, which have a right to bring damage actions in their own name. The passing-on defense is in principle available under German competition law. In addition, under certain circumstances, damage claims and claims for injunctive relief may also be based on the German Act against Unfair Competition and the German Civil Code. **15.87**

According to the 8th amendment to the ARC, consumer associations and industry associations representing customers or suppliers of an undertaking that has violated competition law shall have the right to bring actions requesting remediation or injunctive relief. **15.88**

In order to encourage private litigation, the FCO has intervened as amicus curiae in several private enforcement actions at Federal Supreme Court level. It has also begun to offer specialist training on competition economics to judges. **15.89**

D. Follow-on litigation (includes role of agency determinations of liability for follow-on litigation)

The findings by the FCO are binding on the judge in civil damages proceedings. The passing-on defense is in principle available under German competition law. **15.90**

E. Arbitration and alternative dispute resolution

Under German law, there are no explicit provisions regarding competition matters in arbitration. However, as the competition rules set out in the ARC are compulsory under German law, arbitrators are required to apply those rules in their arbitral awards. **15.91**

F. Remedies

(i) Civil liability

The FCO may impose an administrative fine on undertakings, associations of undertakings or individuals who violate intentionally or negligently the prohibitions of sections referred to in s. 81(4) ARC. In this respect, the FCO just recently amended and republished guidelines on the method of setting fines (June 25, 2013). The guidelines apply to horizontal and vertical restraints of competition as well as unilateral anticompetitive behavior (e.g. abusive practices, unfair hindrance, or boycott). **15.92**

According to the guidelines, the FCO has to set the fine within the statutory framework of fines. According to the statutory framework, the FCO has to set the actual amount of the fine **15.93** in a range between EUR 5 to 10 percent of the worldwide annual turnover achieved by the infringing company including its affiliates. Within this general framework, the FCO sets its fine based on gain and harm potential on the one side and the total turnover of the company on the other. According to its guidelines, the FCO assumes a gain and harm potential of 10 percent of the company's turnover achieved from the infringement during the infringement period, while the turnover achieved from the infringement is the domestic turnover achieved from sales of products and services connected with the infringement over the duration of the infringement. If the expected turnover was not achieved, the FCO uses the turnover the company would probably have achieved without the infringement or the unforeseen course of development to determine the gain and harm potential. Regardless of the actual duration of the infringement, the FCO bases its calculation on a period of twelve months in cases in which the infringement lasted less than twelve months. After establishing the gain and harm potential, the FCO will apply a multiplication factor to account for the size of the respective company. The multiplier used is dependent on the turnover achieved by the company. For instance, if the total turnover achieved by the company was between EUR 10 and EUR 100 billion, a factor of 5–6 will be applied. The scope for setting fines will not be limited by the FCO within the general framework. As an exception, the determined value can be exceeded if this value is obviously too low in the specific case because of a significantly higher gain and harm potential. Within the scope of setting a fine, the FCO also takes into account s. 81(4) sentence 6 ARC and s. 17(3) Code of Administrative Offenses. These are aggravating or mitigating factors concerning offense-related criteria and offender-related criteria. Therefore, such factors as the duration and gravity of the infringement, its effects on the market, the market position of the participating undertakings, and the size and significance of the market affected will also be taken into account. Furthermore, an increase of fine may be permitted in cases of recidivism and serious forms of deliberate intent or if the undertaking concerned played a particularly active role within the cartel like an initiator or ringleader. Individuals (directors and executive employees only) can be fined up to a maximum of EUR 1 million.

15.94 Any positive post-offense behavior in the form of a leniency application is considered by the FCO in a separate stage. Finally, a reduction may be granted if a settlement agreement was reached.

15.95 Apart from fines, the FCO may also confiscate the economic benefit gained by the infringement of competition law (ss. 34 ff ARC) and/or issue an administrative order imposing measures to bring the infringement to an end, for example by means of an administrative order to end the concerted practice in question (s. 32 ARC). Furthermore, the FCO may declare certain commitments offered by the undertakings concerned to be binding (s. 32b ARC). As regards the validity of anticompetitive agreements, contractual provisions violating competition law are null and void.

(ii) Criminal liability

15.96 Under the ARC, the infringement of competition rules constitutes an administrative offense. Therefore, the FCO may not impose criminal sanctions on undertakings or individuals involved in an anticompetitive conduct. However, ss. 263 and 298 of the German Criminal Code impose criminal liability for individuals involved in fraud related to bids or bid rigging. These criminal offenses are punishable by imprisonment or fine. It should be mentioned, that the FCO must refer any proceedings against natural persons to the public prosecutor if the infringement constitutes a criminal offense.

G. Leniency and immunity

15.97 The FCO set up a leniency program under which it may grant companies involved in a cartel immunity from or reduction of fines if they make a decisive contribution to uncover the cartel and cease their anticompetitive behavior. The conditions for immunity or reduction of fines are defined in the FCO's Leniency Notice.[41] In 2012, the FCO received a total of fifty-one leniency applications in thirty-seven proceedings.

The leniency program applies to undertakings, associations of undertakings, and natural persons participating in a cartel (in particular agreements on the fixing of prices or sales quotas, market sharing, and bid-rigging). By way of analogy, the FCO also applies the leniency notice to all kinds of vertical restraints of competition. Corporate leniency applications may be extended to employees involved in the cartel. In this case, the employees may equally benefit from immunity or reduction of fines provided that they immediately cooperate in uncovering the cartel. **15.98**

The conditions to be met for full immunity differ, depending on whether or not the FCO already has sufficient knowledge of a cartel. If the FCO has not yet sufficient evidence to obtain a search warrant at the time of the leniency application, it will grant a cartel participant full immunity if it: **15.99**

- is the first to contact the FCO,
- provides sufficient information or evidence which enables the FCO to obtain a search warrant,
- was not the only ringleader of the cartel and did not coerce others to participate in the cartel, and
- cooperates fully and continuously with the FCO.

If a cartel participant contacts the FCO at a time when it already has sufficient evidence in the case at hand to obtain a search warrant, the FCO will generally not impose a fine on the cartel participant in case: **15.100**

- it is the first to contact the FCO before it has sufficient evidence to prove the existence of the cartel,
- it provides sufficient information or evidence which enables the FCO to prove the cartel offense,
- it was not the only ringleader of the cartel and did not coerce others to participate in the cartel,
- it cooperates fully and continuously with the FCO and
- no other cartel participant has already been granted full immunity pursuant to the procedure described above in para. 15.99.

If the conditions for immunity are not met, the FCO may reduce the fine by up to 50 percent if the cartel participant: **15.101**

- provides sufficient information or evidence which makes a significant contribution to prove the cartel offense and
- cooperates fully and continuously with the FCO.

The amount of reduction depends on the value of the contribution to uncovering the cartel offense and the rank of the leniency application. Undertakings wishing to take advantage of the leniency program should therefore apply for leniency as early as possible. In order to save the rank of the application, the applicant may place a "marker" by declaring its willingness to cooperate. The marker can be placed verbally or in writing, in German or English. Within a given time of putting down a marker, the undertaking must provide information on the type and duration of the infringement, the product and geographic markets affected, the identity of the cartel participants, and at which other competition authorities leniency applications **15.102**

[41] FCO Notice No. 9/2006 of March 7, 2006 ("Leniency Notice").

have been or are intended to be made. If the leniency applicant does not fulfill these obligations within the time limit set by the FCO, he loses his rank and the subsequent applicants move up.

15.103 According to the leniency notice, the FCO will—within the scope of statutory limits—protect the identity of the leniency applicant and business secrets contained until it issues a statement of objection to one of the cartel participants. As regards third-party access to leniency applications in order to prepare a civil action for damages, the FCO refuses such access to guarantee the effectiveness of the leniency program. Recently, the Local Court of Bonn[42] confirmed the lawfulness of such refusal after it referred the matter to the Court of Justice of the European Union[43] seeking clarification on whether European competition law prohibits the disclosure of leniency applications to victims of a cartel. The Local Court upheld the refusal of the FCO arguing that the threat to the effective detection and prosecution of cartels justified denying the access to the leniency applications. This judgment is in line with a decision of the Higher Regional Court of Düsseldorf which also denied third parties access to leniency material.[44] However, these legal opinions have not been adopted in the 8th amendment to the ARC. Therefore, third-party access to leniency material is still to be decided by the courts on a case-to-case basis, while the status quo is that disclosure will not be granted.

15.104 The leniency program has no effect on private enforcement of competition law and it does not grant immunity from enforcement of criminal offenses (such as bid rigging or fraud relating to bids).

H. Document creation and retention

15.105 Under German competition law, there are no explicit provisions regarding document creation and retention. However, although there is no general obligation to retain documents containing incriminating evidence of infringements of competition law, the destruction of such documents is prohibited in proceedings concerning administrative fines once the FCO issued a formal request for information (s. 81(2) ACR). Furthermore, it should be noted that the destruction of evidence may deprive the undertaking of the possibility of benefitting from immunity or a reduction of fine by filing a leniency application if it is therefore unable to provide the FCO sufficient information or evidence of the infringement.

[42] AG Bonn 51 Gs 53/09.

[43] Case C-360/09 *Pfleiderer* [2011] ECR I-05161.

[44] OLG Düsseldorf, Case no. V-4 Kart 5/11 (August 22, 2012).

16

GREECE

Gregory M. Pelecanos, Nancy G. Gerakinis, and Andrew T. Themelis
Ballas Pelecanos & Associates L.P.C.

Introduction

According to article 1 of Law 3959/2011, all agreements between undertakings, all decisions by associations of undertakings, and concerted practices which have as their object or effect the prevention, restriction, or distortion of competition in the Greek territory are prohibited and, in particular, those which: **16.01**

- directly or indirectly fix purchase or selling prices or any other trading conditions;
- limit or control production, markets, technical development, or investment;
- share markets or sources of supply;
- apply dissimilar conditions to equivalent transactions with other trading parties, thereby placing them at a competitive disadvantage, in particular by refusing without valid justification, to sell, purchase, or conclude any other transaction; or

- make the conclusion of contracts subject to acceptance by other parties of additional obligations which, by their nature or according to commercial usage, have no connection with the object of such contracts.

16.02 The prohibition covers both horizontal and vertical agreements. The first category ("cartels") is generally regarded to encompass more "serious" violations. As far as the second category is concerned, the EU block exemption regulations (see also para. 16.05) also apply in Greece. Within the said category, the restriction of passive sales and resale price maintenance (RPM) are two types of practice which raise the most concerns.

16.03 Under article 1(3) of Law 3959/2011, the provisions of article 1(1) may not apply where the disputed agreement between undertakings, decision by associations of undertakings, or concerted practice, actually contributes to improving the production or distribution of goods or to promoting technical or economic progress, while allowing consumers a fair share of the resulting benefit, and does not:

- impose on the undertakings concerned restrictions which are not indispensable to the attainment of these objectives;
- afford such undertakings the possibility of eliminating competition in respect of a substantial part of the products in question.

16.04 Until the enactment of the new competition law (Law 3959/2011), the system of self-assessment was partially adopted in Greece, and a mandatory notification system was in place (as per art. 21 of Law 703/77). The new law has signified the end of this formality and the automatic exemption, so long as the above requirements are (cumulatively) met. The onus of (self-)assessment lies with the undertakings involved.

16.05 Lastly, paragraph 4 of Law 3959/2011 states that all EU regulations relevant to the application of article 101(3) TFEU (i.e. in relation to the block exemption) will accordingly apply to agreements and decisions which are not likely to affect inter-state trade. Essentially, this provision states that the relevant EU regulations also apply in Greece.

16.06 Article 2 prohibits any abuse by one or more undertakings of a dominant position, within the national market or in a part of it. Such abuse may, in particular, consist in:

- directly or indirectly imposing unfair purchase or selling prices or other unfair trading conditions;
- limiting production, markets or technical development to the prejudice of consumers;
- applying dissimilar conditions to equivalent transactions with other trading parties, thereby placing them at a competitive disadvantage;
- making the conclusion of contracts subject to acceptance by the other parties of supplementary obligations which, by their nature or according to commercial usage, have no connection with the subject of such contracts.

16.07 The particular type of abuse of dominance may vary. Every case needs to be evaluated on the basis of its own particular factual background and the competition "map" of the relevant market.

16.08 The Hellenic Competition Commission (HCC) has constructed a set of priorities for the enforcement of competition policy centered on the basic criterion of serving the public interest—this appears to have a particular significance in a period where the Greek market experiences a deep and long recession. Hence, competition policy in Greece has prioritized anticompetitive practices that especially affect end consumers. In achieving this, primary emphasis is given on cases that raise issues of hardcore restrictions of competition; which affect products and services of essential or major importance to Greek consumers; and which affect prices and may have cumulative effects. As such, competition policy in Greece is applied under a certain unique set of criteria which derive from the abovementioned consumer-centric context.

I. Acting alone

Greek law does not provide for a definition of dominance. The HCC follows the path laid down by the EU case-law. Accordingly, the criteria of (i) market share (possibly > 40–50 percent) and (ii) the capacity of an undertaking to act independently of competitors and customers are crucial. Of course, several other factors will be taken into consideration, including barriers to entry, etc. The HCC will assess the instances of abuse on the basis of the established principles of EU case law. In terms of "acting alone," rebates and resale price maintenance are the main areas of enforcement by the HCC. **16.09**

A. Predatory pricing

Predatory pricing covers cases when the dominant undertaking deliberately incurs losses ("sacrifice"), in order to foreclose or be likely to foreclose actual or potential competitors with a view to strengthening or maintaining its market power.[1] **16.10**

The said conduct entails a sacrifice if, by charging a lower price for all or a particular part of its output over the relevant time period, the dominant undertaking is incurring losses that could have been avoided. Proper assessment of such a conduct presupposes a careful cost analysis. The average avoidable cost (AAC) (average variable cost according to *AKZO* case)[2] is the appropriate starting point for assessing whether the dominant undertaking is incurring avoidable losses. If a dominant undertaking charges a price below AAC for all or part of its output, it is not recovering the costs that could have been avoided by not producing that output: it is incurring a loss that could have been avoided. Other than that, each case needs to be examined on an *ad hoc* basis, in the framework of the exact competition conditions of each market. **16.11**

The HCC has not yet ruled on a predatory pricing case, although it is to be noted that the pricing of various bundles of products/services (multi-product rebate schemes) offered by the dominant telecommunication operator are quite frequently under the review of the national regulator—the Hellenic Communications and Post Commission (EETT)—which has rejected various such offers as constituting an abusive practice. Usually, this abusive practice is related to predatory pricing and/or margin squeeze, for example, Decision no. 601/18 of the EETT of April 28, 2011 which prohibited a bundle of products/services (the offer was for the provision of broadband internet connectivity to the speed of 2 Mbps for the period of 6+6 months), since its pricing was considered as constituting predatory pricing and margin squeeze. **16.12**

Sales below cost are also regulated by Greek Law 146/14, as amended "on unfair competition," which prohibits any unfair competitive act. **16.13**

B. Exploitative offenses (excessive pricing, monopoly leveraging)

Article 2 of Law 3959/2011 prohibits a dominant company from abusing its position through imposing excessive prices. The European Community courts have in the past dealt with such cases and the HCC has in a number of occasions relied on these cases. **16.14**

[1] TFEU, art. 102 and Law no. 3959/2011, art. 2.

[2] Case C-62/86 *AKZO v. Commission* [1991] ECR I-3359.

16.15 In a relatively recent decision the HCC rejected the complaint by a number of aeroclubs against EKO (a petroleum company) for allegedly abusing its dominant position through pricing excessively a specific type of fuel for airplanes.[3] The HCC applied the two-stage (cumulative conditions) test on excessive pricing deriving from the *United Brands* case,[4] and concluded that EKO's conduct did not satisfy the first limb of the test, namely that the price difference between EKO's costs and pricing of its customers was neither significant nor was there a significant profit margin available for EKO.

16.16 More recently, in its Decision 528/VI/2011,[5] the HCC—again applying the test in *United Brands* and in *Scandlines Sverige AB*[6]—similarly rejected the complaint made by the Hellenic Army General Staff in relation to the alleged excessive pricing by two maritime transportation companies. The HCC considered the pricing of the two companies in a number of cases and concluded that the higher costs charged by them were not at such a high level that could (compared to other cases on excessive pricing, e.g. *British Leyland*)[7] be considered as constituting an abuse and which could not possibly be objectively justified.

C. Monopsony

16.17 Article 2 of Law 3959/2011 also applies upon conduct by undertakings which are in a dominant position as a buyer, similar to relevant EU case law. It needs, however, to be noted that the creation of such a dominant buyer entity is not prohibited. Quite the opposite, very recently, the Greek state created such a body within the healthcare provision market—the National Organization for Health Care Provision (EOPYY)—in an attempt to enhance price and quality based competition in this sector of the economy. There have not been any monopsony cases yet.

D. Price discrimination

16.18 Article 2 of Law 3959/2011 mirrors article 102 TFEU, and hence it also expressly prohibits both price and non-price discrimination by dominant undertakings.

16.19 Finding that a dominant company has abused its position through discriminatory practices is, of course, not an easy task, especially given that various other factors may well justify the reason behind the difference in the treatment of customers (e.g. lower prices achieved through volume discounts). A relatively recent case on this issue that the HCC had to decide upon, following a complaint by a Greek political party against two companies operating in this sector, was related to the petroleum/fuel market. The complaint was related to the alleged cartel operated by two major petroleum companies (Hellenic Petroleum and Motor Oil) and/or the abuse of dominance; the absolute price alignment; the discriminatory treatment of smaller trading companies in relation to discount policies (i.e. that smaller companies receive far smaller discounts compared to those received by the bigger company—Shell); and on issues related to the lack of transparency in the cost data of the companies/refineries.[8]

16.20 In its Decision, the HCC considered that in relation to the alleged discriminatory conduct, the relevant EU case law on article 102 TFEU, does not prohibit volume discounts. The HCC considered that the discount policy concerned was not related to the Hellenic Petroleum company but to another company—Petrola. Hellenic Petroleum acquired Petrola

---

[3] HCC Decision no. 489/VI/2010 (May 7, 2010).

[4] Case 27/76 *United Brands Company and United Brands Continentaal BV v. Commission* [1978] ECR 207.

[5] HCC Decision no. 528/VI/2011 (September 29, 2011).

[6] *United Brands* (n 4); *Scandlines Sverige AB v. Port of Helsingborg*, COMP/A.36.568/D3 (July 23, 2004).

[7] Case 226/84 *British Leyland plc v. Commission* [1986] ECR 3263.

[8] HCC Decision no. 502/VI/2010 (July 21, 2010).

in 2003 (a company which was not in a dominant position) while these contested discounts were given. The latter's discount policy was a volume discount policy known in advance and applied uniformly to all its customers, based on the economies of scale logic of operation. According to the HCC, the relative variation in the increments between Shell and the other smaller companies were justified since Shell was the larger customer.

E. Dictating or influencing resale prices

(i) Resale price maintenance

Fixed or minimum RPM (i.e. a supplier imposing upon a distributor the products' resale price or setting the minimum price they are to be sold) is considered a serious infringement of article 1 of Law 3959/2011 similar to article 101 TFEU. A maximum or recommended price will not infringe the competition provisions, provided of course that they do not essentially operate as fixed or minimum prices. **16.21**

The former forms of RPM are also caught by the Block Exemption Regulation 330/2010 (BER) as it is considered as a hard core restriction, no matter what the market share of the relevant company is (i.e. even if very low). It is essential to also note that RPM does not necessarily have to be direct; the relevant competition provisions will also be infringed by indirect methods of imposing the resale prices. Nonetheless, the new Guidelines of the BER provide—for the first time—certain examples where RPM could potentially be found to generate efficiencies as a defense. **16.22**

In Greece, the HCC has previously ruled on RPM in several cases. In its Decision 370/V/2007 on spare parts for cars,[9] the HCC found an infringement of article 1 (of the then Law 703/1977) and of article 101 TFEU (then art. 81 EC) and fined a Greek car dealer. However, it is to be noted that the HCC's Decision has been appealed and is currently pending. **16.23**

(ii) Minimum advertised price programs

See above, the discussion in subsection (i) on Resale Price Maintenance. The concept of minimum advertised price (MAP) (in any form, including Internet operated MAP (IMAP)) can be covered by rules on RPM which prohibit both direct and indirect methods of fixing the price or setting a minimum price. **16.24**

F. Tying arrangements

Articles 101(1) (e) and 102(d) TFEU prohibit making a contract conditional on accepting supplementary obligations unrelated to the contract. **16.25**

Pricing practices which have a tying effect could lead to an abuse of the dominant position. The HCC will normally take action where the undertaking is dominant in the tying market and where, in addition: (a) the tying and tied product are distinct products and (b) the tying practice is likely to lead to anticompetitive foreclosure. The anticompetitive foreclosure is assessed under the "as efficient competitor" test. If the "as efficient competitor" who offers only some of the components cannot compete against the discounted "bundle", the rebate scheme may be anticompetitive on the tied or tying market. **16.26**

In the past, tying and bundling practices have been considered by the HCC, for example, in Decision 434/V/2009 which is discussed in Section I.J, and the relevant legislative framework and EU case law is always applied by the EETT as part of its review on offers of "bundles" of products/services in the telecoms sector. **16.27**

[9] HCC Decision no. 370/V/2007 (November 29, 2007).

G. Exclusive dealing

16.28 According to recent case law, a dominant company's practice to provide cabinets on the basis of exclusivity aimed at capturing the available space at smaller retail shops (e.g. kiosks) and raising entry/expansion barriers, to the exclusion of competition and rebates conditional upon the commitment of all or the most substantial part of available shelf/store space for its products, has been held to be a prohibited abusive conduct.[10]

H. Refusal to deal

16.29 Refusal to deal is generally considered abusive, as it limits the customers' operations and prevents access of other competitors to the market of a certain product or service.

16.30 A refusal to supply may be justified by the right of the dominant undertaking "to take such reasonable steps as it deems appropriate to protect its [commercial] interests," although "such behavior cannot be countenanced if its actual purpose is to strengthen this dominant position and abuse it."[11] In other words, the refusal to supply may be legitimate as a commercial response to competitors' attacks, but it must be proportionate to the threat, taking into account the economic strength of the undertakings confronting each other.

16.31 Even if a refusal to supply/deal is deemed not to fall within the restrictions of article 2 of Law 3959/2011 because it is justified, it may still be considered abuse of right according to the general provisions of the Greek Civil Code.

I. Essential facilities

16.32 In its Decision no. 317/V/2006,[12] the HCC found that the company with the exclusive rights of management of the Canal of the Isthmus of Corinth (which is an essential infrastructure) had acted in a manner abusive of its dominant position. The company had the right to set and collect tolls for the passage of vessels from the Canal, while it also had the right to operate as a provider of "bateau mouche" cruises. The company gradually took advantage of this ability and became active "downstream" the market in the relevant geographic area of the Isthmus.

16.33 The abusive conduct came by way of both adjusting and setting the level of fees as well as setting a new categorization of vessels in such a way so as to make it particularly onerous for competing companies to operate in the relevant market for these cruises. The company raised the tolls by 852 percent, and although this was uniformly applied to all passenger vessels, the frequency of the cruises was a factor not taken into consideration. Hence, these arrangements particularly affected those smaller providers of similar Canal cruises which had to pass more frequently from the Isthmus than other passenger vessels, and which could not bear such huge costs resulting from the increased tolls, whilst the dominant company was not paying the tolls. The HCC considered that the dominant company could not use its power resulting from its exclusive right to manage the Canal and to set the tolls so as to further strengthen its position in another relevant market and to make it less favorable for competitors to operate in the same market. The HCC therefore ordered the company to cease its abusive practices and to re-adjust the relevant tolls.

J. Bundling (including loyalty and market share discounts)

16.34 Since tying is a form of bundling, the terms are often used interchangeably. Tying can be seen as a special type of bundling.

---

[10] HCC Decision no. 520/VI/2011 (May 5, 2011); see also the HCC's Press Release on this Decision (in English) available at: <http://www.epant.gr/img/x2/news/news399_1_1328713831.pdf>.

[11] *United Brands* (n 4).

[12] HCC Decision no. 317/V/2006 (July 28, 2006).

Moreover, fidelity rebates (namely cases when, in order to obtain the rebate on past purchases, the customer is unable to switch for future purchases to other suppliers) and loyalty rebates (namely rebates conditional on the customer buying all or most of his requirements from the supplier) foreclose the market and discriminate between dealers. Both can come in various forms and combinations based on the ingenuity of the deviser of the scheme.[13] **16.35**

Target rebates are a particular case. A rebate is given if the customer reaches an individually specified sales target. Most schemes in the market include some element of target rebate/discount. As any rebate scheme it should reward a dealer for producing an economic benefit for the supplier, it must not discriminate between comparable dealers, it must not foreclose competition and it must be transparent. **16.36**

By applying the rulings of the European Courts, the HCC held in its Decision no. 434/V/2009 that the defendant company infringed Greek and EU competition law by abusing its dominant position in the instant coffee market. In particular, the HCC was concerned with: in the retail instant coffee market, regarding trading relations with supermarket chains, the granting of target and fidelity rebates, prohibiting/impeding parallel imports, as well as prohibiting any simultaneous marketing activities of its products and competitive products; and in the HO.RE.CA. instant coffee market, the imposition of exclusive supply and bundling contract arrangements, as well as the granting of fidelity rebates aiming at inducing customer loyalty. **16.37**

In its most recent Decision no. 520/VI/2011,[14] the HCC found that a company that is mainly active in the production and distribution of salty snacks in Greece, infringed Greek and EU competition Law. According to the Decision "the company has adopted and implemented a single, consistent and targeted policy in the market for salty snacks that sought to exclude its competitors from smaller retail outlets (notably kiosks, grocery stores and traditional food stores & mini-markets), and to limit their growth possibilities." To achieve this objective, the company employed various abusive practices including rebates conditional upon the commitment of all, or the most substantial part of, available shelf/store space for its products and target rebates at both wholesale and retail level. **16.38**

As mentioned in Section I.A, the bundling of products/services and their pricing appears in the telecoms sector and is an issue that is frequently reviewed (every offer to consumers during the year is being scrutinized) by the National Regulator for Telecommunications (EETT) in relation to the offers made by the dominant provider in Greece. **16.39**

K. Standard-setting groups (disclosure requirements, licensing arrangements, and licensing pools)

Standard-setting activities have been under the scrutiny of the Commission, with the publication of new guidance on this subject in 2011 which is also applicable in Greece. However, there does not appear to be any relevant extensive activity in Greece. **16.40**

L. Customer termination

Customer termination is a sub-category of "refusal to deal."[15] In case there are valid reasons which justify the termination of a relationship with a customer, it is unlikely that such refusal by a dominant undertaking to supply such customer would give rise to competition law implications, as it would in the opposite case. **16.41**

---

[13] See the discussion of the HCC's Decision no. 434/V/2009 (May 22, 2008) in para. 16.37.
[14] Cited at para. 16.28.
[15] See Section I.H.

16.42 Until recently, article 2a of the previous competition Law 703/77 provided for the prohibition of abuse of a relationship of economic dependence of an undertaking upon another undertaking which was its client or supplier, even if this relationship of dependence concerned only one type of product or service, so long as the "dependant" undertaking did not have an equivalent alternative. However, this provision was abolished and integrated in Law 146/1914 regarding unfair competition. Please note that the HCC has no jurisdiction over the application of the provisions of law 146/1914 on unfair competition, the application of which is in the competence of civil courts.

M. Termination of intermediaries (retailers, wholesalers, dealers, and value-added resellers, agents, and brokers)

16.43 Termination of intermediaries is a sub-category of "refusal to deal"[16] and would not amount to a violation of article 102 TFEU, unless the intermediaries are competing with the dominant undertaking. Moreover, it would not amount to a violation of article 101 TFEU, unless termination represents a tool to strengthen a separate anticompetitive practice, for example, cutting off supplies to distributors who do not comply with a fixed resale price imposed by the dominant undertaking or who disregard an export prohibition. In a recent case, the Athens Court of First Instance ruled that the company that provided certification services abused its dominant position by imposing on several examination centers exclusivity clauses and threatening to terminate the respective agreements in case they did not agree and/or follow such clauses (i.e. in case the examination centers proceeded in concluding agreements with rival companies that provided certification).[17] Moreover, in the famous *Lelos* case, the Athens Court of Appeals (1983/2010),[18] following a preliminary ruling by the Court of Justice of the European Union (CJEU),[19] ruled that the refusal by a pharmaceutical company to fulfill in total the orders of wholesalers engaging in parallel exports constitutes an infringement of article 102 TFEU.

N. Termination of relationships with competitors

16.44 Termination by a dominant undertaking of a relationship with a competitor would not amount to a competition violation, unless the circumstances of the termination point to abusive behavior. In such case, a violation of article 102 TFEU would be established.

O. Exemptions

16.45 As mentioned in para. 16.03, under article 1(3) of Law 3959/2011, the provisions of article 1(1) may be declared inapplicable in the case of any agreement between undertakings, any decision by associations of undertakings, any concerted practice, which contributes to improving the production or distribution of goods or to promoting technical or economic progress, while allowing consumers a fair share of the resulting benefit, and which does not: (a) impose on the undertakings concerned restrictions which are not indispensable to the attainment of these objectives; (b) afford such undertakings the possibility of eliminating competition in respect of a substantial part of the products in question.

16.46 Greece applies the EU block exemption regulations.

---

[16] See Section I.H.

[17] Case 4027/2007 of the Athens Court of First Instance (see rep. in "*Hellenic Justice*" 50(A) 2009, p. 619).

[18] Case 1983/2010 of the Administrative Court of Appeals of Athens (Judgment issued on August 24, 2010).

[19] Joined Cases C-486/06 to C-478/06 *Sot. Lelos kai Sia EE and others v. GlaxoSmithKline AEVE* [2008] ECR I-9139.

II. Dealing with competitors

Greek competition policy does not differ from that of the EU in terms of prioritization of targets. The main focus is to detect and punish all types of agreements that are of an anti-competitive nature and especially those which are considered as hard core infringements of competition (i.e. price fixing, market sharing, etc.). The interest comes with the enforcement aspect of the relevant competition provisions. The HCC has been quite active in the recent years in this area, having demonstrated an upgrade on its enforcement abilities, its investigative powers, and performance in tackling cartels. **16.47**

A. Horizontal price fixing (including advanced announcements of price or product changes)

Horizontal price fixing is considered as a serious threat to competition and to the overall welfare of Greek consumers especially during the economic crisis experienced in Greece. It is worth mentioning that the fight against price-fixing cartels is considered as the first of certain "strategic targets" by the Hellenic Competition Commission in tackling anticompetitive conduct. Law 3959/2011 prohibits horizontal price fixing and the HCC has imposed considerable fines in a number of occasions.[20] Price fixing can take various formations and this may also included advanced announcements of price or product changes. The interpretation of article 1 of Law 3959/2011 will follow EU case law and its interpretation on these subjects. **16.48**

B. Horizontal agreements to allocate customers or territories; agreements not to compete

All agreements which aim at allocating markets or customers as well as agreements to abstain from competing are, similar to price-fixing agreements, dealt with increased hostility by the HCC. **16.49**

A recent *ex officio* investigation initiated by the HCC was triggered by announcements of an association of undertakings in its website asking its members to limit their activities (construction of new buildings/real estate) unless a certain percentage of their available real estate was previously sold. **16.50**

C. Horizontal boycotts

Horizontal boycotts are prohibited by Law 3959/2011 and they are accordingly seen as a hardcore restriction of competition. Both articles 1 and 2 of Law 3959/2011 can apply upon such practice. **16.51**

The HCC discussed the issue of boycotts in its Decision no. 277/IV/2005 (under the previous competition legislation, Law 703/1977) in relation to a supermarket's cartel formation.[21] It considered the possibility of applying article 1 as well as article 2 (arts. 101 and 102 TFEU) with the latter being of interest to the potential of having an abuse of collective dominant position. In that Decision the HCC proceeded in analyzing both bilateral boycotts and tripartite agreements to boycott. The latter category was analyzed from a cartel formation perspective, nevertheless there was absence of evidence that the parties acted in such a manner. **16.52**

[20] See, most recently, HCC Decision no. 520/VI/2011 (February 14, 2011) for a EUR 4 million fine in relation only to art. 1 of Law 3959/2011 and art. 101 TFEU infringements by the dominant company (on appeal, the fine was reduced to EUR 2 million), see Case 869/2013 Administrative Court of Appeals of Athens, Judgment of March 13, 2013.

[21] HCC Decision no. 277/IV/2005 (April 1, 2005).

D. Joint ventures and other competitive collaborations

16.53 On the issue of joint ventures and other collaborations, the Greek competition law similarly follows that of EU law and case law precedent. In addition, and as it is noted in article 1(4) of Law 3959/2011, the EU exemption regulations will also apply, intact, in Greek law, hence this also will cover the specialization agreements and the R&D agreements.[22]

16.54 Joint ventures will be dealt with under the merger control provisions (i.e. non-full function joint ventures are subject to art. 1 of Law 3959/2011 and article 101 TFEU). These provisions are article 5(5) of Law 3959/2011 (art. 5 is titled Concentration of Undertakings), which defines what a joint venture is (i.e. autonomous economic entity), and article 7(3) of Law 3959/2011 (titled as Control of the Concentration of Undertakings) dealing with the appraisal of joint ventures, which mirrors articles 2(4) and 2(5) of Commission Regulation 139/2004.

E. Trade associations

16.55 The HCC has shown a particular interest in the rules of operation and decisions of trade associations in the Greek market in a number of sectors ranging from consumer goods to construction. Undoubtedly, the actual participation within such associations is not contrary to competition law, hence neither are discussions between members (competitors) or decisions applied upon the association's members provided of course that these do not have an anticompetitive target (i.e. fixing prices/commercial policies, etc.). Similarly to EU case law precedent, both decisions by the associations or discussions taking place therein by the members which have as their subject matter the imposition of uniform prices or components and parameters of formulating prices, trading terms and other commercial policies will infringe competition law.

16.56 As an example of its practice, the HCC has previously imposed a fine on the Technical Chamber of Greece for imposing upon its members a minimum price (cost) for the construction of projects thereby resulting in raising the prices charged by engineers/architects.[23] On another occasion, the HCC imposed small fines on a number of associations of estate agents for imposing on their members a direct and indirect minimum price percentage charged to clients (2 percent of the value of the property) as well as imposing restrictions on their members in relation to advertising of prices below that percentage.[24] More recently, the HCC imposed fines against a number of professional associations of foreign language school owners for price-fixing practices as well as other restrictions in the exercise of professional activities of their members.[25]

16.57 It is evident from the various *ex officio* investigations that the HCC monitors trade associations and attempts to gather evidence from various sources.

F. Interlocking directorates

16.58 Article 1 of Law 3959/2011 and article 101 TFEU can be used in cases where an interlocking system is used in order to coordinate prices and other commercial policies. Article 2 of Law 3959/2011 and article 102 TFEU as well as the Merger Control provisions could also apply.

---

[22] See the relevant Commission Regulations Nos. 1218/2010 and 1217/2010.

[23] HCC Decision no. 512/VI/2010 (December 22, 2010).

[24] HCC Decision no. 518/VI/2011 (December 20, 2011).

[25] See the HCC's Press Release on this Decision (October 21, 2013), available at <http://www.epant.gr/img/x2/news/news563_1_1382420810.pdf> (in English).

Overall, this is an area that competition enforcement in Greece is not sufficiently explored in the wider market context. Nevertheless, it is to be emphasized that the HCC is also competent to enforce Law 3592/2007 on Concentration and Licensing of Media Companies and other Provisions, which focuses on the media sector and targets the concentration of control over the media market (art. 2) and also the control of more than one *electronic* media by the same legal or natural person (art. 5). The law encompasses the main competition provisions and it is also applied in conjunction with the existing competition legislation. **16.59**

G. Facilitating practices

There is nothing specific in the Greek legislation on the issue of facilitating practices. Following the Court of First Instance's Decision in *AC-Treuhand AG*,[26] the interpretation of article 1 of Law 3959/2011 can be wide enough so as to apply to undertakings that in any way facilitate cartel formation. Criminal sanctions could hence also apply to natural persons from such facilitating undertakings. **16.60**

H. Information exchange

Similar to EU competition case law precedent and the Commission's Horizontal Cooperation Agreements Guidelines. **16.61**

Recently, the Guidelines were also cited by the HCC (in relation to information exchange) in its Opinion no. 21/VII/2012 in relation to the repeal of article 9 of Market Decree 7/2009 on the obligation to submit wholesale price lists.[27] **16.62**

I. Joint purchasing agreements

Similar to EU competition case law precedent and the Commission's Horizontal Cooperation Agreements Guidelines. **16.63**

J. Joint lobbying/regulatory/legislative efforts

Joint lobbying is not prohibited, provided of course that these joint efforts are not also used as methods of coordinating commercial policies (e.g. in relation to prices).[28] **16.64**

III. General issues

A. Jurisdiction and applicable law (including sector-specific competition regulation)

Law 3959/2011 (for the Protection of Free Competition) is the main legislation. As mentioned earlier, articles 1 and 2 of Law 3959/2011 are equivalent to articles 101 and 102 TFEU. Similarly to the EU legislation, the relevant Law 3959/2011 is not restricted as to its application. This means that it could be applied in all markets (subject of course to the same EU law restrictions) and even to undertakings not situated in Greece but which implement the prohibited practices in Greece (as it follows from the relevant EU Court precedent). **16.65**

Additionally, Law 3592/2007 (on Concentration and Licensing of Media Companies and other Provisions) applies in relation to the media market sector. **16.66**

[26] T-99/04 *AC-Treuhand AG v. Commission* [2008] ECR II-1501.
[27] HCC Opinion 21/VII/2012 (March 22, 2012).
[28] See Section II.E in relation to discussions that may be regarded as anticompetitive in the context of trade associations and Section II.H in relation to information exchange.

B. Antitrust system

(i) Name of agency/agencies

16.67 The Hellenic Competition Commission (HCC)[29] and also the sector-specific Regulatory Authority of the Hellenic Telecommunications and Post Commission (EETT)[30] and the Regulatory Authority for Energy (RAE),[31] which both have regulatory/enforcement powers in their own sectors. According to article 24 of Law 3959/2011, the HCC cooperates with such Regulatory Authorities and may contribute towards the enforcement of both Greek and EU competition legislation.

(ii) Staff size and budget

16.68 The HCC's staff size is approximately 110 people in various positions (this number includes administrative staff). The majority of the personnel are divided into four main Divisions which correspond to four main categories of products and services, i.e.:

(1) Division A deals with markets such as chemicals, mines, quarries, construction, automobiles;
(2) Division B deals with markets such as agriculture, livestock farming, fishery, food, beverages, clothing, pharmaceuticals, electrical, and electronics;
(3) Division C deals with the banking sector, financial services, information technology, tourism, sports sector, culture, catering, and entertainment industry;
(4) Division D deals with the areas of energy, water supply, know-how, transportation, publishing, advertising, intellectual property.

16.69 Beyond these market categories, the HCC operates a Special Division for inspections in the Media market. These Divisions are supported by the Legal Substantiation Directorate and by the Economic Substantiation Directorate.

16.70 The HCC has a separate legal personality and it has administrative and financial autonomy, although it remains subject to auditing by the Court of Audit. Its budget is approved by the Minister of Finance and the Minister of Economy, Competitiveness and Shipping. Its budget for the year 2012 was around EUR 28 million and for 2013 around EUR 30 million.

16.71 Furthermore, according to article 17 of Law 3959/2011, a 1 per mil of the fee imposed on all limited companies which are either being set up in Greece or increase their capital (the fee is imposed on the founding capital or on the capital increase) is deposited to a special account manageable by the HCC.

16.72 Every two years, and following the deduction from any expenses, from the revenue generated—if any—by the HCC, an amount equal to 80 percent is given towards the state budget.

(iii) Recent enforcement actions and trends

Enforcement priorities/HCC's prioritization criteria

16.73 The *HCC* has set certain criteria which are applied for the prioritization of cases:[32]

(1) First, the HCC's basic concern is how to best serve the public interest; the most fundamental criterion assessed in light of the estimated impact upon effective competition and

---

[29] HCC website, <www.epant.gr>.

[30] EETT website <www.eett.gr>.

[31] RAE website <www.rae.gr>.

[32] HCC Decision no. 525/VI/2011 (July 7, 2011). See also HCC Press Release, "Criteria Setting for Enforcement Priorities and Strategic Objectives of the Competition Commission" (August 31, 2011) available at <http://www.epant.gr/img/x2/news/news365_1_1315828654.pdf> (in Greek).

consumers. This translates in giving priority to *ex officio* investigations and/or complaints which focus on and particularly raise the following issues:

- hard core restrictions of competition taking place across the Greek market (i.e. price fixing/market sharing/sale or production limitations—with horizontal agreements (cartels) being on top of the list of priorities) taking into consideration the market position of the undertakings; market structure; and volume of consumers affected;
- the essential nature and importance of the particular products/services for consumers;
- the impact on prices/quality following the anticompetitive practice;
- comparison of these effects felt in the Greek market with other EU member states; and
- potential cumulative effects resulting out of the anticompetitive conduct under investigation;

(2) Second, as to whether a complete leniency application has been made, provided of course that the leniency program criteria are met;

(3) Third, as to the actual necessity to adopt exceptional—and absolutely necessary, suitable, and proportionate—regulatory measures within particular sectors of the economy in order to create (possibly also enhance) the necessary conditions of effective competition; and

(4) Fourth, the HCC's advisory power/competence (e.g. advising in drafting legislation/amendments, etc.).

In addition to these four criteria, the HCC states that for this prioritization procedure it will additionally take into account a number of (internal to its operation) factors, such as the availability on human and financial resources; the necessity to clarify any potential novel legal issues; the HCC's best placement to deal with the case at hand; the result out of the intervention; the comprehensiveness of the submitted complaint. Recently, the HCC has adopted an informal and internal "point system" for the investigation of pending cases.[33] This system essentially covers the points (1)–(4) in the priority procedure aiming to enhance the effectiveness of the procedures and of the investigations of cases which are considered as having a significant impact on competition and/or are of a systemic effect.[34] **16.74**

Recent trends, investigations/cases

Given the particular economic conditions experienced in Greece, there has been much debate as to whether competition policy is to be adapted and applied more leniently. Triggered by certain announcements as well as actions initiated by certain association of undertakings arguing for the validity of crisis cartels alleging the problematic financial market environment and how this affected their operation (e.g. through the rise of raw materials' prices, tax reforms, etc.), the HCC rejected this approach and sought to clear any misconceptions by noting that: **16.75**

> [C]ompetition law…imposes on undertakings to face economic situations framing an autonomous trading policy independently of each other and with means which neither distort nor disrupt free competition. Therefore, any possible pursuit of increase or maintenance of undertakings or shifting financial burdens to consumers by way of cartels, decisions by associations of undertakings or unilateral abusive practices, puts the public interest at risk and harms the consumer, without any offset for society.[35]

Consequently, in preventing any similar considerations and practices by undertakings from arising in the future, the HCC stressed that it will use all potential sources of information to detect such anticompetitive conduct and subsequently to impose upon it severe sanctions. **16.76**

[33] HCC Decision no. 539/VII/2012 (May 24, 2012).

[34] HCC Press Release, "Point System for the investigation of cases by the Directorate-General for Competition" (June 28, 2012), available at <http://www.epant.gr/img/x2/news/news432_1_1340905460.pdf> (in English).

[35] HCC Announcement, "Enforcement of competition rules in special economic conditions" (March 14, 2011), available at <http://www.epant.gr/img/x2/news/news361_1_1311248129.pdf> (in English).

16.77 Following from this, and as a general observation, the HCC has been particularly active during the last two years. It has initiated a number of *ex officio* investigations and issued Opinions; concurrently, certain important decisions have been adopted both in relation to cartels and to abusive of dominance behavior. Most notably, during this period the HCC has amongst others:

- initiated an investigation into the construction sector following numerous press reports and evidence in the website of the Association of Building Manufacturers;
- initiated an investigation into the alleged infringement of article 1 of Law 703/77 and article 101 TFEU in the flour market in relation to the practices of two flour mills associations and in the context of its investigation to this market it imposed a fine for the obstruction of on-site inspections;
- imposed a fine on the Technical Chamber of Greece for the adoption of a "minimum cost for construction projects" thereby increasing fees for architects and engineers;
- adopted an infringement decision against two gas supply companies in relation to abusive of dominance behavior;
- initiated an investigation into alleged infringement of articles 101 and 102 TFEU and articles 1 and 2 of Law 703/77 in the gas market;
- adopted a decision concerning the infringements of both articles 1 and 2 of Law 703/77 and articles 101 and 102 TFEU, by the leading savory/salty snacks producer.

16.78 Moreover, the HCC issued numerous Statements of Objections, for example against the Association of Estate Agents for imposing restrictions and fixing minimum fees; in relation to an exclusivity agreement for satellite broadcasting (subsequently accepting commitments); against the professional associations of foreign language school owners in relation to price-fixing and professional restrictions; against a tank vehicles transport company in relation to an alleged article 1 and 2 of Law 703/77 violation; against various undertakings active in the production and distribution of poultry-meat in relation to an alleged cartel; more recently, against a leading producer of personal care products (for alleged violations of both articles 1 and 2 of Law 703/1977 and of Law 3959/2011, and articles 101 and 102 TFEU); and against a major telecommunications retailer (for violations of article 1 of Law 3959/2011 and of article 101 TFEU).

16.79 Furthermore, and amongst others, the HCC has reviewed and cleared two mergers in the ice-cream and dairy products markets imposing a Monitoring Trustee for the management of the divested branch of chocolate milk business; it has cleared a number of mergers in the banking sector; and also cleared concentrations in the supermarket sector.

16.80 In addition, the HCC issued Opinions in various market sectors, for example concerning the distribution of infant milk; in relation to the professions of actuaries, chartered appraisers, accountants, tax consultants, and many other public security licensed professions; in relation to the market for the production, testing, certification and marketing of cement; and issued an Opinion on numerous provisions of the Greek Market Control Code.

C. Private litigation

16.81 Persons who have suffered a loss due to acts or omissions by undertakings breaching the competition rules may refer the matter to the civil courts for an eventual award of damages. The number of such actions is small.

16.82 The law provides for two forms of compensation: pecuniary and non-pecuniary damages.

16.83 Pecuniary damages are awarded for damage to goods which have an economic value and can be paid through monetary compensation or, not commonly, in kind.

16.84 Non-pecuniary damages are awarded in cases of moral damage, i.e. damage to non-pecuniary goods, such as an undertaking's good will or market reputation.

The law provides for specific means of evidence in case of pecuniary damages, including: 16.85

- confession,
- documents,
- expert opinion,
- witness testimony, etc.

The amount of damages is calculated based on the harm (usually monetary) incurred by the plaintiff. No economic models exist under Greek law for the calculation of damages. The amount of damages is determined by the court on the basis of three basic requirements: the existence of causation, the comparison between the economic situation of the aggrieved party before and after the occurrence of damage, and the actual evaluation of the harm incurred. 16.86

The case law of the Greek courts confirms that violation of articles 1 and 2 of Law 3959/2011 (or previous competition legislation) may amount to tort under articles 914 ff. of the Greek Civil Code and allow private actions for damages.[36] 16.87

The main reason for the limited number of damages actions against companies which have infringed competition rules is the difficulty of the claimant to obtain access to the relevant economic data and files of the defendant, since this usually requires separate legal action and, under Greek procedural law, the claimant must identify in detail the requested documents, which, in practice, may be an insurmountable obstacle. Additionally, Greek civil law rules on determining damages are stringent requiring causality between the infringement and the damage and concrete analysis of the damage. 16.88

D. Follow-on litigation (includes role of agency determinations of liability for follow-on litigation)

By virtue of the law, decisions of the HCC, when final, are binding on national Civil Courts, while decisions of foreign Competition Authorities or foreign Courts are rarely assessed by domestic Courts. The burden, however, of putting forward such statements or decisions as supportive evidence during the proceedings lies with the parties. 16.89

E. Arbitration and alternative dispute resolution

Competition issues may arise in the context of arbitration proceedings and are deemed proper subject matter for arbitration. Following the CJEU's ruling in *Eco Swiss* which pronounced the public policy nature of competition rules,[37] their mandatory nature in domestic private law (*ius cogens*) and in private international law (*lois d'application immediate*) cannot be disputed. Despite the narrow construction of the public order exception under the New York Convention,[38] Greek courts may find that public order is violated if awards violate or do not apply competition law rules. The Greek Supreme Court[39] confirmed that the basic provisions of EU and Greek competition law pertain to Greek public policy and any arbitral award that would run counter to the latter cannot be enforced in Greece. Notably, in this judgment, the Greek Supreme Court limited its review to whether the competition rules had been applied 16.90

[36] See Decision 18743/1992 of the Athens Single Member Court of First Instance (see rep. in "*Commercial Law Review*" (44), 1993, p. 141); Decision 18/2002 of the Patras Administrative Court of Appeal (see rep. in "*Business and Company Law*" 9(5), 2003, p. 524); and Decision 6042/2002 of the Athens Court of Appeal (see rep. in "*Business and Company Law*" 9(3), 2003, p. 282).

[37] C-126/97 *Eco Swiss China Time Ltd v. Benetton International NV* [1999] ECR I-3055.

[38] New York Convention on the Recognition and Enforcement of Foreign Arbitral Awards, done at New York, June 10, 1958; entered into force June 7, 1959, 330 U.N.T.S. 38 (1959).

[39] Areios Pagos Judgment 1665/2009 (Civil, Division D) (published on June 30, 2009); the case is available at the Areios Pagos website: <http://www.areiospagos.gr/en/INDEX.htm> (in Greek).

by the arbitrator, and having found that they had been applied, was satisfied that there was no case of public policy violation despite that the arbitrator had rejected the arguments based on these provisions on their merits.

F. Remedies

(i) Civil liability

16.91 According to article 25 of Law 3959/11, the HCC has the power to impose fines against the violating undertakings which violate competition rules. The fine cannot exceed 10 percent of the gross turnover of the undertaking in the current or preceding financial year.

16.92 Law 3959/2011 provides for three new elements regarding administrative sanctions:

- in case of a group of companies, the aggregate group turnover is considered;
- in case where the economic benefit enjoyed by the undertaking can be measured, the fine cannot be less than that (even if it exceeds the threshold of 10 percent); and
- individuals involved in violations of Law 3595/2011 face a two-fold personal liability:
  - they are jointly liable together with the undertaking for the payment of the above fine; and
  - a separate fine ranging from EUR 200,000 to EUR 2 million may be imposed against them if it is proven that they have participated in the preparation, organization and commitment of the infringement by the undertaking.

16.93 The administrative fines for obstructing the Commission's investigation, for refusing to provide information or copies from required books and records are ranging from EUR 15,000 to 1 percent of the annual turnover.

16.94 Moreover, the HCC is vested with extensive powers in order to ensure compliance with its decisions. The Commission may impose fines or periodic penalty payments, or both, in cases of non-compliance.

16.95 The HCC may impose penalty payments not exceeding the amount of EUR 10,000 per day calculated from the date appointed by the decision for non-compliance with a decision requiring the undertakings concerned to bring an infringement to an end.

16.96 The HCC may impose a penalty payment not exceeding the amount of EUR 5,000 per day in order to compel the undertakings involved to comply with a decision ordering interim measures taken *ex officio* or upon request of the Minister of Development.

(ii) Criminal liability

16.97 The HCC may impose criminal sanctions in case of violation of Law 3959/2011. According to article 44 of Law 3959/2011, criminal sanctions may be imposed on partners/owners, executives or personnel such as imprisonment of at least two years and a criminal penalty from EUR 100,000 up to EUR 1,000,000 (for violations of art. 1 L.3959/2011 and 101 TFEU). A criminal penalty from EUR 30,000 to EUR 300,000 has been introduced against those who implement an abuse of dominant position. Nobody has been found guilty of criminal acts under the competition law yet.

G. Leniency and immunity

16.98 The HCC has recently revised its leniency program in an attempt to offer a more attractive and effective leniency framework which will strengthen its efforts against cartels.[40] According

[40] HCC Decision 526/VI/2011 (August 30, 2011); see further HCC Press Release, "The HCC adopts a revised Leniency Programme" (November 25, 2011), available at <http://www.epant.gr/img/x2/news/news378_1_1326791189.pdf> (in English).

to the HCC, the new leniency program builds upon European and international experience. The most important features of the new Leniency Program are:

(1) The leniency program is offered to both undertakings and natural persons involved that will cooperate with the HCC in relation to violations of article 1 of Law 3959/2011 and/or article 101 TFEU. Hence, it concerns horizontal agreements (cartels) that affect prices (or quantities or market shares etc.), market sharing, restrictions on imports/exports, bid rigging, collective boycott, etc.
(2) It can offer a total immunity or a reduction in the fines following a significant contribution towards the HCC that will assist it to detect cartel formations operating in the Greek market. In addition, for natural persons, a total immunity will absolve them from any potential criminal liability and a fine reduction will be seen as a mitigating circumstance.

A total immunity or reduction depends upon the time of the application; on the usability of the leniency application for the HCC to establish the infringement; as to whether the information/evidence submitted is complete and significant; the additional and probative value of the new evidence assisting the HCC to establish the critical facts of the investigated offense. **16.99**

The HCC's Leniency Program comprises three types: **16.100**

(1) *Type 1A* which offers full immunity from fines to the first to offer sufficient evidence that will allow the HCC to initiate its inspections. This evidence should not be in the HCC's possession prior to the submission.
(2) *Type 1B* which offers full immunity from fines to the first to offer evidence allowing the HCC to establish the cartel infringement—in case the HCC evidence was insufficient.
(3) *Type 2* which offers a reduction from fines following the provision of evidence for a cartel formation. The information must be of significant added value to the information gathered by the HCC.

Importantly, undertakings that have coerced others to participate in the cartel formation are excluded from the Leniency Program—although individuals acting for these undertakings are not. **16.101**

Oral statements can be accepted. Access is possible after the statement of objections serving to the parties. **16.102**

The Leniency Program also introduces a "marker" system. In addition, the HCC can offer advice prior to any official submission of evidence. **16.103**

H. Document creation and retention

Greek competition law does not include any particular provision in relation to document creation or retention. However, it can be noted that Law 3959/2011 places particular emphasis on the full cooperation that companies and their officials must demonstrate while being under investigation by the HCC officials. Full cooperation in relation to this particular issue requires that documents are shown to the HCC investigators and copies of these documents are allowed to be taken. **16.104**

As mentioned above, the relevant competition law provides heavy fines (from EUR 15,000 up to 1 percent of the annual turnover) in the case where the investigation is impeded and the necessary information/books/documents are not provided to the HCC investigators; while the people responsible are faced with an imprisonment for a period of at least 6 months. **16.105**

17

HONG KONG

Stephen Crosswell
Clifford Chance

Introduction

17.01 To date, Hong Kong has pursued a light-handed competition policy consistent with its laissez-faire economic policy. This has consisted of:

- the application of sectoral competition laws in sectors where there was perceived to be a need;
- regulation of utilities and transport through flexible consensual regulatory mechanisms (such as the contractual electricity schemes of control); and
- the establishment of a Competition Policy Advisory Group (COMPAG) to review private and public conduct and to make recommendations to the Hong Kong government where it is considered competition issues have been identified that require a policy response.

This light-handed competition policy has been driven by Hong Kong's strong faith in the ability of markets to self-correct and a recognition of the risks of regulatory error where intervention is considered as a means of addressing perceived market failures. **17.02**

At the time of writing, Hong Kong has enacted a general competition law, the Competition Ordinance (the "Ordinance").[1] The law was gazetted on June 22, 2012, but the prohibitions are not yet in force. The law is to be implemented in phases as the Competition Commission (the "Commission") and Competition Tribunal (the "Tribunal") are established. Provisions concerning the establishment of the Commission were implemented on January 18, 2013 and provisions for the establishment of the Tribunal were implemented on August 1, 2013. **17.03**

The Ordinance will repeal the existing sectoral competition laws that exist under the Telecommunications Ordinance and the Broadcasting Ordinance. From that point, those sectors will be subject to the new law. **17.04**

The Commission is, after consulting with the Legislative Council and others it considers appropriate, required to issue guidelines as to: **17.05**

- the manner in which the Competition Authorities will interpret and give effect to the Conduct Rules;
- the manner and form in which the Competition Authorities will receive applications for block exemptions and decisions and how they expect to make decisions and grant block exemptions;
- the manner and form in which complaints are to be made;
- the procedures they will follow in deciding whether to investigate and in conducting investigations; and
- the manner in which they will interpret the provisions relating to mergers, including how it will be determined mergers substantially lessen competition, when they will fall within the efficiency exclusion and the manner and form in which mergers should be notified.

The prohibitions are only expected to come into force after the above guidelines have been issued. **17.06**

During the Bills Committee debate on the new law and in response to increasing concerns as to the a lack of clarity in the draft law, the Administration tabled draft guidelines in relation to interpretation of the Conduct Rules and the approach that would be taken to market definition. However, the draft guidelines met with some criticism as to the vagueness and failure to provide meaningful guidance on key aspects of the prohibitions. It was also emphasized by the Administration that the draft guidelines had no legal force and in no way fettered the Competition Authorities in the approach to be taken in due course when the law was enacted. **17.07**

Although the draft guidelines do not fetter the approach the Commission may ultimately take, they are referenced to some degree in the following Sections, given the absence of any better indication of the Commission's possible approach under the new law. Where considered useful, reference is also made to the current telecommunications and broadcasting competition guidelines. **17.08**

It remains to be seen whether the law will, on balance, increase Hong Kong's competitiveness. There have been concerns expressed throughout the enactment process that the law was not **17.09**

[1] An Ordinance to prohibit conduct that prevents, restricts or distorts competition in Hong Kong; to prohibit mergers that substantially lessen competition in Hong Kong; to establish a Competition Commission and a Competition Tribunal; and to provide for incidental and connected matters (Cap. 619) E.R. 2 of 2012 ("Competition Ordinance").

tailored to suit Hong Kong's small, open economy and its traditionally laissez-faire market policies. This included criticism of the broad carve-out that the Government proposes for statutory bodies engaging in economic activities in the market. There have also been concerns expressed as to whether the Commission will be adequately resourced with competition law experts with the necessary skills to administer the law to ensure that it is not disproportionate in the costs and uncertainty it potentially introduces.

I. Acting alone

A. The general prohibition against misuse of market power

17.10 When it comes into force, s. 21 of the Ordinance, the Second Conduct Rule, will prohibit undertakings with a substantial degree of market power from engaging in conduct that has the object or effect of preventing, restricting or distorting competition in Hong Kong. Predatory pricing and "limiting production, markets or technical development to the prejudice of consumers" are highlighted as particular conducts that could comprise a breach.

17.11 Having significant market power is not prohibited and nor is striving, through competition, to obtain a position of significant market power. The Ordinance only prohibits conduct that is considered an abuse of that market power, because it has the proscribed object or effect.

(i) Market power

17.12 Until guidelines are published and there is clarity in decisions from the Tribunal and appeal courts, it is difficult to say when an undertaking will be considered to have a "substantial degree of market power."

17.13 The Hong Kong government argued during the Bills Committee debate that the "substantial degree of market power" threshold is lower than the "dominance" threshold used in other jurisdictions, such as Singapore, the UK, and Mainland China and that market shares as low as 25 percent could be indicative of a substantial degree of market power. This is a very low threshold in view of the small and open nature of Hong Kong's economy and it remains to be seen whether the Tribunal and appeal courts agree. By comparison, Singapore, which is an economy with many features in common with Hong Kong, gives an indicative market power threshold of 60 percent.

17.14 In any event, market power is not measured by looking at market share alone.

17.15 The Second Conduct Rule states that market share, power to make pricing decisions, barriers to entry, and other relevant matters specified in the guidelines are factors that should be taken into account.

17.16 The draft guidelines state that market power arises where an undertaking does not face sufficiently strong competitive pressure. Reference is made to the ability to profitably sustain prices above competitive levels or to restrict output or quality below competitive levels over a sustained period of time, clearly alluding to the small but significant and non-transitory increase in price (SSNIP) test used in some other jurisdictions.

17.17 The draft guidelines recognize that entry barriers are an important consideration. The following are listed as examples of barriers to entry:

- sunk costs;
- limited access to key inputs and distribution outlets (including "essential facilities");
- economies of scale; and
- exclusionary behavior by incumbents.

The draft guidelines state that relevant constraints on the ability to exercise market power include actual competitors, potential competitors, and other factors, such as powerful buyers in a market. **17.18**

(ii) Object and effect

The draft guidelines state that it is the objective purpose of the conduct engaged in by the undertaking considered in the economic context in which it is to be applied that is relevant, not the subjective intention of the concerned undertaking. Where a conduct has more than one object, it will be in breach if one of its objects is a proscribed object.[2] **17.19**

Rather unusually in comparison with other major jurisdictions, the Second Conduct Rule further provides that where a conduct has more than one effect, it has the effect of preventing, restricting or distorting competition if one of its effects is to prevent, restrict or distort competition.[3] **17.20**

It remains to be seen whether this provision causes consideration of the effect limb of Hong Kong's prohibitions to be interpreted in a different manner to overseas jurisdictions. There is no logical reason why Hong Kong should depart from international norms when it comes to assessing competition effect. Indeed, with Hong Kong's traditional faith in markets, it should only be where there is very clear evidence of an anticompetitive effect with no overriding benefits that there should be consideration of action against any particular conduct and, even then, only if the proposed remedy is demonstrably superior to the status quo. **17.21**

The draft guidelines list the following as conduct that may have a proscribed effect under the Second Conduct Rule: **17.22**

- anticompetitive foreclosure of competitors;
- raising of barriers to entry; and
- withdrawal of products or services from the market or a reduction in the quality of the services offered.

(iii) Objective justification defense

The draft guidelines reference overseas authority, suggesting that an undertaking may raise a defense to allegations of abuse of market power based on "objective justification." In order to succeed, the guidelines say that the undertaking must demonstrate (a) that the conduct was objectively necessary based on factors relevant to all undertakings in the market and (b) that the conduct must be proportionate. The example given is a refusal to supply based on poor credit worthiness. Such a basis for refusing to supply may be reasonable, but only if proportionate to protect the commercial interests of the supplying undertaking. **17.23**

B. Predatory pricing

The Second Conduct Rule lists predatory behavior towards competitors as one of the two particularized conducts that may constitute an abuse of market power in breach of the Rule. **17.24**

The draft guidelines state that in assessing if predation is taking (or has taken) place, the Competition Authorities will usually first consider whether the undertaking with a substantial degree of market power is pricing below the relevant measure of cost. It is stated that the measure of costs may be fact-specific, but that in general the following benchmarks would apply: **17.25**

- pricing below average variable cost (AVC) of production for a sustained period of time—predation may be presumed in the absence of objective justification for this pricing strategy. Loss-leading (namely an undertaking cutting the price of a single product in order to

[2] Competition Ordinance (n 1) s. 22(1).
[3] Competition Ordinance (n 1) s. 22(3).

increase sales of other products) and short-run promotions (namely an undertaking selling below AVC for a limited period, especially where a new product is introduced to a market) are provided in the draft guidelines as examples of possible legitimate commercial reasons for such conduct;

- pricing above AVC but below average total cost (ATC) of production—this may be evidence of predation, but other evidence will need to be considered to determine if predation is taking (or has taken) place. For example, the Competition Authorities will consider whether the undertaking's strategy is only commercially sensible because it weakens competition. Another example is whether the undertaking implements price cuts against a competitor, while maintaining higher prices elsewhere; and
- where price is above ATC—evidence on costs does not indicate predation.

C. Exploitative offenses (excessive pricing, monopoly leveraging)

17.26 Although not expressly addressed in the Ordinance, on a plain reading it appears that the Second Conduct Rule does not extend to exploitative offenses. However, with no case law or guidelines on this point, it remains to be seen how broadly the Second Conduct Rule is interpreted in practice.

17.27 A new prohibition applicable to "dominant" telecommunications licensees is to be introduced by way of an amendment to introduce by way of a new s. 7Q to the Telecommunications Ordinance (the "Telco Rule").[4]

17.28 Under the Telco Rule, a dominant licensee is prohibited from fixing and maintaining prices or charges at an "excessively high level" and setting "unfair trading terms and conditions."

17.29 This raises a number of issues for telecommunications licensees, including:

- When will they be considered dominant?
- What will be regarded as "excessive pricing" or "unfair" terms?
- How will enforcement of the Telco Rule be managed along-side potential enforcement actions under the Conduct Rules?

D. Dominance

17.30 There has been considerable attention given under the existing telecommunications sector competition law to the question when a licensee will be considered to be in a dominant position. This includes numerous declarations of non-dominance as the industry was liberalized. The Telecommunications Authority (now merged into the Communications Authority) has also published guidelines addressing this issue.[5]

17.31 Essentially, dominance refers to a measure of market power that enables a dominant licensee to behave to an appreciable extent in terms of pricing and output without significant restraint from its existing competitors, potential entrants, upstream input suppliers, or downstream customers.

17.32 Factors which the Telecommunications Authority said that it would take into account in assessing dominance include the licensee's market share, the licensee's power to make pricing and other decisions, any barriers to entry, and the degree of production differentiation.[6]

---

[4] Telecommunication Ordinance: to make better provision for the licensing and control of telecommunications, telecommunications services and telecommunications apparatus and equipment (Cap. 106) E.R. 2 of 2012 ("Telco Rule").

[5] See the Guidelines to Assist Licensees to Comply with the Competition Provisions under the Telecommunications Ordinance issued by the Office of Telecommunications Authority on December 30, 2010 (the "Telco Guidelines"), s. 4 <http://tel_archives.ofca.gov.hk/en/tas/ftn/ta20101230.pdf>.

[6] For detailed discussion, please refer to the Telco Guidelines (n 6) s. 4.

Despite precedent and the Guidelines to Assist Licensees to Comply with the Competition Provisions under the Telecommunications Ordinance issued by the Office of Telecommunications Authority on December 30, 2010 (the "Telco Guidelines"), recent decisions of the Office of Telecommunications Authority have been difficult to reconcile with sound economic analysis. It is hoped that the situation will improve as Hong Kong moves forward with implementation of the new competition law. **17.33**

E. Excessive market regulation

Hong Kong's telecommunications liberalization has been very successful. It now has perhaps the most competitive telecommunications industry in the world, with unparalleled levels of facilities and service-based competition. Most homes and businesses have access to multiple high capacity networks, which offer a variety of fixed line telephone, broadband internet, and media (e.g. TV) services. As a result, in the period through to 2007, steps were taken to roll back regulation to allow market forces to shape the industry and drive innovation. In fact, the liberalization process has been so successful that the telecommunications industry easily ranks alongside other highly competitive markets in Hong Kong. **17.34**

It is not, therefore, clear why the Hong Kong government decided to introduce the new Telco Rule to prohibit "excessive pricing." **17.35**

Price regulation could be a rational competition policy response in markets that are being liberalized (and *ex ante* tariff regulation was applied in the early days of Hong Kong's telecommunications sector liberalization). However, if, and when, liberalization has succeeded in introducing competition, the regulator should step back because competition and markets are far better tools for delivering innovation and other efficiencies. **17.36**

F. Monopsony

There are no specific provisions in the law or draft guidelines addressing this. **17.37**

G. Price discrimination

The draft guidelines on the Second Conduct Rule do not deal with price discrimination specifically. One may seek to draw inferences as to the Competition Authorities' approach from the Telco Guidelines. **17.38**

The Telco Guidelines state that price discrimination will not, in and of itself, be regarded as harmful to the competitive process or to consumers. Consumers may in fact benefit from different pricing, which could be an inherent outcome of competition. The Telecommunications Authority has indicated that it would examine price discrimination only in circumstances where it is plausible that it may have the "purpose or effect of preventing or substantially restricting competition" (the test under the current sectoral telecommunications competition laws). **17.39**

H. Dictating or influencing resale prices

(i) Resale price maintenance

There are no specific provisions in the law or draft guidelines addressing this. **17.40**

(ii) Minimum advertised price programs

There are no specific provisions in the law or draft guidelines addressing this. **17.41**

I. Tying arrangements

The draft guidelines recognize that tying and bundling often have no anticompetitive consequences and that undertakings with or without market power engage in tying and bundling to deliver products to consumers more cost-effectively. **17.42**

17.43 The draft guidelines state that when assessing tying practices, the Competition Authorities will consider factors such as whether the concerned undertaking has a substantial degree of market power in the tying market; whether the tying and tied goods are two distinct products; and whether the practices are likely to have a market distorting foreclosure effect.

17.44 The example given is of an undertaking with a substantial degree of market power reducing the number of potential buyers available for its competitors in the tied market and thereby creating a barrier for new entrants.

J. Exclusive dealing

17.45 There are no specific provisions in the law or draft guidelines addressing this.

K. Refusal to deal

17.46 The draft guidelines state that the starting point for the Competition Authorities will always be that an undertaking, whether having a substantial degree of market power or not, should be free to decide whom they will deal with, or will not deal with. Therefore, a refusal to supply, even by an undertaking with a substantial degree of market power, would not normally be an abuse.

17.47 The draft guidelines state that a refusal to supply by an undertaking with a substantial degree of market power could be considered an abuse when two conditions are satisfied:

- there is evidence of likely substantial harm to competition; and
- the behavior cannot be objectively justified.

17.48 The draft guidelines highlight refusals to supply access to an essential facility as conduct that may constitute an abuse of market power.

L. Essential facilities

17.49 The draft guidelines state that a refusal to allow a rival to have access to an essential facility might constitute abuse under the Second Conduct Rule. A facility will be viewed as essential only where it can be demonstrated that access to it is indispensable in order to compete in a related market, and where duplication is impossible or extremely difficult owing to physical, geographic, economic, or legal constraints.

17.50 The draft guidelines state that an asset will not be regarded as an essential facility, if other similar facilities compete within the same relevant market (i.e. if there are potential substitutes), or if the facility is not indispensable to the provision of the product in question.

17.51 As with refusals to supply in general, it appears that a refusal to allow access to an essential facility should only raise concerns of breach if there is evidence of likely substantial harm to competition and there is no objective justification for the undertaking's behavior. Objective justifications might include constraints in the capacity of the facility; substantial increase in cost resulting from granting access that might jeopardize the economic viability of the facility holder or the undertaking seeking access not being technically able to use the facility in a proper manner.

M. Bundling (including loyalty and market share discounts)

17.52 See Section I.I.

N. Standard-setting groups (disclosure requirements, licensing arrangements, and licensing pools)

17.53 The draft guidelines state that agreements on technical or design standards may lead to an improvement in production by reducing costs or raising quality, or may promote technical or economic progress by reducing waste and consumers' search costs. The draft guidelines go on to state, however, that such agreements may have an appreciable adverse impact on competition in particular, if they include restrictions on what the parties may produce or, in effect, are a means of limiting competition from other sources, for example by raising entry barriers. Another example that is cited is standardization agreements which prevent the parties from developing alternative standards or products that do not comply with the agreed standard.

The draft guidelines state that a scheme is unlikely to have an appreciable adverse impact on competition where certification is available to all manufacturers that meet objective and reasonable quality requirements, but that where manufacturers must accept additional obligations governing the products which they can buy or sell, or restrictions as to pricing or marketing, the scheme will likely have an appreciable adverse impact on competition. **17.54**

O. Customer termination

There are no specific provisions in the law or draft guidelines addressing this. **17.55**

P. Termination of intermediaries

There are no specific provisions in the law or draft guidelines addressing this. **17.56**

Q. Termination of relationships with competitors

There are no specific provisions in the law or draft guidelines addressing this. **17.57**

R. Exclusions and exemptions

(i) Exclusions

Specified persons and activities are excluded under s. 4 of the Ordinance. As yet, no persons or activities have been flagged as falling within this exclusion. There is also a broad exclusion applying to most statutory bodies per s. 5 of the Ordinance. **17.58**

Schedule 1 to the Ordinance sets out various further exclusions. In the case of the Second Conduct Rule, exclusions apply in relation to: **17.59**

- conduct to the extent it is undertaken to comply with any law in Hong Kong (including subsidiary legislation);
- conduct engaged in by an undertaking entrusted by the Hong Kong government with the operation of services of general economic interest in so far as the Second Conduct Rule would obstruct the performance, in law or in fact, of the particular tasks assigned to it; and
- Mergers.

There is a further *de minimis* exclusion. A small or medium-size enterprise (SME) is protected from prosecution under the Second Conduct Rule where its turnover is less than HKD 40 million (approximately USD 5.1 million). This threshold is very low, and provides protection to only the smallest of businesses in Hong Kong. **17.60**

SMEs are defined as to manufacturing enterprises with fewer than a hundred employees and non-manufacturing enterprises with fewer than fifty employees. As of September 2012, there were about 300,000 SMEs in Hong Kong. **17.61**

(ii) Exemptions

Section 31 of the Ordinance provides that the Chief Executive in Council may, by order published in the Gazette, exempt specified conduct or a specified class of conduct from the application of the Second Conduct Rule, if he or she is satisfied that there are exceptional and compelling reasons of public policy for doing so. **17.62**

17.63 Section 32 of the Ordinance provides that the Chief Executive in Council may, by order published in the Gazette, exempt specified conduct or a specified class of conduct from the application of the Second Conduct Rule, if he or she is satisfied that it is appropriate to do so, in order to avoid a conflict between the Ordinance and an international obligation that directly or indirectly relates to Hong Kong.

17.64 Orders made under s. 31 or 32 are subject to negative vetting by the Legislative Council. There is no indication yet as to any conduct to which this exemption may be applied.

(iii) Efficiencies

17.65 As discussed below, there is an efficiency exclusion in Schedule 1 to the Ordinance which is only applicable to the First Conduct Rule, the prohibition in the Ordinance relating to concerted conduct. This leaves open the question how efficiencies will be assessed under the Second Conduct Rule. One must presume that it was not the legislature's intention that efficiencies of conduct engaged in by firms with market power be ignored. Otherwise, the Second Conduct Rule could have the effect of prohibiting a wide range of efficiency enhancing conduct that benefits consumers, simply because that conduct might, *prima facie*, impact in some negative way on competition.

17.66 The most logical inference is that efficiencies must be weighed in the balance when considering whether a conduct which is *prima facie* an "abuse" of market power has had the object or effect of preventing or restricting competition (the fact that this is the approach currently favored by the European Commission should have persuasive force in Hong Kong). However, it will only become clear when guidelines and decisions from the Tribunal and the appeal courts are available.

(iv) Decisions

17.67 Undertakings wanting to clarify whether agreements or conduct are exempt or excluded, may apply to the Competition Authorities for a decision ("Decision"). The Competition Authorities are only required to consider an application for a Decision if:

- the application poses novel or unresolved questions of wider importance or public interest in relation to the application of exclusions and exemptions under the Ordinance;
- the application raises questions for which there is no clarification in existing case law or Decisions; and
- it is possible to make a Decision on the basis of the information provided.

17.68 The Competition Authorities are required to bring applications for Decisions to the attention of other persons they consider likely to be affected and must consider any representations made to them about an application. The process will not, therefore, be private, and interested persons will have an opportunity to object to, or support applications.

17.69 The Competition Authorities may impose conditions or limitations subject to which a Decision is to have effect.

17.70 If a Competition Authority issues a Decision that conduct or agreements are excluded or exempt from the application of the Conduct Rules (or the Merger Rule), then the undertakings named in the Decision have immunity from any action under the Ordinance in relation to the relevant agreements or conduct. This immunity only applies to the extent the undertakings comply with any conditions or limitations in the Decision.

17.71 The Competition Authorities may rescind a Decision if there is a material change of circumstances after the Decision is made or if it is subsequently apparent that the information on which they based the Decision was materially incomplete, false or misleading.

II. Dealing with competitors

A. The general prohibition against anticompetitive concerted conduct

When it comes into force, s. 6 of the Ordinance, the First Conduct Rule, will prohibit agreements, concerted practices and decisions of associations of undertakings that have the object or effect of preventing, restricting or distorting competition in Hong Kong. The prohibition distinguishes between two different categories of agreements: **17.72**

(i) "serious anticompetitive conduct" i.e. price-fixing, market-sharing, output-controls and bid-rigging; and
(ii) "other agreements" i.e. any agreements not falling in category (i).

(i) Efficiency exclusion

Both categories require a two-step assessment: first, as to whether an agreement is, *prima facie*, in breach of the First Conduct Rule; and, if it is, as to whether the agreement has efficiencies that allow it to be excluded from prosecution (per the efficiency exclusion in Schedule 1, s. 1 of the Ordinance). **17.73**

To be excluded from prosecution, an agreement must: (i) contribute to improving production or distribution or (ii) promote technical or economic progress. However, it is also necessary to demonstrate that it does so while "allowing consumers a fair share of the resulting benefit." Finally, the agreement must not impose on the undertakings concerned restrictions which are not indispensable to the attainment of those objectives or which afford the undertakings concerned the possibility of eliminating competition in respect of a substantial part of the goods or services in question. **17.74**

(ii) Serious anticompetitive conduct and warning notices

There is an important procedural distinction between serious anticompetitive conduct and other conduct under the First Conduct Rule. Agreements between undertakings that are not considered "serious anticompetitive conduct" will be subject to a warning notice before the Competition Authorities are allowed to commence a prosecution under the First Conduct Rule. The warning notice must describe the conduct which the Commission says is in breach, identify the undertakings involved, and state the evidence or other materials the Commission relies on in support of its allegations. **17.75**

Warning notices are required to contain a statement that the Commission requires the undertakings involved to bring the conduct identified in the warning notice to an end within a specified period (the warning period) and must also indicate the manner in which the undertakings may cease the conduct (which may, in some commercial arrangements, be quite complex). **17.76**

In setting the length of the warning period, the Commission is required to have regard to the time likely to be required to cease the conduct that is said to be in breach. **17.77**

If the undertakings do not bring the conduct to an end within the warning period, the Competition Authorities are able to take action against the undertakings, but only in relation to conduct engaged in from the expiry of the warning period. **17.78**

(iii) Undertakings

The First Conduct Rule only applies to agreements between two or more separate undertakings. **17.79**

Any entity, regardless of its legal status or the way in which it is financed, could be regarded as an undertaking—the relevant test is whether the entity is engaged in economic activity. Undertakings may include companies, partnerships, individuals operating as sole traders, cooperatives, societies, business chambers, trade associations, and non-profit organizations. **17.80**

17.81 The draft guidelines state that the term "economic activity" is a broad term that refers to any activity consisting in offering goods or services on a market and which could, at least in principle, be carried on to make profits. An entity may engage in economic activity in some of its functions but not others.

17.82 Importantly for group companies, the draft guidelines state that the First Conduct Rule does not apply to agreements between entities which form a single economic unit. Generally, entities will be regarded as a single undertaking if there is a high degree of operational and financial control. The most obvious example is an agreement between a parent company and its subsidiary company, or between two companies under the control of a third company.

(iv) Agreement

17.83 The draft guidelines suggest that Hong Kong will, following other major jurisdictions, take a broad view as to what constitutes an agreement for the purposes of the Ordinance. The definition will include both legally enforceable and non-enforceable agreements, whether written or oral—including "gentlemen's agreements."

(v) Concerted practice

17.84 The Ordinance does not define the term "concerted practice." However, the draft guidelines state that a concerted practice may exist where there is informal cooperation between competitors, without any formal agreement or decision. It is expected that an approach similar to that adopted in Singapore will be taken in Hong Kong, namely that a concerted practice may exist where the parties knowingly substitute the risks of competition with cooperation between them.

17.85 Taking a pragmatic approach, the draft guidelines state that the simple fact that competitors are engaged in similar or parallel behavior does not mean that they are involved in a "concerted practice." Often this will be evidence of quite the opposite, because in a highly competitive market it is to be expected that competitors have no choice but to respond to each other's moves in the market.

17.86 The draft guidelines state that the following are examples of factors that the Commission may consider:

- whether the parties knowingly entered into practical cooperation;
- whether behavior in the market is influenced as a result of direct or indirect contact between undertakings;
- whether parallel behavior results from contact between undertakings leading to conditions of competition which do not correspond to normal conditions of the market; and
- whether the structure of the relevant market and the nature of the product involved are favorable to collusion.

(vi) Object and effect

17.87 Where a conduct has more than one object, it will be in breach if one of its objects is a proscribed object.[7] Rather unusually in comparison with other major jurisdictions, the First Conduct Rule, like the Second Conduct Rule, further provides that where a conduct has more than one effect, it has the effect of preventing, restricting or distorting competition if one of its effects is to prevent, restrict or distort competition.[8]

17.88 The draft guidelines list the same conduct under both the First and Second Conduct Rules as examples of conduct that may have a proscribed effect.

[7] Competition Ordinance (n 1) s. 7(1).

[8] Competition Ordinance (n 1) s. 7(3). See further discussion at paras. 17.19–17.22 in relation to the Second Conduct Rule.

(vii) Block exemptions

The Commission is empowered under s. 15 of the Ordinance to issue a block exemption order in respect of a particular category of agreements if satisfied that they fall within the efficiency exclusion in Schedule 1, s. 1 to the Ordinance. **17.89**

It remains to be seen how the Competition Authorities will use this power in Hong Kong, but it is assumed that some form of block exemption will be applied in relation to vertical agreements. Block exemptions may be granted on the Competition Authorities' own volition or on application by an undertaking. Interested third parties can be heard on whether block exemptions should be granted and any block exemptions granted by the Competition Authorities must be reviewed at least every five years after any grant or renewal. **17.90**

(viii) De minimis carve-out

SMEs have some degree of protection in relation to the First Conduct Rule under the *de minimis* thresholds that have been implemented. It is important to emphasize that the *de minimis* threshold does not apply to what the Ordinance defines as "serious anticompetitive conduct." The thresholds do, however, protect SMEs from prosecution for "other agreements," so long as the combined turnover of all undertakings that have entered into the agreement is no greater than HKD 200 million. **17.91**

(ix) Other exclusions and exemptions

The various other exclusions and exemptions referred to at paras. 17.58–17.59 and 17.62–17.63 that apply in relation to the Second Conduct Rule also apply to the First Conduct Rule. **17.92**

(x) Vertical agreements

The First Conduct Rule makes no distinction between horizontal and vertical agreements. Vertical agreements are those between undertakings at different levels in the production or distribution chain. **17.93**

It is said in the draft guidelines that vertical agreements would be subject to the application of the First Conduct Rule in a "much more limited fashion." The draft guidelines recognize that vertical agreements are generally a legitimate way of influencing how a supplier's products is distributed and marketed. It remains to be seen how the exemption for vertical agreements is structured and how broadly it is applied. **17.94**

B. Horizontal price fixing (including advanced announcements of price or product changes)

Fixing, maintaining, increasing, or controlling the price for the supply of goods or services is specified as one of the serious types of anticompetitive conduct under s. 2 of the Ordinance. The Ordinance defines prices to include any discount, rebate, allowance, price concession, or other advantage in relation to the supply of goods or services. **17.95**

The draft guidelines state that there are many ways in which prices can be fixed, including fixing either the price itself or the components of a price such as a discount, or establishing a range outside which prices are not to move. The draft guidelines also reference recommendations by trade associations and price coordination on any product as examples of price fixing. **17.96**

C. Horizontal agreements to allocate customers or territories; agreements not to compete

Allocating sales, territories, customers, or markets for the production or supply of goods or services is specified as a serious anticompetitive conduct under s. 2 of the Ordinance. Market sharing, in essence, consists of agreements that establish defined markets for particular undertakings (whether by territory, size or product). **17.97**

17.98 The draft guidelines give the following examples of agreements between undertakings that may fall foul of this prohibition:

- not to compete in the production of each other's goods;
- not to sell in each other's geographic "territories";
- not to solicit or sell to each other's customers; or
- not to expand into a market in which another participant is an actual or potential rival.

17.99 Some market-sharing agreements may not be considered serious anticompetitive conduct. For example, the agreements between undertakings to specialize in the manufacture of certain components of a product, in order to produce in longer runs and compete more efficiently might not be considered as serious anticompetitive conduct. It is not yet clear how Hong Kong proposes to approach such agreements. In any event, such conduct—even if not "serious" anticompetitive conduct—may be prohibited under the "other agreements" category if it nevertheless restricts competition in all the circumstances.

D. Horizontal boycotts

17.100 See paras. 17.118–17.120. See further the discussion at paras. 17.19–17.22 in relation to the Second Conduct Rule on joint purchasing. Otherwise, there are no specific provisions in the law or draft guidelines addressing this.

E. Joint ventures and other competitive collaborations

17.101 The Merger Rule (contained in Schedule 7 to the Ordinance) prohibits any merger (whether the agreement was entered into in Hong Kong or overseas) that has, or is likely to have, the effect of substantially lessening competition in Hong Kong. It is, at present, restricted to mergers involving one or more entities that own or control (directly or indirectly) a telecommunications carrier licensee.

17.102 The definition of a merger for the purposes of the Merger Rule extends to full-function joint ventures, i.e. the establishment, on a lasting basis, of a joint venture to perform the functions of an autonomous economic entity.

17.103 The Ordinance provides a carve-out for mergers to prevent them from being attacked under the Conduct Rules. The carve-out is consistent with the Hong Kong government's stated policy position that it is not introducing a general merger control regime at this stage.

17.104 Some joint ventures will enjoy a degree of protection, to the extent that they fall within the definition of a "merger" and can thereby rely on the merger carve out. In order to qualify, it will be necessary to demonstrate that the joint venture is one to "perform, on a lasting basis, all the functions of an autonomous economic entity."

17.105 Joint ventures that do not have the benefit of protection under the merger carve out will be subject to potential challenge, where there is a concern that they have the object or effect of preventing, restricting or distorting competition.

F. Trade associations

17.106 The First Conduct Rule expressly prohibits members of associations (including trade associations) from giving effect to decisions of their association which have the object or effect of preventing, restricting, and distorting competition in a market in Hong Kong.

17.107 Decisions of associations can take many forms, including: the constitution or rules of an association, association recommendations, or resolutions and binding decisions of the association's management or executive committee.

The draft guidelines state that trade associations have continued to function effectively to the benefit of their members in jurisdictions which have had competition laws for many years. They go on to say that the key consideration is whether the object or effect of the decision, whatever form it takes, is to influence the conduct or coordinate the activity of members in some commercial matter. **17.108**

G. Interlocking directorates

There are no specific provisions in the law or draft guidelines addressing this. **17.109**

H. Facilitating practices

There are no specific provisions in the law or draft guidelines addressing this. **17.110**

I. Information exchange

Information sharing between manufacturers, distributors, and retailers can be in breach of the First Conduct Rule, for example, if strategic price information provided to a supplier by a retailer and is then shared by that supplier with a competitor retailer (known as "hub-and-spoke" information exchange which can facilitate the coordination of the retailers' respective prices.) **17.111**

The draft guidelines state that generally there is no objection to the exchange of information between competitors, through a trade association or otherwise. However, they go on to say that competitive pressure in a market is often driven by uncertainty amongst competitors about how each other proposes to compete and their likely responses to each other and that the exchange of information may have an appreciable adverse impact on competition, where it serves to reduce or remove uncertainties inherent in the process of competition. **17.112**

It is not necessarily relevant that the information could have been obtained from other sources—the draft guidelines suggest that the process of exchange directly between competitors may build up a level of predictability and certainty between them that gives rise to a breach of the First Conduct Rule. The draft guidelines suggest an announcement of a proposed price increase may also trigger a breach. **17.113**

Factors the draft guidelines suggest will be relevant include: **17.114**

- the number of undertakings operating in the market;
- the frequency of the exchanges;
- the sensitivity and confidentiality of the information that is exchanged; and
- whether access to information exchanged is limited to certain participating undertakings to the exclusion of their competitors and buyers.

(i) Exchanges of historic pricing information

The draft guidelines state that exchanges of purely historical information that is aggregated, and which cannot be disaggregated, is unlikely to have an appreciable adverse impact on competition. The more recent or current the information exchanged, the more likely that exchange could have an appreciable adverse impact on competition. **17.115**

(ii) How old, anonymous, and aggregated pricing information needs to be

There are no specific provisions in the law or draft guidelines addressing this. **17.116**

(iii) What pro-competitive purposes, if any, exchange needs to help participants achieve; pre-merger due diligence

There are no specific provisions in the law or draft guidelines addressing this. **17.117**

J. Joint purchasing agreements

17.118 The draft guidelines state that where competitors group together to exercise more leverage against sellers, this generally should not be regarded as adversely affecting competition because such conduct usually results in lower prices and better conditions of purchase. In particular, agreements between small and medium-sized enterprises to allow them to obtain favorable buying conditions matching their much larger competitors in the market will normally give rise to no concerns under the Ordinance.

17.119 The draft guidelines indicate that there will be a concern about the impact on competition if the parties to the joint purchasing agreement are exercising their buying power to foreclose competitors or to raise rivals' costs. An example is limiting the access of competing buyers (i.e. competitors which are not part of the buying group) to suppliers.

17.120 The draft guidelines also suggest there will be a concern about the impact on competition where joint selling agreements are, in substance, agreements to restrain competition between the parties. For example, joint selling agreements to coordinate pricing policies of participating undertakings will eliminate price competition between the parties.

K. Joint lobbying/regulatory/legislative efforts

17.121 There are no specific provisions in the law or draft guidelines addressing this.

III. General issues

A. Jurisdiction and applicable law (including sector-specific competition regulation)

(i) Jurisdiction

17.122 The Competition Rules only apply to "undertakings." The key consideration is whether an entity is engaged in "economic activities," i.e. whether it offers goods or services on a market.

17.123 Many statutory bodies are to be exempted from the law even though they may, in whole or in part, carry out economic activities that bring them within the definition of an undertaking.

17.124 The Conduct Rules will apply to conduct regardless of whether it is engaged in within or outside Hong Kong. The critical question to ask is whether the conduct has been engaged in with the object or effect of preventing, restricting or distorting competition in Hong Kong.

(ii) Sectoral regimes

17.125 There are currently two sectoral competition law regimes: one regulating telecommunications licensees and the other regulating broadcasting licensees. Both regimes are, since the amalgamation of the Telecommunications and Broadcasting Authorities in April of 2012, now administered by the Communications Authority.

17.126 The Telecommunications Ordinance[9] contains prohibitions against telecommunications licensees engaging in:

[9] Telco Rule (n 5).

- conduct which in the opinion of the Communications Authority, has the purpose or effect of preventing or substantially restricting competition in a telecommunications market (the s. 7K prohibition);
- abuse of a dominant position, which is deemed to have occurred if, in the opinion of the Communications Authority, a licensee has engaged in conduct which has the purpose or effect of preventing or substantially restricting competition in a telecommunications market (the s. 7L prohibition);
- conduct which, in the opinion of the Communications Authority, is misleading or deceptive in providing or acquiring telecommunications networks, systems, installations, customer equipment or services (the s. 7M prohibition); and
- discrimination by a dominant licensee between persons who acquire services in the market on charges or the conditions of supply, where, in the opinion of the Communications Authority, such discrimination has the purpose or effect of preventing or substantially restricting competition in a telecommunications market (the s. 7N prohibition).

Competition provisions can also be found in certain license conditions, which are generally not inconsistent with the statutory prohibitions outlined above. **17.127**

The Broadcasting Ordinance,[10] contains prohibitions against broadcasting licensees engaging in: **17.128**

- conduct which, in the opinion of the Authority, has the purpose or effect of preventing, distorting or substantially restricting competition in a television program service market (the s. 13 prohibition); and
- abuse of a dominant position, which is deemed to have occurred if, in the opinion of the Authority, a licensee has engaged in conduct which has the purpose or effect of preventing, distorting or substantially restricting competition in a television program service market (the s. 14 prohibition).

Competition provisions can also be found in certain license conditions, for example, the firewall provisions in the licenses of Television Broadcasts Limited (TVB) and TVB Pay Vision Limited. **17.129**

The sectoral competition laws will be withdrawn when the Conduct Rules come into force and the Communications Authority will share concurrent jurisdiction with the Competition Commission to enforce the Conduct Rules under a Memorandum of Understanding to be promulgated between the two regulators. At that point, a new prohibition on excessive pricing and unfair terms (the Telco Rule) will be introduced. The Telco Rule will only apply to telecommunications licensees that are dominant in a telecommunications market. **17.130**

B. Antitrust System

(i) Name of agency/agencies

Competition Rules The Competition Rules will be enforced under a judicial enforcement model. **17.131**

The Competition Commission: with its primary functions being to (i) investigate suspected breaches of the Ordinance; (ii) take pre-prosecution enforcement actions (e.g. to issue decisions, take commitments, and issue infringement/warning notices); and (iii) bring **17.132**

[10] An Ordinance to license companies to provide broadcasting services, to regulate the provision of broadcasting services by licensees, and to provide for matters incidental thereto or connected therewith (Cap. 562) E.R. 2 of 2012 ("Broadcasting Ordinance").

enforcement proceedings in relation to alleged breaches of the Competition Rules. The Commission can also carry out market studies, though it is not clear how extensive this function will be.

17.133 The Communications Authority: with concurrent jurisdiction over cases under the Competition Rules involving telecommunications or broadcasting licensees. The Communications Authority will also have jurisdiction over excessive pricing cases. However, such cases will proceed under an administrative enforcement model whereby the Communications Authority investigates and makes infringement decisions.

17.134 The two regulators are referred to as the Competition Authorities.

17.135 The Competition Tribunal: a division of the High Court competent to (i) review decisions made by the Competition Authorities under the Ordinance; (ii) act as the primary court of first instance to hear and decide competition cases and to impose penalties and other relief orders for contravention of the Competition Rules; and (iii) to hear follow-on private actions.

17.136 The Chief Executive in Council of the Hong Kong SAR Government will appoint a President to lead the Tribunal. Each case is to be led by a presiding Tribunal member, sitting with other judicial members. The Tribunal may also appoint assessors or non-judicial persons to assist in the adjudication of cases.

17.137 It appears that the Tribunal will have its own rules of practice and procedure and it is not bound by the usual rules of evidence that bind the courts.

17.138 The right to legal professional privilege has been expressly preserved, pursuant to s. 58 of the Ordinance.

17.139 Claims related purely to alleged infringement of a Conduct Rule must be brought in the Tribunal, as must Merger Rule claims.

17.140 The *Court of Appeal* hears appeals against Tribunal decisions. Appeals against final decisions are allowed as of right but leave is required to appeal an interlocutory decision. Leave may only be granted where the Tribunal is satisfied the appeal has a reasonable prospect of success or there is some other reason in the interests of justice why the appeal should be heard. There is also a process for stating cases to the Court of Appeal in relation to Tribunal review of the Competition Authorities' decisions.

17.141 *Court of Final Appeal* is Hong Kong's final court of appeal and will, in appropriate cases, hear appeals from decisions of the Court of Appeal.

17.142 **Telco Rule** *Communications Authority*: the Telco Rule is to be brought in under the Telecommunications Ordinance, which adopts an administrative enforcement model. Under this model, the Communications Authority has both the investigative and adjudicative functions.

17.143 *Telecommunications (Competition Provisions) Appeal Board (Competition Appeal Board)* hears appeals against decisions of the Communications Authority.

17.144 Cases may be stated to the Court of Appeal and appealed to the Court of Final Appeal, either during or at the conclusion of Competition Appeal Board hearings by way of application for a case sated.

17.145 Where a case is brought against a telecommunications licensee under the Telco Rule, there is every chance it will be coupled with allegations of abuse of market power. A recent example of such a scenario (though not involving the Telco Rule) is the Telecommunications Authority's

November 2010 decision in *PCCW-HKT Telephone Limited.*[11] Given that the Ordinance provides that allegations of abuse of market power (breaches of the Second Conduct Rule) are to be decided by the Tribunal and that appeals are to be heard by the Court of Appeal, it is not clear how the apparently intractable jurisdictional issues created by such an approach will be resolved.

Judicial review The Commission and the Communications Authority are amendable to judicial review. There were a considerable number of judicial review claims brought against the Office of the Telecommunications Authority before it was subsumed into the new Communications Authority and this trend may continue. **17.146**

Although there is no express prohibition against judicially reviewing the Tribunal, this is likely to be an unusual course to consider in practice, given that the standard procedure for a party aggrieved by a decision of the Courts of First Instance is to appeal to the Court of Appeal. **17.147**

As a statutory appeal board, the Competition Appeal Board is also amenable to judicial review, highlighting a difference between the judicial enforcement model that applies under the Ordinance and the administrative enforcement model that applies under the Telecommunications Ordinance. **17.148**

(ii) Staff size and budget

The Commission will be led by a Chairperson and will consist of between 5 and 16 members (including the Chairperson). Commission members are expected to have expertise or experience in industry, commerce, economics, law, SMEs, or public policy. While it has not been established yet, the Hong Kong government earmarked HKD 80.7 million[12] in the 2012/2013 budget to cater for the recruitment and employment of the Commission's staff, the leasing of the Commission's office accommodation, and research and promotional work of the Commission. **17.149**

As of March 31, 2012, the Office of Telecommunication Authority had an overall staff strength of 327, comprising 202 civil servants, and 125 employed on non-civil service contract terms. Total revenue of the Office of Telecommunication Authority for the financial year 2012 is HKD 411.6 million, with 84.6 percent of it as license fees revenue. **17.150**

(iii) Recent enforcement actions and trends

There has been active litigation under the existing sectoral competition laws in the broadcasting and telecommunications sectors over recent years, including in relation to alleged abuses of dominance and issues arising around changes in the telecommunications regulatory structures. **17.151**

As the Conduct Rules are not yet in force, there are no enforcement trends outside the sectoral regimes. **17.152**

C. Private litigation

The Ordinance does not provide for standalone rights of private action in relation to the Conduct Rules. **17.153**

In relation to the Telco Rule, s. 39 A of the Telecommunications Act provides that: **17.154**

> a person sustaining loss or damage from a breach of section 7K, 7L, 7M or 7N, or a breach of a licence condition, determination or direction relating to that section, may bring an action for damages, an injunction or other appropriate remedy, order or relief against the person who is in breach.

[11] *PCCW-HKT Telephone Limited*, OFTA Case no. T62/08 (November 2008), <http://tel_archives.ofca.gov.hk/en/ca_bd/case_closed/T62_08.pdf>.

[12] See Secretary for Commerce and Economic Development
Session No. 12, Replies to initial written questions raised by Finance Committee Members in examining the Estimates of Expenditure 2012–13, <http://www.legco.gov.hk/yr11-12/english/fc/fc/w_q/cedb-cit-e.pdf>.

D. Follow-on litigation (includes role of agency determinations of liability for follow-on litigation)

17.155 There are follow-on rights of private action under the Ordinance, where it is established that there has been a breach of the Conduct Rules.

17.156 Claimants may seek damages and a wide range of other remedies in follow-on actions, including disgorgement orders, awards of damages, orders for divestiture and a wide range of other orders as specified in Schedule 3 to the Ordinance.

E. Arbitration and alternative dispute resolution

17.157 There are no express provisions in the Ordnance addressing arbitration or alternative dispute resolution (ADR). It remains to be seen whether ADR may be addressed in the guidelines and/or the Tribunal's rules of procedure.

F. Remedies

(i) Commitments

17.158 The Competition Authorities may accept commitments from a person to take any action or refrain from taking any action that they consider appropriate to address their concerns about a possible contravention of a Conduct Rule. If they accept a commitment, they may agree:

- not to commence an investigation or, if they have commenced an investigation, to terminate it; or
- not to bring proceedings in the Tribunal or, if they have commenced proceedings, to terminate them.

17.159 Undertakings need to take care when agreeing to commitments. The Competition Authorities may ask for an admission that one or more of the Conduct Rules was infringed, exposing the undertaking to potential follow-on actions.

(ii) Infringement notices

17.160 The Competition Authorities may, instead of bringing a prosecution for serious anticompetitive conduct or abuse of market power, issue an infringement notice against the person(s) it proposes to prosecute, offering not to bring the proceedings if they agree to make a commitment to comply with the infringement notice. The Competition Authorities are not obliged to take this step and could, in appropriate case, proceed directly to lodging proceedings in the Tribunal.

17.161 An infringement notice must contain details of the alleged contravention, including: the Conduct Rule alleged to have been contravened; the conduct that is alleged to contravene the rule; the person(s) whose conduct is alleged to constitute the contravention; and the evidence or other materials that the Competition Authorities rely on in support of their allegations.

17.162 The notice must also set out the requirements the undertakings must comply with in order to avoid a prosecution being brought. The Competition Authorities may require that undertakings admit to a contravention of the relevant Conduct Rule. If this is the case, this would expose the undertakings to follow-on actions from third parties.

17.163 The Competition Authorities are required to give notice of their intention to issue an infringement notice, and to allow the undertakings concerned a period of no less than fifteen days to make submission on why an infringement notice should not be issued.

17.164 It bears emphasis that infringement notices may only be issued in relation to (i) serious anticompetitive conduct that might be in breach of the First Conduct Rule or (ii) conduct that might be in breach of the Second Conduct Rule. Non-serious conduct under the First Conduct Rule is subject to the warning notice mechanism discussed in the following Section.

(iii) Warning notices

Agreements between undertakings that are not considered "serious anticompetitive conduct" will be subject to a warning notice before prosecution under the First Conduct Rule. **17.165**

Warning notices must describe the conduct that the Competition Authorities say is in breach, identify the undertakings involved and state the evidence or other materials they rely on in support of their allegations. Warning notices are required to contain a statement that the Competition Authorities require the undertakings involved to bring the conduct identified in the warning notice to an end within a specified period (the warning period) and must also indicate the manner in which the undertakings may cease the conduct (which may, in some commercial arrangements, be quite complex). In setting the length of the warning period the Competition Authorities are required to have regard to the time likely to be required to cease the conduct that is said to be in breach. **17.166**

It is not clear whether the Competition Authorities can, within the warning notice, require the undertakings involved to admit liability and agree to commitments. If this is allowed, this could expose undertakings to follow-on private actions. **17.167**

In the event that the undertakings do not comply with the warning notice and the Competition Authorities bring a prosecution, proceedings may not be brought in respect of any period that precedes the warning period. **17.168**

(iv) Injunction

The Tribunal has the power (under s. 95) to issue interim orders (including interim injunctions) if it is satisfied that a person is engaged in or proposing to engage in a contravention of the Competition Rules, pending a final determination on contravention of the Competition Rules. **17.169**

Interim orders may be granted either on the Tribunal's own motion or on application. The Tribunal may make an interim order regardless of whether: **17.170**

- the person against whom the order is to be made intends to engage again or to continue to engage in the conduct the subject of the order;
- the person has previously engaged in the conduct that is to be the subject of the order; or
- there is imminent danger of damage or loss being incurred by the person if the order is made.

(v) Telco Rule

There are no express mechanisms under the Telecommunications Ordinance for infringement notices, warning notices, commitments, or leniency (although the regulator states in its guidelines that consideration will be given to leniency in appropriate cases). In practice, the Telecommunications Authority has tended to deploy a range of remedies, including sometimes just issuing a warning at the conclusion of an investigation if considered appropriate. **17.171**

The Telecommunications Authority has published guidelines as to its investigation procedures in relation to the existing sector-specific telecommunications competition provisions in the Telecommunications Ordinance. However, those guidelines have not always been followed in practice. It is hoped that this trend will not continue under the auspices of the new Communications Authority. **17.172**

As has been noted above, there are likely to be difficult issues as to jurisdiction and procedure to be applied in cases concerning allegations both of breach of the Telco Rule and breach of one or more of the Conduct Rules. It is hoped the guidelines will clarify what is proposed in this regard and it remains to be seen how these jurisdictional issues will be resolved. **17.173**

(vi) Civil liability

17.174 The Tribunal has the power to apply a broad range of remedies for contraventions of the Competition Rules. This includes pecuniary penalties not exceeding 10 percent of the turnover of the undertaking "obtained in Hong Kong" for each year of infringement, up to a maximum of three years. If the period of the infringement exceeds three years, the penalty may be the three years of infringement with the highest turnover.

17.175 The Tribunal may also make disgorgement orders, awards of damages to aggrieved parties; interim injunctions during investigations or proceedings; injunctions and disqualification orders against directors, orders for divestiture, and a wide range of other orders as specified in Schedule 3 to the Ordinance.

17.176 **Indemnity of directors/employees** There are restrictions stipulated under s. 168 of the Ordinance on the ability to indemnify employees against liability from paying pecuniary penalties and costs incurred in defending actions for contempt of the Tribunal, offenses committed under the Ordinance and in defending proceedings in which that person is ordered to pay a penalty for breaching a Competition Rule.

17.177 Any indemnity in breach of these restrictions will be void. Undertakings found in breach of these restrictions will also be subject to financial penalties equating to the value of the indemnity, which could result in a substantial fine in some cases.

17.178 The prohibition on funds for indemnity in defending proceedings is subject to some qualifications, allowing indemnity in certain circumstances, so long as the funds are to be repaid in the event of the employee being required by the Tribunal to pay the pecuniary penalty and if the funds are to be repaid not later than the date when the decision of the Tribunal becomes final.

(vii) Criminal liability

17.179 There is no criminal liability for breach of the Conduct Rules.

17.180 However, ss. 172–175 of the Ordinance provide for criminal penalties, including imprisonment for:

- without reasonable excuse, failing to comply with requirements or prohibitions imposed in relation to obtaining documents and attending before the Competition Authorities;
- intentionally, or recklessly destroying or otherwise disposing of, falsifying, or concealing documents;
- obstructing searches being conducted under warrant;
- knowingly, or reckless, providing false or misleading information to the Competition Authorities; or
- terminating the employment of employees or in any way discriminating against them where they have provided material to the Competition Authorities or agreed to give evidence for them.

G. Leniency and immunity

17.181 The Competition Authorities may enter into leniency agreements with individuals and corporations, agreeing not to pursue penalties against them, in exchange for their cooperation in an investigation or proceedings. The Competition Authorities can enter into such agreements on terms they "consider appropriate." It should be emphasized that such agreements only relate to proceedings for penalties.

17.182 The restriction on the Competition Authorities bringing proceedings for a penalty where there is a leniency agreement in place would also protect employees of a company where it is the company that has entered into the leniency agreement.

There are no express mechanisms under the Telecommunications Ordinance for leniency. However, the Telecommunications Authority states in its guidelines that consideration will be given to leniency in appropriate cases. It is observed that, in practice, the Telecommunications Authority has deployed a range of remedies, including sometimes just issuing a warning at the conclusion of an investigation, if considered appropriate. **17.183**

H. Document creation and retention

The Ordinance does not provide for specific rules in relation to document creation and retention. **17.184**

18

HUNGARY

Gábor Fejes
Oppenheim

Introduction

18.01 Hungarian competition law is modeled on, and—with a few exceptions as detailed below—very much follows, European antitrust law. Thus, similarly to European antitrust law, Hungarian competition law and competition enforcement not only concerns anticompetitive agreements entered into between competitors (as detailed in Section II), but also anticompetitive agreements between non-competitors (such as resale price maintenance) as well as entirely unilateral conduct by an undertaking (as detailed in Section I). This latter set of categories is dealt with by the rules on the prohibition of an abuse of a dominant position (such as refusal to supply or predatory pricing). The fundamental rules on competition are codified by the Hungarian Competition Act (Act No. 57 of 1996) (HCA). Public enforcement of such rules lies exclusively with the Hungarian Competition Authority (*Gazdasági Versenyhivatal*) (GVH), an independent agency which reports solely to the Hungarian Parliament.

I. Acting alone

A. Anticompetitive agreements and understandings with non-competitors

As to the conceptual framework concerning anticompetitive agreements between non-competitors, under Hungarian competition law agreements between non-competitors may also fall under the general prohibition of anticompetitive agreements as contained under article 11 of the HCA. At the same time, such arrangements may escape this prohibition, if the cumulative conditions contained in article 17 of the HCA are fulfilled (such conditions being largely identical to those encapsulated under article 101(3) of the Treaty on the Functioning of the European Union (TFEU)). In addition, there are various block exemption regulations issued by the Hungarian legislator, which are almost word-for-word copies of their EU counterparts, and which make it unnecessary for companies to undertake an individual analysis of their arrangements, provided that the conditions contained in the relevant block exemption regulation are met. **18.02**

B. Abuse of a dominant position

Article 21 of the HCA encapsulates a general prohibition of an abuse of a dominant position. The same provision also provides—without wishing to set forth an exhaustive list—examples for each of the typical forms of abuses (such as unfairly high prices, tying, discrimination, etc.). A position of dominance of a relevant market exists, under the definition of the HCA: "when an undertaking is capable of behaving appreciably independently of the other market operators, without having to have regard to the market conduct of its competitors, suppliers and business partners when it is defining its own market conduct" (art. 22 HCA). The HCA also lists various factors which help determine whether dominance exists, including—as under European law—the market situation of the undertaking (including its market share); the barriers to entry to, and exit from, the market; as well as any competitive pressure exercised by other market players, such as customers or buyers. It is interesting to note that the HCA itself acknowledges the notion of collective dominance, when it states that a dominant position may be held by one undertaking alone or by several undertakings jointly (art. 22(3) HCA). **18.03**

As under European law, enjoying a dominant position in itself is not against the law; it is only the abuse of such a position that falls foul of the Hungarian antitrust rules. There are unfortunately no guidance or general principles issued by the GVH as to the application of the Hungarian rules; nevertheless, the growing practice of the GVH gives a rather good overview of the stance of public enforcement as regards the relevant market practices. **18.04**

The GVH has not been thus far an overly active authority in terms of potential abuses of dominant positions, and the amounts of fines imposed have been significantly below those levied in relation to arrangements between competitors. In terms of the rules pertaining to unilateral conduct, the GVH appears to have intervened the most in certain specific sectors (such as telecommunications), where—mostly due to historic reasons or as a result of the specific legislative background—the harm to consumers was clear and apparent. A possible reason for this less activist approach of the GVH could be the rather high standard that the GVH applied in respect of such infringements: namely, the GVH made it clear from early on that its purpose is not the protection of individual competitors, but rather the safeguarding of the competitive process as such. As a result, a breach of competition law can only be found if it was made clear from the facts of the case that the given conduct entailed an appreciable harm to consumers and could not be objectively justified.[1] **18.05**

[1] See the consistent line of cases starting with *Rónahír*, GVH, Case no. Vj-10/2002 (July 5, 2002).

C. Predatory pricing

18.06 Predatory pricing is an abuse specifically contained in the HCA itself. It is defined as a conduct whereby an undertaking applies low prices (i) that are not based on greater efficiency vis-à-vis competitors and (ii) that are capable of excluding competitors from the market or of hindering their entry or expansion.

18.07 The GVH had the opportunity to consider the issue of predatory pricing in a number of cases, and put emphasis on passing the latter part of the two-tier test (namely the practical capability of the exclusion of competitors). In this respect, the GVH considered the following factors to be relevant: (i) the resources of the dominant undertaking to sustain the low prices, (ii) the barriers to entry to the market in general, and (iii) the time frame of the application of those low prices. Despite numerous attempts, so far there has not been a single case where this type of infringement would have been successfully established by the GVH. For example, on one occasion, the GVH reviewed the pricing and costs of various petrol stations operated by retail chains (such as Tesco or Auchan): it reviewed consumer prices in light of applicable costs (namely average variable costs and average total costs). As the prices applied were, in fact, above costs on the basis of the proper economic calculations, the GVH found against predatory conduct.[2]

D. Exploitative offenses

18.08 Excessive (unfair) pricing and the "imposition of unjustified advantages" can also constitute abuses within the meaning of Hungarian competition law.

18.09 In terms of pricing, the practice of the GVH clearly confirms that unfairly high prices could be abusive. It is also well-established that the issue of unfairness is to be defined on the basis of a comparison of the actual price applied by the given undertaking to the competitive price. Such competitive price could be established either on a cost-based model (taking into account the justifiable costs and a reasonable profit) or on the basis of benchmarks (prices used in a different, but comparable geographical market or prices which were used in the same market in an earlier time period). Like other competition agencies, the GVH has shown a certain reluctance to find for such type of an infringement, most probably since the GVH also does not wish to see itself as a price regulator. For example, in a case concerning electricity distribution fees, even though the GVH found that the relevant fees could very well be excessive in general, it decided not to intervene due to the fact that the regulatory environment has changed in the meantime in favor of consumers.[3]

18.10 With regard to other exploitative practices, the GVH stated that they could cover a wide range of conduct, for example, a failure by a dominant undertaking to provide sufficient time for its customers to adapt to an entirely new and complex method of selling airtime[4] or even a decision by a dominant cable TV operator to change the grouping of TV programs to the detriment of viewers.[5]

E. Monopsony

18.11 A dominant buyer may be held liable for abusing such a position. The GVH confirmed this in a case concerning a failure by the Hungarian national motorway agency to issue a tender for the construction of certain motorways before Hungary's accession to the European

---

[2] See *TESCO/Auchan petrol stations*, GVH, Case no. Vj-168/2004 (March 25, 2005).

[3] See *Electricity companies*, GVH, Case no. Vj-27/2005 (July 27, 2006).

[4] See *RTL pricing*, GVH, Case no. Vj-49/2004 (June 17, 2005).

[5] *Alföld Cable TV*, GVH, Case no. Vj-64/2004 (January 27, 2005).

Union. However, as the GVH did not find the agency to be in a dominant position on the buying side of the market, the case was not pursued any further.[6]

F. Price discrimination

For undertakings in a dominant position, the HCA contains a general prohibition of discrimination (in terms of prices, payment deadlines, or other selling or purchase conditions), provided that such discrimination entails a competitive disadvantage to others. The above definition clearly includes all forms and types of discrimination, including price discrimination. **18.12**

The relevant Hungarian practice makes it clear that, in order for price discrimination to arise, the criterion of competitive disadvantage, and thereby an appreciable/detectable harm to consumers, must be present. In a case concerning fees charged for the distribution of commercial TV programming, the GVH found that there was no evidence of an appreciable distortion of competition on the downstream market, and therefore the difference between the fees charged was not found to be abusive.[7] In addition, if lower/different prices are justified by the different characteristics of the deals (e.g. different volumes entailing different discounts), then discrimination cannot be established. **18.13**

At the same time, if a difference in prices results in higher than normal prices, then this can clearly be regarded as an exploitative abuse,[8] and such differences could also have exclusionary effects.[9] **18.14**

G. Dictating or influencing resale prices

(i) Resale price maintenance

Fixed or minimum resale prices are regarded under Hungarian competition law as a serious infringement. The GVH has confirmed this in a number of cases, consistently holding that agreeing on fixed or minimum resale prices is an "obviously anticompetitive practice,"[10] and negative effects on competition must be "presumed" from the existence of the arrangement itself.[11] From this line of cases, it can be inferred that fixed or minimum resale price arrangements are regarded as being "hard core" restrictions, i.e. having an anticompetitive object within the meaning of competition law. This entails that from the perspective of the existence of an infringement, the sanctions attached to the agreement or the compliance therewith are irrelevant. **18.15**

Fixed or minimum resale prices are also arrangements that cannot be exempted under the Hungarian vertical block exemption regulation, and as a result, the entire agreement falls outside the scope of such block exemption (due to its "hard core" nature). Resale price maintenance (RPM) is not likely to satisfy the efficiency conditions contained under article 17 of the HCA (individual exemption), either. Notwithstanding this, the possibility of such an exemption was emphasized in a seminal case, even for these types of practice, in light of recent developments in European law.[12] **18.16**

At the same time, under the rather generous Hungarian *de minimis* regulation, fixed or minimum resale price arrangements between companies that have a market share below 10 percent are regarded as an arrangement of minor importance falling outside the scope **18.17**

[6] *Nemzeti Autópálya*, GVH, Case no. Vj-41/2002 (June 2, 2003).
[7] *MTM-SBS*, GVH, Case no. Vj-7/2007 (December 4, 2008).
[8] See Section I.D. on excessive pricing.
[9] See Section I.L. on fidelity rebates.
[10] *MOL*, GVH, Case no. Vj-171/2002 (June 24, 2003), para. 52
[11] *Castrol*, GVH, Case no. Vj-7/2008 (March 29, 2010).
[12] *Gekko*, GVH, Case no. Vj-60/2009 (April 27, 2010).

of the prohibition of anticompetitive agreements (this is relevant, however, only if the given arrangement has no effect on trade between EU member states, i.e. if European competition law does not apply).

18.18 Hungarian case law is also indifferent whether an RPM agreement can be established on the basis of a written contract, an oral agreement, or by an exchange of letters. Furthermore, the prohibition on RPM in the GVH's practice extends to both direct and indirect means of influencing the resale prices: examples include a requirement for the manufacturer's prior consent to resale price changes,[13] provisions setting the margin of retailers,[14] and clauses which prohibit application of discounts by the distributor.[15]

18.19 As opposed to fixed or minimum resale prices, maximum or recommended resale prices are not anticompetitive, provided that they do not entail fixed or minimum resale prices (imposed, e.g. through pressure exerted, or incentives offered, by the supplier).

18.20 In terms of sanctions, the GVH has followed a relatively flexible policy concerning RPM arrangements. If the facts of the case showed that the RPM arrangement did not work in practice and the manufacturer/producer was open to cooperation with the GVH in removing any potentially restrictive clauses, generally, no fine was imposed. However, where the RPM agreement was effectively enforced, then higher fines were imposed by the GVH, primarily on the parties that were active on the upstream market (i.e. the manufacturer or the importer). Two cases—both concerning the distribution of the navigational devices—stand out in terms of fines: in *Navi-Gate*,[16] the GVH imposed a fine of HUF 43 million (approx. EUR160,000) and in Mitac/LCP,[17] the GVH imposed a fine of HUF 103 million (approx. EUR 400,000).

(ii) Minimum advertised price programs

18.21 As stated above in Section I.G(i), RPM arrangements under Hungarian law include not only express resale price fixing but also indirect forms achieving the same or equivalent results. It is therefore likely that, as under European law, any requirement by a supplier that a distributor refrain from advertising resale price below the minimum price set by the supplier, will be treated in the same way as direct RPM.

H. Tying arrangements

18.22 Tying as well as bundling arrangements are defined under the HCA. Tying is defined—both in terms of an anticompetitive agreement and as a specific form of abuse of a dominant position—as "making the conclusion of an agreement dependent on the undertaking of such obligations that do not correspond to the subject of the agreement either by their nature or under usual commercial practice" (arts. 11(h) and 21(f) HCA). Bundling is not expressly dealt with by the HCA, but the notion is well known in the practice of the GVH.[18] Such arrangements could thus either fall under the prohibition of anticompetitive agreements or be regarded as abuse of a dominant position (certainly provided that the practice is done by a dominant undertaking).

---

[13] *Hungaropharma*, GVH, Case no. Vj-57/2008 (December 22, 2008); *Navi-Gate and others*, GVH, Case no. Vj-26/2006 (November 5, 2007).

[14] *Euro-Elzett*, GVH, Case no. Vj-147/1999 (February 3, 2000).

[15] *Hungarian Association of Book Publishers*, GVH, Case no. Vj-47/2004 (April 11, 2006); *Kemira GrowHow*, GVH, Case no. Vj-161/2004 (March 21, 2006)

[16] *Navi-Gate* (n 13).

[17] *Mitac/LCP*, GVH, Case no. Vj-166/2006 (September 24, 2009).

[18] *Navi-Gate* (n 13).

A typical case of tying was examined by the GVH in *VIVANet*,[19] when a cable TV operator dominant in a given area offered internet services in that area only on condition that subscribers also subscribe to its cable TV services (the case was finally closed with remedies imposed on the TV operator). **18.23**

I. Exclusive dealing

Exclusive purchasing could be regarded as an abuse and therefore an infringement, if the supplier has a dominant position. The GVH scrutinized an exclusivity arrangement in *Hungarian Post*,[20] whereby the incumbent (and dominant) Hungarian Post concluded an agreement with an important customer of a bulk mail sender (a large telecommunications company), whereby the customer agreed not to procure this type of service from third parties for the duration of the agreement. In *Hungarian Post*, however, the GVH did not establish infringement, as it found that the exclusivity arrangement was incapable of foreclosing competitors, in particular due to the relatively low market share of the telecommunications company in the Hungarian mail services market. The GVH reached similar conclusions (and terminated the proceedings) due to the likely absence of foreclosure in respect of English clauses applied by various dominant electricity service providers in *DÉMÁSZ and others*.[21] At the same time, in *MÁV*,[22] the GVH found that the long-term agreements concluded, shortly before the liberalization of the rail cargo markets, between MÁV (the incumbent Hungarian rail cargo company) and various bulk goods shipping companies, whereby MÁV demanded exclusivity from those companies, constituted an abuse of MÁV's dominant position. **18.24**

In addition, an exclusive purchase clause could also be regarded as an agreement restrictive of competition and thus illegal, even if applied by a non-dominant company. As in the EU rules, an exclusive purchasing clause (or a clause with a similar effect) is defined as a clause requiring the purchaser to source more than 80 percent of its total needs from one supplier. Such a clause may, however, fall under the vertical block exemption regulation, provided that the market share of both the supplier and the purchaser remains below 30 percent and that the duration of the relevant agreement does not exceed five years (noting that exclusive purchasing obligations that are tacitly renewable beyond a period of five years are also not covered). The GVH examined such obligations in its case-law in the framework of franchise agreements[23] and funeral services.[24] **18.25**

J. Refusal to deal

Hungarian competition law acknowledges the principle of contractual freedom as well as the right to property. An intervention which restricts these fundamental rights was held to be justified only in exceptional cases, such as with a view to preventing a dominant company from harming the competitive conditions on the market and/or the interests of consumers by way of artificially limiting its output. **18.26**

Under Hungarian competition law, a refusal to deal with a third party—as under European law—can only be regarded as abusive (i) if such refusal has appreciable negative effects on competition on the market, and (ii) if such refusal cannot be objectively justified.[25] The GVH emphasized in several cases that harming the "mere" individual interest of the third party is **18.27**

---

19 *VIVANet*, GVH, Case no. Vj-37/2005 (April 20, 2006).
20 *Hungarian Post*, GVH, Case no. Vj-174/2005 (October 5, 2006).
21 *DÉMÁSZ and others*, GVH, Case no. Vj-104-109/2006 (September 10, 2008)
22 *MÁV*, GVH, Case no. Vj-22/2005 (December 15, 2003).
23 *GEKKO*, GVH, Case no. Vj-60/2009 (April 27, 2010).
24 *Léthé*, GVH, Case no. Vj-42/2008 (December 4, 2008).
25 *Rónahír*, GVH, Case no. Vj-10/2002 (July 5, 2002).

not equal to harming effective competition on the market, and thus, for example, termination of a distribution relationship by a manufacturer does not in itself suffice for the finding of an abuse.[26] It is also clear that when analyzing the effects of a refusal to deal on the market, both short-term and medium-/long-term effects need to be taken into account.[27]

18.28 The GVH has therefore found infringement in relatively few cases, in particular, when there was a pressing consumer interest at stake: for example, in a unique case from 2000, the main reason for finding an infringement was that, in the GVH's assessment, the refusal to supply threatened the continuous supply of vital consumer services (namely maintenance services of a certain type of electronic goods).[28]

18.29 Margin squeeze, more specifically, is regarded as a special form of anticompetitive conduct under Hungarian competition law. It is not expressly included in the individual list of potential abuses under the HCA. The GVH examined, and for the most part applied, the European test/conceptual framework of margin squeeze cases in the funeral services sector, where such term was not used expressly, but the theory of harm applied was essentially equivalent to margin squeeze; in the telecommunications sector,[29] where the GVH found for an infringement and imposed fines and in the railway sector,[30] where the GVH dropped its case in this respect.

K. Essential facilities

18.30 The notion of "essential facilities" has been applied in the GVH's practice, generally, as a particular case of refusal to deal. For example, the GVH found an infringement when the operator of a telecommunications network refused to provide access to invoicing services for internet service providers,[31] or when a municipality—as the owner of public space—fails to provide approval to the construction of a rival/additional cable TV network.[32]

L. Bundling (including loyalty and market share discounts)

18.31 The evaluation of bundling under Hungarian competition law is very similar to that of tying,[33] and therefore a competition law concern generally arises only in relation to the prohibition of abuse of a dominant position (although a tying practice would also entail an agreement restrictive of competition).

18.32 Loyalty and market share discounts applied by dominant undertakings, which could also constitute an abuse if they have the effect of excluding (equally efficient) competitors, have come to the attention of the GVH only in a relatively small number of cases. In *Holcim*,[34] the GVH found that the rebate given by a (collectively) dominant cement manufacturer to cement wholesalers for not selling foreign/import cement was abusive (it is noteworthy that the decision precedes Hungary's entry into the EU, thus, the theory of harm did not concern the prevention of parallel trade but merely the tying of wholesalers to the dominant manufacturer(s) thereby strengthening its/their dominant position). In the more recent *Hungarian Post* case,[35] the GVH found that some of the various rebate/discount schemes applied by the Hungarian Post could not be regarded as being quantity-based and therefore clearly unobjectionable (for

[26] *Nemzeti Autópálya*, GVH, Case no. Vj-41/2002 (June 2, 2003).
[27] *DÉMÁSZ*, GVH, Case no. Vj-126/2007 (February 14, 2008).
[28] *Philips*, GVH, Case no. Vj-8/2000 (June 8, 2000).
[29] *Matáv*, GVH, Case no. Vj-100/2002 (January 22, 2004).
[30] *MÁV*, GVH, Case no. Vj-35/2008 (April 27, 2012).
[31] *Emitel*, GVH, Case no. V-184/1999 (April 19, 2000).
[32] *Elek City Municipality*, GVH, Case no. Vj-6/2002 (March 4, 2003).
[33] See Section I.H.
[34] *Holcim*, GVH, Case no. Vj-73/2001 (8 October 2002).
[35] *Hungarian Post* (n 20).

example, since one of the discounts was applicable if the customer achieved an increase in its yearly turnover with the Hungarian Post, but with a retroactive effect for the entire value purchased in the new year). In the end, however, the GVH found that the relevant discounts either entailed a very low nominal percentage of the purchases or were regarded by customers as being irrelevant when they made their decision as to their choice of supplier; as a result, the GVH terminated its proceedings without an express finding of infringement.

Despite the lack of clear and consistent indication from the GVH's practice, it can generally be expected that in case discounts applied by a dominant undertakings clearly have the effect of inducing a customer to make most or all of its purchases from the dominant undertaking, then such practice is likely to be found abusive. However, transparent, non-discriminatory, and quantity-based discounts or rebates, which entail that the benefits of economies of scale are being shared with customers, are unlikely to constitute an infringement. **18.33**

M. Standard-setting groups (disclosure requirements, licensing arrangements, and licensing pools)

The GVH has had little enforcement on standard-setting arrangements, and there has been hardly any published case law in this respect. It is nevertheless expected that the GVH would apply Hungarian competition law in conformity with the principles of European law, namely the Horizontal Cooperation Guidelines and the practice of the European Commission and the European Courts. **18.34**

N. Customer termination

The termination of a contract with an existing or potential customer by a dominant undertaking could be regarded as abusive and thus an infringement of Hungarian competition law. Generally, such conduct could be considered as a special situation where "refusal to deal" occurs.[36] The GVH has so far treated such cases under a rather high standard of proof, as stated above, whereby it is emphasized that harming the "mere" individual interest of the third party is not equal to harming effective competition on the market (thus, for example, termination of a distribution relationship by a manufacturer does not in itself suffices for the finding of an abuse). As a result, in the GVH's practice, customer termination has rarely been found to be illegal. **18.35**

If, however, the company terminating a customer relationship is not in dominant position, the termination cannot generally be regarded as a breach of competition law, unless there is an anticompetitive agreement behind such termination (such as a boycott-cartel among horizontal competitors, whereby members of the cartel would agree not to conclude agreements with a certain customer). **18.36**

O. Termination of intermediaries (retailers, wholesalers, dealers, and value-added resellers, agents, and brokers)

Termination of intermediaries is again regarded as a special form of "refusal to deal" and customer termination, therefore the considerations set out above in Sections I.J and I.N apply. **18.37**

P. Termination of relationships with competitors

It cannot be excluded that a termination by a dominant company of its business relations with a competitor may be regarded as abusive, if such termination entails a distortion/restriction of competition on the relevant market(s). In such case, the termination would be regarded as an infringement. **18.38**

[36] See Section I.J.

Q. Exemptions

18.39 Hungarian competition law is industry-neutral, which means that it applies to all sectors of the economy. There is, however, a new—and very much questionable—exception in relation to agricultural products: namely, in cases where trade between member states is not affected, the Hungarian prohibition of anticompetitive agreements is not applicable if the competent Government minister establishes that the distortion of competition resulting from the relevant agreement does not exceed the extent that is necessary for an "economically justifiable and equitable income," and if the players on the relevant market "are not prevented from reaching such income." It is currently unclear how these vague provisions, which are clearly alien to the logic and structure of classic antitrust law, would be applied in practice.

18.40 Like the European regime, as stated in Section I.A, if a conduct falls under the prohibition of anticompetitive agreements, then such conduct may still be exempted if it fulfills the four conditions for exemption as contained in article 17 of the HCA (improvement of technical progress, proportionality, fair share of benefits to consumers, and no exclusion of competition). It is important to note that, in practice, there are rather low chances that a price fixing or market sharing agreement is considered by the GVH to fulfill the exemption criteria.

18.41 There are also several block exemptions, which are almost word-for-word restatements of the European block exemptions: the fulfillment of the criteria contained in the block exemptions entails the assumption that the relevant arrangement is exempted from the prohibition of anticompetitive agreements. The specific block exemptions are as follows: (a) a general block exemption for vertical arrangements (covering distribution agreements);[37] (b) a block exemption for research and development agreements;[38] (c) a block exemption for specialization agreements;[39] and, lastly, (d) sector-specific block exemptions applicable to the motor vehicle aftermarket[40] and insurance.[41]

18.42 It is worth noting that while the Hungarian prohibition of abuse of a dominant position does not contain an express provision for exemption (as in the case of the prohibition of anticompetitive agreements), it is possible for a dominant undertaking to prove that the given conduct has an objective justification (for example, that the refusal to deal occurred as a result of credit unworthiness of a given customer, etc.).

18.43 Furthermore, in the case of the prohibition of anticompetitive agreements, there are also two important exceptions when the prohibition does not apply. First, there is a statutory *de minimis* rule, whereby the Hungarian legislator considered that certain agreements of minor importance should fall outside of the scope of the prohibition. Under article 13 of the HCA, an agreement is regarded as having minor importance if the market share of the parties to the agreement is below 10 percent, which entails that the very same threshold applies for both horizontal and vertical agreements (as opposed to a similar European law rule). At the same time, the HCA makes it clear that the most restrictive ("hard core") types of anticompetitive agreements (namely horizontal price fixing and market sharing) cannot under any

[37] Government Decree No. 205/2011 on Exemptions from the Prohibition of Restriction of Competition in case of Vertical Agreements.

[38] Government Decree No. 206/2011 on exempting certain groups of agreements in the field of research and development.

[39] Government Decree No. 202/2011 on exempting certain groups of specialization agreements from the general prohibition of economic restraints.

[40] Government Decree No. 204/2011 on exempting certain groups of the motor vehicle after-market sector from the general prohibition of restraints.

[41] Government Decree No. 203/2011 on exempting certain groups of agreements in the insurance sector from the general prohibition of restraints.

circumstances avail themselves of the *de minimis* exception. It is important to note here that, due to the wording of the relevant provision of the HCA—as opposed to the relevant EU rules—serious vertical restrictions, such as direct RPM, may still fall under the *de minimis* rule if they satisfy the market share threshold.

Finally, although this is not stated expressly in the HCA as an exception, when an agreement determines the scope of activities of an agent in relation to its principal, the Hungarian prohibition of anticompetitive agreements does not apply. The test whether a genuine agency relationship exists within the meaning of competition law is, like under the EU regime, centered around the allocation of risks and costs between the parties: where the intermediary bears a significant commercial and financial risk in relation to the relevant contracts/goods, it will not qualify as a genuine agent. **18.44**

II. Dealing with competitors

Agreements between competitors that have as their object or effect the restriction of competition are prohibited by article 11 of the HCA. The wording and the interpretation of article 11 HCA by the GVH is very much similar to that of article 101 TFEU. In addition, as a result of Hungary's membership in the European Union, European competition law, and thus also article 101 TFEU, is also directly applicable in Hungary, in accordance with the rules set out in Regulation 1/2003,[42] when trade between member states is affected. **18.45**

Article 11 HCA covers both horizontal agreements (i.e. agreements between competitors) as well as vertical agreements (i.e. agreements between market players acting on different levels of the supply chain, e.g. wholesalers and retailers). Nevertheless, the enforcement priority of the GVH has in recent years clearly been horizontal arrangements. The most serious infringements of competition law by competitors are considered to be horizontal price fixing and market sharing. Such practices are regarded by the GVH as being anticompetitive by their very nature, and hence by their object. Thus, an infringement of competition law may in this respect be established without the need to prove any potential or actual anticompetitive effects of the arrangement on the market. Nevertheless, all types of agreements infringing article 11 HCA, including price fixing and market sharing agreements, may escape the prohibition of article 11 HCA if the conditions of article 17 HCA are fulfilled (being largely identical to those of art. 101(3) TFEU), and hence an individual exemption is available (such safe harbor being an *ex lege* exemption). The fulfillment of those conditions is to be proven by the undertakings concerned, and, in practice, there are very low chances that a price fixing or market sharing agreement is capable of meeting the criteria of an individual exemption. **18.46**

According to article 13 HCA, agreements that—due to the parties' low market share—do not appreciably restrict competition, shall be exempted from the prohibition of article 11 HCA ("*de minimis* rule"). The *de minimis* rule applies if the aggregate market share held by the parties to the agreement does not exceed 10 percent on any of the relevant markets affected by the agreement (contrary to European competition law, there is no separate, lower threshold in cases where there is a network of several similar agreements on the market). It is important to note that the *de minimis* rule may not be applied to horizontal price fixing, market sharing, or output limitation agreements. **18.47**

[42] Council Regulation (EC) No. 1/2003 on the implementation of the rules on competition laid down in Articles 81 and 82 of the Treaty (December 16, 2002).

18.48 An important enforcement priority of the GVH has in recent years been the construction industry, the IT sector, the food industry and the banking sector with special regard to bid-rigging in public procurement and concession procedures.

18.49 The GVH may impose a fine for an infringement of article 11 HCA. According to the general rules on fines (which are applicable to all types of violation of the HCA, not only to agreements between competitors), the maximum fine is 10 percent of the net turnover of the undertakings concerned, achieved in the last closed business year prior to the GVH's decision. There is a special provision in the HCA which allows for imputation of liability: if the undertaking that has participated in the infringement is a member of a group of undertakings, the GVH has the power "to identify the group of undertakings," by naming the ultimate parent company, as a result of which the maximum level of the fine can be increased to 10 percent of the turnover of the given group of undertakings. The HCA does not contain any test which the GVH would be expected to apply when deciding on whether it wishes to impose a fine on the undertaking directly involved in the arrangement or on its ultimate parent. The provision itself is located in the HCA in a way which seems to indicate that the HCA treats this rule as a mere technical norm in relation to the calculation of the fine. The lack of a clear test in connection with a *de facto* liability-allocation rule gives rise to serious constitutional law concerns. Judicial practice has not thus far had the chance to deal with this provision in detail; the GVH has applied it in a very limited number of cases. In those cases, the GVH has not, however, formulated any detailed test, but rather confined itself to stating that the application of the rule was justified under the circumstances. In one case, the GVH went so far as to argue that the only reason it applied this rule, and thereby grossly increased the turnovers relevant for the purposes of the calculation of the fine, was that, without involving the turnovers of the whole group, it could not have imposed a fine with a sufficient deterring effect.[43]

18.50 The GVH has developed a robust fining practice since 2004: it imposed its third largest fine in the *Motorway construction* case already in 2004 (HUF 7 billion, approx. EUR 25 million) (upheld by the courts),[44] the second largest fine imposed to date was in 2010, in the *Railway construction works* case (total amount of fines imposed were HUF 7.2 billion, approx. EUR 25.3 million),[45] while the largest fine to date was imposed in 2013 in the *FX-loan prepayment case* (HUF 9.5 billion, approx EUR 31.9 million).[46]

A. Horizontal price fixing

18.51 Horizontal price fixing agreements have always been an enforcement priority of the GVH. As stated above, price fixing agreements are also considered by the GVH as an infringement of competition law by their object, which in practice means that the GVH may find an infringement and impose a fine without having to prove that the agreement in question had in fact anticompetitive effects on the market.

18.52 The fines imposed by the GVH for participation in a horizontal price-fixing agreement have always been very high. The latest major case concerning horizontal price fixing was the *Rail freight forwarding* case in 2012, where the GVH imposed altogether HUF 1.25 billion (approx. EUR 4.5 million) in fines on the leading rail freight forwarding companies for an alleged price fixing and market sharing agreement (the case is currently under judicial

---

[43] *Vasútépítők and others*, GVH, Case no. Vj-174/2007 (May 14, 2010).

[44] *Motorway construction*, GVH, Case no. Vj-27/2003 (July 23, 2004).

[45] *Vasútépítők* (n 43).

[46] *FX-loan prepayment*, GVH, Case no. Vj-74/2011 (November 19, 2013).

review).[47] Other important decisions regarding horizontal price fixing were the *Railway construction works* case in 2010 (the total amount of fines imposed was HUF 7.2 billion, approx. EUR 25.3 million; and the largest individual fine was HUF 3.4 billion, approx. EUR 12 million);[48] the *Heves-Nógrád counties construction works* case in 2009 (where the total fines imposed was HUF 3.5 billion, approx. EUR 12 million);[49] and the *Mill cartel* case in 2010 where the undertakings concerned faced a fine amounting to HUF 2.3 billion (approx. EUR 8 million).[50] In both the construction as well as the mill cartel cases, one of the participants was granted full immunity based on a successful leniency application.

B. Horizontal agreements to allocate customers or territories; agreements not to compete

Besides horizontal price fixing, allocation of the markets or customers amongst competitors is also considered by the GVH as the most serious infringement of competition law and a violation of competition law by its object. The biggest cases regarding market sharing involved a horizontal price-fixing element, as well; they include: the recent decision in the *Rail freight forwarding case* in 2012 where the GVH found that the cooperation between the rail freight forwarding companies in the system of successive freight forwarding and the alleged unwillingness of the companies to carry out transportation services outside their "traditional railway lines" qualifies as market sharing;[51] as well as a series of cases between 2002 and 2009 in the construction sector (where market sharing took the form of bid-rigging).[52] A classical non-compete type of infringement was found by the GVH in a case concerning an agreement between the incumbent postal service provider (Hungarian Post) and the dominant magazines and newspaper distributor, LAPKER. The parties agreed that Magyar Posta would not enter the classical newspaper and magazines retail market, whereas LAPKER refrains from entering the market of prepaid newspaper home delivery.[53] **18.53**

C. Horizontal boycotts

Agreements between competitors not to deal with certain market players (horizontal boycott agreements) are considered a serious infringement of competition law. Nevertheless, in its ruling concerning the decision by an association of pharmaceutical manufacturers and an association of pharmacists to encourage pharmaceutical manufacturers not to sell certain products to retailers other than pharmacies, the GVH found that such decision may not be regarded as an infringement of competition law by object. On a closer look, the GVH found that certain legislative changes had deprived the pharmaceutical manufacturers of their right to sell certain products to buyers other than pharmacies, the conduct in question was in fact unable to exert any anticompetitive effects on the market.[54] **18.54**

D. Joint ventures and other competitive collaborations

As in EU competition law, under the merger control regime of the HCA, the creation of a full-function joint venture qualifies as a concentration/merger and shall thus be notified **18.55**

---

47 *Rail Cargo/GySEV*, GVH, Case no. Vj-3/2008 (April 27, 2012).
48 *Vasútépítők* (n 43).
49 *Colas and others*, GVH, Case no. Vj-130/2006 (January 29, 2009).
50 *Júlia Malom and others*, GVH, Case no. Vj-69/2008 (October 28, 2010).
51 *Rail Cargo/GySEV* (n 47).
52 *Bartók Road Construction*, GVH, Case no. Vj-138/2002 (March 18, 2004); *Motorway Construction*, GVH, Case No. Vj-27/2003 (July 23, 2004); *Budapest Works*, GVH, Case no. Vj-25/2004 (September 16, 2005); *Municipal Works*, GVH, Case no. Vj-56/2004 (September 22, 2005); *Vasútépítők* (n 43).
53 *Magyar Posta/LAPKER*, GVH, Case no. Vj-140/2006 (November 8, 2007).
54 *Gyógyszerészkamara*, GVH, Case no. Vj-33/2007 (November 4, 2008).

to the GVH if the turnover thresholds laid down in the HCA are met by the founding members. A full-function joint venture is here understood as a joint venture that performs, on a long-term basis, all the functions of an autonomous economic entity, having its own dedicated day-to-day management and access to resources such as finance, staff, and assets, and providing, at least in the long run, goods/services to third-party customers other than the parent companies.

18.56 If a joint venture lacks full functionality (e.g. because it was created for a limited time period only, carries out its activities exclusively for the founding members, or does not possess sufficient resources), the creation of the joint venture will have to be assessed in light of the prohibition of anticompetitive agreements (i.e. art. 11 HCA). When carrying out its analysis under article 11 HCA, the GVH first examines the level of transparency/the scope of information accessible to the founding members regarding each other's activities and the effects of the joint venture on the competition between the founding members. If, based on the assessment under article 11 HCA, the joint venture agreement qualifies as an anticompetitive agreement, it may still escape the prohibition in article 11 if the conditions for an individual exemption as laid down in article 17 HCA are met.

18.57 The Hungarian Government issued block exemption regulations exempting certain categories of agreements from the prohibition laid down in article 11 HCA, which may be applied to certain joint ventures between competitors. Such block exemptions concern specialization agreements and research-and-development agreements. All agreements fulfilling the conditions laid down in those regulations fall outside of the prohibition of article 11 HCA.

E. Trade associations

18.58 Like article 101 TFEU, the prohibition under article 11 HCA extends, besides anticompetitive agreements between competitors, to anticompetitive decisions by associations of undertakings. According to the case law of the GVH, the term "association" covers all organizations/entities the aim of which is (at least in part) to harmonize, align, represent, or protect the interests of its members (in particular professional chambers, e.g. chambers of architects, auditors, public notaries, attorneys, pharmacists etc., or other associations or organizations in the framework of which undertakings cooperate with each other or otherwise align their activities, e.g. farmers' associations).

18.59 The operation of trade associations has long been the focus of the GVH's enforcement. There were numerous decisions delivered, in particular between 2006 and 2010, most of them relating to price recommendations or certain marketing prohibitions issued by associations (examples are the proceedings against the association of auditors, architects, pharmacists, attorneys, journalists, hairdressers, egg producers, cement manufacturers, patient ambulance services etc.).[55]

18.60 In all its rulings concerning decisions by associations, the GVH emphasized that, besides compulsory decisions (i.e. decisions that bind the members), non-binding recommendations (in practice, typically minimum price recommendations), shall be regarded as "decisions of

[55] See *Hungarian Trade Association of Auditors*, GVH, Case no. Vj-16/2005 (July 17, 2006); *Hungarian Trade Association of Architects*, GVH, Case no. Vj-201/2005 (December 11, 2007); *Hungarian Association of Pharmacists*, GVH, Case no. Vj-33/2007 (November 4, 2008); Hungarian Bar Association, GVH, Case no. Vj-180/2004 (June 14, 2006); *Hungarian Association of Journalists*, GVH, Case no. Vj-36/2008 (July 7, 2010); *Hungarian Trade Association of Hairdressers*, GVH, Case no. Vj-51/2008 (June 23, 2010); *Trade Association of Egg Producers*, GVH, Case no. Vj-199/2005 (November 30, 2006); *Hungarian Trade Association of Cement Producers*, GVH, Case no. Vj-73/2001 (October 8, 2002); *National Association of Patient Ambulance Service Providers*, GVH, Case no. Vj-92/2003 (December 16, 2003).

associations" in breach of competition law. It is also important to note that all undertakings that have participated in anticompetitive association meetings or decisions are regarded by the GVH to be in violation of article 11 HCA, including those that did not actively contribute to the discussions. Only those undertakings escape the prohibition of article 11 HCA that can successfully prove to have voted/argued against a given decision and/or left the meeting and/or openly distanced themselves from the decisions taken.

F. Interlocking directorates

Interlocking directorates as such are not prohibited by Hungarian competition law but may raise two issues: (i) they may lead to a control position and thus to concentration within the meaning of the merger control provisions of the HCA (and as such a notification obligation, if the turnover thresholds are met); or (ii) they may fall within the scope of article 11 HCA, in particular with regard to the exchange of sensitive commercial information. In this respect, the GVH would determine whether the multiple directorate leads to a level of transparency which reduces competition between the affected companies. The GVH has not thus far paid special attention to interlocking directorates. A question concernig interlocking directorates is part of the standard merger notification form (where, besides minority shareholding of the participants, personal links between the participants and third independent companies are also to be disclosed). **18.61**

G. Facilitating practices

Facilitating practices are a type of conduct which does not clearly constitute an agreement but helps competitors eliminate strategic uncertainties and coordinate their conduct on the market. The most common form of facilitating practices is information sharing. In the GVH's case law, facilitating practices have so far been analyzed together with horizontal price-fixing and market-sharing agreements, and have been assessed in light of, and as complementary to, an underlying cartel agreement. The same rules will normally apply to facilitating practices as to information exchanges.[56] It is, however, important to note that reciprocity is not automatically considered by the GVH as a necessary element of a violation of competition law; nor is it not necessary that the information be unknown to the public: in the 2007 *Foreign currency exchange outlets* case, the GVH found that, by sending out the actual currency rates to their competitors every morning, the parties violated article 11 HCA, despite of the fact that those exchange rates were then, during the day, made public and available both in exchange outlets as well as on the internet.[57] **18.62**

H. Information exchange

Under the case law of the GVH (similar to that of the European Commission), the exchange of information between competitors may, under certain circumstances, fall under the prohibition of anticompetitive agreements.[58] The reason behind this is that information exchanges may, by increasing transparency, facilitate coordination and collusion between competitors. Apart from collusion, information exchanges can also lead to anticompetitive foreclosure effects by excluding potential competitors from the market and stabilizing the existing competitors' market position. For the applicability of article 11 HCA it is not necessary that an express agreement on information exchange is concluded by the competitors: when a company receives strategic data from a competitor, it will be presumed to have accepted the **18.63**

[56] See Section II.H.

[57] *Northline and others*, GVH, Case no. Vj-83/2005 (January 25, 2007).

[58] *Adeptus and others*, GVH, Case no. Vj-56/2004 (September 22, 2005), or *Holcim and others*, GVH, Case no. Vj-73/2001 (October 8, 2002).

information and adapted its market conduct accordingly, unless it has expressly refused the information.

18.64 An exchange of individual data between competitors regarding future prices and/or future quantities is generally considered as a per se restriction of competition, a restriction of competition by object. In such cases, according to the established case law of the GVH, the competition authority does not have to prove any (actual or potential) anticompetitive effects resulting from the conduct. As opposed to information exchanges restrictive by their object, in the case of any other information exchange schemes, the GVH will have to assess, on a case-by-case basis, whether the exchange may have anticompetitive effects and thus fall within the scope of article 11 HCA. In this respect, the governing principle is that market players are required to act independently of each other; therefore agreements or concerted practices having an effect of eliminating or substantially reducing the uncertainties which would otherwise incentivize participants to adopt a more competitive strategy are likely to be condemned by the GVH. Although it would appear that the burden of proof placed on the GVH is relatively high in such cases, the GVH's practice shows that actual, full-scale and in-depth effects-based analyses are only rarely undertaken. In fact, the GVH generally is satisfied with showing that—in light of the factors and circumstances detailed in para. 18.65—the given conduct is "capable of producing" or "likely to produce" such effects. The most recent leading case in this respect is the *Fx-loan prepayment* case, which concerned exchange of sensitive information by major Hungarian banks in relation to a governmental measure allowing early repayment of foreign exchange loans at a fixed conversion rate.[59]

18.65 When the effects/likely effects of an information exchange are analyzed, the following main circumstances are taken into account by the GVH: (i) the structure of the market; (ii) the nature and type of information exchanged; (iii) the frequency and timing of the information exchange; and (iv) the persons involved in the information exchange. According to established case law, information exchange systems are very likely to result in anticompetitive effects in highly concentrated and transparent oligopolistic markets (e.g. three to four players having an aggregate market share of over 80 percent), where the entry barriers are high and there is a considerable level of brand loyalty. With regard to the nature of the information exchanged, as a general rule, it is the sharing of strategic data that can give rise to restrictive market effects. Strategic data covers, in particular, data related to prices, customer lists, production costs, quantities, turnovers, sales, capacities, marketing plans, and technologies. In contrast, generally, the collection of statistical information giving an aggregate picture of the markets does not give rise to competition concerns, provided that individual undertakings cannot be identified and the relevant data is historic. Whether data is historic depends on the characteristics of the relevant market and in particular the frequency of price re-negotiations in the industry (for example, data can be considered as historic if it is several times older than the average length of contracts in the industry if the latter are indicative of price re-negotiations). As a general rule, it appears that the GVH tends to regard information that is more than one year old as historic and thus its exchange falling outside the scope of article 11 HCA. According to the GVH's case law, the frequency and timing of the information exchange shall also be considered. If data are exchanged on a frequent basis, this is more likely to raise competition concerns than if exchange takes place only sporadically or annually. Whether information exchanges shall be regarded as taking place frequently depends on the characteristics of the market. In markets with long-term contracts and infrequent price negotiations even a less frequent information exchange may be sufficient to lead to a collusive result. In addition to the above circumstances, the involved persons (i.e. recipients of

59 *FX-loan prepayment* (n 46).

the disclosed information) shall also be looked at. If the information is asymmetric, i.e. only a certain circle of businesses profit from it, and other competitors or consumers are hindered from receiving the information, the resulting asymmetric increase in transparency may be regarded as anticompetitive. However, if consumers also benefit from such transparency and if the information providing such transparency is available to all undertakings in a given market, it is likely that this will have a pro-competitive effect.

I. Joint purchasing agreements

Joint purchasing agreements are, as a general rule, not regarded as a per se infringement of competition law (unless certain additional elements of the joint purchasing agreement constitute a per se infringement, i.e. if the parties additionnally agree on sales prices or if they share strategic data with one another). Therefore, when examining whether a given cooperation infringes article 11 HCA, the potential and actual effects of the joint purchasing agreement are reviewed. **18.66**

The GVH analyzes the aggregate market power of the participants on their selling markets as well as on their purchasing markets and finds infringement if the parties' cooperation leads to a substantial lessening of competition on either the selling or the purchasing market. **18.67**

Joint purchasing agreements are currently not the focus of the GVH's enforcement practice; the latest decisions date back to 2002–4 when undertakings had the possibility of requesting that the GVH review their cooperation and state whether it falls under the prohibition of article 11 HCA or grant an individual exemption to the parties.[60] **18.68**

As in the case of other agreements, even if a joint purchasing agreement falls under article 11 HCA, it may escape the prohibition if the conditions of an individual exemption as laid down under article 17 HCA are met. **18.69**

J. Joint lobbying/regulatory/legislative efforts

Joint lobbying/regulatory/legislative efforts in themselves are not prohibited by Hungarian competition law. Nevertheless, as it does to any other meetings and discussions between competitors, article 11 HCA applies to meetings and discussions with lobbying and legislative purposes article 11 HCA shall be applied. Such discussions and meeting may thus not aim at or lead to horizontal price fixing, market sharing, exchange of commercially sensitive information, boycott of certain competitors or any other horizontal agreement with anticompetitive object or effect. This was confirmed by the GVH in its decision regarding the *Egg cartel* case in 2006.[61] **18.70**

III. General issues

A. Jurisdiction and applicable law (including sector-specific competition regulation)

Hungarian competition law applies (*ratione materiae*) to all sectors of the economy with an important and rather questionable exception for agriculture.[62] Competition law extends to economic conduct of undertakings. Conduct which is not of economic nature is thus not captured by the competition provisions. **18.71**

[60] *METSPA*, GVH, Case no. Vj-176/2003 (April 7, 2004), or *CBA*, GVH, Case no. Vj-20/2002 (August 21, 2002).

[61] *Magyar Tojás*, GVH, Case no. Vj-199/2005 (November 30, 2006).

[62] See Section I.Q.

18.72 The law applies (*ratione personae*) to all "undertakings," which includes any entity engaged in economic activity, whatever its legal form. In addition to "undertakings," "associations of undertakings" are also subject to the norms relating to anticompetitive agreements, concerted practices, and decisions restricting competition. To the extent that they are engaged in economic activity, public as well as private entities are subject to these rules.

18.73 When acting as sovereign, the state and its functionalities are not considered to constitute an undertaking within the meaning of competition law. The GVH has dealt with the defense of state action[63] and state inducement[64] in a number of cases in the past.

18.74 Neither are employees and their labor law bodies (trade associations, etc.) considered as undertakings and associations of undertakings, respectively. Households are also not treated as undertakings, hence their activities on the demand side of the markets are not caught by the competition provisions.

18.75 Hungarian competition law applies (*ratione territoriae*), under article 1 HCA, to the conduct of undertakings that has or may have an impact on competition in Hungary. If trade between member states of the EU is also affected, Hungarian and EU competition law will be applied by the GVH in parallel, under the rules of Regulation 1/2003.

18.76 The rules of the HCA are in force (*ratione temporae*) since January 1, 1997. The previous Competition Act (adopted by the Parliament in 1990) entered into force on January 1, 1991 (and was then superseded by the HCA on January 1, 1997). In essence, modern and EU law-based competition law provisions have now been in place in Hungary for more than 20 years.

B. Antitrust system

(i) Name of agency/agencies

18.77 The GVH (*Gazdasági Versenyhivatal*) is the specific state agency which is responsible, under the HCA, for (i) public enforcement of the competition rules; (ii) competition advocacy; and (iii) dissemination of a culture of economic competition.

18.78 The GVH is independent of the government and any other state organs. It cannot be given instructions or directions. It reports directly to the Hungarian Parliament.

18.79 The GVH's internal structure has two main branches. On the one hand, there are "investigative units," such as the Cartel Unit, the Antitrust Unit, the Mergers Unit, the Consumer Protection Unit, as well as the administrative and support units. These units are responsible for opening cases and conducting the investigation which terminates in the adoption of an Investigation Report. On the other hand, there is the internal decision-making body, the Competition Council (*Versenytanács*) (VT). The VT takes over the case once the Investigation Report has been completed. It is the VT which then decides whether to send a statement of objections to the undertakings and then whether to find infringement or to close the case without findings (or to adopt commitments, etc.). The members of the VT are independent and cannot be given instructions or directions, whether internally or from outside of the GVH. They serve a term of six years.

18.80 The GVH is led by the President. The President is nominated by the Prime Minister and appointed by the President of the Republic. His term is six years. The President cannot be recalled (he may lose his position only under exceptional circumstances). The President is supported by two Vice-Presidents: one is responsible for overviewing the work of the investigative units, whereas the other is the head of the VT.

[63] See e.g. *Érd Város*, GVH, Case no. Vj-57/2007 (June 4, 2009), and *Tesco and others*, GVH, Case no. Vj-62/2012 (April 10, 2013).

[64] See e.g. *Rail Cargo/GySEV* (n 47).

The GVH does not have powers to issue legislative measures (only notices, for example, on fining in antitrust cases). **18.81**

With regard to public enforcement, the GVH applies the HCA as well as other competition-law-related acts (such as the Act against Unfair Commercial Practices of 2008, the Act on Commerce of 1995, or the Act on Economic Advertising of 2008), as well as the block exemption regulations issued by the Government in form of Government Decrees. The GVH will also apply EU competition law, as set forth by Regulation 1/2003. **18.82**

The GVH proceeds *ex officio*, for the benefit of the public. It opens a case if (i) it has the powers to start the proceedings in relation to the given conduct; (ii) it has reasonable suspicions of infringement; and (iii) opening an investigation is in the interest of the public, considering all relevant factors (such as the costs of the investigation, likely consumer harm, etc.). **18.83**

The proceedings of the GVH are governed by specific procedural provisions of the HCA and other competition-law-related legal instruments containing procedural provisions (e.g. Regulation 1/2003). As a secondary set of rules, the General Act on Administrative Proceedings of 2004 will be applicable. **18.84**

The decisions of the GVH are subject to judicial review of at least two instances: (i) the Metropolitan Administrative Court hears the appeals against the GVH's decisions as a court of first instance; it has unlimited jurisdiction to review both facts and the legal assessment of the GVH. (ii) The Metropolitan Court proceeds in relation to appeals brought against judgments of the Metropolitan Administrative Court. While no new facts can generally be submitted to the Metropolitan, it has unlimited jurisdiction to review the facts, as well as to conduct legal assessment of the decisions of the GVH and the Metropolitan Administrative Court. (iii) Finally, an application for legal revision may be submitted to the Kúria (the Supreme Court of Hungary) on points of law. **18.85**

With regard to advocacy, the GVH consults with state organs when it comes to issues relevant to competition in the legislative process. In its advocacy role, the GVH draws the attention of the legislative organ to the priorities of competition. On certain occasions, the GVH turns to the public with a view to thwarting legislative proposals which would have a negative impact on competition. On rare occasions, it is the GVH that initiates legislative steps, if it is convinced that a given market failure cannot be resolved by the market itself and individual regulatory intervention is also unlikely to yield proper results (for instance, recently, the GVH has joined forces with the Hungarian National Bank and the Financial Regulatory Authority in order to advocate for legislation relating to the payment of card interchange fees—an issue much debated in a number of jurisdictions). **18.86**

For the purposes of disseminating a culture of economic competition, the GVH has founded a separate institution, the Centre for Competition Culture (*Versenykultúra Központ*) (VKK). The VKK is an independent body within the GVH. Ten percent of all fines imposed by the GVH in antitrust cases are allocated to the budget of the VKK. The VKK uses these funds to support a number of different forms of dissemination of competition culture. It sponsors conferences, university seminars, and other events (participation in which is free for the targeted audience). The VKK also finances research, studies, and reviews of hot topics within competition law and economics. It also publishes books and Hungarian translations of major international competition law treaties. **18.87**

(ii) Staff size and budget

The GVH has approximately 125 staff (including administrative and other staff). Its 2012 budget was HUF 2.3 billion (approximately EUR 6.5 million). **18.88**

(iii) Recent enforcement actions and trends

18.89 Cartels have been for a long time, and remain, the top priority of the GVH. Recently, however, the GVH has suffered some not insignificant defeats in the courts in cases where it tried to argue for a lower standard of proof or in cases where the calculation of the fine was non-transparent or otherwise erroneous. There are signs in the practice that the GVH's approach has, as a result, become more cautious.

18.90 In order to uncover secret cartel activities, the GVH applies two main tools. On the one hand, the GVH has been very active in the use of dawn raids ever since 2001 (when the dawn raid powers of the GVH were introduced into the HCA). On the other hand, the GVH wishes to have more use of the leniency regime which has been in place since 2006 (and so far has yielded much fewer results than expected).

18.91 As of 2012, the GVH has significantly improved its IT infrastructure to detect and prove cartel cases. The GVH has obtained both powerful hardware and software which it can use in dawn raids and which enables it to perform extremely thorough and extensive searches of vast volumes of data in very few days. This in turn means that companies under investigation also need to obtain and analyze the information within a very tight timeframe, and take key strategic decisions such as whether and where to apply for leniency far faster than was the case in the past. In this respect, the "mirror-copying" of full server-contents (the seizure during dawn raids of copies of hard disks or other computer materials without selecting the relevant documents first) remains a controversial issue. As a result, advisers have thus also incentives to equip themselves with forensic IT tools.

18.92 The GVH has also made a number of steps to boost its leniency regime. The GVH, together with the VKK, has invested significant effort in raising awareness of the availability of the leniency regime. Furthermore, the GVH was successful in proposing legislation which supports private persons to become informants of the GVH. They will be eligible for an informant fee in the amount of up to HUF 50 million (approx. EUR 180,000). The GVH expects that the informants' fee regime may successfully supplement, or in certain cases completely substitute, leniency applications.

18.93 The GVH has had, at the same time, a very modest track record under article 21 HCA (abuse cases) in recent years. It seems that the approach of the Chicago School has found its way to the decision-making of the GVH on abuse cases. The GVH seems to be very concerned about "Type II errors" (intervention in cases that would lead to over-enforcement).

C. Private litigation

18.94 A party that has suffered loss as a result of any anticompetitive agreement or conduct may claim damages or indeed the nullity/unenforceability of the agreement in question or other forms of relief such as an injunction, in front of civil courts. This litigation may be started directly in front of civil courts and the plaintiff is not obliged to first turn to the GVH as complainant under article 88/A of the HCA.

18.95 Until recently, the number of such actions was small, but over the past few years it has increased steadily. The vast majority of such actions relate to agreements, rather than other types of restrictive agreements and abuses of dominance.

18.96 The GVH has power to intervene in private litigations by way of submitting an *amicus curiae* brief. The proceeding court is obliged to notify the GVH if article 11 or article 21 of the HCA is invoked by any of the parties to the litigation. The GVH may then submit an *amicus curiae* brief, or may wish to submit oral arguments, or indeed it may also decide to open administrative proceedings to investigate the given conduct. In the latter case, the civil court is obliged to stay proceedings pending the outcome of the GVH administrative proceedings.

There is no system for collective redress under Hungarian law (Hungarian procedural law does not know class actions or similar collective forms of remedies). The GVH has, however, the power to bring actions for the benefit of the public. The GVH has so far used this power in order to have certain general terms and conditions of certain undertakings declared to be anticompetitive and thus null and void by civil courts. Such declaratory judgments have *erga omnes* effects. **18.97**

D. Follow-on litigation

A large proportion of private litigation, and especially damages claims, is follow-on litigation. Hungarian courts, when ruling on an agreement or conduct which is already the subject of a Commission decision or a decision of the GVH cannot take a decision running counter to an existing Commission decision (art. 16 of Regulation 1/2003) or that of the GVH (art. 88/B HCA). They are therefore required to treat the Commission or the GVH infringement decision as proof of the existence of an infringement, but not necessarily of all the factual and legal findings included in the decision. **18.98**

In 2009, the Hungarian legislator introduced two specific provisions into the HCA with a view to foster follow-on damages actions. Article 88/C of the HCA essentially states that, in civil law cases initiated for damages allegedly caused by market sharing or price fixing cartels, it must be presumed that the cartel had influenced the market process by 10 percent. The presumption is rebuttable by the defendant. In other words, plaintiffs are provided with a comfortable position, since they do not have to run the extra mile to show the extent of their harm. They can simply rely on the "10% rule" and invoke the presumption that, as a result of the cartel, their price was 10 percent more, than it otherwise would have been, had the cartel never existed. This unprecedented rule has created a plaintiff friendly environment: since 2009, the number of follow-on damages litigations have increased. **18.99**

Article 88/D HCA wishes to enhance private litigation by removing a disincentive for leniency and hence helping to create situations in which private claimants may rely on the decisions of the GVH. Under article 88/D of the HCA, the leniency applicant will not bear joint or several liability for the damages caused by the cartel. Cartel members have always been perceived by Hungarian civil law as co-tortfeasors. Co-tortfeasors bear joint and several liability for all damages caused by each of them under article 344 of the Civil Code. Without protection against this rule, a leniency applicant could, as in a number of other jurisdictions, easily find itself in the target of private litigation earlier than the other members of the cartel (who will likely fight a long judicial battle against the administrative decision of the GVH, pending of which follow-on cases against them will not fly). **18.100**

E. Arbitration and alternative dispute resolution

Competition issues, and in particular disputes as to the enforceability of contractual terms, may arise in arbitration. Arbitral tribunals are not under an obligation to inform the GVH when article 11 or 21 of the HCA is invoked. **18.101**

Whether arbitral tribunals would be obliged to apply the competition rules on an *ex officio* basis or whether the non-application or a wrong interpretation of the main provisions of the HCA would lead to the annulment of the arbitral award is still open under Hungarian law. **18.102**

F. Remedies

(i) Civil liability

Administrative fines of up to 10 percent of the undertaking's net turnover may be imposed by the GVH under article 78 of the HCA. The limitation period is five years from the end of the infringement, but any enforcement action interrupts the running of the limitation period. **18.103**

18.104 In 2012, the GVH has adopted a new notice on the calculation of the fines. The cornerstones of the 2012 notice are very close to those of the Commission's 2006 Guidelines on the method of setting fines imposed pursuant to article 23(2)(a) of Regulation No. 1/2003.

18.105 In addition to making an infringement finding and imposing a fine, the GVH may issue a cease-and-desist order, or otherwise impose behavioral remedies with a view to restore effective competition.

18.106 As well as imposing fines for substantive infringements, the GVH has power to impose fines for procedural infringements. Fines of up to 1 percent of a company's annual turnover can be imposed in certain circumstances for intentionally or negligently supplying incorrect, incomplete, or misleading information or for non-cooperation with the HCA in the HCA's investigative steps (most particularly dawn raids).

18.107 The GVH may close a case with a formal commitments decision, rather than an infringement decision. Commitments do not involve an infringement finding or any fine. Breach of commitments entered into can lead to the same fines (up to 10 percent of the net turnovers of the preceding business year) as a classical substantive infringement.

18.108 Under exceptional circumstances, the GVH may impose interim measures pending its final decision which require a business to suspend its conduct or the operation of an agreement pending the conclusion of its investigation.

18.109 In addition, any term of agreement or any decision by an association of undertakings which infringes article 11(1) HCA (the cartel prohibition) is automatically void and unenforceable under article 11(3) HCA. Contractual terms infringing article 21 HCA are considered by the judicial practice to be also null and void (art. 21 HCA read in conjunction with art. 93 HCA and art. 200(1) of the Civil Code). Clauses affected by the competition provisions are severable from the rest of the contract (under art. 239 of the Civil Code), unless it is shown that the parties would not have entered into the arrangement without the clauses in question.

(ii) Criminal liability

18.110 Since the 2005 amendment to the Criminal Code, private persons who are involved in price-fixing and market-sharing arrangements (agreements, concerted practices or decisions of associations of undertakings) in relation to public procurement or public concession tenders may be sentenced to a term of up to five years of imprisonment (art. 420 of the New Criminal Code). A person who is the first to report a previously unknown infringement to the authorities receives full immunity from criminal sanctions.

18.111 The Hungarian cartel offense is thus relatively narrow in its scope: it only affects horizontal arrangements in public procurement or public concession tenders. Other cartels or other types of anticompetitive conduct (even if hard core or very harmful to consumers), do not result in criminal liability for private persons.

G. Leniency and immunity

18.112 Corporate leniency has been available under Hungarian competition law since 2003. The leniency-related rules of the HCA very much resemble the 2006 Commission Notice on Immunity from fines and reduction of fines in cartel cases.

18.113 Leniency is only available in horizontal cases under article 11 HCA (hence the benefit of leniency is not applicable to vertical arrangements or unilateral conduct).

18.114 Full immunity from fines is available only to the first company which provides information to the GVH that allows it either (i) to carry out an unannounced inspection, or (ii) to make an infringement finding with respect of the cartel. The immunity applicant will have to make a detailed corporate statement containing all relevant evidence in its possession. There is also the possibility of putting down a "marker" with the GVH for full immunity applicants, and providing the necessary information at a later time. From the moment of the submission of the application, the undertaking must cease participating in the cartel, unless the GVH gives permission for it to continue, and must fully and genuinely cooperate with the GVH throughout the proceedings.

Other companies which subsequently supply the GVH with evidence of "significant added value" to the investigation can obtain reductions in fines they would otherwise have to pay. Like an immunity applicant, they will also have to provide a corporate statement and cooperate continuously. The second applicant (that is, the first to come forward after immunity has been secured) is eligible for a fine reduction of 30–50 percent; the third, 20–30 percent; and any later applicants, up to 20 percent. **18.115**

The GVH's leniency policy has not yielded thus far the expected results. Since 2003, fewer than fifteen cases have been based on a leniency application. Most of the applications were multijurisdictional ones. **18.116**

H. Document creation and retention

Hungarian antitrust law does not include any explicit rules on document creation and retention. However, companies under investigation by the GVH are under a duty to actively cooperate with the GVH. Any negligent or intentional destruction of potentially relevant documents will be treated as a serious failure to cooperate, and may result in significant fines: a fine of up to 1 percent of the undertaking's total turnover can be imposed such a procedural infringement. In 2004, the GVH imposed a fine of HUF 110 million (then almost EUR 0.5 million) on a company which was unable to produce the originals of documents which the GVH had previously copied during a dawn raid on the company premises.[65] It was argued that the originals went missing during the moving of offices which took place after the dawn raid. While the GVH did not want to call the trustworthiness of this statement into question, it simply noted that an undertaking has the duty to fully cooperate with the GVH, which for the purposes of this specific scenario means that special attention must be paid to documents which were searched during dawns raids, since the undertaking ought to know that these documents may be of high relevance at a later stage. The courts agreed with the position of the GVH and confirmed the procedural fine. **18.117**

Documents which were created for the purposes of the defense of an undertaking in ongoing competition cases or documents which may later serve such purpose are protected by legal professional privilege under article 65/B HCA. These documents cannot be seized, reviewed, or copied by the GVH and cannot be used as evidence against the undertaking. **18.118**

[65] *Motorway Construction*, GVH, Case no. Vj-27/2003 (July 23, 2004).

19

INDIA

Naval Satarawala Chopra
Amarchand

Introduction

19.01 The Competition Act, 2002, was enacted in 2003 to prevent anticompetitive conduct, promote competition, and protect the interests of consumers. The enforcement of the Competition Act has been entrusted to the Competition Commission of India (CCI), which consists of a chairperson, 6 members, and their staff. The CCI is vested with inquisitorial, investigative, regulatory, and adjudicatory powers, and to a limited extent even advisory jurisdiction. The Competition Act empowers the CCI to inquire into and regulate anticompetitive agreements, abuses of a dominant position and combinations (i.e. merger control). The CCI is also provided with an investigative arm in the form of the Director General, who has powers to compel production of evidence, record sworn statements, and conduct dawn raids.

19.02 Over the last four and a half years of enforcement, the CCI has not been afraid to flex its muscles as a competition authority. From an early focus on dominant enterprises, the CCI appears to have shifted its focus to cartel activity and, in particular, the activities of trade associations. The Competition Act is increasingly being used as a tool by customers and competitors to protect their rights. The government of India has recognized the same and supports the competition regime. In fact, the government recently recommended a series of changes in the form of a Competition (Amendment) Bill, 2012, based on the experiences of all stakeholders since the enforcement of the Competition Act. Notably, the Competition (Amendment) Bill, 2012, proposes to introduce the concept of "collective dominance" in India.

I. Acting alone

Section 4 of the Competition Act prohibits an enterprise or group from abusing its dominant position. An enterprise is dominant under the Competition Act when it enjoys a position of strength, in the relevant market, in India, which enables it either to operate independently of competitive forces prevailing in the relevant market, or to affect its competitors or consumers or the relevant market in its favor. Dominance per se is not prohibited under the Competition Act; it is the conduct of the dominant enterprise which may be scrutinized to determine whether there has been an abuse of a dominant position. **19.03**

Pure unilateral conduct is covered by s. 4 of the Competition Act. The abuses covered by s. 4 of the Competition Act, however, overlap with some agreements between non-competing enterprises (enterprises in a vertical relation) which are considered anticompetitive under s. 3(4) of the Competition Act where the vertical agreement causes or is likely to cause an appreciable adverse effect on competition (AAEC) in India. Such vertical agreements are prohibited under s. 3(4) of the Competition Act, irrespective of whether the party to the agreement is dominant, provided the agreement causes or is likely to cause an AAEC in India. Accordingly, Section I deals with conduct arising from a dominant enterprise acting alone (i.e. unilateral conduct), including conduct arising from agreements between enterprises in a vertical relation where one party is a dominant enterprise. **19.04**

The CCI does not appear to have any clear enforcement priorities in relation to unilateral conduct. Since the inception of the Competition Act, the CCI has found violations in, amongst others, the stock exchange, real estate and sporting sectors, based on information filed by enterprises. The CCI has dealt with abuses ranging from unfair pricing to unfair terms, leveraging and denial of market access. What is clear, however, is that the CCI has been reluctant to go into detailed cost and economic analysis in its s. 4 assessments, and tends to focus more on conduct as a whole. It is worth noting that the CCI does not consider market share to be the only factor in assessing the dominance of an enterprise nor has it suggested a market share threshold beyond which dominance is assumed. While this means that it has, in a unique manner, found the number-two player in a market to be dominant in the case involving National Stock Exchange of India Ltd.,[1] it also means that it considers a range of factors when assessing the dominance of an enterprise. **19.05**

A. Predatory pricing

Predatory pricing is one of the abuses listed under s. 4 of the Competition Act. Under s. 4(2)(a)(ii), predatory pricing has two elements: first, that the price of goods or services must be below the relevant measure of cost and, second, that the dominant enterprise must engage in below-cost pricing with a view to reducing competition or eliminating competitors (i.e. an **19.06**

[1] *MCX Stock Exchange Ltd. & others v. National Stock Exchange of India Ltd. others*, CCI, Case no. 13/2009 (June 23, 2011) ("*NSE* case").

intent requirement). According to CCI regulations, the default measure of cost to determine whether the price of goods is predatory is the average variable cost. However, the regulations provide that the CCI may use other measures of cost depending on the nature of the industry, market, and technology, including, avoidable cost, long run average incremental cost, and market value.

19.07 In the *NSE* case, the informant had alleged that the NSE had engaged in predatory pricing. In a peculiar order, the CCI has found that, if an enterprise is pricing at zero, it is not necessary to inquire into whether the pricing is predatory, as such a price is unfair. It further held that since predatory pricing is only a subset of "unfair pricing," a zero price can be held to be unfair and hence abusive. In assessing the fairness of NSE's pricing policies, the CCI found that NSE's pricing was unfair to the informant. Both the concept of non-predatory low pricing amounting to an abuse and judging fairness on the basis of effect on existing competitors (as opposed to an equally efficient competitor, or competition, or the consumers) is a departure from international competition law jurisprudence. The NSE case is currently under appeal before the Competition Appellate Tribunal (COMPAT).

19.08 However, in a subsequent case,[2] involving an allegation of predatory bidding by Schlumberger, the CCI acknowledged that the aspect of predatory pricing has to be looked from an appropriate cost benchmark, though it did not analyze any cost data. The CCI also observed that reduction of prices is the essence of competition and that the informant in this case had merely lost out in a competitive bid. Accordingly, the CCI dismissed the claim at the *prima facie* stage.

B. Exploitative offenses (excessive pricing, monopoly leveraging)

19.09 Imposition of unfair or discriminatory conditions/prices in the purchase or sale of goods and services by a dominant enterprise is considered as abusive conduct under the Competition Act. A dominant enterprise can also be found guilty of abuse if it uses its dominant position in one relevant market to enter into, or protect another relevant market (i.e. a leveraging abuse).

19.10 An excessive pricing allegation was raised against Springer India by Prints India[3] in the market for publishing scientific, technical, and medical journals in English. No substantive guidance can be drawn from this case, as the CCI did not find Springer India to be a dominant enterprise. This case is currently under appeal before the COMPAT.

19.11 The CCI has also found that unfair, one-sided terms in contracts entered into by a dominant enterprise amounts to the imposition of an unfair condition in violation of s. 4(2)(a)(i) of the Competition Act.[4] In the *DLF* case, the CCI has recommended amended terms, such as the builder cannot arbitrarily forfeit earnest money without notice to the allottees; the builder cannot change plans without approval of the allottees; provisions for default for both parties on account of delay or abandonment of the project; interest and penalties of equal level can be levied on both sides for default; an allottee who is not agreeable to the terms of the agreement should have the liberty to withdraw his application and the application amount should be refunded. The adjudication of these amended terms is pending before the COMPAT.

19.12 While the law on monopoly leveraging is still developing in India, and the test under the Competition Act suggests that there should be associational links between the market in

[2] *H.L.S. Asia Limited, New Delhi v. Schlumberger Asia Services Ltd. Gurgaon and Oil & Natural Gas Corp. Limited, New Delhi*, CCI, Case no. 80/2012 (February 6, 2013).

[3] *Prints India v. Springer India Private Limited and others*, CCI, Case no. 16/2010 (July 3, 2012).

[4] *Belaire Owner's Association v. DLF Limited*, CCI, Case no. 19/2010 (January 3, 2013) ("*DLF* case").

which an enterprise is dominant and the market in which the abuse has occurred, the CCI appears to have departed from this principle in the *NSE* case. In the *NSE* case, the CCI held that there is no requirement for "associational links" between the market in which the firm has a dominant position and the market that it seeks to enter or protect.[5] Further, it appears that the CCI believes that mere cross subsidization would be an abuse under the Competition Act. As mentioned earlier, the NSE case is under appeal before the COMPAT.

C. Monopsony

A monopsonist, or a dominant buyer, could be found guilty of an abuse under the Competition Act. The definition of a "dominant position" under the Competition Act only refers to a position of strength in the "relevant market" and does not distinguish between a seller's market and a buyer's market. Further unfair prices/conditions imposed in the "purchase" of goods or services are also considered to be abusive under the Competition Act. The Airports Authority of India (AAI) was alleged to have abused its dominant position on the market for procurement of bollards for certain specified airports by specifying unfair technical requirements.[6] However, both the CCI and the COMPAT[7] found that the AAI was not dominant since the relevant market was for the procurement of bollards in general and not limited to the specified airports. **19.13**

D. Price discrimination

The imposition of unfair and/or discriminatory conditions by a dominant enterprise amounts to a violation of s. 4(2)(a)(i) of the Competition Act. The CCI has observed that when different rates of discounts are given to buyers it could amount to unfair and discriminatory conditions.[8] On the facts of the *Schott Glass* case, the CCI observed that the discount was discriminatory because higher discounts were offered to Schott Glass's downstream joint venture company, to the detriment of other players in the downstream market. **19.14**

Further, it was noted that the discount policies of Schott Glass for other players in the downstream market were intended to maintain its dominance in the upstream market. Schott Glass offered two kinds of discounts, volume-based and functional discounts. The volume-based discounts were based on the volume of purchases made at the beginning of the transaction and were adjusted at the end of each quarter. The functional discounts were offered for promoting the products by purchasing agreed quantities. These discount policies forced customers in the downstream market to procure nearly all their requirements of glass tubes from Schott Glass and were held to be "loyalty inducing", to the detriment of other upstream market players. The *Schott Glass* case is currently under appeal before the COMPAT. **19.15**

E. Dictating or influencing resale prices

(i) *Resale price maintenance*

An agreement for resale price maintenance (RPM) under the Competition Act includes any agreement to sell goods on the condition that the resale prices to be charged by the purchaser shall be the prices stipulated by the seller unless it is clearly stated that prices lower than those prices may be charged. Thus, it is noteworthy that, unlike many other jurisdictions, fixing **19.16**

[5] *NSE* case (n 1).

[6] *Kanazia Digital Systems Private Limited v. Airports Authority of India*, CCI, Case no.11/2011 (April 26, 2011).

[7] *Kanazia Digital Systems Private Limited v. Competition Commission of India and others*, COMPAT, Appeal No.14/2011 (July 26, 2012).

[8] *Kapoor Glass Private Limited v. Schott Glass India Pvt. Limited*, CCI, Case no. 22/2010 (March 29, 2012) ("*Schott Glass* case").

or recommending maximum retail prices is excluded from the scope of RPM by statutory definition. If a dominant enterprise imposes RPM, it could be viewed as imposing an unfair condition, which is an abuse under s. 4 of the Competition Act. There have been no substantive decisions of the CCI relating to RPM under s. 4 (or s. 3(4)) of the Competition Act.

(i) Minimum advertised price programs

19.17 Minimum advertised price (MAP) is not defined, or statutorily specified, as conduct which could call for scrutiny under s. 4 (or s. 3(4)) of the Competition Act. Nor has the CCI dealt with this issue in any case so far. It is likely that MAP programs would fall within the ambit of "unfair condition" under s. 4(2)(a)(i) (or as RPM under s. 3(4)(e)) of the Competition Act.

F. Tying arrangements

19.18 A tie-in arrangement is defined under the Competition Act to include any agreement that requires a purchaser of goods to purchase some other goods as a condition of such purchase.[9] The CCI has identified three essential conditions for an agreement to amount to an anticompetitive tie-in arrangement in violation of s. 3(4)(a) of the Competition Act: (1) the presence of two separate products or services capable of being tied; (2) the seller must have sufficient economic power with respect to the tying product to appreciably restrain free competition in the market for the tied product; and (3) the tying arrangement must affect a "not insubstantial" amount of commerce.[10]

19.19 Tying arrangements are also covered by s. 4(2)(d) of the Competition Act which prohibits dominant enterprises from making the conclusion of contracts subject to acceptance by other parties of supplementary obligations which, by their nature or according to commercial usage, have no connection with the subject of such contracts. Tying arrangements under s. 4 were examined in the *Schott Glass* case.[11] The CCI concluded that since both clear and amber products were tied and marketed together, and a bundled discount was offered on the purchase of both variants of glass tubes, Schott Glass infringed s. 4(2)(d) of the Competition Act.

19.20 Although the CCI has not considered many tie-in cases, it has recognized that it is prudent to examine the facts of individual cases holistically to arrive at a conclusion on the net impact on competition.[12]

G. Exclusive dealing

19.21 An exclusive distribution agreement is defined under the Competition Act to include any agreement to limit, restrict, or withhold the output or supply of any goods or allocate any area or market for the disposal or sale of the goods. An exclusive supply agreement is defined to include any agreement restricting in any manner the purchaser in the course of his trade from acquiring or otherwise dealing in any goods other than those of the seller or any other person.

19.22 Where a dominant enterprise imposes exclusivity, it could be held to be abusive under s. 4 of the Competition Act if it is viewed as imposing an unfair condition, limiting production, technology, or markets or denying market access.

19.23 While dealing with an exclusive supply agreement, the CCI has stated that, in general, the buyer's choice of supplier would be given deference, unless it was made in such a manner as to

---

[9] Explanation (a) to s. 3(4) of the Competition Act.

[10] *Shri Sonam Sharma v. Apple Inc. USA and others*, CCI, Case no. 24/2011 (March 19, 2013).

[11] Schott Glass case (n 8).

[12] *Automobiles Dealers Association, Hathras, U.P. v. Global Automobiles Limited and Pooja Expo India Private Limited*, CCI, Case no. 33/2011 (July 3, 2012).

restrict competition in the market.[13] In the *Explosive Manufacturers* case, Coal India Limited (one of the largest procurers of explosives in India), entered into an agreement with one enterprise for a period of five years for supply of up to 20 percent of its annual requirement of explosives. Following a detailed investigation, the CCI found that the agreement was not in violation of the provisions of the Competition Act, as a significant portion of Coal India's requirements were still open to other suppliers.

Similarly, where parties to an exclusivity agreement accounted for a small portion of similar transactions in the market, the CCI has stated that it does not amount to an AAEC.[14] Additionally, a without-cause termination clause with a short notice period of 30 days, coupled with evidence of frequent switching of suppliers by purchasers with similar contracts, may, in CCI's view, negate any adverse effect on competition. **19.24**

Further, different considerations would guide the CCI where long-term exclusive agreements were frequent outcomes in the markets under consideration.[15] In the *Jindal Steel* case, the CCI considered various factors including non-price factors such as safety, the lack of any other suppliers at the time of concluding the contract, the lack of proof of superior efficiency of the product produced by the informant, in making a determination regarding the anti-competitive nature of the agreement under s. 3(4) of the Competition Act. **19.25**

H. Refusal to deal

A refusal to deal is defined under the Competition Act to include any agreement that restricts, or is likely to restrict, by any method, the persons or classes of persons to whom goods are sold or from whom goods are bought.[16] **19.26**

Where a dominant enterprise refuses to deal, it could be held to be abusive under s. 4 of the Competition Act as it could result in limiting production or markets, denial of market access, etc. In the *NSE* case, where access codes were denied to the currency derivative segment of the stock exchange by NSE to a software vendor, the CCI held that this amounted to denial of market access.[17] Where cable TV operators belonging to the Fastway Group had refused to broadcast the Kansan News channel, the CCI found that the Fastway group had effectively denied Kansan News access to the market, in contravention of s. 4(2)(c) of the Competition Act.[18] The *Fastway* case is currently under appeal before the COMPAT. A clause in a media rights agreement for a period of ten years between the Board for Control of Cricket in India (BCCI) and MSM, a media broadcaster, by which the BCCI had bound itself not to organize, sanction, recognize any other private professional domestic league/event which could compete with its private cricket league, the Indian Premier League (IPL), was found to result in the denial of market access to any potential competitor to the IPL.[19] The CCI noted that, by expressly agreeing not to sanction any private cricket league other than the IPL during the **19.27**

---

[13] *Explosive Manufacturers Welfare Association v. Coal India Limited*, CCI, Case no. 04/2010 (July 26, 2011) ("*Explosive Manufacturers* case").

[14] *Cine Prakashakula Viniyoga Darula Sangham v. Hindustan Coca Cola Beverages Pvt. Ltd. and Consumer Guidance Society v. Hindustan Coca Cola Beverages Pvt. Ltd.*, CCI, Case nos. UTPE 99/2009 and RTPE-16/2009 (May 23, 2011).

[15] *Jindal Steel and Power Ltd. v. Steel Authority of India Limited*, CCI, Case no. 11/2009 (December 20, 2011) ("*Jindal Steel* case").

[16] Explanation (d) to s. 3(4) of the Competition Act.

[17] *NSE* case (n 1).

[18] *Kansan News Private Limited v. Fastway Transmission Private Limited*, CCI, Case no. 36/2011 (July 3, 2012) ("*Fastway* case").

[19] *Sh. Surinder Singh Barmi v. Board for Control of Cricket in India*, CCI, Case no. 61/2010 (February 8, 2013).

currency of the media rights agreement, the BCCI had used its regulatory powers to deny market access to competitors in violation of s. 4(2)(c) of the Competition Act. The *BCCI* case is currently under appeal before the COMPAT.

I. Essential facilities

19.28 The doctrine of essential facilities may have limited application under the Competition Act. The CCI has outlined limited circumstances, such as existence of technical feasibility to provide access, possibility of replicating the facility in a reasonable period of time, distinct possibility of lack of effective competition if access is denied, and possibility of providing access on reasonable terms, where the "essential facilities doctrine" could be invoked.[20] The *Arshiya* case had been appealed to the COMPAT but was ultimately dismissed due to non-maintainability of the appeal under the provisions of the Competition Act.[21]

J. Bundling (including loyalty and market share discounts)

19.29 Section 4(2)(d) of the Competition Act prohibits a dominant enterprise from making conclusion of contracts subject to acceptance by other parties of supplementary obligations which, by their nature or according to commercial usage, have no connection with the subject of such contracts. Discounts given by a dominant enterprise can also amount to unfair or discriminatory pricing and hence constitute abuse under s. 4(2)(a) of the Competition Act. An abusive tie or bundle by a dominant enterprise was assessed by the CCI in the *Schott Glass* case. The CCI concluded that since two different products were tied and marketed together, and a bundled discount was offered on the purchase of both variants of glass tubes, Schott Glass had infringed s. 4(2)(d) of the Competition Act.[22]

K. Standard-setting groups (disclosure requirements, licensing arrangements, and licensing pools)

19.30 There is no guidance on the treatment of standard-setting groups in India. However, the CCI has recently passed a *prima facie* order directing an investigation into Ericsson's injunction actions against and failure to enter into FRAND licensing arrangements for its Standard Essential Patents with Micromax Informatics Limited, an Indian mobile handset manufacturer.[23] This case is currently being investigated by the Director General-CCI.

L. Customer termination

19.31 Customer termination was alleged in one of the cases before the CCI[24] but no substantive guidance can be drawn from this case as Transitions India was found not to be dominant in the relevant market. Customer termination is likely to be assessed within the framework of refusals to deal under s. 3(4) of the Competition Act, and if the termination is by a dominant enterprise, it could also be assessed as an abuse by denial of market access under s. 4.

---

[20] *Arshiya Rail Infrastructure Limited v. Ministry of Railways through the Chairman, Railway Board & Container Corporation of India Limited*, CCI, Joined Cases 64/2010, 12/2011, and 02/2011 (August 14, 2012) ("*Arshiya* case").

[21] *Arshiya Rail Infrastructure Limited v. Competition Commission of India and others*, COMPAT, Appeal No. 136/2012 (April 4, 2013).

[22] *Schott Glass* case (n 8).

[23] *Micromax Informatics Limited v. Telefonaktiebolaget LM Ericsson (Publ.)*, CCI, Case no. 50/2013 (November 12, 2013).

[24] *GKB Hi Tech Lenses Private Limited v. Transitions Optical India Private Limited*, CCI, Case no. 01/2010 (May 16, 2012).

M. Termination of intermediaries (retailers, wholesalers, dealers, and value-added resellers, agents, and brokers)

As in the case of customer termination, there is currently no guidance from the CCI on the treatment of termination of intermediaries. Also, termination of intermediaries is likely to be assessed within the framework of refusals to deal under s. 3(4) of the Competition Act, and if the termination is by a dominant enterprise, it could also be assessed as a denial of market access abuse under s. 4(2)(c) of the Competition Act. **19.32**

N. Termination of relationships with competitors

Relationship between competitors is typically problematic under s. 3(3) of the Competition Act and is presumed to cause an AAEC. If there exists a relationship between competitors, a termination thereof can be assessed under s. 4, if any of the enterprises is determined to be dominant. There is, however, currently no guidance on this issue from the CCI. **19.33**

O. Exemptions

As mentioned above, s. 4(2)(a) of the Competition Act prohibits a dominant enterprise from imposing unfair or discriminatory conditions/prices in the purchase or sale of goods and services. However, such prices/conditions will not be considered to be "unfair" or "discriminatory" if they are adopted by dominant enterprises to "meet the competition" (i.e. a "meeting competition" defense). There is currently no substantive guidance available on how the CCI will apply the meeting competition defense. **19.34**

In addition, it should be noted that s. 3(5)(i) of the Competition Act exempts from s. 3 those agreements which impose reasonable conditions for the protection of intellectual property rights conferred upon them by certain specific Indian statutes. Such rights have, however, been held not to be absolute, and s. 3(5)(i) exempts the right holder from the rigors of competition law only to protect his rights from infringement.[25] The CCI has also observed that a refusal to deal by a dominant enterprise with an enterprise that has infringed its intellectual property rights in the past will not be considered to be abusive conduct.[26] **19.35**

Further, agreements which relate exclusively to exports are also exempt from the applicability of s. 3, under s. 3(5)(ii) of the Competition Act. **19.36**

When conduct of a department of the government is under investigation, it is not clear whether the immunity from the applicability of the Competition Act would be available only in cases where the activity of the concerned government department is limited to atomic energy, currency, defense, and space (which fall outside the definition of "enterprise" under the Competition Act), and activities which may be specifically exempt under s. 54(c)[27] of the Competition Act, or if this immunity also extends to other activities of the government. This issue arose in the *Arshiya* case, where the rail freight activity of the Ministry of Railways was alleged to be a non-sovereign function.[28] Whilst the CCI did not provide a conclusive finding on this issue, it held that, when providing railways services to passengers and other customers, the Indian Railways was performing a commercial function, and therefore, was an enterprise, **19.37**

---

[25] *FICCI–Multiplex Association of India v. United Producers/Distributors Forum and others*, CCI, Case no. 01/2009 (May 25, 2011).

[26] *Schott Glass* case (n 8).

[27] Section 54(c) gives the power to the central government to exempt from the application of the Competition Act, or any provision thereof, and for such period as it may specify, any enterprise which performs a sovereign function on behalf of the central government or a state government.

[28] *Arshiya* case (n 20).

and the provisions of the Competition Act applied squarely to its conduct. The CCI has also gone a step further in holding that entities that perform a single economic activity are also enterprises for the purposes of the Competition Act, even if this activity is undertaken on a one-off or stand-alone basis, such as government schools and state education departments inviting tenders for the services of printing, supplying, and distribution of text books.[29]

II. Dealing with competitors

19.38 Section 3(1) of the Competition Act prohibits agreements between persons, enterprises, or associations of persons/enterprises, in respect of the production, supply, distribution, storage, acquisition, or control of goods or provision of services, which causes or is likely to cause an AAEC within India. Section 3(3) of the Competition Act deals with "horizontal agreements" or agreements among enterprises or persons, including cartels, engaged in identical or similar trade of goods or provision of services. Agreements covered by s. 3(3) of the Competition Act are presumed to cause an AAEC. This presumption is, however, rebuttable and the burden of proof lies on the parties to the agreement to prove that the agreement in question does not or is not likely to cause an AAEC.

19.39 Horizontal agreements include agreements that—(i) directly or indirectly determine sale price; (ii) limit or control production, supply, markets, technical development, investment or provision of services; (iii) share the market or source of production or provision of services by way of allocation of geographical area, type of goods or services, or number of customers; and (iv) directly or indirectly result in bid rigging or collusive bidding.

19.40 The CCI has, in several cases, discussed the nature of these agreements, practices, types of conduct, or decisions of associations, and analyzed several issues, such as (i) whether s. 3 would apply to enterprises forming part of the same "group"; (ii) the evidentiary requirements of proving the existence of an agreement; and (iii) considerations/factors to assess where an industry trade association is involved in conduct that falls foul of s. 3(3) of the Competition Act. The conduct of trade associations has been an area of active enforcement for the CCI. In an encouraging move for industry, the CCI does not appear to automatically hold that conduct within and through a trade association is violative of the provisions of the Competition Act, and does consider the facts of individual cases on their own merit.

19.41 The CCI has held that it is not necessary to delineate a relevant market for the purposes of s. 3(3) and it is sufficient that the elements in s. 3(3) are present in order to determine and find a contravention of the Competition Act.[30]

A. Horizontal price fixing

19.42 Horizontal agreements which directly or indirectly determine purchase or sale price are presumed to be anticompetitive. However, where minimum prices were agreed but not implemented, the CCI found that such presumption stands rebutted and there is no violation of s. 3.[31] It appears from the *Sugar Mills* case that, to prove that an agreement is anticompetitive, it must be proved that the agreement has been implemented by the parties. It is not sufficient

[29] *Pitambara Books Private Limited, Delhi v. Primary Education Department, Office of the Director, Andhra Pradesh Open School*, CCI, Case no. 53/2011 (November 30, 2011).

[30] *Varca Druggist & Chemist v. Chemists and Druggists Association, Goa*, CCI, MRTP C-127/2009/DGIR4/28 (June 11, 2012) ("*Varca Druggist* case") and *Builder's Association of India v. Cement Manufacturers' Association of India*, CCI, Case no. 29/2010 (June 20, 2012) ("*Cement Cartel* case").

[31] *In Re: Sugar Mills*, CCI, Case no. 01/2010 (November 30, 2011) ("*Sugar Mills* case").

to show that there had been a meeting to discuss a price change, when the price change was not implemented in the market. However, the CCI is not bound by its own precedent, and this decision is a clear departure from European jurisprudence where price fixing is considered to be a violation of article 101 of the Treaty on the Functioning of the European Union (TFEU), by object. The *Sugar Mills* case is currently under appeal before the COMPAT.

To activate the presumption of anticompetitive effect, the CCI noted in its early decisional practice that the existence of an agreement needs to be unequivocally proven on the basis of precise and coherent evidence.[32] However, the standard of proof to establish the existence of an agreement, in subsequent cases, has been held to be a "preponderance of probability" and not "beyond a reasonable doubt".[33] Further, the CCI has held in the *Cement Cartel* case that evidence of an agreement need not be direct, and in the absence of direct evidence, it may rely on circumstantial evidence.[34] The *Cement Cartel* case is currently under appeal before the COMPAT and once this appeal has been decided, a clearer picture on the standard of proof required to be met by the CCI to prove the existence of a cartel may emerge. **19.43**

In the *Bank Loans* case,[35] the CCI has held that, despite a decision to levy a charge as well as the quantum of the charge being discussed at an association meeting, the fact that the levy of the charge took place at different times suggested that this was not the result of a cartel or an anticompetitive agreement.[36] **19.44**

B. Horizontal agreements to allocate customers or territories; agreements not to compete

Horizontal agreements that limit or control the production, supply, markets, technical development, investment or provision of goods or services are presumed to be anticompetitive. The CCI has looked at several cases concerning limitation of production and dispatch. **19.45**

In the *Cement Cartel* case,[37] the CCI found that the cement manufacturers had limited the production and supply of cement into the market by artificially operating their cement plants at lower capacity and withholding dispatches into the market. Evidence in relation to capacity additions, capacity utilization, production, dispatches, etc., of cement by the cement manufacturers was analyzed by the CCI in coming to this conclusion. **19.46**

Whether market power is an important factor in assessing a violation of s. 3(3)(b) was assessed by the CCI in the context of trade associations. Where a trade association enjoys a position such that it is impossible to do business without being a member of that association and such association prohibits its members from dealing with persons other than its own members, the CCI has found a contravention of s. 3(3)(b). In the *Uniglobe* case,[38] a decision made by a trade association, having sufficient market power, to refuse or reduce the supply of goods, was found by the CCI to be an anticompetitive activity. The CCI's decision in the *Uniglobe* case has been upheld by the COMPAT.[39] **19.47**

---

[32] *Neeraj Malhotra v. Deustche Post Bank Home Finance Ltd.*, CCI, Case no. 06/2009 (May 11, 2011) ("*Bank Loans* case").

[33] *In Re: Aluminium Phosphide Tablets Manufacturers*, CCI, Case no. 2/2011 (April 23, 2012) ("*Aluminium Phosphide* case").

[34] *Cement Cartel* case (n 30).

[35] *Bank Loans* case (n 32).

[36] See further Section II.H on price parallelism and "plus factors."

[37] *Cement Cartel* case (n 30).

[38] *Uniglobe Mod Travels Pvt. Ltd. v. Travel Agents Federation of India*, CCI, Case no. 03/2009 (October 4, 2011) ("*Uniglobe* case").

[39] *Travel Agents Association of India v. Uniglobe Mod Travels (P) Ltd. and others*, COMPAT, Appeal No. 24/2011 (July 10, 2013).

19.48 Collusive bidding or bid-rigging which has the effect of eliminating or reducing competition for bids or adversely affecting or manipulating the process of bidding is presumed to be anticompetitive. However, this presumption only applies to agreements between firms engaged in similar levels of production and not agreements between the party who opens the bid and one or more bidders. Such an agreement or conduct, however, may be covered under s. 3(4) of the Competition Act, which deals with vertical agreements. The CCI has recognized that there are certain factors that, in general, may increase the likelihood of bid-rigging in a market, including a constant and predictable flow of demand, small number of suppliers, few new entrants, an active trade association, repetitive bidding, identical products, few or no substitutes, and no significant technological changes.[40] The *LPG case* is currently under appeal before the COMPAT.

C. Horizontal boycotts

19.49 The CCI has found collective boycotts by associations of travel agents of particular airlines to be violative of s. 3 of the Competition Act, as the travel agents' associations were unable to reverse the presumption that their conduct had caused an AAEC in India, nor were the travel agents' associations able to show that their conduct created efficiencies which were greater than the actual adverse impact on competition.[41] In the *Explosive Manufacturers* case, the CCI found that the firms had contravened s. 3(3)(d) of the Competition Act when they collectively decided to boycott an auction. Some parties had also sent identical letters of objection to the terms of the bid, which the CCI considered to be evidence of a "meeting of minds" between the parties.[42] The CCI also observed that the Explosive Manufacturers' boycott of Coal India's tender resulted in limiting supply of explosives to Coal India, in violation of s. 3(3)(b) of the Competition Act. On appeal, the COMPAT has upheld the CCI's finding of a bid rigging violation under s. 3(3)(d). However, since Coal India's tender had been rescheduled and conducted successfully, the CCI's finding of "limiting supply" in violation of s. 3(3)(b) was rejected.[43]

D. Joint ventures and other competitive collaborations

19.50 The proviso to s. 3(3) of the Competition Act lays down an exemption to the presumption raised in relation to horizontal agreements listed in s. 3(3) of the Competition Act. According to the proviso, a joint venture agreement is not presumed to be anticompetitive if it can be shown that such agreement increases efficiencies in production, supply, distribution, storage, acquisition, or control of goods/provision of services. This provision is yet to be tested by the CCI and currently, there is no substantive guidance on the standard of evidence required to qualify as an efficiency enhancing joint venture under this exemption.

E. Trade associations

19.51 The Indian industry is replete with trade associations. Typically, competition authorities view trade associations with suspicion, as they provide an ideal platform for competitors to coordinate their conduct on the market. The general approach adopted by most competition authorities is that, other than for purposes of discussing issues which affect an industry as a whole, for example, technological advancements, taxation policies, etc., there is no need

[40] *In Re: Suo-Motu Case against LPG Cylinder Manufacturers*, CCI, Case no. 3/2011(February 24, 2012) ("*LPG* case").

[41] *Uniglobe* case (n 38).

[42] *Explosive Manufacturers* case (n 13).

[43] *M/s Gulf Oil Corporation Ltd. and others v. Competition Commission of India and others*, COMPAT, Appeal Nos. 82/2012, 83/2012, 84/2012, 85/2012, 86/2012, 87/2012, 88/2012, 89/2012, and 90/2012 (April 18, 2013).

for competitors to meet. The CCI has dealt with a number of cases involving allegations of anticompetitive agreements through trade associations. It has observed that although trade associations can be legitimate *fora* for promoting standards, innovation and competition, they can also become facilitators for cartel behavior.[44]

The CCI has held that coordination of prices, refusal to supply goods, customer allocation, output restrictions, or rigging of bids achieved through the medium of a trade association, would be in violation of s. 3 of the Competition Act. Rules and regulations governing the operation of a trade association may, by themselves, be adjudged as anticompetitive by the CCI. In fact, the CCI has relied on guidelines, circulars, and rules of trade associations as evidence of an anticompetitive agreement.[45] **19.52**

In the *Cement Cartel* case,[46] where the Cement Manufacturers' Association (CMA) was collecting both retail and wholesale prices and circulating details of capacity utilization, production, and dispatch among all its members, the CCI held that the CMA had provided a platform to the cement companies and facilitated cartelization. A penalty of 10 percent of the total receipts for two years was imposed on the CMA, in addition to the penalties that were imposed on its members. **19.53**

Like in the *Cement Cartel* case, penalties have been imposed on trade associations as well as their constituent members, in other cases. However, in some cases, only the trade associations have been penalized and not their constituent members.[47] **19.54**

Individuals who were primarily involved in the activities of the infringing trade association, by virtue of being members of its executive committee, were also held liable for contravention in the *Varca Druggist* case[48] and the CCI stated that a separate order will be passed against such individuals once certain information is received. No separate order against these individuals has been passed by the CCI as yet. **19.55**

F. Interlocking directorates

There is no restriction under the Competition Act on interlocking directorates. However, if two or more competitors, alleged to be in a cartel in violation of s. 3(3) of the Competition Act, are found to have common directors, it could be viewed by the CCI as one of the relevant factors in assessing the existence of a horizontal agreement and horizontal anticompetitive conduct. **19.56**

G. Facilitating practices

The CCI has dealt with several cases involving "price parallelism" and other parallel behavior across various industries. Parallel prices could indicate cartelization but could also arise from competitive market dynamics and therefore may not be a result of unlawful activity. **19.57**

It has been the CCI's position that mere price parallelism cannot be said to be evidence of the existence of a cartel.[49] In order to arrive at a violation of s. 3(3) of the Competition Act, **19.58**

[44] *In All India Tyre Dealers Federation v. Tyre Manufacturers*, CCI, MRTP Case RTPE No. 20/2008 (October 30, 2012) ("*India Tyre* case").

[45] *Varca Druggist* case (n 30); *Reliance Big Entertainment Ltd. and others v. Karnataka Film Chamber of Commerce and others*, CCI, Joined Cases 25/2010, 41/2010, 45/2010, 47/2010, 48/2010, 50/2010, 58/2010, & 69/2010 (February 16, 2012).

[46] *Cement Cartel* case (n 30).

[47] *Uniglobe* case (n 38).

[48] *Varca Druggist* case (n 30).

[49] *In Re: Glass Manufacturers of India,* CCI, MRTP Case no. 161/2008 (January 24, 2012) ("Glass Manufacturers case").

the CCI has identified certain "plus factors" which would be necessary, in addition to mere parallel pricing. Price parallelism, in the CCI's view, may arise from firms following similar pricing models,[50] or may be a natural consequence of competition in an industry in which prices typically vary only between a particular price band.[51] The CCI has repeatedly exonerated enterprises accused of cartelization based solely on the existence of price parallelism, due to the fact that there was no evidence of an actual agreement.

19.59 Where certain action was undertaken by competitors on a common date, it was held to be insufficient to infer existence of an agreement.[52] In the *Travel Agents* case, the CCI and COMPAT held that the decision of foreign airlines to reduce the commission paid to travel agents starting from the same date did not amount to a cartel as the airlines were independently implementing their global policies, and the only evidence adduced by the informant was a common date, which was deemed insufficient to prove the existence of an agreement.[53] The *Travel Agents* case was appealed to the Supreme Court of India but has been subsequently withdrawn.

19.60 Further, a high degree of correlation must be observed, in CCI's view, to find price parallelism. In the *India Tyre* case,[54] where there was a variation of between 6 to 12 percent between the prices of tyres of various tyre manufacturers, the CCI held that there was no price parallelism. Further, in the *Cement Cartel* case,[55] the CCI found that there need not be complete parallelism for the entire duration of the alleged anticompetitive conduct and, if there are certain durations of coordinated conduct, evidenced through identical patterns, a case for parallelism could be established.

H. Plus factors

19.61 Parallelism in prices cannot, by itself, be considered sufficient to prove the existence of an agreement. There must be other factors in addition to parallel prices, popularly known as "plus factors," in order to arrive at a finding of collusion.

19.62 In the *Cement Cartel* case,[56] price parallelism, along with low capacity utilization, low dispatch figures, higher profitability levels of the cement manufacturers, active trade association, etc., have been found by the CCI to be suggestive of anticompetitive behavior.

19.63 In the *India Tyre* case,[57] fluctuations in market shares were found by the CCI to be inconsistent with cartel conduct where market shares generally remain consistent through the years. Further, it was noted that, in a cartel setup, it would be against rational business behavior to lose market share to a rival, and such trends in market share movements, according to the CCI, are possible only in competitive environments.

19.64 A review of the CCI's jurisprudence in relation to parallel conduct shows interesting insights, as well as inconsistent and contradictory approaches. For example, in the *Cement Cartel* case,[58] the CCI only considered the absolute changes in price when considering price parallelism

[50] *In Re: Domestic Air Lines, CCI,* Reference Case no. 01/2011 (January 11, 2012); *In Re: Domestic Air Lines*, CCI, RTPE Case no. 05/2009 and Suo-Motu Case no. 02/2010 (January 10, 2012).

[51] *Glass Manufacturers* case (n 49).

[52] *Travel Agents Association of India v. Lufthansa German Airlines and others*, CCI, Case no. 14/2009 (October 31, 2011) ("*Travel Agents* case").

[53] *Travel Agents Association of India v. Lufthansa German Airlines and others*, COMPAT, Appeal No. 25/2011 (December 7, 2012).

[54] *India Tyre* case (n 44).

[55] *Cement Cartel* case (n 30).

[56] *Cement Cartel* case (n 30).

[57] *India Tyre* case (n 44).

[58] *Cement Cartel* case (n 30).

whereas in the *India Tyre* case, it looked at percentage changes.[59] Further, the CCI in the *India Tyre* case, considered the fact that the lower capacity utilization by the tyre manufacturers was a result of increased capacity which was not immediately fully available for utilization, while this fact seems to have been ignored by the CCI in the *Cement Cartel* case. In the *Glass Manufacturers* case, the CCI recognized the fact that in a commodity product, prices tend to move in a narrow band, and competitors will not price their products in a manner which is completely out of sync with competitive market conditions, a factor which seems to have not been dealt with in detail in the *Cement Cartel* case.

I. Information exchange

The CCI has provided guidance on what information exchanges between competitors would be in violation of s. 3(3) of the Competition Act in the *Cement Cartel* case.[60] Such information exchanges include (i) commercially sensitive information or strategically useful data, such as detailed and recent sales, production, dispatch information; (ii) non-public information, i.e. information not available in the public domain or not equally easily accessible by other people; (iii) data that is individualized and is non-aggregated; and (iv) information that is not sufficiently historic. **19.65**

(i) Exchanges of historic pricing information

In the *Cement Cartel* case, the CCI indicated that historical exchange of information is permitted.[61] **19.66**

(ii) How old, anonymous, and aggregated pricing information needs to be

No substantive guidance has been provided in the *Cement Cartel* case on how old, anonymous, and aggregated pricing information needs to be in order for such information exchange to be permissible. **19.67**

(iii) What pro-competitive purposes, if any, exchange needs to help participants achieve; pre-merger due diligence

Information exchanges involving the exchange of certain commercially sensitive information between competitors are presumed to cause an AAEC. Such a presumption can be rebutted by the defendant in the case of an alleged claim by showing a pro-competitive rationale and establishing that such conduct does not, and is not likely to, cause an AAEC. **19.68**

Parties that are proposing to enter into a transaction (e.g. acquisition, merger, or amalgamation) may inadvertently share certain information which may be viewed as being anticompetitive. Some safeguards like establishing Chinese walls between the transaction team and other officers of the companies involved, establishing "clean teams" etc., can be adopted to possibly counter any claim of collusion. **19.69**

J. Joint purchasing agreements

There have been no substantive decisions of the CCI relating to joint purchasing agreements and therefore, no guidance is currently available on how the CCI will treat such agreements. **19.70**

K. Joint lobbying/regulatory/legislative efforts

Where the law requires parties to come together to initiate any action (e.g. antidumping laws), such action on its own is unlikely to be viewed as an infringement of the provisions of **19.71**

---

59 *India Tyre* case (n 44).
60 *Cement Cartel* case (n 30).
61 *Cement Cartel* case (n 30).

the Competition Act. In the *India Tyre* case, the association of tyre manufacturers made joint applications, in accordance with the antidumping laws, for levy of antidumping duty for the welfare of the tyre industry.[62] Such an action was not considered by the CCI as amounting to a cartel between the tyre manufacturers, especially as no confidential information in relation to any particular tyre manufacturer was shared with the others.

19.72 Section II deals with agreement/conduct between competitors which is prohibited under s. 3(3) of the Competition Act. Section 3(4) of the Competition Act (which is covered under Section I of this Chapter) prohibits "vertical" agreements or agreements amongst enterprises or persons at different stages or levels of the production chain in different markets, in respect of production, supply, distribution, storage, sale, price, or trade in goods or provision of services, if such an agreement causes or is likely to cause an AAEC in India, and includes, (i) tie-in arrangements, (ii) exclusive supply agreements, (iii) exclusive distribution agreements, (iv) refusals to deal, and (v) resale price maintenance agreements. Vertical agreements are not presumed to be anticompetitive under the Competition Act. There are very few decisions of the CCI on s. 3(4),[63] and therefore, there exists little guidance on how the conduct under s. 3(4) will be scrutinized by the CCI.

III. General issues

A. Jurisdiction and applicable law (including sector-specific competition regulation)

19.73 The CCI has the jurisdiction to inquire into any alleged contravention of the provisions of the Competition Act, the applicable law in India. Such inquiry can be made *suo motu* by the CCI or on receipt of any information from any person, consumer, or their association or trade association, or upon a reference made to it by the central government or a state government or a statutory authority. The CCI is also empowered to inquire into acts taking place outside India if such acts are likely to have an AAEC in India.

19.74 There are no sector-specific competition regulations in India. However, the government of India has by a notification dated January 8, 2013 exempted banking companies from notifying mergers and acquisitions to the CCI for a period of five years, i.e. until January 7, 2018.

19.75 As a general matter, the provisions of the Competition Act apply to "enterprises." According to the Competition Act, an "enterprise" includes any person carrying out any activity relating to the production, storage, supply, distribution, acquisition, or control of articles or goods; the provision of services; or activity relating to investment, acquiring, holding, underwriting, or dealing with shares, debentures, or other securities of any other body corporate, either directly or through its units or divisions or subsidiaries. The definition of an enterprise also includes a department of the government but does not include activities of the government relatable to sovereign functions, including all activities carried on by the government dealing with atomic energy, currency, defense, and space.

19.76 The CCI has had, and continues to have, a fair amount of litigation challenging its jurisdiction on issues such as: (i) whether the CCI has jurisdiction over agreements and conduct that took place prior to the enforcement of ss. 3 and 4 of the Competition Act (i.e. prior to May 20, 2009), and whether the CCI can rely on evidence that predates the enforcement of the Competition Act; (ii) the scope of the term "enterprise" under the Competition Act; and (iii)

[62] *India Tyre* case (n 44).

[63] See Section I.

whether the CCI has jurisdiction in relation to sectors where specialist sectoral regulators already exist.

The provisions of the Competition Act have an overriding effect, notwithstanding any inconsistencies vis-à-vis other laws in force. Recognizing that certain sectors may have specialized regulators and may require sectoral expertise, the Competition Act also gives the power to the CCI to invite and give opinions to other statutory authorities, and obligates the authority to which a reference has been made to consider the opinions issued. With a view to preventing turf wars and inconsistencies between sectoral regulators and the CCI, the current voluntary reference is proposed to be made mandatory, pursuant to a proposed amendment in the Competition (Amendment) Bill, 2012. As a result, when issues that may conflict with the sectoral regulatory framework arise during the CCI's review and, similarly, when competition law issues arise during proceedings before a sectoral regulator, the relevant regulators are "required" to make a reference to one another. This reference is to be time bound to 60 days and the CCI and the statutory authorities are required to give due regard to the opinion sought in coming to their decisions. **19.77**

B. Antitrust system

(i) Name of agency/agencies

The enforcement of the Competition Act has been entrusted with the CCI. The Director General is the investigation arm of the CCI. **19.78**

Final orders of the CCI are appealable to the COMPAT and decisions of the COMPAT are appealable to the Supreme Court of India, which is the apex court of India. **19.79**

(ii) Staff size and budget

The CCI consists of a chairperson and six members and is supported by a staff of approximately eighty-six people. The Director General's office currently has a staff of approximately twenty people. The CCI's annual budget in 2011/2012 was INR 3,792 lakhs (approx. USD 7 million). **19.80**

(iii) Recent enforcement actions and trends

Over the last three and half years of enforcement, the CCI has issued a number of important decisions in the area of cartels and dominance. Targeting hard core cartels has been an enforcement priority for the CCI and significant penalties have been imposed. The CCI has addressed a variety of issues such as the treatment of enterprises in the same group, proof of cartel agreements based on circumstantial evidence, the conduct of trade associations and bid rigging. While cartels are likely to be an enforcement priority in the years to come, the concept of collective dominance, sought to be introduced by including the words "jointly or singly" in s. 4 of the Competition Act, may result in a number of cases being filed under s. 4 of the Competition Act or the CCI itself initiating *suo motu* actions against enterprises that are collectively dominant and have abused their dominant position. **19.81**

C. Private litigation

There is no private right to antitrust litigation in India. The Competition Act specifically supersedes the jurisdiction of civil courts. The CCI is the only authority entrusted with enforcing the provisions of the Competition Act. Appeals, however, lie to the COMPAT and finally to the Supreme Court of India. **19.82**

D. Follow-on litigation (includes role of agency determinations of liability for follow-on litigation)

The CCI does not have the power to grant any compensation. Upon an application made to the COMPAT, the COMPAT can grant compensation for the loss or damage shown to **19.83** have been suffered as a result of any contravention of the provisions of the Competition Act. Where any loss or damage is caused to numerous persons having the same interest, one or more of such persons may, with the permission of the COMPAT, file an application on behalf of all the interested persons. As of the date of writing, there have been no applications for compensation made before the COMPAT.

E. Arbitration and alternative dispute resolution

19.84 Since no private litigation is permitted, an enterprise cannot contractually oust the jurisdiction of the CCI by referring competition claims to arbitration.

F. Remedies

19.85 If an enterprise is found to be in contravention of s. 3 or s. 4 of the Competition Act, the CCI has the power, *inter alia*:

(i) to pass cease-and-desist orders;
(ii) to impose a penalty not exceeding 10 percent of the average turnover for the last three financial years on each enterprise that is a party to an anticompetitive agreement. In the case of cartels, the penalty is higher and can be up to three times of the profit or 10 percent of the turnover of each participating enterprise for each year of continuance of such agreement, whichever is higher; and
(iii) to modify any offending agreement.

19.86 The CCI also possesses the power to order the division of a dominant enterprise which is found guilty of an abuse. The COMPAT has held that the CCI must record reasons while imposing penalties for contraventions of the Competition Act, especially since the CCI is an adjudicatory body, and that penalties imposed must be proportionate to the wrong committed.[64] In dismissing the appeal from the *Aluminum Phosphide* case, the COMPAT reduced the penalty imposed on Aluminum Phosphide tablet manufacturers and held that penalties imposed on multi-product firms should be based on turnover from the relevant market, i.e. the quantum of penalty should be imposed on the relevant turnover.[65] The COMPAT's decision in the *Aluminum Phosphide* appeal is likely to be challenged before the Supreme Court of India and the position on this issue will be settled once the appeal to the Supreme Court of India has been decided.

19.87 Contravention of CCI's orders can invite further penalties, and the CCI can even file a criminal complaint against such contravention which, in turn, could lead to the imposition of additional fines or even imprisonment of up to three years. Further, where a company has contravened the Competition Act with the connivance or consent of any director, manager, or secretary or of any other officer of the company who was responsible and in charge of conduct of business of the company, such persons shall be deemed to be guilty and punished accordingly.

19.88 The CCI has not framed any guidelines or given any guidance, in cases decided so far, on calculating penalties. However, the CCI has not been hesitant to impose significant monetary penalties for violations of the provisions of s. 3 of the Competition Act. In *Varca Druggist* case,[66] the CCI imposed the maximum penalty of 10 percent of the annual turnover of the parties for a contravention of s. 3. In the *Cement Cartel* case,[67] the CCI imposed a penalty of

---

[64] *M/s Sandhya Organic Chemicals (P) Limited v. Competition Commission of India and others*, COMPAT, Appeal No. 80/2012 (October 29, 2013) ("*Aluminum Phosphide* appeal").
[65] *Aluminum Phosphide* appeal (n 64).
[66] *Varca Druggist* case (n 30).
[67] *Cement Cartel* case (n 30).

0.5 times the profit of the companies over two years of the existence of the cartel. The penalty imposed on the cement manufacturers and the cement trade association was approximately USD 1,174.2 million—the highest penalty imposed in any case by the CCI so far. The CCI has also imposed significant fines in abuse of dominance cases. In the *DLF* case, the CCI imposed a fine of 7 percent of turnover (approximately USD 114.5 million) on DLF.[68]

(i) Civil liability

Infringements of the Competition Act attract only civil liability except for when orders of the CCI are not complied with. **19.89**

(ii) Criminal liability

There is currently no criminal liability for infringements of the Competition Act, except where orders of the CCI are not complied with. Members of the CCI have publicly supported the introduction of criminal liability, though this does not appear to be a high priority item on the legislative agenda. **19.90**

G. Leniency and immunity

A member of a cartel can apply for leniency under s. 46 of the Competition Act read with the Competition Commission of India (Lesser Penalty) Regulations, 2009 (Lesser Penalty Regulations). Leniency is not available for cases relating to vertical agreements or abuse of dominance. The Lesser Penalty Regulations prescribe when, and the manner and degree to which, the CCI can reduce the penalties to be imposed on members of a cartel that make a full, true, and vital disclosure to the CCI. So far, no case has been decided based on a leniency application received by the CCI. **19.91**

A party seeking lesser penalty must fulfill the following essential conditions, as set out in Regulation 3 of the Lesser Penalty Regulations, in order to obtain a reduction in penalty: **19.92**

(i) cease from further participation in the cartel, unless otherwise directed by the CCI;
(ii) provide vital disclosure to the CCI;
(iii) provide all relevant information, documents and evidence as may be required by the CCI;
(iv) extend genuine, full, continuous and expeditious cooperation to the CCI throughout its investigation and other proceedings before the CCI; and
(v) must not conceal, destroy, manipulate or remove any relevant documents which may establish the existence of a cartel.

Additionally, the CCI seems to be taking a view that an admission of violation (i.e. being party to a cartel) is a prerequisite to applying for leniency. An enterprise cannot apply for leniency where the report of the Director General, in relation to the alleged infringement(s), has already been received by the CCI.

Further, where an applicant has been granted lenient treatment under the leniency provisions of the Competition Act, such leniency will not extend to any compensation claims by third parties, i.e. a leniency applicant could still be subject to compensation claims before the COMPAT and may be liable to pay damages under s. 53N of the Competition Act. **19.93**

Any reduction in monetary penalty to be paid by a leniency applicant is based on the discretion of the CCI and the CCI's discretion in the matter will be exercised having given due regard to (i) the stage at which the leniency applicant comes forward with its disclosure, (ii) the evidence already in possession of the CCI, (iii) the quality of the information provided **19.94**

[68] *DLF* case (n 4).

by the applicant, and (iv) the facts and circumstances of the case. The first party to make a vital disclosure to the CCI could potentially benefit from a reduction of up to 100 percent of the penalty sought to be imposed, in the event the applicant's disclosure: (i) enables the CCI to form a *prima facie* opinion regarding the existence of a cartel, where the CCI did not have, at the time of the application, sufficient evidence to form such a *prima facie* opinion, or (ii) submits such evidence which enables the CCI to establish a contravention of s. 3 of the Competition Act which the Director General or the CCI did not have in its possession in a matter under investigation. The applicants marked as second and third in the priority status may get a reduction of up to or equal to 50 percent and 30 percent, respectively, upon making a disclosure of evidence that provides *significant added value* to the evidence already in possession of the CCI or the Director General.

H. Document creation and retention

19.95 There are no specific provisions under the Competition Act dealing with document creation and retention. However, s. 45 prescribes a fine in case where documents are willfully altered, suppressed or destroyed. Further, the Competition (Amendment) Bill, 2012, proposes that a raid can be authorized to be conducted by the DG where there is mere "reason to believe" that a person or enterprise will not provide the information relevant to the investigation.

20

IRELAND

Vincent J.G. Power
A&L Goodbody

Introduction

20.01 Competition in Ireland is regulated by: (a) European Union (EU) competition law and (b) Irish competition law. If there is a conflict between the two regimes then the EU one prevails in accordance with the Doctrine of Supremacy of EU law over conflicting member state law. Irish law provides explicitly that it is possible to bring a civil action in the Irish courts for a breach of EU and/or Irish competition law. Moreover, certain breaches of EU competition law have been criminalized by Irish law so it is possible to be prosecuted before the Irish courts under Irish criminal law for a breach of aspects of EU and/or Irish competition law.

20.02 EU competition law involves the competition rules contained in the Treaty on the Functioning of the European Union (TFEU) as well as the secondary rules adopted by the Council, Parliament and/or Commission. EU competition law is described in Chapter 12 in this handbook, so this Chapter concentrates on Irish competition law.

20.03 Irish competition law is primarily legislative (or statutory) in nature with the rules contained primarily in the Competition Acts 2002–2012. The non-legislative rules (i.e. judge-made rules or so-called "common law") apply whenever the legislation does not apply, but typically this only occurs in regard to restrictive covenants in employment agreements. In terms of the Irish legislation, the Competition Act 2002 (the "2002 Act") is the principal statute and sets out the main substantive and procedural rules. Section 4 of the 2002 Act is comparable to article 101 TFEU (all references to "s. 4" in this Chapter are to this section). Section 5 mirrors Article 102 TFEU (all references to "s. 5" in this Chapter are to this section). Part 3 of the 2002 Act establishes a concentration control regime whereby the Irish Competition Authority (the "Authority") examines mergers, acquisitions, and certain types of joint venture to see if the proposed transaction would substantially lessen competition (the "SLC" test). The Competition (Amendment) Act 2006 (the "2006 Act") deals with certain aspects of competition in the grocery sector. The Competition (Amendment) Act 2012 (the "2012 Act") was enacted to enhance enforcement. A further statute is expected to be initiated in the near future and it is anticipated that the statute will consolidate existing legislation and amalgamate the Authority with the National Consumer Agency.

20.04 The Authority is the statutory agency charged with public enforcement of Irish competition law. Unlike many other competition agencies, it does not have the power to impose fines because, under the Irish Constitution of 1937, only courts may impose fines as the power to do so is classified as a judicial function. Enforcement is therefore primarily undertaken by the courts in cases instituted by the Authority (in civil and minor criminal matters) or the Director of Public Prosecutions (DPP) in more serious criminal matters. In the case of hard core breaches of competition law (e.g. price-fixing), the courts may impose: (a) on individuals, jail sentences of up to ten years and/or fines of up to EUR 5 million; and (b) on non-individuals (e.g. companies), fines of up to 10 percent of worldwide turnover.

20.05 To date, public enforcement has been more prevalent than private enforcement. Private actions for damages, exemplary damages, injunctions, and/or damages have been possible since 1991 but such actions have not been commonplace largely because there have been few large-scale public enforcement actions which would lead to follow-on private actions but also because the law is still relatively uncertain with plaintiffs facing significant evidential, jurisprudential, and financial challenges. In terms of public enforcement, the priority is likely to remain on cartels. However, there are indications that the Authority realizes that abuse of dominance (particularly, monopolies) is also worthy of attention. There have been several public enforcement criminal actions but they have related to small-scale matters such as price-fixing among small-scale oil distributors and car dealers so they have not stimulated follow-on actions because the damages which would follow would have been too small. There have been some public enforcement civil actions but they have either not succeeded[1] or have been settled.[2]

20.06 There are many areas of Irish competition law which are underdeveloped in terms of jurisprudence (particularly, in regard to abuse of dominance because the Authority's priority has been the enforcement of cartels). In terms of developing these areas, the basic ground rules are already present (ss. 4 and 5 of the 2002 Act which are comparable to articles 101 and 102 TFEU) so it is very likely that the Irish courts and Authority would follow the EU jurisprudence. Indeed, the "Long Title" to the 2002 Act provides that the statute is "by analogy" with

[1] E.g. *Competition Authority v. O'Regan and others* [2007] IESC 22.

[2] E.g., *Competition Authority v. Beef Industry Development Society*, settled.

the TFEU while the Irish courts have stated that the Irish legislation should be construed by analogy with EU law.

The Irish Supreme Court has stated in *Competition Authority v. O'Regan and others* that **20.07**

> [the] entire aim and object of competition law is consumer welfare. Competitive markets must serve the consumer. That is their sole purpose. Competition law, as is often said, is about protecting competition, not competitors, even if it is competitors who most frequently invoke it. Its guiding principle is that open and fair competition between producers of goods and services will favour the most efficient producers, who will thereby be encouraged to satisfy consumer demand for better quality products, wider choice and lower prices. Their reward is a greater market share. Production of better and newer products may necessitate expensive market research, involving a degree of economic resources and market power.[3]

Ireland can claim two European firsts in the area of enforcement: the first criminal competition law conviction by a jury following a trial;[4] and the first custodial sentence in Europe of a defendant under competition legislation.[5] **20.08**

The administration of competition law in Ireland is very largely free of political involvement or interference with power delegated to the Authority. The Authority has prioritized cartels but anyone involved in any anticompetitive arrangement or practice should know that the Authority is intent on investigating such breaches and has a team of lawyers, economists, and police detectives at its disposal to do so and has shown an increasing resolve and determination to do so. **20.09**

Irish competition law provides a combination of remedies or reliefs (referred to, for convenience, in this Chapter as the "usual remedies"). These remedies are damages, exemplary damages, injunctions and declarations (i.e. a court order setting out the legal position). These usual remedies are available in smaller matters from the Circuit Court or, in all other matters, from the High Court. The maximum award by the Circuit Court is EUR 38,092.14 but this amount can be increased if the parties involved in the case agree in writing. The High Court is a court of unlimited jurisdiction. **20.10**

I. Acting alone

Section 5 controls anticompetitive behavior by an undertaking acting alone where the undertaking has a dominant position in Ireland (or any part of Ireland) and there is an abuse of that dominance. It is comparable to article 102 TFEU and the section should be construed in the context of the jurisprudence on that article. Section 5 only applies to undertakings which have a dominant position in Ireland or any part of Ireland. The terms "dominant position" and "abuse" are not defined in the statute but are construed in the same way as the EU concepts are interpreted. While the term "abuse" is not defined, a non-exhaustive list of abuses is contained in s. 5—this list is the same as that in article 102 TFEU. (It is notable that while art. 102 refers to a dominant position in the internal market or in a *substantial* part of the internal market, the qualifier "substantial" does not apply in s. 5.) **20.11**

In the context of a discussion on "acting alone," it should be noted that s. 4 which controls anticompetitive arrangements and practices requires two or more undertakings to be involved so it is inapplicable where an undertaking is acting alone. **20.12**

[3] *O'Regan* (n 1) para. 106.
[4] *DPP v. Flanagan*, 2006, unreported.
[5] *DPP v. Lambe*, 2005, unreported.

20.13 There is no equivalent in Ireland of the European Commission's Article 102 Guidance.[6] Nonetheless, the Irish Authority and courts would have regard to the Guidance though would not be bound by it. As noted above, Irish enforcement priorities have not been in this area and case law, as a result, remains underdeveloped.

A. Predatory pricing

20.14 Section 5 prohibits predatory pricing by any undertaking having a dominant position in Ireland (or any part of Ireland) where the predatory pricing involves an abuse of that dominance. Irish competition legislation does not deal extensively with predatory pricing but there is no doubt that the practice would be prohibited by s. 5 when practiced by a dominant undertaking and the practice involved an abuse of that dominance. It is likely that EU jurisprudence would be taken into account by an Irish court in considering the meaning of the concept of predatory pricing. It is therefore likely, based on the Court of Justice of the European Union's (CJEU) judgment in *AKZO*[7] that predatory pricing would amount to an abuse of dominance where the price was below average variable cost. If the price was above average variable cost but below average total cost then it would be predatory if there was an intention to eliminate competition. It is also possible that the Irish courts would accept the post-*AKZO* formulation of the concepts: the Commission's reformulated the *AKZO* test in its Guidance on article 102; in paragraph 26 of the Guidelines, the Commission uses the terms "average avoidable cost" and "long run average incremental cost" instead of "average variable cost" and "average total cost." It is also likely that Irish law would not require actual proof that the dominant company will later be able to recoup the losses it incurs while predating.[8]

B. Exploitative offenses (excessive pricing, monopoly leveraging)

20.15 Section 5 prohibits exploitative abuses of dominance (such as excessive pricing or monopoly leveraging) by any undertaking having a dominant position in Ireland or any part of Ireland where the practice involves an abuse of that dominance. Nonetheless, the Irish law on this area remains underdeveloped. If it develops further then it is very likely to do so on the basis of EU jurisprudence. Therefore practices such as excessive pricing could constitute an abuse of dominance contrary to s. 5 when the conditions of the section are met.

C. Monopsony

20.16 Monopsony as such would not be a breach of Irish competition law. This is because dominance due to monopsony is not in breach of s. 5. However, certain monopsonistic practices could constitute an abuse of dominance and thereby beach s. 5. The same considerations would apply to monopsonistic activities and practices as would apply to monopolistic ones. Equally, the EU jurisprudence is likely to be fully applicable in an Irish context.[9]

20.17 In the Irish context, monopsony may well arise in the context of the state acting as the sole purchaser of certain goods and services. In such cases, a claim could only succeed where the state was acting as an undertaking (i.e. an entity engaged "for gain" in the production of foods or services).[10]

---

[6] Guidance on the Commission's enforcement priorities in applying [Article 102 TFEU] to abusive exclusionary conduct by dominant undertakings, OJ C 45, February 24, 2009 ("Article 102 Guidance").

[7] Case 62/86 *AKZO Chemie v. Commission* [1991] ECR I-3359.

[8] This would be in line with the EU law position: Case C-202/07 *France Télécom v. Commission* [2009] ECR I-2369.

[9] E.g. Case C-95/04 *British Airways plc v. Commission* [2007] ECR I-02331.

[10] See *O'Neill v. Minister for Agriculture* [1998] 1 IR 539 and *Lifeline v. Health Services Executive* [2012] IEHC 432.

D. Price discrimination

Price discrimination by dominant undertakings where the discrimination amounts to an abuse of dominance is explicitly prohibited by s. 5.[11] To date, price discrimination has not been a major priority for the Authority and therefore there is no extensive case law to report. However, in its discussion on price discrimination in the energy sector, the Authority has indicated that "price discrimination can either reduce or increase overall consumer welfare and as such, any evaluation of the likely effects of price discrimination must be undertaken on a case-by-case basis."[12] It is quite likely that any development is likely to be on the basis of EU jurisprudence (e.g. the Irish courts are likely to follow the requirement that the price is predatory—i.e. below average total cost—before there could be price discrimination in most circumstances).[13] Price discrimination on the basis of nationality or any other invidious criterion would be outlawed and would be treated as particularly serious where it involved discrimination against nationals of other EU Member States. Equally, price discrimination to carve up the EU or Irish market or drive up prices to higher than normal levels would also be regarded as serious breaches. **20.18**

E. Dictating or influencing resale prices

(i) Resale price maintenance and minimum advertised price programs

Section 5 of the 2002 Act may be used to control resale price maintenance (RPM) and minimum advertised price (MAP) programs, but it would ordinarily be difficult to show that there was an abuse of dominance. RPM cases to date have mainly involved anticompetitive arrangements rather than abuse of dominance. Such arrangements are generally perceived as hard core breaches incapable of exemption. **20.19**

Section 1 of the 2006 Act inserted a new s. 15B of the 2002 Act to the effect that, as a general rule, a grocery goods undertaking shall not directly or indirectly attempt to compel or coerce another grocery goods undertaking, whether by threat, promise or any like means, to resell or advertise for resale any grocery goods at: (a) a price fixed directly or indirectly by the first mentioned grocery goods undertaking, or (b) a price above a minimum price fixed directly or indirectly by the first mentioned grocery goods undertaking. The principal exception to this rule is s. 15B(5) which provides that conduct shall not be prohibited unless it has as its object or effect the prevention, restriction, or distortion of competition in trade in any grocery goods in the state or in any part of the state. **20.20**

The 2012 Act provided for a new type of order under s. 14B of the 2002 Act. Section 14B allows for commitments given to the Authority to be made an order of court. The Authority conducted an investigation into Double Bay Enterprises Ltd, which traded as Brazil Body Sports (BBS), who were the exclusive distributors of the FitFlop brand of footwear in Ireland. Following the investigation, BBS gave commitments to the Authority which were then made an order of the court under s. 14B. The investigation into BBS involved allegations of resale price maintenance. Under the agreement, BBS agreed not to restrict retailers from deciding their own pricing policy in relation to the sale of FitFlop products. **20.21**

F. Tying arrangements

Tying can constitute a breach of s. 5 where the conditions set out in the section are satisfied. The same principles which apply in regard to article 102 TFEU should also apply in the context of s. 5. **20.22**

[11] See s. 5(1) and 5(2)(c).

[12] The Competition Authority, Submission to the Commission for Energy Regulation: Price Discrimination & Customer Protection in the De-regulated Electricity Market, Submission No. S/11/004 (March 2011) <http://www.tca.ie/images/uploaded/documents/S-11-004%20Price%20Discrimination%20Consumer%20Protection.pdf>.

[13] See Case C-209/10 *Post Danmark A/S v. Konkurrencerådet*, 27 March 2012.

For example, the Authority was concerned with what it saw as tying in regard to the Irish League of Credit Unions (ILCU) and instituted proceedings against the ILCU. The Supreme Court dismissed the Authority's claim in the *Competition Authority v. O'Regan* case[14] despite the High Court initially upholding the Authority's case.[15] The Supreme Court held that tying requires the presence of the following elements: (i) the tying and tied goods were two separate products; (ii) the undertaking concerned was dominant in the tying product market; (iii) the undertaking concerned did not give customers a choice to obtain the tying product without the tied product; and (iv) tying foreclosed competition. It also held that distinctness between products presupposed the existence of an independent product market for each of the products in question, from the viewpoint of consumer demand, and further, that there were widespread sales of the tying item in unbundled form. In this case, the unavailability of an independent, commercially provided product, and the lack of willingness on the part of the market to provide such a service, in this particular case signified that the product in question was not a distinct product. Rather, it was an integral part of a bundle of services provided by ILCU to its own members, so the Authority's claim failed.

G. Exclusive dealing

20.23 When an undertaking with a dominant position imposes an exclusive dealing (or exclusive purchase or non-compete) obligation on a customer then the conduct usually amounts to an abuse of the dominance where it obliges the customer to make most or all of its purchases from it or provides current discounts or retrospective rebates which have the same practical effect. It is likely that the Authority and courts would apply the principles developed in cases such as *Intel*.[16]

H. Refusal to deal

20.24 As a general principle, Irish law allows undertakings to deal or not deal with whoever they choose; the Authority stated, as a general principle, "undertakings are entitled to decide how their products shall be distributed to their customers."[17]

20.25 One of the exceptions to this general principle is where an undertaking with a dominant position refuses to deal, and that refusal amounts to an abuse of dominance contrary to s. 5. Another exception would be where a number of undertakings combine to refuse to deal or an undertaking refuses to deal so as to enforce an anticompetitive arrangement then such an arrangement would breach s. 4 irrespective of whether or not the undertakings were dominant.

20.26 The concept of refusal to deal and the concept of essential facilities are often intertwined and seen as one in Irish law. The concepts of refusal to deal/essential facilities are well known in Irish law because of EU cases involving Irish or Irish-based businesses[18] as well as cases before the Irish courts.[19] Much of the Irish jurisprudence was developed prior to *Oscar*

---

[14] *O'Regan* (n 1).

[15] *Competition Authority v. O'Regan and others* [2004] IRLHC 330.

[16] *Intel*, Commission Decision COMP/C-3/37.900 (May 13, 2009).

[17] Competition Authority decision of October 13, 1994 relating to a proceeding under Section 4 of the Competition Act, 1991, Notifications Nos. CA/212/92E and CA/427/92E—*Murphy Brewery/Clada Soft Drinks*, Decision No. 362, para.10

[18] E.g. Joined Cases C-241/91 P and C-242/91 P *RTE and ITP v. Commission ("Magill")* [1995] ECR I-743; Case C-344/98 *Masterfoods Ltd. v. HB Ice Cream Ltd.* [2000] ECR I-11369; Case 27/76 *United Brands Company and United Brands Continental v. Commission* [1978] ECR 207 (the case had an important Irish angle); *Sealink/B & I—Holyhead: Interim Measures* [1992] 5 CMLR 255 ("*Holyhead I*"); *Sea Containers v. Stena Sealink: Interim Measures*, Commission Decision 94/19/EC of December 21, 1993, IV/34.689, OJ 1994 L 15/8, 18.1.1994 ("*Holyhead II*"); *Irish Continental Group v. Chambre de Commerce et Industrie de Morlaix* [1995] 5 CMLR 177 ("*Roscoff*").

[19] E.g. *HB v. Mars* [1993] ILRM 145 (High Court); *Chanelle v. Pfizer* [1997] IEHC 88; *A&N Pharmacy v. United Drug* [1996] 2 ILRM 42; and *Hinde Livestock Exports Ltd. v. Pandoro Ltd* [1997] IEHC 222, [1998] 2 IR 203.

Bronner,[20] *IMS Health*,[21] and *Microsoft Corp.*[22] but it is likely that the three-pronged test there would be applied (i.e. (a) the input which is being refused is indispensable, because duplication is impossible or extremely difficult, (b) the refusal excludes any competition on a secondary market, and (c) there is no objective justification for the refusal). The High Court has been willing to order supply of goods in the case of a refusal to supply: *A&N Pharmacy v. United Drug*.[23]

Margin squeeze has been considered from time to time by the Irish communications regulator: the Commission for Communications Regulation (known as "ComReg") and the EU principles (developed in cases such as *Deutsche Telekom*[24] and *TeliaSonera*[25]) are most likely to apply if the issue of margin squeeze were to come before an Irish court. **20.27**

I. Essential facilities

Closely linked in Irish law to the concept of refusal to supply is the concept or doctrine of essential facilities. The doctrine is well known to Irish-based competition lawyers and officials (e.g., because of the cases cited above such as *Holyhead I, Holyhead II, Roscoff*, and *Hinde*)[26] but it is not referred to explicitly in the Irish competition legislation. Typically, the term "essential facilities" refers to an objectively unjustifiable refusal by a dominant undertaking to provide access to infrastructure or property which is indispensable or "objectively necessary"[27] to the putative user and the refusal distorts competition. It is a specific application (in the context of facilities) of the law on refusal to supply. The concept is construed narrowly[28] but it is perfectly feasible to invoke it. Indeed, the Irish courts have recognized the concept (and unlike the CJEU, named it as a concept in judgments) and applied it, for example, Cooke J in *Island Ferries Teoranta*, where the judge stated (albeit *obiter*): **20.28**

> 76. It is also clear that because of its geographic location, its proximity to the Aran islands and its distance from Galway city as well as its orientation, water depth and other characteristics, Rossaveel harbour is effectively an essential facility for any operator wishing to provide regular sea transport services between the mainland and the islands. The distance by sea to Galway harbour from the islands is such that that harbour is not a viable alternative to the Rossaveel Harbour/bus service to Galway option.
>
> 77. In that regard it is clear that the Minister as operator of the harbour occupies a dominant position in respect of the market for the provision of facilities for the operation of sea transport services and particularly passenger services to the Aran Islands. As such, the Court is satisfied that the prohibition of s. 5 of the Act of 2002 is applicable in principle to the conduct of the Minister in providing the facilities and services at Rossaveel Harbour. In this regard the Minister's position is not materially distinct from that of other comparable harbor authorities or harbour service operators. (See, for example Case C-179/90 *Porto di Genova* [1991] ECR I-5889; the Decisions of the European Commission of October 21, 1997 *on piloting services in the Port of Genoa* (1997) OJ L 301/27; and of December 21, 1993 *on refusal of access to facilities in the Port of Rødby* (1994) OJ L 55/52).[29]

---

[20] Case C-7/97 *Oscar Bronner GmbH v. Mediaprint* [1998] ECR I-7791.
[21] Case C-418/01 *IMS Health GmbH v. NDC Health GmbH* [2004] ECR I-05039.
[22] Case T-201/04 *Microsoft Corp. v. Commission* [2007] ECR II-3601.
[23] *A&N Pharmacy* (n 19).
[24] C-280/08 *Deutsche Telekom AG v. Commission* [2010] ECR I-9555.
[25] Case C-52/09 *TeliaSonera* [2011] ECR I-00527.
[26] *Holyhead I* (n 18); *Holyhead II* (n 18) p. 8; *Roscoff* (n 18); *Hinde* (n 19).
[27] The phrase used by the European Commission in its Article 102 Guidance (n 6) paras. 83–84.
[28] *Oscar Bronner* (n 20).
[29] *Island Ferries Teoranta v. Minister for Communications, Marine and Natural Resources and others* [2011] IEHC 388, paras. 76–77.

J. Bundling (including loyalty and market share discounts)

20.29 The Authority has recognized the possibility of bundling being a breach of s. 5 but there has been little elaboration of the concept but in the Authority's limited commentary on the topic, the Authority has treated bundling and tying as comparable.

K. Standard-setting groups (disclosure requirements, licensing arrangements, and licensing pools)

20.30 The issue of standard setting groups has not been considered at any length by the Irish Authority or courts. It is assumed that when they come to consider the issue then they would apply the EU jurisprudence (including the Commission's Horizontal Cooperation Guidelines[30]).

L. Customer termination

20.31 Customer termination could amount to a breach of s. 5 where the termination was by a dominant undertaking and the termination was an abuse of that dominance. It is quite possible that intermediaries who have their relationship with a supplier terminated (or the terms of it altered) could invoke competition law claiming that the supplier was abusing dominance. It is a sub-species of the refusal to supply and essential facilities doctrine above so the topic has been largely addressed in Sections I.H and I.I. It is quite likely that an Irish court would apply the principles relating to "refusal to deal" and "essential facilities" in this scenario.

M. Termination of intermediaries (retailers, wholesalers, dealers, and value-added resellers, agents, and brokers)

20.32 Termination of intermediaries can be, in certain circumstances, another sub-species of refusal to deal and therefore the principles discussed above would usually be applicable (as well as, in particular circumstances, the principles relating to the essential facilities doctrine).

20.33 If the termination of an intermediary was committed by an undertaking with a dominant position and the termination amounted to an abuse of dominance then s. 5 could be invoked and the victim could seek damages, exemplary damages, injunctions and/or declarations from the Circuit Court or the High Court.

20.34 If the termination of an intermediary was committed by an undertaking without a dominant position but the termination was in pursuance of an anti competitive arrangement then the termination then s. 4 could be invoked and the victim could seek the usual remedies (applying the principles in, e.g., *Telefunken*[31]).

N. Termination of relationships with competitors

20.35 It would be an unusual, but not impossible, claim for an aggrieved person to argue that the termination of their relationship with a competitor amounted to an abuse of dominance. The plaintiff would have to prove each of the ingredients of s. 5 (i.e. the defendant is an undertaking, the defendant undertaking has a dominant position, that dominance relates to a market in Ireland, and the termination amounted to an abuse of that dominance). Plaintiffs could well be cautious about bringing such a claim because it raises questions as to what were they doing engaging with competitors. However, there could be circumstances where such a case would be instituted (e.g. a competitor is dependent on a facility owned by a competitor

[30] Guidelines on the applicability of Article 101 of the Treaty on the Functioning of the European Union to horizontal co-operation agreements, OJ C 11, January 14, 2011 ("Horizontal Cooperation Guidelines"),

[31] Case 107/82 *AEG Telefunken v. Commission* [1983] ECR 3151.

which both competitors use but which the facility owner has decided to preserve for its own downstream operator).

O. Exemptions

As a general rule, unlike s. 4, there are no exemptions possible under s. 5 whenever the section applies. Instead, the Authority or courts would, if they believed that there was no abuse of dominance, probably construe the activity of practice as falling outside the scope of s. 5 altogether either because there was no dominance to abuse or, even if there was dominance, there was no abuse (e.g. because the conduct was justified objectively or it was, on balance, beneficial to the economy because it produced economic efficiencies). The burden of proving that what was otherwise an abuse of dominance was not in fact an abuse of dominance would lie on the party asserting that there was no abuse of dominance. **20.36**

The Competition Acts apply to all economic sectors. There were proposals to exempt some sectors (namely, medical doctors and voice-over actors) but those proposals are not likely to be adopted soon, if at all. **20.37**

The circumstances where Irish competition law would not apply—and they should not be seen as exemptions—would include where there is no effect on trade in Ireland; the arrangement or practice did not prevent, restrict or distort competition; and the arrangement or practice is covered by a statutory exemption. **20.38**

II. Dealing with competitors

Most of the Irish case law and resources of the Authority relate to multilateral activity (i.e., arrangements between undertakings and, in particular, cartels and other arrangements between competitors) rather than unilateral behavior. Equally, the more severe penalties are reserved for multilateral rather than unilateral activities and the vast majority of the cases relate to multilateral activities. **20.39**

Section 4(1) prohibits, as a general rule, all agreements between undertakings, decisions by associations of undertakings and concerted practices involving undertakings which have as their object or effect the prevention, restriction or distortion of competition in Ireland or any part of Ireland. Arrangements may be permitted where they are, on balance, beneficial to the economy according to the criteria set out in s. 4(5) which mirrors article 101(3) TFEU. **20.40**

Section 4 would almost invariably outlaw arrangements between competitors which involve price-fixing, sharing markets, sharing customers, tender sharing, boycotting collectively, or fixing trading terms. Such market sharing arrangements are typically described as cartels and their detection and punishments are the top priority of the Authority. The Irish courts have indicated that they are willing to imprison cartelists.[32] **20.41**

Section 4 would cover arrangements whether written or oral, legally binding or not, and concluded inside and outside Ireland. The Authority would be most concerned about those arrangements which have as their object or effect the fixing of prices, the carving up of markets, the rigging of bids and the boycott of others. These so-called "hard core" breaches are unlikely to be exempted under s. 4 and are more likely to attract severe penalties when they are proven to have occurred. Less serious anticompetitive arrangements may also be investigated and prosecuted by the Authority/DPP but they may also arise in the context of civil **20.42**

[32] E.g. the comments of McKechnie J in *DPP v. Patrick Duffy and Duffy Motors (Newbridge) Limited* [2009] IEHC 208.

proceedings before the courts where one party seeks to enforce the arrangement but the other claims that the arrangement is unenforceable as it is void (in whole or in part).

20.43 It is possible that arrangements which are anticompetitive within the meaning of s. 4 are nonetheless capable of operating lawfully under s. 4 by virtue of being exempted under the section. The criteria by which such arrangements may be exempted are identical to those in article 101(3) TFEU.[33]

A. Horizontal price fixing (including advanced announcements of price or product changes)

20.44 Horizontal price-fixing arrangements among two or more undertakings would breach s. 4(1) where the conditions set out in that section are met. The exemptions conditions in s. 4(5) would not usually apply to price-fixing arrangements. The Authority would regard such arrangements as a top priority for investigation. Equally, the DPP would ordinarily regard such arrangements as a top priority for prosecution. A horizontal price-fixing arrangement would fall within the scope of a breach of competition law by object. Such breaches emerge usually by virtue of a participant availing of the Cartel Immunity Programme.

B. Horizontal agreements to allocate customers or territories; agreements not to compete

20.45 Horizontal arrangements among two or more undertakings to allocate customers or territories would breach s. 4(1) where the conditions set out in that section are met. Horizontal arrangements among two or more undertakings not to compete would breach s. 4(1) where the conditions set out in that section are met. They would be treated as a top priority by the Authority, the DPP, and the courts. Such an arrangement would fall within the scope of a breach of competition law by object.

C. Horizontal boycotts

20.46 The term "boycott" owes its origins to Irish history where tenant farmers collectively decided in 1880 not to deal with a Captain Charles Boycott who was their landlord's agent. Not surprisingly, Irish competition law prohibits boycotts by undertaking where there is a breach of either s. 4 or 5. For example, arrangements between undertakings not to purchase from, or supply to, a particular party or parties would be a breach of the relevant section provided that the conditions of that section are met (e.g. it had the object or effect of preventing, restricting or distorting competition in Ireland or any part of Ireland). The fines would be particularly serious where the boycott was aimed at pursuing an anticompetitive strategy or agenda (e.g. to police a cartel or collectively prevent a new entrant to the market). They ought to include competitors to be a true "boycott" but not all members of the boycott would have to be competitors. Such breaches emerge usually by virtue of a participant availing of the Cartel Immunity Programme.

D. Joint ventures and other competitive collaborations

20.47 Joint venture agreements involving two or more undertakings may be subject to review under either (a) ss. 4 and/or 5, or (b) Part 3 of the 2002 Act. If an arrangement is notified under Part 3 of the 2002 Act then ss. 4 and 5 usually do not apply.

20.48 Section 16(4) of the 2002 Act provides that the creation of a joint venture to perform, on an indefinite basis, all the functions of an autonomous economic entity shall constitute a merger falling within s. 16(1)(b) and therefore fall within the scope of Part 3 of the 2002 Act. This

[33] See Chapter 12, European Union.

has its attractions for some parties: a predictable timetable and certainty as to whether the transaction is compatible with the 2002 Act because otherwise the parties to the arrangement would have to engage in self-assessment. Conversely, if the joint venture agreement falls within the scope of Part 3 then the parties must notify it and comply with the procedures under that Part.

Ancillary restraints (e.g. non-compete covenants) are typically reviewed under s. 4 even where the arrangement itself falls within the scope of Part 3 of the 2002 Act. **20.49**

The test applied to a joint venture in terms of its compatibility with the Competition Acts varies between whether it is subject to Part 3 (where the test is whether the arrangement "substantially lessens competition in markets for goods or services in the State")[34] or whether it is not notified under Part 3 (where the test is whether the arrangement has the object or effect of preventing, restricting or distorting competition in Ireland or any part of Ireland and whether it involves an abuse of dominance by any undertaking having a dominant position in Ireland or any part of Ireland). In reality, it is unlikely that a joint venture would be permissible under one test but not under the other. **20.50**

E. Trade associations

The Authority has been long concerned about some of the activities of certain trade associations. The existence of such bodies is perfectly lawful as a matter of competition law. Equally, the vast majority of their activities are perfectly lawful. However, they can be a forum for anti competitive behavior. Hence, the Authority has dawn raided many associations over time. Indeed, it has taken court actions against several associations (e.g. actions against the Licensed Vintners Association and the Vintners Federation of Ireland[35]). **20.51**

Participants in meetings of trade associations should ensure that their activities comply fully with competition law. In particular, they should pay attention to anticompetitive exchanges of information, market sharing, price fixing, and any other potential anticompetitive arrangement or practice. In particular, exchanging information on pricing, credit terms and so on should be avoided, and if others participate in such activities then the best advice is to leave immediately and have it noted that one is leaving because of the topic under discussion. **20.52**

Most of the leading Irish competition cartel cases have all had their origins in trade associations (i.e. the oil distributors and the motor vehicle dealers cases) so participants need to be particularly vigilant. Particular warning signs would include discussions on prices and withdrawing supply as well as the exchange of competitively sensitive information. The Authority has helpfully issued some guidance which could assist those who attend but care should be taken at all times.[36] **20.53**

F. Interlocking directorates

Irish competition law does not deal explicitly with interlocking directorships. There have been no Irish competition law cases to date on the topic. It is possible that Irish competition law could however address the issue using s. 4 (and, possibly but less likely, s. 5) and, in particular, such headings as the exchange information or collusion. The issue could also arise in the context of merger control where it could be linked with the issue of acquisition of minority stakes. **20.54**

34 The 2002 Act, s. 21(2)(a).

35 E.g. *Competition Authority v. Licensed Vintners Association & Others* [2009] IEHC 439.

36 See Competition Authority, Notice on Activities of Trade Associations and Compliance with Competition Law, November 2009, <www.tca.ie>.

G. Facilitating practices

20.55 Irish competition law does not deal explicitly with the issue of facilitating practices. It is likely that any such practices (e.g. by means of exchanging information about plans or future conduct) would be addressed using s. 4 generally.

H. Information exchange

20.56 In common with other jurisdictions, Irish competition law has become very interested in the area of information exchange but there is not yet any notable decisional practice in the area. It is likely that the Authority and the courts would be influenced by the developing EU jurisprudence and philosophy on the issue. Therefore, they would pay attention to the Commission's Horizontal Cooperation Guidelines.[37] It is possible, but not certain, that the Authority and courts would have regard to the UK decisional practice on the topic (particularly, the decisional practice of the Office of Fair Trading and the Competition Appeal Tribunal).

20.57 Irish legislation does not lay down any rules or guidance on how old the information must be before its exchange does not raise a competition law issue. The best advice is that each case should be analyzed in its own specific context and newer/fresher information could be exchanged in more fast moving sectors where transactions are occurring very frequently; conversely, in sectors where transactions are relatively rare and the information stays fresh for longer, exchanges must be less frequent and fulsome.

20.58 The issue of information exchange arises particularly in the context of due diligence/investigation leading to mergers, acquisitions and joint ventures between actual or potential competitors. Great care should be taken to control the exchange of information in such circumstances and to avoid any breach of s. 4. Ideally, the information exchanged should be the minimum possible and the exchange should be undertaken only between "clean" or "fresh" teams who are not involved in competing in the market (e.g. setting prices) with only the minimum possible amount of information being exchanged, then the information exchanged should be controlled tightly and not used for any purpose other than the purpose of due diligence.

I. Joint purchasing agreements

20.59 Joint purchasing agreements are not unlawful as such but can be unlawful where the arrangement between undertakings has the object or effect of preventing, restricting or distorting competition in Ireland or any part of Ireland but the exemption criteria set out in s. 4(5) (i.e. the Irish equivalent to art. 101(3) TFEU) are not satisfied. Typically, such arrangements would be examined from the perspective of effect than object. It is possible to exempt a joint purchasing arrangement which would otherwise breach s. 4(1) where the criteria under s. 4(5) are satisfied. The issue of the compatibility of a joint purchasing agreement may arise in the context of an Authority investigation but may also be more likely to arise in the context of a court case about the enforceability (or not) of such agreement.

J. Joint lobbying/regulatory/legislative efforts

20.60 In its own right, joint lobbying/regulatory legislation efforts should not raise any competition issue. However, participants should be cautious to ensure that there is no breach of competition law through ancillary ore related activities—for example, there must be no anti competitive exchange of information between actual or potential competitors (e.g. in preparing their case or argument, competitors should not exchange competitively sensitive information or

[37] Horizontal Cooperation Guidelines (n 30) esp. paras. 64–110.

data). There should be no anti competitive activity (e.g. collective boycotts) flowing from, or involved in, the joint lobbying efforts. There have been no Irish cases dealing with the issue explicitly but there have been a number of cases which touch tangentially on the issue and could be used as influential precedent.

III. General issues

A. Jurisdiction and applicable law (including sector-specific competition regulation)

20.61 Irish competition law applies to all economic sectors (including, e.g., agriculture, media and transport). The 2002 Act applies to all sectors but there is a specialist competition regime for the telecommunications sector (administered by ComReg) and a specialist merger control regime for the media sector (administered by the Authority and the Minister for Jobs, Enterprise and Innovation). There is a special regime for groceries (embodied in the 2006 Act), but the 2002 Act also applies to that sector. There is also a special regime for certain transactions in the financial services sector (e.g. where the Credit Institutions Financial Services Act 2008 applies and decisions on merger control is taken by the Minister for Finance rather than the Authority). This regime has been applied on one occasion to date: when AIB acquired EBS (approved by the Minister for Finance on June 27, 2011).

20.62 The Competition Acts apply to the behavior of "undertakings" and "associations of undertakings." Section 3(1) of the 2002 Act defines an undertaking as meaning "a person being an individual, a body corporate or an unincorporated body of persons engaged for gain in the production, supply or distribution of goods or the provision of a service." The legal form, nationality or structure of the entity would be irrelevant. The Irish Supreme Court held in *Deane v. VHI*[38] that an entity can be an undertaking even if it is not profit-making where it at least charges for its services. State bodies can be undertakings where they are engaged in economic activities.[39]

B. Antitrust system

(i) Name of agency/agencies

20.63 The principal competition agency in Ireland is the "Competition Authority."[40] It was established on October 1, 1991 under the Competition Act 1991 (the "1991 Act") and was continued in existence by the 2002 Act. It has had a higher profile internationally than the small size of the jurisdiction would suggest. As mentioned above, it was instrumental in obtaining the first conviction by a jury in Europe for cartel activities and the first custodial sentence in Europe for cartel behavior. It has been very active in the International Competition Network and the European Competition Network. It has attracted staff from around the world and some of its staff has then worked in agencies globally (including the Competition Authority's head, who subsequently became head of the UK's Office of Fair Trading). A number of former US officials also have worked for the Competition Authority, including a former Federal Trade Commissioner and former Federal Trade Commission's General Counsel.

20.64 Unlike agencies such as the European Commission, the Authority may not impose fines. This is because, as a matter of constitutional law, the imposition of fines is a judicial function confined to courts.

---

38 *Deane v. VHI* [1992] 2 IR 319.

39 See Supreme Court in *Deane v. VHI* (n 38) and Competition Authority in Enforcement Decision Series ED/01/008 *Alleged anticompetitive conduct by the Health Service Executive relating to the administration of the Community Drugs Schemes* October 10, 2008.

40 See <www.tca.ie>.

20.65 The Authority is not the only agency or institution involved in the Irish competition law system. First, competition legislation is enacted by the Oireachtas which is the Irish Parliament. Secondly, legislation is proposed by Government (in particular, the Minister for Jobs, Enterprise and Innovation (the "Minister")). Thirdly, competition law is applied and enforced by the courts. In the Irish context, the courts play a critical role. They are also national competition authorities for the purposes of the EU's Regulation 1/2003.[41] They are the only institutions in Irish law which may impose fines and terms of imprisonment. Fourthly, the Minister adopts statutory instruments (or Ministerial orders) which are the delegated legislative instruments which supplement the legislation enacted by the Oireachtas. The Minister also has a limited role in regard to mergers and acquisitions in the media sector. The Irish regime is very largely free from political interference. Finally, it is worth noting that it is the DPP, and not the Authority, which institutes proceedings in the courts.

20.66 The Authority has a role in applying EU competition law as a National Competition Agency within the European Competition Network.[42]

(ii) Staff size and budget

20.67 The Authority had, at the end of 2011, 39 staff members including up to five members (including a chairperson) but the Authority has been granted the right to hire ten extra staff and, by the end of 2012, three had been hired. The vast majority of the staff are professional lawyers, economists, and others with a very small support/administrative/IT staff (around six). In 2012, the Authority was given a grant by the state of EUR 4.54m (down from EUR 5.1m in 2011) but only spent EUR 4.24m (up from EUR 3.6m).

(iii) Recent enforcement actions and trends

20.68 The Authority has focused primarily (but not exclusively) on cartel investigations. This had led to 33 convictions for cartel activity. There have been some acquittals which is a welcome indication that the Authority and the DPP are not just willing to take "sure" convictions but are willing to take some of the harder cases as well. The increasing public awareness of the Cartel Immunity Programme means that there will probably be more immunity applications which is likely to lead to more cartel investigations and possible cartel prosecutions.

20.69 There are indications that the Authority could be increasing its focus on abuse of dominance. The Authority has also shown an interest in resale price maintenance. As the Authority is also the merger control authority and must, as a matter of law, deal with around 40 cases annually, there are some limitations on what other activities that it may undertake. Overall, the Authority has been willing to investigate issues in diverse economic sectors and has not been conservative in its approach.

20.70 A number of trends emerge in regard to the sanctions imposed by the courts. First, the courts have typically imposed relatively modest fines for cartel behavior (i.e. Irish fines have been in the thousands of euro as opposed to the fines running into the millions of euro imposed at an EU level but they are more in line with the level of fines in Ireland in the criminal law generally). Second, there have been some jail sentences imposed but they have been suspended (i.e. the convicted person does not have to serve the jail term provided they do not breach the law for a specified period of time). Third, judges have stated their intention to impose jail sentences which would have to be served in future cases which would come before the courts.

[41] Council Regulation (EC) No. 1/2003 on the implementation of the rules on competition laid down in Articles 81 and 82 of the Treaty OJ 2004 L 1/1 (December 16, 2002).

[42] See the Regulation 1/2003 (n 41) and Ireland's European Communities (Implementation of the Rules on Competition Laid Down in Articles 81 and 82 of The Treaty) Regulations 2004 (Statutory Instrument No. 195 of 2004).

Mr. Justice McKechnie, when he was a judge in the High Court (he is now in the Supreme Court), stated in *DPP v. Duffy* that a cartel crime is:

> ... a crime against all consumers and is not simply against one or more individuals. To that extent it is different from other types of crime and while society has an interest in preventing, detecting and prosecuting all crimes, those which involve a breach of the Competition Act are particularly pernicious. In effect, every individual who wished to purchase, for cash, a vehicle from these dealers [i.e., the persons convicted of operating a price-fixing cartel] over the period which I have mentioned were liable to be defrauded, and many surely were by the scheme and by the practices which unashamedly this cartel operated. These activities in my view have done a shocking disservice to the public at large ... [and] [c]ompetition crimes are particularly pernicious. Coupled with that, and the low likelihood of recidivism amongst perpetuators, this means that in order to be effective, sanctions must be designed and utilised for, and have the purpose of, deterring offenders from committing crimes in the first place.[43]

Finally, the 2012 Act increased the penalties for breaching competition law so it is likely that the courts will impose higher penalties as a result.

The Authority had hoped that Irish law would provide for so-called "civil fines" as part of the 2012 Act reform. These would be fines imposed by courts in cases instituted by the Authority but these civil fines would differ from criminal fines because the standard of proof would be "on the balance of probabilities" (i.e. the civil standard) rather than the higher criminal standard of "beyond reasonable doubt." However, there were concerns that such a proposal would be unconstitutional because it would involve a criminal sanction being imposed on the civil standard so the proposal was not implemented; it is unlikely to be revived any time soon. **20.71**

If the planned amalgamation between the Authority and the National Consumer Agency proceeds (and it is expected to do so in 2013) then it is quite likely that there will be an even greater interest in consumer matters. **20.72**

The enforcement priorities of the Authority and the European Commission have differed over time with the former concentrating on more local issues and not dealing in issues such as arrangements to delay market entry of generics, information technology issues and the like but more traditional cartel-like issues. Some commentators would say that it would be useful if the Authority used its powers to address more structural dominance issues rather just focusing on the more traditional cartel like issues. **20.73**

C. Private litigation

Private litigation by "aggrieved persons" is not only permissible under Irish competition law (e.g. s. 14 of the 1991 Act (now repealed) provided for it) but is encouraged and facilitated (e.g. s. 14 of the 2002 Act as amended by the 2012 Act). The volume of private litigation in Ireland is not high but some private settlements have occurred. **20.74**

The reasons why there have been relatively few private cases include the facts that: (a) the convictions which have occurred have involved relatively small losses to aggrieved persons so there would not be such an incentive to bring private cases; (b) class actions are not feasible in Irish law in the same way that they are feasible in jurisdictions such as the US; and (c) there was relatively little awareness of competition law until recent times. **20.75**

Aggrieved persons (who do not have to be undertakings) may sue for damages, exemplary damages, injunctions and/or declarations. **20.76**

[43] *DPP v. Duffy and Duffy Motors (Newbridge) Ltd* [2009] IEHC 208.

20.77 While there have been relatively few cases before the Irish courts, there have been several cases instituted by Irish connected entities before the European Commission by way of complaints. Examples have included cases such as *United Brands*,[44] *Sealink/B & I—Holyhead: Interim Measures*,[45] and *Roscoff*.[46] As the European Commission has decentralized more cases, it is possible that these types of cases will be more likely to be instituted before Irish courts. Competition law is well known in Ireland as a concept. This higher level of knowledge in Ireland about competition law has meant that complaints and proceedings are more likely to be made and instituted. Equally, the Irish judges are very familiar with EU law having either practiced before the Court of Justice of the European Union (or the General Court) or even been judges or advocates general in Luxembourg.

D. Follow-on litigation (includes role of agency determinations of liability for follow-on litigation)

20.78 Follow-on litigation is possible under Irish competition law. Section 14 of the 2002 Act (as amended) facilitates such actions by providing a statutory basis for them. The section provides that actions may be instituted by "aggrieved persons" in respect of breaches of Irish competition law as well as articles 101 and 102 TFEU. The plaintiffs do not have to be undertakings but they do have to be "aggrieved" even though the statute does not define that term. The actions would typically be in the High Court but if the claim is for a very small amount of damages (less than EUR 38,000) then the claim could be in the Circuit Court. The remedies available to the plaintiff would include any combination of damages, exemplary damages, injunctions, and/or declarations.

20.79 There is no history of class actions in Ireland in the same way as there is in jurisdictions such as the United States. There is a procedure akin to class actions but they have not been used to date in competition law claims.

20.80 In some ways, there would be less follow-on litigation in Ireland relating to breaches of the Irish legislation than one might suspect initially and this is because the finding of a breach is not usually done by the Authority but is done by the court and the plaintiff who brings the case alleging a breach will usually include a claim for damages so the case will be simultaneous rather than following on.

E. Arbitration and alternative dispute resolution

20.81 Competition law claims may be made in arbitration and in alternative dispute resolution (ADR) procedures. Competition claims (e.g. a claim that a provision in a contract is void and therefore unenforceable) might well arise in the context of an arbitration claim. However, there are some limitations to such procedures. For example, if there was an issue arising in an arbitration relating to EU competition law then a preliminary reference from an arbitrator to the Court of Justice of the European Union under rticle 267 TFEU would not be possible because the arbitrator may not constitute a court or tribunal for the purposes of article 267 but would it be possible from a court.[47] It should be presumed that an arbitrator in Ireland is obliged to apply Irish and EU competition law given their public policy nature and the fact that they are part of the law of Ireland.

---

[44] *United Brands* (n 18).
[45] *Holyhead I* (n 18).
[46] *Roscoff* (n 18).
[47] See Case C-126/97 *Eco-Swiss* [1999] ECR I-3055.

F. Remedies

(i) Civil liability

There can be civil remedies for breaches of competition law. First, any arrangement or practice in breach of s. 4 or s. 5 would be void (i.e. it is unenforceable in Irish law). This is a significant remedy or sanction. Void provisions may be severable from the valid provisions of arrangements subject to the rules on severance. Second, aggrieved persons (who do not have to be undertakings) may obtain damages to compensate them for the loss which they suffered. These damages would be awarded by the court (not the Authority). The 2012 Act has facilitated the recovery of damages by providing for certain presumptions (i.e., some findings in earlier cases can be relied upon in subsequent civil proceedings which means that the plaintiff's task is made a little easier). Third, aggrieved persons (who do not have to be undertakings) may obtain exemplary damages which are not based on the need to compensate the plaintiff but rather to make an "example" of the defendant. Exemplary damages would be rare and would be confined to such cases as where the defendant knew it was doing wrong. Fourth, aggrieved persons could obtain declarations which would be court orders confirming the legal position on the matter reviewed by the court (e.g. that a provision was void). Finally, aggrieved persons could obtain injunctions which could be prohibitory (i.e. negative in nature to stop something occurring) or mandatory (i.e. positive in nature to compel something). **20.82**

(ii) Criminal liability

Since 1996, breaches of competition law are criminal offenses in Ireland. (There were earlier offenses under the Restrictive Practices Acts (enacted between 1953 and 1987), the Mergers Acts (enacted between 1978 and 1987) and the Competition Acts 1991–1996 but they are not relevant for present purposes.) The 2002 Act imposed serious penalties for criminal liability and these penalties were increased by the 2012 Act. Now the penalties in Ireland for breaching certain provisions of the 2002 Act (principally hard core anti competitive arrangements) are very severe with: (a) jail sentences of up to ten years for offenses after July 3, 2012; and (b) fines of up to the greater of: (i) 10 percent of worldwide turnover of the undertaking; or (ii) EUR 5 million. (For offenses between July 1, 2002 and the entry into force of the 2012 Act on July 3, 2012, the maximum jail term was five years and the maximum fine was EUR 4 million.) **20.83**

A distinction is drawn between the provisions on anti competitive arrangements and abuse of dominance with, for example, no imprisonment being imposed in respect of an abuse of dominance but there could be a fine of up to EUR 5,000,000. **20.84**

G. Leniency and immunity

Ireland has an immunity regime whereby the first person to approach the Authority with evidence of a cartel may be granted conditional immunity from criminal prosecution by the DPP. The Cartel Immunity Programme[48] was adopted on December 20, 2001 but it is going to be amended shortly. One applies for the immunity to the Authority but the immunity is granted by the DPP because it is she, rather than the Authority, who decides to prosecute for cartel offenses. Notwithstanding the decision to grant the immunity is the DPP's decision, the Cartel Immunity Programme is administered by the Authority. **20.85**

The immunity may be granted to only one applicant—joint or later applications are not permitted under the Irish regime. It is possible that a successful applicant could lose the benefit of the immunity where the conditions of the Cartel Immunity Programme are not met. The Cartel Immunity Programme relates to cartels but it may be possible to have immunity in **20.86**

[48] Competition Authority, Cartel Immunity Programme, <www.tca.ie/EN/Enforcing-Competition-Law/Cartel-Immunity-Programme.aspx>.

respect of any other area or activity provided the DPP grants it. In respect of parties who do not benefit from immunity, the courts would nonetheless probably take into account the level of cooperation (or obstruction) by those third parties to the Authority's investigation. The immunity does not prevent civil damages and other actions being taken successfully against any party including the successful immunity applicant.

20.87 The Irish courts have not yet decided whether the papers lodged as part of the immunity application can be made available to third parties (e.g. plaintiffs in damages actions). The Irish courts would be influenced by such CJEU cases as *Pfleiderer*.[49] It is not yet clear how the courts would decide the matter but there is a reasonable chance that they will side with the preservation and protection of the immunity regime rather than facilitating aggrieved persons to recover damages and therefore not order the Authority and the DPP to release the documentation where there would be a risk to the cartel immunity Cartel Immunity Programme.

H. Document creation and retention

20.88 There may be obligations to retain documents arising from various sources of law (e.g. revenue or company law) but Irish competition law does not have specific rules on the retention or the creation of documents.

20.89 As documentary evidence is so important in many competition cases, it is important that care is taken in creating legitimate documents that there is no impression given that there is no anti competitive intent or practice (e.g. by using loose or misleading language).

20.90 The Authority has extensive search and seizure powers by virtue of s. 45 of the 2002 Act. Therefore, any incriminating document could be seized by the Authority and used against undertakings, associations of undertakings, or individuals suspected of breaching competition law. Anyone subject to such an investigation must cooperate with the investigators because their power is founded on statute (principally, s. 45 of the 2002 Act) and, in the case of dawn raids, a District Court warrant. It is possible that anyone who obstructs the investigation could be charged with obstruction of the administration of justice which is a criminal offense. It is also possible that a jury hearing any charge alleging breaches of competition law may draw a negative inference from any evidence that documents were destroyed, shredded, or deliberately lost. In any event, there should be no attempt to undermine an investigation which is under way (e.g. by destroying documents) and if such a course of action were undertaken then the general criminal law would apply as well as s. 45(10) of the 2002 Act which provides:

> [a] person who obstructs or impedes an authorized officer in the exercise of a power conferred by this section [which deals with investigations/dawn raids] or does not comply with a requirement under this section shall be guilty of an offence and shall be liable on summary conviction to a fine not exceeding €3,000 or imprisonment for a term not exceeding 6 months or to both such fine and such imprisonment.

20.91 In regard to document retention, undertakings and others may retain documents (i.e. not hand them over to investigators) where there is a legitimate claim of privilege. The most relevant form of privilege would be legal professional privilege. Advice given by external legal advisors is usually covered by legal professional privilege. The Irish Authority has indicated informally that, unlike the European Commission, it recognizes in-house/internal legal professional privilege.

[49] Case C-360/09 *Pfleiderer AG v. Bundeskartellamt*, June 14, 2011.

21

ISRAEL

Dr. David E. Tadmor and Shai Bakal
Tadmor & Co.

Introduction

The Restrictive Trade Practices Act (the "Antitrust Law" or the "Law") deals with three types of restraints of trade: restrictive arrangements, merger transactions and abuse of dominant position. Chapter B of the Law provides that restrictive arrangements must be approved in advance by the Antitrust Tribunal (the "Tribunal") unless they fall under a statutory or a block exemption or receive a particular exemption from the Antitrust Commissioner (the "Commissioner"). Chapter C regulates mergers and requires that the Israel Antitrust Authority (IAA the "IAA") be notified in advance of any transaction that falls under the definition of a "merger" (as defined in s. 1 of the Law), if it meets certain thresholds as defined in s. 17 of the Law. Chapter D includes provisions regarding the definition of dominant position, actions that may be regarded as unlawful abuse of such position and powers to regulate monopolies. **21.01**

21.02 The Law was amended in 2011, so that the Commissioner was vested with the power to declare, under certain circumstances, that a small group of competitors constitutes a "concentrated group" and thus a potential target for antitrust enforcement measures under chapter D1 of the Law. The amendment also provided the Commissioner with a wide variety of powers to regulate the activities of such concentrated groups' members in order to preserve or even enhance competition. The Commissioner has already begun making use of these new powers when he announced that he is considering proclaiming that the four suppliers of baby food compounds constitute a concentrated group.

21.03 Another significant amendment to the Law was made in 2012, when the Commissioner was accorded the authority to unilaterally impose administrative fines ("monetary payments") on antitrust violators under chapter G1 of the Law.

21.04 In the passing decade, most of the IAA's enforcement attention was directed at mergers and restrictive arrangements. Influenced by the Chicago School of thought, the IAA took a very liberal view of unilateral practices, taking action against dominant firms only in very few cases where a complicated economic analysis was not required to establish exclusionary effect. However, the IAA is in the midst of a major policy change under its current Commissioner, Prof. David Gilo, and it is expected to pay close attention to unilateral conduct in the coming years. 2012 seems to mark another change of direction in the IAA's approach, towards applying stricter criteria to proposed mergers. This impression is supported by the unprecedented numbers mergers that were either blocked or withdrawn (7–10 percent) in comparison to the IAA's record during the last decade (2–5 percent).

I. Acting alone

21.05 Unilateral conduct is governed by chapter D of the Law, which deals with monopolies. The Law states that a firm is deemed a "monopoly" if it controls more than 50 percent of the supply or the acquisition of a product or a service (i.e. more than 50 percent of a relevant product market).[1] In order to define the relevant market, the Commissioner and the Antitrust Tribunal apply certain quantitative methods, but mainly rely on qualitative "practical indicators".[2] These include the purpose and use (functionality) of the products or services in question, the objective physical properties of the products or services, their price, the structure of supply and demand in the market, and other characteristics of the product that may indicate the extent of substitutability. The views of different market participants are also a significant factor. The IAA and the Tribunal will also take into account market definitions that were applied in previous cases or in other jurisdictions.

21.06 Generally speaking, unilateral conduct may only be illegal if it is carried out by a monopoly. Thus, a firm with considerable market power is often free to engage in exclusionary or exploitive practices, as long as its market share does not cross the 50 percent threshold. The Minister of Industry, Trade and Labor may, under s. 26 of the Law, set a lower market share threshold for certain goods or services. This power, however, has not been executed in practice yet. On the other hand, a firm which controls a market share exceeding 50 percent is subject to unilateral conduct prohibitions (to be detailed below), even if such market share is not accompanied by market power (for instance because entry barriers are low).

[1] *Strauss Elite v. Commissioner*, AT 506/04 (2007) IAA Website, 5000613, para. 12.

[2] See e.g. *Food Club v. Commissioner* App 1/00 (2003) IAA Website, 3017513E.

A. Monopoly Proclamation and abuse of monopoly position

The Israeli unilateral conduct regime is unique not only in substance, but also in terms of procedure. Section 26 of the Law includes a mechanism, by which the Commissioner may declare a certain firm a Monopoly ("Monopoly Proclamation"). According to s. 43 of the Law, a Monopoly Proclamation serves as a *prima facie* evidence that the firm in question is indeed a monopoly, in any legal proceedings, including criminal proceedings.[3] A firm whose market share exceeds 50 percent of a relevant market is a monopoly, even if it has not been declared as such by the Commissioner.[4] **21.07**

Monopolies are not illegal under the Law. However, unilateral conduct by a Monopoly is illegal if it falls under one of the following categories: **21.08**

- Refusal to deal (s. 29 of the Law);
- Abuse of monopoly position (s. 29A of the Law), which is subdivided in the following way: s. 29A(a) of the Law applies an effects based test, according to which any practice employed by a monopoly which may injure competition or the public is an illegal abuse. Section 29A(b) stipulates specific practices which are deemed abusive, when engaged by a monopoly (e.g. tying, predatory pricing, price discrimination). According to the case law, there is an irrefutable presumption of injury to competition with respect to the practices mentioned in s. 29A(b) of the Law.[5]

However, these practices are defined very vaguely, in a way which leaves room for economic analysis.

Section 30 of the Law authorizes the Commissioner to instruct a monopoly to take measures necessary for eliminating harm to competition and to the public. Moreover, according to s. 31 of the Law, the Tribunal might order the separation of a monopoly to different business entities according to the Commissioner's request, if the existence of the monopoly causes substantial harm to the public and if there is no possibility to prevent the harm by issuing instructions according to s. 30 of the Law. **21.09**

B. Predatory pricing

Section 29A(b)(1) of the Law prohibits "the establishment of an unfair buying or selling price of an asset or a service over which a monopoly exists." The Commissioner and the courts have acknowledged that predatory pricing falls within the scope of s. 29A(b)(1) of the Law. Predatory pricing may also be prohibited under the general prohibition of monopoly abuse in s. 29A(a) of the Law. **21.10**

According to several Tribunal decisions,[6] for prices to be considered predatory three cumulative conditions must be met: (a) prices should fall below the monopoly's relevant costs; (b) there should be a reasonable likelihood that such prices would drive competition out of the market; (c) the monopoly should be able to recoup its losses. The Tribunal has acknowledged that recoupment is unlikely if the monopoly does not have market power.[7] Although **21.11**

[3] *State of Israel v. Gibor Sabrina Textile Factories Inc.*, CrimC 4783/93 (1996) IAA Website, 3005974.

[4] *Bezeq The Israeli Telecommunication Corp. Ltd. v. Commissioner*, App. 7/95 (1999) IAA Website 3001553, para. 5.

[5] *Commissioner v. Yediot Ahronot Ltd.* (Partial Ruling), AT (Jerusalem) 2/96 (1999) IAA Website 3006366, para. 56.

[6] See *Food Club* (n 2); *Amana Bonded & Free Warehouse Ltd. v. Commissioner*, App. no. 9/99 (2002) IAA Website 3013742.

[7] *Amana Bonded* (n 6) para. 16.

these principals were outlined by the Tribunal in the context of merger control litigation, they reflect the IAA's policy in the area of unilateral conduct too.

21.12 The case law is ambiguous with respect to the relevant cost standard which should be applied in predatory pricing cases. An Israeli court decision in the matter of *Oto-Kav*[8] refers to *variable costs*, while an IAA's press release refers to *marginal costs*.[9] On some other occasion the IAA suggested *average variable costs* as a possible proxy. It seems that Israeli case law has yet to establish a clear standard, be it a general one or industry specific. This is of no surprise, since the IAA hardly ever investigates predatory pricing claims, let alone acts against monopolies on these grounds.

C. Exploitative offenses

21.13 For more than a decade the IAA had demonstrated little interest in excessive pricing. The IAA's reluctance to investigate excessive pricing was, at least in part, driven by the notion that the IAA was ill equipped to determine the "right" price of products, and that competition, not price regulation, was the best cure for excessive pricing. The current Commissioner, Prof. David Gilo, is of a different view. In November 2013, the Commissioner published Draft Guidelines on the Prohibition of Excessive Pricing by a Monopoly,[10] In these draft guidelines, the Commissioner determined, for the first time, that charging an excessive price constitutes an abuse of monopoly position and violates s. 29A(b)(1) of the Law.

The Commissioner, however, acknowledged the difficulties entailed in applying a rule against excessive pricing, and set several ground rules so as to diminish such difficulties. *Inter alia*, the Commissioner stated that the prohibition of excessive pricing will only be enforced against proclaimed monopolies and that no criminal enforcement will be used, but rather only administrative measures (see Section III.F). The Commissioner also determined that no steps will be taken against a monopoly for excessive pricing when the difference between the price of the product and the cost of its manufacturing is under 20 percent. When such difference is higher than 20 percent, additional methodologies will be used to determine whether the monopoly has violated the prohibition on excessive pricing. Thus, the profitability of the monopoly will be examined against an objective benchmark and the price charged by the monopoly will be compared to prices of competing products, to prices charged from different clients, to prices of similar products in other geographical markets, etc. In addition, the Commissioner outlined different circumstances in which the IAA will be inclined to take measures against excessive pricing (anticompetitive acquisition of monopoly power, unregulated industries, entry barriers, low risk or R&D costs, high market shares, essential goods).

21.14 To date, Israeli courts have been rather reluctant to accept claims which were based on excessive pricing. The Supreme Court ruling in the *Howard Reiss* case[11] left open the question whether such pricing policy violates s. 29A of the Law. The *Howard Reiss* ruling, as well as subsequent decisions, stressed the difficulties in *assessing* whether the pricing is indeed excessive, *inter alia*, since according to s. 29A(b)(1) of the Law the price must not only be "excessive" (if the section indeed covers excessive pricing), but also be "unfairly" so. Israeli

[8] *Oto-Kav Computerized Engineering Ltd v. Taldor Computer Systems (1986), Inc.*, CivC (TA) 42717/99, decision of November 29, 2001, available at <http://www.nevo.co.il/psika_html/shalom/s9942717.htm>.

[9] IAA Press Release, "The IAA allowed 'Nesher' to offer discounts to customers under conditions that will ensure competition is unharmed" (March 12, 2002) IAA Website 3013854.

[10] IAA Draft Guidelines on the Prohibition of Excessive Pricing by a Monopoly (2013) IAA Website 500491.

[11] *Isracard v. Howard Reiss*, LCA 2616/03, ISRSC 59(5) 701, 711 (2005).

courts have noted that "unfairness" must be proven by a well-established economic opinion.[12] Courts were more willing to accept excessive pricing claims where other factors were present, such as price discrimination[13] or deviation from an established benchmark, for example regulated fees.[14] In light of the new Draft Guidelines on the Prohibition on Excessive Pricing by a Monopoly, the courts might be more prone to determine that excessive pricing violates the Law.

D. Monopsony

The special rules that the Law applies to a monopoly are also applicable to unilateral conduct of a monopsony. Like monopoly, monopsony is defined in s. 26 of the Law based on a market share threshold (more than 50 percent of the acquisition of a certain product or service). Section 29 of the Law ("Unreasonable Refusal") has been amended in 2004 to include a specific reference to refusal to purchase. Hence, all monopoly prohibitions and obligations apply, *mutatis mutandis*, to monopsony.[15] **21.15**

E. Price discrimination

Section 29A(b)(3) of the Law specifically prohibits "the establishment of different contractual conditions for similar transactions in a manner which is likely to grant certain customers or suppliers with an unfair advantage vis-à-vis their competitors." **21.16**

This section is based on its European counterpart, article 102(c) TFEU. **21.17**

While s. 29A(b)(3) sets an irrefutable presumption of abuse with respect to price discrimination, it is phrased in a way which requires economic analysis to establish whether it has been breached. Terms like "similar transactions" or "unfair advantage" leave considerable room for interpretation. For instance, it has been determined that different prices may not be deemed discriminatory if the transactions differ in size or levels of risk (assuming that the price gap reasonably correlates with these differences). **21.18**

Price discrimination may also be prohibited under the general prohibition on monopoly abuse in s. 29A(a) of the Law. The courts have acknowledged that not every type of price discrimination is illegitimate, and that price discrimination may increase total welfare.[16] **21.19**

F. Dictating or influencing resale prices

(i) Resale price maintenance

In Israel, resale price maintenance (RPM) *is generally not considered a unilateral conduct*, but rather a concentrated action involving two offenders: the supplier and the retailer. Resale price maintenance is primarily examined under the "restrictive arrangements" chapter of the Law. The definition of "restrictive arrangement" is found in s. 2(a) of the Law. Section 2(b) outlines a number of irrefutable presumptions of agreements which may result in competitive injury. These include price restrictions (s. 2(b)(1)), market allocation (s. 2(b)(3)), and other types of agreements, which are inherently anticompetitive. The IAA and the courts have **21.20**

---

[12] *Howard Reiss* (n 11) para. 26; see also *Menorah Izo Aharon Ltd v. City of Haifa*, Ad.Pet. 1061/05 (2005) IAA Website 5000121, para. 16.

[13] See *Tower Air and others v. Sherutei Teufa, Inc.*, CC (TA) (2007) IAA Website 5000590, para. 131.

[14] *Tower Air* (n 13); see also *The Israeli Records Federation Ltd v. Commissioner*, AT 3457/00 (2004) IAA Website 5000812.

[15] See *Bikur Holim Hospital v. Clalit Health Services*, MCA 4300/07 (decision of April 22, 2007, available at <http://www.nevo.co.il/psika_html/mechozi/m07004300-424.htm>), paras. 19–25; The General Director's position on Commercial Arrangements between Food Suppliers and Retail Chains (2005) IAA Website 5000007, s. 4.1 ("Food Suppliers and Retail Chains").

[16] The Israeli Records Federation (n 14) para. 89.

classified all RPM agreements as restrictive arrangements under s. 2(b)(1) of the Law ("price restrictions").[17]

21.21 However, more recent decisions, such as the Supreme Court's *Wahl* ruling,[18] raise serious doubts as to whether vertical agreements fall within the boundaries of s. 2(b) of the Law. The *Wahl* decision mentions three elements that may distinguish typical s. 2(b) arrangements from other arrangements: (a) whether they include naked restraints; (b) whether they are horizontal or vertical; and (c) whether the restraint is essential to achieve a pro-competitive goal. While the *Wahl* decision casts serious doubts on the applicability of s. 2(b) to vertical agreements, the IAA continues to treat RPM arrangements (maximum and minimum alike) as restrictive arrangements under both s. 2(a) and 2(b) of the Law. Some lower courts follow.

21.22 As we will further explain, restrictive arrangements are not illegal if they fall under a statutory exemption or a block exemption, or if they receive a particular exemption from the Commissioner or are approved by the Tribunal. The Commissioner has rendered several exemptions to maximum RPM arrangements, for instance in the tobacco industry. The IAA also approved certain maximum RPM provisions in Apple's iPhone carrier agreements, pointing out that such practice is legitimate and potentially pro-competitive as it will facilitate Apple's entry to the Israeli cell phone market. According to the new Block Exemption for Non-Horizontal Agreements that do not Include Certain Price Restrictions (see Section I.P), maximum RPM provisions are expressly exempt from the requirement to obtain a particular exemption, as long as they do not reflect serious potential harm to competition.[19]

21.23 A seller is not prohibited from issuing recommended resale price lists. However, any attempt to monitor and enforce the recommendation, including by sanctioning a retailer who deviated from such recommendation, would constitute an illegal RPM.[20] If a recommended price list is uniformly and consistently adopted by the retailers, an inference of illegal RPM is established.

(ii) Minimum advertised price programs

21.24 Any involvement of a supplier in a retailer's decision-making process with respect to prices is considered an RPM agreement. Moreover, any attempt to restrict a distributor's ability to communicate a certain price to its customers, may independently fall under the definition of restrictive arrangement, either through s. 2(a) of the Law (possible injury to competition) and s. 2(b)(1) of the Law ("Price Restrictions"). A less categorical treatment of minimum advertised price (MAP) programs may be possible under the Supreme Court's *Wahl* decision.[21]

G. Tying arrangements

21.25 Tying arrangements are caught by s. 29A(b)(4) of the Law, which prohibits "conditioning a contract regarding an asset or a service over which a monopoly exists with conditions that, by their nature or according to accepted trading practices, are unrelated to the subject matter of the contract." Tying may also be prohibited under the general prohibition of monopoly abuse in s. 29A of the Law. Although s. 29A(b)(4) of the Law sets an irrefutable presumption of abuse, in determining whether the section was breached, economic assessment plays an important role. Tying can be made explicitly by refusing to supply the tying product without

[17] See Food Suppliers and Retail Chains (n 15) s. 3.9; *The State of Israel v. Schulstein*, CrimC 1142/01 (2008) IAA Website 5001304.

[18] *The State of Israel v. Wahl*, CrimA 2560/08 (2009) IAA Website 5001448.

[19] Antitrust Rules (Block Exemption for Non-Horizontal Agreements that do not Include Certain Price Restrictions), 2013.

[20] *Aminach and others v. Commissioner*, AT (Jerusalem) 7014/02 (2005) IAA Website 5000123, para. 65.

[21] *Wahl* (n 18).

the tied product, but it can also take other forms such as physical, technological or "economic tying." Economic tying is a pricing formula, which makes it unreasonable for the customer to source the tying product without the tied product. The most notable enforcement action, which was based on economic tying, was the proceeding launched by the IAA against the daily newspaper Yediot Ahronot.[22] The IAA argued that Yediot Ahronot, a declared monopoly in daily newspapers, offered a bundle of its national and local newspapers for the price of just the national paper. The IAA claimed that given this pricing a rational customer would buy both the national and local newspapers from Yediot, thereby excluding Yediot's competitors in the local newspapers market. The Tribunal accepted the principle that effective tying can be achieved through economic means, where a reasonable customer would not source the tied product apart from the tying product, but dismissed the IAA's claims, based on the fact that similar bundling was common in the industry for years and thus—was an "accepted trading practice."

H. Exclusive dealing

Exclusive dealing is governed by the "restrictive arrangements" chapter of the Law, but may also constitute an illegal abuse of dominant position, when entered into by a monopoly.[23] Partial exclusivity, for example, securing a large portion of the sales or a large portion of purchases in a way which effectively excludes competitors, may also be considered a restrictive arrangement. Exclusive dealing is legal if it falls under a statutory exemption or a block exemption, or if it receives a particular exemption from the Commissioner. **21.26**

There are several block exemptions applying to exclusive dealing, including the exclusive acquisition, exclusive distribution and franchising agreements exemptions.[24] Nevertheless, the block exemptions *would normally not apply* to exclusive arrangements to which a monopoly is party, regardless of whether the arrangement is actually anticompetitive. In fact, particular exemption was needed even for exclusive arrangements, where the foreclosure was well below one percent.[25] **21.27**

Section 3(6) of the Law *exempts mutual exclusivity* agreements, *regardless of any market share threshold*. This exemption is virtually the only way for a monopoly to engage in exclusive dealing without the need to receive a particular exemption from the Commissioner. The exemption will not apply if the arrangement is horizontal, if the exclusivity is incomplete (e.g. supplier retains direct sales to certain customers) or if the agreement contains other restrictions (e.g. price restrictions). **21.28**

The current legal regime was criticized for being too liberal (by exempting *mutual* exclusive arrangements made by monopolies even if such arrangements carry a significant foreclosing effect) and for being too formalistic (by denying exemption for *non-mutual* exclusive arrangements, even without probable foreclosing effect). **21.29**

Against this background, the Commissioner is now advocating the annulment of s. 3(6) of the Law. At the same time, the IAA recently introduced a new block exemption for vertical arrangements, which exempts exclusive dealing as long as it does not significantly endanger competition (and provided that such agreements would not include certain price restrictions).[26] **21.30**

---

[22] *Yediot* (n 5) para. 149.

[23] Food Suppliers and Retail Chains (n 15).

[24] See further Section I.P.

[25] See A Decision to Render an Exemption from the Approval of a Restrictive Arrangement for an Arrangement between M. H. Elissar Distribution Ltd. and Bistop Kiosks Ltd. (2008) IAA Website 5001349.

[26] See Section I.P.

I. Refusal to deal

21.31 The basic rule under the Law is that firms are free to choose with whom to contract and are equally free not to deal with a supplier, a customer or a competitor. However, s. 29 of the Law prohibits "unreasonable refusal to supply or purchase" a product regarding which a monopoly exists. Refusal to deal may also be prohibited under the general prohibition of monopoly abuse in s. 29A of the Law.[27] Both provisions apply only to firms that are deemed a monopoly under s. 26 of the Law, i.e. owning over 50 percent market share.

21.32 To be illegal, the refusal to deal must be "unreasonable." A reasonable refusal to deal is defined as one "that is compatible with the principles of the antitrust laws and free competition."[28] If a refusal to deal has an anticompetitive object or outcome, it cannot be considered reasonable. The courts have acknowledged refusals to deal that stem from a commercial dispute, possible insolvency of the customer, or payment ethics of the client.[29]

21.33 A refusal to deal with rivals is not necessarily "unreasonable." It is commonly agreed that the Law does not impose a sweeping obligation on the monopoly to deal with its rivals.[30]

21.34 In 2004, the IAA brought criminal charges against a monopoly in the aerial photography market for a breach of mergers reporting duties, and for refusing to supply inputs to downstream rivals.[31] The monopoly was convicted by the court. In another case, the Tribunal suggested that harming competition by excluding rivals from a monopolized input is a criminal offense, and therefore one should not assume that it will be undertaken by a monopolist.[32] However, the scope of duty to deal with competitors under the Law is currently unclear. It is especially unclear whether the duty exists only within the boundaries of the "essential facility" doctrine or whether it is broader than that, as suggested in previous IAA decisions.

21.35 A refusal to deal can raise antitrust scrutiny in two other typical ways—when competitors collectively refuse to deal (a boycott) and when the refusal is aimed to "discipline" a supplier or a customer (e.g. as part of an RPM agreement).[33] We note, however, that in such situations it is not the actual refusal that is illegal, but rather the separate arrangement which it serves.

J. Essential facilities

21.36 The essential facilities doctrine was first applied in the *Dubek* decision.[34] In that case, the Tribunal implemented the doctrine in the context of cigarette distribution facilities, stating that small competitors are economically unlikely to reproduce such facilities. Based on this doctrine the Tribunal required *Dubek*, a tobacco monopoly at that time, to share its distribution chain with competitors until they can form an independent supply chain. In the *Egged* case, the Commissioner declared that a central bus station was an essential facility and Egged Company was forced to provide access to such stations to its competitors. The Commissioner conducted a thorough discussion regarding the essential facility doctrine and expressly stated that the doctrine does not require the existence of a natural monopoly and can apply to facilities whose reproduction will take too long or cost too much. The Commissioner stated that

---

[27] Determination of Abuse of Position: Bezeq the Israeli Telecomm Corp. (2007) IAA Website 5000727E.

[28] *Gibor Sabrina* (n 3) para. 10.

[29] *Kilstein v. Fertilizers and Chemical Materials, Inc.*, CivC (Haifa) 12430-07-09, decision of June 21, 2011, para. 42, available at <http://www.nevo.co.il/psika_html/shalom/SH-09-07-12430-766.htm>.

[30] See *Tower Air* (n 13) paras. 76–96; IAA Press Release, "The IAA is considering determining that Bezeq had abused its position in the transmission infrastructure area" (October 11, 2011) IAA Website 5001827.

[31] *State of Israel v. Friedlander*, CrimC 1268/01 (2004) IAA Website 5001746.

[32] *Food Club* (n 2).

[33] See Section I.F.

[34] *Commissioner v. Dubek Ltd.*, Mon 1/93 (1995) IAA Website 3005459, para. 20.

s. 29 (refusal to deal) and s. 29A (abuse) are independent of the essential facility doctrine, but that the doctrine may "create further justification and an even stronger basis" for the Commissioner's intervention.[35] However, in recent years, the IAA has been far less eager to force monopolies to deal with their competitors, especially when the essential facilities doctrine is seemingly not met.

The most recent use of the doctrine was in late 2010, when the IAA announced that it is considering to proclaim the Israeli Postal Company a monopoly with respect to recipients whose mailboxes are located in post distribution centers, and require the Postal Company to allow access to such distribution centers to its competitors.[36] These contemplated actions are still pending before the IAA. **21.37**

K. Bundling (including loyalty and market share discounts)

Incentives in the form of discounts and rebates are normally reviewed as a unilateral conduct under chapter D of the Law which deals with monopolies, although such incentives may, in unusual circumstances, constitute a restrictive arrangement.[37] **21.38**

Incentive programs can roughly be divided into three categories: quantity discounts, loyalty discounts, and target discounts. **21.39**

Quantity discounts are characterized as discounts which are offered by the supplier for the whole purchased quantity, based on objective criteria, that equally apply to all customers.[38] For many years, quantity discounts were deemed legal, but recent action of the IAA may indicate a change in policy. Thus, the Commissioner informed the cement company "Nesher" that he was considering requiring it to cease providing selective discounts, including certain quantity discounts which it currently offers.[39] The Commissioner argued that such discounts diminish the incentive of certain Nesher customers to compete with Nesher as cement suppliers. Another example is the IAA Guidelines on the Use of Monetary Sanctions Proceedings,[40] which mention quantity discount as a possible subject of monetary sanction. **21.40**

Loyalty discounts are defined as contingent discounts, which are only offered if the customer purchases all the required goods, or a significant part of them, from the supplier. Such discounts are intended to bind the purchaser to the supplier and thus are normally regarded as an illegal abuse of dominant position and may also be classified as a form of exclusive dealing, which is a restrictive arrangement.[41] The same applies to incentives granted in return for a certain market share commitment by the customer.[42] **21.41**

Target discounts are discounts which the customer receives if it reaches a certain sales target. The target can be set for a specific product or for the total volume of several products accumulatively (bundled discounts). The Tribunal's decision in *Yediot* states that target discounts **21.42**

[35] Determination of Restrictive Arrangement and Monopoly: Nitzba Holdings 1995 Ltd.—Egged, Israel Transp. Coop. (1999) IAA Website, 3003280E, art. 8.

[36] See IAA Press Release, "The Commissioner is Considering to proclaim the Israel Postal Company a monopoly regarding access to postal distribution services and to instruct it to provide access to such service" (October 17, 2010) IAA Website 5001673.

[37] Food Suppliers and Retail Chains (n 15).

[38] *Commissioner v. Yediot Ahronot Ltd. (Complementary Ruling)*, AT (Jerusalem) 2/96 (2000) IAA Website 3008136, para. 4.

[39] See IAA Press Release, "Advertising cement prices and terms of delivery to customers" (February 16, 2012) IAA Website 5001902.

[40] IAA Guidelines on the Use of Monetary Sanctions Proceeding (n 10).

[41] *Yediot (Complementary Ruling)* (n 38) para. 4.

[42] See Food Suppliers and Retail Chains (n 15) s. 3.6.

will be condemned, if they are likely to exclude competition, if they do not reflect competition on the merits, and are rather intended to unfairly increase the supplier's position or injure its rivals.[43] The IAA's position regarding trade practices between dominant suppliers and major retail chains (the "Food Sector Report"), provides a more analytical guidance on target discounts, according to which such discounts should be banned if an equally efficient competitor cannot match them. The Food Sector Report condemned a specific type of target discount—conditional rebate in the form of "roll-back discount." Roll-back discount is a rebate which is conditioned on the increase of the dominant supplier's volume by a certain amount, but the discount is spread on the entire volume and not just the incremental units. The IAA argued that given the asymmetry in volumes between the dominant supplier and its competitors, spreading the discount this way may be a predatory pricing in disguise. That is, the retailer is offered the marginal quantity (which is subject to competition) at a loss, but this illegitimate pricing practice is camouflaged by spreading the discount over the dominant supplier's total sales.[44] According to the IAA, the proper analysis of conditional rebates requires the supplier to attribute the discount only to the marginal sales and then to verify that the price for each unit is above costs.

21.43 Bundled discounts, which are another type of target discounts, were not analyzed in detail by the courts to date (with the exemption of *Yediot (Complementary Ruling)*[45]), but they are likely to be examined under the rules which apply to tying and price discrimination.

L. Standard-setting groups (disclosure requirements, licensing arrangements, and licensing pools)

21.44 The discussion on standard-setting groups in Israel is fairly limited. In general, standard-setting groups will normally be analyzed like other forms of collaborations among competitors, under the restrictive arrangements chapter. Such a collaboration would often be deemed a restrictive arrangement, which requires a particular exemption by the Commissioner, if other exemptions (namely block exemptions) do not apply (See Section I.P. for a more elaborate discussion on exemptions).

21.45 The IAA's view of standard-setting agreements is illustrated by the exemption which was granted to naval ports operators to use uniform management software applications and forms.[46] The IAA pointed out that the standard was aimed at enabling consumers to use the same procedure when connecting to a port, thereby simplifying communication with the ports. The IAA pointed to three major concerns that may arise in such agreements: that using the same standard will narrow down the variety of services offered and reduce innovation; that the uniform standard will become a pre-condition for operating in the market and can thus be used to exclude competitors; and that the cooperation between the parties will spill over to other areas and may facilitate collusion. The IAA determined that on balance, the pro-competitive aspect of the naval ports agreement outweighs the concerns and approved the agreement.[47] Recently, the IAA addressed the issue of standard setting by competitors in the

---

[43] *Yediot (Complementary Ruling)* (n 38) paras. 17–22.

[44] See Food Suppliers and Retail Chains (n 15) s. 3.5(c).

[45] *Yediot (Complementary Ruling)* (n 38).

[46] A Decision to Render a Conditional Exemption from the Approval of a Restrictive Arrangement: An Arrangement Between Israeli Ports Development and Assets Ltd., Ashdod Port Ltd. and Eilat Port Ltd. (2008) IAA Website 5001292.

[47] For another illustrative case, see A Decision to Render a Conditional Exemption from the Approval of a Restrictive Arrangement: An Arrangement Between Choices International Foundation and Businesses in the Food and Beverage Industry in Israel, 2009 IAA Website 5001365 ("Choices Conditional Exemption").

Draft Guidelines on Trade Associations and Their Operation,[48] which refer to the competitive concerns stated above and outlines practical rules for setting standards by competitors.

M. Customer termination

Customer termination is normally reviewed under the standards applicable to refusal to deal.[49] There is a logical link between the duty to supply and the ability to terminate: where a duty to deal exists, undue termination may infringe such duty. This should not be interpreted as excluding the ability of a monopoly to terminate contracts when there is a legitimate justification to do so, since the Law only forbids an "unreasonable" refusal to deal. **21.46**

Termination may be analyzed differently than a refusal to deal, when the terminated relations are with a competitor. It is arguable that, while a refusal to deal with competitors is illegal only under the essential facility doctrine, a termination of an existing contract may violate the Law on a wider set of circumstances. The reason is that existing relations suggest that dealing with the competitor is economically profitable to the monopoly, which casts doubt on the real motive to terminate the agreement. **21.47**

N. Termination of intermediaries (retailers, wholesalers, dealers, and value-added resellers, agents, and brokers)

Termination of intermediaries is closely affiliated with the rules governing refusal to deal. Thus, if a firm terminates intermediaries as part of a business model which is based on direct sales to customers, the termination should not be objectionable, provided it is not discriminatory. On the other hand, termination that attempts to "discipline" a supplier or a customer (e.g. as part of an RPM agreement, see Section I.F) will be objectionable under the restrictive arrangements chapter of the Law. **21.48**

O. Termination of relationships with competitors

See Section I.M. **21.49**

P. Exemptions

The Law establishes a licensing regime with regard to restrictive arrangements, according to which any arrangement that falls within the scope of the broad definition of "Restrictive Arrangement" set in s. 2 of the Law, must be authorized in advance either by the Commissioner or by the Tribunal, or be otherwise exempted. An arrangement does not require prior authorization if it falls within one of the statutory exemptions or under a block exemption. These exemptions apply to restrictive arrangements and do not exempt unilateral conduct by a monopoly. **21.50**

(i) Statutory exemptions

Section 3 of the Law details several categories of arrangements that would not be deemed a restrictive arrangement (often referred to as "statutory exemptions"). Among the exempted categories are: restrictions that are dictated by statute (s. 3(1) of the Law); certain restraints concerning licensing of intellectual property (s. 3(2) of the Law); certain restraints ancillary to granting rights in real estate (s. 3(3) of the Law); restraints concerning most kinds of locally grown agricultural products (s 3(4) of the Law); agreements between a firm and its subsidiary (s. 3(5) of the Law); mutually exclusive marketing agreements (s. 3(6) of the Law); certain agreements concerning sea or air transportation (s. 3(7) of the Law); a non-compete **21.51**

[48] See Section I.E.
[49] See Section I.I.

commitment ancillary to certain types of mergers; (s. 3(8) of the Law); and certain collective agreements between labor unions and employer unions relating to employment terms (s. 3(9) of the Law).

21.52 The statutory exemptions usually require that all the restrictions in the agreement fall under the exemption. Thus, for instance, an agreement which includes an exempted mutual exclusivity restriction is not exempted if it also includes price restrictions. Some authors maintain, however, that statutory exemptions may be combined, for example a mutual exclusivity agreement including restraints referring to intellectual property.[50] The Tribunal has stated that the statutory exemptions are exceptions to the general rule that such agreements are restrictive arrangements, and should therefore be interpreted narrowly.

(ii) Block Exemptions

21.53 In order to narrow the scope of the Law and focus enforcement only on arrangements that pose actual threat to competition, several block exemption were enacted according to the authority vested in the Commissioner by s. 15A of the Law. The block exemptions exempt certain kinds of restrictive arrangements from the mandatory filing requirement, if such arrangements meet certain conditions, including market shares thresholds.

21.54 Block exemptions were enacted for the following types of arrangements: joint ventures;[51] research and development agreements;[52] agreements that fall under the *de minimis* rule;[53] restraints ancillary to mergers;[54] agreements between air carriers and agreements between marine shipping carriers[55] (these exemptions effectively replaced the statutory exemption, as far as local carriers as concerned); franchise agreements;[56] exclusive distribution;[57] exclusive purchase;[58] and intra-group agreements[59] (this has been enacted due to the IAA's view that the statutory exemption in s. 3(5) of the Law does not extend beyond the strict firm-controlled subsidiary relations). A new Block Exemption for Non-Horizontal Agreements that do not Include Certain Price Restrictions was published in August 2013. The block exemption refers to a broad spectrum of arrangements, is not dependent on market shares, and allows a mechanism of self-assessment. The self-assessment mechanism introduced in this block exemption is precedential, and we believe it will play a crucial role in the development of the Israeli antitrust policy in coming years. It should be noted that a mistake in self-assessment, while unlikely to result in criminal charges if based on an expert advice, may nonetheless result in administrative fines, as well as other civil and administrative implications.

21.55 In general, an agreement between competitors which includes naked restraints such as price fixing, setting quotas, market allocation or horizontal boycott cannot enjoy a block

[50] See Michal (Shitzser) Gal, "Monopolies in Competition: The Balance between Encouraging Innovation and Creativity and Harming Competition in Antitrust Law," *Din U Dvarim Journal* 2 (2006), 425.

[51] Antitrust Rules (Block Exemption for Joint Ventures), 2006.

[52] Antitrust Rules (Block Exemption for Research and Development Agreements), 2006.

[53] Antitrust Rules (Block Exemption for Agreements with *De Minimis* Impact on Competition), 2006.

[54] Antitrust Rules (Block Exemption for Restraints Ancillary to Mergers), 2009 and Draft Amended Antitrust Rules (Block Exemption for Restraints Ancillary to Mergers) 2013 IAA Website 500497.

[55] Antitrust Rules (Block Exemption for Arrangements between Aircraft Carriers), 2013; Block Exemption for Arrangements between Aircraft Carriers (Flight Capacity Marketing Arrangements to Destinations Covered by Open Skies Agreements), 2012; Antitrust Rules (Block Exemption for Operational Arrangements Regarding International Sea Transport), 2012.

[56] Antitrust Rules (Block Exemption for Franchise Agreements), 2001.

[57] Antitrust Rules (Block Exemption for Exclusive Distribution Agreements), 2001.

[58] Antitrust Rules (Block Exemption for Exclusive Purchase Agreements), 2001.

[59] Antitrust Rules (Block exemption for Agreements between Affiliated Firms) (Temporary Order), 2011.

exemption.[60] Unless otherwise stated in a specific exemption, an oral agreement is presumed *not* to fulfill the conditions of a block exemption, but this presumption is apparently rebuttable.

(iii) Tribunal approval and individual exemptions

The Tribunal has the power to approve a restrictive arrangement, even an anticompetitive one, if there are other interests which such agreement furthers, that outweigh the injury to competition. According to s. 10 of the Law, the Tribunal may consider, among other considerations, the following: efficiencies in production or marketing; ensuring better quality, prices of the product or its availability; mitigating anticompetitive behavior by a third party; preventing severe harm in other important areas of the economy; employment and foreign trade balance. **21.56**

A Tribunal approval is generally a rather long and cumbersome process, and Tribunal proceedings may take up to several years. This is the reason why such proceedings are scarce. The Commissioner was vested with the power to grant individual exemptions from the need to obtain the Tribunal's exemption. According to s. 14(a)(1) of the Law, such exemptions may be granted when the restraints in the arrangement do not restrict competition in a large portion of the market, or when they do not reflect serious potential harm to competition. Exemptions will not be granted to "naked" restraints, which are not necessary for realizing the main objectives of the arrangement. **21.57**

(iv) Exemption for matters of foreign relations or national security

According to s. 52 of the Law, the Minister of Industry, Trade and Labor may exempt a restrictive arrangement from some or all of the provisions of the Law, if the exemption is deemed necessary for reasons related to the State's foreign relations or national security. Prior to granting such an exemption, the Minister must consult with the Economic Affairs Committee of the Israeli Parliament (The Knesset). This authority has never been used so far. **21.58**

Q. Concentrated group

Under recently enacted legislation, the Antitrust Commissioner may declare, under certain circumstances, that a small group of competitors dominating more than 50 percent of a market is a "concentrated group" and thus a potential target for antitrust enforcement measures. The Commissioner is not required to prove lack of competition within the oligopoly. In order to proclaim members of an oligopoly a "concentrated group", the Commissioner needs to demonstrate that "conditions supportive of limited competition" exist (s. 31B(a) of the Law), and that there are remedies that can enhance competition or prevent further injury to competition. **21.59**

According to the Law, "conditions supportive of limited competition" would exist, among other things, where there is an entry barrier to the market with two additional components, such as switching costs, cross-holdings between competitors, market share symmetry, homogenous products, or the transparency of terms and conditions in the market. Naturally, these attributes may exist in many oligopolistic markets. **21.60**

In order to regulate activities in such markets the Commissioner may, *inter alia*, take measures to decrease barriers to entry or expansion—for example, by forbidding the use of long-term contracts with consumers or the inclusion of high termination fees in such contracts (s. 31C(a)(1) of the Law) or terminating facilitating practices, such as information exchanges (s. 31C(a)(2)–(3) of the Law). **21.61**

[60] Antitrust Rules (General Instructions and Definitions), 2006, s. 4.

21.62 In addition, the Tribunal is vested with the authority to order a member of a concentrated group to divest its holdings (even minority holdings) in a competing firm, if such measure would prevent significant harm to competition or significantly enhance competition (s. 31C(b) of the Law).

21.63 The Commissioner has recently executed his new powers for the first time. In November 2013, the Commissioner declared the Israeli ports as a concentrated group and issued directives to the ports in order to facilitate the formation and entry of new competitors to the existing ports.[61] In addition, the Commissioner announced his intention to declare and issue directives in several other markets.[62]

II. Dealing with competitors

21.64 Agreements between competitors are governed by the "Restrictive Arrangements" chapter (chapter B) of the Law. The definition of a restrictive arrangement is comprised of two wings:

- s. 2(a) of the Law outlines a substantial test which applies to any arrangement that may decrease competition in the market or between the contracting parties (or between one of them and a third party);
- s. 2(b) of the Law outlines several restrictions which, if included in an arrangement, necessarily render it a restrictive arrangement (price restrictions, market allocation, profit sharing and more). The definition of restrictive arrangement was given a broad meaning, so that almost any form of collaboration between competitors would be deemed a restrictive arrangement.

21.65 While virtually all agreements between competitors may be caught under s. 2(b) of the Law, such agreements can be roughly divided to two categories:

- Bid rigging and cartelistic agreements (market allocation, price fixing, etc.). Such agreements will not be able to enjoy any block exemption, are unlikely to receive a particular approval and will normally be subject to criminal proceedings.
- Other forms of competitor collaborations, such as joint ventures. These agreements may fall under the block exemptions, depending–among other things–on the market shares of the relevant parties. Moreover, such agreements will often receive particular exemptions from the IAA, if they fall outside the block exemptions, insofar as they do not cause real competitive concerns.

A. Horizontal price fixing (including advanced announcements of price or product changes)

21.66 Horizontal price fixing is considered a typical cartelistic practice. It is illegal and might result in criminal sanctions, including imprisonment for up to five years. In practice, actual imprisonment was imposed to date in only few occasions. In one prominent example, the principle

[61] Determination Under Section 43(a)(6) of the Restrictive Trade Practices Act, 1988 Regarding the Existence of a Concentrated Group in Providing Loading and Unloading of Local Containers in Regular Marine Shipping Routes and Directives to the Members of the Concentrated Group (2013) IAA Website 500512.

[62] See IAA Press Release, "A hearing before declaring the baby food compounds market as a concentration group" (February 27, 2013) IAA Website 500351; IAA Press Release, "Hearing before declaring the market for unloading cargo at Ben Gurion Airport as a concentration group" (August 7, 2013) IAA Website 500446.

participants and the coordinator of a cartel between the main tile production companies in Israel were sentenced to imprisonment of several months.[63]

Imprisonment to be served by way of community service was more commonly applied. Nonetheless, the Israeli Supreme Court stressed several times that imprisonment to be served behind bars was the appropriate punishment for antitrust offenses,[64] and the IAA has been very active in investigating, indicting and seeking actual imprisonment for price fixing violations. For example, the IAA indicted companies and employees from the meteorological sector for bid rigging.[65] The IAA also filed an indictment against forty-four suspects from the tree pruning sector for bid rigging.[66] **21.67**

The IAA makes use of technologically advanced and sophisticated investigative methods including wiretapping, computer seizing and other investigative measures. Until recent years, the IAA usually *detained* suspects of antitrust violations for questioning. In 2009, the IAA arrested several suspects as part of an investigation into possible bid rigging in the area of water counters. Since then, arrests were made during several other investigations conducted by the IAA. **21.68**

The IAA stated several times that it views the exchange of forward-looking information between competitors as an offense. Nonetheless, the IAA has yet to indict in cases involving forward-looking transfer of information. Unless such transfer of information is part of a price-fixing scheme (or an attempt to enter into such scheme), it seems more likely to result in an administrative fine.[67] **21.69**

B. Horizontal agreements to allocate customers or territories; agreements not to compete

Like price fixing, horizontal allocation of customers or territories between competitors is regarded as a typical cartelistic practice. As such, it is deemed an illegal restrictive arrangement, which is potentially liable for criminal sanctions. In one famous example, insurance companies were convicted, *inter alia*, of agreeing to allocate certain insurance segments among them. The convicted companies were heavily fined and their managers were sentenced to imprisonment to be served by the way of community service.[68] **21.70**

Somewhat different rules apply to non-compete provisions, that aim at securing a legitimate collaboration between competitors. Such non-compete provisions are deemed ancillary restrictions, and they may be exempted by a block exemption. When such restrictions fall outside the scope of the block exemptions (e.g. for exceeding market shares thresholds), they may receive a particular exemption from the Commissioner, subject to more careful competitive analysis.[69] Typical legitimate non-compete provisions are those that accompany a merger transaction or the forming of a joint venture. The non-compete provisions, even **21.71**

[63] See *Aloni v. State of Israel*, CrimA 2919/03 (2002) IAA Website 3015629; *State of Israel v. Svirsky*, CrimA 2929/02 (2003) IAA Website 3017060.

[64] See e.g. *Aloni* (n 63) para. 4.

[65] See Press Release, "The IAA filed charges against a number of companies in the field of metrology for bid rigging" (March 20, 2012) IAA Website 5001912.

[66] See Press Release, "Hearing letters were sent in the case of bid rigging in the trees pruning sector" (July 5, 2012) IAA Website 5001988.

[67] See Section III.F(i); IAA Guidelines on the Use of Monetary Sanctions Proceeding (n 10). More on the exchange of information between competitors, see Section II.H.

[68] *State of Israel v. Burovich*, CrimA 4855/02 (2005) IAA Website 5000783.

[69] See Section I.P.

when legitimate, must be limited in scope and time. Non-compete provisions may also be legitimate and exempted in a vertical setting.

C. Horizontal boycotts

21.72 Horizontal boycotts were always perceived illegal, and in recent years the IAA launched several enforcement actions against such boycotts. In 2009, the Commissioner determined that a private hospitals organization's actions to convince its members not to participate in a governmental tender, which led all competitors to boycott the tender, were illegal.[70] However, the alleged breach was handled by administrative means and the IAA did not bring any criminal charges. Moreover, the determination concerned only the organization but not its members.

21.73 In 2010, IAA indicted the Contractors Association for recommending its members to refrain from participating in a governmental tender, a recommendation which allegedly led all the members (but one) to boycott the tender.[71] The charges were initially brought against both the Association and the members. However, in 2012, the District Court decided that the charges against the contracting companies are discriminatory and should be dropped, since no measures (not even administrative) were taken against the members of the private hospitals organization in the 2009 case mentioned above, in similar circumstances. The criminal charges against the Contractors Association, on the other hand, remained.

21.74 The Restrictive Trade Practices Rules (General Instructions), 2006, explicitly state in s. 4 that a horizontal boycott cannot enjoy any kind of block exemption. Therefore, such boycott will normally require a particular exemption by the IAA or an approval from the Tribunal. Such particular exemption, however, is unlikely.

D. Joint ventures and other competitive collaborations

21.75 Joint ventures between competitors are sometimes classified as merger transactions and sometimes as restrictive arrangements. The basic distinction is this: if a party to a joint venture receives influence over *existing assets and activities* of another joint venture member—the transaction would most likely be deemed a merger transaction. This would be the case, for instance, when two firms transfer their existing activity in a relevant market to a jointly held joint venture, while remaining independent in other markets. Other situations normally fall under the less favorable restrictive arrangements regime, and require a particular exemption, unless exempted by the Law or by a block exemption.

21.76 The principal exemption that deals with joint ventures is the Restrictive Trade Practices Rules (Block Exemption for Joint Ventures), 2006 (the "JV Block Exemption"). The JV Block Exemption defines a "joint venture" very broadly—as a "contract for collaboration." The JV Block Exemption differentiates between joint ventures that relate to the area of overlap between the competing parents and joint ventures that relate to non-overlapping activity. Joint ventures in the area of overlap directly affect competition between the parents, while for other ventures the effects, if any, are indirect ("chilling effects" or spillover concerns). Thus, different requirements apply to each type of joint venture, in particular different market share thresholds. Like most other block exemptions, the JV block exemption is subject to general requirements.[72]

---

[70] Determination of Restrictive Arrangement: Organization of Private Hospitals for Chronic Patients in Israel (2007) IAA Website 5000740 ("Private Hospitals Restrictive Arrangement").

[71] See Press Release (December 15, 2010) IAA Website 5001700.

[72] See Section I.P.

Joint research and development between competitors may be exempt under the Restrictive Trade Practices Rules (Block Exemption for Research and Development Agreements), 2006 (the "R&D Block Exemption"). Market share thresholds under the R&D Block Exemption are similar to the ones under the JV Block Exemption. **21.77**

Other collaborations among competitors may be exempt under the Restrictive Trade Practices Rules (Block Exemption for Agreements with *De Minimis* Impact on Competition), 2006. In this case, cumulative market shares must not exceed 15 percent in the relevant market for the agreement and 30 percent in markets unrelated to the agreement. **21.78**

There are several segment related exemptions for collaborations between competitors. Section 3(7) of the Law provided a statutory exemption for arrangements made between air carriers and for arrangements made between shipping carriers. This sweeping exemption was narrowed with time and essentially replaced by more narrow block exemptions: the Restrictive Trade Practices Rules (Block Exemption for Arrangements between Aerial Carriers), 2008 and Restrictive Trade Practices Rules (Block Exemption for Operational Arrangements Regarding International Sea Transport), 2012. **21.79**

Section 3(4) of the Law sets another statutory exemption for growing and marketing of domestic agriculture produce of certain types (fruits, vegetables, field crops, milk, eggs, honey, cattle, sheep, poultry, or fish), provided that all the parties to the arrangement are growers or wholesalers. **21.80**

When a joint venture or another form of legitimate cooperation falls outside the scope of the block exemptions and no statutory exemption applies, parties may receive a particular exemption from the Commissioner. In such case they would have to prove that the joint venture is legitimate and that it does not pose real potential competitive harms. Sometimes, the combined share of the parties is very large and the concerns to competition are considerable, but the venture promotes other important interests. In such cases, parties may seek approval from the Tribunal, who is authorized to consider other interests that contradict with the interest of competition. Such was the case with the Israeli recycling corporation, which incorporated all major drinks producers in Israel.[73] **21.81**

E. Trade associations

The establishment of a trade association is not considered, in and of itself, a "restrictive arrangement."[74] The IAA recognizes the legitimate purposes of trade associations, such as updating members on professional literature, methods and technological novelties.[75] The trade association may also serve as the contact point for various governmental bodies to approach the industry.[76] **21.82**

However, trade associations should not serve as platforms for cartels, and should not engage in facilitating practices. Trade associations must refrain from any involvement in commercial matters, including by way of information exchange. Section 5 of the Law explicitly forbids a trade association from initiating a "course of action" which may eliminate or reduce competition between its members. The IAA has explained that when the members of an association jointly discuss the possible implications of a commercial course of action, such as whether **21.83**

---

[73] *Beverage Bottle Collection Corporation Ltd. v. Blue Square Israel Ltd.*, AT (Jerusalem) 508/04 (2005) IAA Website 5000845.

[74] A Decision to Render an Exemption from the Approval of a Restrictive Arrangement: Internet Websites in Israel Association (2002) IAA Website 3015425.

[75] Private Hospitals Restrictive Arrangement (n 70); see also Choices Conditional Exemption (n 47).

[76] Choices Conditional Exemption (n 47).

it is profitable to participate in a tender, such joint discussion may also amount to an illegal "course of action" by the trade association.[77]

21.84 In contrast to commercial activity, trade associations are normally allowed to approach governmental bodies, under the IAA's Guidelines on Collaborations between Competitors Acting before Governmental Agencies,[78] that specify certain "safe harbors" for competitors acting together to promote their regulatory interests. The safe harbors are rather narrow, excluding, for example, any monopoly entity. Conditions include, among others, the presentation of full and accurate information to the relevant government entity and certain limitations on contact between competitors and exchange of information.

21.85 The IAA focused significant resources and launched several criminal investigations in recent years against trade associations, which allegedly facilitated cartel arrangements between their members. Thus, the IAA indicted the Insurance Appraisers Union of Israel and its chairman for recommending the members of the Union's vehicle branch to set fixed fees for their services.[79] The Contractors Association's indictment[80] is another example. The IAA also notified the Travel Agents Association of that it will be prosecuted for recommending its members of strategies to increase the payments received from customers.[81]

21.86 In order to provide better certainty for members of trade associations, in November 2013 the Commissioner issued the Draft Guidelines on Trade Associations and Their Operation,[82] which outline the best practices for the establishment of trade associations and for their conduct. The Draft Guidelines specify, *inter alia*, the optimal mode of conduct during meetings and professional conferences and in acting before governmental agencies. The Draft Guidelines also address the trade association's recommendations in certain areas, joint advertising, dissemination of statistical information, joint conferences, and other types of business activities.

F. Interlocking directorates

21.87 Under certain circumstances, an interlocking directorate may raise antitrust questions, both under the merger review regime and the restrictive arrangements chapter. Section 1 of the Law stipulates that the acquisition of more than 25 percent of the right to appoint directors in a firm is a merger transaction, which will be reviewed under the merger chapter of the Law. Not all mergers, however, are subject to scrutiny. Only if one or more of the filing thresholds set in s. 17 is met, the merger will be subject to antitrust review.

21.88 The Law does not address, at least not directly, interlocking directorates that do not amount to merger transactions. Nor are we familiar with any court ruling or IAA decision, which directly addressed the issue.

21.89 Yet, it seems reasonable that in cases where such interlocking directorates may potentially decrease competition, the IAA will argue that it constitutes a restrictive arrangement. There are several indications in this direction. The IAA has long been in the position that minority acquisitions that are below the merger threshold may be regarded as restrictive arrangements.

---

77 Private Hospitals Restrictive Arrangement (n 70).

78 IAA's Guidelines on Collaborations between Competitors Acting before Governmental Agencies (2000) IAA Website 3007119E.

79 See IAA Press Release, "The IAA has indicted the Insurance Appraisers Union of Israel and its chairman" (June 4, 2012) IAA Website 5001962.

80 See Section II.C.

81 See IAA Press Release (July 12, 2012) IAA Website 5001991.

82 Draft Guidelines on Trade Associations and Their Operation (2013) IAA Website, 500506.

For instance, the IAA's Guidelines regarding the Enforcement of Financial Administrative Sanctions, state that "minority holdings" which do not constitute a merger under the Law constitute a restrictive arrangement that will be financially sanctioned by the IAA. The Antitrust Rules (Block Exemption for Non-Horizontal Arrangements that do not include Certain Price Restrictions), 2013 define a "horizontal arrangement" (for which the exemption does not apply), *inter alia*, as an investment in one's competitor that does not constitute a "merger"). The same logic would seemingly apply to interlocking directorates. Moreover, the Antitrust Rules (Block Exemption for Agreements with *De Minimis* Impact on Competition) 2006, are excluded where the arrangement includes the acquisition of rights in a competing firm (s. 3(2) of the Block Exemption), including the right to appoint directors.

The IAA may find indirect support by the Tribunal's decision in the case of *Baron-Fishman*.[83] In the context of merger litigation, the Tribunal noted that an interlocking directorate might impede competition even more than a mere passive holding.[84] **21.90**

G. Facilitating practices

The term "facilitating practices" describes practices employed by competitors in a concentrated market, which enable or facilitate their ability to achieve and sustain a supra-competitive equilibrium. **21.91**

Facilitating practices are generally examined under the restrictive arrangements chapter of the Law. A facilitating practice may serve as a circumstantial evidence ("plus factor") from which the court may infer, combined with other evidence, the existence of a restrictive arrangement.[85] It is unclear though whether a facilitating practice may constitute an illegal restrictive arrangement by itself. As we will further elaborate below, the IAA's determination regarding illegal exchange of information between major banks provided a positive answer to this question. The IAA argued that when firms have some type of an agreement (or a mutual understanding) to engage in a facilitating practice—this practice is a restrictive arrangement. On the other hand, it seems that when a facilitating practice is a completely unilateral one, it cannot be classified as an "arrangement," and thus cannot be prohibited under the restrictive arrangements chapter. The banks appeal on the IAA's decision is still pending. **21.92**

Another facilitating practice which was classified by the IAA as a restrictive arrangement is the use of "most favored nation" (MFN) provisions. Under certain circumstances, such practice can facilitate explicit or tacit collusion, as it undermines the ability to deviate from the supra-competitive market equilibrium, by offering small and discreet discounts to specific customers. According to the IAA, this practice constitutes a restrictive arrangement regardless of its likely impact on competition, as it falls under the irrefutable presumption set in s. 2(b)(1), which deals with price restrictions.[86] The Supreme Court was less decisive on this matter.[87] **21.93**

As discussed in Section I.Q, in 2011, the Law was amended to include a chapter regarding oligopolies (concentrated groups).The amendment confers in the hands of the Commissioner significant powers to regulate oligopolistic activities, including the authority to instruct members of an oligopoly to stop employing a certain practice which might facilitate collective dominance (s. 31C(a)(2) of the Law). In particular, s. 31C(a)(3) of the Law authorizes the **21.94**

83 *Commissioner v. Baron-Fishman Communications, Ltd.*, CP 916/03 (2012) IAA Website 5001579.

84 *Baron-Fishman* (n 83) para. 10.

85 See *Burovich* (n 68) para. 133; *Wahl* (n 18) (the Supreme Court decided that the examining the "plus factor" was not needed in that case, since there were direct evidences for collaboration).

86 See A Decision to Render a Partial Exemption from the Approval of a Restrictive Arrangement: Agreement between Mirs Communications Ltd. and Telephone Communications Ltd. (2012) IAA Website 5001928.

87 See *Extal, Ltd. v. Kalma V Industry Ltd.*, PCA 6233/02 (2004) IAA Website 5000847.

Commissioner to prohibit the transmission or publication of information, which might facilitate tacit or explicit collusion. Though so far these powers have not been extensively executed by the IAA,[88] it seems that facilitating practices are a major target for such enforcement.

H. Information exchange

21.95 There is some ambiguity in Israeli case Law as to whether the mere exchange of information can be classified as a "restrictive arrangement" under the Law. In several court rulings, where the subject was discussed as an *obiter dictum*, and the courts stated that information exchange between competitors may facilitate collusion between them or may indicate that such collusion exists, but does not in and of itself constitute an illegal restrictive arrangement.[89]

21.96 As aforementioned, in 2009 the Commissioner issued a determination under s. 43(a)(1) of the Law, stating that the mere transfer of information regarding fees between the five largest banks in Israel was an illegal restrictive arrangement.[90] The decision was published after a prolonged investigation which began in 2004. According to the Commissioner's decision, for more than a decade bank officers exchanged information regarding already collected fees, as well as future conduct concerning fees. The Commissioner further argued that the Israeli banking industry suffered from ongoing competitive shortcomings, and that it was characterized by substantial entry barriers for competitors and considerable switching barriers for consumers. While the Commissioner acknowledged that information may play an important role in making markets more competitive, she claimed that such a beneficial outcome was unlikely in the circumstances evolving the supply of banking services to small businesses and households. According to the Commissioner, the information exchanged between the banks was potentially anticompetitive, because it increased transparency in a concentrated market, and thus constituted a restrictive arrangement under s. 2(a) of the Law. Moreover, the IAA argued that since the exchange related to prices (fees) it was also caught by the irrefutable presumptions in s. (2)(b)(1) of the Law. These statements by the IAA are controversial and an appeal process which was launched by the banks is currently pending before the Tribunal.

21.97 Despite the very broad approach and strong language of the IAA's determination in the baking industry, it is unlikely that the IAA will challenge transfer of information which does not reduce uncertainty, such as aggregate or public information. Historic information (especially if it is rather old) is also less sensitive. Market structure is also very important, as information exchange is mostly dangerous in highly concentrated markets. The IAA attributes importance to the purpose of the exchange. If there is a legitimate interest (such as the need to conduct a due diligence process), the IAA is more likely to accept some degree of exchange of information (but in any event not of sensitive one).

21.98 In March 2013, the Commissioner issued draft Guidelines Regarding Information Exchange in the Course of Due Diligence Prior to a Transaction Between Competitors.[91] The Draft Guidelines provide theoretical principles alongside a practical procedural framework for conducting due diligence in transactions that require the transfer of sensitive information. The procedural framework is focused mainly on proper documentation of the transfer and on

[88] See Section I.Q.

[89] *Wahl* (n 18); *State of Israel v. HaPhoenix Insurance Co. Ltd.*, CrimA 417/97 (2001) IAA Website 5000788; *Food Club* (n 2).

[90] See Determination according to the Bank Hapoalim Ltd., Leumi Bank Ltd., Israel Discount Bank Ltd., United Mizrahi Bank Ltd. and the First International Bank of Israel Ltd (Determination of Restrictive Arrangement), 2009 IAA Website, 5001411E, s. 43.

[91] Draft Guidelines Regarding Information Exchange in the Course of Due Diligence Prior to a Transaction Between Competitors, 2013 IAA Website 500364.

limitation of the exposure of competitively sensitive information to the minimum necessary. While the draft guidelines characterize certain types of competitively sensitive information and suggest ways to transfer such data legally, they confer the ultimate discretion regarding the due diligence process—and the potential liability—on the merging parties.

I. Joint purchasing agreements

The IAA generally treats joint purchasing agreements between competitors as restrictive arrangements in and of themselves, subject to chapter B of the Law.[92] The most relevant exemption is the JV Block Exemption,[93] which exempts joint purchasing under certain conditions, in particular market share thresholds. However, joint purchasing could be a code name for a cartel of buyers, in which case the IAA will not approve it. Thus, when the buying group possesses a substantial buying power vis-à-vis the suppliers or when the group consists of significant competitors in the downstream market—antitrust approval is less likely. On the other hand, the IAA provided several exemptions for buying groups whose members were small competitors striving to achieve economies of scale, especially when these buyers faced dominant suppliers. In such circumstances, the IAA believed that the buying group may mitigate the market power of the supplier, and would then pass the savings to the customers, as its members face fierce competition in the downstream market. **21.99**

J. Joint lobbying/regulatory/legislative efforts

The rules applying for joint lobbying, regulatory, or legislative efforts of competitors are the same as those mentioned above in connection with trade associations. The issue is addressed directly by the IAA's Guidelines on Collaborations between Competitors Acting before Governmental Agencies and by the Draft Guidelines on Trade Associations and Their Operation.[94] **21.100**

III. General issues

A. Jurisdiction and applicable law (including sector-specific competition regulation)

In general, the Law applies to all sectors of the Israeli economy. However, the Law includes several caveats to this very broad application. Section 3(4) of the Law provides a sector-specific exemption to regarding domestic agriculture produces. Section 3(7) of the Law provides an exemption to agreements between sea carriers and air carriers. As explained, the exemption was significantly narrowed and was essentially replaced by sector-specific block exemptions.[95] **21.101**

Section 3(1) of the Law exempts restrictive arrangements whose restrictions were imposed by legislation. This exemption was interpreted narrowly by the Israeli Supreme Court and the Antitrust Tribunal. The Supreme Court has ruled that said exemption may apply only when the State, as a part of a specific sector regulation, sets up rules that generate a restrictive arrangement. However, the mere existence of a sector-specific regulation does not rule out the applicability of the Law to that sector.[96] Moreover, in order for a specific regulation to exclude competition regulation, the regulation must be set by a "law," meaning a legislative **21.102**

---

92 See A Decision to Render a Partial Exemption from the Approval of a Restrictive Arrangement: The Fourth Chain Ltd. and its Members (2012) IAA Website 5001971.

93 See Section II.D.

94 See Section II.E.

95 See Section II.D.

96 See *Beverage Bottle Collection Corporation* (n 73) para. 13; *Burovich* (n 68) para. 83; *Moshe Cohen Garage (1989) v. Clal Insurance Company*, CivC (Haifa) 2447/00 (2006) IAA Website 5001248, para. 9.

instruction.[97] An administrative instruction, a license or a government policy decision do not meet this requirement.[98]

21.103 Though s. 3(1) refers to restrictive arrangements, the same logic was applied by the Tribunal to statutory monopolies as well. The Tribunal addressed the question of the relation between the Law and other legislation in the *Bezeq* case,[99] where a statutory monopoly claimed to be immune from the application of the Law and in the *Magal* case, where a patent owner claimed to be exempt from the application of the Law.[100] In both cases, the Tribunal ruled that in the absence of an explicit statutory exemption, the Law should be interpreted in harmony with other applicable law, in a way which does not repeal the application of the antitrust laws.

21.104 Sector-specific regulations may have different objectives, including promoting competition. However, sector-specific competition regulation is generally designated to complement rather than to replace the Law. Some of such regulations note so explicitly. For instance, the Fuel Market (Promotion of Competition) Law, 1994 states that its provisions shall not derogate from the provisions of any other law.

21.105 The issue of the relation between antitrust regulation and sector-specific regulation is especially relevant in the context of concentrated groups.[101] Traditionally, the IAA focused on enforcement and the task of ongoing regulation was vested exclusively in the hands of market regulators (e.g. the Ministry of Telecommunications or the Bank of Israel). Reforms aimed at increasing competition in these markets were led by these regulators, with the IAA merely serving as an adviser. The amendment regarding concentrated groups has vested the Commissioner with authority to use antitrust enforcement measures to change market characteristics and to implement measures aimed at actively increasing competition rather than merely preserving it.

21.106 The amendment attempts to address possible conflicts between market regulators and the Commissioner. It states that in order to implement enforcement measures designed to prevent harm to competition in an industry that is regulated by another regulator, the Commissioner must first consult the relevant regulator. Moreover, if the Commissioner wishes to implement measures in order to promote competition in a regulated industry, he must obtain the relevant regulator's consent. Special arrangements were structured in the area of banking and capital markets.

B. Antitrust system

(i) Name of agency/agencies

21.107 The competition regulator in Israel is the IAA. The IAA is headed by the Commissioner, who is appointed by the Israeli government. While the IAA is formally part of the Ministry of Industry, Trade and Labor, it is independent and has a record of being professional and politically impartial. Judicial review on the Commissioner's decisions is carried out by the Tribunal. The Tribunal's decisions may be appealed to the Israeli Supreme Court. Decisions and actions of the Commissioner which are not subject to appeal before the Tribunal may be contested by a petition to the Supreme Court (in its capacity as the High Court of Justice).

[97] See *The Israel Electric Corporation Ltd. v. Commissioner*, AT (Jerusalem) 491/98 (1999) IAA Website 3002628, paras. 79–82.

[98] *Israel Electric Corporation* (n 97); see also *Arutzei Zahav & Co. v. The Israeli Film and Television Directors Guild*, AT (Jerusalem) 3276/99 (2000) IAA Website 5000785, para. 43.

[99] *Bezeq* (n 4).

[100] *Magal Security Systems Ltd. v. Commissioner*, AT 97/9 (2001) IAA Website 3006703.

[101] See Section I.Q.

The IAA has very broad investigative authorities, including search and seizure in businesses (no warrant needed) and on private premises (with a court's order). The IAA is also authorized to issue very broad requests for information and has a variety of enforcement tools, which we will further detail below. **21.108**

(ii) Staff size and budget

In 2011 the IAA's staff included seventy-nine people, of whom around twenty were attorneys, about fifteen investigators, and about twelve economists. In 2012–13, as part of a more comprehensive reform aim at boosting competition and reducing the costs of living in Israel, the authority received a significant increase of resources and it currently employs around 120 people, of whom nearly thirty are attorneys and around thirty are economists (exact numbers will be published in 2014). **21.109**

The IAA's budget for 2012 was about ILS 41.1 million, currently amounting to a slightly over USD 10 million. **21.110**

(iii) Recent enforcement actions and trends

Over the last three years, the landscape of Israeli antitrust regime has changed significantly. Backed by a surge of social protest over the costs of living, the Israeli Parliament passed several pieces of legislation which further enhance the power of what was already a very powerful authority—the IAA. **21.111**

As part of this legislation, the IAA was vested with the power to regulate oligopolistic markets.[102] The IAA's authority to issue directives to monopolies was also solidified: a provision in the Law—stating that an appeal on Commissioner's directives to monopolies automatically postpones them—was revoked. The IAA was also provided with the authority to unilaterally impose administrative fines ("monetary payments") on antitrust violators. From an institutional point of view, the IAA received vast new resources and practically doubled its staff. A new division, concentrated on market surveys, was formed. **21.112**

These vast changes are only starting to materialize. The IAA has only begun imposing its authority over oligopolies, and has not imposed any monetary payments to date. The IAA did publish two policy documents concerning the monetary payments reform. The first, "The IAA's Guidelines on the Use of Monetary Sanctions Proceedings,"[103] clarifies which violations will be enforced with monetary payments, distinguished from criminal sanctions. The other paper, "A Statement of Opinion on the Commissioner's Considerations in Setting the Size of Monetary Sanctions,"[104] outlines the parameters to be used in determining the size of payment. **21.113**

Finally, the IAA started a process which can lead to a major reform in the supervision over restrictive arrangements, by introducing self-assessment in the marine transportation industry, and the extension of the self-assessment regime to air transport and to non-horizontal arrangement that do not include certain price restrictions.[105] **21.114**

At the same time, the IAA increased enforcement in the areas of trade associations[106] and merger control (where the IAA blocked several mergers, in contrast to a more lenient approach in this field taken by previous Commissioners). **21.115**

102 Section I.Q.
103 See Section I.C.
104 2012 IAA Website 5001999.
105 On this development, see Section I.P(v).
106 See Section II.E.

C. Private litigation

21.116 Section 50(a) of the Law provides that an act or omission contrary to the provisions of the Law shall constitute a tort in accordance with the Israeli Tort Ordinance [New Version] ("Tort Ordinance"). The same applies to any breach of directives issued by the Commissioner, conditions imposed by the Commissioner as part of a merger or a restrictive arrangement approval, any conditions or instructions set by the Tribunal and any violation of consent decrees entered into with the Commissioner. Such violations are the basis for claims for damages or for injunctive relief.

21.117 The Israeli Class Actions Law, 2006 ("Class Action Law") provides that a person, a public entity or a consumers' organization may, under certain conditions, file a class action on behalf of a class of plaintiffs and seek damages for breach of the Law.

21.118 While class actions and antitrust-specific litigation are less frequent (although there is a noticeable increase in recent years), antitrust claims are made quite frequently in the context of contract litigation. A party who seeks to defend against enforcement of a contract will often argue that the contract violates the Law (illegal contracts are normally not enforced). Israeli courts are reluctant to brand contracts that lack obvious anticompetitive characteristics with a mark of illegality.[107] However, if a court comes to the conclusion that a provision in a contract does violate the Law, this provision will normally be unenforceable.[108]

D. Follow-on litigation

21.119 The Law paves the way for two types of follow-on litigation.

21.120 The IAA may issue a "determination of breach" under s. 43(a) of the Law, which can be used as a *prima facie* evidence in a subsequent private litigation. In practice, determinations are indeed usually followed by private enforcement, in particular class actions. Monopoly proclamation also serves as a *prima facie* evidence in any legal proceeding. Therefore, the proclamation plays a pivotal role in abuse of dominance litigation.

21.121 Follow-on litigation may arise when an investigation ends with a criminal conviction. According to s. 77 of the Courts Act [Combined Version], 1984, the same panel which convicted the defendant may, theoretically, hear a civil case concerning the same facts. This track requires the plaintiff to wait until the very lengthy criminal process ends. It is also less relevant for antitrust offenses, which inflict damage on the general public rather than a specific victim. This is the reason why most civil proceedings are tried independently of the criminal proceeding.

E. Arbitration and alternative dispute resolution

21.122 Antitrust claims, particularly in the context of contract disputes, may be raised not only before a court, but also in the course of an arbitration, or another alternative dispute resolution mechanism, which are becoming more and more common. The Israeli Arbitration Act, 1968 (the "Arbitration Act") provides a very broad discretion for the parties to agree on the substantive law and the procedural rules that would apply to the arbitration process. However, s. 3 of the Arbitration Act states that arbitration cannot be a valid mechanism to enforce an illegal contract and such contract cannot be the subject of an arbitration process. Nonetheless, in an attempt to encourage arbitrations, the courts did not categorically disqualify arbitrations, where one party argued that the disputed agreement was, as a whole

[107] See Section III.E.

[108] See *Tivall v. Chef Hayam*, Rehearing 4465/98 (2001) IAA Website 3003022.

or in part, an illegal "restrictive arrangement." In one case, the Supreme Court validated an arbitration clause, even though the agreement in which it was included was argued to be a restrictive arrangement.[109] The members of the panel expressed different opinions as to whether the agreement indeed violated the Law and this question remained open. In another case the Supreme Court rejected a claim of invalidity regarding an arbitration agreement, based on the fact that it was signed after the contractual relations between the parties (which were claimed to constitute a restrictive arrangement) terminated.[110]

It should be noted that Israeli Contracts Act, 1973, in s. 31, provides that while normally an illegal contract is unenforceable, the court may partially enforce the contract, if it finds that such enforcement is required to achieve justice. This exception is applied more narrowly in the context of antitrust illegality. **21.123**

F. Remedies

(i) Civil liability

As mentioned in Section II, any breach under the Law is also a civil tort under the Tort Ordinance, according to s. 50 of the Law. Accordingly, a private party may file a lawsuit against an antitrust offender seeking compensation for damages incurred as a result of an antitrust violation or apply for an injunction to prevent such damages. Consumers may also file class actions under the Class Actions Law, for harm incurred as a result of an antitrust violation. Civil tort proceedings may be issued by any person in any court. **21.124**

In addition to establishing a breach of the Law, civil liability requires proof of harm and of causal link.[111] The Tort Ordinance grants damages according to the harm actually caused, and generally does not grant exemplary or punitive damages. Damages will, however, normally include interest and will be consumer-price index-linked according to the Interest and Linkage Adjudication Law, 1961. **21.125**

On the administrative side, the IAA normally applies one or more of the following tools: **21.126**

(1) *A determination of breach* under s. 43(a) of the Law, which serves as *prima facie* evidence in any court proceeding, thereby facilitating private lawsuits against the parties to the breaching agreements or practices. As mentioned above, the determination may also facilitate subsequent civil proceedings initiated by private plaintiffs or criminal proceedings brought by the IAA. The determination is subject to an appeal process at the Tribunal.

(2) *A consent decree.* Under s. 50(b) of the Law, the IAA may enter into a consent decree with an alleged antitrust offender. Such a decree is an alternative to a criminal or administrative action and it may include fines and undertakings by the alleged offender. The decree is subject to an approval by the Tribunal.

(3) *Injunctive relief.* The IAA may apply to the Tribunal under s. 50(a) of the Law, seeking a restraining order aimed at preventing or terminating violations of the Law.

As explained in Section 21.09, when a monopoly is involved the Commissioner may issue instructions regarding actions necessary to prevent harm to competition or to the public (s. 30 of the Law). In extreme cases, when it is impossible to prevent the harm to the public by issuing instructions or in any other way, the Commissioner might ask the Tribunal to order the separation of the monopoly (s. 31 of the Law). **21.127**

---

[109] See *Extal* (n 87).

[110] *Huri v. A.Y.H*, PCA 1027/11, decision of April 10, 2011, available at <http://www.nevo.co.il/psika_html/elyon/11010270-w01.htm>.

[111] *Tower Air* (n 13) para. 127.

21.128 According to s. 50D of the Law, which was added in 2012, the Commissioner may unilaterally impose significant monetary payments on companies and individuals for a wide range of antitrust offenses, such as illegal restrictive arrangements, gun-jumping violations in mergers and abuse of dominant position. The payment can reach up to ILS 1 million (currently about USD 250,000) for individuals and up to ILS 24 milion (about USD 6 million) for corporations. Monetary sanctions may also be a part of a consent decree, according to s. 50B(a) of the Law. All the offenses for which the Commissioner may impose monetary payments are also subject to criminal enforcement, as well as other administrative measures (e.g. a determination of breach, an injunctive relief or a consent decree).

21.129 The IAA Guidelines on the Use of Monetary Sanctions Proceedings[112] were published by the IAA, in order to clarify when it will resort to monetary payments as the primary enforcement measure (instead of seeking criminal sanctions). According to the Guidelines, monetary payments are relevant for non-horizontal transactions, while for most horizontal transactions, criminal enforcement remains the main enforcement measure. The Guidelines list numerous offenses which will typically be enforced with monetary payments, including non-horizontal restrictive arrangements, information exchange of non-secret information, abuse of dominant position, and failure to comply with data requests.

21.130 The IAA also published its Statement of Opinion on the Commissioner's Considerations in Setting the Size of Monetary Sanctions.[113] This issue was settled to some extent by the legislature, as s. 50E of the Law lists several parameters which must be considered by the Commissioner while determining the size of a payment. These include the duration of the infringement; the potential injury to competitors; the level of involvement the offender had in the offense; prior violations and steps taken by the violator to prevent further violations; the violator's financial means; and personal circumstances (for individuals). However, this list is not exhaustive, and the Commissioner retains a level of discretion. The Statement of Opinion attempts to explain how the different parameters will be implemented in practice, noting that the actual payment amount will be determined on a case-by-case basis. However, the statement of opinion does not explain the relative importance attributed to each parameter; thus, it is difficult to assess the size of potential payments based on these guidelines. Once the IAA begins to implement this new power, a benchmark will be established and parties will be better equipped to predict the IAA's decisions.

21.131 Lastly, the Commissioner published a Notice on the Acts and Omissions Regarding Monetary Sanctions in the Official Journal.[114] The Notice specifies monopolistic acts and omissions for which monetary sanctions might be imposed. These include predatory pricing, excessive pricing, tying and price discrimination.

(ii) Criminal liability

21.132 Criminal liability in Israel applies not only to corporations. A violation of the Antitrust Law might also impose direct personal liability upon corporate officers involved in the antitrust wrongdoing, according to s. 47 of the Law. Moreover, s. 48 of the Law imposes indirect criminal liability on senior officers of a corporation, even if they were unaware of the offense committed, unless they can prove that they had taken all reasonable measures to prevent antitrust violations. In practice, this defense may be best served by a compliance program that meets the IAA guidelines. The IAA issued a rather complex model for adopting a compliance program, which has a methodological approach and lists the necessary elements in

[112] Discussed in Section III.B.
[113] Discussed in Section III.B.
[114] See Section I.C.

a compliance program, such as supervision, control, and intra-corporate punitive measures against offenders.

Criminal penalties include a possible imprisonment of up to three years (five years in aggravating circumstances) and a fine of up to ILS 2,260,000 (about USD 600,000) plus an additional amount of ILS 14,000 (about USD 3,800) for each day that the infringement continues (s. 47 of the Law). The existence of aggravating circumstances is determined by factors such as the defendant's market share and position in the market that was affected by the offense; the period of time over which the offense took place; the harm caused or likely to be caused to the public as a result of the offense; and the benefits gained by the offender as a result of the offense. **21.133**

The IAA is the prosecutorial body responsible for criminal enforcement of the Antitrust Law. While the IAA is authorized to indict corporations and individuals for any violation of the Law, so far it has normally reserved criminal enforcement for hard core cartel offenses, bid rigging and other blunt violations of the Law. For such violations, the IAA's practice was to normally seek imprisonment of any person directly involved in the violations as well as senior officers indirectly liable for such violations, under s. 48 of the Law. All criminal proceedings are adjudicated in the Jerusalem District Court, which ultimately decides the verdict and the penalties to be imposed. The District Court's verdict is subject to an appeal to the Israeli Supreme Court. **21.134**

G. Leniency and immunity

In 2005, the IAA adopted a Leniency Program, which accords a corporation, a director or an employee of a corporation an immunity from criminal prosecution in cartel cases. Immunity is granted provided, among other conditions, that the applicant was the first to move forward, that it was not the leader of the alleged cartel, that it cooperated with the IAA and provided it with complete information before the investigation was made public, and that it had ceased its involvement in the cartel under the IAA's guidance.[115] **21.135**

H. Document creation and retention

(i) Document retention under the model compliance program

The IAA's model compliance program requires several kinds of documents be created and retained. A corporation wishing to enjoy the benefits of a compliance program in Israel should therefore create and retain at least the following documents: the compliance program itself (including a detailed description of the Law and in particular provisions relating to the corporation's activity); statements from all relevant employees that they have read, understood, and are committed to follow the program and its instructions; documentation of consultations, internal investigations, and disciplinary proceedings related to breaches of the Law or the compliance program's instructions. The IAA has committed, in its model compliance program, not to use certain compliance program documents in legal proceedings against the corporation. It is advised to mark these kinds of documents and keep them separately. **21.136**

(ii) Internal documents

The IAA, as well as the courts, attributes great importance to internal documents in the assessments of practices and transactions. The IAA regularly requests, among other things, internal documents such as board meetings protocols, presentations, surveys, and reports that relate to competitors, competition or a concrete contemplated transaction. Such documents must therefore be drafted accurately. **21.137**

[115] See An Immunity Program for Antitrust Offenses (2005) IAA Website 5000097E.

21.138 The IAA is authorized, under s. 46(b) of the Law, to request almost any kind of information that is in the possession of the firm. According to s. 50D(b) of the Law, any failure to respond to such request is a violation of the Law, which is subject to criminal sanctions as well as monetary payments in the amount of up to ILS 300,000 (about USD 75,000) for individuals and small corporations and up to ILS 8 million (about USD 2 million) for large corporations.

22

ITALY

Claudio Tesauro
Bonelli Erede Pappalardo

Introduction

Competition law in Italy is enforced by the Italian Competition Authority (*Autorità Garante della Concorrenza e del Mercato*) (ICA, or the "Authority"), an independent administrative authority that was instituted by Italian Competition Law No. 287 of October 10, 1990 ("Law no. 287"). The ICA enforces competition by prohibiting: (a) any agreement that has as its object or effect, the distortion of competition within the national market, or within a substantial part of it, (b) the abuse of a dominant position within the domestic market; and (c) appraising any planned mergers between undertakings generating a permanent change of control, when the aggregate domestic turnover of all the undertakings concerned is above EUR 482 million, and the target's domestic turnover is above EUR 48 million. **22.01**

Article 1(4) of Law no. 287 has played an essential role in enforcing antitrust law. This article states that the enforcement of antitrust legislation shall be "in accordance with the principles of the European Community competition law." This provision has allowed the ICA **22.02** (instituted in the early 1990s) to be immediately operational and enforce Italian competition law through the application of the *acquis communautaire*.

22.03 From a procedural point of view, in its proceedings, the ICA follows the rules stated by the Decree of the President of the Republic (DPR) No. 217 of April 30, 1998.

22.04 Contrary to what happens in other European jurisdictions, Italian antitrust proceedings always start with a formal decision. This decision has two notable effects: (a) it determines the end date of the proceeding, and (b) it allows the Authority to exercise its penetrating investigative powers (with the help of the fiscal police).

22.05 The transparency of Italian antitrust proceedings is further guaranteed by the right of access to the file, ensured to any interested party, even prior to the ICA's notification of the statement of objections. Moreover, parties can at any time request a meeting with the directorate in charge of the proceedings in order to explain their position and to gain a better understanding of the ICA's concerns.

22.06 Once the ICA has notified the interested parties of the statement of objections, they can request an oral hearing with the ICA's board.

22.07 The final decisions issued by the Authority can be appealed before the Regional Administrative Court of Lazio (*Tribunale Amministrativo Regionale del Lazio*) ("TAR Lazio"), in Rome, within 60 days from the formal communication of the decision. A decision from TAR Lazio can also be appealed before the Supreme Court (*Consiglio di Stato*).

22.08 The ICA is also part of the European Competition Network and—under Regulation 1/2003[1]—enforces competition by applying articles 101 and 102 of the Treaty on the Functioning of the European Union (TFEU), and so, through a coordination mechanism, contributes with other Competition Authorities to the application of European antitrust legislation. In recent years, the ICA, in investigating market abuses, has focused especially on ex-monopolistic markets (energy, post, transports, communication), while, in investigating cartels, it has given particular attention to trade association decisions and information exchanges that might cause price increases and market foreclosures.

I. Acting alone

22.09 Article 3 of Law no. 287 and article 102 TFEU, impose a special responsibility on companies that are dominant in their relevant markets to ensure that they do not abuse their dominant position through their commercial behavior. It is well known that holding a dominant position on a relevant market is not *per se* illegal; only the abuse of this position would infringe competition rules.

22.10 To affirm that a commercial strategy constitutes an abuse of a dominant position the ICA must prove that the subject abusing its market power: (i) is an undertaking; (ii) has a dominant position in the market; and (iii) has abused its market power. In doing so, the ICA might refer to the abovementioned article 1(4) of Law no. 287, and to the criteria stated in the European Commission's Article 102 Guidance.[2]

[1] Council Regulation (EC) No. 1/2003 on the implementation of the rules on competition laid down in Articles 81 and 82 of the Treaty OJ 2004 L 1/1 (December 16, 2002).

[2] Guidance on the Commission's enforcement priorities in applying [Article 102 TFEU] to abusive exclusionary conduct by dominant undertakings, OJ C 45, February 24, 2009 ("Article 102 Guidance").

The notion of an "undertaking" has been broadly interpreted by the Authority as comprising any subject that performs a business activity (foundations and public entities have also been categorized as undertakings under competition law). **22.11**

To date, the ICA has opened about 450 proceedings and imposed fines of millions of euros. The highest fine imposed was EUR 290 million in the *Eni/Trans Tunisian Pipeline* case.[3] **22.12**

In the last two years, the ICA has focused its actions on prosecuting abuses in ex-monopolistic markets by investigating the leading telecom, postal, energy, and transport operators. **22.13**

A. Predatory pricing

The economic criteria used by the ICA to challenge an alleged predatory pricing strategy are those established by the Court of Justice of the European Union (CJEU) in *AKZO*,[4] whereby it held that (a) prices below average variable costs must be regarded as abusive; and (b) prices below average total costs, but above average variable costs, must be regarded as abusive if they are determined as part of a plan to eliminate a competitor. **22.14**

There have been several cases in which the ICA has punished a predatory pricing strategy. The most relevant are *Mercato del calcestruzzo cellulare autoclavato*[5] and *Diano/Tourist Ferry Boat-Caronte Shipping*.[6] **22.15**

Recently, the ICA sanctioned Poste Italiane (the Italian Universal Postal Service operator) for practicing predatory pricing on the customers of its main competitor (TNT).[7] However, the ICA decision was overruled by TAR.[8] **22.16**

B. Exploitative offenses

Under article 3 of Italian competition law, any market behavior whereby a dominant undertaking exploits its market power over its counterparts to gain over-competitive profit constitutes abuse. Typical cases of exploitative offenses are excessive pricing and monopoly leveraging. **22.17**

In cases of abuse of dominant position, the ICA starts the investigation by comparing the behavior under investigation with a benchmark behavior that it assumes to be lawful. This means that, for example, to evaluate if a company can be prosecuted for excessive pricing, it should first be decided what the correct remunerative price would have been, taking into account the effective costs borne by the company. Only once this comparison has been made, it is possible to determine whether the profit is over-competitive or not. **22.18**

Recently the ICA sanctioned SEA (the Company in charge of Milano Malpensa and Milano Linate airports) for its pricing policy related to its airport handling activities, which ICA found to be unfair and excessive. In particular, the ICA assumed that the pricing policy adopted by SEA was not "cost-oriented"; in fact the revenues were 55 percent higher than the economic value of the services sold.[9] **22.19**

[3] *Eni/Trans Tunisian Pipeline*, ICA Bulletin no. 5/2006 (February 15, 2006).
[4] Case 62/86 *AKZO Chemie v. Commission* [1991] ECR I-3359.
[5] *Mercato del calcestruzzo cellulare autoclavato*, ICA, Bulletin no. 40/2007 (October 24, 2007).
[6] *Diano/Tourist Ferry Boat-Caronte Shipping*, ICA, Bulletin no. 16/2002 (April 17, 2002).
[7] *TNT Post Italia v. Poste italiane*, ICA, Bulletin no. 48/2011 (December 14, 2012).
[8] *TNT Post Italia v. Poste italiane*, TAR Lazio, no. 5769 (June 25, 2012).
[9] *SEA v. Tariffe aeroportuali*, ICA, Bulletin no. 45/2008 (November 26, 2008).

22.20 In the *Railway Company/Rete Ferroviaria Italiana (RFI)*,[10] the ICA ruled that the conduct of RFI, which is in charge of the Italian railways, could be qualified as abusive because, by not according a due discount to the Railway Company, a competitor in the same market as Trenitalia (controlled by RFI), RFI imposed an excessive rental fee for the use of the rail infrastructure.

22.21 Other leading cases in this sector include *Ibar/Aeroporti di Roma*[11] and *Morosità pregresse Telecom*.[12]

C. Monopsony

22.22 Though there is no specific case law in Italy regarding monopsony, the principles elaborated under the monopsony theory were applied in the *APCA v. COMPAG*[13] where the ICA sanctioned four Italian sugar producers which had forced beet producers to use a different type of seed than the one they would have otherwise used. According to the ICA, the sugar producers abused their joint dominant position in the purchase of beets, although the dominant position was created by the Italian legislation.

D. Price discrimination

22.23 In general terms, price discrimination occurs when a dominant company applies different conditions to similar transactions with its customers (e.g. different prices for the same product or service). In other words, by applying different conditions to similar transactions a dominant undertaking may—as stated by article 3(1)(c) of Law no. 287—alter competition among its customers.

22.24 Price discrimination assumes specific relevance whenever the dominant undertaking is "vertically integrated" on the market and, on the one hand, sells its products or services to its customers while, on the other hand, competes with them (i.e. directly or through a subsidiary) in the downstream market. In fact, in such cases, the ICA shall evaluate if the price conditions that the dominant undertaking applies to its subsidiary (often difficult to identify) are similar to those it applies to its customers. If there are different price conditions, this conduct might be qualified as anticompetitive (and abusive).

22.25 In its case law, the ICA has often investigated such kinds of abuse and issued important decisions, especially in the postal and in the telecommunications markets. In the telecommunications market the ICA sanctioned, for example, the provider of the Italian telecommunication network, Telecom, for imposing high entry fees on other telecommunication providers, with the effect of impeding them from offering competitive prices to consumers (the fees imposed were in the same amount as the prices directly charged by Telecom to consumers).[14]

E. Dictating or influencing resale prices

22.26 There is no relevant case law regarding the unilateral conduct of dictating or influencing resale prices.

F. Tying arrangements

22.27 The ICA stated that if a dominant undertaking makes the sale of a certain product or service subject to the acquisition of another product or service (known as a "tying" or "tie-in")—that

[10] *Railway Company v. Rete Ferroviaria Italiana-Ferrovie dello Stato*, ICA, Bulletin no. 43/2008 (November 13, 2008).

[11] *Ibar v. Aeroporti di Roma*, ICA, Bulletin no. 6/1993 (March 17, 1993).

[12] *Morosità pregresse Telecom*, ICA, Bulletin no. 32/2008 (August 21, 2008).

[13] *APCA v. COMPAG*, ICA, Bulletin no. 13/1992 (July 6, 1992).

[14] *Infostrada v. Telecom Italia- Tecnologia Adsl*, ICA, Bulletin no.17-17/2011 (May 27, 2011).

is sold as a different product or service—it probably commits abuse of its dominant position if, by doing so, the undertaking intends to use its dominant position in the market to gain market power in another market, and in doing so marginalize other undertakings that already operate in the market of the "tied" products.

Of course, not all joint sales constitute abuse of the dominant position. The ICA verifies whether the two products or services can be sold separately, and if their joint sale entails coercion by means of refusal to sell them separately or by reducing/eliminating discounts or other benefits if they were bought separately. **22.28**

In the leading case *Gruppo Sicurezza v. Aeroporti di Roma (AR)*,[15] the Authority fined AR—the management company of Rome airport—for having abused its dominant position by imposing a flat fee for services "on demand," even if the services were not required. **22.29**

Recently, the ICA prosecuted Toscana Energia, which is active in the distribution of gas for residential use, for imposing on its customers the joint purchase of the connection to the gas network and the construction of a gas pipes installation on private property. However, the ICA did not take a definitive stance on this behavior and accepted the commitments proposed by Toscana Energia.[16] **22.30**

G. Exclusive dealing

In a few cases, the ICA prosecuted agreements between a dominant undertaking and its purchaser by which a "*de facto* exclusive clause" had been agreed upon. In *Enel v. Unapace*,[17] the ICA sanctioned Enel for including a clause in its contracts that allowed Enel to align its commercial proposals with those of its competitors. In doing so, Enel knew its competitors' market strategy and could, therefore, influence competition in the market. For the same reason, the ICA fined Telecom Italia[18] (the decision was confirmed by the Consiglio di Stato) because it had introduced a contractual clause that obliged its customers to communicate to Telecom Italia the offers received by other competing operators. **22.31**

H. Refusal to deal

The refusal to deal may constitute an abuse of market power if a company refuses to sell to another undertaking a product or service required by the latter to enter a specific market, and this refusal is based on the intention to exclude the interested buyer from that market. **22.32**

When investigating this type of abuse, the ICA must, nevertheless, take into consideration the negotiating autonomy of the undertaking, since under Italian law any person or company is completely free to decide whether to deal with other parties or not. Aware of this principle, in determining whether the refusal to deal constitutes market abuse or an expression of commercial autonomy, the Italian Competition Authority has focused its attention on two relevant issues: (i) whether the denial is based on an exclusionary intent; and (ii) whether there is any risk of monopolization of the relevant market once the "refused buyer" has been excluded. **22.33**

One of the most recent decisions concerning a refusal to deal is *Sapec Agro v. Bayer Helm*.[19] The ICA found that Bayer had adopted an exclusionary strategy to the detriment of its competitors, as it blocked their access to studies in Bayer's possession that were essential for obtaining market authorization renewals. The result of this strategy was that Bayer's competitors, who **22.34**

[15] *Gruppo Sicurezza v. Aeroporti di Roma*, ICA, Bulletin no. 13/1993 (November 17, 1993).
[16] *Pace Strade v. Toscana gas*, ICA, Bulletin no. 41/2008 (October 30, 2008).
[17] *Enel v. Unapace*, ICA, Bulletin no. 13-14/1999 (April 9, 1999).
[18] *Comportamenti abusivi di Telecom Italia*, ICA, Bulletin no. 47/2004 (November 16, 2004).
[19] *Sapec Agro v. Bayer Helm*, ICA, Bulletin no. 26/2011 (June 28, 2011).

had even put together a task force to negotiate the access to these studies, were forced out of the market because of their inability to renew the authorizations.

I. Essential facilities

22.35 The principles that regulate the refusal to deal have been used by the ICA to prosecute unjustified denial of access to an essential facility. An "essential facility" is defined as an infrastructure that is not easily duplicable by the competitors and the use of which is essential for those competitors to operate in the same or in a linked market. The ICA has stated in its practice that for an infrastructure to be qualified as "essential" it must be non-duplicable at affordable time and cost. Furthermore, refusal to grant access to such infrastructure does not give rise to an abuse of dominant position if it is based on objective and non-discriminatory reasons.

22.36 However, in Italy, the essential facility doctrine intersects with article 2597 of the Italian Civil Code which obliges the monopolist to deal with all potential purchasers by adopting the necessary measures to face the demand.

22.37 The most relevant decisions are *Eni v. Trans Tunisian Pipeline*[20] and *Tele2 v. Tim-Vodafone-Wind* of September 29, 2009.[21] The ICA, in the first decision, sanctioned Eni for interrupting the expansion of pipeline thus excluding new entrants, and, in the second one, fined Tim-Vodafone-Wind for hindering the resale of termination at the wholesale level, thus eliminating any alternative supply of wholesale termination.

J. Bundling (including loyalty and market share discounts)

22.38 Product bundling occurs when an undertaking offers several products for sale as one combined product at a price that is lower than the sum of the prices of each of the "bundled" products. This marketing behavior may constitute abuse if practiced by a dominant undertaking because—like tying—bundling can be used by a dominant undertaking as a leverage in one market to gain power in another market, to the disadvantage of its competitors operating on the market for the "tied" product.

22.39 Even loyalty discounts may constitute an abuse if the dominant undertaking makes discounts subject to the customer's agreeing not to purchase from the competitors. In doing this, the dominant undertaking forecloses the distribution channels and pushes its competitors out from the market. Furthermore, such conduct is not economically rational since discounts are not granted with regard to the quantity bought but to customer loyalty. However, even discounts based on the quantity acquired (target discounts) may constitute an abuse if the discount aims to acquire the loyalty of purchasers. The typical abuse is when a dominant company gives a discount not only for purchases that exceed the target agreed but also on the initial quantity of products bought. In such cases, the purchaser will not change the supplier because otherwise it would lose the discount granted. That was the case, for example, in the ICA Decision in *Pepsico v. Coca-Cola*.[22]

K. Standard-setting groups (disclosure requirements, licensing arrangements, and licensing pools)

22.40 There is no direct case law on standard-setting groups. However, it is worth noting that, on more than one occasion, the ICA has also applied the essential facility doctrine to intangible assets that are necessary to offer a certain kind of product or service.

---

[20] *Eni v. Trans Tunisian Pipeline*, ICA, Bulletin no. 3/2011 (February 15, 2006).

[21] *Tele2 v. Tim-Vodafone-Wind*, ICA, Bulletin no. 39/2009 (September 29, 2009).

[22] *Pepsico foods and beverages international- IBG Sud v. Coca-Cola*, ICA, Bulletin no. 49/1999 (December 7, 1999).

That was the case, for example, in the decision on Pfizer, a leader in the pharmaceutical market, which was fined EUR 10.6 million for abuse of dominant position because it used an exclusionary strategy to make it more difficult (in terms of time and costs) for generic medicines for glaucoma to enter the market by: (i) prolonging its patent protection from September 2009 to January 2012; and (ii) creating uncertainty among generic drug manufacturers about the possibility of commercializing equivalent specialist drugs by giving numerous warnings concerning administrative and civil disputes that would be brought if the generic medicines were to be commercialized before the new expiration date for its medicine patent protection. **22.41**

L. Customer termination

Customer termination constitutes a variant of refusal to deal. Furthermore, in Italy, this behavior could constitute an abuse of economic dependence on the basis of article 9 of Law No. 192/1998. **22.42**

M. Termination of intermediaries (retailers, wholesalers, dealers, and value-added resellers, agents, and brokers)

There is no relevant case law on this subject. However, the general principles of refusal to deal, explained in Section I.H, are generally applicable. **22.43**

N. Termination of relationships with competitors

There is no relevant case law on this subject. However, general principles of the refusal to deal, explained under Section I.H, are generally applicable. **22.44**

O. Exemptions

The ICA tends to follow the regulations issued by the European Commission on certain categories of horizontal or vertical agreements. These regulations lay down the conditions under which such agreements, though containing restrictions on competition, may qualify for automatic exemption from the provisions of article 101(1) TFEU (also known as "block exemptions"). **22.45**

In general terms, the conditions that allow for exemption concern the market share held by companies party to the agreement, on the one hand, and the absence of certain restrictions on competition that are deemed as being particularly offensive, on the other. **22.46**

However, any agreement, decision, or concerted practice subject to prohibitions pursuant to article 101(1) TFEU that does not benefit from block exemption may be considered compliant with competition law when it meets certain requirements, which are listed in article 101(3) TFEU. **22.47**

The option of voluntarily notifying an agreement to the European Commission in order to be granted individual exemption under article 101(3) TFEU was abolished with the coming into force of Regulation 1/2003. Even absent the Regulation, the ICA's extensive interpretation of the notion of effect on EU trade and consequent application, at the national level, of article 101 TFEU instead of article 2 of Law no. 287 would result in a decline in the number of exemption granted. The ICA thus implicitly recognizes the European principle that abolished individual exemptions. **22.48**

Without an explicit decision by the European Commission or by the ICA certifying that an agreement may be granted exemption, it is now the responsibility of companies and their lawyers to assess whether agreements not covered by block exemption meet requirements set by article 101(3) TFEU. **22.49**

II. Dealing with competitors

22.50 The ICA investigates every agreement or concerted practice between undertakings carried out for anticompetitive purposes, as well as decisions of associations of undertakings, even if adopted on the basis of statutory provisions ("cartels").

22.51 In particular, article 3 of Law no. 287 prohibits any agreement that has as its object (or effect): (a) fixing prices or contractual conditions; (b) foreclosures of production and of technological progress; (c) territorial or customer allocation; (d) discrimination between dealers for similar services; (e) subordination of contracts to the acceptance of supplementary services.

22.52 The application of this legislation, however, needs some clarification. First of all, by the term "undertaking" the ICA means any entity that practices economic activities, irrespective of its qualification. This means that even individuals or associations may be qualified as undertakings on the basis of the analysis of their activities, even if they are not undertakings of the basis of the Italian Civil Code. Recently, for example, the ICA opened a proceeding against the Consiglio notarile di Milano whose purpose is to ensure that notaries respect their duties and professionalism.

22.53 Even the notion of "agreement" has a different meaning from that usually recognized in contractual legislation. In fact, for the ICA, an anticompetitive agreement may occur even if there is only verbal and informal consent between different undertakings—that would not be sufficient to constitute a contractual obligation—by which they decide to act on the market in a predetermined manner.

22.54 This means that even apparently unilateral behavior, normally considered as abuse, might be enforced as cartels if it is carried out in coordination with another undertaking. This is the case of concerted practices that occur when (i) there has been contact between different undertakings, whereby (ii) the undertakings reciprocally lifted any uncertainty about their strategies and (iii) influenced their marketing behavior. That means that the mere parallelism of behavior is not sufficient to prove that a concerted practice has occurred, unless coordination is the only explanation for such a parallelism.

22.55 Cartel enforcement has been a major priority in recent years, with the ICA that focused its enforcement especially on joint purchasing agreements and interlocking directorates. During 2011, the ICA issued fines amounting to approximately EUR 100 million. The highest fine ever issued was EUR 361,229,379.15 in the decision *RC Auto*.[23]

A. Horizontal price fixing (including advanced announcements of price or product changes)

22.56 A horizontal cartel occurs when the undertaking involved competes in the same relevant market. These cartels are assumed to be very dangerous for competition and for consumers.

22.57 The most seriously prosecuted cartels concern price fixing. In fact, agreements on the price of competing products are assumed to be one of the most relevant competition factors and result in an immediate harm to consumers.

22.58 Price fixing may be relevant from different points of view, for example, (i) the direct or indirect fixing of selling or purchasing price, (ii) the agreement on price variations, and (iii) the agreement on price-structure determination.

[23] *RC Auto*, ICA, Bulletin no. 30/2000 (July 28, 2000).

One of the most recent decisions is *Logistica Internazionale*,[24] where the ICA sanctioned nineteen undertakings active in the international freight forwarding market for coordinating price increases during more than twenty meetings of their trade association. **22.59**

B. Horizontal agreements to allocate customers or territories; agreements not to compete

In addition to price fixing, market portioning—with regard to customers or territories—constitutes one of the most dangerous cartels since it is capable to completely eliminate competition between undertakings. These types of conduct assume relevance because they are able to create barriers to the realization of the European market. **22.60**

This was, for example, the case of the ICA decision of May 30, 2012 that sanctioned Repower, EGL, and Tirreno Power for giving rise to an output rotation mechanism that allowed them to eliminate the reciprocal competitive pressure and make over-competitive profits.[25] **22.61**

In another decision, the ICA sanctioned undertaking participating in a cartel for limiting their output. These agreements, in fact, are often linked to price fixing or market portioning cartels, and enable the undertakings involved to maintain constant prices.[26] **22.62**

C. Horizontal boycotts

Italian antitrust law prohibits agreements between competitors not to purchase from, or supply to, specific businesses, with the clear intent of punishing or impeding the market entry or growth of competitors. Horizontal boycotts are also illegal under article 2598 of the Italian Civil Code. **22.63**

A few years ago, the ICA sanctioned the collective boycott by the National Association of Labor Consultants (ANCL, *Associazione Nazionale Consulenti del Lavoro*), which had asked its members (labor consultants) to break off their relation with Inaz Paghe, a company that in 1997 started providing computerized wage and salary management services. The clear intent of the action was to hamper competition from Inaz Paghe on the software market.[27] **22.64**

D. Joint ventures and other competitive collaborations

Under Italian antitrust law, a clear distinction must be made between a cooperative and a concentrative joint venture. The latter, so called *full-function joint venture*, is examined only under the relevant merger regulation. **22.65**

Cooperative joint ventures are scrutinized under articles 2 and 4 of Italian antitrust law to assess the risk of coordination between the parent companies. From this point of view, it must be determined if such companies are actual or potential competitors. In doing so, the ICA also investigates the relationships between the parent companies' market activities and those of the joint venture, the range of the joint venture's activities, and the extent to which the parent companies agree not to compete with the joint venture. **22.66**

However, even joint ventures between competing undertakings are not always prohibited, since, under some circumstances, they are also capable of creating pro-competitive effects. The ICA evaluates these agreements in light of the European block exemption regulations **22.67**

---

[24] *Logistica Internazionale*, ICA, Bulletin no. 24/2011 (June 15, 2011).

[25] *Repower Italia- Prezzo dispacciamento energia elettrica centro sud*, ICA, Bulletin no. 22/2012 (May 30, 2012).

[26] *Mercato del calcestruzzo*, ICA, Bulletin no. 31/2004 (July 29, 2004).

[27] *Inal paghe v. Associazione Nazionale Consulenti del Lavoro*, ICA, Bulletin no. 5/2000 (February 3, 2000).

which cover specialization agreements (Commission Regulation 1218/2010[28]) and research and development agreements (Commission Regulation 1217/2010[29]).

22.68 The analysis of these collaborations is focused on various factors, such as: (a) market shares of the undertakings participating; (b) market structure; (c) possible foreclosure effect on competitors; (d) spill-over effects.

22.69 One of the most recent ICA's investigations into these factors is *FVH-Liquigas-Butangas* in which the undertakings concerned created a joint venture for a warehouse that raised competition concerns for possible foreclosure effects and information exchanges.[30]

22.70 In its investigations, the ICA focused on temporary joint venture arrangements—a particular kind of collaboration between competitors. This collaboration often occurs during public tenders, when competing undertakings collaborate to present a single offer. From the civil law point of view, temporary joint venture agreement can be pro-competitive because it encourages smaller undertakings to participate in these tenders in association with other competitors. However, from a different point of view, this collaboration could be illegal and constitute an anticompetitive cartel because it reduces the number of competitors participating in the tender.

22.71 To settle this issue, in its practice, the ICA stated that a TJV is lawful if a participant was unable to fulfill the object of the tender by acting alone or to meet the technical requisites to participate in the tender.

22.72 To date, three of ICA's most recent five decisions concern participation in tenders. In particular, the ICA sanctioned E.ON Rete and Linea Distribuzione because they jointly participated in a public tender, constituting a temporary joint venture with the intention of sharing the duties on the basis of the *status quo ante*, eliminating competition between them.[31] The same reasons underlie ICA decisions in *Gare Assicurative ASL and Aziende Ospedaliere Campane*[32] and *Gara d'Appalto per la sanità per le apparecchiature per la risonanza magnetica*.[33]

E. Trade associations

22.73 Italian antitrust law does not prohibit companies from attending meetings with competitors on the premise of trade associations. However, resolutions issued by trade associations, in whatever legal form (and irrespective of whether they are binding on the members, consist in the statutory rules of the association, or only consist in recommendations such as circulars, memos, or directives), are deemed to be agreements restricting competition whenever they induce associates effectively to coordinate their market behavior.

22.74 Such effect can be achieved, for example, by decisions that induce the members to coordinate their conduct or require them to adopt specific pricing strategies, regularly exchange confidential information, or refrain from entering into specific markets. It is important to

[28] Commission Regulation No. 1218/2010 on the application of Article 101(3) of the Treaty on the Functioning of the European Union to certain categories of specialisation agreements (December 14, 2010).

[29] Commission Regulation No. 1217/2010 on the application of Article 101(3) of the Treaty on the Functioning of the European Union to certain categories of research and development agreements (December 14, 2010).

[30] *FVH-Liquigas-Butangas-Quiris/I.PE.M.*, ICA, Bulletin no. 20/2009 (May 20, 2009).

[31] *Comune di Casalmaggiore-gara per l'affidamento del servizio di distribuzione del gas*, ICA, Bulletin no. 31/2012 (August 8, 2012).

[32] *Gare Assicurative ASL and Aziende Ospedaliere Campane*, ICA, Bulletin no. 39/2011 (September 28, 2011).

[33] *Gara d'Appalto per la sanità per le apparecchiature per la risonanza magnetica*, ICA, Bulletin no. 33-34/2011 (August 4, 2011).

stress how even informal side meetings held on the occasion of official trade association conventions may be subject to the application of antitrust regulations. Furthermore, it will be necessary to monitor the activities that take place within the trade associations and during other social occasions, even when carried out in an institutional context. In particular, it will be necessary to ensure that any information exchanged in such context does not have the effect of reducing market uncertainty regarding recommended retail prices for the sale of products or services.

Trade associations' decisions have been one of the most investigated cartels. That was the case, for example, of the decision on baby milk of March 2, 2000, whereby the ICA sanctioned many baby milk manufacturers for preventing baby milk from being sold through the major supermarkets and for ensuring that their products would only be sold through pharmacies, charging Italian consumers (up to three times) higher prices than those charged for the same products by the same companies in other European countries. **22.75**

Regarding trade association, the ICA recently sanctioned a number of pasta producers for setting up, with the Italian Pasta Manufacturers Association, an anticompetitive arrangement whereby they agreed to pass on price increases for pasta products to distributors. In this case, the trade associations played a crucial role: they sent out a circular letter encouraging their members to apply uniform price increases and advising the pasta industry, customers, and the public of the increases agreed. **22.76**

F. Interlocking directorates

There is no relevant case law on this issue. **22.77**

G. Facilitating practices

Facilitating practices may be investigated by the ICA if, by adopting softer coordination—different from direct price fixing or market portioning—they infringe Italian antitrust legislation. There is no relevant case law in this area except for cases related to information exchange. **22.78**

H. Information exchange

The only type of facilitating practices investigated by the ICA is exchange of confidential business information, in any given form, whereby competing undertakings try to disguise anticompetitive coordination under lawful communication. **22.79**

In general terms, exchange of confidential data (e.g. production or sales data regarding volume or value, costs or prices, including transportation costs and reference price lists) is viewed as restrictive. As such, it is severely prohibited whenever it reveals future market behavior to be adopted insofar as it allows companies to coordinate their conduct in order to restrict competition. **22.80**

However, it must be noted that information exchange might be lawful and useful if it allows "neutral" knowledge of the market. This kind of information exchange, which often takes place by data room consultations, is even pro-competitive if it fosters competition in the market concerned. Otherwise, usually in oligopolistic markets, even such information exchange may raise concerns about competition when it allows the undertakings to foresee competitors' behaviors. That was the case of the *RC Auto*[34] and *Ras-Generali/IAMA Consulting*.[35] **22.81**

[34] *RC Auto*, ICA, Bulletin no. 30/2000 (July 28, 2000).

[35] *Ras-Generali /IAMA Consulting*, ICA, Bulletin no. 40/2004 (September 30, 2004).

The latter decision was annulled by the TAR Lazio[36] because the information exchanged was public and did not remove the uncertainty as to the future commercial behavior of the competitors.

I. Joint purchasing agreements

22.82 Joint purchasing agreements have been analyzed by the ICA to evaluate if they might strengthen the buying power of the involved undertakings (i.e. if they are an abuse of such power) and eliminate competition through the standardization of the respective costs leading to price alignment.

22.83 The most relevant decision of the ICA is *Coop Italia/Conad/Italia Distribuzione* of March 29, 2001,[37] where the ICA authorized, until 2004, the agreement under which the undertaking Italia Distribuzione treats with suppliers the conditions of purchases made by companies that are part of the cooperative system Coop-Conad.

J. Joint lobbying/regulatory/legislative efforts

22.84 Joint lobbying does not raise antitrust issues in the Italian antitrust law system.

III. General issues

A. Jurisdiction and applicable law (including sector-specific competition regulation)

22.85 The ICA, based in Rome, is responsible for enforcing Italian antitrust law as well as EU competition law through a coordination mechanism with other European Antitrust Authorities (European Competition Network).

22.86 In particular, the ICA exercises its jurisdiction in relation to abuses and cartels that distort competition in Italy. In applying EU competition law, the ICA also assesses whether the abuse or cartel harms inter-European exchanges.

B. Antitrust system

(i) Name of agency/agencies

22.87 In Italy, the ICA enforces antitrust legislation. It is independent from the Government, and ICA Board members are appointed jointly by the presidents of the two chambers of the Italian Parliament. In general, the ICA can investigate any economic sector. This independence gives the ICA a considerable amount of autonomy.

22.88 When the ICA deals with regulated sectors (banks, insurance, communications) it must follow specific procedural rules.

22.89 In fact, when enforcing antitrust legislation in the course of investigations in the telecommunication sector, the ICA must ask, before issuing a final decision, for the (substantially binding) opinion of the regulatory authority, Autorità per le Garanzie nelle Telecomunicazioni (AGCOM). In the case of investigations in the insurance sector, the Authority must ask for the opinion of the Institute for Insurance Supervision (IVASS, *Istituto per la Vigilanza sulle Assicurazioni*).

22.90 Lastly, it is worth analyzing the procedure followed by the Authority when investigating the banking sector. The ICA and the Bank of Italy have signed a cooperation agreement

[36] *Ras-Generali/IAMA Consulting*, TAR Lazio, Case no. 6088 (August 8, 2005).
[37] *Coop Italia/Conad/Italia Distribuzione*, ICA, Bulletin no. 13/2001 (March 29, 2001).

which regulates the relationship between the two institutions with regards to procedures to be undertaken in antitrust enforcement activities dealing with banks and finance companies. The agreement provides for detailed procedures in the case of mergers and, as far as applicable, in the case of abuses and restrictive agreements.

(ii) Staff size and budget

The ICA is a collegiate administrative body headed by a president and composed of two other members (the composition of the Board has been recently reduced from five to three members). It has 277 professional and administrative staff. **22.91**

Since December 2012, the ICA's budget has come from: (i) public coffers (around EUR 17 million per year); (ii) private contributions in the form of fees from undertakings engaged in mergers and/or takeovers; (iii) fines issued for unfair marketing practices; and (iv) contributions from other authorities (around EUR 8 million per year). **22.92**

From 2013, the ICA budget comes from a tax (0.08 per 1,000) that will be imposed on undertakings with an annual turnover of over EUR 50 million. **22.93**

(iii) Recent enforcement actions and trends

In the recent years, the ICA, in investigating market abuses, has focused especially on ex-monopolistic markets (energy, post, transports, communications), while, in investigating cartels, it has given particular attention to trade association decisions and information exchanges that might cause price increases and market foreclosures. **22.94**

C. Private litigation

It is widely acknowledged that "private enforcement" of EU and national competition rules—i.e. actions brought before national courts by private citizens or businesses that have suffered losses as a result of a breach of these rules—plays an important role in the full effectiveness of the antitrust legislation. **22.95**

However, despite the fact that in 2001 the European Court of Justice clarified that any individual is entitled to claim damages caused by a contract (or by a conduct) liable to restrict or distort competition, even if that individual is a party to that contract, actions for damages are still very rare in Italy. **22.96**

Indeed, the first Italian case law interpreted competition rules as being aimed only at protecting undertakings from the unfair conduct of their competitors, while consumers did not have the specific "right to free and fair competition." Only in 2005 did the Supreme Court clarify that the Competition Act is not only "the law of undertakings," but rather a law of every single person in the market, and that consumers also have an interest in the protection of effective competition and may therefore claim damages by alleging the violation of this "specific right." Nevertheless the overall number of judgments regarding damages awarded to consumers has been still relatively low. **22.97**

One of the main problems in the development of private enforcement in Italy is the long period of time needed to obtain a judgment. This time lag benefits the defendants and jeopardizes the chances of effectively recovering the damages suffered as a result of an antitrust infringement, as small undertakings and/or individual consumers who have suffered relatively low-value damage are often deterred from bringing action for damages due to the costs and delays involved. **22.98**

The length of time required for a civil judgment largely depends on the objective complexity of the case (the factual and economic analysis behind the antitrust case), as well as on the need to ensure that all interested parties can fully and effectively exercise their "right of defense." Nonetheless, this time also depends on certain procedural rules which, on the one **22.99** hand, increase legal uncertainty and, on the other, are also improperly used by the defendants and encourage the adoption of delay tactics.

22.100 It must be noted that an important step towards increased effectiveness of "private" enforcement has been the entry into force of "class action," regulated by article 140-bis of the Consumer Code, which allows consumers to bring a collective action before the lower courts (*tribunali*)—through qualified entities, such as consumer associations—and will hopefully contribute to facilitating consumers' access to compensation for damages suffered as a result of antitrust infringement.

D. Follow-on litigation (includes role of agency determinations of liability for follow-on litigation)

22.101 National "private enforcement" case law initially dealt almost exclusively with "follow-on" cases brought by competitors. In the first successful action for damages, a telecommunication Company (Telsystem) alleged that the Italian monopolist (SIP, now Telecom Italia) had abused its dominant position by refusing to connect Telsystem's clients to its direct local network, which was an "essential facility" for Telsystem, necessary for providing new services to "closed users groups" (i.e. services enabling clients belonging to a certain organization to communicate at the cost of a local call even when they are located in different cities). The Court of Appeal of Milan found that the incumbent had abused its dominant position and awarded Telsystem damages amounting to approximately EUR 1.8 million, partly comprising the costs borne by Telsystem to launch its new service and partly representing the lost profits that Telsystem would have made if it had not been for Telecom Italia's abuse.[38]

22.102 The Telsystem action followed a previous ICA infringement decision.[39] Indeed, even if the ICA's decisions are not legally binding, in practice, they play an essential role both as a proof of the infringement and of the causal link between the defendant's conduct and the damage caused.

22.103 In the national case law there are, also, some (isolated) examples of successful "stand-alone" actions. In *Bluvacanze*, a package holiday retailer alleged that certain tour operators had engaged in a concerted practice in violation of article 2 of Law no. 287 by refusing to grant Bluvacanze access to their online reservation system in "retaliation" for the claimant's aggressive pricing policy. Bluvacanze succeeded in providing evidence of the tour operators' restrictive practice, and the Court of Appeal of Milan awarded Bluvacanze damages of approximately EUR 184,000 calculated on the basis of the "before and after method" (i.e. on the basis of the claimant's sales before and after the exclusion, and on the retail margin that had been agreed between the claimant and the defendants), as well as damages of approximately EUR 50,000 for the loss of reputation.[40]

22.104 The most significant actions brought by consumers were those following the ICA's 2000 decision which condemned several insurance companies (representing jointly more than 80 percent of the market) for systematically exchanging information between 1993 and 1999 regarding the car insurance policies market. According to the ICA, this agreement enabled the interested insurance companies to coordinate their commercial strategy and to set the premiums paid by consumers at a level significantly higher than what it would have been without the unlawful conduct. Dealing with an agreement whose purpose was to restrict competition, the ICA did not deem it necessary to investigate the effects of the concerted practice and did not precisely quantify the price increase implemented by each company. Nevertheless, the ICA ascertained, by also taking into account the average price of car insurance policies in

---

[38] *Telsystem S.p.A c. SIP S.p.A*, Court of Appeal Milan (July 18, 1995).

[39] *Telesystem/SIP*, ICA, Bullettin no. 1-2/1995 (January 10, 1995).

[40] *Blucavanze*, Court of Appeal Milan (July 11, 2003).

other EU member states, that the unlawful exchange of information had produced an average increase of 20 percent in the price of premiums.[41] After that decision, several insurance policy holders sued their respective insurance companies to obtain compensation amounting to 20 percent of the policy's premium (i.e. the difference between the premium paid and the premium that they would have paid, without the infringement).

With regard to the assessment of the merits, and in particular the existence of the infringement, case law has, for a long time, made it clear that the findings and the decisions of the administrative authorities have an important authoritative value, especially when delivered by a technically qualified entity such as the ICA. Therefore, since the first actions for damages, the courts have often relied upon the ICA's decisions to prove an infringement, even though those decisions were, in theory, not legally binding. This has enabled the courts to increase the speed of ascertaining a violation, at least in follow-on actions. Nonetheless, the quantification of damages still demands significant effort from the courts, due to the "compensatory" nature of antitrust damages (which excludes any "punitive" quantification and therefore requires that damages must be strictly related to the loss suffered by the plaintiff) and the specific nature of competition authorities' decisions. In fact, even when ascertaining if certain behavior infringes competition rules and damages competition, the authorities' decisions hardly ever give a clear indication of the effects of the behavior on a single competitor (or, even less, on consumers). Therefore, even in follow-on actions, it remains up to the plaintiff to prove both the existence of a significant effect (harm) and the "causality" between the infringement and the harm. **22.105**

E. Arbitration and alternative dispute resolution

Arbitration is not relevant to public enforcement of antitrust legislation. It could, at most, assume relevance in settling private litigation. **22.106**

F. Remedies

Undertakings involved in antitrust proceedings for abuses of dominant position or for participating in an anticompetitive behavior may submit commitments to the ICA in which they state their intention to terminate the anticompetitive activity under investigation within three months from the notification of the start of the proceedings. Following a market test of the commitments, if the ICA considers that the submitted commitments are enough to remove any infringement concerns, it makes the commitments binding and closes the proceedings without ascertaining the infringement. **22.107**

However, the ICA may reject the submitted commitments if the undertakings are involved in serious anticompetitive infringement and/or if the commitments are unsuitable to removing the anticompetitive concerns investigated by the Authority. **22.108**

Furthermore, once the commitments are made binding by the ICA, the undertakings concerned may be sanctioned if these commitments are infringed. The ICA can restart the proceedings if: (i) there is a relevant change in one of the elements on which the decision is based; (ii) there is an infringement of the commitments; or (ii) the information provided by the parties is incomplete, incorrect, or misleading. **22.109**

(i) Civil liability

While commitments are used by undertakings involved in antitrust proceedings to avoid sanctions, the use of these commitments renders private "follow-on" litigation more difficult. In fact, even if commitments decisions do not grant civil immunity, it is more difficult for **22.110**

---

41 *RC Auto*, ICA, Bulletin no. 30/2000 (July 28, 2000).

the parties that want to recover damages arising from an antitrust infringement to prove the anticompetitive relevance of a marketing behavior without a formal finding made by the ICA also because there is a limited access to file information.

(ii) Criminal liability

22.111 Under Italian antitrust legislation there is no criminal liability for anticompetitive behaviors.

G. Leniency and immunity

22.112 The ICA, pursuant to article 15 of Law no. 287, adopted an Immunity and Leniency Program that—in line with the one provided by European Legislation—applies to undertakings that took part in a cartel and that spontaneously provide the ICA with sufficient information to prove the existence of the cartel. The Program focuses on cartels that give rise—through a secret agreement or concerted practice—to price fixing, output foreclosure, or market portioning.

22.113 Leniency applicants, or whistle blowers, are usually rewarded for their collaboration if it allows the ICA to discover and investigate a secret cartel, with full immunity or reduced sanctions.

22.114 However, the Program provides that only the first whistle blower will be awarded such substantial reductions. Undertakings that subsequently collaborate with the ICA may only obtain a reduction if they contribute stronger evidence than the Authority already has at its disposal.

22.115 Leniency applicants must submit a written request to the ICA and give notice of all the evidence they possess that can lead to discovering a cartel. Only complete applications are useful in obtaining full immunity.

22.116 However, applicants can start their collaboration by requesting a marker and asking the Authority to give them a deadline by which they must provide all the other relevant information.

22.117 The Leniency Program obliges leniency applicants to fully cooperate with the ICA during the investigations and the proceedings. They usually have to withdraw from the cartel, unless the Authority asks the applicant to do otherwise so as to collect further evidence. Moreover the applicants could not disclosure their application to the Leniency Program.

22.118 A hotly debated issue related to leniency applications concerns the confidentiality of documents provided by an undertaking at the moment of its application. In fact, while corporate statements are confidential—at least until the statement of the objection—all other document might be disclosed by the Authority to directly interested third parties.

22.119 In recent years leniency applications have given rise to debate in some very important Italian antitrust proceedings. These cases are: *Servizi di agenzia marittima*,[42] *Logistica Internazionale*,[43] and *Vendita al dettaglio di prodotti cosmetici*.[44]

[42] *Servizi di agenzia marittima*, ICA, Bulletin no. 9/2012 (February 22, 2012). The ICA sanctioned fifteen companies and two trade associations, active in the field of maritime agency services, to more than EUR 4 million, for a secret cartel to fix agency's price lasted over five years.

[43] *Logistica Internazionale*, ICA, Bulletin no. 24/2011 (June 15, 2011). The ICA sanctioned nineteen companies operating in the field of international shipments for having restricted competition by agreeing on the price increases to be charged to the customers.

[44] *Vendita al dettaglio di prodotti cosmetici*, ICA, Bulletin no. 49/2010 (December 15, 2010). The ICA fined, for having restricted competition, fifteen cosmetics enterprises that agreed on list-price increases.

H. Document creation and retention

Under Italian antitrust law, companies under investigation can file memorandums, notes, and documents and have the right of access to all the documents retained by the Authority. **22.120**

Contrary to what happens in many other European jurisdictions, as well as at the European Commission level, in Italy, access to the case file, and to all the documents it contains, is very widespread. In fact, all parties "directly involved" in the proceedings have the right to access all documents created or retained by the ICA from the launch of the investigation, rather than from the notification of the statement of objection. **22.121**

Only documents containing sensitive commercial information and other documents redacted (notes, studies, etc.) by the ICA are not accessible. However, parties intending to preserve sensitive commercial information and business secrets contained in a document retained by the Authority shall file a specific and duly motivated request to subtract them to the third party right of access. **22.122**

If the Authority refuses a party access to the case file, or does not examine the request within thirty days from the filing, the party can appeal to the TAR Lazio within thirty days from the expressed or silent refusal. **22.123**

23

JAPAN

Steve Harris and Akira Inoue

Winston & Strawn L.L.P. and Baker & McKenzie L.L.P.

Introduction

23.01 The Japanese antitrust system was largely inspired by the US model as can be seen from its main legislation, the Act on Prohibition of Private Monopolization and Maintenance of Fair Trade (JAA).[1] The infringements covered by the JAA can be broken down into four categories:

(1) private monopolization: exclusion or control of the business activities of other undertakings, which substantially restrains trade (art. 2(5) JAA);

[1] The Law Concerning Prohibition of Private Monopolization and Maintenance of Fair Trade (Law No. 54 of April 14, 1947, as amended).

(2) unreasonable restraints of trade: horizontal restrictions including cartels and bid-rigging (art. 2(6) JAA);
(3) unfair trade practices: specific types of conduct that tend to impede competition, as designated by the JFTC (art. 2(9) JAA), which are enforceable regardless of the firm's market power;
(4) acquisitions or holding of stocks, mergers and acquisitions, transfers of businesses, and similar corporate actions that cause excessive concentration of economic power or that may substantially restrain competition (arts. 9 and 10 JAA).

In this Chapter, the prohibitions contained in the JAA are presented according to whether the firm is acting alone or together with other competitor(s). **23.02**

The JAA was enacted in 1947 and led to the creation of the country's only antitrust agency, the Japan Fair Trade Commission (JFTC), the same year. Amendments to the JAA as well as enforcement guidelines have been introduced over the years to modernize the system, including increasing the amount and scope of administrative surcharges (fines) and creating a leniency regime in 2005. **23.03**

Japan is one of the few jurisdictions where individuals involved in antitrust infringements can be criminally prosecuted. However, no criminal penalties have been imposed to date. In practice, the JFTC enforces the antitrust rules by issuing cease-and-desist orders, and sometimes by imposing fines through surcharge orders. **23.04**

As illustrated below in Section III.B, fines imposed by the JFTC have risen tremendously during recent years. In particular, facing the recent economic downturn, the JFTC has resolved to protect medium-and-small enterprises against exclusionary conduct of bigger companies. The JFTC is expected to remain active in the international antitrust arena, with its investigations of international cartels as well as inter-agency cooperation through the International Competition Network (ICN). **23.05**

Japan's antitrust regime is growing stronger and is now generally seen as a way to establish a more liberal economic society through transparent rules of law. There remain, however, calls for greater predictability of enforcement actions and enhanced protections of procedural due process. The attitude of the government toward antitrust enforcement in the wake of the elections of December 2012 remains to be determined. In 2010, a bill containing proposed amendments to the JAA was submitted to the Diet, which included greater procedural due process guarantees in connection with JFTC proceedings. That bill has not yet been debated in the Diet and is expected to be submitted again in 2013. **23.06**

I. Acting alone

Under the JAA, unilateral conduct may constitute either an unfair trade practice or private monopolization. However, private monopolization alone applies to the assessment of conduct not covered by the Designation of Unfair Trade Practices (discussed below) which has an exclusionary effect. According to a recent summary provided by the JFTC,[2] the JFTC has taken an increasingly aggressive enforcement stance with regard to certain distribution and sales practices, including abuses of a superior bargaining position and unjust low price **23.07**

[2] See: http://www.jftc.go.jp/en/pressreleases/yearly2013/may/AMAinFY2012_Summary.files/AMAinFY2012_Summary.pdf

sales. Both private monopolization and unfair trade practices can apply to exploitative and exclusionary offenses.

A. Predatory pricing

23.08 Article 2(9)(3) of the Act on Prohibition of Private Monopolization and Maintenance of Fair Trade and article 6 of the Designation of Unfair Trade Practices[3] announced by the Japan Fair Trade Commission, classify the following business conduct as unjust low-price sales that constitute an unfair trade practice, and therefore a violation of the JAA:

> [W]ithout justifiable grounds, supplying goods or services continuously for consideration which is excessively below the costs required for the supply, thereby tending to cause difficulties to the business activities of other entrepreneurs.[4]
>
> [I]n addition to any act falling under the provisions of Art. 2, Para. 9, item 3 of the JAA, unjustly supplying goods or services for low consideration, thereby tending to cause difficulties to the business activities of other entrepreneurs.[5]

23.09 According to the Guidelines Concerning Unjust Low Price Sales promulgated by the JFTC pursuant to the JAA (the "Unjust Low Price Guidelines"),[6] the following factors are considered in:

(i) the relationship between price, cost and continuity;
(ii) the tendency of the conduct to cause difficulties to the business activities of other entrepreneurs; and
(iii) lack of justifiable grounds for the price reduction.

23.10 In terms of factor (i), the Unjust Low Price Guidelines state that, while "the costs required for the supply" under article 2(9)(3) of the JAA means the total cost of sales, even where the price of goods is lower than the total cost of the sales of the goods, if the losses pertaining to the supply of the goods will be reduced by continuing to supply the goods, it would be rational to supply the goods at that price. It is also explicitly stated in the Unjust Low Price Guidelines that the total cost of sales corresponds to the sum of all costs required to supply the reduced price goods. For an ordinary manufacturing business, these are the production costs plus the sales costs and the general and administrative costs, whereas for an ordinary sales business, they include the purchasing costs plus the sales costs and the general and administrative costs.

23.11 The second characteristic of unfair price cutting is that it must "tend to cause difficulties to the business activities of other entrepreneurs," meaning that the price cutting need not necessarily create an actual disruption of business operations in order to be determined unfair. It is enough that the price reduction creates a recognized possibility of such a disruption. This

[3] Designation of Unfair Trade Practices, Fair Trade Commission Public Notice No. 15 of June 18, 1982, last revised October 28, 2009 (the "General Designation"). The General Designation lists fifteen types of anticompetitive conduct that may constitute Unfair Trade Practices prohibited by the JAA: Concerted Refusal to Trade, Other Refusal to Trade, Discriminatory Consideration, Discriminatory Treatment on Trade Terms, etc., Discriminatory Treatment, etc. in a Trade Association, Unjust Low Price Sales, Unjust High Price Purchasing, Deceptive Customer Inducement, Customer Inducement by Unjust Benefits, Tie-in Sales, etc., Trading on Exclusive Terms, Trading on Restrictive Terms, Unjust Interference with the Appointment of an Officer by a Fellow Transacting Party, Interference with a Competitor's Transactions, and Interference with the Internal Operations of a Competing Company. The General Designation is available at the following link: <http://www.jftc.go.jp/en/legislation_gls/unfairtradepractices.html>.

[4] JAA (n 1) art. 2(9)(3).

[5] General Designation (n 3) para. 6.

[6] Guidelines Concerning Unjust Low Price Sales under the Antimonopoly Act released by the JFTC (December 18, 2009) (the "Unjust Low Price Guidelines"), <http://www.jftc.go.jp/en/legislation_gls/imonopoly_guidelines.files/unjustlowprice.pdf>.

can be illustrated by the *Maruetsu* case[7] in which two stores sold milk in cartons for several months at significantly below cost, which increased their sales volumes of milk and their total sales during the period. As a consequence of this below-cost pricing, small home-delivery milk sellers in the area lost significant sales volume, though they priced the same products only slightly above cost. The JFTC concluded that the price-cutting conduct had unjustly disadvantaged small competitors, in violation of article 6 of the General Designation.

The impact of price cutting on competitors is determined on a case-by-case basis taking various factors into consideration, including, but not limited to, the size and circumstances of the firm that engaged in the price cutting, the quantity of products subject to the price cut, the duration of the price cut, advertising and publicity associated with the price cut, and the nature of the product. **23.12**

The third important factor that is examined in order to determine the fairness of a price cut is whether there is "proper justification" for it. The JFTC has enumerated specific examples of fact patterns that would not be considered instances of unfair price cutting despite exhibiting the aforementioned characteristics. With perishable goods (the quality of which can decline precipitously) and seasonal goods that have not been sold during periods of peak demand, clearance sales can sometimes be a necessity, in which case, reduced prices are not considered unfair even if they are set below purchase prices. This also holds true when the price of a given product drops due to a change in supply and demand conditions. **23.13**

In the *Tokyo Shibaura Public Slaughterhouse* judgment,[8] the Supreme Court considered that low prices charged by slaughterhouses located in central Tokyo were justified by their general business losses. The Court also held that in order to find predatory pricing, the intention of the firms involved, actual competitive relationships,, and market conditions must all be taken into consideration. **23.14**

The JFTC has frequently enforced the prohibition of predatory pricing during recent years against distributors of liquor and home appliances, as well as gas stations. **23.15**

B. Exploitative offenses (excessive pricing, monopoly leveraging)

The JAA does not specifically prohibit excessive pricing on the sales side. Even the first sentence of article 3 (prohibition of private monopolization) is not generally construed to prohibit excessive pricing, though it is possible to argue that excessive pricing constitutes private monopolization. **23.16**

Meanwhile, whether monopoly leveraging constitutes a violation of the prohibition of private monopolization can be questioned. Among others, low price sales are a typical example of business conduct which may lead a business operator to occupy a monopolistic position. **23.17**

According to the definition of private monopolization under article 2(5) of the JAA, business activities by which any entrepreneur individually excludes the business activities of other entrepreneurs, thereby causing a substantial restraint of competition in any particular field of trade contrary to the public interest, constitute exclusionary private monopolization. Low price sales constitute exclusionary private monopolization when such prices allow an entrepreneur to exclude its competitors from the market and consequently result ultimately in the establishment of an excessive price through subsequent leveraging of its monopoly power. **23.18**

---

[7] *Japan Fair Trade Commission v. Maruetsu*, 29 Shinketsushu 13 (FTC, May 28, 1982).

[8] *Tokyo Shibaura Public Slaughter*, Minshu 43.12.2078 (Supreme Court, December 14, 1989).

23.19 The Guidelines for Exclusionary Private Monopolization under the Antimonopoly Act[9] released by the JFTC classify low prices sales as exclusionary private monopolization. More precisely, according to the guidelines, if a price established by an entrepreneur is too low to allow the entrepreneur to recover the costs associated with supplying a product, the setting of this low price lacks economic rationality except in extraordinary circumstances, since the losses will mount as the supply of the product increases. Accordingly, the guidelines conclude that such low price setting constitutes exclusionary private monopolization if it would cause difficulty to the business activities of an equally or more efficient competitor. When the JFTC analyzes whether such difficulty would be caused to the business activities of an equally or more efficient competitor by the low pricing, it will comprehensively consider such factors as: (i) the circumstances of the entire market for the product; (ii) the positions of the said entrepreneur and its competitors in the market; (iii) the period of the conduct and the transaction value and quantity of the product; and (iv) the intent and purpose of the entrepreneur, the situation in relation to the advertising and publicity associated with the price-cutting and other conditions surrounding the conduct.

C. Monopsony

23.20 Monopsony can constitute a violation of the JAA. Theoretically, when a purchaser in a dominant position in the market individually controls the business activities of other entrepreneurs, and thereby causes a substantial restraint of competition in the market, such conduct constitutes private monopolization as defined by article 2(5) of the JAA.

23.21 However, unlike oligopsony, or the joint purchase agreements mentioned in Section II.I, there has been no substantial discussion of monopsony by the JFTC or prominent commentators; nor have there been any important administrative or court cases involving monopsony in Japan.

D. Price discrimination

23.22 Article 2(9)(2) of the JAA and article 3 of the General Designation state that unreasonable price discrimination constitutes an unfair trade practice. According to the General Designation, the offer to and acceptance by different customers of differential pricing for a commodity or service is included in this category of unfair trade practices. It is generally understood that business activity of this kind is unreasonable only when it is detrimental to competition, which is the case only where there is a tendency for competition to be restrained and where the conduct causes an anticompetitive effect felt by the majority of enterprises in the relevant market.

23.23 It should be noted that since price discrimination means setting different prices for the same commodities or services, the commodities or services in question need to be classified as the same commodity or service. In the judgment of Tokyo High Court in the *Hokkoku Newspaper Press* case,[10] the publisher was ordered to set its prices for two different newspapers, both containing news and opinions and each comprising the same number of pages, at the same price. The court held that products that are substantially the same can be considered for price discrimination, even though they are not physically identical.

23.24 *Toyo Linoleum*[11] is another noteworthy FTC decision which censured conduct involving charging different prices to different customers.

---

[9] Guidelines for Exclusionary Private Monopolization under the Antimonopoly Act <http://www.jftc.go.jp/en/legislation_gls/imonopoly_guidelines.files/guidelines_exclusionary.pdf>.

[10] *Hokkoku Newspaper Press v. JFTC*, 9 Gyosai Reishu 443 (Tokyo High Court, March 18, 1957).

[11] *Japan Fair Trade Commission v. Toyo Linoleum and others*, 26 Shinketsushu 85 (FTC No. 8 of 1979, February 7, 1980).

E. Dictating or influencing resale prices

When wholesalers or retailers are required to set their prices at or above a price designated by the manufacturer, this designation by the manufacturer falls within the scope of resale price maintenance (RPM), a type of unfair trade practice under the JAA. According to article 2(9)(4) of the JAA, RPM is defined as supplying goods to another party who purchases the said goods while imposing, without justifiable grounds, one of the restrictive terms listed below: **23.25**

(a) causing the said party to maintain the sale price of the goods that one has determined, or otherwise restricting the said party's free decision on the sale price for the goods; or
(b) having the said party cause an entrepreneur who purchases the goods from the said party maintain the sale price of the goods that one has determined, or otherwise causing the said party to restrict the said entrepreneur's free decision on the sale price of the goods.

In practice, "...an entrepreneur who purchases the goods from the said party" as used in (b) in para. 23.25, includes an entrepreneur who indirectly purchases the goods from the said party.[12] **23.26**

As stated in the para. 23.25, resale price maintenance is, in principle, unlawful if the parties reselling a product are bound by directions of the manufacturer. The rationale for holding resale price maintenance unlawful in principle is that the conduct can be engaged in only if a manufacturer is able to impose such terms and conditions on distributors, a circumstance that can occur only kesif the relevant market at the manufacturer's level is highly oligopolistic, thus making it possible for the manufacturer to benefit from monopolistic pricing. On the other hand, mere "suggested prices" or "recommended prices" do not amount to resale price maintenance. **23.27**

According to JFTC's Distribution Guidelines,[13] whether resale prices have been restricted is to be determined on the basis of whether any artificial means are used to secure the effectiveness of sales at the price indicated by the manufacturer. Examples of such means include: (i) where a written or oral contact provides that sales are to be made at the price indicated by a manufacturer; (ii) where distributors are required to pledge, in writing, to sell at the price indicted by manufacturer; (iii) where a manufacturer deals only with distributors that agree to sell at the price indicated by the manufacturer;[14] and (iv) where a manufacturer deals with distributors on the condition that they sell at the price indicated by the manufacturer and that unsold goods are to be repurchased by the manufacturer rather than discounted. **23.28**

The prohibition of resale price restriction is enforced regularly by the JFTC through cease-and-desist orders, though there have been very few court decisions in the recent past. The recent JFTC decisions include a cease-and-desist order issued against Adidas Japan in 2012.[15] **23.29**

F. Tying arrangements

A tie-in arrangement is unlawful in principle. Article 10 of the General Designation prohibits unjustly causing another party to purchase a commodity or service from oneself or **23.30**

---

[12] Cease-and-desist order against Nissan Kagaku Kogyo (Heisei 18 (so) No. 4) (May 22, 2008).

[13] Guidelines Concerning Distribution Systems and Business Practices Under The Antimonopoly Act of July 11, 1991 (the "Distribution Guidelines"), <http://www.jftc.go.jp/en/legislation_gls/imonopoly_guidelines.files/distribution.pdf>.

[14] Note that this approach may lead to a different outcome under the JAA under a given approach than would be the case under "Colgate doctrine" under US law, according to which manufacturers may lawfully unilaterally announce resale pricing policies and terminate distributors that fail to adhere to such policies. *United States v. Colgate & Co.*, 250 U.S. 300 (1919).

[15] Cease-and-desist order against Adidas Japan (Heisei 24 (so) No. 7) (March 2, 2012).

from an entrepreneur designated by oneself by tying it to the supply of another commodity or service, or otherwise coercing the said party to deal with oneself or with an entrepreneur designated by oneself. For example, if a seller that enjoys a powerful market position for a certain product requires the purchase of an unwanted tied product before a buyer can buy a wanted product, such a contract may be regarded as unreasonable coercion of consumers and constitute an unfair trade practice.

23.31 According to article 10 of the General Designation, a tie-in arrangement requires both tying and tied products. Sales of, or offers to sell, products which may appear separate but which are treated as a package are not considered to constitute tie-in arrangements under article 10 of the General Designation. For example, if it is indispensable to combine several products as a unit for technical reasons, that combination is unlikely to be regarded as a tie-in arrangement.

23.32 The Distribution Guidelines provide several examples in which tie-in arrangements are deemed to be illegal under the JAA. According to the guidelines, tie-in arrangements are illegal when a party is compelled to purchase products from a firm in the following situations:

(1) Where an influential firm requests another party to purchase the firm's products while indicating that it will terminate or reduce purchases from the other party unless the other party purchases the firm's products;
(2) Where the procurement personnel in the influential firm requests another party to purchase the firm's products while suggesting that the influential firm's purchases will be affected unless the party does so;
(3) Where the influential firm sets a sales target for its products for each transacting party on the basis of the amount of purchases by the latter, indicates that the latter's failure to attain this target will result in a reduction in the volume of purchases by the firm from the latter, and requests that the latter purchase a large enough amount to meet the sales target;
(4) Where the influential firm requests additional purchases by each transacting party by making reference to a comparative list of each transacting party's purchases from and sales to the firm and suggests that it will otherwise purchase only a corresponding volume from the transacting party;
(5) Where, in response to another party's offer to sell, the influential firm indicates that it will do so if the other party purchases services supplied by the firm or a firm designated by it;
(6) Where, even though the other party has expressed its intention not to purchase, the influential firm states that it has purchased services from that party and induces it to purchase the firm's products; or
(7) Where, in spite of the absence of a proposal by the other party to purchase, the firm unilaterally sends its products to that party and offsets the products' total value against an unpaid debt that it owes to the latter.

23.33 There have been a few tying cases during the last two decades, including the *Microsoft* case[16] and the *Toshiba Elevator* case.[17] As can be seen from the *Fujitaya* case,[18] tying is treated as per se infringement.

[16] *JFTC v. Microsoft K.K.*, 45 Shinketsushu 153 (JFTC, December 14, 1998).

[17] *Toshiba Elevator Technos K.K. v. Kousei Denki Yugengaisha*, 833 HANTA 62 (Osaka High Court, July 30, 1993).

[18] *JFTC v. Fujitaya*, 38 Shinketsushu 41 (JFTC, February 28, 1992). In this case, ENIX sold unpopular video games to distributors as a condition to its supplying a highly popular title, Dragon Quest IV. Although the relevant market of video games was too big for ENIX or its popular title to affect the market, the JFTC nonetheless ruled that there was violation of art. 10 of General Designation (n 3).

G. Exclusive dealing

Article 11 of the General Designation defines trading on exclusive terms as unjustly trading with another party on the condition that said party shall not trade with a competitor, thereby tending to reduce trading opportunities for said competitor. Exclusive dealing falling within this definition constitutes an unfair trade practice, and thus, a violation of the JAA.[19] **23.34**

The term "unjustly" is interpreted to mean that exclusive dealing is illegal only in the absence of a justifiable cause and where a likelihood of impeding fair competition exists. **23.35**

The Distribution Guidelines[20] state that where a restriction on the handling of competing products is imposed by an influential manufacturer in a relevant market, and the restriction may result in making it difficult for new entrants or competitors to easily secure alternative distribution channels, such restriction is illegal as a violation of the JAA. **23.36**

Under the Distribution Guidelines, whether a manufacturer is "influential" in a relevant market is determined in principle by whether it has no less than 10 percent of the market share or occupies one of the top three positions in the relevant market. Furthermore, according to the Distribution Guidelines, the JFTC will take into consideration such factors as whether the restriction may result in making it difficult for new entrants or competitors to easily secure alternative distribution channels. On the other hand, if a restriction on the handling of competing products is imposed by a firm which has a market share of less than 10 percent and which is not among the top three firms in its relevant industry in terms of size, the restriction will not usually result in making it difficult for new entrants or competitors to easily secure alternative distribution channels, and will not be found to be illegal under the Distribution Guidelines. **23.37**

The Distribution Guidelines further state that in determining whether a restriction may result in making it difficult for new entrants or competitors to easily secure alternative distribution channels, the following factors are taken into consideration: **23.38**

- the structure of the market;
- the position in the market of the manufacturer that imposes the restriction;
- the number of distributors affected by the restriction and their position in the market; and
- the impact of the restriction on the business activities of the distributors.

On the other hand, according to the Distribution Guidelines, the following cases are not likely to constitute trading on exclusive terms since there is proper justification for restricting transactions with competitors: **23.39**

- where a manufacturer of a finished product commissions parts from manufacturers to produce parts made of materials exclusively for itself; or
- where a manufacturer of a finished product commissions the production of parts by a manufacturer, while supplying the parts manufacturer with materials and know-how that are related to industrial technologies and are secret in nature; and requires the said parts manufacturer to sell the parts exclusively to the finished product manufacturer, if such restriction is deemed necessary to protect the confidentiality of the know-how, or to prevent the unauthorized diversion of the materials and know-how.

The JFTC frequently issues administrative guidance to companies regarding distribution activities about which the JFTC has concerns, but there have been few recent official JFTC or court decisions. **23.40**

[19] *Toyo Seimaiki*, 35 Gyosaireishu 144 (Tokyo High Court, February 17, 1984) is a prominent court precedent concerning exclusive dealing.

[20] Distribution Guidelines (n 13).

H. Refusal to deal

23.41 Unilateral refusal to deal falls within the definition of refusal to trade under article 2 of the General Designation, which is "unjustly refusing to trade, or restricting the quantity or substance of goods or services pertaining to trade with a certain entrepreneur, or causing another entrepreneur to undertake any act that falls under one of these categories."

23.42 According to the Distribution Guidelines, the following conduct typically constitutes refusal to trade under article 2 of the General Designation:[21]

> Where an influential manufacturer in a relevant market prevents its distributors from trading with its competitors, making it difficult for the competitors to find alternative trading partners, and, for the purpose of ensuring the effectiveness of the prohibition, refuses to deal with distributors that do not obey the manufacturer's prohibition.

23.43 According to the Distribution Guidelines, when an influential firm in a relevant market engages in the conduct described as a means of achieving unjust purposes, such as excluding its competitors from a relevant market, and if such conduct may make it difficult for the refused firm to carry on normal business activities, such conduct is illegal under the JAA. For example, the following are considered to constitute unfair trade practices:

- Where the manufacturer of a material influential in a relevant market stops supplying the main materials that it had been supplying to its customers (finished product manufacturers) in an attempt to prevent customers from producing the materials that they had been buying from the manufacturer of a material; or
- Where the manufacturer of a material influential in a relevant market that sells a finished product and has also been supplying the material input to the competing makers of a competing finished product, stops supplying the input to such competitors in an attempt to exclude them from the market, and where the competitors have have established close relationships with the manufacturer.[22]

I. Essential facilities

23.44 Although "essential facility" has not been defined by statutory regulations or court precedents in Japan, it is generally recognized that some types of facilities, such as communication networks or power distribution grids, are indispensable for business operations, and that access to them should not be unjustly refused, to avoid hampering fair competition. If the entities owning or controlling such facilities do not allow their competitors access to them, such conduct raises anticompetitive concerns.

23.45 The regulations typically applicable to anticompetitive conduct related to essential facilities are the prohibition of exclusionary private monopolization[23] and the unfair trade practices known as refusal to deal and discriminatory trading.[24] For an example where regulation by the JAA was enforced in relation to communication networks, please see the *NTT Higashi Nihon* case.[25]

23.46 For example, in recognition of the concept behind the essential facilities doctrine, the Guidelines for Promotion of Competition in the Telecommunications Business Field published jointly by the JFTC and the Ministry of General Affairs defines essential facilities as assets that are required

---

[21] Such conduct also constitutes Dealing on Exclusive Terms as defined by art. 11 of the General Designation (n 3).

[22] For interpretation of influential manufacturers under the Distribution Guidelines, See Section I.G.

[23] JAA (n 1) art. 2(5).

[24] General Designation (n 3) arts. 1–4.

[25] *NTT Higashi Nihon*, 1339 Hanrei Times 55 (Supreme Court, December 17, 2010) (often referred to as the "NTT East" case).

in order to compete effectively in a relevant market and that are difficult or impossible for telecommunications carriers to replicate through their own investments.

The Guidelines further state that if telecommunications carriers with essential facilities reject their competitors' requests to connect to their subscriber networks, and offer unfavorable terms to competitors in such transactions compared with those given to their own departments or affiliates, this conduct may be regarded as private monopolization or an unfair trade practice, and is prohibited by the JAA. **23.47**

J. Bundling (including loyalty and market share discounts)

Bundling distribution channels can constitute a violation of the JAA if it constitutes an unfair trade practice or exclusionary private monopolization, but is more likely to constitute trading on exclusive terms as defined by article 11 of the General Designation. Article 11 of the General Designation defines trading on exclusive terms as unjustly trading with another party on the condition that the it shall not trade with a competitor, thereby tending to reduce trading opportunities for the competitor. It should be noted that no conduct qualifies as trading on exclusive terms unless it satisfies the "unjustly" requirement; in other words, unless bundling conduct is likely to impede fair competition, it will not be considered a violation. **23.48**

For example, while the Distribution Guidelines introduce the following examples of restraints imposed on distributors by manufacturers, these types of conduct are not described as per se illegal: **23.49**

- obliging distributors to handle the manufacturer's products exclusively;
- restricting distributors from handling competitors' products;
- prohibiting or restricting distributors from handling specific products or from handling products from a specific firm;
- restricting distributors from handling competing products by requiring them to sell such a large volume of the manufacturer's products that it approaches or exceeds the distributors' capacities.

According to the Distribution Guidelines, where a restriction on the handling of competing products is imposed by an influential manufacturer in a market, and where the restriction may result in making it difficult for new entrants or competitors to easily secure alternative distribution channels, the restriction is regarded as an illegal instance of dealing on exclusive terms[26] or dealing on restrictive terms.[27] **23.50**

The Distribution Guidelines further provide a basic outline for the analysis of sole distributorships, i.e. cases where firms, domestic or foreign, supply products and grant other firms an exclusive distributorship for such products covering the entire domestic relevant market. Such exclusive distributorship firms are called a sole agent or a sole import distributor. According to the Guidelines, when a distributor becomes a sole distributor, there is a possibility that the distributorship will give rise to an anticompetitive effect, therefore necessitating a detailed analysis using the following factors: **23.51**

(a) The market share and rank of the sole distributor firm and the extent to which its share or rank changes due to the conclusion of the contract;
(b) Overall business capability of the supplier (sales amount, brand value, market position in other markets, etc.);
(c) The market share and rank of the product covered by the contract in the domestic market;

[26] General Designation (n 3) art. 1.

[27] General Designation (n 3) arts. 11 and 12. For an interpretation of what constitutes an influential manufacturer, see Section I.G.

(d) Actual status of competition in the market (number of competitors, fluctuations in market shares, difficulty of new market entry, etc.);
(e) Characteristics of the product covered by the contract, the degree of competition between products produced or marketed by a sole distributor and the product covered by the contract; the presence or absence of closely comparable substitutes, and the sales price of the product covered by the contract; and
(f) Actual status of distribution of the product covered by the contract (difficulty of new entry into distribution, etc.).

23.52 Furthermore, according to the Distribution Guidelines, where an entity to be a sole distributor has the leading market share, which is no less than 25 percent, conclusion of a sole distributorship contract between the entity and a supplier in competition with the firm is considered highly likely to have an anticompetitive effect. In such a case, the distributorship is carefully examined, paying special attention to the following factors:

- whether the overall business capability of the supplier is not large; and
- whether the product covered by the contract already holds a not insubstantial market share in the domestic market.

K. Standard-setting groups (disclosure requirements, licensing arrangements, and licensing pools)

23.53 Japan has recognized that standard-setting activities may pose competition issues. Although there has not been a judicial precedent where standard-setting activities were specifically discussed in relation to the application of the JAA, the JFTC, in recognition of growing concerns about the use of patent pools to facilitate standardization of specifications, published guidelines clarifying principles to be applied under the JAA to examine the standardizing of specifications and the pooling of patents in relation to the specifications in order to license them.[28]

23.54 Many of these activitiesare carried out by trade associations referred to as "standardization associations.". Standard-setting activities conducted by such associations are specificallysubject to article 8 of the JAA, which, inter alia, prohibits trade associations from substantially restraining competition in any particular field of trade.

L. Customer termination

23.55 When an entrepreneur terminates an existing transactional relationship with its customer, there can be a question of whether such termination constitutes a refusal to trade under article 2 of the General Designation.[29] That said, there have been no judicial or administrative decisions under the JAA specifically dealing with customer termination.

M. Termination of intermediaries (retailers, wholesalers, dealers, and value-added resellers, agents, and brokers)

23.56 Termination of transactional relationships with intermediaries can also be considered a type of unilateral refusal to trade under article 2 of the General Designation.

23.57 As described in Section I.H, the Distribution Guidelines specify several types of business conduct which typically constitute refusal to trade under article 2 of the General Designation.

[28] Guidelines on Standardization and Patent Pool Arrangements (September 28, 2007).
[29] See Section I.H for a summary.

Refusal to trade can be interpreted to include termination of existing transactional relationships. In fact, there are several judicial precedents in which such terminations were found to constitute unlawful unilateral refusals to trade.[30] **23.58**

In addition, in civil lawsuits, distributors sometimes argue that the termination of a distributorship agreement by a manufacturer based on a breach by the distributor of restrictions on its activities imposed under the distributorship agreement should be void as a violation of the JAA. In the *Shiseido* case,[31] a distributor sued after Shiseido terminated its supply agreement, asserting that Shiseido's prohibition of selling through mail orders or to other distributors was a violation of the JAA. The Supreme Court upheld the High Court's decision in ruling that, given the nature of the cosmetic products at issue, Shiseido's restrictions on the distributor's sales methods was justifiable, and the termination was therefore deemed valid. **23.59**

N. Termination of relationships with competitors

While the termination of a relationship between an entrepreneur and its competitors is not specifically discussed under the JAA, if an entrepreneur compels its distributors to terminate their relationships with the entrepreneur's competitors, the conduct should be examined as a possible unilateral refusal to trade.,[32] or trading on restrictive terms.[33] **23.60**

O. Exemptions

Exemptions are provided by the JAA explicitly for: (i) acts that can be recognized as lawful exercises of intellectual property rights, (ii) certain actions of cooperatives, and (iii) resale price maintenance for products designated by the JFTC. **23.61**

(i) Exercise of intellectual property rights

Article 21 of the JAA stipulates that the provisions of the Act shall not apply to conduct recognizable as the exercise of any rights under the Copyright Act, the Patent Act, the Utility Model Act, the Design Act, or the Trademark Act. **23.62**

In consequence, the JAA is not applicable to any conduct that is regarded as the proper exercise of intellectual property rights. However, it is not always easy to determine whether specific conduct can be characterized as a proper exercise of intellectual property rights. **23.63**

(ii) Actions of cooperatives

The actions of cooperatives are exempt from article 22 of the JAA. A cooperative qualifies for an exemption when it satisfies the following four-prong test: **23.64**

(1) its purpose is to provide mutual aid among small-scale firms or consumers;
(2) participation in and withdrawal from the cooperative are made on a voluntary basis;
(3) each member has equal voting rights; and
(4) there is a stated limit on the distribution of profit.

Meanwhile, the JAA provides an exception to the exemption. Under this exception, the JAA is applicable to business conduct by cooperatives even when they qualify under the above four-part test when unfair trade practices are employed or when competition in any particular field of trade is substantially restrained, resulting in unjust price increases. **23.65**

---

[30] For example, in *Taisho Pharmaceutical*, 7 Sinketsushu 99 (JFTC, December 10, 1955), the JFTC concluded that termination by Taisho Pharmaceutical, a large Japanese pharmaceutical company, of a transaction with its distributors due to their entry into the supply chains of competing pharmaceutical companies or sales of competing products constituted refusal to trade under the General Designation (n 3).

[31] *Shiseido*, 992 Hanrei Times 94 (Supreme Court, December 18, 1998).

[32] General Designation (n 3) art. 2.

[33] General Designation (n 3) art. 11. For summaries of these regulations, see Sections I.G and I.H.

(iii) Resale price maintenance

23.66 Pursuant to article 23(1) of the JAA, a manufacturer is allowed to maintain the resale price of a consumer commodity designated by the JFTC. It should be noted that as of this writing no commodity has been so designated. Until 1992, some cosmetic and medical products were designated. Pursuant to article 23(4) of the JAA, the publishing of copyrighted materials is exempt from the JAA. A publisher is allowed to maintain the resale prices of copyrighted materials as provided in article 23(4) of the JAA. According to the JFTC, the copyrighted materials governed by article 23(4) of the JAA are CDs, video tapes, records, newspapers, magazines, and books. Meanwhile, article 23(4) of the JAA explicitly states that electronic books do not fall within the scope of copyrighted material since they are distributed as information rather than as tangible products.[34]

II. Dealing with competitors

23.67 The majority of the cases brought by the JFTC are against conduct that involves competitors. These are infringements that restrain competition the most seriously and are enforced vigorously regardless whether the company has any physical presence on the Japanese territory, as long as the conduct substantially restrains competition on the Japanese market. Since the amendments to the JAA enacted in 2002, JFTC can now serve orders to foreign companies through publication by publicly posting the order on the board in front of the JFTC's office. Horizontal collusion, as opposed to legitimate joint ventures or similar collaborations such as lawful information exchanges, is treated most severely and is subject to criminal penalties. In the past decade, the JFTC has frequently coordinated cartel investigations with parallel investigations by antitrust authorities of other jurisdictions, including those of South Korea, the US, the EU, and Canada.

A. Horizontal price fixing (including advanced announcements of price or product changes)

23.68 Horizontal price fixing is classified as an "unreasonable restraint of trade." It is defined by article 2(6) of the JAA as a business activity by which any entrepreneur, by contract, agreement, or any other means irrespective of name, in concert with other entrepreneurs, mutually restricts or engages in business activities in such a manner as to fix, maintain, or increase prices, or to limit production, technology, products, facilities, or counterparties, thereby causing, contrary to the public interest, a substantial restraint of competition in any particular field of trade. Price fixing is considered to be a quintessential violation of the JAA because it is regarded as directly obstructing the functioning of the free market. It is also considered that when price fixing occurs, anticompetitive effects will most likely arise.

23.69 The requirements for unreasonable restraint of trade, including price fixing, consist of (i) conduct by entrepreneurs, (ii) concerted action (i.e. communication of intent, mutual restraint of business activities, and joint execution), and (iii) substantial restraint of competition in any particular field of trade contrary to the public interest.

23.70 Price fixing is considered to be per se illegal; however, this does not mean that price fixing can be deemed illegal without regard to whether it satisfies requirement (iii) in para. 23.69. Indeed the question of whether competition has been restrained has been analyzed in price fixing cases, in contrast to some other jurisdictions, where such harm is presumed to result from such per se conduct.[35]

[34] JFTC, Frequently Asked Questions, answer 14, <http://www.jftc.go.jp/dk/dk_qa.html> (in Japanese).
[35] Tadashi Shiraishi, *Dokusenkinshihou* (2nd edn., 2009) 136.

Every year, between ten to thirty price-fixing and bid-rigging cases are brought by the JFTC. Most cases are local ones, although international cartels have been vigorously investigated. The JFTC also applies the JAA to alleged violators which do not have any physical presence in Japan. **23.71**

B. Horizontal agreements to allocate customers or territories; agreements not to compete

Market division, such as agreements to allocate customers or territories or otherwise not to compete, also constitutes unreasonable restraint of trade under article (2)(6) of the JAA, if: it is engaged in among competitors; competition for customers is restricted; and competition in the market is substantially restrained. **23.72**

According to the Distribution Guidelines, the following types of conduct constitute unreasonable restraint of trade, and thus a violation of the JAA, if they result in a substantial restraint of competition in the relevant market. **23.73**

(1) Allocation of customers:
   (a) Concerted arrangements by manufacturers not to deal with the customers of other firms;
   (b) Concerted restraints by distributors to prevent one another from winning over the customers of other firms by offering lower prices;
   (c) Concerted arrangements by distributors to require payment of a rectification charge when one of the distributors deals with any customers of the other firms;
   (d) Concerted arrangements by manufacturers to prohibit each other from selling their products to customers other than those who are registered in the registry established by the manufacturers; or
   (e) Concerted limitations by distributors of the customers with whom each distributor is permitted to deal.

(2) Market allocation:
   (a) Concerted restrictions by manufacturers of each other's sales territories;
   (b) Concerted arrangements by distributors not to engage in sales activities in any area in which another firm or firms are already engaged in sales activities;
   (c) Concerted restrictions by manufacturers of the standards and types of products to be manufactured by each firm; or
   (d) Concerted arrangements by manufacturers not to manufacture any type of product already being manufactured by another firm or firms.

C. Horizontal boycotts

Concerted refusals to deal can be classified as both unreasonable restraints of trade under article 2(6) of the JAA and as unfair trade practices under article 1 of the General Designation. **23.74**

According to the Distribution Guidelines, the following types of conduct constitute unreasonable restraint of trade if they result in substantial restraints of competition in the relevant market: **23.75**

(a) Concerted refusals by manufacturers to supply products to price cutting distributors in an attempt to exclude them;
(b) Concerted refusals by distributors to supply products to new entrants, or concerted causing by distributors of their suppliers (manufacturers) to refuse to supply products to new entrants, in an attempt to prevent new entry by competitors;
(c) Concerted communications to distributors by manufacturers of the manufacturers' intention to refuse to supply products to distributors that distribute imported goods in an attempt to exclude imports; and
(d) Concerted communications to material suppliers by finished product manufacturers of their intention to refuse to deal with the suppliers if they provide materials to new entrants, in an attempt to prevent competitors from entering a market.

23.76 Note that the guidelines provide several examples of "a substantial restraint of trade" in a relevant market where there is a concerted refusal to deal, such as (i) where it is made very difficult for any firm manufacturing or selling products at high prices and of superior quality to enter the relevant market, or where such a firm is to be excluded from the relevant market; (ii) where it is made very difficult for any firm adopting innovative sales methods to enter the relevant market, or where such firm is to be excluded from the relevant market; (iii) where it is made very difficult for any firm with superior business capabilities to enter the relevant market, or in cases where such a firm is to be excluded from the relevant market; (iv) where it is made very difficult for any firm to enter the relevant market where no active competition is taking place in said market; and (v) where a concerted refusal to deal is the response to any potential entrant to the relevant market.

23.77 On the other hand, under the General Designation, a boycott is regarded as unlawful in principle but possibly justifiable in exceptional cases. According to the Distribution Guidelines, the conduct described above concerning unreasonable restraint of trade shall be an unfair trade practice under the General Designation even when it does not cause a substantial restraint of trade.

D. Joint ventures and other competitive collaborations

23.78 Collaboration among competitors generally poses the issue of whether such collaboration constitutes unreasonable restraint of trade under article 2(6) of the JAA. Although the JAA does not explicitly introduce the concepts of "hard core" and "non-hard core" cartels, such a distinction is generally accepted.[36]

23.79 In practice, price fixing, market or customer allocation among competitors, and bid-rigging are considered to be the typical "hard core" cartels, as these activities usually restrict competition in a particular field of trade. Therefore, detailed analysis of the impact on the relevant market is considered unnecessary in relation to hard core cartels. On the other hand, with regard to non-hard core cartels (e.g. research and development (R&D), joint environmental protection efforts, and other types of collaboration among competitors for socially beneficial purposes), detailed analysis of whether such collaboration constitutes unreasonable restraint of trade under the JAA is usually required.

23.80 In terms of research and development, the JFTC has released its Guidelines Concerning Joint Research and Development under the Antimonopoly Act (the "R&D Guidelines").

23.81 First, the R&D Guidelines provide the JFTC's views on the application of the JAA to R&D activities jointly undertaken by multiple entrepreneurs. According to the R&D Guidelines, where R&D activities are jointly undertaken by multiple entrepreneurs and the individual R&D activities of each member are restricted, such joint R&D activities could constitute unreasonable restraint of trade as defined by article 2(6) of the JAA, as it could substantially restrict competition in the technology or product market. The guidelines also refer to the possibility that joint R&D activities could falls within the scope of regulation of a trade association (art. 8 of the JAA).

23.82 Second, the R&D Guidelines provide the JFTC's views on the regulation of unfair trade practices in relation to arrangements related to implementation of the outcome of joint R&D activities. In this regard, the R&D Guidelines introduce (a) activities considered, in principle, not to constitute unfair trade practices; (b) activities which may constitute unfair trade practices; and (c) activities which are highly likely to constitute unfair trade practices.

[36] E.g. Hienuki Toshifumi, *Chushaku Dokusenkinshihou* (Negishi Akira et al. eds., 2009) 74.

E. Trade associations

Article 8 of the JAA provides regulations that apply to trade associations. As can be seen in the below, these regulations articleshare many factors in common with the regulations imposed on individual entrepreneurs. However, article 8 is considered necessary to directly enforce the JAA against trade associations rather than their individual members. **23.83**

According to article 2(2) of the JAA, "trade association" means any combination or federation of combinations of two or more entrepreneurs having as its principal purpose the furtherance of their common interest as entrepreneurs.[37] **23.84**

The trade association activities prohibited by article 8 are: (i) substantially restraining competition in any particular field of trade; (ii) entering into an international agreement or international contract whose contents constitute unreasonable restraint of trade or unfair trade practices; (iii) limiting the present or future number of entrepreneurs in any particular field of business; (iv) unjustly restricting the functions or activities of the constituent entrepreneurs (meaning an entrepreneur who is a member of the trade association; the same shall apply hereinafter); and (v) inducing entrepreneurs to engage in acts which constitute unfair trade practices. **23.85**

F. Interlocking directorates

Article 13(1) of the JAA explicitly prohibits the directors and employees of an entrepreneur from assuming positions as directors of other companies if doing so would substantially restrain competition in any particular field of trade. **23.86**

A director is defined as a director, executive officer, management member with unlimited liability, inspector, auditor, or person with an equivalent position, or a manager or a business manager of the main or a branch office (art. 2(3) JAA). An employee is defined as a person other than a director engaged in the business of a company on a regular basis (art. 13(1) JAA). According to the Guidelines to Application of the Antimonopoly Act Concerning Review of Business Combinations,[38] a person with an equivalent position means a person who is not a director or auditor, but who has a title such as adviser, counselor, or consultant, and who actually participates in the management of the company by attending meetings of the board of directors or in other ways. **23.87**

The guidelines state that an interlocking directorate requires analysis of its impact on competition in a particular field of trade in the following cases, because it is deemed to form, maintain, or strengthen a joint relationship between interlocking companies and thus may affect competition in the field of trade: **23.88**

(a) the officers or employees of one company comprise a majority of the total number of officers of another company; or

[37] Associations, which typically fall within the definition of a Trade Association, are listed in art. 2(2)(1)–(3), namely: (i) incorporated associations or other associations of which two or more entrepreneurs are members; (ii) any incorporated foundation or other foundation of which two or more entrepreneurs control the appointment and dismissal of directors or managers, the management of affairs or the continuation of its existence; (iii) any partnership of which two or more entrepreneurs are partners; or (iv) any contractual combination of two or more entrepreneurs. Meanwhile, combinations or federations of combinations of two or more entrepreneurs that have capital or contributions made by the constituent entrepreneurs, and whose principal purposes are to operate—and which actually are operating—commercial, industrial, financial or any other businesses for profit are excluded.

[38] Guidelines to Application of the Antimonopoly Act Concerning Review of Business Combinations of May 31, 2004, last revised June 14, 2011, <http://www.jftc.go.jp/en/legislation_gls/imonopoly_guidelines.files/110713.2.pdf>.

(b) the director concurrently assumes a position at two companies and has the authority to represent both companies.

23.89 When an interlocking directorate falls within neither (a) nor (b) in para. 23.88, it is reviewed, first, by taking the following factors into consideration in order to figure out whether it requires further analysis on the grounds that it forms, maintains or strengthens a joint relationship:

(a) whether an interlocking directorate is formed by full-time or representative directors;
(b) the ratio of officers or employees of one of the interlocking companies to the total number of officers of the other interlocking company;
(c) mutual holding of voting rights between the interlocking companies; and
(d) trading relationships (including financial relationships), business alliances and other relationships between the interlocking companies.

23.90 On the other hand, the guidelines state that an interlocking directorate does not constitute a violation of the JAA in principle in the following cases, because it does not then form, maintain, or strengthen a joint relationship:

(a) where any person who concurrently serves as an officer for interlocking companies does not have representative authority at either of them, and where 10 percent or less of an interlocking company's officers are officers or employees of another company;
(b) where any person who concurrently serves as an officer for interlocking companies is not a full-time officer of either of them, where neither interlocking company holds more than 10 percent of the voting rights of another company, and where 25 percent of the directors of neither company are officers or employees of another company.

23.91 Furthermore, according to the guidelines, interlocking directorates among companies which belong to the same group of combined companies[39] in many cases are not considered to constitute violations of the JAA.

23.92 Article 13(2) of the JAA prohibits entrepreneurs from forcing their competitor companies to accept their directors or employees as directors or employees of the competitors by way of unfair trade practices. In addition, article 15 of the General Designation prohibits a corporation from unjustly inducing, abetting, or coercing a stockholder or officer of a corporation with which it is in a domestic competitive relationship or with a corporation of which one is a stockholder or an officer, to engage in an act disadvantageous to such corporation by the exercise of voting rights, transfer of stock, divulging of secrets, or in any other way whatsoever.[40] However, there has not been an actual case in which these regulations have been enforced to date.[41]

G. Facilitating practices

23.93 A facilitating practice can constitute unreasonable restraint of trade under the JAA. However, as discussed in Section II.O, under articles 2(6) and 3 of the JAA, unreasonable restraint of

[39] A group of combined companies is defined to mean a group consisting of a company, its subsidiary companies, its parent company which is not a subsidiary company of another company, and subsidiary companies of the said parent company excluding the said company and subsidiary companies of the said company: JAA (n 1) art. 10(2).

[40] Another type which is relevant to the election of directors is defined by the General Designation (n 3) art. 13: causing a corporation which is one's transacting party to follow one's instructions in advance, or to get one's approval, regarding the appointment of officers of the said corporation unjustly in light of normal business practices by taking advantage of one's superior bargaining position over the party.

[41] Takaji Kanai, *Chushaku Dokusenkinshihou* 287 (Negishi Akira et al. eds., 2009), Takaji Kanai et al., *Dokusenkinshihou* 371 (3rd edn. 2011)

trade requires communication of intent among entrepreneurs; in other words, an agreement among them. Therefore, parallel conduct, i.e. the same actions taken by entrepreneurs without agreement among them, does not constitute unreasonable restraint of trade under the JAA. Therefore, a facilitating practice does not by itself constitute an unreasonable restraint of trade.

However, the JFTC is not always required to prove the existence of an explicit agreement among entrepreneurs when enforcing the regulations on unreasonable restraint of trade. Rather, it is confirmed by the following court precedent that even an implicit understanding can satisfy the requirement of communication of intent. This judgment further confirms that the communication of intent can be presumed to be satisfied by the existence of parallel conduct. **23.94**

As the *Toshiba Chemical Corporation* case[42] shows, while a facilitating practice does not by itself constitute a violation of the JAA, it is evidence of the existence of an unreasonable restraint of trade. **23.95**

In this case, the Tokyo High Court provided the general principle related to the interpretation of communication of intent as follows: **23.96**

> The mere recognition or acceptance of an entrepreneur's price increase by another entrepreneur does not satisfy the requirement of "communication of intent"; however, it does not mean that express, mutually restrictive agreements are unnecessary. Rather, the requirement of communication of intent could be satisfied by mutual acknowledgement and acceptance of a price increase by competitors under an implicit understanding.
>
> Accordingly, where an entrepreneur obtains any information about another entrepreneur's price increase and takes any action identical or similar to the price increase, unless there are exceptional circumstances under which the entrepreneur decided, without regard to the conduct of other entrepreneurs, to take such an action based on its own view that it could survive the price competition, it should be presumed that trust existed among the said entrepreneurs that they would take accommodative action, and thus, the existence of communication of intent should also be presumed.

H. Information exchange

Information exchange, especially communication among competitors as to price, can be illegal under the JAA as an unreasonable restraint of trade. **23.97**

The Guidelines Concerning the Activities of Trade Associations under the Antimonopoly Act released by the JFTC in 1995 state that an exchange of information specifically related to substantial means of business in connection with competition among entrepreneurs is likely to constitute a violation of the JAA. The guidelines also point out that if the parties form implicit understandings or common intentions pertaining to restriction of competition through such information exchange or if the information exchange is used as a means of restricting competition, it constitutes a violation of the JAA in principle. **23.98**

The guidelines also give examples of provision of information by trade associations which do not violate the JAA. These include: (i) provision of information to consumers concerning the proper use of products or services provided by the industry; (ii) provision of general information by governmental organizations or private research institutions concerning trends in technologies and business management information; (iii) provision of general, statistical information concerning business activities (e.g. manufacturing, sales, or investment in **23.99**

[42] *Toshiba Chemical Corporation*, 906 Hanrei Times 136 (Tokyo High Court, September 25, 1995).

facilities) in the past; (iv) provision of general, statistical information concerning prices in the past (excluding any which may provide entrepreneurs with common standards for current or future pricing); (v) provision of documentation or technical standards concerning expense items, difficulty of work, or quality (excluding any which may provide entrepreneurs with common standards for current or future pricing) when comparison of the prices of subject products or services is difficult; (vi) provision of general forecasts concerning the whole industry; and (vii) provision of objective facts related to customers' creditability (excluding those which constitute agreements not to trade with a specific entrepreneur).

I. Joint purchasing agreements

23.100 Under the JAA, joint purchasing is subject to regulation as an unreasonable restraint of trade under article 3 of the JAA in the same manner as joint conduct by sellers.

23.101 The restrictions on unreasonable restraint of trade have been considered applicable to joint purchasing for the following reasons.[43] First, article 2(6), which defines the term "unreasonable restraint of trade," does not distinguish between the activities of sellers and purchasers, and article 2(4) of the JAA, which defines the term "competition,"[44] places competition to purchase in the same category as competition to sell. Second, purchasers can benefit economically by controlling purchase prices when joint purchasing satisfies the requirements provided in article 2(6), and thus joint purchasing should not be distinguished from activities of sellers.

23.102 The applicability of the regulations on unreasonable restraint of trade is made even more concrete by the amendment to article 7-2(1) of the JAA in 2005. After the amendment, article 7-2(1) explicitly refers to the purchase amount of the relevant goods or services as a basis for calculation of a surcharge in the event an unreasonable restraint of trade pertaining to the purchase of goods or services is found.

23.103 The first surcharge payment order which imposed fines on joint purchasing agreements was JFTC's *Mitsubishi Material* decision in 2008.[45] Three metal manufacturers rigged bids during public bids of melt down metal sales and were found to have unreasonably restrained trade under article 3 of JAA.

J. Joint lobbying/regulatory/legislative efforts

23.104 In Japan, there has been no substantial discussion or argument on whether joint lobbying, regulatory, or legislative efforts constitute violations of the JAA to date.

III. General issues

A. Jurisdiction and applicable law (including sector-specific competition regulation)

23.105 Violation of the JAA is subject to administrative orders (cease-and-desist and/or surcharge payment orders), civil litigation, and criminal penalties. Jurisdiction and the material applicable laws in connection with each type of enforcement are summarized in Table 23.1.

[43] Sadaaki Suwazono et al., Heisei 17 Nen Kaisei Dokusenkinshihou 28 (2005).

[44] JAA (n 1) art 2(4) defines "competition" as a state in which two or more entrepreneurs, within the normal scope of their business activities and without making any material change to the facilities for, or kinds of, such business activities, engage in, or are able to engage in, any of the following acts: (i) supplying the same or similar goods or services to the same user; (ii) receiving supplies of the same or similar goods or services from the same supplier.

[45] *Mitsubishi Materials and others*, 55 Shinketsushu 692 (JFTC, October 17, 2008).

Table 23.1. Laws Applicable to Certain Types of Proceedings

Nature of Procedure	Jurisdiction of first instance	Applicable laws
Administrative orders	JFTC	JAA
Civil litigation based on Art. 25 of the JAA	Tokyo High Court	JAA Civil Procedure Code
Civil litigation based on general tort	District Court	JAA Civil Code Civil Procedure Code
Criminal sanctions	District Court	JAA Criminal Code Criminal Procedure Code

With regard to sector-specific regulations, while the JFTC has released the General Designation, which lists fifteen types of unfair trade practices as regulations applicable to business operators without regard to their sectors or industries, it has also released three sets of sector-specific rules designating several types of unfair trade practices applicable to each sector (the "Special Designations"). The Special Designations issued by the JFTC are: (i) Designation of Specific Unfair Trade Practices in the Newspaper Business,[46] (ii) Designation of Specific Unfair Trade Practices by Large-Scale Retailers Relating to Trade with Suppliers,[47] and (iii) Designation of Specified Consigners. 23.106

B. Antitrust system

(i) Name of agency/agencies

The JFTC is the competent authority regarding enforcement of the JAA. It is an independent agency under the Prime Minister's Office, composed of the Chairman, four Commissioners and the General Secretariat. 23.107

(ii) Staff size and budget

Staff sizes and budgets released by the JFTC are provided in Table 23.2. 23.108

Table 23.2 Recent JFTC Statistics

Year	Number of total staff	Number of Investigators	Budget (Billion Yen)
2011	799	452	8.92
2010	791	451	8.96
2009	779	442	8.45
2008	795	429	8.66

[46] Designation of Specific Unfair Trade Practices in the Newspaper Business, Fair Trade Commission Notification No. 9 (July 21, 1999), <http://www.jftc.go.jp/en/legislation_gls/index.files/spaper.pdf>.

[47] Designation of Specific Unfair Trade Practices by Large-Scale Retailers Relating to Trade with Suppliers, Fair Trade Commission Notification No. 11 (May 13, 2005) <http://www.jftc.go.jp/en/legislation_gls/index.files/dsutp.pdf>.

(iii) Recent enforcement actions and trends

23.109 The issuance of cease-and-desist orders and surcharge payment orders by the JFTC has been the primary method for enforcement of the JAA in Japanese practice.

23.110 As shown in the chart below, the surcharge amount has experienced dramatic growth in recent years. According to the JFTC, as of May 31, 2012, the largest surcharge amount imposed in a single case amounted to approximately JPY 27 billion in October 2010, and the largest amount imposed on a single entrepreneur was approximately JPY 9.6 billion. Figure 23.1 shows the recent increase in the total surcharge amount imposed each year.

23.111 Another recent trend seen is internationalization of the enforcement of the JAA by the JFTC. For example, in the automotive parts manufacturer cartel case regarding automotive wire harnesses in 2010, the JFTC started on-site inspections in February 2010, almost simultaneously with the inspections by the EC and the US.

C. Private litigation

23.112 Individuals and corporations can bring legal action to claim compensation for damages arising from violations of the JAA. Such legal actions claiming compensation may be grounded on the general principles of tort law, which is mainly governed by article 709 of the Civil Code. The scope of general tort law is so wide that no violation of the JAA is specifically excluded from its scope, unlike a lawsuit based on article 25 of the JAA.[48] General tort law claims can be filed without regard to the issuance of administrative orders.

23.113 The right to demand compensation for damages based on general tort law is extinguished (i) when the claimant does not exercise the right within three years from the time that he/she became aware of both the occurrence of damages and of the identity of the person who caused the damages or (ii) when twenty years have elapsed from the time of the tortious act.

23.114 The number of private lawsuits has risen significantly since the early 1990s, but cases are still much less common than in the US. Each year between ten and twenty cases are filed, aiming at infringements that mainly involve bid-rigging or unfair trade practices. About a quarter of the claims were successful or partially successful, and the success rate of damage claims is observed to be much higher than that of actions seeking for injunction.[49]

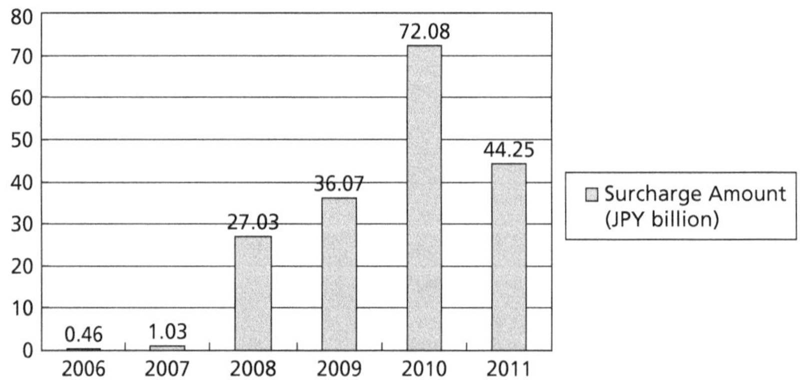

Figure 23.1 Recent increase in total surcharge amount.

[48] See further Section III.D.

[49] Simon Vande Walle, "Private Enforcement of Antitrust Law in Japan: An Empirical Analysis," *Competition Law Review* 8 (2011), 7.

D. Follow-on litigation (including the role of agency determinations of liability for follow-on litigation)

Follow-on litigation—a civil action against an entrepreneur based on a preceding decision by a national competition authority that the entrepreneur infringed competition laws—is prescribed by articles 25 and 26 of the JAA. This is due to the fact that although article 25 of the JAA provides that any entrepreneur that has committed typical violations of the JAA, such as monopolization, unreasonable restraint of trade, and unfair trade practices, shall be liable for damages suffered by the victim thereof, and the fact that article 8(1) provides the same in relation to trade associations that violate the JAA, a civil claim based on article 25 of the JAA can in fact be brought only after the JFTC issues an administrative order declaring the conduct illegal,, and the order becomes final and binding. 23.115

Unlike cases in which plaintiffs' claims are based on article 709 of the Civil Code, violators of the JAA are liable under article 25 of the JAA even where their violations were unintentional or due to negligence. 23.116

The issue of whether a preceding administrative order or declaration of illegality by the JFTC was binding on the courts where claims based on article 25 of the JAA were brought had long been pending. The Supreme Court finally resolved this issue in its judgment in the *Tsuruoka Toyu* case.[50] 23.117

The limitation period for actions claiming compensation for damages under article 25 of the JAA is three years, and commences on the date on which the administrative order or declaration of illegality pertaining to the alleged violation becomes final and binding (art. 26 JAA). The Tokyo High Court has exclusive jurisdiction over actions based on article 25 of the JAA as the court of first instance. 23.118

The JFTC has declared that it will provide relevant documentation to the courts or parties to litigation upon their request in order to support actions for damages by victims of violations of the JAA. Another option that may be used to collect evidence held by the JFTC is to request inspection and copying of the case records. According to article 75-15 of the JAA, after a hearing procedure is commenced, any person interested in the case may request inspection or copying of the JFTC's records with regard to the case in question or delivery of a transcript of a written cease-and-desist or surcharge payment order, written decision of commencement of the hearing, or the written decision, or an extract thereof. 23.119

E. Arbitration and alternative dispute resolution

Arbitration in Japan is governed by the Japanese Arbitration Act (Law No. 138 of 2003, the "JARA"), which is said to be modeled on the United Nations Commission on International Trade Law (UNCITRAL) Model Law on International Commercial Arbitration. 23.120

Arbitration is a possible option for resolving disputes over antitrust-related issues; however, it does not appear to have been used as such. Nevertheless, as the relevant Japanese law was modified in 1996 to allow non-Japanese lawyers to represent their clients in Japanese commercial arbitration proceedings, and also as the number of arbitration institutions in Japan has been increasing, commercial arbitration will be a more attractive forum for those who wish to resolve antitrust-related matters and will be more actively used as a venue to resolve such disputes. 23.121

Mediation, an alternative dispute resolution (ADR) system provided at district courts or summary courts which is governed by the Japanese Civil Mediation Law (Law No. 222 of 1951, as 23.122

---

[50] *Tsuruoka Toyu* (Supreme Court, July 2, 1987).

amended), is another option that may be used to resolve antitrust-related disputes, although it is rarely used for antitrust-related matters.

F. Remedies

(i) Civil liability

23.123 Civil liability for violations of antitrust law takes the form of damages, and violating acts may also be the subject of requests for injunctions.

23.124 The rules of the Civil Code relating to general torts apply to liability for damages. Under these rules, the damages are the difference between the actual situation in which the violation has occurred, and the situation which it is assumed would have arisen if the violation had not occurred.

23.125 Actions for damages based on antitrust law violations can typically be divided into two types, namely (a) actions where a consumer is the plaintiff and (b) actions where a party who was eliminated from the market by competition is the plaintiff. Pursuant to the above method of determining the amount of damages, in principle, in the case of (a), the damages are the difference, from the point of view of the consumer, between the actual price and the assumed price had the anticompetitive act not occurred, and, in the case of (b), the damages are the interest which should have been obtained, from the point of view of the person who was eliminated from the market by the anticompetitive act, compared with the actual situation which it is assumed would have arisen if the anticompetitive act had not occurred.[51]

23.126 It is often difficult to prove the amount of damages caused by a violation of the JAA. In such cases, the courts have discretion to award damages by arriving at a reasonable estimate based on examination of the evidence presented (art. 248 Code of Civil Procedure).

(ii) Criminal liability

23.127 As stated in Section III.B(iii), violations of antitrust law are primarily punished by the issuance of cease-and-desist and/or surcharge payment orders by the JFTC, while criminal penalties are imposed in respect of certain violations. Unreasonable restraint of trade or private monopolization is punishable by up to five years' imprisonment or a fine of up to five million yen where the violation is committed by an individual, and where the violation is committed by a body corporate, a fine of up to five million yen pursuant to dual liability.

23.128 There is no stipulated punishment for violations relating to unfair trade practices. However, where a cease-and-desist order has been issued and is violated after it has become final and binding, the violating individual shall be subject to up to two years' imprisonment or a fine of not more than three million yen, and a body corporate shall be subject to a fine of up to three hundred million yen pursuant to dual liability.

23.129 Furthermore, the penalty for obstructing an inspection is imprisonment for up to one year, or a fine of up to three million yen.

23.130 In order to impose a criminal punishment for a violation of antitrust law, the JFTC must file an accusation with the Prosecutor General. According to the JFTC's Policy on criminal accusations, it will file criminal accusations in the following cases:

23.131 Price-fixing cartels, supply-restraint cartels, market allocation, bid-rigging, joint boycotts, private monopolization, and other violations which substantially restrain competition in certain areas of trade, and which are malicious and serious cases considered to have a widespread impact on people's lives.

[51] Shiraishi (n 34) 674.

Among these acts of violation involving firms or industries which repeatedly commit violations, or those who do not abide by cease-and-desist orders, cases in which it is considered that the purposes of the Anti-Monopoly Act cannot be fulfilled by administrative sanctions imposed by the JFTC alone. **23.132**

As of June 14, 2012, the JFTC has filed criminal accusations in twenty cases. As of October 31, 2011, the maximum fine imposed against any one company was JPY 640 million (a case in which four crimes were consolidated). **23.133**

G. Leniency and immunity

The JAA provides a leniency program.[52] Under the leniency program, a maximum of five violators can file an application for a surcharge reduction or immunity. The rate of reduction of surcharge varies depending on time of filing. **23.134**

The first qualifying applicant who comes forward before the commencement of the JFTC's investigation is entitled to total immunity from administrative surcharges. The second qualifying applicant who comes forward before the commencement of the JFTC's investigation will only be entitled to a fixed 50 percent reduction in the administrative surcharges. The third qualifying applicant who comes forward before the commencement of the JFTC's investigation will only be entitled to a fixed 30 percent reduction in the administrative surcharges. The fourth and fifth qualifying applicants are entitled to a fixed 30 percent reduction in the administrative surcharges if they provide the JFTC with any information which the JFTC had not yet ascertained. **23.135**

Entrepreneurs can file applications for leniency program within 20 days after the commencement of the JFTC investigation. Such applicants are entitled to a 30 percent reduction in their administrative surcharges if: **23.136**

(a) there are no more than five leniency applicants before and after the start of the JFTC's investigation;
(b) there are no more than three leniency applicants after the commencement of the JFTC's investigation; and
(c) they provided the JFTC with information which the JFTC had not yet ascertained.

Two or more of the entrepreneurs can file an application for leniency with the JFTC jointly if they belong to a company group which satisfies the criteria prescribed by article 7-2(13) of the JAA. Such a joint application will be deemed to be a single application and the joint applicants will be accorded the same priority. **23.137**

It should be noted that a leniency applicant should not disclose the fact of its application unless a justifiable reason exists (art. 8 of the Rules on Reporting and Submission of Materials regarding Immunity from or Reduction of Surcharges). Disclosure to a foreign competition authority for the purpose of applying for leniency in the relevant jurisdiction and disclosure to the legal counsel of the parent company for the purpose of consultation are considered to constitute justifiable reasons. **23.138**

[52] The amendments to the JAA which went into effect on January 4, 2006 introduced a leniency program. In 2009, the JAA was further amended to expand the scope of entrepreneurs who would qualify for the reduction of administrative fines (the fourth and fifth applicants were not awarded surcharge reductions before the amendments in 2009) and introduced joint application.

H. Document creation and retention

23.139 According to the Act against Delay in Payment of Subcontract Proceeds, Etc. to Subcontractors,[53] which provides some specific regulations in terms of prohibition of abuse of superior bargaining position, subcontracting entrepreneurs satisfying the threshold prescribed in the Subcontract Act, when concluding subcontract agreement, should:

(a) deliver to the subcontractor a document setting forth the details of work of the contract, the amount of subcontract proceeds, the date of payment, the method of payment and other matters prescribed in the regulation of the JFTC (art. 3 of the Subcontract Act); and
(b) prepare and preserve documents or electromagnetic records,[54] prescribing detail of the work of the subcontractor, the receipt of work, payment of the subcontract proceeds and other matters prescribed in the regulation of the JFTC (art. 5 of the Subcontract Act).

23.140 On the other hand, in the JAA, there are no substantial rules related to document creation and retention, except rules regarding the forms of documents to be created in the course of administrative procedures. For example, the form for an application for the leniency program to be filed with the JFTC is available on the JFTC's web page. Other forms include those for notifications and reports required by the JAA for merger control.

[53] Act No. 120 against Delay in Payment of Subcontract Proceeds, Etc. to Subcontractors of June 1, 1956, last revised June 10, 2009 (the "Subcontract Act").

[54] Defined as a record created in a form that cannot be recognized through one's sense of perception such as in an electronic form or magnetic form that is used for information processing by computer.

24

KOREA

*Steve Harris**
Winston & Strawn Hua Jing-Legrand

Introduction

The Korean antitrust regime regulates traditional fields such as cartels, abuses of dominance, and anticompetitive business combinations. It also contains provisions on unfair trade practices, consumer protection, labeling, and advertising, as well as subcontracting. The Monopoly Regulation and Fair Trade Act (MRFTA),[1] which was enacted in 1980, states in its article 1 that its purpose is to promote fair and free competition by prohibiting abuse of market-dominant positions, preventing excessive concentration of economic power, and regulating improper concerted activities and unfair business practices, thereby stimulating creative business activities, protecting consumers and promoting balanced development of the national economy. **24.01**

The term excessive concentration of economic power refers to the existence of *chaebol* or industrial conglomerate entities. These entities rose after World War II as a result of deliberate **24.02**

* The author would like to thank Hua Jing-Legrand for his contribution to this article.

[1] The Monopoly Regulation and Fair Trade Act, enacted on December 31, 1980; entered into force April 1, 1981 (MRFTA).

governmental intervention to invigorate the economy, and have holdings in many different sectors. While *chaebols* have contributed to Korea's global competitiveness, they have also led the national markets to grow toward monopolistic and oligopolistic concentrations. The making of Korean antitrust policy takes into consideration this phenomenon.

24.03 The Korean antitrust authority is the Korea Fair Trade Commission (KFTC), which was established in 1981 as an independent central administrative organization under the jurisdiction of the Prime Minister.[2] The agency conducts investigations, issues administrative decisions, and imposes fines (surcharges) to punish violations of the MRFTA. Parties may appeal KFTC decisions to the Seoul High Court. The KFTC also has quasi-legislative authority to establish rules, notifications, and guidelines in furtherance of its enforcement of the MRFTA.

24.04 Article 36 of the MRFTA grants jurisdiction to the KFTC for the following types of matters:

(1) matters related to regulating the abuse of market dominance;
(2) matters related to restricting the combination of enterprises and preventing the concentration of economic power;
(3) matters related to regulating illegal cartels or anticompetitive behavior on the part of an enterpriser's organization;
(4) matters related to regulating unfair business practices or resale price maintenance;
(5) matters related to preventing of the conclusion of unfair international contracts;
(6) matters related to competition promotion policies through, for example, consultation or coordination with respect to Acts, subordinate statutes, and administrative measures that restrict competition; and
(7) other matters that shall be handled by the KFTC under other Acts and subordinate measures.

24.05 The KFTC is widely regarded as a particularly active enforcement body among the antitrust authorities in the Asia-Pacific region. Notable developments in enforcement activity, revisions of the law and adoption of numerous regulations and guidelines have been seen in recent years, and collaborative efforts with foreign jurisdictions have become much more common, particularly with regard to international cartel investigations and multi-jurisdictional merger reviews. During the same period, the KFTC has seen its responsibilities and reputation rise significantly within the country, in particular since 2008 when it took over the operation of the Korea Consumer Agency from the Ministry of Strategy and Finance. The KFTC's jurisdiction in the consumer protection field now includes enforcement of the following statutes: the Framework Act on Consumers;[3] the Regulation of Adhesion Contract Act;[4] the Fair Labeling and Advertising Act;[5] the Installment Transactions Act;[6] the Door-to-Door Sales Act;[7] the Act on Consumer Protection in Electronic Commerce;[8] the Consumer's

---

[2] MRFTA (n 1) art. 35.

[3] Act No. 7988, September 27, 2006, as last amended by Act No. 10170, March 22, 2010, available in English at <http://luatcanhtranhvabaovenguoitieudung.wordpress.com/2011/06/01/south-korean-framework-act-on-consumers/>.

[4] Act No. 3922, December 31, 1986, as last amended by Act No. 07491, March 31, 2005, available in English at <http://www.jftc.go.jp/eacpf/01/Korea-adhension.pdf>.

[5] Act No. 5814, February 5, 1999, as last amended by Act No. 10167 of March 22, 2010, available in English at <http://www.wipo.int/wipolex/en/details.jsp?id=12956>. See also the Enforcement Decree of this Act, available in English at <http://eng.ftc.go.kr/bbs.do>.

[6] Act No. 9084, March 28, 2008, available in English at <http://eng.ftc.go.kr/files/static/Legal_Authority/Installment%20Transactions%20Act_Mar%2028%202008.pdf>.

[7] Act No. 5086, December 29, 1995 as last amended by Act No. 5982, May 24, 1999, available in English at <http://eng.ftc.go.kr/bbs.do?command=getList&type_cd=61&pageId=0404>. See also the Enforcement Decree of this Act, available in English at <http://eng.ftc.go.kr/bbs.d>.

[8] Act No. 6687, March 30, 2001, available in English at <http://eng.ftc.go.kr/bbs.do>. See also the Enforcement Decree of this Act, available in English at <http://eng.ftc.go.kr/bbs.do>.

Cooperative Union Act;[9] and the Product Liability Act.[10] The KFTC also protects small and medium-sized enterprises (SMEs) through enforcement of the Fair Subcontract Transactions Act;[11] the Fair Franchise Transactions Act;[12] and the Omnibus Cartel Repeal Act.[13]

I. Acting alone

The MRFTA regulates unilateral anticompetitive behavior through two mechanisms: the prohibition of abuses of dominance and the prohibition of unfair trade practices. **24.06**

A. Abuses of dominance

Chapter 2 of the statute deals with the conduct of "market dominating" firms. Article 3-2 prohibits abuses of market dominance by providing that: **24.07**

> No market-dominating enterpriser shall commit any of the following acts:
>
> (1) Acts of unreasonably determining, maintaining, or changing the price of goods or services
> (2) Acts of unreasonably controlling the sale of goods or provision of services
> (3) Acts of unreasonably interfering with the business activities of other enterprisers
> (4) Acts of unreasonably impeding the participation of new competitors
> (5) Acts to unfairly exclude competing enterprisers or acts that may significantly harm the interest of consumers.

Article 2(7) defines a "market-dominating enterpriser" as: **24.08**

> ... any enterpriser who, as a supplier or customer, individually or jointly with other enterprisers, enjoys Market Dominance and possibly determines, maintains, or changes the prices, quantity, or quality of commodities or services or other terms and conditions of business in a particular business area. Market share, the existence and height of barriers to entry, relative size of competitor businesses, and so forth shall be comprehensively considered in determining [whether a firm is] a market-dominating enterpriser.

In it's landmark decision in *POSCO*[14] the Korea Supreme Court ruled that, in order to determine whether a firm has market dominance, the relevant product and geographical market must first be identified. Article 4 of the MRFTA sets out presumption thresholds of dominance based on market share. Under those presumptions, a single firm is presumed dominant if its market share is 50 percent or more, or if it is one of three enterprisers with a total market share of at least 75 percent, unless its share is less than 10 percent. A *de minimis* rule is also provided in the same article, pursuant to which any enterprisers with annual sales (or in the assessment of buyer dominance, purchases) of less than KRW 4 billion is excluded from being found dominant. **24.09**

---

[9] Act No. 8979, as amended March 21, 2008, available in English at <http://eng.ftc.go.kr/files/static/Legal_Authority/Consumers'%20Cooperative%20Union%20Act_Mar%2021%202008.pdf>.

[10] Act No. 6109, January 12, 2000, available in English at <http://eng.ftc.go.kr/files/static/Legal_Authority/Consumers'%20Cooperative%20Union%20Act_Mar%2021%202008.pdf>.

[11] Act No. 3799, December 31, 1984, as last amended by Act No. 5816, February 5, 1999, available in English at <http://elaw.klri.re.kr/eng_mobile/viewer.do?hseq=22473&type=part&key=19>.

[12] Act No. 6704, May 13, 2002, as last amended by Act No. 10168, March 22, 2010.

[13] Act No. 5815, February 5, 1999.

[14] *POSCO v. The Korea Fair Trade Commission*, Supreme Court of Korea, Decision no. 2002*Du*8626 (November 22, 2007).

24.10 The KFTC's Guidelines for Review of the Abuse of Market Dominant Position[15] set out its approach to determining dominance, which includes the detailed assessment of relevant market conditions such as: entry barriers; the relative size of any competitors to the alleged dominant enterprise; possibility of collusion; substitutable and interchangeable goods and markets; purchasing power; and the financial strength of the enterpriser. The guidelines make it clear that the KFTC's determination of whether a firm is dominant will not be based solely on a firm's market share, but also on the agency's assessment of these market conditions.[16] As cited above, the MRFTA lists five categories of prohibited abusive conducts in article 3-2. These types of conduct are also specified in the article 5 of the Enforcement Decree.[17]

24.11 In its landmark ruling in *POSCO*,[18] the Supreme Court held that the intent and purpose of abusing market dominance as well as the effects of such abuse are legal elements that need to be proven for a finding of abuse of market dominance. The court also held that anticompetitive intent and effect constitute legal standards which are specific to dominance abuse cases, and are not applicable to unfair trade practice cases.

B. Unfair trade practices

24.12 The second category of unilateral conduct prohibited by the MRFTA is unfair trade practices. That prohibition is addressed by chapter 5 of the MRFTA, which applies to all firms regardless of whether they are a "market-dominating enterpriser" as defined in chapter 2.

24.13 Article 23 of the MRFTA prohibits any enterpriser from undertaking any of the following acts:

- Act of unfairly rejecting any transaction or discriminating against a certain transacting partner
- Act of unfairly excluding competitors
- Act of unfairly inducing or coercing customers of competitors to deal with the enterpriser in question
- Act of engaging in a trade with a transacting partner by unfairly taking advantage of its own position in the transaction
- Act of trading under conditions that unfairly restrict the business activities of a transacting partner or disrupt the business activities of another enterpriser
- Act of assisting a person with special interest or other companies by providing advanced payment, loans, manpower, real estate, stocks and bonds, goods and services, intangible assets and such, or by transacting under substantially favorable terms.

24.14 The relevant categories or standards for unfair trade practices are provided in the Enforcement Decree as well as the KFTC's Guidelines for Review of Unfair Trade Practices.[19]

---

[15] Guidelines for Review of the Abuse of Market Dominant Position, enacted on September 8, 2000; last amended October 6, 2009, <http://eng.ftc.go.kr/files/static/Legal_Authority/Guidelines%20for%20Review%20of%20the%20Abuse%20of%20Market%20Dominant%20Position_mar%2014%202012.pdf> ("Abuse of Dominance Guidelines").

[16] In *Hyundai Motor Co.*, KFTC, Decision no. 2007-281 (May 18, 2007); KFTC 2008 Annual Report, p. 48, beyond Hyundai's nearly 50 percent market share and the joint market share of more than 70 percent it held with Kia Motors, KFTC drew attention to other market features such as capital requirements for entry into the market, and the significant economies of scale enjoyed by Hyundai.

[17] Enforcement Decree of the Monopoly Regulation and Fair Trade Act, last amended by Presidential Decree No. 23475 on December 30, 2011, available at <http://eng.ftc.go.kr/bbs.do>.

[18] *POSCO* (n 14).

[19] Guidelines for Review of Unfair Trade Practices, enacted on December 27, 2004; last amended August 12, 2009, <http://eng.ftc.go.kr/files/static/Legal_Authority/Guidelines%20for%20Review%20of%20Unfair%20Trade%20Practices_mar%2014%202012.pdf> ("Unfair Trade Practices Guidelines").

C. Predatory pricing

By referring to article 3-2(1)(5) of the MRFTA which prohibits any "act of unfairly excluding competitive enterprisers, or act that may considerably harm the interest of consumers," article 5(5)(1) of the Enforcement Decree further prohibits any act pertaining to "a possibility of excluding a competitor by supplying goods or services at unreasonably low prices or purchasing goods or services at unreasonably high prices compared to the normal transaction price." **24.15**

The criteria to determine abuse of dominance through predatory pricing are set out in the KFTC's Guidelines. The agency could find that there is abuse if there is concern about unfairly excluding the competitor by supplying goods or services at a lower price or purchasing at a higher price than the normal trading price: **24.16**

(i) Supplying goods or services at a lower price or purchasing at a higher price can be determined by totally considering the difference with the normal trading price, quantity or amount and period of supply or purchase, and characteristics and demand or supply of the item;
(ii) Some concern about excluding the competitor can be determined by globally considering the purpose of the act in question, whether there are similar goods or adjacent market, the market position and the resources of the competitor and an enterpriser in question.

Recent well-known cases include the KFTC's imposition of KRW 26 billion fine (USD 25.4 million) on Intel in 2008[20] for offering large rebates to customers (thus reducing the effective price to ones considered by the KFTC to be unreasonably low), on the condition that the customers purchase a certain percentage of their requirements of the products from Intel instead of a competing supplier. **24.17**

D. Exploitative offenses (excessive pricing, monopoly leveraging)

Article 3-2(1)(3) of the MRFTA prohibits dominant enterprisers from "unreasonably interfering with the business activities of other enterprisers." The provision covers a large range of conduct, including interfering with the purchase of raw materials, and recruiting key personnel from a competitor. **24.18**

In 2007, the KFTC found that Hyundai Motor Co. had violated the MRFTA by obstructing the business relocation of its distributors, as well as restricting salesperson recruitment by entering into an agreement with the trade union that represented its own staff at sales outlets controlled by Hyundai.[21] **24.19**

E. Price discrimination

Article 3-2(1)(1) of the MRFTA, which prohibits dominant firms from "acts of unreasonably determining, maintaining, or changing the price of goods or services," can be applied to price discrimination. Separately, article 23(1)(1) of the MRFTA prohibits any enterpriser from unfairly rejecting any transaction or discriminating against a certain transacting partner. **24.20**

The KFTC's Abuse of Dominance Guidelines recognize that the prohibition of abuse of dominance may be violated by making it difficult for other enterprisers to conduct business by "unfairly discriminating price or the trading conditions or offering to a counterpart **24.21**

---

[20] KFTC sent allegations to Intel Corporation, Intel Semi-Conductor, and Intel Korea; the decision was published on August 8, 2008 and is available in English at <http://eng.ftc.go.kr/utility/quicksearch.jsp?pageId=0601>. The Seoul High Court dismissed Intel's appeal of the KFTC decision on June 19, 2013.

[21] *Hyundai Motor Co.* January 17, 2007; KFTC 2008 Annual Report, p. 48.

unreasonable conditions compared to the normal trading practice."[22] Those guidelines also provide that an enterpriser may engage in an abuse of dominance by "[o]ffering unfair conditions such as the price with striking discrimination...."[23]

24.22 In 2009 the KFTC imposed a KRW 260 billion (USD 208 million) fine on Qualcomm for abusing its dominance position by charging higher royalties for its code division multiple access technologies to companies that bought modem chips from Qualcomm's competitors, while it gave rebates to companies that used Qualcomm chip.[24]

F. Dictating or influencing resale prices

24.23 Resale price maintenance (RPM) is defined by article 2(6) of the MRFTA as "an act of trading goods or services wherein an enterpriser fixes a price in advance in order to force a counterpart enterpriser or another enterpriser at the next stage of transaction to buy from or provide to the enterpriser only at that price or executes transactions under any agreement or binding condition for such purpose."

24.24 Chapter 7 of the MRFTA is a provision separate from chapter 3 (on abuses of dominance) and chapter 5 (on unfair business practices), and provides simply that "[n]o enterpriser shall engage in resale price maintenance."[25] The per se prohibition is further expounded on in the KFTC Guidelines for Review of Resale Price Maintenance.[26] KFTC decisions also make it clear that setting minimum resale prices is per se illegal.[27]

24.25 The MRFTA defines "resale price maintenance" as the "act of trading goods or services wherein an enterpriser fixes a price in advance in order to force a counterpart enterpriser or another enterpriser at the next stage of transaction to buy from or provide to the enterpriser only at that price or executes transactions under any agreement or binding condition for such purpose."[28]

24.26 Maximum RPM is not illegal per se if it can be justified.[29] The RPM Guidelines explain that maximum RPM shall only be considered illegal "if the effect of competition restriction exceeds the enhancement of effectiveness and enhancement of consumer welfare upon ad hoc balancing these effects."[30]

24.27 The guidelines contain two examples wherein justifiable reason is deemed to exist:

(i) When a business with no market dominance concludes an exclusive sales contract with a distribution company, the business does not allow the distribution company to raise the price above a certain level in order to prevent the distribution company from incurring unreasonably high profits;
(ii) The manufacturer sets a maximum price within a set range in light of concern over the fact that the manufacturer sells to only a small number of distributors and these distributors may collude amongst themselves to increase the price, thereby reducing the competitiveness of the manufacturer's products compared to those of its competitors.[31]

---

[22] Abuse of Dominance Guidelines (n 15) s. IV(4)(D)(1).
[23] Abuse of Dominance Guidelines (n 15) s. IV(3)(C)(3)(B).
[24] KFTC decision of July 23, 2009; upheld by the Seoul High Court on June 19, 2013.
[25] MRFTA (n 1) Art. 29(1).
[26] Guidelines for Review of Resale Price Maintenance, amended on December 8, 2009, Fair Trade Commission Established Rule No. 68 ("RPM Guidelines").
[27] See e.g. *KFTC v. Audi Korea*, The Korea Herald (October 17, 2008) p.7
[28] MRFTA (n 1) art. 2(6).
[29] MRFTA (n 1) art. 29(1).
[30] RPM Guidelines (n 26) s. 3(B)(2).
[31] RPM Guidelines (n 26) s. 3(B)(2).

Literary works prescribed by the Enforcement Decree are exempted from RPM prohibition. **24.28**

Article 29(2)(1)–(3) of the MRFTA contains another series of RPM exemptions which are designated in advance by the KFTC. The following conditions must be met: (i) uniformity in the quality of the good must be easily identifiable; (ii) the good must be used "daily by ordinary customers"; and (iii) free competition must exist with respect to the good concerned. Notifications of RPM must be made to the KFTC, which reserves the right to grant the exemption under the reserve that the parties must amend the agreement so as not to "threaten to cause serious harm to the interests of consumers or contradicts public interest." **24.29**

Resale price maintenance is regularly enforced by the KFTC, which appears particularly focused on relationships between suppliers and retailers. In 2012, the KFTC issued two notable RPM decisions. In the first, the agency found that Goldwin Korea, a reseller of North Face® outdoor gear illegally enforced a resale price maintenance policy against retail stores by reducing supplies to, or terminating, retailers that failed to adhere to the policy. It also found that Goldwin's prohibition against online retailer discounting constituted an unfair trade practice. In the second 2012 decision, the KFTC imposed a KRW 1.5 billion (USD 1.2 million) fine on Philips Korea, a subsidiary of Royal Philips Electronics, for preventing online retailers from selling small electronic devices below a certain price.[32] Also, in January 2013, the KFTC fined Fissler Korea LTD KRW 170 million (approx. USD 1.3 million) for prohibiting its franchised, door-to-door distributors from reselling a Fissler pressure cooker below a set price. Fissler imposed penalties for failures to adhere to the policy that included supply suspension and franchise cancellation. **24.30**

Individuals involved in resale price maintenance may be prosecuted for criminal liabilities.[33] **24.31**

G. Tying arrangements

The MRFTA does not have any provision that explicitly prohibits dominant firms from tying products. Nevertheless, article 3-2(1)(5) of the MRFTA prohibits dominant firms from any "act of unfairly excluding competitive enterprisers, or act that may considerably harm the interest of consumers." **24.32**

Article 23(3), which prohibits, as an unfair business practice, any act that unfairly coerces or induces customers to deal with the enterpriser in question, together with article 3-2, has been applied to tying conduct in the December 2005 KFTC case against Microsoft Corp. and Microsoft Korea, which addressed issues of tying of certain types of software in which Microsoft was not dominant to types of software in which Microsoft was dominant.[34] In that decision, the KFTC adopted an approach to tying similar to that applied in the EU, by assessing "whether the tying product and the tied product are separate products, which are traded separately and recognized and perceived separately by consumers, and whether there is sufficient demand for separate purchase of the tied product."[35] **24.33**

H. Exclusive dealing

Article 3-2(1)(5) of the MRFTA, and in particular article 5(4)(1) of the Enforcement Decree prohibits firms with dominant positions from "entering into an exclusive contract with a **24.34**

---

[32] See KFTC 2012 Annual Report, <http://eng.ftc.go.kr/bbs.do?command=getList&type_cd=53&pageId=0301>.

[33] See Section III.F(ii).

[34] *Microsoft*, KFTC, December 7, 2005, <http://ftc.go.kr/data/hwp/micorsoft_case.pdf>. See KFTC 2005 Annual Report, <http://eng.ftc.go.kr/bbs.do?command=getList&type_cd=53&pageId=0301>.

[35] KFTC 2005 Annual Report (n 34).

transaction partner without any justifiable reason." The Guidelines on Review of Abuse of Dominance explain that "exclusive contract" refers to supply goods or services on the condition of dealing only with the goods and services of the designated enterpriser and refraining from dealing with those of other enterprisers.

24.35 The Guidelines further provide that the availability to a substitute client of the competitor, the purpose, period, and counterpart of trading and distribution practices of the business in question shall be totally considered.

24.36 Concerning geographical restrictions, article 23(1)(5) provides that it is illegal to engage in any "act of trading under terms and conditions that unfairly restrict or disrupt business activities." This provision has been applied to acts restricting parallel imports into Korea of trademark-protected items marketed in Korea through a Korean distributor.[36] Another well-known case is *DPK International*[37] in which the KFTC issued a decision condemning Domino's Pizza for imposing territorial restriction on its franchisees although it only had 10 percent of market share.

I. Refusal to deal

24.37 Refusals to deal are dealt with on two bases: prohibition of abuses dominance abuse under article 3-2 of the MRFTA and prohibition of unfair trade practices under article 23(1)(1). For the former provision, refusals to deal by dominant firms are condemned if the product or service involved is an essential factor for the trading party.[38]

24.38 Section V(1)(B)(1)(A)–(D) of the Unfair Trade Practices Guidelines makes it clear that the act of a single business refusing to trade with another specific business constitutes an unlawful refusal to deal if it considerably restricts the number or content of traded goods or services or presents highly disadvantageous trading conditions to a specific business. Refusals to deal with consumers, as opposed to a business, are not included.

24.39 Section V(1)(B)(2)(A)–(B) provides that the illegality of such conduct "shall be determined based on whether the refusal to deal by a single business restricts competition in the related market," specifically identifying the following factors: whether the products declined are essential in the business operations of the other party; whether the business can easily find a substitute trader; whether the degree of competition in the market is expected to be reduced as a result of the refusal to deal; whether market entry of a competitor or potential competitor will be made difficult; and whether the refusal to deal is being used to force prohibited acts (such as resale price maintenance or unlawful collusion). Even if a refusal to deal is deemed to restrict competition under this analysis, s. V(1)(B)(2)(C) provides that it shall not be considered a violation under any the following conditions: a business is unable to supply the amount required by the other business due to lack of inventory and production; there is no other way but to refuse to trade and the other business has a credit flaw, a clear fault, or is on the verge of bankruptcy; the positive effect on consumer welfare is considerably greater than the harm to competition caused by the refusal; the refusal is deemed by the KFTC to have other reasonable justifications.

24.40 Section V(1)(B)(3) provides that, if a refusal to deal is undertaken in order to make it difficult for the other business to engage in business with no other reasonable justification then the

---

[36] *Han-Song Motors Corporation v. Korea Fair Trade Commission*, Supreme Court of Korea, Decision no. 2000*Du*3184 (May 2, 2002).

[37] *DPK International*, KFTC, Decision no. 2000-163 (November 15, 2000).

[38] See Section I.J on essential facilities.

conduct will be considered an "abuse of position" or "obstruction of business activities," and the effect on competition will not need to be analyzed.

Section V(1)(B)(4) creates a "safety zone" under which, if the total market share of the business refusing to trade is below 10 percent, the competition effect shall be considered minimal, and the business is exempted from examination. If the market share cannot be calculated or such calculation is difficult, a business will be exempted if its total annual sales are less than KRW 2 billion (approx. USD 1.8 million). **24.41**

The Unfair Trade Practices Guidelines also address collective refusals to deal, as further discussed in Section II.C. **24.42**

J. Essential facilities

By referring to article 3-2(1)(3) of MRFTA, article 5(3)(3) of the Enforcement Decree prohibits firms with dominant positions from "refusing, discontinuing, or limiting the use of or access to essential facilities for the manufacture, provision, or sale of products or services of other enterprisers without a justifiable reason." **24.43**

By referring to article 3-2(1)(4) of MRFTA, article 5(3)(4) of the Enforcement Decree prohibits: **24.44**

> Unreasonably impeding the participation of new competitors of the Act involves obstructing the entry of new competitors by directly or indirectly engaging in any of the following acts: ... refusing or limiting the use of or access to essential facilities for the manufacture, provision, or sale of products or services of new competitors without a justifiable reason.

The Abuse of Dominance Guidelines include among conduct that may constitute a violation of article 3-2(4)(1), which prohibits unfairly obstructing market entry, an "[a]ct of refusing or restraining the use of or access to the essential factors for production, supply and sales of goods or services of the new competitor without a justifiable reason."[39] The definition of essential factors (or essential facilities) is "material and intangible factors such as network and equipment" which satisfy all of the three following criteria: **24.45**

(i) Without using the factors, it is impossible to manufacture, supply or sale the goods or services in reality; thus an enterpriser cannot enter into the particular business area or its position with a serious inferiority in competition that cannot be avoided in the field of business will continue;
(ii) A specific enterpriser must own or control the factors exclusively;
(iii) It is impossible for an enterpriser intending to use or access to the factors to reproduce the factors or replace the factors with different ones in reality, legally or economically.[40]

An act of refusal to supply an essential input maybe either an outright refusal or imposing unreasonable prices or unfair conditions.[41] **24.46**

The Abuse of Dominance Guidelines recognizes the following justifications: **24.47**

(i) Fair compensation for investment by the enterpriser providing the essential factors is considerably hindered. Note, however, that the reduction of profit caused by intensified competition shall not be considered a hindrance to fair compensation.
(ii) The essential factors cannot be provided without reducing considerably the amount provided to the existing user.
(iii) The quality of service secured in providing the essential factors may be hindered considerably.

---

[39] Abuse of Dominance Guidelines (n 15) s. IV(4)(C).
[40] Abuse of Dominance Guidelines (n 15) s. IV(4)(C)(1)(A)–(C).
[41] Abuse of Dominance Guidelines (n 15) s. IV(4)(C)(3)(A)–(B).

(iv) Providing the essential factors is technically impossible due to the noncompliance with the technical criteria.
(v) There is some concern that it might cause the risk in the safety of the life or the body of the client using a service.[42]

K. Bundling (including loyalty and market share discounts)

24.48 The MRFTA does not have any provision that explicitly bans dominant firm from bundling products (as contrasted with tying). Nevertheless, article 3-2(1)(5) of the MRFTA prohibits dominant firms from any "act of unfairly excluding competitive enterprisers, or act that may considerably harm the interest of consumers." The KFTC decision against Microsoft[43] appears to deal with findings of tying conduct rather than bundling, though the distinction can be a nuanced one and varies somewhat between the usages of different authorities. Also, the discussion of the facts in the decision does not make it entirely clear whether the finding included all the elements of tying as discussed in Section I.G. The rebates in the KFTC case against Intel[44] may also be regarded as loyalty or market share discounts.

L. Standard-setting groups (disclosure requirements, licensing arrangements, and licensing pools)

24.49 On February 1, 2012, the KFTC issued its Model Operating Guidelines for Standard Setting Organizations for Voluntary Compliance with the MRFTA. While these guidelines recognize that standard-setting activities are generally pro-competitive, certain practices, including patent ambush or discriminatory licensing arrangements, are deemed likely to raise competition law concerns.

24.50 In order to reduce risks of infringing competition law, the guidelines state that participation to any standard setting activity should be based on fair and transparent criteria, the decision-making process should be objective and transparent and there should be adequate procedures in place to ensure a fair availability of the standard once it is established. The guidelines further recommend the adoption of early intellectual property rights (IPR) disclosure requirements and fair, reasonable, and non-discriminatory (FRAND) commitments as effective ways to ensure the future availability of standards incorporating essential IPRs.

M. Exemptions

24.51 The Korean competition law is applicable to all business entities and sectors including government entities acting in commercial areas. The MRFTA sets out at chapter 12 three series of general exemptions:

(1) any act which is carried out in accordance with other legislations including any Act and any decree made under any other Act;
(2) any act which is "deemed to be an exercise of rights under the Copyright Act, Patent Act, Utility Models Act, Design Act, or Trademark Act"; and
(3) any act of association which is established in accordance with specified legal requirements including (i) the aim of the association shall be to promote mutual aid among small-scale enterprisers, or consumers; (ii) membership of the association must be voluntary, with free withdrawal; (iii) all members of any such association shall have equal voting rights; and (iv) in the case of any association which makes profits, the distribution of profits to members shall be determined by the articles of incorporation of the association.[45]

---

[42] Abuse of Dominance Guidelines (n 15) s. IV(4)(C)(4)(A)–(E).
[43] *Microsoft* (n 34). See Section I.G for discussion.
[44] *Intel* (n 20). See Section I.C for discussion.
[45] MRFTA (n 1) arts. 58–60.

Exemptions are also provided for resale price maintenance of certain products, including cultural goods and everyday consumer products, as discussed in Section I.F. **24.52**

II. Dealing with competitors

Chapter 4 encompasses the MRFTA's treatment of cartels. The KFTC has issued Guidelines for Concerted Practice Review which seek to enhance the effectiveness and consistency of examining improper concerted practices between competitors by stipulating the general processing principle of "improper concerted practice" in article 19 of the MRFTA.[46] **24.53**

Article 19(1) of the MRFTA enumerates the following behaviors as improper concerted practices: **24.54**

(1) Act of fixing, maintaining, or changing prices.
(2) Act of determining the terms of trade or conditions of payment of goods or services
(3) Act of restricting production, delivery, transportation, or transaction of goods, or transaction of services.
(4) Act of limiting the territory of trade or counterparties to trade.
(5) Act of preventing or restricting the establishment or extension of facilities or installation of equipment required for the production of goods or rendering of services.
(6) Act of restricting the types or specifications of goods or services in producing or transacting goods or services.
(7) Act of jointly carrying out and managing the main parts of a business or establishing a company, and such, to carry out and manage the main parts of a business jointly.
(8) Act of deciding the successful bidder or real estate bidder, bidding price, auctioned price or auctioned real estate price, and other matters that should be prescribed by the Presidential Decree.
(9) Any practice that practices substantially suppressing competition in a particular business area by means other than those under Subparagraphs 1 to 8 that interfere with or restrict the activities or contents of the business of another enterpriser (including the enterpriser performing such act).

Article 19(2) provides a possibility of exemption for the above behaviors. This is when the requirements set out in the Enforcement Decree are fulfilled, when an individual authorization is granted by the KFTC, and if the conduct is undertaken for any of the following purposes: **24.55**

(1) Industrial rationalization.
(2) Research and technology development.
(3) Overcoming economic depression.
(4) Industrial restructuring.
(5) Rationalization of trade terms and conditions.
(6) Enhancement of competitiveness of small and medium enterprises.

Until 2012, the KFTC's position was that hard core cartels—agreements involving price fixing, market sharing, and bid-rigging—whose sole purpose is deemed to restrain competition will be presumed to be per se illegal, and that an analysis of the relevant market is not necessary for such hard core cartel cases. However, on April 26, 2012, the Korea Supreme Court handed down two judgments that contained important clarification on the analytical **24.56**

[46] Guideline for Concerted Practice Review, http://eng.ftc.go.kr/bbs.do?command=getList&type_cd=62&pageId=0401 ("Concerted Practice Guidelines").

framework for concerted conduct cases under article 19(1). In *Kolon Glotech*,[47] the Court clarified the correct sequence of article 19(1) analysis by holding that, first and foremost, a relevant antitrust market must be defined based on a correct set of relevant factors before competitive effects can be ascertained. In *D & T Motors*,[48] the Court held that article 19(1) offenses are not per se illegal but rule of reason offenses and that the KFTC has the burden of proof in establishing a properly defined relevant antitrust market and anticompetitive effects within a properly defined market. On August 21, 2012, the KFTC amended its Concerted Practice Guidelines to provide that a "general market analysis" must be performed even for hard-core concerted conduct (referred to as "firm concerted practice").[49]

A. Horizontal price fixing

24.57 Horizontal price fixing is caught under article 19(1) of the MRFTA as an "improper concerted practice" that unfairly restricts competition. Subparagraph 1 of the article explicitly prohibits enterprisers from agreeing to engage jointly in any "act of fixing, maintaining or changing prices." The Concerted Practice Guidelines recognize horizontal price fixing as a type of "firm concerted practice," as contrasted with "soft concerted practices."[50]

24.58 Enforcement against horizontal price fixing is a key priority for the KFTC. Recent examples include the KFTC's imposition in 2011 of fines totaling KRW 365.3 billion (approx. USD 315 million) on twelve life insurance companies for fixing commission rates of insurance policies.

B. Horizontal agreements to allocate customers or territories; agreements not to compete

24.59 Like price-fixing cartels, market-sharing agreements are prohibited under article 19(1) of the MRFTA and are among the top enforcement target of the KFTC. According to the agency's guidelines, market-sharing agreements are also considered as *prima facie* illegal. The Concerted Practice Guidelines recognize horizontal price-fixing as a type of "firm concerted practice," as contrasted with "soft concerted practices."[51]

24.60 Recent examples include the KFTC's imposition of fines totaling KRW 434.8 billon in May 2011 against four oil refiners for constructing a market-sharing system referred to as the "Original Distributor Control System." In addition to the fines, the KFTC referred three of the players (SK, GS Caltex, and Hyundai Oilbank) to the public prosecutor for criminal enforcement.[52]

C. Horizontal boycotts

24.61 Concerted horizontal boycotts are treated as an unfair trade practice under article 23[53] and are treated as a type of collective refusals to deal in the Unfair Trade Practices Guidelines.[54]

---

47 *Kolon Glotech and others v. KFTC*, Korea Supreme Court, Decision no. 2010*Du*18703 (April 26, 2012).

48 *D & T Motors and others v. KFTC*, Korea Supreme Court, Decision no. 2010*Du*11757 (April 26, 2012).

49 Concerted Practice Guidelines (n 46) s. IV(5).

50 Concerted Practice Guidelines (n 46) s. IV(1)(A)(1) ("Action of deciding and changing the price among competing businesses"). Output restraints are treated in the same manner by the same provision ("Action of deciding and controlling production among competing businesses").

51 Concerted Practice Guidelines (n 46) s. IV(1)(A)(1) ("Action of restriction and allotting a trading counterpart or a trading area among competing businesses").

52 Cartel prosecutions have increased in the past decade.

53 Such conduct is treated most commonly under art. 23(1)(1), which prohibits any act that "unfairly rejects any transaction...."

54 Unfair Trade Practices Guidelines (n 19) III(1)(A).

Such conduct is presumed to be *prima facie* illegal, but justifications are accepted in situations such as market shortage or bankruptcy faced by a potential customer. A safety zone is provided for situations where the combined turnover of the parties imposing the boycott is under 10 percent, or if their combined turnover is less than KWR 2 billion.

D. Joint ventures and other competitive collaborations

Under article 19(1)(7), any "act of jointly carrying out and managing the main parts of a business or establishing a company, and such, to carry out and manage the main parts of a business jointly" is prohibited as an "improper cartel." According to the Concerted Practice Guidelines, this includes acts of "collaboratively operating or managing the production, sale, trade, purchase of raw materials of goods or services as well as other critical parts of operation, and acts of establishing companies, etc. for such purposes." However, joint ventures are permitted if acceptable justifications are provided under article 19(2). The Concerted Practice Guidelines treat joint ventures as a type of "soft concerted practice," which includes joint production, joint research and development, joint marketing, and joint purchase.[55] Those guidelines recognize that "soft concerted practice[s] enhance[s] effectiveness by combining asset[s], knowledge, and experience or distributing risk or reducing repetitive costs, and sometimes have the businesses execute the business that would have been impossible if it was executed individually."[56] However, "soft concerted practice can also cause a competition restriction effect by reducing innovation effort, production, and quality and increasing the price or adjusting the firm concerted practice by maintaining, realizing, and enhancing the market dominance of participating businesses."[57] If it is clear at the first stage of analysis that a joint venture will not restrict competition, the examination by the KFTC can end at that stage.[58] If, however, it is not clear whether a joint venture will have such an effect, the KFTC will assess both the procompetitive and anticompetitive effects of the venture to determine whether competition will be on balance restricted.[59] **24.62**

In the context of restrictions on holding companies under article 8-2 of the MRFTA, the Enforcement Decree defines the term "joint venture" as "an enterprise wherein two or more investors (among those investors in special relation/interest, with the exception of the investor specified by the Presidential Decree, other shall be regarded as one person), with ownership of shares substantial enough to influence the business management, significantly restrict the transfer of stock ownership via any contract or other similar measures thereby making changes in stock ownership among investors difficult."[60] **24.63**

Joint ventures have frequently been approved by the KFTC in the merger review process. Establishments of joint ventures that meet the jurisdictional thresholds for merger reviews must be notified to the KFTC under articles 7(1)(5) and 12(1) of the MRFTA. **24.64**

It should also be noted that, when businesses can be regarded as "de facto one business" as a matter of fact or economically, the Concerted Practice Guidelines provide that agreements between such businesses are not subject to the prohibitions of article 19-1, except for the prohibition of bid-rigging.[61] Criteria for determining whether businesses constitute a "de facto one business" include whether a business possesses all the stock of the other business or **24.65**

55 Concerted Practice Guidelines (n 46) s. IV(B)(1).
56 Concerted Practice Guidelines (n 46) s. IV(B)(2).
57 Concerted Practice Guidelines (n 46) s. IV(B)(2).
58 Concerted Practice Guidelines (n 46) s. IV(B)(3).
59 Concerted Practice Guidelines (n 46) s. IV(B)(4).
60 Enforcement Decree (n 17) ch. 3, art. 8-2.
61 Concerted Practice Guidelines (n 46) s. IV(1).

businesses (in which case all such businesses will be regarded as one business). Even if a business does not possess all stock of another business, they may be considered one business based on an officer holding an additional post in the other business, they engage in consolidated accounting, there are everyday directions from one business to the other business; or if one business in effect controls the other; however, if the businesses compete with each other, they will not be regarded as one business.[62]

E. Trade associations

24.66 Under the MRFTA, a trade association or an "enterprisers organization" is "a juristic combination or federation organized by two or more enterprisers for the purpose of promoting their common interests regardless of the form of organization."[63] The Korean Supreme Court has further interpreted the notion as "an association or affiliation of more than two persons in the manufacturing, service and other businesses established for the promotion of common interest,"[64] and that whether an entity is an enterprisers organization is determined by examining its articles of incorporation as well as its activities as a whole.

24.67 Article 26 of the MRFTA prohibits any trade association from engaging in:

(i) any act of unfairly restricting competition including acts falling under Article 19 (1) [which prohibits improper cartels];[65]
(ii) any act of restricting the present or future number of enterprisers in any business area;
(iii) any act of unreasonably restricting the business matters or activities of a member enterpriser (referring to an enterpriser that is a member of the enterprisers organization; the same shall apply hereinafter);
(iv) any act of inducing a person to engage in unfair trade practices under each item of Article 23(1) [regulating unfair trade practices] or to engage in practices of resale price setting under Article 29 or assist a person in committing such Act.

24.68 The KFTC may impose corrective measures, including ordering the trade association to discontinue the unlawful conduct[66] and/or the imposition of fines,[67] to address any breach of article 26, or publish guidance to be observed by the association.

24.69 A restraint of trade clause contained in a trade association regulation is illegal, unless it is justified by a legitimate purpose.[68]

F. Interlocking directorates

24.70 Interlocking directorates may violate article 7 of the MRFTA, which prohibits companies that meet the thresholds established by the Enforcement Decree, from substantially minimizing competition in a particular business area directly or through a person deemed by the Enforcement Decree to have a "special interest." Specifically, article 7(1)(2) prohibits

---

[62] Concerted Practice Guidelines (n 46) s. IV(2)

[63] MRFTA (n 1) art. 2(4).

[64] *Korean Medical association Inc. v. The Fair Trade Commission*, Supreme Court of Korea, Decision no. 2001*Du*5347 (February 20, 2003).

[65] See e.g. *Gangdonggu Taekwondo Association*, KFTC Decision no. 2005-161 (August 18, 2005) KFTC News, 2005-9.

[66] MRFTA (n 1) art. 27.

[67] MRFTA (n 1) art. 28. Note the maximum fine on the trade association is KRW 500 million, while the KFTC may impose a fine on an enterpriser engaged in violations of article 26 of not more than five percent of turnover, as prescribed by the Enforcement Decree, or in the absence of turnover, a surcharge of not more than KRW 500 million.

[68] *Korea Customs Brokers Associations v. The Fair Trade Commission*, Supreme Court of Korea, Decision no. 2001*Du*175 (June 15, 2001).

the "[c]oncurrent holding of an officer's position in another company...by an officer or an employee...." Addressing that provision, the Enforcement Decree refers to the "[p]ractice of a company's officers or employees...serving on the boards of multiple corporation" as "interlocking directorates." Article 7(1)(5) prohibits the "[p]articipation in the establishment of a new company," except for persons without special interests or a person participates in the establishment of a company by division and merger through the division of an existing company.

Interlocking directorates could conceivably also be reached by article 19(1)(7) of the MRFTA, which prohibits any "act of jointly carrying out and managing the main parts of a business or establishing a company, and such, to carry out and manage the main parts of a business jointly" is a concerted practice. According to the Concerted Practice Guidelines, this includes acts of collaboratively operating or managing the production, sale, trade, purchase of raw materials of goods or services, as well as other critical parts of operation, and acts of establishing companies, etc., for such purposes. **24.71**

G. Information exchange

Information exchange is not illegal per se but direct or indirect information exchange contributes to building up evidence for infringement which are caught under article 19(1). This is particularly the case if information is exchanged through concerted practice and is directly related to competition, price, and production, the possibility of bringing about firm concerted practice increases. According to the Concerted Practice Guidelines, to assess the level of information exchange, the existence of a system for blocking information exchange and duties and organization of the concerted practice performing groups is analyzed. **24.72**

In 2012, the KFTC imposed total fines of KRW 135.4 billion and issued cease-and-desist orders against manufacturers of cup noodles for engaging in price-fixing agreement that was found to have resulted from information exchanges. **24.73**

H. Joint purchasing agreements

Under article 19(1)(7) of the MRFTA, any "act of jointly carrying out and managing the main parts of a business or establishing a company, and such, to carry out and manage the main parts of a business jointly" is a concerted practice. According to the Concerted Practice Guidelines, this includes acts of collaboratively operating or managing the production, sale, trade, purchase of raw materials of goods or services, as well as other critical parts of operation, and acts of establishing companies, etc., for such purposes. These acts are prohibited, unless acceptable justifications are provided. **24.74**

I. Joint lobbying/regulatory/legislative efforts

The Korea Supreme Court ruled in 2012 that, although concerted attempts among competitors to influence government policy or law enforcement may be an exercise of the constitutionally protected rights of free speech and to petition the government, this alone does not mean that such concerted conduct is exempt from the reach of antitrust law. In *Samsung Fire Insurance v. KFTC*,[69] the court held that fourteen life insurance companies and ten casualty insurance companies had violated the MRFTA by holding over twenty meetings during which they agreed to reduce discount rates for preferred corporate clients, reduce or eliminate premium refund rates, and jointly determine risk rates in connection with their group casualty insurance businesses. The court held that the conduct went beyond merely collecting and expressing opinions to the Financial Supervisory Service for its policy formulation, and that **24.75**

---

[69] *Samsung Fire & Marine Insurance Co., Ltd. v. KFTC*, Supreme Court of Korea, Decision no. 2010*Du*375 (May 24, 2012).

the Financial Supervisory Service did not directly and specifically command the companies to agree to reduce discounts or reduce or eliminate refunds of premiums. The court further held that the underlying insurance laws and regulations did not provide an exception to the reach of the MRFTA. However, the court also noted that the companies did not engage in such concerted conduct for the purpose of influencing the Financial Supervisory Service's policy formulation. Consequently, this case (and not other case) addresses the open question of whether the courts may subsequently recognize an exception to the reach of the MRFTA for legitimate joint petitioning activities.

III. General issues

A. Jurisdiction and applicable law (including sector-specific competition regulation)

24.76 The Monopoly Regulation and Fair Trade Act (MRFTA) contains fifteen chapters and a number of addenda, and provides both substantive and procedural rules. It has been amended numerous times.[70]

24.77 Article 2-2 provides that the MRFTA may be applied extraterritorially, as long as the activities taken place overseas have influence on the domestic market. The first time the KFTC applied the Act to overseas conductswas in the graphite electrodes cartel case.[71]

24.78 Any party who is unsatisfied with a KFTC decision may appeal against the measures taken before the KFTC within 30 days of the notification of the decision. If the appeal is made by the party to which the appealed decision applies, it could suspend the execution of the related measures, if the KFTC considers it necessary in order to "prevent irrevocable damage or harm caused by the enforcement of such orders or continuance of procedures."

24.79 The outcome of the appeal to the KFTC can be further contested within 30 days before the Seoul High Court, which has exclusive jurisdiction. Final appeals are made before the Supreme Court.

B. Antitrust system

(i) Name of agency

24.80 The Korea Fair Trade Commission (KFTC) was first created in 1981 following the enactment of MRFTA. It is under the authority of the Prime Minister and is composed of:

(a) the decision-making body: the committee consists of nine commissioners, who deliberate and make decisions on competition and consumer protection issues;
(b) the working body: the secretariat is involved in drafting and promoting competition policies, investigating antitrust issues, and presenting them to the Commission, as well as handling issues in line with the Commission's decision.

24.81 The KFTC has four mandates: promoting competition, strengthening consumers' rights, creating a competitive environment for SMEs, and restraining concentration of economic power. For these purposes, the KFTC enforces a number of laws related to consumer protection including the MRFTA. It has significant powers of investigation including requiring suspected violators and other interested parties to present documents or other materials and

[70] For a detailed discussion of all amendments, see KFTC 2012 Annual Report (n 32) s. III(2).

[71] International Graphite Cartel case, KFTC Decision 2002-07 (April 4, 2002). See KFTC 2002 Annual Report, 13, available at <http://eng.ftc.go.kr/bbs.do?command=getList&type_cd=53&pageId=0301>.

provide oral statements or written answers to investigators, as well as to appoint expert witnesses and request opinions from them. The KFTC investigators are given the rights to enter the offices or other business places of suspected violators to examine books, records and other materials belonging to the suspected violators, and seize any documents or materials which are produced.

(ii) Staff size and budget

The KFTC employs more than 500 people in its head office in Seoul as well as its regional offices in other major metropolitan cities. **24.82**

As of late 2011, the agency's annual budget was KRW 78.8 billion, which was about USD 71 million. The KFTC has seen its budget rise significantly during recent years, in particular since 2008 when it took over the operation of the Korea Consumer Agency from the Ministry of Strategy and Finance.[72] **24.83**

(iii) Recent enforcement actions and trends

During recent decades, the KFTC's enforcement has been active and increasingly tough as there has been a growing awareness for economic democratization in the country. During the year 2012, the KFTC handled 5,316 cases and imposed fines in the total amount of KWR 510.5 billion (about USD 441 million).[73] While the number of measures and orders taken is on steady rise, the agency's case receipt and process records have surged by 54 percent compared to 2011. **24.84**

Since its establishment in 1981, cartel regulation has been one of the primary objectives of the KFTC and this has only become more intensified during the recent period of increased international cartel investigation cooperation. In 2005 the maximum fine on cartels was increased from 5 percent of the relevant revenue to 10 percent. Cartels remain the largest source of fines imposed by the KFTC. The surcharges imposed for cartels alone comprised 84.8 percent of the total fines imposed on 971 enterprises between 2008 and 2011. Seventy-eight percent of the fines in 2012 were imposed on cartel participants. Based on history and recent statements of KFTC officials, cartels are expected to remain the top enforcement priority for the KFTC. **24.85**

Many Korean industries remain oligopolistic or monopolistic as a result of Korea's history of a strong industrial policy in certain sectors. Although the MRFTA prohibits dominance abuses, in reality, the provision has rarely been used in the KFTC's enforcement practice. The KFTC is expected in the future to monitor more closely "unfair" supports among subsidiaries belonging to the same conglomerated groups and to encourage large companies to do more to assist SMEs. **24.86**

C. Private litigation

An amendment to the MRFTA was introduced in 2004 and brought about a radical change in terms of liability to compensate damages. Before the amendment, remedies for damages were provided only to the extent that liability had been found or remedial action had been taken by the KFTC. In other words, only follow-on litigations were available to victims of antitrust infringements. **24.87**

[72] OECD Directorate for Financial and Enterprise Affairs, 2011 Annual Report on Competition Policy Developments in Korea (October 11, 2012), Doc. no. DAF/COMP/AR(2012)38.

[73] KFTC 2012 Annual Report (n 32).

24.88 As a result of the 2004 amendment, article 56 of the MRFTA provides that victims are entitled to compensation unless the defendant can prove that it did not intend to commit any fault and no error is found on its part. This provision, in contrast to circumstances prior to the 2004 amendment, does not require that the KFTC make any prior any decision of a violation or impose any remedy. Such lawsuits are pursued under the general rules of tort liability under which damages are limited to actual damages.

24.89 Seeking injunctive relief is not yet possible within the current legal framework. The only exception is in cases in which an action is possible under the Act on Fair Labeling and Advertising which allows the courts to temporarily suspend misleading labels or advertisements. As already mentioned in Section III.B(iii), proposed legislation is under discussion to pave way for true antitrust private antitrust litigation under the MRFTA, as opposed to the general tort laws, including class actions, injunctions, and treble damages.

24.90 Private civil actions are heard in the first instance by the Korea district court which has geographical jurisdiction over the defendant's residence or the location where the alleged infringement took place. A corporate defendant's residence is deemed to be the location of its principal business office or, if there is no such office, the address of its principal agent. In the case of a foreign company or organization, such location could be its Korean office or branch or, if such office or branch is not available, the address of its agent in Korea. In addition, under the Civil Procedure Act, parties to private antitrust actions may also agree on a court in order to have their case heard in writing. The agreed-upon court may hear the case even if in principle it does not have jurisdiction over it.

24.91 A decision handed down by a district court may be appealed to the High Court that normally reviews decisions of that court. A decision made at the High Court level may be appealed to the Supreme Court of Korea. Appeals made to High Courts are available on both the facts and the law, but appeals made to the Supreme Court are available only on issues of law.

24.92 Notably, in March, 2013, Dao-Young Kim, head of the KFTC International Division, announced that the KFTC has proposed new legislation that would allow for class action lawsuits, treble damages, and injunctions.

D. Follow-on litigation

24.93 Any person may file a lawsuit "in response to" a decision of the KFTC under the MRFTA, pursuant to article 54. In practice, most such lawsuits are appeals seeking to overturn KFTC decisions. Such a lawsuit must be filed within thirty days of the receipt of a notice of the KFTC decision or receipt of a written verdict of the KFTC against the appeal. The Seoul Appellate Court with jurisdiction over the seat of the KFTC has exclusive jurisdiction over such lawsuits,[74] which are referred to as appeals in the MRFTA.

24.94 The Supreme Court of Korea holds that any factual determination made in a confirmed KFTC decision is not necessarily binding on a later decision, but serves as strong evidence. Based on this decision, absent special circumstances, factual determination for the same set of facts in a later decision should not contradict the factual determination made by an earlier decision. Leniency applicants are not protected from follow-on litigation, whether or not leniency is actually granted to them.

[74] MRFTA (n 1) art. 54(2).

E. Arbitration and alternative dispute resolution

In 2007, the KFTC created the Korean Fair Trade Mediation Committee (KFTMC), whose mission is to arbitrate disputes that arise out of provisions related to unfair trade practices as well as the Fair Franchising Act. Within the KFTMC, a Fair Trade Dispute Mediation Council was established to mediate conflicts related to acts charged with violation of unfair trade practices regulated under article 23(1). **24.95**

Any party who alleges that it has suffered injury as a result of a breach of article 23(1) may submit a proceeding-opening request to the KFTMC, unless the KFTC considers that it is more appropriate for it to take action under article 24 (Remedial Measures) or article 51 (Recommendation for the Correction of Violation) of the MRFTA, or if the case is already under investigation by the KFTC. Requests for conflict mediation are forwarded to the KFTMC, which may conduct investigations into the alleged behaviors of violation (e.g. by requesting documents) if necessary, and provide arbitration. Resolution proceedings, that do not preclude the possibility of further bringing a lawsuit under article 56(1), must be resolved within sixty days, beyond which date the procedure is deemed to be abandoned. The procedure can also be ended through withdrawal by either of the parties of if a lawsuit is brought instead. **24.96**

If the parties accept the outcome of the mediation, they will sign the mediation protocol. The resolution then becomes binding and the parties are required to perform as what is agreed in the protocol and submit the result of the performance to the KFTC. **24.97**

Any case that has been subject to such a mediation procedure will not be subject to any correction recommendation (art. 51-1) or remedial measure (art. 24) of the MRFTA. **24.98**

F. Remedies

(i) Civil liability

Whenever the KFTC finds a violation of the MRFTA, the agency may order remedial measures under article 24 of the MRFTA or a corrective recommendation under article 51-1 to be taken by the enterpriser in order to comply with the Act. **24.99**

Financial penalties or fines (usually referred to by the KFTC and the MRFTA as "surcharges") can be imposed under chapter 10-2 of the MRFTA. When assessing the amount of a fine, the KFTC is required to take into consideration the nature and extent of the unlawful practice, the duration and frequency of the unlawful practice, and the amount of benefit accrued from the unlawful practice. Further indications of the standards to be followed in calculating a fine are set forth in the Enforcement Decree. **24.100**

Under article 55(3) of the MRFTA and KFTC guidelines,[75] the calculation of a fine is made through four steps: **24.101**

(1) Determination of the basic surcharge, which is an amount determined according to the criteria for the degrees of violation of respective types of violation after classifying each violation as "weakly significant violation," "significant violation," and "highly significant violation" depending on the nature and extent of the violation. It is the base amount for computing surcharges.
(2) Determination of obligatory adjusted surcharge, which takes into consideration the duration and frequency of violation as well as the amount of unjust enrichment from the violation;

[75] Announcement on Detailed Standards, Etc. for the Imposition of Surcharges (October 20, 2010), <http://eng.ftc.go.kr/files/static/Legal_Authority/Announcement%20on%20Detailed%20Standards,%20Etc%20for%20the%20Imposition%20of%20Surcharges_mar%2014%202012.pdf>.

(3) Determination of optional surcharge: it refers to the amount of further adjustment made to the obligatory adjusted surcharge. It takes into consideration on factors that affect each of the mitigating circumstances under Article 55-3 of the Act, such the intention or negligence of the perpetrator, the nature and circumstance of violation, financial circumstances and market status.
(4) Determination of imposable surcharge: at this stage are taken into account the perpetrator's realistic ability to pay, the effect of the violation on the market, and cases where the surcharge is excessive because other markets or economic circumstances were not sufficiently taken into account.

24.102 The MRFTA provides caps on fines that can be imposed for each type of infringement. An abuse of dominance cannot be punished by more than 3 percent of the enterpriser's sales turnover, or more than KRW 1 billion if the sales data are not available.[76] Cartels are fined up to 10 percent of the enterpriser's sales turnover, or up to KRW 2 billion if sales data are not available.[77] Unfair trade practices can result in fines of up to 2 percent of the enterpriser's sales turnover, or up to KRW 500 million.[78]

24.103 If an enterpriser found to have violated the MRFTA merges with, or is acquired by, another company, the liability arising from the infringement is imputed to the entity which continues to exist after, or is created by, transaction.

24.104 The calculation of fines takes into consideration the fact that the enterpriser in question has implemented a compliance program. Depending on the result and the record of the implementation, 30–50 percent of reduction may be applied to the final amount or surcharge fine imposed. Voluntary termination of infringement before the taking of a final infringement decision as well as cooperation during the KFTC's investigation also contribute be to fine reduction.[79]

(ii) Criminal liability

24.105 Chapter 66 of the MRFTA sets forth its Penal Provisions. Any offense falling under the criminal provisions are prosecuted through public actions only. The KFTC may request that the Prosecutor General prosecute an individual, but the Prosecutor has discretion over whether to proceed.

24.106 Imprisonment for a duration of up to three years or a fine of up to KWR 200 million may be imposed on individuals who have:

(a) committed an abusive act in violation of the provisions of article 3-2 (dominance abuse);
(b) combined enterprises in violation of article 7(1);
(c) violated the provisions of article 8-2(2) to 8-2(5);
(d) established a holding company or converted a company into a holding company in violation of article 8-3;
(e) acquired or owned stocks in violation of the provisions of article 9 or 10(1), excluding the person subject to an order of prohibition as per article 17-2(1) (including the applicable case as per article 4 of the Addenda) from among those violating article 10(1);
(f) guaranteed a debt in violation of the provisions of article 10-2(1);
(g) exercised his/her voting rights in violation of the provisions of article 11 or 18;
(h) evaded the law in violation of the provisions of article 15;
(i) in unfair concerted practices or encouraged others to participate in such in violation of the provision of article 19(1); or

[76] MRFTA (n 1) art. 6.
[77] MRFTA (n 1) art. 22.
[78] MRFTA (n 1) art. 24-2.
[79] *Showa Denko KK v. The Korea Fair Trade Commission*, Supreme Court of Korea, Decision no. 2004*Du*11275 (March 24, 2006).

(j) engaged in prohibited practices involving an enterprisers organization in violation of article 26(1)(1).[80]

Individuals may also be sentenced to a jail term of not more than two years or a fine of not more than KRW150 million, if they have: **24.107**

(a) engaged in unfair trade practices;
(b) violated provisions relating to trade associations;
(c) engaged in illegal resale price maintenance;
(d) concluded an international contract in violation of article 32(1);
(e) failed to comply with the remedial measures or order of prohibition; or
(f) failed to undergo audit by a certified public accountant in violation of article 14(5).[81]

Articles 68 and 69 also provide for fines against individuals and enterprisers for the failure to make certain reports, or make false reports, in violation of various specified provisions of the MRFTA. **24.108**

G. Leniency and immunity

Korea first adopted an antitrust leniency program in 1997. The program has been amended several times and it now helps detect more than half of the cartels cases that the agency brings. The regime is regulated under the Enforcement Decree,[82] as well as the KFTC's Announcement on Implementation of Improper Concerted Acts Leniency Program.[83] **24.109**

Leniency applications may be made orally, by fax, or by email. The first leniency applicant (or "confessor" in the terminology of the Leniency Notification) to expose a cartel to the KFTC is entitled to a full exemption from both correctional orders and surcharges, as well as from criminal liabilities in connection with the cartel. The applicant must, however, report the scheme prior to any existing investigation and provide evidence to establish a case against the cartel, as well as cooperate diligently with the KFTC throughout its investigation and cease the reporting entity's participation in the scheme. **24.110**

If the cartel investigation has already started, the first cartel participant to assist the KFTC by providing evidence necessary to prove the improper concerted practice (deemed a "company cooperating in investigation" in the Leniency Notification) may receive full exemption from surcharge and a partial reduction or full exemption from correctional order. **24.111**

The second participant that reports or assists with the investigation is entitled to 50 percent reduction of surcharge and full immunity of criminal liabilities. However, two conditions must be fulfilled. First, it must have applied for leniency within two years starting from the confession of the first applicant. Second, as of 2012, the 50 percent reduction is no longer granted to any leniency applicant which is second in line and is involved in any two-member cartel. **24.112**

Leniency applicants have 15 to 75 days starting from the initial application to submit any supplementary evidence. Those who file for leniency after the second applicant in line do not benefit from any surcharge reduction, unless they benefit from the "amnesty plus program." **24.113**

In addition, under the KFTC's "amnesty plus program," a leniency applicant in one cartel which also reports its involvement in another cartel (referred to as "other improper cartels" **24.114**

[80] MRFTA (n 1) art. 66.
[81] MRFTA (n 1) art. 67.
[82] Enforcement Decree (n 17).
[83] Announcement on Implementation of Improper Concerted Acts Leniency Program, last amended January 3, 2012, <http://eng.ftc.go.kr/files/static/Legal_Authority/Announcement%20on%20Implementation%20of%20Improper%20Concerted%20acts%20Leniency%20Program_mar%2014%202012.pdf> ("Leniency Notification").

in the Leniency Notice) enjoys up to 20 percent of additional surcharge reduction for the first cartel. The agency has the discretion to decide on the scale of the reduction depending on the significance of the second cartel denounced. The additional confession is only taken into account if, as far as the second cartel is concerned, the applicant is the first to denounce among the participants of that cartel.

24.115 Also, participants who coerced other companies to participate in the scheme cannot benefit from any immunity or fine reduction. Repeated offenders are also excluded from being granted any immunity or fine reduction if, during the past five years, it has been subject to any corrective measure or has already filed for a leniency application.

24.116 Leniency applicants are required to cooperate continuously and with good faith until the completion of the cartel investigation.[84] According to article 5 of the KFTC's Leniency Notification, the applicants must

(i) state every fact they know about the cartel without hesitation;
(ii) promptly submit all materials, which they have or can obtain, related to the concerned cartel;
(iii) answer questions and cooperate with the KFTC's fact-finding exercises;
(iv) ensure that their staff, including where possible former employees cooperate in a sincere and continued manner.

24.117 The Supreme Court has recently held that a notice of non-recognition of leniency status issued by the KFTC constitutes a separate "disposition" by an administrative agency and, accordingly, an applicant that submitted an application for leniency to the KFTC but did not receive a leniency confirmation from the KFTC may appeal such decision by commencing a separate administrative litigation without waiting until the issuance of the final cartel decision from the KFTC.[85]

H. Document creation and retention

24.118 There is no explicit provision regarding document creation or retention contained in the MRFTA. However, failing to make a report or provide materials requested by the KFTC, or presenting falsified materials or information, may be subject to fines under article 69-2.

24.119 As far as confidentiality is concerned, protections are given to information obtained during the course of the application of the MRFTA. Article 62 provides that "no official who commissioner or public official who performs or has performed duties under this Act may neither divulge any secrets of an enterpriser or a enterprisers organization learned in the course of carrying out duties nor use it for purposes other than to enforce this Act." Breaches of this obligation can result in criminal liabilities including up to two years of imprisonment or a fine up to KWR 200 million.

24.120 Pursuant to article 52-2, any party or interested person may request that the KFTC grant "access to or authorization to make copies of data related to measures taken under [the MRFTA]." If the KFTC deems such access necessary for the public interest, or if consent is granted by the person that provided such data to the KFTC, the KFTC must comply with the request.

24.121 Under article 43(1), the KFTC is required to disclose "all trials and resolutions made by the [KFTC]," except when the KFTC deems non-disclosure "necessary to protect the trade secrets of an enterpriser or an enterprisers' organization."

---

[84] Enforcement Decree (n 17) art. 35(1)(1)–35(1)(5).

[85] Supreme Court of Korea, Decision no. 2010*Du*3541 (September 27, 2012).

25

LITHUANIA

Ilona Jančiauskaitė, Marius Juonys, Karolis Kačerauskas, and Arnoldas Puodžius
LAWIN

Introduction

The traditions of Lithuanian competition law could be dated back to 1992, when Lithuania regained its independence and adopted its first Law of Competition. In 1999, the Law on Competition was entirely rewritten by transposing the model of EU competition law. Since then, the prohibition of abuse of dominant position and anticompetitive agreements set out by the Law on Competition are almost identical to articles 101 and 102 of the Treaty on the Functioning of the European Union (TFEU). In turn, the Lithuanian competition council (LCC) issued very few guidelines on interpretation of national competition law, which are supplemented by direct references to the respective guidance instruments adopted by the European Commission. Such harmonization is furthermore extended to case practice which is heavily based on interpretation and application of EU guidelines and precedents. It should be noted, however, that analysis of the EU soft law sometimes results in different conclusions and contributes to the development of national precedents, which are not accepted in **25.01** the EU law. Thus the Lithuanian competition law still contains certain rules which could be considered as purely national.

25.02 The competition policy in Lithuania is given high priority and receives support from the highest governmental institutions. In turn, the LCC is perceived as a sufficiently independent and professional institution and is treated with respect and caution by the business world. The competition policy officially declared by the LCC is based on the premise that authority should focus on cases that could make the highest impact on the consumers and/or concern hard core infringements. As a result, the LCC is currently concentrating its efforts on banking and food sectors, which are subject to complex and long-lasting investigations. In addition, the authority may discover hard core infringements in various sectors either accidentally, or on the basis of operation of leniency program.

I. Acting alone

25.03 Competition law infringements can be the result of unilateral actions as well as conclusion of various types of anticompetitive agreements. Purely unilateral conduct may lead to infringement only if such conduct can be attributed to the undertaking having a "dominant" position on the market, and to that undertaking's decision to exploit its market power for anticompetitive purposes. Nevertheless, it is possible that seemingly unilateral conduct may in fact be also considered as agreement between non-competitors, which makes both parties liable for competition law infringement. The difficulties of legal qualification are well illustrated by the *G4S money management* case,[1] which dealt with the alleged exclusive dealing arrangements made between banks and a provider of money management services having near monopoly power. In this case, the LCC considered that such arrangements could potentially be treated as abuse of dominant position as well as an anticompetitive agreement; however, on the basis of purported efficiency the LCC proceeded only with the allegations of anticompetitive agreement.

25.04 The majority of acting-alone cases, however, are investigated as potential abuses of dominant position. This is evidenced by the fact that during 2010–2012 the LCC resolved thirty-two abuse of dominance cases (three infringement and two settlement decisions) and only six cases concerning vertical anticompetitive agreements (two infringements and one settlement decision). In the majority of those cases, the LCC considered claims concerning allegedly predatory and excessive pricing behavior, and usually rejected such claims without even opening an official investigation. At the same time, the LCC was primarily interested in exclusive dealing, refusal to supply, and discrimination cases, which most usually resulted in infringement and settlement decisions.

A. Abuse of dominant position

25.05 Article 3(2) of the Law on Competition defines dominance as a position on the relevant market held by one or several undertakings (collective dominance), which entitles such undertaking or the group of undertakings to escape direct competition, or enables such undertaking or a group of undertakings to exert unilateral decisive influence on the relevant market by effectively restricting competition.

25.06 The concept of dominance entrenched in Lithuanian law is in principle analogous to the one developed in the context of application of article 102 TFEU, although presumptions of dominance based on market share thresholds are a peculiar feature of Lithuanian law.

[1] *G4S money management* [2012], LCC Decision no. 2S-15.

In particular, the law establishes 40 percent market share as a presumption for single-firm dominance and 70 percent market share held by a group of two or three undertakings as a presumption of collective dominance. These thresholds are reduced specifically for retail trade, where 30 percent market share triggers presumption of single-firm dominance, while 55 percent market share is sufficient to presume collective dominance.

Article 7 of the Law on Competition contains a non-exhaustive list of abusive behavior, which is in principle analogous to the list contained in article 102 TFEU. Thus, the concept of "abuse" of dominant position under Lithuanian law is in principle analogous to the one developed in the context of EU competition rules. **25.07**

In its previous practice, the Lithuanian competition authority allocated its resources mainly to prosecution of abusive conduct of dominant undertakings and cartels. In some years, the LCC even investigated more abuse of dominance cases than cartel cases. However, the current trends suggest that the LCC is ready to take less aggressive stance on abuse of dominance. The new version of the Law on Competition, which entered into effect on May 1, 2012, allows the LCC to set its enforcement priorities. Thus, it is expected that the authority will concentrate its efforts on prosecution of cartels, while investigations of abusive conduct will be less frequent. These expectations are also based on public statements by the present chairman of LCC and on the current version of enforcement priorities adopted by the LCC, declaring that the LCC shall prioritize, *inter alia*, cases which require lower resources. **25.08**

B. Agreements between non-competitors

Agreements between non-competitors are considered under articles 5–6 of the Law on Competition, which are analogous in structure to article 101 TFEU. In particular, article 5 prohibits agreements restricting competition, while article 6 allows for justifications of such agreements, provided that they lead to some efficiencies, which are proportionate and fairly shared with consumers. As a general rule, agreements between non-competitors are perceived less strictly than agreements between competitors. Hence only a few types of agreements between non-competitors are perceived as hard core restrictions of competition, while a majority of agreements lead to competition law infringement only if such agreements actually have negative effect on competition. Such effect-based cases require rather complex and time-consuming analysis. Thus only very limited number of LCC cases concern anticompetitive agreements between non-competitors. **25.09**

C. Predatory pricing

The basic definition of predatory pricing appears in the notice on the concept of dominant position published by the LCC in 2000. As stated in the notice, the concept of predatory pricing refers to the practice of sale below costs having the objective to exclude competitor from the market. The content of such concept is further elaborated in the practice of LCC. **25.10**

The LCC receives predatory pricing claims quite commonly, although the vast majority of such claims are rejected without any official investigation. Such trends are clearly illustrated by numbers: during the period from 2010 to 2012, the LCC resolved 10 cases involving allegations of predatory pricing, which constituted approximately 31 percent of all dominance cases considered by the LCC during this period; however, none of those resulted in infringement decisions. **25.11**

The only instance in which the LCC found a predatory pricing scheme was in the *AGA I* case,[2] which was resolved in 1997. There, the LCC found infringement after determining **25.12**

[2] *AGA I* [1997] LCC Decision no. 1.

that AGA engaged in "sale of goods below production costs." The resolution of LCC did not elaborate on the particular legal tests employed in this case, however it was felt that authority relied on criteria determined by the Court of Justice of the European Union (CJEU) in *AKZO* case.[3] In this case, the LCC imposed a fine on AGA amounting to 3 percent of the company's annual turnover and the obligation to report to LCC prices offered by AGA on the market.

25.13 The LCC provided greater clarity on the legal requirements for predatory pricing claims thirteen years later in the *Vilnius airport IV* case.[4] There, the LCC considered whether an airport operator supplied fuel to aircrafts at unreasonably low prices. Although the LCC found no infringement, it declared that predatory pricing cases shall be considered on the basis of *AKZO* test: (i) pricing below average variable costs (the cost of making one additional item) (AVC) shall be presumed predatory if every sale below AVC leads to losses; (ii) pricing above variable costs, but below average total costs (the total cost of each item) shall be considered predatory only if there is evidence that it constitutes part of a plan to exclude a competitor from the market; (iii) pricing above average total costs shall not be considered predatory.

25.14 The application of the *AKZO* test has been confirmed by the authority in subsequent *TEO LT* and *Lithuanian railways* cases,[5] both of which were terminated without finding infringement.

D. Exploitative offenses

25.15 Exploitative practices mostly concern application of excessive prices. Excessive pricing claims are rather common in the practice of LCC; however, such investigations rarely result in infringement decisions. The latest attempt of the competition authority to prove such kind of infringement concerned pricing employed by the operator of tunnels used for communication cables. In 2007, the LCC declared that prices charged by *Vilniaus energija* were unfair as they have been calculated disproportionately to the space taken by various communication networks in the tunnels.[6]

25.16 In 2010, the Supreme Administrative Court annulled the decision claiming that the LCC had failed to prove the unfairness of prices charged by *Vilniaus energija.* As stated by the court, excessive pricing could be determined by conducting the following analysis:

- the prices charged for the product should be compared with their production costs;
- in the case that the difference between the price and production costs seems *excessive*, it should be considered, whether the prices charged by dominant undertaking could be considered as *unfair*;
- *unfairness* could be determined on the basis of comparison between prices charged by dominant undertaking for certain products and their economic value.

25.17 The court provided little guidance on the determination of economic value of certain products; however, the court suggested that economic value could be determined on the basis of production costs as well as factors, which are not related to costs (such as supply and demand).

25.18 Based on its conclusions, the court remanded the case to the LCC for additional investigation. The renewed attempt of the LCC to prove excessive prices was also annulled by the court in 2012 for the same failure to prove unfairness of prices charged by *Vilniaus energija.*

[3] Case C-62/86 *AKZO Chemie v. Commission* [1991] ECR I-13359.
[4] *Vilnius airport IV* [2010] LCC Decision no. 2S-1.
[5] *TEO LT* [2011] LCC Decision no. 1S-152; *Lithuanian railways* [2011] LCC Decision no. 1S-184.
[6] *Vilniaus energija* [2012] LCC Decision no. 1S-61.

It could be assumed that following six years of unsuccessful litigation in the *Vilniaus energija* case, the LCC will be reluctant to commence excessive pricing cases in the future absent very compelling evidence.

E. Monopsony

25.19 Lithuanian competition law does not exclude the possibility that undertakings could be considered as holding a dominant position on the procurement markets, although the LCC has never brought or investigated a monopsony case.

25.20 In public discussions, the issue of buyer power has been raised in the context of the retail trade sector as there is a general concern that the market power of retail chains has grown excessively and is likely to harm competition. However, for now, Lithuanian authorities have attempted to tackle this problem by introducing a special law restricting certain practices of food retail chains vis-à-vis their suppliers. Nevertheless, the possibility of application of competition law instruments to the growing procurement market power of retail trade chains remains a real concern.

F. Price discrimination

25.21 Price discrimination is considered to be an anticompetitive practice of dominant undertakings. This practice could also be classified as an anticompetitive agreement concluded between two or more undertakings, provided that price discrimination is used to support anticompetitive commitments (e.g. charging reduced prices for customers committing not to engage in parallel trade).

25.22 According to the Lithuanian Law on Competition, price discrimination occurs when a dominant undertaking "applies dissimilar (discriminating) conditions to equivalent transactions with certain undertakings, thereby placing them at a competitive disadvantage." Price discrimination could thus amount to infringement provided three conditions are met: (i) the transactions under investigation are equivalent; (ii) the pricing conditions in such transactions are dissimilar (discriminatory); (iii) such dissimilar (discriminatory) pricing conditions place undertakings at a competitive disadvantage.

25.23 From the Lithuanian law perspective, the "equivalency" of transactions could be established if there are sufficient reasons to conclude that certain transactions are sufficiently similar, rather than identical. For this purpose, the LCC's assessment of "equivalency" is based on the comparison of the nature of agreement (e.g. sale-purchase or distribution contract), object of agreement, and type of distribution of certain products.

25.24 Having determined that transactions are "equivalent," it's necessary to consider whether the conditions applied to different transactions are discriminatory. The prohibition of discriminatory prices does not require that the dominant undertaking apply identical pricing conditions to all transactions. Instead, the law requires that (i) analogous prices be applied to equivalent transactions and (ii) different prices be applied to non-equivalent transactions. Conversely, the differences in pricing can lead to infringement of competition rules if they cannot be objectively justified. In the LCC's practice, a cost-based justification of price difference is the most common example of objective justification (e.g. volume-related price discounts[7]). Nevertheless, there is nothing that could rule out a wider scope of justifications.

25.25 Once it has been determined that a dominant undertaking applies discriminatory conditions to equivalent transactions, it should be ascertained whether such discrimination has led to

[7] *Lietuvos gelezinkeliai* [2001] LCC Decision no. 43.

different competitive conditions for undertakings subject to discrimination. However, as a general rule, the LCC presumes that discriminatory pricing causes competitive disadvantage without having to engage in detailed analysis of the effects.

25.26 To summarizing the practice of LCC in discrimination cases, it could be said that discrimination cases are quite frequent, and the LCC is willingly interfering to remedy the situation. During the period of 2010–2012, the LCC resolved seven cases involving allegations of discriminatory treatment, which constituted approximately 22 percent of all dominance cases considered by the LCC during this period. One of those cases resulted in infringement decision, while two cases were terminated in exchange for commitments proposed by the parties.

G. Dictating or influencing resale prices

(i) Resale price maintenance

25.27 Resale price maintenance (RPM) amounts to a hard core restriction of competition, which eliminates the possibility of *de minimis* and block exemption for vertical restraints. The content of RPM restrictions is generally explained by the EU Regulation 333/2010 on vertical restraints block exemption (VBER)[8] and the explanatory guidelines adopted by the European Commission.[9] Although these pieces of legislation are primarily designed for the application of article 101 TFEU, the application of Regulation 330/2010 is extended by the LCC to purely national situations.

25.28 RPM agreements primarily include contractual arrangements which require that the parties to the agreement follow minimum or fixed prices. Nevertheless, prohibition of RPMs is also applicable to all instruments and arrangements, the combination of which leads to *de facto* the same pricing result, for example fixing the distribution margin, establishing a maximum level of discount that can be provided by the distributor, making incentives (e.g. rebates, bonuses) subject to the observance of certain price level.

25.29 Although the notion of RPM is interpreted broadly, the prohibition of RPM generally does not apply to recommended and maximum resale prices. However, this general rule is subject to certain limits. First, only genuine recommended and maximum prices are excluded from the prohibition, meaning that there should be no positive or negative incentives applied by the supplier, which would *de facto* turn recommended and maximum prices into fixed or minimum prices. Second, the exclusion of maximum and recommended prices from the prohibition of RPM is based on VBER, which does not apply if the market shares of contracting parties exceed 30 percent. If those thresholds are exceeded, it should be considered whether recommended and maximum prices have negative effects on competition and whether such effects could be justified on the basis of the Lithuanian counterpart to article 101(3) TFEU. As stated by the European Commission, the potential of a negative effect on competition directly depends on the market position of the supplier. The stronger the supplier's market position, the higher the risk that resellers follow the recommended or maximum price which functions as a price benchmark.

25.30 Notably, the LCC has brought only one RPM case, which was decided in 2010. In that case, the LCC sanctioned *Forum Cinemas* for contractual vertical price fixing for distributors of DVD movies.[10]

[8] Commission Regulation 330/2010 on the application of Article 101(3) of the Treaty on the Functioning of the European Union to categories of vertical agreements and concerted practices (April 20, 2010), OJ L 102/1.

[9] European Commission, Guidelines on Vertical Restraints, SEC(2010) 411, para. 48 ("Vertical Guidelines").

[10] *Forum Cinemas* [2010] LCC Decision no. 1S-98.

(ii) Minimum advertised price programs

Lithuanian competition law does not provide any specific guidance on the assessment of minimum advertised price (MAP) programs, i.e. the fact of advertising prices below a certain level, which does not extend to restrictions of resale price. Nevertheless, MAP programs are sufficiently likely to result in selling at or above minimum advertised price by a majority of resellers. Such result could already be considered as the establishment of fixed or minimum prices, which amounts to hard core restriction of competition. **25.31**

H. Tying arrangements

As a general rule, tying arrangements could amount to infringement only if such practices are employed by dominant undertakings and, in particular, undertakings dominant on the tying product market. **25.32**

Tying arrangements amount to infringement if (i) the tying and tied products are distinct products; (ii) the tying practice is likely to lead to anticompetitive foreclosure in the tied and/or tying product market; and (iii) tying practices could not be justified by objective reasons or overriding efficiencies. **25.33**

The LCC considered tying arrangements twice in its practice. In the *Funeral company* case,[11] the LCC found that the funeral company held a dominant position in the market for the lease of chapels, which were leased subject to the requirement that customers purchase all funeral goods from the same company. The LCC condemned such actions as tying practice which attempted to eliminate competitors on the funeral goods market and deprived customers of the possibility of choosing alternative suppliers. The LCC reached a similar conclusion in the *Vilnius airport III* case,[12] in which it condemned the lease of galleries meant for access to aircrafts by passengers only in conjunction with services of towing airplanes to and from such galleries. The LCC stated that it would have been willing to accept such bundling if it were is required for technical reasons, but found such technical justifications lacking. **25.34**

I. Exclusive dealing

Exclusive dealing obligations may be explicitly established in contracts or result from the combination of seemingly unrelated contractual arrangements. For example, in the *Orlen Lietuva* case,[13] the LCC envisaged exclusive dealing arrangement stemming from the obligation on the customer to purchase goods in quantities nearly approaching annual needs of the customer (to calculate this, 80 percent threshold was taken as a measurement point). In the *G4S money management* case,[14] on the other hand, the exclusive dealing obligation was stipulated by imposing a penalty on the customer and providing for contract termination by the essential services provider should the customer employ an alternative service provider. **25.35**

Exclusive dealing arrangements could fall under the prohibition of anticompetitive agreements as well as abuse of dominant position. Assessment of exclusive dealing arrangements in light of Lithuanian counterpart to article 101 TFEU (i.e. prohibition of anticompetitive agreements) is based on VBER and Vertical Guidelines, the application of which is extended by the LCC to purely national situations. In particular, exclusive supply arrangements and non-compete arrangements are exempted from the prohibition of article 5 of Law on Competition provided that market share of the supplier on the selling market and the **25.36**

---

11 *Funeral company* [2003] LCC Decision no. 2S-8.
12 *Vilnius airport III* [2009] LCC Decision no. 2S-24.
13 *Orlen Lietuva* [2010] LCC Decision no. 2S-31.
14 *G4S money management* (n 1).

market share of the customer on the procurement market do not exceed 30 percent, and the validity of the non-compete arrangement does not exceed five years. Agreements concluded for indefinite duration and agreements containing automatic renewal clauses are deemed to exceed the five-year limit.

25.37 Exclusive dealing arrangements that do not benefit from the safe-harbor established by VBER may still be justified if it is proven that such arrangements produce some economic efficiencies that could not be reached without exclusive dealing arrangements, and if a fair share of such efficiencies has been passed on to consumers. Such individual assessment should be based on the same principle as assessment of article 101(3) TFEU under EU competition law.

25.38 Exclusive dealing arrangements unilaterally imposed on their business partners by dominant undertakings should be assessed on the basis of article 7 of the Law on Competition, i.e. as abuse of dominant position. In this regard, in the *Orlen Lietuva* case[15] the LCC declared its determination to follow the practice of European Commission by (i) finding such abuses in cases when the network of exclusive dealing arrangements of the dominant undertaking have the effect of preventing the entry or expansion of equally effective competitors, i.e. non-compete obligations foreclose the market, and (ii) holding the position that a foreclosure effect is more likely in the case of long-term exclusive dealing arrangements.

25.39 In the practice of LCC, exclusive dealing cases are not very frequent; however, the ratio of infringement decision is quite high. During the period of 2010–12, the LCC resolved five cases involving exclusive dealing arrangements, and two of them resulted in infringement decisions with the highest fines ever imposed in Lithuanian competition practice. The most valuable precedents with regards to exclusive dealing arrangements have been formulated in the *Orlen Lietuva* and the *G4S money management* cases.[16]

J. Refusal to deal

25.40 As a general rule, competition law does not require undertakings to supply goods and/services to all customers, i.e. undertakings retain discretion in selecting their business partners irrespective of their position in the market. Nevertheless, such discretion may be limited in exceptional cases when refusal to supply risks eliminating or significantly reducing competition on the market.

25.41 The conditions under which refusal to supply leads to a competition law infringement were first established by the LCC in the *KLASKO* case[17] and reiterated in series of *Vilniaus airport* cases.[18] In those cases, the LCC declared that a refusal to supply amounts to infringement when: (i) an undertaking holds a dominant position in the market for the provision of essential facilities to other undertakings; (ii) the undertaking uses the essential facilities in its own business operations; (iii) the undertaking refuses to grant access to such essential facilities to others, or offers access on substantially worse conditions; and (iv) there is no objective reason for justifying such refusal.

25.42 The notion of essential facilities was elaborated by the LCC in the *KLASCO* case,[19] and defined as materials or infrastructure without which an undertaking would not be able to provide services to its clients. Although the LCC did not elaborate in detail on the notion

[15] *Orlen Lietuva* (n 12).
[16] *Orlen Lietuva* (n 12); *G4S money management* (n 1).
[17] *KLASKO* [2002] LCC Decision no. 5/b.
[18] *Vilniaus airport* [2007] LCC Decision no. 2S-14; *Vilniaus airport* [2008] LCC Decision no. 2S-23; *Vilnius airport IV* (n 3).
[19] *KLASKO* (n 16).

of "essential facilities," it could be anticipated that the LCC would follow the EU law and consider as essential only those facilities that could not be effectively duplicated.

In the *GalxoSmithKline* case,[20] the LCC provided a more general insight into the obligation of a dominant undertaking to enter into a contractual relationships with a buyer of its goods or services. More particularly, the LCC noted that even a dominant company must have the freedom to choose its trade partners. Thus, the obligation to deal might be justified only in exceptional circumstances, namely (i) if the purchase of the goods or services at issue is absolutely necessary for a third party in order to remain active in the relevant market; (ii) if the refusal to supply would eliminate the third party from the relevant market; and (iii) if the refusal to deal is not objectively justified. **25.43**

Refusal to deal cases have not been very frequent in the practice of LCC; however, the ratio of interference of LCC is quite high. During the period of 2010–2012, the LCC resolved four cases concerning refusal to supply and two of them resulted in infringement or commitment decisions. In particular, in *Vilnius airport IV* case[21] the LCC issued an infringement decision, and in the *Forum Cinemas* case,[22] the LCC terminated the investigation in exchange for commitments. **25.44**

K. Essential facilities

See Section I.J. **25.45**

L. Bundling (including loyalty and market share discounts)

The Lithuanian competition law practice does not contain any valuable precedents or guidance's with respect to bundling of products and loyalty inducing discounts. Nevertheless, in *Orlen Lietuva*,[23] the LCC directly based its infringement decision referring to the EU Commission Article 102 Guidance,[24] suggesting that the LCC will share the EU Commission's position on exclusionary abuses, including bundling practices and loyalty rebates. **25.46**

Bundling refers to the practice of selling several products only jointly (i.e. in a bundle) or selling products jointly at a lower price than it would cost to purchase them separately. The latter practice is usually referred to as multi-product rebates and might lead to anticompetitive foreclosure provided that the incremental revenue does not exceed the incremental costs for each product in the dominant undertaking's bundle. It is assumed that the sale of some products in a bundle below costs could prevent equally efficient competitors from competing on the tied product market. The remaining elements that need to be taken into account in assessing bundling practices are analogous to those applicable to tying arrangements.[25] **25.47**

The term "loyalty rebates" refers to the practice of providing special discounts that incentivize customers to purchase products exclusively from the dominant undertaking. Loyalty discounts include special rewards for exclusive purchasing and any other discount schemes which force customers to purchase products exclusively from the dominant undertaking. Such discount schemes could include discounts linked to individually determined purchase thresholds, application of sufficiently long period retroactive rebates, etc., all of which restrict an equally efficient competitor from competing with the dominant undertaking on the **25.48**

---

[20] *GlaxoSmithKline* [2009] LCC Decision no. 1S-28.
[21] *Vilnus aiport IV* (n 3).
[22] *Forum Cinemas* (n 9).
[23] *Orlen Lietuva* (n 12).
[24] Guidance on the Commission's enforcement priorities in applying [Article 102 TFEU] to abusive exclusionary conduct by dominant undertakings, OJ C 45, February 24, 2009, para. 23 ("Article 102 Guidance").
[25] See Section I.H.

merits. As a general rule, loyalty rebates are considered to be abuse of dominant position provided that effective competitor cannot match the price offered and still supply goods and/or services profitably.

M. Standard-setting groups (disclosure requirements, licensing arrangements, and licensing pools)

25.49 Lithuanian competition law practice has never dealt with competition restrictions inherent in standard-setting groups. Lithuanian law does not provide any more specific legislation on competition law issues that could arise during the process of standardization. Nevertheless, it could be expected that the LCC would follow the EU practice in this respect.

N. Customer termination

25.50 There are no specific Lithuanian precedents that would distinguish between termination of existing customers and refusal to supply potential customers. In both situations, the LCC is likely to apply the same basic principles, which are applicable for "refusal to supply."[26] Nevertheless, it could be anticipated that the LCC would follow the EU practice in this respect and find infringement more readily in refusal to supply an existing customer, than in refusal to supply new customers.

O. Termination of intermediaries (retailers, wholesalers, dealers, and value-added resellers, agents, and brokers)

25.51 In Lithuania, there is no specific legal provision concerning termination of relations with intermediaries. Nevertheless, it is expected that such termination would be evaluated on the same principles as those applied in the "refusal to supply" cases.[27]

P. Termination of relationships with competitors

25.52 In practice, the "refusal to supply" issue quite often arises in situations when a dominant undertaking cuts off supply to its competitors on the downstream market. Thus, termination of relationships with competitors having effect of eliminating competition from the downstream market will be assessed on the basis of principles outlined in Sections I.J and I.N.

Q. Exemptions

25.53 Unilateral practices by dominant undertaking which raise competition-related concerns, as well as agreements having effect on competition, could be justified under certain circumstances.

25.54 Although there are no "safe harbors" or presumptions of legality designed to justify unilateral practices by dominant undertakings, such potentially restrictive behavior might be justified on a case-by-case basis if the practices are proven to be objectively necessary (e.g. for health or safety reasons) and/or produce economic efficiencies outweighing any negative effects on consumers, provided that the measures employed by the dominant undertaking are proportionate to the aims pursued. It should be noted, however, that the practice of the LCC suggest that the LCC is ready to accept such justifications in very limited instances.

25.55 Unlike unilateral practices of dominant undertakings, anticompetitive agreements are subject to a number of justifications of different kind. In particular, an anticompetitive agreement could be justified as follows: (i) the agreement may fall under the *de minimis* rule, meaning

---

[26] See Section I.J.

[27] For more information on refusal to supply, see Sections I.J and I.N.

that contractual restrictions have no appreciable effect on competition; (ii) the agreement may amount to agency agreement, meaning that the principal should generally be entitled to impose a number of restrictions on the contracts concluded by the agent on its behalf; (iii) the agreement may be individually justified if some restrictions on competition were objectively necessary to produce some efficiencies, which were finally passed on to consumers (Lithuanian counterpart to article 101(3) TFEU); or (iv) the restrictions on competition are subject to block exemptions, meaning *ex ante* presumption that such kind of restrictions satisfy the conditions of Lithuanian counterpart to article 101(3) TFEU.

Notably, all such exemptions correspond to the respective instruments available in the EU competition law. **25.56**

II. Dealing with competitors

Prohibition of anticompetitive agreements is established in articles 5–6 of the Law on Competition, which is modeled after article 101 TFEU. In particular, article 5 of the Law on Competition prohibits conclusion of agreements which actually or potentially restrict competition, and provides a provisional list of agreements which are deemed always to restrict competition. In turn, article 6 provides statutory basis to justify anticompetitive agreements provided that restrictions inherent in such agreements lead to economic efficiencies which are passed on to consumers; that such restrictions are proportionate; and that they do not result in elimination of competition in respect of a substantial part of the products in question. **25.57**

The enforcement of Lithuanian Law on Competition is highly coordinated with EU competition rules, as LCC heavily relies on the precedents adopted by the European Commission and EU courts even in prosecuting purely national infringements. Such coordination is even higher in the area of application of national analogue to article 101(3) TFEU (justifications of agreements restricting competition), as national competition law sanctions direct application of EU regulations ruling upon article 101(3) TFEU even for the purposes of cases having purely national character. **25.58**

Since 2010–11, the LCC has boosted its efforts in prosecuting horizontal anticompetitive agreements. In particular, the LCC officially declared its determination to focus on the most severe hard core agreements between competitors, rather than on vertical agreements or abuse of dominant position. At the same time, the leniency program renewed in 2008 delivered its first results in 2010 (*Small mechanization companies*[28]) and in 2011 (*Orthopedic companies*[29]) and already could be considered as an operational tool to fight hard core horizontal infringements. The LCC also put significant efforts into the prevention of infringements by consulting market players and applying more severe sanctions on restrictive horizontal practices. Such trends are evidenced by the fact that the total amount of fines imposed by the LCC in 2011 was EUR 5 million, whereas in 2007 and 2008 the total amount of fines imposed by LCC did not even reach EUR 1 million. **25.59**

The analysis of trends in the LCC case practice over the past two years also suggests that LCC has clear focus on horizontal agreements, especially those committed within the scope of activity of associations as well as bid-rigging. In particular, in 2012, LCC finalized six cases concerning anticompetitive agreements (with and without infringement decisions), four of which concerned bid-rigging and two—alleged infringements committed with the **25.60**

[28] *Small mechanization companies* [2010] LCC Decision no. 2S-6.

[29] *Orthopedic companies* [2010] LCC Decision no. 2S-2.

involvement of associations. Analogous trends apply for 2011. In 2011, LCC finalized nineteen cases concerning anticompetitive agreements (with and without infringement decisions), ten of which concerned horizontal agreements, five—bid-rigging, and four—alleged infringements committed with the involvement of associations.

A. Horizontal price fixing (including advanced announcements of price or product changes)

25.61 Horizontal price-fixing agreements are considered to be one of the most severe infringements of competition law, and are always deemed to restrict competition. Price fixing covers a wide range of arrangements, all of which concern the pricing behavior of competitors: agreements on selling and buying price rates, agreements on final prices (e.g. minimum, maximum prices), and certain price elements (e.g. margins, rebates), as well as agreements on prices of final and intermediary products (e.g. in *Media agencies*[30]).

25.62 Notably, competition law condemns even the loosest forms of pricing coordination among competitors. For instance, in a number of cases, the LCC condemned price recommendations which by their effect operated as pricing benchmarks for competitors.[31] In turn, in the *Vilnius taxi* case, the LCC declared that price fixing also includes advance notifications of future pricing behavior to competitors.[32]

B. Horizontal agreements to allocate customers or territories; agreements not to compete

25.63 Like price fixing, sharing of markets on the basis of territories, customers, or generally refraining from active competition is considered to be hard core infringement of competition law, and it is always deemed to have the object of restricting competition. The LCC has condemned such arrangements between competitors on a number of occasions.

25.64 The majority of infringements of this kind have been discovered in the context of public procurement procedures, i.e. undertakings coordinating their tender proposals and selecting the ones that would win the particular tender. In most cases, such coordination is rather primitive and proven by the LCC on the basis of analogous grammar and spelling errors in the bids submitted by competing undertakings, discovery of tender material prepared in the name of competitors, as well as unambiguous emails showing coordination of actions between competitors.

C. Horizontal boycotts

25.65 Horizontal boycotts are included in the provisional list of agreements which restrict competition by their object. Hence, once it has determined that competitors had engaged in horizontal boycott practices, the LCC is released from the obligation to prove that such actions actually resulted in negative effects on competition. In the practice of LCC, horizontal boycott has been condemned only once in the *Dog Breeders* case.[33] The LCC condemned actions of a dog breeders' association which restricted its members from selling dogs to customers who planned to resell them. The LCC concluded that the association thereby impeded of the ability of resellers to compete with direct sellers—members of the association in the retail market.

---

[30] *Media agencies* [2009] LCC Decision no. 2S-14.

[31] *Architects* [2001] LCC Decision no. 16/b; *Auditors* [2007] LCC Decision no. 2S-15; *Ship agents* [2011], LCC Decision no. 2S-25.

[32] *Vilnius taxi* [2005] LCC Decision no. 2S-3.

[33] *Dog Breeders* [2010] LCC Decision no. 2S-9.

D. Joint ventures and other competitive collaborations

Competitors may find it in their commercial interest to cooperate with each other on a number of legitimate reasons. The level of such cooperation could range from contractual relations to the establishment of joint ventures specifically designed for joint activity by competing undertakings. 25.66

From the competition law perspective, such joint ventures are subject to merger control procedures or restriction of anticompetitive practices. In particular, merger control procedures apply in cases when competitors establish full-functioning joint ventures (i.e. undertakings which perform all functions of autonomous undertaking, carry out consistent business activity, and have sufficient financial and other recourses to operate on a lasting basis). Cooperation between competitors taking the form of establishment of such full-functioning joint ventures is subject to *ex ante* control, meaning that such cooperation should be notified to the LCC before receiving merger clearance. In practice, a clearance decision means that compliance of the joint venture with competition law should not be an issue provided that the cooperating parties remain within cooperation model cleared by the LCC. 25.67

Any other forms of cooperation are subject to compliance with article 5 of the Law on Competition, which is analogous to article 101 TFEU. The practice of the LCC with respect to pro-competitive forms of collaboration between competitors is very limited. From the legislative perspective, LCC adopted a resolution establishing that, for the purposes of assessment of horizontal cooperation between competitors, the LCC shall directly apply EU regulations, with the exception that turnover thresholds provided in EU regulations shall be reduced tenfold. Generally, the practice of the LCC and national courts suggests that assessment of horizontal cooperation would take into account not only the binding instruments but also "soft law," such as EU Commission's Horizontal Cooperation Guidelines.[34] 25.68

In this regard, it should be noted that the LCC considered two cases concerning horizontal cooperation of competitors. In 2002, the LCC issued an individual exemption for breweries regarding the usage of uniform packaging,[35] and in 2010 the LCC refused to grant a block exemption to the insurance sector claiming that the agreement in question did not meet the required conditions for application of block exemption.[36] 25.69

E. Trade associations

Membership in trade associations is perfectly legal, although such membership may significantly increase the risk of competition law infringement. Such risk is evidenced by the fact that approximately half of anticompetitive practices discovered by the LCC necessarily involve some activity of trade associations. 25.70

From the perspective of Lithuanian competition law, members of trade associations are considered liable for all decisions adopted by the association during the period of their membership as well as any other decisions valid during their membership in the association. Such liability could be invoked irrespective of whether a particular member of an association participated in the decision-making, expressed its will to take part in certain anticompetitive actions, and remained silent during the discussion on such matters. The only possibility of distancing oneself from anticompetitive actions currently accepted by Lithuanian competition law is public and unambiguous declaration to other members of the association 25.71

[34] Guidelines on the applicability of Article 101 of the Treaty on the Functioning of the European Union to horizontal co-operation agreements, OJ C 11, January 14, 2011 ("Horizontal Cooperation Guidelines").

[35] *Breweries uniform packaging* [2002] LCC Decision no. 72.

[36] *Insurance companies* [2010] LCC Decision no. 2S-33.

regarding one's disagreement with anticompetitive actions/decisions taken/adopted by the association, and expression of intention not to comply with practices taken by the association. The practice of the LCC in the *Ship agents* case[37] suggests that only written evidence of such distancing shall be accepted by the LCC in order to release undertakings from liability.

25.72 The Supreme Administrative Court noted in *Media agencies*[38] that members of an association are under the obligation to take an active role within the association and track all decisions and activities of the association. This means that undertakings could be held liable even for anticompetitive actions taken by the association that they were not aware of. Hence, under Lithuanian law, total ignorance of activity of trade association or nominal membership within the association does not release undertaking from liability for anticompetitive actions undertaken by the association.

F. Interlocking directorates

25.73 Interlocking directorates have never been challenged by the LCC. Nevertheless, interlocking directorates could be considered by national competition law as part of anticompetitive practices that facilitate or lead to collusion between competitors.

G. Facilitating practices

25.74 Facilitating practices engaged in by competitors are not subject to any specific regulation of Lithuanian competition law and in most cases would be seen by the competition authority as an integral part of other anticompetitive practices, such as price fixing, market sharing, etc.

25.75 Nevertheless, in certain cases, competition law may invoke liability of undertakings just for facilitating the conclusion of anticompetitive agreements despite the fact that such undertakings provide only certain services to members of cartel agreement. As stated by the LCC in the *Travel agencies* case,[39] liability of such undertakings could be invoked if: (i) the undertaking contributed to the conclusion of an anticompetitive agreement (irrespective of whether such undertaking merely followed instructions, or took an active or passive role); and (ii) the undertaking expressed its express or tacit consent with the anticompetitive purposes of agreement (in this regard, the LCC relied on the criteria established by the EU General Court in *AC-Treuhand AG v. Commission*[40]). In *Travel agencies*, the LCC considered an alleged price-fixing agreement concluded by travel agencies through the operator of an electronic travel reservation system. The operator was been held liable for organizing discussions on the maximum discount that could be provided by travel agencies for travel sold on electronic platform under its operation as well as establishment of technical restrictions to offer higher 3 percent discount on travel.

H. Information exchange

25.76 Sharing of market-specific information between competitors may have a number of legitimate reasons, such as sharing of know-how, understanding business trends, increasing general demand for products, benchmarking performance of competitors, and enabling joint lobbying actions. At the same time, exchange of certain information may result in de-incentivizing vigorous competition and thus amount to competition law infringement.

25.77 Exchange of information between competitors may be challenged by the LCC in two types of situations. First, exchange of information between competitors may be an integral part of

---

[37] *Ship agents* (n 30).

[38] *Media agencies v. LCC* [2011], Supreme Administrative Court of Lithuania, Decision no. A858-294/2011.

[39] *Travel agencies* [2012], LCC Decision no. 2S-9.

[40] Case T-99/04 *AC-Treuhand AG v. Commission* case [2008] ECR II-1501.

more general competition law infringement (e.g. bid-rigging practices always involve disclosure of pricing information). In such cases, information exchange shall be analyzed in the broader context and shall not be considered as a separate infringement of competition law. Second, cooperation between competitors may cover merely information exchange practices, without extending into more intensive cooperation. Such information exchange could be considered as a separate infringement of competition law; however, it would be declared only on certain conditions.

From the perspective of competition law, information exchange is usually considered as having the object of restricting competition if competitors exchange information on their future strategic actions. It is considered that exchange of such strategic information in most cases has no other reasonable commercial explanation than the intention of coordinating actions with competitors. In the remaining cases, information exchange is considered as infringement of competition law if it produces an appreciably negative effect on competition. **25.78**

As explained by the LCC in the *Dairy companies II* case,[41] the potential of negative effect on competition depends on two parameters: (i) the market structure and (ii) the nature of information exchanged. It is considered that negative effect on competition is likely in markets which are sufficiently transparent (i.e. competitors may easily track each other's actions), concentrated (i.e. quite a few competitors on the market), non-complex (i.e. the products are sufficiently homogenous), stable (i.e. the variables of competition are quite constant), and symmetric (i.e. competitors are quite similar in terms of costs, demand, market shares, product range, capacities, etc.). In turn, a negative effect on competition in such markets most likely occurs if undertakings exchange commercially sensitive information which facilitates anticipation of competitors' future behavior or reveals aggressive commercial practices engaged in by the competitors sufficiently early to provide adequate response to such practices in a timely manner and thus de-incentivize vigorous competition. **25.79**

There is no predetermined list of information considered commercially sensitive. As a general rule, commercially sensitive information is taken to include any information that is usually considered by undertakings as their commercial secret (information should be worth protecting) and is sufficiently closely related to commercial activities, for example prices, discounts, sales, and production quantities, market shares, investment projects, commercial strategies. Naturally, such information has a commercially sensitive character only if the exchanged information is still up to date, i.e. is not historical. The LCC does not provide any more specific guidance on separation of relevant from historical information and keeps to the general principle that relevance of information should be assessed on a case-by-case basis, i.e. in dynamic markets the information remains relevant shorter than in stable markets with little innovations. Notably, the LCC has not challenged exchange of information when the information was more than three months old.[42] Nevertheless, in public statements, the LCC has suggested that exchange of information that is one year old may still remain within the ambit of their concern. **25.80**

In addition to the analysis of the nature of information exchanged, one should also take into account the methods of exchange employed by competitors. Even in the case that the competitors decide to exchange commercially sensitive information, commercial sensitivity may be eliminated or significantly reduced by aggregating the information to such an extent that it would not be possible to extract individual data regarding a particular undertaking. As a general rule, such extraction becomes impossible if that exchanged data aggregates individual **25.81**

[41] *Dairy companies II* [2011] LCC Decision no. 2S-13.

[42] *Paper companies* [2006] LCC Decision no. 2S-13.

data from at least three undertakings. Nevertheless, it should not be excluded that a negative effect on competition may still arise in some markets if sharing of aggregated information by three or more competitors allows the competitors to coordinate pricing, as might be the case if two large and one small competitor share aggregated information.

25.82 As noted above, sharing of information between competitors may not necessarily be driven by anticompetitive objectives, and could be justified on the basis of article 6 of the Law on Competition, if the sharing of information leads to some economic efficiencies, which are passed on to consumers, and if the exchange is proportionate and does not result in the elimination of competition in the market.

25.83 In this regard, it should be noted that compliance of information exchange practices should be ensured at all times and even in those cases when receiving information on competitor seems to be intuitively reasonable. For example, from a business perspective, it would seem absolutely rational to receive all information on competitor at the stage of negotiations for its acquisition. Nevertheless, from the perspective of competition law, such intended acquisition cannot be considered as an excuse for exchanging commercially sensitive information. Consequently, in pre-merger situations, undertakings are recommended to appoint independent third parties to aggregate commercially sensitive data on the target, to disclose only such information which is objectively necessary for the purposes of making a decision on the acquisition, and to disclose such limited information only to those people who objectively require it for the purposes of making a decision on the acquisition of the target.

I. Joint purchasing agreements

25.84 Lithuanian competition law does not have any specific national rules, guidance, or case practice which would elaborate on the assessment of joint purchasing agreements from the perspective of competition law. Hence, assessment of joint purchasing agreements under Lithuanian competition law would most likely be based on the principles generally accepted under EU competition law, in particular Horizontal Cooperation Guidelines.

25.85 As a rule of thumb, joint purchasing agreements shall not be perceived as having the object of restricting competition, i.e. they will amount to infringement only if they produce negative effects on competition. Such negative effects may occur in procurement or selling markets, and shall be more likely in the case that parties to the joint purchasing agreement hold significant market shares in these markets. As stated by the EU Commission, negative effects on competition are unlikely if the combined market shares do not exceed 15 percent in the procurement and selling markets (the "safe harbor" rule); however, failure to meet those market shares does not automatically lead to the presumption of negative effect on competition and/or inability to justify joint purchasing arrangements.

25.86 As a general rule, negative effect on competition in the procurement market shall be associated with excessive competitive pressure on suppliers, which leads to a reduction in the output, variety, and quality of their products, as well as foreclosure of the market for alternative purchasers that are unable to secure their supply of raw materials. In turn, negative effects on selling markets of the parties to a joint purchasing organization are associated with the possibility of collusion in the selling markets. Such collusion is more likely if the parties to the joint purchasing agreement have sufficiently high market shares in the downstream markets and high communality of costs.

J. Joint lobbying/regulatory/legislative efforts

25.87 Joint lobbying with regards to regulatory or legislative initiatives is considered to be in line with regular commercial practice, and does not require the intervention of a competition authority. Nevertheless, it should be borne in mind that joint lobbying usually requires collection of specific information on the activity of competitors and/or disclosure of strategic information regarding their future activities. Hence, perfectly legal joint lobbying may easily turn into sharing of commercially sensitive information or some type of concerted practice, which would be considered as the conclusion of an anticompetitive agreement. This concern has been expressed by the LCC in public statements which called business associations established by undertakings with the primary purpose of joint lobbying as one of the main sources of the anticompetitive behavior.

III. General issues

A. Jurisdiction and applicable law (including sector-specific competition regulation)

The Constitution, individual laws, and secondary legislation are the principle sources of national competition law in Lithuania. Despite all the applicable sources of national competition law, the Law on Competition is the main piece of legislation for enforcement of competition law in Lithuania. **25.88**

The Law on Competition encompasses all areas of economic activities, except sector-specific regimes which are regulated by sector-specific laws, for instance, the telecommunications sector, postal services, electric energy, central heating, and gas sectors. These sector-specific laws take precedence over the Law on Competition. **25.89**

The territorial reach of Lithuanian competition policy is based on the extraterritoriality principle which provides for the application of national competition rules to activities by domestic undertakings and activities by undertakings registered outside the territory of the Republic of Lithuania if the said activities restrict competition in the domestic market of Lithuania. The application of this principle also ensures that national competition rules are not applied to activities of undertakings which restrict competition on foreign markets, unless international agreements to which Lithuania is a party provide otherwise. **25.90**

Competition law is applied to all undertakings that exercise any kind of economic activity, i.e. an enterprise, a combination of enterprises (associations, amalgamations, consortiums, etc.), an institution, or an organization, or other legal or natural persons that carry out or may carry out economic activity in the Republic of Lithuania or whose actions or intentions affect or could affect economic activity in the Republic of Lithuania. State and local institutions of the Republic of Lithuania shall be considered to be undertakings if they engage in economic activity. **25.91**

It should be also noted that Lithuania acceded into the European Union in 2004. Since then, Lithuanian competition law has followed the main principles of EU competition law, i.e. national competition law is fully harmonized with EU competition law. **25.92**

B. Antitrust system

(i) Name of agency/agencies

The national authority which exclusively develops and enforces competition law in Lithuania is the Competition Council of the Republic of Lithuania (*Lietuvos Respublikos konkurencijos taryba*). Creation and maintenance of effective competition conditions in regulated markets is entrusted to specialized authorities in specific sectors, i.e. the National Control Commission for Prices and Energy in the energy sector, and the Communications Regulatory Authority in telecommunications sector. **25.93**

(ii) Staff size and budget

The national competition authority is independent from any particular government institution and comprises two divisions—the Competition Council and the Administration. The **25.94**

Competition Council is a decision-making body of the competition authority and consists of up to four members and a chairman. It is entrusted with adopting decisions on behalf of the Competition Council, holding hearings of cases, and imposing sanctions. The Administration of the competition authority is composed of the Head of Administration and eight divisions. The main function of the Administration is to investigate infringements, among others by conducting dawn raids, seizures of documents, and by collecting any relevant information. The divisions of the Administration are also entitled to adopt decisions of minor importance that do not require the attention of the Competition Council and usually are of procedural nature, i.e. deadline extensions for submission of required information, etc. The Administration employs approximately forty-four case-handlers and approximately fourteen members of administrative staff.

25.95 The budget of the Competition Council is approximately EUR 1 million per year.

(iii) Recent enforcement actions and trends

25.96 The Competition Council's enforcement policy has been gradually changing in recent years following legislative amendments. New priority guidelines allow the authority to drop or to refuse to start investigation in cases of lower importance in order to concentrate on major cases that have significant impact on consumer welfare. Recent enforcement actions indicate that the authority concentrates on restrictive horizontal agreements (cartels) and is highly active in investigations of associations' activities. Moreover, the authority is getting stricter in applying sanctions, i.e. it imposes higher fines for infringements of competition rules in order to deter anticompetitive behavior in the future, etc. However, most of investigations in the field of abuse of dominance have now been terminated and no new major investigations are foreseen in the near future.

25.97 Recent and most important enforcement actions of the Competition Council have been retail market investigation concerning food prices, the shipping agents cartel, and investigation into the banking sector concerning interchange fee and outsourcing money management services.

C. Private litigation

25.98 The right of undertakings to private litigation is established in the Law on Competition. A claim might be based on either one or both of the grounds established in the Law on Competition (i.e. claims for determination of illegal actions and/or actions for damages). Undertakings may file claims for the recovery of damages only at the courts of general jurisdiction. The Vilnius District Court has an exclusive jurisdiction in solving private disputes regarding infringements of national competition law and of articles 101 and 102 TFEU.

25.99 According to the Law on Competition, an undertaking found infringing competition law must pay damages to the injured party. The possibility of recovering damages stems from the general principles of civil law. Lithuanian civil law sets high standards for proving lost profit or damages suffered; as a result, not many claims for recovery of damages have been filed.

25.100 There have been only two full-fledged private litigation cases regarding the recovery of damages for anticompetitive behavior in Lithuania. Both claims were filed in the context of abuse of a dominant position. The small number of private litigation competition law-related cases might be due to the fact that the Lithuanian legal system does not provide for the possibility of class action lawsuits or collective or joint claims, and establishes high standards of proof, as mentioned above. Accordingly, private competition law litigation has not been well developed in Lithuania yet. However, there is a trend of cases (small but growing), where parties to a contract dispute the validity of contractual provisions on the basis of a violation of mandatory provisions of competition rules.

D. Follow-on litigation

Follow-on litigation which is based on an earlier infringement decision adopted by a national competition authority is still very rare in Lithuania. According to the existing Lithuanian legal system, follow-on litigation could be assigned to a private litigation institute because the national competition authority does not participate in the proceedings of recovering damages. **25.101**

One of the reasons why follow-on litigation is not very common in the Lithuanian jurisdiction may be the fact that private litigation institute has not been advantageous to the injured parties. For example, in the *Klevo lapas v. Mazeikiu nafta* case regarding recovery of damages, the Lithuanian Supreme Court stated that infringement decisions adopted by the competition authority are not sufficient to prove damage.[43] According to the Court's decision, in the course of civil proceedings the injured party must still prove illegality of actions, harm, and causal nexus. Although there were a few more follow-on litigation cases in Lithuanian, they ended in settlement. **25.102**

E. Arbitration and alternative dispute resolution

The investigation of the Competition Council is an administrative procedure; therefore, the undertakings may only invoke arbitration proceedings in cases related to the recovery of damages caused by the competition law infringement, according to the Law on Commercial Arbitration of the Republic of Lithuania. **25.103**

There have been some theoretical discussions on the application of alternative dispute resolution (ADR) in ongoing competition law-related cases; however, there have been no signs of practical implementation of ADR in such cases so far. **25.104**

F. Remedies

(i) Administrative liability

The Competition Council may impose fines on undertakings of up to 10 percent of annual turnover for the preceding fiscal year for prohibited agreements, abuse of a dominant position, implementation of a notifiable concentration without clearance, continuation of a concentration during suspension period, infringement of concentration conditions or mandatory obligations established by the competition authority. The Competition Council may also impose fines in the amount of up to 5 percent of average annual turnover for the preceding fiscal year for each day of continued infringement when undertakings fail to comply with the obligation to terminate anticompetitive actions or eliminate consequences of the infringement. **25.105**

According to the Law on Competition, with the authorization of the administrative court, the Competition Council may also impose restrictions on economic activity of an undertaking, i.e. temporarily suspend export and import operations, bank operations, validity of relevant licenses, should the undertaking fail to comply with the sanctions imposed by the competition authority. Nevertheless, there is no public data suggesting that the LCC has ever employed such administrative powers. **25.106**

In addition to the fine of up to 10 percent of annual turnover imposed upon undertakings, the Competition Council may impose personal liability on the CEOs of the undertakings. Sanction include a restriction on appointments to the position of the head of a public and/or private legal person, and on membership in a collegial supervisory and/or management body **25.107**

[43] *Klevo lapas v. Mazeikiu nafta* [2010], Supreme Court of Lithuania, Decision no. 3K-3-207/2010.

of a public and/or private legal person for the period of three to five years and a fine of up to approximately EUR 15,000.

25.108 In addition to the above mentioned fines, the Law on Public Procurement of the Republic of Lithuania invests the contracting authority with the right to reject an offer submitted by a potential provider if an undertaking has infringed competition law by participating in an illegal agreement within the last three years.

25.109 The limitation period is five years from the end of an infringement. The enforcement action of the Competition Council as well as court proceedings with reference to the termination of an authority's ongoing investigation or appeal proceedings in relation to the final decision of the competition authority interrupts the running of the limitation period (art. 35(3)(4) of the Law on Competition).

(ii) Civil liability

25.110 According to the Law on Competition, an undertaking found infringing competition law must compensate damages. However, the Competition Council does not initiate the recovery of damages for injured undertakings. Each undertaking that seeks the recovery of damages must individually file a private claim in a civil court.

(iii) Criminal liability

25.111 Lithuanian law does not impose criminal liability for infringement of competition law. Nonetheless, the Lithuanian court has stated that economic sanctions for infringement of competition law, which may be up to 10 percent of annual turnover, are sometimes even higher than criminal fines and can be equated with criminal liability.

G. Leniency and immunity

25.112 Under Lithuanian law, leniency and immunity programs are only applicable to undertakings participating in horizontal agreements (cartels) and vertical agreements regarding direct or indirect price fixing. Possible benefits of cooperation with the Competition Council are total immunity or reduction of a fine of up to 75 percent.

(i) Total immunity

25.113 A participant in a prohibited agreement may be released from fine (total immunity) only if all of the following conditions are satisfied:

(a) the applicant provides information prior to the launching of an investigation;
(b) the applicant is the first party to a prohibited agreement to provide such information;
(c) the applicant provides complete information available to him regarding a prohibited agreement and cooperates with the Competition Council during the investigation;
(d) the applicant was neither the ringleader nor coerced others to participate in the prohibited agreement.

(ii) Reduction of a fine from 50 to 75 percent

25.114 If immunity from a fine is not available, the estimated fine may be reduced by 50 to 75 percent if the applicant:

(a) is the first to provide the Competition Council with all the information relating to a cartel agreement available to him;
(b) presents evidence relating to facts previously unknown to the Competition Council and having significant added value;
(c) was neither the ringleader nor coerced others to participate in a cartel.

(iii) Reduction of a fine by 50 percent

If the applicant was a ringleader or coerced others to participate in a cartel, the estimated fine may be reduced by 50 percent when the applicant satisfies all other conditions (indicated in Section III.G(i)). **25.115**

(iv) Reduction of a fine from 20 to 50 percent

The second and subsequent applicants may benefit from a reduction of fines by 20 to 50 percent, provided that they present evidence having significant added value and relating to the facts previously unknown to the Competition Council. **25.116**

It is noteworthy that if during the investigation an applicant provides additional evidence previously unknown to the Competition Council and such evidence confirms greater gravity or longer duration of an infringement, these new facts that might aggravate the liability of the applicant are not taken into consideration by the Competition Council when calculating the fine. **25.117**

In order to obtain either immunity or fine reduction, an applicant has the duty to cooperate continuously with the Competition Council during the entire duration of the proceedings. The applicant also has the duty to terminate the infringement following the filing of the application, except for what, in the Competition Council's opinion, would be reasonably necessary to preserve the integrity of the investigation. **25.118**

Personal liability for the head of an undertaking is not applicable only if an undertaking has benefited from the total immunity. In other cases (any reduction), the Law on Competition does not provide for any benefits to the head of an undertaking. However, taking into account that the Competition Council has a right and not the obligation to impose sanctions on the head, if an undertaking is found guilty, involvement with the Competition Council may still be very useful for the head of that undertaking. **25.119**

H. Document creation and retention

There are no special rules or principles which should be applied in the creation and retention of documents, and there have been no practical issues regarding document creation or retention in Lithuanian jurisdiction. The same rules and principles should be applied as at EU level. For instance, all correspondence with external counsel should be kept in a separate file marked "confidential—legal professional privilege," the undertaking should be aware of saving communications between competitors, etc. **25.120**

The Competition Council may also fine undertakings in the amount of up to 1 percent of annual turnover for the preceding fiscal year for the failure to provide requested information or for providing false or incomplete information as well as for obstructing dawn raids. **25.121**

26

MALAYSIA

Kamilah Kasim
Rahmat Lim & Partners

Introduction

26.01 Malaysia's competition legislation, the Competition Act 2010 (the "Act") came into force on January 1, 2012. The Act empowers the Malaysian Competition Commission (MyCC) with the administration and enforcement of the Act. The MyCC derives its power from the Competition Commission Act 2010, which came into force on January 1, 2010.

26.02 There are six Parts in the Act and two Schedules as follows:

(1) Part I provides for the interpretation of terms in the Act;
(2) Part II sets out the prohibitions under the Act;
   (a) the chapter 1 prohibition (the "chapter 1 Prohibition") of anticompetitive horizontal and vertical agreements; and
   (b) the chapter 2 prohibition (the "chapter 2 Prohibition") of abuses and dominance.
(3) Part III provides for the investigation and enforcement powers of the MyCC;
(4) Part IV deals with the decisions by the MyCC and leniency;

(5) Part V deals with the establishment of the Competition Appeal Tribunal which hears appeals against the MyCC decisions; and
(6) Part VI deals with the penalty, the right of private action, the powers of the minister in charge of the Domestic Trade and Consumers Affairs ("Minister") to make regulations and the MyCC to issue guidelines under the Act.

The Schedules set out the exclusions from the chapter 1 Prohibition and the chapter 2 Prohibition. **26.03**

Section 65 of the Act allows the Minister to make additional competition regulations. These regulations allow for violations of the Act to be remedied with fines (not to exceed MYR 1 million) or imprisonment (for a term not exceeding five years) or to both. At the date of writing of this chapter, the Minister has not enacted any regulations pursuant to s. 65 of Act.[1] **26.04**

To date, there are four guidelines issued by the MyCC viz; the chapter 1 Prohibition, the chapter 2 Prohibition, the market definition, and the process for complaints. **26.05**

I. Acting alone

A. Applicable law

(i) Anticompetitive Agreements

There are two types of prohibitions in the Act that impact single firm conduct. The chapter 1 Prohibition under s. 4(1) of the Act, provides: **26.06**

> A horizontal or vertical agreement between enterprises is prohibited insofar as the agreement has the object or effect of significantly preventing, restricting or distorting competition in any market for goods or services.

The chapter 1 Prohibition applies to agreements, which are defined under the Act as "any form of contract, arrangement or understanding, whether or not legally enforceable, between enterprises, and includes a decision by an association and concerted practices." **26.07**

For the time being, agreements relating to intellectual property rights are not excluded from the definition of vertical agreements and do not enjoy any specific exemption. The MyCC is in the process of issuing a guideline to address issues relating intellectual property rights. **26.08**

Section 4 applies to horizontal and vertical agreements having the "object or effect" of significantly affecting competition. This means that an agreement will infringe the Act if it has the object of significantly affecting competition, even though such agreement in fact has no significant effect on competition or that the agreement was not implemented. An agreement will also be caught if it has the effect of significantly affecting competition, notwithstanding that such agreement did not have the object to harm competition. **26.09**

(i) Safe harbor

In general, "significant" means the agreements must have more than a trivial impact. It should be noted that impact would be assessed in relation to the identified relevant market. In general, anticompetitive agreements will not be considered "significant" if: **26.10**

- the parties to the agreement are competitors who are in the same market (horizontal agreements) and their combined market share of the relevant market does not exceed 20 percent;

[1] March 2013.

- the parties to the agreement are not competitors (vertical agreements) and all the parties individually have less than 25 percent in any relevant market. For example, an exclusive distribution agreement between a wholesaler and a retailer neither of whom has more than 25 percent of the wholesale market or retail market.

26.11 Paragraph (a) is a safe-harbor in respect of collusion between competitors (b) in respect of vertical agreements including, but not limited to, resale price maintenance (RPM).[2]

(ii) Anticompetitive agreements are void

26.12 By virtue of s. 24 of the Malaysian Contracts Act 1950 ("Act 136"), anticompetitive agreements are void and unenforceable by the parties to the agreements. Section 24 of the Contracts Act provides, *inter alia*:

- The consideration or object of an agreement is lawful, unless—
  - o it is forbidden by a law;
  - o it is of such a nature that, if permitted, it would defeat any law;
- In each of the above cases, the consideration or object of an agreement is said to be unlawful. Every agreement of which the object or consideration is unlawful is void.

26.13 The Contracts Act 1950 provides for general contract laws in Malaysia. The Contracts Act and the Act complement each other. By virtue of s 24 of the Contracts Act, any agreement which infringed and is forbidden by the Act would be unenforceable vis-à-vis the contractual parties, i.e. the enterprises.

B. Abuse of dominant position

26.14 The chapter 2 Prohibition is found in s. 10 of the Act which provides that an enterprise is prohibited from engaging (whether independently or collectively), in any conduct which amounts to an abuse of a dominant position in any market for goods or services.

26.15 Under the Act, an enterprise is in a dominant position where it possesses enough market power to adjust prices, output, or trading terms without effective constraints from actual or potential competitors. The Act usefully clarifies that the fact that the market share held by an enterprise is below or above a particular level is not in itself conclusive of dominance. The guidelines on the chapter 2 Prohibition provide that a market share of 60 percent is likely to indicate dominance, although this will depend on a number of other factors, including the characteristics of the market both from a supply and demand perspective, entry barriers, number and size of competitors, size of the customers, etc. Perhaps it should be mentioned that the Act does not penalize an enterprise for its dominance. It only prohibits any enterprise, independently or collectively with other enterprises, from engaging in any conduct that amounts to an abuse of dominance.

C. Predatory pricing

26.16 In the guidelines on the chapter 2 Prohibition, the MyCC states that predatory pricing, i.e. setting prices below costs, may infringe the Act if a dominant enterprise sets prices below costs to drive other efficient competitors out of the market. In this respect, consumers may benefit in the short term but they may lose out in the long term as once the competitors are driven out of the market, the dominant enterprise is free to raise its price above the original level. However, the MyCC recognizes that enterprises may set prices below cost for many reasons; a new entrant into the market may decide to price below cost to gain initial market share or an existing enterprise may price a new product below cost initially to attract

[2] On RPM please see Section I.G where arguably the safe-harbour may not apply.

consumers. These are acceptable. Therefore the challenge for the MyCC is to determine under what circumstances prices below costs would be predatory. In this connection, under the guidelines on the chapter 2 Prohibition, the MyCC has indicated that it may use several methods (which shall depend on the circumstances and particular conditions in the industry under investigation) which include:

(a) average variable cost (AVC)—a short-term cost concept, which is defined as the sum of all the costs that change as output changes, divided by the total quantity. All fixed costs are excluded;
(b) average avoidable cost (AAC)—all costs (i.e. the variable and fixed costs directly related to the product under investigation) that could have been avoided if the dominant enterprise had not engaged in the predatory strategy. If the dominant enterprise does not cover AAC in its pricing then it is giving up/sacrificing profits;
(c) long-run incremental cost (LRIC) is the change in total costs from the production of an increase in output (which can be either the total output or simply the increase in output due to the predatory conduct), so LRIC includes all the costs associated with the product under investigation even if those costs were sunk (i.e. non-recoverable) before the alleged predatory pricing conduct was engaged in;
(d) average total cost (ATC) is the sum of fixed and variable costs divided by total output.

In assessing predatory pricing, evidence of intent to drive equally efficient competitors out of the market is not by itself indicative of predatory conduct. However, intention could be evidence of effect—i.e. that a predatory strategy is likely to succeed. **26.17**

D. Exploitative offenses

In the guidelines on the chapter 2 Prohibition, the MyCC indicated that excessive pricing may be exploitative. The MyCC also indicated that it will only be concerned with excessive pricing if there is no likelihood that market forces will reduce dominance in a market. This scenario may not be common as many sectors in Malaysia are subject to price control legislation. This suggests that the MyCC does not intend to regulate price but will interfere only if the excessive pricing impedes the competitive process and sought to foreclose a market. **26.18**

E. Monopsony

At the date of writing of this Chapter, the MyCC has not issued guidelines on monopsony. It is likely that an abusive conduct by an enterprise that is in a dominant purchasing position which harms competition would constitute an infringement under s. 10 of the Act. **26.19**

F. Price discrimination

Under s. 10.2(d) of the Act, price discrimination by a dominant enterprise which forces equally efficient competitors out of a market are prohibited. There are two examples set out in the guidelines on the chapter 2 Prohibition on the price discrimination: **26.20**

- a dominant enterprise charging low prices in geographic areas where there is more competition and cover losses by charging more in other areas that lack competition and this would force equally efficient competitors out of the market in the more competitive areas.
- a dominant enterprise charging one buyer more than the other buyer which may impact on competition in the downstream market. In particular, if the dominant enterprise has a subsidiary downstream, then charging a lower price for an important input to the subsidiary will mean other equally efficient competitors downstream cannot compete.

In the guidelines on the chapter 2 Prohibition, the MyCC noted that it will examine excessive pricing on a case-by-case basis. **26.21**

G. Dictating or influencing resale prices

26.22 In the guidelines on the chapter 1 Prohibition with regard to vertical agreements, the MyCC states in no uncertain terms that "it takes a strong stance" against minimum resale price maintenance (RPM) and finds the RPM anticompetitive. It is also to be noted that maximum pricing or recommended retail pricing which serves as a focal point for a downstream collusion would also be deemed anticompetitive.

26.23 In circumstances where retailers request that a manufacturer set a certain price as a way of enforcing a cartel between the retailers, this RPM requirement may have the same impact as a horizontal price fixing agreement. The MyCC would find such an agreement to be anticompetitive.

26.24 It appears that on the plain reading of the guidelines on the chapter 1 Prohibition, anticompetitive "non-price vertical agreements" may not be considered to have a "significant" anticompetitive effect if the individual market share of the seller or buyer does not exceed 25 percent of their relevant market. However, this safe harbor may not apply to price vertical agreements such as the RPM. Arguably, there may be no any safe harbor for the RPM in Malaysia. In this connection, the concept of *de minimis* for now does not exist for the RPM in Malaysia. The rationale for this is not known.

H. Tying

26.25 Tying occurs where a seller refuses to sell a product X unless the buyer also takes Y. An example of tying is provided in the guidelines on chapter 2 Prohibition: a car manufacturer informs a buyer that in order to buy a car he must also take a mobile phone contract. This would force the buyer to buy a product that the buyer may not want. It also means that other mobile phone companies would have part of the market foreclosed to them (i.e. the buyers who buy the cars). If the car manufacturer is dominant, then a significant number of customers will be foreclosed from a significant part of the market for mobile phones.

26.26 Generally, the MyCC would take issue with tying if there is a possibility that an enterprise that is dominant in one market is trying to obtain market power in another market by leveraging its dominance.

I. Exclusive dealing

26.27 An exclusive dealing arrangement between a dominant seller and a buyer may potentially infringe the chapter 2 Prohibition, if such arrangement forecloses a market. For example, a dominant supplier X has 80 percent of the wholesale market and establishes an exclusive dealing arrangement with buyer Y, a retail chain and with this Y gains 80 percent of the downstream market and other buyers are not able to buy the products from X. The competitors of X are prevented from supplying to Y and the market supplied through Y is now foreclosed to them.

26.28 The assessment of whether exclusive dealing arrangements foreclose a significant part of the market which limits the ability of efficient competitors to compete would be examined by the MyCC on a case-by-case basis.

J. Refusal to deal

26.29 The MyCC takes the view that generally enterprises are free to deal with whomever they choose. However, in certain circumstances, a refusal to deal by a dominant enterprise may amount to an abuse.

26.30 In the guidelines on the chapter 2 Prohibition, examples of refusal to deal are *inter alia*, as follows:

(a) a refusal to supply products to a buyer, i.e. where a seller refuses to supply an input to a downstream buyer Y that Y needs and the seller also competes in the downstream market with Y;

(b) a refusal to license intellectual property rights;
(c) a refusal to grant access to infrastructure that is necessary (an essential facility) to supply certain products (e.g. telecommunications services that need access to a telecommunications network that cannot be economically duplicated).

The remedy for a refusal to deal is to force the supplier or the seller to supply at a reasonable consideration. In this respect, the MyCC recognizes that this course of action may reduce the incentive by enterprises to invest in products, intellectual property rights or essential facilities. The challenge for the MyCC is to balance the difficult trade-off involved in forcing supply which leads to a short-term increase in competition but which may harm longer term incentives for innovation and investment. **26.31**

K. Essential facilities

Refusal to supply or grant essential facilities is regarded by the MyCC as part of refusal to deal.[3] **26.32**

L. Bundling (including loyalty and market shares discount)

Products are bundled if they are sold together at a lower price than separately. Bundling would be treated by the MyCC as predatory if the price of one or more of the products in the bundle is set below AVC or LRIC, thus making it difficult for other producers of products to compete. **26.33**

In the guidelines on the chapter 2 Prohibition, the MyCC takes the position that, as a general principle, loyalty rebates and discounts are pro-competitive. If discounts are related to costs, they are justified. However, the loyalty rebates and discounts would infringe the Act if they are used by a dominant enterprise to foreclose a market to equally efficient competitors, in particular non-costs related discounts which are structured in a way where customers are not available to other competitors. **26.34**

M. Standard-setting groups (disclosure requirements, licensing arrangements, and licensing pools)

This standard is not available in Malaysia. At the moment, the law does not contemplate standard-setting issues. **26.35**

N. Customer termination

At the date of writing of this Chapter, there have been no guidelines issued by the MyCC on customer termination. If the customer termination is in fact a refusal to deal and if committed by a dominant enterprise, the termination may potentially be considered abusive and therefore would infringe the chapter 2 Prohibition. **26.36**

O. Termination of intermediaries (retailers, wholesalers, dealers, and value-added resellers, agents, and brokers)

At the date of writing of this Chapter, there have been no guidelines issued by the MyCC on the termination of intermediaries (retailers, wholesalers, dealers, and value-added resellers, agents, and brokers). If the termination is in fact a refusal to deal and if committed by a dominant enterprise, this conduct may potentially be considered abusive and therefore would infringe the chapter 2 Prohibition. **26.37**

---

[3] See Section I.L.

P. Termination of relationships with competitors

26.38 At the date of writing of this Chapter, there have been no guidelines issued by the MyCC on the termination with competitors. If the termination is in fact a refusal to deal and if committed by a dominant enterprise, this conduct may potentially be considered abusive and therefore would infringe the chapter 2 Prohibition.

Q. Exemptions

26.39 Anticompetitive agreements may be exempted from the chapter 1 Prohibition either through an individual exemption or a block exemption granted by the MyCC.

26.40 Under ss. 6 and 8 of the Act, if the MyCC is of the view that a specific agreement notified to the MyCC by an enterprise or a specific category of agreements fulfill certain criteria, it may then grant an exemption with regard to that specific agreement or that particular category of agreements.

26.41 The criteria that an agreement or a category of agreements must meet for an exemption to be granted are set out in s. 5 of the Act. An individual or block exemption (as the case may be) would only be granted by the MyCC where the four (4) cumulative conditions below are met:

(a) there are significant identifiable technological, efficiency, or social benefits directly arising from the agreement;
(b) the benefits could not reasonably have been provided by the parties to the agreement without the agreement having the effect of preventing, restricting or distorting competition;
(c) the detrimental effect of the agreement on competition is proportionate to the benefits provided; and
(d) the agreement does not allow the enterprise concerned to eliminate competition completely in respect of a substantial part of the goods or services.

26.42 The onus of proving the identified technological, efficiency, or social benefits lies with the parties to the agreement. The parties claiming for this relief are required to prove that the benefits gained are passed on to the consumers.

26.43 Enterprises may apply to the MyCC for an individual exemption, which may be granted subject to conditions, obligations, and for a limited duration. It is up to the enterprise to demonstrate the claimed benefits according to the criteria set out in s. 5 of the Act. An individual exemption can be cancelled or varied if there is a material change of circumstances or there is a breach or non-compliance of an imposed condition.

26.44 The MyCC may grant a block exemption to a particular category of agreements. For example, this could be a distribution agreement in a particular industry. The advantage of a block exemption is that similar agreements can be examined at the same time, which will allow the MyCC to provide a better overall assessment of anticompetitive impact and an assessment of the claimed benefits and will also relieve enterprises of having to submit separate applications. As with an individual exemption, a block exemption can be cancelled or varied if there is a material change of circumstances or there is a breach or non-compliance of any imposed condition.

26.45 Enterprises being investigated with possible infringement under the Act may rely on relief of liability under s. 5 of the Act. Similarly, the enterprises can also claim the benefit in litigation.

26.46 It is to be noted that there is no requirement under the Act for an agreement or conduct that may infringe the Act to be notified to the MyCC. Malaysia's competition regime is based on the self-assessment by enterprises of their agreements or conduct as to whether these are permitted by the Act. To this end, the MyCC will not entertain any application for guidance or approval of any potentially anticompetitive agreements unless it is specifically provided for under the Act. Parties are advised to seek independent legal advice.

It is important to note that the Act does not expressly provide for immunity to the enterprises that have applied for exemptions from the MyCC and the Guidelines are also silent on this issue. This is unfortunate as it may deter enterprises with genuine uncertainties about their agreements from seeking guidance from the MyCC. Further, enterprises may be reluctant to enter into agreements, which may result in overall benefits before obtaining an exemption by the MyCC, which could considerably prevent good business initiatives. **26.47**

To date MyCC has received block exemption applications from: **26.48**

(a) the Malaysian Shipowners Association (MASA), the Shipping Association of Malaysia (SAM) and the Federation of Malaysian Port Operators Council (FMPOC);
(b) the Association of Malaysian Hauliers; and
(c) the Life Insurance of Malaysia (LIAM).

Meanwhile, Nestle Products Sdn Bhd is the sole applicant for individual exemption. **26.49**

The MyCC plans to issue a proposed block exemption order (BEO) for liner shipping agreements made within Malaysia or has an effect on the liner shipping services market in Malaysia. **26.50**

It appears that the MyCC may grant the proposed BEO if it is satisfied in that: **26.51**

- there are significant identifiable efficiency benefits arising from the liner shipping agreements;
- the benefits could not reasonably have been provided by the parties to the liner shipping agreement without the agreement having the effect of preventing, restricting or distorting competition;
- the detrimental effect of the liner shipping agreements on competition is proportionate to the benefits provided; and
- the liner shipping agreement does not allow liner operators to eliminate competition completely in respect of a substantial part of the liner shipping services.

The proposed duration of the BEO is three years. After two years, should the need arise, the MyCC may review the exemption. The final BEO is scheduled be announced in June 2013 after the MyCC has evaluated submissions received during the public consultation on the proposal. **26.52**

It should be noted that s. 10 of the Act is not part of the proposed BEO; therefore, parties to a liner shipping agreement can still be found liable for an infringement if they are found abusing their dominant positions in the liner shipping market. The proposed BEO also does not cover inland carriage of goods and warehousing of goods. The proposed BEO additionally allows liner shipping operators to offer, on the basis of individual confidential contracting, their own service arrangements, upon certain conditions that would be attached to the BOE. **26.53**

Further to the exemptions above, the Schedules in the Act set out the exclusions from the chapter 1 Prohibition and the chapter 2 Prohibition. **26.54**

Section 3 of the Act provides that the Act "shall not apply to any commercial activity regulated under the legislation specified in the First Schedule." There are two legislations set out in Schedule 2 and activities thereunder would be excluded from the chapter 1 Prohibition and chapter 2 Prohibition: **26.55**

- Communications and Multimedia Act 1998 [Act 588],
- Energy Commission Act 2001 [Act 610].

26.56 Section 13 of the Act provides that "the prohibitions under Part II shall not apply to the matters specified in the Second Schedule." The Second Schedule specified that the following agreements shall not apply to the chapter 1 Prohibition and the chapter 2 Prohibition:

(a) an agreement or conduct to the extent to which it is engaged in an order to comply with a legislative requirement;
(b) collective bargaining activities or collective agreements in respect of employment terms and conditions and which are negotiated or concluded between parties which include both employers and employees or organizations established to represent the interests of employers or employees;
(c) an enterprise entrusted with the operation of services of general economic interest or having the character of a revenue-producing monopoly in so far as the prohibition under chapter 1 and chapter 2 of Part II would obstruct the performance, in law or in fact, of the particular tasks assigned to that enterprise.

II. Dealing with competitors

26.57 Section 4(2) of the Act states that certain horizontal agreements between competitors with the "object" of engaging in cartel practices are "deemed to have the object of significantly preventing, restricting, or distorting competition." These agreements are:

- fixing, directly or indirectly, a purchase or selling price or any other trading conditions;
- sharing market or sources of supply;
- limiting or controlling:
- production;
- market outlets or market access;
- technical or technological development; or
- investment; or
- performing an act of bid-rigging.

A. Horizontal price fixing

26.58 Under s. 4(2) horizontal price fixing is deemed to have the object of significantly preventing, restricting, or distorting competition. In the guidelines on the Chapter 1 Prohibition, price fixing between competitors is considered by the MyCC as the most anticompetitive agreements and would be closely scrutinized.

B. Horizontal agreements to allocate customers or territories; agreements not to compete

26.59 Market sharing cartels, including geographic market and customer sharing are, like horizontal price-fixing cartels, deemed to have the object of significantly preventing, restricting, or distorting competition under s. 4(2) of the Act.

C. Horizontal boycotts

26.60 At the date of writing of this chapter, there have been no guidelines issued by the MyCC on horizontal boycotts—i.e. agreements between competitors not to purchase from, or supply to, specific businesses. Most likely, the MyCC would only find the horizontal boycotts to be anticompetitive if such arrangements prevent the entry or growth of new competitors, or aim to punish competitors who refuse to cooperate in cartel arrangements.

D. Joint ventures and other competitive collaborations

The Act does not regulate the setting up of joint ventures; but it also does not exclude the setting up of joint ventures or mergers from the purview of the Chapter 1 Prohibition. Therefore, the setting up of joint ventures or mergers, which have the object or effect on competition in any market in Malaysia, may potentially infringe the Chapter 1 Prohibition. As an illustration, the setting up by two or more competitors of a joint venture to market and sell their products or the acquisition by a dominant manufacturer of one or more distributors, which leads to limiting or controlling any market, could infringe the Act. **26.61**

E. Trade associations

Trade and other associations generally fulfill legitimate functions intended to promote the competitiveness of their industries. To this end, participation in trade associations generally is legal. However, in practice, enterprises participating in such associations may collude and coordinate their actions which could infringe the Act and typically trade association meetings and contacts are often at the root of anticompetitive activity. Therefore, it is important to ensure that legitimate meetings and communications between members of trade associations do not become the occasion for anticompetitive cooperation or exchange of information. **26.62**

The guidelines on the Chapter 1 Prohibition clearly state that an agreement, as defined in the Act, could be found where competitors attending a business lunch arranged by their associations listen to a proposal for a price increase without objection. Therefore the MyCC has advised that competitors should avoid meetings or other forms of communication with competitors, particularly where price or anticompetitive exchange of information is likely to be discussed. Mere presence with competitors at an industry association meeting where an anticompetitive decision was made may be sufficient to be later implicated as a party to that agreement. Associations are also advised by the MyCC to inform their members not to discuss the prohibited agreements stipulated in s. 4(2) of the Act, i.e. price fixing, markets sharing, etc. as a way of avoiding liability. **26.63**

F. Interlocking directorates

At the date of writing of this chapter, there have been no guidelines issued by the MyCC on the interlocking directorates. It is likely that, if any acquisition of a minority interest gives an enterprise actual or legal control over the target's commercial conduct, or for some other reason would reduce competition in the market, then the Chapter 1 Prohibition may very well apply. The Chapter 2 Prohibition may apply if a dominant firm acquires an interest in other business in circumstances in which this weakens the competitive structure of the market. **26.64**

G. Facilitating practices

The Act does not deal specifically with the facilitating practices; however, it is likely that conduct such as exchange of information on future pricing or agreements may be caught under the Chapter 1 Prohibition, if they have the object or effect of restricting, preventing or distorting competition. **26.65**

H. Information exchange

Competitors may share non-price information on standards, new technologies that can improve competition in the market. This is perfectly legal and in fact encouraged. However, sharing or exchange of price information would be construed as the agreements having the object or the effect of "significantly preventing, restricting or distorting competition in the market" as provided in s. 4(2) of the Act and therefore would infringe the Act. In general, frequent exchange of confidential information among competitors in a market where very few competitors exist would potentially be viewed by the MyCC to have a significant effect **26.66** on competition. In addition, the exchange of information between competitors that is not provided to consumers is also likely to have a significant effect on competition. Essentially, sharing or exchanging price information which lead to facilitating price fixing would be deemed to be anticompetitive.

I. Joint purchasing agreements

26.67 At the date of writing of this Chapter, there have been no guidelines issued by the MyCC on the joint purchasing agreements. However, it is likely that the joint purchasing agreement may be caught under the Chapter 1 Prohibition, if they have the object or effect of restricting, preventing, or distorting competition.

J. Joint lobbying/regulatory/legislative efforts

26.68 It is likely that, as in many other jurisdictions, joint lobbying concerning regulations or legislations would not raise anticompetition issues. However, as in all contacts with competitors, it is important to ensure that legitimate meetings and communications do not become the occasion for anticompetitive cooperation or exchange of information.

III. General issues

A. Jurisdiction and applicable law (including sector-specific competition regulation)

26.69 The Act applies to enterprise carrying on commercial activities relating to goods or services, save for the exclusions set out in the Schedule 2 of the Act.

B. Antitrust system

(i) Name of agency/agencies

26.70 The MyCC is tasked with the administration and enforcement of the Act. The MyCC has very wide investigating powers under the Act. The Commission officer investigating any commission of an offense under the Act has all the powers of a police officer in relation to police investigation in seizable cases as provided for under the Malaysian Criminal Procedure Code, Act 593.

(ii) Staff size and budget

26.71 The MyCC consists of a chairman, chief executive officer, and nine commissioners. There are five departments in the MyCC, which are the executive arm of the MyCC: (i) management services; (ii) corporate communication; (iii) strategic planning and international affairs; (iv) investigation and enforcement; and (v) legal.

26.72 The MyCC received a development grant under the Tenth Malaysian Plan from the Government of Malaysia in an amount of MYR 10,578,605 to meet its financial liabilities and capital expenditure.

(iii) Recent enforcement actions and trends

26.73 On March 4, 2012, an online portal of local English daily reported that the president of the Cameron Highlands Floculturist Association (CHFA) had announced that its members had agreed to increase the prices of flowers by 10 percent. The announcement led the MyCC to launch its first investigation since the Act came into force.

26.74 Given that the CHFA's case is the MyCC's first enforcement, the MyCC decided to issue a proposed decision to the CHFA prior to making its decision final. The proposed decision was as follows:

(a) the CHFA shall cease and desist the infringing act of fixing prices of flowers;

(b) the CHFA shall provide an undertaking that its members shall refrain from any anticompetitive practices;
(c) the CHFA shall issue a public statement on the above mentioned remedial actions in the mainstream newspapers; and
(d) if a decision is made by the MyCC under s. 40 of the Act and the CHFA fails to comply with the directions issued by the MyCC, a financial penalty amounting to MYR 20,000 may be imposed. An additional MYR 1,000 will be imposed for each or part of each following day that the CHFA fails to comply.

The proposed decision was provided to the CHFA so as to give an opportunity to the CHFA to submit its arguments to the MyCC, and provide any other information for consideration. The final decision recently issued by the MyCC is based on the proposed decision set out above. **26.75**

According to the latest press statement by the MyCC's chief executive officer, moving forward, the MyCC will no longer be lenient as in the CHFA's case in its enforcement for infringement under the Act. **26.76**

The MyCC is also launching another investigation against the Federation of Livestock Farmers Association of Malaysia (FLFAM) after its chairman told a local daily that farmers typically cull about 10 percent of their older layer hens from each cycle (of one to three months, depending on the farm size) to make room for younger, more productive hens. He added that farmers have recently been culling up to 10 percent more hens to reduce production costs. In this connection, the MyCC issued a statement that "unilateral decision by a farmer to reduce production for purposes of prudent costs management may not be an anticompetitive conduct. However, if it is done in agreement with other farmers, then this may be an infringement under the Competition Act 2010." The investigation by the MyCC against the FLFAM is still ongoing. **26.77**

In terms on enforcement priority, it appears that the MyCC is seriously looking at clamping down bid-rigging, especially in bids issued by the Malaysian Government. According to a study carried out by the Organisation for Economic Co-operation and Development (OECD), in most countries, government procurement activities account for more than 15 percent of the country's gross domestic product (GDP). When procurement activities are tainted by bid-rigging, it will definitely give a significantly adverse impact to the country's economy, consequently burdening taxpayers who indirectly have to pay more than the actual price of a product or service. In view of the harmful effects of bid-rigging on the economy, the MyCC has identified bid-rigging as one of the main focus for enforcements. **26.78**

C. Private litigation

Given the Act is only recently enforced, there is no litigation pending. **26.79**

D. Follow-on litigation

See Section III.C. **26.80**

E. Arbitration and alternative dispute resolution

Arbitration and alternative dispute resolution (ADR) by nature are private agreements between contracting parties on how they wish to resolve and settle their disputes in respect of the underlying contracts entered into between the parties. Therefore, it may be unlikely that in Malaysia actions in relation to anticompetitive agreements or abuse of dominance would be referred to arbitration and/or ADR. In this respect, decisions on infringements would be made by the MyCC and thereafter on appeal by the Competition Appeal Tribunal. **26.81**

26.82 Section 64 of the Act states that any person who suffers loss or damage directly as a result of an infringement of the s. 4 or s. 10 prohibitions (regardless of whether such person dealt directly or indirectly with the enterprise) has a right of action for relief in civil proceedings in a court against any enterprise which is or which has at the material time been a party to such infringement. As such private actions must be brought in a court of law in Malaysia. The MyCC and the Competition Appeal Tribunal do not have the power to award damages in such actions.

F. Remedies

(i) Civil liability

26.83 The MyCC may impose financial penalties of up to 10 percent of the infringing enterprise's worldwide turnover for the period of the infringement. The MyCC also has the power to issue any direction it considers appropriate including, *inter alia*, a direction to bring the infringement to an end and, where necessary, require an enterprise to take such action as is specified to bring the infringement to an end. Interestingly, the MyCC also has the power to accept from enterprises, which are being investigated, commitments to do or to refrain from doing anything that the MyCC considers appropriate. In such instance, the MyCC will close the investigation without imposing a penalty. The commitments accepted by the MyCC shall be enforceable against such enterprises as if they had been set out in a MyCC decision.

26.84 In relation to offenses under the Act such as an obstruction of the MyCC in its investigations, an enterprise may be fined up to MYR 5 million for the first offense and up to MYR 10 million for any subsequent offense.

26.85 Section 63 of the Act provides that where a body corporate commits an offense under the Act,

> any person who at the time of the commission of the offence was a director, chief executive officer, chief operating officer, manager, secretary or other similar officer of the body corporate or was purporting to act in any such capacity or was in any manner or to any extent responsible for the management of any of the affairs of the body corporate or was assisting in such management:
> - may be charged severally or jointly in the same proceedings with the body corporate; and
> - if the body corporate is found to have committed the offence, shall be deemed to have committed that offence unless, he may establish that the offence was committed without his knowledge, consent or connivance and he had taken all reasonable precautions and exercised due diligence to prevent the commission of the offence.

(ii) Criminal liability

26.86 There is no personal liability under the Act for infringing the chapter 1 or 2 Prohibitions. However, individuals who commit an offense under the Act may be held personally liable and face imprisonment and/or the payment of fines. Individuals commit an offense if they obstruct an investigation by:

(a) refusing any Commission officer access to any premises;
(b) assaulting, obstructing, hindering, or delaying any Commission officer in effecting entry which the Commission officer is entitled to effect under the Act;
(c) failing to disclose or to give any relevant information, evidence, document, or providing any information, evidence, or document that he or she knows or has reason to believe is false or misleading;
(d) destroying, concealing, mutilating, altering, removing,or conspiring with any person to remove from any premises any record, book, account, document, computerized data, or other thing with the intent to obstruct the investigation;
(e) tipping off or disclosing to any other person any information which is likely to prejudice an investigation or proposed investigation;

(f) without lawful authority breaking or tampering with any seal made by the MyCC to seal any record, book, account, document, computerized data, or other thing.

Such offenses carry a fine not exceeding MYR 1 million and/or imprisonment for a term not exceeding five years. In case of a repeated offense the maximum penalty is a fine of MYR 2 million and/or imprisonment for a term not exceeding five years. **26.87**

G. Leniency and immunity

Section 41 of the Act provides that there shall be a leniency regime with a reduction of up to a maximum of 100 percent of any penalties which would otherwise have been imposed in case of violation of the Chapter 1 prohibition only. In other words, enterprises which disclose a cartel to the MyCC may benefit from immunity from financial penalty or of a reduction in the amount of the financial penalty. **26.88**

Only an enterprise which admits its involvement in an anticompetitive agreement and provides information to the MyCC which significantly assists in the identification or investigation of the cartel may benefit from leniency. **26.89**

The Act specifically provides that the leniency regime to be adopted may permit different degrees in the reduction of fine provided depending on whether: **26.90**

(a) the enterprise was the first to come forward;
(b) the stage of the investigation at which the enterprise provides information; and
(c) when admission was made in respect of the involvement in the cartel agreement.

H. Document creation and retention

When requiring a person to produce document or information, the MyCC may: **26.91**

> (a) take and retain for such duration it deems necessary, possession of any document (the person who provided the document is entitled to be supplied, as soon as practicable, with a copy certified by the MyCC to be a true copy of the document);
> (b) require the person producing the document or information to provide explanations in respect of the document or information so provided; and
> (c) if the document is not produced, require the person served with a notice to produce the document or information to state, to the best of that person's knowledge or belief, where the document may be found, who was the last person who had custody of the document and where person may be found.

It is important to note that the power of the MyCC to seize and retain possession of the original documents differs substantially from other jurisdictions where copies are made and only those copies are retained by the authorities. The retention of original documents by the MyCC may, potentially, have an adverse impact on the continuation of business during an investigation and give rise to various administrative and logistical problems vis-à-vis the handling, preservation, and return of those documents. **26.92**

27

MEXICO

Jesus Gabriel Altamirano, Javier Martinez del Campo L., and Peter Love
Jones Day

Introduction

27.01 Competition law in Mexico comes primarily from four sources:

(1) article 28 of the Federal Constitution and international treaties on antitrust and competition to which Mexico is a party;
(2) the Federal Economic Competition Law;
(3) Regulations to the Federal Economic Competition Law; and
(4) other Mexican federal laws that include antitrust and competition provisions directed to specific industries or areas.

27.02 The Mexican Constitution addresses economic competition and explicitly prohibits monopolies and monopolistic practices, and requires that the law severely punish and authorities effectively prosecute any agreement, procedure, or combination entered into by producers, industries, merchants, or service suppliers, through any means, intended to avoid free commerce or free competition among them and requiring consumers to pay excessive prices.

The Federal Economic Competition Law (*Ley Federal de Competencia Económica*, LFC) seeks to protect the process of competition and free commerce by preventing and eliminating monopolies, monopolistic practices, and other restrictions on the efficient operation of markets for goods and services. To this end, the LFC provides preventive and corrective measures. For prevention, it requires the review of concentrations that may affect the market before they are implemented. For correction, it mandates pursuit of and prosecution of monopolistic practices. **27.03**

As of the drafting of this chapter, Mexican Constitution was amended in the field of competition. **27.04**

As part of the amendment, a new autonomous agency was created to enforce and apply the LFC named Federal Economic Competition Commission (*Comisión Federal de Competencia Económica*, FECC). This new agency will replace and substitute for the current Federal Competition Commission (known as the CFC or Cofeco) in its functions except for broadcasting and telecommunication competition matters. As part of the amendment to the Mexican Constitution, those areas will be entrusted to a new autonomous organism created to regulate those sectors. That regulator will be named the Federal Telecommunication Institute (Instituto Federal de Telecomunicaciones, Ifetel). **27.05**

The new FECC shall have the powers necessary to fulfill effectively its purposes. These powers are being expanded from those the CFC currently possesses and will include the ability to remove entry barriers to competition or barriers to free competition, to regulate access to essential inputs, and to order the divestiture of assets, rights, partnership interests, or actions of economic agents, in the proportions necessary to eliminate anticompetitive effects. **27.06**

As an autonomous entity, the FECC shall be independent in its decisions and performance, professional in their performance, and impartial in its actions. The FECC will be governed according to the following: **27.07**

(i) The Commission shall issue its resolutions completely independently.
(ii) It will exercise its budget independently. The Mexican Congress shall ensure the adequacy of their budget to enable them to exercise their skills effectively and in a timely manner.
(iii) The Commission will issue its own organic statute, through a system of qualified majority voting.
(iv) It may issue general administrative provisions exclusively for the fulfillment of its regulatory function in the area of its competence.

As a consequence of the amendment to the Constitution, the LFC is being reviewed. Because the LFC was amended in 2011 it is not expected that there will be significant modifications of the LFC, but only an adaptation to fit the text of the LFC to the Constitution. The CFC has presented to the Mexican Congress a proposed amendment to the LFC for analysis. **27.08**

The discussion that follows is based on the historical statutes and precedents as enforced by the CFC. Although the FECC will have the power to establish its own governing statute and set its own operating procedures, enforcement and process at the FECC likely will be consistent with past CFC practice. CFC precedents also likely will influence Ifetel on telecommunications matters. **27.09**

I. Acting alone

The LFC distinguishes two types of monopolistic practices: absolute and relative. Absolute monopolistic practices include horizontal agreements that fix prices, restrict output, rig bids, or divide markets. These activities are considered illegal per se and are subject to sanction simply based on proof of their existence. **27.10**

27.11 Relative monopolistic practices are acts, contracts, covenants, procedures, or combinations that have or may have the purpose or effect of improperly displacing other economic agents from the market, substantially preventing their access, or establishing exclusive advantages for one or several persons. According to the LFC, this type of practice includes both unilateral and joint actions such as: (i) predatory pricing, (ii) vertical price restrictions, (iii) tied purchases or sales, (iv) exclusivity, (v) refusals to deal, (vi) boycotts, (vii) vertical segmentation of markets, (viii) discounts based on conditional operations, (ix) cross-subsidies, (x) price discrimination, and (xi) increased costs for a rival.

27.12 In Mexico, relative monopolistic practices are not per se illegal because their use will not always have negative impacts on the competitive process and indeed may even be common due to efficiencies they may generate. The analysis of relative monopolistic practices requires an evaluation of the economic or market power of the actor or actors. The person engaged in the practice must have substantial power in the relevant market, and the practice must relate to goods or services in that market for a relative monopolistic practice to be illegal under the LFC. Such practices may be punishable if they do not generate efficiencies that offset their negative impact. The CFC analyzes relative monopolistic practices on a case by case basis to determine whether or not they violate the law.

27.13 The LFC and the regulations under the LFC set out the basic elements that the CFC evaluates to determine the presence of substantial power in the relevant market. Under article 13 and the regulations thereto, the CFC considers the participation of the relevant economic agents in the market, whether they have the capacity to fix prices or to restrict supply, barriers to entry, the existence and power of competitors, access to input sources, the market positioning of the products in the relevant market, import alternatives and costs, and the costs to consumers if they must find alternative providers.[1] In case of relative monopolistic practices, the CFC also may determine the substantial power in the relevant market of two or more economic agents considered as a whole.[2]

27.14 To determine the market participation of the economic agents, the CFC typically starts with some measure of market shares. In this process, the regulations to the LFC direct the CFC to consider sales indicators, numbers of clients, and productive capacity, but the regulations also allow the CFC to evaluate any other factors the CFC deems relevant.[3] The CFC typically considers high market shares to be indicative of substantial power.

27.15 Fines for engaging in relative monopolistic practices may be as much as 8 percent of the revenues of the economic agent who engaged in the practice and twice as much if the offense is repeated. Fines for engaging in absolute monopolistic practices may be as much as 10 percent of the revenues of the economic agent who engaged in the practice and twice as much if the offense is repeated.

27.16 The CFC has been particularly focused on unilateral conduct in the telecommunications industry that might constitute relative monopolistic practices. Considering the special circumstances of the telecommunications market in Mexico, where a single economic agent may have 70–80 percent market shares in many markets, the CFC has been concerned about practices designed to obstruct competition.

---

[1] Ley Federal de Competencia Económica, *Diario Oficial de la Federación*, December 24, 1992, art. 13 (LFC), and Reglamento de la Ley Federal de Competencia Económica, *Diario Oficial de la Federación*, October, 12, 2007, art. 13 ("LFC's Regulation").

[2] LFC (n 1) art. 13 bis.

[3] LFC's Regulation (n 1) art. 11.

A. Predatory pricing

Under article 10(VII) of the LFC, below cost pricing may be a relative monopolistic practice and constitute predatory pricing when an economic agent with substantial power in the relevant market engages in: (i) a systematic sale of goods or services at prices below the average total cost, or (ii) an occasional sale of goods or services below the average variable cost. In addition, there must be elements to conclude that losses from the below cost pricing will be recovered by future price increases. Under the regulations of the LFC, an economic agent may recover losses from below cost pricing when, in addition to having substantial power in the relevant market, it has enough financial capacity or excess production capacity to maintain below cost pricing, or it has a reputation for affecting free competition in the marketplace. **27.17**

In the case of goods and services produced jointly or divisible for its commercialization, the average total cost and the average variable cost will be distributed among all sub-products and co-products. This distribution must take into consideration the technical characteristic of the production, distribution, or commercialization process as well as the generally accepted accounting principles and financial information norms. **27.18**

In evaluating any relative monopolistic practices, the CFC also considers efficiencies. In the context of below cost pricing, an entity may offer discounts not to displace competitors, but to position its trademark in the market or to facilitate the launch of a new product. Alternatively, excess products may be sold at reduced prices to renew inventory. In these cases, the efficiencies generated may justify temporary below cost pricing that otherwise could violate the LCF. **27.19**

The CFC has had consistent interest in predatory pricing issues and has brought enforcement actions in a number of cases. A landmark case in this area for the CFC involved below cost pricing by Grupo Warner Lambert México, S.A. de C.V. on chewing gum. The CFC found that Warner Lambert had substantial power in the chewing gum market (with a share of sales above 50 percent) and that it had systematically priced one of its brands, Clarks, below average total cost. The below cost pricing created a barrier to entry that displaced a competitor, Canel's, which the CFC judged to be a relative monopolistic practice. The CFC fined Warner Lambert and ordered it to stop the below cost pricing on the Clarks brand.[4] **27.20**

B. Exploitative offenses (excessive pricing, monopoly leveraging)

(i) Excessive pricing

High or even monopoly prices are not illegal themselves. However, article 10(XI) of the LFC considers the action of one or several economic agents for the purpose or effect, direct or indirect, of increasing costs and hindering the productive process or of reducing demand for their competitors a relative monopolistic practice. This type of practice is difficult to prove because it requires substantial power in the relevant market by one of the parties that would obligate market participants to increase their costs to such a degree that they would lose sales. **27.21**

The CFC has brought enforcement actions in a number of cases of excessive pricing where the purpose or effect was to increase costs to competitors. For example, the CFC recently fined Telcel (Radiomovil Dipsa, S.A. de C.V.) for excessive termination fees on Telcel's network. These fees harmed smaller competing networks (both fixed and mobile) by increasing **27.22**

[4] *Grupo Warner Lambert México, S.A. de C.V.*, Comisión Federal de Competencia (México), Case no. IO-016-96 (June 6, 2002).

the costs to interconnect with the Telcel network.[5] On appeal, the fine was withdrawn after Telcel entered into a settlement agreement that reduced interconnection fees.

(ii) Monopoly leveraging

27.23 Under article 10(IX) of the LFC, use of the gains that an entity obtains from the sale, marketing, or supply of a good or service where it has substantial power in the relevant market to finance losses due to the sale, commercialization, or supply of another good or service can be a relative monopolistic practice. In some ways, this offense is similar to predatory pricing except that the source of financing is gains the economic agent receives from participating in another market in which it has substantial economic power.

27.24 An important element of the violation is that the economic agent uses its substantial power in the relevant market in an anticompetitive manner to displace competitors in an effort to monopolize or attempt to monopolize another market. As with other monopolistic practices, efficiencies may justify the use of profits in one market to finance losses in another. Similar to predatory pricing, financing losses resulting from the introduction of a new product would not normally be considered a violation of the law.

27.25 The CFC has considered monopoly leveraging offenses in only a few cases and always in conjunction with other possible relative monopolistic practices. For example, in 2001 the CFC fined Telmex in part for financing the operation of its subsidiary Telcel in the telecommunication market, but this was only one of a number of monopolistic practices that the CFC found.[6] As a result, there is little precedent prohibiting this practice specifically.

C. Monopsony

27.26 In Mexico, the mere possession of monopsony power is not illegal, but the action of one or several buyers against their suppliers or customers could be a relative monopolistic practice under article 10 of the LFC.[7] In the case of several agents who are also competitors, the action may constitute an absolute monopolistic practice.

27.27 To date, the CFC has not brought enforcement actions based specifically on monopsony concerns and has considered such issues only indirectly. In 2002, for example, the CFC investigated the market for the acquisition of supermarket goods and services from distributors. The CFC closed the investigation without taking any action, but mentioned in its resolution that Wal-Mart had committed to issue an internal communication to its buyers reaffirming that negotiations with suppliers must be limited to the cost and conditions of sale to Wal-Mart and that the buyers should not interfere with or suggest the cost or conditions of sale by the suppliers to Wal-Mart's competitors.[8]

D. Price discrimination

27.28 Price discrimination is the differentiation or establishment of different prices or conditions for sale or purchase for different buyers or sellers that are in the same circumstances. Under article 10(X) of the LFC, this practice is prohibited as a relative monopolistic practice if the

---

[5] *Radiomóvil Dipsa, S.A. de C.V., Comisión Federal de Competencia (México)*, Case no. DE-37-2006 (April 7, 2011).

[6] *Teléfonos de México / Radiomóvil Dipsa / SOS Telecomunicaciones / Telecomunicaciones del Golfo*, Comisión Federal de Competencia (México), Case no. DE-16-1995 (July 18, 2001).

[7] See further Sections I.G, II.C, and I.D.

[8] *Wal-Mart de México, S.A. de C.V.*, Comisión Federal de Competencia (México), Case no. IO-02-2002 (March 6, 2003).

economic agent engaging in the practice has substantial power in the relevant market and there are no efficiencies supporting the conduct.

An important aspect of this practice is that the economic agents affected by the conduct should be in the same circumstances. If they have different conditions the sale at different prices could not be considered price discrimination. **27.29**

The CFC has analyzed several price discrimination cases. Most of them have been in the telecommunication market and have imposed fines on the economic agents involved in the practice. The CFC has fined Telmex for committing this practice on more than one occasion,[9] and the CFC currently is investigating several cases involving this practice. **27.30**

E. Dictating or influencing resale prices

Article 10(II) of the LFC treats the imposition of price or other conditions on a distributor or supplier in commercializing or distributing goods or services as a relative monopolistic practice. Nonetheless, suppliers and distributors often desire to see homogeneous prices for the supply of a service or the sale of a product so that buyers find the same product on the same sale conditions and at the same cost regardless of the place where it is acquired. Suppliers and distributors also may desire to establish consistent downstream prices across different outlets as a way to foster non-price competition. As with other relative monopolistic practices, legality depends on whether the actor has substantial power in the relevant market and whether efficiencies offset the negative impact of the practice. **27.31**

(i) Resale price maintenance

If they lack substantial power in the relevant market, manufacturers and distributors may require specific resale prices for their customers under the LFC. This type of practice is common in distribution contracts and often is used with car dealerships and franchises. If the entity setting resale prices has substantial market power in the relevant market, however, the CFC will consider the possible harm to competition and any efficiencies generated that might offset any harm. So far, the CFC has not specifically addressed a situation where a supplier sets resale prices but also competes with its distributors in the relevant market; but if the case were analyzed we expect that the CFC would treat the supplier as a competitor of the distributors and in this sense prohibit the supplier from setting resale prices. **27.32**

(ii) Minimum advertised price programs

The LFC does not specifically address minimum advertised price programs, and the CFC has not specifically considered such a case. Such a program potentially could fall under article 10(II) as the imposition of a sale condition on a distributor and therefore could be illegal as a relative monopolistic practice if done by an entity with substantial power in the relevant market. **27.33**

F. Tying arrangements

Article 10(III) of the LFC specifically identifies tying arrangements as a type of relative monopolistic practice. It prohibits a sale or transaction conditioned on the purchase, acquisition, sale, or provision of another additional service or item, normally different or distinguishable, or a sale or transaction based on reciprocity where the entity providing the tying product or service has substantial power in the relevant market. Absent efficiencies that **27.34**

[9] *Teléfonos de México / Avantel / Alestra*, Comisión Federal de Competencia (México), Case no. DE-07-98 (May 25, 2000); *Teléfonos de México / Avantel / Alestra*, Comisión Federal de Competencia (México), Case no. DE-033-99 (February 20, 2002).

would justify the tie, the CFC views tying arrangements as distorting competition and free commerce in markets and as a means of pressure to inhibit competitive growth.

27.35 The CFC has analyzed tying arrangements in a number of cases. For example, the CFC fined the Sindicato Nacional de Piltos de Puerto (National Union of Port Pilots) in 2005 for tying, on the basis that the union had conditioned the provision of pilot services on a contract for barging services provided by a related company.[10]

G. Exclusive dealing

27.36 The LFC identifies exclusive dealing as another relative monopolistic practice. Article 10(I) specifically describes exclusive dealing as agreements or covenants between entities that are not competitors to set, impose, or establish exclusive distribution of goods or services based on the subject, geographic position, or for a determined period of time. Article 10(I) also includes the division, distribution, or assignment of customers or suppliers or the imposition of an obligation not to manufacture or distribute goods or services for a period of time as relative monopolistic practices.

27.37 Exclusive dealing arrangements are very common among suppliers and distributors, but can constitute a violation of the LFC where one or more of the parties may have substantial power in the relevant market. The CFC has analyzed only a few cases involving exclusive dealings, but has concluded that exclusive dealing arrangements can constitute a barrier entry. As an example, the CFC imposed a fine on Pemex (the Mexican oil company) for requiring gas stations to sell only lubricants and industrial greases of the Pemex brand. In its resolution, the CFC also ordered Pemex to remove this requirement.[11] In another case, the CFC imposed a fine on A.C. Nielsen for executing agreements with convenience stores which included exclusivity clauses. In this case the CFC also ordered A.C. Nielsen to modify such clauses in the agreements executed.[12]

H. Refusal to deal

27.38 Article 10(V) of the LFC treats a unilateral refusal to deal as a relative monopolistic practice. It provides that a unilateral action of refusing to sell or provide goods or services to specific entities where such goods or services are ordinarily offered to third parties is illegal if the entity refusing to sell or provide the goods or services has substantial power in the relevant market.

27.39 The CFC has been very active investigating and sanctioning refusals to deal. One representative refusal to deal case occurred in 2009 when the CFC brought an action against Grupo Televisa for refusing to provide certain television content, including popular channels that Televisa broadcasts on Mexican free television, to a cable television competitor. The CFC fined Televisa MXN 47.5 million (approx. USD 3.7 million) and also had the power to order the suspension of the practice. This proved unnecessary when Grupo Televisa decided to end the practice by itself.[13]

I. Essential facilities

27.40 Denying other market participants access to an essential facility is a relative monopolistic practice under the LFC. It is essentially a unilateral refusal to deal as addressed in article

[10] *Sindicato Nacional de Pilotos de Puerto, Delegación Tampico-Altamira*, Comisión Federal de Competencia (México), Case no. IO-04-2004 (November 23, 2005).

[11] *Pemex Refinación*, Comisión Federal de Competencia (México), Case no. IO-062-97 (July 10, 2003).

[12] *A.C. Nielsen Company*, Comisión Federal de Competencia (México), Case no. IO-22-97 (August 5, 1998).

[13] *Grupo Televisa, S.A.B. and others*, Comisión Federal de Competencia (México), Case no. DE-022-2007 (November 20, 2009).

10(V) and as discussed above. Moreover, there may be a strong implication that an entity has substantial power in the relevant market if it provides a good or service that is essential to other market participants.

The CFC has brought enforcement actions in a number of cases involving essential facilities. A recent case dealing with essential facilities involved Telcel and other telephone service providers. In this case, the CFC concluded that Telcel had increased the cost of its competitors by imposing an interconnection rate higher than those it charged itself for calls within its own network and even higher than the final prices Telcel charged to its customers.[14] **27.41**

J. Bundling (including loyalty and market share discounts)

Bundling may be treated as a relative monopolistic practice under the LFC. If the bundling constitutes a tying arrangement, article 10(III) of the LFC, which addresses tying, would apply. This is discussed above in Section I.F. **27.42**

Alternatively, bundling in the form of discounts for not using or buying the products of third parties (such as loyalty or market share discounts) may be a relative monopolistic practice under article 10(VIII). This section of the LFC discourages the use of discounts or incentives in exchange for not using, purchasing, or selling third parties' products. This section also addresses purchases or transactions conditioned on not selling or providing to third parties the products or services that are the subject of the transaction. As with other relative monopolistic practices, a violation requires a showing that the entity imposing the conditions has substantial power in the relevant market and that efficiencies do not offset the harm to competition from the practice. **27.43**

K. Standard-setting groups (disclosure requirements, licensing arrangements, and licensing pools)

There appear to be no precedents on this issue that have been made available by CFC. **27.44**

Usually, in Mexico, trade associations are very active in promoting industry standard-setting groups. Neither the LFC nor its regulations provide guidelines on the subject. However, standard-setting groups can raise antitrust issues where members: **27.45**

- share competitively sensitive information;
- boycott certain members or standards; or
- adopt discriminatory standards.

The CFC has carefully watched trade associations and fined them and their members when improper practices, especially cartel activities, have been detected. **27.46**

For instance, following a two-year investigation, the CFC found that the National Chamber of Cargo Transportation (Canacar) and representatives of trucking companies had formed an agreement to impose a standard fuel adjustment surcharge on cargo shippers. The surcharge was an attempt to recover increased costs of diesel fuel, for which government-approved prices had risen. The CFC learned that Canacar had used the internet and various traditional publications to announce a standard fuel adjustment surcharge. The CFC viewed the agreement on the surcharge as a clear violation of article 9 of the LFC and an absolute monopolistic practice.[15] **27.47**

[14] *Radiomóvil Dipsa, S.A. de C.V.*, Comisión Federal de Competencia (México), Case no. DE-037-2006 (April 7, 2011).

[15] *Cámara Nacional del Autotransporte and others*, Comisión Federal de Competencia (México), Case no. DE-153-2008 (June 3, 2010).

27.48 Regulations to the LFC consider instructions or recommendations issued by trade associations to its members as indications of a possible absolute monopolistic practice. Not all actions or activities by associations are necessarily illegal, but members of such associations must be alert of possible antitrust concerns when attending meetings. Many Mexican companies have adopted rules that set out basic "do's" and "don'ts" indications as to how to behave in those meetings. Also the CFC has issued guidelines to trade associations to help promote compliance with the LFC.

L. Customer termination

27.49 The CFC has traditionally analyzed customer terminations as a form of refusal to deal. Refusals to deal can be a relative monopolistic practice under article 10(V) of the LFC and is an area where the CFC has been active.[16] For example, the CFC fined a telephone company with substantial power in the relevant market for terminating a service agreement with a client. As a result of its investigation, the CFC determined that the unjustified termination of the agreement resulted in the client's displacement from the market.[17]

M. Termination of intermediaries (retailers, wholesalers, dealers, and value-added resellers, agents, and brokers)

27.50 Termination of intermediaries may create similar antitrust issues as customer termination. The CFC treats these as refusals to deal (discussed above in Section I.H) and has been active in investigating such actions. In one example, the CFC fined a soft drink distributor who stopped supplying product to a retailer that refused to cease selling a competing brand.[18]

N. Termination of relationships with competitors

27.51 Termination of a relationship with competitors may constitute an abusive refusal to deal or potentially the denial of an essential facility. In either case, these would be relative monopolistic practices that require proof of substantial power in the relevant market. Refusals to deal and essential facilities are discussed above in Sections I.H and I.I. Under certain circumstances, the CFC may also view terminating or threatening to terminate a relationship as a means of enforcing, threatening, or inducing other forms of potentially anticompetitive conduct. Such conduct could constitute an absolute monopolistic practice if it entails agreements among competitors about price or output.

O. Exemptions

27.52 As stated above, a relative monopolistic practice is illegal if the actor has substantial power in the relevant market. The LFC lists those activities that are relative monopolistic practices. The only exemptions apply to certain strategic activities conducted by the Mexican government (postal services, oil and other hydrocarbons, basic petrochemical, radioactive minerals and generation of nuclear energy, electricity, and coin minting), labor unions, and temporal privileges granted to authors and inventors rights.

27.53 In addition, the LFC requires that efficiencies be weighed in determining if a given practice is to be punished.

---

[16] For discussion, see Section I.H.

[17] *Teléfonos de México, S.A. de C.V.*, Comisión Federal de Competencia (México), Case no. DE-22-2003 (July 14, 2004).

[18] *Propimex, S.A. de C.V. and others*, Comisión Federal de Competencia (México), Case no. DE-21-2003 (June 30, 2005).

II. Dealing with competitors

Agreements, covenants, arrangements, or combinations between or among competitors may be absolute monopolistic practices under the LFC. Such absolute monopolistic practices are illegal irrespective of their effect on competition. The CFC has construed the language of the LFC to mean that these practices are illegal per se. Absolute monopolistic practices may involve fines or sanctions as well as criminal penalties. Regulations to the LFC consider instructions or recommendations relating to price or other competitive sensitive matters issued by trade associations to its members as indications of a possible absolute monopolistic practice. Anti-cartel enforcement has been and continues to be a key priority for the CFC.[19] **27.54**

A. Horizontal price fixing

Article 9(I) of the LFC makes fixing, increasing, arranging, or manipulating the sale or purchase price of goods or services offered or sought in the markets an absolute monopolistic practice and therefore illegal. The LFC also makes exchanging information for the purpose or effect of fixing prices an absolute monopolistic practice. The regulations to the LFC provide that the following circumstances are indications of this type of practice: (a) the price offered by two or more competitors is significantly different from international prices, unless this is a result of taxes, transportation, or distribution costs; and (b) two or more competitors set maximum or minimum prices or adhere to the prices set by a trade association or any competitor. **27.55**

B. Horizontal agreements to allocate customers or territories; agreements not to compete

Article 9(II) of the LFC considers agreements among competitors to restrict their competition by limiting or fixing the volume of goods or services provided to be absolute monopolistic practices. Similarly, article 9(III) treats agreements among competitors to divide, distribute, or assign portions of the market, whether by customers, suppliers, times, or geography, to be an absolute monopolistic practice. **27.56**

Finally, establishing, arranging, or coordinating bids or withholding bids in public auctions, sales, or competitive bid processes is an absolute monopolistic practice under article 9(IV). The CFC has observed that indications of this practice exist when the bidders in a certain sector "take turns" to win bidding processes. **27.57**

C. Horizontal boycotts

Horizontal boycotts, agreements among competitors not to deal with certain customers or suppliers, are not specifically identified as absolute monopolistic practices under article 9 of the LFC. However, the CFC may treat such an agreement as an absolute monopolistic practice under article 9(III) as an agreement to impose restrictions on the sale to certain parts of the market. Alternatively, the CFC could attack a horizontal boycott as an illegal agreement to refrain from bidding for certain customers. Although there is no specific precedent for it, the CFC might even scrutinize a boycott that falls short of being an absolute monopolistic practice as a refusal to deal, therefore potentially a relative monopolistic practice. **27.58**

D. Joint ventures and other competitive collaborations

The LFC does not specifically regulate joint ventures and other competitive collaborations. However, the CFC may treat such agreements as a special case of concentration where **27.59**

[19] An example of this is discussed in Section I.K.

merger control regulations would apply. For the CFC to review a joint venture or collaboration as a concentration, the arrangement must involve some aspects similar to a merger, acquisition, or other concentration such as establishing a long term relationship beyond the typical commercial relationship or providing for one party to be involved in the decision-making or management of the other, including the appointment of officers or directors. The CFC has even analyzed alliance agreements among airlines as concentrations when notified.

E. Trade associations

27.60 Although not expressly regulated by the LFC, the CFC has carefully watched trade chambers and associations, and in several cases, the CFC has fined such organizations. For instance, in 2010 the CFC found that the National Chamber of Cargo Transportation and representatives of various trucking companies had formed an illegal agreement to impose a standard fuel surcharge.[20] The CFC deemed this an absolute monopolistic practice in violation of Mexican antitrust law.

27.61 By attending meetings of trade associations, competitors may be more likely to engage in monopolistic practices. Therefore, parties should pay close attention to the matters discussed at such meetings and train their officers and employees on actions that must be avoided when attending such meetings. The CFC has issued a Guide for Compliance with the LFC for Associations, Business Chambers, and Professional Organizations.

F. Interlocking directorates

27.62 The issue of interlocking directors is not contemplated under the LFC and is not explicitly prohibited. Where the concept of interlocking directors has come up in CFC cases, it has not been viewed as a separate violation, but only as potential evidence of a concentration between the entities sharing directors.

G. Facilitating practices

27.63 The LFC does not directly address or regulate facilitating practices. Under article 35(X) of the LFC, however, the CFC has the power to fine any person who has "assisted, originated, induced, or participated" in an illegal practice. To exercise this power, the CFC must first establish that an illegal practice under LFC existed. The CFC has actually exercised this power in the past to fine companies and individuals who were co-perpetrators in a monopolistic practice.

27.64 For example, the CFC imposed fines in 2012 on several individuals who had executed a series of agreements to divide the market for tortillas in Tuxtla Gutierrez Chiapas. As part of its investigation, the CFC found that several entities and individuals performed actions that facilitated the implementation of the practice and therefore imposed fines on them under article 35(X) (in addition to that imposed to the individuals who directly committed the practice).[21] The CFC also prohibited the agreements as an absolute monopolistic practice and imposed fines on the individuals directly involved under article 9(III).

H. Information exchange

27.65 The exchange of information between competitors with the purpose or effect to fix, increase, agree to, or manipulate prices is an absolute monopolistic practice. The CFC has actively

---

[20] *Cámara Nacional del Autotransporte and others*, Comisión Federal de Competencia (México), Case no. DE-153-2008 (June 3, 2010).

[21] *José Ramón Salazar Ballinas and others*, Comisión Federal de Competencia (México), Case no. DE-014-2010 (March 22, 2012).

pursued such cases, and combating such cartel activity has been a consistent enforcement focus. Officers of the CFC have even indicated verbally that a strict interpretation of the LFC may make it illegal for only one party to deliver information to another if the purpose or result is to fix, raise, or manipulate prices.

The LFC is not clear regarding the kinds of information that may be exchanged among competitors, and the wording of article 9(I) is broad enough to allow CFC to investigate any case of information exchange. For this reason a case by case analysis is required. **27.66**

Usually, an exchange of information is more likely within a trade association. The CFC guidelines to trade association state that to comply with the LFC, members of trade associations should avoid (i) exchanging price lists or information about the transactions executed by its members, (ii) talking about increasing or decreasing prices or profits, or (iii) issuing recommendations regarding the amount of products produced or sold. **27.67**

Because price information exchanges are not permitted by Mexican law, neither the LFC nor the related regulations provide guidance about whether such information might be exchanged if sufficiently old, anonymous, or aggregated. In addition, the CFC does not appear to have issued any precedents on the subject. **27.68**

One area where some guidance is available relates to information exchanges during due diligence. The provisions of article 19 of the regulations to the LFC, require that parties who are considering a merger or another type of combination that involves a competitor must be extremely careful with respect to exchanges of information that refer to prices and customers. If the merger is not closed and the information exchange was not "protected," there would be a high risk of the practice being considered an absolute monopolistic practice. **27.69**

I. Joint purchasing agreements

A joint purchasing agreement may constitute a relative monopolistic practice if it would lead to monopsony power. Section I.C above addresses this possibility. Although there is no specific precedent for it, the CFC also could view a joint purchasing agreement as an absolute monopolistic practice if it would facilitate collusion among competing parties. **27.70**

J. Joint lobbying/regulatory/legislative efforts

The LFC does not expressly govern joint lobbying, regulatory, or legislative efforts, and there generally is no liability for these actions from an antitrust perspective. Usually these kinds of efforts are made through trade associations that represent the interests of their members. However, liability could arise if such joint activities were used as a means to engage activities that constitute absolute or relative monopolistic practices. See Section II.E regarding trade associations. **27.71**

III. General issues

A. Jurisdiction and applicable law (including sector-specific competition regulation)

The LFC applies generally within the United Mexican States and applies to all areas of economic activity. However, certain strategic activities conducted by the Mexican government are not deemed to be monopolies and are exempt from the LFC in connection with monopolies regulation. These areas are: postal services, oil and the other hydrocarbons, basic petrochemical, radioactive minerals and generation of nuclear energy, electricity, coin minting, labor unions, and temporal privileges granted to authors and inventors rights. **27.72**

27.73 Notwithstanding the above, the agencies and organisms charged with these exempt functions may be subject to the LFC when acting outside their exempt areas.

B. Antitrust system

(i) Name of agency/agencies

27.74 Mexico has a single authority charged with enforcing competition laws and specifically the LFC, the *Comisión Federal de Competencia* (Federal Competition Commission), commonly referred to by either of its acronyms: CFC or Cofeco. The CFC was established in 1993 and is the authority responsible for preventing, investigating, and combating monopolies, monopolistic practices, and concentrations.[22]

27.75 With the recent amendment to the Mexican Constitution (in June 2013) the new agency charged with the application of the LFC will be the Federal Economic Competition Commission (*Comision Federal de Competencia Económica*, FECC) and in broadcasting and telecommunication sectors the authority responsible for competition issues will be the Federal Telecommunication Institute (Instituto Federal de Telecomunicaciones, Ifetel).[23]

27.76 Starting on September 1, 2013, the FECC will come into existence and will have the authority to issue its own its own organic statute, through a system of qualified majority voting. It is not expected that the FECC will depart significantly from past CFC enforcement, but as of the drafting of this Chapter, the FECC has not yet started operation or issued its new its operating statute.

27.77 The Plenum of the new FECC will consist of seven commissioners, one of whom will act as the President of the FECC. The commissioners are appointed to staggered terms by the Mexican President with the ratification of the Mexican Senate. The commissioners will hold office for nine years and cannot under any circumstances serve as a commissioner again.

27.78 The President of the FECC will be appointed by the Senate from among the commissioners, by a vote of two thirds of the members present, for a period of four years, renewable on a single occasion. If a commissioner's term would expire before his four years as President, he would fulfill the role of President only for the duration of his term as a commissioner.

27.79 CFC decisions are taken through majority vote of the commissioners. In extreme cases where the commissioners are unable to exercise their votes or are otherwise prevented from casting their votes, the President of the CFC will have the casting vote to decide the cases submitted to the plenary.

27.80 The CFC has an executive secretary that is in charge of the administrative and operational coordination of the CFC.

27.81 The CFC is integrated by eight departments, including Concentration and Investigation of Monopolistic Practice bureaus.

(ii) Staff size and budget

27.82 The authorized CFC annual budget is MXN 215.1 million for 2012.

27.83 At November 2012 the staff of the CFC is a total of 143 posts.

(iii) Recent enforcement actions and trends

27.84 Since its inception, the CFC has sought to apply strictly competition law in Mexico. Recent amendments to the LFC have given CFC additional tools and powers to act and perform

[22] LFC (n 1) art. 23.

[23] Mexican Constitution, art. 28.

its duties. These amendments to the LFC authorize the CFC to impose significantly higher fines. For example, the CFC may impose fines of up to:

(a) 10 percent of the Mexico originated income of a company in the case of the commission of absolute practices (such as price fixing, bid rigging, and market allocation),
(b) 8 percent of Mexico originated income for engaging in a prohibited concentration or a relative monopolistic practice (which may involve conduct such as tying, price discrimination, the imposition of vertical restrictions, exclusive agreements, and refusals to deal),
(c) 5 percent of Mexico originated income for failing to notify of a concentration when legally required to do so, and
(d) 8 percent of Mexico originated income for failing to comply with an order to refrain from executing a concentration until the Commission issues a favorable decision.

The CFC policy of strict application of the competition laws can be seen in recent decisions where the CFC has not cleared mergers (for instance Nestlè's acquisition of Pfizer's nutritional business) and where the CFC has fined persons who engage in monopolistic practices.[24] An active and effective CFC should result in more competition and better market conditions in Mexico. **27.85**

Persons who have been harmed by a monopolistic practice or prohibited concentration may file an action in defense of their rights or interests independent of the proceedings provided in the LFC. The courts may request the opinion of the Commission on issues within its purview. **27.86**

Actions may be exercised individually or collectively, the latter pursuant to the provisions of Book Fifth of the Federal Civil Procedure Code. **27.87**

C. Private litigation

Anyone, in the case of absolute monopolistic practices, or the affected party, in the case of other practices or prohibited concentrations by the LFC, may file a complaint in writing before the CFC against the entity likely responsible for the prohibited act. The complaint must include the elements that evidence the existence of the prohibited act and that show that the plaintiff has suffered damages or losses. **27.88**

In addition, the CFC may initiate an investigation without request of any person. **27.89**

In general terms, the procedure is divided in two stages: (i) investigation and (ii) administrative procedure. **27.90**

The term of investigation phase takes between 30 and 120 business days. This term may be extended up to four times for 120 additional business days each time. The administrative procedure could take approximately 120 business days. **27.91**

D. Follow-on litigation (includes role of agency determinations of liability for follow-on litigation)

Resolutions issued by the CFC may be challenged through (a) reconsideration petition filed before the CFC, (b) administrative judicial proceedings, or (c) *amparo indirecto* (constitutional review) proceedings. **27.92**

[24] *NESTLÉ, S.A. and PFIZER Inc.*, Comisión Federal de Competencia (México), Case no. CNT-035-2012 (November 8, 2012).

(i) Recurso de reconsideración (reconsideration petition)

27.93 Reconsideration petitions may be filed with the CFC within 30 business days following the challenged decision. The CFC is required to analyze the petition and decide whether to revoke, change, or confirm the challenged decision. The CFC must issue its decision within 60 business days following the filing of the petition. No decision within the period constitutes a confirmation of the challenged decision.

(ii) Administrative judicial proceedings

27.94 A party affected by a CFC decision may elect to challenge the decision before Mexican administrative courts for competition matters in lieu of the reconsideration petition or after the CFC has confirmed its decision in a reconsideration process. This right may be exercised within 30 business days following the decision. The decision by the court may be appealed by either party.

(iii) Amparo indirecto proceedings

27.95 An *amparo indirecto* may be filed when the constitutional rights of a person have been affected by the actions of a Mexican authority. It is the last judicial option in the Mexican legal system. An *amparo indirecto* petition must be filed within fifteen business days following the decision or resolution in question. *Amparo indirecto* proceedings typically take about nine months to obtain a final resolution.

E. Arbitration and alternative dispute resolution

27.96 Not applicable in Mexico.

F. Remedies

(i) Civil liability

27.97 As discussed above in Section III.B, persons who have been harmed by a monopolistic practice or prohibited concentration may file actions in defense of their rights or interests independent of the proceedings provided in the LFC. The courts may request the opinion of the Commission on issues within its purview. The remedy is for direct and immediate damages resulting from the practice.

27.98 Actions may be exercised individually or collectively, the latter pursuant to the provisions of Book 5 of the Federal Civil Procedure Code.

(ii) Criminal liability

27.99 In addition to the economic penalties provided in the LFC, imprisonment of from three to ten years may be ordered for persons who engage in absolute monopolistic practices. The offense is prosecuted by claim made by the CFC when the competent authority has determined by final resolution that an economic agent is responsible for committing an absolute monopolistic practice in the terms of the LFC.

27.100 There will be no criminal responsibility for economic agents who claim the benefit under article 33 bis 3 of the LFC on prior ruling by the Commission that finds it complied with the terms set forth in said provision and other applicable provisions.

27.101 The process followed for this crime can be set aside on petition of the full Commission when the defendants comply with the administrative penalties imposed and further perform the requirements provided in the technical criteria issued by the Commission.

27.102 Criminal action shall prescribe in a period equal to the arithmetical mean term of the penalty of incarceration referred to in para. 27.99.

G. Leniency and immunity

The LFC provides procedures through which the parties involved in prohibited concentrations or in monopolistic practices, may cooperate voluntarily in the investigation by the CFC in order to obtain benefits in imposition of penalties. Hereafter, a general explanation is given how these procedures may apply. 27.103

(i) Prohibited concentrations and relative monopolistic practices

Pursuant to article 33 bis 2 of the LFC, before final judgment is entered in proceedings heard before CFC, whether for relative monopolistic practices or prohibited concentrations, the economic agent involved may file an instrument with CFC by which it agrees to suspend, suppress, correct, or not perform the corresponding concentration or practice. 27.104

The petitioner must evidence in said instrument that: 27.105

(a) the commitment filed has as consequence the restoration or protection of the process of competition and free participation, and
(b) the proposed means are suitable and economically viable to prevent or, as applicable, to void the relative monopolistic practice or the prohibited concentration for which it is deemed presumptively liable, providing the periods and terms for proof.

Once the CFC receives said instrument, it may close the file without imputing any liability whatsoever. It may also allocate liability and impose a fine of up to half of that which would apply without prejudice to a claim for damages.[25] 27.106

Economic agents may only avail themselves of this benefit once every five years. This period shall be computed from and after the notice of resolution by the Commission. 27.107

(ii) Absolute monopolistic practices

For absolute monopolistic practices, pursuant to article 33 bis 3 of the LFC, any economic agent that has engaged in, or is engaged in, an absolute monopolistic practice, has participated directly in absolute monopolistic practices on behalf of legal persons, and the economic agent or individual who has aided, encouraged, induced, or participated in commission of absolute monopolistic practices, may acknowledge it before CFC and claim the benefit of reduced penalties, provided: 27.108

(a) it is the first, among the economic agents or individuals involved in the conduct, to provide sufficient proof that is in its possession and available to it and that, in the judgment of CFC, allows proof of the existence of the practice;
(b) it fully and continuously cooperates with CFC in the proceedings; and
(c) it takes the necessary action to end its participation in the practice which violates the law.

If the foregoing requirements are met, CFC shall issue its resolution and impose a minimum fine. 27.109

Economic agents or individuals who are not the first to come forward may also obtain a fine reduction of as much as 50, 30, or 20 percent of the fine when they provide proof for the investigation in addition to those that CFC already has. 27.110

Individual who have directly participated in absolute monopolistic practices on behalf of the economic agents who receive the benefits from the reduction of penalties may be benefited with the same reduction of penalty, provided they offer the elements of proof they have, 27.111

[25] See Section III.F(i) (civil liability).

cooperate fully and continuously with the proceedings, and undertake the actions necessary to end their participation in the practice.

27.112 CFC shall keep the identity of the economic agent and the individuals who seek to avail themselves of the benefits described above confidential.

I. Document creation and retention

27.113 The powers of the CFC to investigate violations to the LFC can only be exercised within five years. The CFC's powers include the authority to investigate, inspect and request information pertinent to its investigation. Therefore, for competition purposes, parties should retain documents during a period of not less than five years after creation thereof. Other laws may require retention for longer periods.

28

THE NETHERLANDS

Christof Swaak
Stibbe

Introduction

On April 1, 2013, the Dutch Competition Authority (*Nederlandse Mededingingsautoriteit*, NMa) merged with the Netherlands Independent Post and Telecommunications Authority (*Onafhankelijke Post en Telecommunicatie Autoriteit*, OPTA) and the Netherlands Consumer Authority (*Consumentenautoriteit*) to form the Netherlands Authority for Consumers and Markets (*Autoriteit Consument en Markt*, ACM). Unless otherwise stated, we will refer to the Dutch competition authority both before and after April 1, 2013 as the ACM. **28.01**

I. Acting alone

Pursuant to article 24 of the Dutch Competition Act (DCA) undertakings are prohibited from abusing their dominant position. This provision is modeled after its European counterpart article 102 of the Treaty on the Functioning of the European Union (TFEU). European precedents and guidelines are relevant when applying article 24 DCA. For the interpretation of article 24 DCA the case-law of the EU courts is followed and decisions and guidelines of the European Commission are generally considered authoritative. The Dutch government **28.02** did not take the opportunity to introduce stricter rules for abuse of a dominant position than article 102 TFEU.

28.03 When assessing whether or not an undertaking is considered to have a dominant position on a market, the ACM follows the same two-pronged analysis as the EC. First, the ACM defines the relevant geographic and product market. Then, it assesses the economic position of the undertaking concerned. The various forms of abuse are discussed below.

28.04 The main difference between article 102 TFEU and article 24 DCA is the territorial application of these provisions. Article 102 TFEU is only applicable when trade between the member states of the European Union (EU) is potentially affected.

28.05 Cases relating to the abuse of a dominant position are relatively rare in the Netherlands. In 2011 the Ministry of Economic Affairs, Agriculture and Innovation commissioned a report in relation to the low number of interventions by the ACM on the basis of article 24 DCA. Various factors were identified as possible causes: the existence of sector-specific regulation in various industries, the high evidentiary thresholds imposed on the ACM by the Dutch courts and the preference for informal settlement of abuse cases. In response, the ACM pointed out that it would improve its practice regarding the abuse of dominance and that it would consider whether it can make more use of commitment decisions in this regard.

28.06 In view of the alignment of Dutch law with the EU competition rules, the subsequent sections relating to the various forms of abuse of dominance will briefly refer to the European practice if no relevant Dutch example is available. However, it should be noted that enforcement against unilateral practices has not been significant.

A. Predatory pricing

28.07 The DCA does not include an explicit prohibition against sales below purchase price. Selling products at a loss is therefore not prohibited as such. The explanatory memorandum of the DCA refers to the European *AKZO* case.[1] In this judgment the Court of Justice of the European Union (CJEU) held that prices below average variable costs may be regarded as abusive and that prices below total costs but above average variable cost are considered to be abusive if they are part of a strategy to eliminate a competitor. The ACM takes this conduct into account for the purposes of calculating a fine and considers it a "very serious" infringement of the competition rules.

28.08 In 2009, the incumbent Dutch postal operator, PostNL, faced a complaint from a competitor that its low-cost subsidiary had engaged in predatory pricing. However, in its decision, the ACM concluded that in this case there had been no predatory pricing, because the average price was above the long-run average incremental cost (LRAIC), a concept laid down in Article 102 Guidance of the EC.[2]

B. Exploitative offenses

28.09 There are various forms of exploitative offenses. Dominant undertakings may use exploitative offenses to preserve or enforce their dominant position in a certain market or to enhance their position in another market.

28.10 Exploitation may involve practices such as the imposition of excessive prices.

---

[1] Case C-62/86 *AKZO Chemie v. Commission* [1991] ECR I-3359.
[2] *Sandd v. TNT*, NMa Case no. 6207 (December 15, 2009).

In a civil case, the port of Rotterdam was accused of abusing its allegedly dominant position by charging excessive prices to its customers.[3] With reference to the judgment of the Court of Justice in *United Brands*,[4] the Court of Appeal in The Hague considered that prices may be abusive if (i) the difference between the prices and the underlying costs is excessive and, if this first condition is met, (ii) whether the prices are in themselves disproportionate in relation to the economic value of the service delivered. In the case at hand, the Court of Appeal considered that the plaintiffs had provided insufficient evidence to establish excessive prices. **28.11**

The issue of excessive prices is also often raised in the area of collecting societies that charge royalties for copyright-protected works. In the Netherlands, Buma/Stemra is the organization that acts as the Dutch collecting society for composers and music publishers. Buma/Stemra faced a complaint from a commercial broadcasting organization, Fresh FM, that made use of the music repertoire governed by Buma/Stemra.[5] Fresh FM claimed that Buma/Stemra demanded excessive prices for its services. However, the ACM and subsequently the District Court of Rotterdam failed to find any evidence of excessive pricing and dismissed Fresh FM's claim.[6] **28.12**

C. Monopsony

In 2004, the ACM issued a white paper where it stated that its assessment of buyer power was made in accordance with the Commission's decisional practice on this topic. In order to determine whether buyer power constitutes an abuse of a dominant position, the ACM will look at the availability of alternative sales channels. Other important factors include the existence of countervailing power of the suppliers and the role and position that the dominant undertaking has on its own downstream market. **28.13**

From the Dutch cases that assessed this topic, it can be seen that in principle, a dominant undertaking enjoys contractual freedom. The refusal to negotiate, for instance, does not necessarily lead to an abuse. In a case between the Netherlands Association of Dental Hygienists and a health care insurer, the ACM held that the sole fact that the health care insurer only offers non-negotiable standard contracts does not constitute an abuse of a dominant position.[7] Later on, this decision was confirmed by the Trade and Industry Appeals Tribunal (*College van Beroep voor het bedrijfsleven*, CBB) on appeal.[8] **28.14**

D. Price discrimination

Discrimination by the application of different prices to equal parties by an undertaking with a dominant position may amount to an abuse. However, this may be permissible when there is an objective justification for the unequal treatment. **28.15**

A relevant example is the case between Interpay and Superunie.[9] Interpay was the Dutch net clearing and settlement system for payments by switch cards, and Superunie was the purchasing organization representing a number of retailers. Superunie faced higher prices than **28.16**

---

[3] *Rotterdam Port Authority v. Oil sector*, Hof's-Gravenhage, Case no. 105.000.856/01; LJN BM6398 (June 1, 2010).

[4] Case 27/76 *United Brands and United Brands Continentaal v. Commission* [1978] ECR 207.

[5] *Fresh FM v. Buma*, NMa, Case no. 3295 (April 2, 2008).

[6] *Stichting Commerciële Omroep Exploitatie Zuid-Holland v. NMa*, Rechtbank Rotterdam, Case no. AWB 08/2026 MEDED-T1, LJN BJ6328 (August 27, 2009).

[7] *Dutch Association of Dental Hygienists, Nieuwegein (NVM) v. Menzis*, NMa, Case no. 5166 (July 13, 2006).

[8] *NMa v. Dutch Association of Dental Hygienists, Nieuwegein*, CBB Case no. AWB 07/736; LJN BK5722 (November 24, 2009).

[9] *Superunie v. Interpay*, NMa, Case no. 2978 (April 28, 2003).

its main competitor Ahold, the largest supermarket chain in the Netherlands. According to the ACM, the price discrimination was objectively justified. The ACM held it was justifiable that Interpay charged lower prices to Ahold. According to the ACM, the extra discounts that Ahold had received throughout the years could be regarded as a reward for the investments that Ahold made and the risks that it incurred as the first one to switch to this payment system. According to the ACM, these risks justified a special treatment for a certain period. The ACM argued that if it were to have taken a different decision, this could have had the effect of impeding new initiatives and technical innovation.

28.17 Discounts are another example of price discrimination. Discounts often result in a situation in which a customer that purchases a higher volume of certain units pays a lower price than that which a purchaser of a lower volume of units pays. Price schemes that are loyalty-inducing may be prohibited under article 24 DCA. An important precedent in this respect is the ACM decision in relation to CR Delta,[10] the largest supplier of breeding bull sperm to cattle farmers in the Netherlands. The ACM found that CR Delta had abused its dominant position by means of three discount schemes that bound cattle farmers to the company with regard to the purchase of breeding bull sperm. On appeal, the CBB held that although such discount systems can constitute an abuse, in this case the price for bull sperm only accounted for a very small proportion of the costs borne by the cattle breeders.[11] Consequently, the CBB considered that the discount scheme was not capable of removing or restricting the breeders' freedom to choose their sources of supply or of restricting competitors' access to the market. In view thereof, the CBB concluded that the discount scheme did not qualify as an abuse since it could not involve an appreciable restriction of competition.

E. Dictating or influencing resale prices

(i) Resale price maintenance

28.18 Cases in which the ACM assesses the conduct of an undertaking that dictates, influences, or agrees upon resale prices of other undertakings, in particular those of its customers, are rare. The ACM repeatedly stated that it does not consider resale price maintenance (RPM) an enforcement priority. Nonetheless, the ACM may enforce RPM cases in which there are particularly harmful effects, for example, when horizontal collusion is facilitated.

28.19 In the few precedents that are available, the ACM treated RPM as bilateral conduct and assessed this conduct under article 6 DCA. Article 6 DCA prohibits agreements and concerted practices which have as their object or effect the prevention, restriction or distortion of competition.[12] However, an agreement between undertakings may simply constitute the formal confirmation of an economic reality characterized by the fact that an undertaking in a dominant position has succeeded in having resale prices applied by other undertakings. In such a case, the possibility to apply both articles 6 and 24 DCA, the latter prohibiting the abuse of a dominant position, cannot be excluded.[13]

28.20 In the Secon case,[14] the ACM fined clothing producer Secon for applying price recommendations that effectively worked as minimum resale prices for clothing of the G-Star brand. In December 2005, the CBB overturned this decision.[15] Although the CBB held that the agreements between Secon and its customers had the objective to restrict competition, it

---

[10] *CR Delta*, NMa Case no. 3353 (December 31, 2003).

[11] *CRV Holding v. NMa*, CBB Case no. AWB 07/596; LJN: BN9947 (October 7, 2010).

[12] Further discussed in Section II.

[13] Case C-66/86 *Ahmed Saeed* [1989] ECR 803.

[14] *Chilly en Basilicum v. G-Star / Secon Groep*, NMa Case no. 757 (January 12, 2000).

[15] *Secon and G-Star v. NMa*, CBB, LJN AU8309 (December 7, 2005).

overturned the decision as the ACM had not sufficiently demonstrated how the agreements were capable of appreciably restricting competition.

(ii) Minimum advertised price programs

There are no Dutch precedents with regard to agreements between manufacturers and resellers to refrain from advertising the manufacturer's products below a certain minimum price. However, indirect agreements or practices to fix resale prices will be assessed in the same way as RPMs. **28.21**

F. Tying arrangements

Tying may qualify as an abuse of a dominant position if the sale of one product is made conditional on the sale of another product, while there is no objective justification to tie these products. **28.22**

In the assessment of tying arrangements, determining the relevant product market is particularly important. In the KPN case, for example, a telecommunications and ICT service provider in the Netherlands, KPN, lodged a complaint against certain cable companies in 2007. One of the allegations was that the cable operators were abusing their dominant position by bundling analog and digital packages for radio and television. According to the ACM, there was no infringement because the digital and analogue basic packages belonged to the same product market.[16] **28.23**

In the same year, the ACM had to decide on a complaint against Apple, claiming that it abused its dominant position by tying the sales of its portable music player iPod to music services provided by its online music store iTunes. The ACM dismissed the complaint by stating that consumers that purchase music via iTunes are able and permitted to play this music on devices other than an iPod. Furthermore, consumers are allowed to transfer music files bought from other online music stores to an iPod. As a result, the ACM concluded that Apple had not committed an infringement.[17] **28.24**

G. Exclusive dealing

Exclusive dealing arrangements or practices may qualify as an infringement under article 6 DCA, the cartel prohibition, or article 24 DCA, abuse of a dominant position. Within the Netherlands, special attention is paid to exclusive purchase agreements between breweries and owners of hotels, cafés, and restaurants, in the Netherlands referred to as the market for *horeca*. Breweries often offer loans and draft installations to *horeca* entrepreneurs on the condition that no draft beers are purchased from other breweries. However, there are no precedents in which such exclusive dealing arrangement have been found to constitute an abuse of a dominant market position. **28.25**

H. Refusal to deal

In principle, dominant undertakings are free to deal with whichever buyer or supplier they want. A dominant firm is allowed to refuse the supply of products or information to certain buyers. However, if this refusal results in an anticompetitive effect, this conduct may fall under the prohibition of article 24 DCA. In accordance with the Article 102 Guidance of the EC,[18] a particularly important factual question is whether the refused input is objectively indispensable in order to actually compete on the relevant market. **28.26**

---

[16] *KPN v. kabelaanbieders*, NMa Case no. 5702 (July 20, 2007).

[17] *Consumentenbond v. Apple*, NMa Case no. 5981 (September 6, 2007).

[18] Guidance on the Commission's enforcement priorities in applying [Article 102 TFEU] to abusive exclusionary conduct by dominant undertakings, OJ C 45, February 24, 2009 ("Article 102 Guidance").

28.27 In a 2009 judgment, the CBB dealt with the question of when a refusal to deal could qualify as an abuse of a dominant position.[19] With reference to the judgment of the CJEU in the *Bronner* case,[20] the CBB considered that a dominant firm is in principle allowed to refuse the supply of products or information to certain buyers. This type of situation may, however, qualify as an abuse if the refusal (i) excludes every competition on the market, (ii) is not objectively justified, and (iii) if the input is indispensable for the activities of the requesting party.

I. Essential facilities

28.28 Strongly related to the concept of refusal to deal, is the essential facilities doctrine. If an undertaking controls a facility or infrastructure that is necessary for competitors to offer services or products or to reach customers, denying access might constitute an infringement of article 24 DCA.

28.29 In 1998, a Dutch newspaper named *De Telegraaf* was denied access to the program listings of broadcasting organizations. *De Telegraaf* needed this information in order to add a supplement to its newspaper, which listed the programs for the upcoming week. This raised the question of whether this refusal amounted to an abuse of a dominant position by the broadcasting organizations. On final appeal, the CBB ruled, with reference to the *IMS Health* judgment of the CJEU,[21] that this denial of access did not qualify as an abuse of a dominant position. The CJEU held that there was no obstruction to the introduction of a new product since the broadcasting organizations already published their own weekly TV guides listing all radio and TV programs for the entire week.[22] In contrast to the *Magill* judgment of the CJEU,[23] in *De Telegraaf* case, the program listings that would be added to the newspaper in a supplement could not be seen as a new product.[24]

J. Bundling

28.30 The assessment under article 24 DCA of "bundling" is similar to the assessment of "tying."[25] Abuse of a dominant position can also occur through cumulative rebate discount systems, "loyalty rebates," which can have a similar effect to bundling.

28.31 In 2012, the ACM concluded that it had not been established that the incumbent postal service operator PostNL abused its dominant position on the Dutch postal service market by granting discounts for bundles of services.[26] The ACM started its investigation in response to a complaint by PostNL's competitor Sandd. The ACM's investigation showed, among other things, that the purchasers' decision to buy a bundle of services was not influenced by the discount granted by PostNL but by the perceived higher quality of the services. With regard to another aspect of the alleged bundling, the turnover concerned was so low, that a potential effect on competition would be very limited. According to the ACM, bundling only qualifies as an abuse of a dominant position if it would result in foreclosure of competitors. Therefore, the ACM did not establish any abuse because, as a result of the limited effect on competition, there would not be any foreclosure of competitors on the Dutch postal service market.

---

19 *Alarmcentrale Nederland B.V. v. NMa*, CBB, LJN BK6514 (December 3, 2009).

20 Case C-7/97 *Oscar Bronner GmbH v. Mediaprint* [1998] ECR I-07791.

21 Case C-418/01 *IMS Health GmbH v. NDC Health GmbH* [2004] ECR I-05039.

22 *Nederlandse Omroep Stichtin v. NMa*, CBB Case no. AWB 03/132; LJN AQ1727 (July 15, 2004).

23 Joined Cases C-241/91 P and C-242/91 P *RTE and ITP v. Commission ("Magill")* [1995] ECR I-743.

24 *Nederlandse Omroep Stichtin v. NMa*, CBB Case no. AWB 03/132; LJN AQ1727 (July 15, 2004).

25 See Section I.F.

26 *Sandd v. TNT* (n 2).

K. Standard-setting groups

The ACM has given specific attention to recognition schemes in its guidelines on cooperation between undertakings. Under recognition schemes, activities of undertakings are assessed on the basis of qualitative criteria. If an undertaking is recognized on the basis of the recognition scheme, it has the right to publish the recognition. While the ACM acknowledges that recognition schemes can contribute to the quality of products and services of undertakings, it notes that such schemes may violate article 6 DCA, for example by foreclosing undertakings from markets. The latter will be the case if (i) market entrants are not allowed to participate in the scheme on unjustified grounds, (ii) the undertakings that do participate represent a large part of the market and (iii) their customers consider the recognition as an important condition for purchasing the products and services involved. A recognition scheme would normally not violate article 6 if (i) it has an open character, (ii) the requirements for recognition are objective, non-discriminating and clear in advance, (iii) the procure for recognition is transparent and (iv) includes an independent decision about admission to the scheme (either in first instance or on appeal). **28.32**

L. Customer termination

As stated in the EC's enforcement priorities, the refusal to deal is more likely to be considered an abuse of a dominant position if it relates to the termination of an existing supply arrangement. Customer termination will especially raise concerns if the purchaser has made relation-specific investments. If this is the case, the input is more likely to be seen as indispensable. **28.33**

M. Termination of intermediaries

The termination of agreements with *intermediaries* is a special form of the refusal to deal.[27] It is not likely that article 24 DCA will be infringed when the party that terminated the relationship is not competing with the intermediary. Furthermore, this conduct will in general not result in an infringement of the cartel prohibition as found in article 6 DCA. However, if the termination is used to enforce a separate anticompetitive practice, the termination may result in an infringement.[28] **28.34**

N. Termination of relationships with competitors

The termination of a relationship with a competitor will only under certain circumstances constitute an infringement of Dutch competition law. Article 24 DCA may be infringed by an undertaking with a dominant position if the termination in itself amounts to an abuse.[29] **28.35**

O. Exemptions

The prohibition against abuse of a dominant position does not provide for any exemptions but does allow for the specific possibility of obtaining a waiver. Pursuant to article 25 DCA, upon request, a waiver may be granted to undertakings entrusted with the supply of services of general economic interest. Undertakings that wish to obtain a waiver will have to request a decision by the ACM declaring article 24 (1) DCA inoperative in respect to a specific practice. This decision may be issued subject to certain restrictions and/or conditions. Such a request can also be made while a case concerning an alleged abuse of dominance is pending. **28.36**

[27] See Section I.H.

[28] Case C-107/82 *AEG Telefunken v. Commission* [1982] ECR 1179.

[29] See Seections I.H and I.K.

28.37 In the case in which *De Telegraaf* was refused access to program listings by certain broadcasting organizations,[30] the ACM held that article 25 DCA is derived from article 106(2) TFEU. This statement is of importance to the explanation of the concept of "services of general economic interest." Article 25 DCA only slightly differs from its European counterpart. Whereas article 106(2) TFEU automatically exempts the undertaking, article 25 DCA only applies upon request by the undertaking. However, it is unclear whether an undertaking's behavior that qualifies for an article 106 (2) TFEU exemption, would nonetheless have to submit a request for a waiver under article 25 DCA.

II. Dealing with competitors

28.38 Article 6 DCA prohibits agreements and concerted practices which have as their object or effect the prevention, restriction, or distortion of competition. The subsections of article 6 DCA stipulate that infringing arrangements are null and void. However, they also provide for the possibility of exemptions if certain criteria are satisfied. Furthermore, article 6 DCA is modeled after its EU law counterpart, article 101 TFEU. Accordingly, the Dutch legislation stipulates that Dutch courts will follow EU case law, as well as the European Commission's decisional practice when interpreting article 6 DCA. Moreover, pursuant to articles 12 and 13 DCA, the cartel prohibition laid down in article 6 DCA shall not apply to practices to which article 101(1) TFEU is declared inoperative under EU law. This means that the European Commission's Block Exemption Regulations, pertaining to various horizontal and vertical arrangements, are applicable in the Dutch jurisdiction, also in cases where inter-state trade is not affected.

28.39 Following the CJEU's ruling in the *Expedia* case,[31] practices which restrict competition by object and affect inter-state trade are to be considered as appreciably restricting competition. Dutch courts have yet to apply this judgment to purely national cases, that is, cases in which inter-state trade may not be appreciably affected.

28.40 Nevertheless, article 7 DCA contains a *de minimis* regime that excludes the applicability of article 6 DCA to agreements between less than eight competitors, which have a combined aggregate turnover of EUR 5.5 million for undertakings whose core activity is the supply of goods, or a combined aggregate turnover of EUR 1.1 million= for all other undertakings. In addition, according to article 7(2) DCA, agreements, concerted practices, and decisions among competitors or potential competitors in which inter-state trade may not be appreciably affected, are exempt from article 6 DCA if their combined market share on any of the affected markets does not exceed 10 percent. In addition, Dutch competition rules also include two more specific exemptions from article 6 DCA for retail traders. These are laid down in the Cooperation Agreements Retail Trade Exemptions Decree (*Besluit vrijstellingen samenwerkingsovereenkomsten detailhandel*) and the Sector Protection Agreements Exemption Decree (*Besluitvrijstelling branchebeschermingsovereenkomsten*).

28.41 Of great relevance for the relationship between article 6 DCA and article 101 TFEU is article 3 of Regulation 1/2003[32] which asserts that the ACM and the Dutch courts must apply article 101 TFEU to article 6 DCA cases where inter-state trade may be affected. Moreover, the application of Dutch competition law may not lead to the prohibition of conduct which

[30] See Section I.I.
[31] Case C-226/11, *Expedia*, December 13, 2012.
[32] Council Regulation (EC) No. 1/2003 on the implementation of the rules on competition laid down in Articles [101 and 102 TFEU] (December 16, 2002).

may affect inter-state trade but which does not restrict competition under article 101 TFEU or which is exempted from the application of article 101 (1) TFEU pursuant to article 101 (3) TFEU.

Article 6 DCA is commonly known for the fact that it prohibits "hard core cartels," i.e. arrangements entailing price fixing, fixing of other trading conditions, market sharing, bid-rigging (collusive tendering), or collective boycotts. However, just like its EU law counterpart, the scope of application of article 6 DCA is considerably broader. Also included within its scope are various "non-hard core" arrangements between competitors such as joint ventures, joint purchasing arrangements, standard-setting systems, R&D cooperation, as well as various types of vertical agreements, that is, arrangements between parties operating at different levels of the production and supply chain. **28.42**

The enforcement efforts related to article 6 DCA are mainly focused on arrangements between competitors and more particularly hardcore cartels. Actually, a large majority of the fines that are imposed by the ACM relate to cartel cases. Most of these cases are initiated following one or more leniency applications, but the ACM may also act on the basis of complaints or conduct an ex officio investigation. **28.43**

On various occasions—and contrary to other EU member states—the ACM has indicated that resale price maintenance as a purely vertical restriction is not an enforcement priority. There are currently no precedents pertaining to more hybrid forms of collusion, notably "hub-and-spoke" infringements. **28.44**

Contrary to the Commission, the ACM has not yet established a practice of settlements in relation to hard core cartel cases. With a few exceptions, those cases are generally pursued all the way up to the fining stage. In relation to other infringements of the competition rules, both the commitment decision[33] and more "informal" forms of closing an investigation, that is to say *inter partes* without a formal decision being adopted, are often seen. **28.45**

A. Horizontal price-fixing

Horizontal price-fixing is among the most severe infringements under article 6 DCA for which the Dutch fining guidelines allow the gravest fines. The ACM quite regularly prosecutes horizontal price-fixing schemes which are a priority in its enforcement practice. **28.46**

A 2012 example of these practices is the "pepper cartel" for which the participating undertakings that accounted for approximately 30 to 40 percent of the Dutch market for the production of sweet peppers, were fined a total of EUR 14 million. The cartel allegedly sought to artificially keep the purchase price high for their buyers. The participants allegedly agreed upon minimum prices and "respected" each other's customers. **28.47**

B. Horizontal agreements to allocate customers or territories; agreements not to compete

The allocation of customers or territories is another clear example of anticompetitive conduct that is prohibited under article 6 DCA. In 2012, the ACM imposed a fine of EUR 18 million on four major laundry companies for dividing up the market.[34] According to the fining decision, these laundry companies that provided cleaning services for bed linen and work clothes for health care providers, had put in place market sharing arrangements from 1998 until **28.48**

[33] See Section III.F(i).

[34] *Wasserijen*, NMa Case no. 6855 (January 10, 2012).

2009. The concerned laundry companies were each assigned a specific district and agreed not to compete with undertakings in other districts.

C. Horizontal boycotts

28.49 Agreements concluded with the intention of collectively refusing to supply goods or provide services to certain undertakings fall under the cartel prohibition and are considered "hardcore" infringements. In 2004, the ACM assessed a number of anticompetitive agreements on the market for the sale of North Sea shrimp, including a collective refusal to supply to a potential trader of North Sea shrimp that was not able to enter the market because of this boycott.[35] In its decision, the ACM held that a collective boycott of a new participant in the market falls under the cartel prohibition and would typically not fulfill the statutory criteria for exemption.

28.50 Both in its guidelines on the cooperation between undertakings and in its guidelines for the healthcare sector (the latest versions published in 2008 and 2010 respectively), the ACM reiterated that it is unlikely that a collective refusal to supply will not fall under the cartel prohibition. Collectively drafting and exchanging "black lists" of customers or potential customers by undertakings that act on the same market or by an association of undertakings will, in general, not qualify as an infringement of the cartel prohibition as laid down in article 6 DCA.[36] However, this behavior would qualify as a horizontal boycott and thus an infringement of article 6 DCA if such a list is accompanied by obligations or recommendations as a consequence of which the undertakings involved no longer independently decide to whom they supply their products.

D. Joint ventures and other competitive collaborations

28.51 Mirroring EU competition rules, under the DCA, a joint venture will be assessed under the merger control rules if the joint venture performs all the functions of an autonomous economic entity on a lasting basis. These joint ventures are referred to as "full-function" joint ventures. Joint ventures that do not fulfill these requirements will have to be assessed under article 6 DCA.

28.52 Joint ventures can have a large variety of objectives, but absent the scenario in which the joint venture is in reality serving as a cloak for a hardcore cartel, these collaborations are assessed as to their effects on competition. In general, a joint venture will not be considered anticompetitive if the intended cooperation leads to the development of an activity that the collaborating undertakings could not have performed independently. Moreover, pursuant to articles 12 and 13 DCA, joint venture collaborations will often be covered by the EU Block Exemption Regulations.[37]

E. Trade associations

28.53 Decisions of trade associations as object or effect to restrict competition are caught by article 6 DCA. The cartel prohibition is applicable to both formal and informal decisions of trade associations. Also to the extent that recommendations or informal recommendations of trade associations have the objective of aligning members' conduct, they qualify as decisions caught

---

[35] *Noordzeegarnalen*, Case no. 2269 (December 28, 2004).

[36] *Stichting Kredietbeheer Betonindustrie*, Case no. 486 (May 24, 2002).

[37] Commission Regulation No. 1217/2010 on the application of Article 101(3) of the Treaty on the Functioning of the European Union to certain categories of research and development agreements (December 14, 2010); Commission Regulation No. 1218/2010 on the application of Article 101(3) of the Treaty on the Functioning of the European Union to certain categories of specialisation agreements (December 14, 2010).

by article 6 DCA. Moreover, as in all contacts between competitors, it is important to ensure that meetings of trade associations do not form a platform for anticompetitive cooperation or exchange of commercially sensitive information.

Recently, the ACM imposed a fine of nearly EUR 8 million on the Dutch association of general practitioners for recommending its members to only accept new general practitioners in a certain area if the already established general practitioners in that area agreed to such an entry. According to the ACM, this trade association called on its members to restrict the freedom of establishment of general practitioners. Two officials of the association were fined individually for EUR 50,000 and EUR 25,000 respectively, because the ACM held them responsible for the recommendations of the association. In addition, the ACM imposed an order on the association, subject to periodic penalty payments, requiring it to inform all of its members and regional divisions that the illicit recommendations had been revoked. **28.54**

F. Interlocking directorates

Although interlocking directorates and the acquisition of a minority interest will normally be assessed in the context of merger control proceedings, acquisitions of minority shareholdings that do not confer effective control may be analyzed under articles 6 and 24 DCA. **28.55**

In 2004, the ACM assessed whether the participation structure of an asphalt plant would constitute commercial cooperation that would restrict or distort competition on the markets on which the shareholders were active.[38] Three road construction companies participated in this plant, one of them by holding the majority of the shares and the other two by holding a minority interest. According to the ACM, the cartel prohibition would be infringed if these shareholdings would lead the road construction companies to take into account each other's interests when determining their own commercial policy. It would also be an infringement when these shareholdings would influence their commercial behavior in such a way that it would lead to an appreciable negative effect on competition. The ACM came to the conclusion that this was not the case because the shareholders were only active in a few joint projects. In addition, the asphalt plant only disposed of a very limited part of the total production capacity of asphalt in the Netherlands and the joint market share of the majority shareholder and each of the minority shareholders was relatively low. **28.56**

G. Facilitating practices

Facilitating a cartel may qualify as an infringement of article 6 DCA. Any restriction of competition that results from a concurrence of wills between the undertakings involved, may qualify as an anticompetitive agreement between undertakings. The fact that an undertaking with a facilitating role in a cartel is not active on the market, or on a vertically integrated market, on which the restriction of competition materializes does not exempt it from liability for the infringement. Neither is the facilitating undertaking exonerated by the fact that it only participated in a subsidiary, accessory, or passive role. The impact of that contribution may nonetheless be taken into consideration for the purposes of determining the level of the penalty. **28.57**

Recently, the ACM fined a facilitating party that, among other things, organized cartel meetings in the case of the pepper producers cartel.[39] **28.58**

[38] *ACS*, Case no. 318 (February 26, 2003).

[39] See Section II.A.

H. Information exchange

28.59 The ACM recognizes that the exchange of information between undertakings, whether or not via trade associations, may foster the competitive process and benefit consumers. However, it also acknowledges that the exchange of information can be anticompetitive as it can reduce the uncertainty in the market, in particular with regard to the intended market behavior of competitors. The information exchange is specifically problematic when (i) information about prices, customers, and/or production is exchanged, and (ii) the information exchanged is detailed, not in the public domain, and relates to current information of intended market conduct.

28.60 The ACM is known for prosecuting as hardcore cartels "pure" information exchange schemes, in contrast to information exchange as a corollary to, for example, a price-fixing scheme. The key example is the Mobile Operators case which led to the influential judgment of the CJEU in the *T-Mobile* case.[40] In the aftermath of the Mobile Operators case the ACM issued a very interesting decision in which it assessed the unsuccessful argumentthat the mobile operators' market behavior was not influenced by the information exchange.

28.61 The Hospitals case offers another relevant example of a scheme of information exchange assessed by the ACM. In 2010, the ACM launched an investigation into the exchange of statistical data between hospitals in Amsterdam. The information that was shared included information on patient flows and production figures. The ACM concluded that the exchange of information raised concerns, as the hospitals could use the information to coordinate their behavior in negotiations with healthcare insurers. Although ultimately no fines were imposed since the hospitals offered commitments that were accepted and declared binding by the ACM, the commitment decision does offer a detailed look at the framework of assessment applied by the ACM in its effects analysis.[41]

I. Joint purchasing agreements

28.62 In 2008, the ACM contributed to a report of the Organisation for Economic Co-operation and Development (OECD) on monopsony and buyer power. In its submission, the ACM stated that joint purchasing agreements will generally not be prohibited if the undertakings involved would pass on the advantages to their customers.

28.63 If a joint purchasing agreement is concluded between competitors, the question is whether the undertakings involved meet substantial competition from companies that are not engaged in the agreement. If so, according to the ACM, it might be assumed that advantages will be passed on. Otherwise, the agreement might restrict or distort competition and therefore qualify as an infringement under article 6 DCA. The latter may be the case especially if the combined market shares of the buying undertakings that are party to the joint purchasing agreement are high.[42]

28.64 Furthermore it is noteworthy that the ACM, in an "Information Chart" regarding the cooperation of healthcare insurers on the purchasing of health care and emergency care, notes that health care insurers are only allowed to exchange commercially sensitive information as long as it is strictly necessary for their joint purchasing activities. Also, cooperating health care insurers are not allowed to conclude agreements with health care suppliers that exclude other health care insurers.

---

[40] Case C-8/08 *T-Mobile v. NMa* [2009] ECR I-04529.

[41] *Ziekenhuiszorg Amsterdam*, NMa Case no. 6895, December 31, 2010.

[42] *Inkoopsamenwerkingsovereenkomst ziekenfondsen VGZ, OZ en CZ*, NMa, Case nos. 652 and 145 (13 October 2000).

In 2012, the ACM advocated joint purchasing by health care providers on the market for medical equipment in a press release referring to the results of a sector study on medical equipment.[43] Joint purchasing would force manufacturers and suppliers of medical equipment to submit their best offers possible and could lead to cost savings, according to the ACM. In 2007, the ACM took a similar position in a press release with regard to joint purchasing on the market for advertising space.[44] **28.65**

J. Joint lobbying/regulatory/legislative efforts

The mere fact that undertakings jointly engage in lobby activities in order to alter legislation or regulations does not qualify as an infringement of Dutch competition law. However, in light of the cartel prohibition, contacts between competitors will often be heavily scrutinized. In order not to infringe article 6 DCA, the undertakings that participate in these joint efforts should be wary of any spillover effect that might arise from meetings with competitors, such as the illicit exchange of commercially sensitive information or the conclusion of anticompetitive agreements. **28.66**

III. General issues

A. Jurisdiction and applicable law

The DCA, which entered into force in 1998, is applicable to all sectors of the economy. However, specific regulations apply to regulated markets such as the telecommunications, energy, public transport, and financial markets. Some of these specific regulations are enforced by an administrative body other than the ACM, such as the Financial Supervision Act (*Wet op het financieel toezicht*, also referred to as the Wft), which is enforced by the Netherlands Authority for the Financial Markets (*Autoriteit Financiële Markten*, AFM). **28.67**

In accordance with EU competition law, the DCA applies to all "undertakings." Under Dutch and EU competition law, any entity engaged in an economic activity is considered to be an undertaking, whatever its legal form. To the extent that they are engaged in an economic activity, both public and private entities are subject to the Dutch competition rules. **28.68**

Another legislative act of importance to competition oversight is the General Administrative Law Act (*Algemene wet bestuursrecht*, GALA). The GALA contains the general administrative law framework within which the enforcement of the competition rules is embedded. The GALA also sets out rules pertaining to the filing of administrative objections, as well as appeals against decisions of administrative bodies, including fining decisions, like the ACM. **28.69**

B. Antitrust system

(i) Name of agency/agencies

The enforcement of the DCA is entrusted to the Authority for Consumers and Markets (ACM) that was established on April 1, 2013. The ACM is the result of a merger between the Netherlands Competition Authority (*Nederlandse Mededingingsautoriteit*, NMa), the **28.70**

[43] ACM Press Release, "Efficiënt inkopen leidt tot kostenbeheersing medische hulpmiddelen" (February 15, 2012).

[44] ACM Press Release, "Meer inkoopmogelijkheden voor adverteerders" (July 26, 2007).

Independent Post and Telecommunications Authority (*Onafhankelijke Post en Telecommunicatie Autoriteit*, OPTA), and the Netherlands Consumer Authority (*Consumentenautoriteit*).

28.71 The ACM has assumed the powers and tasks of the previously independent enforcement authorities and it is led by a board of three members presided by a Chairman. The ACM will focus on three main themes: consumer protection, sector-specific regulation, and competition oversight.

28.72 The ACM consists of seven directorates, the most relevant of which are the Competition Directorate (*Directie Mededinging*); the Energy Directorate (*Directie Energie*); the Telecommunications, Transport and Postal Services Directorate (*Directie Telecom, Vervoer en Post*); the Consumers Directorate (*Directie Consumenten*); and the Sanctions and Legal Affairs Directorate (*Directie Sancties en Juridische Zaken*). Each of these directorates is headed by a team manager. It is noteworthy that competition law enforcement on the energy markets is assumed by the Energy Directorate, while the energy market for consumers falls under the supervision of the Consumers Directorate. The Sanctions and Legal Affairs Directorate will be entrusted with the imposition of all sanction decisions.

28.73 The formal establishment of the ACM does not yet entail any changes as to the application of the DCA. Changes in and harmonization of the procedures and powers of the different divisions of the ACM will be brought about by separate legislation. It is envisioned that this additional legislation will enter into force on January 1, 2014, only after it has gone through the entire legislative process.

(ii) Staff size and budget

28.74 The current ACM staff consists of around 520 members. At the moment of editing this Chapter (November 2013), the total budget of the ACM had not yet been published. The budget of the NMa in 2012 amounted to approximately EUR 45 million.

(iii) Recent enforcement actions and trends

28.75 The ACM initiates its investigations on the basis of third-party complaints, requests for leniency by an undertaking that participated in an infringement, or on the initiative of the ACM itself. Every year, the ACM publishes its enforcement priorities. When setting these priorities, the ACM is guided by the harm that an issue inflicts on consumers, the public interest that is at stake, and the possibility for the ACM to tackle an issue effectively. The ACM's key priorities for 2013 were, among others, problems in essential basic services for consumers such as energy and telecommunication, housing and health care.

28.76 The total amount of fines imposed by the NMa in 2012 was EUR 36.9 million. The Dutch government set as a "target" for 2013 to receive a total amount of fines for infringements of competition law of EUR 75 million, EUR 100 million in 2014, and after 2014 EUR 125 million, on an annual basis. Afterwards, the Minister of Economic Affairs stated that these amounts have to be considered as an "estimate" of the fines that the ACM was expected to impose, acting independently. In addition, the Minister is currently working on a legislative proposal to increase the statutory maximum of fines that can be imposed for competition law infringements. Nevertheless, even with that increase, the Dutch parliament was informed that it is unlikely that the forecasts mentioned above would be achieved.

28.77 Besides enforcing the DCA, the ACM is entrusted with the oversight and compliance of the Public Enterprises Market Activities Act (*Wet Markt en Overheid*) that came into force on July 1, 2012. This act contains legal provisions on economic activities of public legal entities and publicly owned companies, in order to ensure equal competition between these entities and other providers of goods and services.

C. Private litigation

In civil proceedings, the competition law provisions can be used strategically as a sword, by claiming damages on the basis of harm suffered as a result of the infringement, or as a shield, by claiming that an agreement is null and void, and therefore not enforceable, because it is in violation of competition law. **28.78**

On the basis of article 101(2) TFEU and article 6(2) DCA, agreements, or part thereof, in violation of competition law are null and void. This provision is quite regularly invoked as a defense in Dutch civil proceedings. The burden of proof of a competition law infringement is on the party invoking the infringement and may be relatively high depending on the nature of the infringement and the legal and economic context, as complex economic assessments may be at issue. Where the CJEU has decided that article 101 TFEU is of public order, the Dutch Supreme Court has ruled that the Dutch equivalent article 6 DCA is not of a public order nature. Therefore, parties must actively invoke article 6 DCA in civil proceedings. **28.79**

Article 102 TFEU and article 24 DCA do not provide for a specific nullity sanction. It can be argued that agreements in violation of article 102 TFEU or 24 DCA are nonetheless null and void on the basis of article 3:40 of the Dutch Civil Code (DCC), which stipulates that legal acts in violation of mandatory law are in principle null and void. However, there is no authoritative case law that confirms this. **28.80**

Damages as a result of alleged cartel infringements are usually claimed in civil proceedings following on decisions of competition authorities.[45] However, independent non follow-on claims are also possible. Such claims, which often relate to non-secretive violations of competition law in vertical agreements, are instituted regularly. In recent cases substantial damages have been awarded for non-compete or exclusivity clauses in violation of Dutch and European competition law. **28.81**

D. Follow-on litigation

As a matter of European law, all parties that have suffered harm as a result of an infringement of article 101 or 102 TFEU have the right to claim compensation.[46] **28.82**

Under Dutch law, this right can be exercised by instituting a claim for damages on the basis of the DCC. The Dutch Civil Code does not contain specific provisions with regard to competition law related claims. On the basis of article 6:97 DCC full compensation of actual harm is awarded, which includes suffered losses and deprived profits. In addition, a statutory interest can be claimed, which is calculated on a cumulative basis from the moment of the infringement. Punitive damages are not awarded under Dutch civil law. In line with the principle of compensation, defendants are allowed to argue that direct claimants did not suffer harm, given that any overcharge as a result of a cartel is "passed on" to the next chain in a distribution channel. **28.83**

An infringement of competition law will qualify as a tort (*onrechtmatige daad*) under article 6:162 DCC. Other possible legal grounds for claiming damages are: undue payment (*onverschuldigde betaling*, art. 6:203 DCC), unjust enrichment (*ongerechtvaardigde verrijking*, art. 6:212 DCC), or breach of contract (*wanprestatie*, art. 6:74 DCC). **28.84**

The Dutch Civil Code provides for the possibility of collective claims by interest groups but this option is not used very often because only declaratory judgments can be obtained, and **28.85**

[45] See Section III.D.

[46] See the judgments of the ECJ in Case C-453/99 *Courage and Crehan* [2001] ECR I-06297 and Joined Cases C-295/04–C-298/04 *Manfredi* [2006] I-06619.

no damages can be awarded. Rather, claims are instituted by professional claimant vehicles collecting claims by way of assignment of claims.

28.86 Damage claims on the basis of "hard core" secretive cartel infringements are often initiated as a follow-on claim to decisions of competition authorities. In this way, claimants can benefit from the facts derived from the decision of the European Commission or national competition authorities. In addition, the CJEU has established in the *Masterfoods* case,[47] that national courts cannot render a judgement contrary to Commission decisions, unless the decision is annulled by the European courts. This rule has been laid down in article 16 (1) of Regulation 1/2003. This provision does not apply to decisions of national competition authorities. Nonetheless, administrative decisions of the ACM will be considered strong, although arguably not irrebuttable, evidence of a tort in relation to private claimants.

28.87 There are currently a number of large follow-on collective actions pending before the Dutch courts, including actions in relation to infringements on the paraffin wax market, the air-freight market, and the elevator market. These cases are all based on prior EC infringement decisions. Many of these actions were started by professional claimant vehicles that have collected claims by way of assignment from companies that were allegedly harmed by the cartel. These proceedings are mostly still in a preliminary phase, dealing with issues like jurisdiction and the question of whether the proceedings should be stayed while an appeal against the Commission decision is pending.

28.88 The Dutch Code of Civil Procedure (DCCP) does not provide for US style discovery. However, parties can petition for the disclosure of certain documents and request the court for witness hearings. It should be noted that the Dutch rules with regard to the disclosure of documentary evidence are relatively stringent. Despite these stringent rules, claimants as well as defendants quite regularly try to obtain documents from the other party via this disclosure procedure in the context of competition law claims.

28.89 The Netherlands is, together with the United Kingdom and Germany, a jurisdiction that is favored by claimants bringing private damage actions in the EU. This is related to the fact that it is relatively inexpensive to litigate in the Netherlands, that legislation on the disclosure of possible evidence is available and that it is possible to collectively start civil proceedings and achieve opt-out class settlements. In addition, cumulative statutory interest can be obtained under Dutch law.

E. Arbitration and alternative dispute resolution

28.90 Mediation and arbitration are attractive given that these mechanisms of dispute resolution are well developed in the Netherlands. Arbitration is governed by articles 1020–1076 DCCP and the New York Convention.[48] The arbitration awards are binding on all parties, and in principle they are not open for appeal.

28.91 In recent years, mediation has gained a stronger foothold in the Netherlands. From 2005, referral facilities to mediation were gradually introduced in all courts. If the parties do not reach a compromise during the mediation process, the dispute can still be resolved in court or by using arbitration.

28.92 The Dutch Civil Code and the Dutch Code of Civil Procedure provide for the possibility of a class settlement of mass damages under the collective settlement of mass damages act

[47] Case C-344/98 *Masterfoods and HB* [2000] I-11369.

[48] New York Convention on Recognition and Enforcement of Foreign Arbitral Awards of 1958, 33 UNTS 38.

(*Wet Collectieve Afwikkeling Massaschade*, WCAM). The WCAM provides for the possibility to make generally binding an agreement on damages between plaintiffs and defendants. After a settlement is agreed upon, the Amsterdam Court of Appeal can approve the settlement and declare it generally binding, with a possibility for harmed parties to "opt-out." The Court cannot declare decisions generally binding outside a settlement context, in other words, there is no opt-out class action available under Dutch law.

F. Remedies

(i) Administrative liability

The ACM is authorized to impose administrative fines on undertakings and, under specific circumstances, on natural persons. There are three types of fining rules: **28.93**

(1) rules for the violation of the cartel prohibition (art. 6 DCA and/or art. 101 TFEU) or the prohibition of abuse of a dominant position (art. 24 DCA and/or art. 102 TFEU) committed by undertakings;
(2) rules for the violation of other provisions of the DCA and acts governing specific sectors of industry; and
(3) rules for the violation of competition law committed by natural persons.

In the event of a violation of the cartel prohibition or the prohibition of the abuse of a dominant position, the ACM can impose an administrative fine, an order subject to periodic penalty payments, or a binding instruction to comply with the DCA. **28.94**

The administrative fine can amount to a maximum of 10 percent of the undertaking's turnover (arts. 56–57 DCA). The ACM applies the European concept of "undertaking," including the doctrine of parental liability. The Policy Rules on the Imposition of Administrative Fines 2009 (*Beleidsregels van de Minister van Ecnomische Zaken voor het opleggen van boetes door de NMa* 2009) set out the manner in which the fines are calculated. **28.95**

In addition to fines imposed for infringing the cartel prohibition or the prohibition of the abuse of dominance, the ACM has the power to impose a fine for the violation of the procedural provisions of the DCA. These fines can amount up to 1 percent of the undertaking's turnover. **28.96**

The ACM can impose an administrative fine on natural persons for a failure to cooperate or for infringing the provisions of the DCA, article 101 or 102 TFEU or acts governing specific industry sectors. Depending on what provision is violated, the seriousness of the violation and the income and assets of the natural person, the fine can range up to EUR 450,000. The possibility of fining natural persons is of particular importance to executives who have given instructions with regard to an infringement or have exercised de facto leadership over a violation.[49] **28.97**

As an alternative to a decision establishing an infringement and imposing a sanction, the ACM can adopt a "commitment decision." This instrument is comparable to the instrument laid down in article 9 of Regulation 1/2003. In a commitment decision, the ACM declares binding one or more commitments offered by the undertaking or undertakings under investigation. Such commitments have to prevent, or ensure the discontinuation of, any violation of article 6 or 24 DCA. The ACM can adopt a commitment decision and terminate its investigation if (i) it is ensured that the undertakings involved will act in accordance with articles 6 and 24 DCA as a result of that decision, (ii) the undertakings involved show, within reason, that they will comply with the decision in a verifiable manner, and (iii) it is more effective in enforcement of the law to issue a commitment decision than to impose an administrative **28.98**

[49] See further Section II.E.

fine or an order subject to a penalty. In 2012, the ACM adopted five commitment decisions, a small increase in comparison with the previous two years during which seven commitment decisions were adopted.

28.99 The power of the ACM to impose a fine or an order sanctioned by periodic penalty payments lapses five years after an infringement is committed.

(ii) Criminal liability

28.100 Neither the DCA nor other Dutch legislation allows the ACM to impose criminal liability for the infringement of competition law. Furthermore, charges will be dismissed if the public attempts to charge a criminal offense based on acts directly related to infringements of competition law, such as participation in a criminal organization or forgery of documents to conceal the cartel. The public prosecutor will be allowed to prosecute for offenses that do not relate directly to the infringement of competition law, such as tax evasion.[50] Therefore, in practice, potential violations of the DCA will be investigated by the ACM and will only result in administrative proceedings.

G. Leniency and immunity

28.101 Undertakings or individuals can notify the ACM of their participation in a cartel. In return, the ACM can grant immunity or reduction of a possible fine. The rules regarding leniency and immunity are set out in the Policy Rules of the Minister of Economic Affairs on the Reduction of Administrative Fines in respect to Cartels (*Beleidsregels Minister van Economische Zaken tot vermindering van bestuurlijke boetes betreffende kartels).*

28.102 The ACM may grant a leniency applicant immunity for the fine if the applicant is the first one to apply for leniency and if the application concerns a cartel into which the ACM has not yet started an investigation. However, if the investigation has already started, the applicant may be granted a reduction of its fine between 60 percent and 100 percent. Other applicants may be granted a reduction of their fine between 10 percent and 40 percent and only if the information that is provided by the applicant is of significant added value.

28.103 Apart from fining undertakings for their. involvement in a cartel, the ACM can also impose fines on employees or former employees of these undertakings for having exercised *de facto* leadership over the infringement. It should be noted that a leniency application that is submitted by an employee or former employee of an undertaking involved in a cartel only covers the right of this employee, and not of the undertaking involved, to a possible fine reduction. On the other hand, when an undertaking applies for leniency it should emphasize that the application also relates to the possible *de facto* leadership exercised over the infringement by its current or former employees.

28.104 In order to obtain a reduction of the fine, an applicant for leniency should not have coerced another undertaking into participating in the cartel and has to provide information that enables the ACM to conduct a targeted inspection. Furthermore, the applicant is under an obligation to continuously provide full cooperation to the ACM.

28.105 An applicant who has submitted an incomplete leniency application may qualify for a marker, which in essence stops the clock and allows the applicant to submit additional information without losing its place in the line. A marker is granted if the ACM considers that the leniency application provides a concrete basis for a reasonable suspicion of the applicants' involvement in a cartel. Furthermore, at least a minimum of information has to be provided,

[50] Hof 's-Gravenhage 21 mei 2008, NJFS 2008, 170. S.M.M.C. Vinken & E.C. Scheffers, *Strafrechtelijke handhaving en het mededingingsrecht: het glazenwasserkartel*, Bb 2008-16.

including information on the parties and the products that are involved and on the duration of the cartel. If the ACM provides a marker, it will set a term within which the applicant must complete its leniency application.

The ACM's policy is to keep leniency information confidential. It will not publish citations from leniency applications, nor will it display references in the footnotes. However, the ACM can paraphrase leniency information and no confidentiality will be awarded to documents that existed at the time of the cartel, even if these are supplied by means of a leniency application. **28.106**

H. Document creation and retention; duty to cooperate

There is no rule under either Dutch or European competition law that requires undertakings to retain or store documents for a certain minimum period of time. However, both the DCA and the GALA provide for explicit rules concerning the duty of undertakings and individuals to actively cooperate with the ACM. As soon as an undertaking is subject to an investigation by the ACM, the intentional destruction of potentially relevant documents or the concealment thereof will be treated as a serious failure to cooperate and is subject to fines. **28.107**

Pursuant to article 5:20 GALA, full cooperation with the appointed ACM officials is required. When exercising the powers entrusted to them, ACM officials may demand cooperation within such reasonable time limits as they may specify. The officials cannot demand cooperation when, in line with the principle of proportionality as laid down in article 5:13 GALA, it is not reasonably necessary for the fulfillment of their task. The duty to cooperate relates to all forms of cooperation such as moving furniture, opening doors, opening cupboards, or making available computer records, including the provision of passwords or entry codes. **28.108**

Everyone has a duty to cooperate. Accordingly, the circle of individuals subject to this obligation is not restricted by article 5:20 GALA, but only by the application of the proportionality principle. Normally, the undertakings involved and the employees whose conduct is investigated by the ACM are subject to the duty to cooperate. **28.109**

The duty to cooperate becomes applicable after the ACM has explicitly demanded cooperation in the investigation. There are no formal requirements to such a demand. The only requirement is that the demand is explicitly stated, either verbally or in writing. There is no duty to cooperate in situations where an ACM official merely requests information. The ACM may request information directly from any person that has a connection with the undertaking that is investigated without first demanding this information from the official representative of the undertaking. **28.110**

The ACM may request information by sending a letter but also by initiating an interview. During such an interview, employees of the undertaking concerned, including officials such as members of the board of directors and the supervisory board, have the right to remain silent. The right to remain silent, also referred to as the *nemo tenetur* principle is an application of the "fair trial" right laid down in article 6 of the European Convention on Human Rights (ECHR). Very recently the CBB held that former employees of an undertaking under investigation by the ACM can also invoke the right of the undertaking to remain silent. This would only be the case if a former employee is interrogated by the ACM on the conduct of his former employer at the time that the former employee still worked there.[51] **28.111**

Article 5:20(2) GALA states that any person bound by a professional or statutory duty of secrecy may refuse to cooperate to the extent that their duty of secrecy requires them to do so. **28.112**

[51] *A, B v. NMa*, CBB Case no. AWB 11/555; LJN BY7026 (December 21, 2012).

This statutory exception applies to all powers of the ACM officials. As a result, professionals with legal privilege are not under any obligation to provide information on the conduct of the undertaking involved or to provide access to business information or documents of the undertaking involved; they are exempted from the duty to cooperate. The exception of legal privilege does not apply to professionals who themselves are the subject of an investigation. It follows from the DCA that the protection of legal privilege applies to both external and in-house counsel, as long as the person in question has been admitted to the bar. The Dutch regime of legal privilege therefore diverges from the EU regime in which there is no exemption from the duty to cooperate for in-house counsel that are admitted to the bar. In a recent judgment,[52] the Dutch Supreme Court pointed out that the *AKZO* judgment of the CJEU[53] only relates to the European level and that this does not affect the legal privilege of in-house counsel under Dutch law.

28.113 Under article 69 DCA, failure to comply with the duty to cooperate can result in a fine for the undertaking involved up to EUR 450,000 or 1 percent of its turnover. On individuals, a fine up to EUR 450 000 may be imposed.

28.114 Furthermore, article 5:16 GALA grants the ACM and other regulatory authorities the competence to issue information requests. This provision stipulates that "an inspector is empowered to demand information." According to recent case law, the concept of information as mentioned in article 5:16 GALA only encompasses oral and written information, and not business documents and files, electronic or otherwise. As a result, the duty to cooperate only requires addressees to answer truthfully to the oral or written questions posed by the ACM.

28.115 Article 5:17 GALA provides that a regulator can inspect and make copies of business information and documents. Articles 5:16; 5:17, and 5:20 GALA do not require alleged infringers or third parties to send the requested files to a regulator.

28.116 In practice, the above means that the only way the ACM can obtain the information it needs to establish an infringement, is by conducting a company visit. Pursuant to article 5:15 GALA, ACM officials are allowed to enter all premises of undertakings without an official judicial authorization. Sometimes, ACM officials contact the undertaking involved to make an appointment for such a visit. ACM officials may also conduct a "dawn raid" and visit the undertaking, or several undertaking at the same time, unannounced. Article 5:16 GALA subsequently ensures that alleged infringers, or their employees indicate where the requested data can be found, while article 5:17 GALA authorizes the ACM to inspect and copy them. While the ACM may not demand that documents are sent to it, it may accept an offer to that effect.

[52] *Plaintiff v. Stichting H9 Invest and others*, Hoge Raad, Case no. 12/02667, LJN BY6101 (March 15, 2013).

[53] *AKZO* (n 1).

29

NEW ZEALAND

Torrin Crowther and Glenn Shewan
Bell Gully

Introduction

The Commerce Act 1986 (the Act) sets out New Zealand's competition law rules. The Act has the stated purpose of promoting competition for the long term benefit of consumers within New Zealand. The Commerce Commission (the Commission) is responsible for regulating market competition in New Zealand and the relevant legislation. Part II of the Act contains the relevant prohibitions on restrictive trade practices. **29.01**

The Commission has placed a high priority on investigating and prosecuting cartel arrangements over recent years, with deterrence being the primary objective.[1] The Commission has **29.02**

[1] As stated by Dr. Mark Berry (Commission Chair) in his speech "An Update from the Commerce Commission" at the 12th Annual Competition Law and Regulatory Review Conference, Wellington,

also recently signaled continued active enforcement in the cartels area, indicating that it is currently conducting a number of cartel investigations.[2] The New Zealand courts have shown they are willing to uphold jurisdiction over foreign firms in appropriate cases.

29.03 The New Zealand regulator works closely with the Australian Competition and Consumer Commission (ACCC), and currently there is a trend towards harmonizing competition law across the two jurisdictions. The Commerce (Cartels and Other Matters) Amendment Bill (the Cartel Bill), currently proceeding through Parliament, is likely to see a new definition of "cartel conduct" which will align this aspect of New Zealand's competition law more closely with Australia. While it contemplates criminalizing cartel conduct, it also contains wide exemptions from cartel provisions aimed at ensuring the prohibition does not chill pro-competitive or efficiency-enhancing behavior. At the time of writing, the Bill is expected but has not yet been passed. The two jurisdictions have also recently enhanced their ability to cooperate on matters of common interest, with the Commerce Commission (International Co-operation, and Fees) Amendment Act 2012 and a subsequent cooperation agreement between the Commission and the ACCC.[3]

29.04 While the New Zealand Government seems to be broadly supportive of the current competition regime, it has not included amendments to the misuse of substantial market power prohibition in the Cartel Bill. This is despite concerns expressed by many (including the Commission) that the interpretation of the provision by the courts has significantly narrowed its application. Due to the high threshold required to establish a breach under this prohibition, the Commission has focused more upon merger cases and coordinated conduct, with the changes in the Cartel Bill likely to see cartel conduct remain a focus of the Commission in the coming years.

I. Acting alone

29.05 Section 36 of the Act is designed to target exclusionary conduct: it prohibits firms with "a substantial degree of power in a market" from "tak[ing] advantage of that power for the purpose of restricting the entry of a person... preventing or deterring a person from engaging in competitive conduct... or eliminating a person from that or any other market."[4] As set out in greater detail below, the courts have fairly consistently confirmed that a firm will not misuse its market power where it acts in the same way a firm without substantial market power, but otherwise similarly placed, would have acted. This runs counter to the notion that dominant firms in New Zealand are subject to any special responsibilities to assist their competitors,[5] or that their conduct should be viewed through a "special lens." The prohibition is based on

May 28, 2012: <http://www.comcom.govt.nz/the-commission/media-centre/speeches/keynote-speech-for-the-12th-annual-competition-law-and-regulatory-review-conference-an-update-from-the-commerce-commission/>.

[2] Joint New Zealand Commerce Commission and Australian Competition and Consumer Commission Seminar, Victoria University, Wellington, February 27, 2013.

[3] See further Section II, para. 29.39.

[4] The current test was introduced by an amendment in 2001 which replaced the (then) existing formulation based on a firm using a "dominant" position (rather than taking advantage of substantial market power) for an anticompetitive purpose. The courts have since confirmed that the expressions "use" and "take advantage of" involve the same inquiry. See *Commerce Commission v. Telecom Corporation of New Zealand* [2010] NZSC 111, [2011] 1 NZLR 577 para. 1.

[5] *Union Shipping NZ Ltd. v. Port Nelson Ltd.* [1990] 2 NZLR 662 (HC) at 706, confirmed in *Telecom Corporation of New Zealand v. Commerce Commission* [2012] NZCA 278 para. 124.

three elements: (i) substantial degree of market power; (ii) taking advantage; and (iii) anticompetitive purpose.

Substantial degree of market power: the first step in ascertaining a firm's market power is defining the relevant market.[6] In New Zealand, there is no market-share threshold for determining whether the degree of market power held by a firm is substantial. The Act states that in the context of s. 36, "substantial" should not be interpreted to mean "real or of substance": the courts have interpreted it as "large or weighty." The Commission's view is that a firm will hold a substantial degree of market power where it has the ability to act substantially free from competitive constraints.[7] An alternative formulation is to consider whether a firm is able to raise prices to supra-competitive levels without rivals taking away a sufficient proportion of its customers. **29.06**

Taking advantage: since the *Telecom v. Clear*,[8] Privy Council decision in 1995, demonstrating a causal connection between a firm's market power and the alleged anticompetitive conduct has become of central importance in New Zealand. This sets New Zealand law apart from similar prohibitions in many other jurisdictions. Despite imposing a high threshold to meet in practice, the New Zealand Supreme Court recently confirmed that this so called "counterfactual test" is the sole test for assessing this element of s. 36.[9] In order to demonstrate that a firm has taken advantage of its market power, it must be shown that a hypothetical firm in a workably competitive market, i.e. without market power would not (as opposed to could not) have acted as it did.[10] **29.07**

Anticompetitive purpose: s. 36 proscribes three specific anticompetitive purposes: restricting entry of a firm into a market; preventing or deterring a firm from engaging in competitive conduct in a market; and/or eliminating a firm from a market. It is not necessary for a firm to have market power in the market to which its purpose relates. Further, s. 36B provides that an anticompetitive purpose may be inferred from the conduct of any relevant person, or from any relevant circumstances. That is not to say, however, that purpose necessarily flows from effect. The New Zealand courts have confirmed that, while purpose can often be deduced from effect, it does not follow that they are always the same.[11] Indeed, purpose has been interpreted to require more than a mere intention to engage in an act for which it is known there will be anticompetitive consequences: "purpose requires the conduct to be motivated or inspired by a wish for the occurrence or consequences."[12] Proof of purpose may, however, be inferred from the conduct of any relevant person or circumstances and it may be that a firm taking advantage of its market power can be used to infer the firm's purpose was the effect in fact produced.[13] **29.08**

Section 36 shares some similarity with the Australian equivalent (s. 46 of the Competition and Consumer Act 2010). As a result, the Australian jurisprudence is often relevant. Finally, the Act explicitly exempts persons who seek to enforce a statutory intellectual property right from the application of s. 36. **29.09**

---

6 See Section II.A(i).

7 See Dr Mark Berry's (Chair of the Commission) speech (February, 2011): <http://www.comcom.govt.nz/dmsdocument/11019>.

8 *Telecom Corporation of New Zealand v. Clear Communications Ltd* [1995] 1 NZLR 385 (PC).

9 *Telecom Corporation* [2010] NZSC 111, [2011] 1 NZLR 577 (n 4).

10 *Telecom Corporation* [2010] NZSC 111, [2011] 1 NZLR 577(n 4) para. 34.

11 *NZ Private Hospitals Assn + Auckland Branch (Inc.) v. Northern RHA*, HC Auckland CP440/94 (December 7, 1994) per Blanchard J.

12 *Telecom Corporation* [2012] NZCA 278 (n 5) para. 253.

13 *Telecom Corporation* [2012] NZCA 278 (n 5) para. 253.

29.10 Examples of conduct which may contravene the prohibition are set out in paras. 29.11–29.34. The Commission is focused on particularly egregious cases of margin squeeze and refusing access to facilities, but has signaled that given the current interpretation of s. 36 they are unlikely to take more borderline cases.

A. Predatory pricing

29.11 Predatory pricing is not specifically prohibited in New Zealand. Such conduct instead principally falls for review under s. 36 of the Act. As lower prices typically enhance competition, to date the courts have said a breach requires that goods or services are sold below cost and that recoupment is possible.[14] The relevant counterfactual test asks:[15]

(a) first, whether a firm without a substantial degree of market power—in this case, the financial resources necessary to sustain the losses resulting from pricing below variable cost of production or supply—would have engaged in the same price cutting strategy; and
(b) second, whether it is likely that the firm is capable of recouping such losses in the future.

29.12 The most recent application of s. 36 involved the Court of Appeal considering the conduct of an incumbent telecommunications provider under the Efficient Component Price Rule.[16] In that case the Court confirmed that "whilst predatory prices may create price squeezes, not every price squeeze will involve predatory pricing."[17] It is worthwhile noting that in New Zealand predatory pricing has also been considered under the general prohibition of agreements that substantially lessen competition.[18]

B. Exploitative offenses (excessive pricing, monopoly leveraging)

29.13 In New Zealand there is no general prohibition on charging prices which bear no reasonable relation to the economic value of the product supplied. Because of the purpose element of s. 36, exploitative behavior, including excessive pricing, is prohibited only where a firm engages in the conduct with the aim of restricting, eliminating or deterring a competitor from the market, and where the firm has taken advantage of its market power, e.g. certain margin squeezes/raising a rival's costs. In its most recent decision on this point, the Court of Appeal considered that a telecommunications firm had breached s. 36 in charging downstream competitors disproportionately high access prices. It could not have raised prices to such levels without market power (and hence the causal connection between the market power and the conduct necessary for a "taking advantage" was made out).[19]

C. Monopsony

29.14 A firm which has substantial power as a purchaser is also subject to s. 36. There is limited New Zealand authority on this point, although, the courts have considered s. 36 in the context of a monopsonist health authority. The health authority, as a part of a rationalization process, reduced the number of health providers it contracted with (effectively forcing the

---

[14] *Carter Holt Harvey Building Products Group Ltd v. Commerce Commission* [2004] UKPC 37, [2006] 1 NZLR 145. Note: this case was decided in 2001, prior to the amendment of s. 36. However, the view set out in this decision has subsequently been referred to by the Court of Appeal in *Telecom Corporation* [2012] NZCA 278 (n 5).

[15] *Carter Holt Harvey Building Products* [2004] UKPC 37, [2006] 1 NZLR 145 (n 14).

[16] See Section I.H.

[17] *Telecom Corporation* [2012] NZCA 278 (n 5) para. 123.

[18] *Port Nelson Ltd. v. Commerce Commission* [1996] 3 NZLR 554 (CA). This decision predated the amendment to s. 36 in 2001 (see n 4). The proceedings were brought under s. 27 because it could not be established that the dominant firm had "used" its market power. Refer further to Section II.

[19] *Telecom Corporation* [2012] NZCA 278 (n 5) para. 262.

unsuccessful health providers out of business). However, the Court was not satisfied that the health authority had acted with an anticompetitive purpose, instead believing the rationalization to be for the purposes of focusing on fewer (and better quality) providers.[20] The Court emphasized that "often purpose can be deduced from effect; but it does not follow that effect and purpose are always the same."[21]

D. Price discrimination

Price discrimination is not specifically prohibited by the Act. However, such conduct will fall for review under s. 36 and s. 27. Section 36 cases involving price discrimination have typically arisen in New Zealand in the context of a vertically integrated firm favoring its downstream subsidiary with the effect of raising the costs of competitors. A relevant decision is *Union Shipping NZ Ltd v. Port Nelson Ltd.*[22] A sole supplier of harbor and port facilities was found to have used its dominant position to require a stevedoring company to enter into a port user license agreement (effectively requiring the company to pay for services it did not require) with the purpose of preventing or deterring the competitive activities engaged in by a competitor. **29.15**

E. Dictating or influencing resale prices

(i) Resale price maintenance

Section 37 of the Act specifically prohibits resale price maintenance (RPM) of goods irrespective of proof of any effect on competition in a market. The prohibition prevents suppliers from obtaining agreement from a reseller, or otherwise inducing or attempting to induce a reseller, to adhere to a minimum (or actual) price. This includes through withholding supply (or threatening to do so)[23] or supplying on less favorable terms. The prohibition extends to not only minimum prices, but also to the stipulation of exact prices and specifying prices by reference to a formula or method of calculation.[24] Stipulating maximum prices is not specifically prohibited but may be subject to the general s. 36 and 27 prohibitions.[25] The Cartel Bill will introduce a specific exemption from the prohibition on cartel conduct where: an agreement is between a customer and supplier; the provision relates to the maximum price at which the customer can resell the goods or services; and the provision does not have the dominant purpose of lessening competition. Section 39 of the Act provides that a supplier will not be taken as inducing or attempting to induce another person to sell goods at a price less than that specified where the price is preceded by the words "recommended price" or the supplier gives notification in writing that the price is recommended only and there is no obligation to comply with the recommendation. **29.16**

The prevailing view is that the prohibition does not extend to agency arrangements, on the basis that where title does not pass there is no "supply." The Act defines supplier to include anyone who supplies or re-supplies goods "by way of sale, exchange, lease, hire, or hire purchase," therefore capturing distributors, wholesalers and manufacturers. **29.17**

A supplier or reseller engaged in RPM, or proposing to enter into an RPM arrangement, may seek authorization from the Commission. The Commission will grant authorization where it is satisfied that the RPM will in all the circumstances result, or be likely to result, in a net **29.18**

---

20 *NZ Private Hospitals Assn*, HC Auckland CP440/94 (n 11).

21 *NZ Private Hospitals Assn*, HC Auckland CP440/94 (n 11) 24.

22 *Union Shipping* [1990] 2 NZLR 662 (n 5).

23 *Commerce Commission v. Hewlett Packard* [1993] 3 NZLR 252 (HC).

24 Commerce Act 1986, s. 37(4)(b).

25 *Tru Tone Ltd. v. Festival Records Retail Marketing Ltd.* [1988] 2 NZLR 352 (HC). In this case, the particular maximum price was found not to have breached either s. 27 or 36.

public benefit (i.e. that the efficiency benefits of the RPM outweigh any adverse effects on competition).

(ii) Minimum advertised price programs

29.19 The prohibition on RPM in New Zealand extends to activities relating to the promotion of goods. Section 37(5) of the Act explicitly defines sale to include "advertise for sale, display for sale and offer for sale." Minimum advertised price programs are therefore captured by the broad s. 37 prohibition.[26]

F. Tying arrangements

29.20 The Act does not explicitly prohibit tying (or "third line forcing"). However, such arrangements remain subject to the s. 36 and 27 prohibitions.[27]

G. Exclusive dealing

29.21 Exclusive dealing arrangements are not specifically prohibited in New Zealand. However, parties which *are* in competition may be captured by the explicit s. 29 prohibition.[28] In addition, a firm with substantial market power may be exposed to liability under s. 36 (typically where the exclusive dealing forecloses competitors).

29.22 Further, and most commonly, exclusive dealing is assessed in the context of the substantial lessening of competition test in s. 27.[29] In the leading case of *Fisher & Paykel Ltd. v. Commerce Commission*, Fisher & Paykel imposed product exclusivity terms on its white goods dealers. The High Court emphasized that it is necessary to take into account all of the effects of the exclusive dealing clause (EDC) in determining whether the s. 27 test is met, both pro-competitive and anticompetitive: "[I]f it could be shown that the net effect of the EDC was to promote competition, then there could be no 'substantial lessening of competition' in terms of S.27."[30] Further, "[i]n the absence of artificial barriers to entry, an EDC can have positive pro competitive effects in a market... provided that a significant component, in this case, retail space, has not been foreclosed."[31] The High Court found there were no significant barriers to entry, significant retail space was not foreclosed and the arrangements could be terminated on 90 days' notice without penalty. Further, the arrangement was pro-competitive in that it allowed investment into service and brand promotion. There was, therefore, no substantial lessening of competition in a market.

29.23 In *Shell (Petroleum Mining) Co. Ltd. v. Kapuni Gas Contracts Ltd.*,[32] a long-term agreement (having run for twenty-nine years), tying up the sole benefit in the Kapuni gas field (the only significant on-shore New Zealand gas field), was found to breach s. 27, but not s. 36. The Court accepted that long term contracts can be inherently anticompetitive. However, it also recognized that there can be pro-competitive effects from such arrangements. For example, they can encourage entry into markets where a large capital investment is required, or provide for economies of scale. Such pro-competitive aspects could be taken into account when considering whether the arrangement substantially lessened competition in a market.

---

[26] That the RPM provision was intended to include restrictions on advertising was confirmed in *Hewlett Packard* [1993] 3 NZLR 252 (HC) (n 23).

[27] See Section I.J.

[28] See Section II.E.

[29] For example, *Fisher & Paykel Ltd. v. Commerce Commission* [1990] 2 NZLR 731 (HC), in which the Court considered an exclusive dealing arrangement under s. 27 and 36.

[30] *Fisher & Paykel* [1990] 2 NZLR 731 (n 29) at 740.

[31] *Fisher & Paykel* [1990] 2 NZLR 731 (n 29) at 767.

[32] *Shell (Petroleum Mining) Co. Ltd. v. Kapuni Gas Contracts Ltd.* (1997) 7 TCLR 463 (HC) at 528–31.

Efficiencies in this case were inadequate to overcome the foreclosure in the market as a result of the arrangement, and thus the contract was anticompetitive and breached s. 27.[33]

H. Refusal to deal

The Act does not explicitly prohibit a firm from refusing to deal with a competitor. In the New Zealand context, the Privy Council recorded that firms (even those with monopoly power) are not under a duty to help competitors: "[a] monopolist is entitled, like everyone else, to compete with its competitors: if it is not permitted to do so it 'would be holding an umbrella over inefficient competitors.'"[34] However, a refusal to deal may, depending on the circumstances, amount to a misuse of market power in breach of s. 36—please refer to the discussion of s. 36 in paras. 29.5–29.8. The obligation to supply arises from the counter-factual test, i.e. it will be a breach of s. 36 if a firm without a substantial degree of market power would not rationally have refused supply.[35] Further, a constructive refusal to deal may be found where a firm with substantial market power offers to supply goods or access but at prices so high that it constitutes an effective refusal. **29.24**

A related issue is the setting of access prices by vertically integrated non-regulated firms with substantial market power. The New Zealand Court of Appeal considered such an instance recently. It relied on the Efficient Component Price Rule (ECPR)[36] analysis to find that the incumbent telecommunications access provider had taken advantage of its market power to charge downstream competitors disproportionately high prices for wholesale access to its network (i.e. prices which exceeded the opportunity cost of providing access).[37] The ECPR rule is based on the notion that "the price of access must be selected in a manner that provides compensation to the incumbent for all of its properly incurred costs, *including its foregone profits*, while at the same time the price of access must be sufficiently low that it does not act as a barrier to entry."[38] However, while the Court of Appeal stated it would be reluctant to second guess a genuine attempt to apply ECPR prices, it indicated compliance with ECPR pricing will not necessarily provide immunity from a breach of s. 36.[39] **29.25**

Further, where a refusal to deal is pursuant to any contract, arrangement or understanding, it falls for consideration under s. 29 and s. 27.[40] **29.26**

I. Essential facilities

Access to essential facilities is generally considered in the same terms as set out in Section I.H, rather than under a separate doctrine in New Zealand. Despite early suggestion that the New Zealand courts could adopt the specific essential facilities doctrine,[41] the courts declined to rely on the doctrine in subsequent decisions. Recently, the courts confirmed that no essential facilities doctrine existed, save to provide insights into the consideration of s. 36.[42] **29.27**

---

33 *Shell (Petroleum Mining)* (1997) 7 TCLR 463 (n 32) at 528–31.
34 *Telecom v. Clear* [1995] 1 NZLR 385 (n 8).
35 *Telecom Corporation* [2012] NZCA 278 (n 5) para. 132.
36 *Telecom Corporation* [2012] NZCA 278 (n 5) para. 64.
37 *Telecom Corporation* [2012] NZCA 278 (n 5).
38 *Telecom Corporation* [2012] NZCA 278 (n 5) para. 65 (emphasis added).
39 *Telecom Corporation* [2012] NZCA 278 (n 5).
40 See further Section II.E and Section II para. 29.38 and A.
41 See e.g. *Union Shipping* [1990] 2 NZLR 662 (n 5).
42 Stated by the High Court in *Commerce Commission v. Telecom Corporation of New Zealand Ltd.*, HC Auckland CIV-2004-404-1333 (October 9, 2009) and confirmed by the Court of Appeal in *Telecom Corporation* [2012] NZCA 278 (n 5) para. 132.

29.28 It is worthwhile noting—as in Section I.H—that Part 4 of the Act provides for industry-specific regulation, meaning that essential facilities, like all industries, may be subject to sector-specific regulation if they meet the various thresholds.

J. Bundling (including loyalty and market share discounts)

29.29 Bundling/tying is not explicitly prohibited by the Act. However, such conduct may be an issue under s. 27 and a firm with substantial market power may breach s. 36. There are a number of ways to assess the competitive impact of a bundle. An approach the Commission has adopted previously involved applying the entire bundle discount to only those products in the bundle which are, or could be, offered by competing firms in the market (the competitive bundle test).[43] The rationale underlying this approach is that if an equally efficient competitor—which may not be capable of supplying the entire bundle—could nevertheless neutralize the bundle discount and still operate profitably, then there is no need to intervene on competition law grounds. While there are inevitable debates about the precise measure of evaluation, the underlying policy is to ensure that equally efficient competitors can still compete in the market.

K. Standard-setting groups (disclosure requirements, licensing arrangements, and licensing pools)

29.30 The Act specifically exempts provisions which require a person to comply with or apply standards prepared or approved by the Standards Association of New Zealand (being the only prescribed body thus far).[44]

29.31 Outside of this exemption, standard setting principally falls to be considered under s. 27 of the Act. However, if the arrangement results in a substantial lessening of competition a firm may seek authorization from the Commission on the basis that the standard setting results in net public benefits.[45] In determining whether to grant an authorization, the Commission will weigh the overall efficiencies that will result from the standard setting against the competitive detriments.

L. Customer termination

29.32 Customer termination is a form of refusal to deal.[46] Putting aside termination for selling below a minimum price, in New Zealand a firm will only be liable for unilaterally engaging in such conduct where the three limbs of the s. 36 test are satisfied, i.e. substantial market power, taking advantage, and a prohibited purpose (including deterring the customer from competing in that, or any other market). Where the termination is pursuant to any contract, arrangement or understanding, it falls for consideration under s. 27 and 29.[47]

---

[43] This test was the one favored by the Commission in the *Telecom Bundling of Broadband Services Investigation Report* (December 21, 2007). The Commission did, however, expressly note that the competitive bundle test is the most appropriate test "in the present context."

[44] Commerce Act 1986, s. 44(1)(e).

[45] For example, in 2011 the Commission granted authorization to a refrigerant licensing board which proposed an arrangement under which up to 100 percent of New Zealand refrigerant wholesalers (including new wholesalers who entered the market) would agree to supply refrigerants only to purchasers who meet certain training and certification requirements, on the basis it would increase compliance with New Zealand law. Decision 735: *Refrigerant License Trust Board Authorisation* (Final Determination) (November 25, 2011).

[46] See Section I.H.

[47] For example in *Commerce Commission v. Wrightson NMA Ltd.* (1995) 5 NZBLC 103 (HC) withdrawing custom from a real estate supplement breached s. 29 when done to prevent a rival from competing. Refer also to Sections II.E and II.A, and para 29.38.

M. Termination of intermediaries (retailers, wholesalers, dealers, and value-added resellers, agents, and brokers)

Termination of intermediaries is a form of refusal to deal, and dealt with on the same basis.[48] In New Zealand, a firm will be liable for engaging in such conduct where the three limbs of the s. 36 test are satisfied.[49] Again, where the termination is pursuant to any contract, arrangement or understanding, it falls for consideration under s. 29[50] and s. 27.[51] **29.33**

N. Termination of relationships with competitors

Section 29 of the Act explicitly prohibits contracts, arrangements, or understandings containing exclusionary provisions between competitors (subject to an exemption).[52] To the extent termination is pursuant to a contract, arrangement, or understanding, s. 27 may apply.[53] Further, such conduct may contravene s. 36 where the firm is taking advantage of substantial market power for an anticompetitive purpose in terminating the relationship.[54] **29.34**

O. Exemptions

Generally, the New Zealand competition law regime applies across all sectors of the economy, though there are some limited exceptions. The majority of the exemptions to the regime are set out in s. 44 of the Act. This section includes exemptions in relation to: agreements entered into in the context of a business partnership; employment agreements; provisions to protect business goodwill in sale and purchase agreements; standards prescribed by an industry body or association; and arrangements relating to the export or provision of services outside of New Zealand. Section 44(1A) also provides an exemption from the restrictive trade practice provisions of the Act for arrangements where the only parties are or would be interconnected bodies corporate, with interconnected bodies corporate defined in s. 2 of the Act. This exemption does not apply to s. 36, however. The Act will not apply to conduct of the New Zealand Government unless such conduct is "in trade." Further, only limited remedies are enforceable against the Crown, even when it is acting "in trade." **29.35**

Section 43 of the Act excludes the application of New Zealand's competition law regime (as contained in Part II of the Act) where a statute enacted by Parliament specifically authorizes the act or the class or kind of act at issue. For example, s. 14 of the Shipping Act 1987 excludes Part II and IV of the Act from applying to certain arrangements in relation to shipping. Section 91 of the Civil Aviation Act 1990 excludes ss. 27 and 29 of the Act from applying to contracts and arrangements authorized by the Minister of Transport under s. 88 of the Civil Aviation Act 1990. The Cartel Bill proposes to withdraw the scheme relating to shipping, meaning international shipping will be covered by the Commerce Act. A review of the Civil Aviation Act is also underway at the time of writing, which will assess whether civil aviation should likewise be subject to the general competition regime contained in the Commerce Act. **29.36**

While the Commission itself is able to authorize restrictive trade practices that breach s. 27 of the Act (provided the net public benefit assessment is satisfied), the Commission does not have the same scope to authorize breaches of s. 36. **29.37**

---

48 See Section I.H.

49 While there does not appear to have been any specific cases on this subject matter, see *Telecom Corporation* [2010] NZSC 111, [2011] 1 NZLR 577 (n 4) for guidance on the application of the relevant test.

50 See e.g. *Wrightson* (1995) 5 NZBLC 103 (n 47) and Section II.E.

51 See Section II para. 29.38 and A.

52 See Section II.E.

53 See Section II and e.g. *Commerce Commission v. Ophthalmological Society of New Zealand Incorporated*, HC Wellington CP354/97 (May 4, 2000) regarding an agreement between New Zealand surgeons to refuse to provide the necessary supervision for their Australian counterparts.

54 See paras. 29.5–29.8.

II. Dealing with competitors

29.38 Section 27 of the Act provides a general prohibition on anticompetitive arrangements. More specifically, the prohibition prevents persons from entering into, arriving at, or giving effect to, contracts, arrangements, or understandings containing a provision which has a purpose, effect, or likely effect of substantially lessening competition (SLC) in a market. The prohibition does not distinguish between horizontal and vertical contracts, arrangements or understandings, and it is irrelevant whether the parties to the arrangement are in competition with one another. The crux of the prohibition lies in the SLC test.

29.39 The Commission remains focused on cartel enforcement. Further, Parliament recently passed the Commerce Commission (International Co-operation, and Fees) Act, enabling the New Zealand and Australian competition agencies to work together more effectively, making it easier to tackle trans-Tasman competition, consumer and telecommunications issues. The cooperation agreement between the Commission and the ACCC provides for the agencies' cooperation on matters of common interest, including: notification relating to activities that impact the other jurisdiction; the coordination of enforcement activities; the exchange of information in certain circumstances; and the creation of joint educational programs and publications.[55]

29.40 The number of investigations launched by the Commission into coordinated behavior varies each year. For example, in the 2010/11 year the Commission concluded twenty-one coordinated conduct investigations but in 2011/12 this number dropped to nine overall.

A. Terminology

(i) Market definition

29.41 According to the Act, a market includes goods and services that, as a matter of fact and commercial common sense, are substitutable.[56] A SSNIP (small but significant non-transitory increase in price) analysis is often used as an aid in undertaking market definition. In the recent case of *Commerce Commission v. Air New Zealand Ltd* the High Court stated:

> while we see the heart of a market in economic terms as being the actual and prospective transactions between sellers and buyers, the broader ambit of a "market" looks to the rivalry between sellers for those who will buy their products, and encompasses the factors that directly shape and constrain that rivalry, as a matter of fact and commercial common sense.[57]

(ii) Contract, arrangement, or understanding

29.42 Contracts, arrangements and understandings (describing progressively lower degrees of formality) are not defined by the Act. The courts have, however, treated the three concepts distinctly. The prevailing view is that the following elements are required for an understanding (the least onerous of the three levels):[58]

(a) communication giving rise to a meeting of the minds among the parties;
(b) that embodies an expectation as to the future conduct of at least one of the parties;
(c) such that the parties are under some form of obligation to conduct themselves in a manner in which their communication has indicated.

---

[55] Cooperation arrangement between the New Zealand Commerce Commission and the Australian Competition and Consumer Commission in relation to the provision of compulsorily acquired information and investigative assistance (February 2013).

[56] Commerce Act 1986, s. 3(1A).

[57] *Commerce Commission v. Air New Zealand Ltd.* (2011) 9 NZBLC 103,318 (HC).

[58] See e.g. *Auckland Regional Authority v. Mutual Rental Cars (Auckland Airport) Ltd.* [1987] 2 NZLR 647 (HC) and *Giltrap City Ltd. v. Commerce Commission* [2004] NZLR 608 (CA).

It should also be noted that attempts, falling short of a contract, arrangement or understanding, can also breach the Act. Section 80(1)(b) of the Act allows the Commission to seek pecuniary penalties from parties who attempt to enter into an arrangement in breach of any of the restrictive trade practice provisions. **29.43**

(iii) Substantial lessening of competition

The substantial lessening of competition test is a relative standard. One approach is to ask whether a "firm's market power [has] moved along the spectrum away from perfect competition towards monopoly."[59] The courts have traditionally interpreted the SLC test by analyzing the three elements—substantial, lessening, and competition—separately. **29.44**

Section 2(1A) of the Act defines "substantial" as "real or of substance." It has been interpreted by the courts as meaning "lessening competition in a way which is more than insubstantial or nominal. The merely ephemeral and minimal will not suffice."[60] Further, the courts have noted that "[i]nevitably, that will involve some attention to relativity; and in the end be a question of judgment on a matter of degree."[61] The threshold may be met in either qualitative or quantitative terms. **29.45**

"Lessening" is defined by s. 3(2) of the Act to include "hindering or preventing of competition" indicating that while the effect on competition needs to be substantial, it need not be permanent or absolute. **29.46**

Section 3(1) of the Act defines competition as "workable or effective competition" where firms in a market are constrained by existing and potential competitors. **29.47**

In order to assess an arrangement's impact on competition, the Commission will define a counterfactual. An arrangement will have the effect of substantially lessening competition in a market if there is materially less competition in the factual than there would be but for the relevant arrangement (the counterfactual). **29.48**

B. Horizontal price fixing (including advanced announcements of price or product changes)

Section 30 of the Act imposes a per se prohibition on price fixing arrangements reached between competitors, by deeming such arrangements to breach s. 27. The section states: **29.49**

> [A] provision of a contract, arrangement, or understanding shall be deemed for the purposes of [s. 27] to have the purpose, or to have or to be likely to have the effect, of substantially lessening competition in a market if the provision has the purpose, or has or is likely to have the effect of fixing, controlling, or maintaining, or providing for the fixing, controlling, or maintaining, of the price for goods or services... that are supplied or acquired by the parties... in competition with each other.

The prohibition applies irrespective of any actual impact on competition (i.e. a SLC need not be established). As with other restrictive trade practices, attempts, as well as inducing, or attempting to induce others, to enter into a price fixing arrangement are prohibited.[62]

Price is defined widely by the Act to include valuable consideration in any form.[63] In the s. 30 context it is stated specifically to include "any discount, allowance, rebate, or credit, in relation to goods or services." The New Zealand courts have generously interpreted this element. **29.50**

---

59 Commerce Commission, Mergers & Acquisitions Guidelines (2013) para. 2.20.

60 *Commerce Commission v. Port Nelson Ltd* (1995) 6 TCLR 406 (HC) at 434.

61 *Port Nelson* (1995) 6 TCLR 406 (n 61) at 434.

62 Under ss. 80 and 81. Ancillary liability also attaches to certain other conduct, see s. 80(1).

63 Commerce Act 1986, s. 2(1).

For example, a free car wash with the purchase of petrol was captured, in that an agreement to withdraw the promotion was an agreement, in effect, to increase the price of petrol or to reduce the discount on petrol.[64] Further, other agreements, such as in regard to the allocation of markets or the rigging of bids, can amount to price fixing depending on the circumstances.

(i) Contract, arrangement, or understanding

29.51 Please refer to the explanation of contract, arrangement, or understanding in Section II.A(ii).

(ii) Fixing, controlling, or maintaining

29.52 The courts in New Zealand have indicated that the fixing, controlling, or maintaining threshold is low. Specificity as to price is not essential to satisfy this limb: arrangements that affect price are sufficient to establish liability.[65] For example, references to a formula or other method in setting prices will be caught. Further, permanency of price or method is not required. The Commission (having reviewed a series of cases) took the view that price will be fixed, controlled, or maintained "where there is some artificial interference with, or constraint on, the finding of a price or prices by competitive forces or processes (in particular the interaction of supply and demand)."[66]

(iii) Purpose, effect, likely effect

29.53 Purpose is usually assessed objectively under s. 30. However, purpose, effect, and likely effect are disjunctive terms, and it is sufficient if an arrangement has the effect or likely effect of fixing prices. Therefore, even if the firms involved do not appreciate their behavior will fix prices, and therefore do not have the purpose of fixing prices, or harming competition, they may still be in breach of the prohibition. The New Zealand courts have stated that while purpose is to be primarily assessed objectively, subjective evidence is relevant to that assessment, though it should be used with caution to ensure defendants are not able to use a subjective ascertainment of purpose to avoid liability for conduct that is prohibited absolutely.[67]

(iv) In competition

29.54 The phrase "in competition" is yet to receive definitive judicial direction, although in many cases it will be obvious. The current understanding is that the relevant question to be asked is: whether the parties are actual or likely competitors for the supply or acquisition of the particular goods or services. Despite that the s. 30 prohibition requires only that the parties are "in competition," the High Court has recently confirmed that "the requirement in s 27 that there be a market in New Zealand survives the effect of the deeming provision."[68] However, the Court emphasized that the market need not be pleaded in every s. 30 case, it will likely be assumed that the market is in New Zealand where there is no suggestion otherwise.[69]

C. Joint ventures and other competitive collaborations

29.55 Section 31 of the Act provides a specific exemption from the price fixing prohibition for contracts, arrangements, or understandings between parties to a joint venture. The exemption applies to activities carried out "in trade" and covers two forms of joint venture: those carried on by two or more persons, whether or not in partnership (provided the supply by the parties to the joint venture is in proportion to their respective interests in the joint venture); and

64 *Commerce Commission v. Caltex New Zealand Ltd* (1999) 9 TCLR 305 (HC).
65 *Caltex* (1999) 9 TCLR 305 (n 65).
66 *Electricity Governance Board Limited,* Decision no. 473 (September 30, 2002) at para. 147.
67 *ANZCO New Zealand Ltd. v. AFFCO Foods Waitara Ltd.* [2006] 3 NZLR 351 (CA) paras. 255 and 260.
68 *Air New Zealand* (2011) 9 NZBLC 103,318 (n 58) para. 76.
69 *Air New Zealand* (2011) 9 NZBLC 103,318 (n 58) para. 76.

those carried on by a body corporate for the purpose of enabling two or more persons to carry on a joint activity by means of their joint control or shared ownership of the body corporate.

Where the joint venture is unincorporated, the goods must be jointly produced by the parties in pursuance of the joint venture and in proportion to their respective interests in the joint venture. This suggests that both parties must have had a genuine role in the process of physically producing the goods in order to be exempt. Any marketing arrangement must be connected to the production of the goods, and must be in proportion to the interests in the joint venture arrangement. Services supplied by the joint venture must also be in pursuance of the joint venture, or made available as a result of it and in proportion to the joint venture parties' respective interests. For an incorporated joint venture, the supply must be of goods produced in pursuance of the joint venture and the supply of services must be in pursuance of the joint venture and by the body corporate itself, and not by any interconnected body for example. **29.56**

The s. 31 exemption applies only to the deemed price fixing rule; all joint venture arrangements remain subject to the general s. 27 competition test. This was confirmed in *Commerce Commission v. Bay of Plenty Energy Ltd.*[70] The Court found that while agreements between joint venture parties as to price will not automatically breach the Act under s. 30 where the s. 31 exemption is held to apply, the agreements will still be subject to consideration under s. 27 as to whether they have the purpose, effect or likely effect of a SLC in a market. **29.57**

Parties who intend to enter a joint venture can apply to the Commission for authorization or clearance (where the joint venture is achieved via an acquisition) to protect themselves from proceedings for a contract, arrangement or understanding that would otherwise contravene the Act. **29.58**

The Cartel Bill proposes to widen the existing joint venture exemption by replacing it with a broad exemption for all collaborative activities (please refer to Section III.F). **29.59**

D. Horizontal agreements to allocate customers or territories; agreements not to compete

Current New Zealand law does not contain a per se prohibition on the allocation of customers or territories. A market division arrangement that does not contain an exclusionary provision (which would introduce s. 29) will typically fall for review under s. 27 or s. 30. Whether a contract, arrangement or understanding which involves a restriction on output, or allocates markets, customers, or territories, could breach s. 27 depends on the respective levels of market concentration and any resulting impact on competition in that market. Such arrangements are also subject to the per se price fixing prohibition (s. 30). Whether they amount to price fixing will depend on the circumstances, but the greater the proportion of the market subject to/affected by the agreement, the greater the risk a breach will occur. **29.60**

The new cartel offense proposed by the Cartel Bill seeks to introduce an explicit prohibition on restricting output and allocating markets/customers (please refer to Section III.F). **29.61**

E. Horizontal boycotts

Section 29 of the Act contains a general prohibition on exclusionary provisions. Exclusionary provisions are provisions in an arrangement (of which any two parties are in competition), which has the purpose of preventing, restricting, or limiting, the supply or acquisition of goods or services to or from a competitor (or class of competitors) of a party to the arrangement, **29.62**

[70] *Commerce Commission v. Bay of Plenty Electrical Ltd.*, HC Wellington CIV-2001-485-917 (December 13, 2007).

either generally, in particular circumstances, or on particular conditions.[71] A defendant will avoid liability, however, where they can establish that the relevant provision does not have the purpose, or does not have or is not likely to have the effect, of substantially lessening competition in a market.[72] For example, liability under s. 29 arose when real estate agents refused to advertise in a property supplement if the supplement published the advertisements of a rival agent's reduced commission rates. The agents conceded their purpose in withdrawing their advertisements was to prevent the maverick agent from acquiring advertising space in the supplement and advertising his reduced rates.[73]

29.63 Section 29 is proposed to be repealed under the Cartel Bill given some overlap with the expanded cartel offense and the fact that anticompetitive agreements can also be considered under s. 27.[74]

F. Trade associations

29.64 Trade associations are subject to the Act. In particular, s. 2(8)(a) of the Act deems any arrangement entered into, or recommendation made by, a trade association or body to be an arrangement entered into by the association and those individual members, notwithstanding anything to the contrary in the rules or constitution of the association.[75]

29.65 Though the Cartel Bill proposes its repeal, s. 32 of the Act currently provides an exemption from the s. 30 price fixing prohibition for arrangements recommending price that are entered into by more than 50 persons who supply or acquire goods or services in trade. The exemption specifically contemplates trade associations, though such arrangements will still be subject to the general s. 27 substantial lessening of competition prohibition.

G. Interlocking directorates

29.66 There is no per se rule against interlocking directorates. To the extent they are pursuant to or facilitate a contract, arrangement, or understanding, the ss. 27, 29 and 30 rules will apply. They can also be a relevant consideration in the merger context in terms of assessing the level of constraint firms may impose on each other. For example, in the context of one bus company (New Zealand Bus Limited (NZ Bus)) attempting to acquire the remaining 74 percent of shares in a rival (Mana) that it did not already own, it was relevant that NZ Bus had appointed a director of Mana and that the executive director of NZ Bus regularly attended Mana's board meetings. This information was used in assessing the level of constraint the companies actually imposed on each other.[76] However, this is not an issue that often arises for consideration.

H. Facilitating practices

29.67 The New Zealand competition law regime does not specifically address facilitating practices, though such arrangements will be subject to s. 30 and the general s. 27 prohibition. Practices that fall short of a contract, arrangement or understanding will therefore not be prohibited

---

[71] Commerce Act 1986, s. 29(1).

[72] Commerce Act 1986, s. 29(1A).

[73] *Wrightson* (1995) 5 NZBLC 103 (n 47). This case was decided before the defense to s. 29 was enacted, i.e. that a provision of a contract, arrangement or understanding will not be an exclusionary provision if the defendant can prove the provision does not have the purpose, or does not have or is not likely to have the effect, of substantially lessening competition in a market.

[74] Commerce (Cartels and Other Matters) Amendment Bill (341-1) (explanatory note) at 4.

[75] A member can expressly disassociate themselves in writing.

[76] *Commerce Commission v. New Zealand Bus Ltd.* (2006) 8 NZBLC 101,774 (HC), a finding supported by the Court of Appeal.

in New Zealand, unless they constitute an attempt to enter into an arrangement in breach of s. 30 or 27, or otherwise trigger ancillary liability pursuant to s. 80(1) of the Act.[77] Facilitating practices are relevant to the assessment of whether there is in fact an agreement.

I. Information exchange

The Act does not make specific reference to concerted practices; rather information exchanges are subject to the s. 27 and 30 prohibitions.[78] **29.68**

Information sharing between competitors is less likely to cause concerns broadly where the exchanges relate to general information or only historic pricing information, aggregated over a number of firms, collected independently, provided voluntarily and is anonymous.[79] On the other hand, competitor information as to specific future pricing is likely to cause concerns. **29.69**

J. Joint purchasing agreements

Section 33 of the Act provides an exemption from the s. 30 price-fixing rule for collective purchasing arrangements. In order to make use of the exemption, the purchase must be made collectively (but not necessarily jointly) and can occur directly or indirectly. Further, the exemption extends to joint advertising for the resupply of the collectively acquired goods (though not to services). However, s. 27 will still apply meaning the arrangement will breach the Act if it has the purpose, effect, or likely effect of substantially lessening competition in a market. Firms concerned that a joint purchasing arrangement may be anticompetitive are able to seek authorization from the Commission for such conduct. **29.70**

The Cartel Bill proposes to clarify that individual purchasing at a collectively negotiated price, and the provision for an intermediary to take title to the goods and resell or resupply them to another party to the arrangement, would also attract the exemption—please refer to Section III.F. **29.71**

K. Joint lobbying/regulatory/legislative efforts

Joint lobbying is unlikely to raise competition concerns in New Zealand. Concerns could arise however, where the contact between competitors in aid of the joint lobbying leads to improper information exchanges[80] or results in an arrangement between competitors as to price, or causes a substantial lessening of competition.[81] **29.72**

III. General issues

A. Jurisdiction and applicable law (including sector-specific competition regulation)

Competition law in New Zealand is regulated by the Commerce Act 1986. The stated purpose of this Act is to "promote competition in markets for the long-term benefit of consumers within New Zealand."[82] The Act extends to the engaging in conduct outside New Zealand by any person resident or carrying on business in New Zealand where that conduct affects a New Zealand market.[83] Both the New Zealand courts and the Commission have indicated **29.73**

[77] Commerce Act 1986, s. 80(1)(b).
[78] See Sections II.A and II.B and para. 29.38.
[79] *Re New Zealand Medical Association* (1988) 1 NZBLC (Com) 104,369.
[80] See Section II.I.
[81] See the discussion of ss. 30 and 27 in Sections II.A and II.B, and para. 29.38.
[82] Commerce Act 1986, s. 1A.
[83] Commerce Act 1986, s. 4.

increasing willingness to extend the application of the Act to conduct carried on outside of New Zealand, including via the attribution of conduct involving New Zealand to foreign parents.[84]

B. Antitrust system

(i) Name of agency/agencies

29.74 The Commerce Commission is the statutory body responsible for administering the Commerce Act in New Zealand. The Commission is a combined regulatory and quasi-judicial authority which operates independent of any Government direction. It adjudicates on clearances and authorizations for mergers and acquisitions and authorizations for restrictive trade practices. Aside from adjudicating in respect of clearance and authorization applications, the Commission does not have the power to make enforcement orders. Remedies must be obtained from the court and can be sought by the Commission or private parties. However, the Act does provide the Commission with wide powers to administer its enforcement functions, including the ability to issue cease-and-desist orders.

(ii) Staff size and budget

29.75 The Commission is typically made up of five full Commissioners, a Telecommunications Commissioner, two Cease-and-Desist Commissioners and two Associate Commissioners. Economists, lawyers and industry experts are employed in support of the Commissioners. Commission staff collect information, accept submissions and carry out investigations in order to provide the Commissioners with information and recommendations. The Commission has a total of approximately 180 staff. Only in limited circumstances do businesses and their advisers interact directly with the Commissioners; the majority of communication is with the investigating teams.

29.76 For the 2013/2014 financial year the Commission's operating expenditure budget is around NZD 39.5 million. The Commission also receives income from Commerce Act fees, interest, cost recovery and some court-awarded costs.

(iii) Recent enforcement actions and trends

29.77 The investigation and prosecution of cartels has been a top priority for the Commission in recent years. Dr. Mark Berry (Commission Chair) stated in May 2012 "[a] suite of cartel cases have continued to dominate our Competition program over the past 18 months."[85] Settlements with cartel participants endorsed by the High Court have been common.

29.78 There have been a very limited number of prosecutions of misuse of market power under s. 36 in recent years. Many, including the Commission, have stated dissatisfaction with the very high threshold inherent in the current s. 36 prohibition. The Cartel Bill does not propose amendments to s. 36.

29.79 The Commission has increasingly been open to settlement discussions where they think they can avoid costly court cases. Its Enforcement Response Guidelines emphasize the Commission is "receptive to resolving non-compliance by agreement where a remedy is possible and a negotiated settlement can be achieved that is prompt, easily implemented and in the public interest."[86]

---

[84] *Kuehne + Nagel International AG v. Commerce Commission* [2012] NZCA 221, [2012] 3 NZLR 187.

[85] Berry (n 1).

[86] Commerce Commission, Enforcement Response Guidelines (October 2013) para. 63, <http://www.comcom.govt.nz/the-commission/commission-policies/enforcement-response-guidelines/>.

C. Private litigation

Section 82 of the Act enables a party who has suffered loss as a result of any anticompetitive conduct to institute civil proceedings for damages. Such damages will be limited to any loss or damage caused by the contravening conduct. To date, private actions have not been particularly prevalent in New Zealand. **29.80**

D. Follow-on litigation (includes role of agency determinations of liability for follow-on litigation)

Section 82 of the Act allows compensatory damages to be claimed against parties who have been found to have breached the Act by the courts or by agreement with the Commission. However, in New Zealand there is no equivalent to s. 83 of the Australian Competition and Consumer Act 2010 (Cth) which provides for a finding of fact that has been made by a court in other (specified) proceedings where a contravention has been found to be prima facie evidence of that fact in proceedings for damages (s. 82). That said, as a practical (rather than legal) matter, such a finding by a Court, or admission of liability in a Court-approved settlement, will make proving a breach of the Commerce Act easier. **29.81**

Such cases have seen little court action, with the few instances being thus far settled out of court. A current case is New Zealand Bloom Limited's claim for compensation from Cargolux, alleging cartel conduct resulted in higher freight costs for its exotic flower import business between 2004 and 2006. The Court had sanctioned an earlier cartel settlement between the Commission and Cargolux International Airlines S.A. in relation to cartel conduct. **29.82**

E. Arbitration and alternative dispute resolution

While not very common, private actions can be resolved through the use of arbitration and other means of alternative dispute resolution where the parties agree. Alternative dispute resolution is increasingly popular in New Zealand and the High Court Rules also allow the parties to agree to a judicial settlement conference, in which a Judge conducts what is essentially a mediation. Settlement prior to trial is common in New Zealand. **29.83**

F. The Cartel Bill

The Cartel Bill, before the New Zealand Parliament at the time of writing, proposes to substantially amend the competition law regime in New Zealand by replacing the existing s. 30 with a broad prohibition on entering into or giving effect to a cartel provision.[87] A cartel provision is defined in the Bill as broadly price fixing, restricting output, and market/customer allocating. **29.84**

Alongside this broad prohibition a "collaborative activities" exemption is proposed with the aim of ensuring that enterprises, ventures or other activities which are not carried on for the dominant purpose of lessening competition do not attract "cartel" liability. Based on proposed wording, it will need to be established that the offending provision is an element of a contract, arrangement, or understanding between parties to a collaborative activity, and the provision is reasonably necessary to that activity. The Cartel Bill defines collaborative activities as enterprises, ventures or other activities, in trade, carried on in cooperation between two or more persons. They must not be carried on for the purpose of lessening competition between the parties (rather than the market generally). This exemption is a novel one, and is **29.85**

[87] Commerce (Cartels and Other Matters) Amendment Bill, <http://www.legislation.govt.nz/bill/government/2011/0341/latest/DLM4090009.html>.

intended to be wide in its coverage, to include both ancillary restraints and joint ventures.[88] A clearance regime is also proposed for collaborative activities that do not substantially lessen competition in order to provide certainty.

29.86 The Cartel Bill also proposes to provide a widened joint purchasing exemption for cartel provisions. Not only would collective acquisition and advertising of those goods and services be covered, but individual purchasing at a collectively negotiated price, and the provision for an intermediary to take title to the goods and resell or resupply them to another party to the arrangement, would also be protected.

29.87 Further, the Cartel Bill includes a proposed vertical supply exemption which exempts from the cartel prohibition provisions of a contract between a supplier (or likely supplier) of goods or services and a customer (or likely customer). The cartel provision must relate to the supply of the goods or services and must not have the dominant purpose of lessening competition between parties to the contract. This exemption specifically includes the setting of a maximum price at which a customer may resupply the goods or services.

G. Remedies

(i) Civil liability

29.88 **Restrictive trade practices** Individuals are exposed to a maximum pecuniary penalty of NZD 500,000. Where an individual has breached the price fixing prohibition, a body corporate is prevented from indemnifying the individual for this penalty or the costs incurred. Furthermore, the court has the power to make an order for any individual found in breach of s. 30 or s. 29 to be excluded from the management of a body corporate for a period of five years.[89]

29.89 The court has more flexibility in determining the penalties for a body corporate found guilty of a restrictive trade practice. A body corporate will be exposed to a fine equal to the greater of:

1. NZD 10,000,000; or
2. either—
   (a) if the commercial gain can be readily ascertained, three times the value of any commercial gain resulting from the contravention; or
   (b) if the commercial gain cannot be readily ascertained, 10 percent of the turnover of the body corporate and all of its interconnected bodies corporate (if any) in New Zealand.

29.90 The court may make an order for an injunction to restrain any person from engaging in a restrictive trade practice.[90] Ancillary liability can be brought under the Act, including for (among other things) being in any way knowingly concerned in a contravention of the Act.[91] Finally, exemplary damages may be awarded under s. 82A of the Act even if the court has made, or may make, an order for a pecuniary penalty for the same conduct.

29.91 Fines imposed in recent years have included NZD 12 million for New Zealand's largest telecommunications company for taking advantage of its market power to charge downstream

---

[88] Minster of Commerce, Cabinet Paper: "Proposed Amendments to the Commerce Act in relation to cartels" (January 31, 2012), p. 7: <http://www.med.govt.nz/business/competition-policy/cartel-criminalisation/Cabinet%20paper%20recommending%20criminalisation.pdf/view>.

[89] Commerce Act 1986, s. 80C.

[90] Commerce Act 1986, s. 81.

[91] Commerce Act 1986, ss. 80–84A.

competitors disproportionately high access prices to its network.[92] There have also recently been a number of court sanctioned settlements with airlines for agreements in respect of surcharges on cargo rates to New Zealand. Total fines for that matter reached NZD 42.5 million.

(ii) Criminal liability

The Act does not provide for criminal liability for breach of the restrictive trade practice provisions. However, the Cartel Bill would (if passed) introduce criminal sanctions, (alongside a parallel civil offense), for hard-core cartel behavior (i.e. price-fixing, output restricting and market/customer sharing). It is proposed that the criminal offense provision will come into force two years after royal assent. **29.92**

Cease-and-desist orders Sections 74A to 74D of the Act provide the Commission with the power to obtain orders against firms engaged in anticompetitive conduct. Cease-and-desist orders can be made by the Commission where it is necessary to restrain anticompetitive conduct in breach of s. 27, 36, or 47 (regulating mergers and acquisitions), or it is necessary to require a person to do something to restore competition or the potential for competition in a market. Such an order may be made where a Cease-and-Desist Commissioner (who must be a lawyer) is satisfied that: **29.93**

(a) at first sight, on the face of the evidence, there is anticompetitive conduct that contravenes the Commerce Act; and
(b) it is necessary to act urgently:
    (i) to prevent a particular person or consumers suffering serious loss or damage; and
    (ii) in the interests of the public.

In order to determine whether a cease-and-desist order should be made, the Commission will first commence an investigation into the offending conduct. Where it is satisfied that there has been a contravention of the Act, it will prepare a report to Commissioners including a recommendation that a cease-and-desist order be made. Provided the Commissioners are satisfied that they agree with the report recommendation, an application will be directed to the Cease-and-Desist Commissioner to make the relevant order. Before the order is made, the firm or individual in breach will have the opportunity to review all relevant information and make a written submission to the Cease-and-Desist Commissioner. The Commission may also apply to the courts for other remedies in addition to the cease-and-desist order. **29.94**

H. Leniency and immunity

The Commission operates a Leniency Policy providing immunity from proceedings initiated by the Commission to the first person involved in a cartel who reports the cartel to the Commission and cooperates fully. A "paperless" process is available. Immunity may be available even if the Commission is aware of, or is already investigating the cartel, where the evidence it holds is likely insufficient to be able to initiate proceedings. Immunity can be granted to an individual or a firm, and is available for the "ring leader" of the cartel, but not for a party that has coerced others to participate. Immunity for a firm may extend to any current or former director, officer, or employee of that firm but immunity for an individual acting independently from a firm means immunity will not then be available to the firm. The person must cooperate fully with the Commission. They are subject to a range of obligations, including providing all relevant information, confirming they have ceased the conduct (unless the Commission directs otherwise), and if a firm, using best efforts to: **29.95**

(a) secure the complete and truthful co-operation of current and former directors, officers or employees;

[92] *Telecom Corporation of New Zealand Limited v. Commerce Commission* [2012] NZCA 344.

(b) encourage and facilitate current and former directors, officers or employees to voluntarily provide the Commission with any information, to appear for interviews and to give evidence in court where required by the Commission;
(c) ensure that its related entities provide all assistance reasonably requested by the Commission; and
(d) not disclose to, or communicate with, any third party that they have applied for leniency or whether it has been granted.

29.96 The Commission can be approached for clarification as to whether leniency is available on a "hypothetical" or "off the record" basis. The Commission has stated this will not be considered an application and it will not use the information provided for any other purpose.

29.97 The Commission's cooperation policy may be available to those second in line to formally apply for leniency or where leniency is not otherwise available. The Commission will exercise its discretion to take a lower level of enforcement action, or no action at all, against an individual or firm in exchange for information and full continuing and complete cooperation. A lower level of enforcement action may include a settlement, or a submission made by the Commission to the court for a reduction in penalty on behalf of an individual or firm.

I. Document creation and retention

29.98 Section 98 of the Act provides the Commission with the power to require a person to furnish information, produce documents, or give evidence and s. 98A provides the Commission with the power to search premises to establish a contravention of the Act. The New Zealand courts have confirmed that the Commission's power is not unlimited; a real limitation is imposed via the terms of s. 98 which require that the power must be "for the purposes of carrying out its functions and exercising its powers under this act."

29.99 Section 103 of the Act makes it an offense (carrying a maximum fine of NZD 30,000 for a body corporate, or NZD 10,000 for an individual) to fail to furnish the required information to the Commission via refusal, obstruction, or the provision of false or misleading information. The Cartel Bill proposes to increase these penalties.

29.100 Information gathered via the Commission's s. 98 powers may be subject to proceedings under the Official Information Act 1982, though the Commission has made firm public statements to the effect that it will vigorously protect truly confidential information.

30

NORWAY

Beret Sundet & Eirik Østerud
Bugge, Arentz-Hansen & Rasmussen

Introduction

Norwegian substantive antitrust law consists of two sets of rules: those found in the European Economic Area Agreement (EEA) between the EFTA states (Norway, Iceland and Liechtenstein) and the EU member states, and those under the Norwegian Competition Act ("Competition Act") (2004). **30.01**

Articles 53 and 54 EEA prohibit anticompetitive agreements/concerted practices and abuse of market dominance. The provisions are equivalent to, and shall be interpreted in the same manner as, articles 101 and 102 of the Treaty of the Functioning of the European Union (TFEU). **30.02**

The prohibitions in article 53 and 54 EEA are enforced by the European Commission and the EFTA Surveillance Authority (ESA). The competences between the two agencies are distributed according to the relatively complex jurisdictional criteria (effect on trade criteria combined with geographical allocation of a percentage of overall turnover) set out in article 56 EEA. The Main Part of the EEA Agreement, including the antitrust prohibitions, is **30.03** incorporated in Norwegian law through the Norwegian EEA Act 1992 (Act of November 27, 1992 No. 109 on the implementation of the main part of the EEA Agreement). A procedure for decentralized enforcement of EEA competition law is set out in the Surveillance and Court Agreement (Protocol 4 to the Agreement between the EFTA States on the establishment of a Surveillance Authority and a Court of Justice) and in the Norwegian EEA Competition Act (Act of March 5, 2004 No. 11 concerning implementation and enforcement of the competition rules of the EEA Agreement), providing also the Norwegian Competition Authority (NCA) with the competence to monitor compliance with and enforce articles 53 and 54 EEA.

30.04 The Competition Act (Act of March 5, 2004 No. 12 on competition between undertakings and control of concentrations) entered into force on May 1, 2004. Potential infringements of the prohibitions in the Competition Act are monitored, investigated and, if appropriate, sanctioned by the NCA. The Act brought Norwegian substantive antitrust law in line with EU/EEA competition law by adopting prohibitions against anticompetitive agreements/concerted practices (s. 10) and abuse of dominance (s. 11). The provisions are modeled after the prohibitions in articles 101 and 102 TFEU and articles 53 and 54 EEA. Pursuant to the preparatory works of the Competition Act, case law and decisional practice from the corresponding TFEU and the EEA prohibitions shall be given considerable weight when interpreting and applying ss. 10 and 11 of the Competition Act.

30.05 The purpose of the Competition Act, as stated in s. 1, is "to further competition and thereby contribute to the efficient utilization of society's resources." Furthermore, "special consideration shall be given to the interests of consumers." In so far as EU/EEA antitrust law arguably has broader objectives than the Competition Act, due to the overriding objectives of the EU/EEA (in particular market integration), it cannot be excluded that ss. 10 and 11 of the Competition Act may, in some cases, be interpreted somewhat differently than the corresponding provisions in the TFEU and the EEA Agreement. This may, for example, be the case with practices that restrict cross-border trade. In most cases, however, ss. 10 and 11 of the Competition Act shall be interpreted in the same way as the equivalent EEA and TFEU prohibitions.

30.06 On February 14, 2012, a committee appointed by the Norwegian Ministry of Government Administration, Reform and Church Affairs delivered its report "More efficient competition act."[1] Although the report proposes several procedural and substantive amendments to the Competition Act (predominantly in relation to merger control), the committee did not see the need for any changes with regard to the substantive content of ss. 10 and 11. The report has been on public hearing, and the Ministry presented its proposal for amendments to the parliament March 15, 2013. The bill was passed in parliament on June 3, 2013, and the amendments take effect January 1, 2014.

30.07 The effective use of society's resources is a central and salient element in the Government's policies. Moreover, competition is considered an important instrument for reaching the goal of obtaining a well-functioning and reasonably priced production of goods and services in the private as well as the public sector, to the benefit of the consumers. Albeit with some deviations and minor differences between the political parties, on an overall level there is a general political consensus on these issues in Norway.

30.08 Although the NCA, in the past, has decided relatively few cases finding antitrust infringements, the Authority is currently investigating several high profile cases. Moreover, ESA has decided two cases, in 2010 and 2011, imposing substantial fines for antitrust infringements.

[1] Norwegian Official Report, "More Efficient Competition Act," Doc. No. NOU 2012:7.

Bearing in mind that the sample of cases is too small to draw any definitive conclusions, these developments may nevertheless signal a trend towards increased enforcement of the antitrust rules in Norway.

This Chapter will first and foremost deal with, and highlight, Norwegian and EEA antitrust law and practice. This choice of emphasis undeniably creates a risk of under-communicating the significance of EU antitrust law when interpreting and applying EEA and Norwegian substantive antitrust law. Since EU antitrust law is dealt with extensively elsewhere, however, this Chapter on Norway aims to supplement an informed reader on EU antitrust law with antitrust case law, practice and issues specific to Norway. **30.09**

I. Acting alone

Section 11 of the Competition Act prohibits any abuse by one or more undertakings of a dominant position. The prohibition corresponds to article 54 EEA and article 102 TFEU and should generally be interpreted and applied in the same way. **30.10**

Section 11 only applies to dominant undertakings. The notions of dominance and collective dominance in s. 11 correspond to the equivalent concepts under EU/EEA antitrust law. However, article 102 TFEU requires that the undertaking in question has a dominant position "within the internal market or in a substantial part of it." Similarly, article 54 EEA sets out that the undertaking in question must be dominant "within the territory covered by the EEA Agreements or in a substantial part of it." As the territorial scope of the Competition Act is confined to Norway, such requirements do not apply under s. 11. The concept of "abuse" of dominance in s. 11 should also, generally, be interpreted and applied in accordance with the corresponding concepts in articles 102 TFEU and 54 EEA. Both s. 11 and article 54 EEA contain a non-exhaustive list of abusive conduct. **30.11**

Section 10 of the Competition Act and article 53 EEA prohibit agreements, decisions by associations of undertakings, and concerted practice that have an anticompetitive "object or effect." The prohibitions may not only apply to horizontal collusion among competitors (dealt with in Section II. Dealing with Competitors), but also to agreements and understandings among non-competitors, for instance between undertakings that have a vertical relationship. Section 10(3) of the Competition Act and article 53 (3) EEA set out an exception rule, pursuant to which countervailing efficiencies may render the practice lawful pursuant to certain conditions. **30.12**

With one exception—a decision by ESA where a vertical agreement was considered contrary to both articles 53 and 54 EEA—the NCA's and ESA's infringement decisions have concerned either abuse of dominance or horizontal collusion. Although the NCA's enforcement priority seems to be horizontal cooperation agreements, its outspoken goal is to also intensify its enforcement of abuse of dominance cases. In this regard, on December 4, 2012, the NCA announced that the NCA and ESA conducted joint and unannounced inspections at the Norwegian telecom-incumbent Telenor's premises. The investigation is ongoing. **30.13**

A. Predatory pricing

As with other forms of abusive conduct, EU case law should generally be relied upon when establishing the legal principles for assessing predation cases under s. 11 of the Competition Act and article 54 EEA. **30.14**

The NCA has only decided one predatory pricing case pursuant to s. 11. In 2005, the NCA fined the airline company SAS NOK 20 million for predatory pricing on the domestic **30.15** route Oslo-Haugesund route in the period May and June 2004.[2] The NCA's infringement decision was subsequently annulled by Oslo City Court.[3] Even though the court referred to the "*AKZO*-test" for predation as set out by the Court of Justice of the European Union (CJEU),[4] the court nevertheless did not apply the test criteria to the facts of the case. Instead, the court came to the conclusion that, *even presuming that SAS had failed the AKZO-test,* its pricing practice would nevertheless be justified, *inter alia*, due to SAS's centrally controlled pricing policy, its adaptation to the prevailing market conditions, and to the fact that its prices did not undercut the competitor's prices. The court's interpretation and application of s. 11 in this respect is questionable, given the objective of interpreting the Norwegian antitrust rules in line with EU/EEA antitrust law and practice. The NCA brought an appeal before Borgarting Court of Appeals, but the NCA withdrew the appeal after conducting a renewed assessment of the case whereby the initial decision was reversed. The NCA's new decision maintained that SAS had infringed s. 11, but did not impose a fine.[5]

30.16 ESA has never made any decisions on predatory pricing.

B. Exploitative offenses (excessive pricing, monopoly leveraging)

30.17 Neither the NCA nor ESA has decided any cases on exploitative offenses. As the substantive content of the prohibitions on abuse of dominance is generally harmonized with EU antitrust law, exploitative abuses of dominance are also covered by s. 11 and article 54 EEA. The NCA's and ESA's enforcement activity to date may possibly be taken to indicate a priority of exclusionary over exploitative conduct.

C. Monopsony

30.18 There are no decisions where the NCA or ESA have found an abuse of monopsony purchasing/buying power. On January 14, 2013, however, the NCA announced that it would investigate an agreement between NorgesGruppen and ICA—two of the four largest grocery chains in Norway—concerning joint purchasing and distribution allegedly having the effect of increasing NorgesGruppen's purchasing power. On April 19, 2013, the NCA decided to temporarily suspend the cooperation between the two grocery chains while the case is under investigation.[6] On July 8, 2013, the Ministry (partially) upheld the NCA's decision. The Ministry found that the conditions for ordering an interim suspension were satisfied only with regard to joint distribution, and not with regard to joint purchasing.[7] The NCA's investigation is ongoing.

D. Price discrimination

30.19 There are no decisions, neither from the NCA nor ESA, finding an abuse of dominance due to price discrimination. The NCA's enforcement history may indicate that pure secondary line price discrimination is generally not an enforcement priority, at least unless appreciable anticompetitive effects can be demonstrated. In line with the case law of the CJEU, it cannot, however, be excluded that the NCA may apply s. 11 to for example rebate systems that are both exclusionary and discriminatory, and thus find an abuse of dominance on several

---

[2] *SAS*, NCA Decision no. V2005-9 (June 6, 2005).
[3] *SAS v. NCA*, Oslo City Court decision no. 05-111347TVI-OTIR/06, (July 26, 2006).
[4] Case 62/86 *AKZO Chemie v. Commission* [1991] ECR I-3359.
[5] *SAS*, NCA Decision no. V2007-28 (December 7, 2007).
[6] *ICA/NorgesGruppen*, NCA Decision no. V2013-6 (April 19, 2013).
[7] *ICA/NorgesGruppen*, Decision by the Ministry of Government Administration, Reform and Church Affairs (July 8, 2013).

separate grounds. Price discrimination on the basis of nationality, or in conjunction with practices that limit trade between the Contracting Parties of the EEA Agreement, may well be an enforcement priority for ESA.

E. Dictating or influencing resale prices

To date, neither the NCA nor ESA has decided any cases concerning resale price maintenance (RPM) or minimum advertised price (MAP) programs. Such restrictions will generally be dealt with under s. 10 of the Competition Act or article 53 EEA, pursuant to the same principles as under article 101 TFEU. **30.20**

Agreements or concerted practices having as their direct or indirect object the establishment of a fixed or minimum resale price or price level are considered "hard core" restrictions, and will not be covered by the applicable block exemption regulations on Vertical Restraints. A requirement that the distributor shall not advertise below a certain price level will likely be considered as having the indirect object the establishment of a minimum or fixed resale price. **30.21**

RPM and MAP programs will generally be considered restrictive of competition by their very "object," and thus contrary to s. 10 (1) of the Competition Act and article 53(1) EEA. Furthermore, such restrictions will, normally, not be considered as satisfying the conditions in the exception set out in s. 10 (3) of the Competition Act and article 53 (3) EEA. Generally, such restrictions are considered among the most serious vertical infringements, and may entail severe fines. **30.22**

F. Tying arrangements

There have been no decisions concerning tying arrangements pursuant to the Competition Act and the competition rules in the EEA Agreement. The application of the prohibitions found in the Competition Act and the EEA Agreement to tying arrangements are likely to correspond to the application of the equivalent prohibitions in the TFEU. **30.23**

G. Exclusive dealing

There have been several decisions concerning contractual or *de facto* exclusive dealing, both from the NCA and from ESA. **30.24**

In 2007, the NCA fined Norwegian dairy product producer Tine NOK 45 million (approx. EUR 5.7 million) for violating ss. 10 and 11 of the Competition Act.[8] According to the NCA, Tine in its negotiations with food store chain REMA 1000 in 2004, achieved a position as sole supplier of certain cheese products, *inter alia*, as a result of granting additional discounts, which effectively lead to the exclusion of Tine's sole competitor Synnøve Finden from REMA 1000's grocery stores. The NCA also held that Tine, in the same time period, had attempted to achieve a position as sole supplier to another large food store chain (ICA Norge AS). **30.25**

Tine brought the case before Oslo City Court, which annulled the NCA's decision,[9] finding that Tine had not granted rebates in return for exclusivity, and that the decision to remove Synnøve Finden from its assortment was REMA 1000's unilateral choice. Upon appeal, however, Borgarting Court of Appeals held that Tine's unilateral conduct during its negotiations with REMA 1000 amounted to an abuse of dominance, but did not find Tine guilty of any illegal behavior during its negotiations with ICA Norge AS or any infringement of s. 10 of **30.26**

[8] *Tine*, NCA Decision no. V2007-2 (February 19, 2007).

[9] *Tine v. NCA*, Oslo City Ct no. 07-063120TVI/OTIR/07 (March 25, 2009).

the Competition Act.[10] The fine was set at NOK 30 million (approx. EUR 4.3 million). Tine appealed to the Supreme Court, whereby the court's majority (3:2) finally acquitted Tine of any illegal behavior and confirmed the judgment by Oslo City Court.[11] The Supreme Court's majority vote on the interpretation of s. 11 is generally in line EU/EEA antitrust law. The Supreme Court's minority vote, as well as the judgments in the lower courts, nevertheless illustrate that both the NCA and the Norwegian court system, in some cases, have difficulties maintaining a consistent interpretation and application of Norwegian antitrust law with the corresponding EU/EEA rules and practice.

30.27 ESA's two decisions regarding infringements of EEA competition law so far both concern exclusivity agreements/agreements having similar effect as exclusivity provisions.

30.28 In *Norway Post/Privpak*, ESA imposed a EUR 12.89 million fine on Posten Norge AS.[12] ESA concluded that Posten Norge AS had infringed article 54 of the EEA Agreement by abusing its dominant position in the market for B-C parcel services with over-the-counter delivery in Norway between 2000 and 2006. Posten Norge AS is the national postal operator in Norway and the leading provider of parcel delivery services. ESA found that Posten Norge AS had entered into exclusivity agreements with certain retail groups and outlets (grocery stores, kiosks and petrol stations) for the establishment of a Post-in-Shop network, and that these agreements foreclosed other suppliers of parcel delivery services from establishing a competing delivery network. Posten Norge AS subsequently brought an action for the annulment of ESA's decision before the EFTA Court. The EFTA Court upheld the finding of an infringement, but reduced the fine to EUR 11.112 million as the duration of ESA's investigation had been excessively long.[13] The EFTA Court set out a standard for the application of article 54 EEA according to which "it is sufficient to show that the abusive conduct of the undertaking in a dominant position tends to restrict competition or, in other words, that the conduct is capable of or liable to having that effect" (para. 477).

30.29 In December 2011, ESA issued a decision in the *Color Line* case, concerning ferry operator Color Line's short haul passenger ferry services with tax-free sales between Sandefjord in Norway and Strömstad in Sweden. ESA held that Color Line's long-term exclusive harbour agreements with the Municipality of Strömstad infringed articles 53 and 54 EEA, and imposed a fine of EUR 18.811 million.[14] Color Line did not challenge the decision before the EFTA Court.

30.30 In its decisions against Norway Post and Color Line, ESA has applied a relatively weak standard of likelihood when assessing effects under article 54. According to ESA, it is sufficient to demonstrate that the practice in question "tends to" or is "capable of or liable to" restrict competition. ESA does not consider itself restricted by the more rigorous standard of economic analysis described in the European Commission's Guidance on its enforcement priorities when applying the prohibition on abuse of dominance to exclusionary conduct.

H. Refusal to deal

30.31 There have been no enforcement decisions from the NCA or ESA concerning refusals to deal. Section 11 of the Competition Act and article 54 EEA will generally be interpreted in line with article 102 TFEU also with regard to refusals to deal.

---

[10] *NCA v. Tine*, Borgarting Court of Appeals no. 09-089085ASD-BORG/02 (September 7, 2010).

[11] *Tine v. NCA*, Supreme Court, Rt. 2011 s. 910 (June 22, 2011).

[12] *Norway Post/Privak*, ESA Case no. 34250 (July 14, 2010).

[13] Case E-15/10 *Posten Norge AS v. EFTA Surveillance Authority* (April 18, 2012).

[14] *Color Line*, ESA Case no. 59120 (December 14, 2011).

I. Essential facilities

The NCA and ESA have not decided any cases concerning essential facilities. 30.32

J. Bundling (including loyalty and market share discounts)

Neither the NCA nor ESA has made any infringement decisions concerning bundling 30.33 of two or more different products. The NCA, however, has decided one case concerning loyalty rebates, when it ordered bus company Nettbuss Sør AS to stop offering return ticket discounts and so-called "customer card-rebates" on its express buses serving the route between Oslo and Kristiansand due to the rebates' alleged loyalty-inducing incentives leading to a foreclosure effect on competition.[15] Nettbuss Sør AS complained, and in a subsequent decision, the NCA repealed its initial decisionafter having conducted a new assessment finding that the rebates in question did not qualify as abusive conduct because they did not have loyalty-inducing or foreclosure effects.[16] The NCA's initial decision, being the first decision subsequent to the entry into force of the Competition Act (2004), which adopted prohibitions equivalent to those found in EU/EEA antitrust law, was based on a misinterpretation and misapplication of the prohibition on abuse of dominance to loyalty rebates.

K. Standard-setting groups

There have been no enforcement decisions from the NCA or ESA concerning standard- 30.34 setting groups. Standard setting may raise antitrust issues under both s. 10/article 53 EEA and s. 11/article 54 EEA. In a specific case, ESA and the NCA will likely follow the principles set out in the case law of the CJEU, in the European Commission's decisional practice, and in the European Commission's and ESA's equivalent to EU Horizontal Cooperation Guidelines.[17]

L. Customer termination

Customer termination may constitute an infringement of s. 11 of the Competition Act and/ 30.35 or article 54 EEA. Customer termination may be classified as a form of refusal to deal/essential facilities in so far as the dominant firm and the customer are competitors on the downstream market. Depending on the circumstances, customer termination may also be used as a means to induce exclusivity, to discriminate between various customers, restrict cross-border trade or as a threat or sanction to achieve other forms of anticompetitive behavior such as RPM or absolute territorial protection. To date, neither the NCA nor ESA has decided any cases concerning customer termination.

M. Termination of intermediaries (retailers, wholesalers, dealers, and value-added resellers, agents, and brokers)

Termination of intermediaries may create similar antitrust issues as customer termination. 30.36 In so far as termination is used as a sanction or a threat to enforce a form of anticompetitive practice, it will generally be considered contrary to the competition rules. There have been no decisions by the NCA or ESA concerning termination of intermediaries.

[15] *Nettbuss Sør*, NCA Decision no. V2004-29 (July 19, 2004).
[16] *Nettbus Sør*, NCA Decision no. V2004-34 (December 22, 2004).
[17] Guidelines on the applicability of Article 101 of the Treaty on the Functioning of the European Union to horizontal co-operation agreements, OJ C 11, January 14, 2011 ("Horizontal Cooperation Guidelines").

N. Termination of relationships with competitors

30.37 Termination of relationship with competitors may constitute an abusive refusal to deal/essential facilities under s. 11 or article 54 EEA. As mentioned above, terminating or threatening to terminate a relationship may, depending on the circumstances, also be used as a means of enforcing, threatening, or inducing various other forms of potentially anticompetitive conduct. To date, there have been no decisions by the NCA or ESA concerning termination of relationships with competitors.

O. Exemptions

30.38 The wording of s. 11 of the Competition Act and article 54 EEA does not contain any exemptions. In line with the case law pursuant to article 102 TFEU, however, *prima facie* abusive conduct may nevertheless, and subject to a proportionality test, be "objectively justified." It is for the dominant undertaking to put forward evidence showing that its conduct was objectively justified and therefore legitimate. Such a justification may, *inter alia*, relate to countervailing efficiencies. The proportionality test may, in practice, represent a difficult burden to overcome for dominant undertakings that have engaged in *prima facie* illegal conduct.

30.39 Section 10 of the Competition Act and article 53 EEA only apply to agreements that have an "*appreciable*" effect on competition. ESA has issued a notice on agreements of minor importance (*de minimis*) which is equivalent to the European Commission's notice on the same subject matter. The NCA will generally look to the *de minimis* notice when applying s. 10.

30.40 Section 10(3) of the Competition Act and article 53(3) EEA contain exception rules equivalent to article 101(3) TFEU. An individual exemption requires that (i) the agreement in question contribute to improving the production or distribution of goods or contribute to promoting technical or economic progress; (ii) consumers receive a fair share of the resulting benefits; (iii) the restrictions be indispensable to the attainment of these objectives; and (iv) the agreement afford the parties no possibility of eliminating competition in respect of a substantial part of the products in question. Block exemptions that set out what is covered by s. 10(3) and article 53(3) have been issued, which correspond to the block exemption regulations concerning the application of article 101(3) TFEU.

II. Dealing with competitors

30.41 The first paragraph of s. 10 prohibits all agreements between undertakings, decisions by associations of undertakings and concerted practices which have as their object or effect the prevention, restriction or distortion of competition. The prohibition corresponds to article 53 EEA and article 101 TFEU.

30.42 Pursuant to second paragraph of the provision, any agreements prohibited by s. 10 and article 53 EEA shall be automatically void. The third paragraph of s. 10 and article 53 EEA contains an exception rule, which applies where it is demonstrated that the agreement brings about countervailing efficiencies in an individual case or where the agreement is covered by a block exemption.

30.43 In line with the interpretation of article 101 TFEU, collusion between competitors in the form of price fixing, market sharing, bid-rigging, output restrictions, as well as other forms of obviously anticompetitive practices, are generally considered infringements by "object" within the meaning of s. 10 and article 53 EEA, and will, in most cases, not benefit from an exception. Such practices will normally be treated as serious infringements and receive the strictest sanctions. Other forms of cooperation among competitors may, depending on the circumstances and the concrete effects, be either legitimate or illegal.

There have been no decisions by ESA concerning collusion among competitors contrary to article 53 EEA. A plausible explanation is that larger cartels, where trade between EU member states is affected, are generally handled by the European Commission pursuant to article 56 EEA, while illegal collusion confined to the EEA / EFTA-states is investigated and sanctioned by the respective national competition authorities. **30.44**

A. Horizontal price fixing

Horizontal price fixing agreements or arrangements will generally be considered among the most serious antitrust infringements. Since the entry into force of the Competition Act, in 2004, the NCA has not, however, sanctioned any large price-fixing cartels. **30.45**

In 2008, the NCA imposed fines on plumbing companies Oslo VVS (NOK 500,000) and Håkonrune Rør (NOK 250,000) for illegal bid-rigging, in breach of s. 10, in relation to parties submitting separate bids in a tender process for the renovation of a sheltered housing project in Oslo in 2006.[18] The NCA found that the infringing parties had coordinated their bid prices, evidence of which included the fact that Oslo VVS consistently, and on all separate parts of the tender contract, priced its bid exactly seven percent higher than Håkonrune Rør. **30.46**

With regard to advanced price announcements, it may be noted that the NCA, in its contribution to the Organisation for Economic Co-operation and Developmetn (OECD) Roundtable on Unilateral Disclosure of Information with Anticompetitive Effects (2012), expressed its concern that "the scope of legal unilateral information exchange is not clear.... [T]here can be considerable uncertainty with regard to when a unilateral information exchange can be considered to be a violation of the competition act."[19] In its contribution to the OECD report, the NCA appears to distinguish between announcements of pricing intentions and announcements on binding future price changes, the former being more likely of constituting a violation of the prohibition. **30.47**

B. Horizontal agreements to allocate customers or territories; agreements not to compete

As with horizontal price fixing arrangements, horizontal agreements to allocate customers or territories, and agreements not to compete, are generally considered serious antitrust infringements. **30.48**

In two related decisions, the NCA fined Borregaard and Brenntag NOK 1.6 million (approx. EUR 205,000) and 1.3 million (approx. EUR 166,000) respectively, for sharing the market for technical acetic acid infringing s. 10 and article 53 EEA, during the period from October 1, 2002 to at least April 26, 2006.[20] Jointly, Borregaard and Brenntag controlled almost the entire market for technical acetic acid in Norway. The illegitimate cooperation consisted in an agreement whereby Borregaard would sell acetic acid only in bulk to customers requesting large quantities, while Brenntag would sell acetic acid only to customers requesting smaller quantities, thereby allocating various customer groups between the parties. Borregaard was awarded the larger fine, primarily due to its higher overall turnover on the relevant market. **30.49**

The extent to which the moderate level of fines in the NCA's decisions against Borregaard and Brenntag achieves a sufficient punitive and deterrent effect may be questioned due to the undertakings' substantial overall turnover. In a recent decision, however, the NCA adopted a much more offensive fining policy for a market sharing arrangement. **30.50**

---

[18] *Håkonrune Rør AS og Oslo VVS*, NCA Decision no. V2008-18 (November 19, 2008).

[19] OECD, Policy Roundtables, Unilateral Disclosure of Information with Anticompetitive Effects (2012), p. 146 <http://www.oecd.org/competition/cartels/48379006.pdf>.

[20] *Borregaard Industries Limited*, NCA Decision no. V2008-4 (February 28, 2008) and Brenntag Nordic AS, NCA Decision no. V2008-5 (March 14, 2008).

30.51 In October 2010, the NCA issued a preliminary notification announcing that it had uncovered extensive collusion and bid-rigging between the undertakings Veidekke and NCC, in relation to procurement contracts for asphalt paving between 2005 and 2008. According to the NCA's preliminary view, the two companies had divided large public contracts between themselves and also shared competitively sensitive information in relation to tender competitions. On March 4, 2013, the NCA announced that Veidekke and NCC were fined NOK 220 million (approx. EUR 29 million) and 140 million (approx. EUR 19 million), respectively, for infringements of the prohibition of anticompetitive agreements.[21] As Veidekke had applied for leniency, the undertaking received immunity. The fines are, by far, the largest fines ever imposed by the NCA. NCC has decided to challenge the NCA's decision in court and the case is currently pending.

C. Horizontal boycotts

30.52 Neither the NCA nor the ESA has decided any cases concerning horizontal group boycotts. Horizontal boycotts aimed at reinforcing the implementation of a cartel, for example by refusing to supply customers that purchase goods or services from non-cartel members, or horizontal boycotts designed to exclude competitors from a downstream market by restricting supply of an essential input, will generally be considered contrary to s. 10 and article 53 EEA.

D. Joint ventures and other competitive collaborations

30.53 Jointly controlled full-function joint ventures are considered under the merger control rules. Other forms of joint ventures and competitive collaborations are analyzed under s. 10 of the Competition Act and article 53 EEA, pursuant to the same principles as under article 101 TFEU.

30.54 The NCA has decided several cases concerning joint ventures and other competitive collaborations. In a 2007 decision, the NCA ordered two bus companies, Tide Reiser AS and Veolia Transport Sør AS, to discontinue their collaboration on the express bus "Kystbussen" serving the route between Bergen and Stavanger.[22] In May 2012, however, the Ministry set aside the NCA's decision due to both a finding of anticompetitive effects less adverse and efficiencies larger than what the NCA had considered.[23] The NCA *Taxi Midt-Norge AS* decision concerned an umbrella association for the holders of taxi driving permits in Trøndelag County that had submitted a bid for a tender competition for the purchase of patient transport services by a public health undertaking. The NCA held that the submission of a joint bid on behalf of all the holders of taxi permits was contrary to s. 10. The association incurred a fine of NOK 300,000 (approx. 38,000 EUR).[24] In a similar case, *Ski Follo Taxi*, the NCA held that Ski Follo Taxidrift AS, a company jointly owned by the two competing taxi companies Ski Taxi BA and Follo Taxisentral BA, violated s. 10 by submitting a single joint bid in two tender competitions concerning patient transport services in 2010. Ski Follo Taxidrift AS was fined NOK 2.2 million (approx. EUR 282,000), while Follo Taxisentral BA and Ski Taxi BA received respective fines of NOK 400,000 (approx. 51,000 EUR) and NOK 250,000 (approx. EUR 32,000).[25] The taxi companies brought the NCA's decision before Follo District Court, which annulled the NCA's decision in its judgment from February 8,

---

[21] *VeidekkeASA / VeidekkeIndustri AS and NCC AB / NCC RoadsAS*, NCA Decision no. V2013-3 (March 4, 2013).

[22] *Tide Reiser AS / Veolia Transport Sør AS*, NCA Decision no. V2007-9 (May 15, 2007).

[23] Decision by the Ministry of Government Administration, Reform and Church Affairs (May 4, 2013).

[24] *Taxi Midt-Norge AS*, NCA Decision no. V2009-7 (March 13, 2009).

[25] *Ski Taxi BA, Follo Taxisentral BA and Ski Follo Taxidrift AS*, NCA Decision no. V2011-12 (July 4, 2011).

2013.[26] With regard to the first tender, the court found that the parties were neither actual nor potential competitors as one of the parties lacked the necessary capacity to fulfill the contract unilaterally. With regard to the second tender, the court surprisingly acknowledged that, while the cooperation was restrictive of competition, the effect was negligible and not appreciable. The NCA has appealed, and the case is pending before Borgarting Court of Appeals.

As a general observation, the NCA in its decisions concerning joint ventures between competitors has applied a broad concept of restricting competition by "object," alleviating the NCA of the need to conduct more comprehensive analyses of effects. Contrary to what appears to be the NCA's view, however, the "object" category should arguably be reserved for more obvious restrictions of competition, while cooperative joint ventures and competitive collaborations involving the integration of the involved undertakings' respective resources should generally be considered infringements only where appreciable anticompetitive effects have been demonstrated. **30.55**

E. Trade associations

Membership and participation in a trade association are not, by themselves, contrary to the antitrust rules. Such associations may, in certain cases, nevertheless function as a vehicle for illegal practices among competitors, for example in the form of exchange of competitively sensitive information, facilitation of cartel cooperation or in the form of issuing anticompetitive decisions. **30.56**

In a decision from June 2009, the NCA imposed a NOK 400,000 (approx. EUR 51,000) fine on Norges Turbileierforbund (a trade association for Norwegian tour bus companies) for repeatedly having encouraged its members to increase the price of their services in a printed bulletin. The trade association had also distributed to its members a standard model for calculating prices. The NCA rejected arguments that the trade association's printed statements were protected by the Norwegian Constitution's and the European Convention on Human Right's rules on freedom of expression.[27] The NCA's decision was upheld by Oslo City Court. An appeal was withdrawn after the NCA accepted a reduction of the fine due to the trade association's inability to pay the full amount. Article 23(4) of EC Council Regulation 1/2003,[28] explicitly regulates the liability of the members of a trade association in a situation where the trade association itself is not solvent. In contrast, there are no explicit equivalent rules under Norwegian competition law. **30.57**

F. Interlocking directorates

Neither the NCA nor the ESA has decided any cases finding an infringement of s. 10 or article 53 EEA on the grounds of interlocking directorates. The exchange of commercially sensitive information between competitors, also in the context of interlocking directorates, may, however, constitute an infringement of s. 10, as well as article 53 EEA. Interlocking directorates may also constitute a basis for establishing collective dominance pursuant to s. 11 and article 54 EEA. **30.58**

It may be noted that the committee responsible for the report on "More efficient competition act"[29] briefly considered the pros and cons of prohibiting interlocking directorates in **30.59**

[26] *Ski Taxi BA, Follo Taxisentral BA and Ski Follo Taxidrift AS* v. *NCA*, Follo District Court Case no. 11-202508TVI-FOLL (February 8, 2013).

[27] *Norges Turbileierforbund*, NCA Decision no. V2009-15 (June 30, 2006).

[28] Council Regulation (EC) No. 1/2003 on the implementation of the rules on competition laid down in Articles [101 and 102 TFEU].

[29] More Efficient Competition Act (n. 1).

competing undertakings. The committee did not, however, propose any explicit regulation of the subject matter, *inter alia* considering DG Comp's announced intention to conduct a study on the economic importance of minority shareholdings.

G. Facilitating practices

30.60 The NCA has not issued any infringement decisions concerning facilitating practices. In 2007, however, the NCA investigated a possible infringement of s. 10 of the Competition Act by market analysis company AC Nielsen Norge AS which conducted weekly distribution of detailed price and volume information among the largest Norwegian food store chains. The NCA considered that the practice was likely restrictive of competition and illegal. As a response to the NCA's investigation, AC Nielsen Norge AS and the food chains agreed to alter the arrangement to alleviate the NCA's competition concerns. The NCA therefore closed its investigation without adopting a final decision.

30.61 In line with the case law on the interpretation of article 101 TFEU, an undertaking may be liable as a co-perpetrator, for example as a facilitator, of an infringement of s. 10 and article 53 EEA, even if the undertaking is not by itself active on the relevant market.

H. Information exchange

30.62 The exchange of commercially sensitive information among competitors may, in line with the case law of the CJEU, constitute an infringement of s. 10 of the Competition Act and article 53 EEA. The exchange of information on future prices and quantities will generally be considered an infringement by its very "object."

30.63 In a 2009 decision, the NCA found that two entrepreneurs, Grunnarbeid and Gran & Ekran, had exchanged prices and information prior to submitting separate bids for a tender competition concerning the repair/rehabilitation of five bridges in Trøndelag County. The NCA imposed fines of NOK 5 million (approx. EUR 640,000) on Grunnarbeid and NOK 2 million (approx. EUR 250,000) on Gran & Ekran for violating s. 10.[30] Prior to submitting separate bids, the undertakings had agreed on a reciprocal subcontracting arrangement. The NCA held that the parties had a common understanding that Gran & Ekran should submit a cover bid without having the intention of winning the tender contest.

30.64 The parties brought the NCA's decision before Sør-Trøndelag District Court, which upheld the NCA's finding of infringement as well as the level of fines.[31] Upon appeal, however, Frostating Court of Appeals upheld the finding of infringement, but found that the infringement was only negligent, and not intentional.[32] Subsequently, the Supreme Court, in a unanimous vote, found the undertakings guilty of an intentional infringement.[33] The judgment also clarified that a qualified standard of proof applies to the NCA's decisions imposing fines, although the standard is not as high as in criminal cases.

30.65 In *IcopalTak AS—Fløysand Tak AS*, the NCA held that two roofing companies had violated s. 10 of the Competition Act by exchanging pricing information in relation to a tender competition for the roofing of a Norwegian military building.[34] Two days before the closing date for submitting bids, Fløysand Tak sent an e-mail to IcopalTak with an attachment containing

[30] *Gran & Ekran AS og Grunnarbeid AS*, NCA Decision no. V2009-17 (July 13, 2009).

[31] *Gran & Ekran AS and Grunnarbeid AS v. NCA*, Sør-Trøndelag District Court Case no. 09-143089TVI-STOR (June 2, 2010).

[32] *Gran & Ekran AS and Grunnarbeid AS v. NCA*, Frostating Court of Appeals Case no. 10-139398ASD-FRO (December 8, 2011).

[33] *NCA v. Gran & Ekran AS*, Supreme Court no. HR-2012-01942-A (October 11, 2012)

[34] *IcopalTak AS / Fløysand Tak AS*, NCA Decision no. V2011-11 (June 30, 2011).

both Fløysand Tak's unit prices as well as its total price for the project. A printed copy of the e-mail and the documents attached was later discovered by the NCA in IcopalTak's files. Based on this single piece of evidence, the NCA established an infringement. As a result of a successful leniency application, IcopalTak was granted immunity from fines, while Fløysand Tak received a fine of NOK 350,000 (approx. EUR 45,000). The decision marked the first successful leniency application in Norway.

With regard to the exchange of historic, anonymous and aggregated pricing information, the NCA and ESA will likely follow the European Commission's and ESA's approaches to information exchange as set out in their respective Horizontal Cooperation Guidelines. **30.66**

In a pre-merger due diligence situation, prior to the NCA having cleared a notifiable concentration, the undertakings involved should be careful not to exchange commercially sensitive information, in particular if they are actual or potential competitors. Such information exchange may be contrary to the prohibition on anticompetitive cooperation. The undertakings involved should therefore not exchange more information than necessary for the due diligence process. In some transactions it may be advisable develop mechanisms or impose confidentiality obligations or "clean teams" to restrict access to and prevent distribution of sensitive information that may be exploited for anticompetitive purposes. **30.67**

I. Joint purchasing agreements

Neither the NCA nor ESA has decided any cases concerning joint purchasing agreements. Joint purchasing arrangements will, however, be contrary by s. 10 and article 53 EEA, where the arrangement functions as a disguise for cartel activity, where the joint purchasing agreement involves the exchange of commercially sensitive information or where the arrangement otherwise produces anticompetitive effects. The NCA and ESA will generally follow the analytical principles set out in the European Commission's and ESA's Horizontal Cooperation Guidelines, which also deals with purchasing agreements. **30.68**

J. Joint lobbying/regulatory/legislative efforts

Joint lobbying or joint regulatory or legislative efforts is generally legitimate under Norwegian and EU/EEA competition law. The undertakings involved should, however, make sure that such cooperation does not involve the exchange of commercially sensitive information or other forms of anticompetitive collusion. **30.69**

III. General issues

A. Jurisdiction and applicable law (including sector-specific competition regulation)

Pursuant to s. 5, the Competition Act applies to terms of business, agreements, and actions that are undertaken, have effect, or are liable to have effect within the Kingdom of Norway. **30.70**

Section 3 states that the Competition Act does not apply to terms and conditions relating to work and employment. The exemption primarily aims to exclude collective labor agreements from the scope of the prohibitions in ss. 10 and 11. Pursuant to s. 3, three regulations have been issued that exempt certain forms of cooperation: (a) within the agriculture and fishing sectors; (b) in book sales; and (c) among doctors, psychologists, and physiotherapists. **30.71**

Pursuant to s. 14, the King (in Council) may, if necessary to promote competition in the markets, by regulation intervene against terms of business, agreements, or actions that restrict or are liable to restrict competition contrary to the purpose of the Competition Act. Two **30.72** regulations have been issued: one prohibiting bonus systems on domestic air travels and one requiring undertakings offering internet real estate advertising services to give non-discriminatory access to third parties. The regulation prohibiting bonus systems on domestic air travels was repealed May 16, 2013.

30.73 Several sectors of the Norwegian economy are subject to specific regulation, i.e. postal services, telecommunication services, the sale, marketing and distribution of pharmaceuticals, the energy sector, and the sale and marketing of alcohol. The list is not exhaustive.

30.74 Articles 53 and 54 EEA are subject to a jurisdictional criterion, and are only applicable to agreements and unilateral conduct by dominant firms that "may affect trade between Contracting Parties." In line with the case law of the EU Courts concerning articles 101 and 102 TFEU, the concept of effect on trade is given a broad interpretation. The ESA has published Guidelines regarding the concept of effect on trade in articles 53 and 54 EEA that describe principles and methodology for the interpretation and application of the effect on trade concept. The EEA Agreement generally does not cover common agricultural and fisheries policies.

B. Antitrust system

(i) Name of agency/agencies

30.75 The competition authorities in Norway are the King (in Council), the Ministry (currently the Ministry of Government Administration, Reform and Church Affairs. From January 1, 2014, the Ministry of Trade and Industry will take over responsibility for competition policy.), and the Competition Authority (*Konkurransetilsynet*, NCA).

30.76 The NCA may not be instructed as to decisions in individual cases. The King may, however, order the NCA to deal with a case. The Ministry may reverse decisions by the NCA if they are invalid, even if the decision has not been appealed. Decisions involving administrative fines must, however, be brought before ordinary courts.

30.77 The NCA is given the task of supervising competition in various markets, and among other things: ensuring adherence to the prohibitions and orders of the Competition Act; intervening where necessary against concentrations; implementing measures to promote market transparency; enforcing articles 53 and 54 of the EEA Agreement; and calling attention to any restrictive effects on competition of public measures.

30.78 The EFTA Surveillance Authority (ESA), in conjunction with the European Commission and National Competition Authorities, enforces the competition rules in the EEA Agreement. ESA has equivalent powers and similar functions to those of the European Commission.

(ii) Staff size and budget

30.79 The NCA has approximately one hundred employees. Its budget for 2013 was NOK 96 million (approx. EUR 11.6 million).

30.80 ESA has sixty-eight employees in 2012, whereas approximately seven are dedicated to competition issues. ESA's total budget for 2013 was EUR 12.7 million.

(iii) Recent enforcement actions and trends

30.81 The NCA has, in the past, decided relatively few cases finding infringements of the applicable antitrust rules. Since the entry into force of the Competition Act in 2004, the NCA has decided three s. 11 cases, the most recent in 2007. Of the three decisions, one was repealed;[35]

[35] See *Nettbus Sør* (n 16).

one was annulled by the court before the NCA revised its initial decision and decided not to impose a fine;[36] and one was finally annulled by the Supreme Court.[37] Consequently, no legally binding fines have so far been imposed by the NCA for s. 11 infringements. With regard to s. 10, the NCA has issued nine infringement decisions since 2004. The largest fines imposed for a horizontal infringement of s. 10 (bid rigging) was in the *Asphalt-cartel* case, where the fines were calculated to NOK 220 million (approx. EUR 29 million) and 140 million (approx. EUR 19 million), to Veidekke and NCC for collusion in relation to procurement contracts for asphalt paving.[38]

The NCA's decisions to date cover both horizontal and vertical agreements and abuse of dominance cases. The undertakings involved have been active in various sectors of the economy. Although the NCA's decisional practice is relatively limited, two general trends deserve to be mentioned. First, the level of fines imposed by the NCA has, so far, been moderate, at least in absolute amounts and as compared to the level of fines imposed by the European Commission. This may, in most cases, largely be explained by the involved undertakings' modest turnover. A cautious fining policy on the part of the NCA may, however, also have been a contributing factor in this regard. As of January 1, 2012, however, a new Regulation on the calculation of fines entered into force. An outspoken objective has been to increase the level of fines to the level of fines adopted by the European Commission. The Regulation has therefore adopted the European Commission's method of setting fines. The NCA's decision in the *Asphalt-cartel* case of March 5, 2013 strongly suggests that higher fines for competition law infringements can be expected.[39] Second, the NCA has, since 2010, experienced an increase in the number of leniency applications received. Even though the leniency institute has been in force since 2004, the first successful leniency application was approved as late as 2011. Since 2008, the NCA has received around fifteen leniency applications. It may be expected that the increase in the number of leniency applications will ultimately result in an increase also in the number of infringement decisions under s. 10. Looking beyond the NCA's decisional practice, the NCA has adopted certain surveillance and reporting systems in the dairy product, grocery and electricity sectors. **30.82**

ESA, on its part, appears to have increased its enforcement activities in recent years. Until 2010, ESA had not decided any infringement cases concerning articles 53 and 54 EEA. The two decisions from 2010 and 2011, where ESA imposed substantive fines,[40] show that ESA is prepared to investigate difficult cases, and that it will impose fines comparable to those imposed by the European Commission. **30.83**

C. Private litigation

To date, the Competition Act and the antitrust rules in the EEA Agreement have predominantly been enforced by the NCA and ESA. That said, private parties may bring various claims for infringements of the competition rules, including damages actions, injunctions, and actions for voidness and unenforceability. **30.84**

---

36 See *SAS* (n 5).

37 See *Tine v. NCA* (n 11).

38 See *VeidekkeASA / VeidekkeIndustri AS* (n 21). Veidekke received leniency/immunity from fines. NCC has decided to challenge the decision in court.

39 See *VeidekkeASA / VeidekkeIndustri AS* (n 21).

40 *Norway Post* (n 12): EUR 12.89 million; *Color Line* (n 14): EUR 18.811 million.

30.85 Recent private antitrust litigation cases from 2011 to 2013[41] include: a judgment by Borgarting Court of Appeal[42] (where the court rejected a claim to apply s. 11 (margin squeeze) of the Competition Act in a contractual dispute over a payment obligation *inter alia* due to insufficient evidence; a judgment by Jæren District Court,[43] where the court rejected the claim that a joint venture agreement was invalid for being contrary to s. 10 of the Competition Act; a judgment by Nedre Romerike District Court[44] where a distributor of magazines was held liable for discriminatory distribution conditions on contractual grounds, whereas a claim that the distributor was liable also on the grounds of an infringement of s. 11 of the Competition Act was rejected because the distributor was not found to have a dominant market position; and a judgment by Agder Court of Appeals[45] where the court held that the exclusive right of the plaintiffs to perform customer transportation on behalf of the defendant, a gravel supplier, was not contrary to s. 10 of the Competition Act. On November 29, 2012, Asker & Bærum District Court delivered its judgment in *Telenor v. Network Norway* concerning the content and validity of an agreement concerning national roaming access to telecom incumbent Telenor's network.[46] Based on an interpretation of the contract, the court rejected Telenor's claim that Network Norway was liable for an additional payment of in excess of NOK 165 million (approx. EUR 22.4 million) for violating the contract's restriction on entering into a national roaming agreement with another national network operator in Norway (the so-called "double roaming restriction"). The court, on the other hand, also rejected Network Norway's counterclaim that the "double roaming restriction" was contrary to s. 11 of the Competition Act. An appeal regarding Agder Court of Appeals' judgment,[47] finding that Hovden ski center's decision to discontinue its business relations with a ski school was contrary to s. 11 of the Competition Act, is currently pending before the Supreme Court. It is worth noting that only one final judgment in a stand-alone private enforcement case has found an infringement of the competition rules.[48]

D. Follow-on litigation

30.86 Probably due to the fact that the NCA and ESA have decided relatively few infringement cases, the Norwegian courts have, so far, not finally decided any follow-on litigation cases. In the wake of recent infringement decisions, as well as the increase in the number of leniency applications received by the NCA potentially leading to even more infringement decisions, it is reasonable to expect an increase also in follow-on antitrust lawsuits.

30.87 The Competition Act does not contain any specific rules on follow-on litigation or damages claims.

30.88 The rules on procedure are set out in the Act Relating to Mediation and Procedure in Civil Disputes.[49]

---

[41] Older cases under the Competition Act (2004) include: *Lynghaug & Lynghaug v. Torget i Bergen AS*, Gulating Court of Appeals, Case no. LG-2004-5524 (2005); *Total Waste Management Alliance Plc v. Thermtech AS*, Gulating Court of Appeals, Case no. LG-2004-10668 (2006); *Lødingen Stenindustri AS* (n 42); *Benair AS v. Oslo Lufthavn AS*, Eidsivating Court of Appeals, Case no. RG 2009 s. 188 (2009); *Meltwater News AS v. Mediebedriftenes Klareringstjeneste AS*, Oslo City Court, Case no. TOSLO-2008-156741 (2009); *Datek Løfteteknikk AS v. Tele Radio AB*, Borgarting Court of Appeals, Case no. LB-2009-202293 (2010).

[42] *CargoNet AS v. Cargolink AS*, Case no. LB-2011-164879 (2013).

[43] *Jærkylling AS v. Nortura SA*, Case 10-068972TVI-JARE (2011).

[44] *MP Media Norge AS v. Interpress AS*, Case 11-007278TVI-NERO (2012).

[45] *Reddal Sand AS v. Asbjørn Kristiansen AS and Olav Lindstøl AS*, Case no. LA-2012-3783 (2012).

[46] *Telenor v. Network Norway*, Case no. 12-051158TVI-AHER/2 (2012).

[47] *Arne Johan Mosfjeld v. Hovden Skisenter AS*, Case no. LA-2012-77094 (2013).

[48] *Lødingen Stenindustri AS* (n 42), finding that an exclusivity clause between two undertakings in the concrete industry was contrary to s. 10 of the Competition Act and art. 53 EEA and therefore void.

[49] Act of June 17, 2005 No. 90 Relating to Mediation and Procedure in Civil Disputes.

With regard to legal standing, Norwegian law requires that "[t]he claimant must show a genuine need to have the claim determined against the defendant." This shall be determined based on a total assessment of the relevance of the claim and the parties' connection to the claim. Depending on the specific circumstances of the case, competitors, suppliers, customers and also indirect customers may have legal standing. **30.89**

Class actions are dealt with in chapter 35 of the Act Relating to Mediation and Procedure in Civil Disputes. Generally, class actions require registration of class members (opt-in). Under certain circumstances, the court can decide that persons that have claims shall be class members without registration, unless they register a withdrawal (opt-out). So far, there have been no class actions for infringements of the antitrust rules in Norway. **30.90**

While infringement decisions by the NCA will not be binding upon the courts, such decisions will generally be given substantial evidential weight when determining whether an infringement has taken place. An infringement will not automatically entail that the undertaking has acted culpable, but will generally be considered sufficient in the absence of exceptional circumstances. **30.91**

Pursuant to s. 8 of the EEA Competition Act, when the courts rule on agreements, decisions or practices under article 53 or article 54 EEA which are already the subject of a decision by ESA, they cannot take decisions running counter to the decision adopted by ESA. They must also avoid giving decisions which would conflict with a decision contemplated by ESA in proceedings it has initiated. **30.92**

The award of damages should in principle correspond to the economic loss suffered by the claimant. Punitive damages are not awarded. Indirect customers will likely face difficulties establishing sufficient proximate cause. A pass-on defense is, in principle, applicable based on the principle *compensation lucri cum damno* (reduction of damages due to unjust enrichment). The burden of adducing evidence that an overcharge has been passed-on will be placed on the injuring party. **30.93**

Damages claims for antitrust infringements are subject to the general limitation period set out in s. 9 of the Act Relating to the Limitation Period for Claims.[50] Pursuant to s. 9, claims for damages are subject to a limitation period of three years from the date on which the injured party obtained, or should have himself acquired, necessary knowledge of the damage and the person responsible. The limitation period may thus expire even while the competition authorities are still investigating the case, unless the claimant takes actions to interrupt the limitation period. Pursuant to the amendments to the Competition Act passed in parliament June 3, 2013, a new s. 34, regarding limitation periods, will enter into force January 1, 2014. Under the new s. 34, claims for damages may, even if the limitation period set out in s. 9 of the Act Relating to the Limitation Period for Claims is expired, be brought by a separate action at law instituted within one year after a final decision or a judgment is *res judicata*. **30.94**

E. Arbitration and alternative dispute resolution

Arbitration may, in certain cases, be preferable to litigation to achieve a swifter, more cost-efficient, confidential resolution by expert judges. Section 9 of the Norwegian Arbitration Act[51] explicitly states that "[t]he private law effects of competition law may be tried by arbitration." The court of arbitration, unlike the ordinary courts, is not in a position to request the EFTA-court to give preliminary rulings on the interpretation of EEA law.[52] **30.95**

[50] Act of May 18, 1979, No. 18 Relating to the Limitation Period for Claims.
[51] The Arbitration Act of May 15, 2005.
[52] Case C-126/97 *Eco Swiss* [1999] ECR I-03055.

F. Remedies

(i) Civil liability

30.96 Pursuant to s. 29 of the Competition Act, an undertaking may be subject to administrative fines by the NCA for intentional or negligent infringements of several provisions in the Competition Act, including s. 10 and 11.

30.97 The NCA both investigates infringements and decides over the administrative fine. Undertakings that receive administrative fines may bring an action against the state to contest the decision. Such actions are dealt with by the ordinary courts, and the court may try all aspects of the matter. The Civil Litigation Act pertains insofar as it is relevant.

30.98 Fines for infringements of s. 10 or s. 11 of the Competition Act cannot be imposed after ten years. The statutory limitation period for other infringements is five years. Such time limits are suspended once the Competition Authority takes steps to secure evidence under s. 25 of the Act or informs an undertaking that it is suspected of infringing the Act or decisions made pursuant to the Act.

30.99 Pursuant to s. 29(3) of the Competition Act, when determining the amount of a fine, particular attention should be paid to the turnover of the undertaking, the gravity and duration of the infringement, and leniency pursuant to s. 31.[53]

30.100 The King may by regulation provide more specific rules as to determining administrative fines. As of January 1, 2012, a new Regulation on the calculation of and leniency from administrative fines entered into force.[54] The methodology set out in the new regulation is based on, and largely corresponds to, the principles set out in the European Commission's Guidelines on the method of setting fines.[55] For infringements of ss. 10 and 11, the maximum fine is 10 percent of the undertaking's annual turnover. In June 2012, the NCA sent draft guidelines on the calculation of and leniency from fines on public hearing. To date, final guidelines have not been published.

30.101 Section 29 of the Competition Act, as well as the Regulation on the calculation of and leniency from fines, apply equivalently when the NCA enforces articles 53 and 54 EEA.

30.102 Pursuant to article 23 of Chapter II in Protocol 4 (on the functions and powers of the EFTA Surveillance Authority in the field of competition) to the Surveillance and Court Agreement, ESA may by decision impose fines on undertakings that intentionally or negligently infringe article 53 or 54 EEA. The fine shall not exceed 10 percent of the undertaking's total turnover in the preceding business year. ESA has published Guidelines on the method of setting fines that correspond to the European Commission's Guidelines on the method of setting fines. The limitation period for the imposition of fines for infringements of articles 53 and 54 EEA is five years.

(ii) Criminal liability

30.103 Pursuant to s. 30[56] of the Competition Act, penal fines, or imprisonment of up to three years, may be imposed on anyone who intentionally or through gross negligence infringes

---

[53] Pursuant to the amendments to the Competition Act passed in parliament June 3, 2013, which will enter into force January 1, 2014, full and partial leniency will be dealt with in ss. 30 and 31 respectively. A new s. 29(3) will therefore refer to both ss. 30 and 31.

[54] FOR-2005-08-22-909 amended by FOR-2011-12-19-1400.

[55] Guidelines on the method of setting fines imposed pursuant to Article 23(2)(A) of Chapter II of Protocol 4 to the Surveillance and Court Agreement, OJ 2006/C 314/12 (2006).

[56] Pursuant to the amendments to the Competition Act passed in parliament June 3, 2013, which will enter into force January 1, 2014, s. 30 will be renumbered s. 32.

several provisions of the Competition Act (including the prohibition on anticompetitive agreements, but *not* the prohibition on abuse of dominance). If an infringement of the prohibition on anticompetitive agreements is made under severely aggravating circumstances, imprisonment of up to six years may be imposed.

Penal fines may under the current rules be imposed on both undertakings and persons. Penal sanctions are imposed by the courts pursuant to the procedures set out in the Criminal Procedure Act (2006). The NCA's role is to investigate the possible infringement and report it to the prosecution authority. To date, neither criminal fines nor prison sentences has been imposed pursuant to s. 30. Pursuant to the amendments to the Competition Act passed in parliament June 3, 2013, which will enter into force January 1, 2014, undertakings will, according to a new s. 32(4), no longer be subject to criminal liability. **30.104**

ESA is not competent to impose imprisonment for competition law infringements of the EEA competition rules. Pursuant to article 23(5) of chapter II in Protocol 4 (on the functions and powers of the EFTA Surveillance Authority in the field of competition) to the Surveillance and Court Agreement, ESA's decisions to impose fines shall not be of a criminal law nature. **30.105**

G. Leniency and immunity

Pursuant to s. 29(2) of the Competition Act, in determining the amount of fines for infringements of s. 10 (prohibition on anticompetitive agreements), consideration shall be given as to whether the undertaking has assisted the competition authorities in the detection of its own infringements or those of others. **30.106**

More detailed rules are set out in the Regulation on the calculation of and leniency from administrative fines.[57] Full leniency will be granted if the undertaking, on its own initiative, is the first to submit evidence that is sufficient to acquire a court order to secure evidence in connection with a possible infringement of s. 10, or prove an infringement of s. 10. Full leniency will only be granted if the NCA is not already in possession of sufficient evidence to acquire a court order or prove an infringement. **30.107**

Full leniency will not be given if the undertaking does not fully cooperate with the NCA's investigation, does not end its participation in the infringement no later than when the evidence is submitted, or had sought to coerce other undertakings to participate in the infringement. Only one undertaking may be granted full leniency for the same infringement. **30.108**

Partial leniency will be granted if the undertaking submits evidence that significantly strengthens the Competition Authority's ability to establish an infringement of s. 10 and ends its participation in the infringement no later than when the evidence is submitted. **30.109**

The leniency program only applies to administrative fines pursuant to s. 29 of the Competition Act, and not to penal sanctions pursuant to s. 30. To attempt to alleviate this potential deficiency in the leniency program, the NCA has published a notice stating that it will not report an undertaking applying for leniency to the prosecution authorities. January 1, 2014, a new s. 33 of the Competition Act will take effect, pursuant to which infringements that may result in criminal liability will only be subject to public prosecution either where the NCA petition for prosecution or where strong public interests so require. **30.110**

[57] FOR-2005-08-22-909 amended by FOR-2011-12-19-1400. Pursuant to the amendments to the Competition Act passed in parliament June 3, 2013, which will enter into force January 1, 2014, full and partial leniency will be dealt with in ss. 30 and 31 respectively.

30.111 ESA has published a Notice on immunity from fines and reduction of fines in cartel cases that sets out the framework for rewarding cooperation in the ESA investigation by undertakings which are or have been party to secret cartels affecting the EEA. The Notice corresponds to the European Commission's Notice on immunity from fines and reduction of fines in cartel cases.

H. Document creation and retention

30.112 Undertakings, including their management and employees, should take great care not to use terms, phrases or language that may create the impression that legitimate competitive behavior may be suspicious or even unlawful pursuant to the competition rules.

30.113 Documentary evidence is routinely used in competition cases, and statements both in internal and external correspondence (e-mails, letters, faxes), notes, minutes, presentations, press releases, etc., may be given considerable or even decisive evidentiary significance—both in public and private enforcement cases.

30.114 Both the NCA and ESA have extensive powers of investigation, and may require information and documentation from undertakings, as well as demand access to and secure evidence from premises, means of transport, and even private homes. They also use sophisticated computer investigation systems to discover electronic evidence. Documents that may shed light over the subject-matter of the investigation will likely be discovered. Unfortunate choice of words may result in prolonged investigation, or even result in otherwise legitimate conduct being considered an infringement of the competition rules.

30.115 The exercise of due care with regard to document creation should include, *inter alia*, keeping records contact with competitors; keeping records of sources of information on competitors' market behavior; avoiding statements indicating an exclusionary motive or objective or suggesting a common intention with competitors; avoiding statements indicating or exaggerating market power; and avoiding statements indicating a particular view on the definition of the relevant market.

30.116 Communications with external legal counsel are generally subject to legal professional privilege protection. With regard to in-house legal counsel, Norwegian and EU/EEA competition law differ. Under Norwegian law, in-house lawyers will be protected by legal privilege protection in so far as the subject matter in question concerns employee's role or function as legal counsel. Under EU/EEA competition law, however, confidential information between lawyer and client will only be protected provided that such communications are made for the purposes of the exercise of the client's rights of defense and that they emanate from independent lawyers.

31

PERU

Carlos A. Patrón
Payet, Rey, Cauvi, Pérez, Mur
Pontificia Universidad Católica del Perú

Introduction

The Repression of Anticompetitive Conducts Law enacted by Legislative Decree No. 1034 (the "Competition Law"),[1] lays down the principal competition rules that apply to undertakings in all sectors of economic activities. **31.01**

[1] Legislative Decree No. 1034, published June 25, 2008. The Competition Law abrogated Legislative Decree No. 701, Law Against Monopolistic, Controlist and Restrictive Practices, enacted in November 1991 (as amended by Decree Law No. 25868, published on November 24, 1992; Decree Law No. 26004, published on December 27, 1992; Legislative Decree No. 788, published on December 31, 1994; Legislative Decree No. 807, published on April 18, 1996; and Legislative Decree No. 957, published on July 19, 2004).

31.02 The enforcement of the Competition Law has been charged to INDECOPI (The National Institute for the Defense of Competition and for the Protection of Intellectual Property),[2] an administrative agency with unmatched investigative powers and fining capabilities. Notwithstanding, the competition authority's administrative decisions are subject to judicial review litigation.

31.03 The Peruvian Competition Law prohibits and sanctions certain conducts, unilaterally carried out by a single undertaking, that constitute abuse of a dominant position, as well as coordinated or mutually voluntary conducts among two or more undertakings that constitute horizontal or vertical restraints of trade or collusion.

31.04 Over the past two decades, merger control legislation has been limited to the electricity sector, resulting in a rapid structural transformation of the main sectors of economic activities, which today are relatively concentrated. Notwithstanding, dominance has not been the main concern of INDECOPI largely due to Peru's exceptional openness to trade and foreign investment, which generally has served to discipline the market.

31.05 Enforcement emphasis has traditionally focused on horizontal price fixing cartels. Over the past decade, as modern retail and distribution activities have expanded, enforcement has gradually begun to shift towards vertical restraints.

I. Acting alone

31.06 Peruvian legislation deals with both a single firm's actions that constitute abuse of a dominant position (art. 10 of the Competition Law), as well as coordinated or mutually voluntary conducts among two or more non-competing businesses that operate upstream or downstream in the supply chain that constitute vertical restraints of trade (art. 12 of the Competition Law).

31.07 Enforcement activities pursued *ex officio* by INDECOPI relating to potentially anticompetitive single firm actions have not been significant, with emphasis placed instead on horizontal collusion. Single firm conduct cases have largely been challenged through private enforcement actions, with marginally successful results, with INDECOPI deciding the majority of the cases in favour of the defendants.

31.08 In addition, until recently, vertical restraints have not been actively pursued, either through *ex officio* actions by INDECOPI or through private enforcement.

A. Abuse of dominant position

31.09 Conduct carried out by an undertaking acting alone may constitute a breach of Peruvian competition legislation only if: (i) the undertaking enjoys a "dominant position" in the market and (ii) such conduct is legally characterized as an "abuse."

31.10 Article 7.1 of the Competition Law defines a "dominant position" as an undertaking's ability to substantially restrict, affect, or distort supply or demand in a particular market, independently of its competitors, suppliers, or customers.

31.11 The standard methodology employed by INDECOPI for testing dominance requires, first of all, determining the relevant market, which in turn implies defining the relevant geographic market and product market, and, secondly, the dominance of the firm in said market.

[2] See Section "CC"(i).

Article 7.1 of the Competition Law explicitly states that dominance may be the result of factors such as significant market share, the particular characteristics of supply and demand of the good or services involved, the costs associated with technological developments, competitors' access to sources of finance or other supplies, the existence of economic, legal, or natural barriers to entry, the absence of suppliers, clients, or competitors or their lack of negotiation power, among others. **31.12**

Generally, when determining dominance, INDECOPI heavily relies on a market share test, complemented by an analysis of competitive conditions in the market and ease of market entry. While INDECOPI has not expressly defined a market share threshold above which dominance may be found, a review of the existing administrative precedents reveals that a market share greater than 50 percent may be considered a strong evidence of dominance. **31.13**

Under the Competition Law, it is not illegal for an undertaking to obtain or enjoy a dominant position, but only to abuse such a position. Accordingly, the Law focuses exclusively on "behavioral" controls, and does not contain "structural" control provisions such as restrictions on economic concentrations arising from mergers, acquisitions, or joint-ventures, even if their effect is such as to harm, diminish, or impede competition. **31.14**

The types of practices that may be characterized as abuse are listed in article 10.2 of the Competition Law, although this list is open-ended and allows authorities to consider other types of conducts of similar effects as abusive. Notwithstanding, both the Competition Law and binding precedents issued by INDECOPI explicitly limit the concept of abuse to practices that may have an exclusionary effect on competition,[3] thus barring exploitative abuses, such as excessive pricing or exploitative price discrimination, from the scope of enforcement. Historically, the most commonly investigated practices include refusals to deal, discriminatory prices and conditions, tying arrangements, and exclusive dealing agreements. **31.15**

B. Anticompetitive understandings among non-competing businesses

Anticompetitive understandings among non-competing businesses in the distribution chain are treated under the Competition Law as vertical restraints or mutually voluntary collusive agreements. In order for an anticompetitive vertical collusion to be found, the Competition Law requires: (i) that at least one party to the agreement enjoy a dominant position in its corresponding market and (ii) that the parties enter into practices legally characterized as uncompetitive. **31.16**

The types of practices that may be characterized as uncompetitive are listed in article 12.2 of the Competition Law, although, once again, this list is open-ended and allows authorities to deem unlawful other types of conducts of similar effects. **31.17**

Certain practices, such as the execution of exclusive dealing agreements, are characterized under the Competition Law as both a "unilateral" abuse of dominant position and as a "mutually voluntary" vertical collusion. The Competition Law, however, does not establish criteria to determine when a practice carried out by a dominant undertaking in conjunction with a non-competing business that performs activities upstream or downstream in the distribution chain is to be judged as one or the other. **31.18**

C. Predatory pricing

Predatory pricing is not explicitly listed as a practice that may constitute an abuse of dominant position under the Competition Law or under the competition legislation that preceded **31.19**

[3] *Agencias de Turismo del Cusco v. Consettur Machupicchu S.A.C.*, Ruling No. 052-2007-INDECOPI/CLC (September 14, 2007).

it. Notwithstanding, as previously explained, the Competition Law's list of practices that may be characterized as abuse is open-ended and allows authorities to deem other types of conducts of similar effects as abusive.

31.20 Predatory pricing charges have been brought forward in a handful of cases over the past two decades. In *Wendell v. Proquinsa*,[4] INDECOPI admitted that predatory pricing could qualify as a conduct of similar effect to those explicitly listed in Peruvian legislation as abuse. In this case, INDECOPI defined predation as pricing below a certain level of cost with the intention of eliminating one or several competitors. In addition, in finding in favor of the defendants, INDECOPI established that to determine predation it was necessary to demonstrate (i) selective price undercutting, (ii) unprofitable or very low profit pricing, and (iii) pricing policies targeted to a specific competitor, although specific tests for these purposes were not established.

31.21 All of the predatory pricing cases handled by INDECOPI to this date have resulted from private claims and all rulings issued have favored the defendants.

D. Exploitative offenses (excessive pricing, exploitative discriminatory pricing)

31.22 INDECOPI has been relatively inconsistent on its position concerning exploitative offenses. During a brief span, under the competition legislation that preceded the Competition Law, INDECOPI held that excessive pricing and exploitative discriminatory pricing practices carried out by dominant undertakings could be deemed unlawful.[5]

31.23 Notwithstanding, in 2007, INDECOPI reversed its position and issued a binding precedent explicitly limiting the concept of abuse to practices that may have an exclusionary effect on competition,[6] thus barring exploitative abuses, such as excessive pricing or exploitative price discrimination, from the scope of enforcement. Shortly afterwards, the Competition Law currently in place, enacted in 2008, explicitly defined abusive practices as those that could have a potential exclusionary effect on competition. Since then, INDECOPI has dismissed several private claims that it found to involve exploitative offenses.[7]

E. Monopsony

31.24 As previously mentioned, the Peruvian Competition Law defines a "dominant position" as an undertaking's ability to substantially restrict, affect or distort either supply or demand. Likewise, the catalogue of conducts that could potentially qualify as abuse listed in the Competition Law include, for instance, unjustified refusals to satisfy either purchase or sale requirements. Accordingly, abusive conducts by a business in a dominant purchasing position could constitute an infringement of the Competition Law. Notwithstanding, to date, there is not any relevant case law on the matter.

F. Price discrimination

31.25 Discriminatory practices, whether related to pricing or other commercial terms and conditions, are explicitly stated in article 10.2.b of the Competition Law to be abuses of a dominant position.

---

[4] *Wendell v. Proquinsa*, Ruling No. 070-96-INDECOPI-CLC (September 17, 1996).

[5] *Central Workers' Union v. Private Pension Funds*, Ruling No. 0225-2004/TDC-INDECOPI (June 4, 2004).

[6] *Agencias de Turismo del Cusco* (n 3).

[7] *Armando Kiyan Kiyan v. Unimpro*, Ruling No. 005-2008/ST-CLC-INDECOPI (February 22, 2008); *Asociación de Agencias de Turismo del Cuzco v. CONSETTUR Machu Pichu*, Ruling No. 0027-2008/SC1-INDECOPI (October 16, 2008).

However, for discriminatory practices to be deemed abusive, the Competition Law requires that these have a potentially exclusionary effect. Accordingly, discriminatory practices used by a dominant company to extract prices higher than normal, in so far as they exclusively pursue an exploitative effect, would be excluded from the scope of the Competition Law. **31.26**

Historically, discriminatory practices have been one of the most common claims in private suits relating to potential abuses of dominant positions. However, INDECOPI has sided with the defendants in the majority of these types of cases. **31.27**

The main lines of defense employed to justify discriminatory or differentiated price treatment have involved cost structure (for example, differences in distribution costs) and volume discounts. Other defenses taken into account by INDECOPI include absence of continuity in the discriminatory practice (for example, in *SNI v. Centromín*, INDECOPI considered that the defendant's conduct of charging higher prices to local refined lead buyers, compared to prices charged to international clients, was not unlawful because it was sporadic) and the existence of private commercial arrangements (for example, in *El Comercio v. AreoContinente*, INDECOPI considered it justifiable that an airline impose higher freight charges on a local newspaper compared to other newspapers with which it had entered into commercial agreements to exchange publicity for transportation).[8] **31.28**

The Competition Law explicitly states that the volume discounts and bonuses resulting from generally accepted commercial uses, granted in certain compensatory circumstances, such as advanced payment or large volume or amount purchases, does not constitute abusive discriminatory practices, so long as the discounts and bonuses are generally granted on equal terms. **31.29**

G. Dictating or influencing resale prices

Anticompetitive understandings among non-competing businesses in the distribution chain are treated under the Competition Law as vertical restraints or mutually voluntary collusive agreements. Among the types of practices that may be characterized as a vertical restraint, the Competition Law includes vertical price fixing agreements, which would allow authorities to review resale price maintenance (RPM) agreements. Other indirect forms of achieving a result similar to an explicit price fixing agreement, such as minimum advertised price (MAP) programs, could also be reviewed under the Competition Law, in so far as the practices produce an effect similar to RPM. Notwithstanding, to date, there has been no relevant case law on the matter. **31.30**

As previously mentioned, in order for an anticompetitive vertical collusion to be found, the Competition Law requires that at least one party to the agreement enjoy a dominant position in its corresponding market. Likewise, it is important to note that vertical restraints are not deemed per se illegal under the Competition Law and, accordingly, are subject to a reasonability test. **31.31**

H. Tying arrangements

Tying arrangements are explicitly stated in article 10.2.c of the Competition Law to be abuses of a dominant position. **31.32**

The Competition Law broadly defines tying as subordinating contracts to the acceptance of additional goods or services that, by nature or commercial uses, are not related to the purpose of said contract. **31.33**

---

[8] *SNI v. Centromín*, Ruling No. 001-98-CLC (January 9, 1998); *El Comercio v. AreoContinente*, Ruling No. 004-98-CLC (September 30, 1998).

31.34 Although case law is still sparse, INDECOPI has tended to side with plaintiffs in these types of cases. For instance, in *Servicios Técnicos Marítimos v. ENAPU*, INDECOPI deemed illegal that the State operated monopoly port authority force terminal users to contract its trailer transportation services, prohibiting potential competitors from offering alternative services in the ports.[9] Likewise, in *INDECOPI v. Los Portales*, INDECOPI sanctioned the concessionaire of Lima's international airport's parking services for tying a mandatory two-hour parking fee to all vehicles that entered the airport,[10] although this decision was issued prior to the explicit exclusion of exploitative practices from the scope of the Competition Law referred to above.[11]

I. Exclusive dealing

31.35 The Competition Law defines exclusive dealing as the establishment, imposition, or suggestion of unjustified exclusive distribution or sale agreements, or non-compete or equivalent clauses.

31.36 Under the Competition Law, exclusive dealing arrangements could potentially be judged as either a unilateral abuse of dominant position case or a mutually voluntary vertical restraint case. In the latter case, article 12.3 of the Competition Law requires that at least one party to the agreement enjoy a dominant position in its corresponding market, although if an unreasonable restraint were to be found, both parties to the agreement could result subject to fines. While local case law is scarce, INDECOPI has judged most cases brought to its attention as unilateral abuses of a dominant position.

31.37 In the leading cases on the matter, INDECOPI has held that exclusive dealing arrangements that result in a market foreclosure of less than 15 percent of available distribution channels were not anticompetitive and that a foreclosure rate greater than 30 percent to 40 percent could result harmful to competition.[12] Likewise, INDECOPI has held that exclusive dealing arrangements of three years or less may not be deemed anticompetitive so long as they are commercially justifiable and contract termination costs are not prohibiting.[13]

J. Refusal to deal

31.38 The Peruvian Constitution warrants individuals the right to freely choose its trading partners and determine their contractual obligations. Accordingly, refusals to deal may only be considered unlawful in very specific circumstances and only if such practice is carried out by a dominant undertaking and no commercially reasonable justification may be found. Not surprisingly, a review of existing case law reveals that INDECOPI has largely tended to side with defendants.

31.39 In the few cases that an unjustified refusal to deal has been found, INDECOPI has sanctioned both refusals to deal in which the dominant firm's refusal had an impact in a vertically integrated secondary market and refusals to deal in which the dominant firms did not, directly or indirectly, compete with the plaintiff. Thus, for example, in *Holguín v. Enaco*, INDECOPI sanctioned the state coca-leaf collection monopoly Enaco for refusing to sell coca-leaf to a company the competed in the coca tea market;[14] while in *Cab Cable v. Electrocentro*, INDECOPI sanctioned an electricity distributor for refusing to rent its posts to a local cable company.[15]

---

9 *Servicios Técnicos Marítimos v. ENAPU*, Ruling No. 014-93-CLC (December 23, 1993).
10 *Comisión de Libre Competencia v. Los Portales*, Ruling No. 057-95-CLC (December 29, 1995).
11 See Section I.D.
12 *Ambev v. Backus*, Ruling No. 45-2009-CLC/INDECOPI (June 25, 2009).
13 *Ambev v. Backus* (n 12).
14 *Holguín v. Enaco*, Ruling No. 016-94-CLC (July 27, 1994).
15 *Cab Cable v. Electrocentro*, Ruling No. 869-2002/TDC-INDECOPI (December 11, 2002).

In cases favorable to the defendants, INDECOPI has considered that a refusal to deal may be justified on financial, commercial, or contractual grounds. For example, in *Tele Cable v. Fox and Turner*, INDECOPI considered reasonable that Fox Latin American Channel and Turner Broadcasting System America refuse to grant broadcasting licenses to a local cable operator that had repeatedly breached contractual payment obligations to the defendants.[16] In *IEQSA v. Centromín and Minero Perú*, INDECOPI considered that a refusal to sell refined zinc to the plaintiff was justifiable on the grounds that one of the defendants had already committed its entire production to other buyers, while the other defendant was involved in a privatization process that impeded it from selling the product.[17] **31.40**

K. Essential facilities

While the refusal to grant a competitor access to an essential facility is not explicitly listed as a practice that may constitute an abuse of dominant position under the Competition Law or under the competition legislation that preceded it, INDECOPI has explicitly sanctioned this practice in the past as a conduct similar in effect to an unjustified refusal to deal. **31.41**

An essential facility has been loosely defined under Peruvian case law as an infrastructure that is indispensable for production in another market. In addition, INDECOPI has held that the refusal to grant access to such facility may only be considered anticompetitive when said facility is under the control of a monopolist or an undertaking with a dominant position and it is impossible or unreasonable to replicate the facility.[18] **31.42**

L. Bundling (including loyalty and market share discounts)

Bundling is not explicitly listed as a practice that may constitute an abuse of dominant position under the Competition Law. Notwithstanding, as previously explained, the Competition Law's list of practices that may be characterized as abuse is open-ended and allows authorities to deem other types of conducts of similar effects as abusive. Accordingly, bundling could potentially be reviewed by INDECOPI as a practice of similar effect to an unlawful tying arrangement, although there is no specific case law on the matter. **31.43**

M. Standard-setting groups (disclosure requirements, licensing arrangements, and licensing pools)

Requirements imposed by standard-setting groups are not explicitly listed as practices that may constitute an abuse of dominant position under the Competition Law. Agreements among competitors within such an organization could potentially be considered an anticompetitive collaboration between competitors subject to horizontal collusion rules. **31.44**

Notwithstanding, the Competition Law does explicitly list as an abusive conduct the denial without justification of access or permanence to a competitor to an intermediary association or organization, although there is no specific case law on the matter. **31.45**

N. Customer termination

Customer termination is not explicitly listed as a practice that may constitute an abuse of dominant position under the Competition Law and has in the past been treated by INDECOPI as a special case of an unjustified refusal to deal.[19] **31.46**

[16] *Tele Cable v. Fox and Turner*, Ruling No. 005-2003-INDECOPI/CLC (May 14, 2003).

[17] *IEQSA v. Centromín and Minero Perú*, Ruling No. 013-97-CLC (May 14, 1997).

[18] *AeroContinente S.A. v. Banco de Crédito del Perú*, Ruling No. 870-2002/TDC-INDECOPI (December 11, 2002).

[19] See Section I.J.

O. Termination of intermediaries (retailers, wholesalers, dealers, and value-added resellers, agents, and brokers)

31.47 Termination of intermediaries is not explicitly listed as a practice that may constitute an abuse of dominant position under the Competition Law, and therefore a unilateral termination could potentially be reviewed by INDECOPI as a practice of similar effect to an unjustified refusal to deal, although there is no specific case law on the matter.

31.48 In recent decisions, INDECOPI has considered that an understanding among a dominant supplier and its wholesalers to terminate sells to retailers that carried rival products constitutes a form of vertical collusion.[20]

P. Termination of relationships with competitors

31.49 Termination of relationship with competitors is not explicitly listed as a practice that may constitute an abuse of dominant position under the Competition Law and has in the past been treated by INDECOPI as a special case of an unjustified refusal to deal.[21]

Q. Exemptions

31.50 Peruvian legislation does not contain explicit provisions exempting specific sectors of economic activities from the scope of the Competition Law.

II. Dealing with competitors

31.51 Agreements and arrangements entered into between undertakings that compete in horizontal markets have historically been the main focus of *ex officio* enforcement priorities by INDECOPI and have been deemed the most serious types of infringements to the Competition Law, resulting in some of the highest fines imposed.

31.52 Horizontal collusion is defined under article 11.1 of the Competition Law as agreements, decisions, recommendations, or concerted practices among competing undertakings which have, or may have, as their object or effect to restrict, prevent, or simulate competition. The types of specific practices that may be characterized as forms of horizontal collusion are listed in the Competition Law, although this list is open-ended and allows authorities to deem other types of conducts of similar effects as equally illegal.

31.53 Although, as a general rule, conduct that could potentially constitute an infringement under Competition Law (either as an abuse of a dominant position or a form of collusion) is judged under a rule of reason standard, certain types of horizontal agreements among competitors are considered hard core cartels and are therefore deemed unlawful per se.

A. Horizontal price fixing (including advanced announcements of price or product changes)

31.54 Horizontal price fixing has historically been the main focus of INDECOPI's enforcement priorities. Over half of the horizontal collusion investigations launched over the past two decades have been related to possible price-fixing arrangements, and an additional quarter of the investigations have dealt with possible bid-rigging agreements.

---

[20] *Malva v. Unión Andina de Cementos S.A.A.*, Ruling No. 010-2013/CLC-INDECOPI (January 22, 2013).

[21] *Ambev v. Backus* (n 12).

Article 11.1(a) of the Competition Law defines price fixing as a direct or indirect concerted setting of prices or other commercial or service terms. **31.55**

INDECOPI has consistently held that, absent additional direct or circumstantial evidence of an effective agreement, a "parallel behavior" does not in itself constitute or demonstrate the existence of a price-fixing agreement.[22] Accordingly, to sanction a price-fixing arrangement, authorities must additionally collect direct or circumstantial evidence to demonstrate the existence of such agreement. Advanced announcements of price or product changes, while not explicitly listed as a form of horizontal collusion, may be considered among the circumstantial evidence of a price-fixing agreement. **31.56**

Under article 11.2 of the Competition Law, "naked" horizontal price-fixing arrangements, as well as bid-rigging arrangements, are deemed per se illegal.[23] Inter-brand horizontal agreements among competitors that are not complementary or ancillary to other licit agreements, are characterized as "naked" under the aforementioned provision. **31.57**

B. Horizontal agreements to allocate customers or territories; agreements not to compete

The allocation of clients, suppliers, and territories is explicitly listed as a form of horizontal collusion under the Competition Law. As is the case with price-fixing agreement, article 11.2 of the Competition Law deems "naked" horizontal arrangements of this nature to be per se illegal.[24] **31.58**

C. Horizontal boycotts

Horizontal boycotts are defined in the Competition Law as a concerted unjustified refusal to deal or to satisfy purchase or sale requirements. Unlike price-fixing and market allocation agreements, the legality of potential horizontal boycotts is judged under a rule of reason standard. Accordingly, agreements among competitors not to purchase from, or supply to, specific businesses, will be considered a form of horizontal collusion if entered into without sufficient commercially reasonable justification, although there is no relevant case law on the matter. **31.59**

D. Joint ventures and other competitive collaborations

The Peruvian Competition Law focuses exclusively on "behavioral" controls, and does not contain "structural" control provisions such as restrictions on economic concentrations arising from mergers, acquisitions, or joint ventures, even if their effect is such as to harm, diminish, or impede competition. The only sector of economic activity subject pre-notification and authorization procedures in the event of vertical or horizontal concentrations is the electricity generation, transmission and distribution markets, as a result of specific legislation.[25] **31.60**

Accordingly, joint ventures and other forms of competitive collaborations are generally not considered a form of horizontal collusion in so far as they do not exclusively pursue **31.61**

---

[22] *Municipalidad Provincial de Lambayeque v. Cooperativa de Transportes San Pablo, and others*, Ruling No. 0225-1997/TDC-INDECOPI (September 5, 1997).

[23] Under the competition legislation that preceded the Competition Law, INDECOPI held that all forms of collusion were subject to the rule-of-reason standard. Accordingly, INDECOPI concluded that in order to sanction these infractions, authorities had to, in addition to evidencing the collusion, verify that "the conduct adopted be capable of producing the effect of restricting, impeding or forging competition and that it was in fact implemented in the market" (*Asociación Peruana de Empresas de Seguros* (n 35)).

[24] See para. 31.57.

[25] Law No. 26876, the Antitrust and Anti-oligopoly Law for the Electricity Sector, published on November 19, 1997.

anticompetitive aims on the market. Ancillary restraints of trade among the undertakings collaborating in a joint venture are not considered per se illegal, and will be lawful so long as the principal agreement is deemed licit.

31.62 Under Peruvian case law, INDECOPI has stated that collaborative agreements with the sole purpose of jointly advertising a standard product identified under a common trademark, may be deemed licit so long as they are not ancillary to an agreement to restrict competition, are not employed as a mechanism to implement a price-fixing agreement, and do not limit or restrict each individual undertaking's ability to advertise on its own.[26]

E. Trade associations

31.63 Non-profit private entities, including trade associations and professional bodies, are subject to the Competition Law collusion provisions.

31.64 In determining the individual liability of a trade association in a collusion claim, INDECOPI has held that the separation between a legal entity (i.e. the association) and its members does not hinder the possibility of sanctioning the former when it serves as an instrument for the execution of an illegal horizontal restraint. In such cases, the entity is not punished for the acts of its members but for its own actions and participation in the collusion that stemmed from a different decision-making source.[27] INDECOPI has further held that non-profit entities, such as trade associations, are bound by the general competition rules and, accordingly, that guilds are liable for their participation in price-fixing agreements through actions that serve as incentive, support or props of such infractions.[28]

31.65 Examples of business associations that have been subject to competition investigations or have been sanctioned for having infringed the competition legislation include poultry producers,[29] trucking companies,[30] urban transport companies,[31] moto-taxi,[32] the national bread bakers' guild,[33] port-pilotage,[34] and insurance companies.[35]

31.66 Likewise, INDECOPI has held that professional bodies are subject to the rules set forth in competition legislation, not only for the economic activities directly carried out by them, but also for the binding decisions adopted on behalf of its members while acting as an assemblage of enterprises (i.e. adopting decisions, through its decision-making bodies, that bind its members).[36] In addition, INDECOPI has stated that the autonomy granted to professional bodies under the Peruvian Constitution does not exclude them from the scope of application of competition legislation.

---

[26] *Comisión de Libre Competencia v. Asociación Peruana de Avicultura and others*, Ruling No. 276-97-TDC (November 19, 1997).

[27] *Asociación Peruana de Avicultura* (n 26).

[28] *Asociación Peruana de Avicultura* (n 26).

[29] *Asociación Peruana de Avicultura* (n 26).

[30] *Cámara de Comercio de Lima v. Unión Nacional de Transportistas Dueños de Camiones del Perú, and others*, Ruling No. 032-2005-INDECOPI/CLC (June 20, 2005).

[31] *Comisión de Libre Competencia v. Federación de Choferes del Perú, and others*, Ruling No. 015-1993/CLC (December 30, 1993).

[32] *Comisión de Libre Competencia v. Taxi Tel, and others*, Ruling No. 003-2000-INDECOPI/CLC (June 16, 2000).

[33] *Comisión de Libre Competencia v. Federación Nacional de Industrias Panificadoras del Perú*, Ruling No. 001-1993/CLC (July 15, 1993).

[34] *Maersk Perú S.A.and others v. Pilot Station S.A., and others*, Ruling No. 010-2002-INDECOPI/CLC (June 28, 2002).

[35] *Comisión de Libre Competencia v. Asociación Peruana de Empresas de Seguros, and others*, Ruling No. 0224-2003/TDC-INDECOPI (June 16, 2003).

[36] *Carlos León Madalengoitia v. Colegio Químico Farmacéutico del Perú, and others*, Ruling No. 068-96-INDECOPI-CLC (September 17, 1996).

Examples of professional bodies that have been held to have infringed the Competition Law include the *Colegio Químico Farmacéutico del Perú* (professional body of pharmacists),[37] *Colegio de Abogados de Loreto* (an attorney bar association),[38] as well as the *Colegio de Notarios de Lima* (a professional body of public notaries).[39] **31.67**

F. Interlocking directorates

Interlocking directorates are not explicitly characterized as a form of horizontal collusion under the Competition Law and have not been subject to investigations by INDECOPI in the past. Generally, interlocking directorates do not infringe the Competition Law, to the extent that the conformation of such directorates is not the result of a collusive horizontal agreement (i.e. a mechanism to enforce such an agreement). **31.68**

Furthermore, in numerous occasions, INDECOPI has stated that arrangements among undertakings subject to a common control do not constitute horizontal collusion. Accordingly, interlocking directorates resulting from a common control structure should not give rise to competition concerns. **31.69**

G. Facilitating practices

Facilitating practices are not explicitly characterized as a form of horizontal collusion under the Competition Law. Nevertheless, exchanges of information concerning intended pricing or other types of facilitating practices may be construed as indicative of a restrictive practice and may, together with additional direct or indirect evidence, serve to demonstrate an unlawful collusion. **31.70**

H. Information exchange

The exchange of information among competitors is not explicitly deemed a form of horizontal collusion under the Competition Law, although it could be eventually circumstantial evidence of a price-fixing or other collusive agreement. **31.71**

Under Peruvian case law, INDECOPI has stated that such types of exchanges may be deemed economically favorable and not restrictive of competition when they pursue the exclusive goal of compiling common information required by companies to determine independently and autonomously their future conducts in the market.[40] If, however, the conduct of such competitors is in any way, directly or indirectly, coordinated, or the liberty of such competitors to act is in any way limited, a restriction to competition may be found.[41] **31.72**

Furthermore, INDECOPI has stated that the exchange and publication of production and sale information through trade associations will not be objectionable if such information is aggregated and made available to the general public.[42] **31.73**

I. Joint purchasing agreements

Joint purchasing agreements are not explicitly listed under the Competition Law as a form of horizontal collusion. Notwithstanding, as previously explained, the Competition Law's list of practices that may be characterized as a form of horizontal collusion is open-ended and allows **31.74**

---

[37] *Carlos León Madalengoitia* (n 36).

[38] *AFP Integra v. Colegio de Abogados de Loreto*, Ruling No. 0237-1999/TDC-INDECOPI (July 7, 1999).

[39] *Julio Antonio Del Pozo Valdez v. Colegio de Notarios de Lima*, Ruling No. 003-2003-CLC/INDECOPI (April 23, 2003).

[40] *Asociación Peruana de Avicultura* (n 26).

[41] *Asociación Peruana de Avicultura* (n 26).

[42] *Asociación Peruana de Avicultura* (n 26).

authorities to deem unlawful other types of conducts of similar effects. In such an event, joint purchasing agreement would not be judged to be per se illegal and would need to be analyzed in terms of their effects on competition and commercial reasonability, although there is not any relevant case law on the matter.

J. Joint lobbying/regulatory/legislative efforts

31.75 Joint lobbying in connection with regulation or legislation is not explicitly characterized as a form of horizontal collusion under the Competition Law and has not in the past raised antitrust issues under Peruvian case law.

III. General issues

A. Jurisdiction and applicable law

31.76 The Competition Law's rules are applicable to all economic activities (i.e. productive and commercial activities, as well as the rendering of services). Peruvian legislation does not contain explicit provisions exempting specific sectors of economic activities from the scope of the Competition Law.

31.77 Article 2.1 of the Competition Law broadly defines the addressees of the competition rules contained therein as all natural persons and all public or private legal entities that undertake economic activities, including state-owned enterprises and any other public entity, even non-profit in nature, that offer or demand goods and services in the market.

31.78 The territorial scope of application of the Peruvian Competition Law is defined in s. 4 of the Law. According to this provision, the Competition Law is applicable to all conduct that produces or may produce anticompetitive effects within the national territory, including effects originating in acts carried out abroad. In line with this provision, in prior decisions, the Competition Commission explicitly affirmed the application of the "effects doctrine" to sanction anticompetitive conducts originated outside of the national territory.[43]

B. Antitrust system

(i) Agency

31.79 INDECOPI is the Spanish acronym for Peru's National Institute for the Defense of Competition and for the Protection of Intellectual Property,[44] an independent administrative agency that acts as a multiple registry of intellectual property rights and as an administrative court that enforces competition and trade legislation.[45] The agency comprises under a common administration a series of very different functions loosely connected by the common denominator that they all aim to encourage and strengthen the development of a

---

[43] *Asociación Peruana de Agencias de Viaje y Turismo v. Alitalia, Linee Aeree Italiane, and others*, Ruling No. 043-2004-INDECOPI/CLC (July 19, 2004).

[44] Instituto Nacional de Defensa de la Competencia y de la Protección de la Propiedad Intelectual.

[45] INDECOPI's decision-making or functional area is organized in two tiers. The first tier is divided into three "intellectual property protection" offices: the Trademark Office, the Patents and New Technologies Office, the Copyright Office; three "intellectual property protection" commissions: the Trademark Commission, the Patents and New Technologies Commission, the Copyright Commission; and seven "defense of competition" commissions: the Defense of Free Competition Commission, the Consumer Protection Commission, the Repression of Unfair Competition Commission, the Antidumping and Countervailing Duties Commission, the Patrimonial Restructuring Commission, the Access to Market Commission, and the Technical and Commercial Norms Commission.

well-functioning market economy. Commonly, in most western countries, such regulatory powers are dispersed among different Government entities.[46]

INDECOPI's Defense of Free Competition Commission ("Competition Commission") is charged with enforcing the Competition Law in all fields of economic activity, with the exception of activities that affect or may affect the public telecommunications markets.[47] **31.80**

As a general rule, all of INDECOPI's commissions have the power investigate, prosecute and fine individuals or corporations who are found to have infringed one of the statutes under their specific area of supervision, through an administrative fining procedure. They also have the power to grant interlocutory and permanent injunctions, but may not award damages. Lastly, while these decision-making bodies do not have legislative functions, they are empowered to issue binding administrative precedents and to enact policy guidelines related to the interpretation and application of the statutes entrusted to them. **31.81**

The rulings adopted by the Competition Commissions may be appealed to the Tribunal for the Defense of Competition and Intellectual Property (the "Tribunal"), the second and final administrative decision-making body.[48] **31.82**

The Tribunal's rulings conclude administrative fining proceedings. These rulings can in turn be disputed before the Judiciary through judicial review litigation. **31.83**

Both the Competition Commission and Tribunal are multidisciplinary in their conformation, this meaning that unlike the Judiciary, where decision-makers are exclusively lawyers, the Commission and Tribunal have members with different professional and academic backgrounds. **31.84**

(ii) Staff size and budget

Each commission at INDECOPI is supported by an administrative staff, headed by a Technical Secretariat. The Technical Secretariat and its staff serve as both clerks to its commission, handling day-to-day administrative functions, and as prosecutors in the administrative sanctioning procedures that the commission decides to initiate, collecting evidence, conducting investigations, and drafting reports recommending the rulings to be adopted in each case. **31.85**

[46] Thus, e.g. INDECOPI assumed the responsibilities shared in the Unites States by the Department of Commerce, the National Institute of Standards and Technology, the Patent and Trademark Office, the Department of Justice Antitrust Division, the Federal Trade Commission, the Bankruptcy Courts, the Court of Federal Claims, and the Court of Appeals for the Federal Circuit.

[47] Law No. 27336 (published on August 5, 2000) charges the Peruvian Private Investment in Telecommunications Supervisory Agency (in Spanish known as OSIPTEL) with the enforcement of the Competition Law in matters related to activities that affect or may affect the markets for public telecommunications services. Under current Peruvian legislation, telecommunications services qualify as public if they are supplied to the public in exchange for a fee. Consequently, the concept of "public telecommunications services" excludes services supplied by an individual or corporation to satisfy its own needs (e.g. private communications networks) and services supplied to the public without requiring a fee in exchange (e.g. non-subscription television and radio broadcasting services). As a result, telecommunications services that fall under OSIPTEL's scope of enforcement include public carrier services, public final communications services (e.g. telephone, telex, telegraph, or beeper services), public broadcasting services (e.g. cable television services), and public value-added services (e.g. voice mail, internet, or e-mail services).

[48] The Tribunal is divided into three chambers: (i) the Protection of Intellectual Property Chamber, which handles the appeals of the rulings handed-down by the Offices and IP Commissions; (ii) the Consumer Protection Chamber, which handles the appeals of the rulings handed-down by the Consumer Protection Commissions; and (iii) the Competition Chamber, which handles the appeals of the rulings handed down by the remaining commissions, including the Competition Commission.

31.86 Currently, the Competition Commission's administrative support staff comprises a Technical Secretariat and approximately a dozen attorneys and economists. In addition to the Competition Commission's small staff size, funding is limited, which hinders local authorities' ability to undertake more than a dozen investigations at a time.

(iii) Recent enforcement actions and trends

31.87 Over the past two decades, INDECOPI's *ex officio* antitrust enforcement activities have been mainly focused on coordinated conducts and in particular horizontal price fixing cartels. Traditionally, these enforcement activities have focused on politically sensitive mass consumer consumption goods and services (i.e. public transportation, flour, poultry, etc.). The most recent enforcement actions carried out INDECOPI have dealt with possible horizontal restrictions in the pharmaceutical product distribution and compressed natural gas markets.

31.88 Generally, potential unilateral anticompetitive conducts have been challenged through private enforcement actions.

C. Private litigation

31.89 An administrative fining procedure may be initiated *ex officio* by the Competition Commission, at the request of the Technical Secretariat or at the request of a third-party plaintiff. In determining the initiation of an administrative fining procedure at a plaintiff's request, the Competition Commission must evaluate if there is reasonable circumstantial evidence of an infringement to the Competition Law. If such circumstantial evidence is not found to exist, the Competition Commission may *prima facie* dismiss such requests without prejudice.

31.90 In addition, as explained in Section III.D(ii), the Competition Law authorizes any person harmed by agreements or practices prohibited under said law to file civil liability (tort) suits before the Judiciary in order to recover damages, although these types of actions are rarely promoted.

D. Follow-on litigation (includes role of agency determinations of liability for follow-on litigation)

(i) Judicial review litigation

31.91 Section 148 of the Peruvian Constitution warrants that decisions handed down by the Public Administration's final decision-making bodies may be judicially reviewed. Consequently, decisions handed down by INDECOPI's final decision-making body (i.e. the Tribunal) may be disputed before the Judiciary.

31.92 Judicial review litigation is regulated in the Judicial Review Procedure Law,[49] and supplemented by the Peruvian Code of Civil Procedure.

31.93 Under Peruvian law, the only administrative rulings that may be subject to judicial review are those handed down by final administrative decision-making bodies.[50] As discussed in para. 31.82, rulings handed-down by the Competition Commission may be appealed to the INDECOPI Tribunal. Accordingly, in the case of INDECOPI, the only rulings that may be subject to judicial review are those handed down by the Tribunal. If the parties consent to the Competition Commission's rulings (e.g. implicitly waiving appeal, allowing the deadlines to appeal to lapse), such rulings will be deemed definitive and, hence, their result will be undisputable before the Judiciary.

[49] Law No. 27584, published on December 7, 2001.

[50] The Judicial Review Procedure Law, s. 18, as supplemented by the Decree Law No. 25868, s. 16 and the General Administrative Procedure Law, s. 218.

Under s. 17 of the Judicial Review Procedure Law, the deadline to file judicial review actions against a final administrative ruling, lapses three months from the date that the notice of such ruling is given. Judicial review litigation is rarely bypassed by defendants sanctioned for violating the Competition Law. **31.94**

(ii) Civil recovery litigation

Section 49 of the Competition Law authorizes any person harmed by agreements or practices prohibited under that Law to file civil liability (tort) suits before the Judiciary in order to recover damages, upon the conclusion of administrative fining procedures. **31.95**

Civil liability actions are regulated by ss. 1969–1988 of the Peruvian Civil Code. Peruvian civil legislation allows recovery in cases of damages caused by intentional harm and negligence (s. 1969 of the Civil Code), and subjects damages resulting from hazardous activities to strict liability (s. 1970 of the Civil Code). **31.96**

Section 1985 of the Civil Code allows recovery of compensatory damages, including direct and consequential losses (i.e. direct economic losses and current or future lost earnings) and non-pecuniary injuries (i.e. moral and personal damages). Punitive damages are not allowed under Peruvian civil legislation. **31.97**

The statute of limitations for filing a civil liability suit is two years. **31.98**

Despite that the Competition Law authorizes private enforcement through civil litigation, plaintiffs rarely exercise this option. **31.99**

(iii) Class action litigation

Section 131 of the Peruvian Consumer Protection Code empowers INDECOPI to file class action suits before the Judiciary on behalf of consumers related to any matter that falls under the scope of its jurisdiction.[51] Likewise, INDECOPI is allowed to delegate this power upon consumer associations that are capable of adequately representing consumers' interests. In these actions, INDECOPI is authorized to seek any remedy necessary to protect the affected consumers' rights, including civil liability damages and the recovery of any amounts paid in excess. **31.100**

Pursuant to current legislation, class actions promoted by INDECOPI are adjudicated in summary procedures before Civil Judges. **31.101**

Damage awards granted in the judgment are collected by INDECOPI, which in turn is responsible for distributing these amounts among the members of the class. Any amount that is not claimed within one year from the date of collection by INDECOPI is allocated to a special fund for the promotion of consumer rights administered by the agency. **31.102**

Current legislation establishes that in order for INDECOPI to file class action suits, prior authorization must be issued by the agency's Board of Directors. To this date, however, INDECOPI's Board of Directors has yet to authorize such actions in a case related to infringements to the Competition Law. **31.103**

E. Arbitration and alternative dispute resolution

Competition legislation is deemed public policy under Peruvian Law and, accordingly, is exclusively subject to public enforcement. **31.104**

Civil recovery actions arising from infractions to the Competition Law are private in nature and, thus, could be subjected to arbitration or other types of ADR. Notwithstanding, **31.105**

[51] Law No. 29571, published on September 2, 2009.

arbitration is voluntary and would require that all parties consent to it, which has not occurred to date.

F. Remedies

(i) Administrative fines and injunctive remedies

31.106 Section 43 of the Competition Law authorizes the Competition Commission to sanction infractions to said statute by imposing pecuniary fines on each individual defendant.

31.107 The maximum fines that may be imposed if the infractions are considered to be very severe, must not exceed 12 percent of the gross sales or income earned by the defendant in the fiscal year prior to the Competition Commission's decision.

31.108 As an exception, maximum fines may not exceed a cap of 1,000 Tax Reference Units (approx. USD 1.5 million) if the defendant is a trade association or a professional body or if the defendant initiated its economic, industrial, or commercial activities after January 1 of the calendar year prior to the Competition Commission's decision.

31.109 In addition, if the infringing defendant is a corporation or a legal entity, the Competition Law empowers the Competition Commission to impose ancillary fines of up to 100 Tax Reference Units (approx. USD 150,000) on each of the representatives, directors, or officers who took part in the infractions committed. INDECOPI regularly asserts these types of penalties in horizontal collusion cases. Furthermore, in past decisions, the Tribunal explicitly barred infracting corporations from disbursing or reimbursing the ancillary fines imposed on their directors and officers, mandating that the fines imposed on the latter may not be paid by the former nor affect its assets.[52]

31.110 In addition to its fining capacity, the Competition Commission has the power to grant interlocutory and permanent injunctions. Interlocutory injunctions may be issued *ex parte* at any point during an investigation to secure the performance of final decisions.

31.111 In decisions issued under the competition legislation abrogated by the Competition Law, INDECOPI stated it was empowered to impose on defendants both permanent behavioral or structural remedies (including the breakup or de-bundling of assets), when such remedies "report substantial benefits for competition that exceed the costs associated to their imposition and supervision."[53] The Competition Law in force since 2008, however, only allows the imposition of permanent injunctions of a behavioral nature (i.e. cease-and-desist orders, mandatory contracting obligations, disapplying anticompetitive contractual provisions, etc.).

(ii) Civil liability

31.112 The Competition Commission is not empowered to grant damage rewards. However, as explained in Section III.D(ii), individuals may seek damages before the judiciary upon the conclusion of administrative fining procedures.

(iii) Criminal liability

31.113 Until 2008, (i) the abuse of a monopoly or oligopoly position in the market and (ii) the participation in practices or agreements restrictive of productive, commercial or service activities, with the purpose of impeding, restricting or distorting competition, were criminal

[52] *Asociación Peruana de Operadores Portuarios, and others v. Pilot Station S.A., and others*, Ruling No. 0407-2007-TDC-INDECOPI (March 22, 2007).

[53] *Ferrocarril Santuario Inca Machupicchu S.A.C., and others v. Ferrocarril Transandino S.A.*, Ruling No. 1122-2007-TDC-INDECOPI (July 1, 2007).

offenses under s. 232 of the Peruvian Penal Code. This provision was explicitly abrogated by the Competition Law. Accordingly, under current Peruvian Law, competition offenses may only result in administrative and civil liability.

G. Leniency and immunity

Both leniency and proffer immunity are allowed under the Competition Law. **31.114**

Under the leniency rules, individuals and corporations involved in an administrative fining procedure may voluntarily undertake a commitment (i) to cease-and-desist any conduct subject to a competition investigation or (ii) voluntarily modify or amend certain aspects related thereto, in exchange for an indefinite suspension of the fining procedures. In evaluating such petitions, the Competition Commission will require a formal acknowledgement of all or part of the charges under investigation, evidence that the anticompetitive practices under investigation have not caused severe damage to consumer welfare, and corrective actions that may allow authorities to verify that the anticompetitive practices have ceased and that guarantee that they will not be repeated. **31.115**

The approval of a leniency commitment results in an indefinite suspension of fining procedures. Regardless of the outcome, individuals affected by said practices are still entitled to seek damages before the judiciary. **31.116**

As part of the Competition Commission's standard practices, leniency petitions (including the fact of their filing) are treated as confidential while they are under review and until such time as they are approved. Rulings by the Competition Commission approving leniency commitments are normally accessible to the general public, although authorities may decree part of the background documentation on record as classified. In contrast, the Competition Commission continues to treat leniency petitions that are rejected as confidential. **31.117**

In addition to leniency commitments, a defendant in a competition investigation may request immunity as part of a proffer or confession that serves to identify and evidence illegal competition activities. Proffer immunity petitions may be filed before the Technical Secretariat at any stage during the investigation. If the Technical Secretariat deems that the evidence proffered is sufficient to sanction the illegal practices under investigation, it may propose to the Competition Commission that the petition be accepted. **31.118**

Immunity agreements are executed between the collaborating party and the Technical Secretariat and may, with the approval of the Competition Commission, contain confidentiality provisions as to the source of the evidence proffered, if the nature of such evidence allows it. **31.119**

The execution and fulfillment of an immunity agreement exonerates the defendant of all administrative liability resulting from the illegal practice, barring the Competition Commission from initiating procedures related to the same facts. Notwithstanding, individuals affected by said practice are still entitled to seek damages before the judiciary. **31.120**

H. Document creation and retention

The Competition Law does not include explicit rules on document creation and retention. **31.121**

Notwithstanding, current legislation grants authorities the power to summon individuals and corporations the exhibition and presentation of any kind of documentation, including corporate and accounting books, invoices, commercial correspondence, and any form of electronic media content (including the application software required to process it), as well as to require information related to the organization, the businesses and the shareholder and property structure of any corporation. **31.122**

31.123 To secure collaboration during the investigations, the Competition Commission is empowered to impose coercive fines in the event of refusals to cooperate. Accordingly, authorities may fine individuals or corporations who unjustifiably fail to fulfil their information requests up to 50 Tax Reference Units (approx. USD 75,000), without hindering any criminal liability that may arise. These fines may be duplicated indefinitely in the event of persisting behavior until compliance is secured.

31.124 Furthermore, any information presented or supplied to INDECOPI during the course of an investigation is deemed by law as an affidavit. Accordingly, fines of up to 50 Tax Reference Units (approx. USD 75,000) may be imposed on all those who willfully supply false information or hide, destroy or alter books, records, or documents, without hindering any criminal liability that may arise. These fines may also be duplicated indefinitely in the event of repeated offenses.

32

POLAND

Dorothy Hansberry-Bieguńska and Lech Bieguński
Hansberry Competition

Introduction

Following the political changes of 1989, Poland began its successful transition to a market **32.01**
economy. Within a short time, the Polish parliament enacted the Act on Counteracting Monopolistic Practices.[1] Since that time, the competition law was amended twelve times. The current competition law is the 2007 Act on Competition and Consumer Protection ("the Act").[2] The Chairman of the Polish Office for the Protection of Competition and Consumers (OPCC, or the "Office") is responsible for instituting and conducting investigatory proceedings against undertakings that may have violated the Act.

[1] Act on Counteracting Monopolistic Practices, Journal of Laws No. 14, item 88 (enacted February 24, 1990).

[2] Act on Competition and Consumer Protection, Journal of Laws no. 50, item 331, as amended (enacted February 16, 2007).

32.02 The Act's application extends to the conduct of foreign undertakings, if such conduct causes or may cause effects in the territory of Poland. In addition, from the time Poland joined the European Union (EU) in May 2004, the Chairman of the OPCC has been empowered to investigate violations of articles 101 and 102 of the Treaty on the Functioning of the European Union (TFEU) if such violations affects trade between member states. Article 6 of the Act, prohibiting certain types of agreements, mirrors article 101 TFEU, and article 9, which prohibits the abuse of a dominant position, mirrors article 102 TFEU. The OPCC Chairman often relies upon decisions of the European Commission and judgments of the European courts to support and justify OPCC decisions. In recent years, cartels, abuses of dominance in local markets and resale price maintenance have been the priorities of the Office.

I. Acting alone

32.03 Unilateral conduct falls under the ambit of article 9 of the Act, which mirrors article 102 TFEU and prohibits the abuse of a dominant position.

32.04 A dominant position is defined in article 4 (10) of the Act as

> a position of the undertaking which allows it to prevent the efficient competition within a relevant market thus enabling it to act in a significant degree independently of competitors, contracting parties and consumers; it is assumed that the undertaking holds a dominant position if its market share exceeds 40%.

Although the presumption of dominance at a 40 percent threshold is a rebuttable presumption, the OPCC has often adopted a rigid position and found that dominance is achieved upon the acquisition of a market share of 40 percent or higher.

A. Predatory pricing

32.05 It appears from the scarce number of Office investigations of predatory pricing that enforcement of this form of abuse of a dominant position occurs less frequently in the Polish economy. One such investigation took place with respect to the pharmaceutical industry. Among other things, the OPCC investigated whether GlaxoSmithKline Pharmaceuticals S.A. ("Glaxo") held, and if so, had abused, a dominant position by engaging in predatory pricing.[3] The OPCC's investigation was triggered by a complaint from a competitor of Glaxo, who was admitted as an interested party to the investigatory proceeding. Under the former Act, as mentioned in Section III.A, interested parties were able to be admitted as parties to the proceedings with the right to review case files and appeal a decision of the OPCC.

32.06 Specifically, the OPCC investigated whether Glaxo had imposed glaringly low prices in its bid to a hospital in Krakow. The relevant market was found to be the domestic market for inhaled corticosteroids.

32.07 The OPCC found that the Glaxo's comparative market share, measured according to the Growth Share Matrix of The Product Portfolio methodology of Boston Consulting Group, significantly exceeded—in the year preceding the issuance of the Office's decision—the level of 1.5, recognized as an advantage and indicative of dominance. With regard to the predatory pricing charge, the Office used the Areeda-Turner test and considered whether a dominant company's price was below average variable cost and thus, presumed predatory. It found that the prices offered by Glaxo's in the bid were indeed drastically lower than the purchase price for the medicine, which was imported by Glaxo.

---

[3] *GlaxoSmithKline Pharmaceuticals S.A.*, OPCC Decision no. RPZ 22 [2006].

However, in the course of its investigation, the OPCC noticed that in accordance with the tender specification required by the hospitals, the investigated remedy was offered in packets that included a number of other medicines. The conclusive criterion of a successful tender was the price of the entire packet, not of the particular remedies. Thus, the bidders competed based upon the prices of their respective packets, and not the prices of particular remedies. According to the Office, an evaluation of the alleged use by Glaxo of glaringly low prices in its bid should include proof that the price of the entire packet was lower than the average variable cost of production of all medicines contained in a packet. A comparative analysis of the winning Glaxo bid and the second most competitive offer showed that the price differences among the particular medications in the two bidders' packets did not exceed the Polish currency equivalent of EUR 0.50. Moreover, the second offer under comparison contained lower as well as higher prices of particular medications than those offered by Glaxo. **32.08**

The Office concluded its investigation with the finding that Glaxo had not abused its dominant position in the relevant market by offering glaringly low prices in tenders organized by hospitals. **32.09**

B. Exploitative offenses (excessive pricing, monopoly leveraging)

There are no special rules regulating issues relating to exploitive offenses, excessive prices, or monopoly leveraging. Investigations of these practices occur within the ambit of article 9 of the Act (prohibition of abuses of dominance), which is presented below. **32.10**

C. Monopsony

The Act does not differentiate between a dominant position held by a purchaser and by a seller. A company that holds a dominant purchasing position and exploits its suppliers may be found to have abused its dominant position. There have been a few investigations involving the abuse of dominance by a company on the buying side. In one such case, the Office investigated whether a buyer of sugar beets, Sugar Plant Pelplin (the "Sugar Plant") abused its dominant position by imposing unfair conditions upon growers in its output contracts for sugar beets.[4] The OPCC's investigation was triggered by a request to start an investigation by the National Union of Root Crops' Planters. Once the relevant market was defined—as that of sugar beets purchased by the Sugar Plant in its contract territory—it was clear that the Sugar Plant possessed a dominant position in the market because, on the supply side, there were numerous growers, whereas on the demand side, there was practically only one company, the Sugar Plant. **32.11**

In assessing whether the Sugar Plant's conduct constituted an abuse of dominance, the Office investigated whether the Sugar Plant imposed upon the growers conditions of their contracts, and whether such conditions were anticompetitive. The OPCC noted that according to the Polish law on sugar production, the terms of the output contracts for sugar beets should have been agreed upon with the Union of Sugar Beet Growers. However, in the case at hand, the Sugar Plant ignored that law and simply unilaterally dictated the terms of the agreement in such a way that it abused its position of dominance. **32.12**

The Office undertook a review of whether the agreements between the growers and dominant buyer reflected the principle of equality of parties. According to the terms of the investigated agreements, the Sugar Plant was able to charge a contractual penalty or request compensation for any damages (which were to be understood as at least the incurred additional costs) in the event that a grower failed to deliver the contracted beets. If the Sugar Plant were to refuse, however, without even giving any reason, to receive beets that met the quality requirements, a grower could demand only a limited percentage of the value of such beets. The Sugar Plant limited its own liability to the disadvantage of the suppliers. **32.13**

[4] *Cukrownia Pelplin Sugar Plant*, OPCC Decision no. RGD. 32 [2001]

32.14 The Office concluded that the imposition by the Sugar Plant of the above-described conditions for the purchase of sugar beets was anticompetitive because they allowed for exploitative abuse of the Sugar Plant's dominant position. The OPCC ordered Sugar Plant to abandon the challenged practices.

D. Price discrimination

32.15 Both the EU and Polish prohibitions on abuse of dominance cover the practice of charging different prices to similarly placed customers, or charging the same prices to differently placed customers. Dominant undertakings are not allowed to charge less favorable prices (or offer less favorable terms) to customers under similar circumstances unless there is an objective justification for such a differentiation.

32.16 In 2009, the OPCC Chairman imposed a fine of the equivalent of EUR 15 million on PKP Cargo S.A., a railway freight transportation company for abusing its dominant position by treating its customers differently.[5] The majority shareholder of PKP Cargo S.A. is a state-owned company PKP S.A. Within the EU, PKP Cargo S.A. is the second largest rail carrier. A victim of PKP Cargo's conduct was CTL Logistics S.A., the largest private enterprise in railway transportation of goods in Poland.

32.17 The Office charged PKP Cargo with abusing its dominant position by refusing to give its competitors the same favorable terms (lower rates) as those given to customers who were not competitors. The OPCC found that PKP Cargo had infringed article 8.2.5 of the Competition Law of 2000, by hindering the emergence or development of competition.

32.18 PKP Cargo defended itself by explaining that it had the right to offer competitor companies different conditions from those offered to customers who did not compete, because to do otherwise would be to "support competitors and strengthen their market power at the cost of PKP Cargo." According to the OPCC, this defense in fact demonstrated that the goal of PKP Cargo was to limit competition by depriving competitors of the possibility of transporting goods with PKP Cargo at the otherwise prevailing market conditions. OPCC found that PKP Cargo limited entry into the market and interfered with the ability of competitor carriers to offer a full range of transportation service to their clients.

E. Dictating or influencing resale prices

32.19 Resale price maintenance (RPM) is considered a hard core restriction of competition, and is pursued almost exclusively under article 6's prohibition of anticompetitive agreements rather than under article 9's prohibition of abuse of dominance. Recommended resale prices and maximum retail price agreements are permitted, provided that they are not accompanied by other factors or conduct that cause distributors to treat them as fixed or minimum resale prices.

32.20 For several years, RPM has been one of the enforcement priorities of the OPCC and for this reason, the subject is more widely considered in this section. In one case, the OPCC used the evidence provided by a leniency applicant to a series of vertical price-fixing agreements.[6] The case involved a vertical price agreement among Polifarb Cieszyn-Wrocław S.A. (PCW), a manufacturer of paints and varnishes, and operators of seven chains of Do-It-Yourself (DIY) stores in Poland. The OPCC found that the DIY chains agreed to charge PCW-suggested minimum retail prices for certain PCW products in exchange for special discounts. Withdrawal from the retail price agreement meant that the DIY retailer would lose its discount and, in some cases, would no longer be supplied by PCW. The OPCC established that

[5] *PKP Cargo S.A.*, OPCC Decision no. DOK-3 [2009].

[6] *Polifarb Cieszyn S.A. and others*, OPCC Decision no. DOK-107 [2006].

the vertical agreements had been initiated by PCW, and that it mediated among the DIYs by, for instance, explaining why competitors' prices differed from those that had been initially agreed upon with PCW. Moreover, PCW kept the DIYs informed of the terms and dates on which its suggested retail prices would be introduced by competing DIY chains.

Several appeals were filed by the accused parties. In its judgment, the Court of Competition and Consumer Protection (the "Competition Court") agreed with most of the OPCC's findings. With regard to the fines, the Competition Court decided to decrease significantly the number of fines imposed by the OPCC upon certain DIYs and ruled that the fine imposed on the initiator of an agreement cannot be lower than that set for a passive party to an illegal agreement. According to the Competition Court, not only the percentage of turnover but the specific level of a fine should be taken into consideration by the OPCC when imposing a fine. **32.21**

The Court of Appeals quashed the Competition Court verdict in October 2009. Although the second instance court agreed with some findings of the Competition Court, it found that the lower court's verdict was insufficiently grounded. The Court of Appeals ordered the Competition Court to determine which specific behavior of each DIY chain had allowed the Court to find that they had each agreed to participate in the illegal agreements. **32.22**

Building on the PCW case, the OPCC opened four more investigations of vertical price fixing in the paint and varnish industry in Poland. In each of the cases, there was at least one leniency applicant. Each of the four investigations concluded with a decision that anticompetitive conduct had occurred in the form of illegal vertical price fixing, and often with a horizontal effect. **32.23**

In a 2011 RPM case in a different sector,[7] the OPCC issued a "commitment decision" (a commitment decision is a milder form of Office decision and carries no fine) pursuant to article 12 of the Act, concerning Scotts Poland's distribution agreements on fertilizers and plant protection products. Since 2003, the investigated agreements included a provision that the "distributor will sell Scotts products at prices agreed upon with Scotts." Scotts committed to eliminate and to refrain from the introduction of the questioned clauses. **32.24**

The OPCC accepted the commitment due to Scott's relatively low market share in Poland and because the challenged vertical price clause was not used in practice. The published version of the decision did not contain evidence supporting the two findings. First, evidence concerning Scott's market share was treated as confidential and thus not included in the public version of the decision. Second, evidence that the agreed-upon prices were not charged was based upon the Office's comparison of those prices and the prices actually charged by distributors. Results of this analysis were not included in the decision, either. The decision stands as a deviation from the Office's customary hard-line approach when faced with vertical price fixing, which is forbidden under the Act with no *de minimis* exemption, regardless of whether the effect of agreement has been achieved. Under the Office 2012 Guidelines on Issuances of Commitment Decisions (issued one year after the Scotts Decision), an article 12 commitment decision would likely not be available for the vertical price fixing conduct found in the Scotts Decision. **32.25**

There are no cases of which the authors are aware involving a minimum advertised price program. The obligation of a distributor or retailer not to advertise prices below a certain price level is very likely to be deemed as RPM. If presented with evidence of such a practice, it is likely that the OPCC would investigate the conduct under article 6 (illegal agreements) or article 9 of the Act, if a party held a dominant position. **32.26**

---

[7] *Scotts Poland Sp. z o.o.*, OPCC Decision no. DOK-3 [2011].

F. Tying arrangements

32.27 Tying products or services can be in violation of the Act's article 6(5) (prohibition of illegal agreements) and article 9(4) of the Act, both of which prohibit "making conclusion of an agreement subject to acceptance or fulfilment by the other party of another performance, having neither substantial nor customary relation with the subject of such agreement."

32.28 With regard to the right to public broadcasting of sports events, the OPCC Chairman issued a decision finding that the tying of certain products amounted to an abuse of dominance in violation of article 9.[8] The OPCC investigated the terms of the sale of rights to public broadcasting of Euro 2008, to which Cyfrowy Polsat, one of the DTH satellite television services in Poland, had exclusive rights. Companies that were interested in broadcasting the championships had to conclude a contract with the Cyfrowy Polsat. The OPCC found that Cyfrowy Polsat had a dominant position and made the sale of the rights to the public broadcast of the matches dependent on the purchase of a decoder and technical support services. In this way it obtained unjustified benefits.

32.29 The OPCC decided to issue a commitment decision pursuant to article 12 of the Act and in the decision, obliged Cyfrowy Polsat to repurchase the tied decoders from the affected undertakings and to reimburse all costs of the tied technical support services. Cyfrowy Polsat was obliged to submit a report on the implementation of the commitment decision, *inter alia*, on the occasion of the next three licensed sports events, for which it will acquire the exclusive rights to the sale of rights to public broadcasting.

32.30 In adopting a commitment decision, the OPCC Chairman refrained from imposing a financial penalty. However, sanctions may arise in situations in which an undertaking fails to fulfill its obligations. The maximum financial penalty is EUR 10,000 per each day of delay in the implementation of the decision.

G. Exclusive dealing

32.31 In the context of exclusive distribution, there is a Polish block exemption for vertical agreements. The Regulation of the Council of Ministers of March 30, 2011 on the "exemption of certain types of vertical agreements from the prohibition on competition restricting agreements" (the "Vertical Regulation") replaced the Vertical Regulation of November 19, 2007. Pursuant to the Vertical Regulation, the grant of an exclusive territory or customer group to a distributor—with the commitment by the supplier not to supply other distributors in that territory or customer group—will not infringe the Act, provided that (i) the supplier and the capital group to which it belongs have a share of less than 30 percent of the relevant market for the contract products; (ii) the purchaser and the capital group to which it belongs have a share of less than 30 percent of the market for purchasing such products; and (iii) the arrangement does not contain any "hard core" restrictions, such as resale price maintenance, or restrictions on the ability of the distributor to deal with unsolicited orders from other geographic territories or customer groups, etc. Similarly, the agreement that a distributor will purchase exclusively (or quasi-exclusively) from a particular supplier will fall within the safe harbor exemption if the parties meet the above-mentioned market share thresholds and the agreement does not exceed five years in duration. Arrangements falling outside the safe harbor block exemption must be assessed individually for antitrust compliance.

H. Refusal to deal

32.32 The Office's approach to refusals to deal is consistent with other competition authorities. While the Office recognizes that a refusal to deal can be an abuse of dominant position, the

[8] *Cyfrowy Polsat S.A.*, OPCC Decision no. DOK-1 [2010].

Office also recognises that businesses are generally free to supply, or not to supply, whomever they choose, and that this freedom should be limited if there is evidence of likely substantial harm to competition and if the behavior cannot be objectively justified.

The approach of the Office when it finds that a refusal to deal is an abuse of dominance is reflected in a natural gas industry case. The goal of OPCC's investigation in this case was to determine whether Polish Oil and Gas Company (PGNiG) had abused a position of dominance by refusing to sell and deliver gas to its competitor and vendor of natural gas to end purchasers, DOK-2/2012. PGNiG is the largest vendor of natural gas in Poland and the largest importer of gas. A majority shareholder in this company is Polish government. The OPCC's investigation was triggered by a complaint of New Gas (NG). NG is a company that sells natural gas to end purchasers in central Poland. It does not have its own pipelines and needs access to PGNiG's gas transfer and distribution network in order to operate. **32.33**

In January 2010, NG asked PGNiG to execute an agreement for the sale and delivery of gas to defined points of reception on complex terms of agreement. PGNiG refused to sign such an agreement. It explained that the rules of allocation defined by the Polish energy regulator's Instruction of Movement and Exploitation of Distribution Network (the "Instruction") did not allow for such a settlement of gas. The Instruction is based on the Polish Energy Law, and it was prepared by a distributor (in this case PGNiG) and authorized by the President of the Office of Regulation of Energy (URE). A few weeks later, PGNiG asked URE to accept a proposed change in the Instruction, arguing that the current version did not define the solutions that a distributor should implement in respect of the distribution system trading balance when the supplier has been changed. In a decision issued a few months later, URE refused the proposed change. The reason for the refusal, URE explained, was that the Instruction clearly and precisely described the procedure for the change of supplier and the methods of gas allocation. Despite URE's clear explanation that the Instruction already contained the procedure PGNiG inquired about, PGNiG held its position for another few months until November 2010, when it finally proposed NG new rules of allocation of gas. **32.34**

During its investigation, the Office defined the relevant market in which PGNiG engaged in the questioned practice as the domestic wholesale natural gas market. The share of independent active participants in the wholesale and retail markets does not exceed 2 percent, which means that, undoubtedly, PGNiG was dominant in this market. The OPCC found that PGNiG had abused its dominant position by its refusal to sell natural gas as per the complex agreement regarding NG's planned resale of gas. NG had no alternative sources of gas supply. Moreover, PGNiG's refusal was not justified by any rational arguments. Therefore, the refusal to sell gas led to reduced competition in the domestic market for retail gas. By engaging in this abusive practice, PGNiG transferred its market power to a related market in which it also held a dominant position. PGNiG's refusal to execute a complex agreement, and by extension to sell gas, harmed consumers and contractors. For this violation, the OPCC imposed on PGNiG a fine of PLN 60 million (approx. EUR15 million).[9] **32.35**

More recently, the Office has announced that it opened another investigation in order to determine whether PGNiG had again abused its dominant position. An Office press release described the investigation. The OPCC inspected the agreements concluded between PGNiG and its industrial contractors, representatives buying from PGNiG gas fuel intended for further resale as well as standard forms of agreements applied by PGNiG. The initial analysis of clauses contained therein revealed that they may result in the restriction of competition. The Chairman was concerned, among other things, about clauses restricting the possibility **32.36**

[9] *Polskie Górnictwo Naftowe i Gazownictwo S.A.*, OPCC Decision no. DOK-2 [2012].

of recipients of gas fuel to decrease the amount of gas fuel ordered for subsequent years as compared to the previous orders. Furthermore, the Chairman of the OPCC challenged these clauses which hindered contractors from further resale of gas purchased from PGNiG. The proceedings will be conducted based on EU law as well, declared the Office.

32.37 In a recent case involving the dominant rail freight carrier, PKP Cargo, the Office found that PKP had again abused its dominant position and issued a fine of PLN 16.5 million (EUR 4.1 million).[10] The investigation was initiated by the Office in August 2012, following a complaint filed by Majkoltrans (one of the company's contractors), which operated in the shipping industry. When providing services to its contractors, the company uses, *inter alia*, carriage services by PKP Cargo. The Office found that PKP Cargo refused to render services to the complainant within the area of three stations in a region of Poland located close to coal mines. As a result, the complainant lost its key trading partners who, faced with no alternative, were forced to conclude an agreement with companies belonging to the PKP Cargo capital group. Thus, PKP Cargo's abuse of its dominant market position affected not only Majkoltrans, but also other contractors who were deprived of the choice of carriers. As the Office announced, "this is the next decision concerning the infringement of the antitrust law by PKP Cargo." The company was fined three times before—in 2004 (in June and December), and in 2009 (see para. 32.16).[11]

32.38 As can be seen, the Office carefully monitors the sectors that were subject to prior investigations, and is ready to intervene if necessary.

I. Essential facilities

32.39 A refusal to grant access to an essential facility is in principle treated in the same way as a refusal to deal.

32.40 In 2009, the European Commission investigated the conduct of the Polish telecommunications operator, Telekomunikacja Polska (TP) with regard to TP's refusal to allow competitors access to its facilities.[12]

32.41 In April 2009, the Commission initiated proceedings under article 2(1) of Council Regulation 773/2004[13] and article 11(6) of Council Regulation 1/2003.[14] During the investigation, pursuant to article 18 of Regulation 1/2003, DG Competition sent several requests for information to TP, to alternative operators, which either purchased or were interested in purchasing TP's wholesale broadband Internet access products and to the Polish regulator competent for telecommunications (Office of Electronic Communications). In February 2010, the Commission adopted a statement of objections in which it took the preliminary view that TP held a dominant position in the relevant markets in Poland and had abused it by refusing to supply wholesale broadband Internet access products to alternative operators, thereby inhibiting the development of competition in the retail broadband market in Poland.

32.42 TP denied the existence of the abuse. It admitted certain difficulties in providing access to its wholesale broadband products, in particular in 2006 and 2007, but argued that they could be explained by the technical upgrades which TP had to undergo over a very short time to adapt to the new regulatory environment.

[10] *PKP Cargo S.A.*, OPCC Decision no. RWR 44 [2012].

[11] *PKP Cargo S.A.*, OPCC Decisions no. DOK-50 [2004], No. DOK- 142 [2004], No. DOK-3 [2009].

[12] *European Commission v. Telekomunikacja Polska*, Case no. COMP/39.525 (June 20, 2011).

[13] Commission Regulation (EC) No. 773/2004 relating to the conduct of proceedings by the Commission pursuant to Articles [101 and 102 TFEU] (April 7, 2004) OJ L 123.

[14] Council Regulation (EC) No. 1/2003 on the implementation of the rules on competition laid down in Articles [101 and 102 TFEU] (December 16, 2002).

The Commission found TP's defense to be unpersuasive, and in its decision of June 22, 2011, found that TP committed a single and continuous infringement of article 102 TFEU from August 3, 2005 until at least October 22, 2009 by refusing to give access to its wholesale broadband products. The Commission imposed a fine of EUR 127,554,194 for the infringement.[15] **32.43**

The Commission's decision explained why TP's arguments were not acceptable. The case file included solid evidence of TP's exclusionary conduct. Contemporaneous internal documents of TP confirmed that TP's strategy was designed to impede the access of alternative operators to TP's network. The incumbent had a great deal of time to prepare its internal resources and IT systems for upcoming access obligations (imposed in 2005 and 2006). TP had been aware of these obligations at least since 2003, when Polish telecommunication law identified TP as a significant market power operator. **32.44**

There are significant barriers to entry and expansion in the relevant markets. They arise from the fact that duplicating TP's network is not economically viable. Other barriers include investment and sunk costs, limited product and price differentiation, and the absence of countervailing buying power. The high barriers to entry and expansion are consistent with the market structure observed, where all of TP's competitors are left with a small market share, which, in the case of Netia—TP's largest digital subscriber line competitor—is up to 9 percent (in terms of the number of lines).[16] **32.45**

The decision explained that TP's abusive conduct in the wholesale market had the likely effect of restricting competition in the retail market. The decision relied on empirical evidence that TP's refusal to supply was likely to reduce the rate of entry and expansion of competitors on the retail market for digital subscriber line services, and that TP remains the largest digital subscriber line supplier on the retail market. The low number of unbundled local loops, the Commission found, is a revealing indicator of the likely effect of TP's refusal to supply access to its wholesale products, delaying the growth of competition and thereby the development of alternative infrastructures. **32.46**

In this case, the Office worked closely with the European Commission's investigation. When asked why it had investigated the matter rather than the Office, the Commission explained: **32.47**

> [t]he existence of national sector-specific regulation does not preclude the application of EU competition rules. In the case at hand, despite the regulatory mechanisms put in place by the Polish Office of Electronic Communications obliging TP to give access to its network, competition was restricted due to TP's abusive behavior. The Commission's intervention does not in any case relate to the specific infringements of regulations but to TP's pattern of abusive behavior over more than four years, which constitutes a breach of Art.102 TFEU.[17]

J. Bundling (including loyalty and market share discounts)

There are no specific rules regulating issues relating to bundling in the context of Polish competition law and practice. **32.48**

The OPCC's Regional Offices focus on the protection of competition in local markets, as is exemplified by the decision imposing on EnergiaPro a fine of more than PLN 253,000 (EUR 63,000) for abusing its dominant position in the market of the supply and sales of **32.49**

[15] *European Commission v. Telekomunikacja Polska*, EC Case No. COMP/39.525 (June 20, 2011).

[16] A digital subscriber line is a family of technologies that provide internet access by transmitting digital data over the wires of a local telephone network. This internet service can be delivered simultaneously with wired telephone service on the same telephone line.

[17] See "Commission decision against Telekomunikacja Polska, Frequently asked questions," EC MEMO/11/444 (June 22, 2011), <europa.eu/rapid/press-release_MEMO-11-444_en.htm>.>

electricity in the Lower Silesia and Opole regions of Poland.[18] The Wroclaw Regional Office launched antitrust investigatory proceedings in September 2009, and found that EnergiaPro forced residential and business customers alike to bear the costs of signing a notary deed for the establishment of easements to land zones owned by the respective customers. At the time of the infringement, the fees charged by notaries to all customers of EnergiaPro amounted to PLN 269,000 PLN (approx. EUR 66,000). The executed notary deeds made it possible for EnergiaPro to legally use the areas where the power grids ran, for the purposes of, for instance, maintenance and repair. By law, EnergiaPro was supposed to pay such costs (including notary fees for easements), but instead, it transferred these costs onto its customers.

K. Standard-setting groups (disclosure requirements, licensing arrangements, and licensing pools)

32.50 There are no specific rules regulating issues related to standard setting groups in the context of Polish competition law and practice.

L. Customer termination

32.51 Generally, sellers are free to choose the customers to whom they wish to sell their products and services, and are therefore free to terminate their dealings with those customers at any time. A dominant company may, under certain circumstances, be under the obligation to supply customers, for instance because they are competitors that need access to an essential product or service of the dominant company.

M. Termination of intermediaries (retailers, wholesalers, dealers, and value-added resellers, agents, and brokers)

32.52 It is probable that the Office would treat the termination of contracts with intermediaries in the same way as it would a case of a termination of a contract with a customer.

N. Termination of relationships with competitors

32.53 There may be instances in which a dominant company is required to sell a product or service to a competitor if such sale would be necessary to enable the competitor to either enter the market or compete effectively.[19]

O. Exemptions

32.54 Article 8(1) and (2) of the Act is the Polish equivalent of article 101(3) TFEU, and it exempts agreements and understandings between undertakings from the applicability of article 6 of the Act (prohibition of anticompetitive agreements) if the efficiencies flowing from an agreement outweigh its anticompetitive effects. A charged undertaking has the burden of proving that its conduct meets each of the four criteria of article 8(1) of the Act in order to benefit from the exemption.

32.55 Article 8(3) of the Act specifically empowers the Polish Council of Ministers to enact regulations that exempt from article 6, item 1 prohibition certain types of agreements which meet the conditions referred to in article 8(1) and (2), taking into consideration the benefits resulting from such types of agreements. Currently, there are four block exemption regulations:

(1) block exemption for certain vertical agreements (Regulation of the Council of Ministers of March 30, 2011);

[18] *EnergiaPro S.A.*, OPCC Decision no. RWR 2 [2010].

[19] Please see Section I.I for a discussion of the *TP* case, and Section I.D for a discussion of the *PGNiG* case.

(2) block exemption for certain transfer of technology agreements (Regulation of the Council of Ministers of July 30, 2007);
(3) block exemption for certain specialization and research & development agreements (Regulation of the Council of Ministers of November 19, 2007); and
(4) block exemption for certain motor vehicle distribution agreements (Regulation of the Council of Ministers of October 8, 2010).

No industry-specific offenses, exemptions, or defenses exist with respect to violations of the Act. Separate Polish laws, however, exempt industries such as the state monopoly regulating gaming and lotteries and certain agricultural markets from the general prohibition of anticompetitive practices. The insurance industry enjoys a limited amount of freedom with respect to exchanges of certain information among competitors, and such exchanges are limited in scope. **32.56**

Although there are no exemptions from the offense of abuse of dominance, conduct that can be shown by the dominant company to be objectively necessary and proportionate may be found to be in compliance with the Act. **32.57**

II. Dealing with competitors

As explained in the Introduction, both EU and Polish competition law apply in Poland. The Act follows EU substantive principles and its article 6 is modeled upon article 101 TFEU. Pursuant to the Act, agreements (or clauses in agreements) containing or constituting restrictive practices are invalid *ab initio* in whole or in part. Article 6, which applies both to vertical and horizontal restrictions, prohibits agreements (defined in article 4(5) of the Competition Act as formal or informal agreements, concerted practices, and understandings) which have as their object or effect the elimination or restriction of, or any other harm to, competition in the relevant market. **32.58**

Article 7 of the Act sets out a *de minimis* exemption for certain conduct prohibited by article 6. The *de minimis* rule, however, does not exempt agreements on price fixing, market division, production restriction and collusive tendering, which are always punishable under the Act. Article 8 of the Act both sets out the criteria for a rule of reason defense and refers to block exemptions that the Polish Council of Ministers may enact in the form of a regulation. As mentioned in paragraph 3.55, the Polish Council of Ministers has issued four block exemptions. In addition to being authorized to issue article 8(3) block exemptions, the Polish Council of Ministers is empowered by article 109(5) of the Act to issue a regulation on the procedures for applying for leniency, and it has done so in its leniency regulation of January 26, 2009. **32.59**

A. Horizontal price fixing (including advanced announcements of price or product changes)

To date, the OPCC's major price-fixing case,[20] concerned the cement industry. After a lengthy investigation that drew upon evidence collected from dawn raids and supplied by leniency applicants, the OPCC issued a decision finding that the leading cement producers in Poland had formed a cartel that operated from at least 1998 and through the date of the OPCC's decision, December 8, 2009. Seven cement companies (two of which were granted leniency) were found to have agreed upon the prices or other sale conditions of gray cement; divided the gray cement production and sale markets; and exchanged confidential commercial information, in large part through a trade association. The OPCC concluded that the cement companies intended to stabilize the market by "freezing" their market shares. To do **32.60**

[20] *Lafarge Cement S.A. and others*, OPCC Decision no. DOK-7 [2009].

this, they fixed prices and the levels and dates of price increases and avoided "price wars" among themselves. The exchange of confidential information served to monitor the agreed arrangements regarding the maintenance of a fixed volume of market shares and to ensure full predictability and transparency of the competitors' market moves.

32.61 The first leniency applicant, Lafarge Cement received a waiver of a fine. The fine for the second leniency applicant, for Górażdże Cement, was in the amount constituting 5 percent of its revenue. The remaining five participants of the cartel were each given the maximum fine in the amount of 10 percent of each undertaking's revenue. Altogether, the fines imposed amounted to PLN 411 million (approx. EUR 100 million).[21]

32.62 In a case concerning the setting of interchange banking fees by banks in the MasterCard and Visa payment card systems, the OPCC found a horizontal violation of article 6 of the Act and article 101 TFEU.[22] The case concerned the joint setting by Polish banks of the levels of interchange fees collected on transactions made using Visa and MasterCard cards in Poland. An interchange fee is a component of a four-party payment card systems. In such a system, banks—issuers of payment cards—offer cards to card users, for which they collect fees (usually, such fees are collected annually). Acquiring banks ("acquirers") assure the servicing of a transaction made using a card to pay a merchant (retailers, shops, commercial outlets). The acquirers provide the merchant with equipment facilitating the transaction, conduct settlements of amounts in respect of card transactions and transfer amounts to the merchant's account. Acquirers collect a fee for this service, which is called a merchant service charge. The interchange fee in turn is a payment made by the acquirer to the bank that issues a card to the user.

32.63 The OPCC found that as a result of the challenged agreements, the merchant service charge fee collected from merchants contains a uniform, significant cost component which is the interchange fee, set through multilateral agreements among certain banks. In the OPCC's view, such fee constitutes a minimum threshold for payments collected by acquirers from merchants. Interchange fee agreements, the OPCC concluded, lead to merchants being charged with higher payments for accepting cards at points of sales, which causes an increase in their costs, which may then be shifted in whole or in part to their customers by way of charging higher retail prices. The OPCC did not agree that the interchange fee is indispensable to the functioning of a four-party card system and thus, it did not consider that the parties had satisfied the exemption requirements of article 8 of the Act and article 101(3) TFEU.

32.64 At the conclusion of a five-year investigation, the OPCC issued a decision finding the practice of jointly setting the level of interchange fees collected on transactions made using Visa or MasterCard in Poland as being a restriction of competition and in violation of the prohibition of article 101 TFEU and the Act.

32.65 The OPCC's decision was appealed to the Competition Court. In its judgment, the Competition Court changed the OPCC Chairman's decision, declaring that jointly setting domestic interchange fees does not restrict competition in the relevant market that was defined by the OPCC.

32.66 The OPCC appealed the Competition Court's judgment to the Court of Appeals, who ruled that the OPCC Chairman had defined the correct relevant market and that the challenged conduct had an effect on that market. The case was returned to the Competition Court to examine the defenses put forward by the banks and card systems and, in this context, to determine whether the fines imposed upon the banks are appropriate. On November 21, 2013, the Competition Court announced that it had decided to uphold the OPCC's

[21] *Lafarge Cement* (n 20).

[22] *Visa International Service Association and others*, OPCC Decision no. DAR 15 [2006].

decision, reject all appeals, and lower the fines issued by the OPCC against the banks. The Competition Court will issue its written judgment in early 2014. The judgment can be appealed to the Court of Appeals.

B. Horizontal agreements to allocate customers or territories; agreements not to compete

Market sharing and customer allocation agreements are considered to be a form of hardcore cartel conduct. This conduct is treated in the same way as price fixing: there is no *de minimis* exemption, and the proof of either the intent or the effect of the illegal agreement is sufficient for liability. **32.67**

In an investigation of the market for paper and office supplies, the Office found that two competitors had divided the market by customers. One of the companies, Office Pulse, confessed to concluding an anticompetitive agreement with its competitor, Papier-Hurt, and provided the Office with incriminatory evidence, which was confirmed in the course of antitrust investigatory proceedings. The Office determined that the customer-allocation agreement had been initiated by Papier-Hurt, which forced Office Pulse to refrain from competing against it for five years, and in particular, from making any commercial offers to Papier-Hurt's customers. Breaking the terms of this market allocation agreement would entail financial sanctions. As a result of meeting the Act's leniency requirements, Office Pulse was not fined. Papier-Hurt was fined nearly PLN 90,000 PLN (EUR 22,000). **32.68**

In another case, a branch office of the Polish Post informed the Office about a suspicion of bid-rigging in a bid for the right to produce automated stamps (RWR-24/2010). Two of the bidders were Firma Handlowo-Usługowa "Krystian" K. Kwoczała of Olesnica ("Firma Krystian") and Biuro Grupa Dolny Śląsk S. Kwoczała ("Biuro Grupa Dolny"). Firma Krystian was awarded the bid. The following day, Firma Krystian announced that it could not fulfill the contract as the equipment used to produce automated stamps was broken. Pursuant to the procurement law, the tender organizer should then be able to choose the best offer from among the undertakings who had participated in the tender. In this case, it was Biuro Grupa Dolny. The Office investigated the bidding companies and concluded that the abandonment of the contract took place one day after the winner, Firma Krystian, had learned that the next lowest bid was placed by Biuro Grupa Dolny, the other participant of the bid-rigging agreement. Moreover, the failure of the Firma Krystian's equipment occurred before the company's bid in this tender. The Office fined Firma Krystian over PLN 13,000 (EUR 3,200) and Biuro Grupa Dolny over PLN 2,000 (EUR 500).[23] **32.69**

C. Horizontal boycotts

Agreements between competitors to boycott a rival are viewed as having the object of restricting competition and will therefore breach the civil prohibition on anticompetitive agreements regardless of whether the boycott is successful. This conduct is treated in the same way as price-fixing: there is no *de minimis* exemption and the proof of either intent or the effect of the illegal agreement is sufficient for liability. **32.70**

In a media market decision,[24] the OPCC found that competitors had agreed on how they would behave with regard to purchasing services from a mobile television wholesale provider. In 2009, the Office of Electronic Communications conducted a bid for the reservation of frequencies which would enable, *inter alia*, TV digital video broadcasting via mobile phones **32.71**

[23] *Firma Handlowo-Usługowa "Krystian" Karol Kwoczała and others*, OPCC Decision no. RWR 24 [2010].

[24] *Polkomtel S.A. and others*, OPCC Decision no. DOK 8 [2011].

(DVB-H). There were two bidders—Info-TV-FM and Mobile TV, a joint venture of four mobile network operators (Polkomtel, Polska Telefonia Cyfrowa, PTK Centertel, and P4) (the "Operators"). Earlier, the Operators had formed the joint venture of their intention to place a bid and (if awarded the bid) provide the tendered DVB-H business. The establishment of the joint-venture company was notified to the OPCC, which gave its consent. The winning bidder, Info-TV-FM, was granted the frequencies. In order to conduct the DVB-H business with individual consumers on a large scale, Info-TV-FM first had to execute agreements with the mobile telephony operators that were members of the Mobile TV joint venture. Info-TV-FM was unable to reach an agreement with Operators. After conducting a dawn raid and launching an investigation, the OPCC concluded that the Operators had agreed upon their respective behavior vis-à-vis Info-TV-FM and had exchanged confidential information in this regard. In the OPCC's opinion, the Operators' conduct eliminated any uncertainty needed in a competitive environment as to the commercial behavior of each Operator and its competitors. The development of the services market for television reception in mobile phone handset was hampered, the OPCC President concluded, and consumers were deprived of access to such services. In a decision ordering the cessation of the illegal conduct, the Chairman imposed the following fines: Polkomtel: PLN 33.4 million (EUR 8.1 million); Polska Telefonia Cyfrowa: PLN 34 million (EUR 8.3 million); Polska Telefonia Komórkowa Centertel: PLN 35 million (EUR 8.5 million); and P4: PLN 10.7 million (EUR 2.6 million).

D. Joint ventures and other competitive collaborations

32.72 Joint ventures and other collaborations between competitors that do not fall within the scope of the Polish merger control rules and that do not amount to hard core cartels will be prohibited if they have the effect of appreciably restricting actual or potential competition, and the undertakings parties cannot show that they satisfy the criteria for one of the available block exemptions or, failing that, the criteria for article 8 of the Act or article 101(3) TFEU.

E. Trade associations

32.73 In 2010, there were three decisions issued against the following trade associations: the Polish Journalists Association,[25] the National Council of Notaries,[26] and Beskidzka Chamber of Craft and Entrepreneurship.[27] Other investigations of trade associations are pending. It appears from the Office's investigations of trade associations that this form of cooperation among companies in some cases serves as a platform for reaching agreements restricting competition, for example, by setting uniform or minimum prices, setting the time when such prices will be charged, or by unifying costs such as labor costs.

32.74 In a case involving a trade association and its members in the car repair service sector, the OPCC found a non-binding price recommendation made by a trade association to its members to be anticompetitive and in breach of article 6 of the Act.[28] The price recommendation concerned the hourly rates recommended to garages for repairing broken cars. Broken cars are repaired either on a cash or non-cash basis. If a car owner accepts a cash repair, he is given a certain amount of money and is free to repair his car at any garage. A non-cash repair means that the car owner is obliged to have his car repaired in one of the car service centers selected by the insurance company. A cash settlement follows directly between the insurance company and the garage, and thus it is of no concern to the customer how much and when the insurance company pays. The investigated practice concerned non-cash repairs. The trade

[25] *The Polish Journalists Association*, OPCC Decision no. RPZ-26 [2010].
[26] *National Council of Notaries*, OPCC Decision no. RWA-3 [2010].
[27] *Beskidzka Chamber of Craft and Entrepreneurship*, OPCC Decision no. RKT-4 [2010].
[28] *Częstochowska Chamber of Craft and Entrepreneurship*, OPCC Decision no. RKT-22 [2009].

association recommended that garages should charge insurance companies prices not lower than what it recommended for mechanical, paintwork, and bodywork repairs. The recommendations were given in the form of letters signed by the trade association's authorities.

The OPCC found that the non-binding price recommendations made by the trade association concerning the hourly rates to be charged by its members to insurance companies constituted illegal conduct of association of undertakings. From the Office's perspective, it did not matter whether the price recommendations were binding and whether they were followed. In the OPCC's opinion, price recommendations may have influenced the market activity of garages, acting as a strong signal for them to raise retail prices if the prices charged originally were lower than those recommended. As a consequence, the recommendations could have caused an increase in prices for non-cash repairs covered by insurance firms. Thus, consumers could have been adversely affected as insurance companies may have had to increase their premiums. According to the OPCC, it is clear that the price recommendations made by trade associations may have eliminated uncertainty as to their members' business activities. It could be assumed that the purpose of the price recommendations was anticompetitive in light of the circumstances of this case. It is significant that the price recommendations concerned only non-cash repairs. In this case, consumers did not treat price as a competitive factor as the fees or the price were paid by insurance companies. Furthermore, consumers had a limited choice of garages in which they were allowed to repair their cars. Under such circumstances, it was easier for garages to comply with the recommended retail price, knowing that there was only a limited number of garages which were authorized to repair a given car, and knowing that price was not an issue for the consumer. **32.75**

F. Interlocking directorates

There is no rule explicitly prohibiting interlocking directorates, that is, a situation where a director or a management board member sits on the boards of two or more competitors. Clearly, when the same person sits on competing boards, there should be measures and procedures in place to protect against any inference of an illegal exchange of confidential information or of cartel conduct. **32.76**

G. Facilitating practices

As already mentioned, the OPCC has been active in the pursuit of "hub and spoke" cartels, in which competitors exchange anticompetitive information, as well as complaints on "cheating" on the vertical price agreements through a third party, typically a supplier.[29] **32.77**

H. Information Exchange

Information exchange can be treated as circumstantial evidence of an unlawful price-fixing or market-allocation agreement among competitors. In addition to serving as evidence of an unlawful agreement, information exchange may, under certain circumstances, be illegal in and of itself. **32.78**

As mentioned in Section II.G, in a case involving the cement industry,[30] the OPCC issued a decision finding that the leading cement producers in Poland had formed a cartel that operated from at least 1998 through to December 8, 2009, the date of the decision. Seven cement companies (two of which were granted leniency) were found to have agreed upon the prices or other sale conditions of gray cement; divided the gray cement production and sale markets; and exchanged confidential commercial information, in large part through a trade association. The OPCC concluded that the cement companies intended to stabilize the market by "freezing" their market shares. To do this, they fixed prices and the levels and dates of price increases **32.79**

[29] See the discussion in Sections III.B(iii) and I.E.
[30] *Lafarge Cement S.A. and others*, OPCC Decision no. DOK-7 [2009].

and avoided "price wars" among themselves. The exchange of confidential information served to monitor the agreed arrangements as to the maintenance of a fixed volume of market shares and to ensure full predictability and transparency of the competitors' market moves.

32.80 The exchange of current confidential information within the trade association by all the important actors in the market permitted the monitoring of practically the entire market in terms of changes in the demand levels and, thus, it permitted the adjustment of cement production volumes.

32.81 The OPCC charged the cement producers with exchanging data on the volumes of their monthly production and sales through vehicle of the trade association. The exchange was sometimes frequent and involved up-to-date information, sometimes covering ten-day periods.

32.82 The cement producers had changed the way in which they exchanged data within the trade association in late 2002. As of 2003, the information was to be collected by a law firm, not the trade association, and cement producers only obtained aggregated data concerning the entire sector. Data with the information broken down into individual cement producers were then provided after a year's delay. Relying upon EU case law, the OPCC found that this change was in conformity with the law as the one-year-old data were historic and aggregated. Nevertheless, the OPCC charged the cement companies with illegal exchange of confidential data as there was evidence that a number of the cement companies exchanged current, confidential data among themselves outside of the law firm's collection of historical, aggregated data.

(i) Exchange of historic pricing information

32.83 See paras. 32.78–32.82.

(ii) How old, anonymous, and aggregated pricing information needs to be

32.84 See paras. 32.78–32.82.

(iii) What pro-competitive purposes, if any, exchange needs to help participants achieve; pre-merger due diligence

32.85 There are no special rules or procedures covering the exchange of information in pre-merger due diligence. To the extent that disclosure of confidential information is necessary for due diligence or pre-merger integration planning purposes, it is always advisable to set up certain safeguards such as "Chinese walls" between staff or form "clean teams."

I. Joint purchasing agreements

32.86 There are no Polish guidelines for evaluating the legality of a joint purchasing agreement. It is likely, however, that that OPCC would follow the European Commission Horizontal Guidelines in assessing such an agreement.

J. Joint lobbying/regulatory/legislative efforts

32.87 There is no concept in Polish competition law corresponding to the US Supreme Court's "Noerr–Pennington doctrine," which grants antitrust immunity to the joint efforts of businesses to petition or influence government bodies, even though intended to eliminate competition.[31]

32.88 An example of such legislative efforts is in connection with the Polish government's initiative to regulate the level of interchange fees. The government set up a working group composed of

[31] See *Eastern Railroad Presidents Conference v. Noerr Motor Freight*, 365 U.S. 127 (1961) and *United Mine Workers v. Pennington*, 381 U.S. 657 (1965).

industry stakeholders, such as various ministries, merchant organizations, banks, competing payment card systems, and the OPCC. The working group is tasked with making recommendations and comments on the several versions of draft laws concerning interchange fees.

III. General issues

A. Jurisdiction and applicable law (including sector-specific competition regulation)

The Chairman of the OPCC is authorized to investigate potential violations of the Act. The only way in which an investigation (other than a merger investigation) can be launched is by the OPCC Chairman on an *ex officio* basis. Under the former competition acts, the Chairman was under the duty to act in response to a complaint of anticompetitive conduct. Now, under article 86 of the Act, one can only file with the OPCC Chairman a complaint describing suspected anticompetitive conduct. Such complaint is not binding upon the OPCC Chairman to take action. The Chairman must, however, inform the complainant of the OPCC's position on the complaint within the prescribed time. In the event that the Chairman follows up on the complaint and opens an investigation, the complainant will not be a party. In other words, under the current Act, a complainant has no right to be heard, no access to the case files, and cannot appeal a decision issued by the Chairman of the OPCC. Under the previous Competition Acts, it was possible for an interested party to be admitted as a party with the right to review case files and lodge an appeal of a decision of the OPCC Chairman. A complainant has no right to appeal if the Chairman does not follow the complaint and open an investigation. **32.89**

In 2012, the Office received 438 complaints regarding suspicions of anticompetitive conduct. Of the 290 explanatory proceedings opened, 176 were opened as a result of such complaints. Of the 112 antitrust investigatory proceedings opened, fifty-four were opened as a result of such complaints.[32] Thus, despite the described changes in legislation limiting the rights of complainants during proceedings, the signals and complaints of market participants still play a significant role in the initiation and direction of the Office's work. **32.90**

A brief explanation of the OPCC's investigatory procedures is as follows. Sometimes, investigations begin with what is called "explanatory proceedings." In explanatory proceedings, there are no formal parties. The purpose of such proceedings is for the OPCC to determine whether a violation of the Competition Act has occurred that would justify the opening of antitrust investigatory proceedings, which are formal proceedings with parties. In some cases, the OPCC institutes antitrust proceedings at the outset, without conducting explanatory proceedings. As opposed to explanatory proceedings, a company is notified by the OPCC when it is a subject of an antitrust investigation. The details of such a notification are sparing at best. Usually, they are limited to an announcement that an undertaking is suspected of having violated the Act, for example by fixing the price of given products in a given industry for a given period. **32.91**

During the investigation, the OPCC issues to parties and other companies in the industry formal requests for information and documents. Parties to an investigation have the right of access to the OPCC's case files. They can read the substance of the complaint (if one had been filed in the matter) as well as the written queries and demands of the OPCC and answers of other parties. Not included in the case files are references to documents or written submissions of undertakings that are considered to be trade secrets. Kinds of information that can be trade secrets are described in a separate piece of legislation, the Act on Counteracting Unfair **32.92**

[32] See OPCC, 2012 Activity Report, p. 10 <http://www.uokik.gov.pl/reports_on_activities.php>.

Competition of 1993, article 11(4).[33] With regard to investigations under article 6 of the Act and article 101 TFEU (illegal agreements), only at the close of an investigation are the submissions of a leniency applicant available to the other parties for inspection.

32.93 Once the investigation is officially closed, the OPCC formally notifies the parties of the closure, invites them to review the case files, and—if a party wishes—to submit its written position on the charges and evidence. The "charges" are often unchanged from the vague language used at the outset of the investigation. There are no statements of objections.

32.94 At the conclusion of an investigation, the OPCC Chairman may issue a decision finding a violation of the Act and imposing a fine. Article 106 of the Act empowers the Chairman to impose a fine on an undertaking that violated article 6 or 9 of the Act in an amount of up to 10 percent of the gross revenue earned by the undertaking in the year prior to the date of issuance of the Chairman's decision. Fines are set as a percentage of the undertaking's gross revenue and are not limited to a percentage of the value of the undertaking's turnover affected by the illegal conduct. In this regard, the Office's method of calculating fines significantly differs from that used by the European Commission, which issues fines based on the value of the affected sales.

32.95 On May 16, 2012, the OPCC Chairman published for public comment the agency's proposed amendments to the Competition Act. As of the date of writing this Chapter, the amendments have not been enacted. Under one of the proposed amendments, an individual may be fined up to the equivalent of EUR 500,000 for violating article 6 of the Act, which prohibits illegal agreements.

32.96 As an alternative to issuing a decision finding anticompetitive conduct and imposing a fine, the Chairman can issue a commitment decision pursuant to article 12 of the Act. In July 2012, the OPCC Chairman published the Office's "Clarifications on using a commitment decision in cases of competition-restricting practices and practices infringing collective consumer interests" in order to "enhance the transparency" surrounding the circumstances in which a commitment decision may be appropriate.

32.97 A party to a decision issued by the Chairman of the OPCC has the right to appeal the decision to the Court for Consumer and Competition Protection (the "Competition Court"), a court of first instance. Appeals to the Competition Court are actually filed with the Chairman of the OPCC. The Chairman may abrogate the decision or change the decision in part if the OPCC finds the appeal to be justified. This occurs only rarely, if ever. If the Chairman decides not to change the decision, the OPCC is required to pass the appeal and case files to the Competition Court "without delay." Typically, however, the time between the lodging of an appeal and the time when the Chairman of the OPCC passes the appeal and case files to the Competition Court can vary from several months to over a year.

32.98 The Competition Court judges the merits of, as well as procedural challenges to, the case at hand. Despite its name, besides the Chairman of the Court, judges of the Competition Court do not have background or experience in competition law. In contrast, over a decade ago, the judges of the Competition Court were almost entirely competition law experts.

32.99 Any party can appeal a judgment of the Competition Court to the Court of Appeals, which acts as a second instance court. A decision of the OPCC Chairman, and hence any fine imposed in that decision, is considered final when and if the Court of Appeals upholds the OPCC Chairman's decision.

[33] Act on Counteracting Unfair Competition (enacted April 16, 1993), Journal of Laws of 2003 no. 153, item 1503, as amended.

The Polish Supreme Court may hear an appeal of last resort (referred to as a "cassation") of the judgment of the Court of Appeals. The Supreme Court does not automatically or easily give leave to hear a cassation. It will do so, generally, when a case is in the public interest or if there are legal issues that require the Supreme Court's ruling in order to avoid conflicts or discrepancies in the law. **32.100**

B. Antitrust system

(i) Name of agency/agencies

The OPCC, a central administrative body headquartered in Warsaw, is supported by nine Regional Offices. The Chairman of the OPCC for the Protection of Competition and Consumers (the OPCC) is responsible for enforcing the Competition Act and, since May 1, 2004, has also been authorized to conduct investigations pursuant to article 101(1) TFEU if a suspected violation affects trade between member states. **32.101**

Previously, the Chairman was selected in a competition process and held the position for a five-year term. An amendment dated June 20, 2007, eliminated the competition process for the selection of a chairman and, instead, empowered the Prime Minister to select and dismiss the OPCC Chairman at any time. Another amendment dated March 24, 2009 clarified the selection and eligibility requirements for a candidate to the position of Chairman. In view of the Prime Minister's power to dismiss the Chairman, the OPCC cannot be considered as a truly independent agency, although the current Chairman has demonstrated her independence on a number of occasions. **32.102**

(ii) Staff size and budget

The OPCC employs 465 individuals with a budget of PLN 55 million (approx. EUR 13.5 million).[34] **32.103**

(iii) Recent enforcement actions and trends

In the recent years, the Office conducted annually approximately 130–140 investigations of suspected monopolistic practices and issued approximately hundred decisions. The vast majority of those decisions (approx. 70 percent) were related to abuses of dominance. Looking at the list of decisions concerning abuses of dominance, we can see that a majority concerned local geographic markets and local municipalities or businesses that perform public utility services, for example waste collection or providing water and sewage services. In the national market, Office focused on the rail transport (PKP Cargo's discriminatory practices) and the natural gas market sectors, both of which are practically monopolized. **32.104**

Other recent decisions concerning vertical or horizontal price fixing were issued in the cases of: **32.105**

(1) PPH Konimpex-Plus—vertical price fixing of clothing, footwear, sports, tourist and climbing equipment, as well as commercial partners of the company;[35]
(2) Fabryka Okien i Drzwi Bas from Lublin and its distributors—vertical price fixing of windows and balcony doors;[36]
(3) horizontal price fixing among taxi companies in Bydgoszcz (a city in north central Poland)—MPT Łuczniczka Taxi, Radio Taxi Mercedes and Zrzeszenie Transportu (decision no. RBG-9/2011).[37]

[34] OPCC, 2012 Activity Report (n 32).
[35] *PPH Konimpex-Plus and others*, OPCC Decision no. RKT-16 [2011].
[36] *Fabryka Okien i Drzwi Bas Sp. z o.o. and others*, OPCC Decision no. RLU 9 [2011].
[37] *MPT Łuczniczka Taxi and others*, OPCC Decision no. RBG-9 [2011].

32.106 As discussed in Section III.G, the OPCC's mission is supported by the fact that under article 109 of the Act, violations of article 6 of the Act (and article 101 TFEU) are subject to leniency. Article 6 of the Act prohibits both vertical and horizontal illegal agreements, and thus, leniency is also available to undertakings that have taken part in prohibited vertical agreements. The availability of leniency for anticompetitive vertical conduct has substantially influenced the OPCC's focus on investigating vertical price fixing in the past several years.

32.107 The reason for this trend is understandable. Whereas it is highly unusual in horizontal relations for competitors to meet on a regular and open basis, it is completely customary, and in fact, commercially necessary, for a manufacturer and its distributor(s) to do so in vertical relations. If a supplier and distributor reached an agreement on fixed or minimum retail prices, there is bound to be ample documentary evidence in each of the companies' files evidencing the nature of any manufacturer price recommendations and subsequent retail price agreements. It is the task of the Office to find, among the documents showing continued negotiations between manufacturers and distributors, those that prove RPM; and a leniency applicant can simplify this task. In view of the Office's focus on investigating illegal vertical agreements, companies are likely to consider applying for leniency when finding that they have been involved in vertical price fixing.

C. Private litigation

32.108 Only the OPCC Chairman can enforce the Act through administrative proceedings. Although an injured party can file a civil claim to declare an instance of conduct to be in violation of the competition law and be awarded damages, there are no specific regulations or acts in Polish legislation that regulate private antitrust actions. The legal grounds for private litigants to file civil actions alleging anticompetitive conduct is the Polish Civil Code, the Unfair Competition Act, or the Act on Pursuing Claims in Group Proceeding (as a member of a class). A civil plaintiff (either an individual or an entrepreneur) has the option of filing a damage claim pursuant to the following:

(1) article 405 of the Polish Civil Code, which requires the return of an undue benefit when the economic benefit was obtained at the expense of another;
(2) article 415 of the Polish Civil Code, which requires the redress of damages based upon tort liability and provides that whoever by his or her fault caused damage to another person shall be obliged to redress it; and
(3) article 471 of the Polish Civil Code, which addresses damages due to the failure to perform or due to the improper performance of a contract.

32.109 The Group Claims Act, which came into force on July 19, 2010, concerns claims in cases in which one type of claim is petitioned by at least 10 people (the group). The scope of the Group Claims Act is limited to consumer rights cases, dangerous product liability cases, and tort actions, including infringements of the Competition Act. Excluded from the coverage of the Group Claims Acts are tort actions based on personal interests claims.

32.110 The court (a three-judge panel) decides the admissibility of a group claim. If the court admits a claim, it will order the publication in the press of an appropriate announcement regarding the initiation of proceedings and will allow persons to join the proceedings within a two-month period. Thus, the Group Claims Act uses the opt-in approach, which means that only those persons who expressly agreed to be included can be members of the group.

32.111 To date, there have been no notable reported private damage actions concerning competition law violations.

D. Follow-on litigation (includes role of agency determinations of liability for follow-on litigation)

Polish competition enforcement is based on administrative procedures carried out by the OPCC and civil procedures in the form of private actions. In 2008, the Supreme Court clearly noted the different aims of private and public enforcement and decided that both proceedings are autonomous. A civil court can decide on its own whether an antitrust infringement occurred. The only exception concerns OPCC proceedings concerning the same case in which a decision of the OPCC is final. The finality of a decision occurs when a decision that finishes the antitrust proceedings before the OPCC, if it is appealed, is finally upheld by the Court of Appeals. **32.112**

Similar to other jurisdictions with an antitrust or competition law, the preferable litigation stance in Poland is to file a lawsuit following the issuance of a decision of the OPCC finding anticompetitive conduct. Civil courts are bound to follow a final decision (one that, if challenged, is upheld by the Court of Appeals) of the OPCC in the same case. The OPCC's decisions are often extremely detailed with regard to a description of the evidence of the illegal conduct. Often, the abundance of detailed evidence decisions of the OPCC will also assist a plaintiff and a civil court to better assess the infringement and the level of damages. **32.113**

An award of leniency by the Chairperson of the OPCC does not protect an undertaking from being liable in civil damage actions; however, a leniency applicant's statements to the OPCC, similar to any other documents collected by the OPCC during its proceedings, are not available to civil litigants. Article 73(1) of the Act prohibits the use of "information received during the course of [the OPCC's] proceedings" from being used in "any other proceedings conducted pursuant to separate provisions." The exceptions to this prohibition are listed in article 71(2), but do not include proceedings before civil courts. **32.114**

E. Arbitration and alternative dispute resolution

Arbitration, mediation, and conciliation procedures are available for civil damage actions pursuant to the terms set out in the Code of Civil Procedure. **32.115**

Settlement is recognized in civil proceedings, and thus private antitrust actions before the civil courts can be resolved by a settlement agreement. Settlement agreements in civil proceedings are subject to a court's authorization. A court may deny a request to withdraw a lawsuit if it finds that the proposed settlement agreement is contrary to the law or principles of social coexistence, or is intended to circumvent the law. In such circumstances, a court may also rule that a settlement between the parties is inadmissible. **32.116**

F. Remedies

The OPCC has the power to issue administrative fines for violations of the Act or of articles 101 and 102 TFEU. As of January 1, 2009, the OPCC's Guidelines for setting fines in competition cases (the "Fines Guidelines") are in effect. The Fines Guidelines distinguish among three types of violations: very severe; severe; and "other" violations. A formula for setting a "base amount" is described by the Fines Guidelines as well as the factors which the OPCC Chairman will consider as mitigating or in aggravating an offense and thus, influencing the level of the fine. The Fines Guidelines are not legally binding upon the OPCC; however, the Chairman announced that the OPCC will follow them. **32.117**

In addition, the Act authorities the Chairman of the OPCC to impose a fine in an amount of up to the equivalent of EUR 50 million if an undertaking, even unintentionally, fails to provide information requested by the OPCC, or if the undertaking provides false or misleading information. **32.118**

32.119 If an undertaking, even unintentionally, does not cooperate with the representative of the OPCC during a dawn raid inspection, the Chairman of the OPCC can impose a fine in an amount of up to the equivalent of EUR 50 million. A separate fine may be imposed upon: a person holding a managerial position; a member of the management board; or a person authorized to act on behalf of an undertaking during a dawn raid of up to 50 times the average monthly salary.

(i) Civil liability

32.120 Article 106 of the Act empowers the Chairman of the OPCC to impose an administrative fine on an undertaking taking part in a cartel of up to 10 percent of the gross revenue earned by the undertaking in the year preceding the date of issuance of the decision of the Chairman of the OPCC. As mentioned earlier, fines are set as a percentage of an undertaking's gross revenue and are not limited to a percentage of the value of an undertaking's turnover affected by the illegal conduct, as is the method used by the European Commission, which issues fines based upon the value of the affected sales.

(ii) Criminal liability

32.121 The Act does not provide for criminal sanctions for cartel conduct or for any other anticompetitive conduct. Article 305 of the Polish Criminal Code, however, makes bid-rigging of a public project tender a crime subject to three years' imprisonment.

32.122 On May 16, 2012, the OPCC published for consultation its proposed amendments to the Act. The consultation period has passed and, at the time of writing, Parliament has yet to act on the amendments. One of the proposed amendments concerns the enforcer to be put in charge of investigating bid-rigging on public tenders. The OPCC's proposed amendment provides that in cases in which the OPCC Chairman has decided to waive or mitigate a penalty (leniency), an individual will not be subject to criminal prosecution under article 305 of the Criminal Code for bid-rigging on public tenders.

G. Leniency and immunity

32.123 In May 2012, the OPCC Chairman published for public comment the agency's proposed amendments to the Competition Act. As of the date of writing, the amendments have not been enacted. A number of the proposed amendments concern leniency. As mentioned earlier, in one of the amendments to the Act proposed by the OPCC, an individual would be subject to be fined up to the equivalent of EUR 500,000 for engaging in conduct prohibited by article 6 of the Act. Another amendment would permit individuals to apply for leniency. Currently, only undertakings may seek leniency under the Act.

32.124 In another of the proposed amendments, leniency plus would be introduced to the Polish leniency system. Leniency Plus, which originated in the US, would allow an applicant to provide the OPCC Chairman with evidence of illegal activity in a market other than the one being investigated in exchange for leniency with respect to the conduct in that second market, and a further reduction in the fine in the first investigation.

32.125 The Act provides that the leniency procedure applies to violations of article 6 of the Act or article 101 TFEU. Consequently, a vertical agreement that is in violation of the Act or article 101 TFEU can be subject to a leniency application. To date, the majority of cases investigated in accordance with the leniency procedure have involved vertical agreements. In some decisions, the Chairman of the OPCC found that vertical agreements had a horizontal effect.

32.126 The legal basis for, and instructions on how to file, a leniency application can be found in article 109 of the Act as well as in the Council of Ministers' Leniency Regulation of January 26, 2009 (the "Leniency Regulation"). In 2009, the OPCC also issued its Leniency Guidelines.

Full leniency (a waiver of a fine) will be granted to the first leniency applicant who was not the initiator of a cartel, who meets the statutory requirements, and who provides the OPCC with sufficient evidence either to open an investigation or to issue a decision finding an infringement of article 6 of the Act and/or article 101 TFEU. A leniency applicant who was the initiator of a cartel, however, can still be eligible for a fine reduction not exceeding five percent of its revenue. **32.127**

Subsequent leniency applicants may benefit from the leniency program by receiving reduced fines. The second leniency applicant who meets the statutory requirements is eligible for a fine reduction not exceeding 7 percent of its revenue. The third and subsequent leniency applicants may be eligible for fines not exceeding eight percent of their respective gross annual revenues. **32.128**

The Leniency Regulation introduced a marker system whereby an applicant can file a simplified application (the "marker") and, within a term agreed upon with the OPCC, file the completed leniency application. In this way, the applicant can approach the OPCC early and keep its place (that is, the date it filed its marker) in the leniency queue. **32.129**

Since the introduction of leniency in April 2004, until December 2012, forty-six leniency applications were filed with the Chairman of the OPCC. It is worth noting that in April 2008, almost four years after the introduction of the leniency program, the OPCC Chairman withdrew a conditional leniency grant that had been issued. The case concerned an alleged vertical retail price agreement between a paint and varnish manufacturer and a large do-it-yourself store which was the first to apply for leniency in the case (the "DIY Applicant"). At the close of the investigation, the OPCC Chairman issued a decision withdrawing the conditional leniency granted to the DIY Applicant, and fined both the DIY Applicant and the paint manufacturer.[38] **32.130**

The reason that the DIY Applicant was ineligible for leniency, according to the Office, was that, after seeking leniency, it had continued to charge retail prices that had allegedly been set in collusion with the manufacturer, for two paint products manufactured exclusively for the DIY Applicant. (The DIY Applicant and the paint manufacturer each denied fixing the retail prices on these particular two products.) The OPCC Chairman reasoned that because the DIY Applicant had not fulfilled one of the statutory requirements for leniency, that is, ceasing the illegal conduct no later than the day on which it submitted its leniency application, it could not receive leniency. In its judgment of April 27, 2011, the Competition Court agreed with the Chairman's conclusion that to "cease" illegal conduct means to stop charging the fixed prices. The Competition Court did, however, decrease by two thirds the level of the fine the Chairman had imposed upon the DIY Applicant, in view of the cooperation that the company had provided and the fact that it was not the initiator of the offense.[39] The Court of Appeals upheld the judgment of the Competition Court in June 2012.[40] The DIY Applicant filed a cassation (appeal of last resort) with the Supreme Court. **32.131**

H. Document creation and retention

In administrative proceedings there is a duty to cooperate with the Office. The Chairman of the Office may impose a fine in an amount of up to the equivalent of EUR 50 million if an **32.132**

[38] *Castorama Polska and others*, OPCC Decision no. DOK-1/08 [2008].

[39] *Castorama Polska and others*, Court for the Protection of Competition and Consumers, Decision no. XVII AmA 44/09 [2011], on appeal from *Castorama Polska* (2008) (n 38).

[40] *Castorama Polska and others,* Court of Appeals in Warsaw, Civil Division VI, Decision no. ACa 1339/11 [2012], on appeal from *Castorama Polska* (2011) (n 39).

undertaking, even unintentionally, fails to provide information requested by the Office or if the undertaking provides false or misleading information.

32.133 If an undertaking, even unintentionally, does not cooperate with representative of the Office during a dawn raid inspection, the Chairman of the Office can impose a fine in an amount of up to the equivalent of EUR 50 million. In such case, a separate fine may be imposed upon a person holding a managerial position; a member of the management board; or a person authorized to act on behalf of an undertaking during a dawn raid of up to 50 times the average monthly salary.

32.134 The Office Chairman found that two mobile telephony operators obstructed the Office from carrying out dawn raids in their respective headquarters. Both of the charged acts of obstruction occurred on the same day at the offices of two competing operators. In the case involving Polska Telefonia Cyfrowa (PTC) the Office found that PTC had hindered the inspector's ability to access the premises and to commence inspection activities without delay. The Chairman stressed in her decision the necessity of punctual commencement of inspections, especially when there are simultaneous inspections of several companies. PTC delayed letting the inspectors in and the start of the search for over an hour. For failure to cooperate with the dawn raid, PTC was fined PLN 123 million (approx. EUR 30 million).[41]

32.135 The second operator, Polkomtel, was also found to have hindered the Office's dawn raid by making the inspectors wait for an unreasonably long time, according to the Office, and when the search started, Polkomtel refused to give access to its hard disc. In addition, Polkomtel refused to provide certain documents and instead gave the inspectors with extracts of those documents. For failure to cooperate with the dawn raid, Polkomtel was fined PLN 131 million (approx. EUR 32 million).[42]

[41] *Polska Telefonia Cyfrowa Sp. z o.o.*, OPCC Decision no. DOK-9 [2010].
[42] *Polkomtel S.A.*, OPCC Decision no. DOK-1 [2011].

33

PORTUGAL

Joaquim Caimoto Duarte and Tânia Luísa Faria
Uría Menéndez—Proença de Carvalho

Introduction

The Portuguese competition law framework currently in force has been recently reformed. In fact, Law 19/2012, the new Portuguese Competition Act, was published on 8 May and came into force on July 7, 2012 (the "Portuguese Competition Act"). The current legal framework arose, to a significant extent, from the Memorandum of Understanding on Specific Economic Policy Conditionality, which concerned the granting of financial assistance to Portugal (MoU).[1] The MoU highlighted the need for better enforcement of competition **33.01**

[1] The Memorandum of Understanding on Specific Economic Policy Conditionality (May 17, 2011), <http://ec.europa.eu/economy_finance/eu_borrower/mou/2011-05-18-mou-portugal_en.pdf> ("MoU"), details the general economic policy conditions regarding the granting of financial assistance to Portugal. The European Financial Stabilization Mechanism and the European Financial Stability Facility financial support were provided to Portugal, on the basis of a policy program negotiated with the Portuguese authorities, by the European Commission in liaison with the European Central Bank and the International Monetary Fund.

rules in Portugal by the Portuguese Competition Authority (PCA), as well as a revision of the former competition act to bring it into line with European Union (EU) competition legislation.[2]

33.02 The investigative and sanctioning procedure in Portugal for restrictive practices is of administrative nature (*processo de contraordenação*) and is carried out by the PCA, an independent authority. The PCA is responsible for the investigation, the issuance of a statement of objections and the final decision on antitrust cases. The PCA's decisions are subject to appeal to the Court of Competition, Regulation and Supervision (*Tribunal da Concorrência, Regulação e Supervisão*), a newly established specialized court.

33.03 As a relevant specific feature of the Portuguese legal framework, it should be mentioned that the members of the board of directors of the offending undertaking, as well as those responsible for the management or supervision of areas of activity involving an administrative offense who, with knowledge or a duty to know the existence of an infringement committed, have not adopted appropriate measures to immediately bring the action to an end, are also liable under the Portuguese Competition Act. The fine for natural persons cannot exceed 10 percent of their annual income deriving from the exercise of their functions in the undertaking concerned, accrued in the last full year in which the infraction occurred.

I. Acting alone

33.04 The new Portuguese Competition Act provides a description of the unilateral conducts which are deemed anticompetitive. The statutory provisions on antitrust offenses, including unilateral conducts, have not changed substantially with the enactment of the new law. However, the amendments introduced by the Portuguese Competition Act have brought Portuguese law closer to the European Union's provisions on this matter in particular in relation to exploitative abuses harming consumers.

33.05 The Portuguese Competition Act prohibits the abuse of a dominant position. For this prohibition to apply, two elements must be proven: (i) the existence of a dominant position in a certain market and (ii) an abusive act from the dominant undertaking.

33.06 As to the existence of a dominant position, the PCA, in line with EU case law, will generally consider that an undertaking is dominant in a market if it can decide its commercial policies regardless of the reaction of any other economic agent.

33.07 The ability of a company to behave independently from other economic agents can be rooted in its own characteristics (market share, financial capability, or vertical integration) or in the market features (e.g. the existence of barriers to entry to the market or of network effects).

33.08 In relation to the concept of abuse, there is no legal definition, but the law provides an indicative list of potentially abusive conducts. An undertaking abuses its dominant position when it behaves in a way that is likely to influence the structure of a market where, as a direct result of its presence, competition has already been weakened and which, through the recourse to methods other than those governing normal competition in products or services based on traders' performance, have the effect of hindering the maintenance or development of the degree of competition still existing in the market.

33.09 The conducts that may be considered abuses of a dominant position, according to article 11 of the Portuguese Competition Act, which now essentially mirrors, with the exception of the

[2] See MoU (n 1) paras. 7.9 and 7.17.

last paragraph, article 102 of the Treaty on the Functioning of the European Union (TFEU), include the following:

(a) imposing, directly or indirectly, unfair purchase or selling prices or other unfair trading conditions;
(b) limiting production, markets, or technical development to the detriment of consumers;
(c) applying dissimilar conditions to equivalent transactions with other trading parties, thereby placing them at a competitive disadvantage;
(d) making the execution of contracts subject to acceptance by the other parties of supplementary obligations which, by their nature or according to commercial usage, have no connection with the subject of such contracts;
(e) refusing another undertaking access to a network or other essential facilities that the dominant undertaking controls, when appropriate payment for such is available, in a situation where the other undertaking cannot, therefore, in fact or in law, act as a competitor of the undertaking in a dominant position in the market, upstream or downstream, unless the dominant undertaking can demonstrate that, for operational or other reasons, such access cannot reasonably be provided.

This list is not exhaustive, and thus other conducts not expressly referred to may also be considered abusive when falling within the scope of the definition of abuse. Sections I.A through I.M of this Chapter deal with different kinds of unilateral practices that may amount to an abuse of dominant position. **33.10**

It is worth mentioning that the Portuguese Competition Act also prohibits the abuse of a joint dominant position. Finally, article 12 of the Portuguese Competition Act includes the prohibition of the abuse of economic dependence. In fact, one or more undertakings are prohibited from abusing the economic dependence under which any of its or their suppliers or customers may find itself or themselves as a result of the fact that any equivalent alternative is not available and to the extent that such a practice affects the way the market or competition operate.[3] The conducts referred to above as abuses of a dominant position can also be considered abuses of economic dependence in cases where there is no dominant position. Other examples of such abuse comprise any unjustified total or partial breach in established commercial relations, bearing in mind previous commercial relations, recognized practices in that particular economic activity and the contractual conditions that have been laid down. **33.11**

There have been no publicly available decisions concerning an abuse of economic dependency to date. **33.12**

It should be noted that the PCA, under the previous legal framework, did not make available on its website the decisions regarding antitrust infringements. Therefore, most of our references to the relevant previous decision practice are based on the PCA's press releases. **33.13**

The decision practice of the PCA regarding dominant position consists to date, essentially, of three cases against Portugal Telecom, the main telecommunications company in the country, historically the incumbent in this market. The most significant sanction applied within this context amounted to around EUR 53 million, although this infringement was considered time-barred by the appeal court. The types of conduct, as better explained below, concern primarily pricing and access to essential facilities. **33.14**

[3] According to the applicable Portuguese legal provision, an undertaking is deemed not to have an equivalent alternative when: (a) the supply of goods or services at hand, specifically at the point of distribution, is controlled by a limited number of undertakings; and (b) the undertaking cannot find identical conditions from other commercial partners within a reasonable period of time.

A. Predatory pricing

33.15 Predatory pricing is illegal according to the Portuguese Competition Act; however we are not aware of publicly available decision practice of the PCA on the subject. We understand, however, that the PCA would most likely follow the EU's approach on this matter.

B. Exploitative offenses (excessive pricing, monopoly leveraging)

33.16 The main example of exploitative abuses is represented by the imposition of excessive prices by a dominant undertaking. The Portuguese Competition Authority has not yet specifically addressed this issue.

C. Monopsony

33.17 There are no specific provisions of Portuguese law on monopsony and no specific cases. The abovementioned provisions, regarding the abuse of a dominant position and the abuse of economic dependence also apply when the market is comprised of a single buyer and several producers.

D. Price discrimination

33.18 Price discrimination by dominant companies is considered abusive insofar as it implies applying different conditions to equivalent services. On the contrary, when the different customers are not in a comparable situation, there would be no abuse of dominant position.

33.19 Once the different treatment has been evidenced, the dominant company could prove the existence of an objective difference between the parties that justifies such divergence. This objective justification may result from a number of elements, such as the purchase of different volumes or the existence of a stable preexisting supply relationship.

33.20 In 2008, the PCA sanctioned Portugal Telecom, previously the incumbent in this market, with a fine of EUR 2.1 million for discriminatory pricing practices in the access to digital circuits necessary to the provision of electronic communication services.[4] This undertaking allegedly offered more favorable prices to companies within its group operating in the retail market when compared to the other competing operators, in particular by means of special discounts.

33.21 An extreme form of price discrimination would consist in margin squeeze practices.

33.22 The PCA has already determined that dominant vertically integrated companies can increase the costs of competitors in an upstream market in order to favor their own businesses in competing downstream markets. The PCA has sanctioned several companies of the Portugal Telecom Group (as well as ZON, a company formerly part of the Portugal Telecom Group that had, at the time of the decision, become an independent company) for alleged margin squeeze practices in 2003. Portugal Telecom and ZON were found by the PCA to have artificially increased prices at the wholesale level, while artificially lowering them at the retail level, to allegedly block the entry of new competitors, and were fined a total of EUR 53 million.[5]

33.23 As discussed, this issue has been an area of enforcement in recent years.

---

[4] PCA Press Release September 1, 2008, available at <http://www.concorrencia.pt/vPT/Noticias_Eventos/Comunicados/Paginas/Comunicado_AdC_200815.aspx?lst=1&Cat=2008>. The full decision is not yet published. Please note that the PCA does not publish decisions that have been judicially appealed, while a court decision is still pending, or dismissal decisions.

[5] *Portugal Telecom*, PRC 2003/05 [2009].

E. Dictating or influencing resale prices

(i) Resale price maintenance

Dictating or influencing resale prices is normally a behavior that falls within the rules governing anticompetitive agreements rather than unilateral conducts. In this regard, direct or indirect vertical price fixing has been generally regarded as a violation of competition laws. **33.24**

Pure price recommendations are normally not considered anticompetitive. These conducts may, however, result in antitrust infringements when the supplier tries to enforce the application of the recommended price or most distributors follow the recommended price, turning it into a fixed price (especially if compliance with the recommended price is spurred by the supplier or monitored by competing distributors). **33.25**

Sanctioning resale price maintenance is not frequent in the PCA's practice, but in 2012, the PCA sanctioned Lactogal, a dairy company, with a fine of EUR 341,098 for resale price maintenance practices (minimum price fixing) in the on-trade distribution market for dairy products. However, regardless of this company's substantial position in the dairy market, the PCA considered the infringement a vertical agreement.[6] **33.26**

(ii) Minimum advertised price programs

There have been no publicly available cases concerning minimum advertised price programs in Portugal. **33.27**

F. Tying arrangements

To the best of our knowledge, the PCA has analyzed a situation related to tying practices; however, no sanctions were imposed. In 2009, the PCA closed, subject to certain conditions, a case against the food undertaking Sugalidal, since it had found that Sugalidal had allegedly abused its dominant position in the acquisition of tomato for transformation by requiring its suppliers to use a specific kind of seed produced by a company of its group. Sugalidal has undertaken to remove the illegal clause from its contractual arrangements and to divulge this removal.[7] **33.28**

G. Exclusive dealing

The PCA has not found any infringement corresponding to exclusive dealing by an undertaking in a dominant position, but rather concerning vertical restraints. In 2007, the PCA closed a procedure against Bayer regarding a clause in its contract with wholesalers according to which the wholesaler was allegedly obliged to only carry Bayer products for five years.[8] Bayer removed the clause in question from existing contracts and to submitted relevant amendments to the PCA. **33.29**

H. Refusal to deal

The refusal to supply by a dominant undertaking might in some cases amount to an abuse of dominant position, in particular when it relates to products that are required by its customers to compete and such refusal eliminates competition in the market and harms consumers. **33.30**

---

[6] PCA Press Release, July 19,2012, available at <http://www.concorrencia.pt/vPT/Noticias_Eventos/Comunicados/Paginas/Comunicado_AdC_201208.aspx?lst=1&Cat=2012>. The full decision is not yet published.

[7] See PCA Press Release, October 15, 2009, available at <http://www.concorrencia.pt/vPT/Noticias_Eventos/Comunicados/Paginas/Comunicado_AdC_200920.aspx?lst=1&Cat=2009>. The full decision is not yet published.

[8] See PCA Press Release, October 2, 2007, available at <http://www.concorrencia.pt/vPT/Noticias_Eventos/Comunicados/Paginas/Comunicado_AdC_200716.aspx?lst=1&Cat=2007>. The full decision is not yet published.

33.31 However, a refusal to supply would not be restrictive if it is based on objective and non-discriminatory grounds.

33.32 In what concerns the PCA's decision practice we are only aware of the publicly available case related to essential facilities described below.

I. Essential facilities

33.33 A specific case of refusals to deal concerns essential facilities.

33.34 As mentioned, Portuguese law makes an express reference to the refusal to grant access to another undertaking to a network or other essential facilities that it controls. In 2007, Portugal Telecom was sanctioned with a EUR 38 million fine for refusing to provide competitors access to what the PCA considered to be an essential facility—PT's underground conduit network[9] (a case that was nevertheless overturned on appeal).

J. Bundling (including loyalty and market share discounts)

33.35 We are not aware of publicly available decisions of the PCA concerning the application of discounts by a dominant undertaking.

K. Standard-setting groups (disclosure requirements, licensing arrangements, and licensing pools)

33.36 Agreements creating technical standards must not establish standards that may be deemed to foreclose the market to potential or actual competitors.

33.37 Within this context, in 2010, the Portuguese Chartered Accountants Association (*Ordem dos Técnicos Oficiais de Contas*) was fined for, among others, abusing its dominant position by limiting the entry of potential competitors in the chartered accountancy market, establishing a mandatory training requirement, exclusively controlled by this association.[10]

L. Termination of intermediaries (retailers, wholesalers, dealers, and value-added resellers, agents, and brokers)

33.38 See Section I.M.

M. Termination of relationships with competitors

33.39 Termination of contractual relationships by a dominant company is a form of refusal to deal and, as such, may be considered abusive. This termination would not be abusive if the undertaking can prove that it had objective grounds to terminate the commercial relationships.

33.40 We are not aware of any decisions in Portugal where this issue has been specifically dealt with.

N. Exemptions

33.41 The Portuguese Competition Act establishes no exceptions to restrictive unilateral conducts. However, in principle, in accordance with the "State Action doctrine," any conduct that is imposed by law will be exempt from competition law. Therefore, a dominant undertaking

[9] See PCA Press Release, August 2, 2007, available at <http://www.concorrencia.pt/vPT/Noticias_Eventos/Comunicados/Paginas/Comunicado_AdC_200713.aspx?lst=1&Cat=2007>. The full decision is yet not published.

[10] See PCA Press Release, May 18, 2010 available at <http://www.concorrencia.pt/vPT/Noticias_Eventos/Comunicados/Paginas/Comunicado_AdC_201006.aspx?lst=1&Cat=2010>. The full decision is not yet published. See also the Court of Justice of the European Union (CJEU) preliminary ruling in this case: Case C-1/12—*Portuguese Chartered Accountants Association v. European Commission*, Preliminary ruling (February 28, 2013); and see Section II.E for further discussion of the case.

that is compelled by law to charge certain prices or to apply certain commercial conditions would not in principle, incur in an abuse of dominant position.

There are no exemptions on this matter set forth in the applicable Portuguese law. 33.42

II. Dealing with competitors

According to the Portuguese Competition Act all kinds of agreements between undertakings, concerted practices, and decisions by associations of undertakings which have as their object or effect the prevention, distortion, or restriction of competition in the domestic market, in whole or in part, and to a considerable extent, are prohibited. 33.43

Article 9 of the Portuguese Competition Act gives as examples of anticompetitive agreements, agreements that directly or indirectly fix purchase or selling prices, or any other trading conditions, limit, or control production, markets, technological development, or investment; share markets or sources of supply; apply dissimilar conditions to equivalent transactions with other trading parties, thereby placing them at a competitive disadvantage and make the execution of contracts subject to acceptance by the other parties of supplementary obligations which, by their nature or according to commercial usage, have no connection with the subject of such contracts. 33.44

There are more exemptions regarding anticompetitive agreements than for unilateral conducts. These include: the *de minimis* rule; block exemptions; and economic balance. 33.45

De minimis *rule*: article 9 of the Portuguese Competition Act requires a considerable restriction of competition, and, therefore, concerted practices and agreements that are not capable of significantly harming competition may be excluded. It is worth noting that, following the EU approach, agreements between competitors with a joint market share below 10 percent would be exempted. This percentage becomes 15 percent when it comes to agreements and concerted practices between non-competing operators (e.g. vertical agreements[11]). 33.46

Block exemptions: In Portugal, EU block exemptions regulations are also applied to merely national situations according to article 10.3 of the Portuguese Competition Act. 33.47

Economic balance: Finally, restrictive agreements may also be deemed compatible with competition law, according to article 10 of the Portuguese Competition Act, if they meet certain requirements that mirror those of article 101(3) TFEU: (1) the agreement must contribute to the improvement of production or commercialization and distribution of goods and services or to the promotion of technical or economic progress; (2) consumers must be allowed to participate adequately in the benefits; (3) unnecessary restrictions to achieve the intended objective must not be imposed; and (4) competition in respect of a substantial part of the products or services in question must not be eliminated. 33.48

We should also mention that the state must refrain from promoting arrangements between competitors, as referred to in the case concerning the meetings promoted by the Azores government with several milk producers regarding the sector, where commercial conditions 33.49

[11] As mentioned previously, the PCA has investigated undertakings for vertical restrictions and in certain cases no fines were imposed. In fact, in the case *Nestlé Portugal*, PRC 2004/31 [2006] and [2008], Nestlé was sanctioned for allegedly including exclusive dealing and minimum purchase clauses in its contracts with retailers; a first PCA decision fined Nestlé for this practice, but after the case returned to the referred Authority (further to a decision from the courts), a case that was eventually dismissed further to Nestlé removal of such clauses from its contracts.

could be discussed. The PCA closed the case without imposing any sanctions, but recommended that the government of the Azores put an end the this practice, refraining from conducts that could facilitate potentially collusive behavior in such region.[12]

33.50 The areas of conduct where antirust sanctioning has been more frequent in Portugal concern restrictive practices within trade and professional associations as well as bid rigging.

A. Horizontal price fixing (including advanced announcements of price or product changes)

33.51 Horizontal price fixing agreements will be considered as objectively anticompetitive and, therefore, the authorities would not need to evidence the effect of these agreements. These kinds of agreements (at an EU level) are even excluded from the *de minimis* exemption. The approach of the PCA normally follows the trend of the European Commission (EC).

33.52 It is worth noting that, since 2006, the PCA has an important instrument in the fight against cartels, the leniency regime (originally included in Law No. 39/2006 of 25 August). The leniency regime has now been included in the Portuguese Competition Act (articles 75 ff).

33.53 The PCA has found and sanctioned several cartels. In cases *Abbot and others*, regarding the supply of glucose diagnostic strips, the PCA found that several pharmaceutical companies had engaged in bid rigging agreements, by colluding to fix prices in advance of presenting their bids to hospital public tender offers.[13] The PCA also fined, in *Aeronorte & Helisul*, two air transport companies for alleged bid-rigging because they had presented a joint bid to a public tender offer, but this decision was overturned on appeal.[14] Furthermore, in *Eurest and others*, in the catering services market, the PCA also fined a number of catering services providers for bid rigging, as well as for market allocation. This case was also significant because it was started by a leniency request and it was also the first case where fines were imposed on company directors and not just on companies.[15]

33.54 In *Cerealis and others*, the PCA fined a number of flourmills for fixing the prices of flour. The decision was subsequently overturned on appeal, on procedural grounds. The reversal of the decision was followed by a new fining decision of the PCA, which was also appealed.[16]

33.55 More recently, a number of driving schools were fined for price fixing in the driving school market in Funchal, Madeira;[17] two industrial cleaning companies for bid rigging agreements;[18] and the last cartel sanctioned by the PCA, in 2012, concerned undertakings active in the graphic sector for allegedly fixing prices and allocating clients.[19]

---

[12] See PCA Press Release, June 24, 2011 available at http://www.concorrencia.pt/vPT/Noticias_Eventos/Comunicados/Paginas/Comunicado_AdC_201107.aspx?lst=1&Cat=2011. The full decision is not yet published.

[13] *Abbott, Bayer, Johnson & Johnson, Menarini & Roche*, PRC 2003/06 & 2005/04 [2008].

[14] *Aeronorte & Helisul*, PRC 2005/20 [2007].

[15] *Eurest; Trivalor; Uniself; Ica & Sodexo Portugal*, PRC 2007/02 [2009].

[16] *Cerealis; Moagem Ceres; Granel; Germen; Eduardo e Artur Grilo Pereira; Farlis; Abranches & Filhos; Carneiro, Campos & Companhia; Catelas & Teorgas & Pitorro* PRC 2003/06 [2005].

[17] PRC 2008/06—*Escola de Condução Francisco Pereira, Lda.; Manuel Rodrigues, Lda.; Escola de Condução Infante, Lda.; Escola de Condução do Estreito, Lda.; Alfredo Camacho, Lda.; SMTZ—Ensino da Condução Automóvel, Ld.; & Fernandes Ramos & Nóbrega, Lda.* [2011].

[18] See PCA Press Release, June 3, 2011 available at <http://www.concorrencia.pt/vPT/Noticias_Eventos/Comunicados/Paginas/Comunicado_AdC_201105.aspx?lst=1&Cat=2011>. The full decision is not yet published.

[19] See PCA Press Release, December 20, 2012, available at <http://www.concorrencia.pt/vPT/Noticias_Eventos/Comunicados/Paginas/Comunicado_AdC_201216.aspx?lst=1&Cat=2012>. The full decision is not yet published.

B. Horizontal agreements to allocate customers or territories; agreements not to compete

The allocation of markets and customers is unlawful under Portuguese law. These types of practices are analyzed in a similar manner to horizontal price fixing. It is common for cartel agreements to combine price fixing and market/customer allocation. **33.56**

For instance, in *Vatel and others*, the PCA fined a number of companies for price fixing and market allocation in the salt wholesale market; the decision was upheld on appeal, although the fines were reduced.[20] In addition, in *Rebonave and another*, the PCA fined a number of companies in the maritime towing services market for price fixing and client allocation in the provision of these services in the port of Setúbal. The decision was upheld on appeal, although the fines imposed were reduced.[21] **33.57**

Non-compete agreements may be a mere instrument for market/customer allocation and, as such, may be analyzed as part of these infringements. Beyond these cases, non-compete agreements are, under certain circumstances, generally accepted by the PCA as ancillary restrictions both in relation to merger control cases or to other legitimate agreements (e.g. joint purchasing, distribution). In these cases, however, if the PCA finds that the non-compete agreements falls outside the scope of the ancillary character normally admissible, it will have to assess the clause under article 9 of the Portuguese Competition Act and consider it restrictive of competition. **33.58**

C. Horizontal boycotts

Horizontal boycotts, through which a group of operators agree to implement some measures to exclude a competitor from the market, may also be considered an infringement of the Portuguese Competition Act. There is no public information on boycott in order to exclude competitors. **33.59**

D. Joint ventures and other competitive collaborations

Joint ventures can be considered either as a transaction subject to merger control rules or as a cooperation agreement between economic operators. A joint venture will qualify as a merger when it performs all the functions of an independent economic entity on a permanent basis. If a joint venture meets this requirement (that mirrors full-function requirements under EU merger control regime), it will be subject to the rules on merger control and will be notified if the legal thresholds are met. If such thresholds are not met, the transaction would not have to comply with any other procedure and should not be subject to scrutiny for merger control purposes.[22] **33.60**

A non-full-function joint venture could be analyzed as a vertical or horizontal agreement and would be reviewed using the EC guidelines on vertical or horizontal cooperation. **33.61**

E. Trade associations

There have been a number of cases involving the recommendations and decisions issued by trade associations. In some cases, the infringements are similar to standard antitrust cases (e.g. price fixing). In most cases involving trade associations, however, the investigated behavior covered recommended practices as well as maximum prices which were understood by the associated undertakings as being mandatory. **33.62**

---

[20] *Vatel; Salexpor; Sociedade Aveirense de Higienização de Sal; Vitasal & Salmex*, PRC 2005/25 [2006]

[21] *Rebonave; Lutamar & Rebosado*, PRC 2006/06 [2007].

[22] For an analysis of this matter see the PCA's decisions in cases *Linética/Gescrap Portugal/Ativos Antunes Reciclagem*, Case no. 59/2012 (January 21, 2011) and —*Bencom/Terparque*, Case no. 31/2012 (July 27, 2012).

33.63 For instance, in *AGEPOR*, the PCA fined the Association of Navigation Agents of Portugal (*Associação dos Agentes de Navegação de Portugal*) for alleged price fixing practices; while in *ANTRAM*, this authority stated that the National Association of Freighters (*Associação Nacional de Transportadores Públicos Rodoviários de Mercadorias*) had issued a decision that, in the PCA's view, established a collective refusal to deal with a certain terminal operator.[23] In 2011, the National Association of Parking Lot Companies (*Associação Nacional de Empresas de Parques de Estacionamento*) was fined almost EUR 2 million for its recommendation of pricing criteria in response to the introduction of new legislation on parking lots.[24]

33.64 A separate mention should be made to the investigation of the PCA in relation to professional associations. The PCA has fined several professional associations such as the Veterinaries' Association (*Ordem dos Médicos Veterinários*), the Dentists Association (*Ordem dos Médicos Dentistas*), and the Doctors Association (*Ordem dos Médicos*) as a result of decisions that had an effect on the pricing of their members (including recommended and maximum prices considered by the associates as mandatory).[25] As discussed earlier, in 2010, the Portuguese Chartered Accountants Association (*Ordem dos Técnicos Oficiais de Contas*) was also fined for restrictions in the market for the training of chartered accountants.

33.65 As evidenced above, the PCA has been active in practices related to trade and professional associations.

F. Interlocking directorates

33.66 There are no special provisions on interlocking directorates under Portuguese law. This matter would be dealt with in merger control, in particular as evidence of possible coordination effects.

G. Facilitating practices

33.67 There are no cases in Portugal in which facilitating practices have been declared infringements of the Portuguese Competition Act.

33.68 However, the PCA has recommended that the state should refrain from promoting arrangements between competitors, as mentioned in the case concerning the meetings promoted by the Azores government with several milk producers regarding the sector where commercial conditions could be discussed.[26]

H. Information exchange

33.69 Information exchanges are a particular form of cooperation between companies that may lead to a collusive result. The PCA follows the line marked by the EC and courts.

33.70 Future price information is always sensitive. Information exchanges may take the form of statistics compiled by a third party or a trade association. In these cases, the compatibility of the statistics may be checked on a case-by-case basis, in view of the characteristics of the affected markets and the mechanisms for the preparation of the statistics. As a general rule, the more recent, sensitive and disaggregated the information, the more likely the prohibition

---

[23] *AGEPOR—Association of Navigation Agents of Portugal* PRC 2004/07 [2005]; *ANTRAM—National Association of Freighters* PRC 2004/23 [2009].

[24] See PCA Press Release, January 19, 2011, available at http://www.concorrencia.pt/vPT/Noticias_Eventos/Comunicados/Paginas/Comunicado_AdC_201101.aspx?lst=1&Cat=2011. The full decision is not yet published.

[25] *Veterinaries' Association* PRC 2004/28 [2005]; *Dentists Association* PRC 2004/29 [2005]; *Doctors Association* PRC 2005/07 [2006].

[26] See PCA Press Release, June 24, 2011 available at <http://www.concorrencia.pt/vPT/Noticias_Eventos/Comunicados/Paginas/Comunicado_AdC_201107.aspx?lst=1&Cat=2011>. The full decision is not yet published.

will apply. On the contrary, historic, non-sensitive, and aggregated information should not be a source of concern.

Under the former competition law, the PCA was required to previously assess proposed systems for information exchange under the economic balance provisions in force (art. 5 of former Law No. 18/2003 of June 11, 2003). According to public information, the PCA refused to positively assess the information system being set up by APETRO (*Associação Portuguesa de Empresas Petrolíferas*), the association of the undertakings active in the petrol sector, mainly because the number of members in the system was very limited (five) which could entail, according to the PCA, the segmentation of non-disaggregated information. **33.71**

I. Joint purchasing agreements

The key element for the PCA analysis, following EU practice and guidelines, would be the parties' market share and the position of suppliers and the percentage of shared costs associated to the agreement. Furthermore, purchasing agreements are only compatible with competition rules if they safeguard the freedom of the parties to set the final prices of the acquired products. **33.72**

J. Joint lobbying/regulatory/legislative efforts

In principle, joint lobbying would be considered one of the legitimate objects of professional and sector associations. There are no public available cases regarding this issue in Portugal. **33.73**

III. General issues

A. Jurisdiction and applicable law (including sector-specific competition regulation)

Competition issues in Portugal are governed by Law No. 19/2012 and it entered in force on July 7, 2012 replacing Law No. 18/2003. **33.74**

The jurisdictional test for the application of the Portuguese Competition Act is that the anticompetitive practices have or may have an impact on the Portuguese territory, regardless of the place where the practices took place. It is worth mentioning, however, that the Portuguese authorities have discretion to decide whether or not to investigate certain practices or claims, in view of the evidence they have and their priorities. **33.75**

Sector regulation, particularly in the energy and telecommunications markets, includes references to the need to safeguard a competitive environment, and most sector policies are aimed at increasing competition and protecting new entrants from the market power of incumbent operators managing energy or communications networks. Competition law will apply even in regulated sectors. **33.76**

B. Antitrust system

(i) Name of agency/agencies

The main body in charge of the application of competition law in Portugal is the PCA, which is an independent administrative authority. The decisions of the PCA are subject to appeal to the recently created Court of Competition, Regulation and Supervision (*Tribunal da Concorrência, Regulação e Supervisão*). In turn, the Court of Competition, Regulation and Supervision's ruling may be appealed before the Court of Appeal (*Tribunal da Relação*). **33.77**

Under article 84 of the Portuguese Competition Act, an appeal does not suspend the execution of the decision except for decisions that impose structural remedies, or when implementing the decision may cause considerable harm to the appellant, and the party offers to pay a **33.78** guarantee in its place, in which case the suspension of the decision depends on the guarantee actually being paid within the term set by the court.

33.79 During the analysis of the appeal, the PCA has the right to participate in the court hearing, submit pleadings and evidence and to independently appeal the court's decisions, but it does not conduct the prosecution, for which the public prosecutor (*Ministério Público*) is responsible. However, the public prosecutor cannot drop the charges without the PCA's consent.

33.80 Under article 88 of the Portuguese Competition Act, the Court of Competition, Regulation and Supervision has gained jurisdiction over the PCA's decision, being entitled to review its findings of fact and law, as well as to reduce or increase fines and penalties.

33.81 Historically, courts have actively reviewed the PCA's decisions. Several of the PCA's decisions, especially in its early days, were overturned by the Commercial Court of Lisbon on essentially procedural grounds. Lately, the PCA seems to be consolidating its stance.

33.82 The national courts are becoming increasingly familiar with competition law issues and it is no longer uncommon to come across citations of EU case law in domestic rulings. The establishment of a specialized court for competition, supervision and regulation matters is expected to result in a more comprehensive treatment of competition law issues.

(ii) Staff size and budget

33.83 According to its last public report (2011), the PCA was composed of 81 employees: sixteen senior employees, fifty-two specialist workers, and twelve support and auxiliary employees.

33.84 The PCA's budget in 2011 was EUR 9.4 million.

(iii) Recent enforcement actions and trends

33.85 Contrary to the previous legal framework, the Portuguese Competition Act grants the PCA some discretion over whether or not to pursue alleged infringements of antitrust rules and whether to prioritize specific matters. This modification aims to reduce the PCA's administrative burden associated with its prior obligation to open, in principle, an investigation in connection with every complaint submitted under the previous legal framework.

33.86 According to the Portuguese Competition Act (arts. 7 and 8), the PCA will exercise its power to impose sanctions whenever it is in the public interest to prosecute and sanction an infringement of the applicable competition rules, taking into account the goals sought by its competition policy and the factual and legal elements submitted, as well as the seriousness of the alleged infringement, the probability of establishing its existence and the extent of the investigation.

33.87 In order to enhance the transparency and certainty of the PCA's conduct, it recently published its competition policy priorities for 2013, stating that, in terms of restrictive practices, its priorities are to fight cartels, using the leniency program, and abuses of dominant position.

33.88 In relation to the PCA's supervisory powers, as a matter of policy for 2013, it will monitor the payment card markets, energy, telecommunications and ports.

C. Private litigation

33.89 There have been some cases related to competition law in the Portuguese courts, mainly related to vertical agreements. As regards compensation for damages, damages for anticompetitive practices are to be claimed before the judicial courts through ordinary civil proceedings. Although this option is available, not many private parties have initiated civil proceedings against infringing undertakings and individuals. In this regard, private litigation is still very underdeveloped in Portugal and we are not aware of any damages being awarded.

D. Follow-on litigation

See Section II.C. 33.90

E. Arbitration and alternative dispute resolution

Competition law has been subject to private enforcement in arbitral courts. This application, however, is less publicized, as these decisions are generally not public. However, according to public information available there has recently been an arbitration related to an abuse of dominant position in the pharmaceutical sector. 33.91

F. Remedies

Under the Portuguese Competition Act, remedies against anticompetitive behavior include the possibility of imposing fines and ordering the infringing undertakings to cease-and-desist from their conduct. Undertakings may be fined up to 10 percent of their turnover in the year before the authority's decision. This amount can be doubled (i.e. up to 20 percent) in specific circumstances in which there are several infringements to the Portuguese Competition Act. Fines imposed to date in cartel cases, for example, have amounted to approximately 5 percent of the undertaking's revenue. 33.92

Individuals involved in the illegal practice can be fined up to 10 percent of their annual income deriving from the exercise of their functions in the undertaking in question. 33.93

In addition, the authorities may impose ancillary measures, such as banning undertakings involved in bid rigging from participating in public bids for two years. Also structural commitment can be imposed by the Portuguese authorities if they are deemed necessary and proportional to end the infringement. 33.94

The Portuguese Competition Act also provides for a settlement mechanism whereby the parties acknowledge their participation in the infringement in exchange for a reduction of the fine, similarly to what is established at an EU level in Commission Regulation no. 622/2008,[27] as regards the conduct of settlement procedures in cartel cases and in the Commission Notice on settlement procedures in cartel cases.[28] 33.95

The settlement mechanism provided for in the Portuguese Competition Act seems to be also applicable to other infringements besides cartels, and may take place prior or after the statement of objections, and, contrary to the EU regime, no maximum amount of reduction is established. The amount of the reduction will be determined by the PCA within the settlement procedure. 33.96

This mechanism may prove useful to simplify proceedings and reduce litigiousness, since the facts to which the respondent comes clean may no longer be challenged on appeal, and the reduction of the fine resulting from a settlement may be combined with the reduction of the fine granted according to the leniency rules, referred to above. 33.97

Since no settlement mechanism existed before the entry into force of the Portuguese Competition Act, it has yet to be tested in practice. 33.98

Apart from a settlement mechanism, the Portuguese Competition Act has established another consensual law enforcement instrument, whereby the undertaking concerned may offer commitments, prior or after the statement of objections, capable of eliminating the negative 33.99

[27] Commission Regulation No. 622/2008 amending Regulation (EC) No 773/2004, as regards the conduct of settlement procedures in cartel cases (June 30, 2008) OJ L 171/3.

[28] Commission Notice on the conduct of settlement procedures in view of the adoption of Decisions pursuant to Article 7 and Article 23 of Council Regulation No 1/2003 in cartel cases, OJ 2008/C 167/01.

effects on competition of the practices at hand (in principle less serious practices). Upon the PCA's acceptance of the proposed commitments, the case is closed and no decision is reached on the infringement.

33.100 Failure to observe the commitments entails a fine of up to 10 percent of the concerned undertaking's annual income.

33.101 This solution, despite not being expressly set out in the previous competition law, was already used by the PCA in practice to close some proceedings related to certain competition law infringements (that would, in principle, exclude serious competition infringements such as cartels) when the undertakings were willing to cooperate in bringing to an end the alleged infringement—for example, the PCA in the decision in *Nestlé* (and other undertakings active in the supply of coffee market), concerning distribution agreements in the HORECA channel, closed the investigation subject to certain conditions that included the amendment of the non-competition clauses in the distribution agreements previously in force.[29]

(i) Civil liability

33.102 As mentioned, we are not aware of any publicly available private enforcement dispute related to civil liability (whether comprising stand-alone or follow-on actions) and, except for disputes primarily related to vertical agreements (e.g. termination of distribution agreements), private enforcement of competition law is still significantly unused in Portugal.

(ii) Criminal liability

33.103 No criminal liability arises from violations of the Portuguese Competition Act. The investigative and sanctioning procedure in Portugal is of an administrative nature (*processo de contraordenação*).

G. Leniency and immunity

33.104 Portugal's leniency regime was introduced by Law No. 39/2006 of August 25, 2006. According to public records, the regime has been applied twice, in a case involving bid-rigging in the industrial catering services sector and in a case concerning a cartel in the graphic market. Note, however, that cooperation by some of the undertakings in previous cases, at a time when leniency provisions were not available in Portugal, such as the glucose diagnostic strips and salt cartel cases, led to substantial reductions of fines.

33.105 As discussed above, the former leniency statute was revoked by the Portuguese Competition Act, which now includes (article 75 and following) the Portuguese leniency provisions, further harmonized with the European Union regime included in the Commission Notice on Immunity from fines and reduction of fines in cartel cases.[30]

33.106 Under the Portuguese legal framework, leniency is available to undertakings or individuals that provide the PCA with complete and accurate information and evidence of cartels.

33.107 Immunity from fines is granted to the first person/undertaking that supplies the information required to carry out searches and seizures or to detect an infringement of EU or Portuguese rules on collusive practices provided that, at that point in time, the PCA does not already have sufficient evidence of the infringement. The undertaking/individual requesting immunity must cooperate fully and continuously during the investigation, cease to take part in the infringement and may not have coerced other undertakings to take part in the same.

---

[29] *Nestlé Portugal* (n 11).

[30] Commission Notice on Immunity from fines and reduction of fines in cartel cases (December 8, 2006) OJ C 298.

The reduction of fines is available to undertakings/individuals that fail to meet the requirements for immunity, but that have submitted information and evidence of significant added value (cooperating fully and continuously with the PCA and ending their participation in the infringement). The first person/undertaking to do so benefits from a 30–50 percent reduction in the fine, the second from a 20–30 percent reduction, and subsequent undertakings/individuals from a 20 percent reduction. According to article 78(4) of the Portuguese Competition Act, these percentages are halved if the information or evidence is supplied after the issuance of a statement of objections. **33.108**

According to article 81 of the Portuguese Competition Act, leniency applications and supporting documents are strictly confidential. Even if leniency is denied, the applicant's cooperation with the investigation weighs in favor of the latter when setting the amount of the fine (according to article 69 of the Portuguese Competition Act). **33.109**

H. Document creation and retention

There is no particular rule under Portuguese competition law regarding the creation and withholding of documents. There are general rules related to commercial files, for instance, accountancy documents must be kept for ten years according to the law. **33.110**

It should be noted, however, that the cooperation obligations of a leniency applicant include the preservation of any potential evidence related to the investigation and that a failure to comply with this obligation may lead to the loss of the leniency benefits. **33.111**

34

ROMANIA

Carmen Peli, Manuela Lupeanu, and Mihaela Ciolan
Peli Filip

Introduction

34.01 The Romanian Competition Law no. 21/1996 (the "Competition Law") entered into force in 1997, ten years before Romania's accession to the European Union. In July 2010, the Competition Law was substantially amended, with the aim of bringing procedural improvements and adapting the national rules to the European competition legislation.

34.02 Changes included the replacement of the notification procedure for individual exemptions of potential anticompetitive agreements with a "self-assessment procedure" similar to the one under article 101 of the Treaty on the Functioning of the European Union (TFEU), the change of the merger standard of review from dominance to substantial impediment of effective competition and the introduction of "settlement" and "commitments" procedures. The national block exemption regulations and guidelines have been repealed, and instead the block exemption regulations issued by the EU Council or Commission for the purpose of the application of article 101(3) TFEU became applicable. Basically, the EU block exemption regulations were "imported" into the national legislation and apply to block-exempt agreements or concerted practices under the Romanian rules.

Adjustments have also been made to procedural rules, including a clearer definition of the rules applicable to unannounced inspections and the documents that can be seized, additional rules concerning the admission of guilt as a particular attenuating circumstance and the process for damages actions. **34.03**

Following these adjustments, the Competition Law sets rules that are generally in line with those of the European Union. **34.04**

The Romanian Competition Council (RCC or the "Authority") enforces the Competition Law. The RCC is a very active authority and follows closely the trends and practice of the European Union. **34.05**

In the past five years the RCC has scrutinized several markets with sensitive political and economic impact at the end-consumer level, including the distribution and retail sales of pharmaceutical products (both over the counter products and RX drugs, fully or partially subsidized by public funds), the distribution and retail sale of various fast-moving consumer goods (FMCG) (cosmetics and hygiene products, flour, grains, bread, fruits commercialization through supermarkets), the distribution of mobile telephony prepaid products and the electronic communications sector in general (including call termination fees in another operator's network), self-regulated sectors of professionals activities (accountants, notaries, dentists), as well as the energy sector. **34.06**

Some of these markets have been scrutinized first based on market investigations—the equivalent under the Competition Law of the European Commission's sector inquiries (pharmaceutical sector, FMCG retail) and afterwards individual proceedings have been opened up against specific players. **34.07**

Vertical agreements have been analyzed quite thoroughly by the RCC in the recent years, with a focus on direct and indirect resale price maintenance (RPM) practices, vertical market or client allocations, and monitoring practices used by suppliers in respect of the distributors or other resellers of their products. However, some of the trends in this respect are not fully clarified due to the fact that the Authority accepted commitments in the most relevant of these cases, and the commitments decisions were sometimes stricter than the competition rules. **34.08**

Cartels have also been sanctioned on various markets, the largest fine to date (amounting to approx. EUR 200 million) being applied to cartelists in the oil products distribution sector in 2011.[1] Another focus of the Authority is on bid-rigging, and several investigations in various infrastructure markets (roads, energy/gas infrastructure) have either been finalized or ongoing for alleged bid-rigging behavior. Another cartel investigation in the banking sector was closed in May 2013 without any findings of infringement.[2] **34.09**

Abusive unilateral practices have been sanctioned particularly in the communications sector, both regarding electronic communications and postal services. **34.10**

[1] RCC decision not published at 1 December 2013.

[2] *Banking and inter-banking services investigation*, RCC, Order no. 260 (May 23, 2013).

I. Acting alone

34.11 A company acting "alone" in the Romanian market may be subject to the prohibitions under the Competition Law only if it holds a dominant position which it uses abusively to act independently from its clients and competitors.

34.12 The abuse of dominant position rules (article 6 of the Competition Law) follow to a great extent the provisions of article 102 TFEU. There are, however, two distinct entries in article 6 which supplement the prohibitions in article 102 TFEU, by bringing stricter rules for certain situations. These rules concern an express prohibition of exploitation of economic dependency[3] and a prohibition on exporting below costs with the recoupment of expenses from the increase of prices for national buyers. Additionally, the Competition Law has sometimes generated practical application difficulties, due to the express and separate prohibitions of unfair prices, excessive prices, and predatory prices.

34.13 The current practice of the RCC is oriented towards complete harmonization with the EU competition practice; however, the above differences in the rules may entitle the Authority to apply stricter sanctions to unilateral practices of dominant companies.

34.14 Usually, in its application of article 6, the RCC follows the Guidance Paper published by the EU Commission on its enforcement priorities in applying article 102 TFEU to abusive exclusionary conduct by dominant undertakings and the case law provided by the European Commission and the Court of Justice of the European Union and the General Court (the "European Courts").

34.15 Importantly, the Competition Law sets a (rebuttable) dominance presumption for companies holding 40 percent market share or above.

A. Predatory pricing

34.16 Predatory pricing issues are addressed in article 6(1)(e) of the Competition Law prohibiting abuse of a dominant position by way of application of excessive or predatory prices with the purpose of eliminating competitors. Additionally, article 6(1)(a), mirroring article 102 TFEU, prohibits the practice of directly or indirectly imposing unfair purchase or selling prices or unfair commercial conditions. These two provisions have therefore the vocation of being applied together or to similar behaviors. The relation between the two provisions was not expressly clarified in practice so far: therefore, there is no indication of the limit where a price can be so low as to be qualified as unfair, without being nevertheless predatory, according to the standard test developed under the article 6 Guidance Paper.[4]

34.17 On the other hand, pricing below costs is prohibited under Romanian laws applicable to the commercialization of products and services, with specific exceptions provided for certain categories of products or for sale in specified conditions. Due to this legislative choice, the

[3] The Competition Law defines this behavior as the exploitation by a dominant undertaking of the economic dependence of another undertaking towards it, where the latter undertaking does not benefit from an equivalent alternative solution for the supply of goods or the provision of services. The abusive behavior also extends to termination of contractual relations for the sole reason that the partner refuses to submit to unjustified commercial conditions.

[4] Communication from the Commission—Guidance on the Commission's enforcement priorities in applying Article 82 of the EC Treaty to abusive exclusionary conduct by dominant undertakings, OJ C 45/7, February 24, 2009, <http://eur-lex.europa.eu/LexUriServ/LexUriServ.do?uri=OJ:C:2009:045:0007:0020:EN:PDF>.

Authority had very scarce opportunity to analyze and potentially sanction predatory pricing behavior.

The RCC, in a case concerning cable television,[5] laid down the cumulative conditions necessary for the predatory pricing to fall within the scope of article 6(1)(e): (i) the company must hold a dominant position on the relevant market; (ii) the predatory pricing practice must have the aim of eliminating competition; and (iii) such practice must have an actual or potential negative effect on the economy or on consumers. **34.18**

However, the Authority has scarcely dealt with predatory pricing practices so far. The few cases brought based on complaints have generally lacked sufficient evidence or were rejected at an early stage of the procedure, as dominance could not be identified. **34.19**

A case in point is the RCC's decision concerning abusive practices in the tobacco industry.[6] The case was brought as a result of a complaint by TDG against NSRT for alleged abuse by the latter of its dominant position through the termination of exclusive distribution agreements concluded with entities in the TDG group. **34.20**

Ironically, the abuse of dominance through predatory pricing in the tobacco industry was a decision rendered by the Authority against TDG. TDG was a dominant company at the distribution level of the tobacco market and sold the cigarettes produced by NSRT below distribution costs with the aim of eliminating competition from other distributors. **34.21**

In its economic analysis, the RCC took into account such concepts as average total cost or average variable cost to establish the existence of a predatory pricing practice. Other concepts used in the European practice, such as average avoidable cost or long-run average incremental cost, have not been mentioned in the RCC's activity so far. **34.22**

B. Exploitative offenses (excessive pricing, monopoly leveraging)

(i) Excessive prices

Excessive prices are expressly prohibited under article 6(1)(e). However, there is also a provision under article 6(1)(a) which covers unfair prices. The decisions of the RCC are sometimes contradictory on this point, although they offer some guidance regarding unfair versus excessive prices. **34.23**

A case concerning the cable television market raised the issue as to what prices would be unfair without being excessive or predatory.[7] In this case, the high prices charged by some of the cable operators in various periods between 2002 and 2005 have been found to be unfair, without being excessive. In fact, the RCC found that the operators abused their dominant position through unfair pricing practices when they raised the level of prices to consumers even though the cable operators' costs were not increasing or were actually decreasing. The prices were not, however, considered excessive; they were just unfair. Thus, Romanian law is more onerous than the EU law on this point. **34.24**

A more recent decision of the Authority seems to lead to an approach more harmonized with the EU practice, without bringing however express clarifications or rejection of the previous RCC practice. **34.25**

---

[5] *Astral Telecom*, RCC, Case no. 46 (March 15, 2005).

[6] *The National Society "Romanian Tobacco" (NSRT) and Total Distribution Group Romania (TDG)*, RCC, Case no. 11 (February 4, 2003).

[7] *UPC Romania, Hi-Fi Quadral, Astral Telecom and Cablevision of Romania*, RCC, Case no. 237 (December 12, 2006).

34.26 The RCC took the opportunity to express at some length its opinion on excessive pricing in a 2010 case concerning a state-owned player on the Romanian mail delivery services market.[8]

34.27 The Post was a national mail operator enjoying state monopoly on this market until the market was liberalized. At the time of the investigation, it held special and exclusive rights for certain postal deliveries (expired at the end of 2012). The Post was accused of having abused its dominant position through excessive pricing practices by unilaterally increasing the tariffs for postal services in commercial correspondence and marketing mail delivery. The Post raised prices and modified the discounting grid available for the standard services previously mentioned, without any input from clients or customers. The companies acting as intermediaries between printing houses or direct marketing companies and the postal operator, claimed that the price increases were unjustified, and that they were significantly harmed by this practice. The Post was found to hold a *de facto* monopoly on some of the relevant markets, but it was determined that it did not abuse its position through the use of excessive pricing. On the contrary, the RCC found that the Post had abused its dominant position by applying dissimilar conditions to equivalent transactions on the market for the supply of postal services in commercial correspondence and marketing mail delivery.

34.28 In this case, the RCC followed the approach taken by the EC in *Scandlines Sverige AB v. Port of Helsingborg*[9] where it stated that:

> it is important to note that the decisive test in United Brands focuses on the price charged, and its relation to the economic value of the product. While a comparison of prices and costs, which reveals the profit margin, of a particular company may serve as a first step in the analysis (if at all possible to calculate), this in itself cannot be conclusive as regards the existence of an abuse under Article 82.

Therefore, the EC took the view that in order to conduct a conclusive assessment on the existence of an excessive pricing practice, two steps should be followed: (i) an assessment of costs actually incurred in providing the products/services in question (the costs of production) and a comparison with the prices actually charged, and (ii) an assessment of whether the prices are unfair when compared to prices charged to other users or by other ports.

34.29 The two-stage approach followed by the RCC seems to require, first, a proof that the price charged is actually excessive (given the high profit obtained by the company in question) and, second, establishing whether the price is unfair and whether it could have anticompetitive effects.

34.30 The economic value of the service will be expressed not only by the costs involved by its performance: other factors shall be taken into consideration by the RCC, such as the supply and demand dynamic on the relevant market.

34.31 The Post decision is likely to be representative of the type of analysis to be applied by the RCC to exploitative offenses. Monopoly leveraging combined with discriminatory treatment applied to specific clients on an upstream market, have been also identified in this case. These practices were found to lead to the exclusion of the dominant undertaking's competitors from one of the upstream markets for the preparation of mail deliveries—a behavior that guaranteed the preservation of the *de facto* monopoly of the Post on the delivery services market.

C. Monopsony

34.32 Monopsony is not a concept addressed in any specific manner by the Competition Law or any other Romanian legislation in the competition field. The situation would likely be dealt with

[8] *The Romanian Post National Company—The Post*, RCC, Case no. 52 (December 16, 2010).

[9] *Scandlines Sverige AB v. Port of Helsingborg*, EC Case COMP/A.36.568/D3 (July 23, 2004).

based on article 6 provisions. The analysis is likely to be performed in the area of the theory of economic dependency of companies, tying, unfair trading conditions, or discrimination.

In a relatively recent decision[10] regarding the cold drawn alloy steel bars market, the RCC had the opportunity to express its opinion on the matter. **34.33**

COST, the only cold drawn alloy steel bars manufacturer on the Romanian market, was accused of abusing its dominant position through exploitative practices. The accusations were made by STEROM, the only client on the market for cold drawn alloy steel bars. The RCC stressed that the existing monopoly was countervailed by the correlative monopsony, and it concluded that both companies had the power to negotiate every contractual provision. Therefore, the RCC stated that, as long as there is a balance on the market and there is a countervailing buyer power, the monopolist manufacturer cannot be accused of abusing its dominant position through exploitative conduct. **34.34**

The economic analysis in this case was straightforward, and the RCC did not get the chance to develop extensively its positions concerning monopsony and monopsony's potential anti-competitive effects on the market. However, it can be said that the RCC is familiar with the concept and would be able to develop it rapidly in its assessments in future cases. **34.35**

D. Price discrimination

The abusive practice of price discrimination is addressed by article 6(1)(c) prohibiting the application of dissimilar conditions to equivalent transactions with other trading parties, thereby placing them at a competitive disadvantage. Similar to the EU structuring of the anticompetitive prohibitions, the Competition Law recognizes that price discrimination may appear despite the absence of a dominant position in the form of an agreement between companies, which is prohibited under article 5(1)(d) of the Competition Law. **34.36**

The Competition Law establishes two cumulative conditions for the existence of the discriminatory pricing practice under article 6(1)(c), identical to the conditions provided by the TFEU. These are: (i) the application of dissimilar conditions to equivalent transactions and (ii) the existence of a competitive disadvantage as a result of such application. **34.37**

The RCC analyzed a price discrimination conduct in the Post case concerning the mail services market.[11] **34.38**

A preferential treatment has been granted by the Post to specific clients in the form of (i) price reductions and (ii) preferential payment term conditions for services performed on upstream markets to the market where the Post was nearly monopolist. The RCC found that the different treatment distorted competition between the clients of the dominant firm, and led to—or at least had as its purpose—the exclusion of competitors from upstream markets. **34.39**

The step-by-step analysis put forward by the RCC in order to prove the existence of an abuse of dominance in the form of price discrimination comprised (i) the proof of the existence of the dominant position; (ii) the proof of discrimination, performed through the application of a difference of regime to competing clients; and (iii) the proof that the services provided by these clients in exchange of the regime obtained could be qualified as representing equivalent transactions. **34.40**

In identifying the existence of discrimination, before it analyzed the above conditions, the authority held that the following factors are likely to be found in discriminatory behaviors: a) the dominant company is an unavoidable commercial partner, if not a monopolist; b) discrimination is **34.41**

[10] *COST S.A. (COST)*, RCC, Case no. 55 (December 22, 2010).

[11] See Section I.B.

usually significant in value and persistent over time; and c) the product/service supplied by the dominant company must have an important place in the total cost of the discriminated buyer.

34.42 Discriminatory pricing will most likely be dealt with in Romania in the context of anticompetitive agreements. Article 5(1)(d) of the Competition Law prohibits (using the same wording as article 6) the application of dissimilar conditions to equivalent transactions concluded by a supplier with its customers. When discrimination is the object or effect of an agreement or concerted practices, all the parties involved may face sanctions. There have been several complaint cases in which one distributor alleged discriminatory treatment in the form of price reductions. However, most cases were either closed for procedural reasons or were not sufficiently supported by evidence provided by the complainants. Thus, they did not generate an extensive and comprehensive analysis of the notion of equivalence of transactions.

E. Dictating or influencing resale prices

34.43 Dominant undertakings on the Romanian market have traditionally had the ability to control and manage the distribution of their products throughout the entire distribution chain.

34.44 The RCC has detected such practices but in most instances, it dealt with them under the provisions prohibiting anticompetitive agreements (article 5) rather than under the abuse of dominance provisions (article 6). Consequently, influencing resale prices would not amount to a simple unilateral practice, and the most significant consequences are that (i) companies may be sanctioned for such practices regardless of whether they are dominant or not (in fact there is no *de minimis* threshold or other safe harbor rule) and (ii) the suppliers and resellers (wholesalers, retailers, etc.) would be all sanctioned for agreeing on resale price fixing.

(i) Resale price maintenance

34.45 Under the Romanian law, resale price maintenance (RPM) is a hard core restriction, which infringes the Competition Law irrespective of whether the supposed agreement between the parties has been implemented or whether the practice had little or no anticompetitive effect.

34.46 RPM may appear in the form of setting/agreeing fixed or minimum resale prices. The practice (i) may be manifest—the parties agree on the resale price, or (ii) it can result from indirect controlling actions of the parties—for example, agreement on discounts to be passed on, imposition of standard discounts grids, or recommendation of resale prices coupled with strong enforcement of the "recommendation."

34.47 One relevant case in the RCC's practice concerns Wrigley Romania and its distributors.[12] Wrigley held a 90 percent market share on the Romanian chewing gum market.

34.48 The distribution agreements concluded by Wrigley included clauses requiring the products to be resold at prices which would not exceed the range of recommended resale prices indicated by the supplier. These clauses were later replaced with ones that stated that the supplier's delivery price to the distributor was to be the maximum recommended price at which the distributors to resell the products.

34.49 In addition, Wrigley had also given discounts grids to be followed by the distributors.

34.50 The RCC found that the combination of the pricing strategies showed the parties' intent to set the resale prices, considering particularly that distributors would have no incentive to ignore "recommendations" from a 90-percent market share supplier. Wrigley and the distributors were fined with approximately EUR 5.5 million.

[12] *Request for exemption made by Wrigley Romania—Produse Zaharoase and 15 distributors*, RCC, Case no. 224 (December 19, 2005).

(ii) Minimum advertised price programs

As discussed in Section I.E(i), indirect RPM is prohibited under Romanian law. **34.51**

Therefore, in an arrangement with distributors, it will be possible to have *recommended advertised prices*, but never minimum ones. Furthermore recommended prices can be treated as hardcore restrictions if they are applied uniformly, becoming *de facto* fixed prices. **34.52**

Advertised recommended prices will likely be acceptable if they are indicated for a limited duration (the promotional period) and they are not so low as to function as fixed prices. The recommended level of resale price will need to be set in such a way as to allow the resellers to recoup their costs and gain a sufficient profit margin even if they were to sell at a price below the recommended level. When the recommended price is set too low, barely allowing them to recoup the expenses and, particularly when the volumes sold in the promotion are not likely to bring significant income, it is highly possible that all the resellers will apply the recommended level of the price. They will not have sufficient incentives to set a lower price, as no significant gains would result from that. They would not set a higher price either, because they may estimate that the supplier could be displeased or that the competitors would observe the supplier-recommended price and thus sell the same products cheaper. **34.53**

F. Tying arrangements

Tying arrangements are caught by article 6(1)(d) of the Competition Law which prohibits a dominant undertaking from engaging in an abusive conduct consisting in the conclusion of agreements on the condition that the partner assumes supplementary obligations, which neither by their nature nor based on commercial usage have any connections with the object of the agreement. **34.54**

Significant tying practices have not been the focus of any RCC investigation as of yet. **34.55**

An interesting case involving potential tying practices has been analyzed by the RCC from a different perspective in a recent decision regarding the supply of natural gas.[13] According to the provisions of the Romanian natural gas legislation, authorized gas suppliers in Romania have to sell to customers a mix of nationally produced gas and imported gas. The purpose of the "mix rule" is to allow customers to benefit from cheaper, domestic gas. In the case at hand, a large gas industrial consumer, Interagro, argued that Romgaz, a state-owned dominant gas producer, conditioned the supply of natural gas on the acquisition of foreign gas. The complainant argued that Romgaz used its dominance to force it to conclude an agreement including conditions not related to its object. The RCC limited itself to rejecting the complaint on the basis of particular gas market rules invoked by the complainant and so did not deal with the compatibility of the competition legislation with the "mix rule." Consequently, the RCC did not have the chance of entering into a deeper analysis of the dominant's potential anticompetitive practice and potential market failure, because of the legislative framework applicable to not fully deregulated markets in Romania. The gas market offers an example of the Authority's limitations in addressing and sanctioning potential abusive behavior of incumbent companies still present on the partially deregulated markets in Romania. The RCC could only recommend changes in the relevant gas legislation without any enforcement being possibly attached to that recommendation. **34.56**

G. Exclusive dealing

The Competition Law does not contain an express prohibition of exclusivity or single branding. These practices are dealt with under article 5 of the Competition Law regarding **34.57**

[13] *Interagro SA (Interagro) and SNGN ROMGAZ SA (Romgaz)*, RCC, Case no. 2 (February 6, 2012).

anticompetitive agreements and concerted practices, and are therefore examined in the context of vertical agreements. The RCC applies the EU block exemption regulations and guidelines on vertical agreements and vertical restraints. The issue of exclusivity and single branding has not been analyzed by the RCC as a unilateral conduct. As for RPM practices, both the supplier and the distributor that are found to have entered into exclusive arrangements illegally would be sanctioned (not just the dominant undertaking).

34.58 An example in this area deals with Cadbury Romania and its twenty-one exclusive distributors.[14] Cadbury notified its distribution system to the RCC in order to obtain an exemption (before the amendment of the Competition Law in 2010 the companies were allowed to request individual exemptions from the RCC for such practices, while now they have to carry out their own assessment). The contracts included territorial exclusivity and single branding both in the form of prohibition of sale of competing products and minimum acquisitions targets. Due to confidentiality reasons in the decision, the market share held by Cadbury Romania was not mentioned, but as no block exemption applied, it is clear that it was at around 30 percent or more. Although Cadbury was the market leader, it was not dominant, and the Authority found that the efficiencies of the system outweighed the competition restrictions and therefore the exclusive dealing was cleared (individually exempted). The RCC considered in its analysis the market context, as the second large supplier on the market (Kraft Foods Romania) applied a similar exclusive system.

H. Refusal to deal

34.59 A dominant undertaking's refusal to deal is prohibited under article 6(1)(a) and 6(1)(f) of the Competition Law. The Romanian Competition Law may therefore be stricter than the similar article 102 TFEU rules dealing with refusal to supply.

34.60 Article 6(1)(a) covers the prohibition of refusal to deal with certain specific suppliers or beneficiaries, while article 6(1)(f) sanctions the interruption of contractual relations for the sole reason that the partner refuses to adhere to unjustified commercial conditions. The latter prohibition refers mainly to the refusal to continue dealing with an existing commercial partner, and it falls under article 6 point which further prohibits the exploitation of economic dependency.

34.61 To date, the RCC has not been called to analyze a large number of cases concerning the refusal to deal. However, the issue has been raised in the context of the market for heating mechanisms.[15] The case concerned the activities of Saunier Duval which was the only supplier of a certain type of heating mechanism on the market. The company used a quantity forcing mechanism compelling the distributors to acquire a minimum number of its products. As a result, the complainant was not able to meet the requirements. The RCC held that, even though Saunier Duval was a monopolist on the market for the commercialization of Saunier Duval heating systems and spare parts in Romania, because it was the only authorized representative of the group importing its products to Romania, the Authority could not intervene in the trading policy of a private company where the policy does not hinder competition. While the company had a dominant position, it did not abuse that position by organizing its distribution network. The complaining company, Multiservice, had an economically viable alternative and could acquire the specific types of heating mechanisms from other distributors who would have been able to satisfy the conditions imposed by the supplier.

---

[14] *Cadbury Romania and its distributors,* RCC, Case no.12 (March 3, 2009).

[15] *Multiservice SRL (Multiservice) and Saunier Duval Distributie SRL (Saunier Duval)*, RCC, Case no. 12 (April 6, 2007).

Overall, based on the available practice dealing mainly or partially with the refusal to deal, refusal to provide access to essential facilities or termination of customer relations,[16] it seems that, in its analysis, the RCC adopts the criteria used at EU level and puts significant emphasis on the existence of an economically viable alternative on the market in question, in order to establish the existence or, on the contrary, the absence of the practice of refusal to deal. **34.62**

I. Essential facilities

Romanian Competition Law does not expressly provide a definition of essential facilities. This concept has entered the Romanian doctrine and competition practice following the intense benchmarking with the EU competition rules, particularly after the accession to the European Union. The essential facilities doctrine is discussed and applied in relation to article 6(1)(a) refusal to deal cases and also in correlation with article 6(1)(f) prohibitions of exploitation of economic dependency or unjustified termination of relations. **34.63**

In its Guidelines on the application of competition rules to access agreements in the telecom sector, the RCC defines the concept of essential facilities as a facility or an infrastructure or a services package which are essential in order to assure (provide) connectivity with consumers and/or in order to allow competitors to carry out their activities, and which cannot be reproduced by economically viable means. Indeed, the RCC applied the doctrine to that sector in cases concerning the access to call termination services on specific markets.[17] **34.64**

The RCC's investigation followed a complaint submitted by Netmaster, a new entrant on the telecom market which did not own technical infrastructure. Netmaster alleged that the three market players in Romania at that time (2006): Orange, Vodafone, and Romtelecom, refused to grant access to calls originating in Netmaster's network and terminating in their own. The initial refusal later evolved into a failure to agree on the tariffs to be applied to call termination services. In its analysis, the RCC took into consideration the criteria established by EU case law and examined how the refusal affected competition. It established that Vodafone and Orange had the obligation to provide call termination service each at its own network, given that such service is an essential facility and that each operator held a natural monopoly with respect to its own network. Overall the analysis was aligned with the EU Commission's approach. **34.65**

In addition to the review by the RCC, the telecom cases had also been considered by the national regulatory authority in telecommunications and by the Romanian courts. **34.66**

J. Bundling (including loyalty and market share discounts)

Romanian Competition Law mirrors the provisions of article 102 TFEU and applies to discounts and bundling. **34.67**

With respect to discounts and loyalty rebates, the RCC follows the European Commission's approach, without ignoring, however, the developments and the practice of the European courts. **34.68**

The RCC has yet to investigate practices involving tying, bundling and discounts. **34.69**

---

[16] See the cases discussed in Section I.I, i.e. *Vodafone Romania S.A. and Netmaster Communications S.R.L.*, RCC, Case no. 1 (February 14, 2011) ("*Vodafone*"); *Orange Romania S.A. and Netmaster Communications S.R.L.*, RCC, Case no. 2 (February 14, 2011) ("*Orange*"); and *Arcelor Mittal Galati S.A. and Comvex S.A.*, RCC, Case no. 31 (June 22, 2012) ("*Comvex*").

[17] *Vodafone* (n 16) and *Orange* (n 16).

K. Standard-setting groups (disclosure requirements, licensing arrangements, and licensing pools)

34.70 The RCC has yet to investigate practices involving standard-setting groups. Such practices would fall within the scope of article 5 (agreements and concerted practices) of the Competition Law if they restrict, prevent, or distort competition and are either carried out in, or produce effects on, the territory of Romania.

L. Customer termination

34.71 Customer termination may be addressed under either article 6(1)(a), which prohibits refusal to deal, or article 6(1)(f), which prohibits abuse of economic dependency or termination of contractual relations for the sole reason that the partner refuses to accept unjustified commercial conditions.

34.72 An illustrative case involving customer termination concerned the market for port services for solid bulk cargo goods.[18] The market in question was characterized by limited capacity as Comvex was the only port operator in Romania capable of meeting Arcelor Mittal's entire cargo demand.

34.73 The RCC's investigation followed Arcelor Mittal's decision to terminate the contract it had with Comvex and to subsequently use port services offered by other companies in Bulgaria. Because Arcelor Mittal was the most important buyer of Comvex's services, the latter alleged that the termination of the contract amounted to an abuse of dominance. This situation presented a particular interest as both parties were dominant on their respective upstream and downstream market.

34.74 The RCC focused on the notion of "unavoidable business partner" and economic dependency as they were expressed by the Court of Justice of the European Union (CJEU),[19] and it concluded that Comvex was able to maintain its profitability despite the loss of the contract with Arcelor Mittal.

34.75 Interestingly enough, the RCC took into consideration the fact that the purpose of the Comvex port was not exclusively to serve the interests of Arcelor Mittal, even though the presence of the steel factory nearby was of relevance in the development of Comvex under the centralized economy period. Comvex's monopoly position was not achieved in the conditions of liberalized economy, and therefore one cannot assume the state of a unilateral dependency of Comvex. Moreover, the RCC considered the existence of a monopsony and countervailing power in the market and concluded that Arcelor Mittal did not abuse its dominant position when it decided to terminate its contract with Comvex.

M. Termination of intermediaries (retailers, wholesalers, dealers, and value-added resellers, agents, and brokers)

34.76 Termination of intermediaries is governed by article 6(1)(a) and article 6(1)(f) mentioned above. Due to the dynamic growth of Romanian economy over the past fifteen years, practices relating to termination of intermediaries have become more frequent, particularly in relation to the distribution segment of the market, in various sectors such as trade of FMCG or pharmaceuticals.

---

[18] *Comvex* (n 16).

[19] Case 85/76 *Hoffmann-La Roche & Co. AG v. Commission* [1979] ECR 461; Case T-219/99, *Virgin v. British Airways* [2003] ECR II-05917.

A significant number of complaints have been submitted to the RCC by various distributors and other type of intermediaries against their suppliers for alleged abusive termination of the commercial relations. One of the cases concerned Colgate Romania, which at the time of the decision held 60 percent market share for oral care products in Romania. The company terminated a distribution agreement with one of its distributors for lack of results. The distributor filed a complaint against Colgate Romania for having been discriminated and eventually driven out of the distribution market. After an extensive investigation, the RCC did not hold the complaint to be true and considered that Colgate did not abuse its position. The distributor had claimed that it was discriminated as compared with Metro Cash & Carry. The RCC analyzed the commercial conditions offered to Colgate Romania's traditional distributors and those offered to Metro, and concluded that (i) the overall discount received by traditional distributors was higher than the one received by Metro and that, in any case, (ii) the trading performance of Metro and of traditional distributors are not fully interchangeable, due to Metro's retail activities (as a cash & carry company, Metro sold products not only to retailers but also to end-customers). However, Colgate and its other traditional distributors were sanctioned for anticompetitive agreements consisting in setting up and implementing an indirect minimum price fixing scheme. **34.77**

A similar complaint of alleged abusive termination by Unilever Romania was submitted by a company belonging to the same group of companies as the complainant in the Colgate case. The RCC rejected the complaint and found that Unilever, even if potentially dominant on some markets, had not abused its position when deciding to terminate the relation with the less efficient distributor in its network. **34.78**

N. Termination of relationships with competitors

The termination of commercial relations with a direct or indirect competitor has not come in the competition spotlight so far, even if this type of situations may have occurred on the Romanian market. **34.79**

The only case that became public so far, but which has not been analyzed under the abuse of dominance rule, is the termination by Orange Romania of an existing commercial relation with a mobile telephony prepaid products distributor, Proton Tehnologies, after the latter had been acquired and became part of the group of a competing operator. After the termination of the distribution agreement, Proton asked Orange Romania and several of its main wholesalers to supply Orange prepaid products. **34.80**

The investigation was carried out under the anticompetitive agreements rules, as the RCC was concerned that Orange and its distributors may have agreed to boycott the acquisition by Proton Tehnologies of Orange products. The RCC accepted commitments regarding the rules to be applied when selecting a distributor/sub-distributor, even if the latter is controlled by a competitor. As such, Orange offered to establish objective and non-discriminatory criteria based on which to select the wholesalers of its prepaid products, namely: (i) the number of points of sale owned or controlled by the potential distributor (minimum 500); (ii) the distributor's financial capabilities (capital owned, turnover obtained, financial health, bank guarantee letter); (iii) the lack of conflict of interests and the distributor's adherence to "ethical principles"; (iv) the wholesaler's distribution experience with particular types of products; and (v) the ownership of distribution management systems. As far as the commercial relation with a distributor that is wholly owned by one of its competitors is concerned, Orange committed to accept it in its network but with the application of certain restrictions to ensure that sensitive commercial information would not be disclosed by such distributor to Orange's competitors. In particular, the competition-owned distributor will receive pre-sale information regarding new products or promotions only 24 hours before their launch by **34.81**

Orange. The post-sale information required by the distributor for the issuance of invoice for electronic products to Orange will not be obtained in real time (as would be the case of the electronic system provided to any other distributor), but it would be offered with the delay of days or weeks, so that the competitor would be unable to assess in real time the marketing efficiency and success of Orange products and campaigns.

O. Exemptions

34.82 Abusive unilateral behavior by dominant undertakings could be accepted if objective justifications can be identified, however, keeping in mind that the RCC is of the opinion that dominant companies hold a special responsibility in their relations with partners or clients.

34.83 Bilateral behaviors by dominant undertakings will not benefit from block exemptions (such as the vertical block exemption regulation) due to their large market shares. Individual exemption may be granted to agreements entered into by dominant undertakings if the Romanian conditions in this respect are met (article 5(2) of the Competition Law).

II. Dealing with competitors

34.84 Lawful or unlawful cooperation with competitors in Romania is addressed by article 5 of the Competition Law, concerning the prohibition of anticompetitive agreements, concerted practices, or decisions by associations of undertakings (all to be covered below by the general term of *agreement*). Following the EU-wide trend in recent years, the RCC has created two separate divisions within the RCC, dealing specifically with the types of cooperative practices usually used by competitors: one dealing with *cartels* and the other with *bid-rigging*. The Authority has also declared on various occasions that its future focus will be on these types of horizontal practices which are so harmful to clients and customers on the Romanian market.

34.85 In line with European Regulation 1/2003, when performing its article 5 analysis, the RCC will follow the European Commission and the European courts' practice. In recent years, the RCC has paid more attention towards cartels, identifying and sanctioning certain horizontal agreements in various sectors, such as the energy sector, the market for taxi services, the market for accounting services, etc.

A. Horizontal price fixing (including advanced announcements of price or product changes)

34.86 Price fixing between competitors is addressed specifically in article 5(1)(a) of the Competition Law. The article prohibits agreements affecting competition on the Romanian market or a part thereof, which directly or indirectly set the purchase or selling prices, or other trading conditions.

34.87 The RCC has dealt with a number of price-fixing cartel cases during its long practice and in various sectors of activity: the meal voucher sector, the cement production sector, bread manufacturing sector in specific regions of Romania, the provision of driving school services in Bucharest. Some of the markets where the sanctioning decisions have been applied may be seen as having a rather limited impact on the overall Romanian market (driving school services); however some decisions had real impact either because of the effect they had on the entire market (the cement producers' cartel) or because of the state's involvement in the creation of the cartels at a certain point in time (the meal voucher services providers' cartel).

In the cement producers' cartel[20] the Authority found, among other things, that the three players in the Romanian market colluded to maintain artificial price levels for cement sold in Romania. The RCC rejected the parties' claims that the high price was the result of the oligopolistic nature of the market and not the result of collusion. The main evidence used by the authority was an internal handwritten note made by the manager of one of the producers describing a price increase scenario. The evidence was subsequently rejected in court and the decision annulled with respect to one of the cement producers. However, by that time, two of the sanctioned parties had paid the fine applied by the RCC and had decided not to appeal the RCC decision. **34.88**

In the meal voucher services decision,[21] the Authority found that the companies issuing meal vouchers in Romania agreed on a minimum price level to be paid by employers for the acquisition of meal vouchers. The value voucher sectors are regulated in Romania. The issuers are issuing meal vouchers to employers; the vouchers are distributed by the employers to their employees as an alternative means of payment, benefitting from certain tax incentives. The issuers conclude agreements with retailers for the acceptance of these vouchers, and the employees may use their vouchers to buy food from various restaurants and retail stores. The case concerned an agreement made by all the issuers, upon the initiative of the Romanian Ministry of Finance (which was also issuing annual authorizations for the conduct of the meal voucher activity by issuers). The undertakings were sanctioned for this practice. Naturally, the meal vouchers issuers raised during the procedure the argument of the state regulatory authority's initiative and involvement in setting up the minimum commission levels. The RCC rejected the defense of state involvement in the perpetuation of the cartel, for the reason that any pressure or involvement of state or public authorities is not a justifying argument for private undertakings' anticompetitive behavior. The state authority involved was not sanctioned or fined for its behavior, as the RCC had no legal basis for applying sanctions to another regulatory authority. However, the RCC's position was particularly inflexible in this case, as even though the facts were quite explicit, and written proofs were available, the RCC concluded that the breach of competition law was not imposed in any way by the Ministry of Finance which does not regulate relations between undertakings and it does not intervene in normal business environment. **34.89**

Another interesting horizontal price-fixing practice took place on the market of driving schools services.[22] The RCC noted that despite the large number of market players, the agreement between thirty-two driving schools had the ability to significantly impede competition on the market in question. **34.90**

The horizontal agreement involved price fixing of instructors' fees coupled with monitoring of enforcement and advanced announcements of price increases. The RCC concluded that the price increase was not directly linked to the increase in costs and that the advanced announcement of such increase resulted in a better coordination between market players. **34.91**

The fine imposed by the RCC on the cartel members was up to 8 percent of the total turnover for the year prior to when the sanction was applied and included aggravating factors for the companies which advanced the price increase announcement. In terms of percentage, this has been one of the highest sanctions applied by the RCC in a cartel case to date. **34.92**

[20] *Lafarge Romcim SA, Holcim Romania SA and Carpatcement Holding SA, sanctions for infringing article 5(1)(a) of the Competition Law,* RCC, Case no. 94 (May 26, 2005).

[21] *Sodexho Pass, infringement of article 5(1)(a),* RCC, Case no. 270 (September 29, 2004).

[22] *Thirty-two driving instructions schools,* RCC, Case no. 35 (June, 2009).

34.93 It is important to note that the RCC has a very harsh attitude towards cartels and it does not seem to be willing to accept commitments from companies involved in horizontal agreements.

B. Horizontal agreements to allocate customers or territories; agreements not to compete

34.94 Horizontal market sharing agreements are prohibited under the article 5(1)(c) of the Competition Law. The RCC has scarcely dealt with market sharing practices among competitors, as they usually appeared incidentally in a wider vertical agreement context.

34.95 The largest fine applied to non-compete agreements amounted to over EUR 200 million. It was imposed in 2012, in a case in which certain oil companies agreed to withdraw some of their products from the market. The formal decision was not yet released, and the reasoning was therefore not publicly available. It is expected that the decision will focus on the non-compete agreement and unlawful cooperation between the five large gasoline suppliers in Romania: OMV Petrom, LukOil, Rompetrol, Mol Romania, and Eni Romania. The companies coordinated to withdraw from the market a less expensive type of gasoline fuel, which allegedly would have been withdrawn anyway following the adoption of stricter environmental standards.

34.96 In 2006, the RCC investigated the allocation of markets between certain cable companies.[23] The case concerned the local cable TV market on which only two companies operated. The companies decided to eliminate the competition between them by allocating the available territory. The RCC's investigation revealed that the companies either shared a given territory of that particular market or each of the companies gained a *de facto* monopoly in parts of the market.

34.97 Non-compete agreements were also investigated by the RCC as part of bid-rigging agreements in the pharmaceutical sector. The acquisition of any pharmaceutical products or devices by hospitals in the framework of a public health program implies the application of public procurement legislation and most of the times a tendering process. One of the cases dealt with by the RCC in this area concerned the market of medical devices for dialysis.[24] The three companies cooperated in bid-rigging regarding a tendering process, on a healthcare market where at least fourteen companies were active in the distribution of dialysis related products. However, not all of them participated in the tender for each lot of products and thus, on most of the very narrow relevant markets identified, the three companies under investigation were the only ones present with offers. The factor which worsened the effect on the market of this anticompetitive conduct was that the relevant authorities had not organized any other tendering process after the one in question. Instead, the authorities kept renewing the contracts already signed. The RCC noted that on a regulated market where acquisitions are made through a tendering process, the competition on the market takes place only during the tender and it is therefore essential to avoid bid-rigging.

34.98 In another case, the RCC found the existence of a hub-and-spoke market sharing practices on the markets for distribution of diabetes products (insulin and other medicines).[25] The Authority found clear evidence to support the identification of a vertical market sharing practice initiated by the supplier. As for the distributors, however, the existence of an agreement/concerted practice between them was deducted indirectly from the fact that each of

[23] *SC UPC Romania SA and SC HI-FI Quadral SRL*, RCC, Case no. 237 (December 12, 2006).

[24] *SC Fresenius Medical Care SRL, SC Alsifcom Intermed SRL and SC Opremi Medfarm SRL*, RCC, Case no. 12 (March 3, 2008).

[25] *Eli Lilly Export SA and its distributors Mediplus Exim SRL, A&AMedical SRL and Relad Pharma SRL*, RCC, Case no.15 (March 12, 2008).

them accepted to participate to tenders with only one type of insulin products manufactured by Eli Lilly, while before the tender, all the wholesalers involved were distributing the entire portfolio of diabetes products manufactured by Eli Lilly.

C. Horizontal boycotts

Horizontal boycotts are dealt with under article 5(1)(g) of the Competition Law. In practice, the concept of collective boycott is seldom used directly and is usually treated as ancillary to other anticompetitive practices. **34.99**

An interesting case in which the issue of collective boycotts has been brought up concerned the dialysis market.[26] The colluding parties tried to improve their position at the tender procedure, and filed an ungrounded complaint against one of their most important competitors alleging fraudulent conduct. They managed in this way to exclude any possible barrier to the implementation of a bid-rigging practice with respect to the public tenders organized on the dialysis market. The RCC started an investigation against the three colluding companies and in addition to the bid-rigging practice, found that the colluders cooperated with the purpose of eliminating an important competitor, without however pursuing the issue further. All three companies were sanctioned with a fine of approximately EUR 1.5 million. **34.100**

D. Joint ventures and other competitive collaborations

Cooperation between competitors in Romania is permitted and subject to rules similar to those adopted by the European Commission. **34.101**

National rules distinguish between full-function joint ventures and non-full-function joint ventures. The first category would be subject to analysis under both the control of economic concentration rules and under the article 5 of the Competition Law, regarding agreements between undertakings, if the creation of the joint venture has as its object or effect the coordination of the competitive behavior of undertakings that remain independent. Non-full function joint ventures might be in certain circumstances examined under merger control rules, although a clear and consistent practice has not yet taken shape. **34.102**

The non-full-function joint venture would generally remain to be dealt with and assessed under article 5 of the Competition Law and according to the European guidelines on horizontal cooperation between potential or actual competitors (research and development, technology transfer, joint commercialization, etc.).[27] **34.103**

It should be also mentioned that in 2010, the legal framework has suffered some adjustments. On the one hand, the Competition Law expressly defined joint ventures which are economic concentrations (i.e. a joint venture which, on a lasting basis, fulfills all the functions of an autonomous economic entity); on the other hand, the Law repealed the national rules on horizontal agreements, replacing them with a direct application of the European Commission's relevant legislation. The practical manner in which these EU regulations and guidelines will be applied with respect to the Romanian competition legislation has not yet taken shape in any decisions. **34.104**

In the cement producers cartel case discussed at para. 34.88,[28] the Authority used as evidence of anticompetitive cooperation the sale of a production unit from one producer to the other **34.105**

---

[26] *Fresenius and others* (n 24).

[27] Guidelines on the applicability of Article 101 of the Treaty on the Functioning of the European Union to horizontal co-operation agreements, OJ C 11, January 14, 2011 ("Horizontal Cooperation Guidelines"), <http://eur-lex.europa.eu/LexUriServ/LexUriServ.do?uri=OJ:C:2011:011:0001:0072:EN:PDF>.

[28] *Lafarge Romcim and others* (n 20).

and the intended creation by the three players on the market of a new company, responsible for providing consulting services to the three companies and for identifying new external market opportunities and suppliers.

E. Trade associations

34.106 Anticompetitive decisions of associations of undertakings are prohibited by article 5 of the Competition Law. The RCC has dealt with decisions of associations of undertakings hindering competition law on several occasions. The cases mainly concerned actions of professional bodies in various Romanian markets such as: dental technicians, accountants, taxi drivers, real estate evaluation professionals, psychiatrists, the union of real estate agencies, grain storage merchants in Romania, bailiffs and notaries. The activities of associations from the cosmetics market, cement market, grain depositories market, ship-owners have been analyzed in the context of identification of various anticompetitive practices performed mainly by the members.

34.107 To illustrate, note the RCC's investigation of trade association active in the market for accountancy services.[29] In Romania, the accounting profession is self-regulated by CECCAR, a professional autonomous body with the ability to enforce the rules of this profession (i.e. to revoke the accountant's title). The RCC examined price recommendations given by the CECCAR to all its members as well as the price monitoring enforced subsequently by CECCAR.

34.108 The RCC's analysis focused on the idea that a price fixing agreement did not constitute a part of CECCAR's prerogatives and such recommendation was not necessary in order to achieve any quality standard of the accountancy services.

34.109 It is worth noting that the fine imposed in this case amounted to 9.2 percent of the association's total turnover. This sanction, which applied nearly the maximum level of fines permitted under the Competition Law (i.e. 10 percent of the association's total turnover) is the highest percentage applied so far by the RCC as a result of the long duration of this particular agreement.

F. Interlocking directorates

34.110 Interlocking directorates have not been examined so far by the RCC. It is not excluded, however, that such practices may be viewed (although not directly contemplated under the antitrust rules) as favoring anticompetitive behavior.

G. Facilitating practices

34.111 Practices that may facilitate anticompetitive behavior are rarely analyzed as a stand-alone concept. They are usually addressed alongside the main anticompetitive activity and may have an impact in the determination of the final fine applied, when taken into consideration as aggravating circumstances.

34.112 Practices facilitating other illegal behaviors could appear under the form of a horizontal or vertical exchange of information, category management, recommendations made in relation to trade conditions, interlocking directorates etc.

34.113 However, when these practices have a direct anticompetitive effect on the market, they could be addressed and sanctioned as independent offenses under the Competition Law.

---

[29] *The Body of Expert and Authorized Accountants of Romania (CECCAR)*, RCC, Case no. 47 (November 2, 2010).

H. Information exchange

Information exchanges performed in the Romanian market are subject to competition rules and practice developed at the EU level and reflect the approach as outlined in the European Commission Guidelines on the applicability of article 101 TFEU to horizontal cooperation agreements. **34.114**

Accordingly, information exchange is not prohibited when it does not concern sensitive, individualized and recent market information. The exchange may raise concerns when it supports the creation or implementation of an anticompetitive practice such as cartels, or when it concerns price fixing. **34.115**

Information exchanges have been addressed by RCC representatives on various public occasions (i.e. interviews, conferences), suggesting that in a vertical relation the Authority would likely be concerned with the increase of market transparency and the possibility of control that can be exercised by a supplier over a distributor's business independence. **34.116**

I. Joint purchasing agreements

Joint purchase activities performed by competitors are assessed under article 5 of the Competition Law and Horizontal Cooperation Guidelines. Cooperation might be acceptable as long as the competitors are able to prove that the efficiencies generated by the agreement exceed the negative competitive effects. **34.117**

There has been little practice in relation to joint purchasing activities in Romania. **34.118**

One interesting case concerned the acquisition of harbor services by a ship-owners' association in sea and Danube harbors in Romania.[30] That association negotiated for ten years the pricing and other acquisition conditions for port services on behalf of its members, over twenty-five operators and ship owners. The association was vested with the power to represent its members and negotiate tariffs and price reduction for port services offered by the port administration companies. The members of the association considered that the joint negotiation of tariffs and other acquisition conditions were necessary in order to countervail the potential negotiation power held by the port administrations. The RCC qualified the practice as horizontal price-fixing understanding. **34.119**

In an older case (not reported) the RCC prohibited cement companies from jointly acquiring a raw material (slag) from Sidex Mittal (which was the super-dominant producer of steal and slag as a by-product). **34.120**

J. Joint lobbying/regulatory/legislative efforts

Romanian competition rules have not been used so far to limit joint activities of undertakings aiming to affect legislation or regulatory process in Romania. However, such practice will most likely be examined under the "best practice" rules issued by the RCC in 2013, regarding lobbying activity. According to these best practice rules, lobbying activities might be examined both from the perspective of the purpose of the lobbyists (e.g. supporting the introduction of certain administrative barriers to entry or minimum prices might require the analysis under the antitrust rules), as well as from the perspective of collateral effects (such as the exchange of sensitive information). **34.121**

---

[30] *Association of Ship-owners and Port-River Operators, infringement of art. 5(1)(a) of the Competition Law*, RCC, Case no. 95 (May 26, 2005).

III. General issues

A. Jurisdiction and applicable law (including sector-specific competition regulation)

34.122 The Competition Law entered into force in 1997 and applies to acts having impact on competition that are undertaken, have effect, or are likely to have effect on the Romanian market, even though the triggering act may not actually have taken place in Romania. While the main goal of the law is to protect the overall market welfare, particularly consumer well-being (through the stimulation of the overall market competitiveness), the Competition Law has also evolved as a useful tool for the accomplishment of other multiple purposes, such as the protection of competitors (perceived as an indirect tool for protecting consumer welfare). For example, when dealing with a restriction of exports to non-EU countries by a medicines supplier, the RCC explained that such ban would risk affecting the local wholesale market structure (i.e. the respective distributors would be restricted from expanding their business and gain additional revenues from volume discounts from the export activity), and indirectly, the Romanian consumers. The RCC argues that, in the absence of the exports outside the European Economic Area (EEA), the distributors would not be able to allocate some of such potential revenue gains as discounts to the Romanian consumers.[31]

34.123 The RCC is also generally interested in safeguarding the overall market functionality mostly in specifically regulated sectors, such as the telecommunications, pharmaceuticals, or banking. Also, starting with 2007, the RCC sought to contribute to the integration of the national market within the internal EU market, by fighting parallel trade infringements, as well as of any other unlawful behavior affecting trade between Romania and other member states. In light of this policy goal, in recent years, the RCC has applied significant fines to several manufacturers of medicinal products for having banned parallel trade.

34.124 The Competition Law is concerned with: (i) agreements between competitors (e.g. market sharing, price fixing, non-competition, output restriction, etc.) or between firms at different levels of the market (e.g. resale price maintenance, customer and market allocation, etc.) having as their object of effect the restriction of competition; (ii) unilateral abusive behavior by monopolist or dominant undertakings (e.g. price squeezing, discrimination, unlawful pricing, predatory pricing, etc.); as well as (iii) mergers between firms that could be harmful to the competitive environment. Competition rules also apply to public authorities legally responsible for restriction and distortion of competition by public decision in their powers (e.g. sector regulations, individual decisions, subsidies, etc.).

34.125 When an agreement or a unilateral conduct also affects trade between member states, the enforcement of national competition rules is accompanied by an application of article 101 or 102 TFEU to the respective infringement.

34.126 Starting with 2011, the Competition Law has expressly followed EU case law when defining the notion of "*undertaking*"—a concept generally referring to any economic operator offering goods or services on a given market while performing an economic activity.

34.127 Sector-specific competition rules exist in relation to communications and energy. Various other sectors including financial services, transport, pharmaceuticals, etc. also contain regulations that may be relevant from a competition standpoint. Market regulation generally occurs by the setting of standard sector-specific rules, as well as by the adoption of individual corrective measures.

[31] *Bayer SRL and six Romanian distributors*, RCC, Case no. 98 (December 29, 2011).

B. Antitrust system

(i) Name of agency/agencies

The enforcement of the competition rules mainly lies with the Romanian Competition Council (RCC) and secondarily with the Romanian courts of law. **34.128**

The RCC is an autonomous administrative authority enjoying wide discretion to obtain information from undertakings, carry out dawn-raids, issue decisions, and impose penalties. The RCC powers in competition matters are wide-ranging, embodying regulatory powers (i.e. enactment of mandatory regulations and guidelines on competition matters), decisional powers (i.e. sets fines, accepts commitments, applies leniency procedures, etc.), investigational powers as well quasi-judicial powers (i.e. the first tier review of the act of accusation prepared by the investigation team is carried out by the RCC Board which takes the final decision). It also advises the relevant authorities in the legislative process in order to avoid the enactment of legislation that contradicts the competition rules. **34.129**

Before Romania's accession to the European Union, the RCC had also dealt with state aid matters. Since 2007, most of its cases have been transferred to the European Commission. The RCC remained the national contact authority on state aid between the European Commission and the public bodies, state aid providers and beneficiaries. **34.130**

The RCC has also enforcement powers against unfair competition practices. However—in the absence of clear and updated guidelines about the types of unfair acts to be pursued and the sanctions to be applied in this field, this competence has not been explored so far. Draft proposals for revived unfair competition rules are currently on the RCC's table. Also, the RCC gained particular competence in the railway sector, where surveillance of competitive mechanism in the railway sector was passed on from the relevant ministry to the RCC. **34.131**

Where the RCC shares competition enforcement powers with specific regulatory agencies (e.g. telecommunications or energy), the relations between the RCC and specialized regulatory agencies are usually ruled by inter-institutional bilateral arrangements. **34.132**

Romanian judicial courts also enjoy competences to deal with competition cases. Courts can either be called to decide whether there has been an antitrust infringement in the context of private claims—procedure scarcely popular at local level—or in the context of judicial review of the RCC's administrative decisions. In this second scenario, any of the RCC's decisions—with few exceptions—may be challenged before the Bucharest Court of Appeal, which could at its turn be reviewed—if appealed—by the High Court of Justice. **34.133**

There are no specialized courts dealing with competition cases. Challenges to the RCC's decisions are submitted to court departments dealing with general administrative cases. Private claims are dealt with by the civil/commercial section of the various courts. **34.134**

In terms of power of review, the local judicial courts enjoy full jurisdiction to assess the RCC's decisions. This includes full powers to reexamine all facts and legal merits of an RCC's decision, including authorizing the parties to bring additional proofs against the antitrust decision. Courts may quash the RCC's decisions in whole or in part, they may even force the RCC to issue a new decision or start an investigation, as well as award pecuniary or moral compensatory damages. However, by virtue of the legal separation between the judiciary and executive powers, judges cannot themselves take a new decision replacing an RCC existing decision. A relevant example where the court made a thorough reexamination of the facts is the cement cartel decision,[32] where the courts concluded that there was no sufficient evidence **34.135**

[32] *SC Carpatcement Holding SA*, Supreme Court of Justice, Decision no. 1358 (March 5, 2007).

to prove the cartel, while the market parallelism could have been caused by other lawful market conditions.

34.136 In the current overall enforcement of competition rules, however, courts generally tend to perform a marginal assessment of the actual sometimes sophisticated merits of the cases, while predominantly looking at procedural irregularities usually incidental in ordinary administrative cases.

(ii) Staff size and budget

34.137 In 2011, the RCC's overall staff consisted of 286 employees (other than members of the Board) distributed among several specialized directorates (Services, Industry and Energy, Consumption Goods, State Aid, Research, Legal, Public and International Relations), as well as territorial directorates. In 2011, case handlers counted for more than half of the personnel, among whom 67.5 percent are economists, while approximately 20 percent have a legal background. Budgetary constraints triggered small cuts in the overall staff size (by 3 percent compared to 2010 and by 4 percent compared to 2009).

34.138 The RCC staff passed intensive training under the auspices of the European Commission DG Competition, or in cooperation with peer national competition agencies.

34.139 At the head of the RCC is the Board, which is a collegial body made up by seven members (President, two Vice-Presidents, and four counsellors) appointed by the President of Romania.

34.140 In 2011, the RCC's budget amounted to approximately EUR 8 million. Due to the economic downturn, the budged registered a decreasing trend.

(iii) Recent enforcement actions and trends

34.141 While the financial downturn has led to a substantial reduction in the total number of merger control procedures, the RCC has proved an increasing interest in investigating agreements and unilateral practices. There has been an overall increase in the number of antitrust investigations. In fact, in 2011, there were seventy ongoing investigations, with twenty-seven cases started by the RCC in 2011.

34.142 The RCC's sanctioning policy has not been constant through the years. Its peak was reached in 2011, with historic fines applied in cases concerning mobile telephony, gasoline, and pharmaceutical markets.

34.143 In a number of cases, investigations and infringement decisions originated in the RCC's analysis in relation to sector inquiries carried out in specific industries (e.g. banking and insurance, retail, pharmaceutical, energy, and infrastructure).

34.144 There has been an increased interest in bid-rigging cases, with a focus on specific sectors: the tendering procedures in public hospitals, the public road infrastructure sector, and energy constructions. In order to prioritize such cases, a distinct unit has been recently established especially dedicated to investigating bid-rigging. Another unit is dedicated to investigating cartels.

34.145 Also, in its advocacy interventions, the RCC focused on raising different stakeholders' awareness about bid-rigging in public procurement procedures.

34.146 Another increase in the volume of antitrust work was triggered by the RCC's increased interest for the leniency program. Such a program was available starting with 2004, but has been substantially reshaped in 2009 so as to also apply to market sharing and price fixing vertical arrangements. Leniency has not been used significantly so far, but the RCC encourages companies to apply for the program and benefit from immunity or reduction of fines.

Commitments and fine reduction instruments have also facilitated the RCC's practice. Firms under the RCC's scrutiny have an additional option to admit guilt leading to up to 30 percent fine reduction under the "settlement" procedure.[33] The RCC also promotes antitrust compliance by rewarding firms implementing actual corporate competition compliance programs with a fine reduction.[34] **34.147**

The RCC has also declared increased interest in the criminal liability, as well as in the private enforcement of competition claims. Starting with 2010, the RCC has referred to the competent prosecution bodies a number of individuals involved in several big-rigging and cartel antitrust infringements under the RCC's investigation. Also, the RCC is actively lobbying to the Romanian legislator for hardening criminal sanctions for persons involved in antitrust offenses. On the basis of available information so far, no criminal sanctions have been applied so far in connection with antitrust infringements. **34.148**

In its strategy paper for 2010–14, the RCC set up its main goals to promote compliance with competition rules: deterrence, positive rewards, advocacy, increased transparency, and legal certainty of the competition policy and development. **34.149**

C. Private litigation

In line with the European Commission's strategy, the RCC has been committed to encourage private competition law actions. As of 2010, the Competition Law expressly provides the possibility for any person who has suffered damages from anticompetitive practices to seek compensation in court. **34.150**

Private claims can be filed either independently ("stand-alone" actions) or after the issuance of a sanctioning decision by the RCC ("follow-on" claims[35]). **34.151**

Actions for damages due to breach of national or EU competition rules are generally governed by national tort law. It would be necessary for any plaintiff to demonstrate that damages were caused by the infringement in order to recover damages, i.e. one has to prove: (i) the illegal practice, (ii) the damage incurred, (iii) the defendant's fault, and (iv) the link of causality between the damage and the fault. **34.152**

Private parties are generally entitled to full compensation of the damages incurred as a consequence of the anticompetitive practice (i.e. actual damages as well as lost profits; material, as well as moral damages). **34.153**

Colluders may be held jointly liable (i.e. up to the full amount of the damage) irrespective of their individual fault and/or involvement in the infringements. **34.154**

Interestingly, Romanian Competition Law expressly incorporated a clear-cut prohibition of the "passing-on" defense. Anticipating the great obstacle that claimants would face otherwise, the national rules allow purchasers to sue for antitrust overcharge damages and to recover losses (e.g. volume sales decrease) irrespective of them passing-on the overcharge to their customers. The RCC is currently working on an effective mechanism allowing customers to recover overcharges from unlawful cartel or abuse of dominance practices. This would be performed through actual guidance sections in the sanctioning decisions informing consumers about the availability of the damage claim procedure, while also providing computation methods for quantifying the actual damage levels. **34.155**

[33] For more details see para. 34.185.
[34] For more details see para. 34.186.
[35] See Section III.D.

34.156 The deadline for bringing a stand-alone private antitrust claim in court is within three years from the date when the damage resulting from the antitrust infringement actually occurred or the damaged party learnt of such damage. The legal time limits for claiming the recovery of damages resulting from an infringement fined by an RCC decision is of maximum two years as of the date when the RCC decision remained final (either not challenged in court or confirmed by a definitive and irrevocable court decision).

34.157 As there are no specialized courts to hear actions for damages in private antitrust litigations, the amended Competition Law vested the RCC with the power to become involved as *amicus curiae* in private litigations concerning both national and EU competition matters. Additionally, anytime a private case regards the enforcement of article 101 or 102 TFUE, a copy of the court decision must be communicated—through the RCC—to the European Commission.

34.158 Despite the RCC encouragement for firms to detect and treat antitrust wrong-doing by means of private claims, the main enforcement path of competition rules still remains administrative. According to cases reported so far, there have been no court decisions awarding damages in private antitrust litigations.

34.159 It should be noted, however, that an important drawback to the judicial system is the fact that not all court decisions are publicly available. In many cases, the decisions (whether administrative or commercial) are available to the parties only.

D. Follow-on litigation (includes role of agency determinations of liability for follow-on litigation)

34.160 Damages arising from antitrust infringements can be recovered through follow-on claims. Such actions follow an infringement decision issued by the RCC.

34.161 The main attractiveness of such claims is that plaintiffs would no longer need to prove the existence of the infringement. The RCC's final decision creates a legal presumption with regards to the existence of the anticompetitive act. The presumption may be rebutted if, for example, the challenge of the RCC decision was accepted by the administrative appeal court. Otherwise, the complainant would generally need to prove the causal link and the existence of damage and level of the damage. Given the lack of practice so far, it cannot be assessed if the courts would be generally satisfied with the proof of these conditions only.

34.162 Courts remain entirely responsible to quantify the damage. The RCC fining decisions have made no reference so far to the actual determination of liability for follow-on litigations.

34.163 Interestingly, the RCC is currently instructing its chief economists to deliver computations on market damages in antitrust files. Also, from observations submitted by the RCC following the European Commission public consultation on the matter,[36] the RCC appears to embrace the model of the representative customer (buyer) for harm quantification. This method entails the quantification of damages as a difference between the actual market outcome and a hypothetical situation where there would have been no anticompetitive conduct. This model is based on the consumer surplus whereas the damage is estimated as the monetary equivalent to the welfare loss caused by the infringement. The RCC sees the following advantages arising from this computation method: courts would enjoy a common framework of analysis, the plaintiffs would no longer be needed to quantify the damage by own methods,

[36] Romanian Competition Council, *Romania: Standpoint on quantification of harm suffered because of an infringement of Article 101 and/or Article 102 of the Treaty regarding the functioning of the European Union*, <http://ec.europa.eu/competition/consultations/2011_actions_damages/romanian_competition_council_en.pdf>.

and collective redress would be facilitated. In line with these proposals and the RCC's interest in developing effective damage computation methods, we could expect the RCC to play in the future a more active role in the actual determination of liability for follow-on claims.

Further, one vice-president of the RCC recently declared that the RCC would not exclude applying methods for mitigating the administrative fine level on a case-by-case basis whenever public fines are also accompanied by stand-alone civil damage claims. **34.164**

Post-issuance of a decision, RCC's assistance in follow-on litigations would be further needed. Judicial courts are expected to ask for documents and any needed information from the antitrust case file, while the RCC could also voluntarily become involved in the case file as *amicus curiae*. Local courts are theoretically permitted to adjudicate in a stand-alone claim for damages arising from an anticompetitive infringement even though the RCC has not issued a final decision in an ongoing antitrust investigation having the same object. However, given the local court's reluctance in dealing with such type of relatively specialized claims, they would likely tend to postpone dealing with the court file until having received a decision from the RCC. **34.165**

The deadline for bringing a follow-on action is of two years starting from the date when RCC's sanctioning decision had remained final. **34.166**

Despite the RCC meritorious efforts, the legal availability to recover damages through follow-on actions has been scarcely explored. **34.167**

E. Arbitration and alternative dispute resolution

Administrative offenses and liability cannot be subject to arbitration. Both administrative and criminal liability is personal and cannot make the object of transaction between the parties. **34.168**

However, the arbitrability of antitrust private disputes (e.g. follow-on actions, damage claim share between cartelists, merger remedies enforcement share, arguing the nullity *ab initio* of the agreement under which the claimant is seeking to bring a claim, etc.) is not precluded by national rules. Other alternative methods, such as mediation or expert determination of the damage may be equally explored as useful dispute resolution mechanisms. However, the parties may agree on arbitration only post-infringement, which generally would prevent an intensive use of alternative dispute resolution (ADR) methods. **34.169**

Although the popularity of arbitration—mostly before foreign arbitration bodies—has grown the past years in Romania, given the relatively high costs of arbitration procedures, disputes are more frequently brought before ordinary courts. **34.170**

There have been no significant disclosed arbitration precedents in antitrust matters. *Ex ante* arbitration clauses have been rarely used. We are not aware of any *ex post* arbitration agreements so far. **34.171**

F. Remedies

(i) Civil liability

According to article 51 of the Competition Law, undertakings may be sanctioned by fines of up to 10 percent of their turnover of the year preceding the sanctioning decision. **34.172**

Under the Civil Code rules and depending on the relevant company's internal rules, a company subjected to administrative fines or civil claims for antitrust wrong-doing can seek redress against directors or other corporate officers whose actions caused firms knowingly to undertake the unlawful course of conduct. **34.173**

Also, the civil liability of legal or economic advisers providing wrongful antitrust counselling could not be excluded. **34.174**

(ii) Criminal liability

34.175 Companies are not subject of criminal sanctions for antitrust infringements (only administrative fines apply).

34.176 According to article 60(1) of the Competition Law, directors or any other corporate officers found guilty of wilfully triggering or contributing to the setting of an unlawful agreement (cartels as well as concerted practices or vertical infringements) may be sentenced to up to three years imprisonment or heavy penalty fine payments. Personal criminal contribution to collusive tendering particularly materializing in bid-rigging is differently and more severely looked for by criminal rules (article 60(2) of the Competition Law).

34.177 The RCC does not have the power to prosecute suspected criminal offenses by way of an investigation even if such offenses are related to antitrust infringements. Such conducts must normally be referred to the competent criminal prosecution bodies. To date, there have been no such criminal sanctions applied. However, the RCC has indicated that it will intensify its activity in reporting infringements that may result in criminal sanctions.

G. Leniency and immunity

34.178 As of 2010, companies having committed an anticompetitive infringement can apply for leniency subject to (i) recognition of guilt and (ii) bringing additional evidence of the infringement. A leniency unit advising firms and managing leniency applications has been created as an integrated part of the RCC.

34.179 The local leniency mechanism resembles the EU leniency system. The effect of applying for leniency is a clearance from fines or a substantial reduction of the fine.

34.180 *Type A immunity.* Fine immunity is available to firms that provide information and evidence that allow the RCC to start an investigation and carry out dawn-raids.

34.181 *Type B immunity.* This type of immunity is available to firms providing information and evidences that allow the RCC to prove an infringement when an investigation has already been triggered and provided that: (i) no Type A immunity had been granted to other whistleblower, and (ii) the RCC has no sufficient evidence supporting the infringement.

34.182 *Fine reduction.* Alternatively to fine immunity, a system of fine reduction is implemented by the RCC. Potential reductions range from 20 percent to 50 percent and may be granted to firms providing additional significant information not available to the RCC during the course of the investigation.

34.183 The initiator of an infringement can at most obtain a fine discount.

34.184 Unfortunately, despite the effervescent advertising of this procedure by the RCC, to date, the leniency regime did not have a wide application as the prospect of obtaining concrete benefits is uncertain. In particular, there is no practical guidance as to how the evidence provided would be actually assessed by the RCC. The procedure has been applied only once so far, in a case involving a very small local company and the decision did not contain any explanation as to the type of evidence provided by the applicants.

34.185 *Settlement.* Another interesting procedure regards the possibility of obtaining a reduction in fine of up to 30 percent if firms under investigation expressly admit having committed the infringement under investigation. Firms admitting guilt would have a limited ability to challenging the fining decisions in court. Although this procedure has been applied by the RCC in several cases in 2011, no details or guidance have been yet made available by the RCC.

34.186 *Fine mitigation.* As of 2011, acknowledging that the success of competition rules is substantially linked to the setting of effective implementation of corporate compliance culture, the RCC set an up to 10 percent fine reduction to firms proving the existence and actual implementation of a competition law compliance program. The RCC has not provided so far guidance on how eligible antitrust compliance programs are expected to take place. No fine reductions based on effective compliance programs have been applied so far. The RCC has recently promised to bring further guidance on this matter.

H. Document creation and retention

The destruction by an undertaking of incriminating business documents—while not being expressly sanctioned by the Competition Law—is generally deemed as a form of unlawful opposition to the RCC's unexpected inspections which usually take place at the business premises of investigated undertakings. Any such behavior may risk a sanction of up to 1 percent of the respective undertaking's overall turnover in the year preceding the date of the inspection. Based on this legal incrimination, the RCC has applied once a relatively high fine to a local resort of warm mineral baths attempting to destroy relevant documents during inspections seeking to find proof of unlawful cartel on the respective market.[37] **34.187**

Despite the existence of this severe legal sanction, Romanian undertakings had not—until very recently—consider putting in place an actual corporate policy related to the creation and retention of documents having a potential competition involvement. **34.188**

The absence of any such protection favored the increase in the number of successful antitrust investigations where the RCC has been able to fully evidence the existence of incriminating antitrust arrangements exclusively relying on hard copy or electronic documents (correspondence, e-mails, reports, presentations, drafts, memos, agenda notes, etc.) which have been relatively easily collected during unexpected inspections at the business premises of the investigated undertakings. Frequently, such documents supported the existence of express hard core restrictions, such as price fixing or parallel trade bans. **34.189**

However, the intense advertising of competition compliance by the RCC followed by the introduction of a legal fine mitigation to firms putting in place effective competition compliance programs,[38] as well as the intensification of antitrust investigations and the increase in the incidence and value of sanctions have recently increased market participants' interest for effective competition compliance with focus on a more prudent document creation and retention. **34.190**

[37] *S.C. OLANESTI RIVIERA S.A.*, RCC, Case no. 34 (June 19, 2009).

[38] See comments in para. 34.186.

35

RUSSIA

Alexander Viktorov
Freshfields

Introduction

35.01 The first Russian competition law was enacted in 1991 and was subsequently replaced by a new one—Federal Law No.135-FZ on the Protection of Competition of July 26, 2006 (LPC). The LPC, as amended, is currently the key law governing competition issues in Russia. The competition legislation and practice have developed significantly since the enactment of the LPC. However, although in certain areas, generally accepted approaches have been worked out, some issues still lack clarity and consistent interpretation, leaving therefore much room for discretion. The LPC has an exterritorial effect and applies to agreements or actions carried out outside Russia if such agreements or actions may impact on competition in Russia.

35.02 The LPC is enforced by the Federal Antimonopoly Service (the FAS) and a large network comprising eighty-three local agencies established in various Russian regions. The current government is supportive of the competition regime and has vested strong investigative and enforcement powers in the FAS. The Russian authority cooperates with competition authorities globally including within the International Competition Network and also by way of bilateral and multilateral agreements.[1]

The FAS's attention is currently focused on the unilateral behavior of dominant enterprises restrictive of competition, cartels, and anticompetitive vertical agreements. The markets which attract particular scrutiny are the markets for energy products, food, chemicals, pharmaceuticals, telecommunications, transportation, financial services, among others. The number of cases initiated by the FAS in connection with antitrust infringements increases yearly. **35.03**

I. Acting alone

The most serious antitrust infringements in Russia involve cartels entered into between competitors.[2] However, there is also a broad range of other types of conduct that can infringe antitrust law, some of which can attract heavy sanctions. **35.04**

This range includes, first, agreements or understandings entered into with other, non-competing, businesses in the supply chain (e.g. resale price maintenance, exclusivity, quantity forcing, non-compete). These are analyzed under article 11 of the LPC. In recent years, attention has been given to markets of importance to consumers, such as, for example, food products, pharmaceuticals, and telecommunications. **35.05**

Second, the range of scrutinized conduct includes purely unilateral conduct characterized as an "abuse" (e.g. using a monopoly position to impose high (exploitative) or low (predatory) prices, refusal to deal, discrimination in contractual conditions). Such abusive unilateral conduct is only illegal if it is carried out by a business in a "dominant position," in which case it infringes article 10 of the LPC. Recent enforcement action has involved a broad range of sectors, but some have received particular attention. One of these is oil products, where the FAS has brought proceedings concerning issues such as establishing and maintaining monopoly high prices and discrimination in contractual conditions. There have also been a number of cases in electric and heat power, transportation, telecommunications markets concerning behavior that excludes competing suppliers, or the charging of excessive prices. **35.06**

A. Anticompetitive agreements and understandings with non-competitors

Agreements between business entities that have, or may potentially have, a restrictive impact on competition are prohibited. **35.07**

The LPC prohibits any agreements (except for franchise agreements and vertical agreements where the parties' market shares do not exceed 20 percent in any market[3]), if they lead or may lead to a limitation of competition and in particular provide for: **35.08**

- imposing on a counterparty terms and conditions which are onerous or unrelated to the subject matter of the agreement (e.g. an unjustified requirement to provide funds or assets, or to purchase products which the purchaser does not need);

[1] It is noteworthy that in February 2012, the Eurasian Economic Commission of the Customs Union of Belarus, Kazakhstan, and Russia was created. It is intended to act as a single supranational regulatory body for the Customs Union in a manner similar to the European Commission for the European Union and is expected to start fully functioning in 2014–15.

[2] See Section II.

[3] Note that the market may be any market, and need not be necessarily relevant to the agreement concerned.

- setting different prices (tariffs) for one and the same product, if this is not economically, technologically or otherwise justified;
- impeding access to or exit from a product market for other business entities; or
- setting conditions for membership in professional and other associations.

35.09 Many of the prohibitions are not applicable to agreements if they qualify as vertical agreements (i.e. agreements between buyer and seller). The list of bans applicable to vertical agreements is limited to just two (and these two only apply if either party's market share exceeds 20 percent in any market): (i) setting resale prices, except for maximum resale prices; and (ii) prohibiting the sale of competing goods (except for agreements for the sale of products under the seller's trademark).

35.10 Vertical agreements made between parties whose market share does not exceed 20 percent are exempt from any prohibitions which otherwise would have been applicable.

35.11 The above prohibitions do not apply, as a general rule, to agreements or concerted actions between parties that belong to the same group and where one party controls the other one(s) or where the parties are under common control. There is another exemption for concerted actions (but not for agreements): the prohibitions do not apply to concerted actions between parties the market share of each of which does not exceed 8 percent and whose aggregate market share does not exceed 20 percent.

35.12 There are some exceptions. In order for an agreement to be permitted, its draft, and also certain information about the parties, have to be submitted to the FAS in a special filing. After reviewing the filing the FAS issues a decision saying whether the agreement is permissible. The FAS has thirty calendar days, extendable by another twenty days, to issue such a decision. The decision can be issued subject to certain behavioral conditions imposed on the parties.

35.13 The particular situations where anticompetitive behavior is permitted may be generalized by the Russian Government in its regulatory acts by adoption of general exceptions.[4]

B. Abuse of a dominant position

35.14 "Dominant position" is defined under the LPC as a position of one or several companies (a group) in the market for specific goods or services which allows it or them to have a decisive influence on the general terms of trade (e.g. sale or purchase) of such goods or services in this market sector, so as to exclude other companies from or impede other companies' access to this market sector.

35.15 It is not illegal for a business to have a dominant position, but it is illegal to abuse it. Article 10 of the LPC prohibits any abuse of a dominant market position.

35.16 Determining whether a particular entity enjoys a dominant position involves a complex evaluation of various factors, the most important of which is the entity's market share. There is a presumption of market dominance for entities with a market share of more than 50 percent and below this threshold, it is presumed that there is no market dominance. However, the FAS may still find that an entity holding a share of 35–50 percent holds a dominant position on the basis of the stability of the entity's market share, its competitors' market shares, barriers to market entry, and/or other factors. An entity holding a market share of 35 percent or less can also be found dominant if it can "dictate" prices, and access to the market for new players is impaired and there is no substitute for the goods and/or services provided by that company.

[4] See Section I.P.

Furthermore, there is a presumption of collective dominance of the top three to five companies in a market if their aggregate market share exceeds 50–70 percent, provided that (i) the market share of each of these companies is at least 8 percent; (ii) market shares are stable over time and there are high barriers to entry for new competitors; (iii) such companies' products have no substitutes; and (iv) the information about the prices and the terms of the sale or purchase of the respective goods on the corresponding markets is accessible to an indefinite number of parties. **35.17**

The FAS has different methods for identifying dominant companies. It constantly monitors the market and tracks any conduct or other factors leading to dominance. It also obtains relevant information from other governmental agencies, interested organizations and companies, law enforcement authorities, courts, and also in the course of merger control reviews and dealing with competition law offenses. The FAS maintains the Russian register of legal entities having a market share over 35 percent for particular products or services (the Register). Approximately 9,700 entities are listed on the Register. As a general rule, there is no political or any other aspects in this, and those companies that are listed objectively and indeed possess market power. However, the list is not complete, as there exist other companies (e.g. purely trading rather than production companies, and thus less "conspicuous"), whose market share is in fact more than 35 percent but which are not listed. **35.18**

The Register is a database of business entities (and their groups) which is used to allow state control over such entities (and groups) to ensure their compliance with antitrust laws and regulations. Inclusion on the Register implies certain reporting obligations. At present, such obligations consist of regularly providing the anti-monopoly bodies with information on key performance results. **35.19**

The fact of inclusion on the Register does not prove that a company is dominant in the respective market. However, the risk of companies listed in the Register being considered dominant is significant, especially for the companies with a market share of more than 50 percent. **35.20**

C. Predatory pricing

Predatory pricing is an abuse of the LPC if committed by an undertaking with a dominant position in the market. Predation consists of imposing monopoly low prices and is aimed at weakening or excluding competitors from the market. **35.21**

The price is considered "monopoly low" according to the LPC if it is below the cost and the price existing in a "comparable" competitive market (i.e. where competition is not restricted). The LPC does not require actual proof that the dominant company will later be able to recoup the losses it incurs while predating. Generally, predatory pricing is not common in Russia. Analysis of court practice shows that that enforcement in the area of "monopoly low" prices is less frequent that in the area of "monopoly high" prices. Still, the FAS brings such cases from time to time. **35.22**

By way of example, in June 2006, the FAS brought proceedings against a Russian airline, following a complaint by its competitor, for violating the LPC by introducing a special price for certain customers, which was one third of the general price on the route. The competitor alleged that the Russian airline's prices were predatory and that the volume of the competitor's transportation services substantially decreased.[5] The case was closed when the Russian airline stopped these low pricing practices. The LPC does not provide for any specific guidance on the appropriate measure of cost. Another example is the case held by *FAS against* **35.23**

[5] *Sibir Airline*, FAS (June 27, 2006) <http://fas.gov.ru/fas-in-press/fas-in-press_7158.html>.

AKADO-Stolitsa. In 2009, the FAS held that AKADO-Stolitsa, a telecommunication provider, infringed the LPC by introducing and maintaining a monopoly low price for technical support services in the South-East Administrative District of Moscow, which could lead to excluding competitors from the relevant market. The FAS decision was upheld by court in three instances.[6]

D. Exploitative offenses

35.24 Excessive pricing (or, using the Russian term, imposing monopoly high prices by a dominant undertaking) constitutes abuse and is an infringement of article 10 of the LPC.

35.25 Generally, any price increase or decrease by a dominant undertaking may be subject to a whole set of restrictions and conditions. Even maintaining prices at the same level can be deemed a violation of the LPC if conditions exist for their reduction. At the same time, a price set by a dominant undertaking cannot be deemed monopoly high if it does not exceed the price existing in a comparable competitive market (inside or outside of Russia) and if it does not exceed the price for such product set at a commodity exchange provided that the applicable antimonopoly rules are complied with.

35.26 The FAS brings exploitative pricing cases quite often, the most "notorious" ones having been a series of cases in the market for oil products brought by the FAS in the period from 2008 to 2012. In particular, in 2008, oil prices in the world market considerably decreased but Russian oil companies and fuel retailers were reluctant to lower domestic prices. The FAS initiated a number of proceedings with regard to such violations and a significant number of oil companies were held liable and fined.[7] A second and the third "wave" of cases against oil companies with respect to their oil and oil product pricing was initiated by the FAS in 2009—2012.[8] The reason why the oil industry enjoys this special attention is because oil companies make high profits, and increases in prices for gasoline and other fuels are very noticeable and affect everyone—hence the relevant proceedings. However, the FAS takes action against companies in other industries as well—it's just that the fines are not as high (in particular because the turnover which is the basis for fine calculation is lower) and the proceedings are less conspicuous. The fines paid by oil companies within the three "waves" of cases totaled over RUB 20 billion.

E. Monopsony

35.27 The LPC applies to dominant purchasers. There are no particular differences in legal treatment between dominant purchasers and dominant suppliers. However, the legal methodology for defining the dominant position focuses on the seller rather than the purchaser.

35.28 The issue of abuse by a dominant purchaser was raised, however, in the following case. In April 2011, the FAS determined that the State Corporation for Organizing Air Traffic violated the LPC by refusing to enter into an agreement with ZAO Aircompany Skytest. The case was initiated following an application filed by ZAO Aircompany Skytest. The company stated that the State Corporation refused to enter into an agreement with the applicant for the provision of services for the examination of ground facilities, flight radio technical support, air

---

[6] *Akado-Stolitsa,* 2009, FAS Case no. 7-37/2009 (August 26, 2009).

[7] *Lukoil, NK Rosneft, TNK-BP Holding, Gazprom Neft, Surgutneftegaz,* FAS (2008) <http://fas.gov.ru/fas-in-press/fas-in-press_21515.html>.

[8] *Gazprom Neft, TNK-BP Holding, Lukoil, NK Rosneft, Surgutneftegaz, Tatneft, Bashneft, Alliance Oil,* FAS (2009), <http://fas.gov.ru/fas-in-press/fas-in-press_28375.html>; *Gazprom Neft, Lukoil, NK Rosneft, Bashneft,* FAS (2011), <http://fas.gov.ru/fas-news/fas-news_32609.html>; *Lukoil-Severo-Zapadnefteprodukt,* FAS (2012), <http://fas.gov.ru/fas-news/fas-news_33374.html>.

telecommunications, and lighting facilities for civil aerodromes. The State Corporation is the dominant purchaser of such services as it operates about 95 percent of such equipment that is located in civil aerodromes in Russia. After the agreement with ZAO Aircompany Skytest had been terminated in 2009, the State Corporation entered into a contract for equipment inspection with its affiliate and refused to extend the agreement or enter into a new one with ZAO Aircompany Skytest. The FAS imposed a fine on the State Corporation for Organizing Air Traffic in the amount of RUB 100,000 and obliged it to enter into an agreement with ZAO Aircompany Skytest.[9] The relevant FAS decision was upheld by both first and second instance courts. Enforcement in this area is not frequent.

F. Price discrimination

Article 10 of the LPC specifically states that imposing discriminatory terms is an abuse if it is used by a dominant company. In particular, the LPC prohibits setting different prices (tariffs) for the same goods unless this is economically, technologically or otherwise justified. There is no formal guidance in the LPC or subordinate legislation as to what can serve as sufficient justification. As follows from the analysis of court decisions, the following reasons can, *inter alia*, be viewed by courts as appropriate: duration of the contractual relationship; volume discounts; monthly production volume; volume and cost of raw materials; the technological output of finished products from raw materials; different market circumstances, including offers from other vendors; and breach of the terms of payment by a consumer. A number of cases initiated by the FAS that resulted in very high fines imposed on oil companies focus on abuse of a dominant position carried out by applying discriminatory price terms to certain customers in the wholesale market for oil products.[10] Enforcement is very frequent in this area and covers, in addition to the oil sector, many other industries. **35.29**

G. Dictating or influencing resale prices

(i) Resale price maintenance

An agreement which leads or may lead to setting fixed or minimum resale prices is explicitly prohibited under the LPC. The prohibition does not apply if neither party to the vertical agreement has a market share in excess of 20 percent in any market. The law talks about any market, not necessarily covered by the agreement. Court practice is inconsistent: some precedents support the logical approach (only the share in the relevant market should matter); others pursue the letter of law approach: since the law says "any," this must indeed mean "any." **35.30**

The seller is allowed to set (i) a maximum resale price or (ii) a recommended resale price. Maximum or recommended resale price clauses will not infringe the LPC provided they do not in practice operate as fixed or minimum resale price, because of pressure from or incentives offered by the seller. If the agreement contains such provisions it should be expressed very explicitly in writing that the prices are only recommended. If the agreement contains a provision on recommenced prices and yet another provision obliging the distributor to report on the resale prices which it applies when selling goods further to its buyers, or introducing sanctions on a distributor for failure to comply with recommenced prices or additional benefits for compliance with them, such provisions can be viewed by the FAS as enabling the seller to monitor the resale prices which, in turn, can lead to price fixing. Still, if neither party to the agreement has a market share exceeding 20 percent, such agreement is permissible. **35.31**

[9] *State Corporation for Organizing Air Traffic*, 2011, FAS Case no. 1 10/92-10.

[10] *Lukoil, NK Rosneft, TNK-BP Holding, Gazprom Neft, Surgutneftegaz*, FAS (2011) <http://fas.gov.ru/fas-in-press/fas-in-press_34086.html>.

35.32 A maximum resale price is expressly permitted to be set only for the immediate party to the agreement. Setting maximum resale prices for further resellers (i.e. for any companies that are not parties to the particular agreement), if the market share of either party to the distribution agreement in any market exceeds 20 percent, may be considered anticompetitive and fall under prohibitions set out in article 11.4 of the LPC.

35.33 An example of an RPM case might be a case brought in June 2011 whereby the FAS held that the entry by LLC Russol Trading, OJSC Bassol, and LLC Iletsksol (all members of the same group) into a vertical agreement which led to the setting of a resale price that exceeded the price for a similar type of salt by 76.6 percent—98.3 percent constituted a breach of the LPC.[11] This decision was upheld by a court. The FAS imposed a fine on LLC Russol Trading in the amount of more than RUB 27 million (but this was subsequently reduced by a court decision). It is noteworthy that due to the 2012 amendments to the LPC which introduced an exemption for agreements between companies belonging to one group, currently this case would no longer amount to an infringement of the LPC.

35.34 Another example is a case examined in November 2012, the FAS initiated proceedings against OJSC United Trading Company and its nine distributors operating in the Russian baking soda market. The FAS revealed, during the dawn raids conducted from October 2011 through October 2012, that OJSC United Trading Company had been imposing fixed resale prices for baking soda on its distributors.[12] Generally, RPM is an area of significant enforcement.

(ii) Minimum advertised price programs

35.35 Minimum advertised price (MAP) may be considered an indirect form of resale price maintenance. There is no formal guidance in this regard in the LPC and subordinate legislation. However, it is likely that a requirement by a supplier that a distributor refrain from advertising any resale price below the minimum price set by the supplier will be treated in the same way as direct RPM and thus constitute an infringement of the LPC, if either party's market share (in any of its markets) exceeds 20 percent. There have been no MAP-related cases to date.

H. Tying arrangements

35.36 Tying is abusive under the LPC. Whilst the LPC does not use the term "tying," this falls under the concept of imposing on a counterparty terms that are onerous or unrelated to the subject matter of the agreement—which is expressly prohibited. Accordingly, tying practices may constitute an infringement of article 10 if an undertaking that is tying has a dominant position or article 11 if it does not. Tying arrangements may be exempt from the restrictions set by the LPC if there is no abuse of dominance and both contracting parties' market share is below 20 percent in any market.

35.37 In November 2009, the FAS held that a bank and some insurance companies violated the law by imposing on borrowers contractual terms which were onerous to the counterparty or did not relate to the subject matter of the contract. When issuing loans, the bank compelled its clients to purchase insurance against certain risks that were not relevant to the subject matter of the contract, including life insurance for themselves and their guarantors. The FAS has found a number of similar violations in the financial services market in the past few years.[13]

---

[11] *LLC Russol Trading, OJSC Bassol and LLC Iletsksol*, 2010, FAS Case no. 1 11/219-09.

[12] *OJSC United Trading Company, LLC Kashtan M, LLC Kashtan SPb, LLC Celting, LLC Agros 2003, LLC Potok, LLC Trading House Sibsol, LLC Chelyabkhimprodukt, LLC Stav Tris, LLC Agroresurs, LLC Penzenskaya Bakaleynaya Kompaniya*, FAS (2012) <http://fas.gov.ru/fas-news/fas-news_34097.html>.

[13] *Raiffeizenbank and 10 insurance companies*, 2009, FAS Case no. 1 11/81-09.

In 2009, the FAS held that OJSC MMZ Znamya, a dominant manufacturer of spare parts for military and civil aircraft, had infringed article 10.1 of the LPC. The FAS found that Znamya was imposing on its counterparties onerous terms that were not connected with the subject matter of the agreements.[14] The claim was filed by a company engaged in the provision of repair services for aircraft with which Znamya had entered into an agreement on the condition that it would buy from Znamya so-called "author supervision" services. The FAS decision was upheld by courts at three instances and the fine paid by Znamya for that infringement exceeded RUB 1 million. **35.38**

In March 2012 the FAS initiated proceedings against LLC BMW Rusland Trading for its entry into an agreement pursuant to which BMW's dealers and service centers had to purchase corporate identification units, furniture, and service equipment only from one supplier—LLC TD Ekvinet. Prior to this, the dealers had not been limited in their choice of suppliers and could buy from producers directly—which had been much more efficient. The limitation imposed on the dealers was not economically or technologically justified and caused extra costs to the dealers.[15] **35.39**

Automotive dealers have also come under the FAS's scrutiny. They require, under threat of the car owner losing the manufacturer's warranty, that maintenance and repairs of the car be carried out at the facilities of, and that the relevant spare parts be purchased from, the official dealer—although the official dealers' prices for such parts and services are, as a rule, much higher than those available in the market. Following an analysis of numerous claims submitted to the FAS, in September 2012, the authority published on its website recommendations to automotive dealers and manufacturers containing, *inter alia*, a recommendation not to hinder establishment of independent service centers which are not involved in car distribution, and the establishment of distribution centers which do not offer maintenance or repair services.[16] **35.40**

I. Exclusive dealing

As a general rule, Russian law finds exclusive dealing, non-compete provisions, and single branding abusive, but which in some circumstances may nevertheless be permissible.[17] If the exemptions do not apply, such clauses in contracts are usually deemed invalid by Russian courts. **35.41**

Set out below are some examples of FAS cases dealing with such violations (and, generally, this is an area of considerable enforcement). **35.42**

A subsidiary of sportswear company Adidas was ordered by the FAS to remedy its offense in 2005 after it imposed an obligation on its distributors to sell ski bindings manufactured only by Salomon and Rottefella.[18] **35.43**

The FAS initiated two cases in 2005 against Coca-Cola and Pepsi which used an exclusive dealing provision in their agreements with restaurants, cinemas, circuses, and other places of entertainment which imposed obligations on the purchasers not to sell competitors' products. The case against Coca Cola was closed by the FAS because the company amended the agreements by removing the illegal provisions.[19] The case against Pepsi was also closed.[20] **35.44**

[14] *OJSC MMZ Znamya*, 2009, FAS Case no. 1 10/109-08.

[15] *LLC BMW Rusland Trading*, 2012, FAS Case no. 1 11/26-12.

[16] Recommendations of the FAS of Russia to automotive dealers and manufacturers of automotive products in the Russian Federation, <http://fas.gov.ru/clarifications/clarifications_30389.html>.

[17] See e.g. Section II.D.

[18] *Adidas*, FAS (2005) <http://fas.gov.ru/fas-news/fas-news_1869.html>.

[19] *Coca-Cola*, FAS (2005) <http://fas.gov.ru/fas-in-press/fas-in-press_2910.html>.

[20] *Pepsi*, FAS (2005) <http://fas.gov.ru/fas-in-press/fas-in-press_2830.html>.

35.45 In November 2006, Russian Standard Invest and Cardiff SA operating in the insurance services market were found liable for including in a shareholders' agreement a provision establishing an exclusive dealing relationship between their joint venture company—Russian Standard Insurance—and Russian Standard Bank.[21]

35.46 One of the largest Russian producers specializing in the manufacture of internal combustion engines for cars and buses, Zavolzhskiy Motorniy Zavod (ZMZ), violated antimonopoly law by coordinating economic activity by means of agreements binding dealers to prevent the products of other organizations (competitors of ZMZ) from entering the market. In October 2007, the FAS required ZMZ to introduce amendments to all signed manufacturer–dealer agreements, specifying that dealers, distributors, and sub-dealers of ZMZ can buy, sell, store, and advertise component parts, units, or assemblages of other suppliers of the same product mix as supplied by ZMZ.[22]

35.47 In October 2009, the FAS initiated proceedings against a producer of microcontrollers for entry into an exclusive agreement: the producer granted the purchaser an exclusive right to purchase its products and agreed not to sell them to any other customer without prior consent of the purchaser. Following its investigation the FAS concluded that the microcontrollers were indispensable parts of equipment widely used in Russia and such exclusivity could therefore result in a significant restriction of competition in the relevant market. The FAS closed the case after the parties voluntarily amended the agreement to remove the exclusivity.[23] The offender brought court proceedings seeking annulment the FAS's decision to the effect that the agreement was illegal, but the courts of all instances upheld the position of the FAS.

35.48 In 2011, the FAS found LLC Spetstekhnika—Gruppa Gaz liable for concluding agreements with it dealers which imposed on the dealers an obligation not to enter into similar dealer contracts with other producers. This decision of the FAS was upheld in court in March 2012.[24]

J. Refusal to deal

35.49 Refusal to deal may infringe the LPC if practiced by a dominant company or, in the context of an agreement, if either party's market share in any covered market is in excess of 20 percent.

35.50 One prominent case of 2004 dealt with the unjustified refusal by a group of companies possessing the only ammonia pipeline in Russia to enter into a contract to connect another company to that ammonia pipeline (Minudobreniya had filed a claim with the FAS against Togliattiazot and Transammiak). The FAS deemed the refusal an abuse of dominance and ordered the defendant to conclude the contract, and also imposed a fine.[25]

35.51 In July 2008, the FAS found the Russian Railways (RZD) to have breached the LPC by requiring the booking clerks of RZD not to sell insurance policies of insurance companies that had no contracts with RZD. As a result, these companies were forced out of the market for voluntary insurance of railway passengers.[26]

---

[21] *Russian Standard Invest and Cardiff SA*, FAS (2006) <http://fas.gov.ru/fas-news/fas-news_9851.html>.

[22] *Zavolzhskiy Motorniy Zavod*, FAS (2007) <http://fas.gov.ru/fas-news/fas-news_15819.html>

[23] *Angstrem and Smartronics projects PTE LTD*, FAS (2009) <http://fas.gov.ru/fas-news/fas-news_27233.html>.

[24] *LLC Spetstekhnika—Gruppa Gaz*, 2011, FAS Case no. 1 11/112-10.

[25] *Togliattiazot and Transammiak*, FAS (2004) <http://fas.gov.ru/solutions/solutions_349.html>.

[26] *Russian Railways (RZD)*, 2008, FAS Case no. 1 10/468-07.

K. Essential facilities

The issue of refusal to grant access to essential facilities always arises in Russian law in the context of natural monopolies' unilateral conduct. There is a special regulation in relation to natural monopolies—Federal Law No. 147-FZ on Natural Monopolies dated August 17, 1995 and a number of sector-specific Federal Laws and subordinate legislation. Under these laws and regulations the natural monopolies are obliged to grant access to their facilities on a non-discriminatory basis. The FAS, to the extent applicable, exercises control over the activities of natural monopolies and has brought a number of cases on refusals to grant access to essential facilities, which constitutes abusive conduct, with respect to the natural monopolies, which are deemed "dominant" per se. Such cases are brought on the formal grounds of breaching article 10 of the LPC (the unjustified refusal to enter into agreements with certain sellers or customers), since the LPC does not contain a specific provision with respect to refusal to grant access to essential facilities. **35.52**

By way of example, in November 2006, the FAS initiated a case against the Russian airport Koltsovo. The airport was purportedly refusing to grant slots to an airline company, Ural Airlines, and to extend a lease of Ural Airlines' premises in the airport building.[27] **35.53**

In another case, on November 27, 2006, a Federal arbitration court of Moscow district upheld a decision of the FAS against Mashinostroitelny Zavod Mayak. The company was found liable for stopping the supply of electric power to and refusing to make an electricity supply agreement with ATON Group, and was ordered to desist.[28] **35.54**

In May 2011, the FAS held LLC Krasnoyarsk Regional Energy Company liable for abuse of dominance by refusing to enter into an agreement for power supply with LLC Montazh-Stroi. The Company was fined for RUB 7 million.[29] The FAS ruling was upheld by the court. **35.55**

L. Bundling (including loyalty and market share discounts)

The term "bundling" is not used in the LPC, however, such practices may fall under the concept of "impeding access to a product market for rivals," which is abusive under article 10 if an undertaking that is bundling has a dominant position or may constitute an infringement under article 11 if it does not. If the agreement containing bundling arrangement is made between parties whose market share does not exceed 20 percent in any of its markets it is permissible. **35.56**

M. Customer termination

Customer termination is a special case of "refusal to deal."[30] Refusal by a dominant company to supply an existing customer is treated as an abuse, unless such refusal can be economically or technologically justified. **35.57**

N. Termination of intermediaries (retailers, wholesalers, dealers, and value-added resellers, agents, and brokers)

Termination of intermediaries is a special case of "refusal to deal."[31] **35.58**

Recent examples of the FAS enforcement in this area include cases against pharmaceutical companies. In particular, the FAS has been increasingly focusing its attention on relationships **35.59**

[27] *Airport Koltsovo*, FAS (2006) <http://fas.gov.ru/fas-in-press/fas-in-press_10291.html>.

[28] *Mashinostroitelny Zavod Mayak*, 2006, FAS Case no. 7-2/2006, Court Case no. KA-A40/11364-06.

[29] *LLC Krasnoyarsk Regional Energy Company*, 2011, FAS Case no. 1 10/78-11.

[30] See Section I.J.

[31] See Section I.J.

with distributors in the Russian pharmaceutical market and has found that most of the players in that market did not have established policies determining relationships between pharmaceutical companies and distributors or clearly defined criteria for the assessment of distributors and making decisions on entering into/renewal of agreements with distributors. All this, in the FAS's view, leads to violations of the LPC such as unreasonable refusals to cooperate, or avoidance of entry into supply agreements with particular distributors in the markets where the relevant pharmaceutical company holds the dominant position.

O. Termination of relationships with competitors

35.60 Termination of a relationship with a competitor can only constitute an antitrust infringement in circumstances in which the termination is abusive. Such termination is a special case of "refusal to deal" and may fall under the prohibitions set by articles 10 and 11 of the LPC.[32]

P. Exemptions

35.61 Article 12 of the LPC exempts from any restrictions vertical agreements if they are franchise agreements or if the market shares of the parties to them in any market does not exceed 20 percent. Also exempt are agreements between non-competitors which relate to intellectual property or which are entered into between companies belonging to the same group where one of the parties controls the other one or where the parties are under common control.

35.62 Article 13.1 of the LPC provides that conduct of a dominant entity or an agreement which qualifies as restricting competition under the LPC can be permitted if it does not eliminate competition in the relevant market, or impose on its parties or third parties restrictions inconsistent with the goals of such agreement and if it has some positive effects, i.e. results or may result in: (i) improvement in the production or distribution of products, promoting technical or economic progress or enhancing competitiveness of Russian products in global markets; and (ii) receipt by the buyers of benefits that are comparable with the benefits received by the parties to the agreement.

35.63 It is not clear from the LPC whether the agreement has to meet each of these conditions or if meeting either of them is sufficient.

35.64 Under article 13.2 of the LPC, the Russian Government may adopt exemptions in relation to certain types of agreements on the basis of the above criteria. Exemptions in relation to agreements between sellers and buyers are provided for by Resolution of the Russian Government No. 583 dated July 16, 2009, which entered into force on July 31, 2009 and is effective for five years from this date (the Decree). The Decree, with due regard to the recent amendments to the LPC, provides that agreements between sellers and buyers may be permitted if each of the following conditions are met: (i) the seller sells products to two or more purchasers and its market share does not exceed 35 percent or, if it sells products to one purchaser only, such purchaser's market share does not exceed 35 percent; (ii) the seller and the buyer do not compete with each other; and (iii) the buyer does not manufacture products competing with the products sold by the seller under the agreement. The permissibility of the agreements is subject to limitations, e.g. the term of certain agreements may not exceed three years. If these specific conditions are met, the general prohibitions are inapplicable.

35.65 Generally, reliance on such exemptions where they make permissibility contingent on the parties' market shares is risky, as there are different approaches to defining markets, and there is always a risk that the FAS will not necessarily share the parties' views on the size of their market shares.

---

[32] See Section I.J.

In addition, the Russian Government adopted general exceptions applying to agreements between credit and insurance companies (April 2009) and to agreements on joint scientific research and its use (July 2009). **35.66**

II. Dealing with competitors

The January 2012 amendments to the LPC formally introduced the term "cartel", which is defined as an agreement between competitors which leads or may lead to: (i) setting or maintaining prices (tariffs), discounts, mark-ups, etc.; (ii) increasing, reducing or maintaining prices at tenders; (iii) market sharing; (iv) limiting or terminating production; and (v) refusing to enter into agreements with certain sellers or customers. Before the amendments were enacted, the term "cartel" had not been used, but agreements or actions leading to the consequences now included in the definition of the cartel were still prohibited. **35.67**

Cartels are prohibited per se, i.e. on an absolute basis and irrespective of whether they are implemented and have an actual impact on competition. The FAS views a cartel as the most serious type of infringement. No exemptions with respect to cartels are available. **35.68**

The LPC prohibits also concerted actions between competitors. In particular, the activities of several undertakings (in the absence of an agreement) would qualify as concerted actions when all of the following conditions are met: (i) the result of such activities corresponds to the interests of each of the economic undertakings concerned; (ii) their activities are known to each other beforehand through the public announcement by one of them of the intention to act in a certain way; (iii) the activities of each of the undertakings are caused by the actions of the other undertakings participating in concerted actions rather than by circumstances equally influencing all economic undertakings in the respective product market. Such circumstances may, in particular, include a change in regulated tariffs, a change in prices for raw materials, a change in prices in the world market, a significant change in the demand for the product within no less than one year or within the period of existence of the respective product market (if the period in question is less than one year). **35.69**

Concerted actions which lead to a limitation of competition, including in the form of the consequences listed in para 35.67, constitute infringements of the LPC. Note that concerted actions are not prohibited on a per se basis and may be found permissible. **35.70**

The recent amendments to the LPC introduced the procedure whereby the antimonopoly authority may issue a warning of the impermissibility of certain actions. Such a warning notice would be given if an officer of a business entity publically announced planned market-related actions which could lead to an antitrust offense, but there are no grounds to initiate proceedings or an investigation into an antitrust offense. **35.71**

The above prohibitions do not apply, as a general rule, to agreements/concerted actions between parties that belong to the same group and where one party controls the other one(s) or where the parties are under common control. There is another exemption for concerted actions (but not for agreements): the prohibitions do not apply to concerted actions between parties the market share of each of which does not exceed 8 percent and whose aggregate market share does not exceed 20 percent. **35.72**

Cartel enforcement in Russia is significant: the FAS has officially declared fighting cartels as its priority. Cartel enforcement is focused primarily on domestic cartels, although there is some cooperation in this area between the FAS and the competition authorities of other jurisdictions. **35.73**

A. Horizontal price fixing

35.74 Horizontal price fixing is expressly prohibited by article 11 of the LPC and price fixing cartels are among the most serious of all antitrust law infringements. The FAS brings many cases and imposes very high fines for price fixing.

35.75 As FAS put it, a "classic" cartel, aiming at price fixing and limitation of production volumes, was proved by the FAS in 2009 on the basis of documents obtained in dawn raids which were undertaken simultaneously in six Russian regions. For approximately ten years, nine Russian, Ukraininan, and Belorussian match manufacturers, holding in aggregate 95 percent of the Russian market for match production, met quarterly and made decisions, which were fixed in the written minutes of the meetings, setting out prices, volumes of production of matches at the same level for determined periods, as well as territories or sales. All participants in the cartel acknowledged having infringed antitrust law and volunteered to end the arrangements.[33]

35.76 In another case, in December 2011, the FAS found twenty-three participants in a cartel in the market for caustic soda to have violated the law. The cartel lasted from 2005 to 2011. One of the largest FAS fines ever was imposed in this case in April 2012. A fine of over RUB 912 million was imposed on OJSC United Trading Company for organizing and entering into a cartel agreement.[34] The agreement led to price fixing in the wholesale market for caustic soda, market sharing and unreasonable refusal to deal with customers. The FAS also forwarded the case to law enforcement bodies for criminal proceedings against the company's officers.

35.77 One of the latest major "concerted actions" cases is *FAS v. MTS and VympelCom* which was settled in April 2012. In the period from October 2011 to April 2012, the FAS investigated these two major Russian mobile operators in connection with allegations of price fixing for the smart phone Apple iPhone 4, which led to the prices for such models being much higher than in other countries. The FAS came to the conclusion that there was no agreement between MTS and VympelCom but that the parties had engaged in concerted actions. Accordingly, the FAS ruled that MTS and VympelCom violated article 11.1.1 of the Russian Competition Law. However, having received sufficient evidence that the parties stopped such concerted actions in April 2012, the FAS terminated the proceedings without imposing any behavioral conditions on them.[35] Still it is expected that a fine for the violation which actually took place will be imposed.

B. Horizontal agreements to allocate customers or territories; agreements not to compete

35.78 Market sharing cartels, including geographic market and customer sharing, are, like horizontal price-fixing cartels, among the most serious of all antitrust law infringements. The FAS brings many cases and imposes high fines for this type of infringement. The most high profile of the recent cases was the 2011 case which involved over ten companies in the Russian chlorine market, which entered into a market sharing agreement with regard to the volume of sales and list of buyers, determining the market share of each party. Under the agreement, each chlorine producer (and its dealers) could only sell products to the "allocated" buyers. To ensure mutual control, the parties to the agreement exchanged information on their buyers and the volumes of sales on a monthly basis. A special coordination board was established to coordinate the activities of the parties.[36]

---

[33] *Plitspichprom and others*, FAS (2009) <http://fas.gov.ru/fas-in-press/fas-in-press_30853.html>.
[34] *OJSC United Trading Company,* 2011, FAS Case no. 1 11/139-11.
[35] *MTS and VympelCom,* 2012, FAS Case no. 1 11/188-11.
[36] *Kaustik, Khimprom, Khloraktiv and other parties,* 2011, FAS Case no. 1 11/2-11.

This cartel was proved by the FAS on the basis of documents and information obtained in the course of more than 10 dawn raids carried out over one year. The total fines imposed amounted to approximately RUB 51 million. **35.79**

C. Horizontal boycotts

Agreements between competitors not to purchase from, or supply to, specific businesses, if entered into for an anticompetitive purpose, are a serious infringement of article 11 of the LPC. **35.80**

Although the LPC does not use the term "horizontal boycott," it generally falls under the concept of an agreement between competitors on refusal to enter into contracts with certain sellers or purchasers which qualifies as a cartel. One of early drafts of the "Third Antimonopoly Package" of amendments to the LPC contained a reference to a "boycott." Such wording, however, was not included in the text of the amendments which was ultimately enacted. Still, when commenting on the Third Antimonopoly Package FAS officials often use the term "boycott" to characterize the relevant anticompetitive agreements. **35.81**

D. Joint ventures and other competitive collaborations

There are no specific rules in Russian antitrust law with respect to joint ventures. Joint ventures can take a wide variety of forms and their creation may fall under the mandatory merger control rules in articles 27–29 of the LPC. The relevant joint venture agreements (JVAs) may also be analyzed under article 11 of the LPC. The key point of the analysis of the joint venture agreement from an antitrust perspective is whether it has anticompetitive effects on the market. **35.82**

The recent amendments to the LPC introduced an exemption with respect to joint venture agreements which may lead to restriction of competition. They can be permissible if they do not eliminate competition in the relevant market, or impose on the parties or third parties restrictions inconsistent with the goals of such agreement and if they result or may result in: (i) an improvement in the production or distribution of products, promoting technical, or economic progress, or the parties making direct investments in the territory of Russia (including putting into operation of new production facilities or modernization of existing production facilities); and (ii) the receipt by the buyers of benefits that are comparable with the benefits received by the parties to the agreement. **35.83**

It is not clear from the LPC whether the agreement has to meet each of these conditions or meeting either of them is sufficient. **35.84**

In order for an agreement to be found permissible, its draft, and also certain information about the parties to the agreement, has to be submitted to the FAS in a special filing. After reviewing the filing, the FAS issues a decision saying whether the agreement is permissible. The FAS has thirty calendar days extendable by another twenty days to issue such a decision. The decision can be issued subject to certain behavioral conditions on the parties. **35.85**

A practical question which arises quite often alongside with exclusive dealing,[37] is whether or not the non-compete provisions commonly included in JVAs, shareholders agreements (SHAs), or other agreements between joint venture partners are permissible. **35.86**

As a matter of law a voluntary commitment by companies not belonging to the same group not to be active in the market is viewed as a "sign" of limitation of competition and thus, as **35.87**

[37] See Section I.I.

a general rule, prohibited. Accordingly, there is a risk that under Russian law a non-compete clause would be held invalid and unenforceable and could even subject the parties to sanctions.

35.88 The clarification from the FAS received in response to our query whether non-compete provisions are permissible in JVAs stated that each agreement has to be reviewed on a case-by-case basis, and that in order to get a specific response one has to submit a full scale filing to the FAS. Therefore, the solution that offers as much comfort as possible in the circumstances (but which nevertheless does not eliminate legal risks completely) is to submit a filing and get the FAS's official response prior to entry into a joint venture non-compete arrangement.

E. Trade associations

35.89 Participation in trade associations is in principle perfectly legal. However, in practice, trade association meetings and contacts are often at the origin of anticompetitive activity, so it is important to ensure that legitimate meetings and communications do not become the occasion for anticompetitive cooperation.

35.90 Trade association gatherings should not be used as an opportunity to agree with any competitor on prices or other trading terms, or even discuss prices with them. Nor should price information or other commercially sensitive information be exchanged. It is important to avoid any meetings with competitors where prices (including recommended retail prices) or components of prices (including rebates, discounts, credit terms, or allowances) or other trading terms are discussed.

F. Interlocking directorates

35.91 Interlocking directorates as such are not regulated by articles 10 or 11 of the LPC. The issue, however, may be relevant in the context of merger control. Under the LPC, companies, more than 50 percent of whose directors are the same persons, form a group. Given that special merger control rules apply to some intragroup transactions, interlocking directorates may in certain circumstances help to avoid the need to obtain prior consent to a concentration (though as a general rule the LPC provides that even intragroup share transfers require prior consent).

G. Facilitating practices

35.92 Facilitating practices are not subject to specific rules in Russia, but if they are aimed at or have the effect of restricting competition, they will likely fall under the relevant prohibitions of anticompetitive agreements and concerted actions in articles 11 and 11.1 of the LPC, respectively.

H. Information exchange

35.93 Information exchange itself does not normally give rise to antitrust issues, unless the antitrust authority can prove that this exchange was part of an anticompetitive agreement or concerted actions. This may be of particular relevance to an exchange of information regarding prices, price elements, and other commercially sensitive information, which can be seen as a preparatory step towards price fixing and/or coordination, which are expressly prohibited.

I. Joint purchasing agreements

35.94 There are no specific rules in Russian antitrust law with respect to joint purchasing agreements. Generally, such agreements should be analyzed from the standpoint of their potential or actual impact on competition in the relevant market, and the provisions of article 11, including those applicable to cartels, may apply.

J. Joint lobbying/regulatory/legislative efforts

Joint lobbying in connection with regulation or legislation does not normally raise antitrust issues. However, as in all contacts with competitors, it is important to ensure that legitimate meetings and communications do not become the occasion for anticompetitive cooperation or exchange of information.[38] **35.95**

III. General issues

A. Jurisdiction and applicable law (including sector-specific competition regulation)

The main applicable law is Federal Law No. 135-FZ "On the Protection of Competition" dated October 26, 2006 (LPC) and was last amended by the so-called "Third Antimonopoly Package" of amendments which came into force in January 2012. **35.96**

The LPC regulates, from a competition perspective, the conduct of all companies (both Russian and foreign) and individuals (including individual entrepreneurs) operating in Russia. The LPC also applies to agreements made outside Russia (between Russian and/or foreign entities), which may have an impact on Russian markets. **35.97**

Furthermore, the LPC applies to actions of Russia's federal and regional governments and municipal authorities and stipulates in detail the rules on state aid, defining what state aid includes and the situations in which it can be granted. Pursuant to the LPC, governmental authorities are prohibited from engaging in anticompetitive practices when entering into contracts. **35.98**

The sanctions (penalties) for the violations of the Antitrust Law are fixed in the Code on Administrative Offenses of the Russian Federation and as regards certain types of abuse of dominant position and cartels—also in the Criminal Code of the Russian Federation. **35.99**

There is a special regulation in relation to natural monopolies—Federal Law No. 147-FZ on Natural Monopolies dated August 17, 1995. In addition, antimonopoly provisions regarding equal access to, and the transparent distribution of, natural resources are included in sector-specific legislation, such as the Water Code, Forest Code, and Land Code. **35.100**

B. Antitrust system

(i) Name of agency/agencies

The applicable legislation is enforced by the Federal Antimonopoly Service of Russia (the FAS) and a large network of its local agencies established in all of eighty-three Russian regions. The FAS is subdivided into several divisions, each of which deals with a specific economic sector.[39] **35.101**

The core functions of the FAS are control over compliance with antimonopoly laws in both commodity and financial markets, control over economic concentration, control over procurement for government needs, control over state and municipal aid, detection and prevention of offencses, investigations, imposing sanctions, all in relation to the above and also with respect to abuse of dominant position, cartels, and unfair competition (advertisement, IP, trade secrets). **35.102**

---

38 See Section II.H.

39 More detailed information on the FAS can be found on its website <http://www.fas.gov.ru>.

(ii) Staff size and budget

35.103 The FAS has the staff of about 3,200 employees (including local agencies). The budget for 2011 was about RUB 2.3 billion (approximately EUR 57 million).

(iii) Recent enforcement actions and trends

35.104 The FAS has recently published a report on the results of its activities in the period from 2004 to 2012. According to the report, the number of cases initiated by the FAS in connection with antitrust infringements increases yearly. By way of example, the total number of cases initiated in 2011 exceeds by 2.4 times the total number of cases in 2007. In 2011, the FAS fines for antitrust infringements totaled RUB 21,026.4 million (approx. EUR 525 million).

35.105 The FAS views a cartel as the most serious type of infringement and in 2012 it declared combating cartels to be its top priority. In this context the FAS is actively developing its cooperation with law enforcement bodies. In 2012, the highest fine imposed for a cartel amounted to over RUB 912 million (approx. EUR 27.8 million) (the fine was imposed on OJSC United Trading Company operating in the caustic soda market).

35.106 Also, the FAS regularly brings abuse of dominance proceedings and traditionally focuses on such sectors as energy, oil products, pharmaceuticals, and telecommunications, although other sectors (e.g. foodstuffs, construction materials, automotive) are often the focus of the FAS's attention. One of the latest high-profile cases settled in July 2011 is *FAS v. Novo Nordisk*. The violation was an abuse by the Russian subsidiary of Novo Nordisk of its dominant position on the wholesale market for insulin in the form of refusal to supply to, and discrimination against, certain distributors. It is noteworthy that the FAS initially ruled that distributors' engagement in corrupt practices was an invalid justification of Novo Nordisk's refusal to supply to such distributors, and this decision raised much debate about the conflict between Russian competition law and foreign anticorruption rules. Finally, the FAS clarified that engagement in corrupt practices may be a valid ground for a supplier to refrain from dealing with a distributor that engages in such practices. An amicable settlement was entered into in July 2011 and the fine imposed on Novo Nordisk was decreased from approximately EUR 2.1 million to approximately EUR 1.3 million.[40] When negotiating the amicable settlement agreement with the FAS, Novo Nordisk, in cooperation with the FAS, designed a new policy in relation to commercial partners containing clear criteria and terms of assessment for potential commercial partners, and a new form of supply agreement which does not contain provisions that lead to discrimination between potential and existing partners. It was proposed that such documents be posted on the website of the Novo Nordisk group and thus be available to any interested party. The policy has already been posted. The FAS has started to apply the same approach (i.e. requiring publication of a distributor policy) to other dominant pharmaceutical companies.

35.107 The general trend is that the FAS is becoming increasingly active in enforcing the LPC.

C. Private litigation

35.108 An individual or private entity may file a lawsuit with a court against any company which has violated antitrust law. The right to claim civil damages is generally governed by Russian Civil Code, but also by article 37.3 of the LPC which provides that the parties whose rights and interests were impaired as a result of infringement of antitrust law have the right to claim damages, including loss of profit. This might be, for instance, against a dominant company if the abuse affected the claimant's interests (e.g. if the individual or private entity was forced to purchase goods at an unreasonably high price or was squeezed out of the market by the

[40] *Novo Nordisk,* 2011, FAS Case no. 1 10/91-10.

dominant company). In a private action, the court can award damages and the court (and also the FAS, but within its own administrative proceedings) can order the dominant company to grant access, supply goods or services or conclude, amend or terminate a contract.

As far as damages are concerned, the key in such proceedings would be to prove that the loss in the amount claimed was indeed caused, and caused in that amount, by a breach of antitrust law. In practice, this is difficult, and as a result private enforcement in Russia is not significant. However, such cases exist, and their number is growing. **35.109**

One of the cases was the claim of OAO Voskresenskie Mineralniye Udobreniya against OAO Apatit. The court found for the claimant and ordered that the respondent (the dominant company) shall pay more than RUB 1 billion in damages (actual loss) in 2010, caused to the claimant by setting monopoly high price for the respondent's products. The amount of damages was calculated as difference between the price actually paid by the claimant and the price recommended by the FAS (which it considers a fair price).[41] Another example is a private litigation case in 2011 whereby OAO Russian Railways was ordered to pay over RUB 3 million in damages caused by the abuse of dominance.[42] One of the latest cases (2012) was the claim for damages against the Ministry of Agriculture of the Tula Region. The court of first instance ruled that the claim shall be satisfied in full (the damages that were to be paid from the state budget amounted to almost RUB 43 million), but the court of second instance lowered them to approximately RUB 25 million.[43] Another case initiated in 2012 was the claim of a car dealer against a car distributor seeking to make the latter enter into a dealership agreement with the claimant and pay damages caused by the refusal to deal. The court of first instance satisfied this claim in full and the damages awarded amounted to approximately RUB 2 million.[44] **35.110**

D. Follow-on litigation

The recognition of violation by the FAS is the basis for a private entity's claim against the company which violated antitrust law, in a private court action. Alternatively, the claimant can join the FAS as a third party to the case. **35.111**

If the claimant files a lawsuit in connection with a violation of antitrust law without first bringing administrative proceedings within the FAS, the court informs the FAS accordingly to ensure the authority's participation in the case, and the procedural status of the FAS under such circumstances is determined by the court depending on the nature of the case under review. **35.112**

This means that a private court action depends very much on the cooperation of the FAS. If there is no support from the FAS, in practice there is little chance of succeeding with private court action. **35.113**

E. Arbitration and alternative dispute resolution

In Russia, jurisdiction over disputes arising out of commercial activities of companies and individual entrepreneurs, both Russian and foreign, and also disputes related to competition infringements is granted to so-called "arbitrazh" courts which are state commercial courts and should not be confused with arbitration tribunals. The "arbitrazh" courts also consider claims **35.114**

---

41 *Voskresenskie Miniralnye Udobreniya v. Apatit*, 2010, Moscow Arbitrazh Court, Case no. A40-64377/08-77-496.

42 *OOO Kompania Stal v. RZD*, 2011, Federal Arbitrazh Court of the Moscow District, Case no. A40-2196/11-50-19.

43 *CJSC Mosselprom v. Ministry of Agriculture of the Tula Region*, Arbitrazh Court of the Tula Region, Case no. A68-4924/12, Arbitrazh Court of the City of Moscow, Case no. A40-129919/12 (2012).

44 *OOO Modus Novorossiisk v. Hyundai Motors CIS*, Moscow Artibrazh Court, Case no. A40-84943/12-56-783 (2012).

of companies to invalidate actions of government authorities that infringe their rights and violate their lawful interests and also claims of government authorities against companies. By way of example, in the competition context, the most common cases reviewed by the "arbitrazh" courts are those initiated by companies against the FAS seeking to challenge its decision imposing a fine or to reduce the amount of the fine.

35.115 Parties to a contract may agree, by including in the contract an arbitration clause, to submit their disputes to arbitration tribunals. However, given that competition law is public law, only the "arbitrazh" courts are entitled to review competition-related disputes on the merits. Arbitration tribunals, however, may award damages on the basis of a decision of an "arbitrazh" court confirming that there was a breach of antitrust law.

F. Remedies

(i) Civil liability

35.116 General rules of civil liability under Russian law apply, i.e. a party that incurred loss (which includes actually incurred loss, future loss and lost profits) as a result of a breach of antitrust law by another party or parties can bring proceedings against such other party/parties seeking compensation. However, for the reasons explained in para. 35.109, there are very few such private actions in Russia.

(ii) Administrative liability

35.117 Administrative liability is imposed for all types of infringement of the LPC, including, *inter alia*, abuse of dominance, entering into anticompetitive agreements, concerted actions and coordination.

35.118 Abuse of dominance may be penalized by the following sanctions:

- for officers:
  - o a fine of up to RUB 20,000 (if the abuse has not led and may not lead to a restriction of competition or if the dominant entity holds less than 35 per cent in the relevant market); or
  - o a fine of up to RUB 50,000 or disqualification (i.e. prohibition to hold a management position) for up to three years;
- for legal entities:
  - o a fine of up to RUB 1 million (if the abuse has not led and may not lead to a restriction of competition or if the dominant entity holds less than 35 per cent in the relevant market); or
  - o a turnover-based fine of 1 percent to 15 percent of the offender's proceeds in the market where the offense occurred, but not more than 2 percent of the total amount of the offender's proceeds in all markets where it operates on a worldwide basis, and not less than RUB 100,000. The relevant period for defining the amount of the fine is the calendar year preceding the year in which the offense was revealed or, if the offender did not make any sales in such preceding year, part of the current calendar year preceding the date on which the FAS discovered the infringement. The amount of a fine may not exceed RUB 1 million if the dominant entity holds less than 35 percent in the relevant market;

35.119 Entry into agreements restricting competition, participation in concerted actions or conducting coordination of business may be penalized by the following sanctions:

- for officers:
  - o a fine of up to RUB 50,000; or
  - o disqualification for up to three years;

and

- for legal entities:
  - o a fine of 1 percent to 15 percent of the offender's revenues in the market where the offense occurred, earned in the year preceding the year in which the offense occurred; or
  - o a fine of 0.3 percent to 3 percent of the revenues in the market where the offense occurred if more than 75 percent of the offender's overall revenues are earned in that market,
  - o but in either case not more than 4 percent of the offender's total revenues (i.e. in all markets where it is active) and not less than RUB 100,000.

In addition to the fines discussed above, the FAS has the right to order that the parties in breach of the LPC pay to the Russian State budget their revenues earned as a result of the breach. As a matter of practice, however, the FAS imposes this sanction rarely and primarily where the turnover-based fines cannot be calculated. **35.120**

(iii) Criminal liability

Criminal liability for abuse of dominance may involve imprisonment for up to seven years and a fine that, in particularly serious cases, can reach a maximum of RUB 1 million or five years' salary or income of the relevant officer. **35.121**

In the context of anticompetitive agreements, coordination, and concerted actions, criminal liability applies for cartels only. Individuals/officers involved in a cartel which caused a large (over RUB 1 million loss to individuals, business entities or the state), or a large (over RUB 5 million) benefit to the cartelists, may be penalized by a fine of up to RUB 1 million or an amount equivalent to five years' salary/income or imprisonment for up to seven years with or without disqualification for up to three years. Prior to 2009, the article in the Criminal Code of Russia establishing criminal liability for violating the LPC existed, but did not work. In 2009, that article was amended, which gave rise to criminal enforcement. Currently there is no reliable statistics on this issue and the data available from public sources is limited to the number of cases passed by the FAS to the police which is empowered to initiate criminal proceedings and impose criminal liability. Thus, in 2010 the FAS passed twenty-three cases to the police. **35.122**

G. Leniency and immunity

Russian law provides for the following leniency rules. **35.123**

(i) Administrative liability

A person who voluntarily provides the FAS with information on an anticompetitive agreement or concerted actions shall be released from administrative liability if the following conditions are met: **35.124**

- at the time of the application for leniency the FAS did not have the relevant information and documents;
- the person stopped participating in the agreements or concerted actions; and
- the information and documents are sufficient to establish the fact of the offense.

Only the first person to apply for leniency and satisfy these conditions will be released from administrative liability. **35.125**

"Admission of guilt" shall be kept confidential, accepted by an authorized FAS officer and evidenced by a special acknowledgement receipt. **35.126**

(ii) Criminal liability

A cartelist will be released from criminal liability if he or she facilitated the investigation of the cartel and paid compensation for the loss caused, provided that his or her actions did not result in any other criminal offense. **35.127**

H. Document creation and retention

35.128 The LPC sets out explicit rules for provision of information and documents to the FAS in audits, dawn raids, investigation proceedings or if reasonably requested by the FAS in the context of performing any of its tasks (such as, for example, conducting a market analysis, or reviewing merger filings). The terms "information" and "documents" are understood broadly and mean any documents and information (including of confidential nature), including any deeds, agreements, statements, correspondence and other documents and files in digital format or recorded on electronic media. Information or documents submitted to the FAS can be designated as confidential, and the submission will then enjoy a stricter confidentiality regime. A failure to provide information or documents to the FAS leads to imposition of a fine.

35.129 The LPC does not provide for any specific rules on document creation or retention. However, destruction or concealment of documents when an investigation is ongoing may be qualified by the FAS as hindering the investigation and lead to an increase of the base fine for infringement by 50 percent.

35.130 It is worth noting that the FAS actively uses special equipment and software allowing it to copy information stored on hard discs of PCs, including (according to a FAS officer) damaged or deleted files.

36

SOUTH AFRICA

Heather Irvine and Candice Upfold
Norton Rose Fulbright

Introduction

South Africa has a strong, established competition law enforcement regime and an active regulator. The South African economic system is predominantly based upon the principles of a free market economy. However, as in most developed economies, competition in South Africa is regulated both by the common law and the Competition Act, 1998 ("the Act"). This antitrust legislation applies not only to economic activity conducted in South Africa, but also to all economic activity having an effect in South Africa. **36.01**

In the years after the legislation first came into effect in late 1999, the South African competition authorities focussed on merger review. However, the emphasis has gradually shifted to enforcement, and in particular, to detecting and prosecuting cartels and abuses by dominant firms. **36.02**

36.03 The Act imposes an outright prohibition on price-fixing, market allocation and collusive tendering (bid rigging) by competitors and potential competitors, and even a first time offense can attract a fine of up to 10 percent of a firm's annual turnover in, into or from South Africa. Substantial fines have been imposed on cartels operating in South Africa to date, particularly in the food, chemical, manufacturing, and construction industries. The Commission introduced a corporate leniency policy (CLP) in 2004, and this has significantly enhanced the Commission's ability to detect and prosecute cartels.

36.04 The Act prohibits various anticompetitive practices by dominant firms, including price discrimination; predatory pricing; refusing to give a competitor access to an essential facility when it is economically feasible to do so; refusing to supply a competitor with scare goods when it is economically feasible to do so; buying up a scarce supply of intermediate goods or resources required by a competitor; requiring or inducing a supplier or customer not to deal with a competitor; selling goods or services on condition that the buyer purchases separate goods or services unrelated to the object of a contract; excessive pricing and selling goods or services below their marginal or average variable cost. To date, the competition authorities have considered cases involving unilateral conduct by several dominant South African companies, including South African Airways, Sasol, Telkom, and Mittal.

36.05 In 2009, significant pressure was placed on the South African government and the competition authorities by trade unions and consumer groups to amend the Act, after a spate of high profile cartel cases involving companies supplying basic goods to poor and vulnerable consumers, like Pioneer (maize), Tiger Consumer Brands (bread), Adcock Ingram (pharmaceuticals), and Clover (milk). In particular, there were calls to criminalize participation in cartels and give the Commission wider powers to investigate sectors of the economy which remained concentrated despite enforcement of the existing legislation. The Competition Amendment Act was passed in August 2009, but has yet to be signed into effect by the President. It will enable the Commission to conduct market inquiries akin to those conducted in Europe, as well as to prosecute conscious parallel or coordinated conduct by competitors in highly concentrated markets (termed "complex monopoly conduct"). Individual managers or directors who participate or knowingly acquiesce in price fixing, market division or collusive tendering will face fines in South Africa of up to ZAR 500,000 and/or prison sentences of up to ten years.

36.06 The South African government has repeatedly emphasized its commitment to the enforcement of competition law and the importance of the Commission's work to addressing historical inequalities in the economy and combating anticompetitive practices which impact on consumers in South Africa, particularly those from poor and previously disadvantaged backgrounds. Although the Economic Development Department has the right in terms of the Act to participate in all merger reviews, it has exercised this power very sparingly and the only significant merger in which it has actively participated in a Tribunal merger hearing to date was the acquisition by global retail giant Walmart of Southern African retailer Massmart, which was ultimately approved by the South African Competition Appeal Court subject to several conditions relating to preserving employment and the local manufacturing base in South Africa.

36.07 South Africa is slowly recovering from the global recession and local and cross-border merger activity is likely to rise. Fairly uniquely, the Competition Act requires the South African authorities to consider not only whether a proposed merger will result in a lessening of competition in South Africa, but also whether it will impact on a range of specified public interest factors. Specifically, this refers to the impact that a merger will have on a particular industry sector or region, employment, the ability of small businesses or firms controlled or owned by historically disadvantaged persons to become competitive, and the ability of national industries to compete in international markets. In the Walmart decision, the Competition Appeal

Court (CAC) emphasized that the competition authorities must consider not only whether any workers employed by the merging companies will lose their jobs, but also whether their working conditions will deteriorate. In addition, job losses in the broader South African supply chain also need to be assessed and, if these effects are substantial, they must be addressed by imposing appropriate conditions. This aspect of the Commission's jurisdiction is likely to continue to be an area of focus, although it is not clear to what extent the Government will participate in large mergers to the extent it did in this transaction. Firms that are party to notifiable transactions in South Africa should consider the wider public interest implications of their transaction, not only whether the merger may lead to job losses in the merging firms. It is clear that in the world post-the Walmart case, companies who need a quick clearance for their transaction must find solutions to potential public interest problems.

The Commission is likely to prioritize cartel investigations. Administrative fines of approximately ZAR 731 million were paid by companies that engaged in price fixing, market allocation, or collusive tendering in the 2012/2013 financial year. For example, Lafarge Industries South Africa paid ZAR 148.7 million for its participation in a cement cartel; Foodcorp paid ZAR 88.5 million for its involvement in a white maize milling and wheat milling cartel; and Oceana Brands paid ZAR 34.7 million for its role in fixing prices in the pelagic fishing market. The Commission has finalized several existing cartel cases, including a settlement process relating to bid-rigging in the construction industry which goes back to February 2011. The construction settlements amounting to approximately R 1.5 billion will be reflected in the Commission's 2013/2014 annual report. The Commission has established a dedicated cartel unit to enhance its ability to detect and prosecute cartels, and it referred several new complaints about price fixing to the Tribunal for adjudication (including in the steel and oil industries). **36.08**

The Commission is likely to continue to focus on prosecuting anticompetitive practices by dominant companies in concentrated South African industries like fuel, telecommunications and chemicals. For example, it is currently prosecuting chemical and fuels manufacturer Sasol in relation to alleged excessive pricing of polymers; and a market study on competition in the healthcare sector is planned by the Commission in the near future (although terms of reference indicating the nature and scope of this study have yet to be published). **36.09**

I. Acting alone

The Act prohibits various forms of unilateral conduct by dominant firms which result in substantial lessening or prevention of competition. **36.10**

Section 7 provides that a firm is dominant if it has a market share of 45 percent or more, or if it has less than 45 percent but it has market power. Market power is defined in the Act as "the power of a firm to control prices, or to exclude competition or to behave to an appreciable extent independently of its competitors, customers or suppliers." **36.11**

Dominant firms are furthermore prohibited from engaging in any "exclusionary act" if the anticompetitive effect of that act outweighs technological, efficiency, or other pro-competitive gains. An exclusionary act is defined as "an act that impedes or prevents a firm entering into, or expanding within, a market." **36.12**

The following exclusionary acts are furthermore specifically prohibited by s. 8(d) of the Act, unless the dominant firm can prove that the efficiency, technological, or other pro-competitive gains outweigh the anticompetitive effects of such conduct: **36.13**

(i) requiring or inducing a supplier or customer not to deal with a competitor;
(ii) refusing to supply scarce goods to a competitor, when such supply is economically feasible;

(iii) selling goods or services on condition that the buyer purchases separate goods or services unrelated to the object of the contract, or forcing a buyer to accept a condition unrelated to the object of the contract (known as "tying" or "bundling");
(iv) selling goods or services below their marginal or average variable cost (known as "predatory pricing"); or
(v) buying up a scarce supply of intermediate goods or resources required by a competitor.

36.14 Under s. 9, price discrimination by a dominant firm is prohibited. As such, a dominant firm may not discriminate between different customers buying the same product in terms of:

(i) the price charged;
(ii) any discount, allowance, rebate or credit given or allowed;
(iii) the provision of services in respect of the product; or
(iv) payment for services provided in respect of the product.

A. Predatory pricing

36.15 Predatory pricing is the practice of a dominant firm charging low, unsustainable prices with the object of driving out less resourced or resilient competitors. It could also act as a barrier to the entry of new competitors. Once the competitors have been driven out of the market, the dominant firm then raises its prices to recoup its losses.

36.16 The Act does not refer to the term "predatory pricing" but does prohibit it as an exclusionary act generally under s. 8(c), and specifically in s. 8(d)(iv) which prohibits a dominant firm from selling goods or services below their marginal or average variable cost. Predatory pricing is presumed to be prohibited unless the dominant firm can show technological, efficiency or pro-competitive gains which outweigh the anticompetitive effect.

36.17 The leading case in South Africa is *Nationwide Airlines (Pty) Limited v. South African Airways (Pty) Limited*, Nationwide alleged that South African Airways' failure to increase their air fares in accordance with fuel price increases and the depreciation of the Rand against the US Dollar, amounted to pricing below marginal or average variable cost.[1]

36.18 The Tribunal acknowledged that there were difficulties in determining whether predation was the motive behind a firm's price decrease and also the dangers in potentially disincentivizing firms from lowering their prices, even as a result of competitive forces, for fear of being accused of predatory pricing. The Tribunal's approach in such cases is therefore to limit the scope of s. 8(d)(iv). Unless the record shows unequivocally that a respondent is pricing below the prescribed cost levels the Tribunal should not make a finding under s. 8(d)(iv) but should consider the complaint under s. 8(c).

B. Exploitative offenses (excessive pricing, monopoly leveraging)

36.19 Dominant firms may not charge an excessive price to the detriment of consumers (s. 8(a)). An excessive price is defined in s. 1 of the Act as a price for a good or service which bears no reasonable relation to the economic value of that good or service and is higher than the value referred to above.

36.20 The nature and scope of this prohibition was considered by the Tribunal and the CAC in the *Mittal Steel* case (2009).[2] Harmony Gold and Durban Roodepoort Deep complained

[1] Nationwide Airlines (Pty) Limited and Another v. South African Airways (Pty) Limited (80/CR/Sept06) [2010] ZACT 13 (February 13, 2010).
[2] Mittal Steel South Africa Limited and others v. Harmony Gold Mining Company Limited and another (70/CAC/Apr07) [2009] ZACAC 1 (May 29, 2009).

that the import parity price charged by Mittal Steel in South Africa for flat steel market was excessive. The Tribunal emphasized that the task of the South African competition authorities is not to determine what the right price would be, but rather, to defend competitive market structures. The Tribunal emphasized that there are significant hurdles to be cleared by a complainant who alleges that it has been charged an excessive price by a dominant supplier:

(1) Firstly, it must be shown that the supplier is a "super-dominant" firm, or one of overwhelming size relative to the market in which it participates, and that the structure of this market enables it to charge excessive prices. The s. 8(a) prohibition thus only applies in rare markets.
(2) Secondly, the complainant must demonstrate that the dominant supplier has in fact taken advantage of these market conditions by imposing excessive prices on its customers.

The Tribunal held that Mittal met the first leg of this test, because its dominance in the South African flat steel market is indeed absolute in that there are no meaningful constraints on Mittal's ability to unilaterally determine prices and no prospects of new entry into this market. Mittal's conduct also met the second leg of the test because it had imposed a pre-determined price (the import parity price) on South African customers by withholding supplies of flat steel from the domestic market, purposefully preventing arbitrage, and maintaining the segmentation of its markets. The Tribunal characterized this as "the most fundamental and egregious monopolistic conduct." **36.21**

On appeal, however, the CAC found that the Tribunal had erred by interpreting the Act to require that only a super-dominant firm could engage in excessive pricing. The CAC held that the Tribunal should have determined the economic value against which Mittal's prices should be assessed. However, the CAC did not prescribe the correct test for economic value. Although excessive pricing cases in South Africa remain quite rare, the Commission is currently involved in a complaint referral concerning the alleged excessive pricing of propylene and polypropylene, polymers used in plastic packaging and automotive components. **36.22**

There is no explicit reference to monopoly leveraging (the use of monopoly power in one market to gain a competitive advantage in another) in the Act, but this is addressed by the broad prohibition on exclusionary acts by dominant firms set out in s. 8 of the Act. In *The Competition Commission v. Telkom SA Ltd.*,[3] the Tribunal found that telecommunications provider Telkom had leveraged its upstream monopoly in the infrastructure market in order to advantage its own subsidiary in the competitive value added network market through various non-price, restrictive practices in violation of ss. 8(b), 8(c), and 8(d)(i) of the Act. **36.23**

C. Monopsony

A monopsony entails a form of market dominance by a downstream firm as the only purchaser of a good or service. The monopsonist may dictate terms to its suppliers in the same manner that a monopolist controls the market for its buyers. **36.24**

There is no South African case law involving an abuse of dominance by a monopsonist. However, the concept has been considered by the Tribunal in the merger context. Monopsony power was one of the anticompetitive affects identified by the Tribunal in the proposed large merger between Southern African retailers *JD Group Ltd. and Profurn*.[4] In considering the merger, the Tribunal referred with approval to the US Horizontal Merger Guidelines, which demonstrates an appreciation of the dangers of monopsony. The Tribunal ultimately **36.25**

[3] The Competition Commission v. Telkom SA Ltd. (11/CR/Feb04) [2012] ZACT 66 (August 7, 2012).
[4] JD Group Limited and Profurn Limited (60/LM/Aug02) [2003] ZACT 23 (April 29, 2003).

approved the merger, however, on the condition that JD Group continues to buy supplies from independent furniture manufacturers in the same proportion as they did pre-merger.

D. Price discrimination

36.26 Price discrimination is allowed where the dominant firm can show good grounds for the differential treatment, such as differences in cost or likely cost of manufacture, distribution, sale, promotion, or delivery resulting from the different places to which, methods by which or quantities in which products are supplied to different customers. In addition, dominant firms may act in good faith to meet a price or benefit offered by a competitor and may also engage in price discrimination in response to changing conditions affecting the market, such as closing down sales or sales of perishable goods which are about to go off, or sales of goods which have become obsolete.

36.27 Price discrimination by a dominant firm is prohibited if it is likely to have the effect of substantially preventing or lessening competition; it relates to the sale, in equivalent transactions, of goods or services of like grade and quality to different purchasers; and it involves discriminating between those purchasers in terms of the price charged for the goods or services; any discount, allowance, rebate, or credit given or allowed in relation to the supply of goods or services; the provision of services in respect of the goods or services; or payment for services provided in respect of the goods or services. However, a dominant firm can defend differential treatment of purchasers if it can show that this makes only reasonable allowance for differences in cost or likely cost of manufacture, distribution, sale, promotion, or delivery resulting from the differing places to which, methods by which, or quantities in which, goods or services are supplied to different purchases; is constituted by doing acts in good faith to meet a price or benefit offered by a competitor; or is in response to changing conditions affecting the market for the goods or services concerned.

36.28 In the *Nationwide Poles* case,[5] the complainant alleged that Sasol Oil (Pty) Ltd. was charging more to small purchasers of creosote, a wood preservative used in pine pole treatment. The Tribunal held that the phrase "likely to have the effect of substantially preventing or lessening competition" must be interpreted in accordance with considerations of equity and the participation of small and medium enterprises in the economy. The Tribunal concluded that the discount structure for the sale of creosote exhibited a material differentiation between the most and least favored customers. Creosote constituted a significant input cost for firms such as respondent which competed in the treated poles market against rivals who benefited from the price discrimination. Furthermore, the Tribunal concluded that it was likely that the complainant and firms similarly situated in the market, as well as new entrants, would be less effective competitors as a result of this pricing practice, particularly in a market where small firms, absent price discrimination, could be effective competitors to their larger rivals. The Tribunal accepted that Sasol had engaged in prohibited price discrimination.

36.29 On appeal, however, the CAC held that the ability of small businesses to become competitive was a public interest consideration, rather than a factor which should be used to interpret the prohibition set out in s. 9 of the Act.[6] The CAC held that there was no evidence to suggest that Sasol Oil's pricing was capable of having, or likely to have, an anticompetitive effect in the market for pole treatment, which had remained highly competitive. Nationwide Poles was still able to compete and continue to operate in the relevant market, which remained

[5] Nationwide Poles CC v. Sasol Oil (Pty) Ltd. (72/CR/Dec03) 2006 (3) SA 400 (CAC)

[6] Sasol Oil (Pty) Ltd. v. Nationwide Poles CC (49/CAC/Apr05) [2005] ZACAC 5 (December 13, 2005).

one in which small firms could effectively compete against their large rivals. The CAC accordingly held:

> [O]n the evidence, this Court is not able to conclude that there is a reasonable possibility that competition has been significantly prevented or lessened. Putting the evidence in the best possible light for Respondent, Respondent suffers a disadvantage by way of an additional cost of purchases of creosote pursuant to Appellant's pricing policy. However, competition law does not protect the competitor, it protects competition. Evidence which goes no further than suggesting that one competitor may be prejudiced is insufficient to bring the impugned conduct within the scope of section 9(1)(a).

E. Dictating or influencing resale prices

(i) Resale Price Maintenance

Section 5(2) of the Act imposes an outright prohibition on minimum resale price maintenance (RPM). It is not necessary for a complainant to demonstrate that the practice of minimum resale price maintenance actually had anticompetitive effects, and parties to a vertical price fixing arrangement cannot justify it on the basis that it leads to pro-competitive or other efficiency gains. The s. 5(2) prohibition applies equally to dominant firms and those without market power. **36.30**

Section 5(3) of the Act does however permit suppliers to recommend a resale price, on two conditions. First, the supplier or producer must make it clear to the reseller that the recommendation is not binding. Second, if the product has its price stated on it, the words "recommended price" must appear next to the stated price. **36.31**

In the *Federal Mogul* case, the Tribunal noted that s. 5(2) states that the "practice" of minimum resale price maintenance is prohibited, with no reference to any "agreement" to maintain minimum prices.[7] All that the section therefore requires is a unilateral determination of a minimum resale price, backed up by a sanction for non-compliance. This decision was upheld by the CAC, which observed that "the drafters of the Act clearly regarded resale price maintenance as an egregiously anticompetitive activity and wished to state so in terse and clear terms. The wording of the section indicates that to establish a contravention thereof, it suffices to produce evidence which shows that a supplier has imposed on its distributors a price at which its goods are to be resold and the distributors are thereby induced to comply with this minimum price on pain of a sanction for non-compliance."[8] **36.32**

(ii) Minimum advertised price programs

Like minimum resale price maintenance, minimum advertised price (MAP) programs are implemented through vertical agreements that seek to prohibit resellers and dealers from advertising the supplier or producer's goods below a certain minimum price. There is no South African case law dealing specifically with MAP programs. However, where MAP programs effectively result in minimum resale price maintenance, this will be prohibited outright in terms of s. 5(2) of the Act. **36.33**

F. Tying arrangements

Tying arrangements constitute an abuse of dominance when a dominant firm makes the supply of one good subject to the purchase of another, unrelated good. The dominant firm therefore leverages its dominance in one market, to gain an unfair advantage in another. **36.34**

---

[7] The Competition Commission of South Africa and Federal Mogul Aftermarket Southern Africa (Pty) Ltd. Federal Mogul Friction Products (Pty) Ltd. T & N Holdings Ltd T & N Friction products (Pty) Ltd. (08/CR/Mar01) [2003] ZACT 43 (August 21, 2003).

[8] Federal-Mogul Aftermarket Southern Africa (Pty) Ltd. v. Competition Commission (33/CAC/Sep03) [2003] ZACAC 9; [2004] 1 CPLR 25 (CAC) (December 3, 2003).

36.35 Section 8(d)(iii) of the Act prohibits tying arrangements by a dominant firm. In *Sappi Fine Papers*, the Tribunal identified two distinct practices, both of which are prohibited by this section of the Act.[9] Firstly, the Act defines tying arrangements as they are classically understood in academia and other competition regimes like the US and UK. The defining feature is the linking of two unrelated products or markets. Secondly, the Act prohibits the imposition of a *condition* which is unrelated to the object of the contract. The Tribunal remarked that this will not automatically result in anticompetitive effects, and distinguished it from the other practices listed in s. 8(d). The Tribunal held that the imposition of a condition which is unrelated to the object of a contract will only be prohibited in terms of s. 8(d)(iii) if it can be shown that the condition had the effect of linking two separate markets.

G. Exclusive Dealing

36.36 Exclusive dealing entails an agreement between a supplier and purchaser in which the purchaser is bound to purchase from a single supplier to the exclusion of every other supplier on the market. There has been extensive debate regarding the merits of exclusive dealing particularly from a business efficiency perspective.

36.37 In South Africa, this conduct is addressed by the prohibitions on exclusionary acts by dominant firms set out in s. 8(c) and (d) of the Act, as well as the general prohibition on anticompetitive agreements between customers and suppliers (or both) which substantially prevent or lessen competition set out in s. 5(1) of the Act. In both cases, however, this practice may be defensible if it leads to technological, efficiency or other pro-competitive gains which outweigh its anticompetitive effects.

36.38 In the *Patensie Sitrus Beherend* case,[10] the complainant alleged that Patensie Sitrus's articles of association contravened the Competition Act in that they contained a number of exclusive supply provisions which locked farmers into an exclusive supply agreement thus excluding potential competitors from the market for the packing and distribution of citrus fruit. This application followed an earlier High Court application by Patensie Sitrus in which it sought an urgent interdict compelling the complainant and another citrus farmer, to comply with their contractual supply obligations in terms of the company's articles of association. The two farmers wanted to sell their fruit to an alternative packer who offered them a better price. The Tribunal found that these clauses excluded competition and allowed the respondent to exert market power in order to raise prices. The lack of competition in the market also lowered the incentive for the respondent to keep its production costs low.

H. Refusal to deal

36.39 Section 8(d)(ii) also prohibits a particular kind of refusal to deal by a dominant firm, namely, refusing to supply scarce resources to a competitor when it is economically feasible to do so. In *York Timbers v. South African Forestry Company*,[11] the Tribunal (following the view expressed by US antitrust scholars Areeda and Hovenkamp) held that an arbitrary refusal to deal by a monopolist cannot in itself be unlawful unless it extends, preserves, creates or threatens to create significant market power in some related market.[12] The Tribunal held that in order to find an abuse of dominance from a refusal to supply, market power must be shown

[9] Sappi Fine Papers and Competition Commission (62/CR/Nov01) [2002] ZACT 26 (April 17, 2002).

[10] JJP Bezuidenhout Patensie and Sitrus Beherend Limited (66/IR/May00) [2000] ZACT 32 (July 19, 2000).

[11] York Timbers Ltd. v. SA Forestry Ltd. (09/CAC/May01) [2001] ZACAC 3; [2001–2002] CPLR 94 (CAC) (September 18, 2001).

[12] Phillip E. Areeda and Herbert Hovenkamp, Antitrust Law (Boston: Little, Brown and Company, 1996), vol. 3a, 167.

to have been extended or created. This is crucial in order to give expression to the requirement in this section of the Act that it is the refusal to supply to a *competitor* that offends. In the Tribunal's words, action against a competitor is only prohibited when it is anticompetitive and this will be measured by its capacity to extend or create market power.

In *The Bulb Man* case,[13] The Bulb Man applied to the Competition Tribunal on the basis that Hadeco, a supplier of flower bulbs, had refused to supply them. The Tribunal noted that in order to sustain a complaint, it must be shown that a refusal to deal enhanced Hadeco's market power. In this case, the Tribunal held that the refusal to supply did not amount to a dominant firm flexing its anticompetitive muscle, but rather was simply an instance of a supplier divorcing its customer based on irretrievable breakdown in their relationship. **36.40**

I. Essential facilities

A dominant firm may not refuse to give a competitor access to an essential facility when it is economically feasible to do so. An "essential facility" is defined as an infrastructure or resource that cannot reasonably be duplicated, and without access to which, competitors cannot reasonably provide goods or services to their customers. This conduct is prohibited outright, and a dominant firm cannot raise any efficiency defense. Even a first time contravention may result in a fine of up to 10 percent of the turnover of the dominant firm. **36.41**

In the *Telkom* case,[14] the Tribunal held that Telkom, the dominant provider of fixed line telecommunications facilities in South Africa, had refused independent value-added network service providers (VANS) (including internet service providers) access to facilities required to enable them to compete in the downstream value added network services market. Telkom refused to supply the essential facility to the VANS providers unless they agreed to certain conditions, which were based on Telkom's interpretation of the Telecommunications Act and its license. Telkom also intermittently froze the networks of a number of VANS providers. Telkom was fined ZAR 449 million, or approximately 2 percent of Telkom's annual turnover for 2010/2011. However, the Tribunal did not define precisely what constitutes an essential facility, and in what circumstances a good or service will be regarded as one. The Tribunal also did not deal with the meaning of "economically feasible." Telkom has indicated that it will appeal to the CAC. **36.42**

It is noted that the conduct in s. 8(b) is prohibited outright with no provision for the offending firm to raise a defense while in contrast; denying a competitor a scarce resource (a refusal to deal) is prohibited subject to the offending firm being unable to demonstrate a benefit outweighing the anticompetitive effect of its refusal. **36.43**

J. Bundling (including loyalty and market share discounts)

Bundling is closely related to tying arrangements. It entails the selling of two or more goods together at more attractive prices than would be paid if a customer purchased the goods separately. Bundling may therefore have the same effect as tying-in. A distinction is made between pure bundling where the individual bundled goods are not made available separately and mixed bundling where the goods are available separately albeit at a higher cost. **36.44**

Similar to tying arrangements, it is argued that the anticompetitive effect of bundling lies in the possibility that a dominant firm can leverage their market power in the sale of one item to gain market power in the bundled market. One of the distinctions between bundling and **36.45**

[13] *The Bulb Man (SA) (Pty) Ltd. and Hadeco (Pty) Ltd.* (81/IR/Apr06) [2006] ZACT 86 (November 28, 2006).

[14] *Competition Commission v. Telkom SA Ltd.* (n 3).

tying is that the bundled items are often related in some way which makes any anticompetitive effect more difficult to discern. Indeed, bundling can often have positive effects. For example, bundling can allow suppliers to achieve economies of scale which can be reflected in the discount offered to customers. The bundle may also simply be more attractive and of greater value to consumers than the individual items sold separately or to offer a bundle which is more attractive (and of greater value) to consumers than the sum of its separate parts.[15]

K. Standard-setting groups (disclosure requirements, licensing arrangements, and licensing pools)

36.46 Standard setting is analyzed differently by the South African competition authorities depending on whether it is undertaken by parties in a horizontal relationship (competitors) or in a vertical relationship (between customers and suppliers or both).

36.47 In the *Netstar* case,[16] the Commission referred a complaint against competing vehicle tracking companies, Netstar, Matrix Vehicle Tracking, and Tracker Network (representing over 90 percent of the industry) and the industry association, the Vehicle Security Association of South Africa (VESA). This case involved the setting of standards by VESA, an industry association, for motor vehicle tracking devices and suppliers of such devices. The complainant, Tracetec, complained that the standards impeded its entry because South African Insurance Association and the insurers who were members of it would only insure tracking devices and suppliers which complied with VESA standards. The Tribunal held that it is necessary to consider the following questions: (i) Does the standard-setting body have market power? If yes, it is likely to have an exclusionary effect. (ii) Who is the driver of the standards? If it is rivals driving the standards, it is more problematic than if consumers are driving the standards. (iii) What is the effect of the standard? The more effective the standard is, i.e. creating barriers to entry, the more restrictive the standard is. And (iv) Is the standard reasonable? This relates to whether the standard is consistent with the rationale behind it and whether a reasonably efficient firm could comply with the standard.

36.48 The Tribunal held that the standard setting had resulted in a prevention or lessening of competition because it was not possible for firms to expand in the stolen vehicle recovery market without complying with the standards, because short-term insurers would not use the motor vehicle tracking devices that did not comply with VESA standards. Secondly, consumers were denied the benefit of lower prices, greater choices and technological development offered by products which did not meet the standards. This decision was overturned by the CAC on appeal.[17] The CAC held that although the factors identified by the Tribunal were generally useful, the Tribunal had failed to properly consider the evidence presented in this particular case. The CAC ultimately held that it was the stance which insurance companies took to the standards, rather than the standards set by the competing companies, which created the anticompetitive effects.

L. Customer termination

36.49 In South Africa, this is treated as a species of refusal to deal, on the same basis as discussed above. There have not been any decided cases thus far dealing specifically with customer termination.

---

[15] EU Competition Law (4th edn.), 455.

[16] *Competition Commission and another v. Netstar (Pty) Ltd. and others* (17/CR/Mar05) [2010] ZACT 29 (April 19, 2010).

[17] *Netstar (Pty) Ltd. and others v. Competition Commission South Africa and another* (99/CAC/MAY10, 98/CAC/MAY10, 97/CAC/MAY10) [2011] ZACAC 1; 2011 (3) SA 171 (CAC) (February 15, 2011).

M. Termination of intermediaries (retailers, wholesalers, dealers, and value-added resellers, agents, and brokers)

The Tribunal considered termination of intermediaries in *National Association of Pharmaceutical Wholesalers* (the Manufacturers) and *Glaxo Wellcome* (2003) (the Wholesalers).[18] **36.50**

The Tribunal held that the conduct of wholesalers was as a response to *market conditions*. The "cost" associated with a large number of retailers interacting with a few big manufacturers and vice versa provided a need which they proceeded to fill. However, recent market developments had been putting the squeeze on pharmaceutical companies and had prompted manufacturers to look at where costs could be lowered. In this regard, the manufacturers turned to their mode of distribution and decided to undertake the process in a way that differed to the traditional wholesalers model. The court remarked that there was nothing sinister about this even though it operated to the detriment of the middlemen. In the end, the Tribunal felt that the wholesalers needed to react to the move with innovation rather than a resort to regulation. **36.51**

The Tribunal found that the Act had not been contravened, primarily because the termination (or, the replacement) of the intermediary in this case arose as a result of market forces, which is precisely what the Commission attempts to protect. **36.52**

N. Termination of relationships with competitors

As explained in Section I.H, s. 8(d)(ii) contains a specific prohibition on a dominant firm refusing to supply scarce resources to a competitor, when supplying these goods is economically feasible. **36.53**

O. Exemptions

There is no provision in the Act for block exemptions. However, s. 10 of the Act provides that the Commission may grant an exemption from the prohibitions on anticompetitive conduct in chapter 2 of the Act, if the applicant can demonstrate that an agreement or practice is required for: **36.54**

- the maintenance or promotion of exports;
- the promotion of the ability of small businesses or firms controlled or owned by historically disadvantaged persons to become competitive;
- a change in productive capacity necessary to stop decline in an industry; or
- the economic stability of an industry designated by the Minister of Trade and Industry after consulting with the Minister responsible for that industry.

The Commission may also exempt an agreement or practice, or category of agreements or practices, that relates to the exercise of a right acquired or protected in terms of intellectual property legislation (such as copyrights, patents, and trademarks). **36.55**

Schedule 1 provides that a professional association may apply to the Commission to have all or part of its rules exempted from the provisions of chapter 2 of the Act, provided that the rules do not contain any restriction that has the effect of substantially preventing or lessening competition in the market, an exemption may be granted provided that, and having regard to internationally applied norms, the restrictions are reasonably required to maintain professional standards or to maintain the ordinary function of the profession. **36.56**

[18] *Pharmaceutical Wholesalers and Glaxo Wellcome (2)* (68/IR/JUN00) [2003] ZACT 37 (June 18, 2003).

36.57 The Commission may grant conditional or unconditional exemption, for a specified period of time. Before granting an application for exemption, the Commission must give notice of the application in the Government Gazette, and interested parties will be given an opportunity to comment.

36.58 To date, relatively few applications for exemption have been successful, and the application process typically takes some months, or even years, to complete.

II. Dealing with competitors

36.59 The South African authorities regard cartels as the most egregious contravention of the Act and have prioritized the prosecution of firms involved in the direct or indirect fixing of prices or trading conditions, market allocation, and collusive tendering.

A. Horizontal price fixing (including advanced announcements of price or product changes)

36.60 Section 4 of the Act regulates restrictive horizontal practices, or practices involving competitors. Depending on their effect, horizontal agreements can be classified as prohibited practices in two broad categories, namely "non-per se," or, "rule of reason" horizontal agreements; and "per se," or "outright" prohibited practices.

36.61 The first category, dealt with in s. 4(1)(a), consists of those practices which are prohibited if the agreement between competitors has the effect of substantially preventing or lessening competition in the market, unless the parties to the agreement can show that there is a pro-competitive gain that outweighs the anticompetitive effect. This category is judged according to its effects, by way of a "rule of reason" test.

36.62 The second category, set out in s. 4(1)(b) of the Act, describes the so-called per se practices which cannot be justified in accordance with any rule of reason test. These consist of agreements between competitors which involve:

- the direct or indirect fixing of a purchase of selling price or any other trading condition (generally referred to as price-fixing);
- the division of markets by allocating customers, suppliers, territories or specific types of goods or services (market allocation); or
- collusive tendering.

36.63 In the *Nedschroef* case,[19] the Tribunal held that s. 4 of the Act applies not only to actual, but also to potential competitors.

36.64 Any agreement or understanding, whether formal or informal, verbal or in writing, between two or more competitors to fix either the selling price or the purchase price of a product is illegal. Section 4(1)(b) prohibits both agreements and "concerted practices," which are defined as "co-operative, or co-ordinated conduct by firms, achieved through direct or indirect contact, that replaces their independent action but does not amount to an agreement."

36.65 In the *Patensie* case,[20] the Tribunal held that the term "trading conditions" in s. 4(1)(b) relates to any condition which impacts on the price, quantity or quality of a product or service.

[19] *Nedschroef Johannesburg (Pty) Ltd. and Teamcor Ltd. / Waco International Ltd. / CBC Fasteners (Pty) Ltd. / Avlock International (Pty) Ltd.* (95/IR/Oct05) [2006] ZACT 7 (February 1, 2006).

[20] *Competition Commission v. Patensie Sitrus Beherend Beperk; Bezuidenhout and another v. Patensie Sitrus Beherend Beperk* [2002] ZACT 18 (April 8, 2002).

Once an agreement between competitors falls within the per se prohibition in s. 4(1)(b), the practice is prohibited outright and is considered illegal without regard to any pro-competitive or efficiency benefits it might produce. Parties to agreements caught by this section cannot raise any arguments or evidence in justification of the practice, although they may be able to argue that their practice should not be characterized as one which falls within the scope of s. 4(1)(b) of the Act. **36.66**

However, in the *American Natural Soda Ash Corporation (ANSAC)* case,[21] the Supreme Court of Appeal (SCA) observed that s. 4(1)(b) of the Act did not necessarily prohibit every form of horizontal cooperation between competitors. The SCA recognized that it was permissible for competitors to lead evidence about whether or not their agreement should be "characterized" as the kind of conduct to which s. 4(1)(b) of the Act should apply. There is accordingly some limited scope for competitors to enter into efficiency enhancing joint ventures in South Africa, although the Tribunal has yet to pronounce on the nature and limits of this defense. **36.67**

Even if an agreement, understanding or concerted practice by competitors does not fall within the per se offenses in s. 4(1)(b), it may still be prohibited in terms of s. 4(1)(a), if has the effect of "substantially preventing, or lessening, competition in a market." In the *Vehicle Security Association of South Africa*[22] case, for example, the Commission alleged that the setting of membership criteria and technical standards by vehicle tracking and recovery companies and the manufacturers of gear locks, alarms and immobilizers contravened s. 4(1)(a) of the Act, because it raised barriers to entry in the industry. However, this complaint was dismissed on appeal by the (CAC),[23] on the basis that the standards were in fact set by the insurance industry rather than the competing vehicle tracking and security device manufacturers. **36.68**

B. Horizontal agreements to allocate customers or territories; agreements not to compete

As explained above, the Act imposes an outright prohibition on the division of markets by competitors by allocating customers, suppliers, territories, or specific types of goods or services. **36.69**

The Tribunal has considered the application of this prohibition on restraints of trade in agreements between competitors. Although restraints may be sought in order to protect legitimate strategic commercial interests and are frequently requested, particularly in the context of joint ventures and sale of business agreements, any agreement between parties who are actual or potential competitors not to compete with one another in South Africa potentially constitutes a form of division of markets which is prohibited outright by s. 4(1)(b)(ii) of the Act. As explained above, this section imposes an outright prohibition on market allocation by competitors and agreements or understandings of this nature cannot be defended on the basis that they are pro-competitive or give rise to efficiency or other legitimate commercial benefits. In the *Nedschroef* case,[24] the Tribunal confirmed a consent order in which potential competitors who had concluded a restraint consequent upon a sale of business admitted that their restraint constituted a contravention of s. 4(1)(b)(ii) of the Act and paid administrative penalties. However, in the *Gallo* case,[25] the Tribunal held that a restraint concluded between **36.70**

---

[21] American Natural Soda Ash Corporation and another v. Competition Commission of South *Africa* (554/2003) [2005] ZASCA 42; [2005] 1 CPLR 1 (SCA); [2005] 3 All SA 1 (SCA) (May 13, 2005).

[22] *Competition Commission v. Netstar* (n 16).

[23] *Netstar (Pty) Ltd v. Competition Commission South Africa* (n 17).

[24] *Nedschroef* (n 19).

[25] *Replication Technology Group (Pty) Ltd. v. Gallo Africa Limited* (92/IR/Sep07) [2007] ZACT 99 (December 10, 2007).

the seller of a business and the purchaser which precluded the purchaser from providing competing services in the Republic for a two-year period after the sale did not contravene s. 4(1)(b). The Tribunal noted that this was "a common garden variety restraint of trade normally associated with the sale of a business" which was "limited as to duration." The Tribunal accepted that these kinds of restraints are mechanisms for protecting the goodwill acquired by a purchaser when it purchases a business. In particular, the Tribunal noted that this restraint did not require that the restrained party refrain from participation in the market altogether, and the terms of the restraint "did not seem unduly restrictive relative to restraints of this type." Most importantly, it was a temporary and partial restraint, which was necessary to protect the value of the investment made by the purchaser.

36.71 Several companies have admitted to market allocation in contravention of the Act. Examples include Afrisam which admitted that it had entered into agreements and arrangements which had the affect of dividing the cement market through the allocation of market shares;[26] construction group Aveng which geographic areas in the market for pipes and culverts, customers and contracts;[27] and Marley Pipes which admitted to attending a series of meetings where agreements, arrangements, and/or understandings to divide the markets for pipes products in South Africa were reached.[28]

C. Horizontal boycotts

36.72 Horizontal boycotts may be analyzed as a form of abuse of dominance or a contravention of the prohibition on fixing of a trading condition by competitors in contravention of s. 4(1)(b) of the Act. In the *United South African Pharmacies (USAP)* case,[29] USAP agreed to pay an administrative penalty of ZAR 250,000 in relation to an alleged boycott of the Anglo American Corporation Medical Scheme and Engen Medical Fund after they refused to accept the discount USAP's members offered on chronic and acute medication.

D. Joint ventures and other competitive collaborations

36.73 Joint ventures which constitute a "merger" as defined in s. 12(2) of the Act are required to be notified to the South African competition law authorities if the monetary thresholds for compulsory notification as an intermediate or a large merger in South Africa are met. The Commission has issued a notice on joint ventures[30] which sets out the Commission's approach to notification of joint ventures and some practical guidance on calculating whether the monetary thresholds for notification are met.

36.74 Joint ventures between firms which are competitors (or potential competitors), which are not approved by the competition authorities as a merger, may potentially be scrutinized in terms of the outright prohibition on the fixing of prices and trading conditions and market allocation by competitors set out in s. 4 of the Act. As explained above, in the *American Natural Soda Ash Corporation* case,[31] the SCA observed that s. 4(1)(b) of the Act did not necessarily prohibit every form of horizontal cooperation between competitors. The SCA recognized

[26] *Competition Commission v. Afrisam (South Africa) (Pty) Ltd.* (93/CR/Nov11) [2011] ZACT 98 (November 16, 2011).

[27] *Competition Commission v. Aveng (Africa) Ltd.* (24/CR/Feb09).

[28] *Competition Commission v. Marley Pipes Systems (Pty) Ltd., Competition Commission v. DPI Plastics (Pty) Ltd. and others* (15/CR/Feb09) [2010] ZACT 24 (March 31, 2010).

[29] *Competition Commission of South Africa and others and United South African Pharmacies and others* (04/CR/Jan02) [2003] ZACT 4 (January 22, 2003).

[30] Competition Commission, "Issue 3. The application of merger provisions of the Competition Act 89 of 1998, as amended, to joint ventures," <http://www.compcom.co.za/assets/Uploads/AttachedFiles/MyDocuments/Practitoner-Update-Joint-Ventures-Published-version.doc>.

[31] *American Natural Soda Corporation* (n 21).

that it was permissible for competitors to lead evidence about whether or not their agreement should be "characterized" as the kind of conduct to which s. 4(1)(b) of the Act should apply. There is accordingly some limited scope for competitors to enter into efficiency enhancing join ventures in South Africa, although the Tribunal has yet to pronounce definitely on when joint ventures between competitors which fix prices or trading conditions, or divide markets, are defensible.

E. Trade associations

Participation by competitors in trade associations by competitors is not prohibited by the Act. However, the South African competition authorities are concerned that such associations may provide platforms for collusion which result in contraventions of the provisions of s. 4 of the Act. **36.75**

Several complaint referrals have focused on price fixing by industry associations. In 2002, for example, the Commission initiated an investigation into the activities of the South African Medical Association (SAMA), the Hospital Association of South Africa (HASA), and the Board of Healthcare Funders (BHF). The Commission concluded that all three industry associations had contravened the s. 4(1)(b) prohibition on price fixing by publishing pricing tariffs, even though these were simply a guideline. HASA,[32] SAMA,[33] and BHF[34] concluded consent orders with the Commission in which they agreed to pay administrative penalties of ZAR 4.5 million, ZAR 900,000, and ZAR 500,000 respectively. **36.76**

F. Interlocking directorates

Interlocking directorates are not expressly prohibited by the Act. **36.77**

However, s. 4(2) creates the presumption that a firm which has at least one director (defined broadly in the Act) in common with a competing firm, has engaged in a contravention of the outright prohibition on price fixing and market allocation in s. 4(1)(b) of the Act. The onus to lead evidence to rebut this presumption lies with the party accused of contravening this section of the Act. **36.78**

G. Facilitating practices

The law does not recognize facilitating practices. **36.79**

H. Information exchange

Several cases involving the exchange of commercially sensitive pricing or other strategic information between competitors (either directly, or indirectly through industry associations) have been prosecuted by the Commission to date. In the *cement industry* case for example, *Afrisam*[35] and *Lafarge*[36] agreed to pay administrative penalties of ZAR 124,878,870 and ZAR 148,724,400, respectively, and admitted that they had exchanged detailed, disaggregated monthly sales information via the Cement and Concrete Institute of South Africa, which had enabled the South African cement producers to maintain agreed market shares. **36.80**

---

[32] *Competition Commission and Hospital Association of South Africa* (24/CR/Apr04) [2004] ZACT 29 (April 26, 2004).

[33] *Competition Commission and South African Medical Association* (23/CR/Apr04) [2004] ZACT 28 (April 26, 2004).

[34] *Competition Commission and The Board of Healthcare Funders of Southern Africa* (07/CR/Feb05) [2001] ZACT 5 (March 12, 2001).

[35] *Afrisam* (n 26).

[36] *The Competition Commission v. Lafarge Industries South Africa (Pty) Ltd.* (23/CR/Mar12) (March 28, 2012).

(i) Exchanges of historic pricing information

36.81 Even historic information exchange may potentially be problematic if the data is disaggregated and provides insight into competitors' future pricing or strategy.

(ii) How old, anonymous, and aggregated pricing information needs to be

36.82 Generally, an exchange of pricing or other commercially sensitive information is most likely to be problematic where the information is exchanged in advance or where the sensitive information relates to future pricing, the level of price increases, future costs, and customer data. An exchange of historical data may also be problematic where this information gives competitors detailed insight into the pricing philosophy of rivals. Generally, historical information, such as information that is more than a year old can be shared, provided such information is sufficiently aggregated to ensure that a competitor is unable to use the information to influence their pricing strategy.

(iii) What pro-competitive purposes, if any, exchange needs to help participants achieve; pre-merger due diligence

36.83 Provided appropriate safeguards are in place, there is no legal prohibition against coordinating an industry approach on the enactment of new legislation; programs to promote product safety or environmental protection or other matters of general interest to the industry; industry wide quality control education and training programs or the joint compilation of general industry studies.

I. Joint purchasing agreements

36.84 Joint purchasing agreements may operate to create buying power amongst competitors, which may generate efficiencies which benefit consumers in the form of lower prices. However, this practice is prohibited outright by s. 4(1)(b)(i). Unless such arrangements are capable of being characterized as outside of the scope of this prohibition in terms of the approach suggested by the SCA in the ANSAC[37] case (dealt with above), or the parties have obtained an exemption in terms of s. 10 of the Act, competitors who fix purchase prices may face a fine of up to 10 percent of their turnover, even for a first time offense.

J. Joint lobbying/regulatory/legislative efforts

36.85 There is no express prohibition on joint lobbying or other regulatory/legislative efforts by competitors. However, it is important to ensure that this activity does not result in any contravention of the prohibition on price fixing and market allocation in s. 4(1)(b) of the Act.

K. Agreements between customers and suppliers or both

36.86 Section 5(1) of the Act regulates agreements between customers and suppliers or both. It provides that "an agreement between parties in a vertical relationship is prohibited it if has the effect of substantially preventing or lessening competition in the market, unless a party to the agreement can prove that any technological, efficiency or other pro-competitive, gain resulting from that agreement outweighs that effect."

36.87 In terms of s. 5(1) of the Act, the standard against which a vertical agreement must be tested is whether or not it has the effect of substantially preventing or lessening competition in any relevant market. If so, the parties to the agreement would need to prove that

[37] *ANSAC* (n 21).

any technological, efficiency, or other pro-competitive gain resulting from the agreements outweigh its detrimental effects. This inquiry is essentially a factual one which involves the balancing of any pro-competitive effects of the vertical agreement against negative or anti-competitive effects.

III. General issues

A. Jurisdiction and applicable law (including sector-specific competition regulation)

The Act applies to all economic activity within, or having an effect within, South Africa, with limited exceptions for collective bargaining between employers and employees and agreements in terms of the Labour Relations Act, as well as concerted conduct which is designed to achieve a non-commercial socio-economic objective or similar purpose. **36.88**

To the extent that they are engaged in economic activity, public as well as private entities are subject to the Act. **36.89**

Section 3(1A) of the Act provides that the competition authorities have concurrent jurisdiction with other regulatory authorities that regulate particular sectors of the economy, such as energy, postal services, and telecommunications. **36.90**

B. Antitrust system

(i) Name of agency/agencies

The Act establishes three regulatory bodies which are charged with enforcing its provisions: the Competition Commission, the Competition Tribunal, and the Competition Appeal Court. **36.91**

The main functions of the Commission are to investigate complaints about alleged prohibited practices, to consider applications for exemption from certain provisions of the Act, to decide on intermediate mergers and to make recommendations to the Tribunal on large mergers. The Commission has extensive powers, which include the power to subpoena witnesses to give evidence under oath and produce documents, and the power to enter business premises and conduct searches and seizures. **36.92**

The Commission is obliged to investigate complaints from the public, but can also initiate its own complaints. However, a complaint in respect of a prohibited practice may not be initiated more than three years after the practice has ceased (s. 67). **36.93**

The ability of the Commission to amend its complaints subsequent to referral to the Tribunal has been considered by CAC in two cases in 2012, one involving an alleged fertilizer cartel (*Yara*)[38] and the other an alleged polyurethane foam cartel (*Loungefoam*).[39] The Commission sought direct access to the Constitutional Court in both of these cases, but its applications were dismissed. On appeal to the SCA, the SCA held that although the Commissioner must "initiate" a new complaint not covered by the original complaint submitted by a complainant in terms of s. 49B(2)(b), this initiation can be informal or even tacit. In this case, the SCA held that the Commission had in fact tacitly initiated the cartel complaint which was not **36.94**

[38] *Yara South Africa (Pty) Ltd. v. Competition Commission and Others in re: Competition Commission v. Sasol Chemical Industries Ltd. and others; Omnia Fertilizers v. Competition Commission* [2011] ZACAC 9; [2011] ZACAC 2 (March 14, 2011)

[39] *Competition Commission v. Loungefoam (Pty) Ltd. and others* (102/CAC/Jun 10) [2012] ZACAC 10 (December 14, 2012).

covered by the original abuse of dominance complaint. The referral by the Commission was thus not invalid, and so the CAC should not have struck it out.[40]

36.95 The Tribunal adjudicates complaints about prohibited practices, confirms settlement agreements entered into by the Commission as consent orders, hears appeals against decisions of the Commission and decides on large mergers. A complaint may not be referred to the Tribunal against any firm that has been a respondent in any completed proceedings before the Tribunal.

36.96 Parties can appeal decisions of the CAC to the SCA, and if there is a constitutional issue, also to the Constitutional Court.

(ii) Staff size and budget

36.97 The Commission's Annual Report for 2012/13 indicates that it employs approximately 68 staff in its Merger, Enforcement and Exemptions, Policy and Research, and Legal divisions. Its budget for the financial year was around ZAR 157 million.

(iii) Recent enforcement actions and trends

36.98 Cartels remain the Commission's top enforcement target. Commission fines for cartels in 2012/2013 year exceeded ZAR 731 million, although the majority of cases are settled by the companies involved in terms of the consent order procedure, rather than proceeding to a hearing by the Tribunal.

36.99 The CLP remains a powerful weapon in the Commission's arsenal, and the Commission has also employed dawn raids (for example, in the tyre and cement cartel cases), in order to obtain documents and electronic data which evidence price fixing and market allocation by competitors. The Commission is currently finalizing a substantial investigation into bid-rigging in the South African construction sector, which is likely to result in a significant number of companies being find substantial amounts for colluding on tenders to construct sports stadiums and roads.

36.100 The Commission has also pursued a number of complex abuse of dominance cases, particularly in the sectors of the South African economy which it has identified as priority sectors for investigation, such as telecommunications (Telkom), petrochemicals (Sasol), and construction (Mittal), but also in sectors such as airlines (SAA). Administrative penalties of approximately R 449 million were paid by dominant firms for various abuses in the 2012/2013 financial year. The Commission's focus continues to be on products and services which are essential to poor South Africans.

C. Private litigation

36.101 The Tribunal and the CAC have exclusive jurisdiction in respect of the interpretation and application of, *inter alia*, chapter 2 (prohibited practices) of the Act. However, s. 62(5) provides that the Tribunal and the CAC have no jurisdiction over "the assessment of the amount, and awarding, of damages arising out of a prohibited practice." The substantive requirements for instituting civil actions are set out in s. 65 of the Act. A civil court "must not consider an issue concerning conduct that is prohibited in terms of the Act" but must refer that issue to the Tribunal "to be considered on its merits" unless the issue is one in respect of which the Tribunal or the CAC has made an order, in which case the court must apply such determination (s. 65(2)).

[40] *Competition Commission v. Yara (South Africa) (Pty) Ltd. and others* (784/12) [2013] ZASCA 107; [2013] 4 All SA 302 (SCA) (September 13, 2013).

These provisions indicate that a finding by the competition authorities regarding a prohibited practice is a pre-requisite for a civil claim for damages and cannot be reconsidered by a civil court. Sections 62 and 65(2) contemplate that the competition authorities have exclusive jurisdiction to determine prohibited practices under the Act, but the civil courts have exclusive jurisdiction to determine whether a claimant is entitled to damages and if so, how much. A person who has suffered loss as a result of a prohibited practice may not commence an action for damages if that person has already been awarded damages in a consent order. To date, however, no such claims have been determined. **36.102**

Any person *who has been affected* by prohibited conduct (not only a complainant or an intervener) may rely upon a certificate issued under s. 65(6)(b) of the Act in order to claim damages. **36.103**

Few civil claims for damages have been brought to date in South Africa (one example is the claim by South African airline Nationwide against national carrier South Africa Airways,[41] arising from certain anticompetitive agreements it entered into with South African travel agents). However, private actions may increase following a recent decision by the Supreme Court of Appeal in the Pioneer bread cartel case, which clarified the requirements for bring a class action. The matter related to a bread cartel which was successfully prosecuted by the Commission in 2010.[42] A number of non-government organizations and five individuals have attempted to launch a class action against food giants Tiger Brands, Pioneer Foods, and Premier Foods. The SCA sent[43] the case back to the High Court for consideration after it refused to certify the applicants as a class (a prerequisite to bringing a class action in South African law). The High Court will now decide based on the SCA precedent whether a class should be certified. If successful, this will be the first claim of its kind in South Africa. **36.104**

D. Follow-on litigation

The South African Constitution makes provision for class actions, but the South African courts have yet to rule whether this kind of action is available in cases involving a contravention of the Act. This is likely to be determined in the Pioneer decision. **36.105**

E. Arbitration and alternative dispute resolution

There is no reason why parties in South Africa cannot agree to arbitration or other means of alternative dispute resolution (ADR) in order to address a complaint about anticompetitive conduct. However, arbitration and ADR are relatively expensive in South Africa, and this is not common. **36.106**

F. Remedies

(i) Administrative penalties

Administrative fines of up to 10 percent of a firm's annual turnover can be imposed for even a first time contravention of the prohibitions on price fixing, market allocation and collusive tendering in contravention of s. 4(1)(b) of the Act; minimum resale price maintenance in terms of s. 5(2) of the Act, and if a dominant firm engages in excessive pricing, refusing to give a competitor access to an essential facility when it is economically feasible to do so or any of the exclusionary acts set out in s. 8(d) of the Act. **36.107**

[41] This case was ultimately settled by means of a confidential out of court settlement.

[42] *Competition Commission v. Pioneer Foods (Pty) Ltd.* (91/CAC/Feb10) [2010] ZACAC 2 (October 15, 2010).

[43] *Children's Resource Centre Trust v. Pioneer Food* (50/2012) [2012] ZA SCA 182 (November 29, 2012).

36.108 Section 59 of the Act provides that when determining an appropriate penalty, the Tribunal or the appeal courts must take into account the nature of the conduct, duration, gravity and extent of the contravention; the loss or damage resulting from the conduct; the degree of the firm's cooperation with competition authorities; the firm's behavior, market circumstances; the level of profit derived from the contravention; and whether the firm is a repeat offender. The application of these factors has been considered by the Tribunal in abuse of dominance cases (for example, the *SAA* case,[44] and in cartel cases (for example, the *Southern Pipeline*[45] and *Aveng*[46] cases).

36.109 In addition to making an infringement finding, the Commission may impose behavioral or structural remedies (s. 58(1)).

(ii) Criminal liability

36.110 Sections 70–73 create various offenses of a procedural nature, mainly relating to hindering the Commission's administration of the Act.

36.111 The Amendment Act will introduce criminal liability for individual managers or directors who participate or knowingly acquiesce in price fixing, market division or collusive tendering in contravention of s. 4(1)(b) of the Act. Individuals will face administrative penalties of up to ZAR 500,000, and/or prison sentences of up to ten years, if found guilty. Firms will be prohibited from paying these fines or procuring insurance to cover their representatives convicted of these offenses.

(iii) Civil liability

36.112 Parties who have suffered loss as a result of the contravention of the Act may commence action in the civil courts to recover their loss once the Tribunal has certified that the Act has been contravened. As explained above, few civil claims for damages have been brought to date in South Africa. However, following the consent order in the SAA abuse of dominance case, both Nationwide and Comair instituted action in the High Court for damages arising from SAA's anticompetitive conduct.

G. Leniency and immunity

36.113 In 2004, the Commission published a Corporate Leniency Policy (CLP), which was amended in 2008.[47] The CLP is a compliance tool that outlines a process in terms of which the Commission is able to grant the first cartel member to approach the Commission with information about cartel immunity from prosecution in terms of the Act. The Commission may grant conditional or total immunity.

36.114 Leniency is only available for cartel conduct (the direct or indirect fixing of prices or trading conditions, market allocation or collusive tendering which contravenes s. 4(1)(b) of the Act). In summary, in order to qualify for leniency, an applicant must:

- honestly provide the Commission with complete and truthful disclosure;
- be the first cartel member to come forward and provide the Commission with information;
- offer full and expeditious cooperation to the Commission;
- immediately stop the cartel activity, or act as directed by the Commission.

[44] *Nationwide Airlines (Pty) Ltd.* (n 1).

[45] *Competition Commission v. Southern Pipeline Contractors Conrite and another* (23/CR/Feb09) (November 29, 2010).

[46] *Competition Commission v. Aveng (Africa) t/a Steeldale and others* (84/CR/Dec09) [2012] ZACT 32 (May 7, 2012).

[47] Competition Commission, "Corporate Leniency Policy" <http://www.compcom.co.za/assets/Uploads/CLP-public-version-12052008.pdf>.

In addition the applicant must not: 36.115

- alert other cartel members about its application for leniency;
- destroy, falsify or conceal evidence, documents and information; and
- make any misrepresentations concerning the cartel activity, or act dishonestly.

There is provision for applicants to apply for a marker, and for statements to be provided orally to the Commission. There is no "blanket immunity"—an applicant must apply in relation to each separate contravention of s. 4 of the Act. Immunity granted by any another competition authority will not automatically qualify the applicant for immunity in South Africa. 36.116

Other companies which subsequently supply the Commission with evidence of "significant value" to the investigation can obtain reductions in the fines which they would otherwise have paid. Like an immunity applicant, they will also have to provide a corporate statement and cooperate continuously. 36.117

Leniency in terms of the CLP does not protect the applicant from civil or criminal liability. 36.118

The SCA confirmed the validity of the CLP when it dismissed an appeal by *Agri Wire*[48] in which it argued that the CLP was invalid because the Commission is not empowered by the Act to grant leniency, and therefore, any evidence in terms of the CLP was unlawfully obtained. 36.119

H. Document creation and retention

In *Arcelormittal*,[49] the CAC ruled that respondents in a complaint referral to the Tribunal are entitled to discovery of the documents produced by a leniency applicant in support of a leniency application, unless these documents constitute information which is defined as "confidential information" in terms of the Act. 36.120

[48] *Agri Wire (Pty) Ltd and another v. Commissioner of the Competition Commission and others* (660/2011) [2012] ZASCA 134; [2012] 4 All SA 365 (SCA); 2013 (5) SA 484 (SCA) (September 27, 2012).

[49] *Arcelormittal South Africa Ltd. and another v. Competition Commission and others* (103/CAC/Sep10) [2012] ZACAC 1 (April 2, 2012).

37

SPAIN

Edurne Navarro Varona
Uría Menéndez Abogados

Introduction

37.01 Cartel investigations are considered the main priority for national and regional competition authorities in Spain. According to the data published by the National Competition Commission (NCC) in its 2011–2012 Report (November 2011 to July 2012) decisions involving anticompetitive agreements represented 68 percent of the cases ending with a sanction and 74 percent of the total amount of fines. The second area of interest is abuse of dominant position (mainly in relation to the behavior of dominant companies in regulated sectors and the fees charged by intellectual property collecting societies). The rest of the activity of the NCC has focused on unfair competition practices with impact on the public interest.

37.02 The current Spanish competition law framework entered into force in 2007, following a modernization process that was widely supported by all political parties in Spain. In addition, by virtue of Act 3/2013[1] there was a significant change in the enforcement bodies. As a result the NCC has merged with other sector regulators (energy, telecommunications, air transport, etc.). Although this change has not affected substantive regulation, it has had an impact on the authority, but whether it will change its priorities remains to be seen.

I. Acting alone

Anticompetitive unilateral conducts under Spanish competition law may be addressed under both article 2 and article 3 of Act 15/2007.[2] **37.03**

Article 2 declares illegal the abuse of a dominant position. For this prohibition to apply, two elements must be proven: (i) the existence of a dominant position in a certain market and (ii) an abusive act from the dominant company. **37.04**

As to the existence of a dominant position, the Spanish authorities, in line with the EU case law, have steadily identified dominance and commercial independence, holding that a company would be dominant in a market if it can decide its commercial policies without being concerned by the reaction of any other economic agent. **37.05**

As the precedents show, it is not always easy to assess the existence of a dominant position.[3] Traditionally, the first and main reference to identify a dominant position is the market share of the allegedly dominant company: the higher the market share, the more likely that the company may be dominant. However, as dominance is rooted in commercially independent behavior, the Spanish national and regional authorities seldom rely solely on market shares for declaring a dominant position, but also assess other related circumstances. These circumstances include mainly the following: evolution and structure of the market, existence of barriers to entry that refrain other operators from challenging the alleged dominant position, potential competition, vertical integration, or the degree of bargaining power held by the customers. **37.06**

In relation to the concept of abuse, article 2 does not provide a legal definition, but merely prohibits abuse and provides an indicative list of potentially abusive conducts. The abuse has long been defined as the use by a dominant company of its privileged market position to yield commercial advantages that would not be available in a competitive market and that is harmful to the interests of other operators or consumers. **37.07**

Article 2 of the Spanish Competition Act includes an indicative list of conducts that may be considered abuses of a dominant position and that include the following: **37.08**

(a) imposition of unfair prices or other commercial conditions (this category includes excessive pricing and similar behavior);
(b) limitation of production, distribution, or technical development;
(c) refusal to supply products or services;
(d) application of different commercial conditions to equivalent services, placing some competitors at a disadvantage compared to others; and
(e) bundling and tying.

This list is non-exhaustive, meaning that other conducts not expressly referred to in said provision may also be considered abusive if falling within the scope of the definition of abuse. **37.09**

[1] Act 3/2013 on the creation of the National Markets and Competition Commission (June 4, 2013).

[2] Act 15/2007 on the Defense of Competition (July 3, 2007) (the "Spanish Competition Act"). English versions of the Spanish Competition Act and Regulation are available at <http://www.cncompetencia.es/Default.aspx?TabId=81&pag=1>.

[3] Case R 362/99, *Bacardi* (September 30, 1999).

Sections I.A through I.N below deal with different kinds of unilateral practices that may amount to an abuse of dominant position.

37.10 Finally, it is worth mentioning that article 2 also prohibits the abuse of a joint dominant position. In these cases, although the dominant position is collective, the abuse is unilateral (even if there are parallel separate abuses by all the dominant companies). Under Spanish law, however, it is not always easy to draw the line between the abuse of a dominant position and conscious parallelism or even tacit collusion in oligopolistic markets. In recent times there have been few cases involving this kind of behavior. The NCC has recently revisited this concept in a case involving collective dominance in relation to mobile telephony services.[4] The arguments of the NCC supporting collective dominance in that case, however, are not particularly clear in the decision.

37.11 The Spanish Competition Act provides for another category of individual actions that may be considered restrictive and, as such, subject to the scrutiny of the competition enforcement authorities. Article 3 of this Act includes within the scope of anticompetitive behavior any act of unfair competition (*competencia desleal*) which (i) distorts competition in the market and (ii) affects the public interest.

37.12 Under the Spanish Unfair Competition Act, unfair behavior would include a wide range of conducts, such as selling at a loss, slandering or confusing advertising, legal infringements, etc.

37.13 Article 3 of the Competition Act has been scarcely applied due to the fact that in most cases the complaints under this provision refer to merely private disputes not affecting the public interest. In the last months, however, article 3 has been the basis of a series of decisions in the energy sector. These involved a behavior of certain electricity distributors that following an intended liberalization of the commercialization of electricity in Spain, would have automatically referred some customers that were formerly supplied by them to commercialization companies of their same group. This practice would be a violation of an energy regulation and, therefore, an act of unfair competition towards other commercialization companies that are not allowed to compete for these customers.[5]

37.14 In the last two years, the areas where the NCC has been more active in relation to abuse cases have been the collective management of intellectual property rights[6] and the transfer of the advantages enjoyed by certain energy companies in a regulated activity to other activities.[7] Aside from these cases, there has not been a significant amount of cases involving unilateral conduct in the last two years, as the authority is more focused in investigating cartel-type offenses.

A. Predatory pricing

37.15 Predatory pricing is among the conducts which have been traditionally considered abusive under the Spanish Competition Act without being included in the express list of abuses. The NCC has considered that a price set by a dominant undertaking may be predatory when (i) the price is set below costs, (ii) the dominant company pretends to exclude competitors (i.e. anticompetitive intent), and (iii) the behavior is suitable for excluding efficient competitors from the market.[8] More recently, the NCC has supported the full application in Spain of the Guidance on the EU Commission's enforcement priorities in applying article 102 of the

[4] Case S/0248/10, *SMS* (December 19, 2012).
[5] Case S/0213/10, *Iberdrola SUR* (February 24, 2012) and Case S/0304/10, *Endesa* (June 11, 2012).
[6] Case S/0220/10, *SGAE* (July 3, 2012) or Case S/0297/10, *AGEDI* (November 19, 2010).
[7] Case S/0003/07, *E.On* (November 8, 2011), or Case S/2795/07 *Hidrocantábrico* (September 20, 2011).
[8] Case R 718/07, *Puertos de Andalucía* (March 13, 2008).

Treaty on the Functioning of the European Union (TFEU) to abusive exclusionary conduct by dominant undertakings.[9] However, the number of abuse investigations in Spain remains lower than cases on restrictive agreements.

B. Exploitative offenses (excessive pricing, monopoly leveraging)

The difficulties appraising the excessive or abusive nature of the conditions applied by a dominant company have led to a relatively scarce case law in this area in Spain. **37.16**

In one of the leading cases in this area,[10] the NCC summarized the practice of the authority in determining the existence of excessive pricing. The NCC would consider the existence of excessive pricing in view of (i) the relation between prices and stand-alone costs (the broader the difference, the more likely the prices are abusive), (ii) comparison with prices for similar products in other geographic markets, and (iii) the absence of an economic rationale for the price level charged by the dominant company. **37.17**

In other cases, the comparison with previous pricing levels in the same market has also been used as a reference.[11] **37.18**

A significant number of excessive pricing cases have taken place in the field of management of intellectual property rights by collecting societies. In these cases, the NCC has insisted in the need to take into account the real economic value of the IP rights. **37.19**

Leveraging is another exploitative offense that has been analyzed by the Spanish competition authorities. These conducts include the behavior of a company that uses its dominant position in a market to gain influence in other related non-dominated markets. This kind of conducts may benefit the dominant company itself[12] or third companies associated to the dominant company.[13] **37.20**

C. Monopsony

There is no specific precedent in Spain regarding monopsonies. Before the entry into force of the Spanish Competition Act, the law also prohibited so-called abuses of economic dependence (which would in theory cover the restrictive behavior engaged in by monopsonies). However, this prohibition was almost never applied by the authorities and, therefore, was removed from the current Spanish Competition Act. It must be said, however, that the abuse of economic dependence is considered an act of unfair competition. Therefore, under article 3 of the Spanish Competition Act, such behavior may be punished if it has an impact on the public interest. **37.21**

D. Price discrimination

Price discrimination by dominant companies is considered abusive insofar as it implies applying different conditions to equivalent services. On the contrary, when the different customers are not in a comparable situation and the different conditions are related to the different position of the customers, there would be no abuse of dominant position.[14] **37.22**

Once the different treatment has been evidenced, the dominant company could prove the existence of an objective difference between the parties which justifies it. This objective **37.23**

[9] Case 2748/06, *Axion/Abertis II* (March 30, 2011).

[10] Case 626/07, *Explosivos Canarias* (February 12, 2008).

[11] *Iberdrola Generación*, Judgment of the Spanish National Court (*Audiencia Nacional*) (July 2, 2009).

[12] Case S/0089/08, *Unión Fenosa Instalación* (September 20, 2011).

[13] Case 513/01, *Tubogas/Repsol* (March 7, 2002).

[14] Case R 644/05, *Estaciones de Servicio* (May 19, 2005).

justification may result from a number of elements, such as the purchase of different volumes or the existence of a stable supply relationship with a customer against isolated orders from others.

37.24 The Spanish case law had traditionally admitted price discrimination favoring companies of the dominant undertaking's group. However, this traditional line has been recently amended by the NCC in the sense that the dominant undertaking may only favor its own subsidiary when the more favorable treatment is the result of normal competition tactics and was not aimed at foreclosing competitors from the market.[15]

37.25 An extreme form of price discrimination would consist in margin squeeze practices. In these cases, dominant vertically integrated companies raised the costs of competitors in an upstream market in order to favor their own businesses in competing downstream markets. Spanish competition authorities have also acted in this kind of cases.[16] As the NCC has only recently focused on cartel-type infringements, there has not been a significant amount of cases in this area.

E. Dictating or influencing resale prices

(i) Resale price maintenance

37.26 Under Spanish law, dictating or influencing resale prices is normally a behavior falling within the rules governing anticompetitive agreements rather than unilateral conduct. In this regard, direct or indirect vertical price fixing has been generally regarded by the Spanish competition authority as a serious violation of EU and Spanish competition law. This principle has been recently highlighted by the NCC in cases related to the automotive sector.[17]

37.27 Although this infringement results from an agreement rather than unilateral behavior, the NCC usually considers that the responsibility of the supplier in the infringement is generally more serious than the responsibility of the distributors, and sets fines accordingly.[18]

37.28 Pure price recommendations are normally not considered anticompetitive by the Spanish competition authorities. These conducts may, however, result in antitrust infringements when the supplier tries to enforce the application of the recommended price or most distributors follow the recommended price, turning it into a fixed price (especially if compliance with the recommended price is spurred by the supplier or monitored by competing distributors). Examples of such incentives may include cases where the wholesale price depends on the degree of compliance with the recommended price.[19]

37.29 Recently, there have been some cases involving vertical price-fixing in the automotive sector. In *Suzuki*,[20] for example, the NCC imposed fines on a vehicle manufacturer and its resellers in two Spanish provinces for agreements aiming at fixing the margin of agents and distributors.

(ii) Minimum advertised price programs

37.30 There have been no cases of minimum advertised price programs in Spain.

[15] Case S/0153/09, *Mediapro* (March 17, 2011).
[16] Case S/0207/09, *Transporte Televisión* (February 8, 2012).
[17] Case S/0237/10, *Motocicletas* (March 27, 2012).
[18] Case 612/06, *Aceites 2* (June 21, 2007).
[19] Case 652/07, *Repsol/CEPSA/BP* (July 30, 2009).
[20] Case S/0237/10, *Suzuki* (March 27, 2012).

F. Tying arrangements

As with leveraging,[21] the risk posed by this conduct is that the dominant company may extend its dominance to other markets to the detriment of its competitors. The NCC has stated that when the tied-in supplementary services are objectively justified and relate to the main products or services, tying may not be abusive.[22] **37.31**

Tying does not only include an imposition of acquiring both products, but it is enough for the dominant company to offer better conditions in the first (and dominated) product if the second is acquired.[23] Since the NCC has recently focused on cartel-type infringements, there has not been a significant amount of cases in this area. **37.32**

G. Exclusive dealing

The Spanish competition authorities have stated that the restrictive effect of the exclusivity clause in dominance cases becomes abusive when it entails a significant impact on competition.[24] **37.33**

In this regard, the NCC has considered that one of the main criteria for determining the abusive character of exclusivity clauses is the duration of the clauses. Long-term exclusive agreements are obviously suitable for foreclosing the market to competitors, while minor terms could be compatible with competition law (again, if objectively justified).[25] There is no clear-cut rule as to the acceptable duration of these obligations. It would largely depend on the market in question and the commercial and economic rationales supporting the need for an exclusive arrangement. As in recent times the NCC has focused on cartel-type infringements, there has not been a significant amount of cases in this area. **37.34**

H. Refusal to deal

Article 2 expressly includes a general obligation on dominant undertakings to deal with third parties. Thus, the refusal to supply by a dominant undertaking might in some cases amount to an abuse of dominant position. **37.35**

Starting from the principle that companies should be free to decide what commercial relationships they wish to engage in, the refusal to supply from a dominant company is abusive when it refers to products that are required by its customers to compete and such negative eliminates competition in the market and harms consumers.[26] **37.36**

However, a refusal to supply would not be restrictive if it is grounded on objective and non-discriminatory reasons (such as, for example, requiring certain qualifications for the supply or timely payment of invoices). **37.37**

The Spanish competition authorities also admit partial refusals to deal when the dominant company evidences that there are objective limitations to the full supply (such as a shortage). Also, there is no refusal to supply when the dominant company accepts to negotiate a supply agreement, but the negotiations between the parties fail due to the impossibility of reaching reasonable terms. As in recent times the NCC has focused on cartel-type infringements, there has not been a significant amount of cases in this area. **37.38**

---

21 See Section I.C.
22 Case S/0078/08, *eBay* (February 23, 2009).
23 Case 412/97, *BT v. Telefónica* (January 21, 1999).
24 Case 413/97, *Airtel v. Telefónica* (February 26, 1999).
25 Case 646/08, *Axión/Abertis* (May 19, 2009).
26 Case S/0176/09, *Sedifa* (June 9, 2010).

I. Essential facilities

37.39 A special case of refusals to deal is the application of the essential facilities doctrine. The Spanish competition authorities have admitted the principles of this doctrine as applied by the EU Commission and courts.[27]

37.40 Most of the references made by the Spanish antitrust authorities to essential facilities do not involve physical facilities, but access to information. It has been deemed abusive for a dominant company to refuse third parties access to commercial information that constitutes a competitive advantage and that is used by the dominant company's subsidiaries or affiliates.[28]

37.41 The Spanish competition authorities have held that the essential facilities doctrine would not apply when the relevant assets can be replicated or are not really necessary for competing.[29] An example of this unnecessary (though certainly convenient) asset that is not an essential facility would be the access to a quality brand.[30] As in recent times the NCC has focused on cartel-type infringements, there has not been a significant amount of cases in this area.

J. Bundling (including loyalty and market share discounts)

37.42 The Spanish competition authorities have held that pure loyalty discounts granted by dominant companies are always abusive. An example of this would be a discount scheme whereby the advantage was linked to the total acquisitions made through a particular channel rather than linked to the volume of sales of the product subject to the rebate.[31]

37.43 In relation to growth discounts (i.e. discounts granted in relation to the increase in the acquisitions made to the dominant undertaking within a certain period), the Spanish competition authorities have indicated that it is relevant to assess the real fidelity-enhancing effect of the scheme (i.e. its suitability for foreclosing the market to competitors). This fidelity-enhancing effect would depend on the structure and level of the discount and its ability to induce the acquirer to increase its sales to enjoy the benefit of the discount.[32] The same fidelity-enhancing effect may be found when a dominant firm uses discount policies to reward the attainment of certain level of sales obtaining a *de facto* exclusivity.[33]

37.44 A discount policy may be also abusive when it hides a predatory strategy.[34] It can pose a risk to the company involved if it falls within the scope of the guidelines provided by the European Commission's Article 102 Guidance.[35]

K. Standard-setting groups (disclosure requirements, licensing arrangements, and licensing pools)

37.45 In the past, the Spanish competition authorities have not opposed to agreements creating technical standards in the telecommunications sector[36] or metal trading.[37] These agreements or groups must not, however, establish standards that may be deemed to foreclose the market to potential or actual competitors.

---

[27] Case 518/01, *Internautas v. Telefónica* (April 29, 2002).
[28] The most significant case in this regard is *Tubogas/Repsol* (n 13).
[29] Case R 35/08, *Distribución de Gas Alicante 2* (May 4, 2009).
[30] Case S/0087/08, *AENOR* (May 5, 2009).
[31] Case 470/99, *COFAS* (September 1, 2000).
[32] Case 514/01, *Iberia* (April 1, 2002).
[33] Case 568/03, *Asempre/Correos* (February 7, 2003).
[34] See Section I.B.
[35] Guidance on the Commission's enforcement priorities in applying [Article 102 TFEU] to abusive exclusionary conduct by dominant undertakings, OJ C 45, February 24, 2009 ("Article 102 Guidance").
[36] Case A 304/01, *Pagos por Móvil* (September 15, 2002).
[37] Case A 267/99, *Almacenistas de Hierros* (April 12, 2000).

L. Termination of intermediaries (retailers, wholesalers, dealers, and value-added resellers, agents, and brokers)

See Section I.N. **37.46**

M. Termination of relationships with competitors

Termination of contractual relationships by a dominant company is an extreme form of refusal to deal and, as such, may be considered abusive under Spanish law. Again, it would be possible for a dominant undertaking to escape the charges of abuse by evidencing the existence of an objective justification for terminating commercial relationships. Among accepted justifications may be a change in the economic balance between the parties[38] or a sudden change in the pattern of supply to wholesalers.[39] As the NCC has recently focused on cartel-type infringements, there has not been a significant amount of cases in this area. **37.47**

N. Exemptions

The Spanish Competition Act only provides for two exemptions for restrictive unilateral conducts: the application of the *de minimis* rule and the so-called legal exemption. **37.48**

De minimis rule. Under article 5 of the Spanish Competition Act any restrictive behavior (including potential abuses) that has not enough entity as to affect competition in the market is considered exempted under a *de minimis* rule. In practice, however, from a conceptual perspective, it seems difficult to imagine a *de minimis* abuse of dominant position in view of the very concept of dominance. **37.49**

Legal exemption. Article 4 of the Spanish Competition Act provides that any conduct that is imposed by law is automatically exempt from competition law. Therefore, a dominant company that is compelled by law to charge certain prices or to apply certain commercial conditions would not incur in an abuse of dominant position. **37.50**

II. Dealing with competitors

Article 1 of the Spanish Competition Act prohibits all kind of "agreements, decisions, collective recommendations, or concerted or consciously parallel practices that have as their object, produce or may produce the effect of impeding, restricting or distorting competition in all or part of the national market." Spanish law and its enforcer follow the path of EU competition law in relation to restrictive agreements (with the exception of the prohibition of consciously parallel conducts). **37.51**

For an agreement to be restrictive it must have an object contrary to competition (i.e. per se restrictions such as horizontal price fixing or market allocations) or a negative effect on competition. But the anticompetitive intent is not a legal requisite for the prohibition to apply. **37.52**

In relation to the different forms assigned to restrictive behaviors involving competitors, Spanish law includes the following: **37.53**

- First of all, anticompetitive agreements cover all range of contracts or covenants between two parties, from legally binding contracts to gentlemen's agreements, verbal or in writing. To this effect, a concurrence of at least two separate wills must operate (this requisite leaves outside the scope of the prohibition intra-group agreements).

[38] Case R 424/00, *Distribuidora Peña Sagra* (June 23, 2000).
[39] Case R 611/04, *Spain Pharma/Glaxo* (October 13, 2004).

- Second, collective decisions or recommendations mainly refer to the action of professional associations or bodies (although technically they may be unilateral, the associative and representative nature of the association may be equivalent to an agreement between competitors).
- Third, concerted practices are a looser version of collusion, where an anticompetitive behavior is followed by the participant in a market without an express agreement between them.
- Finally, the Spanish Competition Act forbids acts of so-called "conscious parallelism." The prohibition of this behavior is the main substantive difference between Spanish and EU competition law. It implies situations where operators do not reach any kind of express or tacit agreement, but act in the market with the aim of avoiding discordance with other operators, being able to know in advance the position of its competitors.[40] This figure, however, is seldom used in practice, and its application resembles to that of tacit coordination under EU law.

37.54 The Spanish Competition Act offers a range of exemptions to anticompetitive agreements broader than in the case of unilateral conducts:

37.55 De minimis *rule*. Article 5 of the Spanish Competition Act foresees that agreements that are not suitable for significantly harming competition are exempted from the article 1 prohibition. To this effect, the Competition Regulation has established some exceptions resembling those of the EU Commission's Notice on the same object. It is worth noting that normally agreements between competitors with a joint market share below 10 percent are exempted. This percentage is raised to 15 percent in relation to agreements between non competing operators (vertical agreements).

37.56 *Legal exemption*. As indicated above, any conduct that is imposed by law is automatically exempt from competition law.[41] The Supreme Court has pointed out that it is not necessary that the law imposes the anticompetitive behavior, but it is enough that it allows it.[42]

37.57 *Block exemptions*. In Spain, EU block exemption regulations are also applied to merely national situations. In addition, the Government can pass national block exemptions. This possibility has been used only once, with an exemption for default registries that was in force between 2006 and 2011.

37.58 *Individual exemptions*. Finally, restrictive agreements may also be declared compatible with competition law if they meet certain criteria that mirror those of article 101.3 TFEU: (1) the agreement must contribute to the improvement of production or commercialization and distribution of goods and services or to the promotion of technical or economic progress; (2) consumers must be allowed to participate adequately in the benefits; (3) unnecessary restrictions to achieve the intended objective must not be imposed; and (4) competition in respect of a substantial part of the products or services in question must not be eliminated.

37.59 As indicated, article 1 investigations represent most of the cases investigated by the Spanish authorities, especially in relation to horizontal agreements between competitors and cartels. According to the NCC 2011–12 report, during this period, article 1 investigations represented roughly two thirds of all cases resulting in the imposition of fines.

A. Horizontal price fixing (including advanced announcements of price or product changes)

37.60 The Spanish competition authorities regard competition in prices as a cornerstone of a competitive market. Therefore, any agreement between competitors regarding horizontal

[40] Case R 437/00, *Laboratorios Farmacéuticos* (January 26, 2005).
[41] Case R 722/07, *Video Clubs de Cataluña* (May 19, 2008).
[42] Case 3821/2010, *Repsol*, Supreme Court Judgment (July 6, 2010).

price-fixing is considered by the enforcers as one of the most serious infringements of Spanish competition law.

Horizontal price-fixing agreements will be considered as objectively anticompetitive and, therefore, in face of evidence of the existence of any of these agreements, the authorities would not need to evidence the effect of these agreements. These kinds of agreements are even excluded from the *de minimis* exemption. **37.61**

Horizontal price-fixing agreements reach its most crude expression in hard core cartels, where companies directly agree on the application of a certain level of prices.[43] In recent years, the fighting against this kind of practices has greatly benefited from the entry into force of the leniency program in 2008. However, the Spanish competition authorities closely examine any complaint or indicia of horizontal price fixing. **37.62**

Price-fixing agreements also include any kind of arrangement aiming at unifying prices in a given market, including indirect strategies, such as agreeing on elements of the price (such as discounts). They also include horizontal price recommendations (including recommendations issued in the context of a professional association[44]) and even maximum prices.[45] **37.63**

B. Horizontal agreements to allocate customers or territories; agreements not to compete

Market and customers allocation follow horizontal price fixing in the scale of priorities of the Spanish competition authorities and is expressly forbidden by article 1(1)(c) of the Spanish Competition Act. This kind of agreement is normally investigated as part of a cartel.[46] **37.64**

The assessment of this type of practice is similar to horizontal price fixing. It is common that cartel agreements combine price-fixing and market/customer allocation.[47] However, market or customer allocation may also be considered as independent infringement where, for example, some competitors allocate turns to serve certain customers.[48] **37.65**

Non-compete covenants may be a mere instrument for market/customer allocation and, as such, may be analyzed as such infringements. Outside these cases, non-compete covenants are generally accepted by the NCC as ancillary restrictions both in relation to merger control cases or to other licit agreements (joint purchasing, distribution, etc.). In these cases, however, if the NCC finds out that the non-compete covenant falls outside the scope of the ancillary character normally admissible, it will assess the clause under article 1 of the Competition Act and consider it restrictive of competition.[49] In this regard, as a general rule, the Spanish competition authorities rely on EU competition law for guidance as to the concept of ancillary restrictions. **37.66**

C. Horizontal boycotts

Horizontal boycotts, whereby a group of operators agree to implement some measures to exclude a competitor from the market, have also been considered a serious infringement of the Spanish Competition Act. The Spanish competition authorities focus their assessment **37.67**

[43] Case S/0179/09, *Hormigón y productos relacionados* (January 12, 2012) or Case S/0244/10, *Navieras Baleares* (November 20, 2012).

[44] Case 387/96, *Películas Video* (May 11, 1998).

[45] Cases A 364/07, *Tasas Intercambio/Sistema 4B* (October 10, 2012) and S/0198/09, *ANCCE* (May 17, 2011).

[46] Cases S/0287/10, *Postensado y Geotecnia* (August 2, 2012) or S/192/09, *Asfaltos* (October 26, 2011).

[47] Case 648/08, *Hormigones Cantabria* (July 22, 2009).

[48] Case 639/08, *Colegios Farmacéuticos Castilla-La Mancha* (June 18, 2012).

[49] Case S/0014/07, *Gestión de Residuos Sanitarios* (January 18, 2010).

on the likelihood of this kind of behavior to limit the commercial freedom of the boycotted operators and to foreclose markets to open competition.[50] To date, the Spanish competition authorities have identified and sanctioned boycotts in all kind of sectors.

37.68 It must be noted that a boycott may take place at the recommendation from a trade association. In this case, the NCC may decide to focus only on one infringement and consider that the acts of the association aimed at excluding competitors from the market are more appropriately addressed as a restrictive collective recommendation.[51] As in recent times the NCC has focused on cartel-type infringements, there has not been a significant amount of cases in this area.

D. Joint ventures and other competitive collaborations

37.69 Joint ventures can be considered either a transaction subject to merger control rules or a cooperation agreement between economic operators. A joint venture will qualify as a merger when it performs all the functions of an independent economic entity on a permanent basis. If a joint venture meets this requirement (that mirrors full-function requirements under EU merger control regime), it will be subject to the rules on merger control and will be notified if the legal thresholds are met. If such thresholds are not met, the transaction would not have to comply with any other procedure and should not be subject to scrutiny as an anticompetitive agreement.

37.70 When full-function is not achieved, the agreement will qualify as cooperation between economic operators.[52] In its assessment, the NCC takes into account the provisions of the EU block exemption regulations and even the possibility of applying an individual exemption under article 1(3) of the Spanish Competition Act.[53]

37.71 In case of doubt, Spanish merger control rules allow the parties to submit a formal consultation on the existence of a merger to the NCC. These cases are especially sensitive, as there is a risk that the consultation may lead to the opening of infringement procedures against the parties.[54]

E. Trade associations

37.72 The activities of trade associations have been a focus of the NCC in recent years. In December 2009, the NCC published a Guide for Trade Associations providing guidance in order to avoid potentially restrictive practices.[55]

37.73 There have been a number of cases involving the recommendations and decisions issued by this kind of entities. In some occasions the infringements can be assimilated to typical antitrust cases (price fixing, boycotts, etc.). In most cases involving trade associations, however, the investigated behavior covered recommended practices (both in relation to prices and commercial conditions).

37.74 A separate mention should be made to the investigation of the NCC in relation to trade associations involving professionals (such as engineers, lawyers, architects, etc.). These associations have traditionally had certain self-regulating powers in the organization of the

---

50 Case 423/98, *Asisa* (November 22, 2001).
51 Case 649/08, *Productos Farmacéuticos Genéricos* (March 24, 2009).
52 Case A 365/07, *Cargill/Piema* (August 2, 2007).
53 *Press Clipping*, Supreme Court, Judgment of May 17, 2011.
54 Case S/0232/10, *Prisa/Zeta* (November 24, 2011).
55 NCC Guide to Competition Assessment, <http://www.cncompetencia.es/Inicio/Informes/GuiasyRecomendaciones/tabid/177/Default.aspx>.

professional activities of their members. The Spanish competition authorities have acted to avoid that these faculties do not protect unnecessary restrictions of competition.[56]

F. Interlocking directorates

There is no provision under Spanish law regarding interlocking directorates. However, it is worth noting that this fact would be taken into account in merger control as an indicium of possible coordination effects. **37.75**

Therefore, in some merger control cases, the NCC has expressly conditioned the clearance of the transaction to the avoidance of interlocking directorates.[57] A recent judgment has also indirectly addressed this problem in confirming the refusal of a company to deliver commercial information to one shareholder that was also a competitor, and even having a legal right to that information under Spanish Company Law, on the grounds that the access to that information may lead to an infringement of competition law.[58] **37.76**

G. Facilitating practices

There are no cases in Spain where facilitating practices have been declared infringements of the Spanish Competition Act. **37.77**

H. Information exchange

Information exchanges are a particular form of cooperation between companies that may lead to a collusive result. Historically, Spanish antitrust authorities have followed the line marked by the EU Commission and Courts. Recently, however, the Spanish approach to this practice has become more rigid, to the point of considering that certain long-term information exchanges on strategic issues could be identified with a hard core cartel.[59] **37.78**

It must be noted that the NCC considers that future price information is always sensitive and, as such, even a slight interchange of information in this regard may lead to sanctions.[60] **37.79**

Information exchanges may take the form of statistics compiled by a third party or a trade association. In these cases, the compatibility of the statistics may be checked on a case-by-case basis, in view of the characteristics of the affected markets and the mechanisms for the preparation of statistics. As a general rule, the more recent, sensitive and disaggregated the information, the more likely the prohibition will apply.[61] On the contrary, historic, non-sensitive and aggregated information should not be a source of concern.[62] **37.80**

In this regard, the Spanish competition authorities consider that an exchange of information between competitors is restrictive when the information is relevant to the commercial strategy of any competitor (which would depend on the market) and facilitates coordination.[63] **37.81**

Finally, it is worth noting that until December 2011 there was a national exemption regulation in Spain on information exchanges regarding bad debtors which allowed companies to share recent information in certain cases. In recent months, exchanges of information have **37.82**

---

[56] Cases S/0292/10, *Colegios Procuradores* or S/0357/11, *Colegios Agentes Propiedad Inmobiliaria* (April 17, 2012).

[57] Case C/0098/08, *Gas Natural/Unión Fenosa* (September 20, 2010).

[58] Case 14866/2011, *Takata Petri A.G.*, Judgment of the Court of Appeal of Madrid (November 25, 2011).

[59] Case S/0086/08, *Peluquería Profesional* (March 2, 2011).

[60] Case S/0280/10, *Suzuki/Honda* (January 19, 2012).

[61] Case A 360/06, *Estadística Cerveceros 2* (July 11, 2007).

[62] Case A 296/01, *Anuario Videográfico* (March 17, 2005).

[63] Case 588/05, *Distribuidores de Cine* (March 26, 2013).

appeared as one particular focus of interest to the CNC, either as stand-alone cases or (more commonly) as part of wider anticompetitive practices.

I. Joint purchasing agreements

37.83 Joint purchasing agreements have been analyzed by the Spanish competition authorities in a number of cases. Although the perspective of two competitors jointly covering their needs for supply may be anticompetitive (as it eliminates uncertainty as to a cost element and may create incentives for coordination), this kind of agreement may also have efficiencies as it may help to balance the otherwise strong bargaining power of suppliers. In this regard, the key element in the assessment would be the parties' market share and the position of suppliers[64] and the percentage of shared costs associated to the agreement. In any event, joint purchasing agreements are only compatible with competition rules if they preserve the freedom of the parties to set the final prices of the acquired products (otherwise it would become a horizontal price-fixing agreement).

37.84 Joint selling agreements are more rarely tolerated by the NCC, as the risk of coordination is normally higher (involving avoiding competition in sales). In these cases, the NCC normally requires the parties to remove any concern regarding future coordination and guarantee the commercial freedom of the parties.[65] Joint selling agreements have also been subject of interest in merger control cases, as it is not uncommon that the NCC limits the joint commercialization of the products of the resulting entity.[66]

J. Joint lobbying/regulatory/legislative efforts

37.85 In principle, joint lobbying should be considered the legitimate object of a professional association. In areas subject to regulation by public authorities, the possibility that the representatives of all interested parties may have the chance of intervening in the regulatory process could be even considered as desirable.

37.86 Although there are not many cases where the Spanish competition authorities have investigated lobbying activities under antitrust law, they have indicated that the intervention of a professional association before the public authorities in an effort to influence future regulation on prices may be anticompetitive. This would be the case if there is an asymmetry between the information available to the companies and to the public administration and the companies do not provide reliable information with the purpose of obtaining a more favorable pricing environment.[67]

III. General issues

A. Jurisdiction and applicable law (including sector-specific competition regulation)

37.87 The substantive legal framework of competition law in Spain is determined by both articles 101 and 102 TFEU (applicable by Spanish enforcement agencies and courts through articles 5 and 6 of EU Regulation 1/2003) and the Spanish Competition Act.

[64] Case A 320/02, *Cinesa* or Case 605/05, *Juguetes Cataluña.*
[65] Case S/0246/10, *Vocento/Godó* (June 30, 2011).
[66] Case C 0432/12, *Antena 3/La Sexta* (March 21, 2012).
[67] Case S/0256/10, *Inspecciones Periódicas de Gas* (July 30, 2012).

The jurisdiction test for the application of the Spanish Competition Act is that the anticompetitive practices have or may have an impact on any Spanish market, regardless the place where the practices took place. 37.88

Sector regulation, particularly in the energy and telecommunications markets, include references to the need to safeguard a competitive environment and most sector policies are aimed at increasing competition and protecting new entrants from the market power of incumbent operators managing energy or communications networks. In spite of the foregoing, competition law is common to all sectors and is uniformly applied by the NCC (and when applicable the regional competition authorities). The interaction between competition law and sector regulation is expected to develop as the NCC merged with other regulators.[68] 37.89

B. Antitrust System

(i) Name of agency/agencies

The main body in charge of the application of competition law in Spain was the NCC, recently replaced by the National Market and Competition Commission (NMCC) (see para. 37.98). The latter comprises the Competition Directorate (*Dirección de Competencia*) is in charge of investigating cases and handling complaints and leniency applications, and the Council (*Consejo*) which is in charge of adopting the final decisions. 37.90

In addition, Spanish law provides for the existence of regional enforcement agencies, which are competent to investigate restrictive behaviors that do not exceed the territory of one Spanish region. As of January 2014, eight Spanish regions have independent regional competition enforcement agencies (Andalucía, Aragón, Castilla y León, Cataluña, Extremadura, Galicia, País Vasco, and Valencia) and three others (Madrid, Canarias, and Murcia) have investigation agencies, referring the cases to the Council of the NMCC for decision. The regional enforcement agencies must coordinate their actions with the NMCC. 37.91

Finally, Spanish civil courts may also directly apply competition.[69] 37.92

(ii) Staff size and budget

According to its last public report (covering 2010 and 2011), the NCC's staff includes 189 persons: 22 senior staff, 84 technical staff, and 83 support and auxiliary staff. 37.93

In 2011, the NCC's budget amounted to EUR 12,647,850, representing a EUR 600,000 decrease from 2010. The budget is allocated as follows: human resources, 77 percent; material resources, 19 percent; and institutional activities, 4 percent. Regional antitrust agencies differ in size and resources, from large well-organized institutions to smaller ones. 37.94

(iii) Recent enforcement actions and trends

In recent years, the NCC had identified some particular priorities in the enforcement of competition law. 37.95

First, the NCC investigated compliance with its past decisions. To this effect, it created a particular division within the Investigation Directorate entrusted with ensuring that all the decisions taken by the Council were effectively applied. This trend resulted in a number of infringement proceedings and economic sanctions. 37.96

Second, the NCC focused on the compliance with competition law of public bodies. To this effect, it declared that public bodies participating in anticompetitive agreements are 37.97

[68] See Section III.B(iii).
[69] See Section III.F.

also liable and subject to fines.[70] It also published a guide on public procurement and competition, indicating how public tenders should be organized and a set of recommendations to public authorities for more efficient and pro-competitive market regulation.[71] Finally, it started challenging in the Spanish administrative courts public tenders organized by regional governments that may have excluded competitors from the bid.

37.98 Lastly, the biggest challenge of antitrust enforcement in Spain has been the substitution of the NCC by another body, that merges the former NCC with other seven sector regulators (energy, telecommunications, postal services, railways, airports, audiovisual activities and game) in order to create a National Market and Competition Commission. This new institution, that has been widely criticized, started operating on October 4, 2013.

37.99 There is a risk that the new body, in charge of a number of sectors, loses the focus on competition issues and that the enforcement of competition law in Spain may be affected. Also, it is expected that the new institution results in a reduction of the staff currently devoted to competition enforcement.

C. Private litigation

37.100 Private litigation is still a pending issue in competition law enforcement in Spain. Since the entry into force of the Spanish Competition Act, the number of civil cases involving the enforcement of competition law has increased. However, these cases are still rare. Claimants in these cases normally request that the courts award them damages for an anticompetitive harm or (more often) confirm that a clause deemed anticompetitive is null and void. Interim injunctions can also be sought for the courts in order to avoid anticompetitive damage while the process is pending.

37.101 It is worth noting, however, that there has been abundant recourse to private litigation in cases against gas stations and oil companies. Indeed, as early as 1993, the Spanish civil courts have decided on stand-alone actions based on competition law regarding the long-term exclusivity agreements in the retail distribution of fuel.[72]

D. Follow-on litigation (includes role of agency determinations of liability for follow-on litigation)

37.102 Before the entry into force of the current Spanish Competition Act, follow-on actions were possible but rare, due to the fact that a final administrative decision was required for the plaintiff to be able to claim damages. In follow-on cases, the Spanish civil courts do not challenge the findings of the NCC in its decisions.

37.103 It is worth noting a recent series of judgments in a famous follow-on set of actions in relation to a decision of the Spanish antitrust authority in relation to the sugar markets.[73] These judgments have completely supported the findings of the administrative decisions and have resulted in interesting findings. In particular, and although it is common in other areas, it has been the first time that a Spanish court has expressly admitted the passing-on defense in a competition case.[74]

---

[70] Case S/0167/09, *Productores Uva y Mosto de Jerez* (October 6, 2011), decision partially overturned by the Spanish Courts.

[71] Both documents are available in English at <http://www.cncompetencia.es/Default.aspx?TabId=81&pag=1>.

[72] From the first Judgment of the Supreme Court in this area, Case 9269/1993, *Campsa*, (December 30, 1993) to the last one, Case 6211/2012, *Total España S.A.U.* (September 28, 2012).

[73] Case 426/1998, *Sugar* (April 15, 1999).

[74] Judgments of the Court of Appeal of Valladolid of October 9, 2009 (case 1185/2009, *Nestlé España and others*) of the Supreme Court of June 8, 2012 (case 5462/2012, *Galletas Gullón and others*) and of November 7, 2013 (case 659/2013, *Nestlé España and others*).

E. Arbitration and alternative dispute resolution

Competition law has been also subject to private enforcement in arbitral courts. This application, however, is less publicized as the decisions of the arbiters are not public. In this regard, it is worth noting that, in at least one case, the Spanish courts have annulled the arbitral decision applying competition law because the parties had not included competition law pleadings in their submissions.[75] **37.104**

F. Remedies

Under the Spanish Competition Act, the most direct remedy against anticompetitive behavior is provided by the intervention of the NCC and includes the possibility of imposing fines and ordering the infringing companies to cease-and-desist from their conduct. Almost all decisions declaring the existence of an infringement include these two remedies. In addition, the NCC may impose on the parties affirmative obligations aimed at avoiding future antitrust concerns, such as modifying existing contracts with third parties.[76] **37.105**

(i) Civil liability

In addition to the intervention of the NCC (or a regional competition authority), the parties may seek relief against an anticompetitive behavior from civil courts. Since the entry into force of the Competition Act in 2007, Spanish civil courts have competence to declare the existence of antitrust infringements and declare the civil liability of the alleged infringing party. They already had this possibility in applying EU law since the entry into force of Regulation 1/2003. **37.106**

So far, the role of Spanish civil courts in the enforcement of competition law has been limited, in part due to the difficulty of evidencing the existence of certain antitrust infringements before a civil court and in part to the traditionally restrictive application of tort law in Spain. **37.107**

Any person who has been harmed by a competition infringement is entitled to damages, covering both the actual and the potential losses (i.e. *damnum emergens* and *lucrum cessans*). The injured person would have to evidence before the court (i) the existence and extent of the damage, (ii) the existence of an illicit behavior of the plaintiff, and (iii) the causal link between this behavior and the alleged damages. **37.108**

(ii) Criminal liability

Spanish competition law is exclusively administrative and, therefore, infringers are not subject to criminal liability. It must be noted, however, that the Spanish Criminal Code includes certain offenses that are related to competition infringements and may eventually lead to imprisonment. These offenses include manipulating the offer of raw materials and essential products to cause a shortage in the market and applying price increases resulting from (i) the provision of false information or (ii) the use of violence, threats, or privileged information. Bid-rigging may also be subject to prison sentences. **37.109**

These provisions have been scarcely applied by the criminal courts and never within the context of an antitrust offense. **37.110**

G. Leniency and immunity

Since 2007 Spain has had a leniency program for cartel cases. It has been very successful, leading to several dawn raids and investigations. **37.111**

---

[75] Judgment of the Court of Appeals of Madrid of March 30, 2007 (*Cespa/Athisa*).

[76] *Axión/Abertis* (n 24).

37.112 The first company requesting leniency may obtain a 100 percent exemption from the fine if it can provide the NCC with sufficient relevant evidence to support a cartel charge. Further leniency applicants may obtain fine reductions from 50 percent to 10 percent, according to the order of their requests. Leniency applications entail the obligation for the companies to fully cooperate with the investigation and not challenging the facts that the NCC may include in the Statement of Facts and the Proposed Decision. It also entails that the leniency applicant cannot destroy any document that may be evidence of the investigated behavior.

37.113 Leniency applications are dealt with by a special division within the Investigation Directorate.

H. Document creation and retention

37.114 There is no particular rule under Spanish competition law regarding the creation and retention of documents. As a general rule, companies are required by law to preserve any commercial communications and documents for five years. Once this time has lapsed, the companies are free to destroy these documents.

37.115 There is a particular rule imposing the retention of documents: the cooperation obligation on a leniency applicant including the preservation of any potential evidence related to the investigation. Failure to comply with this obligation may lead to the withdrawal of the leniency.

37.116 The NCC has never challenged a document retention policy implemented by a company.

38

SWEDEN

Marcus Glader

Vinge

Introduction

The Swedish competition law rules are laid down in the Swedish Competition Act (2008:579) (the "Competition Act"). **38.01**

Sections 2:1–2:2 and 2:7 of the Competition Act contain two main prohibitions: a ban against agreements or concerted practices among undertakings which restrict competition and a ban against the abuse of a dominant position. **38.02**

These provisions mirror their EU counterparts in articles 101 and 102 of the Treaty on the Functioning of the European Union (TFEU), with the exception that a practice does not have to affect trade between member states to contravene Swedish competition law. According to the preparatory works underlying the Competition Act, the Swedish rules shall also be applied in a consistent manner with EU competition law. Furthermore, EU block exemption regulations have been made applicable under the Swedish rules and the Swedish Competition Authority (SCA) has issued a notice similar to the EU Commission's *de minimis* **38.03**

Notice.[1] In addition, where conduct by one or several undertakings may affect trade between EU member states and the EU rules apply, the Swedish Competition Authority and relevant courts shall also apply articles 101 and 102 TFEU (Council Regulation 1/2003, art. 3(1)).

38.04 The Competition Act also lays down the Swedish merger control rules (ss. 4:1–4:21), and includes specific rules governing sales activities conducted by public entities (ss. 3:27–3:32).

38.05 The public enforcement remedies available to the SCA include injunctions ordering an undertaking to terminate a competition law infringement (s. 3:1) and decisions to accept voluntary commitments to bring a perceived infringement to an end (s. 3:4). However, the SCA does not have the authority to impose administrative fines unless the company accepts such a fine (ss. 3:16–3:18). In disputed cases, the SCA must bring an action seeking administrative fines before the Stockholm City Court, and this court's decision may subsequently be appealed to the Market Court.

38.06 With regard to enforcement priorities and trends, the SCA has increased its dawn raid activities during the past few years. In most of cases the SCA has nevertheless closed its investigations fairly quickly, which suggests that the evidentiary threshold for carrying out a surprise inspection is relatively low. These inspections have involved suspected cartel infringements as well as abuses of dominance. Abuse investigations are particularly complex and resource consuming, and the SCA has only brought a few cases in recent years. A particular feature of the Swedish system is the possibility for a complainant, in cases where the SCA has closed its investigation, to bring the matter before the Market Court. A number of private litigants have successfully brought such claims, in which the Market Court essentially becomes the first and last instance. Another feature is the specific rules applicable to sales activities by public entities (see paras 38.10–38.11) which were recently introduced in the Swedish Competition Act. The SCA is currently pursuing the first court cases under these provisions.

38.07 In the following, a brief overview of different abuse categories is provided in Section I; agreements among undertakings are discussed in Section II; and general issues are presented in Section III. Given the close relationship between the EU and Swedish competition law, and to avoid too much repetition, EU practice will be used as the backdrop for this presentation. Consequently, the following overview is best read in conjunction with the chapter on EU competition law (Chapter 12).

I. Acting alone

A. Dominance

38.08 Unilateral conduct by a firm that occupies a dominant position may infringe s. 2:7 of the Competition Act. Relevant factors for determining dominance include high (absolute and relative) markets shares, barriers to entry, financial strength, the power and position of counterparties, the maturity of the market, etc. (see Chapter 12).

38.09 Furthermore, under specific rules applicable to public sales entities, unilateral conduct may also infringe the Competition Act despite the absence of dominance on part of the entity involved.

[1] Commission Notice on agreements of minor importance which do not appreciably restrict competition under Article 81(1) of the Treaty establishing the European Community (*de minimis*), OJ C 368, December 22, 2001, pp. 13–15 ("*de minimis* Notice").

B. Specific rules against anticompetitive sales activities by public entities

The Competition Act was recently amended to include specific rules regarding anticompetitive sales activities by public entities. Sales activity occurs where a public entity offers products or services in a market. Examples of sales activities recently reviewed by the SCA include the operation of gyms, hotels, or restaurants. Under these rules, which are set forth in ss. 3:27–3:32 of the Competition Act, the manner in which a sales activity is conducted may be prohibited if it (i) distorts, by object or effect, the conditions for effective competition within the market, or (ii) impedes, by object or effect, the occurrence or the development of such competition. Examples of conduct that typically may be prohibited include predatory pricing, the refusal to provide access to essential facilities on reasonable terms, discrimination, and other selective behavior. An injunction may nevertheless not be imposed in relation to conduct that can be justified by public interest considerations. **38.10**

These rules are applicable to sales activities conducted by the state, a municipality, or a county council, (including legal persons over whom these public bodies have a decisive influence). Furthermore, sales activities carried out by municipalities or county councils (but not by the state) can *as such* also be prohibited under these same conditions unless they are compatible with law (primarily the Swedish Local Government Act (1991:900) and the Municipal Competency Act (2009:47) (*Lag om vissa kommunala befogenheter*)). Cases are tried by the Stockholm City Court on application by the SCA. If the SCA decides not to apply for an injunction in a particular case, an application may be brought by a private undertaking that is affected by the conduct or activity in question. So far the SCA has brought a handful of cases which are currently pending before the Stockholm City Court, and which can be expected to contribute to clarifying the scope of application of these rules. **38.11**

C. Predatory pricing

Practices whereby a dominant undertaking sells below cost may constitute an abuse of a dominant position under s 2:7 of the Competition Act. **38.12**

Following, *inter alia*, the Court of Justice of the European Union's (CJEU) approach in *AKZO*,[2] different approaches have been used in order to establish such abuses. Accordingly, a price policy by a dominant undertaking is generally abusive if the price applied is below the average variable costs; or, if the price is above the average variable cost but below its average total cost *and* is part of scheme to eliminate a competitor.[3] **38.13**

There is no recent Swedish case law in this area. Generally, the SCA and courts could be expected to apply concepts developed in the EU Commission's practice and guidance paper (Article 102 Guidance[4]), focusing on the possible exclusion of competitors that are "as-efficient" as the dominant undertaking and using cost benchmarks such as "average avoidable cost" and "long-run average incremental cost" (see Chapter 12). **38.14**

D. Exploitative offenses

Practices whereby a dominant undertaking, directly or indirectly, imposes unfair purchase or selling prices or other unfair trading conditions may be considered abusive. **38.15**

---

[2] Case 62/86 *AKZO Chemie v. Commission* [1991] ECR I-3359.

[3] See e.g. *Statens Järnvägar v. SCA*, Market Court, Judgment, (MD 2000:2) (February 1, 2000), p. 23.

[4] Guidance on the Commission's enforcement priorities in applying [Article 102 TFEU] to abusive exclusionary conduct by dominant undertakings, OJ C 45, February 24, 2009 ("Article 102 Guidance").

38.16 In order to determine whether the price charged by a dominant firm is excessive, the SCA and Swedish courts have referred to the tests established in *United Brands*.[5] Under *United Brands*, a price can be unfair where it bears no reasonable relationship to the economic value of the product or service supplied. For this purpose, the court considered (i) whether the difference between the costs actually incurred and the price actually charged is excessive, and, if so, (ii) whether the price is unfair in itself or when compared to competing products. These standards, which are inherently difficult to apply in practice, have been loosely followed in Swedish cases.[6] More recently, the SCA conducted a thorough analysis into district heating prices applied by Fortum Värme but ultimately closed the investigation. In the meantime, Fortum Värme had pledged to make certain changes to its pricing policy.[7]

38.17 Notably, with regard to unfair trading conditions, the Market Court recently ordered an airport operator, and the company tasked with organizing the taxi operations at Stockholm Arlanda Airport, not to impose a certain additional service fee from taxi operators.[8] This fee applied where customers who had pre-ordered a taxi requested that the driver meet them at the arrivals hall with a sign indicating the customer's name. Whereas the regular fee for organizing pre-bookings was accepted, the Market Court held that the additional fee for using a sign constituted an unfair trading condition (not necessarily an excessive price), since there was no requisite connection between the fee and the relevant service. The court noted that it had not been shown that the service fee would lead to increased efficiency and shorter waiting times, and thereby increased customer satisfaction. Potential logistical problems at the airport could rather be solved by other means.

E. Monopsony

38.18 A dominant purchaser may infringe s. 2:7 of the Competition Act. For example, with respect to exclusivity obligations, dominant purchasers have been treated in similar way as dominant sellers (see Section I.I).

F. Price discrimination

38.19 Abusive discrimination may occur when a dominant undertaking applies dissimilar conditions to equivalent transactions with other trading parties, thereby placing them at a competitive disadvantage. This applies insofar as there is no objective justification for the dissimilar treatment. For example, in a case brought before the Stockholm City Court,[9] Preem, active in the petroleum business, claimed that Gävle Hamn, a port operator, abused its dominant position by discriminating against Preem vis-à-vis an alleged competitor, A Flygbränslehantering AB ("Afab"). The Stockholm District Court considered the services rendered as technically equivalent. The court also found that factors such as other contractual differences, which could motivate the price differences, had not been sufficiently demonstrated. However, as the court did not consider Preem and Afab to be competitors in any upstream or downstream market, this alone meant that no competitive disadvantage could be established.

38.20 In a rather particular case, *Luftfartsverket v. Scandinavian Airlines Systems*,[10] the Göta Court of Appeals found that Luftfartsverket, a public airport operator, had abused its dominant position by levying fees on Scandinavian Airlines Systems (SAS) for the financing of a terminal

---

[5] Case 27/76 *United Brands and United Brands Continentaal v. Commission* [1978] ECR 207.

[6] See e.g. *Uppsala Taxi 100 000 AB v. Swedavia AB and others*, Market Court, Case no. A 6/10 (MD 2011:28), Judgment, November 23, 2011; and *FAC Flygbussarna Airport Coaches AB and others v. Luftfartsverket and the SCA*, Market Court, Case no. A 3/99 (MD 2005:27), Judgment, August 30, 2005.

[7] See *Fortum Värme*, SCA Docket no. 521/2007 (November 10, 2010).

[8] *Uppsala Taxi* (n 6).

[9] *Preem Aktiebolag v. Gävle Hamn AB*, Stockholm City Court, Case no. T 5995-09.

[10] *Luftfartsverket v. Scandinavian Airlines Systems*, Göta Court of Appeal, Case no. T 33-00.

building at Arlanda airport, in addition to the regular fees applicable to both SAS and other aircraft carriers for their operations at the airport. The court found that this differential treatment was not objectively justified and disadvantaged SAS. The Court ordered Luftfartsverket to reimburse SAS for the additional fees that had been paid and that SAS should not be obliged to pay the disputed additional fees in the future.

Discrimination may also concern non-price conditions. For example, the SCA issued an interim decision ordering Luftfartsverket not to apply a planned system for the allocation of lanes for taxis at Stockholm Arlanda Airport.[11] According to the SCA, the allocation of the lanes benefited certain larger taxi companies at the expense of smaller rivals since they were given separate lanes closer to the terminal building. The SCA considered the allocation discriminatory, distortive of competition, and lacking objective justification. The decision was upheld on appeal by the Market Court.[12] **38.21**

G. Dictating or influencing resale prices

As discussed in Chapter 12, resale price maintenance (RPM) is considered a serious infringement of article 101 TFEU. These principles also apply under s. 2:1 of Competition Act. **38.22**

Minimum advertised price (MAP) programs are likely to be treated in a similar way as RPM.[13] **38.23**

H. Tying arrangements

The main theory of harm in tying or bundling is that these arrangements may lead to anticompetitive foreclosure of competitors by limiting their abilities to supply products that are part of the tie or bundle, limiting the customers' ability to purchase substitutes and to receive more attractive terms. **38.24**

In *Norra Åsby Renhållnings AB*,[14] the SCA investigated Norra Åsby Renhållnings AB (NÅRAB), which was the sole operator entrusted by a number of municipalities to gather certain types of waste from households. NÅRAB was also active in the collection of certain other types of waste—a segment that was open to competition. The SCA suspected that NÅRAB had abused its dominance by offering a rebate on the services covered by the monopoly if the customers also used NÅRAB for services that were open to competition. The SCA considered the rebate exclusionary since an as-efficient competitor would not be able to compete with NÅRAB in the market that was open for competition. The SCA nevertheless closed the investigation after NÅRAB had modified the rebate in question. **38.25**

I. Exclusive dealing

A common form of exclusive dealing involves an obligation on the customer to purchase the whole or large parts of its requirements from the dominant undertaking. Such obligations may be abusive primarily where they lead to anticompetitive foreclosure of competitors by limiting their access to the market, and may infringe s. 2:7 as well as s. 2:1 of the Competition Act. Under Swedish case law, relevant factors for the assessment include the duration and the scope of the exclusivity obligation, the possibility of termination, and the size/importance of the customer(s) concerned. **38.26**

In *the SCA v. Nitro Nobel AB*,[15] the Market Court considered that eight separate agreements with six different customers which included purchasing commitments cumulatively **38.27**

[11] *Luftfartsverket*, SCA Joined Cases nos. 542, 547, and 561/2009 (October 23, 2009).
[12] *SCA v. Luftfartsverket*, Market Court, Case no. A 3/09 (MD 2010:5), Judgment February 5, 2010.
[13] See Chapter 12.
[14] *Norra Åsby Renhållnings AB*, SCA Docket no. 536/2011 (September 27, 2012).
[15] *SCA v. Nitro Nobel AB*, Market Court (MD 1999:17).

amounted to an abuse. The purchasing commitments ranged from all or virtually all of the customers' purchasing requirements to the majority of their needs, for periods of eight to twelve months. In *Ticnet AB*,[16] the SCA closed its investigation after concluding that the exclusive agreements, which covered a substantial part of the market but were of limited duration, did not result in such exclusionary effects that they should be considered abusive.

38.28 In *SCA v. AGA Gas AB*,[17] the Market Court analyzed the effects of a non-compete clause in a standard agreement applied by a dominant firm in relation to its independent agents/resellers. The court did not consider this exclusivity arrangement abusive since the competitors had various possibilities to organize their distribution through other agents than those of the dominant undertaking. Furthermore, the Market Court took into account the legitimate interest of the firm to protect its investments in its dealers' businesses.

J. Refusal to deal

38.29 Freedom of contract is a fundamental principle that also applies to dominant undertakings. A dominant firm must therefore generally be free to organize and develop its business activities and decide with whom it wishes to contract. Similar to the situation at the EU level, case law nevertheless demonstrates that there are limits to this freedom. A refusal to deal may, under specific circumstances, infringe s. 2:7 of the Competition Act.

38.30 In *Scandinavian Airlines System v. the SCA*,[18] the Market Court assessed whether Scandinavian Airlines System (SAS) was under an obligation to enter a so-called interline-agreement with a competing airline for a specific domestic flight. SAS used to be the statutory monopolist in a market that recently had been opened for competition. The court concluded that although dominant firms are generally under no duty to contract, a refusal may be abusive where it is aimed at preventing a competitor from either entering the market or from sustaining a current market presence, provided that such refusal is not objectively justified on commercial grounds. SAS's refusal to enter the agreement could, according to the court, have a detrimental effect on smaller airlines inclination to commence competing operations.

38.31 The pricing by a dominant company may be abusive where it results in a margin squeeze irrespective of whether the company had a duty to supply in the first place. This is illustrated in the recent landmark case *TeliaSonera*, where the Stockholm City Court, following a preliminary ruling by the CJEU,[19] ordered TeliaSonera to pay a fine of SEK 144 million for abusing its dominant position by conducting a margin squeeze.[20] The court found that TeliaSonera abused its dominant position since the prices applied to competitors at the wholesale level for ADSL-broadband connectivity and to end-customers at the retail level meant that an as-efficient competitor would have a negative, or at least insufficient, margin. On appeal, the Market Court upheld the judgment in part and lowered the administrative fine to SEK 35 million.[21, 22]

[16] *Ticnet AB*, SCA Docket no. 444/2005 (March 7, 2007).
[17] *SCA v. AGA Gas AB*, Market Court Case no. A 4/99 (MD 2000:6), Judgment February 29, 2000.
[18] *Scandinavian Airlines System v. the SCA*, Market Court (MD 1999:22).
[19] C-52/09 *TeliaSonera Sverige* [2011] ECR I-527.
[20] *SCA v. TeliaSonera AB*, Stockholm City Court, Case no. T 31862-04 (December 2, 2011).
[21] *TeliaSonera v. SCA*, Market Court, Case no. A 8/11 (MD 2013:5), Judgment (April 12, 2013).
[22] See also Section I.N.

K. Essential facilities

For a general discussion, see Chapter 12. In *Övertorneå kommun and others v. Ekfors Kraft AB and others*,[23] a dominant undertaking, Ekfors Kraft AB (EKAB) was the owner and operator of an electric grid to which the street lighting in the two municipalities was connected. EKAB also owned the street lighting system. Following a dispute over a price increase the municipalities refused the pay more than they deemed reasonable. As a consequence, EKAB turned off the street lighting. The municipalities claimed that the street lighting constituted an essential facility, without which the safety of the local residents was put at risk. In addition, the costs of erecting a parallel street light network would be very high. According to the majority of the court, the street lighting did not constitute an essential facility, and the municipalities had failed to show that the conduct would weaken competition in any market. Two judges dissented concluding that the electric grid was an essential facility and that there were no objective justifications for switching off the electricity to enforce payment of disputed claims. **38.32**

After a few dark years, one of the municipalities erected its own network. When EKAB refused to connect the system to its electric grid, the SCA imposed interim measures which were upheld by the Market Court.[24] According to the court, the grid constituted an essential facility and the refusal prevented the entry of a new market participant in the market for street lighting. **38.33**

L. Bundling (including loyalty and market share discounts)

Bundling and various types of discount schemes by a dominant undertaking may be abusive where they have exclusionary effects. Rebate schemes may also lead to discrimination.[25] **38.34**

Loyalty-inducing discounts can be considered exclusionary, particularly where they apply retroactively. In *Bring City Mail Sweden AB v. Posten Meddelande AB*,[26] the court ordered Posten Meddelande AB ("Posten") not to apply a discount scheme whereby Posten's customers would be granted a discount on all items in a delivery provided that the total number exceeded a certain quantity and the mail had been pre-sorted in accordance with Posten's requirements. The case was brought to the Market Court by Bring City Mail Sweden AB (BCM), a challenger to the incumbent Posten and active in certain areas of the country, predominantly in and around the three largest cities. According to BCM, the rebate was exclusionary since it applied to deliveries in the whole country and provided that the customer purchased a large quantity. This meant that certain customers would lose the entire rebate if they split the order and used BCM in the areas where there was competition. The SCA had investigated the matter but closed the case after having analyzed Posten's costs and prices under the analytical framework in the EU Commission's Article 102 Guidance. Notably, the Market Court held that it was not necessary to conduct an as-efficient-competitor analysis in order to determine an infringement. The court pointed to the extensive responsibility of Posten as a dominant undertaking (a former statutory monopolist with high market shares), that the discounts applied by Posten had an exclusionary effect or, in any event, tended to restrict competition, and that Posten had failed to show that the discounts were economically motivated and did not go beyond what is necessary to achieve the possible benefits of the discounts. **38.35**

[23] *Övertorneå kommun and others v. Ekfors Kraft AB and others*, Market Court, Case no. A 4/06 (MD 2007:26), Judgment, November 15, 2007.

[24] *Ekfors Kraft AB v. the SCA*, Market Court, Case no. A 4/09 (MD 2010:07) Judgment, February 26, 2010, upholding the SCA's decision in *Ekfors Kraft*, SCA Docket no. 533/2009 (November 25, 2009).

[25] See Section I.F(i).

[26] *Bring City Mail Sweden AB v. Posten Meddelande AB*, Market Court, Case no. A 3/10 (MD 2011:14), Judgment June 8, 2011.

38.36 In a subsequent investigation of rebate schemes the SCA continued to focus on whether the rebate in question was likely to foreclose an as-efficient-competitor.[27]

M. Standard-setting groups

38.37 No Swedish case law exists in this area. See Chapter 12.

N. Customer termination

38.38 It may be abusive for a dominant undertaking to terminate (or threaten to terminate) an existing customer when the measure is aimed at restricting competition, for example as retaliation against a customer that has purchased supplies from a competitor. In other situations where the termination of an established customer tends to restrict competition in the market, the dominant firm may often have to show that the measure is objectively justified. Consideration may also be given to whether the dominant firm has given sufficient notice to allow the customer to make appropriate adjustments.

38.39 In *Europe Investor Direct AB and others v. VPC AB*,[28] the plaintiff was a group of companies processing and selling various forms of investor information. The plaintiff brought a damages claim against VPC, the Swedish central securities depository, for terminating the supply of address information for shareholders in listed companies. Stockholm City Court found for the plaintiff, concluding that VPC had abused its dominant position by refusing to continue the supply. The company was a monopolist in the market for the supply of information contained in share registers of listed companies, and the refusal tended to restrict competition and could not be objectively justified. On appeal, the Svea Court of Appeals shared the district court's assessment in these respects.[29]

38.40 Occasionally, the Market Court has also considered that termination of a customer relationship may amount to an abuse in situations where the conduct did not restrict competition, but rather amounted to exploitation. In *Saint-Gobain Isover AB v. Nordvästra Skåne Södra Halland Energi AB* (NVSH),[30] the Market Court held that NVSH had abused its dominant position by threatening to disconnect Saint-Gobain Isover ("Isover") from a high-voltage electricity network, unless Isover paid certain disputed network fees. NVSH held a *de facto* a monopoly, and Isover was a long-standing customer. According the court, Isover's objections in respect of the fees were not unfounded, and a disconnection from the network would entail a long-term interruption in the company's operations that would cause severe economic loss. Since NVSH could not show any objectively justified reasons for its actions, NVSH was found to have abused its dominant position.[31]

O. Termination of intermediaries

38.41 Termination of intermediaries is a special case of refusal to deal or termination of customers (see Sections I.J and I.N).

P. Termination of relationships with competitors

38.42 See para 38.41 and Chapter 12.

[27] *Posten AB*, SCA Docket no. 262/2011 (May 3, 2012).

[28] *Europe Investor Direct AB and others v. VPC AB*, Stockholm City Court, Joined Cases nos. T 32799-05 and T 34227-05 (November 20, 2008).

[29] *Euroclear Sweden AB v. Europe Investor Direct AB and others*, Svea Court of Appeals, Case no. T 10012-08 (January 19, 2011).

[30] *Saint-Gobain Isover AB v. Nordvästra Skåne Södra Halland Energi AB*, Market Court, Case no. A 6/01 (MD 2002:11), Judgment April 19, 2002.

[31] See also *Ventelo Sverige AB*, SCA Docket no. 681/2010 (January 10, 2011).

Q. Exemptions

There is no formal exemption to the abuse prohibition in s. 2:7 (as is the case with respect to s. 2:1).[32] A form of conduct which otherwise could constitute an abuse will nevertheless not be regarded as abusive if it is shown to be objectively justified, for example where it is economically motivated on sufficient efficiency grounds. A dominant undertaking is allowed to protect its legitimate commercial interests. In some situations it is also possible that a certain type of conduct could be motivated by reasons such as consumer protection, health and safety and therefore should not constitute an abuse. **38.43**

II. Dealing with competitors

Section 2:1 of the Competition Act prohibits agreements between undertakings if there is an appreciable prevention, restriction or distortion of competition. This applies to all types of "agreements," whether formal or informal, written or oral. Although agreements between competitors are most prone to restrict competition, the prohibition also applies in other settings such as vertical agreements between suppliers and retailers. **38.44**

If an anticompetitive object can be established it is not necessary to further investigate the likely effects. As described in Chapter 12, the most serious infringements such as price fixing or bid-rigging, export prohibitions and minimum RPM are considered to restrict competition by object. Classical cartels and similar hard core infringements have also been the main enforcement priority of the SCA over the years. **38.45**

Similar to the development at the EU level, there are indications that Swedish courts may take a rather broad view of potential restrictions by object, even in vertical agreements (i.e. between non-competitors). A recent example is found in *Sveriges Bildelsgrossisters förening v. KIA Motors Sweden AB*,[33] concerning certain warranty terms applied by KIA Motors AB (KIA). New cars were sold with a seven-year warranty, provided the customer regularly serviced the vehicle at a garage authorized by KIA. If the customer used a non-authorized garage for servicing, then the warranty would only apply for three years. The Market Court considered that this condition restricted competition by object. **38.46**

If an agreement involves an appreciable restriction of competition, it may still be exempted under s. 2:2 of the Competition Act if the agreement gives rise to sufficient economic efficiencies. This provision mirrors article 101(3) TFEU and includes four conditions. The agreement must (i) improve the production or distribution or to promote technical or economic progress; (ii) allow consumers a fair share of the resulting benefit; (iii) only impose restrictions which are indispensable to the attainment of the objective referred to under (i); and (iv) not afford the possibility of eliminating competition in respect of a substantial part of the utilities in question. In practice, agreements that are considered restrictive by object are rarely exempted. **38.47**

Certain categories of agreements have been formally exempted from the prohibition in s. 2:1, provided that certain conditions are met. This applies to taxi services, vertical agreements, specialization agreements, agreements concerning research and development, agreements in the motor vehicle sector, agreements in the insurance sector, and technology transfer agreements. These exemptions are set out in separate laws, which, with the exception of taxi **38.48**

[32] See Section II.

[33] *Sveriges Bildelsgrossisters förening v. KIA Motors Sweden AB*, Market Court Case no. A 3/11 (MD 2012:13), Judgment December 4, 2012.

services, essentially incorporate the corresponding EU block exemption regulations. Finally, ss. 2:4–2:5 of the Competition Act provide for further exceptions for certain agreements between taxi companies and agreements within agricultural associations.

A. Horizontal price fixing (including advanced announcements of price or product changes)

38.49 Section 2:1 of the Competition Act prohibits, in particular, agreements which directly or indirectly fix purchase or selling prices or any other trading conditions. Agreements or concerted practices among competing undertakings which aim to establish prices, rebates and/or bonuses almost always constitute serious infringements.

38.50 Examples of Swedish cartel cases include:

- the *Asphalt cartel*,[34] where eight undertakings were fined approximately SEK 500 million for bid-rigging in connection with procurements of asphalt construction work;
- the *Gas cartel*,[35] where five gas companies were fined approximately SEK 112 million for fixing rebates; and
- the *Car dealers' cartel*,[36] where eight car dealers were fined an amount of approximately SEK 21 million for fixing prices and rebates.

B. Horizontal agreements to allocate customers or territories; agreements not to compete

38.51 Horizontal agreements to allocate markets among competitors are, along with horizontal price fixing, considered one of the most serious contraventions of Swedish competition law. Common forms of market sharing include the division of customers and agreements to only operate within certain geographic territories or products. Notably, over the last few years the SCA has conducted a number of dawn raids on the suspicion of bid-rigging in connection with public or private tenders in various industry sectors.[37] The *Asphalt cartel* and the *Car dealers' cartel*, mentioned above, also included elements of market sharing.

C. Horizontal boycotts

38.52 As under EU competition law, agreements between competitors not to supply to or purchase from certain undertakings may constitute an infringement of s. 2:1 of the Competition Act. Swedish case-law not particularly well developed in this respect. However, in 2011, the SCA investigated a suspected collective boycott concerning the supply of spare parts for boat engines. The SCA suspected that a number of sellers of spare parts had coordinated the termination of deliveries to an undertaking which had been acquired by a competitor in the aftermarket for repairs. According to SCA, the authority failed to find sufficient evidence establishing any mutual understanding to adopt the parallel behavior.[38]

D. Joint ventures and other competitive collaborations

38.53 Certain joint ventures, which are classified as "full-function," fall under the Swedish merger control rules. Section 2:1 of the Competition Act applies to other joint ventures and

[34] E.g. *NCC AB and others v. the SCA*, Market Court Case no. A 2/07 (MD 2009:11), Judgment May 28, 2009; *SCA v. Kvalitetsasfalt i Mellansverige AB and others*, Stockholm District Court, Case no. T 5467-03 (July 10, 2007).

[35] *SCA v. Norsk Hydro Olje AB and others*, Marker Court, Case no. A 2/03 (MD 2005:7), Judgment February 22, 2005.

[36] *SCA v. AB Bil-B and others*, Markert Court Case no. A 3/06 (MD 2008:12), Judgment September 10, 2008.

[37] See Section III.B.

[38] *Brunswick Marine in Sweden AB and others*, SCA Docket no. 399/2011 (December 19, 2011).

collaborations. Such collaborations between competitors may take many different forms, such as joint research and development, production, purchasing or commercialization. The principles developed under EU competition law, as set out in, *inter alia*, in the Horizontal Cooperation Guidelines, are also applied under Swedish competition law.

Generally, in its assessment of joint ventures the SCA has focused on whether (i) the joint venture restricts actual or potential competition between the parents of the joint venture, or between one of the parents and the joint venture, (ii) the cooperation is likely restrict competition between the parents in markets not concerned by the joint venture, and (iii) if the joint venture restricts competition vis-à-vis third parties. **38.54**

Where the collaboration leads to some appreciable restriction of competition, it must be considered whether the exemption in s. 2:2 applies. **38.55**

E. Trade associations

It is common that undertakings in Sweden are organized within trade organizations. Since the members are often actual or potential competitors, the activities within such organizations are nevertheless particularly sensitive from a competition law perspective. The formation of the organization is generally not restrictive in itself as long as objective membership criteria apply. Activities such as the monitoring of legal developments in the industry, contacts with public authorities, and the publishing of industry statistics in appropriate forms[39] are generally not unlawful, either. However, any disguised cartel activities will be prohibited and various forms of information exchanges or discussions about costs, prices or other sensitive trading terms must be avoided.[40] **38.56**

F. Interlocking directorates

There are no Swedish cases concerning interlocking directorates as such. However, undertakings that are jointly owned by competitors have been considered a possible venue for information exchange.[41] **38.57**

G. Facilitating practices

Facilitating practices (i.e. practices which help competitors to eliminate strategic uncertainty and coordinate conduct more effectively) are not subject to specific rules.[42] Various types of facilitating conduct, such as information exchanges, may nevertheless infringe s. 2:1 of the Competition Act.[43] **38.58**

H. Information exchange

Information sharing regarding prices, costs, customers, and other sensitive commercial terms between competitors are often prohibited. It is likely that the SCA will apply the principles set out in the Horizontal Cooperation Guidelines.[44] **38.59**

With regard to market data and statistics gathered and supplied (e.g. by trade associations), this has generally not been considered restrictive of competition provided that the information gathered concerns historical conditions and the market data is made available in **38.60**

---

39 See Section I.H.

40 See Chapter 12.

41 See e.g. *Telia AB*, SCA Docket no. 321/2001 (March 12, 2002) and *Konsortiet Scandinavian Airlines*, SCA Joined Cases nos. 726/2001 and 768/2001 (January 4, 2002).

42 See further Chapter 12.

43 See Section II.H.

44 See Chapter 12.

a sufficiently aggregated form. Factors such as the age of the data and how frequently it is delivered are relevant. The market conditions are also of importance for the assessment. Information exchanges are generally more likely to be considered restrictive where the market is concentrated, there are high barriers to entry and/or products are homogenous.[45]

I. Joint purchasing agreements

38.61 Joint purchasing agreements may be prohibited where they restrict competition among the participating undertakings and/or third parties, for example by foreclosing competing purchasers by limiting their access to efficient suppliers. Joint purchasing agreements where the undertakings are not competitors in downstream selling markets are less likely to raise concerns, at least unless the undertakings have significant market power in the purchasing market. Joint purchasing agreements are likely to be assessed under the principles set out in the Horizontal Cooperation Guidelines.[46]

J. Joint lobbying/regulatory/legislative efforts

38.62 Joint lobbying and other similar efforts have not been an enforcement priority in Sweden and are generally not prohibited, provided they are undertaken in a manner that does not raise other concerns, such as the exchange of sensitive information.[47]

III. General issues

A. Jurisdiction and applicable law (including sector-specific competition regulation)

38.63 The Competition Act is applicable to all sectors of the economy. Specific exceptions apply to agricultural associations and taxi services. It follows expressly from s. 2:1 of the Competition Act that it is not applicable to agreements between employers and employees relating to wages and other conditions of employment. Some sectors, such as telecoms and utilities, are also subject to sector-specific regulation.

B. Antitrust system

(i) Name of agency/agencies

38.64 The Swedish Competition Authority (*Konkurrensverket*) is the state authority responsible for the enforcement of the Competition Act as well as the rules on public procurement. The current Director General of the SCA is Mr. Dan Sjöblom.

(ii) Staff size and budget

38.65 The SCA has about 140 full-time equivalent employees, most of whom are lawyers or economists. About 90 percent of the employees hold an academic degree. The annual budget of the SCA amounts to about EUR 16 million. In 2010–2011, approximately 70 percent of the budget covered personnel costs. About 80 percent of the budget was allocated to the enforcement of competition law, and 20 percent to public procurement.

(iii) Recent enforcement actions and trends

38.66 In recent years, the number of cases brought before the courts by the Competition Authority has increased. This is partly due to the recent amendments to the Competition Act with rules

[45] See e.g. *Sweboat*, SCA Docket no. 414/2012 (December 18, 2012).
[46] See further Chapter 12.
[47] See Sections II.E and II.H.

regarding sales activities by public entities[48] and to the growing number of public procurement matters.

The Competition Authority has taken an active approach to dawn raids, assisting the Commission and other national competition authorities when required, and carrying out an increasing number of inspections on its own. The inspections have concerned both suspected abuses and anticompetitive practices among undertakings in sectors such as financial services, postal services, boat engine spare parts, and hotels. Many of the investigations in which the SCA carried out dawn raids were closed rather quickly. This suggests that the evidentiary threshold for conducting surprise inspections is rather low. **38.67**

Recent case law from the Market Court shows that plaintiffs may successfully bring cases to the court after the SCA has decided to close an investigation into the same practice. In some of these cases, the SCA has closed the docket without detailed investigation, for example due to lack of priority, and in others following an extensive analysis.[49] **38.68**

C. Private litigation

The Competition Act stipulates that an undertaking that has intentionally or negligently infringed ss. 2:1 or 2:7 of the Competition Act or article 101 or 102 TFEU shall compensate the damage that is caused thereby. **38.69**

The Competition Act does not contain specific provisions on standing. In practice, the need to show an identifiable and indemnifiable injury as well as a causal link between the injury and the competition law violation will limit the scope for claims. **38.70**

Plaintiffs who have suffered damages as a result of a competition law infringement may choose to bring a claim in damages after the infringement has been established in a decision or a judgment (see Section II.D), or bring a claim in damages that also includes proving the infringement for the first time. **38.71**

Section 3:25 of the Competition Act provides that the right to damages lapses "if no action is brought within ten years from the date when the damage was caused." It is also possible to bring cases claiming that certain clauses or agreements are null and void. **38.72**

Two principal fora are available for a private action. First, under general procedural law, the competent court for civil cases is the court for the place where the defendant resides. Group actions brought pursuant to the Group Proceedings Act are handled by specifically designated district courts in each Swedish county. Second, under a special forum provision in s. 3:26 of the Competition Act, Stockholm City Court is always competent to examine cases relating to damages pursuant to s. 3:25. **38.73**

A limited number of damages cases have been brought before courts, including *Preem v. Gävle Hamn*[50] and *Euroclear v. Europe Investor Direct*.[51] In the latter case, the claimant was awarded damages after having successfully established that the defendant had abused its dominant position by refusing to supply the claimant, who was a long-standing customer. **38.74**

Furthermore, if the SCA decides not to require an undertaking to terminate an infringement of s. 2:1 or 2:7 of the Competition Act or article 101 or 102 TFEU, the Market Court may require an undertaking to do so at the request of an undertaking that is affected by the infringement. **38.75**

---

48 See Section I.

49 See e.g. *Bring City Mail* (n 26); *Uppsala Taxi* (n 6); and *Sveriges Bildelsgrossisters förening v. KIA Motors Sweden AB* (n 33).

50 *Preem* (n 9).

51 *Euroclear* (n 29).

D. Follow-on litigation (includes role of agency determinations of liability for follow-on litigation)

38.76 A limited number of follow-on claims have been brought before the Swedish courts, the majority of which have been settled. These include follow-on actions with respect to the *Asphalt cartel*.[52] Currently, a civil action for damages is pending before the Stockholm City Court following the *TeliaSonera* case.[53]

38.77 As a result of the limited case law, the precise status of a decision by the SCA, or a court judgment following such a decision, has not been fully determined. The Swedish courts are at liberty to evaluate all evidence in order to determine what has been proven in the case at hand. As a practical matter, the outcome of a previous public action concerning the same conduct is nevertheless highly relevant from an evidentiary perspective. A prior decision or judgment can thus be expected to be important for follow-on actions.

E. Arbitration and alternative dispute resolution

38.78 An arbitration agreement may constitute a bar to (general) court proceedings, if invoked by the defendant upon receiving a summons application. It follows from s. 1 of the Swedish Arbitration Act (1999:116) that arbitrators may rule on the civil law effects of competition law as between the parties. They may thus assess the validity of an agreement and the right to damages under competition law. However, the arbitrators' jurisdiction does not, for example, include actions for fines or issuing an order against a competition law infringer.

38.79 The SCA is not bound by an arbitration award. Furthermore, arbitrators are not directly bound by a decision of the SCA, although in practice it is unlikely that the arbitrators would be able to ignore it when rendering an award.

F. Remedies

(i) Civil liability

38.80 **Obligations and commitments** The SCA may require an undertaking to terminate an infringement of s. 2:1 or 2:7 of the Competition Act or article 101 or 102 TFEU. The SCA may also impose interim measures for the period until a final decision has been taken, if there are particular reasons for doing so.

38.81 Furthermore, an undertaking may offer commitments with respect to an alleged infringement of s. 2:1 or 2:7 of the Competition Act or article 101 or 102 TFEU. If such a commitment has been offered, the SCA may adopt a decision stating that there are no longer grounds for action with respect to the suspected infringement. Such a decision may be combined with a default fine if the undertaking fails to fulfill its commitment.

38.82 For example, in *Rationella Kontors Varuinköp AB* (RKV),[54] a purchase and marketing organization consisting of members active in office supplies, distributed sales catalogues that included recommended prices. The SCA found that the catalog prices in this horizontal setting were restrictive of competition. After RKV gave a commitment not to include recommended prices in future catalogs, the SCA considered that there were no longer grounds for an intervention. The commitment was combined with a default fine.

---

[52] See para. 38.51.

[53] *TeliaSonera* (nn. 20 and 21).

[54] *Rationella Kontors Varuinköp AB*, SCA Docket no. 607/211 (June 18, 2012).

Administrative fines The SCA may request the Stockholm City Court to order an undertaking to pay an administrative fine where the undertaking, or a person acting on its behalf, intentionally or negligently infringed the prohibitions in s. 2:1 or 2:7 of the Competition Act or article 101 or 102 TFEU. Administrative fines may not exceed ten percent of the group turnover in the preceding business year. Further details on how the SCA determines what administrative fine to request are set out in chapter 3 of the Competition Act and the SCA's communication on its method of setting fines.[55] **38.83**

Fine order Under s. 3:16 of the Competition Act, the Competition Authority may issue a fine order instead of instigating proceedings for an administrative fine. A fine order may only be issued if the Competition Authority considers that the circumstances concerning the infringement are clear. It is up to the undertaking in question to accept a fine order or to determine whether it would prefer proceedings for an administrative fine. If the undertaking consents to a fine order within the time specified by the SCA, proceedings may not be instituted. The possibility of a fine order has been available since November 1, 2008 but has rarely been applied.[56] In practice, the fine orders have not amounted to more than SEK 2 million for an individual undertaking. **38.84**

Penalty of a fine An injunction ordering the termination of an infringement of s. 2:1 or 2:7 of the Competition Act or article 101 or 102 TFEU, or a decision regarding a commitment by an undertaking in relation to the mentioned provisions can be made subject to a default fine. Furthermore, certain investigative measures by the SCA can also be made subject to a default fine. **38.85**

(ii) Criminal liability

According to the Trading Prohibitions Act (1986:436) (TPA), a trading prohibition may under certain circumstances, and if called for in the public interest, be imposed for hardcore horizontal cartel infringements under s. 2:1 of the Competition Act or article 101 TFEU. **38.86**

A trading prohibition may primarily be imposed on individuals (e.g. on the CEO, the deputy chief executive, or a board member) who are formal representatives of an undertaking, or in practical terms, those persons who exercise management of the business operations of an undertaking that participated in a horizontal cartel. The duration of a prohibition may extend from three to ten years, during which the individual may not conduct business activities or undertake senior roles within an undertaking, for example as a CEO, deputy chief executive, or board member. If the prohibition is violated, the person may be liable to pay a fine or be sentenced to a term of imprisonment for up to two years. **38.87**

The SCA may bring proceedings for a trading prohibition before the Stockholm City Court, either stand-alone or in conjunction with proceedings for administrative fines. A person who cooperates with the SCA, the Commission, or a national competition authority, may escape a trading prohibition. **38.88**

G. Leniency and immunity

Leniency or immunity from fines may be granted with respect to infringements of s. 2:1 of the Competition Act or article 101 TFEU, but is not available for infringements of s. 2:7 of **38.89**

[55] *Method of setting administrative fines*, SCA Docket no. 394/2009 (November 19, 2009).

[56] See *Rundvirke Poles AB*, SCA Docket no. 237/2007 (June 30, 2009); *Björn Hägglunds Maskiner AB*, SCA Docket no. 327/2010 (December 1, 2011); and *Fonus ek för and others*, SCA Docket no. 20/2009 (July 2, 2010).

the Competition Act or article 102 TFEU. Only one of the undertakings that have participated in an infringement may be granted leniency in the form of immunity from fines.

38.90 According to s. 3:12 of the Competition Act, the SCA may grant an undertaking leniency from fines if (i) the undertaking is the first to notify the infringement to the SCA and (ii) if owing to the information contained in the notification, the SCA had obtained a sufficient amount of information to take action against the infringement.

38.91 When the SCA has already received sufficient information to take action, leniency may be granted provided that (i) the undertaking was the first to provide information that leads to the establishment that the infringement has occurred, or (ii) the undertaking has, in some other way, to a very significant extent, facilitated the investigation of the infringement.

38.92 Leniency may not be granted if the undertaking has compelled another undertaking to participate in the infringement.

38.93 Furthermore, a fine *reduction* may be granted if an undertaking provides the SCA with information that facilitates the SCA's investigation to a significant extent.

38.94 In each case, the applicant must, among other things, cooperate on a continuous basis with the SCA during the investigation and submit all available information about the infringement.[57]

H. Document creation and retention

38.95 Under Swedish competition law there are no explicit rules regarding the creation or retention of documents. However, undertakings are often required to supply information, documents or other material during an investigation by the SCA. Such disclosures may be subject to a default fine. Furthermore, if an infringement is established, the SCA may take into account when determining the magnitude of the administrative fine whether the undertaking in question has cooperated with the SCA during the course of the investigation.

---

[57] For further information see *The General Guidelines of the Swedish Competition Authority on immunity from fines and reduction of fines*, English version, KKVFS 2012:1 (September 6, 2012).

39

SWITZERLAND

Marcel Meinhardt, Astrid Waser, Michael Cabalzar, and Roman Kern

Lenz & Staehelin

Introduction

Swiss competition law is governed by the Federal Law on Cartels and Other Restraints of Competition of October 6, 1995, as amended ("the Cartel Act"). The regulatory framework is complemented by several federal ordinances and general notices and communications of the Competition Commission (the "ComCo"). The Cartel Act came into effect on July 1, 1996. After five years, the Act was reviewed by a team of experts, and subsequently amended in 2003. In April 2004, the revised Cartel Act entered into force. Over the past few years, the ComCo has had a particular enforcement priority regarding bid rigging cartels and vertical restraints focusing on resale price maintenance and market foreclosure. Open and free markets are also the main focus of the current activities of the ComCo. **39.01**

I. Acting alone

39.02 An undertaking is deemed dominant in a specific market, if it is able, as supplier or consumer, to behave to an appreciable extent independently of the other participants (competitors, suppliers or consumers) in the market. Two or more undertakings can have a collective dominant position.

39.03 Article 7 Cartel Act states as a general rule that dominant undertakings behave unlawfully if, by abusing their position in the market, they hinder other undertakings from starting or continuing to compete, or disadvantage trading partners. Market dominance usually emerges as the result of competition. Therefore, also under the Cartel Act, market dominance as such is not unlawful. Only the abuse of a dominant position is unlawful.

39.04 The problem inherent in this provision is that competitive behavior on the one hand and abusive behavior on the other can hardly be distinguished on a phenomenological level. The Cartel Act therefore provides a non-exhaustive catalogue of six types of abusive practices. However, the statutory examples are not unlawful either per se or by a refutable presumption. If an undertaking has legitimate business reasons, a behavior that would otherwise be deemed abusive can be justified.

39.05 Except for its catalogue of abusive practices, the Cartel Act does not provide further clarification on the concept of dominance. The determination whether a specific behavior is competitive or abusive has therefore to be made with regard to economic criteria on a case-by-case basis.[1]

39.06 In recent years, the ComCo has investigated several acting-alone cases regarding potentially dominant behavior in the watch, telecom, media and entertainment industry including news, cinema, radio, and TV.

39.07 In exceptional cases where an abusive behavior is in the public interest, it may be authorized by the Federal Council (executive branch of the Swiss federal government) on request of the undertakings concerned (art. 8 Cartel Act).

39.08 In Swiss cartel law, dictating or influencing resale prices is not organized as an abuse of market dominance. The framework for these vertical agreements restricting competition is discussed in Section I.E(i) (dictating and influencing resale prices) and Section II (paras. 39.41–39.49).

A. Predatory pricing

39.09 Article 7(2)(d) Cartel Act provides that any undercutting of prices or other conditions by a dominant undertaking directed against specific competitors is a potentially unlawful practice.

39.10 Under Swiss law, the effects of pricing are scrutinized rather than pricing as a behavior. In order to test predatory pricing, the ComCo has tested whether (i) a specific price is economically irrational (measured at costs, most likely average variable cost); (ii) there is sufficient promise for recoupment; and (iii) there are no objective legitimate business reasons justifying such prices.[2]

---

[1] Compare *Terminierung Mobilfunk*, Recht und Politik des Wettbewerbs (RPW) [Competition Law and Policy] 2007/2, 241 ff.; *Publigroupe*, Swiss Federal Supreme Court, Decision no. 139 I 72 (June 29, 2012).

[2] *Radio- und TV-Markt St. Gallen*, RPW 2002/3, 431 ff.; *Cornèr Banca SA/Telekurs AG*, RPW 2004/4, 1002 ff.

B. Exploitative offenses (excessive pricing, monopoly leveraging)

Article 7(2)(c) Cartel Act prohibits the imposition of unfair prices or other unfair conditions of trade by a dominant undertaking. This covers both the imposition of unreasonably high prices on consumers and unreasonably low prices on suppliers. The key element of this prohibition is "imposition," which means that the trading partner is left with no other choice than to accept the conditions set by the dominant undertaking. The Cartel Act does not, however, protect business partners that do have a choice and merely accept such offers.[3] **39.11**

In a recent decision that is currently on appeal, the ComCo discussed monopoly leveraging in connection with refusal to deal or unfair pricing in neighboring markets as well as tying arrangements.[4] **39.12**

C. Monopsony

Swiss competition law regulates market power on the supply and the demand side through (i) control of abusive market behavior and (ii) merger control. In both cases, the law only becomes applicable if the market power amounts to a dominant position. **39.13**

A buyer is deemed dominant if it is (individually or collectively) able to behave to an appreciable extent independently of other participants (competitors, suppliers, or consumers) in the market. **39.14**

So far, there have been no cases concerning abuse of market power by monopsonies. However, buyer power has often been considered in merger control cases. **39.15**

D. Price discrimination

As stated in article 7(2)(b) Cartel Act, a dominant undertaking abuses its position if it discriminates among business partners through prices or other terms of business. Accordingly, dominant undertakings are bound by the principle of non-discrimination. Discrimination means unequal treatment of comparable situations without legitimate business reasons. If there are legitimate grounds (e.g. different transportation or distribution costs), cases can be treated differently. A business partner may be an actual or potential customer or a competitor. It is required that the unequal treatment hinders the business partner to compete.[5] **39.16**

E. Dictating or influencing resale prices

(i) Resale price maintenance

In Swiss competition law, the rules on resale price maintenance (RPM) are independent from market dominance. **39.17**

According to article 5(4) Cartel Act, agreements between undertakings operating at different levels of the market, designed directly or indirectly to fix resale prices, are presumed to eliminate effective competition in a given market. This presumption may be rebutted if it can be shown that, on the contrary, effective competition is not eliminated by this agreement. Both agreements on minimum prices and agreements on fixed resale prices fall under the presumption. Recommended retail prices as well as agreements on maximum prices are in principle lawful, provided that they do not have the effect of a minimum or fixed resale price, enforced by applying pressure or providing financial incentives. Prices may be fixed directly **39.18**

---

[3] *Terminierung Mobilfunk*, RPW 2011/4, 522 ff.; see as well the final report on the ComCo's preliminary investigation regarding *Acquiring fees for Maestro transactions*, RPW 2012/4, 749 ff.

[4] *SIX/Terminals mit Dynamic Currency Conversion*, RPW 2011/1, 96 ff.

[5] *Publigroupe*, Swiss Federal Supreme Court, Decision no. 139 I 72 (June 29, 2012).

(e.g. through a contractual agreement on such prices) or indirectly (e.g. through fixed rebate and bonus systems). The ComCo has decided several cases regarding RPM.[6] Retail price maintenance has been one of its enforcement priorities. Several RPM cases have, however, been appealed and are pending.[7]

39.19 Any undertaking that participates in RPM may be sanctioned with a fine of up to 10 percent of its turnover in Switzerland in the preceding three financial years.

39.20 An exception to the prohibition of RPM may exist with regard to agency contracts if the agent is merely permitted to resell goods (i) either in its own name or in the principal's name and (ii) on the principal's account and bears no economic risk. In such case, it can be assumed that competition law does not apply to the relationship between the principal and the agent. However, there has been no case law of the ComCo in this respect which would have clarified the conditions for agency contracts.

(ii) Minimum advertised price programs

39.21 Under the Cartel Act, there are no provisions on minimum advertised price (MAP) programs. Article 5(4) Cartel Act also extends to MAP programs (see Section I.E(i)).

F. Tying arrangements

39.22 According to article 7(2)(f) Cartel Act, tying is concluding a contract on the condition that the other contracting party agrees to accept or deliver additional goods or services. In tying arrangements, two sorts of goods are being distinguished by doctrine: A tying good is a good that the customer actually demands. A tied good, on the other hand, is a good that has to be purchased in order to buy the tying good. While the tied good can also be purchased individually, the tying good is only offered in combination with the tied good. Tying can be arranged both by contract and through technological and/or physical combination of two separate goods.

39.23 In principle, it is allowed to tie two or more products or services. However, if the company is dominant in the market of the tying good, tying arrangements bear the risk of (i) unfair hindrance of competitors, (ii) exploitative offenses, and (iii) adverse effects on secondary markets.

39.24 According to the case law of the ComCo, tying arrangements by a dominant undertaking are illegal if (i) the tying and tied goods are actually two goods; (ii) the purchase of the tied good is a condition set by the seller for the purchase of the tying good; (iii) the tying arrangement has an adverse effect on competition; and (iv) there is no objective justification for such tying arrangement.[8]

G. Exclusive dealing

39.25 Exclusive dealing is not explicitly mentioned in the Cartel Act as an unlawful practice by dominant undertakings. In the case law, the imposition of exclusivity has been discussed with regard to the imposition of unfair trade conditions.[9] On the one hand, the imposition of exclusivity can be a disadvantage for the business partner on which it is imposed. On the other hand, exclusive dealing also prevents competitors from concluding contracts with businesses that are bound by exclusivity.

---

[6] E.g. *Sécateurs et ciscailles*, RPW 2009/2, 143 ff.

[7] E.g. *Hors-Liste Medikamente: Preise von Cialis, Levitra und Viagra*, RPW 2010/4, 649 ff; Decision of the Federal Administrative Tribunal B-364/2010 of December 3, 2013.

[8] *SIX/Terminals* (n 4).

[9] Cartel Act art. 7(2)(a); *Ticketcorner*, RPW 2005/4, 672 ff.

H. Refusal to deal

According to article 7(2)(a) Cartel Act, refusals to deal are prohibited as a potentially unlawful practice by dominant undertakings if the refusal cannot be justified based on legitimate business reasons. It covers both refusals to supply and to purchase goods or services. It also includes termination, interruption and limitation of business relations. **39.26**

However, a dominant position does not create a duty to establish business relationship with another party. The dominant undertaking is free in its decisions as long as it does not abuse its dominant position. **39.27**

With regard to refusals to deal, the ComCo tests whether (i) the dominant undertaking refuses a deal; (ii) the refused good or service is essential for the business activities of the other party; (iii) the refusal leads to an elimination of effective competition; and (iv) the refusal can neither be objectively justified nor be based on efficiency reasons.[10] Moreover, in its most recent decision regarding clockwork elements, the ComCo has prior to these criteria examined the historical background of the dominant position. In accordance with the EU practice it stated that an obligation to supply must be considered very carefully unless the dominant position was initially based on exclusive or special rights or governmental support.[11] **39.28**

I. Essential facilities

The Cartel Act provides no specific rules for essential facilities. The provisions on refusals to deal apply *mutatis mutandis* to essential facility cases. **39.29**

In particular, important and non-duplicable infrastructures such as airports or networks may be qualified as essential facilities. **39.30**

In practice, the ComCo applies the same set of rules to refusals to deal cases as to cases regarding denial of access to an essential facility. According to the Swiss Supreme Court, denial of access to an essential facility and a common refusal to deal do not differ to such an extent that different criteria should apply, i.e. the fact that in a refusal to deal case an actual facility is concerned rather than a good or service does not justify the application of stricter rules.[12] **39.31**

J. Bundling (including loyalty and market share discounts)

Bundling practices are not expressly addressed in article 7 Cartel Act. The doctrine distinguishes between (i) pure bundling and (ii) mixed bundling. Pure bundling means that two goods are only offered as a bundle, i.e. together. Neither good can be procured individually. According to the doctrine, the rules for tying also apply to pure bundling.[13] **39.32**

In case of mixed bundling, the bundled goods can also be procured individually from a given seller, i.e. there is no coercion to buy both goods. The procurement of the bundled goods, however, usually entails price reductions or other advantages. Mixed bundling can have the effect of pure bundling if the price for at least the good for which the company holds a dominant position is unreasonably high. In such a case, the rules for pure bundling apply. **39.33**

---

[10] See e.g. *ETA SA Manufacture Horlogère Suisse*, RPW 2005/1, 128 ff; *Swatch Group Lieferstopp*, RPW 2011/3, 400 ff.

[11] Swatch Group Lieferstopp, Decision of the ComCo of October 21, 2013.

[12] *Watt Suisse AG/Migros*, RPW 2003/4, 925 ff. For more on this topic, please refer to Section I.H.

[13] See Section I.F.

K. Standard-setting groups (disclosure requirements, licensing arrangements, and licensing pools)

39.34 The Cartel Act does not provide for any specific rules governing standard-setting organizations. Therefore, the general competition rules are applicable to standard-setting organizations. In the case law, standards have so far only been discussed in connection with other forms of abusive behavior of dominant firms.[14]

39.35 In general, standard setting may raise a series of competition issues. If several undertakings form a group to set up a standard, there is a risk of facilitating collusion or quantity restraints. Also, access to the standard might be restricted. Furthermore, there is the risk of lock-in effects once the standard has been established. Thus, innovation could be harmed.

39.36 Without market power (mainly where competing standards exist), restrictive effects on competition are unlikely. Competition issues increase the more important a standard becomes. Control over an indispensable standard may be equivalent to a dominant position which can be held by a single entity or collectively by a group of entities. Competition law risks for standards can be minimized by implementing unrestricted participation in the standard adoption procedure, the creation of a transparent standard adoption procedure, by not imposing an obligation to comply with the standard, and, if applicable, by establishing a clear and balanced policy regarding implemented intellectual property rights.

L. Customer termination

39.37 The rules on refusals to deal also include customers. Therefore, please refer to Section I.H.

M. Termination of intermediaries

39.38 The rules on refusals to deal also include intermediaries. Therefore, please refer to Section I.H.

N. Termination of relationship with competitors

39.39 The rules on refusals to deal also include competitors. Therefore, please refer to Section I.H.

O. Exemptions

39.40 Article 7(1) Cartel Act does not provide for specific exemptions. It applies across all sectors of the economy. Article 3 Cartel Act provides that where a statute (enacted by Parliament) specifically does not allow for competition in a market for certain goods or services, such rules take precedence over the provisions of the Cartel Act. Such statutory provisions include in particular provisions that establish an official market or price system (art. 3(1)(a) Cartel Act) and provisions that grant special rights to specific undertakings for the fulfillment of public duties (art. 3(1)(b) Cartel Act).

II. Dealing with competitors

39.41 The general provision on agreements of horizontal or vertical nature set forth in article 5(1) Cartel Act establishes that all agreements that significantly restrict competition in a market for specific goods or services and that are not justified on grounds of economic efficiency, as well as all agreements that eliminate effective competition, are unlawful.

---

[14] *SIX/Terminals* (n 4).

The regulatory framework of the Cartel Act is governed by the principle of abuse. The mere existence of an anticompetitive agreement does not in itself mean that such agreement is unlawful. To qualify as unlawful, an agreement must either eliminate effective competition or significantly impede effective competition without being justified on economic efficiency grounds. For certain categories of agreements, which are considered to be particularly detrimental to competition, articles 5(3) and 5(4) Cartel Act impose a statutory presumption that these restraints *eliminate* effective competition. This presumption covers horizontal agreements that directly or indirectly fix prices; restrict quantities of goods or services to be produced, purchased, or supplied; or allocate markets geographically or according to trading partners (art. 5(3) Cartel Act) and vertical agreements that contain minimum or fixed resale prices or foreclose geographical markets (art. 5(4) Cartel Act). **39.42**

For article 5(3) Cartel Act to apply, the anticompetitive horizontal agreement must be entered into between actual or potential competitors. Undertakings are actual competitors if their goods or services are offered or requested on the same market level (horizontal relationship). The inclusion of potential competitors shall ensure that undertakings that may immediately, or in a short timeframe of approximately two to three years, enter the affected market and consequently exercise competitive pressure on the existing players are also covered by the scope of the legal presumption. The mere possibility of a limitation of potential competition may already satisfy the thresholds of article 5(3) Cartel Act and cannot be justified by grounds of economic efficiency as set out in article 5(2) Cartel Act. **39.43**

If all requirements of article 5(3) Cartel Act are established, the legal presumption applies and effective competition is deemed eliminated. Provided the presumption is not rebutted as described below, the restraint is unlawful and may not be justified on grounds of economic efficiencies. **39.44**

The legal presumption can be rebutted if the undertakings involved successfully demonstrate that, as a matter of fact, effective competition has not been eliminated by the agreement. If the presumption is successfully rebutted, the test of whether the agreement between competitors significantly restricts competition applies. A significant restriction of competition requires the parties to such an agreement to reach a certain minimal market power. Moreover, agreements significantly restricting competition are only unlawful if they cannot be justified on grounds of economic efficiencies (art. 5(2) Cartel Act). These economic efficiencies may include reduction in production or distribution costs, an improvement in products or production processes, promotion of research into, or the dissemination of, technical or professional know-how, and more effective exploitation of resources. **39.45**

In order to rebut the presumption, the undertakings must establish sufficient residual competition on the market(s) affected by the restraint, i.e. sufficient residual internal competition (between the undertakings involved) or external competition (between the undertakings not involved). This assessment is done on the basis of quantitative and/or qualitative criteria. **39.46**

To establish residual *external* competition on the basis of quantitative criteria, the number and characteristics of competitors is of particular relevance. The market position of the undertakings involved in a restrictive practice is compared to the position of other, actual or potential, competitors on the relevant market. In a qualitative assessment, the competitive parameters not affected by the restraint are weighted against those affected by the restraint. Sufficient residual competition exists as long as the compensating (i.e. unaffected) parameters are of similar relevance as those affected by the restraint. In general, sufficient external competition exists if the supply or demand of the other undertakings is a real option for the trading partners of the undertakings involved in the restraint. Therefore, the market share and the number of competitors are of particular importance. **39.47**

39.48 Sufficient residual *internal* competition prevails on a relevant market if the agreement is not followed by the participating undertakings, or if effective competition persists with regard to other competitive parameters not affected by the agreement.[15]

39.49 Finally, in such cases, direct sanctions pursuant to article 49a(1) Cartel Act apply, and an undertaking participating in an unlawful agreement under article 5(3) Cartel Act risks being charged a fine in the amount of up to 10 percent of the turnover generated in Switzerland in the preceding three financial years. In its practice, the ComCo imposes direct sanctions under article 49a(1) Cartel Act also in cases where the presumption of article 5(3) Cartel Act is rebutted, but the agreement to share markets, fix prices, or quantities is still regarded as impeding effective competition under article 5(1) Cartel Act. The threshold for justifying such agreements on the ground of economic efficiencies is high. This was confirmed recently in the *Music Distribution* case and in the *ASCOPA* decision.[16]

A. Horizontal price fixing (including advanced announcements of price or product changes)

39.50 As outlined above, agreements to fix prices between actual or potential competitors are presumed to eliminate effective competition pursuant to article 5(3) Cartel Act. Authorities tend to interpret the notion of price broadly. It may not only cover the price itself, i.e. the monetary amount paid for specific goods or services, but also price elements or components. It covers prices on upstream markets as well as prices on downstream markets. On the supply side, it may concern, for example, wholesale prices and, in particular, purchasing cooperatives, common price policies.[17]

39.51 A broad range of means may be used to coordinate prices. Under the Cartel Act, the effect of price coordination is relevant but not the means by which it is achieved. Accordingly, decisions of trade associations, market price information systems, registries in public procurement proceedings, or even joint ventures, may serve as a means for unlawful price coordination.

39.52 Prices can be fixed either directly or indirectly. Direct price fixing includes agreements in which any deviation from the agreed price is prohibited and where the undertakings involved are left no room for competing on prices. Usually, it involves the setting of minimum or maximum prices. Indirect price fixing arrangements may cover, for example, agreements on discounts and rebates; the setting of price relations between separate products; the determination of price mark-ups; or agreements on clearing or commission models. Advanced announcements of prices or product changes are particularly sensitive if the audience is not simultaneously and non-discriminatorily informed about the planned change.

B. Horizontal agreements to allocate customers or territories; agreements not to compete

39.53 Horizontal agreements between competitors on the allocation of customers or territories are also covered by the legal presumption of article 5(3) Cartel Act.

39.54 An agreement on the allocation of territories or customers can be entered into directly by agreeing not to supply the territories or customers allocated to the other undertaking. The same foreclosure effects can also result for example from licensing or similar agreements. Indirect market sharing also falls within the scope of article 5(3) Cartel Act. In *Markt für Strassenbeläge*,[18] exclusivity arrangements between manufacturers not to supply customers

[15] *Buchpreisbindung*, RPW 2002/4, 731 ff.
[16] *Music Distribution*, RPW 2012/4, 820 ff.; *ASCOPA*, RPW 2011/4, 529 ff.
[17] *Tarifverträge Zusatzversicherung Kanton Luzern*, RPW 2008/4, 554 ff.
[18] *Markt für Strassenbeläge*, RPW 2000/4, 588 ff.

in the territory of other manufacturers, or to supply via these manufacturers only, were deemed unlawful. Customer protection and non-compete provisions were held unlawful in *Reine Gase und Mischgase.*[19] Other cases involved agreements not to solicit customers[20] or prohibiting passive sales.[21] In *Swico/Sens*,[22] ComCo considered an agreement between two entities, where one partner assumed the task of disposing electric office equipment and the other partner was responsible for the disposal of household appliances, as an agreement on the allocation of customers and, therefore, declared it unlawful. In two bid rigging cases, *Strassenbeläge Tessin* and *Wettbewerbsabreden im Strassen- und Tiefbau im Kanton Zürich*[23] ComCo also identified a market sharing agreement in the form of a customer allocation between the undertakings involved. In a recent settlement decision on music distribution,[24] ComCo held that the agreement among the members of a record producers' association to refrain from parallel imports qualified as horizontal market sharing within the meaning of article 5(3) Cartel Act.

C. Restrictions on quantities of goods or services to be produced, purchased, or supplied

The third category of agreements presumed to eliminate effective competition consists in agreements on the restriction of quantities of goods or services to be produced, purchased, or supplied. On downstream markets, quotas may be allocated by defining production output,[25] and on upstream markets supply volumes[26] or purchase cooperations may be agreed upon. **39.55**

On the basis of an effects-based approach, the restriction on quantity must be suitable for affecting effective competition. The benchmark must not necessarily be the actual level of production, purchase, or supply, since for example an agreement not to increase capacity irrespective of increased demand is covered by the presumption. A refusal to supply by a group of competitors (horizontal boycott) with the aim of preventing a customer or supplier from entering a market may also fall within the scope of this category. **39.56**

D. Joint ventures and other competitive collaborations

The analysis of horizontal cooperation agreements shares common elements with merger control rules. The merger control regime applies if horizontal cooperation is established in the form of a full-function joint venture, i.e. where the parties acquire joint control over an undertaking that performs on a lasting basis all functions of an independent economic entity. **39.57**

Where the full-functionality of the joint venture cannot be established, the horizontal cooperation will be scrutinized under article 5 Cartel Act. In a recent case on cooperation with regard to the construction and operation of a fibre-to-the-home network between the incumbent Swiss telecommunications service provider and a local energy supply company, ComCo concluded that the full-functionality test was not satisfied and, subsequently, opened a preliminary investigation against the two companies.[27] **39.58**

---

[19] *Reine Gase und Mischgase*, RPW 1999/1, 67 ff.

[20] *Kooperationsvorhaben UBS/Postfinance—Die Schweizerische Post*, RPW 2003/2, 262 ff.

[21] *Livres en langue française, Decision of the ComCo of* May 27, 2013.

[22] *Swico/Sens*, RPW 2002/2, 265 ff.

[23] *Strassenbeläge Tessin*, RPW 2008/1, 96 ff.; *Wettbewerbsabreden im Strassen- und Tiefbau im Kanton Zürich*, Decision of the ComCo of April 22, 2013.

[24] *Music Distribution* (n 16).

[25] See *Accords sur les prix/repartition des ventes sur le marché des vitamins*, RPW 2000/2, 186 ff.

[26] *Markt für Strassenbeläge*, RPW 2000/4, 588 ff.

[27] *FTTH Fribourg*, RPW 2012/2, 171 ff.

39.59 Accordingly, agreements between competitors on cooperation or collaboration in research and development, joint manufacturing, marketing, or purchasing must be drafted with a particular view to horizontal price fixing, market sharing, or restrictions on quantities, and with a particular focus on issues relating to the exchange of competitively sensitive information.[28]

E. Trade associations

39.60 Decisions of trade associations may also qualify as an agreement falling under article 5 Cartel Act. Interactions between competitors in the framework of trade associations were the subject matter of several decisions of the ComCo. Recent examples include a settlement decision in the field of music distribution,[29] where the members of a record producers' association mutually agreed to refrain from parallel imports of records of other members of the association. This declaration and the fact that no parallel imports were in fact made was qualified as horizontal market sharing within the meaning of article 5(3) Cartel Act. While the legal presumption was successfully rebutted, the agreement could not be justified under article 5(2) Cartel Act, and ComCo imposed fines on the trade association representing its members.

39.61 In general, trade associations must not offer their members a platform to collude, and liability may not be avoided by interposing a trade association. In this respect, market price information systems generally increase price-transparency and, in the end, may even lead to a situation where the undertakings involved implicitly align prices in breach of article 5(3) Cartel Act. Also, reporting platforms operated by trade associations may be deemed unlawful. In a 2003 decision against the Swiss Contractors Association,[30] ComCo came to the conclusion that the operation of a platform on which contractors registered procurement projects and where competitors had access to such registration could raise competition law concerns.

F. Interlocking directorates

39.62 Interlocking directorates may give rise to concerns from various angles, be it with regard to concerted practices, dominance, or merger control. In the present context, however, the focus is on the potential risk of liability for information exchange through interlocking directorates, i.e. concerted practices.[31]

39.63 So far, interlocking directorates have not been sanctioned in ComCo's case practice. Nevertheless, the appointment of common members in the executive bodies of competing undertakings may be viewed as a means to facilitate coordination. The main concern is about systematic exchange of certain market data allowing undertakings to anticipate their competitors' market behavior. Already the participation in meetings during which competitively sensitive topics are discussed may qualify as concerted practice. A particularly high risk, however, exists where such interlocking directorates are established between undertakings active in the same product and geographic markets, i.e. which are in a horizontal relationship.

G. Facilitating practices

39.64 There is no case law on facilitating practices similar to the cases against *AC Treuhand* in the EU.[32]

---

[28] See Section II.H.

[29] *Music Distribution* (n 16).

[30] *Wettbewerbsreglement des Schweizerischen Baumeisterverbandes*, RPW 2003/4, 72 ff.

[31] See also Section II.H.

[32] T-99/04 *AC-Treuhand v. Commission* [2008] ECR II-01501 and T-27/10 *AC-Treuhand v. Commission*, pending. However, in the *Music Distribution* case (n 16) one party was fined for supporting an illegal agreement.

H. Information exchange

In general, exchange of information raises competition concerns if the exchange of specific information prevents competitors from acting independently and autonomously from each other because their actions are influenced by the information received from competitors. The exchange of information is particularly likely to be qualified as unlawful in case of concentrated, stable and symmetric markets. **39.65**

The relevant criteria include, in particular, the content of the exchanged information, i.e. whether the information is competitively sensitive. Such data may for instance consist of price-related information, such as actual prices or discounts. Moreover, the level of detail and aggregation will be taken into account, as well as the age of the data (i.e. whether it is historic or current) and the frequency of exchanges. Finally, publicly available information that is equally accessible to all competitors or customers is not likely to cause concerns from a competition law perspective. **39.66**

In a recent decision of October 31, 2011 in the field of luxury cosmetics,[33] the ComCo prohibited the exchange of information on prices, turnovers, advertising expenses, and sales terms between several undertakings. The ComCo held that the information exchange between the participating undertakings infringed the Cartel Act because the exchanged information allowed the participants to adjust their market behavior to one another. However, the ComCo considered that this information exchange could not be regarded as a hard-core cartel and, therefore, did not impose a penalty on the undertakings involved. The decision provides general guidance on the ComCo's practice in relation to information exchange. In the *ASCOPA* case, the undertakings involved shared information on sales figures and turnovers, gross sell-in prices charged to their respective retailers, marketing channels, advertising expenses, and general sales conditions. **39.67**

The exchanges involving gross sell-in prices and marketing expenses occurred regularly on a semi-annual basis. Whilst having a different level of detail, information on sales figures and turnovers occurred on a monthly, quarterly, and annual basis. As a result, ASCOPA members were able to integrate this data into their cost analyses for new products, but also to adjust pricing policies in response to the other members' strategies. The ComCo concluded that such information exchange went beyond "benchmarking" activities and that the ASCOPA members were enabled to adjust their market behavior relative to each other. **39.68**

I. Joint purchasing agreements

Joint purchasing agreements concern the joint purchase of products through, for example a jointly controlled company, a company in which other companies hold non-controlling stakes, a contractual arrangements, or similar forms. The main goal of joint purchasing agreements is to create or strengthen buyer power. Whilst this may be beneficial to consumers if it results in lower prices or better quality, buyer power may also give rise to competition law concerns from a horizontal and vertical perspective. If horizontal and vertical agreements are involved, a two-step analysis becomes necessary. First, the horizontal agreements between the undertakings engaged in joint purchasing have to be assessed. Second, the relevant vertical agreements need to be reviewed. **39.69**

Generally speaking, joint purchasing may lead to restraints of competition on the purchasing and/or downstream selling market, including increased prices, reduced output, product quality or variety, or innovation, market allocation, or foreclosure of competing purchasers. **39.70**

[33] *ASCOPA* (n 16).

Joint purchasing arrangements are particularly likely to restrict competition if they do not actually concern joint purchasing, but serve as a means to engage in cartelistic behavior—i.e., otherwise prohibited price fixing, output limitation or market allocation.

J. Joint lobbying/regulatory/legislative efforts

39.71 These kinds of activities are not likely to fall within the scope of the Cartel Act and there is no particular case law on this.

III. General issues

A. Jurisdiction and applicable law (including sector-specific competition regulation)

39.72 Competition law in Switzerland is regulated by the Cartel Act and its implementing ordinances. Furthermore, the ComCo issues general notices and communications. The objective of the Cartel Act is to prevent the harmful economic or social effects of cartels and other restraints of competition and, by doing so, to promote competition in the interests of a liberal market economy.

39.73 It applies to any private or public undertaking engaged in an economic process that offers or acquires goods or services. Neither the organization nor the legal form of an undertaking is relevant. The Cartel Act applies to practices that have an effect in Switzerland, even if they originate in another country.

39.74 The ComCo's general notices set out the conditions under which agreements affecting competition are as a general rule deemed justified on grounds of economic efficiency. They relate in particular to vertical agreements in general, vertical agreements in the automotive sector, small and medium-sized businesses, homologation and sponsoring of sporting goods and use of calculation tools.

B. Antitrust system

(i) Name of agency/agencies

39.75 The federal authorities administering the Cartel Act are the ComCo and the Secretariat of the Competition Commission ("Secretariat"). The ComCo consists of twelve members (usually lawyers, economists, and, importantly, also representatives of business associations and consumer organizations) who are elected by the Federal Council. The majority of the ComCo members must be independent experts.

39.76 The Secretariat is institutionally separate from the ComCo. Its main task is to investigate and prepare the cases to be decided by the ComCo.

(ii) Staff size and budget

39.77 The ComCo consists of twelve (part-time) members. Its full-time Secretariat on the other hand has—after a significant staff increase in 2012—an equivalent of approximately seventy full-time employees at its disposal. For 2013, the ComCo has a budget of approximately CHF 13 million.

(iii) Recent enforcement actions and trends

39.78 The ComCo has been concerned that despite the revaluation of the Swiss Franc, imported goods have not become cheaper. In this regard, the ComCo has intensified investigations of horizontal price fixing, resale price maintenance, as well as restrictions on parallel imports into Switzerland.

A particular enforcement priority is the action against cartels in the construction sector. For this purpose, the ComCo has established a new service, which only treats cases in the field of the construction market. 39.79

C. Private litigation

According to article 12 Cartel Act, a person hindered by an unlawful restraint on competition from entering or competing in a market is entitled to request (i) the elimination of, or desistance from, the restraint on competition; (ii) damages and satisfaction in accordance with the Swiss Federal Code of Obligations; and (iii) surrender of unlawfully earned profits. Such restraints on competition include in particular the refusal to deal and discriminatory measures. 39.80

In order to enforce the right to elimination and desistance, the courts may, at the plaintiff's request, rule that contracts are null and void in whole or in part. In addition, the undertaking engaging in unlawful restraints of competition may be bound to conclude contracts with the plaintiff on terms that are in line with the market or the industry standard. 39.81

So far, there have been only a few private litigation cases. This might be due to the fact that the claimant bears the burden of proof, in particular of the damages incurred. In one past cartel case decided by the ComCo,[34] the parties settled their dispute on damages in an extra-judicial agreement. 39.82

D. Follow-on litigation (includes role of agency determinations of liability for follow-on litigation)

An injured party can bring an action for damages in civil courts. The Swiss Civil Procedure Code does not provide for class action. 39.83

If the legality of a restrictive practice is questioned in the course of civil proceedings, the case is referred to the ComCo for an expert report. 39.84

E. Arbitration and alternative dispute resolution

Private action can be resolved through arbitration or other means of alternative dispute resolution. According to the Swiss Civil Procedure Code, parties to a dispute can agree on arbitration. The arbitration agreement may relate to existing or future disputes arising from a specific legal relationship. 39.85

The Swiss Civil Procedure Code also provides for mediation. The parties may at any time make a joint request for mediation. The court proceedings remain suspended until the request is withdrawn by one of the parties or until the court is notified of the end of the mediation. Mediation proceedings are confidential and separate from the court proceedings. So far, there have been no published mediation cases in competition law. 39.86

F. Remedies

(i) Civil liability

From a civil law point of view, cartel activities result in the total or partial nullity of the agreement in question. Although generally accepted by the doctrine, it has not yet been confirmed by the courts that the nullity of the agreements applies *ex tunc*. 39.87

Third parties affected by a cartel may sue the cartel members for damages in civil courts, claiming damages and reparations or restitution of unlawful profits obtained from the illegal cartel 39.88

34 *Strassenbeläge Tessin* (n 23) 85 ff.

activity. However, since the claimant bears the burden of proof, under Swiss law, the main difficulty that arises in practice is providing sufficient evidence of the damage incurred and establishing a causal link between the anticompetitive agreement and such damage. Class actions are not yet available under Swiss law. Consumers and consumer organizations may participate in investigations before the Commission but, in general, have no standing before civil courts. Whether and to what extent trade associations have standing is a matter of dispute.

39.89 From an administrative law point of view, the maximum administrative sanction the ComCo can impose is a fine in the amount of up to 10 percent of the (cumulative) turnover realized in Switzerland during the last three financial years. The amount of the fine is calculated by taking into account the duration and gravity of the unlawful agreements or practices, as well as the presumed profit gained from the unlawful agreements or practices. Aggravating factors (such as recidivism, a leading role in the cartel, or non-cooperation with the authorities) or mitigating factors (such as a passive role in the cartel, effective cooperation with the authorities, or severe and effective compliance programs) also have an influence.

39.90 Furthermore, an undertaking that, to its own advantage, violates an amicable settlement, a legally enforceable decision of the ComCo, or a judgment either of the Federal Administrative Tribunal or the Federal Supreme Court, can be fined by the ComCo in the amount of up to three times the profit generated from such non-compliance. If such profit cannot be calculated or estimated, the amount may not exceed 10 percent of the undertaking's most recent annual turnover in Switzerland.

39.91 Finally, an undertaking that fails to provide information or produce documents, or that only partially complies with its obligations during an ongoing investigation, can be fined up to CHF 100,000.

(ii) Criminal liability

39.92 There are no direct criminal sanctions for individuals participating in cartel activities unless acting as undertakings on their own. However, individuals acting on behalf of an undertaking and violating an amicable settlement, a legally enforceable decision, or a court judgment may be fined in the amount of up to CHF 100,000. Individuals who intentionally fail to comply or only partly comply with the obligation to provide information in an ongoing investigation can be fined up to CHF 20,000. Individuals who can be fined include executives and board members as well as all de facto managers and directors. These sanctions are, nevertheless, time-barred after five years following the incriminating act. In contrast to various other European jurisdictions, there is no express criminal provision on bid rigging.

G. Leniency and immunity

39.93 The Cartel Act contains a leniency/immunity program as well as an opposition procedure. If the undertaking assists in the discovery and elimination of the restraint of competition, a charge may be waived in whole or in part. Only the first whistle-blower may enjoy full immunity. The threshold for full immunity is rather high, and requires in particular that the Commission as yet has no information on the case at issue, and that the undertaking in question does not qualify as the ringleader.

39.94 Although under the Cartel Act, immunity is limited to the "first in," cooperating in investigations can help limit the level of the sanction or fine. Thus, going in second will not secure total immunity from a fine but it may be an element in view of obtaining partial immunity of up to 50 percent. Further, the amount of the fine can be reduced by up to 80 percent if an undertaking provides information to the Commission about other hard core restraints of competition, if such hard core restraints on competition were unknown to the Commission at the time of disclosure (amnesty plus program).

In addition to the leniency program, immunity is granted if (i) the undertaking notices the restraint on competition before it takes effect (opposition procedure). If the undertaking is informed of the opening of a procedure within five months following its notification but continues to implement the anticompetitive behavior, the immunity is lost. It is also granted if (ii) the restraint on competition has not been exercised for more than five years by the time an investigation is opened; or (iii) the Federal Council has authorized a restraint on competition. However, no such authorization has been granted to date. **39.95**

H. Document creation and retention

With respect to competition regulations, parties to agreements, undertakings with market power, undertakings involved in concentrations, as well as affected third parties have to provide the competition authorities with all the information required in the investigation, and produce all the necessary documents (duty of cooperation). **39.96**

Moreover, other federal and cantonal government offices are also required to cooperate with the competition authorities in their inquiries, and to make any necessary documents available to them. The competition authorities may publish their decisions. **39.97**

While in principle the duty to cooperate covers all documents, there are nevertheless some exemptions. The most important one relates to legal privilege and the protection against self-incrimination. **39.98**

It is also important to note that the right of access to witness statements, minutes of hearings and other documents relevant to the investigation may be limited to protect cooperating parties and business secrets. **39.99**

40

TAIWAN

*Matt Liu, Tim Chou, and Yawen Yang**

Tsaw & Tsai Law Firm

Introduction

40.01 The Fair Trade Act of Taiwan (TFTA) is the antitrust legislation in Taiwan. The TFTA regulates, *inter alia*, both unilateral conduct and cartels. Among all anticompetitive behaviors, international companies should pay particular attention to the risk of violation of the prohibition of concerted actions. The Fair Trade Commission of Taiwan (TFTC) has been very active in taking enforcement actions against concerted actions. Companies with a dominant or significant market power should be cautious when determining their pricing. Such legal risk is greater for companies supplying consumer products because the TFTC regularly watches the price change of certain important consumer products.

* Matt Liu, Integrated Partner, Tsar & Tsai Law Firm; Tim Chou, former Associate Partner, Tsar & Tsai Law Firm; Yawen Yang, former Senior Associate, Tsar & Tsai Law Firm.

In November 2011, the TFTA was amended to introduce a leniency program. In September 2012, the TFTC issued its first international cartel decision, in which it sanctioned several global optic disk drive suppliers for participating in bid-rigging concerning certain online biddings of HP and Dell. In this case, the TFTC heavily relied on the statements and evidence submitted by a leniency applicant. The TFTC indicated in a press conference that it will strengthen its enforcement actions against international cartel. Currently, a bill for amendment to the TFTA, which will grant the search and seizure power to the TFTC, is pending in the Taiwan legislature. If the amendment is passed by the Taiwan legislators, it is expected that the TFTC's enforcement against concerted action will be stronger and more effective. **40.02**

I. Acting alone

Abuse of dominance is an infringement under the TFTA. Article 10 of the TFTA prohibits any monopolistic enterprise from (1) directly or indirectly preventing any other enterprises from competing by unfair means; (2) improperly setting, maintaining, or changing the price for goods or the remuneration for services; (3) obtaining preferential treatment from a trading counterpart without justification; and (4) engaging in any other abuse of market power. **40.03**

"Dominance" under the TFTA is defined as an enterprise which (1) has market power to exclude competition in a relevant market; (2) generates TWD 1 billion or more in its total turnover in the preceding fiscal year; and (3) enjoys a of local market share of 50 percent or more. If the market is subject to special legal or technological restraints, the TFTC may disregard the thresholds of turnover and market share set forth above to determine the dominance.[1] Furthermore, if two or more enterprises do not in fact engage in price competition with each other and they as a whole meet the definition of dominance, the enterprises would be deemed as monopolistic enterprises.[2] **40.04**

While article 10 of the TFTA only applies to unilateral conduct of a dominant enterprise, article 19 of the TFTA may apply to dominant and non-dominant enterprises with respect to unreasonable restraint of competition. Article 19 prohibits any enterprise from engaging in any of the following activities which are likely to lessen competition or to impede fair competition: (1) boycott; (2) offering discriminatory treatments to other enterprises without a justifiable ground; (3) forcing the trading counterparts of the competitor to do business with itself by means of coercion, seduction, or any other improper means; (4) causing other enterprises to refrain from competing with itself by means of coercion, seduction, or any other improper means; and (5) imposing improper restrictions on the business activities of one's trading partners as a condition of business partnership, such as unreasonable tying arrangement, allocation of customers or territory, and exclusive dealing. Historically, the TFTC brought many more abuse of dominance cases pursuant to article 19 than to article 10 because it is difficult to prove the monopolistic position of the violator. In recent years, the TFTC paid a lot of attention to unreasonable allocation of territory and/or customers. In 2012 alone, the TFTC brought three cases in this regard.[3] The violators were fined TWD 2 million and TWD 3.5 million respectively. In addition, the TFTC brought many cases on **40.05**

---

[1] *Trade-Van Information Services Co.*, Kung-Chu-Tzu Case no. 094017 (2005).

[2] *Koninklijke Philips Electronics, N.V., Sony Corporation, and Taiyo Yuden Co., Ltd.*, Kung-Chu-Tzu Case no. 098156 (2009).

[3] *Hotai Motor Co., Ltd.*, Kung-Chu-Tzu Case no. 101031 (2012); *Merida Industry Co., Ltd.*, Kung-Chu-Tzu Case no. 101063 (2012); and *Giant Manufacturing Co., Ltd.*, Kung-Chu-Tzu Case no. 101153 (2012).

resale price maintenance and causing other enterprises to refrain from competing. Notable resale price maintenance cases include *Nestle baby formula*,[4] in which Nestlé was fined TWD 2.5 million, and *IMEI soybean milk*,[5] in which IMEI was fined TWD 1 million. In a case concerning the act of forcing other enterprises to refrain from competing, the violators were imposed an administrative fine up to TWD 3 million.[6]

A. Predatory pricing

40.06 Predatory Pricing is a type of abuse of dominance and therefore violates article 10 of the TFTA. Guidelines on the Business Practices of Cross-Ownership and Joint Provision among 4C Enterprises ("4C Guidelines") promulgated by the TFTC provide that predatory pricing constitutes abuse of dominance. The 4C Guidelines also specify that predatory pricing is composed by three elements: (1) the product or service is priced below the average variable cost or the average incremental cost; (2) the enterprise intends to impede or exclude its competitors by such pricing policy; and (3) the enterprise is capable of recovering its losses and raising its prices to the level of monopolistic price after its competitors have been impeded or excluded from the market. However, such conduct could be regarded as reasonable when the lower prices are used as part of a short-term promotion method, or when an unexpected fall in the costs results in lower prices. In recent years, the TFTC hasn't brought any predatory pricing cases.

B. Exploitative offenses

40.07 Excessive pricing or imposing other exploitative conditions on the trading partners can constitute abuse of dominance and therefore violates article 10 of the TFTA.

40.08 Monopolistic enterprises' concealment of material information from consumers, or provision of improper pricing information to consumers, can be regarded as abuse of dominance. In Case No. 83/2000,[7] a gas company with a dominant position was found in violation of article 10 of the TFTA because it did not disclose certain material information to its customers and provided the customers with improper type of meters which cost the customers higher monthly fees. To determine if the price is reasonable, the TFTC may also compare the price with those in other geographic markets, and consider whether the enterprise has any business justification.[8] Generally speaking, the TFTC does not bring exploitative cases frequently.

C. Monopsony

40.09 Under the TFTA, dominance refers to both dominant selling position and dominant purchasing position. Article 10 of the TFTA applies to monopoly as well as monopsony if an enterprise conducts business by abusing its dominant position. In particular, article 10 (3) of the TFTA provides that no monopolistic enterprises shall "make a trading counterpart give preferential treatment without justification," which specifically indicates that monopsony shall be regulated under article 10 of the TFTA. Nevertheless, there have been no monopsony cases brought by the TFTC as of today.

D. Price discrimination

40.10 Dominant enterprises conducting business by way of price or non-price-related discrimination will be in violation of article 10 of the TFTA. Non-dominant enterprises conducting

4 *Nestle Taiwan Limited*, Kung-Chu-Tzu Case no. 096102 (2007).
5 *Shine Mei Foods Marketing & Distribution Co., Ltd.*, Kung-Chu-Tzu Case no. 101076 (2012).
6 *New Century Advertising Corp.*, Kung-Chu-Tzu Case no. 101009 (2012).
7 *The Great Taipei Gas Corporation*, Kung-Chu-Tzu Case no. 083 (2000).
8 *Ji-Ding Development Co., Ltd.*, Kung-Chu-Tzu Case no. 085 (2000).

business by way of price or non-price-related discrimination will be in violation of article 19(2) of the TFTA.

Dominant enterprises are prohibited from implementing price discrimination between its customers in order to maintain their dominant position. In 1999, a monopolistic oil company implementing price discrimination between its customers was found in violation of article 10 of the TFTA.[9] The oil company lowered the supply price of liquefied natural gas to customers who were exclusively supplied by the oil company so as to punish those engaged in business with new importers, i.e. new competitors of the oil company. **40.11**

Non-dominant enterprises with a substantial market position conducting business by way of price or non-price-related discrimination without business justifications can be found in violation of article 19(2) of the TFTA. Based on the TFTC's precedents, enterprises with a market share of 25 percent or more are very likely to be regarded as having a substantial market position.[10] Enterprises with a market share between 10 percent and 25 percent may be regarded as having a substantial market position in terms of price discrimination. However, this is not to say that enterprises with a market share below 10 percent would not be deemed as having a substantial market position. The TFTC has exercised discretion in determining the market share threshold for finding of a substantial market position on a case-by-case basis. Generally speaking, the TFTC does not bring price discrimination cases frequently. **40.12**

E. Dictating or influencing resale prices

(i) Resale price maintenance

Minimum resale price maintenance (RPM) is illegal per se under article 18 of the TFTA. Under article 18, a supplier shall allow its distributors to decide the resale prices based on their own business considerations so as to maintain competition at the distributor level. If a supplier sets minimum resale prices of its products and takes measures to request the distributors to follow, such action would deprive distributors of their freedom to set their own prices, and it would impede price competition among distributors. The TFTC regularly brings minimum RPM cases.[11] Just like price fixing among competitors, fixed resale price is strictly scrutinized by the TFTC. **40.13**

However, a recommended resale price set forth by a supplier without compelling measures to force distributors to employ such recommended resale price is not in violation of the RPM provision. Nevertheless, the concept of compelling measures would not be limited to actual disadvantage imposed on distributors. As long as distributors are hindered in their activities by the actions or schemes engaged in by the supplier, these actions or schemes can be regarded as compelling measures depriving the distributors of their freedom to make their own price decision.[12] Compelling measures include refusal to deal, termination of relationship with the distributor, punishment schemes or other actions with a similar effect. Recent significant resale price maintenance cases include *Nestle baby formula*,[13] in which Nestle was fined TWD 2.5 million, and *IMEI soybean milk*,[14] in which IMEI was fined TWD 1 million. **40.14**

---

[9] *CPC Corporation, Taiwan*, Kung-Chu-Tzu Case no. 091050 (2002).

[10] *Filmate International Incorporation*, Kung-Chu-Tzu Case no. 038 (1998); *Nan I Book Enterprise Co., Ltd.*, Kung-Chu-Tzu Case no. 087 (1998).

[11] See e.g. *Chung Hsiang Foods Industry Co., Ltd.*, Kung-Chu-Tzu Case no. 101068 (2012); *Shine Mei Foods Marketing & Distribution Co., Ltd.* (n 5); *Commonwealth Publishing Co., Ltd.*, Kung-Chu-Tzu Case no. 101137 (2012); and *Giant Manufacturing Co., Ltd.* (n 3)

[12] *Hocheng Corporation*, Kung-Chu-Tzu Case no. 100005 (2011).

[13] Nestle Taiwan Limited (n 4).

[14] Shine Mei Foods Marketing & Distribution Co., Ltd (n 5).

40.15 Maximum resale price maintenance is also caught by article 18 of the TFTA, and thus shall be scrutinized under the per se illegal rule.[15] However, maximum RPM and minimum RPM may have different effects on the competition. It would be reasonable to apply different levels of scrutiny to these two types of RPM. Nevertheless, the TFTC has not brought any maximum RPM case since its decision in.[16]

40.16 In the latest draft Amendment to the TFTA proposed by the TFTC in December 2012, RPM is proposed to be scrutinized by the "rule of reason," instead of the "per se illegal" rule. The draft amendment is pending review by the Taiwanese legislative body.

(ii) Minimum advertised price programs

40.17 Taiwan law does not distinguish between minimum advertised prices (MAP) and RPMs. As indicated in Section I.E(i), as long as suppliers impose compelling measures on distributors to deprive distributors' freedom of price decision, such compelling measures can be in violation of RPM law.

F. Tying arrangements

40.18 In principle, tying arrangements can be caught by article 10 of the TFTA if the seller has dominant market power. However, in practice, the TFTC usually brings such cases pursuant to article 19(6) of the TFTA, regardless of whether the seller has dominant market power. Under article 19 of the TFTA, tying arrangements are scrutinized under the rule of reason.

40.19 The TFTC will consider the following five elements with respect to the legitimacy of tying arrangements: (1) there are two separate products; (2) the buyer is prevented from purchasing the products separately; (3) the seller has market power in the tying product market; (4) whether the seller has any business justification to employ the tying arrangement; and (5) how competition of the tied product market is affected by the tying arrangement.[17] Generally speaking, the TFTC does not bring tying cases frequently.

G. Exclusive dealing

40.20 Similar to tying arrangements, suppliers having dominant market power and conducting exclusive dealing can be subject to article 10 of the TFTA. However, in practice, the TFTC usually brings exclusive dealing cases pursuant to article 19(6) of the TFTA, regardless of whether the suppliers have dominant market power.[18] Based on this practice, exclusive dealings will be scrutinized under the rule of reason. Generally speaking, the TFTC does not bring tying cases frequently.

40.21 A separate type of unreasonable restraint is restrictions on the territory or customers, which are also subject to article 19(6) of the TFTA. In recent years, the TFTC paid a lot of attention to unreasonable restraint of territory and customers. The TFTC brought several cases with respect to territorial restrictions in 2012, especially focusing on the restrictions in online sales by distributors.[19] The violators were fined TWD 2 million to TWD 3.5 million respectively.

H. Refusal to deal

40.22 An enterprise with a dominant position refusing to deal with its trading partners can be in violation of article 10 of the TFTA. Through such practice, a monopolistic enterprise

[15] *Harvestman Industrial Co., Ltd.*, Kung-Chu-Tzu Case no. 013 (1996).
[16] *Harvestman Industrial Co., Ltd.* (n 15)
[17] *Taiwan Tobacco & Liquor Corporation*, Kung-Chu-Tzu Case no. 095142 (2006).
[18] *CPC Corporation, Taiwan*, Kung-Chu-Tzu Case no. 079 (1995).
[19] *Merida Industry Co., Ltd.* (n 3); *Giant Manufacturing Co., Ltd.* (n 3).

may extend its upstream market dominance to the downstream market. For example, an oil company with a dominant position in the domestic fueling market was found in violation of article 10 of the TFTA because it refused to supply aviation fuel to a distributor in order to preclude that distributor from the aviation fueling service market.[20]

A separate type of abuse is price squeeze. An enterprise can be in violation of article 10 of the TFTA if it has dominant market power in the upstream market and adopts unreasonable and unjustified measures in dealing with its distributors that compete in the downstream market. The measures include setting unreasonable supply price, reducing the supply of necessary parts to the distributors, or other actions with similar effect. The distributors risk being driven out of the market in the long run and the competition in the downstream market may be impeded. The TFTC indicated that the following factors should be considered in determining whether the practice is in violation of the TFTA: the dominant enterprise's intent in engaging in such practices, its cost structure, anticompetitive effects on the downstream market, etc.[21] **40.23**

Generally speaking, the TFTC does not bring refusals to deal cases frequently. **40.24**

I. Essential facilities

"Essential facilities" is not a term used in the TFTA. In the 4C Guideline, the TFTC defines essential facilities as those meeting the following elements: (1) essential facilities are controlled by a monopolist; (2) competitors (including potential competitors) are unable to duplicate equivalent essential facilities in an economically reasonable way within a short period of time; (3) competitors will be unable to compete with the controller of such essential facilities if the facilities are not accessible to the competitors; and (4) it is feasible for the controller to provide competitors with the facilities. **40.25**

Enterprises controlling essential facilities could have the dominant power to impede or exclude competitors from competition. Hence, if such enterprises, without justification, preclude competitors from having access to the facilities, cease to provide competitors with the facilities, or provide the facilities in a discriminative way which may impede competition, such actions can be in violation of article 10 of the TFTA. So far, the TFTC has not brought any essential facilities cases. **40.26**

J. Bundling (including loyalty and market share discounts)

Bundling can be caught by the article 10 of the TFTA if the enterprise engaging in bundling has dominant market power. The TFTC has stated in the 4C Guidelines that meeting consumers' habits, the convenience of one-stop shopping, and other pro-competitive effects on the economy can be business justifications. While bundling is similar to tying, it is not clear whether a non-dominant enterprise engaged in bundling can be caught by article 19(6), as it would in the case of tying. So far, the TFTC has not brought any cases involving bundling. **40.27**

Loyalty discounts can constitute an abuse of dominance in violation of article 10 of the TFTA if the enterprise engaging in such practice has dominant power. In 2005, a loyalty discount scheme imposed by a dominant enterprise was found to be an abuse of dominance. In the rebate scheme, the dominant enterprise offered its dealers a loyalty discount if the dealers exclusively purchased services provided by the dominant enterprise. If any of the dealers purchased services provided by competitors of the dominant enterprise, the dealer had to pay a penalty equal to the difference between the loyalty discount and the original rate to **40.28**

[20] *CPC Corporation, Taiwan*, Kung-Chu-Tzu Case no. 170 (2000).
[21] *The TFTC's Interpretation* No. 073 (1993).

the dominant enterprise. The TFTC has found that the penalty provision was in violation of article 10(1) of the TFTA because it increased the switching cost to the dealers, precluded competitors from the market, and impeded competition. The TFTC imposed an administrative fine of TWD 1.5 million on the infringing enterprise.[22] So far, this is the only one loyalty discount case brought by the TFTC.

K. Standard-setting groups (disclosure requirements, licensing arrangements, and licensing pools)

40.29 Pursuant to article 5 of the TFTA, two or more enterprises shall be deemed monopolistic if they do not engage in price competition with each other, and such enterprises as a whole have a dominant position in the relevant market. Therefore, the participants in a standard-setting group may be deemed to be monopolistic enterprises if the standard (including the intellectual property involved) has a dominant market power in the relevant market. As such, actions taken by the participants of the standard-setting group may be involved in excessive pricing, price discrimination, refusal to deal, or other forms of abuse of dominance.

40.30 In the lengthy CD-R case, all three members of a standard-setting group, Philips, Sony, and Taiyo Yuden, were found to be abusing their dominant power in the CD-R technology licensing market because they (1) maintained unreasonable high license fee; (2) refused to provide the licensees with material information on the licensed patent technologies, such as patent contents, scope, and duration; and (3) prohibited the licensees from contesting the validity of the licensed patents.[23] So far, this has been the only case involving standard-setting group brought by the TFTC.

L. Customer termination

40.31 The TFTA does not distinguish between customer termination and refusal to deal.[24] Absent any justification, a dominant enterprise's refusal to deal with a potential customer[25] or an existing customer would be in violation of article 10 of the TFTA.[26]

M. Termination of intermediaries (retailers, wholesalers, dealers, and value-added resellers, agents, and brokers)

40.32 The TFTA does not distinguish between termination of intermediaries and refusal to deal,[27] i.e. termination of intermediaries by a dominating enterprise can be caught by article 10 of the TFTA. However, the TFTC has not brought any cases involving termination of intermediaries.

N. Termination of relationships with competitors

40.33 Termination of relationships with competitors would not be in violation of the TFTA, unless the enterprise terminating the relationship held essential facilities.[28]

O. Exemptions

40.34 In principle, the TFTA applies to all sectors of the economy in Taiwan. Only limited exceptions provided under statutes can be exempted from the competition law. However, an

[22] *Trade-Van Information Services Co.* (n 1).
[23] *Koninklijke Philips Electronics, N.V., Sony Corporation, and Taiyo Yuden Co., Ltd.* (n 2).
[24] See Section I.H.
[25] *CPC Corporation, Taiwan* (n 20).
[26] *CPC Corporation, Taiwan,* Kung-Chu-Tzu Case no. 091050 (2002).
[27] See Section I.H.
[28] See Section I.I.

exemption is usually designed to exempt certain specific situations in an industry, not to exempt a certain industry, from the competition law. Some exemptions are:

(i) Bank Mergers in certain situations

Article 19 of the Financial Holding Company Act provides that, in certain urgent situations, with the approval from the competent authorities, a merger involving financial holding companies and their subsidiaries can be exempted from merger control regime prescribed under the TFTA. Similarly, article 13 of the Financial Institutions Merger Act provides that, in certain emergent situations with an approval from the competent authorities, a merger involving farmers association or fishers association can be exempted from the merger control regime prescribed under the TFTA. **40.35**

(ii) State action

Pursuant to article 9(2) of the TFTA, with respect to any matters involving the authority of other government agencies, the TFTC shall consult with such government agencies when dealing with such matters. In practice, if business activities taken by enterprises are approved by other government agencies, such activities would normally be exempted from TFTC's action. **40.36**

(iii) Government procurement

Matters of government procurement are not expressly exempted from the TFTA in accordance with statutes. However, after the Government Procurement Act took effect in 1999, the TFTC and the Public Construction Commission reached an agreement that government procurement matters taking place on or after the effective date of the Government Procurement Act shall be handled by the Public Procurement Commission in accordance with the Government Procurement Act. The practice was conducted since then, despite of criticism from the public. **40.37**

II. Dealing with competitors

Under article 7 of the TFTA, a concerted action refers to any contract, agreement, or any other means of collusion between horizontal competitors to jointly determine price, or limit quantity, technology, products, facilities, trading counterparties, or to allocate trading territory, etc., of their goods or services which is sufficient to affect the market functions. Concerted actions which are not significant enough to affect market functions are not regulated. Note also that under the TFTA, a trade association is considered as an "enterprise" on its own right and thus may be fined for being involved in a concerted action. **40.38**

Under article 7 of the TFTA, a concerted action which is likely to affect the market functions is prohibited, unless the participants in such concerted action have obtained the TFTC's approval based on any of the exemption grounds set forth in article 14 of the TFTA. Under article 14 of the TFTA, certain types of concerted action which may enhance efficiency, reduce costs, help enterprises to go through economic difficulty, protect small and medium-sized enterprises' survival, etc., would be permissible upon the TFTC's prior approval. In such cases, enterprises may seek the TFTC's prior approval; a decision is made by the TFTC within three months from the submission of the complete application. **40.39**

The TFTC has issued 180 decisions against concerted action since 1992. In 2012 alone, the TFTC issued eighteen decisions against concerted action. There is a trend of intensified enforcement against concerted action in the TFTC. Further, a bill granting the TFTC the power of search and seizure, which will raise the effectiveness of enforcement, is now under **40.40** the legislator's review. It is expected that such power, if granted, will give the TFTC teeth to fight concerted action.

40.41 Taiwan introduced a leniency program on November 23, 2011 in the hope to overcome the difficulty in collecting direct evidence for concerted actions. However, before the leniency program was introduced, the TFTC had a history of relying on indirect evidence in prosecuting concerted actions, which was not challenged by most courts. It is thus worth asking whether the introduction of the leniency program will lead the courts to raise the TFTC's burden of proof in fact findings.

40.42 When a concerted action is found, the TFTC may order the infringing enterprise to cease or to rectify its conduct, or to take any necessary corrective action and, in addition, it may impose an administrative fine between TWD 50,000 and TWD 25 million. A concerted action would be considered a serious infringement if: (1) the turnover of one of the participating enterprises during the infringement period exceeds TWD 100 million, or (2) the profits obtained from the illegal concerted action exceed TWD 25 million. If an infringing enterprise fails to cease its conduct or take the necessary corrective action within the time period ordered by the TFTC, or if it commits the same infringement again, it would be subject to a cease-and-desist order and consecutive administrative fines ranging from TWD 100,000 to TWD 50 million until such infringement is cured. If the second infringement is deemed by the TFTC to be serious, the administrative fine would be increased up to the total of 10 percent of the turnover of the infringing enterprise in the preceding fiscal year (which is expected to be higher than the administrative fine imposed for the first infringement). Also, if an infringing enterprise fails to cease its conduct or take the necessary corrective action within the time period ordered by the TFTC, or it engages in the same or a similar conduct again, the individuals who are responsible for such infringement would be subject to imprisonment of up to three years and/or a criminal fine of TWD 100 million.

A. Horizontal price fixing (including advanced announcements of price or product changes)

40.43 Horizontal price fixing which is sufficient to affect the market function is punishable under article 14 of the TFTA. The TFTC does not have definite rules governing under which circumstances the market function would be deemed to be affected, but it generally considers: (1) the number of enterprises involved in the price fixing, and (2) the aggregate market share of the participating enterprises.

40.44 Legally speaking, the TFTC is obligated to bear the burden of proof for the existence of enterprises' agreement or any kind of communication on tactic or explicit price fixing. However, in many cases, the TFTC relies on indirect evidence such as facilitating practices[29] to demonstrate the enterprises' communication regarding price fixing. When competing enterprises adjust prices of the same goods in parallel with each other, without sufficient evidence of independent business rationale, the TFTC would assume that the enterprises had reached mutual understanding about price setting. The acceptance of indirect evidence lowers the TFTC's burden of proof and practically shifts the burden of proof to enterprises.

40.45 Pursuant to article 14 of the TFTA, a group of small competing enterprises may, via their trade association, apply for the TFTC's approval on fixed prices (especially price ceilings) for certain goods or services. The TFTC may grant approval if: (1) the price fixing may improve market transparency and trade efficiency, (2) the total sales amounts in such transactions are not high, and (3) such transactions often occur contingently. For instance, the Taiwan

[29] See Section II.G.

Federation of Rubber Product Industries Associations was granted an approval on price ceilings for tire repairs because the ceilings would avoid a driver who has flat tires from being ripped off due to the unexpected situation.[30] However, according to the TFTC statistics, very few cases have been filed by small enterprises, even though approval may not be difficult to obtain.

B. Horizontal agreements to allocate customers or territories; agreements not to compete

Horizontal agreements to allocate customers or territories, and agreements not to compete, are banned under article 14 of the TFTA. For instance, twenty-one cement suppliers faced high fines because they had entered into non-compete agreements with a foreign cement supplier, agreeing not to sell cement in each other's current sales territory. They also entered into agreements to fix prices, to limit the supply quantities, and to eliminate market participants.[31] **40.46**

C. Horizontal boycotts

Boycotts may be regulated under either article 14 or 19 of the TFTA. An enterprise compelling another enterprise not to supply to or purchase from a specific enterprise in order to inflict damage on that specific enterprise is in breach of article 19 of the TFTA if such an actions are likely to be anticompetitive. Boycotts initiated by a single enterprise are regulated under article 19 as a sort of unfair competition practice, while agreements made by competing enterprises to boycott are regulated under article 14. **40.47**

Generally speaking, the TFTC is not active in the enforcement against boycotts. A notable example of an article 14 boycott is the Taiwan Bar Association which notified all local bar associations that attorneys-at-law shall refrain from joining an internet legal service company.[32] The internet company provided an online platform through which potential clients could search for suitable lawyers and contact the selected lawyer via a designated toll phone number charged at a high rate. The phone charges collected would be distributed among the internet company, the phone company, and the lawyers who provided legal advises. Since under the Lawyers Act only licensed lawyers are allowed to provide certain legal services in Taiwan, and the company was not run by licensed lawyers, the Taiwan Bar Association believed that the business model of the internet company violated the Lawyers Act. However, the TFTC believed that the Taiwan Bar Association, by sending the notice, was boycotting the internet company and preventing the new service platform from entering into the legal service market. Yet the TFTC's decision was rebutted by the Executive Yuan, the highest executive authority in Taiwan, which held that the Taiwan Bar Association had the authority to express its view on ethical legal practices and the notice was a due exercise of such an authority. This case may weaken the TFTC's authority in its enforcement against associations of professionals.[33] **40.48**

D. Joint ventures and other competitive collaborations

Joint ventures in Taiwan are mostly regulated under merger control rules. A joint venture which reaches the regulatory threshold shall be notified to the TFTC and can only be commenced if the TFTC does not object to the joint venture within thirty days after the filing of a complete notification. In addition to merger control rules, a joint venture entity shall not be used as a **40.49**

[30] *Taiwan Federation of Rubber Product Industries Associations*, Kung-Lien-Tzu Case no. 004 (1997).
[31] *Taiwan Cement Corporation and others*, Kung-Chu-Tzu Case no. 094136 (2005).
[32] *R.O.C. National Federation of Bar Associations*, Kung-Chu-Tzu Case no. 101053 (2012).
[33] See Section III.E.

vehicle for anticompetitive behaviors; otherwise participants in the joint venture may be penalized pursuant to article 14, despite the fact that they had complied with merger control rules.

40.50 Many joint ventures are established to facilitate product research and development. Innovation-oriented joint ventures may apply for the TFTC's prior approval if they need to conduct concerted actions. For instance, eleven motorcycle manufactures set up a joint venture entity, through which they jointly researched and developed electronic motorcycles and purchased spare parts. The TFTC gave the joint venture entity the green light to purchase jointly on behalf of the eleven manufactures, because joint purchasing is vital for the much anticipated technology innovation and product standardization, as the technology of electronic motorcycles is still under development. However, the TFTC also ordered that the joint venture entity shall not abuse its market power. Nor can it become a platform for other concerted actions such as price fixing or joint selling.[34]

E. Trade associations

40.51 Joining trade associations is not per se susceptible to antitrust challenge. However, many article 14 infringements are committed through trade associations. Traditionally, trade associations fulfill the function of providing information about suggested retail prices, service price standards, and analytical data on commodities and costs, which used to be widely accepted. The TFTC has issued regulatory letters to prohibit trade associations' behaviors involving price fixing and information exchange. Meanwhile, the TFTC seeks to amend the TFTA to expand the scope of offenders. If the association engages in concerted action, current law imposes administrative sanctions only on the trade association but not on members. However, members of a trade association would become punishable if the drafted amendment is passed by the legislators.

40.52 In Taiwan, certified professionals, such as architects, lawyers, accountants, actuaries, etc., have to be admitted by professional associations to practice legally. Many professional associations have issued suggested service rates for members to charge their clients. On some occasions, such practices are accepted by courts if the professional associations are vested by law with a self-regulatory power. For instance, both the Taipei Institute of Certified Public Accountants and the Taipei Bar Association were fined for providing members signs or posters, which stated "consultation services will be provided for fees." The TFTC believed that the two associations, through such signs or posters, were imposing a ban against their members' offering free service. The two associations argued that the target audiences are clients rather than members; and that their members are free to decide whether or not to display the signs or posters.[35] Both associations succeeded in appeal.[36] These cases suggest that associations of certified professionals, protected by the self-regulatory power granted by laws, are less likely to be prosecuted by the TFTC for concerned action. However, this conclusion should not be generalized to all kinds of trade associations.

F. Interlocking directorates

40.53 Interlocking directorates are not considered a concerted action under article 14 of the TFTA, but are generally regulated through merger control rules, provided the interlocking directorates occur due to a merger as defined by the TFTA, which reaches the filing threshold.

[34] *Tuntex Corporation,* Kung-Chu-Tzu Case no. 008 (2000).

[35] *Taipei Institute of Certified Public Accountants,* Kung-Chu-Tzu Case no. 100015 (2011); *Taipei Bar Association,* Kung-Chu-Tzu Case no. 100016 (2011).

[36] *Taipei Bar Association v. Taiwan Fair Trade Commission,* Executive Yuan Administrative Appeal Decision, Yuan-Tai-Su-Tzu Case no. 1000104923 (2011); *Taiwan Fair Trade Commission v. Taipei Institute of Certified Public Accountants,* Supreme Administrative Court Judgment, Pan-Tzu Case no. 705 (2012).

G. Facilitating practices

Although facilitating practices per se do not necessarily infringe article 14 of the TFTA, many high-profile antitrust cases in Taiwan are prosecuted by the TFTC based on indirect evidence of enterprises' facilitating practices. For instance, the TFTC imposed a large fine on the only two petroleum suppliers in Taiwan for price fixing. The TFTC did not find any direct evidence showing that the two suppliers had communicated about prices or entered into an agreement on price fixing. However, infringement was found by the TFTC because, when one leading petroleum supplier had released news on future price adjustments, the other would soon follow. As the two suppliers had different cost structures and yet maintained generally synchronic price levels, the TFTC found that, since the two suppliers were unable to justify their price setting patterns based on any independent commercial judgment, their price adjustments constituted the strategy of price fixing.[37] Similar approaches can be found in cases where four convenient store chains and the main milk suppliers were fined because they had announced, roughly at the same time period, price adjustments for their brewed coffee and milk respectively.[38] Any businesses selling consumer goods should be particularly careful when adjusting prices because the TFTC has been very active in enforcing against price fixing of consumer goods. **40.54**

H. Information exchange

Any form of collusion which might result in price fixing or limiting the supply quantity, trading counterparties, territory, etc. is prohibited under article 14 of the TFTA. As information exchange is likely to facilitate such collusive practices, the TFTC explicitly bans enterprises from exchanging any competition-sensitive information, such as price, cost structures, business strategies, quotes to customers, etc. In several precedents, the TFTC found the existence of price fixing based on information exchange between competitors.[39] **40.55**

I. Joint purchasing agreements

In principle, joint purchasing agreements are considered as concerted actions and banned by article 14 of the TFTA. However, participants to joint purchasing agreements which will enhance trading efficiency in import of goods may apply for the TFTC's prior approval. For instance, dozens of wheat purchasers have been repeatedly granted approvals, valid for three years, to import wheat jointly.[40] The TFTC believes that the joint wheat import agreement is beneficial to Taiwan's economy, necessary for domestic wheat purchasers' survival, and in line with domestic agricultural and trade policies. On the other hand, the TFTC also orders that any new competitor shall be able to join the agreement if it desires. And the parties to the agreement shall not take advantage of the agreement to fix prices or undergo any other concerned actions. **40.56**

---

[37] *CPC Corporation, Taiwan and Formosa Petrochemical Corp.*, Kung-Chu-Tzu Case no. 093102 (2004).

[38] *Wei Chuan Corporation, Uni-President Enterprises, Corp, and Kuang Chuan Dairy Co., Ltd.*, Kung-Chu-Tzu Case no. 100204 (2011); *President Chain Store Corp, Taiwan Family Mart Co., Ltd, Hi-Life International Co., Ltd., and Lai Lai Convenient Stores Company*, Kung-Chu-Tzu Case no. 100220 (2011).

[39] E.g. *Hsinyi Happy Cable Broadcasting System Co., Ltd. and others*, Kung-Chu-Tzu Case no. 070 (1999);*Leo Shyun Pharmacy and others*, Kung-Chu-Tzu Case no. 163 (2000); *Kang Hsuan Educational Publishing Co., Ltd., Nan I Book Enterprise Co., Ltd., Han Lin Publishing Co., Ltd., and Newton Education & Publishing Corporation*, Kung-Chu-Tzu Case no. 095138 (2006); and *Tofu Association of Kaohsiung City*, Kung-Chu-Tzu Case no. 097107 (2008).

[40] E.g. *Formosa Oilseed Processing Co., Ltd. and 35 other enterprises*, Kung-Lien-Tzu Case no. 101001 (2012); *Lien Hwa Industrial Corporation and 6 other Enterprises*, Kung-Lien-Tzu Case no. 096004 (2007).

J. Joint lobbying/regulatory/legislative efforts

40.57 Joint lobbying efforts are generally not regulated under the TFTA. In principle, joint lobbying efforts do not raise competition law concerns if participants do not, by means of the joint efforts, set prices, exchange price-related information, or engage in concerted actions. So far, there has been no reported investigation by the TFTC in this respect.

III. General issues

A. Jurisdiction and applicable law (including sector-specific competition regulation)

40.58 The Taiwan competition law is composed by the Taiwan Fair Trade Act (TFTA), which was enacted on February 4, 1991 and came into effective on February 4, 1992, and the relevant regulations and guidelines promulgated by the TFTC pursuant to the TFTA. Taiwan competition law applies to all sectors of the economy, with limited exceptions, as set out in Section I.O.

40.59 The TFTA applies to all "enterprises," including companies, partnership, sole proprietorships, trade associations, persons and other organizations, public or private, engaging in trading of goods or services.

40.60 Although there is no express provision in the TFTA, the TFTC has claimed extra-territorial jurisdiction of the TFTA as long as an infringing conduct that takes place outside of Taiwan produces a local effect on Taiwan's economy.

B. Antitrust system

(i) Name of agency/agencies

40.61 The Taiwan Fair Trade Commission (TFTC) is responsible for the enforcement of competition law in Taiwan. The TFTC has the power to request information from enterprises (domestic or foreign), interview relevant enterprises, conduct on-site inspections, impose administrative fines, issue cease-and-desist orders, and issue orders requiring the infringing enterprise to rectify its conduct or take necessary corrective actions.

(ii) Staff size and budget

40.62 In 2012, the TFTC had around 220 staff, including law-enforcement staff and administrative staff. The TFTC staff are mainly responsible for investigating cases concerning single firm conduct, cartel, merger control, unfair competition (such as false advertisement and deceptive trade practices), and multilevel sales.

40.63 The TFTC's budget for 2012 is around TWD 355 million.

(iii) Recent enforcement actions and trends

40.64 Cartels have been a focal area enforced by the TFTC since its establishment in 1992. After the leniency program took effect on November 23, 2011, it is expected that the TFTC will intensify its cartel enforcement. In September 2012, the TFTC sanctioned four optical disk drive (ODD) suppliers for participating in bid-rigging in its first international cartel enforcement case. Notably, the TFTC initiated this investigation after learning about the United States Department of Justice's press release on its plea agreement with an ODD supplier. Further, this case also involved the first leniency application in Taiwan. The TFTC concluded this investigation by heavily relying on the evidence provided by the leniency applicant.[41]

[41] Kung-Chu-Tzu Case no. 101132 (2012).

In 2011, the TFTC established an Information and Economic Analysis Office, with the mission to build up thorough market databases to enhance the TFTC's ability to review merger filings and conduct antitrust investigations. **40.65**

Regarding single firm conduct, while the number of article 10 cases (abuse of dominance) is small, the TFTC has brought many article 19 cases (unfair competition of dominant and non-dominant enterprises). Article 19 of the TFTA applies to several types of anticompetitive conduct, such as tying, exclusive dealing, restrictions on territory or customers, etc. It is noted that the TFTC brought three cases involving restriction of distribution territory in 2012, which signals that the TFTC is paying more attention to single firm conduct. **40.66**

C. Private litigation

According to the TFTA, any enterprise that infringes any of the provisions of the TFTA, and thereby causes damages to another enterprise shall be liable for such damages. In addition, if the infringement is intentional, the infringed enterprise may claim up to three times of the proven damage amount. Furthermore, the infringed enterprise may request the court to issue orders requiring the infringing enterprise to cease the existing infringing conduct or to abstain from taking potential infringing conduct. **40.67**

In Taiwan, infringement of the TFTA is oftentimes asserted as a defense in some private actions, especially in patent infringement actions. In some private actions, infringement of the TFTA is asserted by the plaintiff as one of the legal grounds (other being torts or violation of other laws) to claim compensation. In Taiwan, private enforcement is not significant. The major enforcement actions are from the TFTC. **40.68**

D. Follow-on litigation (includes role of agency determinations of liability for follow-on litigation)

In Taiwan, follow-on private litigation is rare. This is mainly due to two reasons. First, infringing enterprises normally cease their infringing conducts after the TFTC has issued its decision, leaving the aggrieved parties fewer incentives to pursue private action. Second, due to the high burden of proof imposed by the courts, it is difficulty for a plaintiff to prove the actual damage and the causation between such damage and the infringement. **40.69**

In a follow-on civil action, while civil courts are not legally bound by the TFTC's decisions, they usually accept the factual and legal findings of those decisions, unless the defendants can successfully challenge them in administrative appeal proceedings. **40.70**

E. Arbitration and alternative dispute resolution

Competition issues may arise from the disputes, especially as to the enforceability of the terms of a contract, adjudicated by arbitration. The arbitration tribunal generally has discretion to apply the rule of equity instead of the provision of the TFTA. In addition, if an arbitral award is rendered based on a TFTC's decision which is subsequently reversed by the court, the losing party may appeal the arbitral award to the court. It is rather rare for arbitration cases in Taiwan to involve antitrust issues. **40.71**

F. Remedies

(i) Civil liability

Under the TFTA, an infringed party may file a damages claim with the court against the infringing enterprise. The compensation that the infringed party may claim includes its damage and loss of profits caused by the infringement. In addition, if the infringement is intentional, the infringed party may claim up to three times of the proven damage amount. Furthermore, the infringed party may request the court to issue orders requiring the **40.72** infringing enterprise to cease the on-going infringing conduct or to abstain from taking potential infringing conduct.

(ii) Criminal liability

40.73 Regarding the infringement of article 10 of the TFTA (abuse of dominance), if an infringing enterprise fails to cease its conduct or take the necessary corrective action within the time period ordered by the TFTC, or it commits the same or similar conduct again, the individuals who are responsible for such infringement would be subject to imprisonment of up to three years and/or a criminal fine of TWD 100 million.

40.74 Regarding the infringement of article 19 of the TFTA (unfair competition by dominant or non-dominant enterprises), if an infringing enterprise fails to cease its conduct or take the necessary corrective action within the time period ordered by the TFTC, or it engages in the same or a similar conduct again, the individuals who are responsible for such infringement would be subject to imprisonment of up to two years and/or a criminal fine of TWD 50 million.

G. Leniency and immunity

40.75 In Taiwan, the leniency legislation came into effect on November 23, 2011. The TFTC promulgated the detailed leniency regulations on January 6, 2012. Under the leniency regulations, the TFTC will grant full immunity from cartel fines to the first leniency applicant and a reduction of cartel fines to up to four additional leniency applicants. Specifically, the second to fifth leniency applicants will be entitled to a reduction, respectively, of 30–50 percent, 20–30 percent, 10–20 percent, and less than 10 percent in the amount of fines imposed by the TFTC. However, leniency is not available to parties that: (i) force competitors to participate in a cartel or prevent competitors from exiting the cartel; (ii) destroy, forge, alter, or withhold evidence; (iii) directly or indirectly disclose the fact that they are going to apply for leniency or the contents of their leniency application; or (iv) do not cooperate with the TFTC's investigations or other conditions imposed by the TFTC when granting the permission for leniency application.

H. Document creation and retention

40.76 Pursuant to article 43 of the TFTA, enterprises that, without any justification, refuse to respond to inquiries, to appear before the TFTC, or to submit relevant documents or other evidence will be seen as being uncooperative and thus subject to an administrative fine of up to TWD 250,000. Any negligent or intentional destruction of potentially relevant documents may be deemed as a failure to submit relevant documents. In addition, the TFTC will impose higher fines for infringement of the TFTA than it would have otherwise on enterprises refusing to cooperate in the TFTC's investigation.

41

TURKEY

Gonenc Gurkaynak
Elig

Introduction

Law No. 4054 on Protection of Competition ("Law No. 4054"), which entered into force on December 13, 1994, is designed to prevent agreements, decisions and practices that have as their purpose or effect the prevention, restriction or distortion of competition in the markets for goods or services within Turkey; the abuse of dominance by undertakings dominant in a relevant market; and concentrations creating or strengthening a dominant position and significantly lessening the competition in the whole territory of Turkey or a part thereof. **41.01**

According to a recent report published by the Competition Authority ("the Authority") dated on February 5, 2013, summarizing the investigations carried out by the Authority since its inception, 146 investigations out of a total of 189 were conducted on the basis of allegations regarding violations of article 4 of Law No. 4054 which prohibits all agreements between undertakings, decisions by associations of undertakings, and concerted practices that have (or may have) as their object or effect the prevention, restriction, or distortion of competition within a Turkish product or services market or a part of thereof; while thirty-eight investigations have been conducted out on the basis of allegations regarding violation of article 6 of **41.02**

Law no. 4054 which prohibits "any abuse on the part of one or more undertakings, individually or through joint agreements or practices, of a dominant position in a market for goods or services within the whole or part of the country." The remaining five investigations have been initiated on the basis of both article 4 and article 6 concerns. Accordingly, it would be justified to assert that cooperative offenses, referring to both horizontal and vertical arrangement, have traditionally been the area of heaviest enforcement under Turkish competition law. That said, the number and volume of abuse of dominance cases in Turkey has hit all-time highs in 2011. Over the last two years, the Competition Board ("the Board") has relatively shifted its focus from merger control cases to concentrate more on the fight against cartels and cases of abuses of dominance. As a reflection of this trend, the Board has also shown an increased interest in the unilateral pricing behavior of undertakings, as exemplified by recent high-profile predatory pricing investigations involving Turkish Airlines[1] where there was ultimately no finding of an abuse of a dominant position, and the shipping company UN Ro Ro[2] where UN Ro Ro was fined in the amount of 0.4 percent of its 2011 turnover which amounted to TRY 841,199.70.

41.03 It is also clearly observable that the Turkish Competition Authority has been putting substantial efforts into enriching the secondary legislation over the last four years. Main reason behind this trend is that the legislation on the Turkish merger control regime is heavily inspired by the regulations of EU Commission. Furthermore, Turkey is an official candidate for the European Union since the Helsinki summit (which took place in December 10–11, 1999), there has been an ongoing negotiation process between Turkey and European Union, and the competition chapter is one of the most of important chapters for the harmonization process, which inevitably leads to the close observation (and adaptation) of the competition law related developments at the European Commission's end.

I. Acting alone

41.04 Unilateral activities which are prohibited by Turkish Competition Law generally fall under the ambit of article 6 of Law No. 4054. The concept of "dominant position" is defined under article 3 of Law No. 4054 as "the capacity of an undertaking or a group of undertakings in a given market to determine economic parameters such as price, output, supply and distribution independently from competitors and customers." As a provision concerning the behavior of dominant firms, article 6 prohibits the activities falling under its ambit only in the context of a dominant firm. Among the types of offenses covered below, those with heaviest enforcement track record are vertical offenses such as resale price maintenance (RPM) or exclusive dealing arrangements which are covered under article 4 of Law No. 4054, and therefore also include the conduct of non-dominant firms.

A. Predatory pricing

41.05 Predatory pricing is analyzed under article 6(a) of Law No. 4054 which prohibits activities that directly or indirectly impede the entry of another firm into the market or impede the activities of those already within the market. The Board's most recent predatory pricing decision, UN Ro Ro,[3] in which the dominant undertaking was fined in the amount of TRY 841,199.70 has done much to clarify the legal standard with respect to predatory pricing

[1] *Turkish Airlines*, Case no. 11-65/1692-599 (December 30, 2011).
[2] *UN Ro Ro*, Case no. 12-47/1412-474 (October 1, 2012).
[3] *UN Ro Ro* (n 2).

under Turkish competition law. In *UN Ro Ro*, the Board identified the elements of predatory pricing as follows: (1) being in a dominant position in the relevant market, (2) a pricing scheme in where products are consistently priced below cost, (3) the intent to engage in a predatory pricing scheme, and (4) a reasonable probability of anticompetitive market foreclosure through exclusion of equally efficient competitors from the market.

UN Ro Ro has significantly clarified the existing case law as it includes a detailed discussion of the appropriate measure of cost whereas past decisions such as *Goldaş*,[4] *Feniks*,[5] and *Turkish Airlines*[6] simply referred to "pricing below cost" without clearly sprcifying the appropriate measure. In line with the Draft Guidelines on the Evaluation of Exclusionary Abuses by Dominant Undertakings ("Draft Guidelines on Exclusionary Abuses") which has yet to be formally adopted by the Authority, the *UN Ro Ro* decision has opted for the use of average avoidable cost, also mentioning that long run average incremental cost could be a more appropriate measure in certain exceptional cases. Where prices are below average total cost but higher than average avoidable cost, predatory pricing complaints may still go forward but the intent to engage in predatory pricing needs to be shown by clear evidence. On the other hand, if the price is below average avoidable cost, a predatory intent is presumed and the burden is on the defending party to rebut this presumption. Unlike certain past cases,[7] the *Un Ro Ro* decision has stated that the possibility of recoupment is not a necessary element of predatory pricing. Instead, in accordance with the Draft Guidelines on Exclusionary Abuses, the fourth element considered in the relevant decision is a reasonable likelihood of anticompetitive market closure. Simply showing a reasonable likelihood of closing the market to equally efficient competitors is sufficient to satisfy this element and the relevant competitor does not need to have been in fact excluded from the market. Furthermore, the Draft Guidelines on Exclusionary Abuses states that this element may also be satisfied through showing that the predatory pricing scheme led to the disciplining of a vigorous competitor by the dominant undertaking and therefore led to an anticompetitive outcome. **41.06**

Due to its reluctance to micro-manage pricing behavior, the Board requires high standards for predatory pricing claims and has frequently dismissed past complaints alleging this issue. On the other hand, the recent *UN Ro Ro* decision has shown that the Board will not hesitate to step in when confronted with cases of clear predation. **41.07**

B. Exploitative offenses

Exploitative pricing or supply terms may fall under the prohibition of article 6. There have been past cases where excessive or exploitative pricing behavior has been condemned by the Competition Board;[8] however, complaints on this basis are frequently dismissed, as the Competition Authority is reluctant to micro-manage pricing behavior. In particular, the Board's past decisions in this regard show that (a) the dominant undertaking in question needs to be a monopoly; (b) there need to be substantial barriers to entry in the relevant market as a result of legal or natural factors; (c) the relevant market must not be otherwise regulated in terms of price; (d) the prices charged must be in excess of the economic value of the product based on the consideration of a variety of factors, such as the relationship between the cost and price, prices charged by the relevant undertaking in similar markets, and/or the prices charged by other undertakings in the relevant market. Particularly, in its recent *TMST* decision, the **41.08**

[4] *Goldaş*, Case no. 07-29/259-90 (March 29, 2007).

[5] *Feniks*, Case no. 07-67/815-310 (August 23, 2007).

[6] *Turkish Airlines* (n 1).

[7] See *Goldaş* (n 4); *Feniks* (n 5)

[8] See e.g. *TTAŞ*, Case no. 02-60/755-305 (October 2, 2002); *Belko*, Case no. 01-17/150-39 (April 6, 2001); *HAVAŞ*, Case no. 08-01/5-4 (January 3, 2008).

Board explained that in the absence of substantial barriers to entry, the presence of excessive prices in a market will create a greater incentive for competitors to enter that market which will lower prices without governmental interference.[9] Accordingly, in *Belko*, where the Board found an article 6 violation, it emphasized that Belko was a legal monopoly so the barriers to entry in the particular market were absolute, and that Belko acted carelessly in its commercial affairs due to its reliance on its monopoly position.[10] In *HAVAŞ*, where the Board condemned HAVAŞ's pricing scheme (even though it postponed enforcement), it pointed out that excessive prices become truly exploitative when there is a group of customers who are "locked in" as a result of the barriers to entry which sustains the relevant firm's monopoly position.[11] Similarly, in the *Tüpraş* and *Ataköy Marina* cases, where there were no findings of infringement, the Board emphasized the undesirability of interference with private commercial pricing decisions and reiterated the need for substantial barriers to entry in the relevant market.[12]

C. Monopsony

41.09 While Law no. 4054 does not contain specific references to monopsony markets, the Board has not declined jurisdiction over claims of abuse by dominant purchasers in the past[13] and it remains possible that abusive acts of dominant purchasers may fall under the prohibitions of Law no. 4054. However, to date there have been no article 6 cases involving a finding of infringement and imposition of monetary fines on dominant purchasers.

D. Price discrimination

41.10 Price discrimination falls under the ambit of article 6(b) which prohibits direct or indirect discriminatory practices towards equally situated purchasers by a dominant firm. In the past, the Board has found incumbent undertakings to have infringed article 6 by engaging in discriminatory behavior concerning prices and other trade conditions.[14] In *Coca Cola / Burger King*, the Competition Board stated that in order for a finding of abuse through discriminatory conduct, (i) the undertakings that receive dissimilar conditions must be competitors, (ii) dissimilar conditions must be imposed on equivalent transactions, and (iii) the supplier's conduct must put one of the relevant competitors at a competitive disadvantage.[15] Price discrimination is an offense which is frequently alleged and constitutes one of the significant areas of enforcement activity in the context of abuses of a dominant position, since price discrimination by a dominant undertaking carries a significant risk of altering the market structure in an anticompetitive manner.

41.11 It must be emphasized that unequal terms do not automatically translate into abusive conduct. Rather, different transactions must be analyzed as a whole with reference to differing parameters such as the size of the shipment, characteristics of the product in question, the level of the purchaser within the production chain, the characteristics of the geographic region that the transaction takes place in and the commercial history between the relevant parties.[16] Differing terms become discriminatory when the buyers are truly equally situated and thus difference

[9] See *TMST*, Case no. 2010, 10-42/756-243 (June 10, 2010).

[10] *Belko* (n 10).

[11] *HAVAŞ* (n 10).

[12] See *Tüpraş*, Case no. 09-52/1246-315 (November 4, 2009); *Ataköy Marina*, Case no. 08-30/373-123 (April 24, 2008).

[13] See e.g. *ÇEAŞ*, Case no. 03-71/874-373 (November 10, 2003); *Tüpraş*, Case no. 02-24/243-98 (February 16, 2002).

[14] See e.g. *TTAŞ* (n 10); *Türk Telekom/TTNet*, Case no. 08-65/1055-411 (November 19, 2008).

[15] *Coca Cola / Burger King*, Case no. 05-36/453-106 (May 26, 2005).

[16] See e.g. *Emek Ecza Deposu*, Case no. 11-25/470-141 (April 21, 2011); *Dystar Tekstil Boya*, Case no. 07-53/579-190 (June 20, 2007).

between the offered terms does not depend on objective, reasonable grounds. To explain by way of example, in *Uludağ Gazoz*, the Board found that an individual store and a giant retail chain were not equally situated based on a number of factors ranging from the big chain store's market power, to the role that such stores could play in the launching of the product.[17]

That said, the Board's decisional practice also includes certain examples where the discriminatory imposition of excessively burdensome conditions on smaller market players was found to constitute abusive discrimination. For example, in *Sanofi Aventis*, the imposition of extremely short maturity dates for wholesalers with purchase volumes less than TRY 250,000 was condemned by the Board as there was no commercial justification for the TRY 250,000 mark except to prioritize larger players and the disadvantegous terms threatened to put significant numbers of smaller players out of business in the downstream market.[18] **41.12**

E. Dictating or influencing resale prices

(i) Resale price maintenance

Dictating or influencing resale prices falls within the ambit of article 4 of Law no. 4054 which prohibits price-fixing agreements. The prohibition against price maintenance set forth in article 4 is a per se restriction; as a result, the Board may adopt a finding of infringement without going into the analysis of whether the actions of the supplier have resulted in anticompetitive effects.[19] **41.13**

While the Block Exemption Communiqué no. 2002/2 on Vertical Agreements ("Communiqué no. 2002/2") exempts certain vertical conduct, such as setting a maximum retail price or mere recommendation of an area of activity, conduct which negates the freedom of the purchaser to set its own prices or impose minimum resale prices does not fall under the exemption and is therefore prohibited. Furthermore, Communiqué no. 2002/2 does not apply to the activities of the undertakings possessing more than 40 percent share in the relevant market. **41.14**

As far as vertical demands by non-dominant firms are concerned, it is necessary to go into greater detail concerning the requirements of the Communiqué no. 2002/2. According to the Guidelines on Vertical Agreements, any conduct fixing the resale price or setting up a minimum price is clearly outside the exemption and therefore prohibited. Furthermore, while the Communiqué no. 2002/2 permits the determination of a maximum resale price, or a simple resale price recommendation, it is necessary that any such recommendations or maximum prices do not turn into the fixing of a specific resale price, or the determination of a minimum price. To that effect, any price lists which are published or communicated to the buyer must clearly state that the relevant prices are only maximum prices or mere recommendations with no binding effect. The foregoing prohibitions also apply to cases where the maintenance of resale prices is accomplished through indirect methods. Conduct such as discriminatory prices towards the buyer for refusals to comply with the supplier's demands, the awarding of discounts based on compliance, late deliveries to the relevant buyer to punish non-compliance, or the discontinuation or suspension of the relevant buyer for the same purpose constitute examples of attempts to maintain resale prices indirectly. **41.15**

RPM is one of the most significant areas of enforcement activity in the Turkish competition law system. The Board considers it an essential characteristic of competitive markets that undertakings be independent in their pricing decisions. Accordingly, interferences (falling out of the limits set out in the legislation) by suppliers in the pricing decisions of their customers receive **41.16**

[17] See *Uludağ Gazoz*, Case no. 2011, 11-59/1519-544 (November 24, 2011).

[18] Sanofi Aventis, Case no. 09-16/374-88 (April 20, 2009).

[19] See e.g. *3M*, Case no. 07-22/207-66 (March 13, 2007); *Nobel Pazarlama*, Case no. 03-10/114-52 (February 18, 2003)

heavy. Law no. 4054 aims at eliminating all mechanisms targeting to achieve resale price maintenance, through direct (such as explicit contractual obligations to observe the supplier's price policy) or indirect (such as fixing the distribution margin, fixing the maximum level of discount the distributor can grant from a prescribed price level, making the grant of rebates, or reimbursement of promotional costs by the supplier subject to the observance of a given price level, etc.) means of dictating trade parameters to the distributor. It is the Board's established practice to adopt a very sensitive approach in connection with all resale price maintenance arrangements. If there is a direct resale price maintenance arrangement, anticompetitive conduct will readily be inferred and the undertakings concerned will be condemned.

(ii) Minimum advertised price programs

41.17 The Board has not yet made any rulings concerning minimum advertised price (MAP) programs. Furthermore, while the Guidelines on Vertical Agreements go into great depth concerning varieties of vertical arrangements which may violate article 4 of Law no. 4054, MAP programs have not been mentioned explicitly in this source either.

F. Tying arrangements

41.18 Article 6(c) specifically refers to tying arrangements among practices which constitute an abuse of a dominant position. However, the enforcement track record indicates no cases where the incumbent firms were fined as a result of tying arrangements.

G. Exclusive dealing

41.19 Exclusive dealing arrangements are dealt with within the context of article 4 of Law No. 4054. Communiqué no. 2002/2 includes exclusive dealings arrangements within the vertical agreements which may benefit from the block exemption. However, Communiqué no. 2002/2 also lays down a number of conditions which such agreements must comply with. In general, undertakings may grant their distributors exclusive rights with respect to certain territories, or groups of customers. However, such arrangements may only impede competition with respect to active sales. Any restriction of passive sales, whether on the basis of customer groups or territories, is outside the scope of the exemption and constitutes a violation of article 4. Moreover, the restrictive arrangements must only cover the sales by those who are party to the exclusive dealing agreement. In other words, although an ultimate supplier may divide the territories of its immediate distributors, the active or passive sales of their customers can't be restricted. There are two exceptions to this rule: (1) it is permitted for a company to set up a selective distribution chain where only authorized personnel may engage in the marketing of a certain product; and (2) where a supplier sells parts of its products to downstream parties to be assembled before sale, it may restrict its buyers from selling the relevant parts to its competitors. With respect to the latter exemption, the relevant parties must still be able to sell such parts to the final consumer, or to parties authorized to perform maintenance of the products to be used as spare parts.

41.20 Furthermore, it must be emphasized that conduct of enterprises possessing more than 40 percent market share in the relevant market fall outside the exemption provided by Communiqué no. 2002/2. As a result, exclusive dealing arrangements have a significant potential to present problems if undertaken by dominant firms and will be deemed legal only if they merit an individual exemption under article 5 of Law no. 4054. Examples of enforcement decisions by the Board concerning exclusive dealing arrangements by dominant undertakings include *Unilever*, *Mey İçki*, and *Coca Cola*.[20] All three cases cited above involve the revocation of negative clearances in favor of exclusive dealing arrangements by dominant firms prior to 2007

[20] *Unilever*, Case no. 08-33/421-147 (May 15, 2008); *Mey İçki*, Case no. 07-70/863-326 (September 10, 2007); and *Coca Cola*, Case no. 07-70/864-327 (September 10, 2007).

when Communiqué no. 2002/2 was amended to exclude undertakings possessing more than 40 percent market share from its coverage. In these cases, the Board ruled that the undertakings in question were no longer covered by the block exemption provided by Communiqué no. 2002/2 and therefore conducted an individual exemption analysis under article 5 of Law no. 4054 whereby it found that the exclusive dealings arrangements in question generally did not merit an individual exemption as they (a) did not involve instances involving transfers of significant know-how or individualized investments into the facilities of the buyers which would necessitate exclusivity arrangements; and (b) the arrangements in question impeded competition more than what was necessary to achieve the desired pro-competitive effects. However, the Board did carve out certain arrangements for individual exemptions where it found that the above factors were in existence such as exclusivity arrangements for Algida café-shops where Unilever made individualized investments in the facilities of the buyers.

As may be understood from the cases presented above, the Board pays close attention to exclusive dealing arrangements, especially in the case of dominant firms. Since the introduction of the 40 percent market share threshold for the application of Communiqué no. 2002/2, the Board has been very active in its policing of exclusive dealing arrangements. **41.21**

H. Refusal to deal

Refusals to deal are generally analyzed under article 6 of Law No. 4054 as a form of abuse of a dominant position. Indeed, this is an abuse which is alleged often and there are a number of Board decisions concerning the issue.[21] **41.22**

In order for a refusal to deal to constitute an abuse of a dominant position, the required elements are as follows: (a) the enterprise engaging in the refusal must be in a dominant position; (b) the enterprise must continue to supply certain customers while refusing to deal with others; (c) there must be a long-term commercial relationship between the dominant firm and the relevant purchaser; (d) the refusal to deal must not be justified by objective, reasonable grounds; and (e) the refusal to deal must be motivated by anticompetitive intent. Among these factors, the Board seems to place special emphasis on the fourth element both in itself and as an indicator of anticompetitive intent.[22] Furthermore, when evaluating anticompetitive intent, the Board also looks at whether the undertaking refusing to deal with a certain party is active in the upstream or downstream market which the relevant party is active in. If this is not the case, the Board is less likely to find that the conduct was motivated by a desire to disrupt competition.[23] **41.23**

I. Essential facilities

Refusal of access to essential facilities falls within the ambit of article 6(a) of Law. No 4054 which prohibits conduct which purports to, directly or indirectly, obstruct the entry of new undertakings in the relevant market. The Board has recognized the concept in a number of decisions and has laid down a number of factors which justifies a finding of an article 6 violation with respect to a refusal to supply within the context of the essential facilities doctrine in its *Çukurova Elektrik* decision.[24] Under the test provided in the decision, in order for a given facility to be regarded as "essential," (a) the essential facility must be controlled by an **41.24**

[21] See e.g. *POAŞ*, Case no. 01-56/554-130 (November 20, 2001); *Ak-Kim*, Case no. 03-76/925-389 (December 4, 2003); *Çukurova Elektrik*, 03-72/874-373 (November 10, 2003); *Göltaş*, Case no.10-71/1483-569 (November 10, 2010).

[22] See, e.g. *TKİ*, Case no. 04-66/949-227 (October 19, 2004); *POAŞ*, 01-56/554-130 (November 20, 2001).

[23] See *TKİ* (n 25).

[24] See *Çukurova Elektrik*, Case no. 03-72/874-373 (November 10, 2003).

undertaking which is a monopoly or in a dominant position within the relevant market, and (b) the independent production or establishment of the relevant facility by competitors must be impossible under reasonable conditions. For a finding that the refusal to the essential facility constitutes an abuse of a dominant position under article 6(a), it is further required that the refusal not depend on objectively reasonable justifications.

J. Bundling (including loyalty and market share discounts)

41.25 Turkish Competition Law generally does not make a distinction between cases of tying and bundling. Both are subject to the prohibitions of article 6(c) which mark tying and bundling as forms of abuse of a dominant position. However, as mentioned above in the Section I.F, there is no record of enforcement against incumbent firms for tying or bundling.

K. Standard-setting groups

41.26 A number of trade associations in Turkey (e.g. Turkish Dentists Association, Association of Turkish Bars) are authorized by law to set professional standards for their relevant industries. Such authority often includes powers that clearly limit competition such as establishing minimum fees for certain services provided in the relevant industry. However, where such powers are vested in the relevant organization by law, the Competition Board is generally unable to impose any sanctions against this conduct.[25] However, in case a trade association which is not authorized by law engages in the same sort of conduct, it would not enjoy any legal protection against sanctions by the Competition Board. Article 4 of Law no. 4054 which prohibits collective action in restraint of trade expressly includes the decisions of trade associations within its ambit and as a result any trade association decision would be subject to an article 4 analysis which is set out in greater detail below in Section II.E.

L. Customer termination

41.27 Cases of customer termination are analyzed according to the general "refusal to deal" framework. As explained above, in order for a refusal to deal to constitute an abuse of a dominant position under an article 6 analysis, (a) the enterprise engaging in the refusal must be in a dominant position; (b) the enterprise must continue to supply certain customers while refusing to deal with others; (c) there must be a long-term trade relationship between the dominant firm and the relevant purchaser; (d) the refusal to deal must not be justified by objective, reasonable grounds; and (e) the refusal to deal must be motivated by anticompetitive intent. To provide an example of this in the customer termination context, in the Board's *POAŞ* decision,[26] it was found that Petrol Ofisi did not engage in abuse when it terminated a customer with whom it had only a short-term, irregular trade relationship based on reasonable grounds.

M. Termination of intermediaries

41.28 As with cases of customer terminations, terminations of intermediaries are also analyzed within the general "refusal to deal" framework. The Board's *TKİ* decision[27] provides an example of a case where it was alleged that a dominant firm distorted competition in the downstream market when it started supplying to exclusive dealers determined through a bidding process. In this case, the Board found that there was no abuse because the change in the supply system was based on objective, reasonable grounds and was not motivated by anticompetitive intent.

---

[25] See e.g. *Türkiye Barolar Birliği*, Case no. 03-73/876 (November 13, 2003).

[26] *POAŞ*, 01-56/554-130 (November 20, 2001).

[27] *TKİ* (n 25).

N. Termination of relationships with competitors

The termination of relationships with competitors may become problematic depending on the exact character of the relationship. Most importantly, if a company has a vertical relationship with another firm in addition to its horizontal competitive relationship, then the termination of the vertical relationship will be subject to the sort of analysis provided above with respect to the termination of customers or intermediaries. For example, in its *BIRYAY* decision,[28] the Board found that BIRYAY, a distribution joint venture established by the two dominant newspaper and magazine distribution firms in the market—themselves owned by two large media conglomerates—violated article 6 when it offered unfavorable terms to or refused to distribute those publications which did not belong to the controlling conglomerates.[29] BIRYAY was fined in the amount of TRY 128,427.64 while its parents, BBD and YAYSAT, were fined in the amount of TRY 268,662.2515 and TRY 495,126.185 for various article 6 violations. Unless there is a vertical relationship of some sort between the relevant competitors, the unilateral termination of a relationship with a competitor is unlikely to be problematic. **41.29**

O. Exemptions

As stated in the introductory section, unilateral activities generally fall under the ambit of article 6 which prohibits abuses of a dominant position. As a result, the activities of non-dominant are exempted from article 6 enforcement. **41.30**

Furthermore, there are a number of communiqués which provide exemptions within the context of vertical arrangements and sector-specific contexts. The block exemption rules currently applicable are: (i) the Block Exemption Communiqué no. 2002/2 on Vertical Agreements; (ii) the Block Exemption Communiqué no. 2005/4 on Vertical Agreements and Concerted Practices in the Motor Vehicle Sector; (iii) the Block Exemption Communiqué No. 2003/2 on R&D Agreements; (iv) the Block Exemption Communiqué No. 2008/3 for the Insurance Sector; (v) the Block Exemption Communiqué No. 2008/2 on Technology Transfer Agreements; and (vi) the Block Exemption Communiqué No. 2013/3 on Specialization Agreeements. **41.31**

II. Dealing with competitors

Violations that take place at the horizontal level are generally governed by article 4 of Law No. 4054 which prohibits all agreements between undertakings, decisions by associations of undertakings and concerted practices that have (or may have) as their object or effect the prevention, restriction, or distortion of competition within a Turkish product or services market or a part of thereof. **41.32**

It must be further emphasized that article 4 does not refer to limitations such as "appreciable effect" or "substantial part of a market" and thereby does not contain any *de minimis* exceptions. Furthermore, as indicted by the formulation of the prohibition, the ban also reaches agreements which "may have the effect of" preventing, restricting, or distorting competition. This feature of the Turkish Competition Law provides a wide range of discretion to the Turkish Competition Authority. **41.33**

[28] *BIRYAY*, Case no. 00-26/292-162 (July 17, 2000).

[29] *BIRYAY* (n 31).

41.34 Cartel investigations have been on the rise as a part of the Authority's strategy of devoting more resources from merger control to policing competition law violations more effectively. Indeed, cartel enforcement has become especially prominent as exemplified by recent fining decisions such as *Peugeot* and *Cement*.[30]

A. Horizontal price fixing

41.35 Article 4 of Law No. 4054 brings a non-exhaustive list of prohibited restrictive agreements, and horizontal price fixing is prohibited under paragraph (a) which stipulates that agreements "fixing the purchase or sale price of goods or services, elements such as cost and profit which form the price, and any terms of purchase or sale" are illegal. Price fixing is one of the most common forms of cartel agreements. Prices may be fixed through determining maximum or minimum prices as well as through standardization of various rebate systems. Therefore, not only direct agreements that result in price control constitutes competition law violation but also practices that induce price control mechanism in an indirect manner may fall under the scope of the horizontal price fixing prohibition.

41.36 In addition, besides the agreements concluded between the competitors, price fixing may occur by decisions of trade association which will be further discussed below as well as by concerted practices. To provide an example of enforcement against a price-fixing arrangement under article 4, in a recent decision several Peugeot dealers were fined in the sum of 0.5 percent of their turnover by the Board for engaging in concerted determination of prices and allocation of territories.[31] This decision came as a result of an investigation which spinned off of an earlier investigation where a large group of Peugeot dealers were fined in the amount of sums between 1 percent and 4 percent of their turnovers.[32]

B. Horizontal agreements to allocate customers or territories; agreements not to compete

41.37 Article 4(b) of Law No. 4054 expressly prohibits horizontal agreements which have as their object, have the effect of, or may have the effect of, directly or indirectly "sharing of the markets in goods or services, or the allocation or control of any sources of supply or other elements within the markets." This wording reaches both the allocation of territories and the allocation of specific customer groups between competitors. This is confirmed by decisional practice. For example, in a 1999 decision by the Competition Board, several undertakings active in the cement industry who allocated territories within western Turkey and also formed an export cartel mandating the export of production above a certain level were found to have violated article 4(a)–(c).[33] In a more recent decision, several suppliers of gas were found to have violated article 4 of Law No. 4054 when they conspired to share hospital tenders among themselves to make sure each supplier could bid high prices with respect to the allocated customer.[34]

41.38 As indicated by the foregoing, horizontal agreements not to compete with respect to a group of customers or a geographical territory are expressly caught by the prohibitions of article 4. Vertical agreements not to compete may benefit from the Block Exemption Communiqué no. 2002/2 on Vertical Agreements under certain circumstances. However, where the vertical agreement foresees a competition restriction which continues after the vertical agreement

[30] *Peugeot*, Case no. 12-20/557-141 (April 12, 2012); *Cement*, 12-17/499-140 (April 6, 2012).
[31] *Peugeot* (n 33).
[32] *Peugeot*, Case no. 10-53/1057-391 (August 6, 2010).
[33] See *Cement*, Case no. 99-30/276-166 (June 17, 1999).
[34] See *Gas*, Case no. 10-72/1503-572 (November 11, 2010).

is terminated and may become a de facto horizontal restraint, an exemption is no longer available.

C. Horizontal boycotts

Horizontal boycotts are one of the most frequently encountered competition law violations. According to article 4(c) of Law No. 4054 "complicating and restricting the activities of competing undertakings, or excluding undertakings operating in the market by boycotts or other behavior, or preventing potential new entrants to the market" are prohibited. The cases brought before the Competition Board regarding horizontal boycotts were primarily related to the practices of associations of undertakings such as regularly increasing the membership fees[35] or excluding undertakings from participating in the expositions.[36] **41.39**

The enforcement record also includes horizontal boycotts where a number of undertakings concertedly boycotted certain buyers in order to raise prices in the relevant markets. An example of this is the *Fako* case where a number of pharmaceutical distributors acted in concert to boycott tenders relating to teaching hospitals.[37] The Board decided that the conduct was a clear violation of article 4 and levied monetary fines against the concerned undertakings. **41.40**

D. Joint ventures and other competitive collaborations

Under the Turkish competition law regime, joint ventures are primarily reviewed under merger control rules as they may raise concentration risks. Such joint ventures are governed under article 7 of Law No. 4054 and article 5(3) of Communiqué No. 2010/4 which provide that in order to qualify as a full-function joint venture, first, joint control must be established, second, the joint venture must perform all the functions of an autonomous economic entity, and third, no anticompetitive purpose or effect should arise out of the transaction. Accordingly, joint ventures are reviewed under article 4 of Law No. 4054 only if they are cooperative in nature and therefore do not satisfy the aforementioned conditions. While determining whether the joint ventures result in cooperation or not, the Competition Board takes several factors into consideration such as whether the joint venture operates in the same market as the parent undertakings or markets neighboring thereto, whether the joint venture acquired the existing activities of its parents or whether it has sufficient resources to operate as an independent entity. **41.41**

Without forming a separate legal entity as joint ventures, undertakings operating at the same level in the market may collaborate with each other for R&D or distribution purposes. As these types of collaborations primarily purport to supplement the insufficiencies of the parties, they may also aim towards the provision of a new product line or the development of a specific product. Strategic cooperation between competitors is mostly reviewed under article 4 of Law No. 4054 and some of them may also be subject to individual exemption according to article 5 of Law No. 4054. Furthermore there is also block exemption legislation for R&D agreements. Therefore, it could be said that as these forms of collaborations contribute to the technological development, distribution, and competition, they are not reviewed in detail and mostly discussed within the meaning of individual exemption or negative clearance with minor amendments. **41.42**

E. Trade associations

Article 4 of Law no. 4054 expressly includes the decisions of trade associations within its ambit. A decision by a trade association may become subject to sanctions for any of the **41.43**

[35] See *TÜRSAB*, Case no. 03-80/967-397 (December 17, 2003).

[36] See *BIRYAY*, Case no. 00-49/529-291 (December 14, 2000).

[37] *Fako and others*, Case no. 07-07/43-12 (January 19, 2007).

prohibited activities indicated in article 4 in the same manner as other agreements between undertakings. The decision by the relevant trade association does not need to be binding, and mere recommendations are also actionable.[38] In cases where the conduct of a trade association violates article 4, such as issuing a decision or a recommendation allocating territories or determining sale prices, the association itself becomes subject to the penalties, in the form of fines or otherwise, levied by the Competition Board. This will be true regardless of whether the relevant trade association has separate legal personality. For example, in its *Engines* decision,[39] the Board issued a fine against an association without separate legal personality for issuing an "agreement protocol" involving recommended prices, and the fine was divided equally between the members.

41.44 There are numerous examples of actions against trade associations in the enforcement record based on various grounds. For example, TÜRSAB (Turkish Association of Travelling Agencies) was found to violate article 4 by impeding entry of new firms to the market when it set excessive fees to join the Association.[40] In another case, concerted decisions by several trade associations active in the petroleum industry were deemed to have committed a violation.[41]

41.45 It is also possible for undertakings which are members of the trade association to be fined in their individual capacity. For example, in the *Automobiles* decision,[42] a large group of undertakings active in the auto industry were fined by the Board as a result of improper informational exchanges conducted through the trade associations that the undertakings belonged to.

F. Interlocking directorates

41.46 While interlocking directorates do not violate competition law in and of themselves, this issue may come up in relation to broader investigations. For example, in its *Erdemir* decision concerning regular exchange of current information concerning prices and supply sizes between several undertakings in the steel industry, the Board talked at length about the facilitating effect of the interlocking ownership structure present in the steel industry.[43] The Board also mentioned the fact that Erdemir's shares in its competitors provided it with the right to appoint a director on the boards of its competitors. As a result, in addition to the monetary fines imposed on the relevant firms, the Board ordered Erdemir to release its shares in its competitors.

G. Facilitating practices

41.47 The enforcement record with respect to conduct traditionally studied under the facilitating practices heading, such as most-favored nation (MFN) or most-favored customer (MFC) clauses and informational exchanges, is relatively scarce, and the vast majority of enforcement decisions in this front concern informational exchanges which are analyzed in the next section.

H. Informational exchange

41.48 The enforcement history contains a number of enforcement decisions based on informational exchanges between competitors. For example, in *Erdemir*, regular informational exchanges

[38] See e.g. *Turkish Union of Banks*, Case no. 02-46/563-229 (August 01, 2002).
[39] *Engines*, 01-10/100-24 (February 27, 2001).
[40] *TÜRSAB*, Case no. 03-80/967-397 (December 17, 2003).
[41] See *Petroleum*, Case no. 00-35/392-219 (September 18, 2000).
[42] *Automobiles*, Case no. 11-24/464-139 (March 18, 2011).
[43] See *Erdemir*, Case no. 09-28/600-141 (September 16, 2009).

concerning current shipment sizes and prices were deemed to be clear violations of article 4 as they had the object of restraining competition and fixing prices and supply volume in the industry.[44]

The Board's decisional practice does not provide clear guidelines as to how old or aggregated pricing information or other types of commercial information which may be exchanged needs to be. In its recent *Petder* decision, the Board emphasized that the anticompetitive effects of informational exchanges may be minimized where (a) the gathering and publishing of information is carried out by a third party, (b) the information in question is gathered from public sources, and (c) the information in question pertains to the sector in general and doesn't include firm-specific information.[45] The informational exchanges in *Petder* were found to merit negative clearance because they satisfied the above criteria, and the level of transparency in the sector was already very high so that the information in question didn't cause the relevant market to become significantly more transparent. In another recent negative clearance decision, the Board emphasized that information exchanges are considered under a rule of reason inquiry and a number of factors including the level of concentration in the market, the level of transparency in the market, the homogeneity of the relevant product, the frequency with which information is exchanged and the characteristics of the information which is exchanged may be considered.[46] Particularly, in its *UND* decision, the Board granted negative clearance with respect to publishing of current changes in fuel prices in UND's (International Carriers' Association) website; however, it refused to grant negative clearance to the publishing of "estimated increases in the costs of carriers" as a result of the fuel increases as it found a greater potential to function as recommended prices. **41.49**

The Board went into greater detail regarding the character of information which may be exchanged in its decisions concerning information exchanges in the automotive industry.[47] Particularly, in *ODD & OSD*, the Board declined to find a violation in regard to frequent information exchanges between competitors concerning sales projections, estimated market shares, and even current prices; whereas in *Automobiles*, the Board imposed a monetary penalty against certain dealers who exchanged information concerning current stocks, pricing strategies, and sales strategies which it considered commercial secrets. In declining enforcement in *ODD & OSD*, the Board relied on the fact that the market for automobiles was already very transparent, and the information which was exchanged could also have been obtained by the parties themselves, whereas the information exchanges in *Automobiles* was deemed to constitute trade secrets. **41.50**

Comparisons between the cases cited above shows that the most determinative issue for the Board seems to be whether the information exchange significantly alters the current level of transparency within the market. Accordingly, the Board was tolerant of even the exchange current price information where it finds that such information is independently obtainable (*ODD & OSD*), whereas in a relatively non-transparent market the exchange of information with mere potential to become recommended prices was found to be objectionable (*UND*[48]). **41.51**

Lastly, the Board has noted in a variety of decisions that perfectly competitive markets presuppose fully informed buyers and sellers, and accordingly informational exchanges which are unlikely to lead to collusion will generally result in pro-competitive outcomes as the **41.52**

---

44 See *Erdemir* (n 46).

45 *Petder*, Case no. 11-48/1215-428 (September 22, 2011).

46 See *UND*, Case no. 12-13/389-118 (March 21, 2012).

47 See *ODD*, Case no. 11-43/916-285 (July 14, 2011); *Automobiles* (n 38); *ODD & OSD*, Case no. 09-41/998-255 (September 9, 2009).

48 *UND* (n 49).

markets will balance themselves faster where buyers and sellers are fully informed of the terms of trade prevalent in the relevant market. As a result, where the Board finds that information exchanges in question do not pose substantial anticompetitive concerns, it will not engage in the further inquiry of the pro-competitive purposed served by the exchanges in question.

I. Joint purchasing agreements

41.53 Unlike cartel agreements which are per se illegal under Turkish competition law regime, joint purchasing agreements concluded between competing undertakings are assessed in terms of whether they have pro-competitive effects by contributing to efficiency or whether they embody certain competition law risks. At the horizontal level, these risks are primarily associated with coordination through information exchange and concerted practice through harmonizing the price or cost structures. As these types of agreements are likely to lead to more concerns at the horizontal level, the Competition Board opts for analyzing the horizontal risks first before the vertical ones (*Zer*).[49] There are no decisions on record where the Board has prohibited a joint purchasing agreement.

J. Joint lobbying/regulatory/legislative efforts

41.54 The enforcement record in Turkey does not include any cases where undertakings were found to have violated competition law based on joint lobbying or legislative/regulatory efforts.

III. General issues

A. Jurisdiction and applicable law (including sector-specific competition regulation)

41.55 The foundation stone of the Turkish competition law regime is the Law on Protection of Competition No. 4054 of December 1994. Its purpose is to prevent agreements, decisions, and practices preventing, distorting, or restricting competition in markets for goods and services, and the abuse of dominance by the undertakings dominant in the market, and to ensure the protection of competition by performing the necessary regulations and supervisions to this end. Law No. 4054 applies to undertakings and associations of undertakings. An undertaking is defined as a single integrated economic unit capable of acting independently in the market to produce, market, or sell goods and services. Law No. 4054 also does not discriminate between sectors. In other words, transactions limiting competition by undertakings and associations of undertakings in all markets for goods and services are deemed to be covered, without exception. It is worth mentioning that Turkey is one of the "effect theory" jurisdictions where the decisive factor behind the scope of application of the Turkish competition law solely depends on whether the anticompetitive conduct has produced effects on Turkish markets. Furthermore, as the Competition Authority is authorized to issue communiqués and make the necessary regulations as to the implementation of the Law No. 4054, there are many regulations and guidelines that relate to the implementation of the competition law matters as well as the internal structure of the Competition Authority.

B. Antitrust system

(i) Name of agency/agencies

[49] *Zer*, 11-60/1559-552 (December 7, 2011).

In Turkey, the national competition agency that enforces competition law is the Turkish Competition Authority which possesses administrative and financial autonomy. The Turkish Competition Authority was established as per article 20 of the Law no. 4054 which reads as "... in order to ensure the formation and development of markets for goods and services in a free and sound competitive environment, to observe the implementation of this Act, and to fulfil the duties assigned to it by the Act." Its main duty is to prevent any threats to the competitive process in the markets for goods and services through the use of the powers granted by law. In this respect, the Competition Authority holds the following powers in order to achieve its aim under article 20 of the Law No. 4045: **41.56**

- conducting examination and investigations;
- granting exemptions and secondary legislations with respect to actions which in principle fall within the prohibitions of Law No. 4054, but which could be deemed to be a benefit for the economy and the consumers;
- reviewing mergers, acquisitions and joint-ventures which meet the jurisdictional thresholds in order to prevent monopolies and conducting examinations on the privatization processes;
- reviewing, regulating, and monitoring the markets in order to prevent anticompetitive agreements, abuses of dominant positions and mergers and acquisitions which significantly impede competition;
- promoting the competition policy and taking necessary measures to guide the administration to act in line with the competition policy; and
- conducting research in competition law, economics and policies, developing policies and contributing to the development of macroeconomic policies in terms of competition policy.

(ii) Staff size and budget

The Competition Authority consists of the Competition Board, Presidency, and Main Service Units. In its capacity as the competent body of the Competition Authority, the Competition Board is responsible for, *inter alia*, reviewing and resolving notifications concerning mergers, acquisitions, and joint-ventures. The Competition Board consists of seven members and is seated in Ankara. The Main Service Units consist of five supervision and enforcement departments with sector-specific work distribution that handle competition law enforcement work through approximately 120 case handlers along with department of decisions, economic analyses and research department, information management department, external relations, training, and competition advocacy department, strategy development, regulation, and budget department and cartel on-the-spot inspections support division. **41.57**

According to the 13th Annual Report,[50] the budget of the Competition Authority for year 2011 was TRY 45,750,000.00. **41.58**

(iii) Recent enforcement actions and trends

In 2011, the Competition Board decided on a total of 283 antitrust infringement cases (158 cases on article 4; ninety-five cases on article 6 (abuse of dominant position); thirty mixed). Out of 188 article 4 cases, 108 relate to horizontal infringements, seventy-five to vertical infringements, and five to both. Moreover, the number of finalized negative clearance/exemption decisions is fifty-four and merger/acquisition decisions was 253 in 2011 consisting of three mergers, 168 acquisitions, sixty-eight joint ventures, and fourteen privatizations. **41.59**

In 2011, the total amount of fines related to substance was TRY 459,508,920 where article 4 cases accounted for almost all of the monetary fines imposed on substantive grounds. The **41.60**

[50] Competition Authority, 13th Annual Report, <http://www.rekabet.gov.tr/File/?path=ROOT/Documents/Faaliyet+Raporlar%c4%b1/falRap27.pdf> (in Turkish).

most recent landmark decision is the *Turkish Airlines/Pegasus* decision[51] as it concerns the two major airline operators in Turkey. The case was brought before the Turkish Competition Authority by Pegasus Airlines with the allegation that Turkish Airlines had abused its dominant position through exclusionary practices. Pegasus Airlines' claim was based primarily on predatory pricing in the context of abuse of dominance under article 6. The Competition Board, in its conclusion, reached no finding of an abuse of dominance under article 6 and decided not to impose any fines on Turkish Airlines. Instead, the Competition Board decided to deliver an opinion on slot allocation and bilateral air service agreements.

41.61 In the light of the foregoing case concerning predatory pricing, coupled with recent pre-investigations launched by the Competition Board,[52] it could be concluded that the Competition Board has increased its interest in pricing behaviors of the undertakings operating in the respective markets.

C. Private litigation

41.62 In Turkey, competition law is primarily enforced by Turkish Competition Authority and public enforcement is also supplemented with private actions as well. Articles 57 ff. of Law no. 4054 entitle any person who is injured in his business or property by reason of anything prohibited in the antitrust laws to sue the violators for three times their damages plus litigation costs and attorney fees. Therefore, Turkey is one of the exceptional jurisdictions where law permits a court to triple the amount of damages to be awarded. In private actions, the incumbent firms are adjudicated before the competent general civil courts. Because the treble damages clause allows litigants to obtain three times their loss as compensation, private antitrust litigations increasingly make their presence felt in article 6 and article 4 arenas. The applicable periods of limitation in private suits are subject to the general provisions of the Turkish Code of Obligations, according to which the right to sue violators on the basis of an antitrust-driven injury claim terminates upon the lapse of ten years from the event giving rise to the damage of the plaintiff. Moreover, the general cost rules for civil law claims apply also in private action concerning antitrust claims. Antitrust-based private lawsuits have been rare but increasing in practice. The majority of the private lawsuits in Turkish antitrust enforcement rely on refusal to supply allegations. Civil damage claims have usually been settled among the parties involved, before the court rendering its judgment. That said, there are no statistical studies or reports that set out magnitude of the settlements in question.

D. Follow-on litigation

41.63 Although there is no explicit provision governing the relationship between the decision of the Competition Board and private actions, in practice, courts usually do not engage in an analysis as to whether there is actually a condemnable action, and wait for the Board to render its opinion on the matter, therefore treating the issue as a prejudicial question. Since courts usually wait for the Board to render its decision, the court decision can be obtained in a shorter period in follow-on actions.

E. Arbitration and alternative dispute resolution

41.64 Under Turkish competition law regime, there is no explicit provision regarding arbitration or ADR. Therefore, the question of whether there is a room for arbitration and ADR remains uncertain. The main hurdle behind the application of arbitration to competition law cases was that whether competition law satisfies the condition of "suitability for arbitration"

51 *Turkish Airlines* (n 1).

52 See e.g. *İDO*, Case no. 12-29/854-254 (May 31, 2012).

required under the relevant legislations governing the institution of arbitration. On the other hand, presently, it is accepted that as the competition law infringements are torts by their nature, and as torts are suitable for arbitration, competition law disputes can also be resolved through arbitration.

F. Remedies

In the case of a proven competition law violation, the companies concerned shall be separately subject to fines of up to 10 percent of their Turkish turnover generated in the financial year preceding the date of the fining decision (if this is not calculable, the turnover generated in the financial year nearest to the date of the fining decision will be taken into account). Employees and/or managers of the undertakings/association of undertakings that had a determining effect on the creation of the violation are also fined up to 5 percent of the fine imposed on the undertaking/association of undertaking. **41.65**

After the recent amendments, the new version of the Competition Law makes reference to article 17 of the Law on Minor Offenses to require the Board to take into consideration factors such as the level of fault and the amount of possible damage in the relevant market, the market power of the undertaking(s) within the relevant market, duration and recurrence of the infringement, cooperation or driving role of the undertaking(s) in the infringement, financial power of the undertaking(s), compliance with the commitments etc., in determining the magnitude of the monetary fine. In line with this, the Regulation on Monetary Fines for Restrictive Agreements, Concerted Practices, Decisions and Abuses of Dominance (the Regulation on Fines) was recently enacted by the Turkish Competition Authority. The Regulation on Fines sets out detailed guidelines as to the calculation of monetary fines applicable in the case of an antitrust violation. The Regulation on Fines applies to both cartel activity and abuse of dominance, but illegal concentrations are not covered by the Regulation on Fines. According to the Regulation on Fines, fines are calculated by first determining the basic level, which in the case of cartels is between 2 and 4 percent of the company's turnover in the financial year preceding the date of the fining decision (if this is not calculable, the turnover for the financial year nearest the date of the decision); aggravating and mitigating factors are then factored in. The Regulation on Fines also applies to managers or employees who had a determining effect on the violation (such as participating in cartel meetings and making decisions that would involve the company in cartel activity), and provides for certain reductions in their favor. **41.66**

In addition to the monetary sanction, the Board is authorized to take all necessary measures to terminate the restrictive agreement, remove all de facto and legal consequences of every action that has been taken unlawfully, and to take all other necessary measures in order to restore the level of competition and status as before the infringement. Furthermore, such a restrictive agreement shall be deemed as legally invalid and unenforceable with all its legal consequences. Similarly, the Competition Law authorizes the Board to take interim measures until the final resolution on the matter, in case there is a possibility for serious and irreparable damages. **41.67**

(i) Civil liability

The legal consequences of the restriction of competition in the civil law arena are provided in articles 56 to 59 of Law no. 4054. Article 56 stipulates that "any agreements, and decisions of associations of undertakings, contrary to article 4 of this Act are invalid. The performance of acts arising out of such agreements and decisions may not be requested. In case a request is made for reclamation due to the invalidity of the previous acts fulfilled, the return obligation of the parties is subject to articles 63 and 64 of the Code of Obligations." Therefore, the **41.68** sanctions envisaged for civil liability are nullity, actions for damages, and unjust enrichment. Furthermore, sanctions under civil law are subject to the principles of law of obligations.

(ii) Criminal liability

41.69 The sanctions that could be imposed under the Competition Law are administrative in nature. Therefore, the Competition Law leads to administrative fines (and civil liability) but no criminal sanctions. That said, there have been cases where the matter had to be referred to a public prosecutor after the competition law investigation is complete. On that note, bid-rigging activity may be criminally prosecutable under ss. 235 ff. of the Turkish Criminal Code. Illegal price manipulation (i.e. manipulation through disinformation or other fraudulent means) may also be condemned by up to two years of imprisonment and a civil monetary fine under s. 237 of the Turkish Criminal Code.[53] In the Board's *Cardiological Medical Consumables*[54] decision, a large group of sellers of medical consumables related to cardiology were subject to fines ranging from 2 percent to 5 percent of their 2001 turnover, in relation to cartel activity which involved boycotts and sharing of public tenders and was already prosecuted by the criminal system. In effect, the evidence collected through the criminal investigation constituted the backbone of the Board's investigation.

G. Leniency and immunity

41.70 Leniency program is firstly introduced in 2008 by Law No. 5728 ("Law No. 5728") Amending Certain Laws for the Harmonization with the Fundamental Criminal Laws which made substantial amendments mainly on article 16 of Law No. 4054. Following, implementation steps for the immunity regime and leniency program have been taken by way of issuance of the Regulation on Active Cooperation for Discovery of Cartels ("Regulation on Leniency"), which has come into force in 2009. The Regulation on Leniency which empowers the Board to institute and delegate a sub-division in charge for leniency/immunity to deal with leniency applications/affairs ("Leniency Division") can be summarized as follows.

41.71 The leniency program is solely available for "cartelists," and therefore the regulation does not apply to other forms of antitrust infringement. Section 3 of the Regulation on Leniency provides for a definition of cartel, which encompasses price fixing, customer/supplier/market sharing, restricting output or placing quotas, and bid-rigging.

41.72 A cartelist may apply for leniency until the "investigation report" is officially served. Depending on the application order, there may be total immunity from, or reduction of a fine:

(1) The first incumbent undertaking to file an appropriately prepared application for leniency until the "investigation report" is officially served may benefit from total immunity. Employees/managers of the first applicant would also be totally immune. However, for there to be total immunity, the applicant must not be the "ring-leader." If this is the case, i.e. if the applicant has coerced the other cartelists to participate in the cartel, there would be a mere reduction of 33–50 percent for the undertaking and 33–100 percent for the employees/managers.
(2) The second incumbent undertaking to file an appropriately prepared application would receive a 33–50 percent reduction of the fine. Employees/managers of the second applicant that actively cooperate with the Competition Authority would benefit from a reduction of 33–100 percent.

---

[53] See also s. 8 for private suits, which may also become an exposure item against the defendant.
[54] *Cardiological Medical Consumables*, Case no. 07-24/236-76 (March 16, 2007).

(3) The third applicant would receive a 25–33 percent reduction. Employees/managers of the third applicant that actively cooperate with the Competition Authority would benefit from a reduction of 25 percent up to 100 percent. Subsequent applicants would receive a 16–25 percent reduction. Employees/managers of subsequent applicants would benefit from a reduction of 16 percent up to 100 percent.

In order to benefit from immunity or reduction of fines the following conditions must be satisfied. The applicant must submit: (i) information on the products affected by the cartel; (ii) information on the duration of the cartel; (iii) names of the cartelists; (iv) dates, locations, and participants of the cartel meetings; and (v) other information/documents about the cartel activity. The required information may be submitted verbally. The applicant must avoid concealing/destroying the information/documents on the cartel activity. Unless the Leniency Division decides otherwise, the applicant must cease to take part in the cartel. Unless the Leniency Division instructs otherwise, the application must be kept confidential until the investigation report has been served. The applicant must continue to actively cooperate with the Competition Authority until the final decision on the case has been rendered. **41.73**

Although there have not been many decisions of the Competition Board where leniency was granted in a recent investigation launched in order to determine whether Güneş Ekspres Havacılık A.Ş. and Condor Flugdienst GmbH violated Law No. 4054 have restricted competition through various agreements. The investigation was triggered by a leniency application made by Güneş Ekspress. Therefore, although the Competition Board decided that the investigated parties indeed violated Law No. 4054, Güneş Ekspress was granted a total immunity from the administrative monetary fines.[55] **41.74**

H. Document creation and retention

The Competition Board has relatively broad investigative powers. According to article 14 of Law No. 4054, it may request all information it deems necessary from all public institutions and organizations, undertakings and trade associations. Officials of these bodies, undertakings, and trade associations are obliged to provide the necessary information within the period fixed by the Board. Failure to comply with a decision ordering the production of information may lead to the imposition of a turnover-based fine of 0.1 percent of the turnover generated in the financial year preceding the date of the fining decision (if this is not calculable, the turnover generated in the financial year nearest to the date of the fining decision will be taken into account). The minimum amount of fine is TRY 13,591. Where incorrect or incomplete information has been provided in response to a request for information, the same penalty may be imposed. **41.75**

In this respect, article 15 of Law No. 4054 also authorizes the Board to conduct on-site investigations. Accordingly, the Board can examine the books, paperwork, and documents of undertakings and trade associations, and, if need be, take copies of the same; request undertakings and trade associations to provide written or verbal explanations on specific topics; and conduct on-site investigations with regard to any asset of an undertaking. **41.76**

The Law provides vast authority to the Competition Authority on dawn raids. A judicial authorization is obtained by the Board only if the subject undertaking refuses to allow the dawn raid. While the wording of the law allows for employes to be compelled to give oral testimony, case handlers do allow delaying an answer so long as there is a quick written follow-up correspondence. Therefore, in practice, employees can avoid providing answers on issues that are uncertain to them, provided that a written response is submitted in a mutually **41.77**

[55] See *Güneş Ekspress*, Case no. 11-54/1431-507 (October 27, 2011).

agreed timeline. Computer records are fully examined by the experts of the Competition Authority, including deleted items.

41.78 Officials conducting an on-site investigation need to be in possession of a deed of authorization from the Board. The deed of authorization must specify the subject matter and purpose of the investigation. The inspectors are not entitled to exercise their investigative powers (copying records, recording statements by company staff, etc.) in relation to matters that do not fall within the scope of the investigation (i.e., that which is written on the deed of authorization). Refusing to grant the staff of the Competition Authority access to business premises may lead to the imposition of a periodic daily-based fine of 0.5 percent of the turnover generated in the financial year preceding the date of the fining decision (if this is not calculable, the turnover generated in the financial year nearest to the date of the fining decision will be taken into account). The minimum amount of fine is 13.591 Turkish liras. It may also lead to the imposition of a periodic day fine of 0.05 percent of the turnover generated in the financial year preceding the date of the fining decision (if this is not calculable, the turnover generated in the financial year nearest to the date of the fining decision will be taken into account) for each day of the violation.

42

UNITED KINGDOM

Alex Nourry, Greg Olsen, and Dan Harrison
Clifford Chance

Introduction

42.01 Antitrust laws in the UK are made up of four components: (i) a civil prohibition on anti-competitive agreements; (ii) a civil prohibition on abuse of dominance; (iii) a criminal cartel offense; and (iv) the market investigation regime. The first three of these are enforced primarily by the Office of Fair Trading (OFT), although a number of sectoral regulators also have concurrent enforcement powers in respect of the civil prohibitions.[1] As regards the market investigation regime, the relevant UK agency is the Competition Commission (CC), with the OFT or one of the sectoral regulators selecting markets and referring them to the CC for in-depth investigation. With the exception of prosecutions under the criminal cartel offense, these agencies have independent powers to impose penalties or remedies (as appropriate), without prior recourse to a court. From 1 April 2014, the OFT and CC will be merged into a

[1] See Section III.B.

new single authority—the Competition and Markets Authority (CMA)—which will assume responsibility for enforcing the antitrust prohibitions (alongside the sectoral regulators) as well as conducting market investigations.

42.02 The civil prohibition on anticompetitive agreements exists under both EU law—article 101 of the Treaty on the Functioning of the EU (TFEU), previously known as the EC Treaty—and UK law, in chapter I of the Competition Act 1998. The civil prohibition on abuse of dominance is contained in article 102 TFEU and chapter II of the Competition Act. The EU prohibitions are almost identical to their UK counterparts. The principal differences are that the EU prohibitions apply only in so far as the conduct in question has an actual or potential effect on trade between EU countries and, as regards the prohibition on abuse of dominance, is carried out by an undertaking with a dominant position in the EU or a substantial part of it. In contrast, the UK prohibitions apply even if there is no such cross-border impact, and if the dominant position exists in any market in the UK, no matter how small. This means that the UK prohibitions may be applied to highly localized markets which would escape the EU prohibitions. This is often reflected in the mix of cases pursued by the UK agencies.

42.03 Whether a form of conduct is caught by both the EU and UK prohibitions, or the UK prohibition alone, can have certain procedural implications, such as the sharing of case information with agencies of the EU and other EU countries. However, there is no difference in the substance of the EU and UK prohibitions. The Competition Act requires the UK prohibitions to be interpreted and applied by the UK agencies and UK courts consistently with the EU prohibitions, their application by the EU Courts (the General Court and the EU Court of Justice). They must also "have regard to" any relevant decision or statement of the European Commission, and avoid judgments or decisions that are inconsistent with a European Commission decision involving the same facts and parties. Consequently, for the prohibitions on anticompetitive agreements and abuse of dominance, the substantive law set out in the European Union chapter of this handbook is of equal relevance to the UK. This Chapter focuses on UK cases that have built upon and developed the EU case law, and references to the "prohibition on anticompetitive agreements" and the "prohibition on abuse of dominance" refer to both the EU and UK versions of these prohibitions, as appropriate. In contrast, the criminal cartel offense—which applies only to price-fixing, market sharing, customer allocation bid-rigging between rivals—has no EU equivalent.

42.04 As regards the fourth regime referred to above—market investigations under the Enterprise Act 2002—the UK is unusual. While many jurisdictions (including the EU) confer powers on their antitrust agencies to gather information on markets, the UK is one of the few that also confers powers on the agency to remedy any antitrust problems that are identified. The regime is entirely independent of the prohibitions on anticompetitive agreements and abuse of dominance. Companies can become subject to far-reaching remedies—including divestments, price controls, and injunctions (but not fines)—even if there is no suggestion that they have breached any law. The CC need only come to the conclusion that a particular feature of a market—such as its structure, or conduct of one or more market players—is likely to have an adverse effect on competition in the UK. Moreover, there is little democratic or parliamentary scrutiny of the agency's market investigations, and the Competition Appeal Tribunal (CAT)—the UK court which hears first instance appeals of the UK agencies' decisions—applies a much lighter standard of review when judging appeals against market investigation decisions of the CC than it does when judging appeals against the OFT's findings that a company has breached the laws prohibiting anticompetitive conduct.

42.05 With the exception of the criminal cartel offense (which has seen convictions in only one case), there is a relatively high level of enforcement of antitrust laws in the UK. Since the civil antitrust prohibitions came into force in 2000, the trend has been from a large number of small cases in the early years to a focus in more recent years on cases involving larger firms or widespread infringements.[2] Market investigations have been less common, with only sixteen markets referred to the CC for investigation (as of December 2013) since the current version of the regime came into force in 2003. However, such references are often avoided by firms offering formal or informal undertakings to modify their conduct, following a "market study" carried out by one of the agencies with powers to refer a market for investigation by the CC. Moreover, with five market investigations currently ongoing (as of December 2013) there are indications that the referring agencies are making more frequent use of this enforcement tool. The Government has sought to encourage this trend with amendments to the regime (in the Enterprise and Regulatory Reform Act 2013) which in April 2014 will introduce, among other things, powers for the CMA to conduct market investigations into practices that are common to multiple markets and greater scope for consideration of public interest issues.

I. Acting alone

The OFT has been at the forefront of moves by European agencies to focus infringement findings on those cases in which it can be shown that harmful competitive effects are likely, and away from a form-based approach that treats certain types of conduct of dominant companies as being *prima facie* unlawful. While judgments of the EU Courts—which are binding on courts of the UK in this area—have been slow to follow this trend, conduct for which there is no evidence of harmful effects is unlikely to give rise to substantial third party litigation risk in practice, given the principle that damages must be based on proven losses. **42.06**

Large, cross-border abuse of dominance cases tend to be pursued by the European Commission, (whose investigations prevent national agencies of EU countries from conducting parallel investigations into the same facts. Consequently the cases that have been pursued by the UK agencies since the prohibition came into force in 2000 have tended to concern markets of relatively small value (advertising space in local newspapers, in-clinic veterinary analyzers) or local travel markets (local bus services, regional air travel). Indeed, in the *Cardiff Bus* case, the OFT issued an infringement decision despite the dominant company having a turnover below the statutory GBP 50 million threshold that triggers the OFT's powers to impose a fine.[3] It did so to enable harmed rivals to bring damages actions against the dominant company for loss they had suffered as a result of its abuse (which they subsequently did, resulting in the first damages award for a competition infringement by a UK court). **42.07**

Between March 2000 and December 2013, the UK agencies have found infringements of the prohibition on abuse of dominance in seven cases, resulting in fines of between GBP 1.38 million (reduced to GBP 1 million on appeal) and GBP 41.6 million (reduced to GBP 15 million on appeal) and the UK courts have identified breaches in a further three cases. Around eighty cases have been investigated and closed without a finding of infringement, due to lack of evidence of a breach, the case falling outside the relevant agency's enforcement priorities or (in several instances) because the agency accepted formal or informal commitments from the parties to modify their conduct. The majority of cases are investigations by sectoral regulators into the conduct of regulated utilities. **42.08**

[2] See Section III.B for more details on enforcement trends and cases.

[3] *Cardiff Bus*, CA98/01/2008, OFT decision of November 18, 2008.

42.09 As regards the market investigation regime, the agencies' policy line is that single firm conduct will, where necessary and possible, generally be dealt with under the prohibitions on anticompetitive conduct or under sector-specific regulation. However, they have on occasion carried out market investigations that have principally concerned the activities of a single market player (for example, the *BAA airports* market investigation in 2009).[4] Invoking the market investigation regime has certain advantages for the agencies over opening an abuse of dominance investigation, as it is often easier—both legally and procedurally—to establish that the relevant test for enforcement action is met. Moreover, market investigation findings and remedies are less susceptible to successful appeal before the courts, given the lighter standard of review that is applied to appeals against such decisions.

A. Predatory pricing

42.10 There are various examples of cases in which predatory pricing has been found by the UK agencies to infringe the UK prohibition on abuse of dominance. In line with the case law of the EU Courts, the UK agencies consider whether pricing is below "average avoidable cost" (AAC, a measure which is broadly similar to average variable costs) or, if a plan to eliminate a competitor is shown, the "long-run average incremental cost" (a measure which is broadly similar to average total costs).

42.11 The OFT usually takes a measured approach to assessing whether aggressive language in a dominant company's internal documents is really indicative of an exclusionary intent, or merely representative of a given employee's competitive mindset. For example, in both *First Edinburgh/Lothian*,[5] and *Flybe*,[6] the OFT concluded that while the accused companies probably were pricing below AAC, their behavior was directed at establishing themselves firmly in the market rather than at driving out competitors.

42.12 The underlying philosophy is that dominant companies should not be penalized if they are able to charge lower prices than their competitors as a result of their superior efficiency and lower costs, but may be found to have acted unlawfully where their conduct is liable to exclude from the market an equally efficient competitor. In neither case is it necessary to show that the dominant company was likely to have been able to recoup profits sacrificed during the period of predation, once its rival(s) had been successfully squeezed out of the market. However, a dominant company can escape liability if it can show that its conduct was "objectively justified," or likely to lead to substantial efficiencies to the ultimate benefit of consumers. Examples identified by the OFT of potentially legitimate commercial reasons for below-cost pricing include:

- loss leading, so that the supply of a product at a low price or for free may not be predatory if such supply will lead to sufficient profits on related products (see e.g. *IDEXX Laboratories*[7]) unless those profits resulted from the elimination of a rival;
- isolated short run promotions and launches of new products;
- the addition of new customers to a network, the expansion of which benefits all network customers; and/or
- responses to unanticipated market shocks, such as temporary cost spikes.

---

[4] *The supply of airport services by BAA in the UK*, final report of the Competition Commission, March 19, 2009.

[5] *First Edinburgh / Lothian*, CA98/05/2004, OFT decision of April 29, 2004.

[6] *Alleged abuse of a dominant position by Flybe Limited*, OFT1286, OFT decision of November 5, 2010.

[7] *Alleged abuse of a dominant position by IDEXX Laboratories Limited*, OFT1387, OFT decision of November 17, 2011.

However, the European Commission's guidelines on exclusionary abuses are more skeptical, stating that it is "considered unlikely that predatory conduct will create efficiencies," but that it will consider claims that low pricing enables a dominant company to achieve economies of scale or efficiencies related to expanding the market. In addition, in line with the case law of the EU courts, it is not a defense that a dominant company was simply meeting low prices offered by a non-dominant rival. **42.13**

The OFT has been prepared to extend theories of predatory harm by assessing the impact of a low-pricing strategy in one market (or market segment) on competition in another, including in circumstances in which the dominant company is not dominant in the market in which the below-cost pricing occurs.[8] **42.14**

Where established, predatory pricing has resulted in fines: GBP 1.328 million in *Aberdeen Journals*, reduced to GBP 1 million on appeal[9] and GBP 3.21 million in *Napp Pharmaceuticals*, reduced to GBP 2.2 million on appeal.[10] In addition, the Water Services Regulation Authority (Ofwat) closed an investigation into predatory pricing and cross-subsidy of water supply analysis services following commitments by the company under investigation that it would divest the business that had been engaging in the relevant conduct.[11] **42.15**

Predatory pricing has not been dealt with under the current market investigation regime, although it was the subject of investigations under the similar preceding regime, many of which concerned the bus transport sector. **42.16**

B. Exploitative offenses (excessive pricing, monopoly leveraging)

The UK agencies are generally reluctant to bring pure exploitative abuse cases, particularly where these would necessitate price regulation and establishment of an appropriate market price. To date, cases that have been pursued by the agencies have invariably involved an element of exclusion, for example where excessive prices amounted to a refusal to supply, or margin squeeze (these are described below, under "refusals to deal"). Draft "assessment of conduct" guidance issued by the OFT (but never finalized) recognized that high prices may be an integral part of the competitive process, as they may "reflect short term shifts in demand or supply, provide a fair return on earlier investments, or act as a signal for existing and potential competitors, respectively, to expand output and to enter a market." Accordingly, the OFT will not usually investigate excessive prices unless there is evidence that they are substantially higher than would be expected in a competitive market, and that there is no effective competitive pressure to bring them down to competitive levels, nor is there likely to be. **42.17**

The OFT's decision in relation to *Napp Pharmaceuticals*[12] is an example of excessive pricing that resulted in fines and the imposition of directions as to future pricing. In contrast, the November 2001 decision of the Office of Rail Regulation (ORR), regarding pricing of fares for passenger rail services provided by *Virgin West Coast*, is an example of a decision in which an allegation of excessive pricing was rejected, in part because the tender process which took place at the time when Virgin was awarded the franchise to operate the relevant services acted **42.18**

[8] See *Flybe* (n 6).

[9] See *Aberdeen Journals*, CA98/5/2001, Director General of Fair Trading decision of July 16, 2001; and *Aberdeen Journals v. Director General of Fair Trading (II)* [2003] CAT 11.

[10] *Napp Pharmaceutical v. Director General of Fair Trading* [2002] CAT 1.

[11] *Decision to accept binding commitments from Severn Trent PLC, Severn Trent Water Limited and Severn Trent Laboratories Limited*, Ofwat decision of January 17, 2013.

[12] *Napp Pharmaceuticals*, CA98/2/2001, Director General of Fair Trading decision of March 30, 2001.

to ensure that, overall, the operator was not able to earn excessive profits over the life of the franchise, notwithstanding the level of individual fares.[13]

42.19 The UK courts often take a dim view of litigants' attempts to secure capped prices through the use of antitrust law. In *Attheraces*,[14] the Court of Appeal stated that a price only becomes abusive at the level at which it would affect competitors' or customers' ability to compete, and is not abusive merely because it exceeds the cost of producing the product by more than a reasonable amount. Similarly, in *Humber Oil Terminals*,[15] the High Court ruled (and the Court of Appeal confirmed) that Associated British Ports could not be said to have abused a dominant position merely by putting forward high prices during negotiations.

42.20 In contrast, an example of a case in which a court agreed that there had been excessive pricing is the CAT's judgment in *Albion Water*.[16] In that case, the CAT upheld a finding of Ofwat that Dŵr Cymru (a provider of water and sewerage services) had charged unfair "access" prices for the transportation of water, as there was a clear disparity between the access price and both the cost and economic value of services to be supplied. The CAT stated that the assessment of whether a price is excessive—and the appropriate economic methodology for that assessment—are matters of judgment to be applied with regard to the specific circumstances of each case, such that it is not appropriate to specify a particular amount by which a price must exceed the economic value of a product or service in order to breach the prohibition on abuse of dominance.

42.21 A wariness of intervening in pricing is also broadly reflected in the CC's policy on the formulation of remedies in market investigations. However, a number of market investigations have sought to address market-wide practices that were perceived to exploit customers, through the use of remedies other than price controls. For example, in its 2006 *home credit* market investigation, the CC imposed a combination of remedies to increase price transparency and decrease information asymmetries between market operators "in the belief that an increase in competitive pressure will serve to remove the detriment of high prices."[17] Similarly, the CC's 2009 *payment protection insurance* market investigation resulted in a market-wide ban on the sale of such products at the point-of-sale of the underlying loan.[18]

C. Monopsony

42.22 The prohibition on abuse of dominance can, in principle, extend to a dominant company's treatment of its suppliers. However, in its decision on a complaint by *BetterCare* (following annulment of an earlier decision by the CAT), the OFT took the view that paying excessively low purchase prices is only likely to amount to an abuse in exceptional circumstances.[19] In the absence of barriers to exit by suppliers from the relevant market, a purchaser which paid excessively low prices would be unable to obtain supplies beyond the short term, even if it was a monopolist. The OFT therefore considered that excessively low purchase prices will normally be self-correcting and would not, absent price discrimination, usually justify action under the prohibition on abuse of dominance. In the *BetterCare* case, the OFT did not consider such exceptional circumstances to have arisen, in part because there was evidence that

[13] *Virgin Fares Cases*, ORR decision of November 30, 2001.

[14] *Attheraces Limited v. the British Horseracing Board* [2007] EWCA Civ 38.

[15] *Humber Oil Terminals Trustee Ltd. v. Associated British Ports* [2011] EWHC 352 (Ch).

[16] *Albion Water v. Water Services Regulation Authority* [2008] CAT 31.

[17] *Home credit market investigation*, final report of the Competition Commission, November 30, 2006.

[18] *Market investigation into payment protection insurance*, final report of the Competition Commission, January 29, 2009.

[19] *BetterCare Group Ltd/North & West Belfast Health & Social Services Trust (Remitted case)*, CA98/09/2003, OFT decision of December 18, 2003.

at least one of BetterCare's rivals had been able to operate profitably on the basis of the prices paid by the dominant downstream company.

D. Price discrimination

Both the EU and UK prohibitions on abuse of dominance can catch the practice of charging different prices to similarly placed customers, or charging the same prices to differently placed customers. To date, UK cases have all involved exclusionary discrimination resulting in foreclosure of a competitor to the dominant company (e.g. the November 2006 *EWS* decision of the ORR[20]), as opposed to the exploitation of market power by charging discriminatory prices that distort competition between customers who are not rivals of the dominant company. The OFT recognizes that discriminatory pricing is often beneficial, for example if it allows the efficient recovery of fixed costs, expands demand or opens up new market segments. In its *Post Danmark* judgment,[21] the Court of Justice of the European Union (CJEU) expressed the view that selective price-cutting could not be considered to give rise to anticompetitive exclusion if the resulting prices remained above the dominant company's average total costs. **42.23**

Some discriminatory conduct may also appear to amount to a refusal to supply access to an essential facility, which will normally only be considered abusive if a more stringent test is met.[22] The UK High Court ruled on which test to apply in these circumstances in *Purple Parking v. Heathrow Airport*,[23] in which Heathrow Airport Limited (HAL) had refused to allow competing providers of "meet and greet" parking services to operate from its terminal forecourts. The High Court recognized that the claimants would have had difficulties in showing that the stricter conditions for an "essential facilities" abuse were satisfied, but concluded that in this case HAL had instead committed the abuse of discrimination. An important factor in the court's reasoning appears to have been that the terminal forecourts were developed to serve the central purpose of the airport, i.e. to allow airplanes to take off and land with passengers. They were not developed so that HAL could run a meet and greet operation from them. Consequently, the court considered that this was not a case in which HAL was being required to share with a competitor the "real fruits of ownership" of a facility that it had created and in which it had invested. **42.24**

E. Dictating or influencing resale prices

(i) Resale price maintenance

Resale price maintenance (RPM) is considered a hard core restriction of competition, and is invariably pursued under the prohibition on anticompetitive agreements (rather than the prohibition on abuse of dominance). The UK agencies' enforcement of RPM has been relatively limited in recent years, but increased sharply in the second half of 2013. In August 2013, the OFT issued an infringement decision relating to a ban on online reselling and price advertising of mobility scooters[24] and, in a separate case, issued a notice of its intention to accept commitments by certain operators of hotels and online travel agents to limit (but not eliminate) restrictions on the ability of the online travel agents to discount the price of hotel accommodation sold on their websites.[25] The following month, the OFT issued a statement **42.25**

[20] *English Welsh and Scottish Railway Limited (EWS)*, ORR decision of November 17, 2006.

[21] Case C-209/10 *Post Danmark A/S v. Konkurrencerådet*, 27 March 2012.

[22] See Section I.H.

[23] *Purple Parking Ltd. and Meteor Parking v. Heathrow Airport Ltd.* [2011] EWHC 987 (Ch).

[24] *Roma-branded mobility scooters: prohibitions on online sales and online price advertising*, CE/9578-12, OFT decision of August 5, 2014.

[25] *Hotel online booking: Notice of intention to accept binding commitments to remove certain discounting restrictions for Online Travel Agents and Invitation to comment*, OFT1500, OFT notice of August 9, 2013.

of objections to DB Apparel and a number of retailers, alleging that they had engaged in RPM in the sale of sports bras.[26] Before these cases, the OFT had not pursued enforcement action against RPM for a number of years. In earlier cases involving purely vertical arrangements (such as the investigations into *Lladró Comercial, Swarovski, Yamaha*, and *Oakley*),[27] the OFT has tended to refrain from imposing fines in return for a formal or informal undertaking to cease engaging in RPM, with the notable exception of *Hasbro*, which was fined GBP 4.9 million for RPM in relation to the resale of toys.[28] However, cases in which RPM has been combined with horizontal collusion[29] have invariably resulted in fines, such as the GBP 6.6 million fine imposed on Umbro regarding pricing of replica football shirts (reduced to GBP 5.3 million on appeal, in *Umbro v. OFT*)[30] and the GBP 33,737 fine imposed on an importer and resellers of motor vehicle components.[31]

42.26 RPM can, in principle, be excepted from the prohibition on anticompetitive agreements where it can be shown to result in countervailing consumer benefits (see Chapter 12, European Union for some examples). The UK agencies have never, to date, found the exception to apply to an instance of RPM, although the OFT indicated that there appeared to be potential justifications in this respect in the online hotel booking case referred in para. 42.25.

42.27 Recommended resale prices (RRP) are, in principle, permitted, provided they are not accompanied by other factors that cause distributors to treat them as fixed or minimum resale prices (e.g. threatened penalties for pricing below the RRP). RRPs for a variety of domestic electrical goods were prohibited in 1998, as a result of an investigation under the predecessor to the current market investigation regime. However, those prohibitions were recently abolished and the alignment of EU and UK competition law means that it is now unlikely that RRPs will be prohibited under the market investigation regime again, at least in sectors involving significant cross-border sales.

(ii) Minimum advertised price programs

42.28 MAP programs are viewed as hardcore restrictions of competition law, in the same way as for other forms of RPM. In *Lladró Comercial*,[32] the OFT stated that "any provision which restricts a retailer's freedom to inform potential customers of discounts which are being offered removes a key incentive for, and constitutes an obstacle to, price competition between retailers…The mere existence of such provisions amounts to a serious infringement of the Chapter I prohibition."

F. Tying arrangements

42.29 Tying arrangements have been found to breach the UK prohibition on abuse of dominance, but only once. In 2003, the OFT imposed a fine of GBP 6.8 million (reduced to GBP

---

[26] *OFT issues Statement of Objections to sports bra supplier and three UK department stores*, Press release 64/13 (September 20, 2013).

[27] *Agreements between Lladró Comercial S.A. and UK retailers fixing the price of porcelain and stoneware figurines*, CA98/04/2003, OFT decision of March 31, 2003; *OFT receives assurances from Swarovski over retail prices*, Press release 86/04 (May 18, 2004); *OFT closes investigation into Yamaha musical instruments*, Press release 132/06 (September 8, 2006); *Alleged price-fixing of Oakley sunglasses*, CE/2471/03, OFT case closure summary of March 22, 2007.

[28] *Agreements between Hasbro UK Ltd. and distributors fixing the price of Hasbro toys and games*, CA98/18/2002, Director General of Fair Trading decision of November 28, 2002.

[29] See Section II.G.

[30] *Umbro Holdings Limited and others v. Office of Fair Trading* [2005] CAT 22.

[31] *John Bruce (UK) Limited, Fleet Parts Limited and Truck and Trailer Components*, CA98/12/2002, Director General of Fair Trading decision of May 13, 2002.

[32] *Lladró Comercial* (n 27).

3 million on appeal) on Genzyme for—among other things—tying together the supply of its pharmaceutical drug Cerezyme with delivery and homecare services. The OFT believed that this essentially tied the purchaser—the UK's National Health Service (NHS)—to Genzyme for the supply of homecare services and foreclosed third party suppliers. On appeal, the CAT concluded that the OFT had not sufficiently proven that the bundled price had an adverse effect on competition, as there was no evidence that the NHS had wished to obtain the relevant homecare services from anyone else, or had approached Genzyme to suggest that the pricing of Cerezyme was adjusted accordingly.[33]

If widespread in a particular market, tying may also be viewed as a market distorting "feature" that is susceptible to remedy under the market investigation regime. For example, in its 2009 *payment protection insurance (PPI)* market investigation, the CC found that banks' practice of bundling PPI with merchandise cover was one factor that inhibited the development of the market for standalone PPI in the UK, and therefore prohibited the banks from offering such bundles unless they also offered a standalone PPI product.[34] **42.30**

G. Exclusive dealing

Exclusive dealing—whether through express exclusivity requirements or practices which prevent customers from switching in practice—can amount to an abuse when carried out by a dominant company, if it prevents the entry or expansion of rivals. However, enforcement action in the UK has been limited to two cases pursued by the sectoral regulators: an infringement finding by the Office of Rail Regulation against a rail haulage company that had imposed volume purchasing obligations amounting to around 80 percent of customers' requirements (*EWS*); and a finding by the Office of Gas and Electricity Markets (Ofgem, the energy regulator) that National Grid (NG) had abused its dominance by entering into long term contracts for the servicing of gas meters which included (among other things) payments for early termination and contractual limits on replacements of NG's meters.[35] **42.31**

Exclusive dealing can also breach the prohibition on anticompetitive agreements, even if carried out by a non-dominant company. For example, the OFT investigated street furniture advertising contracts entered into by *Clear Channel UK* and *JCDecaux* due to concerns that certain exclusivity clauses, "first refusal" clauses, and tacit renewal clauses in these contracts had the effect of protecting the position of incumbents and restricting competition. It closed the investigation in 2012 on the basis of informal assurances that these clauses would not be enforced.[36] **42.32**

In the context of exclusive distribution, the European Commission's block exemption for vertical agreements applies in the UK. Consequently, the grant of an exclusive territory or customer group to a distributor—with a commitment by the supplier not to supply other distributors in respect of that territory or customer group—will not infringe antitrust laws, provided: (i) the supplier has a share of less than 30 percent of the relevant market for the contract products; (ii) the purchaser has a share of less than 30 percent of the market for purchasing such products; and (iii) the arrangement does not contain certain "hard core" restrictions, such as resale price maintenance, a ban on sales over the internet, or restrictions on the ability of the distributor to satisfy unsolicited orders from other geographic territories or customer groups. Similarly, an agreement that a distributor will purchase exclusively (or **42.33**

[33] *Genzyme Limited v. Office of Fair Trading* [2004] CAT 4.

[34] *Payment Protection Insurance market investigation*, final report of the Competition Commission of January 29, 2009.

[35] EWS (n 20) and *Investigation into National Grid*, CA98/STG/06, Ofgem decision of February 21, 2008.

[36] *OFT acts to boost competition in outdoor advertising*, Press release 39/12 (May 17, 2012).

quasi-exclusively) from a particular supplier will fall within the safe harbor if the parties meet the above market share thresholds and the agreement does not exceed five years in duration. Exclusive purchasing agreements of longer duration will fall outside the scope of the safe harbor, but will often be permissible if the purchaser is also an exclusive distributor of the products in question. Arrangements falling outside the safe harbor of the block exemption must be assessed individually for antitrust compliance.

42.34 Exclusivity arrangements that are prevalent throughout the market are commonly targeted by market investigations. For example, in its 2006 report on the *supply of bulk liquefied petroleum gas*, the CC concluded that the need for suppliers to cover installation costs and customer-acquisition costs justified the use of exclusivity clauses, but only for durations of up to two years.[37]

H. Refusal to deal

42.35 The OFT's approach to refusals to deal is consistent with that of the European Commission. It recognizes that businesses are generally free to supply, or not to supply, whomever they choose, and that this freedom should be curtailed only if there is evidence of likely substantial harm to competition and if the behavior cannot be objectively justified.

42.36 In line with the principles set out in the 2007 *Microsoft* judgment of the General Court,[38] a refusal to deal will, if carried out by a dominant company, amount to an abuse if:

- the refusal relates to a product or service that is objectively necessary to be able to compete effectively on a downstream market (this downstream market can be a potential or hypothetical one);
- the refusal is likely to lead to the elimination of effective competition on the downstream market; and
- the refusal is likely to lead to consumer harm, in particular because it prevents the appearance of a new or improved product for which there is potential consumer demand.

42.37 The above test applies to refusals to supply products and services, refusals of access to an essential facility, and refusals to license intellectual property rights. An offer to supply at a price which is excessive will be treated as a constructive refusal to supply. As regards the difference between refusing to supply a new customer and an existing customer, the CAT indicated in *J.J. Burgess & Sons*[39] that a stricter test may apply in cases concerning a refusal to supply access to facilities that were developed for the exclusive use of the undertaking that created them. However, the subsequent *Microsoft* judgment suggests that, in principle, such a case should be treated no differently to a cessation of supplies to an existing customer, although in practice it may be more difficult to demonstrate likely consumer harm in such circumstances.

42.38 While there have been numerous investigations into allegedly abusive refusals to supply, the *J.J. Burgess* case—which concerned the supply of crematoria services to funeral directors—is a rare example of one that resulted in a finding of infringement. No fine was imposed in that case, as the dominant company agreed to supply unrestricted access to its crematoria as a result of the CAT's judgment.

42.39 As regards the distinction between the abuse of refusal to supply and the abuse of discrimination, see Section I.D.

---

[37] *Market investigation into supply of bulk liquefied petroleum gas for domestic use*, final report of the Competition Commission of June 29, 2006.

[38] Case T-201/04 *Microsoft Corp. v. Commission* [2007] ECR II-3601.

[39] *J.J. Burgess & Sons v. Office of Fair Trading* [2005] CAT 25.

I. Essential facilities

A refusal to grant access to an essential facility is in principle treated in the same way as a refusal to deal (see Section I.H). **42.40**

J. Bundling (including loyalty and market share discounts)

In certain circumstances, a dominant company's rebate and discount schemes can breach the prohibition on abuse of dominance, whether they apply across multiple product lines (bundled rebates, or "mixed" bundling) or to a single product line ("loyalty," "fidelity," or "growth" rebates). The broad test applied by the OFT in such cases is whether an equally efficient rival could match the dominant company's effective prices. **42.41**

(i) Single line rebates

Where rebates are based on purchases of a single product line (or products within a single market), the OFT will assess whether there is a non-contestable portion of customers' demand which will always be supplied by the dominant company in practice (e.g. because of capacity constraints of rivals, or because the dominant company supplies a "must stock" product) and, if so, the effect of the dominant company's rebates on the ability of equally efficient rivals to compete for that contestable portion of demand. In particular, it will ask whether the rebate results in a predatory price for the contestable portion of customers' demand. Rebate structures will tend to give rise to a greater risk of foreclosure if they include retroactive (or "rolled-back") rebates—which are applied to all purchases in a given period once a particular threshold is reached (as opposed to only incremental purchases after the threshold)—and rebates that are set individually for each customer, and so are more likely to correspond to that customer's contestable demand. **42.42**

From a compliance perspective, it is important to understand that it is not just a dominant company's contractual rebate structures that can give rise to these risks, but also conduct which allows customers to develop the *perception* that rebates on offer by the dominant company would be withdrawn in the event of purchases from rivals, even if the relevant contracts expressly state otherwise. This was the case for *Intel*, which received a EUR 1.06 billion fine from the European Commission for such conduct in 2009.[40] **42.43**

The effects-based approach outlined above was applied by the ORR to find that EWS' volume rebates were abusive[41] and by the OFT to support its decision to close an investigation into growth and qualitative rebate schemes operated by Walkers Snacks Limited.[42] **42.44**

(ii) Multi-product rebates

Where rebates are conditional on bundled purchases of multiple product lines, and rivals of the dominant undertaking are not able to sell identical bundles, the agencies will look at the incremental price that is paid for each product in the bundle compared to its standalone price, and ask whether that price is lower than the cost of producing the product in question. For example, if products A and B are each priced at GBP 10, but available in a bundle for GBP 15, a breach of the prohibition could arise if the cost of producing A or B is more than GBP 5, as an equally efficient rival with only one of those products on offer would be unable to match that price. **42.45**

In *IDEXX*,[43] the OFT investigated various multi-product rebates, including discounts on in-clinic analyzers that were conditional on purchases of external lab services, and bundled **42.46**

---

[40] *Intel*, COMP/C-3/37.990, European Commission decision of May 13, 2009.

[41] *EWS* (n 20).

[42] *Walkers Snacks*, CE/1604-02, OFT case closure summary of May 3, 2007.

[43] *IDEXX Laboratories* (n 7).

discounts of two types of specialist external lab test. While it considered that IDEXX was likely to be dominant in the supply of some of these products and services, their effective prices within the bundled price were not below IDEXX's average avoidable costs and, therefore, an equally efficient competitor would have been able to compete profitably with IDEXX for their supply. In addition, even if the discounts had foreclosed an equally efficient competitor, they applied to less than 5 percent of the market, so that any such foreclosure was unlikely to impair effective competition.

K. Standard-setting groups (disclosure requirements, licensing arrangements, and licensing pools)

42.47 Arrangements for setting technology-related standards typically have cross-border impact and for this reason are usually dealt with by the European Commission (see the EU chapter for details of the Commission's approach, including the conditions in which standard-setting arrangements will benefit from the Commission's safe harbor). To date, the OFT has not investigated a standard-setting organization of this nature. Were it to do so, it would likely follow the same approach as the European Commission.

L. Customer termination

42.48 As a general rule, businesses are free to choose the customers to whom they supply their products and services and are therefore free to terminate their dealings with customers as they see fit. However, this is subject to two qualifications.

42.49 First, dominant companies may, in certain circumstances, be under an obligation to supply customers, either because they are rivals who need access to an essential product or service of the dominant company,[44] or because the dominant company continues to supply other similar customers, such that a termination of supplies to one would be discriminatory (for the reasons set out in Section I.B, this latter type of conduct is less likely to be the subject of enforcement action by the agencies and has not been, to date).

42.50 Second, termination of dealings with customers could be viewed as evidence that the supplier is seeking to ensure compliance with a prohibited anticompetitive agreement, such as a resale price maintenance agreement or a restriction on passive sales to customers located outside a distributors' allocated territory.[45]

M. Termination of intermediaries

42.51 The termination of contracts with intermediaries is treated the same way as the termination of a contract with a customer (Section I.L).

N. Termination of relationships with competitors

42.52 As explained in Section I.H, there may be instances in which a dominant company is required to supply a product or service to a rival, where this is necessary to enable the rival to compete effectively and innovatively in the market. Other than these, companies have no obligations under UK or EU antitrust law to deal with their competitors, or to maintain such dealings.

42.53 If, however, a particular contractual relationship with a competitor is in breach of the antitrust rules, the relevant contractual provisions will be automatically void and unenforceable, regardless of whether one or both parties have taken steps to terminate the agreement.[46]

---

[44] See Section I.G.
[45] *John Bruce* (n 31).
[46] See e.g. *Jones v. Ricoh UK Limited* [2010] EWHC 1743 (Ch).

O. Exemptions

The relevant legislation does not provide for a procedure whereby conduct can be individually or automatically exempted from the prohibition on abuse of dominance. There are, however, a number of general and sector-specific exclusions and defenses, many of which serve as forms of exemption in practice: **42.54**

- Conduct that can be shown by the dominant company to be objectively necessary and proportionate. For example, the protection of health and safety may justify various forms of otherwise abusive conduct, the commercial need to sustain losses for an initial period in order to stimulate demand may justify pricing strategies that may otherwise be deemed predatory, and a refusal to supply a long-standing customer may be justified if the customer has a poor credit rating and is unable to fulfill their contractual obligations.
- Conduct that is indispensable for the generation of efficiencies (e.g. technical improvements in the quality of goods, or a reduction in the cost of production or distribution) that outweigh the negative effects of the conduct on competition and consumer welfare in the affected markets.
- Mergers, acquisitions, or joint ventures within the meaning of the EU or UK merger control rules (under the EU Merger Regulation and the Enterprise Act 2002 respectively). Transactions of a type that are reviewable under the relevant merger control rules cannot be investigated under the antitrust prohibitions. This is the case even if they do not meet the turnover or (in the UK) market share thresholds that trigger the agencies' jurisdiction under the applicable merger control rules, subject to a limited exception in the case of joint ventures that result in the coordination of their parents' activities. This exclusion extends to ancillary restrictions that are directly related and necessary to the implementation of the transaction.
- Activities of an undertaking entrusted with the operation of services of general economic interest or having the character of a revenue-producing monopoly, insofar as the prohibition would obstruct the performance of the particular tasks assigned to that undertaking. Services of a "general economic interest" include, for example, universal postal services. This exclusion is construed narrowly by the EU Courts.
- Conduct engaged in to comply with a legal requirement (although the availability of this defense may be limited if the legal requirement is itself in breach of EU laws).
- Conduct specified in an order made by the UK's Secretary of State for Business, Innovation and Skills to avoid a conflict with international obligations or where there are exceptional and compelling reasons of public policy why the chapter II prohibition ought not to apply. This exclusion relates to the UK prohibition only and there has only been one such order to date, in respect of certain agreements in the defense sector (now revoked).
- Finally, an undertaking found to be in breach of the prohibition on abuse of dominance will nevertheless be immune from fines if it its annual turnover is less than GBP 50 million, although this immunity can be withdrawn by the OFT after a finding of breach. This immunity does not extend to third party claims for damages. Indeed, the fact that a fine was not imposed may be taken into account by the courts as a reason to justify the award of exemplary damages to a third party claimant, in addition to those awarded to compensate for harm suffered by a third party (as was the case for a claim against *Cardiff Bus* in a private follow-on damages action[47]).

The market investigation regime does not provide for exemptions from its scope. The only significant restriction on the CC's powers to remedy competitive harms that it identifies is **42.55**

[47] *2 Travel Group Plc v. Cardiff City Transport Services Limited* [2012] CAT 19.

the requirement that its remedies (if imposed) are proportionate to the degree of competitive harm that it is seeking to address.

II. Dealing with competitors

42.56 Dealings between competitors are assessed principally under the civil prohibition on anti-competitive agreements. This prohibits agreements, concerted practices and decisions of associations of undertakings that have as their object or effect the prevention, restriction or distortion of competition within the EU or UK and which affect trade between EU Member States, or within the UK. Such agreements will however fall outside the prohibition if they satisfy the criteria for individual exception—broadly, that they are necessary for the achievement of substantial efficiencies that will be passed on to consumers and do not eliminate competition in respect of the products in question—or the criteria set out in one of the various EU and UK "block" exemptions. The burden of proving that these criteria are met lies with the parties to the arrangement and it is not possible to notify an agreement to obtain confirmation from the agencies that the criteria are met. However, comfort of varying degrees can be obtained in certain circumstances by seeking an informal opinion from the OFT or European Commission, in particular for cases raising novel or unresolved legal issues.[48]

42.57 Collusion between competitors, and cartel conduct in particular, is an enforcement priority of the OFT. Such cases form the majority of its case-load[49] and typically result in very high fines. In addition, the UK is one of the few European countries to criminalize all forms of cartel conduct, with impending legislative changes likely to result in higher levels of prosecution in the future.[50]

42.58 As regards the market investigation regime, dealings between competitors can be investigated by the CC, but this is rare. If evidence of a breach of the prohibition on anticompetitive agreements arises during a market investigation, it is passed to the OFT for a separate investigation under that prohibition.

A. Horizontal price fixing (including advanced announcements of price or product changes)

42.59 Cartel conduct—and price fixing in particular—is the enforcement priority of the OFT.[51] In practice, the sectoral regulators do not investigate such breaches. Individuals who participate in an agreement to engage in cartel conduct (price-fixing, market sharing, customer allocation, and bid-rigging) will be liable to prosecution under the criminal cartel offense. At present, criminal liability only arises if it can be shown that the individual in question acted dishonestly. However, the Enterprise and Regulatory Reform Act 2013 will remove that requirement for conduct taking place after April 1, 2014 and replace it with certain exclusions and defenses for individuals that entered into the relevant agreement "openly," i.e. with the intention that it would be disclosed to customers, the agencies or professional legal advisers.

42.60 As regards the civil prohibition, price fixing is deemed to have the object of restricting competition, and so will result in civil antitrust liability for corporate entities regardless of its effects on competition and whether or not it was implemented successfully. While it is theoretically possible for price-fixing arrangements to qualify for exception from the prohibition

[48] See e.g. *P&H/Makro Joint Purchasing Agreement*, OFT, short form opinion of April 27, 2010.
[49] See Section III.B for a discussion of enforcement trends.
[50] See Section II.A.
[51] See Section III.B for examples of recent enforcement in this area.

if they are necessary for the creation of substantial efficiencies that will be passed on to consumers (e.g. for a "crisis cartel" to reduce excess capacity with welfare-enhancing results), no exemptions have been granted for "crisis cartels" since the 1980s. The OFT did, however, recently issue a "short form opinion" that the publication by an agricultural trade association of recommended prices for the sale of certain land-use rights by its members satisfied the relevant criteria.[52]

The law and enforcement approach to public price signaling is less developed. There have not yet been any cases at EU or UK level in which such conduct has been found to amount to an antitrust breach, in the absence of any non-public communications between the relevant parties. However, the European Commission has indicated in its guidelines on horizontal agreements that public announcements of intended future price changes can infringe antitrust law in certain circumstances, and it recently opened an investigation into price signaling by a number of shipping companies.[53] In addition, in its market investigation into the aggregates, cement, and ready-mix concrete market, the CC has decided (provisionally, at the time of writing) to prohibit the sending of generalized price announcement letters by companies operating in that market, partly because of concerns that such letters facilitate price signaling.[54] **42.61**

B. Horizontal agreements to allocate customers or territories; agreements not to compete

Market sharing and customer allocation agreements are considered to be a form of hardcore cartel conduct and are treated in the same way as price-fixing arrangements, including as regards criminal liability.[55] **42.62**

C. Horizontal boycotts

Agreements between competitors to boycott a rival are viewed as having the object of restricting competition and will therefore breach the civil prohibition on anticompetitive agreements regardless of whether the boycott is successful. For example, in 2009, the OFT announced that it had fined six recruitment agencies a total of GBP 39.27 million (reduced to GBP 7.9 million on appeal), in part for having agreed a collective boycott of a new market entrant.[56] **42.63**

Such conduct does not, however, fall within the scope of the criminal cartel offense. **42.64**

D. Joint ventures and other competitive collaborations

Joint ventures and other collaborations between rivals that do not fall within the scope of the merger control rules and do not amount to hardcore cartels will be prohibited if they have the effect of appreciably restricting actual or potential competition, and the parties cannot show that they satisfy the criteria for one of the available block exemptions or, failing that, the criteria for individual exception.[57] When assessing such agreements against this test, the OFT follows the practice of the European Commission (as set out in its guidelines on horizontal cooperation, which are described in more detail in Chapter 12 of this handbook). The most **42.65**

---

[52] *Rural Broadband Wayleave Rates*, OFT short form opinion of August 23, 2012.

[53] *Commission opens proceedings against container liner shipping companies*, Press release IP/13/1144 (November 22, 2013).

[54] *Aggregates, cement and ready-mix concrete market investigation*, provisional findings of the Competition Commission, May 21, 2013 and provisional decision on remedies, October 8, 2013.

[55] See Section II.A.

[56] *Construction Recruitment Forum*, CE/7510-06, OFT decision of September 29, 2009.

[57] See paras. 42.56–42.58.

relevant block exemptions are the EU exemptions for certain specialization and production joint ventures, R&D arrangements, and agreements involving transfer or licensing of patents, knowhow and software copyrights.

42.66 The UK merger regime covers a wider range of joint ventures than are caught by the EU Merger Regulation, and these joint ventures fall outside the scope of the UK prohibition on anticompetitive agreements. In particular, transactions involving pooling of the parents' productive assets are (voluntarily) notifiable under the merger regime, and therefore fall outside the scope of the UK prohibition, even if the joint venture will primarily serve its parents.[58]

E. Trade associations

42.67 Trade associations can give rise to antitrust risks in three ways: first, as a forum for anticompetitive coordination of their members' activities. There are numerous examples of cartel activity that originated at trade association meetings. Where discussions at such meetings stray into prohibited territory—for example, pricing, production volumes/capacity, or other terms of trade—all other attendees present will render their respective companies liable for antitrust fines if they do not actively distance themselves from the discussion by leaving the meeting and asking for their departure, and its reasons, to be recorded in the minutes of the meeting. Moreover, individual representatives who participate actively in those discussions may become subject to criminal prosecution.

42.68 Second, decisions by a trade association that relate to its members' market activities—such as those relating to standard terms and conditions of sale to be used by members, or pricing recommendations—can attract antitrust liability not only for the trade association itself, but also for members which implemented the decision, or which were aware of its existence without having distanced themselves from it. The OFT has taken action against numerous trade bodies to force them to abandon such practices, in sectors ranging from legal services to construction.

42.69 Third, trade associations can breach the prohibition on anticompetitive agreements if membership of the body is required for market access, and its criteria for admission to membership are unjustifiably discriminatory.[59]

F. Interlocking directorates

42.70 There is no general rule prohibiting interlocking directorates. While some companies have been required to unwind interlocking directorates as a condition of merger control clearance, the issue has not, to date, arisen under the behavioral antitrust prohibitions or the market investigation regime. However, where a director sits on the boards of two or more competitors, it is prudent to put in place appropriate measures to mitigate the risk of anticompetitive disclosures of information by that director, such as confidentiality requirements and restrictions on access to competitively sensitive data.

G. Facilitating practices

42.71 The OFT has been particularly active in the pursuit of so-called "hub and spoke" cartels, in which rivals exchange anticompetitive information through the medium of a third party, typically a supplier. Fines for such conduct have been imposed on suppliers of toys, football

[58] See e.g. the OFT's clearance of the joint venture combining the parties' base station sites and site management businesses of Vodafone and Telefónica: *Anticipated joint venture between Vodafone Limited and Telefónica UK Limited*, ME/5556/12, OFT decision of September 28, 2012.

[59] See e.g. *Glasgow Solicitors Property Centre rules*, OFT press release 154/03 (December 1, 2003).

kits and, most recently, dairy products.[60] The UK courts have established that a hub and spoke infringement will arise where:

- retailer A discloses to supplier B its future pricing intentions;
- A may be taken to intend that B will make use of that information to influence market conditions by passing that information to other retailers (of whom C is, or may be, one);
- B does, in fact, pass that information to C;
- C may be taken to know the circumstances in which the information was disclosed by A to B; and
- C cannot prove that it did not, in fact, use the information in determining its own future pricing intentions.

Careful compliance training in this area is important, as opinions about likely market reactions (e.g. "if you increase your prices your rivals will follow") can easily be misinterpreted as a disclosure of information regarding a third party's pricing intentions. **42.72**

H. Information exchange

An exchange of information that does not extend to an agreement to coordinate rivals' market conduct will not breach the criminal cartel offense, but may amount to an infringement of the civil prohibition on anticompetitive agreements. As regards the latter prohibition, the OFT was heavily involved in the crafting of the guidance on information exchange that is contained in the European Commission's guidelines on horizontal agreements, and may therefore be expected to follow closely the approach described in those guidelines (see Chapter 12 for a summary). **42.73**

In addition to the hub-and-spoke information exchange cases,[61] two recent OFT cases illustrate its approach in this area. In the first—*Professional Loans*—RBS agreed to pay a GBP 28.5 million fine for the disclosure of its future pricing intentions by certain of its employees to certain employees of Barclays. While Barclays received immunity from fines for having reported the case to the OFT, its employees were considered to have committed an infringement for having accepted the information, notwithstanding that they had not disclosed any confidential information to RBS employees.[62] This highlights that under EU and UK antitrust laws, there is no need for an "exchange"—unilateral disclosure alone may amount to an infringement. **42.74**

The second case illustrates the OFT's approach to exchanges of historic and aggregated pricing data. In the *Motor Insurers Data Exchange* case, the OFT accepted binding commitments from six insurance companies and two IT software and service providers to address competition concerns regarding their use of a software tool that allowed regular exchange of non-public and individualized information about their future pricing. The commitments serve as a useful guide to the types of information exchange that the OFT is likely to consider acceptable. They required the parties to limit exchanged information to that which is less than six months old, anonymized, aggregated across at least five insurers and already "live" in policies sold by brokers.[63] **42.75**

---

60 See *Argos Limited and Littlewoods Limited v. Office of Fair Trading and JJB Sports plc v. Office of Fair Trading* [2006] EWCA Civ 1318 and *Tesco plc v. Office of Fair Trading* [2012] CAT 31.

61 See Section II.G.

62 *Professional Loans*, CA98/01/2011, OFT decision of January 20, 2011.

63 *Decision to accept binding commitments to modify a data exchange tool used by Motor Insurers*, OFT1395, OFT decision of December 2, 2011.

42.76 In the context of due diligence for a merger (or indeed any transaction that is not inherently anticompetitive), the OFT and the European Commission recognize that it is often objectively necessary to exchange competitively sensitive information. The degree of caution depends on the nature of the information and the competitive relationship between the parties, but competitors must be particularly careful to avoid the disclosure of non-public information relating to future and current pricing, production volumes, capacities, strategic plans, and proprietary technologies. To the extent that disclosure of such information is necessary for due diligence or integration planning purposes, appropriate safeguards—such as "clean teams"—must be put in place.

I. Joint purchasing agreements

42.77 Joint purchasing is generally recognized as pro-competitive, provided the parties do not have market power on the upstream purchasing market or the downstream market(s) on which they are active. The European Commission's horizontal guidelines state that this is unlikely to be the case where the parties' combined share of any such market does not exceed 15 percent. The OFT has also issued a short-form, non-binding opinion to two wholesale grocery suppliers that their joint purchasing arrangement was antitrust-compliant, notwithstanding that their market shares exceeded 15 percent, primarily because they would remain subject to a substantial degree of competition on downstream markets.[64]

J. Joint lobbying/regulatory/legislative efforts

42.78 There is no concept in the UK or EU antitrust regimes analogous to the US "Noerr–Pennington" doctrine, which grants antitrust immunity to the joint efforts of businesses to petition or influence Government bodies, even if the laws/regulation they advocate would have anticompetitive effects. However, there are various indications in the case law of the EU Courts that the act of joint lobbying in itself is not sufficient to amount to an infringement of EU antitrust law, provided there is no coordination of the parties' market activities or anticompetitive information exchange.

III. General issues

A. Jurisdiction and applicable law (including sector-specific competition regulation)

42.79 See the Introduction to this Chapter for a description of the relevant legal and jurisdictional framework. The antitrust laws are not sector-specific and various sectoral regulators have concurrent powers to apply them.[65] These sectors are also subject to detailed *ex ante* regulation which often seeks to achieve the same objectives, primarily through licensing regimes and access conditions.

B. Antitrust system

(i) Name of agency/agencies

42.80 The primary enforcers are the OFT (for the prohibitions on anticompetitive agreements and abuse of dominance and the criminal cartel offense) and the CC (for the market investigation regime). Sectoral regulators having concurrent powers to apply the civil antitrust prohibitions are Ofcom (telecoms and media), Ofwat (water and sewerage), Ofgem (gas and electricity),

---

64 *P&H/Makro* (n 48).

65 See Section III.B.

the Office of Rail Regulation (ORR, rail), Monitor (healthcare), the Civil Aviation Authority (aviation), and the Northern Ireland Authority for Utility Regulation (gas, electricity, water, and sewerage in Northern Ireland). In addition, the Government has announced that it intends to confer concurrent powers on the Financial Conduct Authority (financial services) and the Payment Systems Regulator (payment systems), from April 2015.

On 1 April 2014, a new agency—the Competition and Markets Authority (CMA)—will **42.81** become operational, replacing both the OFT and the CC (but not the sectoral regulators).

(ii) Staff size and budget

The OFT's budget for the financial year ending March 31, 2013 was around GBP 49 mil- **42.82** lion, falling to around GBP 40 million for the following year. This is partly due to substantial cuts to its budget in recent years, and partly due to the transfer of certain consumer functions (and the associated funding) to other organizations. As of May 31, 2013, it employed a total of 518 full-time equivalent staff, plus a further 101 consultants and temporary contractors. Many of these are in roles that relate to the OFT's consumer protection functions, rather than antitrust. An up-to-date breakdown is not available, but in previous years (when the OFT had more consumer functions) roughly half of the OFT's staff were involved in antitrust work.

The CC's total budget for the year ending March 31, 2013 was GBP 17.1 million, but this **42.83** was later revised to GBP 19.4 million due to the pressure of an increased caseload. Its forecast of expenditure for the year ending March 31, 2014 was GBP 21.3 million. As of March 31, 2013, it employed a total of 154 full-time equivalent staff. The CC also has a number of "members" (forty-eight, as of December 9, 2013) who are appointed for their experience and skills in antitrust economics, law, finance, and business. Groups of at least three members are selected to undertake and decide upon each market investigation, with the support of the CC's staff.

Budgets and staff sizes of the sectoral regulators vary considerably, but as a general rule the **42.84** budget and staff that attach to antitrust-related work make up a relatively small proportion of overall numbers, with regulatory and consumer protection functions accounting for a much greater share.

(iii) Recent enforcement actions and trends

As regards the civil antitrust prohibitions, the trend since those prohibitions came into force **42.85** in 2000 has been from a large number of small cases in the early years—including a glut of abuse of dominance investigations into regulated utilities and investigations into localized cartels (e.g. flat roofing contractors, which were fined a total of GBP 1.6 million[66])—to a focus in more recent years on cases involving larger firms or widespread infringements. In the years 2001 to 2007 inclusive, the agencies concluded an average of twenty-five cases per year, while the period since then has averaged only seven cases per year.

Examples of the larger cases of recent years include the fixing of fuel surcharges by British **42.86** Airways and Virgin, for which BA was fined GBP 58.5 million[67] and the investigation into bid-rigging in the construction industry, which imposed fines on over a hundred separate undertakings for almost 200 distinct infringements.[68] However, the complexity of these larger cases may have contributed to a larger number of decisions being overturned on

[66] *OFT fines roofing contractors in England and Scotland*, Press release 34/06 (February 23, 2006).

[67] *British Airways to pay £58.5 million penalty in OFT fuel surcharge decision*, Press release 33/12 (April 19, 2012).

[68] *Bid Rigging in the Construction Industry in England*, CA98/02/2009, OFT decision of September 21, 2009.

appeal—notably the collapse in 2011 of the OFT's case against various retailers and suppliers of tobacco products for the use of "price parity" clauses[69]—and substantial reductions in fines, such as the Court of Appeal's reduction of National Grid's record GBP 41.6 million fine to GBP 15 million,[70] and the average 85 percent reduction in fines enjoyed by those companies that appealed against their fines for bid-rigging in the construction sector.[71] Perhaps in response to these setbacks, cases commenced and concluded by the OFT during 2013 have involved smaller markets and more straightforward theories of harm, such as RPM in the market for sports bras,[72] bid-rigging for access control and alarm systems[73] and market sharing and price coordination in the distribution of commercial vehicles.[74]

42.87 The OFT's record of enforcement of the criminal cartel offense is much more limited. Prison sentences of between twenty and thirty months were imposed on three executives in 2008 for their participation in a marine hose cartel, but that was the result of a plea bargaining agreement that those executives entered into with the US Department of Justice. The only criminal case that proceeded to trial—of British Airways executives involved in the fixing of air passenger fuel surcharges—collapsed in 2010 when evidence came to light during the trial that had not previously been disclosed to the defense.[75] As of December 2013, the OFT has published details of only one ongoing criminal investigation, which relates to the supply of products to the construction industry.

42.88 It remains to be seen whether the creation of the CMA in April 2014 will impact enforcement levels. Combining the different working cultures of the OFT and CC is likely to be challenging, and the uncertain transition period together with a demanding initial workload will also have some effect.

42.89 In the meantime, the investigative failings that were exposed in the appeals against the *BA* and *Tobacco* decisions have prompted the OFT to introduce various procedural reforms with a view to improving transparency, due process and "robustness" (i.e. susceptibility to successful appeal) of its decisions. It is also reviewing its case load to ensure that it hands over a "full and varied" portfolio of cases to the new CMA.

C. Private litigation

42.90 The courts of England and Wales (the other parts of the UK—Scotland and Northern Ireland—have separate legal systems) are popular forums for private antitrust claims. This can be attributed to a number of features of the English legal system, such as its relatively extensive disclosure rules, the presence of a specialist court—the Competition Appeal Tribunal (CAT)—and its rules on costs and fee arrangements, which allow for claims to be brought with a relatively low or predictable degree of risk.

42.91 Until recently, most antitrust law claims were raised in the context of wider commercial litigation with a view to securing a ruling that a given contractual restriction—often in a distribution arrangement—was void and unenforceable. Most such efforts are unsuccessful,

---

[69] *Imperial Tobacco and others v. Office of Fair Trading* [2011] CAT 41.

[70] *National Grid v. Gas and Electricity Markets Authority* [2010] EWCA Civ 114.

[71] *Kier Group and others v. Office of Fair Trading* [2011] CAT 3; *GF Tomlinson Group and others v. Office of Fair Trading* [2011] CAT 7.

[72] *DB Apparel UK Limited* (n 26).

[73] *Retirement home security suppliers breached competition law, OFT decides,* Press release 81/13 (December 6, 2013).

[74] *OFT issues five infringement decisions in the distribution of Mercedes-Benz commercial vehicles investigation*, Press release 30/13 (March 27, 2013).

[75] *OFT withdraws criminal proceedings against current and former BA executives,* Press release 47/10 (May 10, 2010).

with judges sometimes dismissive of parties' efforts to avoid contractual obligations in this way, although there are a number of notable exceptions, such as *Calor Gas Ltd.* (restrictions in contracts for the distribution of bulk and cylinder liquefied petroleum gas)[76] and *The Football Association Premier League* (restrictions on cross-border sales of TV decoder cards).[77]

Recent years have seen a strong growth of cartel damages actions. These are either "follow-on" actions (which rely on a prior agency decision to establish the breach[78]) or "standalone" claims, in which the breach must be proved by the claimant. At present, many damages claims are initially brought as standalone claims before the High Court, so that they can be launched before the agency has issued its infringement decision. Curiously, the CAT does not have jurisdiction to hear standalone claims, although the Government has published a draft Consumer Rights Bill for consultation, which would rectify this, if enacted in its current form. **42.92**

Instances of parties bringing standalone actions claiming antitrust infringements in the absence of any ongoing agency investigation are rare, and examples of successful claims rarer still (one is *Purple Parking*[79]). There are also numerous reports of competition claims having been settled out of court.[80] **42.93**

D. Follow-on litigation

A finding of infringement of the EU or UK prohibition by the European Commission or a UK agency is (subject to appeals against the infringement decision) binding proof of the existence of a breach. Armed with such a decision, claimants need only demonstrate the extent of the losses that they have suffered as a result of the breach. **42.94**

Notwithstanding the popularity of the English legal system for antitrust litigation, cases to date have usually settled out of court, and only two have resulted in a formal award of damages by a court. One for a relatively meager GBP 93,818.79,[81] and the other for GBP 1,854,493, plus interest.[82] **42.95**

The Government has published for consultation a draft Consumer Rights Bill which includes proposed changes to certain aspects of antitrust litigation in the UK, including extending the CAT's jurisdiction to hear stand-alone actions, introducing a limited opt-out collective actions regime, promoting alternative dispute resolution (ADR) to ensure that court actions are an option of last resort and ensuring that private actions complement the public enforcement regime. **42.96**

E. Arbitration and alternative dispute resolution

Arbitration and alternative dispute resolution are available in the UK. Antitrust law issues are arbitrable if the claim alleging an antitrust breach falls within the scope of a contractual arbitration clause. **42.97**

In appropriate cases, the courts of England and Wales are required to encourage parties to litigation to use an ADR procedure, and the Court of Appeal has highlighted the benefits of arbitrating antitrust disputes.[83] However, the CAT has pointed out that proceedings before it **42.98**

[76] *Calor Gas Ltd. v. Express Fuels (Scotland) Ltd.* [2008] CSOH 13.
[77] *The Football Association Premier League Ltd. v. QC Leisure & others* [2008] EWHC 44 (Ch).
[78] See Section III.D.
[79] *Purple Parking* (n 23), and see para. 42.24 for discussion.
[80] See e.g. Philip Stafford, "LSE and Plus resolve legal dispute," *Financial Times* (UK Edition) (May 30, 2009).
[81] *Cardiff City Transport* (n 47).
[82] See *Albion Water v. Dŵr Cymru* [2013] CAT 6.
[83] *Attheraces* (n 14).

are for the purpose of protecting not only the parties' commercial interests, but also the general public interest,[84] which suggests that it may be more inclined to probe the justifications for any transfer of a dispute from it to a private arbitration (such a move requires the CAT's permission, unless it is with the defendant's consent).

42.99 The Government has decided to introduce legislation that will strongly encourage ADR in antitrust cases, but stop short of making it mandatory. Among other things, the reforms (under consultation in the draft Consumer Rights Bill, at the time of writing) will introduce a new opt-out collective settlement regime (to complement the new regime for opt out collective claims), and possibilities for the new CMA to certify (but not impose) a voluntary redress scheme following an antitrust investigation, resulting in lower fines for those offering the scheme.

F. Remedies

(i) Civil liability

42.100 The financial penalties for breach of the UK civil prohibitions on abuse of dominance and anticompetitive agreements are identical to those applicable under the EU prohibition. The undertaking may be fined up to 10 percent of its worldwide group turnover; ordered to cease or modify its conduct; and third parties may bring an action for damages or, in appropriate cases, an injunction in the civil courts. Parent companies can be (and usually are) held liable for the actions of their subsidiaries on the sole ground that they exercised general powers of control over them at the relevant time, regardless of whether they were aware of their subsidiaries' infringing conduct, or did anything to encourage it.

42.101 If conduct falls solely under the UK prohibition (i.e. where there is no impact on trade between EU countries), the UK agencies cannot impose fines for anticompetitive agreements (except price fixing) between companies with a combined group turnover of less than GBP 20 million, or for abuse of dominance by a company with a group turnover of less than GBP 50 million.

42.102 The UK agencies (unlike their EU counterpart) also have powers to apply to the UK High Court for an order disqualifying individuals from acting as a director of a UK company for up to fifteen years, where the company is guilty of an infringement of any of the EU or UK prohibitions. The OFT has indicated that it may seek such an order not only against individuals involved in the infringing conduct, but also those who did not know, but ought to have known, about the infringement.

(ii) Criminal liability

42.103 Under the criminal cartel offense, individuals involved in cartel conduct (price fixing, output restrictions, bid-rigging, market sharing, or customer allocation) can be imprisoned for up to five years and/or subject to unlimited criminal fines and disqualification from acting as a director of a UK company for up to fifteen years.

G. Leniency and immunity

42.104 The UK has an active leniency program, which covers civil fines that may be imposed by the UK agencies for breach of the EU and/or UK prohibitions on anticompetitive agreements, as well as the criminal penalties that apply to individuals under the UK criminal cartel offense.

42.105 As regards fines under the civil regime:

- total "Type A" immunity from fines is guaranteed for the first party to provide the OFT with sufficient evidence of a cartel before the agency has commenced an investigation into that cartel, provided various other conditions are met;

[84] See *Claymore Dairies Limited and Arla Foods UK plc v. Office of Fair Trading* [2006] CAT 3.

- the OFT has a discretion to reduce fines by up to 100 percent for the first party to provide it with evidence of a cartel that genuinely advances an investigation that has already commenced, provided various other conditions are met ("Type B" immunity and leniency); and
- the OFT has a discretion to reduce fines by up to 50 percent for any other party that provides evidence of a cartel that genuinely advances the investigation, provided various other conditions are met ("Type C" leniency).

The grant of immunity or leniency by the OFT does not protect against fines imposed by the European Commission or any national agency of another EU country. It is therefore common for leniency applicants to apply for leniency to the OFT, European Commission and national agencies of any other jurisdiction potentially affected by the cartel. Unlike the EU leniency regime, it is possible to apply for UK immunity or leniency in respect of vertical RPM agreements. **42.106**

The OFT can also grant immunity from criminal prosecution in England, Wales and Northern Ireland, in the form of a "no-action" letter. Scottish prosecutors will give "serious weight" to any OFT recommendation that immunity should be granted. Undertakings qualifying for Type A immunity from civil fines will also obtain guaranteed "blanket" immunity from criminal prosecution for all cooperating current and former employees and directors of the undertaking, as well as protection from director disqualification proceedings for all cooperating directors. The OFT has a discretion to issue blanket or individual no-action letters in relation to employees and directors of undertakings qualifying for Type B immunity. **42.107**

H. Document creation and retention

Disposal of documents (in any format) that are the subject of a statutory information request of a UK agency can give rise to penalties, including criminal penalties. Destruction of documents after the commencement of an investigation by a UK or EU agency can also result in increased fines for lack of cooperation. In addition, obligations to preserve disclosable documents apply from the moment that litigation is contemplated. **42.108**

Outside these circumstances, a company has no general obligation under EU or UK antitrust laws to retain documents that it has uncovered which evidence its employees' participation in a cartel. However, such destruction will usually be inadvisable. In particular, the loss of relevant documents may compromise a company's ability to secure immunity or leniency. Moreover, those documents will often be in the possession of other cartel participants, so that their destruction would merely hand those rivals an advantage should they decide to apply for leniency. In addition, if the company decides to apply for immunity itself, destruction of documents—particularly when inconsistent with the company's normal document retention policies—might well be considered by the OFT or the European Commission as a failure of continuous cooperation, potentially resulting in a refusal or withdrawal of immunity. **42.109**

As regards document creation, the extensive disclosure rules of the EU courts and agencies mean that there are very limited categories of documents that can be withheld from disclosure. Care must therefore be taken when creating any internal documents (e.g. internal reports, board minutes and emails) discussing an actual or potential antitrust infringement. The most important category of documents that may be withheld from disclosure to an agency or a litigant is that of documents covered by legal professional privilege (LPP). The UK agencies, unlike the European Commission, are bound to respect the application of LPP to documents created by in-house counsel, as well as those created by lawyers qualified in a non-EU jurisdiction. Two primary forms of privilege apply in the UK: **42.110**

- Legal advice privilege attaches to confidential communications (and evidence of those communications) between a client and its lawyers which were created for the purpose of giving or obtaining legal advice. For these purposes, the UK courts have adopted a narrow legal definition of who the "client" is, such that not every company employee can be assumed to be included. For this reason, all internal investigations and evidence-gathering exercises that might uncover evidence relating to the UK should be carried out by suitably experienced lawyers.

- Litigation privilege attaches to confidential documents that were created for the dominant purpose of actual or pending legal proceedings. This covers communications with third parties, as well as clients. The CAT has indicated (*obiter*) that legal proceedings might reasonably be contemplated from the moment that the OFT issues a statement of objections to parties under investigation.[85]

[85] *Tesco Stores Limited and others v. Office of Fair Trading* [2012] CAT6.

43

UNITED STATES

Fiona Schaeffer, Craig Waldman, Keira Campbell,
Molly Wilkens, and Christina Bennett
Jones Day

Introduction

The antitrust laws of the United States encompass both federal statutes, which are concurrently enforced by the Antitrust Division of the Department of Justice (DOJ), the Federal Trade Commission's (FTC) Bureau of Competition state attorneys general, and private persons with standing, as well as state antitrust laws, which are enforced by state attorneys general and private persons. **43.01**

Certain offenses (such as agreements between competitors to raise prices, reduce output, or divide markets) are considered per se *illegal*, meaning that no justification can be offered to rebut their illegality. Under certain circumstances, such offenses may be prosecuted criminally by the DOJ. Offenses that are not per se illegal are assessed under the *rule of reason*, whereby any anticompetitive effects are balanced against procompetitive effects. **43.02**

43.03 The first federal antitrust law, and still the most important US antitrust statute, is the Sherman Act of 1890. Section 1 of that Act addresses concerted action—contracts, combinations and conspiracies—that unreasonably restrain trade. Section 2 prohibits the actual or attempted acquisition of monopoly power through anticompetitive means, i.e. unilateral or concerted predatory or exclusionary conduct.

43.04 Other federal antitrust laws in the US include the Clayton Act, the Robinson–Patman Act, the Federal Trade Commission Act (the "FTC Act"), and the Hart–Scott–Rodino Act. The Clayton Act proscribes certain exclusive dealing and tying arrangements, as well as mergers and acquisitions that may tend to create a monopoly or substantially lessen competition. The Robinson–Patman Act is principally known for its prohibition on price discrimination in the sale of commodities. The relevant sections of the FTC Act proscribe certain practices, including unfair methods of competition. Under the Hart–Scott–Rodino Act, mergers and acquisitions that meet certain thresholds must be notified to the federal antitrust agencies and suspended during a period of review, or waiting period, before they can close.

43.05 The criminal prosecution of cartels and other per se illegal "hard core" conduct remains a top priority for the DOJ. In addition, the DOJ and the FTC have been focusing on a variety of civil conduct, including monopolization, horizontal and vertical restraints, exclusionary conduct,[1] the use of standard essential patents (SEPs) to hold up patents,[2] and the potential anticompetitive effect of most-favored-nation (MFN) clauses.[3]

43.06 Private plaintiffs continue to actively pursue antitrust claims, incentivized by the prospect of treble damages and (in some cases) the class action vehicle.[4] The types of actions initiated by private plaintiffs vary significantly, often filling the gaps of agency enforcement. For example, private plaintiffs are far more likely than the agencies to allege price discrimination under the Robinson–Patman Act[5] or bring cases challenging alleged exclusionary conduct, such as bundling.[6] In addition, private plaintiffs regularly initiate follow-on class action litigation seeking treble damages arising from cartels that have been or are under investigation by the DOJ or antitrust agencies internationally.[7]

I. Acting alone

43.07 Antitrust claims based on unilateral conduct are most frequently brought under s. 2 of the Sherman Act, which prohibits predatory or exclusionary conduct that enables a company to unlawfully obtain or maintain monopoly power. Specific types of anticompetitive conduct are addressed below. First, however, some key terms require elaboration.

43.08 In antitrust terms, *monopoly power* is the power to control prices or exclude competitors. Under US antitrust law, achieving or maintaining monopoly power,

> and the concomitant charging of monopoly prices, is not only not unlawful; it is an important element of the free-market system. The opportunity to charge monopoly prices—at least for a short period—is what attracts "business acumen" in the first place; it induces risk taking that produces innovation and economic growth. To safeguard the incentive to

1 See Section I.
2 See Section I.K.
3 See Section II.G.
4 See Section III.C.
5 See Section I.D.
6 See Section I.J. See also *ZF Meritor v. Eaton Corp.* 696 F.3d 254 (3d Cir. 2012).
7 See Section III.D.

> innovate, the possession of monopoly power will not be found unlawful unless it is accompanied by an element of anticompetitive conduct.[8]

In short, monopoly power is a necessary, but not a sufficient, condition of a s. 2 claim.

In assessing monopoly power, courts consider a variety of factors, including market structure, market shares, barriers to entry, and performance over time. Courts have rarely found monopoly power where a company's market share is less than 50 percent. However, a stable market share of 70 percent or more may raise a rebuttable presumption of monopoly power. **43.09**

To determine market share, one must first define the *relevant product and geographic markets.* The standards for defining the relevant markets are substantially similar under the various federal antitrust statutes. In defining a product market, courts have explained " '[b]ecause the ability of consumers to turn to other suppliers restrains a firm from raising prices above the competitive level,' the relevant market must include all products 'reasonably interchangeable by consumers for the same purposes.' "[9] The relevant geographic market is "the 'area of effective competition . . . in which the seller operates and to which the purchaser can practicably turn for supplies.' "[10] **43.10**

Entry conditions (or barriers to entry) are the prerequisites for entering a particular market, such as the need to acquire permits, build manufacturing facilities, create distribution networks, or create or acquire intellectual property. The existence of significant barriers to entry, which prevented or impeded other players from entering or expanding their business within the market, tend to support a finding of monopoly power. **43.11**

Finally, *exclusionary conduct* (or predatory conduct) is conduct that "not only (1) tends to impair the opportunities of rivals, but also (2) either does not further competition on the merits or does so in an unnecessarily restrictive way."[11] Such conduct must "harm the competitive *process* and thereby harm consumers. In contrast, harm to one or more *competitors* will not suffice."[12] **43.12**

In recent years, the antitrust agencies have demonstrated a renewed interest in enforcing s. 2 claims, as evidenced in the DOJ's 2011 complaint and settlement against United Regional Health Care System of Wichita Falls.[13] The DOJ alleged United Regional maintained its monopoly for hospital services by entering into contracts that improperly prohibited commercial health insurers from contracting with United Regional's competitors. The case was ultimately settled by consent decree, which required, among other things, that United Regional cease conditioning the prices and discounts it offered to commercial health insurers on whether those insurers contract with other healthcare providers. Similarly, in late 2010, the DOJ filed a civil antitrust lawsuit against Blue Cross Blue Shield of Michigan (BCBSM) alleging that certain MFN provisions of its agreements with hospitals raised hospital prices, prevented other insurers from entering the marketplace, and discouraged discounts. In **43.13**

[8] *Verizon Communicationns Inc. v. Law Offices of Curtis V. Trinko LLP*, 540 U.S. 398, 407 (2004).

[9] *United States v. Microsoft Corp.*, 253 F.3d 34, at 51–52 (D.C. Cir. 2001) (quoting *Rothery Storage & Van Co. v. Atlas Van Lines, Inc.*, 792 F.2d 210, 218 (D.C. Cir. 1986) and *United States v. E. I. du Pont de Nemours & Co.*, 351 US 377, 395 (1956)).

[10] *United States v. Philadelphia National Bank*, 374 U.S. 321, 359 (1963) (quoting *Tampa Elec. v. Nashville Coal Co.*, 365 U.S. 320, 327 (1961)) (emphasis omitted).

[11] *Aspen Skiing Co. v. Aspen Highlands Skiing Corp.*, 472 U.S. 585, 605 & n.32 (1985).

[12] *Microsoft Corp.*, 253 F.3d (n 9) 58 (emphasis in original).

[13] *See United States v. United Reg'l Health Care Sys.*, No. 7:11-cv-00030 (E.D. Tex. 2011) (the DOJ's first s. 2 case since 1999 challenging a monopolist for engaging in traditional anticompetitive unilateral conduct).

March 2013, the DOJ moved to dismiss its suit because a Michigan state law was passed that prohibited the use of MFN provisions.[14]

A. Predatory pricing

43.14 US antitrust law recognizes that low prices, by themselves, often enhance competition and benefit consumers. "[C]utting prices in order to increase business often is the very essence of competition. Thus, mistaken inferences... are especially costly, because they chill the very conduct the antitrust laws are designed to protect."[15]

43.15 In *Brooke Group*,[16] the Supreme Court established that predatory pricing may be unlawful where a defendant (1) prices below an appropriate measure of its costs, (2) has monopoly power or the dangerous probability of achieving monopoly power, and (3) has a reasonable probability of recouping any short-term losses (generally by increasing its prices after driving out competitors).

43.16 The Supreme Court has not defined what an "appropriate measure of cost" is, and the lower courts have not adopted a uniform approach to the issue. Some lower courts examine marginal cost (i.e. the cost of producing an additional unit of output), while others consider average variable cost (i.e. a firm's variable costs divided by the number of units produced).

43.17 Predatory pricing claims are rarely successful in the US. For example, the DOJ brought a predatory pricing claim against American Airlines which was dismissed before trial (on a motion for summary judgment) because the DOJ failed to meet the *Brooke Group* standards.[17]

43.18 For a discussion of predatory bidding, see Section I.C.

B. Exploitative offenses (excessive pricing, monopoly leveraging)

(i) Excessive pricing

43.19 Under US antitrust law, high prices and even monopoly prices will not, by themselves, establish an antitrust violation. Supra-competitive prices may be evidence of monopoly power and even a s. 2 violation, but in order to establish the violation, the plaintiff must show that the defendant engaged in exclusionary or predatory conduct resulting in actual or probable monopoly power.

(ii) Monopoly leveraging

43.20 Prior to the Supreme Court's decision in *Trinko*,[18] it was unclear whether the use of monopoly power in one market to gain a competitive advantage in another market without threatening to monopolize that other market, so-called "monopoly leveraging," was an independent violation of s. 2 of the Sherman Act. In *Trinko*, the Supreme Court held that it is insufficient to merely allege that the defendant gained a *competitive advantage* in the second market. Instead, the plaintiff must show that the defendant (1) possessed monopoly power in one market, and (2) used that power in an anticompetitive manner to monopolize or attempt to monopolize a second market.

C. Monopsony

43.21 Under US law, the mere possession of monopsony power, like monopoly power, is not unlawful.

---

[14] *See United States v. Blue Cross Blue Shield*, No. 10-cv-14155-DPH (E.D. Mich.).

[15] *Matsushita Elec. Indus. Co. v. Zenith Radio Corp.*, 475 U.S. 574, 594 (1986).

[16] *Brooke Group v. Brown & Williamson Tobacco Corp.*, 509 U.S. 209 (1993).

[17] *See United States v. AMR Corp.*, 140 F. Supp. 2d 1141 (D. Kan. 2001), *aff'd*, 335 F.3d 1109 (10th Cir. 2003).

[18] *Trinko*, 540 U.S. 398 (n 8).

A monopsony concern arises in the context of predatory bidding. *Predatory bidding*, or predatory buying, occurs not when a dominant firm pays "too little," but rather when it pays "too much" for inputs. By paying too much for inputs, the predatory buyer can drive up the costs of inputs for its rivals, making it unprofitable for them to compete in the downstream market in which the inputs are used. **43.22**

To establish a claim of predatory bidding, the Supreme Court held in *Weyerhaeuser* that the following three elements must be shown: **43.23**

(i) the dominant firm sold the product it manufactures from those inputs below "an appropriate measure" of its costs (including the high costs reflected in the "too high" prices it paid for the inputs);
(ii) the conduct allowed the firm to maintain, or come dangerously close to acquiring, monopsony power in the market for the output product or service (that is, the product or service in which the inputs for which the dominant firm overpaid are used); and
(iii) there is a dangerous probability that the dominant firm could recoup its overpayment for the inputs by subsequently selling its products at supracompetitive prices.[19]

Establishing all three of these elements, especially the probability of recoupment, has proven extremely difficult in practice. **43.24**

D. Price discrimination

Price discrimination claims are primarily asserted under the Robinson–Patman Act, which applies only to sales of tangible goods and commodities (i.e. not services or licenses). To assert a claim of price discrimination under the Robinson–Patman Act, the following must be shown: (1) a price difference (2) in reasonably contemporaneous sales, at least one of which crosses state lines (3) from a single seller to multiple buyers, (4) involving commodities of similar grade and quality, (5) the effect of which may be to substantially lessen competition. Price is defined broadly to mean actual net price after all discounts, rebates, coupons and other factors affecting price, including credit terms. *Primary-line injury* is injury to competition between a discriminating seller and the seller's direct competitors; *secondary-line injury* is injury to competition among or between the discriminating seller's customers. **43.25**

The following defenses exist to liability for price discrimination: **43.26**

- functional availability: there is no actionable price discrimination where the discount is known to and, as a practical matter, available to all competing customers;
- changing conditions: a seller may offer a different price in response to changing conditions affecting the marketability of, or the market for, goods, such as the imminent deterioration of perishable items;
- meeting competition: a seller, acting in good faith, may match (but not beat) a competitor's equally low price; and
- cost justification: a seller may adjust prices based on differences in costs of sale, manufacture, or delivery resulting from different methods or quantities in which the goods are sold or delivered.

The Robinson–Patman Act was enacted to protect smaller retailers that have difficulty competing with larger retailers. This purpose contrasts sharply with the enforcement of other federal antitrust laws, which protect the competitive process, rather than specific competitors. As such, the Supreme Court has emphasized that the Robinson–Patman Act must be interpreted narrowly.[20] **43.27**

---

[19] *Weyerhaeuser Co. v. Ross-Simmons Hardware Lumber Co.*, 549 U.S. 312 (2007).

[20] See e.g. *Volvo Trucks N. Am. v. Reeder-Simco GMC, Inc.*, 546 U.S. 164 (2006) (holding that a manufacturer may not be held liable for secondary-line price discrimination absent a showing that the manufacturer discriminated between dealers competing to resell its product to the same retail customer).

43.28 Although the DOJ and the FTC have concurrent jurisdiction to enforce the Act, in practice, the DOJ does not exercise this jurisdiction, and the FTC has brought very few cases since the 1980s, most recently in 2000. Thus, price discrimination claims, by and large, are initiated by private plaintiffs.

43.29 State laws regarding price discrimination vary significantly. Some states model their statutes on the Robinson–Patman Act, others have statutes that only apply to specific products or industries, and still others address conduct excluded from the Robinson–Patman Act, such as price discrimination in the sale of services.

E. Dictating or influencing resale prices

(i) Maximum resale price maintenance

43.30 Maximum resale price maintenance imposes a ceiling on resale prices and is generally permissible under the rule of reason.[21] In *State Oil*, the Supreme Court noted that such policies could affect competition where (1) the policy depresses reseller margins to such an extent that the resellers cannot economically offer services that customers desire, (2) distribution becomes consolidated among fewer, more efficient distributors, or (3) the policy actually acts as a minimum resale price scheme. Indeed, the Court noted that maximum resale price maintenance may lead to lower prices, which benefits consumers so long as they are above predatory levels.[22]

(ii) Minimum resale price maintenance

43.31 For many years in the US, *minimum resale price maintenance* (i.e. creating a floor on resale prices) was per se illegal. However, in 2007, the Supreme Court recognized that minimum resale price maintenance may promote inter-brand competition and held that such agreements should be evaluated under the rule of reason.[23] In applying the rule of reason, the Court noted that the following factors were relevant to determining the net procompetitive or anticompetitive effect of a minimum resale price maintenance policy:

(i) whether the manufacturer or retailers driving the practice possess market power;
(ii) whether the restraint comes at the behest of retailers or the manufacturer; and
(iii) the number of manufacturers engaged in the practice in the market.[24]

43.32 Minimum resale price maintenance policies are likely to fail a rule of reason analysis where they facilitate "[a] horizontal cartel among competing manufacturers or competing retailers that decreases output or reduces competition in order to increase its price" or where "[a] dominant retailer…request[s] resale price maintenance to forestall innovation in distribution that decreases costs."[25]

43.33 Before *Leegin*, a manufacturer potentially could avoid liability under s. 1 by employing a so-called "Colgate policy"; that is, unilaterally deciding to deal only with resellers that sell at recommended prices. Much of the case law surrounding such resale price maintenance therefore focused on whether or not there was an agreement between the manufacturer and the retailer(s) to charge a minimum price.

43.34 It is generally permissible for a manufacturer to condition receipt of promotional payments on a reseller's adherence to suggested advertised prices. Examples of programs found to be

---

[21] See *State Oil Co. v. Kahn*, 522 U.S. 3, 17–18 (1997).
[22] *Kahn*, 522 U.S. (n 21) 15.
[23] See *Leegin Creative Leather Prods., Inc. v. PSKS, Inc.*, 551 U.S. 877 (2007).
[24] *Leegin Creative*, 551 U.S. (n 23) 897–8.
[25] *Leegin Creative*, 551 U.S. (n 23) 892–4.

lawful include direct-to-consumer rebates, promotions discounting the cost to resellers, and promotions requiring that the reseller "pass-through" the discounts it receives from the manufacturer to the end consumer. Manufacturers may also provide suggested price lists to dealers, advertise suggested resale prices to dealers' customers, and print suggested resale prices on products or price tags, so long as dealers may independently decide whether to observe the suggested retail prices.

However, some states, such as California, Kansas, Maryland, New Jersey, and New York, continue to maintain that minimum resale price maintenance is per se illegal under their state antitrust laws. Because of the risk of liability under state law, many companies continue to use Colgate policies rather than minimum resale price restrictions. **43.35**

F. Tying arrangements

Tying arrangements are not limited to physical goods but can also apply to services, leases, franchises, and licenses to intellectual property. Although tying agreements typically involve the same party selling both the tying and tied products, a tie may also be found when the seller of the tying product stipulates that a product be purchased from a specified third party. **43.36**

Antitrust concerns may arise where a customer has no choice but to buy both products from the one seller even though they would prefer to purchase one of the products from a competing seller. This lack of choice can foreclose competing sellers from the marketplace and adversely impact competition as a whole. A tie involving two different sellers will tend to raise antitrust concerns where the first seller has an economic interest in the sale of the tied product, such as receiving a substantial rebate for mandating that its customers purchase the products from the second seller. **43.37**

Tying arrangements may be challenged under s. 1 of the Sherman Act, s. 3 of the Clayton Act, s. 5 of the FTC Act, and they may support a monopolization claim under s. 2 of the Sherman Act. The US antitrust laws historically condemned tying arrangements as per se illegal. Today, however, tying arrangements are per se illegal in name only. In *Jefferson Parish*,[26] the Supreme Court identified four factors that must be considered when evaluating the extent to which any tying arrangement creates antitrust risks. These factors are considered below. **43.38**

(i) Does the arrangement involve two separate products or services?

There can be no unlawful tie unless the arrangement involves two separate products or services. In most cases, this is relatively easy to determine. However, in other cases, particularly those involving software, hardware, and other technology products, it is less obvious whether the two products allegedly being tied are separate and distinct products. A technological tie involves making two complementary products inseparable or virtually inseparable through "bolting" products together, property interfaces, or communication protocols. The bolting of Microsoft's web browser, Internet Explorer, with its Windows operating system is a classic example of a technological tie. **43.39**

The most important factor in determining whether two products are separate is the existence of independent consumer demand for each product. Other factors include whether the two products can be consumed or used separately (or have to be used together for compatibility or technological reasons), whether the seller has offered them separately in the past, and whether competitors offer competing products separately. **43.40**

[26] *Jefferson Parish Hosp. Dist. No. 2 v. Hyde*, 466 U.S. 2 (1984).

(ii) Is there coercion?

43.41 If there is no coercion or conditioning and the buyer is free to take either product by itself, no tying problem will arise. However, coercion may be found even if there is no express requirement to purchase the two products together if the prices or terms on which the products are sold separately make it economically irrational for customers to purchase them separately. Courts in some cases have found that *substantial* differences between the prices and terms of the bundled purchase vis-à-vis the standalone products may constitute conditioning or coercion sufficient to sustain a violation.

(iii) Does the seller have substantial economic/market power in the tying product market?

43.42 In most cases, a reasonable proxy for evaluating market power is the seller's market share in the tying product market. The risk of a tying violation is low if the seller's market share is 30 percent or less.

(iv) Is a substantial amount of interstate commerce in the tied product affected?

43.43 This prerequisite is met in most cases, with courts finding that dollar amounts as low as USD 10,000 constitute a substantial amount.

43.44 Complicating the tying analysis, in *United States v. Microsoft Corp.*, the D.C. Circuit declined to apply the per se rule to arrangements involving the bundling of a computer operating system and a web browser.[27] The court reasoned that tying arrangements involving computer software may have procompetitive efficiencies, which are not considered in the traditional tying test established in *Jefferson Parish*. However, the D.C. Circuit cautioned against reading its decision as "setting a precedent for switching to the rule of reason every time a court identifies an efficiency justification for a tying arrangement."[28]

G. Exclusive dealing

43.46 Exclusive dealing is prohibited by s. 3 of the Clayton Act when the effect of the arrangement may be to substantially lessen competition or to tend to create a monopoly. Such arrangements may also be challenged under s. 1 of the Sherman Act, s. 5 of the FTC Act, and as conduct evidencing a violation of s. 2 of the Sherman Act.

43.47 Exclusive dealing arrangements can offer several procompetitive benefits, such as the improvement in dealer services arising from their devotion to the one seller's product; avoiding free riding by dealers who use another seller's services and efforts to support a competing brand; ensuring that dealers do not pass off inferior products as their own; and creating a reliable and steady distribution channel for the supplier, thus facilitating efficiency enhancing investments by the supplier and the dealer.

43.48 Like tying arrangements, exclusive dealing arrangements can raise competitive concerns by foreclosing competing sellers from marketing their products to the exclusively contracted dealer. To challenge an exclusive dealing arrangement, there must be evidence that the seller and dealer actually operated an exclusive arrangement. However, it is not necessary to have a written agreement conferring exclusivity; it is sufficient if the factual circumstances surrounding the arrangement infer exclusivity (so-called "de facto" exclusive dealing). Recently, the Third Circuit in *ZF Meritor LLC v. Eaton Corp.* held that certain market share discounts could amount to "de facto partial exclusive dealing."[29] In a 2:1 decision, the majority acknowledged "that 'partial' exclusive dealing is rarely a valid antitrust theory" but found that the long-term

---

[27] *Microsoft Corp.*, 253 F.3d 34 (n 9).
[28] *Microsoft Corp.*, 253 F.3d 95 (n 9).
[29] *ZF Meritor LLC*, 696 F.3d 254 (n 6).

contracts with every direct purchaser in the market which "locked up over 85% of the market for at least five years" were unlawful de facto partial exclusive dealing.[30]

Once exclusivity has been shown, the competitive effects of the agreement are evaluated under the rule of reason. As the first step in this analysis, courts will assess the percentage of the downstream market foreclosed to competing sellers by the arrangements. If this foreclosure is less than 30 percent, the agreement generally is presumed lawful. Courts have also assessed whether competitors are still able to reach ultimate consumers by other means (even though some distributors are unavailable due to the exclusive dealing restriction), such as via direct sales. **43.49**

Finally, in evaluating the competitive effect of an exclusive dealing arrangement, a court may consider the length of the exclusive arrangement (including termination provisions and penalties for the same). Short term agreements (i.e. for one year or less) have often been upheld on the premise that any short-term foreclosure is likely to have minimal anticompetitive effects. Similarly, longer term contracts that can be easily terminated on short notice have been upheld. However, provisions allowing termination on short notice will not save an otherwise anticompetitive exclusive dealing agreement where, as a practical matter, termination is difficult or infeasible. **43.50**

Courts also consider the justifications for, and procompetitive effects of, exclusive dealing arrangements. However, there is no definitive standard for determining how much or what kinds of procompetitive benefits are sufficient to outweigh the potential anticompetitive effect of an exclusive dealing arrangement. Ultimately, liability for exclusive dealing is a significant risk for any business with market power whose entry into a long-term exclusive arrangement substantially forecloses competition. **43.51**

H. Refusal to deal

In general, a firm—even a monopolist—has no duty to sell or license its products to others, including its downstream customers, upstream suppliers, or rivals. The Supreme Court emphasized in *Trinko* that "the Sherman Act does not restrict the long recognized right of [a] trader or manufacturer engaged in an entirely private business, freely to exercise [its] own independent discretion as to parties with whom [it] will deal."[31] Forcing a firm to deal with others (especially competitors) may reduce the firm's incentives to invest and innovate and ultimately goes against the Sherman Act's objective of promoting vigorous competition. Except in rare circumstances, even monopolists are not required to create competition against themselves by dealing with others. The circumstances in which a monopolist is required to deal with a competitor are limited, but have included the following factual scenarios: **43.52**

In *Otter Tail Power*, the Supreme Court required a dominant firm to sell its wholesale power to municipalities that formerly were served by the firm but later sought to establish their own electric distribution systems.[32] **43.53**

In *Aspen Skiing*,[33] the Supreme Court held that a company's decision to terminate a long-standing joint marketing arrangement and to refuse to deal on any terms with its rival was exclusionary because of the parties' prior course of dealing. The Supreme Court in *Trinko* described the holding in *Aspen Skiing* as "at or near the outer boundary of § 2 liability."[34] **43.54**

30 *ZF Meritor LLC*, 696 F.3d (n 6) 18, 21.
31 *Trinko*, 540 U.S. (n 8) 408 (quoting *United States v. Colgate & Co.*, 250 U.S. 300, 307 (1919)).
32 *United States v. Otter Tail Power Co.*, 410 U.S. 366 (1973).
33 *Aspen Skiing*, 472 U.S. 585 (n 11).
34 *Trinko*, 540 U.S. 409 (n 8).

43.55 The federal antitrust agencies' pursuit of unilateral refusals to deal remains exceptional, rather the norm, even in the case of monopolists. However, the FTC has entered into a number of consent decrees and settlement orders where firms have agreed to cease-and-desist from refusing to deal with customers that deal with rivals. For instance, in 2011 the FTC challenged the conduct of PoolCorp, the largest distributor of swimming pool products in the United States, over its refusal to deal with manufacturers. PoolCorp threatened manufacturers of pool products that it would not sell their products if they also sold their products to PoolCorp's rivals. PoolCorp entered into a settlement order with the FTC in which it agreed, *inter alia*, to cease to refuse to deal with any manufacturer.[35]

I. Essential facilities

43.56 The essential facilities doctrine is very rarely invoked in the US and has never been recognized by the Supreme Court. Instead, a firm that is denied access to a competitor's resource that is essential to compete would likely rely on refusal to deal concepts, such as those in *Aspen Skiing*.[36] Nonetheless, in theory, the essential facilities doctrine imposes liability upon a firm that denies a second firm reasonable access to a product or service that the second firm needs in order to compete.

J. Bundling (including loyalty and market share discounts)

(i) Bundled discounts

43.57 *Bundled discounts* are discounts made available to customers that purchase multiple products from more than one of a seller's product lines, typically by reducing the prices of the products in the "bundled purchase" below the combined prices a customer would pay if each of the products in the bundle was purchased separately. Such discounts can be offered at the time of the sale or rebated after a period of time. Courts have tended to treat bundled pricing as distinct from single product loyalty discounts.

43.58 Bundling, like tying, can adversely impact competition through foreclosure of rivals. A bundled discount offered by a dominant firm with diverse product lines may foreclose rivals if the bundled discount makes it more difficult for competitors, especially those that only make one of the products in the bundle, to match those discounts or access customers.

43.59 The courts have taken a variety of approaches to determining the legality of bundling, including:

- that bundled discounts do nothing more than provide options to purchasers; they do not compel purchasers to accept the package;
- that bundled pricing ought to be evaluated under a modified test for predatory pricing;[37]
- that bundled pricing claims should only proceed if they exclude equally or more efficient competitors; and
- that bundled discounts should be viewed as part of a "monopoly broth" supporting a s. 2 claim even if foreclosure is not quantitatively significant.

43.60 In addition, the FTC has asserted that certain forms of bundling can violate s. 5 of the FTC Act. Such claims were made by the FTC against Intel and later settled by consent decree. As part of this decree, a modified test for predatory pricing was applied to certain bundled

[35] See FTC Complaint, No. C-4345, *In the Matter of the Pool Corp.* (January 13, 2012); see also FTC Complaint, No. C-4289, *In the Matter of Transitions Optical, Inc.* (April 27, 2010) (defendant refused to deal with distributors who did not sell its lenses exclusively).

[36] See Section I.H.

[37] For a further discussion of predatory pricing, see Section I.A.

discounts. Intel agreed not to offer certain bundled discounts if any product in the bundle was priced below its costs after the entire amount of the bundled discount was attributed to any product ("the discount attribution test").[38]

Bundling claims continue to be popular with private plaintiffs who will seek to file cases in a plaintiff friendly forum, such as the Third Circuit. **43.61**

(ii) Loyalty and market share discounts

As opposed to bundled discounts, *loyalty discounts* are discounts a seller may offer to reward customers for maintaining or increasing their purchases of a single product from that seller over time. **43.62**

Loyalty and market share discounts are distinct from simple volume discounts that are predicated on the amount of units purchased. Above-cost volume discounts generally do not raise issues under the Sherman Act even if the seller has market power, although they can raise Robinson–Patman issues.[39] **43.63**

When offered by a seller that lacks market power, loyalty and market share discounts generally do not raise antitrust issues. However, when offered by a dominant seller, loyalty discounts can raise similar concerns to tying and bundling arrangements by foreclosing competing sellers' access to customers or distribution channels. Antitrust concerns are more likely where customers depend on a dominant firm for at least some portion of their purchases.[40] In *Advanced Micro Devices*, AMD alleged that Intel had unlawfully maintained its monopoly power in violation of s. 2 by offering customers a system of rebates that could only be attained by purchasing at such high levels that customers could not purchase any significant volumes from competitors, including AMD. **43.64**

Like bundling, there is no settled US legal standard for assessing loyalty and market share discounts: **43.65**

- the court's analysis may turn on whether the prices that result after the discount amount to predatory pricing (Section I.A); or
- the court may analyze the loyalty discounts as actual or de facto exclusive dealing (Section I.G).

Discounts that are expressly contingent on the purchaser buying exclusively from the seller are often treated as exclusive dealing contracts.[41] Courts are split on whether to apply an exclusive dealing analysis where the discounts do not require exclusivity but provide financial inducements to distributors to purchase most or all of their needs from the defendant. **43.66**

Like bundling, loyalty and market share discounts by firms with market power have been challenged by private plaintiffs and antitrust agencies.[42] **43.67**

As noted in Section I.G, the Third Circuit recently held in *ZF Meritor LLC v. Eaton Corp.* that certain market share discounts could amount to "de facto partial exclusive dealing."[43] The majority emphasized the combination of the seller's dominance and the market share discounts in reasoning that this dominance meant buyers were coerced into meeting the **43.68**

---

[38] See *Intel Corp.*, Decision and Order, s. IV(A)(6), No. 9341 (F.T.C. October 29, 2010). In adopting the discount attribution test, the FTC followed the Ninth Circuit's decision in *Cascade Health Solutions v. PeaceHealth*, 502 F.3d 895 (9th Cir. 2007).

[39] For a discussion of the Robinson–Patman Act, see Section I.D.

[40] See e.g. *Advanced Micro Devices Inc. v. Intel Corp.*, No. 1:05-cv-00441 (D. Del.).

[41] For a discussion of the approach to exclusive dealing, see Section I.G.

[42] *See Intel Corp.*, Decision and Order (n 38).

[43] *ZF Meritor LLC*, 696 F.3d (n 6) 281–4.

market share targets.[44] Several other courts had found that market share discounts on a single product line are procompetitive and do not violate the antitrust laws unless the discounted price amounted to predatory pricing.[45]

K. Standard-setting groups (disclosure requirements, licensing arrangements, and licensing pools)

43.69 Industry standard-setting groups do not inherently raise antitrust concerns. The Supreme Court recognized in *Allied Tube* that significant procompetitive advantages can flow from unbiased standard-setting groups.[46] Collaborative standard setting not only can improve product safety through the testing of products but can also foster competition by enhancing the interoperability of products. However, standard-setting groups can raise antitrust issues where members:

- share competitively sensitive information (Section II.E);
- boycott certain members or standards (Section II.C);
- adopt discriminatory standards (e.g. favoring one group of competitors over another); or
- enter into anticompetitive intellectual property arrangements.

43.70 Recent litigation has focused on situations where it has been alleged that a participant in a standard-setting group failed to disclose or misrepresented the fact that its intellectual property rights applied to a proposed standard, and then exercised those rights against other participants after they had adopted the standard (known as a "patent hold-up"). Private plaintiffs and the FTC are also increasingly challenging conduct where the participants disclosed their intellectual property rights, but allegedly later reneged on commitments to license those rights on "fair, reasonable, and non-discriminatory" (FRAND) terms.

(i) Licensing arrangements and licensing/patent pools

43.71 Cross-licensing agreements typically provide reciprocal licenses between licensors. That is, they allow each party (and owner of the relevant patent or license) to use the other party's license or patent. Where the parties to the cross licensing agreement compete with each other, cross licensing restrictions may raise horizontal antitrust issues. For example, if a cross licensing agreement limits the areas or customers to which each party can or cannot use the applicable license or patent, this could amount to a per se illegal agreement to allocate customers or territories. However, such arrangements can frequently result in procompetitive benefits, including the integration of complementary technology, a significant reduction in royalty and negotiation costs involved in commercializing a product, the avoidance of expensive infringement litigation, a promotion of innovation, or encouragement of capital investment. Such arrangements are usually analyzed under the rule of reason, so long as they are not simply a device to mask arrangements that are facially anticompetitive. In this way, the antitrust analysis of cross licensing arrangements is similar to that of joint ventures.[47]

43.72 Patent or licensing pools, which typically involve the cross licensing of patents among a group as well as collective licensing to third parties, are usually formed to combine multiple patented technologies into a single license. Like cross-licensing arrangements, patent pools are generally analyzed under the rule of reason, although again naked restraints on price or output may be deemed illegal per se. Patent pools that combine competing or substitute patents

---

[44] *ZF Meritor LLC*, 696 F.3d (n 6) 281–4.

[45] See *Concord Boat Corp. v. Brunswick Corp.*, 207 F.2d 1039 (8th Cir. 2000); *Cascade Health Solutions v. PeaceHealth*, 502 F.3d 895 (9th Cir. 2007).

[46] *Allied Tube & Conduit Corp. v. Indian Head, Inc.*, 486 U.S. 492, 501 (1988).

[47] See Section II.D.

(i.e. patents that claim alternative non-infringing means of accomplishing the same end) are more likely to raise antitrust concerns than pools that combine blocking or complementary patents (which cover different aspects of the same technology, process, or product), because collectively setting a royalty rate for access to the competing pooled patents is analogous to horizontal price fixing.[48] The DOJ and FTC assert that "[p]ooling agreements typically warrant greater antitrust scrutiny than do cross-licensing agreements due to the collective pricing of pooled patents, greater possibilities for collusion, and generally a larger number of market participants."[49] In short, patent pools are an area of significant litigation risk.

L. Customer temination

Under US antitrust laws, there is no duty to deal with downstream customers, upstream suppliers, or rivals. "[T]he Sherman Act does not restrict the long recognized right of [a] trader or manufacturer engaged in an entirely private business, freely to exercise [its] own independent discretion as to parties with whom [it] will deal."[50] However, terminating customers or suppliers because they do business with a competitor can give rise to liability under s. 2 of the Sherman Act if the termination rises to the level of predatory or exclusionary conduct.[51] **43.73**

M. Termination of intermediaries (retailers, wholesalers, dealers, and value-added resellers, agents, and brokers)

Terminating a distributor or reseller generally does not raise antitrust concerns so long as the supplier's decision to terminate is made independently (i.e. not by agreement with other distributors or competitors) and for legitimate business reasons. Examples of legitimate business reasons may include poor performance, unsatisfactory credit or poor payment record, poor customer relations, or failure to meet quality standards. **43.74**

A company's decision to terminate independent distributors in favor of direct distribution may be based on such legitimate business reasons as giving the manufacturer's personnel greater sales expertise, achieving operating efficiencies and reducing resale prices, securing additional promotional activities or providing better services, and reducing costs. **43.75**

Where a supplier terminates or threatens to terminate a distributor solely because the distributor is also dealing with the supplier's competitors, the termination may be evidence that the supplier is operating a de facto exclusive dealing policy.[52] A termination that merely reinforces a restriction on distribution is analyzed in the same manner as the underlying restriction. For example, a vertical termination that reinforces a horizontal agreement to exclude rivals will be analyzed in the same manner as the underlying horizontal agreement.[53] **43.76**

N. Termination of relationships with competitors

Like termination of intermediaries, termination of relationships with competitors rarely raises antitrust concerns where there are legitimate business reasons for doing so. However, a termination may result in antitrust liability where it is part of a collective boycott of a competitor.[54] **43.77**

---

[48] See Section II.A.

[49] See *Antitrust Enforcement and Intellectual Property Rights: Promoting Innovation and Competition*, Jointly issued by the DOJ and FTC (April 2007), 58.

[50] *Trinko*, 540 U.S. (n 8) 408 (quoting *United States v. Colgate & Co.*, 250 U.S. 300, 307 (1919)).

[51] *Aspen Skiing*, 472 U.S. 585 (n 11). See also Section I.H.

[52] See Section I.G.

[53] See Section II.B.

[54] See *Nw. Wholesale Stationers v. Pac. Stationery & Printing Co.*, 472 U.S. 284 (1985). For a discussion of the antitrust analysis of refusals to deal with competitors, see Section I.H.

O. Exemptions

43.78 A number of industries benefit from legislative exemptions from the antitrust laws. Such industries include certain sectors in labor, agriculture, energy, insurance, finance, healthcare, communications, and professional sports. Determining precisely how these antitrust exemptions apply to particular conduct often requires a detailed examination of industry specific statutes and regulatory schemes, and therefore an antitrust expert should always be consulted to determine if and when these exemptions apply.

43.79 In addition to the exemptions established by the legislature, the judiciary has created two further exemptions: (1) the Noerr–Pennington doctrine and (2) the state action doctrine.

(i) Noerr–Pennington Doctrine

43.80 The Noerr–Pennington doctrine provides immunity from antitrust liability for certain genuine conduct involving constitutional (First Amendment) petitioning rights, such as government lobbying, joint petitioning, and litigation.[55]

(ii) State action doctrine

43.81 The state action doctrine (or *Parker* immunity) protects actions taken pursuant to a state regulatory scheme that evidences or reflects an intention to replace competition with government supervised regulation.[56]

43.82 To qualify for state action doctrine protections: (1) the challenged conduct must have been undertaken pursuant to a "clearly articulated and affirmatively expressed state policy" to replace competition with regulation; and (2) the policy must have been "actively supervised" by the state. In recent years, courts have strictly applied the active supervision prong of the state action doctrine. For instance, courts have refused to grant state action immunity where the plaintiffs could not show that the state had power to review the specific actions at issue and disapprove those that did not accord with state policy.

43.83 The scope of the state action doctrine was recently revisited by the Supreme Court.[57] In *Phoebe Putney*, the Supreme Court unanimously reversed the 11th Circuit and held that because the State had not clearly articulated and affirmatively expressed a policy allowing the hospital authority to make acquisitions that substantially lessen competition, state-action immunity does not apply.

II. Dealing with competitors

43.84 Antitrust claims based on horizontal conduct, that is agreements between competitors, are most frequently brought under s. 1 of the Sherman Act, which prohibits concerted action—contracts, combinations, and conspiracies—that unreasonably restrain trade.

43.85 Per se s. 1 offenses, such as price fixing, bid-rigging, and market or customer allocation among horizontal competitors, are considered hard core violations of the US antitrust laws and will often be treated by the DOJ as criminal offenses. The DOJ pursues such hard core violations aggressively and will assume that participation in such conduct is consistent with a criminal intent to violate the antitrust laws and is thus appropriate for criminal prosecution.

---

[55] For further discussion of the Noerr–Pennington doctrine, see Section II.J.

[56] See *Parker v. Brown*, 317 U.S. 341 (1943) (articulating the doctrine in the first instance).

[57] See *FTC v. Phoebe Putney Health Sys., Inc.*, 663 F.3d 1369 (11th Cir. 2011), *cert. granted*, 133 S. Ct. 1003 (2013).

The penalties arising from criminal prosecution are severe. In 2012, AU Optronics Corp. was fined USD 500 million for its participation in a liquid crystal display price-fixing cartel. Along with the criminal fine, AU Optronics Corp. was required to print advertisements in three major trade publications in the United States and Taiwan acknowledging its convictions and punishments and the remedial steps it has taken as a result of its conviction. The company and its American subsidiary, AU Optronics Corporation America, were also placed on probation for three years, required to adopt an antitrust compliance program and required to appoint an independent corporate compliance monitor. Last but not least, three of AU Optronics Corp. executives received terms of imprisonment of up to three years for their participation in the cartel. Further discussion of criminal penalties is found in Section III.F.

A. Horizontal price fixing

Agreements among competitors to raise, lower, stabilize, or otherwise set or determine prices that are not ancillary to some legitimate efficiency enhancing or other procompetitive activity are per se illegal under s. 1 of the Sherman Act. Such agreements are termed *"naked" price fixing agreements* and no justifications can be offered to rebut their illegality. However, an agreement to fix prices that is ancillary to a legitimate efficiency enhancing joint venture or other procompetitive collaboration is not per se illegal and will be subject to a rule of reason analysis. **43.86**

Generally, a firm is permitted to make advance price announcements. Nevertheless, antitrust concerns may arise if such announcements or communications were, in reality, done to solicit common action or price coordination among competitors. If such evidence of "signaling" is coupled with evidence of parallel actions by competitors that cannot otherwise be justified as being in their individual legitimate interests, a court could infer an unlawful horizontal price fixing agreement.[58] **43.87**

B. Horizontal agreements to allocate customers or territories; agreements not to compete

Like naked price fixing, agreements that operate only to divide territories and allocate customers between competitors, and that are not ancillary to a procompetitive integration of the parties' activities, are per se unlawful. An agreement with respect to industries, customers, or geographic areas may be held valid where it is narrowly focused to the activities of a legitimate joint venture.[59] **43.88**

Similarly, naked agreements not to compete, or market or customer allocation agreements among potential or actual competitors that are not ancillary to legitimate economic integrations are per se unlawful. **43.89**

C. Horizontal boycotts

Horizontal boycotts or unlawful concerted refusals to deal can arise in various contexts, including refusals to enter into new business relationships, terminations of existing relationships, refusals by trade associations to admit new members or expulsions of existing members, and refusals by associations to approve or certify products or services. **43.90**

The circumstances in which a concerted refusal to deal will constitute a per se unlawful horizontal boycott have not been clearly articulated by the courts. As the Supreme Court **43.91**

[58] See Section II.G.

[59] For a discussion of joint ventures and the antitrust analysis applicable to such arrangements, see Section II.D(ii).

observed in *Nw. Wholesale Stationers*,[60] there "is more confusion about the scope and operation of the per se rule against group boycotts than in reference to any other aspect of the per se doctrine."

43.92 The Supreme Court has generally applied the per se approach to cases which have:

> involved joint efforts by a firm or firms to disadvantage competitors by "either directly denying or persuading or coercing suppliers or customers to deny relationships the competitors need in the competitive struggle." ... In these cases, the boycott often cut off access to a supply, facility, or market necessary to enable the boycotted firm to compete, and frequently the boycotting firm possessed a dominant position in the relevant market.... In addition, the practices were generally not justified by plausible arguments that they were intended to enhance overall efficiency and make markets more competitive.[61]

Today, however, most horizontal boycotts are subject to the rule of reason.

D. Joint ventures and other competitive collaborations

43.93 Broadly, a joint venture is any collaborative activity, short of a full merger, by which companies pool resources to pursue a common objective. Thus, participants typically remain at least potential competitors and may be actual competitors in related upstream and downstream activities. For example, competitors may collaborate on research and development or for the production, marketing, or sale of a product. Procompetitive justifications for competitor collaborations may include achieving economies of scale, sharing costs, or attaining other efficiencies that enable the parties to compete more effectively. The following questions are helpful to analyze the antitrust implications of joint ventures in the US.

(i) Is the joint venture acting as a single firm or as a collaboration of independent competitors?

43.94 A joint venture may involve such substantial and permanent integration of activities that the parties, in effect, operate as a single firm (akin to a merger), or it may encompass various forms and degrees of collaboration between independent competitors. Competitor collaborations, unlike mergers, usually preserve some form of competition among the participants. However, the fact of reduced competition necessitates examining whether there are any anticompetitive restraints on the remaining competition.

43.95 The US federal antitrust agencies analyze joint ventures as a horizontal merger falling under the Horizontal Merger Guidelines where:

- the participants are competitors in that relevant market;
- the formation of the collaboration involves an efficiency-enhancing integration of economic activity in the relevant market;
- the integration eliminates all competition among the participants in the relevant market; and
- the collaboration does not terminate within a sufficiently limited period by its own specific and express terms.[62]

(ii) If the joint venture is acting as a collaboration of independent competitors, then is its conduct of a type that always or almost always tends to raise price or to reduce output?

43.96 Naked agreements to raise price or reduce output are a per se violation of the antitrust laws.[63]

---

60 *Nw. Wholesale Stationers*, 472 U.S. (n 54) 294.

61 *Nw. Wholesale Stationers*, 472 U.S. (n 54) 293–5 (internal citations omitted).

62 See *Antitrust Guidelines for Collaborations Among Competitors* (2000) ("Competitor Collaboration Guidelines"); see also *Texaco v. Dagher*, 547 U.S. 1 (2006).

63 See Sections II.A and II.B.

However, parties to a legitimate efficiency enhancing joint venture or other procompetitive collaboration are generally free to agree on the scope of the venture, provided that their agreements are reasonably related to the joint venture. Agreements that are reasonably ancillary to a legitimate joint venture are subject to a rule of reason analysis. **43.97**

(iii) If not, then is the joint venture causing or likely to cause anticompetitive harm?

Competitor collaborations may harm competition and consumers by, for example, increasing the participants' ability or incentive to raise prices, or to reduce output, quality, or service below what would likely prevail absent the agreement, or otherwise decreasing participants' ability or incentive to compete independently. Such anticompetitive effects may arise through agreements that limit independent decision making or combine the control of or financial interests in competitively sensitive decisions such as price or output. Less antitrust exists where (1) sufficient economic integration exists, and (2) any competitive restraints are reasonably necessary for the collaboration to function. **43.98**

Competitor collaborations may also aid explicit or tacit collusion in the relevant market or related markets through facilitating practices.[64] **43.99**

(iv) Is the overall competitive effect of the joint venture such that its procompetitive benefits outweigh its anticompetitive harms?

Competitor collaborations provide efficiency gains where participants combine different capabilities or resources. Likewise, collaborations can result in economies of scale beyond that which any single participant could achieve, such as in research and marketing activities. Such collaborations benefit consumers because the participants are able to lower prices, improve quality, or bring products to market sooner. **43.100**

The FTC and the DOJ have adopted the following "safety zones" for competitor collaborations that are highly unlikely to lead to competitive harm: **43.101**

- collaborations in which the market shares of the collaboration and its participants collectively account for no more than 20 percent of each relevant market; and
- research and development joint ventures in which three or more independently controlled research efforts, in addition to those of the collaboration, constitute a close substitute for the research and development activity of the venture.[65]

Some joint ventures may be reportable transactions under the Hart–Scott–Rodino Act ("HSR Act"). If relevant thresholds are met, one or more of the joint venture participants may be required to make an HSR filing. Even joint ventures that are not subject to the premerger reporting requirements of the HSR Act may be investigated and ultimately challenged by federal and state antitrust enforcers. Recently, the DOJ and the Attorney General of the State of New York challenged a joint venture between two New York City tour bus companies that effectively merged their operations and eliminated competition between them.[66] **43.102**

E. Trade associations

The Supreme Court has rejected the notion that mere participation in a trade association, by itself, provides evidence of a conspiracy unlawfully restraining trade.[67] However, trade associations raise antitrust concerns because they can provide a forum for competitors to **43.103**

---

[64] See Section II.G.

[65] See *Competitor Collaboration Guidelines* (n 62) for specific antitrust analysis of particular types of joint ventures.

[66] See *United States v. Twin America, LLC*, No. 1:12-cv-8989 (S.D.N.Y. Dec. 11, 2012) (complaint filed).

[67] See *Bell Atlantic Corp. v. Twombly*, 550 U.S. 544, 567 n.12 (2007).

exchange competitive information, which can in turn be perceived as reaching an anticompetitive agreement.

(i) Trade association membership rules

43.104 The courts have recognized that trade associations may have some type of membership rules, criteria, or disciplinary procedures which, when invoked, incidentally restrain trade. Antitrust objections are minimized if these rules, criteria, and disciplinary procedures relate to the purpose of the organization and are objective and reasonable.

43.105 Absent very unusual circumstances, exclusion from a trade association or any other joint organization—with the possible exception of a standard-setting body—will not raise antitrust issues, whether due process is followed or not. Nevertheless, because of the potential for the exclusion to be attacked as an unlawful group boycott, many trade associations follow due process procedures.

F. Interlocking directorates

43.106 Section 8 of the Clayton Act prohibits any person from simultaneously serving as an officer or director of two or more corporations that are competitors if each corporation's combined capital, surplus, and profits exceed an inflation-indexed threshold (USD 28,883,000 in 2013). In such a case, both the interlocked corporations and the directors themselves risk liability under s. 8 of the Clayton Act. The most likely remedy for a s. 8 violation is the elimination of the overlap by the resignation of the person from one of the boards.

43.107 Section 8 provides certain *de minimis* exemptions where:

- either corporation's competitive sales, i.e. gross revenues for all products and services for which both companies compete for the same buyers, are less than a *de minimis* threshold (USD 2,888,300 in 2013);
- *each* corporation's competitive sales are less than 4 percent of that corporation's total sales; or
- competitive sales of *either* corporation are less than 2 percent of the corporation's total sales.

43.108 The DOJ and the FTC have taken the position that a "person" under s. 8 includes not only individuals, but also corporations and associations.[68] As such, a corporation or association with representatives serving on the boards of competing corporations may violate s. 8, even though the representatives are not the same individual.

43.109 Section 8 does not apply to interlocks involving members of the same corporate group, such as parents and their wholly owned subsidiaries.

G. Facilitating practices

43.110 *Facilitating practices* are actions that facilitate competitors in coordinating on price, input, output, or other behavior. While such practices may not be unlawful under the Sherman Act and in some circumstances may even enhance competition, the FTC may challenge such practices under s. 5 of the FTC Act. Neither the DOJ nor private plaintiffs may enforce the FTC Act. Although several remedies are available under the Act, the FTC has traditionally sought cease-and-desist orders.

43.111 The FTC has brought s. 5 claims challenging facilitating practices such as:

- price signaling, i.e. direct or indirect advance notice of a price change to the press, existing or potential customers, or other individuals;[69]

---

[68] See Brief for the United States as Amicus Curiae, *Reading Int'l v. Oaktree Capital Mgmt.*, 317 F. Supp. 2d 301 (S.D.N.Y. 2003).

[69] See *Ethyl Corp.*, 101 F.T.C. 425, 428 (1983).

- MFN clauses, for example promises by a seller to charge a customer prices that are no higher than the prices charged to any other customer;[70] and
- invitations to collude, i.e. private or public communications from a firm to an actual or potential competitor that the firm is willing and ready to coordinate on output or price, even though the communications do not rise to the level of an agreement.[71]

Facilitating practices are increasingly subject to antitrust scrutiny. In 2010, the FTC alleged that U-Haul had engaged in invitations to collude in violation of s. 5. In *In the Matter of U-Haul and AMERCO*, the FTC cited both private and public price statements by U-Haul which attempted to encourage Budget, its competitor, to raise its prices. These statements included that U-Haul should "show rate leadership" and that competitors should not "throw away money" by lowering prices. Importantly, the FTC did not allege that other competitors had accepted U-Haul's suggestions to raise their price, or that U-Haul's conduct alone had any actual or likely anticompetitive effects. The case was settled by FTC Order.[72] Additionally, in late 2012 the DOJ and FTC held a joint public workshop examining the legality of MFNs.[73] **43.112**

H. Information exchange

Exchanges of competitively sensitive information may in some circumstances violate s. 1 of the Sherman Act or constitute evidence of an unlawful agreement under s. 1. The most competitively sensitive information includes current or future information regarding prices, capacity, costs, bids, or customers. **43.113**

Albeit in the context of healthcare, the DOJ and the FTC have articulated the following "safety zones" where anticompetitive harm from information exchanges is highly unlikely: **43.114**

- a third party manages the exchange;
- the information exchanged is at least three months old;
- there are five or more sources of information, and the data is presented in aggregated form; and
- no individual company's data represents more than 25 percent of the statistics on a weighted basis.[74]

These statements, despite arising in the healthcare context, are generally considered pertinent for other industries.

It may be necessary to exchange competitively sensitive information in connection with the evaluation or operation of a joint venture or proposed merger or acquisition. To minimize the risk of antitrust issues parties should consider: **43.115**

- who receives the information: parties should avoid disclosure to employees who are directly responsible for the marketing, pricing, sales, or research and development of competing products;
- the form in which the information is provided: parties should take steps to preclude the misuse of competitively sensitive information by, for example, masking specific customer

[70] See *Ethyl Corp.* (n 69) 470.

[71] See *Precision Moulding Co.*, 61 Fed. Reg. 32824 (FTC June 25, 1996) (proposed consent and aid to public comment), 122 F.T.C. 104 (1997) (decision and order).

[72] See *In the Matter of U-Haul Int'l, Inc. and AMERCO*, No. C-4294 (July 20, 2010).

[73] See DOJ Workshop, "Most-Favored-Nation Clauses and Antitrust Enforcement and Policy" (September 12, 2012), available at <http://www.justice.gov/atr/public/workshops/mfn>.

[74] See e.g. *Statements of Health Care Antitrust Enforcement Policy*, jointly issued by the DOJ and FTC (July 8, 2009).

names from sales contracts, using an independent third party to summarize the salient terms or analyze potential exposure, etc.;
- how current the information is: where possible, parties should use historical information, i.e. information that is at least 90 days old;
- whether the information exchange is one way or reciprocal; and
- the purpose of the information exchange: parties should exchange only information that is truly necessary for due diligence or integration planning.

I. Joint purchasing agreements

43.116 Joint purchasing agreements can provide economies of scale for purchasing and storing supplies. They may also ensure access to a stock of goods that might otherwise be unavailable.[75] However, a risk of antitrust liability arises where (1) the joint purchasing agreement may create or increase monopsony power and depress output, thereby harming competition; or (2) the agreement may facilitate collusion among the participants by standardizing costs or making it easier for competitors to estimate or monitor each other's production levels through knowledge of their input levels.

43.117 In evaluating joint purchasing agreements under the rule of reason, the agencies consider:

- the nature and purpose of the agreement;
- whether the participants have market power;
- whether the participants have the ability and incentive to compete independently;
- whether the agreement is exclusive; and
- the duration of the agreement.[76]

Generally, there is little antitrust risk where the parties do not have market power.

43.118 The DOJ and the FTC generally will not challenge joint purchasing arrangements where the purchases account for no more than 35 percent of the total purchases in the relevant market and the cost of the purchases accounts for less than 20 percent of the participants' revenues.[77] Antitrust risks are also reduced if the joint purchasing agreement is not exclusive, i.e. participants may purchase outside of the buying group.

J. Joint lobbying/regulatory/legislative efforts

43.119 Under the Noerr–Pennington doctrine, private efforts to influence legislative, administrative, or adjudicative processes are immunized from antitrust liability even if pursued by competitors collectively. Courts relying on the doctrine tend to base their opinions on the First Amendment right to petition and a narrow construction of the Sherman Act that Congress did not intend to bring petitioning action within the scope of the antitrust laws. However, *Noerr* does not immunize sham litigation or petitioning that involves bribery or other corruption of public officials. In addition, *Noerr* protection generally does not extend to efforts to influence non-governmental or private organizations.

43.120 Legislative and public policy activities cannot be used as a vehicle for reaching agreements about the business activities of industry members. In particular, competitors participating in such activities should avoid:

- reaching any agreement on the price, availability, marketing, or characteristics of their products;

[75] See *Competitor Collaboration Guidelines* (n 62) s. 3.31(a).
[76] See *Competitor Collaboration Guidelines* (n 62) s. 3.3.
[77] See e.g. *Statements of Health Care Antitrust Enforcement Policy* (n 74).

- reaching any agreement to do or not to do business with any individual or firm; and
- exchanging any confidential business information that might facilitate an unlawful agreement, for example business plans, cost data, or customer lists.

To minimize the risk of any antitrust challenge, the companies involved should document the proper scope and nature of their cooperative legislative activities. Agendas should be established and followed in meetings, minutes of such meetings should be kept, and no other activities should be undertaken without consulting legal counsel.[78] **43.121**

III. General issues

A. Jurisdiction and applicable law (including sector-specific legislation)

The Foreign Trade Antitrust Improvements Act (FTAIA) governs the extraterritorial application of US antitrust laws. The FTAIA allows a foreign plaintiff to sue in US district courts for US antitrust violations with respect to conduct involving trade or commerce with foreign nations if: **43.122**

- such conduct has a "direct, substantial and reasonably foreseeable effect" on domestic commerce or US import trade, or on the export commerce of a person engaged in such commerce in the US; and
- such effect "gives rise to" a claim under the Sherman Act.

In *Hoffmann-La Roche*,[79] the Supreme Court considered the question of when foreign conduct "gives rise" to a Sherman Act claim. The Court clarified this requirement where the defendants' conduct had effects in both US and foreign markets by holding that the FTAIA bars foreign purchasers from bringing suit under the Sherman Act when the foreign effects of "wholly foreign" conduct are *independent* of any domestic anticompetitive effects. This means that a foreign plaintiff seeking redress under the US antitrust laws must assert a claim arising from the effects of the alleged anticompetitive conduct on US commerce, and not simply from the alleged effects in some jurisdiction outside the US. Thus, a foreign plaintiff can sue for damages suffered in the US, or potentially for damages suffered outside the US, but only if those damages arise from the effects in the US. It could not sue for damages suffered outside the US, even from the same conduct, if those damages were merely cumulative of any damages suffered in the US. **43.123**

(i) Sector-specific legislation

Several statutes provide industry regulators, such as those in the energy, communication, and banking sectors, with concurrent yet specialized jurisdiction to assess the impact of mergers and acquisition on competition within their regulated industry. For instance, s. 203 of the Federal Power Act requires that the Federal Energy Regulatory Commission authorize mergers and acquisitions involving public utilities within its jurisdiction. Additionally, the Bank Mergers Acts of 1960 and 1966 and the Bank Holding Company Act Amendments of 1970, while prescribing that bank mergers are subject to the Clayton Act, provide unique procedures for banks' mergers and acquisitions. As with sector-specific exemptions, an antitrust expert should be consulted if a transaction arises in these industries. **43.124**

[78] See Section II.E.

[79] *F. Hoffmann-La Roche Ltd. v. Empagran S.A.*, 542 U.S. 155 (2004).

B. Antitrust system

43.125 The DOJ is a cabinet-level department within the executive branch of the US government. By contrast, the FTC is an independent agency. Although the FTC's five commissioners are appointed by the US President, they are not subject to explicit oversight by the executive branch once they are in office. However, the FTC does provide a yearly report of its activities to the legislative branch. Neither the FTC nor the DOJ is devoted solely to antitrust; rather, they have particular divisions responsible for antitrust enforcement—the Antitrust Division of the DOJ and the Bureau of Competition at the FTC.

43.126 Generally, the DOJ and the FTC have concurrent jurisdiction to enforce US antitrust laws; however, only the DOJ may bring criminal enforcement actions under the Sherman Act, and only the FTC may enforce s. 5 of the FTC Act. The FTC's jurisdiction over non-profit entities is also limited.

43.127 Further, the DOJ and the FTC tend to devote their resources to different industries. For example, the FTC focuses on the food, internet, and energy industries, while the DOJ devotes its resources to the insurance, banking, telecommunications, and airline industries.

43.128 In 2011, the DOJ was staffed by 721 employees, and its total budget was USD 162 million. The DOJ's 2011 activities included obtaining more than USD 1 billion in fines and restitution (a 78 percent increase from 2010), filing ninety criminal antitrust cases, strengthening its endeavors to enhance cooperation with international counterparts, and suing to block several transactions, such as AT&T's acquisition of T-Mobile USA and H&R Block's acquisition of TaxACT.[80]

43.129 The FTC was staffed by 1,043 employees and had a total budget of USD 134 million in 2011. Of this total 301 employees were engaged in competition enforcement. The FTC estimates that in 2011, it saved US consumers USD 531 million through merger enforcement activities and USD 445 million from non-merger enforcement activities. It challenged seventeen transactions in industries including health care, energy, and pharmaceuticals. Non-merger enforcement activity included suits regarding patent "hold-ups," i.e. the improper use of SEPs—those patents that cover inventions used as industry-wide standards—to exclude competition.[81]

43.130 Many states have their own antitrust laws. Staff attorneys in state attorney general's offices typically conduct antitrust investigations and enforcement actions. In doing so, they may collaborate with other state attorneys general, a federal enforcement agency, or both. In recent years, states have challenged a variety of mergers (often in conjunction with the federal and other state agencies) and conduct involving tying arrangements, horizontal price fixing and bid-rigging conspiracies, and other anticompetitive conduct, especially in the health care industry.

C. Private litigation

43.131 Private plaintiffs that can establish antitrust standing may bring suit at both the state and federal level, whether or not a competition agency has taken action. Class actions are also permissible. Section 4 of the Clayton Act allows private plaintiffs to recover treble damages and costs, and plaintiffs may seek injunctive relief under s. 16 of the Clayton Act.[82]

---

80 See US Department of Justice's Antitrust Division, *Global Competition Review* (May 29, 2012).

81 See US Federal Trade Commission, *Global Competition Review* (May 29, 2012).

82 For further discussion of the remedies available under US antitrust laws, see Section III.F.

A private plaintiff seeking damages must demonstrate that it has suffered injury-in-fact to its property or business, while a private plaintiff seeking injunctive relief need only show threatened loss or damage. Private antitrust plaintiffs must also show antitrust injury, i.e. "(1) injury of the type the antitrust laws were intended to prevent and (2) that flows from that which makes defendants' acts unlawful."[83] Such conduct must "harm the competitive *process* and thereby harm consumers. In contrast, harm to one or more *competitors* will not suffice."[84] **43.132**

Generally, only direct purchasers may seek damages under US federal antitrust laws.[85] However, an indirect purchaser may have standing to proceed with a claim if the seller and the direct purchaser are alleged to be co-conspirators. Various states also allow indirect purchasers to bring claims under certain circumstances. In addition to satisfying standing requirements, plaintiffs must also meet the plausibility pleading standard set forth by the Supreme Court in *Bell Atlantic*.[86] **43.133**

D. Follow-on litigation

Follow-on litigation occurs where a private plaintiff or putative class of plaintiffs brings suit based on a previously filed suit or investigation by the competition agencies. Plaintiffs pursuing follow-on litigation generally seek damages, and in the US they need not wait to file suit until the competition agencies complete their investigation. At the request of the DOJ or a defendant, a federal civil court judge may stay follow-on civil litigation while a criminal investigation is pending if the judge finds the civil litigation may prejudice the criminal investigation. **43.134**

Under s. 5 of the Clayton Act, final judgments entered against a defendant in a suit brought by the competition authorities under antitrust laws may be used as *prima facie* evidence in a subsequent suit by a private plaintiff where: **43.135**

- the judgment is final;
- the judgment was entered in a criminal or civil proceeding brought on behalf of or by the United States;
- the proceeding was brought under antitrust laws; and
- the judgment is not a consent judgment or decree entered before any testimony has been taken.

For example, a criminal conviction based on a plea of *nolo contendere* is considered to be a consent judgment and would not be admissible as *prima facie* evidence in a subsequent litigation, while a conviction based on a guilty plea is considered final and may be admissible as *prima facie* evidence. **43.136**

E. Arbitration and alternative dispute resolution

The Supreme Court held in *Mitsubishi Motors* that arbitration provisions in contracts involving international disputes, including antitrust claims, were enforceable.[87] Since then, federal courts have generally extended *Mitsubishi*'s reasoning to domestic contracts requiring arbitration of antitrust disputes. Moreover, the Supreme Court in *AT&T Mobility* held that the Federal Arbitration Act of 1925 (FAA) preempted state laws that prohibited contracts from disallowing class-wide arbitration.[88] **43.137**

---

[83] *Brunswick Corp. v. Pueblo Bowl-O-Mat, Inc.*, 429 U.S. 477, 489 (1977).

[84] *Microsoft Corp.*, 253 F.3d (n 9) 58. For a discussion of private actions by foreign plaintiffs, see Section III.A.

[85] See *Illinois Brick Co. v. Illinois*, 431 U.S. 720, 729 (1977).

[86] *Bell Atlantic*, 550 U.S. 544 (n 67).

[87] *Mitsubishi Motors Corp. v. Soler Chrysler-Plymouth, Inc.*, 473 U.S. 614 (1985).

[88] *AT&T Mobility LLC v. Concepcion*, 131 S. Ct. 1740 (2011).

43.138 In 2013, the Supreme Court held that the FAA does not permit courts to invalidate arbitration agreements on the ground that they do not permit class arbitration of a federal law claim. In *American Express*, the plaintiff contended that arbitration clauses within its merchant agreements prohibit merchants from bringing class actions against it. The appeals court had twice ruled that American Express could not force the merchants' claims into arbitration even though their agreements with the credit card company contained class action waivers.[89] The Supreme Court reversed.

F. Remedies

(i) Civil liability

43.139 The DOJ, FTC, and state attorneys general can seek a number of civil remedies, the most commonly sought being a cease-and-desist order that halts the offending conduct and prevents the defendant from continuing it in the future. Both agencies and the state attorneys general may seek other relief in civil conduct cases, such as restitution or disgorgement of unlawful gains. The DOJ and state attorneys general may also seek to recover treble damages suffered by the US as a consumer.

43.140 Section 4 of the Clayton Act permits a successful plaintiff to recover treble damages and costs, including reasonable attorney fees. Because damages are automatically enhanced by the statutory award of treble damages, a private plaintiff may not recover punitive damages in an antitrust case. A private plaintiff may also sue for and seek injunctive relief against "threatened loss or damage" caused by violations of the federal antitrust laws pursuant to s. 16 of the Clayton Act.

(ii) Criminal liability

43.141 The current maximum Sherman Act corporate fine is USD 100 million per violation; the maximum individual fine is USD 1 million per violation. The maximum Sherman Act jail term is ten years per violation.

43.142 In addition, criminal antitrust actions frequently include other charges, such as wire or mail fraud, that may expose the defendants to additional penalties. For example, the statutory penalty for wire or mail fraud is USD 250,000 and twenty years in prison per violation, and it is not uncommon to see multiple counts of wire or mail fraud based on individual incidents involving telephone or mail communications.

43.143 Finally, the Alternative Sentencing Act provides that if the defendant derives pecuniary gain from the offense (or others experience pecuniary loss), the defendant may be fined up to twice the gross gain or twice the gross loss.

43.144 In fiscal year 2012, the DOJ obtained criminal fines totaling USD 1.14 billion—a record high and a significant increase from prior years. By contrast, in 2003 the DOJ's criminal fines totaled only USD 107 million. Similarly, the duration of jail terms continues to grow. In the period 2010–12, the average jail term was twenty-five months, while in the period 1990–99, it was eight months.[90]

---

[89] See *American Express Co. v. Italian Colors Restaurant*, 667 F.3d 204 (2d Cir. 2012), *rev'd* 133 S. Ct. 2304 (June 20, 2013).

[90] *See* DOJ, *Division Update*, Spring 2013, available at <http://www.justice.gov/atr/public/division-update/2013>.

G. Leniency and immunity

The DOJ offers a formal leniency program providing complete immunity from criminal prosecution for a corporation or individual involved in a cartel upon satisfying certain requirements. In certain circumstances, a successful leniency applicant may also be able to limit private damages in follow-on civil litigation.[91] Two types of corporate leniency are available—"Type A" and "Type B." Type A leniency is applicable where a corporation comes forward *before* the DOJ initiates an investigation of the reported conduct and the following conditions are met: **43.145**

- the DOJ has not received information from another source about the illegal activity;
- when the corporation discovers its involvement in the activity, it takes prompt and effective action to end its involvement;
- the corporation reports the activity completely and with candor and provides full, continuing, and complete cooperation during the investigation;
- the admission is a corporate act, rather than isolated confessions of individual employees;
- the corporation makes restitution, where possible; and
- the corporation was not the leader or originator of the activity and did not coerce another party to participate in the illegal activity.

Type B leniency, which applies only after the DOJ has begun its investigation, is available in limited circumstances, namely where: **43.146**

- the corporation is the first to come forward and to qualify for leniency;
- at the time the corporation comes forward, the DOJ does not have evidence against the company likely to result in a sustainable conviction;
- when the corporation discovered its involvement in the activity, it took prompt and effective action to end its involvement;
- the corporation reports the wrongdoing completely and with candor and provides full, continuing, and complete cooperation that advances the investigation;
- the admission is a corporate act, rather than isolated confessions of individual employees;
- the corporation makes restitution, where possible; and
- the DOJ decides that it would not be unfair to others to grant the corporation leniency, considering the nature of the illegal activity, the confessing corporation's role, and when it came forward.

Importantly, both Type A and Type B leniency are only available to the first leniency applicant. A leniency applicant can hold a position as the first in line by reporting the conduct to the DOJ and putting down a "marker" for leniency. A marker gives a leniency applicant a finite period of time to hold its place as the first applicant for leniency while the applicant gathers the information needed to perfect the application. **43.147**

A company or individual implicated in an antitrust cartel can still obtain favorable treatment from the DOJ enforcers even if it is not the first in line if it provides useful information and pledges cooperation with the investigation. Such favorable treatment can include a reduction in any fine but will not extend to complete immunity. **43.148**

Finally, the DOJ offers an "amnesty plus" program in which a cartel member who discloses previously undetected antitrust offenses involving a cartel *different* from the one that first brought that cartelist to the prosecutors' attention can obtain immunity with respect to the **43.149**

[91] See the Antitrust Criminal Penalty Enhancement and Reform Act of 2004, Pub. L. No. 108-237, Title II, 118 Stat. 661 (2004).

second cartel. The DOJ has stated that approximately half of its international cartel investigations are initiated by evidence obtained through amnesty plus.

H. Document creation and retention

43.150 Contemporaneous company documents are a primary source of evidence of many issues in antitrust cases, including business intent, market power, competitive effects, and relevant market definitions. Private parties and US antitrust enforcement agencies bringing antitrust actions may request only non-privileged matters that are relevant to a party's claim or defense, and the discovery requests must also be reasonably calculated to lead to the discovery of admissible evidence. Copies of both paper and electronic documents may be requested. Antitrust agencies and private plaintiffs scrutinize company documents for antitrust "buzz words" that they can use as evidence, such as "entry barriers," "market," "market power," "monopolize," or "dominate."

43.151 The scope of US discovery is very broad. Courts generally do not limit discovery requests to narrow geographic areas. In addition, if more than one aspect of a business or industry may be relevant, courts typically allow full discovery as to all relevant product lines. Finally, courts generally permit discovery for a reasonable period of time prior to the first possible date of the actionable conduct.

43.152 Document retention policies limit the volume of documents a company retains and can provide an explanation as to why certain documents were not preserved. When litigation is reasonably anticipated, pending, or threatened, however, a company typically must suspend its usual document retention policy and implement a litigation hold, which requires the company to retain relevant documents until the matter concludes. A reasonableness standard applies to a litigation hold, which means a company may not be required to freeze all of its documents. A company also may be able to reduce the scope of document preservation by court order or an agreement with the opposing party.

43.153 If a company fails to adequately preserve or produce documents, it may be liable for serious civil and criminal discovery sanctions. Examples of sanctions include the use of an adverse inference instruction for destroyed or lost evidence, admitting evidence of discovery misconduct or excluding evidence at trial, and in extreme cases, entering a default judgment in favor of the non-offending party. Parties that either willfully fail to comply with a court order or intentionally destroy evidence face the most severe sanctions. The HSR Act allows agencies to compel discovery from merging parties through issuance of a so-called "second request," which requires an in-depth production of documents and data. The agencies tailor second requests to the specific products or services at issue in the investigation; however, second requests also often include certain standard document requests, such as requests for organizational charts and personnel information. Issuance of a second request generally extends HSR Act's mandatory waiting period until thirty days after the parties have substantially complied with the request.

43.154 In addition to or instead of voluntary means, the FTC and the DOJ may issue subpoenas or civil investigative demands as means of pre-complaint compulsory process. Part 3 of the FTC's Rules of Practice outlines specific discovery procedures to be used in FTC litigation.[92]

[92] See 16 C.F.R. pt. 3 [Code of Federal Regulations].

INDEX

The manufacturer's authorised representative in the EU for product safety is Oxford University Press España S.A. of el Parque Empresarial San Fernando de Henares, Avenida de Castilla, 2 – 28830 Madrid (www.oup.es/en or product.safety@oup.com). OUP España S.A. also acts as importer into Spain of products made by the manufacturer.

www.ingramcontent.com/pod-product-compliance
Lightning Source LLC
LaVergne TN
LVHW081957200926
848481LV00010B/2757
9780198703846